Sexual Orientation, Gender Identity, and the Constitution

Sexual Orientation, Gender Identity, and the Constitution

Peter Nicolas

Jeffrey & Susan Brotman Professor of Law
Adjunct Professor of Gender, Women, and Sexuality Studies
University of Washington

Carolina Academic Press
Durham, North Carolina

Library of Congress Cataloging-in-Publication Data

Nicolas, Peter.
  Sexual orientation, gender identity, and the constitution / Peter Nicolas.
    p. cm.
  Includes bibliographical references and index.
  ISBN 978-1-59460-991-6 (alk. paper)
1. Sexual orientation--United States. 2. Homosexuality--Law and legislation--United
States. 3. Gay rights--United States. 4. Sex discrimination--Law and legislation--
United States. I. Title.

  KF4754.5.N53 2012
  342.7308'7--dc23

                          2012023673

Carolina Academic Press
700 Kent Street
Durham, North Carolina 27701
Telephone (919) 489-7486
Fax (919) 493-5668
www.cap-press.com

Printed in the United States of America

To Mike

Contents

Table of Principal Cases

Preface

When I first started teaching a course in sexual orientation, gender identity, and the law over a decade ago, I would have never imagined that the legal landscape for sexual minorities would change as quickly and dramatically as it has. Back then, *Bowers v. Hardwick*—the U.S. Supreme Court's 1986 decision upholding the constitutionality of sodomy laws—was still the law of the land, and it was regularly invoked by lower courts as a basis for upholding the constitutionality of laws discriminating against sexual minorities in virtually every aspect of life, including laws denying them custody of their children and laws allowing them to be discriminated against in public employment. Back then, not a single state permitted same-sex couples to marry, sexual minorities were not permitted to serve openly in the military, and public support from elected officials was rare.

Today, by contrast, *Bowers* is no longer the law—having been overturned in 2003 by *Lawrence v. Texas*—and *Lawrence* is with increasing frequency invoked by lower courts as a basis for striking down laws discriminating against sexual minorities. Six states plus the District of Columbia currently allow same-sex couples to marry, while another dozen states permit same-sex couples to enter into domestic partnerships, civil unions, and other substitute relationship recognition schemes. Voters in three states—Maine, Maryland, and Washington—will decide whether to extend the right to marry to same-sex couples in the November 2012 election, with polls showing all of them standing a reasonable chance of being approved. In 2011, Don't Ask, Don't Tell—the military's policy banning open service by gay, lesbian, and bisexual servicemembers—was repealed. Elected officials from both major political parties have recently voted in support of extending marriage and other rights to sexual minorities, and the President of the United States in 2012 became the first U.S. President to publicly back marriage rights for same-sex couples.

Despite this progress, sexual minorities continue to face significant legal obstacles. Thirty states have amended their constitutions to prohibit same-sex marriage, and in some cases, domestic partnerships and civil unions as well. The Federal Defense of Marriage Act prevents same-sex couples lawfully married under state law from receiving federal rights, such as joint income tax filing and survivor social security benefits. Sexual minorities are still largely unprotected against employment discrimination. Moreover, some Members of Congress seek to reinstate Don't Ask, Don't Tell, and military service by transgendered persons is still prohibited. And new state laws are constantly being proposed or adopted to limit the rights of sexual minorities. Accordingly, constitutional litigation regarding the rights of sexual minorities is certain to continue into the foreseeable future.

I decided to write this textbook to fill an important gap in the existing collection of textbooks in the fields of constitutional law and sexual orientation, gender identity, and the law. Textbooks in the field of constitutional law cover so many topics that they can provide only limited coverage of constitutional litigation regarding the rights of sexual minorities. On the flip side, existing textbooks in the field of sexual orientation, gender identity, and the law provide only limited coverage of constitutional law, as they seek to cover all areas of common and statutory law impacting the rights of sexual minorities, such as family, employment, and tax law. Moreover, because constitutional law books are not typically written from the perspective of sexual minorities, they often omit cases—and edit out language in foundational cases—that are of critical importance in litigating the constitutional rights of sexual minorities. And because books on sexual orientation, gender identity, and the law are not typically written from the perspective of a constitutional litigator, they likewise omit critical cases and excerpts from cases. Given their respective broad scopes, both types of textbooks provide only limited coverage of lower state and federal court constitutional law decisions. Finally, neither type of book takes into account the many procedural obstacles that are typically covered in textbooks on federal courts and that have played an increasingly prominent role in constitutional litigation involving the rights of sexual minorities.

As someone who has written and taught in the fields of constitutional law, federal courts, and sexual orientation, gender identity, and the law, I have written this textbook so as to incorporate all three perspectives. The result is a book narrower in focus but greater in depth that is designed to teach students all of the procedural and substantive aspects of constitutional litigation regarding the rights of sexual minorities.

The book is divided into six chapters. Chapter 1 addresses threshold questions regarding the definitions of sexual orientation, sex, and gender, raising the question whether they are about status, conduct, desire, biology, self-identification, or some combination of all of these, and thus setting the stage for the question of "immutability" and the status-conduct and speech-conduct lines that arise in the equal protection, substantive due process, and First Amendment materials that follow. Chapter 2 addresses the various procedural obstacles that arise in constitutional litigation, such as standing, mootness, abstention, and the precedential weight of prior summary affirmances by the U.S. Supreme Court. The next four chapters address each of the three key constitutional doctrines that arise in litigation regarding the rights of sexual minorities. Chapter 3 introduces students to substantive due process, while Chapter 4 introduces them to equal protection principles. Chapter 5 then provides in-depth coverage of both substantive due process and equal protection principles working in tandem in cases involving marriage, parenting, and public employment. Finally, Chapter 6 examines the application of First Amendment principles in cases involving the rights of sexual minorities.

The six chapters are not completely independent, but are instead carefully integrated with one another. Thus, excerpts from the same case might appear in all six chapters, as students consider the threshold definitional questions and procedural obstacles, followed by substantive constitutional challenges on equal protection, substantive due process, and First Amendment grounds. The book thus replicates the stages of analysis that arise when litigating any such case from start to finish.

Throughout the book, I try to use a balanced mix of cases, problems, textual narrative, and explanatory notes. Thus, each section of the textbook typically begins with introductory narrative designed to introduce students to the concept or constitutional principle covered in that section. That narrative is often followed by a problem designed for use in class as a vehicle for raising and addressing the conceptual ambiguities that arise in applying that concept or constitutional principle. Resources for answering the problem are provided by the materials following the problems, usually a set of cases followed by a series of explanatory notes.

The extensive use of problems throughout the textbook—twenty in-depth problems in all—is a key feature of this book designed to help students to master the *application* of constitutional law. By the time law students take constitutional law, most of them have learned how to read cases and to recite the holdings of those cases. Yet many students find it difficult to apply those principles when presented with alternative factual scenarios. These problems thus provide students with ample opportunity to hone their skills in applying constitutional law and to receive feedback on the same.

Because the book covers basic constitutional law doctrine as well as more focused case law regarding the constitutional rights of sexual minorities, it can be used effectively in three different types of courses. First, it can be used in a stand-alone course on sexual orientation, gender identity, and the law. Second, it can be used in a traditional, rights-based constitutional law course by a faculty member who wishes to teach the course with greater focus on the constitutional rights of sexual minorities. Finally, the book is sufficiently comprehensive that it can be used in non-law school courses as well.

In putting this textbook together, I am indebted to my student research assistants, Walter Smith, Chris Olah, Daniel Richards, and Mark Tyson. Walter has worked with me on the book since its inception, comparing all of the edited cases and cited materials with the original sources to ensure accuracy, as well as providing me with valuable research assistance and substantive feedback throughout the drafting process. Chris—in addition to providing me with valuable research assistance—meticulously proofread the entire book from cover-to-cover. Daniel and Mark proofread the final draft of the book from cover-to-cover. I also wish to thank Visiting Professor Ronald K.L. Collins (University of Washington School of Law) and Professor David Skover (Seattle University School of Law)—both experts on the First Amendment—for their invaluable feedback and suggestions regarding Chapter 6. Finally, I wish to thank the students in my Winter 2011 and Spring 2012 courses in GLBT Rights & the Constitution, who gave these materials a trial run and provided me with extremely valuable feedback and suggestions as I prepared these materials for press.

Peter Nicolas
Seattle, Washington
September 2012

Sexual Orientation, Gender Identity, and the Constitution

Chapter 1

Terminology

Throughout American history, numerous laws have been enacted that in explicit terms discriminate on the basis of one's sexual orientation, and more specifically, against those who are gay or lesbian (although the laws typically use the more clinical term "homosexual"). In addition, some such laws discriminate against those who are transgendered or bisexual. Examples of such explicit discrimination include current, proposed, or repealed laws providing that individuals who are "homosexual" are ineligible to adopt children or hold certain types of jobs (such as operators of day care centers or teachers), as well as federal laws and regulations making transgendered persons ineligible to serve in the United States military and providing that those who are openly gay or bisexual cannot serve in the military. Furthermore, even when not explicitly banned from serving in particular public-sector jobs, some employees are fired from those jobs by their supervisors because of their sexual orientation or gender identity.

Other laws, while not explicitly discriminating on the basis of sexual orientation or gender identity, nonetheless *effectively* discriminate against gays, lesbians, and transgendered persons. Thus, for example, laws and constitutional amendments enacted in a majority of states refuse to permit or recognize marriages between persons of the same "sex." Similarly, so-called "sodomy laws" in some states criminalized certain types of sexual activity, but only if they occurred between persons of the same "sex" (other such laws, while applicable without regard to the sex of the individuals involved, nonetheless effectively discriminated against gays and lesbians by prohibiting the only methods of sexual expression available to them).

While most laws discriminating on the basis of sexual orientation or gender identity discriminate against sexual minorities and in favor of "straight" or "heterosexual" persons, some discriminate against the latter group. Thus, for example, some jurisdictions have laws extending benefits to the same-sex partners of unmarried employees but not to the opposite-sex partners of unmarried employees. Moreover, some employers or schools may consider an individual's status as a sexual minority a "plus" factor in deciding whether to hire them or admit them into an educational program.

In the chapters that follow, this book will assess the constitutionality of laws that discriminate on the basis of one's sexual orientation or gender identity, with a particular focus on the guarantees of equal protection, due process, and freedom of association and expression found in the U.S. Constitution as well as analogous guarantees found in state constitutions.

But before assessing the constitutionality of such laws, it is first worthwhile (and necessary) to ask exactly what these laws *do*. In other words, when a law says that a "homosexual" cannot adopt children or serve in a particular type of job, or that marriages between persons of the same "sex" are prohibited, what do those terms mean? Stated somewhat differently, what does it *mean* for someone to be a "homosexual," or a "man," or a "woman"?

In almost all cases, laws of the sort described above do not define such terms, leaving it to those applying the laws (and, to the extent that litigation ensues, the courts) to determine their meaning. Thus, a necessary prelude to addressing the constitutionality of such laws is a question of statutory interpretation. Moreover, *how* those terms are defined may have a bearing on whether they are constitutional or not, and courts—applying canons of construction that require them to interpret laws where possible in a way that upholds their constitutionality—will thus approach the question of statutory construction with the constitutional questions in mind.

Before reading the materials that follow, identify your *own* sexual orientation and gender identity: Are you purely gay, purely straight, or something in between? Are you a man, a woman, or something in between? If the answer to either of those questions is "something in between," what terms do you use to describe your sexual orientation and gender identity, and what terms do you use if forced to make a binary choice (i.e., gay versus straight, man versus woman)? Moreover, *what* are you relying upon in making that assessment? Now think of a friend, acquaintance, or classmate and assess their sexual orientation and gender. What did you conclude, and what did you rely upon in reaching that conclusion?

Section A of this chapter examines the various ways in which one can define an individual's sexual orientation, while Section B examines the various factors that one can rely on to define an individual's gender. Each section begins with a problem that places you in the role of applying a law that takes an individual's sexual orientation or gender into account in determining her ability to exercise a particular type of right. The problems are followed by cases and other materials that present competing ways of defining sexual orientation and gender identity. The final section of this chapter, Section C, takes a closer look at sodomy laws and the interpretive challenges that courts have historically confronted in applying such laws.

A. The Meaning of "Sexual Orientation"

Problem 1-A: No Adoption by Homosexuals!

Assume that you work at a state agency that regulates adoptions. A state statute provides in pertinent part as follows: "No person eligible to adopt under this statute may adopt if that person is a homosexual."

You are charged with reviewing applications by persons who wish to adopt to determine whether or not allowing them to adopt would violate the terms of the statute. During their intake interviews, the applicants state in pertinent part as follows:

Applicant A (a male)—"I am in a committed emotional and sexual relationship with another man."

Applicant B (a female)—"I sometimes have sex with men, and I sometimes have sex with women."

Applicant C (a male)—"I am a heterosexual man, but when I was in college, I had sex with a guy once when I was a little wasted."

Applicant D (a male)—"I have 'made out' with other guys, but I have not gone 'all the way' with anyone yet."

Applicant E (a female) — "I have never dated or engaged in sexual activity with anyone, but I find myself physically attracted exclusively to other women."

Applicant F (a female) — "I am a lesbian, but I am celibate."

Applicant G (a female) — "I have never dated or engaged in sexual activity with anyone, but I recently was tested as part of a university study, and I was told that I carry the gene that scientists believe to be associated with homosexuality."

Applicant H (a male) — "I am a heterosexual man dating a woman who was born with male genitalia but recently completed sex-reassignment surgery."

Which of the applicants are qualified to adopt under the statute, and which of them are not?

Department of Health & Rehabilitative Services v. Cox
627 So.2d 1210 (Fla. Dist. Ct. App. 1993)

ALTENBERND, Judge.

[Same-sex couple wishing to adopt bring challenge to the constitutionality of a Florida statute that prohibits adoption by "homosexual[s]."]

III. THE QUESTION OF VAGUENESS: HOMOSEXUAL ORIENTATION V. HOMOSEXUAL ACTIVITY

Section 63.042(3) does not define "homosexual." Despite the fact that the statute has been in effect since 1977, there are no reported cases in which a litigant has ever alleged that the term "homosexual" in section 63.042(3) is unconstitutionally vague. We have not been provided with any legislative history suggesting that anyone has ever attempted to amend this statute because of any perceived ambiguity. Mr. Cox and Mr. Jackman have admitted that they are homosexual and have never alleged that they found the term to be unconstitutionally vague. Thus, we are troubled by the trial court's unilateral amendment of the plaintiffs' complaint to add a constitutional due process theory that the parties had not chosen to litigate. The plaintiffs have not established that this statute is unconstitutionally vague.

The only other state that has enacted a similar statute is New Hampshire. *See* N.H.Rev.Stat.Ann. § 170-B:4 (1991). That statute has withstood constitutional scrutiny. *See Op. of the Justices,* 530 A.2d 21 (N.H.1987). The New Hampshire statute defines "homosexual" as "any person who performs or submits to any sexual act involving the sex organs of one person and the mouth or anus of another person of the same gender." N.H.Rev.Stat.Ann. § 170-B:2 (1991). In upholding its statute, the New Hampshire Supreme Court limited its definition to persons voluntarily engaging in homosexual activity reasonably close in time to the filing of the adoption application. *Op. of the Justices,* 530 A.2d at 294–295.

HRS argues that the Florida statute can be reasonably interpreted to include the same concepts as those employed in the New Hampshire definition. HRS does not claim that the statute applies to persons who merely have some degree of homosexual orientation or to people who have experimented with homosexual activity in the past. HRS does not intend to bar adoption based on homosexual orientation, but only when it knows of current, voluntary homosexual activity by an applicant.

The legislature need not define every word in a statute to survive a vagueness challenge. It is merely necessary for the legislature to give adequate notice of what conduct is prohibited by the statute and to provide clarity sufficient to avoid arbitrary and discriminatory enforcement. This analysis is performed from the perspective of a person of common understanding and intelligence. This standard is less stringent when the statute is not a criminal statute.

If possible, this court must construe section 63.042(3) in a manner that upholds the statute. A reasonable construction of a statute by an agency charged with its administration is entitled to great weight. We conclude that HRS has reasonably construed the statute to apply only to applicants who are known to engage in current, voluntary homosexual activity. We conclude that an ordinary person would realize that the legislature had not created a rule concerning a person's thoughts, but rather a person's conduct.[6] On the basis of this record, we cannot hold that the legislature was required to use precise anatomical language in order for a person of common understanding and intelligence to appreciate that the homosexual activity intended by the Florida statute is the same as that described in the New Hampshire statute....

We recognize that a definition of "homosexual," limited to applicants who are known to engage in current, voluntary homosexual activity, draws a distinction between homosexual orientation and homosexual activity. We understand that some people have concluded that it is unreasonable or unfair to distinguish homosexual orientation from homosexual activity. They believe that the activity is nothing more than an inevitable expression of the orientation. They believe that both homosexual orientation and activity are caused by biological or environmental factors beyond the control of the individual. In their opinion, homosexual conduct is not a voluntarily chosen lifestyle. From this perspective, a rule which discriminates against the activity is no different than a rule which discriminates against the orientation.

In contrast, other people maintain that homosexual activity is severable from homosexual thought. They believe that homosexual conduct should be regulated by the state. As a result, some types of homosexual conduct have long been the subject of criminal statutes. The United States Supreme Court has held that statutes regulating homosexual sodomy do not violate federal due process. *Bowers v. Hardwick,* 478 U.S. 186 (1986).

At this time, the orientation/activity question is simply a matter upon which reasonable persons can and do disagree — as a matter of scientific fact and as a matter of moral, religious, and legal opinion. Certainly, the record presented to the trial court and to this court does not end the debate. Under these circumstances, the legislature is constitutionally permitted to reach its own conclusions on the validity of the distinction between homosexual orientation and activity without any mandate from this court....

---

6. We have obtained and reviewed the legislative history concerning chapter 77-140. At various hearings, legislators expressed some concern about the need for a definition. One legislator observed that a dictionary definition of "homosexual" was based on sexual desire and not on sexual activity. In rejecting the need for a statutory definition, the legislature appears to conclude that sexual desire is not the controlling issue and that citizens did not need a definition to know the nature of the conduct that was being regulated in the best interests of children.

Meinhold v. United States Department of Defense

34 F.3d 1469 (9th Cir. 1994)

RYMER, Circuit Judge:

    . . . .

I

Meinhold had served for twelve years as an enlisted member of the United States Navy. On May 19, 1992, he acknowledged on television that he was gay. The next day the United States Navy initiated discharge proceedings. . . .

At the hearing, both the Navy Recorder and the Legal Advisor to the administrative discharge board took the position that the board must recommend discharge if it found that Meinhold is homosexual, and that a member of the service is homosexual if he says he is whether or not he has engaged in homosexual conduct. The board so found, due to Meinhold's televised statement. As a result, Meinhold was given an honorable discharge on August 12, 1992.

Meinhold brought this action for a declaration that the Department of Defense's then-existing policy regarding homosexuals was unconstitutional, and sought reinstatement in the Navy on the ground that his discharge was procedurally defective, the Navy was estopped from separating him on the basis of status, and the relevant regulations were constitutionally infirm. . . .

III

On the merits of Meinhold's equal protection claim, DOD contends that since it is constitutionally permissible to conclude that homosexual conduct adversely affects the military, *Beller v. Middendorf,* 632 F.2d 788, 811–12 (9th Cir.1980), *cert. denied,* 452 U.S. 905 (1981), it is equally permissible for the regulations to target those who are likely to engage in homosexual conduct. DOD faults the district court's definition of the pertinent classification for purposes of its equal protection analysis as "gays and lesbians who do not engage in prohibited conduct," arguing instead that under the regulations, the relevant classification is persons who the military reasonably concludes either have committed or are likely to commit homosexual acts based on their admitted "desire" and "propensity" to engage in homosexual conduct. In holding to the contrary, DOD believes the district court failed to test the policy "in light of the purposes [the Navy] sought to achieve," as courts are obliged to do under *Rostker v. Goldberg,* 453 U.S. 57, 75 (1981). DOD then suggests that simply by acknowledging his homosexuality, Meinhold admitted under the regulations that he had a "desire" and "propensity" to commit homosexual acts. From this, it urges, the Navy could permissibly infer that he would probably commit such acts, if he had not done so already.

We believe that both the Navy's application of its regulations and the district court's equal protection analysis start a step too far down the path. When the constitutional validity of a statute or regulation is called into question, it is a cardinal rule that courts must first determine whether a construction is possible by which the constitutional problem may be avoided. "[W]here an otherwise acceptable construction of a statute would raise serious constitutional problems, the Court will construe the statute to avoid such problems unless such construction is plainly contrary to the intent of Congress." *Edward J. DeBartolo Corp. v. Florida Gulf Coast Bldg. & Constr. Trades Council,* 485 U.S. 568, 575 (1988). . . . Thus, it is incumbent on us to see whether there is some way the regulation can be construed to resolve the matter on a nonconstitutional ground.

As we consider the regulation in this case, however, we are guided by another long-settled rule: The military's "considered professional judgment," *Goldman v. Weinberger*, 475 U.S. 503, 508 (1986), is "not lightly to be overruled by the judiciary," *Pruitt v. Cheney*, 963 F.2d 1160, 1166 (9th Cir.1991), *cert. denied*, 506 U.S. 1020 (1992).

> "[I]t is difficult to conceive of an area of governmental activity in which the courts have less competence. The complex, subtle, and professional decisions as to the composition, training, equipping, and control of a military force are essentially professional military judgments, subject *always* to civilian control of the Legislative and Executive Branches."

Rostker, 453 U.S. at 65–66. Our review, therefore, is as deferential as our constitutional responsibilities permit. *Id.* at 70.

To accommodate both principles, we start with the Navy's professional judgment. It is that "[h]omosexuality is incompatible with military service. The presence in the military environment of persons who engage in homosexual conduct or who, by their statements, demonstrate a propensity to engage in homosexual conduct, seriously impairs the accomplishment of the military mission." DOD Directive 1332.14(H)(1)(a).

The regulation, in turn, defines "homosexual" as "a person, regardless of sex, who engages in, desires to engage in, or intends to engage in homosexual acts." DOD Directive 1332.14(H)(1)(b)(1). "A homosexual act means bodily contact, actively undertaken or passively permitted, between members of the same sex for the purpose of satisfying sexual desires." DOD Directive 1332.14(H)(1)(b)(3). Eliminating from the equation a person who has previously engaged in homosexual acts because acts were not at issue in Meinhold's proceeding, a "homosexual" according to the regulations is someone who "desires" or "intends" to engage in bodily contact with members of the same sex for the purpose of satisfying sexual desires.

Separation may be based on homosexuality due to conduct or statements. DOD Directive 1332.14(H)(1)(c). "*Conduct*" consists of engaging in, attempting to engage in, or soliciting another to engage in a homosexual act;[6] a "*statement*" that the member is a homosexual is the basis for separation unless the board finds the member is not a homosexual. *Id.*

There is no dispute in this case that the Navy's policy is constitutionally permissible to the extent it relates to homosexual *conduct*. However, the issue in Meinhold's separation proceeding was his *classification* as a homosexual. Thus, our task is to decide whether this application raises constitutional concerns that can be obviated by construing the regulations differently, but still consistently with the purposes DOD sought to achieve.

Construing the regulation to apply to the "classification of being homosexual" clearly implicates equal protection. We recognized that the Army's discharge of a servicemember because of her acknowledged homosexuality states an equal protection claim in *Pruitt*, 963 F.2d at 1164. Here, the regulation as applied to Meinhold assumes that persons who say they are gay, but who have not acted in accordance with their propensity in the past, will nevertheless act in accordance with their propensity in the future—whether or not

---

6. If such conduct is found, the servicemember must be separated unless the board finds that it was a departure from usual behavior, is unlikely to recur, was not accomplished by force, the member's continued presence is consistent with the interest of proper discipline, and the member does not "desire" or "intend" to engage in homosexual acts. DOD Directive 1332.14(H)(1)(c)(1).

to do so is lawful or acceptable military behavior. Yet no similar assumption is made with respect to servicemembers who are heterosexual.[10] Although courts defer to the military's judgment about homosexual conduct, and classifications having to do with homosexuality may survive challenge if there is any rational basis for them, at least a serious question is raised whether it can ever be rational to presume that one class of persons (identified by their sexual preference alone) will violate regulations whereas another class (identified by their preference) will not.[11]

Equating status or propensity with conduct or acts that are prohibited is problematic as well. The Supreme Court has long recognized the constitutional infirmity of penalizing status alone. *See, e.g., United States v. Brignoni-Ponce,* 422 U.S. 873, 885–87 (1975) (ethnicity is insufficient basis to believe persons are illegal aliens); *Robinson v. California,* 370 U.S. 660, 665–67 (1962) (unconstitutional to criminalize narcotics addiction in absence of proof of use); *cf. Powell v. Texas,* 392 U.S. 514, 532–34 (1968) (recognizing *Robinson* rule that criminal penalties may be inflicted only if accused has committed act by contrast with status). While not controlling because the discharge process is not a criminal proceeding and does not impose punishment, *Robinson, Powell* and *Brignoni-Ponce* nevertheless point out the constitutionally significant danger of making status a surrogate for prohibited conduct. As Justice Black's concurring opinion in *Powell,* joined by Justice Harlan, observed:

> Punishment for a status is particularly obnoxious, and in many instances can reasonably be called cruel and unusual, because it involves punishment for a mere propensity, a desire to commit an offense; the mental element is not simply one part of the crime but may constitute all of it....
>
> ... Perhaps more fundamental is the difficulty of distinguishing, in the absence of any conduct, between desires of the day-dream variety and fixed intentions that may pose a real threat to society; extending the criminal law to cover both types of desire would be unthinkable, since "[t]here can hardly be anyone who has never thought evil. When a desire is inhibited it may find expression in fantasy; but it would be absurd to condemn this natural psychological mechanism as illegal."

Powell, 392 U.S. at 543–44 (Black, J., concurring). And as Justice Harlan wrote in *Robinson:*

> Since addiction alone cannot reasonably be thought to amount to more than a compelling propensity to use narcotics, the effect of this instruction was to authorize criminal punishment for a bare desire to commit a criminal act.
>
> If the California statute reaches this type of conduct, ... it is an arbitrary imposition which exceeds the power that a State may exercise in enacting its criminal law.

Robinson, 370 U.S. at 678–79 (Harlan, J., concurring). The effect of the regulation as applied in Meinhold's case is much the same.

---

10. Prohibited conduct includes adultery, indecent assault, wrongful co-habitation, fraternization, indecent language, indecent acts with another, pandering and prostitution, sodomy and bigamy. Articles 120, 125, 134, Uniform Code of Military Justice, 10 U.S.C. §§ 920, 925, 934 (Supp.1994).

11. We acknowledge the force of DOD's argument that it need not take the risk of a person with homosexual desire or propensity acting on it because of the critical nature of the military mission. However, DOD is prepared to take the risk that a servicemember who has committed a homosexual act but isn't homosexual won't do so again. For that reason, its argument is not wholly rational. In any event, the risk factor alone does not eliminate equal protection difficulties.

Thus, whether the regulation passes constitutional muster is a close question only because of the greater license we give the military to control the military environment. Constitutional tensions may be avoided, however, if the regulation can reasonably be construed to mandate separation due to a statement of homosexuality only when that statement itself indicates more than the inchoate "desire" or "propensity" that inheres in status. We believe it can be.

DOD's policy judgment hinges on *conduct*[12] — whereas the separation provisions include "conduct *or statements.*" DOD contends that a statement admitting homosexuality under the regulation admits "desire" and "propensity" to commit homosexual acts. Arguably it does, in the abstract, because the regulatory definition of "homosexual" is a person who "engages in, desires to engage in, or intends to engage in homosexual acts."[13] But as DOD's brief also acknowledges: "[A] service member's *expressed* 'desire' to commit homosexual [acts] evidences more than an abstract, ephemeral, or suppressible whim. Like acts themselves and like intentions, 'desire' in the relevant sense evidences a 'propensity,' or an 'often intense natural inclination,' *Webster's New Collegiate Dictionary* 943 (9th ed. 1990), to commit serious *regulatory violations*" (emphasis added). Taking DOD's suggestion at face value, the "statement" prong for separation may turn on something more than status: a concrete, expressed desire to commit homosexual acts which are, in turn, prohibited.

This interpretation is consistent with the military's judgment that the presence of persons who engage in homosexual conduct, or make a statement indicating their propensity for engaging in, or attempting to engage in, or soliciting someone else to engage in homosexual acts, impairs the military mission. Nothing in the policy states that the presence of persons who *say* they are gay impairs the military mission. Rather, the focus is on prohibited conduct and persons likely to engage in prohibited conduct. Construing the regulation to reach only statements which manifest a fixed or expressed desire to commit a prohibited act not only coincides with the military's concern for its mission, but gives content to "desire" apart from the defining characteristic of sexual orientation.

We therefore hold that the regulation under which Meinhold was processed need not be construed so broadly as to raise constitutional concerns. It can reasonably be construed to reach only statements that show a concrete, fixed, or expressed desire to commit homosexual acts despite their being prohibited. The Navy applied its regulation to Meinhold's statement of orientation alone and based his separation solely on his classification as a homosexual. His statement — "I am in fact gay" — in the circumstances under which he made it manifests no concrete, expressed desire to commit homosexual acts. The Navy's presumption that Meinhold desires or intends to engage in prohibited conduct on the basis of his statement alone therefore arbitrarily goes beyond what DOD's policy seeks to prevent. Accordingly, Meinhold's discharge on that basis cannot stand....

---

12. "The presence in the military environment of persons who engage in homosexual conduct or who, by their statements, demonstrate a propensity to engage in homosexual conduct, seriously impairs the accomplishment of the military mission." DOD Directive 1332.14(H)(1)(a). Our conclusion in *Pruitt* that the regulation targets homosexual status, 963 F.2d at 1163, is not to the contrary because we were concerned there with whether it targeted speech or status in Pruitt's case.

13. There is no evidence that Meinhold "engaged" in homosexual acts and DOD doesn't argue that he "intended" to.

10 U.S.C. § 654 (1993)

Policy concerning homosexuality in the armed forces

....

(a) **Findings.** Congress makes the following findings:

....

(15) The presence in the armed forces of persons who demonstrate a propensity or intent to engage in homosexual acts would create an unacceptable risk to the high standards of morale, good order and discipline, and unit cohesion that are the essence of military capability.

(b) **Policy.** A member of the armed forces shall be separated from the armed forces under regulations prescribed by the Secretary of Defense if one or more of the following findings is made and approved in accordance with procedures set forth in such regulations:

(1) That the member has engaged in, attempted to engage in, or solicited another to engage in a homosexual act or acts unless there are further findings, made and approved in accordance with procedures set forth in such regulations, that the member has demonstrated that—

(A) such conduct is a departure from the member's usual and customary behavior;

(B) such conduct, under all the circumstances, is unlikely to recur;

(C) such conduct was not accomplished by use of force, coercion, or intimidation;

(D) under the particular circumstances of the case, the member's continued presence in the armed forces is consistent with the interests of the armed forces in proper discipline, good order, and morale; and

(E) the member does not have a propensity or intent to engage in homosexual acts.

(2) That the member has stated that he or she is a homosexual or bisexual, or words to that effect, unless there is a further finding, made and approved in accordance with procedures set forth in the regulations, that the member has demonstrated that he or she is not a person who engages in, attempts to engage in, has a propensity to engage in, or intends to engage in homosexual acts.

(3) That the member has married or attempted to marry a person known to be of the same biological sex.

....

(f) **Definitions.** In this section:

(1) The term "homosexual" means a person, regardless of sex, who engages in, attempts to engage in, has a propensity to engage in, or intends to engage in homosexual acts, and includes the terms "gay" and "lesbian."

(2) The term "bisexual" means a person who engages in, attempts to engage in, has a propensity to engage in, or intends to engage in homosexual and heterosexual acts.

(3) The term "homosexual act" means—

(A) any bodily contact, actively undertaken or passively permitted, between members of the same sex for the purpose of satisfying sexual desires; and

(B) any bodily contact which a reasonable person would understand to demonstrate a propensity or intent to engage in an act described in subparagraph (A).

Conaway v. Deane

932 A.2d 571 (Md. 2007)

[Same-sex couple wishing to marry brought suit seeking a declaration that a state law limiting marriage to opposite sex couples violated, *inter alia*, the equal protection guarantee set forth in the Maryland Constitution.]

HARRELL, J.

....

III. Equal Protection under Article 24 of the Declaration of Rights

A. A Statute That Discriminates on the Basis of Sexual Orientation Does Not Trigger Strict or Heightened Scrutiny.

....

That Family Law § 2-201 draws a distinction based on sexual orientation is undisputed. The actual controversy here, therefore, is what level of constitutional scrutiny should be applied to a statute that treats citizens differently on that basis (i.e., whether sexual orientation constitutes a suspect or quasi-suspect class, thereby triggering one of the heightened levels of scrutiny iterated above). We find that sexual orientation is neither a suspect nor quasi-suspect class, and Family Law § 2-201 therefore is subject to rational basis review. We explain.

There is no brightline diagnostic, annunciated by either this Court or the U.S. Supreme Court, by which a suspect or quasi-suspect class may be recognized readily. There are, however, several indicia of suspect or quasi-suspect classes that have been used in Supreme Court cases to determine whether a legislative classification warrants a more exacting constitutional analysis than that provided by rational basis review. These factors include: (1) whether the group of people disadvantaged by a statute display [] readily-recognizable, "obvious, immutable, or distinguishing characteristics …" that define the group as a "discrete and insular minorit[y];" (2) whether the impacted group is "saddled with such disabilities, or subjected to such a history of purposeful unequal treatment, or relegated to such a position of political powerlessness as to command extraordinary protection from the majoritarian political process;" and (3) whether the class of people singled out is "subjected to unique disabilities on the basis of stereotyped characteristics not truly indicative of their abilities [to contribute meaningfully to society]." We have identified a similar, although not as comprehensive, set of criteria by which we may analyze allegedly new suspect classes. Because Article 24 is construed at least to the same extent as the Fourteenth Amendment, we find useful in our analysis those additional criteria used by the Supreme Court in assessing claims of a new suspect or quasi-suspect classification.

....

2. Evidence that homosexuality is an immutable characteristic.

The term "immutability" defines a human characteristic that is determined "solely by the accident of birth," *Frontiero,* 411 U.S. at 686 (explaining that "sex, like race and national origin, is an immutable characteristic [that is] determined solely by the accident of birth," and that defines a particular group), or that the possessor is "powerless to escape or set aside." *Regents of Univ. of Cal. v. Bakke,* 438 U.S. 265, 360 (1978) (quoting *Weber v. Aetna Cas. & Surety Co.,* 406 U.S. 164 (1972)). *See also Plyler v. Doe,* 457 U.S. 202, 216–17 n. 14 (1982) ("Legislation imposing special disabilities upon groups disfavored by virtue of circumstances beyond their control suggests the kind of 'class or caste' treatment that the Fourteenth Amendment was designed to abolish."). Based on the scientific and sociological evidence currently available to the public, we are unable to take judicial notice that gay, lesbian, and bisexual persons display readily-recognizable, immutable characteristics that define the group such that they may be deemed a suspect class for purposes of determining the appropriate level of scrutiny to be accorded the statute in the present case.

.... Appellees point neither to scientific nor sociological studies, which have withstood analysis for evidentiary admissibility, in support of an argument that sexual orientation is an immutable characteristic.[57]

---

57. No party addresses in its brief the immutability of sexual orientation and the implications of an answer to that query in determining the correct level of constitutional review to be applied to Family Law § 2-201. The issue of the immutability of sexual orientation, however, is the subject of a multitude of recent studies and nationwide debate. *See* J. Michael Bailey & Richard C. Pillard, *A Genetic Study of Male Sexual Orientation,* 48 ARCHIVES GEN'L PSYCHIATRY 1089, 1093 (1991) (studying the similarities in sexual orientation between twin, non-twin, and adopted siblings, and concluding that identical twins are more likely than other types of siblings to have a similar homosexual orientation); Dean H. Hamer, Stella Hu, Victoria L. Magnuson, Nan Hu & Angela M.L. Pattatucci, *A Linkage Between DNA Markers on the X Chromosome and Male Sexual Orientation,* 261 SCIENCE 321 (1993) (finding evidence that there is a connection between male sexual orientation and a particular gene found on the X chromosome and suggesting that male sexual orientation may be linked to maternal relatives); Simon LeVay, *A Difference in Hypothalamic Structure Between Heterosexual and Homosexual Men,* 253 SCIENCE 1034–37 (1991) (finding that the interstitial nuclei of the anterior hypothalamus (INAH) 3, one of four cell groups found within the anterior hypothalamus region of the brain, is twice as large in heterosexual men as compared to homosexual men, and concluding that, at least in men, a heterosexual brain is structurally dimorphic from a homosexual brain). These reports, considered three of the most important in the field, however, are not without challenge. Their imperfections and limitations are well-documented. *See generally* Janet E. Halley, *Sexual Orientation and the Politics of Biology: A Critique of the Argument from Immutability,* 46 STAN L.REV. 503, 529–46 (1994) (reviewing the limitations and flaws within the leading studies on the link between biology and sexual orientation); Ingrid Wickelgren, *Discovery of the "Gay Gene" Questioned,* 284 SCIENCE 571 (1999); Eliot Marshall, *NIH's "Gay Gene" Study Questioned,* 268 SCIENCE 1841 (1995). Other studies have found contrary indicia and have concluded that culture and environment, at least in part, play a factor in the development of an individual's sexual orientation. *See, e.g.,* Dean H. Hamer, et al., *Genetics and Male Sexual Orientation,* 285 SCIENCE 803a (1999) ("Sexual orientation is a complex trait that is probably shaped by many different factors, including multiple genes, biological, environmental, and socio cultural influences."); J. Michael Bailey, Michael P. Dunne, Nicholas G. Martin, *Genetic and Environmental Influences on Sexual Orientation and its Correlates in an Australian Twin Sample,* 78(3) J. OF PERSONALITY & SOC. PSYCHOL. 524 (2000). Even the authors, most notably Simon LeVay, have indicated that the biological studies do not establish that biology is the primary indicator of sexual orientation. LeVay, *supra,* at 1036 ("The discovery that a nucleus differs in size between heterosexual and homosexual men illustrates that sexual orientation in humans is amenable to study at the biological level, and this discovery opens the door to studies of neurotransmitters or receptors that might be involved in regulating this aspect of personality. Further interpretation of the results of this study must be considered speculative. In particular, the results do not allow one to decide if the size of INAH 3 in an individual is the cause or the consequence of that individual's sexual orientation, or if the size of INAH 3 and sexual orientation co-vary under the influence of some third, unidentified variable."). We by no means are able to form any sort of merits-driven conclusion based on the forgoing studies. We note only that there does not appear to be a consensus yet among "experts" as to the origin of an individual's sexual orientation.

Based on our research, no studies currently available to the public have been subjected to rigorous analysis under the *Frye-Reed* standard in order to determine the scientific reliability of the methodology, principles, and resultant conclusions of the foregoing studies for the purposes of evidentiary admissibility. Nor were we able to locate any analyses of the studies under the *Daubert/Kumho Tire/Joiner* standard for admissibility applied in the federal courts and certain of our sister state court systems.

In the absence of some generally accepted scientific conclusion identifying homosexuality as an immutable characteristic, and in light of the other indicia used by this Court and the Supreme Court in defining a suspect class, we decline on the record in the present case to recognize sexual orientation as an immutable trait and therefore a suspect or quasi-suspect classification....

[The opinion of Judge Raker, concurring in part and dissenting in part, and the dissenting opinions of Judges Battaglia and Bell, are omitted.]

Lawrence v. Texas
539 U.S. 558 (2003)

[At issue in this case is a challenge to the constitutionality of a Texas statute that criminalizes same-sex, but not opposite-sex, sodomy. The majority opinion—which struck the statute down on substantive due process grounds—as well as Justice O'Connor's full concurrence and the dissents of Justices Scalia and Thomas, can be found in Chapters 3 and 4. Excerpted below is a portion of Justice O'Connor's concurring opinion, in which she addresses the question whether the statute discriminates on the basis of sexual orientation.]

Justice O'CONNOR, concurring in the judgment.

. . . .

Texas argues ... that the sodomy law does not discriminate against homosexual persons. Instead, the State maintains that the law discriminates only against homosexual conduct. While it is true that the law applies only to conduct, the conduct targeted by this law is conduct that is closely correlated with being homosexual. Under such circumstances, Texas' sodomy law is targeted at more than conduct. It is instead directed toward gay persons as a class. "After all, there can hardly be more palpable discrimination against a class than making the conduct that defines the class criminal." ....

Indeed, Texas law confirms that the sodomy statute is directed toward homosexuals as a class. In Texas, calling a person a homosexual is slander *per se* because the word "homosexual" "impute[s] the commission of a crime." The State has admitted that because of the sodomy law, *being* homosexual carries the presumption of being a criminal. Texas' sodomy law therefore results in discrimination against homosexuals as a class in an array of areas outside the criminal law....

Hernandez v. Robles
855 N.E.2d 1 (N.Y. 2006)

[A group of same-sex couples who applied for and were denied marriage licenses filed a suit contending that the marriage statutes do not limit marriage to opposite-sex couples, and that if they are so construed, they violate the equal protection and due process guarantees of the New York constitution. After concluding that same-sex couples are not permitted to marry under the state's marriage statutes, one of the judges on the court addresses the question whether the statute discriminates on the basis of sexual orientation.]

GRAFFEO, J. (concurring).

Nor does the statutory scheme create a classification based on sexual orientation. In this respect, the Domestic Relations Law is facially neutral: individuals who seek marriage licenses are not queried concerning their sexual orientation and are not precluded from marrying if they are not heterosexual. Regardless of sexual orientation, any person can marry a person of the opposite sex. Certainly, the marriage laws create a classification that distinguishes between opposite-sex and same-sex couples and this has a disparate impact on gays and lesbians. However, a claim that a facially-neutral statute enacted without an invidious discriminatory intent has a disparate impact on a class (even a suspect class, such as one defined by race) is insufficient to establish an equal protection violation (*see Washington v. Davis*, 426 U.S. 229, 240 [1976]). Plaintiffs concede that the Domestic Relations Law was not enacted with an invidiously discriminatory intent — the Legislature did not craft the marriage laws for the purpose of disadvantaging gays and lesbians (*cf. Romer v. Evans*, 517 U.S. 620 [1996]). Hence, there is no basis to address plaintiffs' argument that classifications based on sexual orientation should be subjected to intermediate scrutiny....

[The majority opinion of Judge Smith and the dissenting opinion of Chief Judge Kaye are omitted.]

In re Marriage Cases
183 P.3d 384 (Cal. 2008)

[At issue in this case is a challenge to a California law prohibiting same-sex marriage. The opinion is examined in greater detail in Chapter 5. Excerpted below is a portion of the majority opinion, in which the court addresses the question whether the ban constitutes discrimination on the basis of sexual orientation.]

GEORGE, C.J.

In arguing that the marriage statutes do not discriminate on the basis of sexual orientation, defendants rely upon the circumstance that these statutes, on their face, do not refer explicitly to sexual orientation and do not prohibit gay individuals from marrying a person of the opposite sex. Defendants contend that under these circumstances, the marriage statutes should not be viewed as directly classifying or discriminating on the basis of sexual orientation but at most should be viewed as having a "disparate impact" on gay persons.

In our view, the statutory provisions restricting marriage to a man and a woman cannot be understood as having merely a disparate impact on gay persons, but instead properly must be viewed as directly classifying and prescribing distinct treatment on the basis of sexual orientation. By limiting marriage to opposite-sex couples, the marriage statutes, realistically viewed, operate clearly and directly to impose different treatment on gay individuals because of their sexual orientation. By definition, gay individuals are persons who are sexually attracted to persons of the same sex and thus, if inclined to enter into a marriage relationship, would choose to marry a person of their own sex or gender.[59] A

---

59. As explained in the amicus curiae brief filed by a number of leading mental health organizations, including the American Psychological Association and the American Psychiatric Association: "Sexual orientation is commonly discussed as a characteristic of the *individual*, like biological sex, gender identity, or age. This perspective is incomplete because sexual orientation is always defined in relational terms and necessarily involves relationships with other individuals. Sexual acts and romantic attractions are categorized as homosexual or heterosexual according to the biological sex of the individuals involved in them, relative to each other. Indeed, it is by acting — or desiring to act — with another person that individuals express their heterosexuality, homosexuality, or bisexuality.... Thus, sexual orientation is integrally linked to the intimate personal relationships that human beings form with others to meet their deeply felt needs for love, attachment, and intimacy. In addition to sexual behavior, these bonds encompass nonsexual physical affection between partners, shared goals and values, mutual support, and ongoing commitment. [¶] Consequently, sexual orientation is not merely a personal characteristic that can be defined in isolation. Rather, one's sexual orientation defines the

statute that limits marriage to a union of persons of opposite sexes, thereby placing marriage outside the reach of couples of the same sex, unquestionably imposes different treatment on the basis of sexual orientation. In our view, it is sophistic to suggest that this conclusion is avoidable by reason of the circumstance that the marriage statutes permit a gay man or a lesbian to marry someone of the opposite sex, because making such a choice would require the negation of the person's sexual orientation. Just as a statute that restricted marriage only to couples of the same sex would discriminate against heterosexual persons on the basis of their heterosexual orientation, the current California statutes realistically must be viewed as discriminating against gay persons on the basis of their homosexual orientation....

[The concurring opinion of Justice Kennard, and the opinions of Justices Baxter and Corrigan, concurring in part and dissenting in part, are omitted.]

Notes and Questions

1. The New Hampshire statute referenced in *Cox* not only prohibited "homosexuals" from adopting children, but also prohibited them from serving as foster parents and operating day care centers. *See Opinion of the Justices*, 530 A.2d 21, 23 (N.H. 1987).

2. Assuming that whether one is deemed homosexual or not turns on his *behavior*, what sorts of behavior count? Must the person engage in oral or anal intercourse, or do such things as kissing or holding hands count? *Compare Opinion of the Justices*, 530 A.2d 21, 24 (N.H. 1987) (citing the statutory language, which defined the term "homosexual" as "any person who performs or submits to any sexual act involving the sex organs of one person and the mouth or anus of another person of the same gender"), *with* 10 U.S.C. § 654(f)(3) (defining "homosexual act" as "(A) any bodily contact, actively undertaken or passively permitted, between members of the same sex for the purpose of satisfying sexual desires; and (B) any bodily contact which a reasonable person would understand to demonstrate a propensity or intent to engage in an act described in subparagraph (A)."). *See also Watkins v. U.S. Army*, 875 F.2d 699, 714 (9th Cir. 1989) (Norris, J., concurring in the judgment) (noting that hand-holding and kissing constitute "homosexual acts" under the military's policy).

3. If one's sexual orientation is defined solely by reference to one's behavior, is it relevant that the behavior even be knowing and voluntary? *See Opinion of the Justices*, 530 A.2d 21, 24 (N.H. 1987) ("This very narrow definition of homosexual behavior contains no requirement that the acts or submission thereto be uncoerced.... Therefore, we assume for purposes of our analysis ... that one who performs or submits to the acts described in the definition does so both voluntarily and knowingly; by doing so, we are able to avoid the patently absurd result of the inclusion of a victim of homosexual rape within the scope of the definition and his or her consequent preclusion from adopting, from becoming a foster parent, and from operating a child care agency."). What about those who voluntarily engage in same-sex sexual activity only for situational reasons, say, because they are confined to a single-sex environment such as a prison for an extended period of time? *See* Laumann et al., The Social Organization of Sexuality 291 (1994).

4. In his famous studies on human sexuality, Alfred Kinsey developed a scale for categorizing an individual's sexuality, with 0 representing exclusive heterosexuality, 6 rep-

---

universe of persons with whom one is likely to find the satisfying and fulfilling relationships that, for many individuals, comprise an essential component of personal identity."

resenting exclusive homosexuality, and 1 through 5 representing various mixed degrees of heterosexuality and homosexuality. *See generally* Alfred Kinsey et al., Sexual Behavior in the Human Male (1948); Alfred Kinsey et al., Sexual Behavior in the Human Female (1953). How do the statutes described in this section deal with those represented by the ratings 1 through 5 on the Kinsey scale?

5. Should the *role* one plays when engaging in sexual activity have a bearing on whether one is deemed a "homosexual"? *Compare* 10 U.S.C. §654(f)(3)(a) (defining "homosexual act" as "any bodily contact, actively undertaken or passively permitted, between members of the same sex for the purpose of satisfying sexual desires"), *with* Stephen O. Murray, *Homosexual Characterization in Cross-Cultural Perspective*, in Stephen O. Murray, Latin American Male Homosexualities 11 (1995) (noting that, in Latin American culture, men who take on the "active" role in male-male sexual activity are not considered to be homosexual).

6. The *Cox* and *Meinhold* cases appear to suggest that defining "homosexuality" in a particular way provides a fairer basis for subjecting the group so defined to differential treatment. What is it about the alternative definitions that make them seem less fair by comparison?

7. As indicated in *Conaway*, the U.S. Supreme Court has identified a variety of types of discrimination that are "suspect" (e.g., race) or "quasi-suspect" (e.g., sex) and has held that classifications on such bases are subject to heightened judicial scrutiny. Chapter 4 takes a closer look at the types of classifications that trigger heightened scrutiny as well as the question whether sexual orientation discrimination merits such heightened scrutiny.

8. Which is more persuasive, the conduct-status divide as articulated in cases such as *Cox*, *Meinhold*, and *Hernandez* or the conduct-status convergence as articulated in cases such as *In re Marriage Cases* and in Justice O'Connor's concurring opinion in *Lawrence v. Texas*? In assessing the two approaches, of what relevance is it that, at the time *Cox* and *Meinhold* were decided, the U.S. Supreme Court's decision in *Bowers v. Hardwick*, 478 U.S. 186 (1986) — upholding the constitutionality of sodomy laws as applied to private, consensual activity between two persons of the same sex — was still good law?

9. The *Hernandez* and *In re Marriage Cases* opinions identify and distinguish three categories of laws: (a) those that, on their face, discriminate on the basis of sexual orientation; (b) those that, on their face, do not discriminate on the basis of sexual orientation, but that were designed with the intent of so discriminating; and (c) those that, on their face, do not discriminate on the basis of sexual orientation and that were not designed with the intent of so discriminating. As will be seen in Chapter 4, which category a law falls into is a threshold inquiry for determining whether a party has stated a valid equal protection claim.

10. Once one selects a definition of "homosexuality," one needs to employ evidence to prove or disprove that an individual is or is not "homosexual." Do some definitions of homosexuality require more or less invasive forms of evidence? Are some definitions more or less easy to prove? To what extent do lawmakers and courts appear to take those concerns into account in deciding how to define the term?

11. Note that the *Meinhold* decision was decided under an earlier version of the military's policy regarding gays in the military. The policy was revised in 1993 and codified at 10 U.S.C. §654, which is excerpted immediately following the *Meinhold* decision (in 2011, the entire policy was repealed). To what extent does the 1993 revision clear up the ambiguities identified by the *Meinhold* court?

12. Under 10 U.S.C. §654(b)(2), a servicemember is subject to discharge for making a statement about his sexual orientation. To what extent might such a law raise freedom of speech concerns under the First Amendment? The First Amendment aspects of the statute are considered in Chapter 6.

13. Note 57 in *Conaway* contrasts scientific studies suggesting a genetic or biological explanation for human sexual orientation with those suggesting that cultural and environmental factors may play a significant role in shaping sexual orientation. Suppose that scientists were eventually to conclude that genetic and biological factors play *no role* in determining human sexual orientation, and that cultural and environmental factors fully determine sexual orientation. How would such a conclusion impact the question whether sexual orientation is "immutable"? How, if at all, would it matter that one's sexual orientation—once determined by cultural and environmental factors—remains fixed, or at least is extremely resistant to change? If such factors fully determined one's sexual orientation while one was still a child?

14. In her *Lawrence* concurrence, Justice O'Connor states that the conduct targeted by the Texas statute is "conduct that is closely correlated with being homosexual," and that "there can hardly be more palpable discrimination against a class than making the conduct that defines the class criminal." Justice O'Connor goes on (as will be seen in Chapter 4) to hold that Texas's sodomy statute violates the Equal Protection Clause. Of course, all criminal laws divide people into classes and make the conduct that defines the class criminal, do they not? Thus, for example, laws that criminalize theft target conduct that is closely correlated with being a thief, and make the conduct that defines the class (thieves) criminal. Moreover, laws that criminalize polygamy target conduct that is closely correlated with being a polygamist, and make the conduct that defines the class (polygamists) criminal. Accordingly, unless all criminal statutes are to be deemed unconstitutional, there must be some limiting principle that differentiates those classifications that the Equal Protection Clause tolerates and those that it does not. What limiting principle—if any—differentiates thieves and polygamists on the one hand from homosexuals on the other?

B. The Meaning of "Sex" or "Gender"

Problem 1-B: "One Man, One Woman"

Assume that you work at a county clerk's office that is responsible for issuing marriage licenses. State law provides in pertinent part as follows: "Marriage is limited to the union of one man and one woman. Marriage between two persons of the same sex is prohibited."

The county clerk has charged you with drafting guidelines for determining when an applicant is a "man" and when an applicant is a "woman."

Draft a memo for the clerk explaining the various ways in which the terms can be defined, and the consequences of each way of so defining them.

Littleton v. Prange
9 S.W.3d 223 (Tex. App. 1999)

OPINION

Opinion by: PHIL HARDBERGER, Chief Justice.

This case involves the most basic of questions. When is a man a man, and when is a woman a woman? Every schoolchild, even of tender years, is confident he or she can tell the difference, especially if the person is wearing no clothes. These are observations that each of us makes early in life and, in most cases, continue to have more than a passing interest in for the rest of our lives. It is one of the more pleasant mysteries.

The deeper philosophical (and now legal) question is: can a physician change the gender of a person with a scalpel, drugs and counseling, or is a person's gender immutably fixed by our Creator at birth? The answer to that question has definite legal implications that present themselves in this case involving a person named Christie Lee Littleton.

FACTUAL BACKGROUND

A complete stipulation of the facts was made by the parties in this case.

Christie is a transsexual. She was born in San Antonio in 1952, a physically healthy male, and named after her father, Lee Cavazos. At birth, she was named Lee Cavazos, Jr. (Throughout this opinion Christie will be referred to as "She." This is for grammatical simplicity's sake, and out of respect for the litigant, who wishes to be called "Christie," and referred to as "she." It has no legal implications.)

At birth, Christie had the normal male genitalia: penis, scrotum and testicles. Problems with her sexual identity developed early though. Christie testified that she considered herself female from the time she was three or four years old, the contrary physical evidence notwithstanding. Her distressed parents took her to a physician, who prescribed male hormones. These were taken, but were ineffective. Christie sought successfully to be excused from sports and physical education because of her embarrassment over changing clothes in front of the other boys.

By the time she was 17 years old, Christie was searching for a physician who would perform sex reassignment surgery. At 23, she enrolled in a program at the University of Texas Health Science Center that would lead to a sex reassignment operation. For four years Christie underwent psychological and psychiatric treatment by a number of physicians, some of whom testified in this case.

On August 31, 1977, Christie's name was legally changed to Christie Lee Cavazos. Under doctor's orders, Christie also began receiving various treatments and female hormones. Between November of 1979 and February of 1980, Christie underwent three surgical procedures, which culminated in a complete sex reassignment. Christie's penis, scrotum and testicles were surgically removed, and a vagina and labia were constructed. Christie additionally underwent breast construction surgery.

Dr. Donald Greer, a board certified plastic surgeon, served as a member of the gender dysphoria team at UTHSC in San Antonio, Texas during the time in question. Dr. Paul Mohl, a board certified psychiatrist, also served as a member of the same gender dysphoria team. Both participated in the evaluation and treatment of Christie. The gender dysphoria team was a mutli-disciplinary team that met regularly to interview and care for transsexual patients.

The parties stipulated that Dr. Greer and Dr. Mohl would testify that their background, training, education and experience is consistent with that reflected in their curriculum vitaes, which were attached to their respective affidavits in Christie's response to the motions for summary judgment. In addition, Dr. Greer and Dr. Mohl would testify that the definition of a transsexual is someone whose physical anatomy does not correspond to their sense of being or their sense of gender, and that medical science has not been able to identify the exact cause of this condition, but it is in medical probability a combination of neuro-biological, genetic and neonatal environmental factors. Dr. Greer and Dr. Mohl would further testify that in arriving at a diagnosis of transsexualism in Christie, the program at UTHSC was guided by the guidelines established by the Johns Hopkins Group and that, based on these guidelines, Christie was diagnosed psychologically and psychiatrically as a genuine male to female transsexual. Dr. Greer and Dr. Mohl also would testify that true male to female transsexuals are, in their opinion, psychologically and psychiatrically female before and after the sex reassignment surgery, and that Christie is a true male to female transsexual.

On or about November 5, 1979, Dr. Greer served as a principal member of the surgical team that performed the sex reassignment surgery on Christie. In Dr. Greer's opinion, the anatomical and genital features of Christie, following that surgery, are such that she has the capacity to function sexually as a female. Both Dr. Greer and Dr. Mohl would testify that, in their opinions, following the successful completion of Christie's participation in UTHSC's gender dysphoria program, Christie is medically a woman.

Christie married a man by the name of Jonathon Mark Littleton in Kentucky in 1989, and she lived with him until his death in 1996. Christie filed a medical malpractice suit under the Texas Wrongful Death and Survival Statute in her capacity as Jonathon's surviving spouse. The sued doctor, appellee here, filed a motion for summary judgment. The motion challenged Christie's status as a proper wrongful death beneficiary, asserting that Christie is a man and cannot be the surviving spouse of another man.

The trial court agreed and granted the summary judgment. The summary judgment notes that the trial court considered the summary judgment evidence, the stipulation, and the argument of counsel. In addition to the stipulation, Christie's affidavit was attached to her response to the motion for summary judgment. In her affidavit, Christie states that Jonathon was fully aware of her background and the fact that she had undergone sex reassignment surgery.

THE LEGAL ISSUE

Can there be a valid marriage between a man and a person born as a man, but surgically altered to have the physical characteristics of a woman?

OVERVIEW OF ISSUE

This is a case of first impression in Texas. The underlying statutory law is simple enough. Texas (and Kentucky, for that matter), like most other states, does not permit marriages between persons of the same sex. In order to have standing to sue under the wrongful death and survival statues, Christie must be Jonathon's surviving spouse. The defendant's summary judgment burden was to prove she is not the surviving spouse. Referring to the statutory law, though, does not resolve the issue. This court, as did the trial court below, must answer this question: Is Christie a man or a woman? There is no dispute that Christie and Jonathon went through a ceremonial marriage ritual. If Christie is a woman, she may bring this action. If Christie is a man, she may not.

Christie is medically termed a transsexual, a term not often heard on the streets of Texas, nor in its courtrooms. If we look at other states or even other countries to see how they treat marriages of transsexuals, we get little help. Only a handful of other states, or foreign countries, have even considered the case of the transsexual. The opposition to same-sex marriages, on the other hand, is very wide spread. Only one state has ever ruled in favor of same-sex marriage: Hawaii, in the case of *Baehr v. Lewin,* 852 P.2d 44 (1993). All other cases soundly reject the concept of same-sex marriages. Congress has even passed the Defense of Marriage Act (DOMA), just in case a state decides to recognize same-sex marriages.

DOMA defines marriage for federal purposes as a "legal union between one man and one woman," and provides that no state "shall be required to give effect to any public act, record, or judicial proceeding of any other state respecting a relationship between persons of the same sex that is treated as a marriage under the laws of such other State … or a right or claim arising from such relationship." So even if one state were to recognize same-sex marriages it would not need to be recognized in any other state, and probably would not be. Marriage is tightly defined in the United States: "a legal union between one man and one woman." *See id.* § 3(a).

Public antipathy toward same-sex marriages notwithstanding, the question remains: is a transsexual still the same sex after a sex-reassignment operation as before the operation? A transsexual, such as Christie, does not consider herself a homosexual because she does not consider herself a man. Her self-identity, from childhood, has been as a woman. Since her various operations, she does not have the outward physical characteristics of a man either. Through the intervention of surgery and drugs, Christie appears to be a woman. In her mind, she has corrected her physical features to line up with her true gender.

"Although transgenderism is often conflated with homosexuality, the characteristic, which defines transgenderism, is not sexual orientation, but sexual identity. Transgenderism describes people who experience a separation between their gender and their biological/anatomical sex."

Nor should a transsexual be confused with a transvestite, who is simply a man who attains some sexual satisfaction from wearing women's clothes. Christie does not consider herself a man wearing women's clothes; she considers herself a woman wearing women's clothes. She has been surgically and chemically altered to be a woman. She has officially changed her name and her birth certificate to reflect her new status. But the question remains whether the law will take note of these changes and treat her as if she had been born a female. To answer this question, we consider the law of those jurisdictions who have previously decided it.

CASE LAW

The English case of *Corbett v. Corbett*, 2 All E.R. 33 (P.1970), appears to be the first case to consider the issue, and is routinely cited in later cases, including those cases from the United States. April Ashley, like Christie Littleton, was born a male, and like Christie, had undergone a sex-reassignment operation. April later married Arthur Corbett. Arthur subsequently asked for a nullification of the marriage based upon the fact that April was a man, and the marriage had never been consummated. April resisted the nullification of her marriage, asserting that the reason the marriage had not been consummated was the fault of her husband, not her. She said she was ready, willing, and able to consummate the marriage.

Arthur testified that he was "mesmerised" by April upon meeting her, and he dated her for three years before their marriage. He said that she "looked like a woman, dressed like a woman and acted like a woman." Arthur and April eventually married, but they were never successful in having sexual relations. Several doctors testified in the case, as they did in the current case.

Based upon the doctors' testimony, the court came up with four criteria for assessing the sexual identity of an individual. These are:

(1) Chromosomal factors;

(2) Gonadal factors (i.e., presence or absence of testes or ovaries);

(3) Genital factors (including internal sex organs); and

(4) Psychological factors.

Chromosomes are the structures on which the genes are carried which, in turn, are the mechanism by which hereditary characteristics are transmitted from parents to off-spring. An individual normally has 23 pairs of chromosomes in his or her body cells; one of each pair being derived from each parent. One pair of chromosomes is known to determine an individual's sex. The English court stated that "[T]he biological sexual constitution of an individual is fixed at birth (at the latest), and cannot be changed, either by the natural development of organs of the opposite sex, or by medical or surgical means. The respondent's operation, therefore, cannot affect her true sex." The court then reasoned that since marriage is essentially a relationship between man and woman, the validity of the marriage depends on whether April is, or is not, a woman. The court held that the criteria for answering this question must be biological and, having so held, found that April, a transsexual, "is not a woman for the purposes of marriage but is a biological male and has been so since birth," and, therefore, the marriage between Arthur and April was void. The court specifically rejected the contention that individuals could "assign" their own sex by their own volition, or by means of an operation. In short, once a man, always a man.

The year after *Corbett* was decided in England, a case involving the validity of a marriage in which one of the partners was transsexual appeared in a United States court. This was the case of *Anonymous v. Anonymous,* 67 Misc.2d 982 (N.Y.Sup.Ct.1971).

This New York case had a connection with Texas. The marriage ceremony of the transsexual occurred in Belton, while the plaintiff was stationed at Fort Hood. The purpose of the suit was to declare that no marriage could legally have taken place. The court pointed out that this was not an annulment of a marriage because a marriage contract must be between a man and a woman. If the ceremony itself was a nullity, there would be no marriage to annul, but the court would simply declare that no marriage could legally have taken place. The court had no difficulty in doing so, holding: "The law makes no provision for a 'marriage' between persons of the same sex. Marriage is and always has been a contract between a man and a woman."

Factually, the New York case was less complicated than *Corbett,* and the instant case, because there had been no sexual change operation, and the "wife" still had normal male organs. The plaintiff made this unpleasant discovery on his wedding night. The husband in *Anonymous* was unaware that he was marrying a transsexual. In both *Corbett* and the instant case, the husband was fully aware of the true state of affairs, and accepted it. In fact, in the instant case, Christie and her husband were married for seven years, and, according to the testimony, had normal sexual relations. This is a much longer period of time than any of the other reported cases.

The next reported transsexual case came from New Jersey. This is the only United States case to uphold the validity of a transsexual marriage. In *M.T. v. J.T.,* 355 A.2d 204, 205 (1976), a transsexual wife brought an action for support and maintenance growing out of her marriage. The husband interposed a defense that his wife was male, and that their marriage was void (and therefore he owed nothing). M.T., the wife, testified she was born a male, but she always considered herself a female. M.T. dated men all her life. After M.T. met her husband-to-be, J.T., they decided that M.T. would have an operation so she could "be physically a woman."

In 1971, M.T. had an operation where her male organs were removed and a vagina was constructed. J.T. paid for the operation, and the couple were married the next year. M.T. and J.T. lived as husband and wife and had sexual intercourse. J.T. supported M.T.

for over two years; however, in 1974, J.T. left the home, and his support of M.T. ceased. The lawsuit for maintenance and support followed.

The doctor who had performed the sex-reassignment operation testified. He described a transsexual as a person who has "a great discrepancy between the physical genital anatomy and the person's sense of self-identity as a male or as a female." The doctor defined gender identity as "a sense, a total sense of self as being masculine or female; it pervades one's entire concept of one's place in life, of one's place in society and in point of fact the actual facts of the anatomy are really secondary." The doctor said that after the operation his patient had no uterus or cervix, but her vagina had a "good cosmetic appearance" and was "the same as a normal female vagina after a hysterectomy."

The trial court, in ruling for M.T. by finding the marriage valid, stated:

> It is the opinion of the court that if the psychological choice of a person is medically sound, not a mere whim, and irreversible sex reassignment surgery has been performed, society has no right to prohibit the transsexual from leading a normal life. Are we to look upon this person as an exhibit in a circus side show? What harm has said person done to society? The entire area of transsexualism is repugnant to the nature of many persons within our society. However, this should not govern the legal acceptance of a fact.

The appellate court affirmed, holding:

> If such sex reassignment surgery is successful and the postoperative transsexual is, by virtue of medical treatment, thereby possessed of the full capacity to function sexually as male or female, as the case may be, we perceive no legal barrier, cognizable social taboo, or reason grounded in public policy to prevent the persons' identification at least for purposes of marriage to the sex finally indicated.

Ohio is the last state that has considered this issue. *See In re Ladrach,* 513 N.E.2d 828 (Ohio Probate Ct.1987). *Ladrach* was a declaratory judgment action brought to determine whether a male who became a post-operative female was permitted to marry a male. The court decided she may not.

Like Christie, Elaine Ladrach started life as a male. Eventually, she had the transsexual operation which removed the penis, scrotum and testes and constructed a vagina. The doctor who performed the operation testified that Elaine now had a "normal female external genitalia." He admitted, however, that it would be "highly unlikely" that a chromosomal test would show Elaine to be a female. The court cited a New York Academy of Medicine study of transsexuals that concluded: " … male to female transsexuals are still chromosomally males while ostensibly females." The court stated that a person's sex is determined at birth by an anatomical examination by the birth attendant, which was done at Elaine's birth. No allegation had been made that Elaine's birth attendant was in error. The court reasoned that the determination of a person's sex and marital status are legal issues, and, as such, the court must look to the statutes to determine whether the marriage was permissible. The court concluded:

> This court is charged with the responsibility of interpreting the statutes of this state and judicial interpretations of these statutes. Since the case at bar is apparently one of first impression in Ohio, it is this court's opinion that the legislature should change the statutes, if it is to be the public policy of the state of Ohio to issue marriage licenses to post-operative transsexuals.

The court denied the marriage license application.

OTHER AUTHORITIES

In an unreported case, a court in New Zealand was convinced that a fully transitioned transsexual should be permitted to marry as a member of his new sex because the alternative would be more disturbing. *See* Mary Coombs, *Sexual Dis-Orientation: Transgendered People and Same-Sex Marriage,* 8 UCLA WOMEN's L.J. 219, 250 & n. 137 (1998) (citing *M. v. M.* (unreported) 30 May 1991, S.Ct. of NZ). That is, if a post-operative transsexual female was deemed a male, she could marry a woman, in what would to all outward appearances be a same-sex marriage. The question would then become whether courts should approve seemingly heterosexual marriages between a post-operative transsexual female and a genetic male, rather than an apparent same-sex marriage between a post-operative transsexual female and a genetic female....

DISCUSSION

....

It would be intellectually possible for this court to write a protocol for when transsexuals would be recognized as having successfully changed their sex. Littleton has suggested we do so, perhaps using the surgical removal of the male genitalia as the test. As was pointed out by Littleton's counsel, "amputation is a pretty important step." Indeed it is. But this court has no authority to fashion a new law on transsexuals, or anything else. We cannot make law when no law exists: we can only interpret the written word of our sister branch of government, the legislature. Our responsibility in this case is to determine whether, in the absence of legislatively-established guidelines, a jury can be called upon to decide the legality of such marriages. We hold they cannot. In the absence of any guidelines, it would be improper to launch a jury forth on these untested and unknown waters.

There are no significant facts that need to be decided. The parties have supplied them for us. We find the case, at this stage, presents a pure question of law and must be decided by this court.

Based on the facts of this case, and the law and studies of previous cases, we conclude:

(1) Medical science recognizes that there are individuals whose sexual self-identity is in conflict with their biological and anatomical sex. Such people are termed transsexuals.

(2) A transsexual is not a homosexual in the traditional sense of the word, in that transsexuals believe and feel they are members of the opposite sex. Nor is a transsexual a transvestite. Transsexuals do not believe they are dressing in the opposite sex's clothes. They believe they are dressing in their own sex's clothes.

(3) Christie Littleton is a transsexual.

(4) Through surgery and hormones, a transsexual male can be made to look like a woman, including female genitalia and breasts. Transsexual medical treatment, however, does not create the internal sexual organs of a wom[a]n (except for the vaginal canal). There is no womb, cervix or ovaries in the post-operative transsexual female.

(5) The male chromosomes do not change with either hormonal treatment or sex reassignment surgery. Biologically a post-operative female transsexual is still a male.

(6) The evidence fully supports that Christie Littleton, born male, wants and believes herself to be a woman. She has made every conceivable effort to make herself a female, including a surgery that would make most males pale and perspire to contemplate.

(7) Some physicians would consider Christie a female; other physicians would consider her still a male. Her female anatomy, however, is all man-made. The body that Christie inhabits is a male body in all aspects other than what the physicians have supplied.

We recognize that there are many fine metaphysical arguments lurking about here involving desire and being, the essence of life and the power of mind over physics. But courts are wise not to wander too far into the misty fields of sociological philosophy. Matters of the heart do not always fit neatly within the narrowly defined perimeters of statutes, or even existing social mores. Such matters though are beyond this court's consideration. Our mandate is, as the court recognized in *Ladrach*, to interpret the statutes of the state and prior judicial decisions. This mandate is deceptively simplistic in this case: Texas statutes do not allow same-sex marriages, and prior judicial decisions are few.

Christie was created and born a male. Her original birth certificate, an official document of Texas, clearly so states. During the pendency of this suit, Christie amended the original birth certificate to change the sex and name. Under section 191.028 of the Texas Health and Safety Code she was entitled to seek such an amendment if the record was "incomplete or proved by satisfactory evidence to be inaccurate." Tex. Health & Safety Code Ann. § 191.028 (Vernon 1992). The trial court that granted the petition to amend the birth certificate necessarily construed the term "inaccurate" to relate to the present, and having been presented with the uncontroverted affidavit of an expert stating that Christie is a female, the trial court deemed this satisfactory to prove an inaccuracy. However, the trial court's role in considering the petition was a ministerial one. It involved no fact-finding or consideration of the deeper public policy concerns presented. No one claims the information contained in Christie's original birth certificate was based on fraud or error. We believe the legislature intended the term "inaccurate" in section 191.028 to mean inaccurate as of the time the certificate was recorded; that is, at the time of birth. At the time of birth, Christie was a male, both anatomically and genetically. The facts contained in the original birth certificate were true and accurate, and the words contained in the amended certificate are not binding on this court.

There are some things we cannot will into being. They just are.

CONCLUSION

We hold, as a matter of law, that Christie Littleton is a male. As a male, Christie cannot be married to another male. Her marriage to Jonathon was invalid, and she cannot bring a cause of action as his surviving spouse.

We affirm the summary judgment granted by the trial court.

KAREN ANGELINI, Justice, concurring.

I concur in the judgment. Given the complete absence of any legislative guidelines for determining whether Texas law will recognize a marriage between a male-to-female transsexual and a male, this court is charged with making that determination. This case involves no disputed fact issues for a jury to decide, but presents this court with pure issues of law and public policy.

In his opinion, Chief Justice Hardberger has concluded, based on an analysis of other cases considering this issue, that Texas law will not recognize Christie Lee Littleton's marriage to John Mark Littleton. In doing so, Chief Justice Hardberger notes his agreement with the *Ladrach* decision, which indicates that this is a matter best left to the legislature. He further notes, in accordance with the *Corbett* case, that because we lack statutory guidance at this time, we must instead be guided by biological factors such as chromosomes, gonads, and genitalia at birth. According to Chief Justice Hardberger, such biological considerations are preferable to psychological factors as tools for making the decision we must make. In this case, I must agree.

I note, however, that "real difficulties ... will occur if these three criteria [chromosomal, gonadal and genital tests] are not congruent." *Corbett v. Corbett,* 2 All E.R. 33, 48 (P.1970). We must recognize the fact that, even when biological factors are considered, there are those individuals whose sex may be ambiguous. *See* Julie A. Greenberg, *Defining Male and Female: Intersexuality and the Collision Between Law and Biology,* 41 Ariz. L.Rev. 265 (1999). Having recognized this fact, I express no opinion as to how the law would view such individuals with regard to marriage. We are, however, not presented with such a case at this time.

The stipulated evidence in the case that is before us establishes that Christie Lee Littleton was born Lee Edward Cavazos, Jr., a male. Her doctors described her as a true transsexual, which is "someone whose physical anatomy does not correspond to their sense of being or their sense of gender...." Thus, in the case of Christie Lee Littleton, it appears that all biological and physical factors were congruent and were consistent with those of a typical male at birth. The only pre-operative distinction between Christie Lee Littleton and a typical male was her psychological sense of being a female. Under these facts, I agree that Texas law will not recognize her marriage to a male.

[The dissenting opinion of Justice López is omitted.]

In re Heilig
816 A.2d 68 (Md. 2003)

WILNER, Judge.

Petitioner was born in Pennsylvania in 1948. His birth certificate, issued by the Department of Health of that State, records his name as Robert Wright Heilig and his sex as male.

In March, 2001, Mr. Heilig filed a petition in the Circuit Court for Montgomery County, in which he alleged that he was then a Maryland resident and that he was "transitioning from male to female." Invoking the equitable jurisdiction of the court, he asked for an order that would change his name to Janet Heilig Wright and change his "sexual identity" designation from male to female. He noted in his petition the existence of Maryland Code, § 4-214(b)(5) of the Health-General Article, which directs the Secretary of Health and Mental Hygiene, upon receipt of a court order indicating that the sex of an individual born in Maryland "has been changed by surgical procedure," to amend that person's Maryland birth certificate accordingly, but he did not ask the court to order the alteration or amendment of his Pennsylvania birth certificate or, indeed, of any other document.

No answer or opposition of any kind was filed to the petition. Nonetheless, although ultimately entering an order that changed petitioner's name, the court refused to enter an order changing his sexual identity, concluding that (1) gender had physical manifestations that were not subject to modification, and (2) there was no authority for the court to enter such an order. The effect of the order was to give petitioner a woman's name but to retain his official gender as male. Petitioner did not contest the change in name but appealed the part of the judgment denying his request for recognition of his change in gender.

The Court of Special Appeals affirmed that decision....

We granted *certiorari* to consider whether a Maryland Circuit Court has jurisdiction to grant the kind of relief sought by petitioner, and, if so, whether, on the record in this case, petitioner has established a right to that relief....

BACKGROUND

Perhaps because there was no opposition to the petition, the factual evidence in support of petitioner's request for a legal determination of gender change was rather skimpy. Attached to the petition was a copy of petitioner's birth certificate and two letters, each addressed "To Whom It May Concern." The first, from Dr. Michael Dempsey, an endocrinologist, stated that petitioner had been under his care for eighteen months as a "transgendered person," that her treatment consisted of female hormones and anti-androgens "designed to maintain her body chemistry and bring about anatomical changes within typical female norms," that the hormonal therapy had resulted in "hormonal castration," and that, in Dr. Dempsey's medical opinion, the gender designation on petitioner's driver's license and other documents should be changed to female to "accurately reflect both her appearance and the hormonal changes of her body."[1] The second letter, from a licensed social worker named Ellen Warren, stated that petitioner "is in psychotherapeutic treatment ... as a transsexual woman," that it was Ms. Warren's professional opinion that petitioner's name and gender should be legally changed to reflect "her true gender identity, which is female," and that such change was "in accordance with the Standards of Care of the Harry Benjamin International Gender Dysphoria Association."

....

The hearing conducted by the Circuit Court dealt entirely with the issue of jurisdiction. No inquiry was made as to whether petitioner had undergone any sex reassignment surgery, whether and to what extent the hormonal therapy noted by Dr. Dempsey was permanent and irreversible, or what, if any, criteria had been generally accepted in the medical or legal community for determining when, if ever, a complete, permanent, and irreversible gender change has occurred....

DISCUSSION

Transsexualism: Medical Aspects

One of the dominant themes of transsexualism,[3] which, to some extent, is reflected in the two letters and the Standards offered by petitioner, is the belief that sex/gender is not,

---

1. The letter from Dr. Dempsey used the feminine pronoun in describing petitioner. Because of our conclusion that petitioner has not yet established an entitlement to a determination that his gender has been effectively changed from male to female, we shall use the masculine pronoun. We do so not to disparage petitioner's undoubtedly sincere belief that his transition is, indeed, complete, but simply to be consistent with our conclusion that he has yet to offer sufficient evidence to warrant that determination as a legal matter. We note that, in the petition and other papers filed with the Circuit Court, petitioner also used the masculine pronoun to describe himself.

3. Several different terms have been used, and misused, in describing persons whose sexual identity is inconsistent with their assigned gender. We shall use the term "transsexual," notwithstanding that it, too, has been defined in different ways. STEDMAN'S MEDICAL DICTIONARY 1865 (27th ed. 2000) defines a "transsexual," in relevant part, as "[a] person with the external genitalia and secondary sexual characteristics of one sex, but whose personal identification and psychosocial configuration is that of the opposite sex." That definition, in the context before us in this case, may be too limiting, at least with respect to persons who, as a result of hormone therapy and sex reassignment surgery, have brought their genitalia and some secondary sexual characteristics into conformity with their personal identification. Persons who have undergone those procedures may no longer regard themselves as transsexual but as having achieved a consistent gender. That, however, is the issue. For pure convenience and without implying anything substantive, we shall use the term as descriptive of the person

in all instances, a binary concept—all male or all female. Transsexuals, as petitioner claims to be, seek to achieve recognition of the view that a person's gender/sex is determined by his or her personal sexual identity rather than by physical characteristics alone.[4] Sex reassignment surgery, under that view, merely harmonizes a person's physical characteristics with that identity.

This Opinion is not intended to be a medical text. Apart from our own incompetence to write such a text, it appears that some of the concepts that underlie the views espoused by transsexuals who seek recognition of gender change are the subject of debate, in both the medical and legal communities. The literature, in both communities, is extensive and daunting, and, unguided by expert testimony, there is no way that we could evaluate it properly. It is, however, necessary to understand those underlying concepts in order to determine what gender is and whether, or how, it may be changed.

There is a recognized medical viewpoint that gender is not determined by any single criterion, but that the following seven factors may be relevant:

(1) Internal morphologic sex (seminal vesicles/prostate or vagina/uterus/fallopian tubes);

(2) External morphologic sex (genitalia);

(3) Gonadal sex (testes or ovaries);

(4) Chromosomal sex (presence or absence of Y chromosome);

(5) Hormonal sex (predominance of androgens or estrogens);

(6) Phenotypic sex (secondary sex characteristics, e.g. facial hair, breasts, body type); and

(7) Personal sexual identity.

Blackburn notes that the initial development of a fetus is asexual. The fetus first forms rudimentary sexual organs—gonads, genital ridge, and internal duct system—that later develop into sexually differentiated organs: testes or ovaries, penis/scrotum or clitoris/labia, and fallopian tubes or seminal vesicles/vas deferens, respectively. This initial differentiation, according to Blackburn, is governed by the presence or absence of a Y chromosome inherited from the father. If present, the Y chromosome triggers the development of testes, which begin to produce male hormones that influence much of the fetus's further sexual development. Those hormones cause the development of male genitalia and inhibit the development of the fetus's primitive fallopian tube system. If the Y chromosome is not present, the fetus continues on what has been characterized as the "default" path of sexual development. The gonads develop into ovaries, and, freed from the inhibiting influence of male hormones, the fetus's primordial duct system develops into fallopian tubes and a uterus.

Most often, it appears, a fetus's sexual development is uneventful, and, because all of the sexual features are consistent and indicate one gender or the other, the person be-

---

both before and after any medical procedures. Transsexualism has also been referred to as gender dysphoria. It is a condition to be distinguished from transvestism (cross-dressing) and homosexuality (sexual attraction to persons of one's own gender).

4. In the context before us, the terms "sex" and "gender" are not necessarily synonymous for all purposes, and, indeed, the perceived distinctions between them, to some extent, lie at the core of transsexualism. The term "sex" is often used to denote anatomical or biological sex, whereas "gender" refers to a person's psychosexual individuality or identity. Much of the debate concerns whether "gender," which takes greater account of psychological factors, is the more relevant concept deserving of legal recognition. The source material uses both terms, and, without implying anything of substance, we shall use the terms interchangeably.

comes easily identifiable as either male or female. When this development is changed or interrupted, however, the situation may become less clear, and people may be born with sexual features that are either ambiguous (consistent with *either* sex) or incongruent (seemingly inconsistent with their "assigned" sex).

Individuals who have biological features that are ambiguous or incongruent are sometimes denoted as intersexed or hermaphroditic.[5] The variety of intersexed conditions encompasses virtually every permutation of variance among the seven factors considered in determining gender. These various ambiguities, moreover, may occur both within a specific factor (e.g., ambiguous, unclassifiable genitalia) or between two or more different factors (e.g., chromosomal sex is incongruent with morphological sex).

Generally, these conditions are classified into three "theoretical types": male pseudo-hermaphroditism, female pseudohermaphroditism, and true hermaphroditism. The true hermaphrodite consists of an individual with at least some ovarian tissue and some testicular tissue, and is the most rare. Female pseudohermaphrodites often have XX chromosomes and ovaries, but exhibit "masculinized" external genitalia. The "masculinization" of the genitalia can take many forms, including the enlargement of the clitoris or swelling of the labia (thus resembling a scrotum).

Male pseudohermaphroditism describes an individual who is chromosomally male (XY) and has testes, but who also has external genitalia that have become feminized. In one condition, called androgen insensitivity syndrome (AIS), the feminization of the genitalia is the result of the body's inability to respond to the developmental influences of androgen. Without the effects of the male hormone, the genitalia develop along the "default" path of feminity. This process continues through puberty, resulting in a person with (undescended) testes and male chromosomes who is very feminine. Because the condition may be detectable only upon an internal examination, it is often undiagnosed until puberty, when the presumed woman fails to menstruate.

A condition that produces similar results is known as 5-alpha-reductase deficiency (5AR). Like AIS, the individual with 5AR deficiency has testes but fails to respond to androgen in the womb, resulting in feminine external genitalia. With the onset of puberty, however, the individual *does* begin to respond to the increased production of testosterone, and the body begins to masculinize. The individual grows tall and muscular, begins to grow facial hair, and the genitals become more masculine. Some of these types of ambiguities, as noted above, may go largely unnoticed by the individual manifesting them, and may go undiagnosed for years.

In other cases, the individual's sexual ambiguity may be the result of a mistaken "sex assignment" at birth. The official designation of a person as male or female usually occurs at or immediately after birth, and is often based on the appearance of the external genitalia. Sometimes, when the genitalia are abnormal, doctors have erred in determining the baby's sex, mistaking an enlarged clitoris for a small penis, or *vice versa*. The criteria for determining sex at birth, one researcher has argued, are simply too rudimentary to be entirely accurate. He notes that,

> "Past clinical decisions about gender identity and sex reassignment when genitalia are greatly abnormal have by necessity occurred in a relative vacuum because of inadequate scientific data. Clinical decisions have been constructed largely on the predicted adequacy of the genitalia for adult sexual function. But

---

5. Although these terms too are sometimes given distinct meanings within the medical literature, the distinction is unimportant for the purposes of this case. We shall use the terms interchangeably.

the human may not be so easily deconstructed. Sex chromosome anomalies, gender identity disorder, genital malformations, metabolic adrenal or testicular errors—these conditions imply a sexual plasticity of great complexity."

In the past, it was not uncommon, if a doctor examining the neonatal child observed what appeared to be ambiguous genitalia and concluded that the genitalia so observed would be incapable of functioning in the male capacity, for the doctor to recommend that the child be surgically altered and raised as a girl. It was previously believed that a person was psychosexually neutral at birth, and that subsequent psychosexual development was dependent on the appearance of the genitals. Thus, it was assumed, the altered male would psychologically respond, adapt to the new genitalia, and develop into a functional and healthy female.

That view appears no longer to be generally accepted. Individuals who have undergone such surgical alterations as a result of abnormal genitalia often have rejected their "assigned" gender and ultimately request that the alterations be surgically negated so that they may assume their original gender. In this regard, the medical community seems to have concluded that human brains are not psychosexually neutral at birth but are "predisposed and biased to interact with environmental, familial, and social forces in either a male or female mode."[6]

The medical community's experience with patients born with ambiguous genitalia has led many researchers to believe that the brain "differentiates" *in utero* to one gender or the other and that, once the child's brain has differentiated, that child cannot be made into a person of the other gender simply through surgical alterations. Some scientists have argued that such medical developments now offer a robust biological explanation of transsexualism—that the brain has differentiated to one sex while the rest of the body has differentiated to another.

Transsexualism was once regarded as a form of sexual or psychological deviance and, in some quarters, is still considered so today.

Recent studies have suggested that this condition may be associated with certain conditions in the womb and certain processes in the developing pre-natal brain. As noted, there is evidence suggesting that the brain differentiates into "male" and "female" brains, just as the fetus's rudimentary sex organs differentiate into "male" and "female" genitalia. These studies, the authors assert, "clearly support the paradigm that in transsexuals sexual differentiation of the brain and genitals may go into opposite directions and point to a neurobiological basis of gender identity disorder." Researchers theorize that the developing brain may differentiate in response to hormonal levels in the womb—"intrauterine a[n]drogen exposure." This hypothesis has been tested with animals. Research has indicated, for instance, that the sexual differentiation of primates may be manipulated by controlling prenatal hormone exposure. Such experimental results have been cited by at least one court.

The studies imply that transsexualism may be more similar to other physiological conditions of sexual ambiguity, such as androgen insensitivity syndrome, than to purely psychological disorders. Reiner posits:

"What can be stated is that the absence of prenatal androgen exposure, whether a child is XX, XO, has an androgen insensitivity syndrome, and so on, may

---

6. As a result of this more recent experience and knowledge, doctors and clinicians seem now to be more skeptical about surgical alteration of ambiguous genitalia in very young children. Some doctors and advocates have proposed a moratorium on all surgical reconstruction prior to the patient becoming capable of consenting. Others argue that surgical alteration of the genitalia should be an absolute last resort, performed only if all available alternatives fail.

render the brain to the default, or female, position. Within the potential for transformation from the default brain to the virilized brain is the opportunity for errors of incomplete or improperly timed androgen exposure. Such errors, in addition to acquired, sometimes iatrogenic, post-natal injuries … may lead to the misassignment or reassignment of sex at birth from the genetic sex."

The ultimate conclusion of such studies, which, as noted, is the central point sought to be made by transsexuals, is that the preeminent factor in determining gender is the individual's own sexual identity as it has developed in the brain. Reiner continues:

> "In the end it is only the children themselves who can and must identify who and what they are. It is for us as clinicians and researchers to listen and to learn. Clinical decisions must ultimately be based not on anatomical predictions, nor on the 'correctness' of sexual function, for this is neither a question of morality nor of social consequence, but on that path most appropriate to the likeliest psychosexual developmental pattern of the child. In other words, the organ that appears to be critical to psychosexual development and adaptation is not the external genitalia, but the brain."

Regardless of its cause, the accounts from transsexuals themselves are startlingly consistent. They grow up believing that they are not the sex that their body indicates they are. They believe that they have mistakenly grown up with the wrong genitalia. These disconcerting feelings often begin early in childhood, as early as three or four years. These individuals often rebel against any attempt to impose social gender expectations that are inconsistent with what they believe they are — they may refuse to wear the "appropriate" clothes and refuse to participate in activities associated with their assigned gender. That kind of behavior has become one of the determining factors for a diagnosis of gender identity disorder.

A transsexual wishing to transition to a different gender has limited options. Generally, the options consist of psychotherapy, living as a person of the desired sex, hormonal treatment, and sex reassignment surgery. Although psychotherapy may help the transsexual deal with the psychological difficulties of transsexualism, courts have recognized that psychotherapy is not a "cure" for transsexualism. Because transsexualism is universally recognized as inherent, rather than chosen, psychotherapy will never succeed in "curing" the patient:

> "Most, if not all, specialists in gender identity are agreed that the transsexual condition establishes itself very early, before the child is capable of elective choice in the matter, probably in the first two years of life; some say even earlier, before birth during the fetal period. These findings indicate that the transsexual has not made a choice to be as he is, but rather that the choice has been made for him through many causes preceding and beyond his control. Consequently, it has been found that attempts to treat the true adult transsexual psychotherapeutically have consistently met with failure."

Hormonal treatment has been shown to be more effective, and, for the male-to-female transsexual, results in breast growth, feminine body fat distribution, a decrease in body hair, and softening of the skin. Although most of these effects are reversible upon termination of the treatment, the individual's breast growth may not reverse entirely. Hormonal treatment for female-to-male transsexuals results in deepening of the voice, enlargement of the clitoris, breast atrophy, increased upper body strength, weight gain, increased facial and body hair, baldness, increased sexual arousal, and decreased hip fat.

Surgical options for the male-to-female transsexual include orchiectomy (removal of gonads), vaginoplasty (construction of vagina), and mammoplasty (construction of breasts). Some patients elect to undergo additional cosmetic surgeries to enhance other secondary sex features, such as facial structure or voice tone. Surgical options for the female-to-male transsexual include mastectomy, hysterectomy, vaginectomy, and phalloplasty. As most health insurance companies currently exclude coverage for transsexual treatment, the out-of-pocket cost is often prohibitively expensive. One commentator has asserted that a male-to-female operation costs an average of $37,000, whereas the average female-to-male operation costs $77,000. Another estimate describes the cost as "easily reach[ing] $100,000." Contributing to the much higher cost of female-to-male sex reassignment surgery is the increased technical difficulty of phalloplasty, estimates for which range from $30,000 to $150,000. The procedure may require several operations.

Estimates of the number of intersexed individuals vary considerably, from 1 per 37,000 people to 1 per 2,000 to as high as 3 per 2,000. It seems to be a guess, although Dreger suggests that "the frequency of births in which the child exhibits a condition which today could count as 'intersexual' or 'sexually ambiguous' is significantly higher than most people outside the medical field (and many inside) assume it is."

In reviewing the medical literature, we have avoided making pronouncements of our own, but have simply recounted some of the assertions and conclusions that appear in that literature — assertions and conclusions which, when presented in the form of testimony in court, have evoked differing responses from the courts, both in the United States and elsewhere. Notwithstanding that this remains an evolving field, in which final conclusions as to some aspects may be premature, the current medical thinking does seem to support at least these relevant propositions: (1) that external genitalia are not the sole medically recognized determinant of gender; (2) that the medically recognized determinants of gender may sometimes be either ambiguous or incongruent; (3) that due to mistaken assumptions made by physicians of an infant's ambiguous external genitalia at or shortly after birth, some people are mislabeled at that time as male or female and thereafter carry an official gender status that is medically incorrect; (4) that at least some of the medically recognized determinants of gender are subject to being altered in such a way as to make them inconsistent with the individual's officially declared gender and consistent with the opposite gender; and (5) whether or not a person's psychological gender identity is physiologically based, it has received recognition as one of the determinants of gender and plays a powerful role in the person's psychic makeup and adaptation.

For our purposes, the relevance of these propositions lies in the facts that (1) gender itself is a fact that may be established by medical and other evidence, (2) it may be, or possibly may become, other than what is recorded on the person's birth certificate, and (3) a person has a deep personal, social, and economic interest in having the official designation of his or her gender match what, in fact, it always was or possibly has become. The issue then becomes the circumstances under which a court may declare one's gender to be other than what is officially recorded and the criteria to be used in making any such declaration. . . .

What Must Be Shown?

Most courts and other agencies that have dealt with establishing the gender of transsexuals have done so in particular contexts and have set the requirements for such recognition accordingly. To warrant amending a birth certificate, Maryland (and most States that permit such a change at all) requires by statute a finding that gender *has been changed* "by surgical procedure."[11] Those courts that have permitted transsexuals to marry someone of their former gender have also uniformly required surgery as a condition to recognizing a change in gender.

Surgery seems to be a requirement for recognition of gender change in other contexts as well. The Social Security Administration apparently will alter its records to record a change of gender but requires "[c]linical or medical records or other combination of documents showing the sex change surgery has been completed." .... In the Federal prison system, pre-operative transsexuals are housed with inmates of their birth gender, but post-operative transsexuals are housed with inmates of their acquired gender. It has been reported, although there seems to be no official documentation, that the State Department will issue a temporary passport with a change of gender upon a certified letter from a physician stating that the applicant is about to undergo sex reassignment surgery and will issue a regular new passport showing such a change upon a certified letter stating that the applicant has undergone such surgery.

The statutes or regulations that make surgery a condition to recognition of gender change rarely, if ever, specify the kind of surgery that will suffice, although in the court cases there is usually considerable evidence regarding the nature and effect of any surgery that is undertaken and both the medical and legal literature describe it as well. The point, or relevance, of the requirement of surgery seems to lie in the assumption that, if the person has undergone sex reassignment surgery, the change has been effected, in that at least (1) the person's external genitalia have been brought into consistency with that indicative of the new gender and with other determinants of gender, and (2) the change is regarded as permanent and irreversible. Hormonal therapy alone, which usually can be terminated or perhaps even reversed, has not, to our knowledge, been recognized as effecting either a sufficient change or a permanent one.

Almost all courts have recognized that the question of whether and how gender can be changed is one where the law depends upon and, to a large extent, must follow medical facts (medical facts, in this context, to include relevant psychological facts). Any reasoned legal conclusion respecting an asserted change in one's gender must therefore be based on admissible evidence of medical fact—the factors that actually should be considered in determining gender and what the person's gender status is when viewed in the context of those factors. We have examined the literature available to us and recounted some of the evidence that other courts have found relevant, but only to establish the basis for our conclusion that the court has jurisdiction over petitions seeking recognition of gender change. None of what we have recounted is evidence in this case and therefore does not establish, by itself, petitioner's entitlement to the order he seeks.

This is, clearly, an evolving area. As noted, aside from the two unsworn letters attached to the petition and the Standards of Care of the Harry Benjamin International Gender Dysphoria Association, no medical evidence was presented to the Circuit Court with respect to petitioner's gender status. Because we believe (1) that the court had jurisdiction to consider the petition, and (2) that, on the record before it, the court erred in broadly concluding, apparently as a matter of law, that gender was not subject to modification or adjustment, we shall direct that the case be remanded for the court to consider admissi-

---

11. It appears to be undisputed that no surgery, however extensive, can make a transsexual fertile in his/her "new" gender. Neither male-to-female nor female-to-male transsexuals are capable of conceiving children once sex reassignment surgery has been completed. The fact that §4-214(b)(5) recognizes that surgery *can* effect a change in gender indicates, at least in the context of amending birth certificates, that infertility is not a basis for refusing to recognize the change.

ble evidence relevant to the issue and to make a determination of whether the relief requested by petitioner should be granted based on that evidence. As the seeker of relief,
petitioner has the burden of establishing his entitlement to it, and it will therefore be incumbent upon him to present sufficient medical evidence of both the relevant criteria
for determining gender and of the fact that, applying that criteria, he has completed a
permanent and irreversible change from male to female.…

Notes and Questions

1. As the *Littleton* and *In re Heilig* cases take pains to note, one's gender identity is distinct from one's sexual orientation. Yet as both Problems 1-A and 1-B demonstrate, the
two can interact in important ways when applying laws that draw distinctions based on
sexual orientation or gender. For example, Applicant H in Problem 1-A is a man dating
someone who was born with male genitalia but who has recently completed sex-
reassignment surgery to become a female. Despite the fact that Applicant H considers
himself to be heterosexual and probably has engaged in sexual intercourse exclusively
with women, whether he will be deemed "homosexual" for purposes of adoption, military service, and the like turns on the determination whether the person he is dating is
deemed to be "male" or "female."

Similarly, Texas's "Homosexual Conduct" law (struck down by the U.S. Supreme Court
in 2003 and examined in closer detail in Chapters 3 and 4) provides that "[a] person commits an offense if he engages in deviate sexual intercourse with another individual of the
same sex." TEX. PENAL CODE ANN. §21.06(a). Thus, whether someone is guilty of committing the offense of "homosexual conduct" turns upon how one assesses the sexes of the
two persons involved.

2. Consider the necessary result of holdings such as that in *Littleton*: does it not, in
effect, hold that two individuals who by all appearances are the same sex are nonetheless
permitted to marry? In other words, by making genetics and anatomy at birth the acid
test for determining one's sex, does it not seem to sanction what looks to others as a same-
sex marriage? Does that seem consistent with what the drafters of laws banning same-
sex marriage had in mind? Do you suppose that they even had individuals such as Christie
Littleton in mind?

3. Assume that the reasoning of the majority in *Littleton* is sound with respect to
those whose sex at birth is unambiguous, save perhaps for their psychological identity.
How does one address Justice Angelini's concerns with respect to those whose sex at
birth is ambiguous?

4. As in the case of selecting among various definitions of "homosexuality," one can imagine arguments regarding fairness, ease of proof, and invasiveness so far as the various definitions of sex are concerned. How do the various definitions discussed in the *Littleton*
and *In re Heilig* cases fare?

5. Recall that one way the court in *Conaway* distinguished sexual orientation from sex was
by noting that sex is an "immutable" characteristic while sexual orientation has not been
proven to be immutable. Which definition of the term "sex" is the court in *Conaway* referring to? Depending on the definition employed, to what extent do cases such as *Littleton* and
In re Heilig undermine the premise that "sex" is immutable? Moreover, what, if anything,
is the distinction between "sex" and "gender"? Assuming that there is a distinction between
the two, are they both equally "immutable," and if not, of what consequence is that (or
should that be) for assessing the constitutionality of laws that discriminate on those bases?

C. The Meaning of "Sodomy"

Problem 1-C: Prosecuting "Crimes against Nature"

The state of Oklahoma has for some time had a statute on the books, entitled "Crimes against nature," which provides in pertinent part as follows:

> Every person who is guilty of the detestable and abominable crime against nature, committed with mankind or with a beast, is punishable by imprisonment in the custody of the Department of Corrections not exceeding ten (10) years....

See 21 OKL. ST. § 886. A second statute, entitled "Crime against nature, what penetration necessary," provides as follows:

> Any sexual penetration, however slight, is sufficient to complete the crime against nature.

See 21 OKL. ST. § 887.

You are a judge sitting on the Oklahoma Court of Criminal Appeals in cases raising the following questions:

(1) What *sorts* of sexual acts are covered by the statutes? Would they, for example, encompass:

    a.   One person inserting his penis into the mouth of another person? Into the anus of another person?

    b.   One person inserting her tongue into the anus of another person? Into the vagina of another person?

    c.   One person inserting his or her finger into the anus of another person? Into the vagina of another person?

(2) Of what relevance is it under the statutes that the individuals engaging in such acts are married to one another?

(3) Of what relevance is it under the statutes that the individuals engaging in such acts are (a) both men; (b) both women; (c) a man and a woman?

(4) How, if at all, would your answers differ if:

    a.   The phrase "the detestable and abominable crime against nature, committed with mankind or with a beast," were replaced with the word "sodomy?"

    b.   You were instead applying Georgia law, which at the time it was upheld by the U.S. Supreme Court in 1986 provided that "A person commits the offense of sodomy when he performs or submits to any sexual act involving the sex organs of one person and the mouth or anus of another." *See* GA. CODE ANN. § 16-6-2(a) (1984).

    c.   You were instead applying Texas law, which at the time it was struck down by the U.S. Supreme Court in 2003 provided that "A person commits an offense if he engages in deviate sexual intercourse with another individual of the same sex," and defined "[d]eviate sexual intercourse" to include "(A) any contact between any part of the genitals of one person and the mouth or anus of another person; or (B) the penetration of the genitals or the anus of another person with an object." *See* Tex. Penal Code Ann. §§ 21.01(1), 21.06(a) (2003).

Warner v. State

489 P.2d 526 (Okla. 1971)

BUSSEY, Presiding Judge.

Wilma Jean Warner and James Lewis Warner, hereinafter referred to as defendants, were charged, tried and convicted in the District Court of Oklahoma County for the offense of Oral Sodomy; their punishment was fixed at four years imprisonment, and from said judgments and sentences, a timely appeal has been perfected to this Court.

Briefly stated, the evidence at the trial revealed that on September 16, 1970, Miss Jerry Sellars was 18 years old. She testified that she was walking home after purchasing a package of cigarettes, when the defendants offered her a ride home. She got into the car, because she did not think anything would happen and because they were nice enough to stop. They asked her if she would like to get a beer, and she agreed. The defendant, James Warner, went into a tavern to get the beer, wherein defendant Wilma Warner, attempted to get Miss Sellars to kiss her. She started to get frightened, and was relieved to see defendant James Warner return to the car.

She told them that she needed to return home, and defendant James Warner agreed, as soon as he checked a party. He drove to their house and forced the girl to go inside, stating that she was going to have to make love to them. She attempted to lock herself in the bathroom, but was unsuccessful. The defendants forced her to leave the bathroom, and in the struggle, the toilet seat broke.

She, thereafter, described numerous acts of sexual intercourse and oral sodomy which she was forced to perform with both the defendants. The sordid unnatural acts testified to by this witness are such that little value could be gained by setting them forth in detail in this opinion. They finally agreed to take her home, and on the way home, defendant James Warner required her to commit a further act of oral sodomy. They let her out near her home, and she told a friend what had happened. She was taken to the police station, and then to the hospital....

The first two propositions assert that the court erred in overruling defendant Wilma Warner's Demurrer to the evidence, and the court erred in instructing the jury in that it would be legally impossible for two women to commit the "crime against nature." This is a case of first impression in that an exhaustive search reveals that this issue has never been decided in Oklahoma. The testimony of the victim revealed that the defendant Wilma Warner performed copulation per os on the victim, and in turn, had the victim perform copulation per os on her, the defendant. This Court, in 1917, recognized the distinction between copulation per anum. and copulation per os in the case of Ex parte DeFord, 14 Okl.Cr. 133, 168 P. 58, wherein the Court stated:

> "For the reason that it is the opinion of this court that section 2444, Rev.Laws 1910, supra, meant to cover sodomy in its broader definition as hereinabove indicated, *copulation between human beings through the mouth is included within its prohibitions*, and the judgment of the district court of Bryan county pronounced on the petitioner's plea of guilty to the aforesaid charge is valid" [emphasis added].

In LeFavour v. State, 77 Okl.Cr. 383, 142 P.2d 132 (1943), this Court stated in the second paragraph of the Syllabus:

"The word 'mankind' * * * includes both male and female. 21 O.S.1941 §886."

This state's judicial history in dealing with sexual perversion reflects a slow and painful process wherein the Court of Criminal Appeals has attempted to discreetly define the multiple acts encompassed in the offense of Crime Against Nature. Going one step further, we specifically hold that copulation per os between two females is a violation of 21 O.S. §886....

The final proposition contends that the statute under which the defendants were convicted is unconstitutional. This contention is based on the premise that 21 O.S. §886 is so vague as to be invalid, and further that it is broad enough to cover consensual marital acts. The Nevada Court faced the same contention as to the unconstitutional vagueness of their similar Crime Against Nature Statute in Hogan v. State, 84 Nev. 372, 441 P.2d 620, wherein the Court stated:

"It should be noted that this court is not unique in this interpretation of the infamous crime against nature. At least twenty-one other states define it similarly. See 2 Wharton's Criminal Law and Procedure, §752, pg. 575. The phrase 'infamous crime against nature' indicates an offense against nature and the laws of nature, and is as inherently understandable as are such words as 'robbery', 'larceny', 'burglary', and even 'murder.' All are 'words of art' disclosing their full meaning through interpretation, usage and application."

We concur with the opinion of the Nevada Court, and specifically rule that the language of 21 O.S. §886 is definite in that men or women of common knowledge can reasonably understand the conduct prohibited by said statute....

Franklin v. State
257 So.2d 21 (Fla. 1971)

PER CURIAM:

We here consider these consolidated appeals transferred by the District Court of Appeal, Second District, 243 So.2d 440, because the trial judge passed upon and upheld the constitutionality of Fla.Stat. §800.01, F.S.A., reading as follows:

"Whoever commits the abominable and detestable crime against nature, either with mankind or with beast, shall be punished by imprisonment in the state prison not exceeding twenty years."

The renewed attack on the language of this statute for constitutional vagueness and overbreadth is not surprising in view of the guarded wording used in such statutes in 1868 when it was drafted. A very serious question is raised as to whether the statute meets the recognized constitutional test that it inform the average person of common intelligence as to what is prohibited so that he need not speculate as to the statutory meaning. If the language does not meet this test, then it must fall and the matter must be left to legislative correction. This statute and others relating to a variety of sex offenses need immediate legislative review and action. We urgently commend this important area of great social concern for appropriate remedial legislation.

We have over a long period of time upheld the statute despite earlier constitutional challenges. We are persuaded that these holdings and this statute require our reconsideration. One reason which makes this apparent is the transition of language over the span of the past 100 years of this law's existence. The change and upheaval of modern times are of drastic proportions. People's understandings of subjects, expressions and experiences are different than they were even a decade ago. The fact of these changes in the land must be taken into account and appraised. Their effect and the reasonable reaction and understanding of people today relate to statutory language.

The blindfold upon our Lady of Justice is symbolic of impartiality, as being blind to all outside influences which would divert from the material facts and law applicable to the case in which justice is being sought upon its merits. Her blindfold in no wise suggests that justice should be blind to the facts of life and of the times in which it functions; for the law, to be vibrant, must be a living thing, responsive to the society which it serves, and to which that society looks as the last true depository of truth and justice.

A further reason dictating our reexamination here is the expansion of constitutional rulings on the invasion of private rights by state intrusion which must be taken into account in the consideration of this statute's continuing validity. The language in this statute could entrap unsuspecting citizens and subject them to 20-year sentences for which the statute provides. Such a sentence is equal to that for manslaughter and would no doubt be a shocking revelation to persons who do not have an understanding of the meaning of the statute.

Those who are versed in the law may understand the statute's meaning because of their knowledge of legal interpretations in court opinions, but it seems to us that if today's world is to have brought home to it what it is that the statute prohibits, it must be set forth in language which is relevant to today's society and is understandable to the average citizen of common intelligence which is the constitutional test of such language.

We do not, of course, here sanction historically forbidden sexual acts, homosexuality or bestiality. We only say that in this, as in any other conduct which is made a crime by statute, the forbidden conduct must be stated in terms which meet the constitutional test, i.e., that it is understood by the average man of common intelligence.

It is authoritatively recognized that:

> "This statute provides a penalty for a crime, but *fails to delin[e]ate what conduct* will violate its terms" [emphasis added].

Common law definitions are of course resorted to when the forbidden conduct is not defined. This may supply the deficiency for a *legal* understanding of a vague statute, but it cannot meet the constitutional requirement that the language of the statute be understandable to the common man.

The offense charged is what is often referred to as a homosexual act, between the two appellants, under this statute. According to the testimony, the two were apprehended by a police lieutenant in the commission of the act in a parked car in a public place. The police lieutenant testified that he observed appellants leaving a public restroom on the Municipal Pier in St. Petersburg, Florida, at approximately 2:45 a.m., drive in their separate cars in the same direction, park them together out on a fill area and get together in one of the cars. The time of their apprehension was approximately 2:50 or 2:55 a.m. When the officer walked up to the car and shined his flashlight inside, he observed appellants committing "a crime against nature." If the statutory prohibition of § 800.01 was intended to be oral or anal sex activity between consenting partners, as seems to be indicated from *Delaney, supra,* then this should be made clear in such a statute.

Legislative action is long past due in this and related fields of personal relationships, as we have so strongly pointed out in the disturbing matter of the abortion statutes and with great restraint have left to its proper place in the Legislature the correction which is so sorely needed. The courts would much prefer appropriate legislative action, where proper conditions and restraints can be set forth. We strive to observe the d[e]lineation of our branches of government, but in the case before us here there is no doubt on its face that this statute as worded cannot withstand the constitutional onslaught and must fall. We are thoroughly in accord with upholding proper statutes, but a court must guard equally against those which offend constitutional standards and which constitute an infringement by the state upon the private rights of citizens. The statute, § 800.01, is void on its face as unconstitutional for vagueness and uncertainty in its language, violating constitutional due process to the defendants....

[The concurring opinion of Chief Justice Roberts and the dissenting opinion of Justice Boyd are omitted.]

Virgin v. State
792 P.2d 1186 (Okla. Crim. App. 1990)

PARKS, Presiding Judge:

Herbert A. Virgin, appellant, was tried by jury for the crimes of Forcible Oral Sodomy (Count I), Forcible Anal Sodomy (Count III), both in violation of 21 O.S.1981, § 886 and 21 O.S.Supp.1982, § 888....

In his first assignment of error, appellant asserts that 21 O.S.1981, § 886 and 21 O.S.Supp.1982, § 888, are unconstitutionally vague as applied to his conviction for Forcible Anal Sodomy because neither provision explicitly proscribes the act of inserting one's finger into another's rectum. These provisions are set forth below.

> Section 886:
>
> Every person who is guilty of the detestable and abominable crime against nature, committed with mankind or with a beast, is punishable by imprisonment....
>
> Section 888:
>
> Any person who forces another person to engage in the detestable and abominable crime against nature, pursuant to Section 886 of this title, upon conviction, is guilty of a felony punishable by imprisonment.... This crime may also be known as forcible sodomy.

As both the State and appellant correctly submit, this is a case of first impression. Never before has this Court been asked to interpret these provisions as proscribing an act which did not involve either the genitalia or the vagina. These statutes have been applied only to cases in which the defendant performed fellatio on the victim, *see Golden v. State*, 695 P.2d 6 (Okl.Cr.1985), where the defendant forced the victim to perform fellatio on him, *see Phillips v. State*, 756 P.2d 604 (Okl.Cr.1988), where the defendant performed cunnilingus on the victim, *see Casady v. State*, 721 P.2d 1342 (Okl.Cr.1986), where the defendant forced the victim to perform cunnilingus on her, *see Salyers v. State*, 755 P.2d 97 (Okl.Cr.1988), and where the defendant inserted his penis into the victim's rectum, *see Miller v. State*, 751 P.2d 733 (Okl.Cr.1988).

It is a well established rule of statutory construction that statutes are to be construed according to the plain and ordinary meaning of their language. 25 O.S.1981, § 1. *See also Glass v. State*, 701 P.2d 765, 768 (Okl.Cr.1985). Crime against nature is defined as "[d]eviate sexual intercourse...." *Black's Law Dictionary*, 334 (5th ed.1979). Of greater importance, 21 O.S.1981, § 887 provides that "sexual penetration" is required to sustain a conviction for such crime. Although there is no doubt that the crime herein committed was detestable and abominable, we must rule that the act of inserting one's finger into another's rectum does not constitute "sexual penetration." Accordingly, appellant's conviction for Forcible Anal Sodomy is reversed....

[The concurring opinion of Judge Lumpkin is omitted.]

State v. Stiller

590 S.E.2d 305 (N.C. Ct. App. 2004)

HUDSON, Judge.

Defendant was charged with sexual misconduct with his son, stepdaughter and niece, some twenty-five years before the trial. A jury found defendant guilty of eight counts of second-degree rape and eleven counts of crime against nature, and the court entered judgment 9 May 2002. Defendant appeals, alleging the court erred in the jury instructions on crime against nature and sustaining the State's objections to evidence of defendant's good character. For the reasons discussed below, we find no prejudicial error.

The State's evidence tended to show that Anita Stiller Blackwelder, defendant's estranged stepdaughter, after seeing him with a little girl at a family funeral, recalled that defendant molested her as a child and she went to the police. Ms. Blackwelder testified that defendant had forced her to engage in various sexual acts with himself and with her brother, Richard. Defendant's niece, son, and two other women also testified that, when they were children, defendant had sexually assaulted them or forced them to engage in sexual activity with each other.

Defendant testified in his own behalf, denying the charges against him. Patricia Simmons, defendant's former live-in companion, testified for defendant. Ms. Simmons and her young daughter, the child Ms. Blackwelder saw at the funeral with defendant, lived with defendant for two years. After the Department of Social Services contacted Ms. Simmons, she had her daughter examined for sexual abuse, but no evidence of abuse was found. Defendant's cousin and a family friend who spent time with defendant as a child testified that defendant had never been inappropriate with them. The jury convicted defendant of eight counts of second-degree rape and eleven counts of crime against nature, and defendant appeals.

Defendant first argues that the jury instructions on crime against nature were erroneous and allowed for his conviction on an improper theory. In charging the jury, the court defined a crime against nature as follows:

> An unnatural sexual act would include cunnilingus, which is any touching, however slight, by the lips or tongue of one person to any part [of] the female sex organ of another; fellatio which is any touching by the lips or tongue of one person to the male sex organ of another and *any penetration, however slight, by an object, such as a piece of candy, into the genital opening of a person's body.*

While this jury instruction is consistent with the pattern instruction on crime against nature, defendant argues that this offense is limited to oral and anal sex, and thus, the final part of the instruction given, regarding penetration, was error. For the reasons discussed below, we disagree.

Crime against nature is defined by the common law and interpreted by our courts. At the time of these offenses in 1976 and 1977, crime against nature was defined to "include[ ] all kindred acts of a bestial character whereby degraded and perverted sexual desires are sought to be gratified." *State v. Harward,* 264 N.C. 746, 746, 142 S.E.2d 691, 692 (1965). Our Supreme Court has stated that "though penetration by or of a sexual organ is an essential element of the crime, the crime against nature is not limited to penetration by the male sexual organ." *State v. Joyner,* 295 N.C. 55, 66, 243 S.E.2d 367, 374 (1978) (internal citations omitted). Instead, the offense is broad enough to include all forms of oral and anal sex, as well as unnatural acts with animals. *Id.* While no case in our State has specifically included penetration of the genital opening by an object in its definition of crime against nature, such an act is entirely consistent with the language of *Joyner.* Thus, we do not believe the court's instruction was erroneous....

Notes and Questions

1. What is the rationale for using the non-specific phrase "the detestable and abominable crime against nature" instead of the more specific language employed by the Georgia and Texas statutes? *See Bowers v. Hardwick,* 478 U.S. 186, 197 (1986) (Burger, C.J., concurring) (quoting 4 WILLIAM BLACKSTONE, COMMENTARIES *215) (describing the conduct proscribed as "a heinous act 'the very mention of which is a disgrace to human nature,' and 'a crime not fit to be named'").

2. On the question whether the phrase "crime against nature" is sufficiently clear to give people fair notice of what is proscribed, or unconstitutionally vague under the due process clause of the U.S. Constitution (and its state court analogues) for failing to do so, do you find the reasoning of the *Franklin* or the *Warner* court more persuasive? Shortly after *Franklin* and *Warner* were decided, the U.S. Supreme Court weighed in on the question:

> All the Due Process Clause requires is that the law give sufficient warning that men may conduct themselves so as to avoid that which is forbidden.

Viewed against this standard, the phrase "crimes against nature" is no more vague than many other terms used to describe criminal offenses at common law and now codified in state and federal penal codes. The phrase has been in use among English-speaking people for many centuries, and a substantial number of jurisdictions in this country continue to utilize it. Anyone who cared to do so could certainly determine what particular acts have been considered crimes against nature....

Rose v. Locke, 423 U.S. 48, 50 (1975).

3. The due process challenges described in the previous note are "procedural" in nature, meaning that they do not challenge the legislature's ultimate *power* to criminalize such conduct, but rather the means employed and—specifically in these cases—the question whether the public was given sufficient notice of what the statutes encompass. In Chapter 3, we will examine cases in which a different type of due process challenge is brought against statutes criminalizing sodomy. In this latter group of cases, the statutes are clear about what they criminalize, and thus no question of *procedural* due process is involved. Rather, the contention is that the due process clause prevents the government from interfering with an individual's liberty in this manner, a challenge that goes to the substance of the law itself and is commonly referred to as a "substantive" due process challenge.

4. Does the word "sodomy," standing alone, refer only to anal intercourse or also to oral intercourse? Note that, at common law, the phrase referred solely to anal intercourse, and it was only in the late nineteenth century that states began to expand the definition of sodomy to encompass oral intercourse. *See* Richard A. Posner, Sex and Reason 343 (1992).

5. On their face, most sodomy laws do not and historically did not distinguish between sexual activity involving two men and sexual activity involving a man and a woman; it was not until the 1970s that any states singled out same-sex sodomy for criminal prosecution, and only nine states ultimately did so. *See Lawrence v. Texas*, 539 U.S. 558, 570–71 (2003). However, historically, sexual activity between two women was not punished by sodomy laws. *See, e.g., Commonwealth v. Wasson*, 842 S.W.2d 487, 491 (Ky. 1992) ("Unlike the present statute our common law tradition punished neither oral copulation nor any form of deviate sexual activity between women."); *Thompson v. Aldredge*, 200 S.E. 799, 800 (Ga. 1939). *See generally* William N. Eskridge, Jr., *Hardwick and Historiography*, 1999 U. Ill. L. Rev. 631, 643–46.

Nor have sodomy laws historically distinguished between those who are unmarried and those who are married, *see* Ariela R. Dubler, *Immoral Purposes: Marriage and the Genus of Illicit Sex*, 115 Yale L.J. 756, 778 & n.80 (2006), for the laws were targeted primarily at the non-procreative nature of the sex acts involved rather than the marital status of the participants, *see Lawrence v. Texas*, 539 U.S. 558, 568–69 (2003).

6. Sodomy laws, until recently, were prevalent throughout the United States. In 1961, all U.S. states had such laws on the books. *See Bowers v. Hardwick*, 478 U.S. 186, 193 (1986). By 1986, when the U.S. Supreme Court first considered a substantive challenge to the constitutionality of sodomy laws, about half of those laws had either been repealed or struck down on state constitutional grounds. *See id.* at 193–194. And by 2003, when the U.S. Supreme Court again considered a substantive challenge to the constitutionality of sodomy laws, such laws remained enforceable in only about a dozen states. *See Lawrence v. Texas*, 539 U.S. 558, 573 (2003). Although—as you will see in Chapters 3 and 4—the U.S. Supreme Court in *Lawrence* held unconstitutional the application of sodomy laws to certain types of private, consensual conduct between two adults, sodomy

laws remain on the books today and are still enforced (and enforceable) in contexts falling outside the protected zone identified by the *Lawrence* Court.

7. Given the facts of cases such as those excerpted above, one might wonder why prosecutors in such cases would charge the defendants with sodomy instead of (or in addition to) a charge of rape or sexual assault. One key reason is the difference in proof: rape or sexual assault requires the prosecution to prove absence of consent, while no such proof is required for the offense of sodomy. Thus, prosecutors frequently charge defendants with the lesser crime of sodomy in addition to the crime of rape or sexual assault where proof of the absence of consent is difficult, making it easier to convict the defendant either at trial or in plea bargaining. *See generally* Laurence H. Tribe, Lawrence v. Texas: *The "Fundamental Right" That Dare Not Speak Its Name*, 117 Harv. L. Rev. 1893, 1896 n.11 (2004); *Developments in the Law—Sexual Orientation and the Law*, 102 Harv. L. Rev. 1508, 1520 (1989). A second key reason is that sodomy statutes often served as "gap-fillers" that encompassed conduct not covered by rape statutes:

> A substantial number of sodomy prosecutions and convictions for which there are surviving records were for predatory acts against those who could not or did not consent, as in the case of a minor or the victim of an assault. As to these, one purpose for the prohibitions was to ensure there would be no lack of coverage if a predator committed a sexual assault that did not constitute rape as defined by the criminal law.... Instead of targeting relations between consenting adults in private, 19th-century sodomy prosecutions typically involved relations between men and minor girls or minor boys, relations between adults involving force, relations between adults implicating disparity in status, or relations between men and animals.

Lawrence v. Texas, 539 U.S. 558, 569 (2003).

Chapter 2

Procedural Obstacles to Adjudication on the Merits

While it is tempting in a book about constitutional rights to jump directly into the substance of the constitution, the truth is that, in practice, there are so many procedural obstacles to having a court (particularly a federal court) reach the merits of one's claims that the parties and the court address the constitutional issues—if at all—only after navigating a series of complex procedural doctrines. Because this book aims to provide students with a realistic view of what constitutional litigation involving the rights of sexual minorities looks like in practice, this chapter examines in close detail various procedural doctrines that have the effect of preventing a court from reaching the merits of constitutional claims.

Invoking procedural doctrines has, historically, been a means by which the state and federal governments have successfully prevented sexual minorities from having a court reach the merits of their constitutional claims. Procedural doctrines have also historically been successfully invoked by state governments to prevent having federal constitutional claims adjudicated in federal courts, which traditionally had been more hospitable than the state courts to rights-based claims by historically disadvantaged groups.

But in recent decades, attorneys advocating on behalf of sexual minorities have mastered and in some cases made successful use of these same procedural doctrines, primarily to keep cases out of the federal court system. The rationale: the historical hospitability of federal courts to rights-based claims by disadvantaged groups did not extend to claims by sexual minorities (in part because the federal bench became more conservative over time), while progressive state court judges started to robustly interpret their constitutions to provide significant protections for sexual minorities. Accordingly, hoping to prevent the development of negative precedent (such as the infamous 1986 decision in *Bowers v. Hardwick* upholding the constitutionality of sodomy laws), gay rights groups began to structure their cases in the 1990s and 2000s in such a way as to prevent adjudication in a federal court or review by the U.S. Supreme Court. Indeed, the groups went so far as to intervene in federal litigation brought by gay individuals unaffiliated with the major gay rights organizations to advocate for dismissal on procedural grounds.

Recently, some gay rights groups have returned to federal court, most notably, to challenge the constitutionality of Proposition 8 in California, which overturned a state court decision holding that same-sex couples had a right to marry under the California Constitution. Having successfully won at the trial court level, gay rights advocates have invoked a key procedural doctrine—standing—as a means of insulating the trial court decision from appellate review by higher federal courts. In turn, opponents of the trial court decision have invoked another key doctrine—regarding the weight of "summary affirmances" by the U.S. Supreme Court—to contend that the trial court had no authority to reach the merits in the first place.

In sum, procedural rules, for better or for worse, represent a key aspect of constitutional litigation generally and gay and transgender rights litigation specifically. Accordingly, the sections that follow examine those procedural doctrines that have arisen or are likely to arise in cases adjudicating the rights of sexual minorities.

A. Justiciability

1. Standing

Problem 2-A: I Can't Stand This Denial of Rights!

The state legislature in the State of New Condon (a mythical state located in the United States) amends its marriage laws so as to permit same-sex couples to marry. After a one-year period during which same-sex couples are permitted to marry in New Condon, voters amend the state constitution to limit marriage to opposite-sex couples.

A group of citizens file suit against the relevant state officials in federal court, contending that the state constitutional amendment denying same-sex couples the ability to marry violates the Equal Protection and Due Process Clauses of the Fourteenth Amendment to the U.S. Constitution. The plaintiffs consist of the following:

(1) Doris and Tanya, a same-sex couple who applied for and were denied a marriage license a month after the constitutional amendment was voted into law.

(2) Donna and Phyllis, a same-sex couple who want to marry but who did not bother to apply for a license after learning that the state constitutional amendment had been approved.

(3) Tom and David, a same-sex couple who have been dating for two months and describe themselves as in love. They are not sure yet whether they will get married, but they wish to have that option should their relationship continue to blossom.

(4) Mike, a gay man who is currently single but hopes to fulfill his dream of meeting and marrying his Prince Charming.

(5) Molly, a heterosexual woman who is offended by the idea of living in a state that denies important federal constitutional rights to gays and lesbians.

(6) Equal Rights New Condon, a nonprofit organization that advocates in favor of marriage equality for same-sex couples in the State of New Condon.

(7) Fred, the owner of *My Big Gay New Condon Wedding*, a company located in New Condon that specializes in wedding planning for same-sex couples.

Which of the plaintiffs, if any, have standing to bring suit in federal court?

a. Standing Generally

U.S. Constitution, Article III, § 2

The judicial Power shall extend to all Cases, in Law and Equity, arising under this Constitution, the Laws of the United States, and Treaties made, or which shall be made, under their Authority;—to all Cases affecting Ambassadors, other public Ministers and Consuls;—to all Cases of admiralty and maritime Jurisdiction;—to Controversies to which the United States shall be a Party;—to Controversies between two or more States;—between a State and Citizens of another State;—between Citizens of different States;—between Citizens of the same State claiming Lands under Grants of different States, and between a State, or the Citizens thereof, and foreign States, Citizens or Subjects....

Valley Forge Christian College v.
Americans United for Separation of Church & State, Inc.
454 U.S. 464 (1982)

Justice REHNQUIST delivered the opinion of the Court.

[A group claiming to represent 90,000 taxpayers brought an action in federal court seeking to enjoin the federal government from transferring federal property to a nonprofit religious college at no financial cost to the college, contending that the action violated the Establishment Clause of the First Amendment. The issue facing the Court is whether the group had standing to bring the suit.]

   ....

II

Article III of the Constitution limits the "judicial power" of the United States to the resolution of "cases" and "controversies." The constitutional power of federal courts cannot be defined, and indeed has no substance, without reference to the necessity "to adjudge the legal rights of litigants in actual controversies." The requirements of Art. III are not satisfied merely because a party requests a court of the United States to declare its legal rights, and has couched that request for forms of relief historically associated with courts of law in terms that have a familiar ring to those trained in the legal process. The judicial power of the United States defined by Art. III is not an unconditioned authority to determine the constitutionality of legislative or executive acts. The power to declare the rights of individuals and to measure the authority of governments, this Court said 90 years ago, "is legitimate only in the last resort, and as a necessity in the determination of real, earnest and vital controversy." Otherwise, the power "is not judicial ... in the sense in which judicial power is granted by the Constitution to the courts of the United States."

As an incident to the elaboration of this bedrock requirement, this Court has always required that a litigant have "standing" to challenge the action sought to be adjudicated in the lawsuit. The term "standing" subsumes a blend of constitutional requirements and prudential considerations, and it has not always been clear in the opinions of this Court whether particular features of the "standing" requirement have been required by Art. III *ex proprio vigore*, or whether they are requirements that the Court itself has erected and which were not compelled by the language of the Constitution.

A recent line of decisions, however, has resolved that ambiguity, at least to the following extent: at an irreducible minimum, Art. III requires the party who invokes the court's authority to "show that he personally has suffered some actual or threatened injury as a result of the putatively illegal conduct of the defendant," and that the injury "fairly can be traced to the challenged action" and "is likely to be redressed by a favorable decision." In this manner does Art. III limit the federal judicial power "to those disputes which confine federal courts to a role consistent with a system of separated powers and which are traditionally thought to be capable of resolution through the judicial process."

The requirement of "actual injury redressable by the court" serves several of the "implicit policies embodied in Article III." It tends to assure that the legal questions presented to the court will be resolved, not in the rarified atmosphere of a debating society, but in a concrete factual context conducive to a realistic appreciation of the consequences of judicial action. The "standing" requirement serves other purposes. Because it assures an actual factual setting in which the litigant asserts a claim of injury in fact, a court may decide the case with some confidence that its decision will not pave the way for lawsuits which have some, but not all, of the facts of the case actually decided by the court.

The Art. III aspect of standing also reflects a due regard for the autonomy of those persons likely to be most directly affected by a judicial order. The federal courts have abjured appeals to their authority which would convert the judicial process into "no more than a vehicle for the vindication of the value interests of concerned bystanders." Were the federal courts merely publicly funded forums for the ventilation of public grievances or the refinement of jurisprudential understanding, the concept of "standing" would be quite unnecessary. But the "cases and controversies" language of Art. III forecloses the conversion of courts of the United States into judicial versions of college debating forums. As we said in *Sierra Club v. Morton*, 405 U.S. 727, 740 (1972):

> "The requirement that a party seeking review must allege facts showing that he is himself adversely affected ... does serve as at least a rough attempt to put the decision as to whether review will be sought in the hands of those who have a direct stake in the outcome."

The exercise of judicial power, which can so profoundly affect the lives, liberty, and property of those to whom it extends, is therefore restricted to litigants who can show "injury in fact" resulting from the action which they seek to have the court adjudicate.

The exercise of the judicial power also affects relationships between the coequal arms of the National Government. The effect is, of course, most vivid when a federal court declares unconstitutional an act of the Legislative or Executive Branch. While the exercise of that "ultimate and supreme function" is a formidable means of vindicating individual rights, when employed unwisely or unnecessarily it is also the ultimate threat to the continued effectiveness of the federal courts in performing that role. While the propriety of such action by a federal court has been recognized since *Marbury v. Madison*, 1 Cranch 137 (1803), it has been recognized as a tool of last resort on the part of the federal judiciary throughout its nearly 200 years of existence:

> "[R]epeated and essentially head-on confrontations between the life-tenured branch and the representative branches of government will not, in the long run, be beneficial to either. The public confidence essential to the former and the vitality critical to the latter may well erode if we do not exercise self-restraint in the utilization of our power to negative the actions of the other branches."

Proper regard for the complex nature of our constitutional structure requires neither that the Judicial Branch shrink from a confrontation with the other two coequal branches of the Federal Government, nor that it hospitably accept for adjudication claims of constitutional violation by other branches of government where the claimant has not suffered cognizable injury. Thus, this Court has "refrain[ed] from passing upon the constitutionality of an act [of the representative branches] unless obliged to do so in the proper performance of our judicial function, when the question is raised by a party whose interests entitle him to raise it." The importance of this precondition should not be underestimated as a means of "defin[ing] the role assigned to the judiciary in a tripartite allocation of power."

Beyond the constitutional requirements, the federal judiciary has also adhered to a set of prudential principles that bear on the question of standing. Thus, this Court has held that "the plaintiff generally must assert his own legal rights and interests, and cannot rest his claim to relief on the legal rights or interests of third parties." In addition, even when the plaintiff has alleged redressable injury sufficient to meet the requirements of Art. III, the Court has refrained from adjudicating "abstract questions of wide public significance" which amount to "generalized grievances," pervasively shared and most appropriately addressed in the representative branches. Finally, the Court has required that the plaintiff's complaint fall within "the zone of interests to be protected or regulated by the statute or constitutional guarantee in question."

Merely to articulate these principles is to demonstrate their close relationship to the policies reflected in the Art. III requirement of actual or threatened injury amenable to judicial remedy. But neither the counsels of prudence nor the policies implicit in the "case or controversy" requirement should be mistaken for the rigorous Art. III requirements themselves. Satisfaction of the former cannot substitute for a demonstration of "'distinct and palpable injury'... that is likely to be redressed if the requested relief is granted." That requirement states a limitation on judicial power, not merely a factor to be balanced in the weighing of so-called "prudential" considerations.

We need not mince words when we say that the concept of "Art. III standing" has not been defined with complete consistency in all of the various cases decided by this Court which have discussed it, nor when we say that this very fact is probably proof that the concept cannot be reduced to a one-sentence or one-paragraph definition. But of one thing we may be sure: Those who do not possess Art. III standing may not litigate as suitors in the courts of the United States. Article III, which is every bit as important in its circumscription of the judicial power of the United States as in its granting of that power, is not merely a troublesome hurdle to be overcome if possible so as to reach the "merits" of a lawsuit which a party desires to have adjudicated; it is a part of the basic charter promulgated by the Framers of the Constitution at Philadelphia in 1787, a charter which created a general government, provided for the interaction between that government and the governments of the several States, and was later amended so as to either enhance or limit its authority with respect to both States and individuals....

[The dissenting opinions of Justices Brennan and Stevens are omitted.]

Hardwick v. Bowers

760 F.2d 1202 (11th Cir. 1985)

JOHNSON, Circuit Judge:

The Atlanta Police arrested Michael Hardwick on August 3, 1982, because he had committed the crime of sodomy with a consenting male adult in the bedroom of his own home. Charges were brought as a result of the arrest and after a hearing in the Municipal Court of Atlanta Hardwick was bound over to the Superior Court. At that point the District Attorney's office decided not to present the case to the grand jury unless further evidence developed.

Hardwick then filed this suit asking the federal district court to declare unconstitutional the Georgia statute that criminalizes sodomy, O.C.G.A. § 16-6-2 (1984). Hardwick alleged in his complaint that he is a practicing homosexual who regularly engages in private homosexual acts and will do so in the future. He was joined in bringing the suit by John and Mary Doe, a married couple acquainted with Hardwick. They claimed that they desired to engage in sexual activity proscribed by the statute but had been "chilled and deterred" by the existence of the statute and the recent arrest of Hardwick.

The complaint named as defendants Michael Bowers, Attorney General of Georgia; Lewis Slaton, District Attorney for Fulton County; and George Napper, Public Safety Commissioner of Atlanta....

I. STANDING

A federal court may not hear a legal claim unless it arises from a genuine case or controversy. A case or controversy requires a plaintiff with a personal stake in the outcome sufficient to assure an adversarial presentation of the case. Hence, a plaintiff must demonstrate that he or she has suffered an actual or threatened injury caused by the challenged conduct of the defendant.

The State is not currently prosecuting Hardwick or the Does under the sodomy statute. The Does have never been arrested under the statute and Hardwick cannot rely solely on his past arrest to confer upon him standing to challenge the constitutionality of the statute. This suit, therefore, presents an anticipatory challenge to the statute. The standing of each of the plaintiffs will depend on whether the threat of prosecution under this statute is real and immediate or "imaginary" and "speculative."

A court can estimate the likelihood of prosecution by examining the identity and interests of each of the parties. The interest of the State in enforcing the statute, along with past enforcement patterns, provides one indication; the interest of the plaintiff in engaging in the prohibited activity provides another.

The interest of the State in prosecuting these plaintiffs need not take the form of a specific threat of prosecution against them individually, although such a threat will often suffice to give a plaintiff standing. A general threat of prosecution against an identifiable group may confer standing in some instances. For instance, in *Lake Carriers' Association v. MacMullan,* 406 U.S. 498 (1972), the Court ruled that a group of bulk cargo vessel owners had standing to challenge a state law, about to go into effect, mandating certain sewage disposal methods for cargo vessels. Even though the State had threatened no particular owner with prosecution under the statute, it announced that it would prosecute violators as soon as the statute became effective.

The past enforcement of the statute against Hardwick is especially significant in measuring the State's intentions of prosecuting him in the future. Hardwick alleges that his arrest resulted from a situation in which he regularly places himself, one that will recur often in the future.... A past enforcement effort often will confirm the reasonableness of a plaintiff's subjective fear of prosecution. This is particularly true in Hardwick's case if one accepts as true his allegation that the Atlanta Police enforce the statute in a way that places all practicing homosexuals in imminent danger of arrest.

A second indicator of threatened harm to these plaintiffs comes from the nature of their interest in violating the statute. Each of them claims that their normal course of activity will lead them to violate the statute, completely apart from their desire to have it invalidated. Hardwick's status as a homosexual adds special credence to his claim. While a plaintiff hoping only to challenge a statute might overestimate his or her willingness to risk actual prosecution, a plaintiff who genuinely desires to engage in conduct regardless of its legal status presents a court with a more plausible threat of future prosecution.

In some cases, the authentic interest of the plaintiff in engaging in the prohibited conduct can establish standing even though the only threat of enforcement by the State comes from the very existence of the statute. The Supreme Court in *Babbitt v. United Farm Workers National Union,* 442 U.S. 289, 302–03 (1979), held that a union could challenge a state law prohibiting deceptive advertising relating to farm products because the union planned to sponsor advertising campaigns in the future and the State had not disavowed any intention of enforcing the statute. The risk that the State would detect the inadvertent use of an inaccuracy in an advertisement by the union and would prosecute for that offense was a threat immediate enough to give the union standing....

The past arrest of Hardwick, combined with the continuing resolve on the part of the State to enforce the sodomy statute against homosexuals and the authenticity of Hardwick's desire to engage in the proscribed activity in the future, leads us to agree with the district court that Hardwick has standing to bring this lawsuit. The issue of the Does' standing is less straightforward. They have not been arrested or threatened with arrest for sodomy. At first glance, they appear to be in the same position as several of the plaintiffs in *Younger v. Harris,* 401 U.S. 37, 40–42 (1971), who intervened in a federal suit filed by an acquaintance who had been prosecuted by the state under a criminal syndicalism law. The intervenors, teachers, alleged that the existence of the statute and the prosecution of Harris had "inhibited" their teaching and had left them "uncertain" as to their legal rights. The Court ruled that the intervenors had no standing.

The Does argue that they do not stand in precisely the same position as the intervenors in *Younger* because the defendants in that case brought their appeal after the entry of final judgment in the three-judge district court. The intervenors had been given an opportunity to present evidence of a realistic probability of prosecution apart from their unsupported fears; they had presented no such evidence. The Does, on the other hand, have not had an opportunity to engage in discovery and to present evidence relating to the enforcement of this statute against married couples.

The lack of evidence related to threat of injury should in many cases lead a court to permit discovery and to make factual findings before dismissing a suit for lack of standing. The Does, however, did not allege in their complaint that they faced a serious risk of prosecution. They stated only that the existence of the statute along with the arrest of Hardwick had "chilled and deterred" them and had "interfered" with decisions regarding their private lives. In resisting the defendants' motion to dismiss for lack of standing, the Does never claimed membership in a group especially likely to be prosecuted. Throughout the proceedings in the district court, including the motion for reconsideration of the judgment, the Does claimed that the existence of the statute, its literal applicability to their situation, and the refusal of the State to disavow any intent to prosecute them combined to give them standing. At no time before this appeal did they request discovery or an evidentiary hearing to determine the likelihood of future prosecution; they filed no affidavit to establish any realistic threat. Under these circumstances, *Younger v. Harris, supra,* controls and we affirm the district court's dismissal of the Does' complaint for lack of standing....

[The opinion of Judge Kravitch, concurring in part and dissenting in part, is omitted.]

Smelt v. County of Orange
447 F.3d 673 (9th Cir. 2006)

FERNANDEZ, Circuit Judge.

....

BACKGROUND

It is agreed: Smelt and Hammer are both males who wish to obtain a California marriage license and to marry each other in that state. They applied to the County Clerk of Orange County, California, for issuance of a marriage license on two occasions. They were denied a license both times "because [they] are of the same gender." Were it not for that, "[they] meet the qualifications for issuance of a marriage license. [They] applied for and received a Declaration of Domestic Partnership from the State of California dated January 10, 2000."

Smelt and Hammer then brought this action....

[T]he complaint raised federal constitutional challenges to DOMA. Specifically, it alleged that Section 2 of DOMA (28 U.S.C. § 1738C)[10] violates the United States Constitution's Due Process Cause (Fifth Amendment), equal protection rights (Fifth Amendment), the Right to Privacy, and the Full Faith and Credit Clause. Finally, it alleged that Section 3 of DOMA (1 U.S.C. § 7)[11] violates the "liberty interests protected by the Due Process Clause"; discriminates "on the basis of gender" and "sexual orientation" in violation of equal protection; and violates "the privacy interests protected by the Right to Privacy."

....

The district court ultimately issued a published order ... (2) deciding that Smelt and Hammer have no standing to challenge Section 2 of DOMA (28 U.S.C. § 1738C); and (3) finding that Smelt and Hammer have standing to challenge Section 3 of DOMA (1 U.S.C. § 7), but that the section does not violate the United States Constitution.

Needless to say, Smelt and Hammer disagreed; this appeal followed....

DISCUSSION

....

II. DOMA; Standing

As we earlier noted, Smelt and Hammer have attacked both of the operative sections of DOMA. However, no state has determined that they are married for state purposes, and they do not suggest that they have applied for and been denied some federal benefit. Thus, we are necessarily faced with the issue of standing....

"Over the years," the Supreme Court has "established that the irreducible constitutional minimum of standing contains three elements." *Lujan v. Defenders of Wildlife*, 504 U.S. 555, 560 (1992). Those are:

---

10. "No State, territory, or possession of the United States, or Indian tribe, shall be required to give effect to any public act, record, or judicial proceeding of any other State, territory, possession, or tribe respecting a relationship between persons of the same sex that is treated as a marriage under the laws of such other State, territory, possession, or tribe, or a right or claim arising from such relationship." 28 U.S.C. § 1738C.

11. "In determining the meaning of any Act of Congress, or of any ruling, regulation, or interpretation of the various administrative bureaus and agencies of the United States, the word 'marriage' means only a legal union between one man and one woman as husband and wife, and the word 'spouse' refers only to a person of the opposite sex who is a husband or a wife." 1 U.S.C. § 7.

First, the plaintiff must have suffered an "injury in fact"—an invasion of a legally protected interest which is (a) concrete and particularized, and (b) "actual or imminent, not 'conjectural' or 'hypothetical.'" Second, there must be a causal connection between the injury and the conduct complained of—the injury has to be "fairly ... trace[able] to the challenged action of the defendant, and not ... th[e] result [of] the independent action of some third party not before the court." Third, it must be "likely," as opposed to merely "speculative," that the injury will be "redressed by a favorable decision."

Id. at 560–61. The burden of showing that there is standing rests on the shoulders of the party asserting it.

But there is still more to standing requirements because, beyond constitutional standing, there are prudential standing principles to which "the federal judiciary has also adhered." *Valley Forge Christian Coll. v. Ams. United for Separation of Church & State, Inc.*, 454 U.S. 464, 474 (1982). As the Supreme Court has put it:

[T]his Court has held that "the plaintiff generally must assert his own legal rights and interests, and cannot rest his claim to relief on the legal rights or interests of third parties." In addition, even when the plaintiff has alleged redressable injury sufficient to meet the requirements of Art. III, the Court has refrained from adjudicating "abstract questions of wide public significance" which amount to "generalized grievances," pervasively shared and most appropriately addressed in the representative branches. Finally, the Court has required that the plaintiff's complaint fall within "the zone of interests to be protected or regulated by the statute or constitutional guarantee in question."

Id. at 474–75 (citations omitted).

With those principles in hand, we can approach Smelt and Hammer's attacks on DOMA. We must decide whether Smelt and Hammer have established constitutional and prudential standing as to either of the two relevant DOMA sections. They have not.

We first consider Section 2 of DOMA (28 U.S.C. § 1738C), which, in effect, indicates that no state is *required* to give full faith and credit to another state's determination that "a relationship between persons of the same sex ... is treated as marriage." The insurmountable hurdle that Smelt and Hammer face here is the requirement that they show some actual or imminent injury as opposed to a mere conjectural or hypothetical one.

No state has determined that Smelt and Hammer are married. In fact, as matters now stand California will not do so. Were they to change their residence to Massachusetts, their situation might change, but they have placed nothing before us to suggest that they have gone, or intend to go, to that state. In sum, while Section 2 may affect someone who has been declared married in some state, Smelt and Hammer do not come within that category of people. That being so, we agree with the district court that Smelt and Hammer lacked standing to attack Section 2 of DOMA. But, when it comes to Section 3 of DOMA, we depart from the district court's opposite conclusion.

Section 3 of DOMA (1 U.S.C. § 7) is definitional. The word "marriage" and the word "spouse" are defined for the purposes of federal statutes, rules and regulations. Marriage, it declares, "means only a legal union between one man and one woman as husband and wife." It does not purport to preclude Congress or anyone else in the federal system from extending benefits to those who are not included within that definition.

Here, as with Section 2 of DOMA, Smelt and Hammer are not even married under any state law, or, for that matter, under the law of any foreign country. No doubt they wish they could be, but, again, they are not. We, therefore, do not see how they can claim standing to object to Congress's definition of marriage for federal statutory and regulatory purposes. It certainly is not a question of Congress's refusal to recognize *their* status. DOMA itself simply does not injure them or exclude them from some undefined benefit to which they might have been or might someday be entitled. In fact, they do not suggest that they have applied for any federal benefits, much less been denied any at this point. That they might someday be married under the law of some state or ask for some federal benefit which they are denied is not enough. In short, they have not spelled out a legally protected interest, much less one that was injured in a concrete and particularized way.…

But even if Smelt and Hammer were able to establish constitutional standing, their case stumbles on at least one of the prudential standing hurdles. It is easy to discern that Smelt and Hammer are asking the court to decide "'abstract questions of wide public significance' which amount to 'generalized grievances,' pervasively shared and most appropriately addressed in the representative branches."[34]

While a scry of the complaint might lead one to think that the issue here is not general, a true perscrutation leads to the opposite conclusion. Section 3 of DOMA is merely definitional, and we are told that the words it defines are found in well over one thousand federal statutory enactments. Again, Smelt and Hammer are not in a relationship that has been dubbed marriage by any state, much less by the State of California. True, they are in a relationship, but their attack on DOMA in its multitude of applications is one that every taxpayer and citizen in the country could theoretically bring on the basis that the definition does not include some favorite grouping within its definition of marriage. Thus, anyone could argue that some federal statute might deprive some person in some group of some benefit. Any citizen[36] or taxpayer could as easily claim that some application or other of the DOMA definition to some as yet undesignated statute, which confers some public benefit or right, might exclude that person because DOMA requires a legal union, a man, and a woman.

Because of the generality of the abstract facial attack made here, neither we, nor anyone else, can know whether in the context of some particular statute as applied to some particular person in some particular situation Congress's use of the word "marriage" will amount to an unconstitutional classification. Thus, Smelt and Hammer's facial attack on Section 3 of DOMA is foreclosed because countenancing it would ignore "unambiguous limitations on taxpayer and citizen standing." *Valley Forge,* 454 U.S. at 488. They cannot establish prudential standing at this juncture. In so stating, we do not question the "'sincerity of [their] stated objectives and the depth of their commitment to them.'" *Id.* at 486 n. 21. "[B]ut standing is not measured by the intensity of the litigant's interest or the fervor of his advocacy." *Id.* at 486. Motivation alone is not enough. *Id.* at 486 n. 21. No doubt Smelt and Hammer find DOMA "personally offensive," but that does not suffice to give them standing.

---

34. We recognize that Congress did already address the definition of marriage in DOMA, but Smelt and Hammer's generalized attack remains a fit topic for that body rather than the courts. For example, legislation about same-sex couples is currently pending in Congress. *See* Domestic Partnership Benefits and Obligations Act, H.R. 3267, 109th Cong. (2005); Family and Medical Leave Inclusion Act, H.R. 475, 109th Cong. (2005); Marriage Protection Amendment, S.J. Res. 1, 109th Cong. (2005).

36. That could be a polygamist, a polyandrist, one or both of two roommates or friends (perhaps loving friends), any member of a group of two or more people, a member of a partnership, a corporation, and—as the latter suggests—even a single person.

If it be thought that this approach will insulate Section 3 from attack because nobody can, or will, have standing to bring an action, we must respond as has the Supreme Court. In the first place, "[t]he federal courts were simply not constituted as ombudsmen of the general welfare." *Valley Forge,* 454 U.S. at 487. Secondly, as the Court said:

> But "[t]he assumption that if [appellants] have no standing to sue, no one would have standing, is not a reason to find standing." This view would convert standing into a requirement that must be observed only when satisfied. Moreover, we are unwilling to assume that injured parties are nonexistent simply because they have not joined [appellants] in their suit. The law of averages is not a substitute for standing.

Id. at 489. Similarly, we will not assume that, considering all of the individuals affected by all of the statutes that include the word "marriage," nobody will be able to complain. Certainly, we cannot say that there is no person who will or can bring an action when some particular statute is applied to that person in some particular way. As it is, however, not only are Smelt and Hammer's claims excessively generalized, but also it is impossible to ascertain whether Smelt and Hammer will ever be within the zone of interest of some particular enactment.

In fine, Smelt and Hammer lack standing to attack the constitutionality of Section 3 of DOMA....

[The opinion of Judge Farris, concurring in the result, is omitted.]

Finstuen v. Crutcher
496 F.3d 1139 (10th Cir. 2007)

EBEL, Circuit Judge.

Defendant-Appellant Dr. Mike Crutcher, sued in his official capacity as the Commissioner of Health (hereinafter referred to as "Oklahoma State Department of Health ('OSDH')") appeals a district court judgment that a state law barring recognition of adoptions by same-sex couples already finalized in another state is unconstitutional. OSDH also appeals the district court's order requiring it to issue a revised birth certificate for E.D., a Plaintiff-Appellee who was born in Oklahoma but adopted in California by a same-sex couple....

I.

Three same-sex couples and their adopted children have challenged the following amendment to Oklahoma's statute governing the recognition of parent-child relationships that are created by out-of-state adoptions.

§ 7502-1.4. Foreign adoptions

A. The courts of this state shall recognize a decree, judgment, or final order creating the relationship of parent and child by adoption, issued by a court or other governmental authority with appropriate jurisdiction in a foreign country or in another state or territory of the United States. The rights and obligations of the parties as to matters within the jurisdiction of this state shall be determined as though the decree, judgment, or final order were issued by a court of this state. Except that, this state, any of its agencies, or any court of this state shall not recognize an adoption by more than one individual of the same sex from any other state or foreign jurisdiction.

Okla. Stat. tit. 10, § 7502-1.4(A) (the "adoption amendment").

Each of the three families has a different set of circumstances. Mr. Greg Hampel and Mr. Ed Swaya are residents of Washington, where they jointly adopted child V in 2002. V was born in Oklahoma, and pursuant to an "open" adoption agreement with V's biological mother, the men agreed to bring V to Oklahoma to visit her mother "from time to time." However, they do not state any plans to move to Oklahoma or have any ongoing interactions with the state of Oklahoma. After V's adoption, Mr. Hampel and Mr. Swaya requested that OSDH issue a new birth certificate for V. OSDH did so on July 7, 2003, but named only Mr. Hampel as V's parent. Mr. Hampel and Mr. Swaya contested that action, prompting OSDH to seek an opinion from the Oklahoma attorney general as to whether it must fulfill the request to list both fathers on the birth certificate. The attorney general opined that the U.S. Constitution's Full Faith and Credit Clause required Oklahoma to recognize any validly issued out-of-state adoption decree. OSDH subsequently issued V a new birth certificate naming both men as parents. The state legislature responded one month later by enacting the adoption amendment.

Lucy Doel and Jennifer Doel live with their adopted child E in Oklahoma. E was born in Oklahoma. Lucy Doel adopted E in California in January 2002. Jennifer Doel adopted E in California six months later in a second parent adoption, a process used by step-parents to adopt the biological child of a spouse without terminating the parental rights of that spouse. OSDH issued E a supplemental birth certificate naming only Lucy Doel as her mother. The Doels have requested a revised birth certificate from OSDH that would acknowledge Jennifer Doel as E's parent, but OSDH denied the request.

Anne Magro and Heather Finstuen reside in Oklahoma with their two children. Ms. Magro gave birth to S and K in New Jersey in 1998. In 2000, Ms. Finstuen adopted S and K in New Jersey as a second parent, and New Jersey subsequently issued new birth certificates for S and K naming both women as their parents.

These three families brought suit against the state of Oklahoma seeking to enjoin enforcement of the adoption amendment, naming the governor, attorney general and commissioner of health in their official capacities. The Doels also requested a revised birth certificate naming both Lucy Doel and Jennifer Doel as E's parents.

On cross-motions for summary judgment, the district court found that Mr. Hampel, Mr. Swaya and their child V lacked standing to bring the action. The court concluded their claimed injury—refraining from future visits to Oklahoma due to a fear that the state would not recognize their parent-child relationship—was too speculative. However, the district court granted summary judgment for the remaining plaintiffs, determining that they had standing and that the Oklahoma adoption amendment violated the Constitution's Full Faith and Credit, Equal Protection and Due Process Clauses. The court enjoined enforcement of the amendment, and ordered that a new birth certificate be issued for E.D. On August 29, 2006, we stayed, pending this appeal, the order to issue a revised birth certificate.

OSDH appeals from the district court's conclusion that the Doels and the Finstuen-Magro family have standing and its ruling that the adoption amendment is unconstitutional. The Oklahoma governor and attorney general did not appeal. In addition, Mr. Hampel, Mr. Swaya and their child V timely appeal from the denial of standing, and reassert their claim that the Oklahoma amendment violates their constitutional right to travel.

A. Jurisdiction

We have statutory jurisdiction over this appeal pursuant to 28 U.S.C. §§ 1291, 1331. However, prior to reaching the merits, we must also establish whether the plaintiffs possess Article III standing, which requires that a plaintiff establish injury-in-fact, causation and redressability. "While the rules for standing are less stringent for a facial challenge to a statute, a plaintiff must still satisfy the injury-in-fact requirement." The injury-in-fact must be "concrete in both a qualitative and temporal sense. The complainant must allege an injury to himself that is 'distinct and palpable,' as opposed to merely 'abstract,' and the alleged harm must be actual or imminent, not 'conjectural' or 'hypothetical.'"

The Supreme Court elaborated on the "imminence" requirement in *Lujan v. Defenders of Wildlife*: "[a]lthough 'imminence' is concededly a somewhat elastic concept, it cannot be stretched beyond its purpose, which is to ensure that the alleged injury is not too speculative for Article III purposes—that the injury is *certainly* impending.'" 504 U.S. 555, 564 n. 2 (1992). In a plea for injunctive relief, a plaintiff cannot maintain standing by asserting an injury based merely on "subjective apprehensions" that the defendant might act unlawfully. *City of Los Angeles v. Lyons*, 461 U.S. 95, 107 n. 8 (1983). "The emotional consequences ... simply are not a sufficient basis for an injunction absent a real and immediate threat of future injury by the defendant." *Id.*

"Whether a plaintiff has standing is a legal question, which we review de novo." The district court here decided the questions of standing on cross-motions for summary judgment. "On cross-motions for summary judgment, our review of the summary judgment record is de novo and we must view the inferences to be drawn from affidavits, attached exhibits and depositions in the light most favorable to the party that did not prevail." ....

We agree with the district court that the Hampel-Swaya family lacks an injury sufficiently immediate to establish standing. Mr. Hampel and Mr. Swaya argue that they are obligated under the open adoption agreement with V's mother to bring V to Oklahoma, and have refrained from this travel because of a fear that something will happen during their visit that could require Oklahoma agencies to consider the legality of their parent-child relationship. They contend that the potential harm from a failure to recognize Mr. Hampel and Mr. Swaya as V's parents infringes on their constitutional right to travel.

However, the Hampel-Swaya plaintiffs do not establish the circumstances in which the non-recognition of the adoption would arise. Oklahoma has already issued a revised birth certificate for V, and the Hampel-Swaya family does not claim that it is seeking additional benefits from the state. Ordinary travel generally does not require a state to examine the legitimacy of an asserted parent-child relationship. Although a medical emergency might create a scenario in which parental consent is required, such a situation is merely hypothetical, as opposed to an actual or impending contact with Oklahoma authorities that could jeopardize the rights of any member of the Hampel-Swaya family. Such guesswork invokes *Lyons'* admonition that "[i]t is the *reality* of the threat of repeated injury that is relevant to the standing inquiry, not the plaintiff's subjective apprehensions." The Hampel-Swaya family's alleged injuries are simply too speculative to support Article III's injury-in-fact requirement for standing.

The Finstuen-Magro family, though residing in Oklahoma, similarly fails to satisfy the injury-in-fact requirement for standing. Ms. Magro is the biological mother of children S and K. Therefore, her parental rights cannot be jeopardized by the Oklahoma amendment, and S's and K's rights that flow from that relationship are not threatened. Ms. Finstuen states that she fears having her parent-child relationship invalidated, and this fear causes her to avoid signing forms and papers—such as school permission slips or medical releases—that could trigger a question about her legitimacy as a parent. She also states that S and K are fearful due to her uncertain parental status, and that they have become more "clingy" and are "increasingly concerned about when and whether she will come home."

But Ms. Finstuen recites no encounter with any public or private official in which her authority as a parent was questioned. Most importantly, she has not established that the amendment creates an actual, imminent threat to her rights as a parent or the rights of her adopted children, because she is not presently seeking to enforce any particular right before Oklahoma authorities. The Finstuen-Magro plaintiffs, therefore, also fail to state a sufficient injury to confer standing under Article III for this suit.

In contrast, the district court correctly held that the Doels have standing under Article III. OSDH has refused to revise E's birth certificate to add Jennifer Doel's name as a parent, and thus both Jennifer and E state an injury-in-fact. In addition, Jennifer and Lucy Doel recount an encounter with medical emergency staff in which they were told by both an ambulance crew and emergency room personnel that only "the mother" could accompany E and thus initially faced a barrier to being with their child in a medical emergency. This incident too constitutes a concrete, particularized injury.

In addition to stating an injury-in-fact, the Doels must meet the causation and redressability prongs of Article III standing. "[T]here must be a causal connection between that injury and the challenged action of the defendant — the injury must be 'fairly traceable' to the defendant ... it must be likely, not merely speculative, that a favorable judgment will redress the plaintiff's injury." OSDH argues that the Doels sought a birth certificate for E just before the legislature enacted the adoption amendment, and that OSDH denied the request because of a separate statutory requirement that only the name of E's father be placed in the "father" designation on a birth certificate. Under OSDH's theory, the Doels would lack standing, because the adoption amendment did not cause the state to issue a one-parent, rather than a two-parent, birth certificate.[3]

We are not persuaded that OSDH's rationale for denying a new birth certificate was unrelated to the adoption amendment. As an initial matter, we do not assume for the purposes of standing analysis that OSDH's stated reason for denying the birth certificate was the only cause — or even an actual cause — of OSDH's action, particularly given that the statute governing the identity of fathers on birth certificates appears to apply to live births rather than supplemental adoptive birth certificates. Indeed, when the Oklahoma attorney general opined in March 2004 that the Full Faith and Credit Clause required OSDH to issue a new birth certificate to same-sex adoptive parents who adopt an Oklahoma-born child, that opinion referred to the statute governing supplemental, rather than original, birth certificates. Moreover, correspondence in the record on appeal indicates that OSDH received and denied Jennifer Doel's initial request while OSDH was waiting for the attorney general's opinion as to whether it must issue new birth certificates for same-sex parent adoptions. The Doels responded by renewing their request two months after the legislature enacted the adoption amendment, and OSDH again denied the request. The Doels then wrote OSDH through counsel to explain the validity of Jennifer Doel's request to be listed on E's birth certificate, but apparently to no avail.

Nothing in the record refutes the Doels' claim that the adoption amendment is the reason why OSDH has not yet issued a new birth certificate for E. To the contrary, the record before us strongly suggests that the amendment was the reason for the denial. OSDH's argument that a separate statute bars issuance of a new birth certificate is undermined by

---

3. OSDH did not raise this argument before the district court. "[T]he general rule [is] that an appellate court will not consider an issue raised for the first time on appeal...." However, jurisdictional issues are among the exceptional questions that we will hear even though they were not raised below. To the extent OSDH's new arguments implicate our Article III jurisdiction, we will therefore address them....

the clear language of the statute itself. Instead, by asserting that OSDH had an entirely different reason for denying the Doels' birth certificate request, OSDH attempts to insert a new "fact" in its appeal from summary judgment. "Unsupported conclusory allegations ... do not create an issue of fact." We therefore conclude that the Doels' stated injury is "fairly traceable to the defendant," and that a judgment invalidating the adoption amendment and ordering a new birth certificate will make it "likely, not merely speculative, that a favorable judgment will redress the plaintiff's injury."

Moreover, the Doels brought an equal protection claim claiming that Jennifer and Lucy Doel were injured when they were told that only "the mother" could accompany child E in a medical emergency. In equal protection claims, "the injury is the imposition of the barrier itself." We have not decided this appeal on equal protection grounds, but that is irrelevant for purposes of our standing analysis. "We do not address the merits of plaintiff's claims in our determination of standing." It is clear that the adoption amendment is the codification of a general policy not to recognize the parent-child relationship of same-sex parents, and the Doels have stated that this policy caused their injury. Thus, the Doels have standing under Article III to claim that the Oklahoma adoption amendment is unconstitutional and to request a revised birth certificate for E naming Jennifer Doel as a parent. . . .

[The opinion of Judge Hartz, concurring in part and dissenting in part, is omitted.]

Notes and Questions

1. Must one actually expose himself to the risk of arrest and prosecution in order to challenge the constitutionality of a criminal statute such as a sodomy law? Consider the following description by the U.S. Supreme Court of what is required:

> When contesting the constitutionality of a criminal statute, "it is not necessary that [the plaintiff] first expose himself to actual arrest or prosecution to be entitled to challenge [the] statute that he claims deters the exercise of his constitutional rights." *Steffel v. Thompson*, 415 U.S. 452, 459 (1974). When the plaintiff has alleged an intention to engage in a course of conduct arguably affected with a constitutional interest, but proscribed by a statute, and there exists a credible threat of prosecution thereunder, he "should not be required to await and undergo a criminal prosecution as the sole means of seeking relief." *Doe v. Bolton*, 410 U.S. 179, 188 (1973). But "persons having no fears of state prosecution except those that are imaginary or speculative, are not to be accepted as appropriate plaintiffs." *Younger v. Harris*, 401 U.S. 37, 42 (1971); *Golden v. Zwickler*, 394 U.S. 103 (1969). When plaintiffs "do not claim that they have ever been threatened with prosecution, that a prosecution is likely, or even that a prosecution is remotely possible," they do not allege a dispute susceptible to resolution by a federal court. *Younger v. Harris, supra*, at 42.

Babbitt v. United Farm Workers Nat'l Union, 442 U.S. 289, 298–99 (1979).

2. When challenging the constitutionality of a law that clearly prevents a particular class of individuals from engaging in a particular type of conduct (such as obtaining a marriage license), must the challengers first go through the motions of applying for and being denied a license to engage in the conduct in order to establish standing? *See Hailes v. United Air Lines*, 464 F.2d 1006, 1008–09 (5th Cir. 1972) (plaintiff not required to engage in "futile" act); *accord Howard v. N.J. Dept. of Civil Serv.*, 667 F.2d 1099, 1103 (3d Cir. 1981).

3. Although seldom *directly* enforced against those who engaged in consensual, non-commercial sodomy with other adults, sodomy laws nonetheless had an indirect effect on such individuals, as the *fact* that sexual activity associated with gays and lesbians was criminalized was frequently cited by courts as a basis for denying a gay parent custody of their children upon divorce, or for justifying discriminatory employment practices against a gay employee. Is that sort of injury sufficient to give a litigant standing to challenge the constitutionality of sodomy laws? *See* Christopher R. Leslie, *Standing in the Way of Equality: How States Use Standing Doctrine to Insulate Sodomy Laws from Constitutional Attack*, 2001 Wis. L. Rev. 29, 69–83 (arguing that these are sufficient injuries to justify standing to challenge the sodomy laws).

4. When a party seeks *damages* for past harms, those past harms alone are sufficient to establish standing. But when the party seeks either injunctive or declaratory relief to prevent *future* conduct by the individual or entity that caused the plaintiff harm in the past, that past harm alone does not suffice to establish standing. Rather, the plaintiff must show that it is sufficiently likely that he or she *personally* will suffer *future* harm if the defendant continues to engage in the challenged conduct. *See City of L.A. v. Lyons*, 461 U.S. 95, 101–13 (1983) (individual who had been placed in a "chokehold" by police during an arrest could not bring suit to enjoin the practice in the future or have it declared unconstitutional absent a showing that he personally was likely to be subjected to such a chokehold again in the future).

In *Hardwick v. Bowers*, no claim for damages was asserted. Why wouldn't a plaintiff in such a case routinely seek damages as a way to minimize the risk that a court will find her to lack standing? *See* Donald A. Dripps, Bowers v. Hardwick *and the Law of Standing: Noncases Make Bad Law*, 44 Emory L.J. 1417, 1425 (1995) (noting that such a claim would not typically succeed even if the underlying statute were unconstitutional, since the arrest was independently supported by a valid warrant and the officer would be shielded from liability by the doctrine of qualified immunity).

b. Organizational Standing

Irish Lesbian & Gay Organization v. Giuliani
143 F.3d 638 (2d Cir. 1998)

OAKES, Senior Circuit Judge:

The Irish Lesbian and Gay Organization ("ILGO") appeals from the judgment of the United States District Court for the Southern District of New York, John G. Koeltl, *Judge,* dismissing their suit against the City of New York, its Mayor, and its Police Commissioner (collectively, "the Defendants"). ILGO sued the Defendants under 42 U.S.C. § 1983 for violating ILGO's free speech and equal protection rights by denying ILGO a permit to hold a parade on 5th Avenue in advance of the 1996 annual St. Patrick's Day parade put on by the New York County Board of the Ancient Order of Hibernians ("AOH")....

ILGO, a group of lesbians and gay men of Irish descent, has since 1991 sought to participate in the annual St. Patrick's Day Parade ("the Parade") hosted by AOH. In 1992 and 1993 ILGO filed suit in federal district court to compel AOH to allow it to march in the Parade. These challenges were denied under reasoning anticipating the Supreme Court's decision in *Hurley v. Irish-American Gay, Lesbian and Bisexual Group*, 515 U.S. 557 (1995). ILGO has since then sought to stage a protest march on the morning of the same day and along the same route as the Parade. In every year since 1992, the police have opposed allowing ILGO to march along the Parade route prior to the Parade, and ILGO has refused to consider alternative times or venues for its march. In 1993 and 1994, ILGO attempted to stage a march without police approval, and several hundred ILGO supporters were arrested.

On December 10, 1994, ILGO applied for a formal permit to conduct a parade on 5th [A]venue from 42nd to 86th Street a few hours before the 1995 Parade. This application was made pursuant to New York City Administrative Code § 10-110, which requires the police commissioner to grant parade permit requests subject to two broad restrictions. The first makes it "unlawful" for the commissioner to grant a permit if "the commissioner has good reason to believe that the proposed procession … will be disorderly in character or tend to disturb the public peace." The second forbids the use of any street which is subject to "great congestion or traffic" and is "chiefly of a business or mercantile character." Section 10-110 specifically exempts parades, such as the AOH Parade, which have been marching annually for "more than ten years prior to July seventh, nineteen hundred fourteen," from compliance with its provisions.

ILGO received no response to its 1995 permit request, and filed an Article 78 petition in New York State Supreme Court to compel the City to grant the permit and to enjoin the city from denying similar permits in future years. Defendants removed the case to federal district court. The District Court (Keenan, *J.*) denied ILGO's motion for a preliminary injunction and dismissed the case. ILGO appealed the denial of the preliminary injunction to this Court, which affirmed. ILGO also brought a motion under Fed. R. Civ. Proc. § 59(e) seeking clarification as to whether the District Court's judgment applied to ILGO's request for a permanent injunction concerning future permit requests. The District Court refused to amend the judgment, but stated that the decision referred only to the denial of a permit to march on St. Patrick's Day, 1995, since claims regarding future permit applications were not yet ripe. On October 11, 1995, ILGO again applied for a permit to stage an earlier parade on St. Patrick's Day, 1996, using substantially the same route as the AOH parade. The permit request was denied, as was ILGO's motion for a preliminary injunction. The District Court (Koeltl, *J.*) then granted the Defendants['] motion for judgment on the pleadings pursuant to Fed.R.Civ.P. 12(c) on December 24, 1996.…

The district court dismissed ILGO's…. claim for compensatory damages on the ground that the organization lacked standing to sue for damages on behalf of its members.…

An organization may have standing in either of two ways. It may file suit on its own behalf "to seek judicial relief from injury to itself and to vindicate whatever rights and immunities the association itself may enjoy." *Warth v. Seldin*, 422 U.S. 490, 511 (1975). It may also assert the rights of its members under the doctrine of associational standing. *See Hunt v. Washington State Apple Advertising Comm'n*, 432 U.S. 333, 343–45 (1977). To bring suit on behalf of its membership, the organization must demonstrate that "(a) its members would otherwise have standing to sue in their own right; (b) the interests it seeks to protect are germane to the organization's purpose; and (c) neither the claim asserted nor the relief requested requires the participation of individual members in the lawsuit." *Id.* at 343.

ILGO's complaint stated that it sought "damages to redress the deprivation by the Defendants of the rights secured to ILGO under the Constitution and laws of the United States." Specifically, ILGO alleged that its "inability lawfully to protest [its] exclusion [from the Parade has] injured ILGO … in many ways.…" Among the alleged injuries, ILGO asserted that,

> [m]embers of ILGO have been subjected to family rejection and public ridicule, have been told they are not Irish, have been arrested and have lost their jobs. Perhaps most significantly, the exclusion of and related hostility toward ILGO have divided and isolated ILGO from the rest of the Irish community.

The district court evaluated ILGO's damages claim only under the rubric of associational standing and found that ILGO failed to meet the third prong of the *Hunt* test. The court concluded that to establish the injuries alleged in the complaint—that members had suffered humiliation, had lost their jobs, been arrested, and been told they were "not Irish"— would require the participation of individual members in the lawsuit. This determination was obviously correct, but was incomplete because the court failed to evaluate whether ILGO could bring suit on its own behalf.

It is well established that "organizations are entitled to sue on their own behalf for injuries they have sustained." To do so, the organization must "meet[ ] the same standing test that applies to individuals.... [by] show[ing] actual or threatened injury in fact that is fairly traceable to the alleged illegal action and likely to be redressed by a favorable court decision."

The denial of a particular opportunity to express one's views can give rise to a compensable injury. An organization, as well as an individual, may suffer from the lost opportunity to express its message. That Defendants offered to provide ILGO with other venues and opportunities to express its message may lessen the amount of damages due to ILGO, but ILGO is still entitled to recover if the City unlawfully denied the organization the opportunity to express its message in the way it preferred.[5]

Even if ILGO's lost opportunity for expression were not a compensable injury, a denial of First Amendment rights may give rise to more tangible harms. Although an association like ILGO cannot suffer humiliation or other emotional distress, ILGO's complaint sets forth sufficient general factual allegations of harm to its reputation arising from the Defendants' conduct to show standing. ILGO alleged in its complaint that among the "many ways" ILGO had been harmed by its inability to protest lawfully its exclusion from the Parade, "[p]erhaps most significantly, the exclusion of and related hostility toward ILGO have divided and isolated ILGO from the rest of the Irish community." Although AOH's exclusion of ILGO from the Parade is not traceable to the Defendants' conduct, and would not be redressed by a favorable decision in this case, ILGO's complaint, broadly interpreted, does allege that the City's refusal to allow ILGO lawfully to protest its exclusion from the Parade has damaged ILGO's reputation among the Irish community in New York. Such an injury is sufficient to demonstrate standing to sue for compensatory damages, especially since one of ILGO's stated purposes is to combat prejudice against its members within the Irish community.

Finally, ILGO also has standing to assert a claim for nominal damages. Nominal damages are available in actions alleging a violation of constitutionally protected rights, even without proof of any actual injury. Although ILGO did not specifically request nominal damages in its pleadings, we have not precluded the award of nominal damages in the past

---

5. Although the loss of an opportunity to express oneself is a compensable injury, ILGO does not have standing to request damages on behalf of its members to redress this harm. "[W]hether an organization has standing to invoke the court's remedial powers on behalf of its members depends in substantial measure on the nature of the relief sought." *Warth,* 422 U.S. at 515. An association generally cannot seek relief in damages for injuries to its members because unless the alleged injury is "common to [its] entire membership, [and] shared by all to an equal degree ... both the fact and extent of injury would require individualized proof." *Id.* at 515–16. ILGO contends that the deprivation of constitutional freedoms complained of here was shared equally by its entire membership. However, any recovery must be based on actual loss, and not on "the abstract value of a constitutional right." Therefore, the testimony of individual members would still be required to establish the extent of reasonably quantifiable loss suffered by each. For instance, any member who had not planned to participate in the protest parade might not be entitled to recover any compensatory damages.

if the complaint explicitly sought compensatory damages. Therefore, even if ILGO is not able to produce specific facts demonstrating an actual injury at successive stages of the litigation, ILGO may still be entitled to nominal damages upon proof of discrimination by the Defendants.

....

[The opinion of Judge Real, concurring in part and dissenting in part, is omitted.]

Notes and Questions

1. As indicated by the *Irish Gay and Lesbian Organization* court, under some circumstances, an association or organization has standing to bring a suit not only on its own behalf, but also on behalf of its members. Specifically, it may do so when:

> (a) its members would otherwise have standing to sue in their own right; (b) the interests it seeks to protect are germane to the organization's purpose; and (c) neither the claim asserted nor the relief requested requires the participation of the individual members in the lawsuit.

Hunt v. Wash. State Apple Adver. Com'n, 432 U.S. 333, 343 (1977). The Supreme Court has in cases decided both prior and subsequent to *Hunt* clarified that the first element of the test for associational standing requires only that *at least one* of the members of the organization would have standing to sue in her own right, *not* that all such members would have standing to sue. *See United Food & Commercial Workers Union Local 751 v. Brown Grp., Inc.*, 517 U.S. 544, 554–55 (1996); *Warth v. Seldin*, 422 U.S. 490, 511 (1975).

2. Under the third element of the *Hunt* test, an association lacks standing to sue on behalf of its membership where the suit "requires the participation of the individual members in the lawsuit." Under what circumstances would an action require the participation of the individual members? *See Hunt*, 432 U.S. at 344 (noting that this would occur in cases requiring "individualized proof"). *Accord Warth v. Seldin*, 422 U.S. 490, 515–16 (1975).

Given the third element of the *Hunt* test, when an association sues on behalf of its members, will it *ever* have standing to sue for damages? *See United Food & Commercial Workers Union Local 751 v. Brown Grp., Inc.*, 517 U.S. 544, 553–54 & n.5 (1996) (noting that the Court has only found associational standing in cases seeking injunctive or declaratory relief, not those seeking damages, but leaving open the possibility that standing might exist where the damages were simple to calculate); *Warth v. Seldin*, 422 U.S. 490, 515 (1975) (leaving open the possibility of standing to seek damages on behalf of members where the damages are "common to the entire membership" and "shared by all in equal degree").

3. As indicated above, as a general matter, a plaintiff can only assert her own rights, and lacks standing to assert the rights of third parties. Nonetheless, because this is an aspect of prudential rather than Article III standing, the Court has

> recognized the right of litigants to bring actions on behalf of third parties, provided three important criteria are satisfied: The litigant must have suffered an "injury in fact," thus giving him or her a "sufficiently concrete interest" in the outcome of the issue in dispute; the litigant must have a close relation to the third party; and there must exist some hindrance to the third party's ability to protect his or her own interests.

Powers v. Ohio, 499 U.S. 400, 410–11 (1991) (holding that criminal defendant has standing to assert equal protection rights of jurors excluded from jury service by the state on account of their race).

The second *Powers* factor—that there be a "close relation" between the litigant and the third party—focuses not so much on the intimacy of the relationship but rather whether "'the relationship between the litigant and the third party may be such that the former is fully, or very nearly, as effective a proponent of the right as the latter.'" *Powers*, 499 U.S. at 413 (quoting *Singleton v. Wulff*, 428 U.S. 106, 115 (1976)).

Moreover, regarding the third *Powers* factor—that there be a "hindrance" to the third party protecting her own interests—the focus is not merely on actual *ability* to bring an action on her own behalf, but also the practical likelihood that she would do so in light of the financial stakes involved. *Powers*, 499 U.S. at 414–15; *see also Singleton*, 428 U.S. at 116 n.6 (rejecting a contention that third party standing is appropriate only when "assertion by the third parties themselves would be 'in all practicable terms impossible.'").

4. In a case pre-dating *Powers*, the Supreme Court held that "vendors and those in like positions have been uniformly permitted to resist efforts at restricting their operations by acting as advocates of the rights of third parties who seek access to their market or function." *Craig v. Boren*, 429 U.S. 190, 195 (1976) (holding that bar owners had standing to raise equal protection claims of males between the ages of 18 and 21 who were barred from purchasing liquor under state law setting a minimum drinking age of 18 years for females and 21 years for males). Does this general statement in *Craig* survive *Powers*, or is it correct only if the three *Powers* factors are satisfied?

In answering this question, consider the other types of cases in which the Court has found third-party standing. *See, e.g., Carey v. Population Servs., Int'l*, 431 U.S. 678, 682–84 (1977) (sellers of mail-order contraceptives have standing to assert constitutional rights of potential customers); *Eisenstadt v. Baird*, 405 U.S. 438, 443–46 (1972) (distributors of contraceptives to unmarried persons have standing to assert constitutional rights of potential recipients); *Barrows v. Jackson*, 346 U.S. 249, 254–60 (1953) (white sellers of land have standing to assert constitutional rights of potential African-American purchasers).

c. Standing to Appeal

Problem 2-B: Declining to Defend

Assume the same facts as in Problem 2-A. Assume further that a plaintiff with standing has filed suit, and that the trial court rules in the plaintiff's favor. Assume further that the state officials against whom the action is brought decide not to appeal the adverse judgment against the state.

John Wilson—the leader of the citizen group that collected the signatures to get the constitutional amendment on the ballot and ran the campaign in support of the amendment—seeks to intervene and appeal the adverse judgment to the appropriate circuit of the U.S. Court of Appeals.

Does Wilson have standing to bring the appeal?

Arizonans for Official English v. Arizona
520 U.S. 43 (1997)

Justice GINSBURG delivered the opinion of the Court.

[In litigation between a citizen and state officials regarding the constitutionality of an amendment to Arizona's constitution making English the state's official language, Arizonans for Official English—a citizen group that campaigned in favor of the amendment—and its Chairman, Robert Park, sought to intervene as defendants to urge the constitutionality of the amendment on appeal after the governor announced that she would not pursue an appeal.]

III

Article III, §2, of the Constitution confines federal courts to the decision of "Cases" or "Controversies." Standing to sue or defend is an aspect of the case-or-controversy requirement. *Northeastern Fla. Chapter, Associated Gen. Contractors of America v. Jacksonville,* 508 U.S. 656, 663–664 (1993) (standing to sue); *Diamond v. Charles,* 476 U.S. 54, 56 (1986) (standing to defend on appeal). To qualify as a party with standing to litigate, a person must show, first and foremost, "an invasion of a legally protected interest" that is "concrete and particularized" and "'actual or imminent.'" *Lujan v. Defenders of Wildlife,* 504 U.S. 555, 560 (1992). An interest shared generally with the public at large in the proper application of the Constitution and laws will not do. See *Defenders of Wildlife,* 504 U.S., at 573–576. Standing to defend on appeal in the place of an original defendant, no less than standing to sue, demands that the litigant possess "a direct stake in the outcome." *Diamond,* 476 U.S., at 62.

The standing Article III requires must be met by persons seeking appellate review, just as it must be met by persons appearing in courts of first instance. *Diamond,* 476 U.S., at 62. The decision to seek review "is not to be placed in the hands of 'concerned bystanders,'" persons who would seize it "as a 'vehicle for the vindication of value interests.'" *Ibid.* An intervenor cannot step into the shoes of the original party unless the intervenor independently "fulfills the requirements of Article III." *Id.,* at 68.

In granting the petition for a writ of certiorari in this case, we called for briefing on the question whether AOE and Park have standing, consonant with Article III of the Federal Constitution, to defend in federal court the constitutionality of Arizona Constitution Article XXVIII. Petitioners argue primarily that, as initiative proponents, they have a quasi-legislative interest in defending the constitutionality of the measure they successfully sponsored. AOE and Park stress the funds and effort they expended to achieve adoption of Article XXVIII. We have recognized that state legislators have standing to contest a decision holding a state statute unconstitutional if state law authorizes legislators to represent the State's interests. See *Karcher v. May,* 484 U.S. 72, 82 (1987). AOE and its members, however, are not elected representatives, and we are aware of no Arizona law appointing initiative sponsors as agents of the people of Arizona to defend, in lieu of public officials, the constitutionality of initiatives made law of the State. Nor has this Court ever identified initiative proponents as Article-III-qualified defenders of the measures they advocated....

We thus have grave doubts whether AOE and Park have standing under Article III to pursue appellate review....

[The Court goes on to find that it lacks jurisdiction for a different reason, obviating the need to definitively resolve the issue.]

Perry v. Brown
671 F.3d 1052 (9th Cir. 2012)

REINHARDT, Circuit Judge:

Prior to November 4, 2008, the California Constitution guaranteed the right to marry to opposite-sex couples and same-sex couples alike. On that day, the People of California adopted Proposition 8, which amended the state constitution to eliminate the right of same-sex couples to marry. We consider whether that amendment violates the Fourteenth Amendment to the United States Constitution....

Before considering the constitutional question of the validity of Proposition 8's *elimination* of the rights of same-sex couples to marry, we first decide that the official sponsors of Proposition 8 are entitled to appeal the decision below, which declared the measure unconstitutional and enjoined its enforcement. The California Constitution and Elections Code endow the official sponsors of an initiative measure with the authority to represent the State's interest in establishing the validity of a measure enacted by the voters, when the State's elected leaders refuse to do so. *See Perry v. Brown,* 134 Cal. Rptr. 3d 499 (2011). It is for the State of California to decide who may assert its interests in litigation, and we respect its decision by holding that Proposition 8's proponents have standing to bring this appeal on behalf of the State....

I

....

B

In 2004, same-sex couples and the City and County of San Francisco filed actions in California state courts alleging that the State's marriage statutes violated the California Constitution. Proposition 22 was among the statutes challenged, because as an initiative statutory enactment, it was equal in dignity to an enactment by the Legislature and thus subject to the restrictions of the state constitution. The consolidated cases were eventually decided by the California Supreme Court, which held the statutes to be unconstitutional [under the due process and equal protection provisions of the California Constitution].... Following the court's decision, California counties issued more than 18,000 marriage licenses to same-sex couples.

C

Five California residents — defendants-intervenors-appellants Dennis Hollingsworth, Gail J. Knight, Martin F. Gutierrez, Hak-Shing William Tam, and Mark A. Jansson (collectively, "Proponents") — collected voter signatures and filed petitions with the state government to place an initiative on the November 4, 2008, ballot.... [T]his was an initiative constitutional amendment, which would be equal in effect to any other provision of the California Constitution.... The Proponents' measure, designated Proposition 8, proposed to add a new provision to the California Constitution's Declaration of Rights, immediately following the Constitution's due process and equal protection clauses. The provision states, "Only marriage between a man and a woman is valid or recognized in California." According to the official voter information guide, Proposition 8 "[c]hanges the California Constitution to eliminate the right of same-sex couples to marry in California." Following a contentious campaign, a slim majority of California voters (52.3 percent) approved Proposition 8. Pursuant to the state constitution, Proposition 8 took effect the next day, as article I, section 7.5 of the California Constitution.

Opponents of Proposition 8 then brought an original action for a writ of mandate in the California Supreme Court. They contended that Proposition 8 exceeded the scope of the People's initiative power because it revised, rather than amended, the California Constitution. The opponents did not raise any federal constitutional challenge to Proposition 8 in the state court. The state officials named as respondents refused to defend the measure's validity, but Proponents were permitted to intervene and do so. Following argument, the court upheld Proposition 8 as a valid initiative but construed the measure as not nullifying the 18,000-plus marriages of same-sex couples that had already been performed in the State. *Strauss v. Horton,* 207 P.3d 48, 98–110, 119–22 (Cal.2009)....

II

A

Two same-sex couples — plaintiffs Kristin Perry and Sandra Stier, and Paul Katami and Jeffrey Zarrillo — filed this action under 42 U.S.C. §1983 in May 2009, after being denied marriage licenses by the County Clerks of Alameda County and Los Angeles County, respectively. Alleging that Proposition 8 violates the Fourteenth Amendment to the United States Constitution, they sought a declaration of its unconstitutionality and an injunction barring its enforcement. The City and County of San Francisco ("San Francisco") was later permitted to intervene as a plaintiff to present evidence of the amendment's effects on its governmental interests. The defendants — the two county clerks and four state officers, including the Governor and Attorney General — filed answers to the complaint but once again refused to argue in favor of Proposition 8's constitutionality. As a result, the district court granted Proponents' motion to intervene as of right under Federal Rule of Civil Procedure 24(a) to defend the validity of the proposition they had sponsored.

The district court held a twelve-day bench trial, during which it heard testimony from nineteen witnesses and, after giving the parties a full and fair opportunity to present evidence and argument, built an extensive evidentiary record.... The court held Proposition 8 unconstitutional under the Due Process Clause because no compelling state interest justifies denying same-sex couples the fundamental right to marry. The court also determined that Proposition 8 violated the Equal Protection Clause, because there is no rational basis for limiting the designation of 'marriage' to opposite-sex couples. The court therefore entered the following injunction: "Defendants in their official capacities, and all persons under the control or supervision of defendants, are permanently enjoined from applying or enforcing Article I, §7.5 of the California Constitution."

B

Proponents appealed immediately, and a motions panel of this court stayed the district court's injunction pending appeal. The motions panel asked the parties to discuss in their briefs, as a preliminary matter, whether the Proponents had standing to seek review of the district court order. After considering the parties' arguments, we concluded that Proponents' standing to appeal depended on the precise rights and interests given to official sponsors of an initiative under California law, which had never been clearly defined by the State's highest court. We therefore certified the following question to the California Supreme Court:

> Whether under Article II, Section 8 of the California Constitution, or otherwise under California law, the official proponents of an initiative measure possess either a particularized interest in the initiative's validity or the authority to assert the State's interest in the initiative's validity, which would enable them to defend the constitutionality of the initiative upon its adoption or appeal a judgment invalidating the initiative, when the public officials charged with that duty refuse to do so.

The state court granted our request for certification in February 2011, and in November 2011 rendered its decision. *See Perry v. Brown* (*Perry VII*), 134 Cal. Rptr. 3d 499 (2011). We now resume consideration of this appeal.

III

We begin, as we must, with the issue that has prolonged our consideration of this case: whether we have jurisdiction over an appeal brought by the defendant-intervenor Proponents, rather than the defendant state and local officers who were directly enjoined by the district court order. In view of Proponents' authority under California law, we conclude that they do have standing to appeal.

For purposes of Article III standing, we start with the premise that "a State has standing to defend the constitutionality of its [laws]." *Diamond v. Charles,* 476 U.S. 54, 62 (1986). When a state law is ruled unconstitutional, either the state or a state officer charged with the law's enforcement may appeal that determination. Typically, the named defendant in an action challenging the constitutionality of a state law is a state officer, because sovereign immunity protects the state from being sued directly. In such cases, if a court invalidates the state law and enjoins its enforcement, there is no question that the state officer is entitled to appeal that determination. Moreover, there is no reason that a state itself may not also *choose* to intervene as a defendant, and indeed a state *must* be permitted to intervene if a state officer is not already party to an action in which the constitutionality of a state law is challenged. *See* 28 U.S.C. § 2403(b); Fed.R.Civ.P. 5.1; *cf.* Fed. R.App. P. 44(b). When a state does elect to become a defendant itself, the state may appeal an adverse decision about the constitutionality of one of its laws, just as a state officer may. In other words, in a suit for an injunction against enforcement of an allegedly unconstitutional state law, it makes no practical difference whether the formal party before the court is the state itself or a state officer in his official capacity.

Whether the defendant is the state or a state officer, the decision to assert the state's own interest in the constitutionality of its laws is most commonly made by the state's executive branch—the part of state government that is usually charged with enforcing and defending state law. Some sovereigns vest the authority to assert their interest in litigation *exclusively* in certain executive officers.

The states need not follow that approach, however. It is their prerogative, as independent sovereigns, to decide for themselves who may assert their interests and under what circumstances, and to bestow that authority accordingly. In *Karcher v. May,* 484 U.S. 72 (1987), for example, the Supreme Court held that the State of New Jersey was properly represented in litigation by the Speaker of the General Assembly and the President of the Senate, appearing on behalf of the Legislature, because "the New Jersey Legislature had authority under state law to represent the State's interests." Principles of federalism require that federal courts respect such decisions by the states as to who may speak for them.... It is not for a federal court to tell a state who may appear on its behalf.... Who may speak for the state is, necessarily, a question of state law. All a federal court need determine is that the state has suffered a harm sufficient to confer standing and that the party seeking to invoke the jurisdiction of the court is authorized by the state to represent its interest in remedying that harm.

Proponents claim to assert the interest of the People of California in the constitutionality of Proposition 8, which the People themselves enacted. When faced with a case arising in a similar posture, in which an Arizona initiative constitutional amendment was defended only by its sponsors, the Supreme Court expressed "grave doubts" about the sponsors' standing given that the Court was "aware of no Arizona law appointing initiative sponsors as agents of the people of Arizona to defend, in lieu of public officials, the constitutionality of initiatives made law of the State." *Arizonans for Official English v. Arizona (Arizonans),* 520 U.S. 43, 65–66 (1997). Absent some conferral of authority by state law, akin to the authority that the New Jersey legislators in *Karcher* had as "elected representatives," the Court suggested that proponents of a ballot measure would not be able to appeal a decision striking down the initiative they sponsored. *Id.* at 65.

Here, unlike in *Arizonans,* we *do* know that California law confers on "initiative sponsors" the authority "to defend, in lieu of public officials, the constitutionality of initiatives made law of the State." The California Supreme Court has told us, in a published opinion containing an exhaustive review of the California Constitution and statutes, that it does. In answering our certified question, the court held

> that when the public officials who ordinarily defend a challenged state law or appeal a judgment invalidating the law decline to do so, under article II, section 8 of the California Constitution and the relevant provisions of the Elections Code, the official proponents of a voter-approved initiative measure are authorized to assert the state's interest in the initiative's validity, enabling the proponents to defend the constitutionality of the initiative and to appeal a judgment invalidating the initiative.

"[T]he role played by the proponents in such litigation," the court explained, "is comparable to the role ordinarily played by the Attorney General or other public officials in vigorously defending a duly enacted state law and raising all arguable legal theories upon which a challenged provision may be sustained." The State's highest court thus held that California law provides precisely what the *Arizonans* Court found lacking in Arizona law: it confers on the official proponents of an initiative the authority to assert the State's interests in defending the constitutionality of that initiative, where the state officials who would ordinarily assume that responsibility choose not to do so.

We are bound to accept the California court's determination. Although other states may act differently, California's conferral upon proponents of the authority to represent the People's interest in the initiative measure they sponsored is consistent with that state's unparalleled commitment to the authority of the electorate.... As the California Supreme Court explained in answering our certified question, "[t]he initiative power would be significantly impaired if there were no one to assert the state's interest in the validity of the measure when elected officials decline to defend it in court or to appeal a judgment invalidating the measure." The authority of official proponents to "assert[] the state's interest in the validity of an initiative measure" thus "serves to safeguard the unique elements and integrity of the initiative process."

It matters not whether federal courts think it wise or desirable for California to afford proponents this authority to speak for the State, just as it makes no difference whether federal courts think it a good idea that California allows its constitution to be amended by a majority vote through a ballot measure in the first place. The People of California are largely free to structure their system of governance as they choose, and we respect their choice. All that matters, for federal standing purposes, is that the People have an interest in the validity of Proposition 8 and that, under California law, Proponents are authorized to represent the People's interest. That is the case here.

In their supplemental brief on the issue of standing, Plaintiffs argue for the first time that Proponents must satisfy the requirements of third-party standing in order to assert the interests of the State of California in this litigation. Litigants who wish "to bring actions on behalf of third parties" must satisfy three requirements. *Powers v. Ohio,* 499 U.S. 400, 410–11 (1991). First, they "must have suffered an 'injury in fact,' thus giving [them] a 'sufficiently concrete interest' in the outcome of the issue in dispute." *Id.* at 411. Second, they "must have a close relation to the third party." *Id.* Third, "there must exist some hindrance to the third party's ability to protect his or her own interests." *Id.* Plaintiffs contend that Proponents cannot satisfy these requirements with respect to the State of California as a third party.

The requirements of third-party standing, however, are beside the point: the State of California is no more a "third party" relative to Proponents than it is to the executive officers of the State who ordinarily assert the State's interest in litigation. As the California Supreme Court has explained, "the role played by the proponents" in litigation "regarding the validity or proper interpretation of a voter-approved initiative measure … is comparable to the role ordinarily played by the Attorney General or other public officials in vigorously defending a duly enacted state law." When the Attorney General of California appears in federal court to defend the validity of a state statute, she obviously need not satisfy the requirements of third-party standing; she stands in the shoes of the State to assert its interests in litigation. For the purposes of the litigation, she speaks to the court *as* the State, not as a third party. The same is true of Proponents here, just as it was true of the presiding legislative officers in *Karcher,* 484 U.S. at 82. The requirements of third-party standing are therefore not relevant.

Nor is it relevant whether Proponents have suffered a *personal* injury, in their capacities as private individuals. Although we asked the California Supreme Court whether "the official proponents of an initiative measure possess either a *particularized interest* in the initiative's validity or the authority to assert the *State's interest* in the initiative's validity," the Court chose to address only the latter type of interest. The exclusive basis of our holding that Proponents possess Article III standing is their authority to assert the interests of the State of California, rather than any authority that they might have to assert particularized interests of their *own.* Just as the Attorney General of California need not satisfy the requirements of third-party standing when she appears in federal court to defend the validity of a state statute, she obviously need not show that she would suffer any *personal* injury as a result of the statute's invalidity. The injury of which she complains is the State's, not her own. The same is true here. Because "a State has standing to defend the constitutionality of its [laws]," *Diamond,* 476 U.S. at 62, Proponents need not show that they would suffer any personal injury from the invalidation of Proposition 8. That the *State* would suffer an injury, *id.,* is enough for Proponents to have Article III standing when state law authorizes them to assert the State's interests.

To be clear, we do not suggest that state law has any "power directly to enlarge or contract federal jurisdiction." "Standing to sue in any Article III court is, of course, a federal question which does not depend on the party's … standing in state court." *Phillips Petroleum Co. v. Shutts,* 472 U.S. 797, 804 (1985). State courts may afford litigants standing to appear where federal courts would not, but whether they do so has no bearing on the parties' Article III standing in federal court.

State law does have the power, however, to answer questions antecedent to determining federal standing, such as the one here: who is authorized to assert the People's interest in the constitutionality of an initiative measure? Because the State of California has Article III standing to defend the constitutionality of Proposition 8, and because both the California Constitution and California law authorize "the official proponents of [an] initiative … to appear and assert the state's interest in the initiative's validity and to appeal a judgment invalidating the measure when the public officials who ordinarily defend the measure or appeal such a judgment decline to do so," we conclude that Proponents are proper appellants here. They possess Article III standing to prosecute this appeal from the district court's judgment invalidating Proposition 8.…

[The opinion of Judge N.R. Smith, concurring in part and dissenting in part, is omitted.]

Notes and Questions

1. In *Perry*, same-sex couples negatively impacted by California's Proposition 8 — which amended the California Constitution to ban same-sex marriages — brought a challenge against the law in a federal district court, asserting that it violated the equal protection and due process guarantees of the Fourteenth Amendment. The named defendants — the Governor and Attorney General of California and two counties — were somewhat "friendly" defendants in that they generally agreed with the plaintiffs' challenge and did not mount a vociferous defense, and they opted not to appeal the district court's ruling in the plaintiffs' favor. Does it seem right that a state constitutional amendment can be overturned by a lone district court judge and be insulated from further review in the federal court system because state officials have opted not to mount a strong defense of a voter-initiated law that they do not agree with? In that circumstance, should the sponsors of the ballot initiative have standing to step into the shoes of the state? Suppose instead the situation were reversed: a ballot initiative was passed that *granted* rights to same-sex couples, was challenged in federal court, and was struck down as unconstitutional. If the Governor and Attorney General were hostile to the rights granted by the ballot initiative, does it seem right that they (and a lone district court judge) could effectively nullify the law without further appellate review?

2. In *Perry*, the Ninth Circuit interprets *Arizonans* to hold that whether proponents of a ballot initiative have standing under state law to defend the initiative (and to appeal from an adverse ruling) when state officials fail to do so is both a necessary *and* sufficient condition for a finding that there is Article III standing to do so in the federal courts. Is that the *only* way to interpret *Arizonans*?

3. When the Ninth Circuit certified the standing question to the California Supreme Court, Judge Reinhardt, in a concurring opinion, wrote as follows:

> [T]he issues concerning standing were wholly avoidable in this case.
>
> There can be little doubt that when the Plaintiffs filed this action their purpose was to establish that there was a constitutional right to gay marriage, and to do so by obtaining a decision of the Supreme Court to that effect. Yet, according to what their counsel represented to us at oral argument, the complaint they filed and the injunction they obtained determines only that Proposition 8 may not be enforced in two of California's fifty-eight counties. They next contend that the injunction may not be appealed but that it may be extended to the remaining fifty-six counties, upon the filing of a subsequent lawsuit by the Attorney General in state court against the other County Clerks. Whether Plaintiffs are correct or not, it is clear that all of this would have been unnecessary and Plaintiffs could have obtained a statewide injunction had they filed an action against a broader set of defendants, a simple matter of pleading. Why preeminent counsel and the major law firms of which they are a part failed to do that is a matter on which I will not speculate.
>
> Next, the problem of standing would have been eliminated had the Governor or the Attorney General defended the initiative, as is ordinarily their obligation. Because they believed Proposition 8 to be unconstitutional, they did not do so here. Whether their decision not to defend the initiative was proper is a matter of some debate, although I sympathize with their view that in extraordinary circumstances they possess that right....

Perry v. Schwarzenegger, 628 F.3d 1191, 1201 (9th Cir. 2011) (Reinhardt, J., concurring).

Although Judge Reinhardt is unwilling to speculate as to why "preeminent counsel" failed to sue a broader class of defendants, are you willing to venture a guess as to whether the omission of certain defendants was inadvertent or intentional? Do you agree with Judge Reinhardt's statement that plaintiffs necessarily filed the action with the purpose of obtaining a Supreme Court ruling on the issue?

4. In *Perry*, the Ninth Circuit addressed another procedural issue separate from the merits: whether the trial court judge—who was gay—should have recused himself:

> Finally, we address Proponents' motion to vacate the district court's judgment. On April 6, 2011, after resigning from the bench, former Chief Judge Walker disclosed that he was gay and that he had for the past ten years been in a relationship with another man. Proponents moved shortly thereafter to vacate the judgment on the basis that 28 U.S.C. § 455(b)(4) obligated Chief Judge Walker to recuse himself, because he had an "interest that could be substantially affected by the outcome of the proceeding," and that 28 U.S.C. § 455(a) obligated him either to recuse himself or to disclose his potential conflict, because "his impartiality might reasonably be questioned." Chief Judge Ware, to whom this case was assigned after Chief Judge Walker's retirement, denied the motion after receiving briefs and hearing argument.
>
> The district court properly held ... that Chief Judge Walker had no obligation to recuse himself under either § 455(b)(4) or § 455(a) or to disclose any potential conflict. As Chief Judge Ware explained, the fact that a judge "could be affected by the outcome of a proceeding[,] in the same way that other members of the general public would be affected, is not a basis for either recusal or disqualification under Section 455(b)(4)." Nor could it possibly be "reasonable to presume," for the purposes of § 455(a), "that a judge is incapable of making an impartial decision about the constitutionality of a law, solely because, as a citizen, the judge could be affected by the proceeding." To hold otherwise would demonstrate a lack of respect for the integrity of our federal courts....

Perry v. Brown, 671 F.3d 1052, 1095–96 (9th Cir. 2012). Do you agree with the Ninth Circuit's conclusion? What would be the consequences for civil rights litigation generally had the Ninth Circuit ruled otherwise on the recusal question? *See Perry v. Schwarzenegger*, 790 F. Supp. 2d 1119, 1125 (N.D. Cal. 2011) ("In regards to non-pecuniary benefits reaped by judges solely by nature of their membership in a minority group, courts have cautioned against mandating recusal 'merely because of the way in which the attorneys in the case decided to frame the class,' noting ripe grounds for manipulation. Further, such a standard 'would come dangerously close to holding that minority judges must disqualify themselves from all major civil rights actions.'"). Moreover, if a case touches on race, sex, or sexual orientation, aren't *all* judges—regardless of whether they are white or black, male or female, gay or straight—in some way impacted by the outcome of the decision? If so, why only focus on the alleged interests of the minority group members?

How, if at all, would the result have differed if Judge Walker had married his same-sex partner in California prior to the adoption of Proposition 8? What if he had not married during that time period but intended to do so once any legal impediments to marriage were removed? *Cf. id.* at 1124 (noting the absence of any evidence that Judge Walker intended to marry).

2. Mootness

Problem 2-C: Moot Court?

A group of same-sex couples file a lawsuit in federal court challenging the constitutionality of a state law limiting marriage to opposite-sex couples. While the challenge is pending, the state legislature revises its marriage laws to permit same-sex couples to marry. The plaintiffs still wish to have the constitutionality of the state's pre-existing ban on same-sex marriage adjudicated, but the state objects.

Will the court proceed to adjudicate the plaintiffs' claim?

Friends of the Earth, Inc. v.
Laidlaw Environmental Services (TOC), Inc.
528 U.S. 167 (2000)

Justice GINSBURG delivered the opinion of the Court.

[A group of citizens brought suit against the holder of a National Pollution Discharge Elimination System permit, alleging that the holder of the permit exceeded the permit's limits on mercury discharges.]

II

A

The Constitution's case-or-controversy limitation on federal judicial authority, Art. III, § 2, underpins both our standing and our mootness jurisprudence, but the two inquiries differ in respects critical to the proper resolution of this case, so we address them separately....

B

Satisfied that FOE had standing under Article III to bring this action, we turn to the question of mootness.

The only conceivable basis for a finding of mootness in this case is Laidlaw's voluntary conduct—either its achievement by August 1992 of substantial compliance with its NPDES permit or its more recent shutdown of the Roebuck facility. It is well settled that "a defendant's voluntary cessation of a challenged practice does not deprive a federal court of its power to determine the legality of the practice." "[I]f it did, the courts would be compelled to leave '[t]he defendant ... free to return to his old ways.'" In accordance with this principle, the standard we have announced for determining whether a case has been mooted by the defendant's voluntary conduct is stringent: "A case might become moot if subsequent events made it absolutely clear that the allegedly wrongful behavior could not reasonably be expected to recur." The "heavy burden of persua[ding]" the court that the challenged conduct cannot reasonably be expected to start up again lies with the party asserting mootness.

The Court of Appeals justified its mootness disposition by reference to *Steel Co.,* which held that citizen plaintiffs lack standing to seek civil penalties for wholly past violations.

In relying on *Steel Co.,* the Court of Appeals confused mootness with standing. The confusion is understandable, given this Court's repeated statements that the doctrine of mootness can be described as "the doctrine of standing set in a time frame: The requisite personal interest that must exist at the commencement of the litigation (standing) must continue throughout its existence (mootness)."

Careful reflection on the long-recognized exceptions to mootness, however, reveals that the description of mootness as "standing set in a time frame" is not comprehensive. As just noted, a defendant claiming that its voluntary compliance moots a case bears the formidable burden of showing that it is absolutely clear the allegedly wrongful behavior could not reasonably be expected to recur. By contrast, in a lawsuit brought to force compliance, it is the plaintiff's burden to establish standing by demonstrating that, if unchecked by the litigation, the defendant's allegedly wrongful behavior will likely occur or continue, and that the "threatened injury [is] certainly impending." Thus, in *Lyons ...* we held that a plaintiff lacked initial standing to seek an injunction against the enforcement of a police chokehold policy because he could not credibly allege that he faced a realistic threat arising from the policy. Elsewhere in the opinion, however, we noted that a citywide moratorium on police chokeholds—an action that surely diminished the already slim likelihood that any particular individual would be choked by police—would not have mooted an otherwise valid claim for injunctive relief, because the moratorium by its terms was not permanent. The plain lesson of these cases is that there are circumstances in which the prospect that a defendant will engage in (or resume) harmful conduct may be too speculative to support standing, but not too speculative to overcome mootness.

Furthermore, if mootness were simply "standing set in a time frame," the exception to mootness that arises when the defendant's allegedly unlawful activity is "capable of repetition, yet evading review," could not exist. When, for example, a mentally disabled patient files a lawsuit challenging her confinement in a segregated institution, her post-complaint transfer to a community-based program will not moot the action, despite the fact that she would have lacked initial standing had she filed the complaint after the transfer. Standing admits of no similar exception; if a plaintiff lacks standing at the time the action commences, the fact that the dispute is capable of repetition yet evading review will not entitle the complainant to a federal judicial forum.

We acknowledged the distinction between mootness and standing most recently in *Steel Co.:*

> "The United States ... argues that the injunctive relief does constitute remediation because 'there is a presumption of [future] injury when the defendant has voluntarily ceased its illegal activity in response to litigation,' even if that occurs before a complaint is filed.... This makes a sword out of a shield. The 'presumption' the Government refers to has been applied to refute the assertion of mootness by a defendant who, when sued in a complaint that alleges present or threatened injury, ceases the complained-of activity.... It is an immense and unacceptable stretch to call the presumption into service as a substitute for the allegation of present or threatened injury upon which initial standing must be based."

Standing doctrine functions to ensure, among other things, that the scarce resources of the federal courts are devoted to those disputes in which the parties have a concrete stake. In contrast, by the time mootness is an issue, the case has been brought and litigated, often (as here) for years. To abandon the case at an advanced stage may prove more wasteful than frugal. This argument from sunk costs[5] does not license courts to retain jurisdiction over cases in which one or both of the parties plainly lack a continuing interest, as when the parties have settled or a plaintiff pursuing a nonsurviving claim has died. See, *e.g., DeFunis v. Odegaard*, 416 U.S. 312 (1974) *(per curiam)* (non-class-action challenge to constitutionality of law school admissions process mooted when plaintiff, admitted pursuant to preliminary injunction, neared graduation and defendant law school conceded that, as a matter of ordinary school policy, plaintiff would be allowed to finish his final term); *Arizonans,* 520 U.S., at 67 (non-class-action challenge to state constitutional amendment declaring English the official language of the State became moot when plaintiff, a state employee who sought to use her bilingual skills, left state employment). But the argument surely highlights an important difference between the two doctrines....

Laidlaw also asserts, in a supplemental suggestion of mootness, that the closure of its Roebuck facility, which took place after the Court of Appeals issued its decision, mooted the case. The facility closure, like Laidlaw's earlier achievement of substantial compliance with its permit requirements, might moot the case, but—we once more reiterate—only if one or the other of these events made it absolutely clear that Laidlaw's permit violations could not reasonably be expected to recur. The effect of both Laidlaw's compliance and the facility closure on the prospect of future violations is a disputed factual matter. FOE points out, for example—and Laidlaw does not appear to contest—that Laidlaw retains its NPDES permit. These issues have not been aired in the lower courts; they remain open for consideration on remand....

[The concurring opinions of Justices Stevens and Kennedy, and the dissenting opinion of Justice Scalia, are omitted.]

Federal Election Commission v. Wisconsin Right to Life, Inc.
551 U.S. 449 (2007)

Chief Justice ROBERTS announced the judgment of the Court and delivered the opinion of the Court with respect to Parts I and II, and an opinion with respect to Parts III and IV, in which Justice ALITO joins.

Section 203 of the Bipartisan Campaign Reform Act of 2002 (BCRA), 116 Stat. 91, 2 U.S.C. §441b(b)(2) (2000 ed., Supp. IV), makes it a federal crime for any corporation to broadcast, shortly before an election, any communication that names a federal candidate for elected office and is targeted to the electorate....

I

Prior to BCRA, corporations were free under federal law to use independent expenditures to engage in political speech so long as that speech did not expressly advocate the election or defeat of a clearly identified federal candidate.

BCRA significantly cut back on corporations' ability to engage in political speech. BCRA §203, at issue in these cases, makes it a crime for any labor union or incorporated entity—whether the United Steelworkers, the American Civil Liberties Union, or General Motors—to use its general treasury funds to pay for any "electioneering communication." BCRA's definition of "electioneering communication" is clear and expansive. It encompasses any broadcast, cable, or satellite communication that refers to a candidate for federal office and that is aired within 30 days of a federal primary election or 60 days

---

5. Of course we mean sunk costs to the judicial system, not to the litigants....

of a federal general election in the jurisdiction in which that candidate is running for office. §434(f)(3)(A).

Appellee Wisconsin Right to Life, Inc. (WRTL), is a nonprofit, nonstock, ideological advocacy corporation recognized by the Internal Revenue Service as tax exempt under §501(c)(4) of the Internal Revenue Code. On July 26, 2004, as part of what it calls a "grassroots lobbying campaign," WRTL began broadcasting a radio advertisement entitled "Wedding." The transcript of "Wedding" reads as follows:

> "'PASTOR: And who gives this woman to be married to this man?

> "'BRIDE'S FATHER: Well, as father of the bride, I certainly could. But instead, I'd like to share a few tips on how to properly install drywall. Now you put the drywall up ...

> "'VOICE-OVER: Sometimes it's just not fair to delay an important decision.

> "'But in Washington it's happening. A group of Senators is using the filibuster delay tactic to block federal judicial nominees from a simple "yes" or "no" vote. So qualified candidates don't get a chance to serve.

> "'It's politics at work, causing gridlock and backing up some of our courts to a state of emergency.

> "'Contact Senators Feingold and Kohl and tell them to oppose the filibuster.

> "'Visit: BeFair.org

> "'Paid for by Wisconsin Right to Life (befair.org), which is responsible for the content of this advertising and not authorized by any candidate or candidate's committee.'"

On the same day, WRTL aired a similar radio ad entitled "Loan." It had also invested treasury funds in producing a television ad entitled "Waiting," which is similar in substance and format to "Wedding" and "Loan."

WRTL planned on running "Wedding," "Waiting," and "Loan" throughout August 2004 and financing the ads with funds from its general treasury. It recognized, however, that as of August 15, 30 days prior to the Wisconsin primary, the ads would be illegal "electioneering communication[s]" under BCRA §203.

Believing that it nonetheless possessed a First Amendment right to broadcast these ads, WRTL filed suit against the Federal Election Commission (FEC) on July 28, 2004, seeking declaratory and injunctive relief before a three-judge District Court. WRTL alleged that BCRA's prohibition on the use of corporate treasury funds for "electioneering communication[s]" as defined in the Act is unconstitutional as applied to "Wedding," "Loan," and "Waiting," as well as any materially similar ads it might seek to run in the future....

II

Article III's "case-or-controversy requirement subsists through all stages of federal judicial proceedings.... [I]t is not enough that a dispute was very much alive when suit was filed." *Lewis v. Continental Bank Corp.,* 494 U.S. 472, 477 (1990). Based on these principles, the FEC argues (though the intervenors do not) that these cases are moot because the 2004 election has passed and WRTL "does not assert any continuing interest in running [its three] advertisements, nor does it identify any reason to believe that a significant dispute over Senate filibusters of judicial nominees will occur in the foreseeable future."

As the District Court concluded, however, these cases fit comfortably within the established exception to mootness for disputes capable of repetition, yet evading review. See *Los Angeles v. Lyons,* 461 U.S. 95, 109 (1983); *Southern Pacific Terminal Co. v. ICC,* 219 U.S. 498, 515 (1911). The exception applies where "(1) the challenged action is in its duration too short to be fully litigated prior to cessation or expiration; and (2) there is a reasonable expectation that the same complaining party will be subject to the same action again." *Spencer v. Kemna,* 523 U.S. 1, 17 (1998). Both circumstances are present here.

As the District Court found, it would be "entirely unreasonable ... to expect that [WRTL] could have obtained complete judicial review of its claims in time for it to air its ads" during the BCRA blackout periods. The FEC contends that the 2-year window between elections provides ample time for parties to litigate their rights before each BCRA blackout period. But groups like WRTL cannot predict what issues will be matters of public concern during a future blackout period. In these cases, WRTL had no way of knowing well in advance that it would want to run ads on judicial filibusters during the BCRA blackout period. In any event, despite BCRA's command that the cases be expedited "to the greatest possible extent," *two* BCRA blackout periods have come and gone during the pendency of this action. "[A] decision allowing the desired expenditures would be an empty gesture unless it afforded appellants sufficient opportunity prior to the election date to communicate their views effectively." *First Nat. Bank of Boston v. Bellotti,* 435 U.S. 765, 774 (1978).

The second prong of the "capable of repetition" exception requires a "'reasonable expectation'" or a "'demonstrated probability'" that "the same controversy will recur involving the same complaining party." *Murphy v. Hunt,* 455 U.S. 478, 482 (1982) (*per curiam*). Our cases find the same controversy sufficiently likely to recur when a party has a reasonable expectation that it "will again be subjected to the alleged illegality," *Lyons, supra,* at 109, or "will be subject to the threat of prosecution" under the challenged law, *Bellotti, supra,* at 774–775 (citing *Weinstein v. Bradford,* 423 U.S. 147, 149 (1975) (*per curiam*)). The FEC argues that in order to prove likely recurrence of the same controversy, WRTL must establish that it will run ads in the future sharing all "the characteristics that the district court deemed legally relevant."

The FEC asks for too much. We have recognized that the "'capable of repetition, yet evading review' doctrine, in the context of election cases, is appropriate when there are 'as applied' challenges as well as in the more typical case involving only facial attacks." *Storer v. Brown,* 415 U.S. 724, 737, n. 8 (1974). Requiring repetition of every "legally relevant" characteristic of an as-applied challenge—down to the last detail—would effectively overrule this statement by making this exception unavailable for virtually all as-applied challenges. History repeats itself, but not at the level of specificity demanded by the FEC. Here, WRTL credibly claimed that it planned on running "'materially similar'" future targeted broadcast ads mentioning a candidate within the blackout period, and there is no reason to believe that the FEC will "refrain from prosecuting violations" of BCRA, *Bellotti, supra,* at 775. Under the circumstances, particularly where WRTL sought another preliminary injunction based on an ad it planned to run during the 2006 blackout period, we hold that there exists a reasonable expectation that the same controversy involving the same party will recur. We have jurisdiction to decide these cases.

. . . .

[The concurring opinions of Justices Alito and Scalia, and the dissenting opinion of Justice Souter, are omitted.]

Irish Lesbian & Gay Organization v. Giuliani
143 F.3d 638 (2d Cir. 1998)

OAKES, Senior Circuit Judge:

[At issue in this case—excerpted in greater detail above—is a challenge to the constitutionality of the exclusion of The Irish Lesbian and Gay Organization ("ILGO") from the annual St. Patrick's Day parade in New York City.]

The [district] court found that ILGO's requests for declaratory and injunctive relief with respect to the 1996 permit had become moot because the date on which ILGO sought to hold its march, March 16, 1996, had passed....

The mootness doctrine is derived from the constitutional requirement that federal courts may only decide live cases or controversies. *See* U.S. Const. art. III; *Liner v. Jafco, Inc.*, 375 U.S. 301, 306 n. 3 (1964). A case becomes moot when interim relief or events have eradicated the effects of the defendant's act or omission, and there is no reasonable expectation that the alleged violation will recur. *See County of Los Angeles v. Davis*, 440 U.S. 625, 631 (1979). However, a case is not moot if the underlying dispute between the two parties is "capable of repetition, yet evading review." *Nebraska Press Ass'n v. Stuart*, 427 U.S. 539, 546 (1976) (citation omitted). To show that a case falls within this exception, a party must demonstrate that "'(1) the challenged action was in duration too short to be fully litigated prior to its cessation or expiration, and (2) there was a reasonable expectation that the same complaining party would be subjected to the same action again.'" *Granato v. Bane*, 74 F.3d 406, 411 (2d Cir.1996) (quoting *Murphy v. Hunt*, 455 U.S. 478, 482 (1982))....

ILGO's claims fall within the "capable of repetition, yet evading review" exception. In the last two years, ILGO has had only a few weeks between being notified that its application for a permit was denied and the date of the Parade in which to obtain judicial review. This time period is clearly insufficient for full litigation of ILGO's claims. Given the annual nature of the Parade, and ILGO's repeated attempts to stage a march prior to it, the conduct complained of is almost certain to be repeated. Accordingly, we find that ILGO's claims for declaratory and injunctive relief are not moot....

[The opinion of Judge Real, concurring in part and dissenting in part, is omitted.]

Log Cabin Republicans v. United States
658 F.3d 1162 (9th Cir. 2011)

PER CURIAM:

We are called upon to decide whether the congressionally enacted "Don't Ask, Don't Tell" policy respecting homosexual conduct in the military is unconstitutional on its face.

I

A

In 1993, Congress enacted the policy widely known as Don't Ask, Don't Tell. The policy generally required that a service member be separated from the military if he had engaged or attempted to engage in homosexual acts, stated that he is a homosexual, or married or attempted to marry a person of the same sex.

The nonprofit corporation Log Cabin Republicans brought this suit in 2004, challenging section 654 and its implementing regulations as facially unconstitutional under the due process clause of the Fifth Amendment, the right to equal protection guaranteed by that Amendment, and the First Amendment right to freedom of speech. Log Cabin sought a declaration that the policy is facially unconstitutional and an injunction barring the United States from applying the policy. The district court dismissed the equal protection claim under *Witt v. Department of the Air Force,* 527 F.3d 806 (9th Cir.2008) (upholding section 654 against a facial equal protection challenge), but allowed the due process and First Amendment challenges to proceed to trial.

After a bench trial, in October 2010 the district court ruled that section 654 on its face violates due process and the First Amendment. The court permanently enjoined the United States from applying section 654 and its implementing regulations to anyone. The United States appealed; Log Cabin cross-appealed the dismissal of its equal protection claim.

B

While the appeal was pending, Congress enacted the Don't Ask, Don't Tell Repeal Act of 2010 ("Repeal Act"). That statute provides that section 654 would be repealed 60 days after: (1) the Secretary of Defense received a report determining the impact of repealing section 654 and recommending any necessary changes to military policy, and (2) the President, Secretary of Defense, and Chairman of the Joint Chiefs of Staff certified that they had considered the report's recommendations and were prepared to implement the repeal consistent with military readiness, military effectiveness, and unit cohesion. The Repeal Act left section 654 in effect until the prerequisites to repeal were satisfied and 60 days had then passed.

The report was issued November 30, 2010, and certification occurred July 21, 2011. Section 654 was thus repealed September 20, 2011.

II

A

Because section 654 has now been repealed, we must determine whether this case is moot. "[I]t is not enough that there may have been a live case or controversy when the case was decided by the court whose judgment" is under review. *Burke v. Barnes,* 479 U.S. 361, 363 (1987). Article III of the United States Constitution "requires that there be a live case or controversy at the time that" a reviewing federal court decides the case. *Id.*

Applying that limitation, the Supreme Court and our court have repeatedly held that a case is moot when the challenged statute is repealed, expires, or is amended to remove the challenged language. In determining whether a case has become moot on appeal, the appellate court "review[s] the judgment below in light of the ... statute as it now stands, not as it ... did" before the district court. *Hall v. Beals,* 396 U.S. 45, 48 (1969) (per curiam); *see Burke,* 479 U.S. at 363.

In *Hall v. Beals,* for example, the Supreme Court deemed moot a challenge to a six-month residency requirement imposed by Colorado for eligibility to vote in the 1968 presidential election. 396 U.S. at 46–48. After the district court rejected the challenge and the Supreme Court noted probable jurisdiction, the Colorado legislature reduced the residency requirement to two months, which the plaintiffs would have met at the time of the 1968 election. *Id.* at 47–48. The case was moot because, "under the statute as ... written" when the Supreme Court reviewed the district court's judgment, "the appellants could have voted in the 1968 presidential election." *Id.* at 48. Similarly, in *United States Department of the Treasury v. Galioto,* after the Supreme Court had noted probable jurisdiction to review a ruling that federal firearms legislation unconstitutionally singled out mental patients, the case became moot because Congress amended the statute to remove the challenged language. 477 U.S. 556, 559–60 (1986). And in *Burke v. Barnes,* where several congressmen challenged the President's attempt to "pocket-veto" a bill, the Supreme Court deemed the case moot because the bill expired by its own terms before the Court could rule on the case. 479 U.S. at 363. As in cases dealing with repealed legislation, the Court "analyze[d] th[e] case as if [the plaintiffs] had originally sought to litigate the validity of a statute which by its terms had already expired." *See id.*

Following the Court's lead, we have routinely deemed cases moot where "a new law is enacted during the pendency of an appeal and resolves the parties' dispute." Under these precedents, when a statutory repeal or amendment gives a plaintiff "everything [it] hoped to achieve" by its lawsuit, the controversy is moot.

This suit became moot when the repeal of section 654 took effect on September 20. If Log Cabin filed suit today seeking a declaration that section 654 is unconstitutional or an injunction against its application (or both), there would be no Article III controversy because there is no section 654. The repeal, in short, gave Log Cabin "everything" its complaint "hoped to achieve." There is no longer "a present, live controversy of the kind that must exist" for us to reach the merits. *Hall,* 396 U.S. at 48.

B

Log Cabin concedes that "the injunctive relief awarded by the district court [has] become moot" due to the repeal, but contends that its quest for declaratory relief is live under either of two exceptions to mootness.

We are not persuaded. When a statutory repeal or amendment extinguishes a controversy, the case is moot. There is no exception for declaratory relief.

In any event, no exception to mootness applies here. Log Cabin notes that generally "a defendant's voluntary cessation of a challenged practice does not deprive a federal court of its power to determine the legality of the practice." *City of Mesquite v. Aladdin's Castle, Inc.,* 455 U.S. 283, 289 (1982). But voluntary cessation is different from a statutory amendment or repeal. Repeal is "usually enough to render a case moot, even if the legislature possesses the power to reenact the statute after the lawsuit is dismissed." Cases rejecting mootness in such circumstances "are rare and typically involve situations where it is virtually certain that the repealed law will be reenacted."

We cannot say with "virtual[ ] certain[ty]" that the Congress that passed the Repeal Act— or a future Congress whose composition, agenda, and circumstances we cannot know— will reenact Don't Ask, Don't Tell. We can only speculate, and our speculation cannot breathe life into this case.

A second exception to mootness applies when a party faces "collateral consequences" from a challenged statute even when the statute is repealed. Log Cabin cites several benefits that discharged service members may have lost as a result of their separation. But because these missed benefits are not legal penalties from past conduct, they do not fall within this exception.

III

Having determined that this case is moot, we must "direct the entry of such appropriate judgment, decree, or order, or require such further proceedings to be had as may be just under the circumstances." 28 U.S.C. § 2106.

The "established" practice when a civil suit becomes moot on appeal is to vacate the district court's judgment and remand for dismissal of the complaint. *See United States v. Munsingwear, Inc.,* 340 U.S. 36, 39 (1950). Vacatur ensures that "those who have been prevented from obtaining the review to which they are entitled [are] not ... treated as if there had been a review." *Id.* It "prevent[s] an unreviewable decision 'from spawning any legal consequences,' so that no party is harmed by what [the Supreme Court has] called a 'preliminary' adjudication." *Camreta v. Greene,* 131 S.Ct. 2020, 2035 (2011) (quoting *Munsingwear,* 340 U.S. at 40–41)....

We therefore vacate the judgment of the district court. Because Log Cabin has stated its intention to use the district court's judgment collaterally, we will be clear: It may not. Nor may its members or anyone else. We vacate the district court's judgment, injunction, opinions, orders, and factual findings—indeed, all of its past rulings—to clear the path completely for any future litigation. Those now-void legal rulings and factual findings have no precedential, preclusive, or binding effect. The repeal of Don't Ask, Don't Tell provides Log Cabin with all it sought and may have had standing to obtain. (We assume without deciding that Log Cabin had standing to seek a declaration that section 654 is unconstitutional and an injunction barring the United States from applying it to Log Cabin's members. *See Arizonans for Official English,* 520 U.S. at 66–67 (court may assume without deciding that standing exists in order to analyze mootness).) Because the case is moot and the United States may not challenge further the district court's rulings and findings, giving those rulings and findings any effect would wrongly harm the United States....

[The opinion of Judge O'Scannlain, concurring specially, is omitted].

Notes and Questions

1. Suppose that the challenge at issue in *Log Cabin Republicans* involved a group of discharged gay military personnel seeking reinstatement and lost wages, benefits and status. How, if at all, would that impact the mootness determination?

2. If a class action is brought challenging the constitutionality of a law, the case is now moot as to the named plaintiff, and there is no likelihood of repetition with respect to the *named* plaintiff, is the class action now moot? *See Sosna v. Iowa,* 419 U.S. 393, 397–403 (1975) (holding that the case is not moot so long as the named plaintiff had a live case or controversy at the time the action was filed and there remain class members who have a live case or controversy).

3. In addition to election controversies and those involving parades, cases involving pregnancy present another paradigmatic example of situations falling within the "capable of repetition, yet evading review" exception to mootness:

> The usual rule in federal cases is that an actual controversy must exist at stages of appellate or certiorari review, and not simply at the date the action is initiated.

> But when, as here, pregnancy is a significant fact in the litigation, the normal 266-day human gestation period is so short that the pregnancy will come to term before the usual appellate process is complete. If that termination makes a case moot, pregnancy litigation seldom will survive much beyond the trial stage, and appellate review will be effectively denied. Our law should not be that rigid. Pregnancy often comes more than once to the same woman, and in the general population, if man is to survive, it will always be with us. Pregnancy provides a classic justification for a conclusion of nonmootness. It truly could be "capable of repetition, yet evading review."

Roe v. Wade, 410 U.S. 113, 125 (1973).

3. Facial vs. As-Applied Challenges

Los Angeles Police Department v. United Reporting Publishing Corp.

528 U.S. 32 (1999)

Chief Justice REHNQUIST delivered the opinion of the Court.

California Govt. Code Ann. § 6254(f)(3) (West Supp.1999) places two conditions on public access to arrestees' addresses—that the person requesting an address declare that the request is being made for one of five prescribed purposes, and that the requester also declare that the address will not be used directly or indirectly to sell a product or service.

The District Court permanently enjoined enforcement of the statute, and the Court of Appeals affirmed, holding that the statute was facially invalid because it unduly burdens commercial speech. We hold that the statutory section in question was not subject to a "facial" challenge....

Respondent's primary argument in the District Court and the Court of Appeals was that § 6254(f)(3) was invalid on its face, and respondent maintains that position here. But we believe that our cases hold otherwise.

The traditional rule is that "a person to whom a statute may constitutionally be applied may not challenge that statute on the ground that it may conceivably be applied unconstitutionally to others in situations not before the Court." *New York v. Ferber*, 458 U.S. 747, 767 (1982).

Prototypical exceptions to this traditional rule are First Amendment challenges to statutes based on First Amendment overbreadth. "At least when statutes regulate or proscribe speech ... the transcendent value to all society of constitutionally protected expression is deemed to justify allowing 'attacks on overly broad statutes with no requirement that the person making the attack demonstrate that his own conduct could not be regulated by a statute drawn with the requisite narrow specificity.'" *Gooding v. Wilson*, 405 U.S. 518, 520–521 (1972) (quoting *Dombrowski v. Pfister*, 380 U.S. 479, 486 (1965)). "This is deemed necessary because persons whose expression is constitutionally protected may well refrain from exercising their right for fear of criminal sanctions provided by a statute susceptible of application to protected expression." *Gooding v. Wilson, supra,* at 520–521. See also *Thornhill v. Alabama,* 310 U.S. 88 (1940).

In *Gooding,* for example, the defendant was one of a group that picketed an Army headquarters building carrying signs opposing the Vietnam war. A confrontation with the police occurred, as a result of which Gooding was charged with "'using opprobrious words and abusive language ... tending to cause a breach of the peace.'" 405 U.S., at 518–519. In *Thornhill,* the defendant was prosecuted for violation of a statute forbidding any person to "'picket the works or place of business of such other persons, firms, corporations, or associations of persons, for the purpose of hindering, delaying, or interfering with or injuring any lawful business or enterprise....'" 310 U.S., at 91.

This is not to say that the threat of criminal prosecution is a necessary condition for the entertainment of a facial challenge. We have permitted such attacks on statutes in appropriate circumstances where no such threat was present.

But the allowance of a facial overbreadth challenge to a statute is an exception to the traditional rule that "a person to whom a statute may constitutionally be applied may not challenge that statute on the ground that it may conceivably be applied unconstitutionally to others in situations not before the Court." *Ferber, supra,* at 767. This general rule reflects two "cardinal principles" of our constitutional order: the personal nature of constitutional rights and the prudential limitations on constitutional adjudication. 458 U.S., at 767. "By focusing on the factual situation before us, and similar cases necessary for development of a constitutional rule, we face 'flesh and blood' legal problems with data 'relevant and adequate to an informed judgment.'" *Id.,* at 768.

Even though the challenge be based on the First Amendment, the overbreadth doctrine is not casually employed. "Because of the wide-reaching effects of striking down a statute on its face at the request of one whose own conduct may be punished despite the First Amendment, we have recognized that the overbreadth doctrine is 'strong medicine' and have employed it with hesitation, and then 'only as a last resort.'" *Id.,* at 769. "'[F]acial overbreadth adjudication is an exception to our traditional rules of practice and ... its function, a limited one at the outset, attenuates as the otherwise unprotected behavior that it forbids the State to sanction moves from "pure speech" toward conduct and that conduct—even if expressive—falls within the scope of otherwise valid criminal laws....'" 458 U.S., at 770.

The Court of Appeals held that §6254(f)(3) was facially invalid under the First Amendment. Petitioner contends that the section in question is not an abridgment of anyone's right to engage in speech, be it commercial or otherwise, but simply a law regulating access to information in the hands of the police department.

We believe that, at least for purposes of facial invalidation, petitioner's view is correct. This is not a case in which the government is prohibiting a speaker from conveying information that the speaker already possesses. The California statute in question merely requires that if respondent wishes to obtain the addresses of arrestees it must qualify under the statute to do so. Respondent did not attempt to qualify and was therefore denied access to the addresses. For purposes of assessing the propriety of a facial invalidation, what we have before us is nothing more than a governmental denial of access to information in its possession. California could decide not to give out arrestee information at all without violating the First Amendment....

[The concurring opinions of Justices Scalia and Ginsburg, and the dissenting opinion of Justice Stevens, are omitted.]

United States v. Lemons
697 F.2d 832 (8th Cir. 1983)

HEANEY, Circuit Judge.

Charles Loyd Lemons, Jr., appeals his conviction by the district court on one count of violating the Arkansas "sodomy" statute, Ark.Stat.Ann. § 41-1813 (1977). Lemons contends that the statute under which he was convicted, on its face, violates his constitutional right to privacy....

I. FACTS.

On February 19, 1982, in the early afternoon, Terry Gross, a ranger for the Department of the Interior National Parks Service, observed Lemons and another male in vehicles parked next to each other in Hot Springs National Park, Hot Springs, Arkansas. Approximately five minutes after this observation, Gross noticed that both vehicles apparently had been abandoned and that the radio in one of them was playing loudly. He decided to investigate the situation and found that both vehicles were unoccupied.

Gross then proceeded to a public restroom which was in the vicinity. He heard groaning-type utterances coming from the restroom, entered the men's section of the facility, and saw the legs of two persons beneath the partition of one stall in the restroom. Through the opening in the partially closed door to the stall, he saw two individuals. He opened the unlocked door to find Lemons and another male engaging in oral sex. Gross arrested the men and issued a violation notice against Lemons charging him with violating the Arkansas sodomy statute.[3]

The district court tried Lemons without a jury for violating Arkansas law on federal land under the assimilative crimes statute. Immediately prior to trial, Lemons filed a motion to dismiss, with a supporting memorandum, claiming that the Arkansas sodomy statute was unconstitutional on its face for the same reasons he now presses on appeal....

II. DISCUSSION OF ISSUES.

A. *Right to Privacy.*

On appeal, Lemons thoroughly develops his argument that the Arkansas sodomy statute, on its face, prohibits private, adult, consensual sexual conduct between persons of the same sex. He claims this prohibition violates his right to "decisional" privacy, that is, the right to make private affectional choices, a right which he asserts is protected by the federal Constitution. Although the specific source of the constitutional right to privacy is unclear, *see Roe v. Wade,* 410 U.S. 113, 152–153 (1973), Lemons relies on several recent lower court cases which have held that the right extends to private, adult, consensual sexual conduct between persons of the same sex. The conduct for which the district court convicted Lemons, however, occurred in a public restroom. Because we only examine the constitutionality of the Arkansas sodomy statute as the court applied it to Lemons,

---

3. Ark.Stat.Ann. § 41-1813 (1977) reads:

    Sodomy.—(1) A person commits sodomy if such person performs any act of sexual gratification involving:

      (a) the penetration, however slight, of the anus or mouth of an animal or a person by the penis of a person of the same sex or an animal; or

      (b) the penetration, however slight, of the vagina or anus of an animal or a person by any body member of a person of the same sex or an animal.

    (2) Sodomy is a class "A" misdemeanor.

we do not reach the question whether the statute is constitutional under all hypothetical applications.[4]

We limit our inquiry to the constitutionality of the statute as applied in this case pursuant to the prudential rule of judicial self-restraint established by the Supreme Court which requires federal courts to limit their constitutional scrutiny of statutes to the particular facts of each case. The Supreme Court characterizes this rule as an element of standing to raise constitutional questions. *See County Court of Ulster County v. Allen,* 442 U.S. 140, 154–155 (1979); *Singleton v. Wulff,* 428 U.S. 106, 112 (1976); *United States v. Raines,* 362 U.S. 17, 21 (1960). The rule, however, is an expression of judicial self-restraint apart from the "case or controversy" requirement in Article III of the federal Constitution which is the basis of much standing doctrine.... Thus, although Lemons has constitutional standing under Article III to attack the Arkansas sodomy statute, the scope of his attack is limited by this prudential rule to the circumstances under which the statute was applied to him.

The prudential doctrine of judicial self-restraint which we apply here is "separability"—when possible, we must narrowly read a statute to be constitutional as applied to the facts of the case before us and cannot consider other arguably unconstitutional applications of that statute. The Supreme Court has recognized specific exceptions to this doctrine: a court may entertain facial attacks on statutes when an aggrieved third person could not properly raise an issue on her or his behalf, when the statute itself has an inhibitory effect on freedom of speech, when a limiting construction of a criminal statute would make the statute unconstitutionally vague, when a state court has pronounced that the statute is constitutional in all its applications, or in the rare case when a court can determine that the legislature would not want the statute to stand unless it could stand in all its applications. *United States v. Raines, supra,* 362 U.S. at 22–23. None of these exceptions apply to allow Lemons to avoid the separability doctrine in the present case.

First, persons who seek to raise the privacy issue as it relates to the application of the Arkansas sodomy statute to acts done in private may do so outside the confines of the present litigation. Indeed, Lemons relies heavily on a recent federal district court decision striking down a similar provision of the Texas Penal Code in the context of a request for declaratory judgment. We have no indication that a similar request for declaratory judgment in Arkansas by persons fearing prosecution for private acts under the sodomy statute would not be feasible or would prove fruitless. We express no opinion on the merits of such an action.

Secondly, the "chilling effect" exception to the separability doctrine, which is traditionally called "overbreadth," consistently has been applied only to claims that a statute, though constitutional in its present application, tends to "chill" the constitutional free speech rights of others, in different contexts, in violation of the first amendment. Although some commentators have argued that this exception should extend to facial attacks based on other constitutional protections, the Supreme Court has tended to limit this exception to traditional free speech cases. We follow this precedent and find that the overbreadth exception does not apply to Lemons' privacy claim.

---

4. Lemons vigorously argued in his briefs and at oral argument that his right to privacy claim does not rest on the location of his acts, but on his right to freely decide matters of affectional choice. He asserts that the location of his acts is therefore irrelevant in this case. We understand the argument, but disagree with the conclusion. The location of Lemons' conduct is relevant to the question of the circumstances under which the district court applied the statute to Lemons. The scope of our constitutional inquiry is limited to those circumstances. Thus, we only decide whether the Arkansas sodomy statute as applied to sexual acts between members of the same sex in a public restroom—the circumstances of Lemons' conviction—is constitutional.

Third, our limited review of the Arkansas sodomy statute will not render the statute unconstitutionally vague. The statute gives fair warning that certain sexual acts are prohibited. Our restricted reading that, at least as to those acts done in public, the statute does not violate any constitutional provision falls within the clear prohibition derived from this statutory language. In such a situation, Lemons cannot legitimately claim that our reading of the statute makes it unconstitutionally vague.

Fourth, we are aware of no state decision which has held that the Arkansas sodomy statute applies to the proscribed conduct when performed either in private or in public. Lemons' counsel at trial indicated that this case apparently was the first prosecution under that statute, much less the first case to question its constitutionality. Our research supports that assertion. Thus, in the absence of state court directions that the statute applies to both public and private acts, we limit our inquiry to the facts before us.

Finally, this is not the "rare case" in which we can determine that the Arkansas legislature would not want the statute to stand if it could not stand in all of its applications. Even assuming that the legislature intended the sodomy statute to reach private homosexual activity if constitutionally permitted, we have no evidence that the legislature would wish the provision excised from the criminal code if a court should limit its application in any way. Thus, our consideration of the major exceptions to the separability doctrine indicates that none of them apply in this case, and we are limited by prudential concerns to deciding the constitutionality of the Arkansas sodomy statute only as it has been applied to Lemons.

Having decided to limit our constitutional scrutiny of the Arkansas sodomy statute to the facts of Lemons' conviction, we hold that the statute, as applied to him, does not violate his constitutional right to privacy, whatever the outer bounds of that right may be. None of the cases cited by Lemons hold that a "decisional" right to privacy extends to a decision to express one's affectional choice in the form of public oral sexual conduct. Lemons contends that public sexuality is not the issue here. To the contrary, we find that Lemons' public sexual conduct is the sole issue here. We remain unconvinced that the constitutional right to privacy extends to Lemons' conduct, much less that the State of Arkansas does not have a compelling interest in limiting public sexuality, even if arguably given some constitutional protection, to prohibit oral sex in a public restroom within the confines of a national park....

[The concurring opinion of Judge Fagg, and the dissenting opinion of Judge Henley, are omitted.]

Notes and Questions

1. As demonstrated by *Lemons*, the general rule that federal courts will consider only as-applied rather than facial challenges—coupled with the relative difficulty of finding a challenger who was arrested and/or prosecuted for engaging in sodomy in a setting that would likely be encompassed by the federal right to privacy—made it fairly difficult to challenge the application of sodomy laws in the private, consensual context. The *Hardwick* case (and the Court's subsequent decision in *Lawrence v. Texas* reversing *Hardwick*) was thus a rare example of a situation in which someone was actually arrested for engaging in consensual, non-commercial sodomy with another adult in private, and thus could challenge a sodomy law as applied in that setting. *See generally* Christopher R. Leslie, Lawrence v. Texas *as the Perfect Storm*, 38 U.C. Davis L. Rev. 509, 531–541 (2005).

2. In recent years, the U.S. Supreme Court has been somewhat inconsistent on when it is willing to entertain a facial challenge to a law and when it is not. Thus, despite prior

precedent that appeared to more freely permit facial challenges where statutes restricting abortion were involved, *see, e.g.*, *Sabri v. United States*, 541 U.S. 600, 609–10 (2004); *Janklow v. Planned Parenthood, Sioux Falls Clinic*, 517 U.S. 1174 (1996) (Stevens, J., dissenting from denial of petition of writ for certiorari), the Supreme Court recently announced in just such a case that "the 'normal rule' is that 'partial, rather than facial, invalidation is the required course.'" *Ayotte v. Planned Parenthood of N. New England*, 546 U.S. 320, 329 (2006); *accord Gonzales v. Carhart*, 550 U.S. 124, 167–68 (2007). Subsequent to that decision, the Court announced — in a case involving a First Amendment challenge — that "[f]acial challenges are disfavored." *Wash. State Grange v. Wash. State Republican Party*, 552 U.S. 442, 450 (2008). Yet in one of its most recent cases involving standing, the majority brushed aside arguments that it should entertain an as-applied challenge and instead considered a facial challenge to the constitutionality of a campaign finance law, *see Citizens United v. Fed. Election Com'n*, 130 S. Ct. 876, 890–96 (2010), leading to charges by the dissent that the majority was not following its own recent precedents, *see id.* at 932–36 (Stevens, J., dissenting).

B. Abstention

1. *Younger* Abstention

Younger v. Harris
401 U.S. 37 (1971)

Mr. Justice BLACK delivered the opinion of the Court.

Appellee, John Harris, Jr., was indicted in a California state court, charged with violation of the California Penal Code §§ 11400 and 11401, known as the California Criminal Syndicalism Act.... He then filed a complaint in the Federal District Court, asking that court to enjoin the appellant, Younger, the District Attorney of Los Angeles County, from prosecuting him, and alleging that the prosecution and even the presence of the Act inhibited him in the exercise of his rights of free speech and press, rights guaranteed him by the First and Fourteenth Amendments. Appellees Jim Dan and Diane Hirsch intervened as plaintiffs in the suit, claiming that the prosecution of Harris would inhibit them as members of the Progressive Labor Party from peacefully advocating the program of their party, which was to replace capitalism with socialism and to abolish the profit system of production in this country. Appellee Farrell Broslawsky, an instructor in history at Los Angeles Valley College, also intervened claiming that the prosecution of Harris made him uncertain as to whether he could teach about the doctrines of Karl Marx or read from the Communist Manifesto as part of his classwork. All claimed that unless the United States court restrained the state prosecution of Harris each would suffer immediate and irreparable injury. A three-judge Federal District Court, convened pursuant to 28 U.S.C. § 2284, held that it had jurisdiction and power to restrain the District Attorney from prosecuting, held that the State's Criminal Syndicalism Act was void for vagueness and overbreadth in violation of the First and Fourteenth Amendments, and accordingly restrained the District Attorney from "further prosecution of the currently pending action against plaintiff Harris for alleged violation of the Act." ....

In this Court the brief for the State of California, filed at our request, also argues that only Harris, who was indicted, has standing to challenge the State's law, and that issuance of the injunction was a violation of a longstanding judicial policy and of 28 U.S.C. § 2283, which provides:

> "A court of the United States may not grant an injunction to stay proceedings in a State court except as expressly authorized by Act of Congress, or where necessary in aid of its jurisdiction, or to protect or effectuate its judgments."

Without regard to the questions raised about … the constitutionality of the state law, we have concluded that the judgment of the District Court, enjoining appellant Younger from prosecuting under these California statutes, must be reversed as a violation of the national policy forbidding federal courts to stay or enjoin pending state court proceedings except under special circumstances.[2] We express no view about the circumstances under which federal courts may act when there is no prosecution pending in state courts at the time the federal proceeding is begun.

I

Appellee Harris has been indicted, and was actually being prosecuted by California for a violation of its Criminal Syndicalism Act at the time this suit was filed. He thus has an acute, live controversy with the State and its prosecutor. But none of the other parties plaintiff in the District Court, Dan, Hirsch, or Broslawsky, has such a controversy. None has been indicted, arrested, or even threatened by the prosecutor. About these three the three-judge court said:

> "Plaintiffs Dan and Hirsch allege that they are members of the Progressive Labor Party, which advocates change in industrial ownership and political change, and that they feel inhibited in advocating the program of their political party through peaceful, nonviolent means, because of the presence of the Act 'on the books', and because of the pending criminal prosecution against Harris. Plaintiff Broslawsky is a history instructor, and he alleges that he is uncertain as to whether his normal practice of teaching his students about the doctrines of Karl Marx and reading from the Communist Manifesto and other revolutionary works may subject him to prosecution for violation of the Act."

Whatever right Harris, who is being prosecuted under the state syndicalism law may have, Dan, Hirsch, and Broslawsky cannot share it with him. If these three had alleged that they would be prosecuted for the conduct they planned to engage in, and if the District Court had found this allegation to be true—either on the admission of the State's district attorney or on any other evidence—then a genuine controversy might be said to exist. But here appellees Dan, Hirsch, and Broslawsky do not claim that they have ever been threatened with prosecution, that a prosecution is likely, or even that a prosecution is remotely possible. They claim the right to bring this suit solely because, in the language of their complaint, they "feel inhibited." We do not think this allegation even if true, is sufficient to bring the equitable jurisdiction of the federal courts into play to enjoin a pending state prosecution. A federal lawsuit to stop a prosecution in a state court is a serious matter. And persons having no fears of state prosecution except those that are imaginary or speculative, are not to be accepted as appropriate plaintiffs in such cases. Since

---

2. Appellees did not explicitly ask for a declaratory judgment in their complaint. They did, however, ask the District Court to grant "such other and further relief as to the Court may seem just and proper," and the District Court in fact granted a declaratory judgment. For the reasons stated in our opinion today in Samuels v. Mackell, 401 U.S. 66, we hold that declaratory relief is also improper when a prosecution involving the challenged statute is pending in state court at the time the federal suit is initiated.

Harris is actually being prosecuted under the challenged laws, however, we proceed with him as a proper party.

II

Since the beginning of this country's history Congress has, subject to few exceptions, manifested a desire to permit state courts to try state cases free from interference by federal courts.... [F]rom 1793 to 1970 the statutory exceptions to the 1793 congressional enactment have been only three: (1) "except as expressly authorized by Act of Congress"; (2) "where necessary in aid of its jurisdiction"; and (3) "to protect or effectuate its judgments." In addition, a judicial exception to the longstanding policy evidenced by the statute has been made where a person about to be prosecuted in a state court can show that he will, if the proceeding in the state court is not enjoined, suffer irreparable damages.

The precise reasons for this longstanding public policy against federal court interference with state court proceedings have never been specifically identified but the primary sources of the policy are plain. One is the basic doctrine of equity jurisprudence that courts of equity should not act, and particularly should not act to restrain a criminal prosecution, when the moving party has an adequate remedy at law and will not suffer irreparable injury if denied equitable relief. The doctrine may originally have grown out of circumstances peculiar to the English judicial system and not applicable in this country, but its fundamental purpose of restraining equity jurisdiction within narrow limits is equally important under our Constitution, in order to prevent erosion of the role of the jury and avoid a duplication of legal proceedings and legal sanctions where a single suit would be adequate to protect the rights asserted. This underlying reason for restraining courts of equity from interfering with criminal prosecutions is reinforced by an even more vital consideration, the notion of "comity," that is, a proper respect for state functions, a recognition of the fact that the entire country is made up of a Union of separate state governments, and a continuance of the belief that the National Government will fare best if the States and their institutions are left free to perform their separate functions in their separate ways. This, perhaps for lack of a better and clearer way to describe it, is referred to by many as "Our Federalism," and one familiar with the profound debates that ushered our Federal Constitution into existence is bound to respect those who remain loyal to the ideals and dreams of "Our Federalism." The concept does not mean blind deference to "States' Rights" any more than it means centralization of control over every important issue in our National Government and its courts. The Framers rejected both these courses. What the concept does represent is a system in which there is sensitivity to the legitimate interests of both State and National Governments, and in which the National Government, anxious though it may be to vindicate and protect federal rights and federal interests, always endeavors to do so in ways that will not unduly interfere with the legitimate activities of the States. It should never be forgotten that this slogan, "Our Federalism," born in the early struggling days of our Union of States, occupies a highly important place in our Nation's history and its future.

This brief discussion should be enough to suggest some of the reasons why it has been perfectly natural for our cases to repeat time and time again that the normal thing to do when federal courts are asked to enjoin pending proceedings in state courts is not to issue such injunctions....

In all of these cases the Court stressed the importance of showing irreparable injury, the traditional prerequisite to obtaining an injunction. In addition, however, the Court also made clear that in view of the fundamental policy against federal interference with state criminal prosecutions, even irreparable injury is insufficient unless it is "both great and immediate." Certain types of injury, in particular, the cost, anxiety, and inconvenience of having to defend against a single criminal prosecution, could not by themselves be considered "irreparable" in the special legal sense of that term. Instead, the threat to the plaintiff's federally protected rights must be one that cannot be eliminated by his defense against a single criminal prosecution....

This is where the law stood when the Court decided Dombrowski v. Pfister, 380 U.S. 479 (1965), and held that an injunction against the enforcement of certain state criminal statutes could properly issue under the circumstances presented in that case. In *Dombrowski*, unlike many of the earlier cases denying injunctions, the complaint made substantial allegations that:

> "the threats to enforce the statutes against appellants are not made with any expectation of securing valid convictions, but rather are part of a plan to employ arrests, seizures, and threats of prosecution under color of the statutes to harass appellants and discourage them and their supporters from asserting and attempting to vindicate the constitutional rights of Negro citizens of Louisiana."

The appellants in *Dombrowski* had offered to prove that their offices had been raided and all their files and records seized pursuant to search and arrest warrants that were later summarily vacated by a state judge for lack of probable cause. They also offered to prove that despite the state court order quashing the warrants and suppressing the evidence seized, the prosecutor was continuing to threaten to initiate new prosecutions of appellants under the same statutes, was holding public hearings at which photostatic copies of the illegally seized documents were being used, and was threatening to use other copies of the illegally seized documents to obtain grand jury indictments against the appellants on charges of violating the same statutes. These circumstances, as viewed by the Court sufficiently establish the kind of irreparable injury, above and beyond that associated with the defense of a single prosecution brought in good faith, that had always been considered sufficient to justify federal intervention. Indeed, after quoting the Court's statement in *Douglas* concerning the very restricted circumstances under which an injunction could be justified, the Court in *Dombrowski* went on to say:

> "But the allegations in this complaint depict a situation in which defense of the State's criminal prosecution will not assure adequate vindication of constitutional rights. They suggest that a substantial loss of or impairment of freedoms of expression will occur if appellants must await the state court's disposition and ultimate review in this Court of any adverse determination. These allegations, if true, clearly show irreparable injury."

And the Court made clear that even under these circumstances the District Court issuing the injunction would have continuing power to lift it at any time and remit the plaintiffs to the state courts if circumstances warranted. Similarly, in Cameron v. Johnson, 390 U.S. 611 (1968), a divided Court denied an injunction after finding that the record did not establish the necessary bad faith and harassment; the dissenting Justices themselves stressed the very limited role to be allowed for federal injunctions against state criminal prosecutions and differed with the Court only on the question whether the particular facts of that case were sufficient to show that the prosecution was brought in bad faith.

It is against the background of these principles that we must judge the propriety of an injunction under the circumstances of the present case. Here a proceeding was already pending in the state court, affording Harris an opportunity to raise his constitutional claims. There is no suggestion that this single prosecution against Harris is brought in bad faith or is only one of a series of repeated prosecutions to which he will be subjected. In other words, the injury that Harris faces is solely "that incidental to every criminal proceeding brought lawfully and in good faith," and therefore under the settled doctrine we have already described he is not entitled to equitable relief "even if such statutes are unconstitutional." . . . .

There may, of course, be extraordinary circumstances in which the necessary irreparable injury can be shown even in the absence of the usual prerequisites of bad faith and harassment. For example, as long ago as the *Buck* case, *supra*, we indicated:

> "It is of course conceivable that a statute might be flagrantly and patently violative of express constitutional prohibitions in every clause, sentence and paragraph, and in whatever manner and against whomever an effort might be made to apply it."

Other unusual situations calling for federal intervention might also arise, but there is no point in our attempting now to specify what they might be. . . . Because our holding rests on the absence of the factors necessary under equitable principles to justify federal intervention, we have no occasion to consider whether 28 U.S.C. § 2283, which prohibits an injunction against state court proceedings "except as expressly authorized by Act of Congress" would in and of itself be controlling under the circumstances of this case. . . .

[The concurring opinions of Justices Brennan and Stewart, and the dissenting opinion of Justice Douglas, are omitted.]

Baker v. Wade

553 F. Supp. 1121 (N.D. Tex. 1982)

BUCHMEYER, District Judge.

[Action brought by a gay man challenging the constitutionality of a Texas law that criminalizes sodomy between individuals of the same sex. In the course of its opinion, the court addresses the issue of *Younger* abstention in the context of sodomy laws.]

In *Buchanan v. Batchelor,* 308 F.Supp. 729 (N.D.Tex. 1970), a three-judge panel (Goldberg, Circuit Judge; Hughes and Taylor, District Judges) held that the Texas sodomy statute (Article 524) — which then prohibited *all* oral and anal sex, whether by heterosexuals or homosexuals — was unconstitutional because it violated the right of privacy of married couples by subjecting them to felony prosecution for private acts of sodomy, "an intimate relation of husband and wife." . . . .

The court permanently enjoined the defendant Wade from enforcing Article 524, which "was declared void on its face for unconstitutional overbreadth." . . . .

On appeal, the Supreme Court did not reach the merits, 401 U.S. 989 (1971), but remanded the case for consideration as to whether abstention was proper in light of its then-recent decision in *Younger v. Harris,* 401 U.S. 37 (1971). However, the three judge panel had specifically noted that "there have been no prosecutions under the Act of married persons for private acts of sodomy"; that it was unclear from the record "whether there have been prosecutions of homosexuals for private acts of sodomy"; that no cha[r]ges were pending against the intervenors, a married couple (the Gibsons) and a homosexual male (Strickland); but that the homosexual plaintiff, Buchanan, "had twice been arrested and charged" with acts of sodomy with another male in public restrooms.

Therefore, even if a *Younger* abstention problem was presented in *Buchanan* by the homosexual plaintiff, who sought an injunction against two pending state prosecutions for public offenses — none was presented by either of the intervenors, the married couple (who had prevailed in their right of privacy claim) and the homosexual Strickland (who had not prevailed in his)....

Notes and Questions

1. Once a federal court abstains on *Younger* abstention grounds, the party that initially brought the action into federal court lacks the opportunity to return there, and is forced to raise his federal claims in the state courts, with the only opportunity for federal court review of his federal constitutional claims occurring in the rare event that the U.S. Supreme Court agrees to review the decision.

2. Can *Younger* abstention be invoked if there is no pending state criminal prosecution at the time the federal action is filed, but such a prosecution is *subsequently* initiated? *See Hicks v. Miranda*, 422 U.S. 332, 349 (1975) (noting that the issue was left open in *Younger* and its progeny, and holding that "where state criminal proceedings are begun against the federal plaintiffs after the federal complaint is filed but before any proceedings of substance on the merits have taken place in the federal court, the principles of Younger v. Harris should apply in full force.")

3. When you combine the *Younger* abstention doctrine with the factual prerequisites needed to establish standing, do you see why few challenges to the constitutionality of sodomy laws could be successfully litigated in federal court? *See generally* Christopher R. Leslie, *Procedural Rules or Procedural Pretexts?: A Case Study of Procedural Hurdles in Constitutional Challenges to the Texas Sodomy Law*, 89 Ky. L.J. 1109 (2001).

2. *Pullman* Abstention

Problem 2-D: Justice Delayed ...

A same-sex couple, Peter and Michael, seek to obtain a marriage license from their county clerk, but the clerk refuses to give them the license, contending that marriage licenses are available only to opposite-sex couples. Peter and Michael file suit in federal court, contending that the denial of a marriage license violates their rights under the equal protection and due process clauses of the Fourteenth Amendment of the U.S. Constitution.

The law of the state in which Peter and Michael seek to marry does not define marriage as limited to persons of the opposite sex, but various other provisions in the state's marriage laws use gendered terms such as "husband" and "wife."

Can the federal district court proceed to adjudicate the merits of the claims brought by Peter and Michael?

Railroad Commission of Texas v. Pullman Co.
312 U.S. 496 (1941)

Mr. Justice FRANKFURTER delivered the opinion of the Court.

In those sections of Texas where the local passenger traffic is slight, trains carry but one sleeping car. These trains, unlike trains having two or more sleepers, are without a Pullman conductor; the sleeper is in charge of a porter who is subject to the train conductor's control. As is well known, porters on Pullmans are colored and conductors are white. Addressing itself to this situation, the Texas Railroad Commission after due hearing ordered that "no sleeping car shall be operated on any line of railroad in the State of Texas * * * unless such cars are continuously in the charge of an employee * * * having the rank and position of Pullman conductor." Thereupon, the Pullman Company and the railroads affected brought this action in a federal district court to enjoin the Commission's order. Pullman porters were permitted to intervene as complainants, and Pullman conductors entered the litigation in support of the order. Three judges having been convened, the court enjoined enforcement of the order. From this decree, the case came here directly.

The Pullman Company and the railroads assailed the order as unauthorized by Texas law as well as violative of the Equal Protection, the Due Process and the Commerce Clauses of the Constitution. The intervening porters adopted these objections but mainly objected to the order as a discrimination against Negroes in violation of the Fourteenth Amendment.

The complaint of the Pullman porters undoubtedly tendered a substantial constitutional issue. It is more than substantial. It touches a sensitive area of social policy upon which the federal courts ought not to enter unless no alternative to its adjudication is open. Such constitutional adjudication plainly can be avoided if a definitive ruling on the state issue would terminate the controversy. It is therefore our duty to turn to a consideration of questions under Texas law.

The Commission found justification for its order in a Texas statute which we quote in the margin.[1] It is common ground that if the order is within the Commission's authority its subject matter must be included in the Commission's power to prevent "unjust discrimination * * * and to prevent any and all other abuses" in the conduct of railroads. Whether arrangements pertaining to the staffs of Pullman cars are covered by the Texas concept of "discrimination" is far from clear. What practices of the railroads may be deemed to be "abuses" subject to the Commission's correction is equally doubtful. Reading the Texas statutes and the Texas decisions as outsiders without special competence in Texas law, we would have little confidence in our independent judgment regarding the application of that law to the present situation. The lower court did deny that the Texas statutes sustained the Commission's assertion of power. And this represents the view of an able and experienced circuit judge of the circuit which includes Texas and of two capable district judges trained in Texas law. Had we or they no choice in the matter but to decide what is the law of the state, we should hesitate long before rejecting their forecast of Texas law. But no matter how seasoned the judgment of the district court may be, it

---

1. Vernon's Anno. Texas Civil Statutes, Article 6445:
  "Power and authority are hereby conferred upon the Railroad Commission of Texas over all railroads, and suburban, belt and terminal railroads, and over all public wharves, docks, piers, elevators, warehouses, sheds, tracks and other property used in connection therewith in this State, and over all persons, associations and corporations, private or municipal, owning or operating such railroad, wharf, dock, pier, elevator, warehouse, shed, track or other property to fix, and it is hereby made the duty of the said Commission to adopt all necessary rates, charges and regulations, to govern and regulate such railroads, persons, associations and corporations, and to correct abuses and prevent unjust discrimination in the rates, charges and tolls of such railroads, persons, associations and corporations, and to fix division of rates, charges and regulations between railroads and other utilities and common carriers where a division is proper and correct, and to prevent any and all other abuses in the conduct of their business and to do and perform such other duties and details in connection therewith as may be provided by law."

cannot escape being a forecast rather than a determination. The last word on the meaning of Article 6445 of the Texas Civil Statutes, and therefore the last word on the statutory authority of the Railroad Commission in this case, belongs neither to us nor to the district court but to the supreme court of Texas. In this situation a federal court of equity is asked to decide an issue by making a tentative answer which may be displaced tomorrow by a state adjudication. The reign of law is hardly promoted if an unnecessary ruling of a federal court is thus supplanted by a controlling decision of a state court. The resources of equity are equal to an adjustment that will avoid the waste of a tentative decision as well as the friction of a premature constitutional adjudication.

An appeal to the chancellor, as we had occasion to recall only the other day, is an appeal to the "exercise of the sound discretion, which guides the determination of courts of equity." The history of equity jurisdiction is the history of regard for public consequences in employing the extraordinary remedy of the injunction. There have been as many and as variegated applications of this supple principle as the situations that have brought it into play. Few public interests have a higher claim upon the discretion of a federal chancellor than the avoidance of needless friction with state policies.... These cases reflect a doctrine of abstention appropriate to our federal system whereby the federal courts, "exercising a wise discretion," restrain their authority because of "scrupulous regard for the rightful independence of the state governments" and for the smooth working of the federal judiciary. This use of equitable powers is a contribution of the courts in furthering the harmonious relation between state and federal authority without the need of rigorous congressional restriction of those powers.

Regard for these important considerations of policy in the administration of federal equity jurisdiction is decisive here. If there was no warrant in state law for the Commission's assumption of authority there is an end of the litigation; the constitutional issue does not arise. The law of Texas appears to furnish easy and ample means for determining the Commission's authority. Article 6453 of the Texas Civil Statutes gives a review of such an order in the state courts. Or, if there are difficulties in the way of this procedure of which we have not been apprised, the issue of state law may be settled by appropriate action on the part of the State to enforce obedience to the order. In the absence of any showing that these obvious methods for securing a definitive ruling in the state courts cannot be pursued with full protection of the constitutional claim, the district court should exercise its wise discretion by staying its hands.

We therefore remand the cause to the district court, with directions to retain the bill pending a determination of proceedings, to be brought with reasonable promptness, in the state court in conformity with this opinion....

Smelt v. County of Orange

447 F.3d 673 (9th Cir. 2006)

FERNANDEZ, Circuit Judge.

....

BACKGROUND

It is agreed: Smelt and Hammer are both males who wish to obtain a California marriage license and to marry each other in that state. They applied to the County Clerk of Orange County, California, for issuance of a marriage license on two occasions. They were denied a license both times "because [they] are of the same gender." Were it not for that, "[they] meet the qualifications for issuance of a marriage license...."

Smelt and Hammer then brought this action against the County of Orange and the Orange County Clerk (collectively the County); and the State Registrar of Vital Statistics, California Department of Health Services (the State). The amended complaint alleged that to the extent that California Family Code sections 300,[6] 301,[7] and 308.5[8] preclude them from obtaining a marriage license, those sections violate: equal protection; due process; "the Right to Life, Liberty and the Pursuit of Happiness"; "the right to be free from an undue invasion of the Right to Privacy; ... the Ninth Amendment Right of Reservation of all Rights not Enumerated to the People, and the Right to Travel, and The Right of Free Speech." The complaint also asserted that section 308.5 violates the Full Faith and Credit Clause of the United States Constitution....

....

The State Defendants then filed an abstention motion based on pending litigation in the California state courts on the issue of whether the California Family Code sections that limit marriage to couples consisting of an unmarried man and an unmarried woman comply with the provisions of the California constitution (the Marriage Cases). Equality California, which is involved in the Marriage Cases, filed an amicus brief in support of abstention. The district court took the motion to abstain under submission. In addition, cross motions for summary judgment were filed by Smelt and Hammer, the County, the United States, Prop 22 Fund, and CCF.

The district court ultimately issued a published order: (1) abstaining pursuant to *Railroad Commission of Texas v. Pullman Co.,* 312 U.S. 496 (1941), from deciding the constitutionality of the challenged sections of the California Family Code until the Marriage Cases had been concluded....

Needless to say, Smelt and Hammer disagreed; this appeal followed....

DISCUSSION

I. *The California Family Code Sections; Abstention*

As already noted, the district court abstained on Smelt and Hammer's attacks on the California Family Code Sections. It did so pursuant to the *Pullman* abstention doctrine. The source of the doctrine is found, not surprisingly, in a case involving Pullman sleeping cars, where the federal courts were asked to restrain an order of the Texas Railroad Commission regarding the use of attendants in railroad sleeping cars. A three-judge court (one circuit judge and two district judges) issued an injunction, and an appeal to the Supreme Court followed. The Court noted that the Supreme Court of Texas would have the last word on whether the Commission had even acted within the scope of authority given to it by the laws of Texas. It saw nothing to preclude an action which could be "brought with reasonable promptness, in the state court." Thus, the Supreme Court determined that the federal courts should retain the action, but abstain while that state court process went forward, because the case touched a sensitive area of social policy, the state decision could obviate the need for federal constitutional adjudication, and any fed-

---

6. Cal. Fam.Code § 300 reads as follows, in pertinent part: "Marriage is a personal relation arising out of a civil contract between a man and a woman, to which the consent of the parties capable of making that contract is necessary. Consent alone does not constitute marriage. Consent must be followed by the issuance of a license and solemnization...."

7. Cal. Fam.Code § 301 reads as follows: "An unmarried male of the age of 18 years or older, and an unmarried female of the age of 18 years or older, and not otherwise disqualified, are capable of consenting to and consummating marriage."

8. Cal. Fam.Code § 308.5 reads as follows: "Only marriage between a man and a woman is valid or recognized in California."

eral construction of the state law might, at any time, be upended by a decision of the state courts. That, over time, has been distilled into the factors that go into a determination of whether the *Pullman* abstention doctrine can be utilized. Those factors are usually rendered as follows:

> (1) The complaint touches a sensitive area of social policy upon which the federal courts ought not to enter unless no alternative to its adjudication is open.
>
> (2) Such constitutional adjudication plainly can be avoided if a definitive ruling on the state issue would terminate the controversy.
>
> (3) The possibly determinative issue of state law is doubtful.

And it is not even necessary that the state adjudication "obviate the need to decide all the federal constitutional questions" as long as it will "reduce the contours" of the litigation.…

We must first consider whether the complaint touches a sensitive area of social policy upon which we should not enter unless we have no real alternative. It does, for it cannot be gainsaid that in our social and legal traditions the institution of marriage has been considered to be an integral part of the foundation of a well-ordered and viable society, the sinew that strengthens society, the glue that holds society together. In an unbroken line of cases, the Supreme Court has recognized that.…

Because of its vital importance to society, while the people through their governments have always encouraged marriage, they have always regulated it. Generally that has been at the state level.…

California has exercised that undoubted police power, and in so doing has expressed its concerns and beliefs about this sensitive area. Thus, as this case shows us, the people of the State of California have defined what marriage is, *viz.* a consensual, contractual personal relationship between "a man and a woman," which is solemnized. By the same token, California has regulated and limited the institution in a number of ways. For example: those under 18 cannot marry without somebody else's consent; to marry, you must be unmarried (in other words, no polygamy or polyandry); marriages within certain degrees of consanguinity are forbidden.

But as important as the institution of marriage is, our purpose here is not to write a paean to its past and contemporary glories; it is the more mundane purpose of pointing to the fact that it is difficult to imagine an area more fraught with sensitive social policy considerations in which federal courts should not involve themselves if there is an alternative. In short, the first *Pullman* factor is easily met, and we now turn to the second one.

When we do so, we think it is equally apparent that the resolution of the Marriage Cases in the California courts may not only narrow, but even eliminate, any need for federal constitutional adjudication regarding Smelt and Hammer's attacks on the California statutory provisions in this case. If the California courts ultimately determine that the sections in question violate the California constitution, we will have no need to consider the federal constitutional claims regarding those sections. That brings us to the third *Pullman* factor.

Again, the third factor is easily satisfied in the context of this case. We simply "cannot predict with any confidence how [the California Supreme Court] would decide" the state constitutional questions. Especially is that true where, as here, the California Supreme Court will be faced with a constitutional issue that presents difficult questions of state constitutional law, which it has not yet passed upon. Added to that is the fact that a California Superior Court has found the state statutes to be unconstitutional, and review of that decision is now pending in a California Court of Appeal in the Marriage Cases.

Therefore, all factors in the *Pullman* analysis point toward abstention. Nor have we any reason to assume that the California Supreme Court will construe the California Constitution in the same way as the federal courts construe the United States Constitution.[24] That makes this a particularly good case for *Pullman* abstention....

[The opinion of Judge Farris, concurring in the result, is omitted.]

Notes and Questions

1. When a litigant files an action in state court after the federal court abstains pursuant to *Pullman*, it is not enough to merely present the question of state law to the state court: one must ask the state court to consider the question of state law "in light of" the federal constitutional claims raised in federal court, as that knowledge may cause the state court to interpret state law in a way that avoids a potential confrontation with federal law. *See Gov't and Civic Emps. Org. Comm., CIO v. Windsor*, 353 U.S. 364 (1957).

2. When a federal court abstains pursuant to *Pullman*, the litigants have the option of either having the state court also address the merits of their federal constitutional claims, or returning to federal court to have the federal court address those claims if the state court's consideration of the state law question does not resolve the dispute between the parties. In this sense, *Pullman* abstention is much less draconian than is *Younger* abstention. But a party cannot have it both ways: if she "freely and without reservation" submit their federal claims for decision to the state court, she will be unable to return to the federal district court, with the only possibility of federal court review of her federal constitutional questions available by means of a petition for a writ of certiorari seeking U.S. Supreme Court review of the decision from the state's highest court. Thus, if a litigant wishes to return to federal district court, she should make clear on the record to the state court that she is bringing to the court's attention the federal constitutional claims only so that the state court can interpret the state law issue in light of those claims pursuant to the *Windsor* procedure, and that she intends to return to federal district court. *See England v. La. State Bd. of Med. Exam'rs*, 375 U.S. 411 (1964).

3. If the federal court abstains on *Pullman* grounds, it is not enough to file an action in a state trial court and obtain an opinion; the litigants are required to appeal the case all the way to the state's highest court before returning to federal district court.

4. Some states have a procedure whereby a federal court can certify a question of state law directly to the state's highest court. If such a procedure exists, the federal court may utilize that in lieu of requiring the parties to file a separate action in state court. *See Arizonans for Official English v. Arizona*, 520 U.S. 43, 75–76 (1997).

5. The *Pullman* case involved only an unclear question of state *statutory* law. Yet in *Smelt*, the statutory language seems clear: it unequivocally prohibits marriage between persons of the same sex. So what is the unclear question of state law in *Smelt*? According to the *Smelt* court, it is the possibility that the state statute might violate provisions of the *state* constitution. Is that a valid basis for *Pullman* abstention? The Supreme Court has held that under *Pullman* abstention, the litigants may be required to ask the state court to consider the question whether the state law at issue is inconsistent with provisions in the state's constitution "where the challenged statute is part of an integrated scheme of related constitutional provisions, statutes, and regulations." *Harris Cnty. Com'rs Court*

---

24. For example, California's constitutional law on privacy is different from federal law on that subject.

v. Moore, 420 U.S. 77, 84 n.8 (1975). In contrast, the Court has held that *Pullman* abstention is not required to permit a state court to consider the constitutionality of the state law in light of parallel state constitutional provisions that might, in theory, be interpreted more broadly than their federal counterparts. *See Hawaii Hous. Auth. v. Midkiff*, 467 U.S. 229, 237 n.4 (1984); *Examining Bd. v. Flores de Otero*, 426 U.S. 572, 598 (1976). Into which category does the constitutional provision cited by the *Smelt* court fall?

6. Note that, in *Smelt*, Equality California, a pro-gay rights organization litigating the state court challenge to California's marriage laws, filed an amicus brief in support of the state's motion to abstain under *Pullman*. Why would Equality California (which challenged the state's marriage laws in state court solely on state constitutional grounds) seek to prevent Smelt and Hammer from pursuing their independent federal constitutional challenge to those same laws? Reconsider your answer to this question when you get to Section D of this chapter, which examines the Supreme Court's jurisdiction to review state court decisions.

7. What purpose is served by *Pullman* abstention, and does that purpose justify what is likely to be a significant delay in obtaining federal court adjudication of one's federal constitutional rights?

C. The Precedential Value of Summary Decisions

In 1910, in response to a growing number of cases in which federal district court judges issued injunctions against enforcement of state statutes determined by the district court judge to violate some provision of the U.S. Constitution, Congress enacted the Three-Judge Court Act. Under the Act, when a litigant sought to enjoin enforcement of a state statute on the ground that it was somehow unconstitutional, a three-judge court—consisting of two district court judges and one circuit court judge—would convene to hear and dispose of the application for an injunction, with their decision subject to mandatory, direct review by the U.S. Supreme Court. Although the Act initially applied only to applications for temporary injunctions and only when the challenged law was a state statute, it was later expanded to encompass applications for permanent injunctions as well as challenges to the constitutionality of federal statutes. The rationale for the Act was a belief that the bias, caprice, or imprudence of a single judge should not stop a federal or state statute from being enforced, and that requiring three judges to hear and consider such applications would reduce the risk of these factors resulting in the delay in implementation of a valid federal or state law. *See* ERWIN C. SURRENCY, HISTORY OF THE FEDERAL COURTS 350–51 (2d ed. 2002); Note, *Judicial Limitation of Three-Judge Court Jurisdiction*, 85 YALE L.J. 564, 564–65 (1976).

In addition, the U.S. Supreme Court also had mandatory appellate jurisdiction over two types of cases coming from the state court system: those in which the state courts invalidated a treaty or Act of Congress on federal grounds, or those in which the state courts upheld the validity of a state law attacked on federal grounds.

One result of the Supreme Court's mandatory appellate jurisdiction over these types of cases was that its docket—which otherwise was determined by its discretionary grant of writs of certiorari—began to be dominated by these sorts of cases, making it difficult for the Court to write carefully reasoned opinions about all of the cases it was required to hear as well as those that it chose to review. The U.S. Supreme Court dealt with this unwelcome increase in the size of its docket by issuing "summary" decisions in cases falling within their mandatory appellate jurisdiction, in which it simply "affirmed" or "reversed" the opinion of the lower court without a written opinion, or would dismiss the appeal for "want of a substantial federal question."

In two cases relevant to the subject matter of this course, the U.S. Supreme Court summarily dealt with appeals from lower courts. First, in 1972, the U.S. Supreme Court dismissed for want of a substantial federal question a decision by the Supreme Court of Minnesota rejecting a claim that the U.S. Constitution provided same-sex couples a right to marry. *See Baker v. Nelson*, 191 N.W.2d 185 (Minn. 1971), *appeal dismissed*, 409 U.S. 810 (1972). Second, in 1976, the U.S. Supreme Court summarily affirmed a lower federal court decision upholding the constitutionality of a state sodomy law. *See Doe v. Commonwealth's Attorney for City of Richmond*, 403 F. Supp. 1199 (E.D. Va. 1975), *aff'd* 425 U.S. 901 (1976).

In 1976, Congress repealed the mandatory appeal provisions of the Three-Judge Court Act for almost all types of cases, and in 1988, it eliminated the Supreme Court's mandatory appellate review of state court decisions. Nonetheless, a critical question remains: what is the precedential value of a U.S. Supreme Court decision that either summarily affirms a lower court decision or that dismisses the appeal for "want of a substantial federal question"?

Hicks v. Miranda

422 U.S. 332 (1975)

Mr. Justice WHITE delivered the opinion of the Court.

[Theater owner brought action in federal court challenging the constitutionality of a California obscenity statute. At issue was the question whether the federal district court should have considered itself bound by an earlier decision in *Miller II*, in which the U.S. Supreme Court summarily affirmed without opinion a state court decision sustaining the constitutionality of the very same statute.]

The first question emerges from our summary dismissal in *Miller II*. Appellants claimed in the District Court, and claim here, that *Miller II* was binding on the District Court and required that court to sustain the California obscenity statute and to dismiss the case....

We agree with appellants that the District Court was in error in holding that it would disregard the decision in *Miller II*. That case was an appeal from a decision by a state court upholding a state statute against federal constitutional attack. A federal constitutional issue was properly presented, it was within our appellate jurisdiction under 28 U.S.C. §1257(2), and we had no discretion to refuse adjudication of the case on its merits as would have been true had the case been brought here under our certiorari jurisdiction. We are not obligated to grant the case plenary consideration, and we did not; but we were required to deal with its merits. We did so by concluding that the appeal should be dismissed because the constitutional challenge to the California statute was not a substantial one. The three-judge court was not free to disregard this pronouncement. As Mr. Justice Brennan once observed, "[v]otes to affirm summarily, and to dismiss for want of a substantial federal question, it hardly needs comment, are votes on the merits of a case...," Ohio ex rel. Eaton v. Price, 360 U.S. 246, 247 (1959); cf. R. Stern & E. Gressman, Supreme Court Practice, 197 (4th ed. 1969) ("The Court is, however, deciding a case on the merits, when it dismisses for want of a substantial question …"); C. Wright, Law of Federal Courts 495 (2d ed. 1970) ("Summary disposition of an appeal, however, either by affirmance or by dismissal for want of a substantial federal question, is a disposition on the merits"). The District Court should have followed the Second Circuit's advice, first, in Port Authority Bondholders Protective Committee v. Port of New York Authority, 387 F.2d 259, 263 n.3 (1967), that "unless and until the Supreme Court should instruct otherwise, inferior federal courts had best adhere to the view that if the Court has branded a question as unsubstantial, it remains so except when doctrinal developments indicate otherwise"; and, later, in Doe v. Hodgson, 478 F.2d 537, 539 (1973), that the lower courts are bound by summary decisions by this Court "'until such time as the Court informs [them] that [they] are not.'" ….

[The concurring opinion of Chief Justice Burger, and the dissenting opinion of Justice Stewart, are omitted.]

Hardwick v. Bowers
760 F.2d 1202 (11th Cir. 1985)

JOHNSON, Circuit Judge:

[In this case, excerpted earlier in the chapter, Michael Hardwick brought suit asking the federal district court to declare unconstitutional a Georgia statute that criminalizes sodomy after he was arrested on charges of violating the statute.]

II. THE EFFECT OF *DOE V. COMMONWEALTH'S ATTORNEY*

In 1975 a three-judge district court in Virginia upheld the constitutionality of that state's sodomy law, *Doe v. Commonwealth's Attorney for City of Richmond,* 403 F.Supp. 1199 (E.D.Va.1975). The plaintiffs, homosexuals who had neither been arrested nor threatened with prosecution, argued that the statute violated their rights to due process, freedom of expression, privacy, and freedom from cruel and unusual punishment. They appealed the adverse decision of the district court to the Supreme Court. The Court summarily affirmed the judgment. 425 U.S. 901 (1976). The district court in this case dismissed Hardwick's complaint for failure to state a claim upon which relief could be granted, relying exclusively on *Doe.*

A. The Bounds of the Original Holding in *Doe*

A summary affirmance of the Supreme Court has binding precedential effect. *Hicks v. Miranda,* 422 U.S. 332, 344 (1975). Yet because the Court disposes of the case without explaining its reasons, the holding must be carefully limited. A summary affirmance represents an approval by the Supreme Court of the judgment below but should not be taken as an endorsement of the reasoning of the lower court. *Mandel v. Bradley,* 432 U.S. 173 (1977); *Fusari v. Steinberg,* 419 U.S. 379 (1975).

Despite this general admonition, finding the precise limits of a summary affirmance has proven to be no easy task. Courts seeking to identify the issues governed by a summary affirmance should examine the issues necessarily decided in reaching the result as well as the issues mentioned in the jurisdictional statement. *Illinois State Board of Elections v. Socialist Workers Party,* 440 U.S. 173, 181–83 (1979). These two criteria conflict in this case. The jurisdictional statement in *Doe* presented the question of whether Virginia's sodomy statute violated constitutional rights to privacy, due process, and equal protection under the First, Fourth, Fifth, Ninth, and Fourteenth Amendments. Yet the Court could have approved of the result reached by the district court without addressing those constitutional issues because the plaintiffs in *Doe* plainly lacked standing to sue.[5] Hence, the constitutional issues presented in *Doe* were issues listed in the jurisdictional statement but not necessary to the disposition of that case.

Several reasons lead us to conclude that the mention of constitutional issues in the jurisdictional statement in *Doe* does not override the clear availability of a narrower ground of decision. To begin with, the Supreme Court has generally referred to the two indicia, necessity to the decision and presentation in the jurisdictional statement, as if both were necessary. Furthermore, if the jurisdictional statement could expand a summary affirmance beyond the scope of issues necessarily decided, it would give the litigants considerable control over the scope of summary dispositions. While a jurisdictional statement prevents speculation as to what issues the Court actually considered, it is only a tool in determining the ultimate question: the most narrow plausible rationale for the summary decision.

Lower courts may rely upon the jurisdictional statement as an outside limit on the [precedential] scope of a summary decision but Supreme Court precedent does not allow us to consider the jurisdictional statement as both a minimum and a maximum formulation of the issues decided. Where, as in the *Doe* case, the facts of the case plainly reveal a basis for the lower court's decision more narrow than the issues listed in the jurisdictional statement, a lower court should presume that the Supreme Court decided the case on that narrow ground. We therefore construe *Doe* as an affirmance based on the plaintiffs' lack of standing and not controlling in this case.

B. Doctrinal Developments after *Doe*

Even if *Doe* had been resolved on the constitutional grounds now asserted by Hardwick,[6] the Supreme Court has indicated since that time that the constitutionality of statutes such as the one in question here is not governed by *Doe* but, rather, remains an open question. Since a summary disposition binds lower courts only until the Supreme Court indicates otherwise, *Hicks v. Miranda,* 422 U.S. 332, 344–45 (1975), developments subsequent to the *Doe* decision undermine whatever controlling weight it once may have possessed.

Doctrinal developments need not take the form of an outright reversal of the earlier case. The Supreme Court may indicate its willingness to reverse or reconsider a prior opinion with such clarity that a lower court may properly refuse to follow what appears to be binding precedent. Even less clear-cut expressions by the Supreme Court can erode an earlier summary disposition because summary actions by the Court do not carry the full precedential weight of a decision announced in a written opinion after consideration of briefs and oral argument. The Court could suggest that a legal issue once thought to be settled by a summary action should now be treated as an open question, and it could do so without directly mentioning the earlier case. At that point, lower courts could appropriately reach their own conclusions on the merits of the issue.

At least two actions by the Supreme Court demonstrate that it now considers the constitutional issues purportedly determined in *Doe* to be unsettled. The first indication

---

5. The plaintiffs there had not been arrested for violation of the statute, nor did they present any evidence of threatened prosecutions or past prosecutions under the statute. At most, the plaintiffs had a "generalized grievance" regarding the statute and its enforcement that was insufficient to allow a federal court to reach the merits of their claim....

6. The *Doe* affirmance could not control all of Hardwick's legal claims. He alleges that the Georgia statute violates his First Amendment freedom of association, a claim not addressed by the jurisdictional statement or the district court opinion in *Doe.*

came in the decision in *Carey v. Population Services,* 431 U.S. 678 (1977). The Court there held, *inter alia,* that a state could not prevent the sale of non-prescription contraceptives to adults by persons other than licensed pharmacists. Justice Powell stated in a concurring opinion that the majority had employed an unnecessarily broad principle that subjected all state regulation affecting "adult sexual relations" or "personal decisions in matters of sex" to the strictest standard of judicial review. The majority responded in footnote 5 that its holding only applied to state regulation that burdens an individual's right to decide to prevent conception by substantially limiting access to the means of effectuating that decision. It then went on to state the following: "As we observe below, 'the Court has not definitively answered the difficult question whether and to what extent the Constitution prohibits state statutes regulating [private consensual sexual] behavior among adults,' n. 17, *infra,* and we do not purport to answer that question now" (brackets in original). Footnote 17, although joined only by a plurality, casts some light on the nature of the "private consensual sexual behavior among adults" referred to in footnote 5 because it cites a law review comment that discusses the possible application of Supreme Court precedent to criminal statutes outlawing private consensual sexual activities, including sodomy. Justice Rehnquist, in a dissenting opinion, criticized the language of footnote 5 because he considered it to be in conflict with *Doe,* which in his view had definitively established the constitutional validity of state prohibitions of certain consensual activities.

The implications of footnote 5 could hardly be clearer. The plain meaning of the phrase "private consensual sexual behavior among adults" encompasses acts of sodomy carried out between consenting adults in private. The identical phrase in footnote 17 is accompanied by a reference to just that sort of activity. The ability of the state to regulate conduct as Georgia has attempted to do, according to the Court in *Carey,* is now an open question. Obviously *Carey* does not provide much guidance as to the proper analysis of the constitutional claims presented in this case; just as obviously, it calls on lower courts to analyze such claims rather than relying on *Doe.*

A second development in the Supreme Court occurred more recently when the Court granted certiorari in *New York v. Uplinger,* 464 U.S. 812 (1983), and later dismissed the writ as improvidently granted. The New York Court of Appeals had ruled in that case that federal constitutional law invalidated a New York statute prohibiting persons from loitering in a public place for the purpose of engaging, or soliciting another person to engage, in "deviate sexual behavior." The decision was premised on an earlier ruling by that court in *People v. Onofre,* 51 N.Y.2d 476 (1980), *cert. denied,* 451 U.S. 987 (1981), where it held that the federal constitution invalidated a state statute criminalizing any act of sodomy between two persons. Hence, the petitioner for writ of certiorari in *Uplinger* urged the Supreme Court to consider the constitutionality of state regulations prohibiting consensual sodomy among adults.

After the Supreme Court received the briefs of the parties and heard oral argument in *Uplinger,* it dismissed the writ of certiorari as improvidently granted. In a per curiam order, the Court stated that the case presented an "inappropriate vehicle" for resolving the "important constitutional issues" raised by the parties. The Court also indicated that the constitutionality of state laws against consensual sodomy was one of the most important of those issues; it explained that several impediments to consideration of the constitutional issues presented in the *Onofre* decision figured heavily in its decision to dismiss the writ. Those impediments included the belated decision of the petitioner not to challenge the *Onofre* decision and the fact that the state court decision in *Uplinger* was subject to varying interpretations, leaving uncertainty as to the precise federal constitutional issue the state court decided.

It is fair to conclude from this order that the Supreme Court was prepared to address the constitutionality of state regulations like Georgia's sodomy statute but chose to address the issue when presented more directly in another case. While the Court may have meant that it was prepared to reconsider the *Doe* affirmance, which would have remained binding precedent until overruled, such a possibility is unlikely because the Court never referred to *Doe* in the *Uplinger* proceedings or indicated in any way that the underlying constitutional issue was settled, even temporarily. Under these circumstances, we interpret the order as an indication that the constitutional questions presented by Hardwick are still open for consideration by the Supreme Court and by this Court. This order, together with the Court's observation in *Carey,* deprives *Doe v. Commonwealth's Attorney* of whatever controlling weight it once may have had. The district court erred in dismissing Hardwick's claim.…

[The opinion of Judge Kravitch, concurring in part and dissenting in part, is omitted.]

In re Kandu

315 B.R. 123 (Bankr. W.D. Wash. 2004)

PAUL B. SNYDER, Bankruptcy Judge.

[Same-sex couple — U.S. citizens who married one another in Canada — filed petition seeking bankruptcy protection. At issue in the case is the constitutionality of the Defense of Marriage Act, which does not recognize same-sex marriages for purposes of any federal statute, including the bankruptcy laws.]

IV

DUE PROCESS AND EQUAL PROTECTION

The Debtor asserts that DOMA violates both the due process and equal protection guarantees of the Fifth Amendment to the U.S. Constitution. Specifically, she argues that the fundamental right to marry includes the right to marry someone of the same sex and that the classification created by DOMA is entitled to heightened scrutiny by the courts. The [United States Trustee ("UST")] asserts that there is no controlling authority to support either of the Debtor's contentions, and that moreover, there is controlling authority by the Supreme Court to the contrary, articulated in *Baker v. Nelson,* 409 U.S. 810 (1972).

A. Baker v. Nelson

The UST contends that in *Baker,* the Supreme Court considered the Debtor's constitutional challenges to legislation restricting marriage to a man and a woman, and held that this restriction violates neither due process nor equal protection. The UST argues that, because no Supreme Court or Ninth Circuit decision has reached a different conclusion since *Baker,* that case is binding precedent and dispositive of the issues before this Court.

In the underlying case, *Baker v. Nelson,* 291 Minn. 310 (1971), *appeal dismissed,* 409 U.S. 810 (1972), the Minnesota Supreme Court considered a constitutional challenge under the First, Eighth, Ninth, and Fourteenth Amendments to the U.S. Constitution limiting marriage to one man and one woman. The couple at issue had been denied a marriage license on the basis that the couple was of the same sex. The court rejected the argument that the right to marry without regard to the sex of the parties is a fundamental right. In so holding, the court concluded that the statute did not violate the Due Process Clause. Likewise, the court rejected the argument that the state statute violated the Equal Protection Clause.

Invoking the Supreme Court's mandatory appellate jurisdiction (since repealed), the same-sex couple sought review of the state court ruling, arguing that denial of the marriage license violated the Due Process and Equal Protection Clauses of the Fourteenth Amendment. The Supreme Court, which had no discretion to refuse adjudication of the case on its merits, *see Hicks v. Miranda,* 422 U.S. 332, 344 (1975), summarily decided the case and dismissed the appeal "for want of a substantial federal question." *Baker,* 409 U.S. 810.

With respect to the effect of the Supreme Court's summary decision in *Baker,* the Supreme Court has explained that lower courts are bound by summary actions on the merits by the Court. *Hicks,* 422 U.S. at 344–45.

> Summary affirmances and dismissals for want of a substantial federal question without doubt reject the specific challenges presented in the statement of jurisdiction and do leave undisturbed the judgment appealed from. They do prevent lower courts from coming to opposite conclusions on the precise issues presented and necessarily decided by those actions.... Summary actions, however, ... should not be understood as breaking new ground but as applying principles established by prior decisions to the particular facts involved.

Mandel v. Bradley, 432 U.S. 173, 176 (1977). When the Supreme Court summarily affirms, it " 'affirm[s] the judgment but not necessarily the reasoning by which it was reached.' " *Mandel,* 432 U.S. at 176.

Nonetheless, the Supreme Court has limited the scope of the precedential value of such summary decisions. "[T]he precedential effect of a summary affirmance can extend no farther than 'the precise issues presented and necessarily decided by those actions.' " *Illinois State Bd. of Elections v. Socialist Workers Party,* 440 U.S. 173, 182 (1979). Furthermore, "[q]uestions which 'merely lurk in the record,' ... are not resolved, and no resolution of them may be inferred." *Illinois State Bd. of Elections,* 440 U.S. at 183. One court has explained that "the precedential value of a summary disposition by the Supreme Court is to be confined to the exact facts of the case and to the precise question posed in the jurisdictional statement." *Lecates v. Justice of the Peace Court No. 4 of Del.,* 637 F.2d 898, 904 (3rd Cir. 1980). Thus, before deciding a case on the authority of a summary disposition by the Supreme Court, a judge must,

> (a) examine the jurisdictional statement in the earlier case to be certain that the constitutional questions presented were the same and, if they were,
>
> (b) determine that the judgment in fact rests upon decision of those questions and not even arguably upon some alternative nonconstitutional ground.... "[A]ppropriate, but not necessarily conclusive, weight" is to be given this Court's summary dispositions.

Mandel, 432 U.S. at 180 (Brennan, J., concurring). When "a summary disposition is applicable, it is a binding precedent." *Lecates,* 637 F.2d at 904.

The UST argues that this Court is bound by *Baker* on both the Debtor's due process and equal protection arguments. Before this Court can apply *Baker* as binding precedent, it must examine the jurisdictional statements presented to the Supreme Court that are as follows:

> 1. Whether appellee's refusal to sanctify appellants' marriage deprives appellants of their liberty to marry and of their property without due process of law under the Fourteenth Amendment.
>
> 2. Whether appellee's refusal, pursuant to Minnesota marriage statutes, to sanctify appellants' marriage because both are of the male sex violates their rights under the equal protection clause of the Fourteenth Amendment.
>
> 3. Whether appellee's refusal to sanctify appellants' marriage deprives appellants of their right to privacy under the Ninth and Fourteenthe Amendments.

Juris. Statement in *Baker v. Nelson,* October Term, 1972, p. 3.

Determining whether a summary disposition by the Supreme Court is binding precedent is anything but a clear and certain task. The issue in *Baker* was whether a state licensing statute limiting marriage to opposite-sex couples, and thereby excluding same-sex marriage, violated the due process and equal protection provisions of the Constitution. At first impression, this appears to be the same issue the Debtor brings before this Court now: whether DOMA that limits the term "marriage" to two individuals of the opposite sex, and thereby excludes couples of the same sex, violates the due process and equal protection provisions of the Constitution. Yet there are differences that could sufficiently distinguish *Baker* from the current case. For instance, the appellants in *Baker* sought review of the constitutionality of a state marriage licensing statute, while the Debtor here seeks review of subsequently-enacted federal legislation with its own Congressional history that concerns exclusively federal benefits. Additionally, the appellants in *Baker* challenged the statute under the Equal Protection and Due Process Clauses of the Fourteenth Amendment; the Fifth Amendment is at issue here.

The Debtor also argues that even if *Baker* is applicable, intervening Supreme Court decisions have altered the legal landscape so drastically that the case now has little, if any, precedential value regarding the constitutionality of excluding all same-sex couples from the federal rights and benefits associated with marriage. *See Hicks,* 422 U.S. at 344 (holding that federal courts must rely on cases summarily decided by the Supreme Court until "doctrinal developments indicate otherwise"). The Debtor relies on *Lawrence v. Texas,* 539 U.S. 558 (2003), *Romer v. Evans,* 517 U.S. 620 (1996), and *Zablocki v. Redhail,* 434 U.S. 374 (1978) as support for her supposition that the legal landscape has been drastically altered.

Since *Baker,* there has been no decision by the Supreme Court or the Ninth Circuit addressing the constitutionality of a statute limiting marriage to opposite-sex couples. It is recognized, as discussed below, that there has been no binding federal case law holding that same-sex marriage is a fundamental right, that same-sex couples are a suspect or quasi-suspect class, or that marriage laws distinguishing between same-sex and opposite-sex couples cannot pass rational basis review. The Supreme Court's approach to the constitutional analysis of same-sex conduct, however, at least arguably appears to have shifted. This is particularly apparent in light of the Supreme Court's decision in *Lawrence. See Lawrence,* 539 U.S. at 586–606 (Scalia, J., dissenting).

The Supreme Court decision in *Illinois State Bd. of Elections* clarifies that "summary dispositions are to be narrowly interpreted and are of limited precedential value." William J. Schneier, *The Do's and Don'ts of Determining the Precedential Value of Supreme Court Summary Dispositions, League of Women Voters v. Nassau County Board of Supervisors,* 51 Brook. L.Rev. 945, 959 (1985). Given the enumerated statutory differences between *Baker* and DOMA, subsequent Congressional history related to DOMA, the limited scope of precedential value of summary affirmations and dismissals, and the possible impact of recent Supreme Court decisions, particularly as articulated in *Lawrence,* this Court concludes that *Baker* is not binding precedent on the issues presented by the Debtors....

Wilson v. Ake

354 F. Supp. 2d 1298 (M.D. Fla. 2005)

MOODY, District Judge.

[Same-sex couple who lawfully married one another in Massachusetts filed suit contending that State of Florida was required to recognize their marriage, and sought a declaration that both the federal Defense of Marriage Act and Florida's statute refusing to recognize same-sex marriages violated various provisions of the U.S. Constitution.]

BAKER v. NELSON

The United States argues that this Court is bound by the United States Supreme Court's decision in *Baker v. Nelson,* 291 Minn. 310 (1971), *appeal dismissed,* 409 U.S. 810 (1972). In *Baker v. Nelson,* two adult males' application for a marriage license was denied by the Clerk of the Hennepin County District Court because the petitioners were of the same sex. The plaintiffs, following the quashing of a writ of mandamus directing the clerk to issue a marriage license, appealed to the Minnesota Supreme Court. Plaintiffs argued that Minnesota Statute § 517.08, which did not authorize marriage between persons of the same sex, violated the First, Eighth, Ninth and Fourteenth Amendments of the United States Constitution. The Minnesota Supreme Court rejected plaintiffs' assertion that "the right to marry without regard to the sex of the parties is a fundamental right of all persons" and held that § 517.08 did not violate the Due Process Clause or Equal Protection Clause.

The plaintiffs then appealed the Minnesota Supreme Court's ruling to the United States Supreme Court pursuant to 28 U.S.C. [§] 1257(2). Under 28 U.S.C. [§] 1257(2), the Supreme Court had no discretion to refuse to adjudicate the case on its merits. *Hicks v. Miranda,* 422 U.S. 332, 344 (1975). The Supreme Court dismissed the appeal "for want of a substantial federal question." *Baker,* 409 U.S. at 810.

Plaintiffs assert that *Baker v. Nelson* is not binding upon this Court because the Supreme Court did not issue a written opinion and because the case was decided thirty-two (32) years ago, before the "current civil rights revolution." This Court disagrees. A dismissal for lack of a substantial federal question constitutes an adjudication on the merits that is binding on lower federal courts. *See Hicks,* 422 U.S. at 344. As Justice White noted, the Court was "not obligated to grant the case plenary consideration ... but [the Court was] required to deal with its merits." *Id.*

Although *Baker v. Nelson* is over thirty (30) years old, the decision addressed the same issues presented in this action and this Court is bound to follow the Supreme Court's decision.

The Supreme Court's holding in *Lawrence* does not alter the dispositive effect of *Baker.* The Supreme Court has not explicitly or implicitly overturned its holding in *Baker* or provided the lower courts, including this Court, with any reason to believe that the holding is invalid today. Accordingly, *Baker v. Nelson* is binding precedent upon this Court and Plaintiffs' case against Attorney General Ashcroft must be dismissed....

Notes and Questions

1. When the *Bowers* case was heard in the U.S. Supreme Court, the State of Georgia argued that the Court of Appeals erred in holding that the district court was not obligated to follow the summary affirmance in *Doe.* The Supreme Court held as follows: "We need not resolve this dispute, for we prefer to give plenary consideration to the merits of this case rather than rely on our earlier action in *Doe.*" *See Bowers v. Hardwick*, 478 U.S. 186, 189 n.4 (1986). Thus, although *Hicks* made it clear that *lower* courts are bound by the Supreme Court's summary decisions, the Court itself clearly does not give them the same weight. *See also Edelman v. Jordan*, 415 U.S. 651, 671 (1974) ("[S]ummary affirmances obviously are of precedential value.... Equally ob-

viously, they are not of the same precedential value as would be an opinion of this Court treating the question on the merits. Since we deal with a constitutional question, we are less constrained by the principle of stare decisis than we are in other areas of the law.").

2. *Perry v. Brown*, 671 F.3d 1052 (9th Cir. 2012), struck down as unconstitutional California's Proposition 8, which amended the California Constitution to limit marriage to unions of a man and a woman. In dismissing an argument that the court was bound by the U.S. Supreme Court's prior summary dismissal in *Baker v. Nelson*, 409 U.S. 810 (1972), the Ninth Circuit reasoned as follows:

> Because we do not address the question of the constitutionality of a state's ban on same-sex marriage, the Supreme Court's summary dismissal of *Baker v. Nelson,* 409 U.S. 810 (1972) (mem.), is not pertinent here.
>
> In *Baker,* the Court "dismissed for want of a substantial federal question" an appeal from the Minnesota Supreme Court's decision to uphold a state statute that did not permit marriage between two people of the same sex. *Id.* Such dismissals "prevent lower courts from coming to opposite conclusions on the precise issues presented and necessarily decided by" them, *Mandel v. Bradley,* 432 U.S. 173, 176 (1977) (per curiam), "'except when doctrinal developments indicate otherwise,'" *Hicks v. Miranda,* 422 U.S. 332, 344 (1975). "[N]o more may be read into" them, however, "than was essential to sustain th[e] judgment. Questions which 'merely lurk in the record' are not resolved, and no resolution of them may be inferred." *Ill. State Bd. of Elections v. Socialist Workers Party,* 440 U.S. 173, 183 (1979).
>
> Whether or not the constitutionality of any ban on same-sex marriage was "presented and necessarily decided" in *Baker,* and whether or not *Baker* would govern that question in light of subsequent "doctrinal developments," we address no such question here. We address a wholly different question: whether the people of a state may by plebiscite strip a group of a right or benefit, constitutional or otherwise, that they had previously enjoyed on terms of equality with all others in the state. That question was not present in *Baker* and is squarely controlled by *Romer,* which postdates *Baker* by more than two decades.

Perry, 671 F.3d at 1082 n.14.

3. Nearly all other recent cases involving challenges to either bans on same-sex marriage or the application of the Defense of Marriage Act have determined that the Supreme Court's summary affirmance in *Baker v. Nelson* is not binding for one reason or another. *See, e.g.*, *Golinski v. U.S. Office of Pers. Mgmt.*, 824 F. Supp. 2d 968, 982 n.5 (N.D. Cal. 2012) (in considering challenge to application of DOMA to deny federal benefits to same-sex couple married under state law, noting that *Baker v. Nelson* was about whether same-sex couples had the right to marry, while the instant case addresses the different question whether a couple so married under state law is entitled to federal benefits); *Garden State Equal. v. Dow*, 2012 WL 540608, at *3–*7 (N.J. Super. Ct. 2012) (citing doctrinal developments subsequent to *Baker v. Nelson*, including *Frontiero v. Richardson*, 411 U.S. 677 (1973) (sex discrimination), *Lawrence v. Texas*, and *Romer v. Evans*).

4. In the next two chapters, you will examine a number of due process and equal protection precedents decided after the U.S. Supreme Court's summary decisions in *Baker v. Nelson* and *Doe v. Commonwealth's Attorney for City of Richmond* were issued. After doing so, return to this section and consider whether those doctrinal developments permit lower courts to ignore the holdings in these earlier precedents.

D. Supreme Court Review of State Court Decisions

Recall that Article III, §2 of the U.S. Constitution defines the judicial Power of the United States as encompassing a variety of "Cases" and "Controversies."

Since the enactment of the Judiciary Act of 1789, the U.S. Supreme Court has been given a grant of jurisdiction by Congress to review decisions by state courts. Does that grant of jurisdiction encompass only *federal* questions decided by the state courts, or does it also permit the U.S. Supreme Court to review a state court's interpretation of *state* law?

In 1875, the U.S. Supreme Court interpreted its then-existing grant of jurisdiction to review state court decisions as extending *only* to federal questions, and not to questions of state law. *See Murdock v. City of Memphis*, 87 U.S. (20 Wall.) 590 (1875). In so holding, the Court found it unnecessary to reach "the question whether, if Congress had conferred such authority, the act would have been constitutional." *Id.* at 633. Since the Supreme Court's decision in *Murdock*, it has been firmly accepted that the U.S. Supreme Court lacks jurisdiction to review a case decided purely on state law grounds by a state court.

Moreover, the U.S. Supreme Court has held that, in certain circumstances, it lacks jurisdiction to review a case that contains a mixture of federal and state law claims. Specifically, the Court has stated that:

> where the judgment of a state court rests upon two grounds, one of which is federal and the other nonfederal in character, our jurisdiction fails if the nonfederal ground is independent of the federal ground and adequate to support the judgment.

Fox Film Corp. v. Muller, 296 U.S. 207, 210 (1935).

The materials that follow explore what it means for a nonfederal ground to be independent of the federal ground and adequate to support the judgment.

Problem 2-E: I'll See You in the Supreme Court (or Will I?)

Assume that same-sex couples who have sought and been denied marriage licenses have filed lawsuits in state courts in New Jersey, New York, and Rhode Island. Assume further that in none of these three states does state law *explicitly* limit marriage to opposite-sex couples. The lawsuits make the following claims: (1) that the marriage laws of the state should be interpreted to permit same-sex couples to marry; and (2) if they are construed otherwise, then they violate the equal protection clause of the 14th Amendment to the U.S. Constitution, as well as the equal protection clause of the state constitution.

Assume that the cases are eventually appealed to the highest courts in each of these states, which have held as follows:

New Jersey—The state's highest court has interpreted the marriage laws of that state as not allowing same-sex marriage, and concluded that the laws, so construed, violate both the equal protection clause of the 14th Amendment of the U.S. Constitution and the equal protection clause of the New Jersey constitution.

New York—The state's highest court has interpreted the marriage laws of that state as not allowing same-sex marriage, and has concluded that the laws, so construed, violate neither the equal protection clause of the 14th Amendment of the U.S. Constitution nor the equal protection clause of the New York constitution.

Rhode Island—The state's highest court issued a brief opinion that reads as follows:

"The marriage laws in this state are at best ambiguous on the question whether or not marriage is limited to opposite-sex couples. Yet in light of the serious constitutional question that might arise if construed to bar same-sex couples from marrying, especially given recent decisions by the U.S. Supreme Court, *see Lawrence v. Texas*, 539 U.S. 558 (2003); *Romer v. Evans*, 517 U.S. 620 (1996), we feel that we must construe our marriage laws to allow both same-sex and opposite-sex couples to marry."

To what extent, if any, does the U.S. Supreme Court have jurisdiction to review these decisions?

Michigan v. Long
463 U.S. 1032 (1983)

Justice O'CONNOR delivered the opinion of the Court.

In *Terry v. Ohio*, 392 U.S. 1 (1968), we upheld the validity of a protective search for weapons in the absence of probable cause to arrest because it is unreasonable to deny a police officer the right "to neutralize the threat of physical harm," when he possesses an articulable suspicion that an individual is armed and dangerous. We did not, however, expressly address whether such a protective search for weapons could extend to an area beyond the person in the absence of probable cause to arrest. In the present case, respondent David Long was convicted for possession of marihuana found by police in the passenger compartment and trunk of the automobile that he was driving. The police searched the passenger compartment because they had reason to believe that the vehicle contained weapons potentially dangerous to the officers. We hold that the protective search of the passenger compartment was reasonable under the principles articulated in Terry and other decisions of this Court....

I

[The Court describes the procedural history of the case, which involves a criminal conviction for possession of marihuana in a state trial court in Michigan following a decision to reject the defendant's claim that the search of his car that uncovered the marihuana was illegal, a decision that was ultimately reversed by the Michigan Supreme Court.]

II

Before reaching the merits, we must consider Long's argument that we are without jurisdiction to decide this case because the decision below rests on an adequate and independent state ground. The court below referred twice to the state constitution in its opinion, but otherwise relied exclusively on federal law.[3] Long argues that the Michigan courts have provided greater protection from searches and seizures under the state constitution than is afforded under the Fourth Amendment, and the references to the state constitution therefore establish an adequate and independent ground for the decision below.

---

3. On the first occasion, the court merely cited in a footnote both the state and federal constitutions. On the second occasion, at the conclusion of the opinion, the court stated: "We hold, therefore, that the deputies' search of the vehicle was proscribed by the Fourth Amendment to the United States Constitution and art. 1, § 11 of the Michigan Constitution."

It is, of course, "incumbent upon this Court ... to ascertain for itself ... whether the asserted non-federal ground independently and adequately supports the judgment." Although we have announced a number of principles in order to help us determine whether various forms of references to state law constitute adequate and independent state grounds,[4] we openly admit that we have thus far not developed a satisfying and consistent approach for resolving this vexing issue. In some instances, we have taken the strict view that if the ground of decision was at all unclear, we would dismiss the case. In other instances, we have vacated, or continued a case, in order to obtain clarification about the nature of a state court decision. In more recent cases, we have ourselves examined state law to determine whether state courts have used federal law to guide their application of state law or to provide the actual basis for the decision that was reached. In *Oregon v. Kennedy,* 456 U.S. 667, 670–671 (1982), we rejected an invitation to remand to the state court for clarification even when the decision rested in part on a case from the state court, because we determined that the state case itself rested upon federal grounds. We added that "[e]ven if the case admitted of more doubt as to whether federal and state grounds for decision were intermixed, the fact that the state court relied to the extent it did on federal grounds requires us to reach the merits."

This ad hoc method of dealing with cases that involve possible adequate and independent state grounds is antithetical to the doctrinal consistency that is required when sensitive issues of federal-state relations are involved. Moreover, none of the various methods of disposition that we have employed thus far recommends itself as the preferred method that we should apply to the exclusion of others, and we therefore determine that it is appropriate to reexamine our treatment of this jurisdictional issue in order to achieve the consistency that is necessary.

The process of examining state law is unsatisfactory because it requires us to interpret state laws with which we are generally unfamiliar, and which often, as in this case, have not been discussed at length by the parties. Vacation and continuance for clarification have also been unsatisfactory both because of the delay and decrease in efficiency of judicial administration, and, more important, because these methods of disposition place significant burdens on state courts to demonstrate the presence or absence of our jurisdiction. Finally, outright dismissal of cases is clearly not a panacea because it cannot be doubted that there is an important need for uniformity in federal law, and that this need goes unsatisfied when we fail to review an opinion that rests primarily upon federal grounds and where the *independence* of an alleged state ground is not apparent from the four corners of the opinion. We have long recognized that dismissal is inappropriate "where there is strong indication ... that the federal constitution as judicially construed controlled the decision below."

---

4. For example, we have long recognized that "where the judgment of a state court rests upon two grounds, one of which is federal and the other non-federal in character, our jurisdiction fails if the non-federal ground is independent of the federal ground and adequate to support the judgment." *Fox Film Corp. v. Muller,* 296 U.S. 207, 210 (1935). We may review a state case decided on a federal ground even if it is clear that there was an available state ground for decision on which the state court could properly have relied. *Beecher v. Alabama,* 389 U.S. 35, 37, n. 3 (1967). Also, if, in our view, the state court "'felt compelled by what it understood to be federal constitutional considerations to construe ... its own law in the manner it did,'" then we will not treat a normally adequate state ground as independent, and there will be no question about our jurisdiction. *Delaware v. Prouse,* 440 U.S. 648, 653 (1979). Finally, "where the non-federal ground is so interwoven with the [federal ground] as not to be an independent matter, or is not of sufficient breadth to sustain the judgment without any decision of the other, our jurisdiction is plain." *Enterprise Irrigation District v. Farmers Mutual Canal Co.,* 243 U.S. 157, 164 (1917).

Respect for the independence of state courts, as well as avoidance of rendering advisory opinions, have been the cornerstones of this Court's refusal to decide cases where there is an adequate and independent state ground. It is precisely because of this respect for state courts, and this desire to avoid advisory opinions, that we do not wish to continue to decide issues of state law that go beyond the opinion that we review, or to require state courts to reconsider cases to clarify the grounds of their decisions. Accordingly, when, as in this case, a state court decision fairly appears to rest primarily on federal law, or to be interwoven with the federal law, and when the adequacy and independence of any possible state law ground is not clear from the face of the opinion, we will accept as the most reasonable explanation that the state court decided the case the way it did because it believed that federal law required it to do so. If a state court chooses merely to rely on federal precedents as it would on the precedents of all other jurisdictions, then it need only make clear by a plain statement in its judgment or opinion that the federal cases are being used only for the purpose of guidance, and do not themselves compel the result that the court has reached. In this way, both justice and judicial administration will be greatly improved. If the state court decision indicates clearly and expressly that it is alternatively based on bona fide separate, adequate, and independent grounds, we, of course, will not undertake to review the decision.

This approach obviates in most instances the need to examine state law in order to decide the nature of the state court decision, and will at the same time avoid the danger of our rendering advisory opinions. It also avoids the unsatisfactory and intrusive practice of requiring state courts to clarify their decisions to the satisfaction of this Court. We believe that such an approach will provide state judges with a clearer opportunity to develop state jurisprudence unimpeded by federal interference, and yet will preserve the integrity of federal law. "It is fundamental that state courts be left free and unfettered by us in interpreting their state constitutions. But it is equally important that ambiguous or obscure adjudications by state courts do not stand as barriers to a determination by this Court of the validity under the federal constitution of state action."

The principle that we will not review judgments of state courts that rest on adequate and independent state grounds is based, in part, on "the limitations of our own jurisdiction." *Herb v. Pitcairn,* 324 U.S. 117, 125 (1945). The jurisdictional concern is that we not "render an advisory opinion, and if the same judgment would be rendered by the state court after we corrected its views of federal laws, our review could amount to nothing more than an advisory opinion." Our requirement of a "plain statement" that a decision rests upon adequate and independent state grounds does not in any way authorize the rendering of advisory opinions. Rather, in determining, as we must, whether we have jurisdiction to review a case that is alleged to rest on adequate and independent state grounds, we merely assume that there are no such grounds when it is not clear from the opinion itself that the state court relied upon an adequate and independent state ground and when it fairly appears that the state court rested its decision primarily on federal law.

Our review of the decision below under this framework leaves us unconvinced that it rests upon an independent state ground. Apart from its two citations to the state constitution, the court below relied *exclusively* on its understanding of *Terry* and other federal cases. Not a single state case was cited to support the state court's holding that the search of the passenger compartment was unconstitutional. Indeed, the court declared that the search in this case was unconstitutional because "[t]he Court of Appeals erroneously applied the principles of *Terry v. Ohio* … to the search of the interior of the vehicle in this case." The references to the state constitution in no way indicate that the decision below rested on grounds in any way *independent* from the state court's interpretation of federal law. Even if we accept that the Michigan constitution has been interpreted to provide independent protection for certain rights also secured under the Fourth Amendment, it fairly appears in this case that the Michigan Supreme Court rested its decision primarily on federal law.

Rather than dismissing the case, or requiring that the state court reconsider its decision on our behalf solely because of a mere possibility that an adequate and independent ground supports the judgment, we find that we have jurisdiction in the absence of a plain statement that the decision below rested on an adequate and independent state ground. It appears to us that the state court "felt compelled by what it understood to be federal constitutional considerations to construe … its own law in the manner it did." ….

[The concurring opinion of Justice Blackmun, and the dissenting opinions of Justices Brennan and Stevens, are omitted.]

Notes and Questions

1. What does it mean for a state ground to be "adequate" for purposes of the adequate and independent state ground rule? Consider the following definition:

> A decision based on state law is adequate if the judgment in the case would necessarily be affirmed even if any decision on federal law were reversed. For example, suppose in a state criminal prosecution the defendant moves to exclude evidence under both the fourth amendment of the United States Constitution and under a state's constitution. If a state court rules in favor of the defendant under the state constitution, its decision will be adequate to support the judgment regardless of the outcome on the federal issue. It is adequate because the state is free to extend rights under its own constitution beyond federal law, unless state law is preempted. If, however, the state court ruled against the defendant, its decision ordinarily would not be adequate, since a reversal on the federal constitutional claim would change the outcome of the case.

Richard A. Matasar & Gregory S. Bruch, *Procedural Common Law, Federal Jurisdictional Policy, and Abandonment of the Adequate and Independent State Grounds Doctrine*, 86 Colum. L. Rev. 1291, 1292 n.2 (1986).

2. Under what circumstances is a state law ground not independent of federal law? One circumstance is when the state constitution has a provision analogous to a provision

in the U.S. Constitution — such as an equal protection or due process clause — and the state courts have held that the state constitutional provision is identical in scope to that found in the U.S. Constitution. *See, e.g., Fitzgerald v. Racing Ass'n of Cent. Iowa*, 539 U.S. 103, 106 (2003). A second circumstance is when a state court interprets state law in a particular way, but feels that it is compelled to do so because a different interpretation would result in the state law violating the federal constitution. *See, e.g., Zacchini v. Scripps-Howard Broad. Co.*, 433 U.S. 562, 568 (1977).

3. In Chapter 5, you will examine a variety of recent state high court decisions recognizing that same-sex couples have a right under the state's constitution to marry. Note that, in many of the more recent cases, a *strategy* of gay rights advocates has been to structure their claims for relief so as to avoid the possibility of U.S. Supreme Court review, due to apprehension about a same-sex marriage case getting to the Court too soon and the attendant risk of an unfavorable decision. Accordingly, in most of these cases, gay rights advocates have pled *only* state, not federal, constitutional claims.

When you review these decisions, reconsider them in light of the adequate and independent state ground rule. Do the decisions in fact rest on adequate and independent state grounds? How would they fare under Justice O'Connor's test in *Michigan v. Long*?

4. In some instances, in accordance with the suggestion in *Michigan v. Long*, state high courts insert a "plain statement" in their opinions asserting that their decisions rest on adequate and independent state grounds to avoid the risk that the U.S. Supreme Court will view the question as unclear and review the decision. *E.g., State v. Knapp*, 700 N.W.2d 899, 901 n.3 (Wis. 2005) ("Our decision rests on bona fide separate, adequate, and independent state grounds."); *State v. Carty*, 790 A.2d 903, 915 (N.J. 2002) ("[O]ur decision rests exclusively on 'bona fide separate, adequate, and independent [state] grounds.' 'To the extent that we rely on federal precedents in reaching our state-law decision, we do so only for the purpose of guidance, recognizing that those precedents may not compel the result that we reach today.'"). *See also Florida v. Powell*, 130 S. Ct. 1195, 1202, 1206 (2010) (re-affirming *Long*'s "plain-statement rule").

E. Jurisdiction Stripping

Problem 2-F: Checks and Balances

On July 22, 2004, the United States House of Representatives passed a bill, H.R. 3313, to amend title 28, United States Code, by adding Section 1632, which would read as follows:

"No court created by Act of Congress shall have any jurisdiction, and the Supreme Court shall have no appellate jurisdiction, to hear or decide any question pertaining to the interpretation of, or the validity under the Constitution of, section 1738C or this section."

Section 1738C, to which the bill refers, provides as follows:

"No State, territory, or possession of the United States, or Indian tribe, shall be required to give effect to any public act, record, or judicial proceeding of any other State, territory, possession, or tribe respecting a relationship between persons of the same sex that is treated as a marriage under the laws of such other State, territory, possession, or tribe, or a right or claim arising from such relationship."

Is the proposed bill, in whole or part, a constitutionally valid exercise of congressional power?

U.S. Constitution, Article I, § 8, cl. 9

The Congress shall have the Power.... To constitute Tribunals inferior to the supreme Court....

U.S. Constitution, Article III

SECTION 1. The judicial Power of the United States, shall be vested in one supreme Court, and in such inferior Courts as the Congress may from time to time ordain and establish....

SECTION 2. The judicial Power shall extend to all Cases, in Law and Equity, arising under this Constitution, the Laws of the United States, and Treaties made, or which shall be made, under their Authority;—to all Cases affecting Ambassadors, other public Ministers and Consuls;—to all Cases of admiralty and maritime Jurisdiction;—to Controversies to which the United States shall be a Party;—to Controversies between two or more States;—between a State and Citizens of another State;—between Citizens of different States;—between Citizens of the same State claiming Lands under Grants of different States, and between a State, or the Citizens thereof, and foreign States, Citizens or Subjects.

In all Cases affecting Ambassadors, other public Ministers and Consuls, and those in which a State shall be Party, the supreme Court shall have original Jurisdiction. In all the other Cases before mentioned, the supreme Court shall have appellate Jurisdiction, both as to Law and Fact, with such Exceptions, and under such Regulations as the Congress shall make.

Sheldon v. Sill

49 U.S. 441 (1850)

Mr. Justice GRIER delivered the opinion of the court.

The only question which it will be necessary to notice in this case is, whether the Circuit Court had jurisdiction.

Sill, the complainant below, a citizen of New York, filed his bill in the Circuit Court of the United States for Michigan, against Sheldon, claiming to recover the amount of a bond and mortgage, which had been assigned to him by Hastings, the President of the Bank of Michigan.

Sheldon, in his answer, among other things, pleaded that "the bond and mortgage in controversy, having been originally given by a citizen of Michigan to another citizen of the same state, and the complainant being assignee of them, the Circuit Court had no jurisdiction."

The eleventh section of the Judiciary Act, which defines the jurisdiction of the Circuit Courts, restrains them from taking "cognizance of any suit to recover the contents of any promissory note or other chose in action, in favor of an assignee, unless a suit might have been prosecuted in such court to recover the contents, if no assignment had been made, except in cases of foreign bills of exchange."

The third article of the Constitution declares that "the judicial power of the United States shall be vested in one Supreme Court, and such inferior courts as the Congress may, from time to time, ordain and establish." The second section of the same article enumerates the cases and controversies of which the judicial power shall have cognizance, and, among others, it specifies "controversies between citizens of different states."

It has been alleged, that this restriction of the Judiciary Act, with regard to assignees of choses in action, is in conflict with this provision of the Constitution, and therefore void.

It must be admitted, that if the Constitution had ordained and established the inferior courts, and distributed to them their respective powers, they could not be restricted or divested by Congress. But as it has made no such distribution, one of two consequences must result — either that each inferior court created by Congress must exercise all the judicial powers not given to the Supreme Court, or that Congress, having the power to establish the courts, must define their respective jurisdictions. The first of these inferences has never been asserted, and could not be defended with any show of reason, and if not, the latter would seem to follow as a necessary consequence. And it would seem to follow, also, that, having a right to prescribe, Congress may withhold from any court of its creation jurisdiction of any of the enumerated controversies. Courts created by statute can have no jurisdiction but such as the statute confers. No one of them can assert a just claim to jurisdiction exclusively conferred on another, or withheld from all.

The Constitution has defined the limits of the judicial power of the United States, but has not prescribed how much of it shall be exercised by the Circuit Court; consequently, the statute which does prescribe the limits of their jurisdiction, cannot be in conflict with the Constitution, unless it confers powers not enumerated therein.

Such has been the doctrine held by this court since its first establishment. To enumerate all the cases in which it has been either directly advanced or tacitly assumed would be tedious and unnecessary....

The judgment of the Circuit Court must therefore be reversed, for want of jurisdiction....

Ex parte McCardle
74 U.S. 506 (1868)

[McCardle, a newspaper editor, was arrested by U.S. Army officials on charges of publishing articles alleged to be incendiary and libelous. He sought release by bringing an action for a writ of habeas corpus in a federal Circuit Court in Mississippi. The court denied his petition, and he appealed the denial to the U.S. Supreme Court. Three days after the appeal was argued on its merits, Congress enacted a statute repealing the appellate jurisdiction that it had previously given the U.S. Supreme Court in habeas corpus cases.]

The CHIEF JUSTICE delivered the opinion of the court.

The first question necessarily is that of jurisdiction; for, if the act of March, 1868, takes away the jurisdiction defined by the act of February, 1867, it is useless, if not improper, to enter into any discussion of other questions.

It is quite true, as was argued by the counsel for the petitioner, that the appellate jurisdiction of this court is not derived from acts of Congress. It is, strictly speaking, conferred by the Constitution. But it is conferred "with such exceptions and under such regulations as Congress shall make."

It is unnecessary to consider whether, if Congress had made no exceptions and no regulations, this court might not have exercised general appellate jurisdiction under rules prescribed by itself. For among the earliest acts of the first Congress, at its first session, was the act of September 24th, 1789, to establish the judicial courts of the United States. That act provided for the organization of this court, and prescribed regulations for the exercise of its jurisdiction.

The source of that jurisdiction, and the limitations of it by the Constitution and by statute, have been on several occasions subjects of consideration here. In the case of *Durousseau* v. *The United States*, particularly, the whole matter was carefully examined, and the court held, that while "the appellate powers of this court are not given by the judicial act, but are given by the Constitution," they are, nevertheless, "limited and regulated by that act, and by such other acts as have been passed on the subject." The court said, further, that the judicial act was an exercise of the power given by the Constitution to Congress "of making exceptions to the appellate jurisdiction of the Supreme Court." "They have described affirmatively," said the court, "its jurisdiction, and this affirmative description has been understood to imply a negation of the exercise of such appellate power as is not comprehended within it."

The principle that the affirmation of appellate jurisdiction implies the negation of all such jurisdiction not affirmed having been thus established, it was an almost necessary consequence that acts of Congress, providing for the exercise of jurisdiction, should come to be spoken of as acts granting jurisdiction, and not as acts making exceptions to the constitutional grant of it.

The exception to appellate jurisdiction in the case before us, however, is not an inference from the affirmation of other appellate jurisdiction. It is made in terms. The provision of the act of 1867, affirming the appellate jurisdiction of this court in cases of *habeas corpus* is expressly repealed. It is hardly possible to imagine a plainer instance of positive exception.

We are not at liberty to inquire into the motives of the legislature. We can only examine into its power under the Constitution; and the power to make exceptions to the appellate jurisdiction of this court is given by express words.

What, then, is the effect of the repealing act upon the case before us? We cannot doubt as to this. Without jurisdiction the court cannot proceed at all in any cause. Jurisdiction is power to declare the law, and when it ceases to exist, the only function remaining to the court is that of announcing the fact and dismissing the cause. And this is not less clear upon authority than upon principle.

Several cases were cited by the counsel for the petitioner in support of the position that jurisdiction of this case is not affected by the repealing act. But none of them, in our judgment, afford any support to it. They are all cases of the exercise of judicial power by the legislature, or of legislative interference with courts in the exercising of continuing jurisdiction.

On the other hand, the general rule, supported by the best elementary writers, is, that "when an act of the legislature is repealed, it must be considered, except as to transactions past and closed, as if it never existed." And the effect of repealing acts upon suits under acts repealed, has been determined by the adjudications of this court. The subject was fully considered in *Norris* v. *Crecker*, and more recently in *Insurance Company* v. *Ritchie*. In both of these cases it was held that no judgment could be rendered in a suit after the repeal of the act under which it was brought and prosecuted.

It is quite clear, therefore, that this court cannot proceed to pronounce judgment in this case, for it has no longer jurisdiction of the appeal; and judicial duty is not less fitly performed by declining ungranted jurisdiction than in exercising firmly that which the Constitution and the laws confer.

Counsel seem to have supposed, if effect be given to the repealing act in question, that the whole appellate power of the court, in cases of *habeas corpus*, is denied. But this is an error. The act of 1868 does not except from that jurisdiction any cases but appeals from Circuit Courts under the act of 1867. It does not affect the jurisdiction which was previously exercised.

The appeal of the petitioner in this case must be

DISMISSED FOR WANT OF JURISDICTION.

Notes and Questions

1. *Sheldon* appears to stand for the proposition that Congress is not obligated to put all cases falling within the scope of the judicial power within the lower federal courts, and historically, they have not. Thus, for example, although Article III provides that the judicial power extends to "Controversies … between Citizens of different States," the lower federal courts have had such jurisdiction only when the amount in controversy exceeds a given amount, currently $75,000. *See* 28 U.S.C. § 1332. Indeed, the U.S. Supreme Court has cited *Sheldon* in support of its conclusion that the grant of diversity jurisdiction to the lower federal courts excludes discrete categories of cases. *See, e.g., Ankenbrandt v. Richards*, 504 U.S. 689, 698 (1992) (domestic relations cases not within the scope of the jurisdictional grant).

2. In *Webster v. Doe*, 486 U.S. 592 (1988), an employee of the Central Intelligence Agency brought a suit against its director, claiming that he was fired because he was gay, and contending that this action violated both his federal statutory and constitutional rights. The Court, while interpreting a federal statute to preclude a lower federal court from adjudicating his statutory claims, held that the statute did not preclude adjudication of his constitutional claims, reasoning as follows:

> where Congress intends to preclude judicial review of constitutional claims its intent to do so must be clear.... We require this heightened showing in part to avoid the "serious constitutional question" that would arise if a federal statute were construed to deny any judicial forum for a colorable constitutional claim.

Id. at 603. In light of *Sheldon*, why would such an action by Congress raise a "serious constitutional question" at all? *See id.* at 612–13 (Scalia, J., dissenting) (contending that the statute probably bars not only the federal courts, but also the state courts, from adjudicating such claims).

3. Are there reasons to distinguish between situations in which Congress strips *both* the U.S. Supreme Court and the lower federal courts of jurisdiction over certain types of matters, and situations in which it strips only one or the other of jurisdiction? In other words, is there an argument that—although there is no obligation to create lower federal courts— the whole judicial power must be vested in *some* federal tribunal? *See Martin v. Hunter's Lessee*, 14 U.S. 304, 331 (1816) (opinion of Story, J.) (contending that "the whole judicial power of the United States should be, at all times, vested either in an original or appellate form, in some courts created under its authority."); *see also* Akhil Amar, *A Neo-Federalist View of Article III: Separating the Two Tiers of Federal Jurisdiction*, 65 B. U. L. Rev. 205 (1985) (distinguishing between those categories of judicial power that are preceded by the word "all" and those that are not to conclude that only the former must be vested in a federal tribunal).

4. What do you make of the last paragraph in *McCardle*? Does it, to any extent, cast doubt on Congress's ability to strip the U.S. Supreme Court of appellate jurisdiction? Note, however, that there exists a separate constitutional provision — The Suspension Clause — that prohibits Congress from suspending the writ of habeas corpus, which was implicated in the *McCardle* decision. *See* U.S. Const. art. I, § 9, cl. 2 ("The Privilege of the Writ of Habeas Corpus shall not be suspended, unless when in Cases of Rebellion or Invasion the public Safety may require it.").

5. If lower federal courts and/or the U.S. Supreme Court are stripped of jurisdiction, that does not necessarily mean that *no* court will have jurisdiction to adjudicate the claims; rather, it means that federal rights will be adjudicated in state tribunals. Are there reasons to believe that state courts will be less protective of federal constitutional rights than would be the federal courts?

6. What is the *purpose* of the Exceptions Clause? After all, the framers of the Constitution must have had some reason for giving Congress such authority over the appellate jurisdiction of the U.S. Supreme Court. *See* Charles E. Rice, *Limiting Federal Court Jurisdiction: The Constitutional Basis for the Proposals in Congress Today*, 65 Judicature 190 (1981) (contending that it is one of the "checks and balances" that Congress has against "judicial excess" on the part of the Supreme Court).

7. Of what significance are the last three words in the bill proposed in Problem 2-F? Do those words in any way alter your assessment of the constitutionality of the bill as written?

Chapter 3

(Substantive) Due Process

A. Introduction

In the United States, a debate that began during the drafting and ratification of the Constitution has persisted to the present day: does the U.S. Constitution only protect those rights *specifically* enumerated within its text, or are there other rights not in terms spelled out in the Constitution that it also protects? Moreover, if unenumerated constitutional rights do exist, is there a textual basis for recognizing and enforcing such rights? And how do courts go about determining what, exactly, those rights are?

In part because of a concern that the Constitution as initially drafted appeared to leave certain rights unprotected, a Bill of Rights was proposed and ultimately ratified that—among other things—secured such rights as freedom of speech, religion, and assembly; protection against cruel and unusual punishment; and freedom from unreasonable searches and seizures.

However, there was a debate amongst the founders over whether even to include such a list, the fear being that it would be virtually impossible to enumerate all the rights that government should not infringe, and that a detailed list would imply that anything not enumerated was thus not protected. (Some also did not believe that the Constitution as drafted gave the federal government sufficient power to infringe on such rights in the first place, and that the enumeration of such rights implied that the federal government was granted greater powers than the Constitution actually granted to it.) In part to address these concerns, the drafters of the Constitution included the Ninth Amendment, which provides that "[t]he enumeration in the Constitution, of certain rights, shall not be construed to deny or disparage others retained by the people."

Soon after the Constitution was ratified, two Justices of the U.S. Supreme Court expressed diametrically opposed views on the question whether unenumerated rights were in any form protected by the Constitution. In *Calder v. Bull*, 3 U.S. 386 (1798)—a case involving a challenge to the constitutionality of a state law—Justice Chase wrote as follows:

> I cannot subscribe to the omnipotence of a State Legislature, or that it is absolute and without control; although its authority should not be expressly restrained by the Constitution, or fundamental law, of the State.... An ACT of the Legislature (for I cannot call it a law) contrary to the great first principles of the social compact, cannot be considered a rightful exercise of legislative authority. The obligation of a law in governments established on express compact, and on republican principles, must be determined by the nature of the power, on which it is founded. A few instances will suffice to explain what I mean. A law that punished a citizen for an innocent action, or, in other words, for an act, which, when done, was in violation of no existing law; a law that destroys, or impairs, the lawful private contracts of citizens; a law that makes a man a Judge in his own

cause; or a law that takes property from A. and gives it to B: It is against all reason and justice, for a people to entrust a Legislature with SUCH powers; and, therefore, it cannot be presumed that they have done it.

Id. at 387–88. In response, Justice Iredell wrote:

If, then, a government, composed of Legislative, Executive and Judicial departments, were established, by a Constitution, which imposed no limits on the legislative power, the consequence would inevitably be, that whatever the legislative power chose to enact, would be lawfully enacted, and the judicial power could never interpose to pronounce it void. It is true, that some speculative jurists have held, that a legislative act against natural justice must, in itself, be void; but I cannot think that, under such a government, any Court of Justice would possess a power to declare it so....

In order, therefore, to guard against so great an evil, it has been the policy of all the American states, which have, individually, framed their state constitutions since the revolution, and of the people of the United States, when they framed the Federal Constitution, to define with precision the objects of the legislative power, and to restrain its exercise within marked and settled boundaries. If any act of Congress, or of the Legislature of a state, violates those constitutional provisions, it is unquestionably void.... If, on the other hand, the Legislature of the Union, or the Legislature of any member of the Union, shall pass a law, within the general scope of their constitutional power, the Court cannot pronounce it to be void, merely because it is, in their judgment, contrary to the principles of natural justice. The ideas of natural justice are regulated by no fixed standard: the ablest and the purest men have differed upon the subject; and all that the Court could properly say, in such an event, would be, that the Legislature (possessed of an equal right of opinion) had passed an act which, in the opinion of the judges, was inconsistent with the abstract principles of natural justice.

Id. at 398–99. Although their views on the matter were not necessary to resolution of the case, they represent the divide that has persisted among Justices of the U.S. Supreme Court through to the present day.

As the cases in this Chapter will demonstrate, the Court eventually settled on the Due Process Clauses of the Fifth and Fourteenth Amendments as vehicles for enforcing unenumerated rights against the federal and state governments, respectively. *See* U.S. CONST. Amend. V ("No person shall ... be deprived of life, liberty, or property without due process of law...."); *id.* Amend. XIV ("nor shall any State deprive any person of life, liberty, or property, without due process of law"). In the context of gay rights litigation, the use of the Due Process Clauses to enforce unenumerated rights plays a critical role in both challenges to the constitutionality of sodomy laws as well as challenges to laws prohibiting same-sex marriage. The early history of invoking the Due Process Clauses to enforce unenumerated rights from *Calder v. Bull* through the middle of the twentieth century is summarized in the following concurring opinion by Justice Souter.

Washington v. Glucksberg
521 U.S. 702 (1997)

[A group of physicians and terminally ill patients as well as a nonprofit organization brought suit against the State of Washington, seeking a declaration that its law banning physician-assisted suicide violates the Due Process Clause of the Fourteenth Amendment.]

Justice SOUTER, concurring in the judgment.

....

When the physicians claim that the Washington law deprives them of a right falling within the scope of liberty that the Fourteenth Amendment guarantees against denial without due process of law, they are not claiming some sort of procedural defect in the process through which the statute has been enacted or is administered. Their claim, rather, is that the State has no substantively adequate justification for barring the assistance sought by the patient and sought to be offered by the physician. Thus, we are dealing with a claim to one of those rights sometimes described as rights of substantive due process and sometimes as unenumerated rights, in view of the breadth and indeterminacy of the "due process" serving as the claim's textual basis. The doctors accordingly arouse the skepticism of those who find the due process clause an unduly vague or oxymoronic warrant for judicial review of substantive state law, just as they also invoke two centuries of American constitutional practice in recognizing unenumerated, substantive limits on governmental action. Although this practice has neither rested on any single textual basis nor expressed a consistent theory (or, before *Poe v. Ullman,* a much articulated one), a brief overview of its history is instructive on two counts. The persistence of substantive due process in our cases points to the legitimacy of the modern justification for such judicial review found in Justice Harlan's dissent in *Poe,* on which I will dwell further on, while the acknowledged failures of some of these cases point with caution to the difficulty raised by the present claim.

Before the ratification of the Fourteenth Amendment, substantive constitutional review resting on a theory of unenumerated rights occurred largely in the state courts applying state constitutions that commonly contained either due process clauses like that of the Fifth Amendment (and later the Fourteenth) or the textual antecedents of such clauses, repeating Magna Carta's guarantee of "the law of the land."[5] On the basis of such clauses, or of general principles untethered to specific constitutional language, state courts evaluated the constitutionality of a wide range of statutes....

Even in this early period, however, this Court anticipated the developments that would presage both the Civil War and the ratification of the Fourteenth Amendment, by making it clear on several occasions that it too had no doubt of the judiciary's power to strike down legislation that conflicted with important but unenumerated principles of American government. In most such instances, after declaring its power to invalidate what it might find inconsistent with rights of liberty and property, the Court nevertheless went on to uphold the legislative Acts under review. See, *e.g., Wilkinson v. Leland,* 2 Pet. 627, 656–661 (1829); *Calder v. Bull,* 3 Dall. 386, 386–395 (1798) (opinion of Chase, J.); see also *Corfield v. Coryell,* 6 F. Cas. 546, 550–552 (CC ED Pa.1823). But in *Fletcher v. Peck,* 6 Cranch 87 (1810), the Court went further. It struck down an Act of the Georgia Legislature that purported to rescind a sale of public land *ab initio* and reclaim title for the State, and so deprive subsequent, good-faith purchasers of property conveyed by the original grantees. The Court rested the invalidation on alternative sources of authority: the specific prohibitions against bills of attainder, *ex post facto* laws, laws impairing contracts in Article I, §10, of the Constitution; and "general principles which are common to our free institutions," by which Chief Justice Marshall meant that a simple deprivation of property by the State could not be an authentically "legislative" Act. *Fletcher, supra,* at 135–139.

---

5. Coke indicates that prohibitions against deprivations without "due process of law" originated in an English statute that "rendred" Magna Carta's "law of the land" in such terms. See 2 E. Coke, Institutes 50 (1797); see also E. Corwin, Liberty Against Government 90–91 (1948).

Fletcher was not, though, the most telling early example of such review. For its most salient instance in this Court before the adoption of the Fourteenth Amendment was, of course, the case that the Amendment would in due course overturn, *Dred Scott v. Sandford,* 19 How. 393 (1857). Unlike *Fletcher, Dred Scott* was textually based on a Due Process Clause (in the Fifth Amendment, applicable to the National Government), and it was in reliance on that Clause's protection of property that the Court invalidated the Missouri Compromise. 19 How., at 449–452. This substantive protection of an owner's property in a slave taken to the territories was traced to the absence of any enumerated power to affect that property granted to the Congress by Article I of the Constitution, *id.,* at 451–452, the implication being that the Government had no legitimate interest that could support the earlier congressional compromise. The ensuing judgment of history needs no recounting here.

After the ratification of the Fourteenth Amendment, with its guarantee of due process protection against the States, interpretation of the words "liberty" and "property" as used in Due Process Clauses became a sustained enterprise, with the Court generally describing the due process criterion in converse terms of reasonableness or arbitrariness. That standard is fairly traceable to Justice Bradley's dissent in the *Slaughter-House Cases,* 16 Wall. 36 (1873), in which he said that a person's right to choose a calling was an element of liberty (as the calling, once chosen, was an aspect of property) and declared that the liberty and property protected by due process are not truly recognized if such rights may be "arbitrarily assailed," *id.,* 16 Wall., at 116.[6] After that, opinions comparable to those that preceded *Dred Scott* expressed willingness to review legislative action for consistency with the Due Process Clause even as they upheld the laws in question.

The theory became serious, however, beginning with *Allgeyer v. Louisiana,* 165 U.S. 578 (1897), where the Court invalidated a Louisiana statute for excessive interference with Fourteenth Amendment liberty to contract, *id.,* at 588–593, and offered a substantive interpretation of "liberty," that in the aftermath of the so-called *Lochner* Era has been scaled back in some respects, but expanded in others, and never repudiated in principle. The Court said that Fourteenth Amendment liberty includes "the right of the citizen to be free in the enjoyment of all his faculties; to be free to use them in all lawful ways; to live and work where he will; to earn his livelihood by any lawful calling; to pursue any livelihood or avocation; and for that purpose to enter into all contracts which may be proper, necessary and essential to his carrying out to a successful conclusion the purposes above mentioned." *Id.,* at 589. "[W]e do not intend to hold that in no such case can the State exercise its police power," the Court added, but "[w]hen and how far such power may be legitimately exercised with regard to these subjects must be left for determination to each case as it arises." *Id.,* at 590.

Although this principle was unobjectionable, what followed for a season was, in the realm of economic legislation, the echo of *Dred Scott. Allgeyer* was succeeded within a

---

6. The *Slaughter-House Cases* are important, of course, for their holding that the Privileges and Immunities Clause was no source of any but a specific handful of substantive rights. 16 Wall., at 74–80. To a degree, then, that decision may have led the Court to look to the Due Process Clause as a source of substantive rights. In *Twining v. New Jersey,* 211 U.S. 78, 95–97 (1908), for example, the Court of the *Lochner* Era acknowledged the strength of the case against *Slaughter-House*'s interpretation of the Privileges or Immunities Clause but reaffirmed that interpretation without questioning its own frequent reliance on the Due Process Clause as authorization for substantive judicial review. See also J. Ely, Democracy and Distrust 14–30 (1980) (arguing that the Privileges and Immunities Clause and not the Due Process Clause is the proper warrant for courts' substantive oversight of state legislation). But the courts' use of Due Process Clauses for that purpose antedated the 1873 decision, as we have seen, and would in time be supported in the *Poe* dissent, as we shall see.

decade by *Lochner v. New York,* 198 U.S. 45 (1905), and the era to which that case gave its name, famous now for striking down as arbitrary various sorts of economic regulations that post-New Deal courts have uniformly thought constitutionally sound. Compare, *e.g., id.,* at 62 (finding New York's maximum-hours law for bakers "unreasonable and entirely arbitrary"), and *Adkins v. Children's Hospital of D.C.,* 261 U.S. 525, 559 (1923) (holding a minimum-wage law "so clearly the product of a naked, arbitrary exercise of power that it cannot be allowed to stand under the Constitution of the United States"), with *West Coast Hotel Co. v. Parrish,* 300 U.S. 379, 391 (1937) (overruling *Adkins* and approving a minimum-wage law on the principle that "regulation which is reasonable in relation to its subject and is adopted in the interests of the community is due process"). As the parentheticals here suggest, while the cases in the *Lochner* line routinely invoked a correct standard of constitutional arbitrariness review, they harbored the spirit of *Dred Scott* in their absolutist implementation of the standard they espoused.

Even before the deviant economic due process cases had been repudiated, however, the more durable precursors of modern substantive due process were reaffirming this Court's obligation to conduct arbitrariness review, beginning with *Meyer v. Nebraska,* 262 U.S. 390 (1923). Without referring to any specific guarantee of the Bill of Rights, the Court invoked precedents from the *Slaughter-House Cases* through *Adkins* to declare that the Fourteenth Amendment protected "the right of the individual to contract, to engage in any of the common occupations of life, to acquire useful knowledge, to marry, establish a home and bring up children, to worship God according to the dictates of his own conscience, and generally to enjoy those privileges long recognized at common law as essential to the orderly pursuit of happiness by free men." 262 U.S., at 399. The Court then held that the same Fourteenth Amendment liberty included a teacher's right to teach and the rights of parents to direct their children's education without unreasonable interference by the States, *id.,* at 400, with the result that Nebraska's prohibition on the teaching of foreign languages in the lower grades was "arbitrary and without reasonable relation to any end within the competency of the State," *id.,* at 403. See also *Pierce v. Society of Sisters,* 268 U.S. 510, 534–536 (1925) (finding that a statute that all but outlawed private schools lacked any "reasonable relation to some purpose within the competency of the State"); *Palko v. Connecticut,* 302 U.S. 319, 327–328 (1937) ("[E]ven in the field of substantive rights and duties the legislative judgment, if oppressive and arbitrary, may be overridden by the courts." "Is that [injury] to which the statute has subjected [the appellant] a hardship so acute and shocking that our polity will not endure it? Does it violate those fundamental principles of liberty and justice which lie at the base of all our civil and political institutions?").

After *Meyer* and *Pierce,* two further opinions took the major steps that lead to the modern law. The first was not even in a due process case but one about equal protection, *Skinner v. Oklahoma ex rel. Williamson,* 316 U.S. 535 (1942), where the Court emphasized the "fundamental" nature of individual choice about procreation and so foreshadowed not only the later prominence of procreation as a subject of liberty protection, but the corresponding standard of "strict scrutiny," in this Court's Fourteenth Amendment law. See *id.,* at 541. *Skinner,* that is, added decisions regarding procreation to the list of liberties recognized in *Meyer* and *Pierce* and loosely suggested, as a gloss on their standard of arbitrariness, a judicial obligation to scrutinize any impingement on such an important interest with heightened care. In so doing, it suggested a point that Justice Harlan would develop, that the kind and degree of justification that a sensitive judge would demand of a State would depend on the importance of the interest being asserted by the individual. *Poe,* 367 U.S., at 543.

The second major opinion leading to the modern doctrine was Justice Harlan's *Poe* dissent just cited.... The dissent is important for.... Justice Harlan's respect for the tradition of substantive due process review itself, and his acknowledgment of the Judiciary's obligation to carry it on. For two centuries American courts, and for much of that time this Court, have thought it necessary to provide some degree of review over the substantive content of legislation under constitutional standards of textual breadth. The obligation was understood before *Dred Scott* and has continued after the repudiation of *Lochner*'s progeny.... This enduring tradition of American constitutional practice is, in Justice Harlan's view, nothing more than what is required by the judicial authority and obligation to construe constitutional text and review legislation for conformity to that text. See *Marbury v. Madison*, 1 Cranch 137 (1803). Like many judges who preceded him and many who followed, he found it impossible to construe the text of due process without recognizing substantive, and not merely procedural, limitations. "Were due process merely a procedural safeguard it would fail to reach those situations where the deprivation of life, liberty or property was accomplished by legislation which by operating in the future could, given even the fairest possible procedure in application to individuals, nevertheless destroy the enjoyment of all three." *Poe, supra,* at 541.[7] The text of the Due Process Clause thus imposes nothing less than an obligation to give substantive content to the words "liberty" and "due process of law." ....

[The majority opinion of Chief Justice Rehnquist and the concurring opinions of Justices O'Connor, Stevens, Ginsburg, and Breyer, are omitted.]

Notes and Questions

1. As Justice Souter points out in his concurring opinion, the phrase "substantive due process" is somewhat oxymoronic, in that the phrase "process" is normally associated with challenges to the procedures associated with denying one of life, liberty, or property rather than with a challenge to the substance of the laws themselves. Thus, for example, the due process challenges to the sodomy statutes examined in Chapter 1 were procedural, in that they focused on the arguable lack of adequate notice regarding what those statutes criminalized. In contrast, later in this chapter we will examine cases in which due process challenges are brought against statutes criminalizing sodomy. In these latter cases, the statutes are clear about what they criminalize, and thus no question of *procedural* due process is involved. Rather, the contention is that the Due Process Clauses prevent the government from interfering with an individual's liberty in this manner, a challenge that goes to the substance of the law itself.

For a particularly strong indictment of the concept of "substantive due process," *see* JOHN HART ELY, DEMOCRACY AND DISTRUST: A THEORY OF JUDICIAL REVIEW 18 & n.* (1980) (writing "that 'substantive due process' is a contradiction in terms — sort of like 'green pastel redness'" and that "[b]y the same token, 'procedural due process' is redundant").

---

7. Judge Johnson of the New York Court of Appeals had made the point more obliquely a century earlier when he wrote that "the form of this declaration of right, 'no person shall be deprived of life, liberty or property, without due process of law,' necessarily imports that the legislature cannot make the mere existence of the rights secured the occasion of depriving a person of any of them, even by the forms which belong to 'due process of law.' For if it does not necessarily import this, then the legislative power is absolute." And, "[t]o provide for a trial to ascertain whether a man is in the enjoyment of [any] of these rights, and then, as a consequence of finding that he is in the enjoyment of it, to deprive him of it, is doing indirectly just what is forbidden to be done directly, and reduces the constitutional provision to a nullity." *Wynehamer v. People,* 13 N.Y. 378, 420 (1856).

2. Justice Souter cites *Dred Scott*, which is most commonly studied for that portion of the opinion in which the Supreme Court holds that a slave was not a "citizen" of the United States and thus that the federal courts lacked jurisdiction to adjudicate his suit for freedom. But as Justice Souter points out, the *Dred Scott* Court alternatively held that Congress lacked the power to prohibit slavery in the federal territories, and in the course of so doing, invoked the Due Process Clause substantively:

> The Territory being a part of the United States, the Government and the citizen both enter it under the authority of the Constitution, with their respective rights defined and marked out; and the Federal Government can exercise no power over his person or property, beyond what that instrument confers, nor lawfully deny any right which it has reserved.

> A reference to a few of the provisions of the Constitution will illustrate this proposition.

> For example, no one, we presume, will contend that Congress can make any law in a Territory respecting the establishment of religion, or the free exercise thereof, or abridging the freedom of speech or of the press, or the right of the people of the Territory peaceably to assemble, and to petition the Government for the re-dress of grievances.

> Nor can Congress deny to the people the right to keep and bear arms, nor the right to trial by jury, nor compel any one to be a witness against himself in a criminal proceeding.

> These powers, and others, in relation to rights of person, which it is not necessary here to enumerate, are, in express and positive terms, denied to the General Government; and the rights of private property have been guarded with equal care. Thus the rights of property are united with the rights of person, and placed on the same ground by the fifth amendment to the Constitution, which provides that no person shall be deprived of life, liberty, and property, without due process of law. *And an act of Congress which deprives a citizen of the United States of his liberty or property, merely because he came himself or brought his property into a particular Territory of the United States, and who had committed no offence against the laws, could hardly be dignified with the name of due process of law.*

Dred Scott v. Sandford, 60 U.S. 393, 449–50 (1857) (emphasis added).

3. After the U.S. Supreme Court repudiated its *Lochner*-era cases, it set forth a very permissive standard for reviewing the constitutionality of regulatory legislation under the Due Process Clause: such laws are presumed to be constitutional, and will be struck down only if no "rational basis" for justifying them exists. *See United States v. Carolene Prods. Co.*, 304 U.S. 144, 152 (1938). The Court subsequently described the standard as follows:

> [T]he law need not be in every respect logically consistent with its aims to be constitutional. It is enough that there is an evil at hand for correction, and that it might be thought that the particular legislative measure was a rational way to correct it.

Williamson v. Lee Optical of Okla., 348 U.S. 483, 487–88 (1955).

The *Williamson* Court's formulation of the rational basis fit thus requires only the loosest of fits between the end sought by the government and the means employed to achieve it:

> [U]nder the deferential standard of review applied in substantive due process challenges to economic legislation there is no need for mathematical precision in the fit between justification and means.

Concrete Pipe and Prods. of Cal., Inc. v. Constr. Laborers Pension Trust for S. Cal., 508 U.S. 602, 639 (1993).

Moreover, note the *Williamson* Court's use of the phrase "might be thought." That means, does it not, that the "end" justifying the law need not actually be the one that motivated the legislature to enact it? *See Malmed v. Thornburgh*, 621 F.2d 565, 569 (3d Cir. 1980) ("The court may even hypothesize the motivations of the state legislature to find a legitimate objective promoted by the provision under attack.") (citing *Williamson v. Lee Optical of Okla.*, 348 U.S. 483 (1955)).

4. The Due Process Clause of the Fourteenth Amendment has played a particularly critical role in enforcing even those individual rights that are enumerated in the Bill of Rights so far as challenges to the conduct of *state* governments are concerned. Early on, the U.S. Supreme Court established that the Bill of Rights itself was merely a restraint on the *federal* government, and in no way restricted the conduct of state governments. *See Barron v. Mayor & City Council of Balt.*, 32 U.S. 243 (1833).

After the Fourteenth Amendment was adopted, the Supreme Court—in a long series of cases—has used the Due Process Clause as a vehicle for "incorporating" and applying most of the rights found in the Bill of Rights against the states. *Palko v. Connecticut*, 302 U.S. 319, 325–26 (1937)—cited by Justice Souter above as well as in many of the cases that follow—held that those protections found in the Bill of Rights that are "implicit in the concept of ordered liberty" such that "neither liberty nor justice would exist if they were sacrificed" are thereby incorporated by the Due Process Clause of the Fourteenth Amendment and thus enforceable against the states.

5. *Poe v. Ullman*, whose dissent is cited by Justice Souter, involved a challenge to the constitutionality of a Connecticut statute prohibiting the use of contraceptives. The case itself was dismissed by the majority on the ground that a justiciable controversy was lacking, given the statute's long-standing history of non-enforcement. *See Poe v. Ullman*, 367 U.S. 497, 498–509 (1961). The constitutionality of that same statute is addressed in *Griswold v. Connecticut*, the next main case in this chapter.

B. The Contraception and Abortion Rights Cases

Griswold v. Connecticut
381 U.S. 479 (1965)

Mr. Justice DOUGLAS delivered the opinion of the Court.

Appellant Griswold is Executive Director of the Planned Parenthood League of Connecticut. Appellant Buxton is a licensed physician and a professor at the Yale Medical School who served as Medical Director for the League at its Center in New Haven—a center open and operating from November 1 to November 10, 1961, when appellants were arrested.

They gave information, instruction, and medical advice to *married persons* as to the means of preventing conception. They examined the wife and prescribed the best contraceptive device or material for her use. Fees were usually charged, although some couples were serviced free.

The statutes whose constitutionality is involved in this appeal are §§ 53-32 and 54-196 of the General Statutes of Connecticut (1958 rev.). The former provides:

> "Any person who uses any drug, medicinal article or instrument for the purpose of preventing conception shall be fined not less than fifty dollars or imprisoned not less than sixty days nor more than one year or be both fined and imprisoned."

Section 54-196 provides:

> "Any person who assists, abets, counsels, causes, hires or commands another to commit any offense may be prosecuted and punished as if he were the principal offender."

The appellants were found guilty as accessories and fined $100 each, against the claim that the accessory statute as so applied violated the Fourteenth Amendment....

We think that appellants have standing to raise the constitutional rights of the married people with whom they had a professional relationship. Tileston v. Ullman, 318 U.S. 44, is different, for there the plaintiff seeking to represent others asked for a declaratory judgment. In that situation we thought that the requirements of standing should be strict, lest the standards of "case or controversy" in Article III of the Constitution become blurred. Here those doubts are removed by reason of a criminal conviction for serving married couples in violation of an aiding-and-abetting statute. Certainly the accessory should have standing to assert that the offense which he is charged with assisting is not, or cannot constitutionally be a crime....

The rights of husband and wife, pressed here, are likely to be diluted or adversely affected unless those rights are considered in a suit involving those who have this kind of confidential relation to them.

Coming to the merits, we are met with a wide range of questions that implicate the Due Process Clause of the Fourteenth Amendment. Overtones of some arguments suggest that Lochner v. State of New York, 198 U.S. 45, should be our guide. But we decline that invitation.... We do not sit as a super-legislature to determine the wisdom, need, and propriety of laws that touch economic problems, business affairs, or social conditions. This law, however, operates directly on an intimate relation of husband and wife and their physician's role in one aspect of that relation.

The association of people is not mentioned in the Constitution nor in the Bill of Rights. The right to educate a child in a school of the parents' choice — whether public or private or parochial — is also not mentioned. Nor is the right to study any particular subject or any foreign language. Yet the First Amendment has been construed to include certain of those rights.

By Pierce v. Society of Sisters, the right to educate one's children as one chooses is made applicable to the States by the force of the First and Fourteenth Amendments. By Meyer v. State of Nebraska, the same dignity is given the right to study the German language in a private school. In other words, the State may not, consistently with the spirit of the First Amendment, contract the spectrum of available knowledge. The right of freedom of speech and press includes not only the right to utter or to print, but the right to distribute, the right to receive, the right to read and freedom of inquiry, freedom of thought, and freedom to teach — indeed the freedom of the entire university community. Without those peripheral rights the specific rights would be less secure. And so we reaffirm the principle of the Pierce and the Meyer cases.

In NAACP v. State of Alabama, 357 U.S. 449, 462, we protected the "freedom to associate and privacy in one's associations," noting that freedom of association was a peripheral First Amendment right. Disclosure of membership lists of a constitutionally valid association, we held, was invalid "as entailing the likelihood of a substantial restraint upon the exercise by petitioner's members of their right to freedom of association." In other words, the First Amendment has a penumbra where privacy is protected from governmental intrusion. In like context, we have protected forms of "association" that are not political in the customary sense but pertain to the social, legal, and economic benefit of the members....

The foregoing cases suggest that specific guarantees in the Bill of Rights have penumbras, formed by emanations from those guarantees that help give them life and substance. Various guarantees create zones of privacy. The right of association contained in the penumbra of the First Amendment is one, as we have seen. The Third Amendment in its prohibition against the quartering of soldiers "in any house" in time of peace without the consent of the owner is another facet of that privacy. The Fourth Amendment explicitly affirms the "right of the people to be secure in their persons, houses, papers, and effects, against unreasonable searches and seizures." The Fifth Amendment in its Self-Incrimination Clause enables the citizen to create a zone of privacy which government may not force him to surrender to his detriment. The Ninth Amendment provides: "The enumeration in the Constitution, of certain rights, shall not be construed to deny or disparage others retained by the people." ....

The present case, then, concerns a relationship lying within the zone of privacy created by several fundamental constitutional guarantees. And it concerns a law which, in forbidding the *use* of contraceptives rather than regulating their manufacture or sale, seeks to achieve its goals by means having a maximum destructive impact upon that relationship. Such a law cannot stand in light of the familiar principle, so often applied by this Court, that a "governmental purpose to control or prevent activities constitutionally subject to state regulation may not be achieved by means which sweep unnecessarily broadly and thereby invade the area of protected freedoms." Would we allow the police to search the sacred precincts of marital bedrooms for telltale signs of the use of contraceptives? The very idea is repulsive to the notions of privacy surrounding the marriage relationship.

We deal with a right of privacy older than the Bill of Rights—older than our political parties, older than our school system. Marriage is a coming together for better or for worse, hopefully enduring, and intimate to the degree of being sacred. It is an association that promotes a way of life, not causes; a harmony in living, not political faiths; a bilateral loyalty, not commercial or social projects. Yet it is an association for as noble a purpose as any involved in our prior decisions.

Reversed.

Mr. Justice GOLDBERG, whom THE CHIEF JUSTICE and Mr. Justice BRENNAN join, concurring.

I agree with the Court that Connecticut's birth-control law unconstitutionally intrudes upon the right of marital privacy, and I join in its opinion and judgment. Although I have not accepted the view that "due process" as used in the Fourteenth Amendment includes all of the first eight Amendments, I do agree that the concept of liberty protects those personal rights that are fundamental, and is not confined to the specific terms of the Bill of Rights. My conclusion that the concept of liberty is not so restricted and that it embraces the right of marital privacy though that right is not mentioned explicitly in the Constitution is supported both by numerous decisions of this Court, referred to in the Court's opinion, and by the language and history of the Ninth Amendment. In reaching the conclusion that the right of marital privacy is protected, as being within the protected penumbra of specific guarantees of the Bill of Rights, the Court refers to the Ninth Amendment. I add these words to emphasize the relevance of that Amendment to the Court's holding....

This Court, in a series of decisions, has held that the Fourteenth Amendment absorbs and applies to the States those specifics of the first eight amendments which express fundamental personal rights. The language and history of the Ninth Amendment reveal that the Framers of the Constitution believed that there are additional fundamental rights, protected from governmental infringement, which exist alongside those fundamental rights specifically mentioned in the first eight constitutional amendments.

The Ninth Amendment reads, "The enumeration in the Constitution, of certain rights, shall not be construed to deny or disparage others retained by the people." The Amendment is almost entirely the work of James Madison. It was introduced in Congress by him and passed the House and Senate with little or no debate and virtually no change in language. It was proffered to quiet expressed fears that a bill of specifically enumerated rights could not be sufficiently broad to cover all essential rights and that the specific mention of certain rights would be interpreted as a denial that others were protected.

In presenting the proposed Amendment, Madison said:

> "It has been objected also against a bill of rights, that, by enumerating particular exceptions to the grant of power, it would disparage those rights which were not placed in that enumeration; and it might follow by implication, that those rights which were not singled out, were intended to be assigned into the hands of the General Government, and were consequently insecure. This is one of the most plausible arguments I have ever heard urged against the admission of a bill of rights into this system; but, I conceive, that it may be guarded against. I have attempted it, as gentlemen may see by turning to the last clause of the fourth resolution (the Ninth Amendment)." I Annals of Congress 439 (Gales and Seaton ed. 1834).

Mr. Justice Story wrote of this argument against a bill of rights and the meaning of the Ninth Amendment:

> "In regard to * * * [a] suggestion, that the affirmance of certain rights might disparage others, or might lead to argumentative implications in favor of other powers, it might be sufficient to say that such a course of reasoning could never be sustained upon any solid basis * * *. But a conclusive answer is, that such an attempt may be interdicted (as it has been) by a positive declaration in such a bill of rights that the enumeration of certain rights shall not be construed to deny or disparage others retained by the people." II Story, Commentaries on the Constitution of the United States 626–627 (5th ed. 1891).

He further stated, referring to the Ninth Amendment:

> "This clause was manifestly introduced to prevent any perverse or ingenious misapplication of the well-known maxim, that an affirmation in particular cases implies a negation in all others; and, *e converso*, that a negation in particular cases implies an affirmation in all others." Id., at 651.

These statements of Madison and Story make clear that the Framers did not intend that the first eight amendments be construed to exhaust the basic and fundamental rights which the Constitution guaranteed to the people.

While this Court has had little occasion to interpret the Ninth Amendment, "[i]t cannot be presumed that any clause in the constitution is intended to be without effect."

Marbury v. Madison, 1 Cranch 137, 174. In interpreting the Constitution, "real effect should be given to all the words it uses." The Ninth Amendment to the Constitution may be regarded by some as a recent discovery and may be forgotten by others, but since 1791 it has been a basic part of the Constitution which we are sworn to uphold. To hold that a right so basic and fundamental and so deep-rooted in our society as the right of privacy in marriage may be infringed because that right is not guaranteed in so many words by the first eight amendments to the Constitution is to ignore the Ninth Amendment and to give it no effect whatsoever. Moreover, a judicial construction that this fundamental right is not protected by the Constitution because it is not mentioned in explicit terms by one of the first eight amendments or elsewhere in the Constitution would violate the Ninth Amendment, which specifically states that "[t]he enumeration in the Constitution, of certain rights shall not be *construed* to deny or disparage others retained by the people" (emphasis added).

A dissenting opinion suggests that my interpretation of the Ninth Amendment somehow "broaden[s] the powers of this Court." With all due respect, I believe that it misses the import of what I am saying. I do not take the position ... that the entire Bill of Rights is incorporated in the Fourteenth Amendment, and I do not mean to imply that the Ninth Amendment is applied against the States by the Fourteenth. Nor do I mean to state that the Ninth Amendment constitutes an independent source of rights protected from infringement by either the States or the Federal Government. Rather, the Ninth Amendment shows a belief of the Constitution's authors that fundamental rights exist that are not expressly enumerated in the first eight amendments and an intent that the list of rights included there not be deemed exhaustive. As any student of this Court's opinions knows, this Court has held, often unanimously, that the Fifth and Fourteenth Amendments protect certain fundamental personal liberties from abridgment by the Federal Government or the States. The Ninth Amendment simply shows the intent of the Constitution's authors that other fundamental personal rights should not be denied such protection or disparaged in any other way simply because they are not specifically listed in the first eight constitutional amendments. I do not see how this broadens the authority of the Court; rather it serves to support what this Court has been doing in protecting fundamental rights.

Nor am I turning somersaults with history in arguing that the Ninth Amendment is relevant in a case dealing with a *State's* infringement of a fundamental right. While the Ninth Amendment — and indeed the entire Bill of Rights — originally concerned restrictions upon *federal* power, the subsequently enacted Fourteenth Amendment prohibits the States as well from abridging fundamental personal liberties. And, the Ninth Amendment, in indicating that not all such liberties are specifically mentioned in the first eight amendments, is surely relevant in showing the existence of other fundamental personal rights, now protected from state, as well as federal, infringement. ...

In determining which rights are fundamental, judges are not left at large to decide cases in light of their personal and private notions. Rather, they must look to the "traditions and [collective] conscience of our people" to determine whether a principle is "so rooted [there] * * * as to be ranked as fundamental." Snyder v. Com. of Massachusetts, 291 U.S. 97, 105. The inquiry is whether a right involved "is of such a character that it cannot be denied without violating those 'fundamental principles of liberty and justice which lie at the base of all our civil and political institutions' * * *." Powell v. State of Alabama, 287 U.S. 45, 67. "Liberty" also "gains content from the emanations of * * * specific (constitutional) guarantees" and "from experience with the requirements of a free society." Poe v. Ullman, 367 U.S. 497, 517 (dissenting opinion of Mr. Justice Douglas).

I agree fully with the Court that, applying these tests, the right of privacy is a fundamental personal right, emanating "from the totality of the constitutional scheme under which we live." Id., at 521....

The Connecticut statutes here involved deal with a particularly important and sensitive area of privacy—that of the marital relation and the marital home. This Court recognized in Meyer v. Nebraska that the right "to marry, establish a home and bring up children" was an essential part of the liberty guaranteed by the Fourteenth Amendment. 262 U.S., at 399. In Pierce v. Society of Sisters, 268 U.S. 510, the Court held unconstitutional an Oregon Act which forbade parents from sending their children to private schools because such an act "unreasonably interferes with the liberty of parents and guardians to direct the upbringing and education of children under their control." As this Court said in Prince v. Massachusetts, 321 U.S. 158, at 166, the Meyer and Pierce decisions "have respected the private realm of family life which the state cannot enter." ....

The entire fabric of the Constitution and the purposes that clearly underlie its specific guarantees demonstrate that the rights to marital privacy and to marry and raise a family are of similar order and magnitude as the fundamental rights specifically protected.

Although the Constitution does not speak in so many words of the right of privacy in marriage, I cannot believe that it offers these fundamental rights no protection. The fact that no particular provision of the Constitution explicitly forbids the State from disrupting the traditional relation of the family—a relation as old and as fundamental as our entire civilization—surely does not show that the Government was meant to have the power to do so. Rather, as the Ninth Amendment expressly recognizes, there are fundamental personal rights such as this one, which are protected from abridgment by the Government though not specifically mentioned in the Constitution....

The logic of the dissents would sanction federal or state legislation that seems to me even more plainly unconstitutional than the statute before us. Surely the Government, absent a showing of a compelling subordinating state interest, could not decree that all husbands and wives must be sterilized after two children have been born to them. Yet by their reasoning such an invasion of marital privacy would not be subject to constitutional challenge because, while it might be "silly," no provision of the Constitution specifically prevents the Government from curtailing the marital right to bear children and raise a family. While it may shock some of my Brethren that the Court today holds that the Constitution protects the right of marital privacy, in my view it is far more shocking to believe that the personal liberty guaranteed by the Constitution does not include protection against such totalitarian limitation of family size, which is at complete variance with our constitutional concepts. Yet, if upon a showing of a slender basis of rationality, a law outlawing voluntary birth control by married persons is valid, then, by the same reasoning, a law requiring compulsory birth control also would seem to be valid. In my view, however, both types of law would unjustifiably intrude upon rights of marital privacy which are constitutionally protected.

In a long series of cases this Court has held that where fundamental personal liberties are involved, they may not be abridged by the States simply on a showing that a regulatory statute has some rational relationship to the effectuation of a proper state purpose. "Where there is a significant encroachment upon personal liberty, the State may prevail only upon showing a subordinating interest which is compelling." The law must be shown "necessary, and not merely rationally related to, the accomplishment of a permissible state policy."

Although the Connecticut birth-control law obviously encroaches upon a fundamental personal liberty, the State does not show that the law serves any "subordinating [state] interest which is compelling" or that it is "necessary * * * to the accomplishment of a per-missible state policy." The State, at most, argues that there is some rational relation be-tween this statute and what is admittedly a legitimate subject of state concern — the discouraging of extra-marital relations. It says that preventing the use of birth-control de-vices by married persons helps prevent the indulgence by some in such extra-marital re-lations. The rationality of this justification is dubious, particularly in light of the admitted widespread availability to all persons in the State of Connecticut, unmarried as well as married, of birth-control devices for the prevention of disease, as distinguished from the prevention of conception. But, in any event, it is clear that the state interest in safeguard-ing marital fidelity can be served by a more discriminately tailored statute, which does not, like the present one, sweep unnecessarily broadly, reaching far beyond the evil sought to be dealt with and intruding upon the privacy of all married couples. Here, as elsewhere, "[p]recision of regulation must be the touchstone in an area so closely touching our most precious freedoms." The State of Connecticut does have statutes, the constitutionality of which is beyond doubt, which prohibit adultery and fornication. These statutes demon-strate that means for achieving the same basic purpose of protecting marital fidelity are avail-able to Connecticut without the need to "invade the area of protected freedoms."

Finally, it should be said of the Court's holding today that it in no way interferes with a State's proper regulation of sexual promiscuity or misconduct. As my Brother Harlan so well stated in his dissenting opinion in Poe v. Ullman,

> "Adultery, homosexuality and the like are sexual intimacies which the State for-bids * * * but the intimacy of husband and wife is necessarily an essential and ac-cepted feature of the institution of marriage, an institution which the State not only must allow, but which always and in every age it has fostered and protected. It is one thing when the State exerts its power either to forbid extra-marital sex-uality * * * or to say who may marry, but it is quite another when, having ac-knowledged a marriage and the intimacies inherent in it, it undertakes to regulate by means of the criminal law the details of that intimacy."

In sum, I believe that the right of privacy in the marital relation is fundamental and basic — a personal right "retained by the people" within the meaning of the Ninth Amend-ment. Connecticut cannot constitutionally abridge this fundamental right, which is pro-tected by the Fourteenth Amendment from infringement by the States. I agree with the Court that petitioners' convictions must therefore be reversed.

Mr. Justice HARLAN, concurring in the judgment.

I fully agree with the judgment of reversal, but find myself unable to join the Court's opin-ion. The reason is that it seems to me to evince an approach to this case very much like that taken by my Brothers BLACK and STEWART in dissent, namely: the Due Process Clause of the Fourteenth Amendment does not touch this Connecticut statute unless the enact-ment is found to violate some right assured by the letter or penumbra of the Bill of Rights.

In other words, what I find implicit in the Court's opinion is that the "incorporation" doc-trine may be used to restrict the reach of Fourteenth Amendment Due Process. For me this is just as unacceptable constitutional doctrine as is the use of the "incorporation" approach to impose upon the States all the requirements of the Bill of Rights as found in the provi-sions of the first eight amendments and in the decisions of this Court interpreting them.

In my view, the proper constitutional inquiry in this case is whether this Connecticut statute infringes the Due Process Clause of the Fourteenth Amendment because the en-actment violates basic values "implicit in the concept of ordered liberty," Palko v. State of Connecticut, 302 U.S. 319, 325. For reasons stated at length in my dissenting opinion in

Poe v. Ullman, I believe that it does. While the relevant inquiry may be aided by resort to one or more of the provisions of the Bill of Rights, it is not dependent on them or any of their radiations. The Due Process Clause of the Fourteenth Amendment stands, in my opinion, on its own bottom.

A further observation seems in order respecting the justification of my Brothers BLACK and STEWART for their "incorporation" approach to this case. Their approach does not rest on historical reasons, which are of course wholly lacking, but on the thesis that by limiting the content of the Due Process Clause of the Fourteenth Amendment to the protection of rights which can be found elsewhere in the Constitution, in this instance in the Bill of Rights, judges will thus be confined to "interpretation" of specific constitutional provisions, and will thereby be restrained from introducing their own notions of constitutional right and wrong into the "vague contours of the Due Process Clause."

While I could not more heartily agree that judicial "self restraint" is an indispensable ingredient of sound constitutional adjudication, I do submit that the formula suggested for achieving it is more hollow than real. "Specific" provisions of the Constitution, no less than "due process," lend themselves as readily to "personal" interpretations by judges whose constitutional outlook is simply to keep the Constitution in supposed "tune with the times." ....

Judicial self-restraint ... will be achieved in this area, as in other constitutional areas, only by continual insistence upon respect for the teachings of history, solid recognition of the basic values that underlie our society, and wise appreciation of the great roles that the doctrines of federalism and separation of powers have played in establishing and preserving American freedoms. Adherence to these principles will not, of course, obviate all constitutional differences of opinion among judges, nor should it. Their continued recognition will, however, go farther toward keeping most judges from roaming at large in the constitutional field than will the interpolation into the Constitution of an artificial and largely illusory restriction on the content of the Due Process Clause.

Mr. Justice WHITE, concurring in the judgment.

In my view this Connecticut law as applied to married couples deprives them of "liberty" without due process of law, as that concept is used in the Fourteenth Amendment. I therefore concur in the judgment of the Court reversing these convictions under Connecticut's aiding and abetting statute....

[S]tatutes regulating sensitive areas of liberty do, under the cases of this Court, require "strict scrutiny," Skinner v. State of Oklahoma, 316 U.S. 535, 541, and "must be viewed in the light of less drastic means for achieving the same basic purpose." Shelton v. Tucker, 364 U.S. 479, 488. "Where there is a significant encroachment upon personal liberty, the State may prevail only upon showing a subordinating interest which is compelling." Bates v. City of Little Rock, 361 U.S. 516, 524....

As I read the opinions of the Connecticut courts and the argument of Connecticut in this Court, the State claims but one justification for its anti-use statute. There is no serious contention that Connecticut thinks the use of artificial or external methods of contraception immoral or unwise in itself, or that the anti-use statute is founded upon any policy of promoting population expansion. Rather, the statute is said to serve the State's policy against all forms of promiscuous or illicit sexual relationships, be they premarital or extramarital, concededly a permissible and legitimate legislative goal.

Without taking issue with the premise that the fear of conception operates as a deterrent to such relationships in addition to the criminal proscriptions Connecticut has against such conduct, I wholly fail to see how the ban on the use of contraceptives by married couples in any way reinforces the State's ban on illicit sexual relationships. Connecticut does not bar the importation or possession of contraceptive devices; they are not considered contraband material under state law, and their availability in that State is not seriously disputed. The only way Connecticut seeks to limit or control the availability of such devices is through its general aiding and abetting statute whose operation in this context has been quite obviously ineffective and whose most serious use has been against birth-control clinics rendering advice to married, rather than unmarried, persons. Indeed, after over 80 years of the State's proscription of use, the legality of the sale of such devices to prevent disease has never been expressly passed upon, although it appears that sales have long occurred and have only infrequently been challenged. This "undeviating policy * * * throughout all the long years * * * bespeaks more than prosecutorial paralysis." Poe v. Ullman, 367 U.S. 497, 502. Moreover, it would appear that the sale of contraceptives to prevent disease is plainly legal under Connecticut law.

In these circumstances one is rather hard pressed to explain how the ban on use by married persons in any way prevents use of such devices by persons engaging in illicit sexual relations and thereby contributes to the State's policy against such relationships. Neither the state courts nor the State before the bar of this Court has tendered such an explanation. It is purely fanciful to believe that the broad proscription on use facilitates discovery of use by persons engaging in a prohibited relationship or for some other reason makes such use more unlikely and thus can be supported by any sort of administrative consideration. Perhaps the theory is that the flat ban on use prevents married people from possessing contraceptives and without the ready availability of such devices for use in the marital relationship, there will be no or less temptation to use them in extramarital ones. This reasoning rests on the premise that married people will comply with the ban in regard to their marital relationship, notwithstanding total nonenforcement in this context and apparent nonenforcibility, but will not comply with criminal statutes prohibiting extramarital affairs and the anti-use statute in respect to illicit sexual relationships, a premise whose validity has not been demonstrated and whose intrinsic validity is not very evident. At most the broad ban is of marginal utility to the declared objective. A statute limiting its prohibition on use to persons engaging in the prohibited relationship would serve the end posited by Connecticut in the same way, and with the same effectiveness, or ineffectiveness, as the broad anti-use statute under attack in this case. I find nothing in this record justifying the sweeping scope of this statute, with its telling effect on the freedoms of married persons, and therefore conclude that it deprives such persons of liberty without due process of law.

Mr. Justice BLACK, with whom Mr. Justice STEWART joins, dissenting.

. . . .

The Court talks about a constitutional "right of privacy" as though there is some constitutional provision or provisions forbidding any law ever to be passed which might abridge the "privacy" of individuals. But there is not. There are, of course, guarantees in certain specific constitutional provisions which are designed in part to protect privacy at certain times and places with respect to certain activities. Such, for example, is the Fourth Amendment's guarantee against "unreasonable searches and seizures." But I think it belittles that Amendment to talk about it as though it protects nothing but "privacy." To treat it that way is to give it a niggardly interpretation, not the kind of liberal reading I think any Bill of Rights provision should be given. The average man would very likely not have his feelings soothed any more by having his property seized openly than by having it seized privately and by stealth. He simply wants his property left alone. And a person can be just as much, if not more, irritated, annoyed and injured by an unceremonious public arrest by a policeman as he is by a seizure in the privacy of his office or home.

One of the most effective ways of diluting or expanding a constitutionally guaranteed right is to substitute for the crucial word or words of a constitutional guarantee another word or words, more or less flexible and more or less restricted in meaning. This fact is well illustrated by the use of the term "right of privacy" as a comprehensive substitute for the Fourth Amendment's guarantee against "unreasonable searches and seizures." "Privacy" is a broad, abstract and ambiguous concept which can easily be shrunken in meaning but which can also, on the other hand, easily be interpreted as a constitutional ban against many things other than searches and seizures.... I like my privacy as well as the next one, but I am nevertheless compelled to admit that government has a right to invade it unless prohibited by some specific constitutional provision. For these reasons I cannot agree with the Court's judgment and the reasons it gives for holding this Connecticut law unconstitutional....

The due process argument which my Brothers HARLAN and WHITE adopt here is based, as their opinions indicate, on the premise that this Court is vested with power to invalidate all state laws that it consider to be arbitrary, capricious, unreasonable, or oppressive, or this Court's belief that a particular state law under scrutiny has no "rational or justifying" purpose, or is offensive to a "sense of fairness and justice." If these formulas based on "natural justice," or others which mean the same thing, are to prevail, they require judges to determine what is or is not constitutional on the basis of their own appraisal of what laws are unwise or unnecessary. The power to make such decisions is of course that of a legislative body. Surely it has to be admitted that no provision of the Constitution specifically gives such blanket power to courts to exercise such a supervisory veto over the wisdom and value of legislative policies and to hold unconstitutional those laws which they believe unwise or dangerous. I readily admit that no legislative body, state or national, should pass laws that can justly be given any of the invidious labels invoked as constitutional excuses to strike down state laws. But perhaps it is not too much to say that no legislative body ever does pass laws without believing that they will accomplish a sane, rational, wise and justifiable purpose. While I completely subscribe to the holding of Marbury v. Madison, 1 Cranch 137, and subsequent cases, that our Court has constitutional power to strike down statutes, state or federal, that violate commands of the Federal Constitution, I do not believe that we are granted power by the Due Process Clause or any other constitutional provision or provisions to measure constitutionality by our belief that legislation is arbitrary, capricious or unreasonable, or accomplishes no justifiable purpose, or is offensive to our own notions of "civilized standards of conduct." Such an appraisal of the wisdom of legislation is an attribute of the power to make laws, not of the power to interpret them. The use by federal courts of such a formula or doctrine or whatnot to veto federal or state laws simply takes away from Congress and States the power to make laws based on their own judgment of fairness and wisdom and transfers that power to this Court for ultimate determination—a power which was specifically denied to federal courts by the convention that framed the Constitution.

Of the cases on which my Brothers WHITE and GOLDBERG rely so heavily, undoubtedly the reasoning of two of them supports their result here—as would that of a number of others which they do not bother to name.... The two they do cite and quote from, Meyer v. State of Nebraska, 262 U.S. 390, and Pierce v. Society of Sisters, 268 U.S. 510, were both decided in opinions by Mr. Justice McReynolds which elaborated the same natural law due process philosophy found in Lochner v. New York....

My Brother GOLDBERG has adopted the recent discovery that the Ninth Amendment as well as the Due Process Clause can be used by this Court as authority to strike down all state legislation which this Court thinks violates "fundamental principles of liberty and justice," or is contrary to the "traditions and [collective] conscience of our people." He also states, without proof satisfactory to me, that in making decisions on this basis judges will not consider "their personal and private notions." One may ask how they can avoid considering them. Our Court certainly has no machinery with which to take a Gallup Poll. And the scientific miracles of this age have not yet produced a gadget which the Court can use to determine what traditions are rooted in the "[collective] conscience of our people." Moreover, one would certainly have to look far beyond the language of the Ninth Amendment to find that the Framers vested in this Court any such awesome veto powers over lawmaking, either by the States or by the Congress. Nor does anything in the history of the Amendment offer any support for such a shocking doctrine. The whole history of the adoption of the Constitution and Bill of Rights points the other way, and the very material quoted by my Brother GOLDBERG shows that the Ninth Amendment was intended to protect against the idea that "by enumerating particular exceptions to the grant of power" to the Federal Government, "those rights which were not singled out, were intended to be assigned into the hands of the General Government [the United States], and were consequently insecure." That Amendment was passed, not to broaden the powers of this Court or any other department of "the General Government," but, as every student of history knows, to assure the people that the Constitution in all its provisions was intended to limit the Federal Government to the powers granted expressly or by necessary implication. If any broad, unlimited power to hold laws unconstitutional because they offend what this Court conceives to be the "[collective] conscience of our people" is vested in this Court by the Ninth Amendment, the Fourteenth Amendment, or any other provision of the Constitution, it was not given by the Framers, but rather has been bestowed on the Court by the Court. This fact is perhaps responsible for the peculiar phenomenon that for a period of a century and a half no serious suggestion was ever made that the Ninth Amendment, enacted to protect state powers against federal invasion, could be used as a weapon of federal power to prevent state legislatures from passing laws they consider appropriate to govern local affairs. Use of any such broad, unbounded judicial authority would make of this Court's members a day-to-day constitutional convention.

I repeat so as not to be misunderstood that this Court does have power, which it should exercise, to hold laws unconstitutional where they are forbidden by the Federal Constitution. My point is that there is no provision of the Constitution which either expressly or impliedly vests power in this Court to sit as a supervisory agency over acts of duly constituted legislative bodies and set aside their laws because of the Court's belief that the legislative policies adopted are unreasonable, unwise, arbitrary, capricious or irrational. The adoption of such a loose, flexible, uncontrolled standard for holding laws unconstitutional, if ever it is finally achieved, will amount to a great unconstitutional shift of power to the courts which I believe and am constrained to say will be bad for the courts and worse for the country. Subjecting federal and state laws to such an unrestrained and unrestrainable judicial control as to the wisdom of legislative enactments would, I fear, jeopardize the separation of governmental powers that the Framers set up and at the same time threaten to take away much of the power of States to govern themselves which the Constitution plainly intended them to have.

I realize that many good and able men have eloquently spoken and written, sometimes in rhapsodical strains, about the duty of this Court to keep the Constitution in tune with the times. The idea is that the Constitution must be changed from time to time and that this Court is charged with a duty to make those changes. For myself, I must with all deference reject that philosophy. The Constitution makers knew the need for change and provided for it. Amendments suggested by the people's elected representatives can be submitted to the people or their selected agents for ratification. That method of change was good for our Fathers, and being somewhat old-fashioned I must add it is good enough for me. And so, I cannot rely on the Due Process Clause or the Ninth Amendment or any mysterious and uncertain natural law concept as a reason for striking down this state law. The Due Process Clause with an "arbitrary and capricious" or "shocking to the conscience" formula was liberally used by this Court to strike down economic legislation in the early decades of this century, threatening, many people thought, the tranquility and stability of the Nation. See, e.g., Lochner v. State of New York, 198 U.S. 45. That formula, based on subjective considerations of "natural justice," is no less dangerous when used to enforce this Court's views about personal rights than those about economic rights....

Mr. Justice STEWART, whom Mr. Justice BLACK joins, dissenting.

Since 1879 Connecticut has had on its books a law which forbids the use of contraceptives by anyone. I think this is an uncommonly silly law. As a practical matter, the law is obviously unenforceable, except in the oblique context of the present case. As a philosophical matter, I believe the use of contraceptives in the relationship of marriage should be left to personal and private choice, based upon each individual's moral, ethical, and religious beliefs. As a matter of social policy, I think professional counsel about methods of birth control should be available to all, so that each individual's choice can be meaningfully made. But we are not asked in this case to say whether we think this law is unwise, or even asinine. We are asked to hold that it violates the United States Constitution. And that I cannot do.

In the course of its opinion the Court refers to no less than six Amendments to the Constitution: the First, the Third, the Fourth, the Fifth, the Ninth, and the Fourteenth. But the Court does not say which of these Amendments, if any, it thinks is infringed by this Connecticut law.

We *are* told that the Due Process Clause of the Fourteenth Amendment is not, as such, the "guide" in this case. With that much I agree. There is no claim that this law, duly enacted by the Connecticut Legislature, is unconstitutionally vague. There is no claim that the appellants were denied any of the elements of procedural due process at their trial, so as to make their convictions constitutionally invalid. And, as the Court says, the day has long passed since the Due Process Clause was regarded as a proper instrument for determining "the wisdom, need, and propriety" of state laws....

As to the First, Third, Fourth, and Fifth Amendments, I can find nothing in any of them to invalidate this Connecticut law, even assuming that all those Amendments are fully applicable against the States. It has not even been argued that this is a law "respecting an establishment of religion, or prohibiting the free exercise thereof." And surely, unless the solemn process of constitutional adjudication is to descend to the level of a play on words, there is not involved here any abridgment of "the freedom of speech, or of the press; or the right of the people peaceably to assemble, and to petition the Government for a redress of grievances." No soldier has been quartered in any house. There has been no search, and no seizure. Nobody has been compelled to be a witness against himself.

The Court also quotes the Ninth Amendment, and my Brother GOLDBERG's concurring opinion relies heavily upon it. But to say that the Ninth Amendment has anything to do with this case is to turn somersaults with history. The Ninth Amendment, like its companion the Tenth, which this Court held "states but a truism that all is retained which has not been surrendered," United States v. Darby, 312 U.S. 100, 124, was framed by James Madison and adopted by the States simply to make clear that the adoption of the Bill of Rights did not alter the plan that the *Federal* Government was to be a government of express and limited powers, and that all rights and powers not delegated to it were retained by the people and the individual States. Until today no member of this Court has ever suggested that the Ninth Amendment meant anything else, and the idea that a federal court could ever use the Ninth Amendment to annul a law passed by the elected representatives of the people of the State of Connecticut would have caused James Madison no little wonder.

What provision of the Constitution, then, does make this state law invalid? The Court says it is the right of privacy "created by several fundamental constitutional guarantees." With all deference, I can find no such general right of privacy in the Bill of Rights, in any other part of the Constitution, or in any case ever before decided by this Court.[7]

At the oral argument in this case we were told that the Connecticut law does not "conform to current community standards." But it is not the function of this Court to decide cases on the basis of community standards. We are here to decide cases "agreeably to the Constitution and laws of the United States." It is the essence of judicial duty to subordinate our own personal views, our own ideas of what legislation is wise and what is not. If, as I should surely hope, the law before us does not reflect the standards of the people of Connecticut, the people of Connecticut can freely exercise their true Ninth and Tenth Amendment rights to persuade their elected representatives to repeal it. That is the constitutional way to take this law off the books.

Eisenstadt v. Baird
405 U.S. 438 (1972)

Mr. Justice BRENNAN delivered the opinion of the Court.

Appellee William Baird was convicted at a bench trial in the Massachusetts Superior Court under Massachusetts General Laws Ann., c. 272, § 21, first, for exhibiting contraceptive articles in the course of delivering a lecture on contraception to a group of students at Boston University and, second, for giving a young woman a package of Emko vaginal foam at the close of his address.[1] The Massachusetts Supreme Judicial Court unanimously set aside the conviction for exhibiting contraceptives on the ground that it violated Baird's First Amendment rights, but by a four-to-three vote sustained the conviction for giving away the foam.…

Massachusetts General Laws Ann., c. 272, § 21, under which Baird was convicted, provides a maximum five-year term of imprisonment for "whoever … gives away … any drug, medicine, instrument or article whatever for the prevention of conception," except as authorized in § 21A. Under § 21A, "[a] registered physician may administer to or prescribe for any married person drugs or articles intended for the prevention of pregnancy or conception. [And a] registered pharmacist actually engaged in the business of pharmacy may furnish such drugs or articles to any married person presenting a prescription from a registered physician." As interpreted by the State Supreme Judicial Court, these provisions make it a felony for anyone, other than a registered physician or pharmacist acting in accordance with the terms of § 21A, to dispense any article with the intention that it be used for the prevention of conception. The statutory scheme distinguishes

---

7. …. The Court does not say how far the new constitutional right of privacy announced today extends. I suppose, however, that even after today a State can constitutionally still punish at least some offenses which are not committed in public.

1. The Court of Appeals below described the recipient of the foam as "an unmarried adult woman." However, there is no evidence in the record about her marital status.

among three distinct classes of distributees—*first*, married persons may obtain contraceptives to prevent pregnancy, but only from doctors or druggists on prescription; *second*, single persons may not obtain contraceptives from anyone to prevent pregnancy; and, *third*, married or single persons may obtain contraceptives from anyone to prevent, not pregnancy, but the spread of disease....

We agree [with the Court of Appeals] that the goals of deterring premarital sex and regulating the distribution of potentially harmful articles cannot reasonably be regarded as legislative aims of §§ 21 and 21A. And we hold that the statute, viewed as a prohibition on contraception *per se*, violates the rights of single persons under the Equal Protection Clause of the Fourteenth Amendment....

II

The basic principles governing application of the Equal Protection Clause of the Fourteenth Amendment are familiar. As The Chief Justice only recently explained in Reed v. Reed, 404 U.S. 71, 75–76 (1971):

> "In applying that clause, this Court has consistently recognized that the Fourteenth Amendment does not deny to State the power to treat different classes of persons in different ways. The Equal Protection Clause of that amendment does, however, deny to State the power to legislate that different treatment be accorded to persons placed by a statute into different classes on the basis of criteria wholly unrelated to the objective of that statute. A classification 'must be reasonable, not arbitrary, and must rest upon some ground of difference having a fair and substantial relation to the object of the legislation, so that all persons similarly circumstanced shall be treated alike.'"

The question for our determination in this case is whether there is some ground of difference that rationally explains the different treatment accorded married and unmarried persons under Massachusetts General Laws Ann., c. 272, §§ 21 and 21A.[7] For the reasons that follow, we conclude that no such ground exists.

First. Section 21 stems from Mass. Stat.1879, c. 159, § 1, which prohibited without exception, distribution of articles intended to be used as contraceptives. In Commonwealth v. Allison, 227 Mass. 57, 62 (1917), the Massachusetts Supreme Judicial Court explained that the law's "plain purpose is to protect purity, to preserve chastity, to encourage continence and self restraint, to defend the sanctity of the home, and thus to engender in the State and nation a virile and virtuous race of men and women." Although the State clearly abandoned that purpose with the enactment of § 21A, at least insofar as the illicit sexual activities of married persons are concerned, the court reiterated in Sturgis v. Attorney General, that the object of the legislation is to discourage premarital sexual intercourse. Conceding that the State could, consistently with the Equal Protection Clause, regard the problems of extramarital and premarital sexual relations as "[e]vils ... of different dimensions and proportions, requiring different remedies," Williamson v. Lee Optical Co., 348 U.S. 483, 489 (1955), we cannot agree that the deterrence of premarital sex may reasonably be regarded as the purpose of the Massachusetts law.

---

7. Of course, if we were to conclude that the Massachusetts statute impinges upon fundamental freedoms under *Griswold*, the statutory classification would have to be not merely *rationally related* to a valid public purpose but *necessary* to the achievement of a *compelling* state interest. But just as in Reed v. Reed, 404 U.S. 71 (1971), we do not have to address the statute's validity under that test because the law fails to satisfy even the more lenient equal protection standard.

It would be plainly unreasonable to assume that Massachusetts has prescribed pregnancy and the birth of an unwanted child as punishment for fornication, which is a misdemeanor under Massachusetts General Laws Ann., c. 272, § 18. Aside from the scheme of values that assumption would attribute to the State, it is abundantly clear that the effect of the ban on distribution of contraceptives to unmarried persons has at best a marginal relation to the proffered objective. What Mr. Justice Goldberg said in Griswold v. Connecticut, 381 U.S., at 498 (concurring opinion), concerning the effect of Connecticut's prohibition on the use of contraceptives in discouraging extramarital sexual relations, is equally applicable here. "The rationality of this justification is dubious, particularly in light of the admitted widespread availability to all persons in the State of Connecticut, unmarried as well as married, of birth-control devices for the prevention of disease, as distinguished from the prevention of conception." Like Connecticut's laws, §§ 21 and 21A do not at all regulate the distribution of contraceptives when they are to be used to prevent, not pregnancy, but the spread of disease. Nor, in making contraceptives available to married persons without regard to their intended use, does Massachusetts attempt to deter married persons from engaging in illicit sexual relations with unmarried persons. Even on the assumption that the fear of pregnancy operates as a deterrent to fornication, the Massachusetts statute is thus so riddled with exceptions that deterrence of premarital sex cannot reasonably be regarded as its aim.

Moreover, §§ 21 and 21A on their face have a dubious relation to the State's criminal prohibition on fornication. As the Court of Appeals explained, "Fornication is a misdemeanor [in Massachusetts], entailing a thirty dollar fine, or three months in jail. Massachusetts General Laws Ann. c. 272 § 18. Violation of the present statute is a felony, punishable by five years in prison. We find it hard to believe that the legislature adopted a statute carrying a five-year penalty for its possible, obviously by no means fully effective, deterrence of the commission of a ninety-day misdemeanor." Even conceding the legislature a full measure of discretion in fashioning means to prevent fornication, and recognizing that the State may seek to deter prohibited conduct by punishing more severely those who facilitate than those who actually engage in its commission, we, like the Court of Appeals, cannot believe that in this instance Massachusetts has chosen to expose the aider and abetter who simply *gives away* a contraceptive to *20* times the *90-day* sentence of the offender himself. The very terms of the State's criminal statutes, coupled with the *de minimis* effect of §§ 21 and 21A in deterring fornication, thus compel the conclusion that such deterrence cannot reasonably be taken as the purpose of the ban on distribution of contraceptives to unmarried persons.

Second. Section 21A was added to the Massachusetts General Laws by Stat. 1966, c. 265, § 1. The Supreme Judicial Court in Commonwealth v. Baird, held that the purpose of the amendment was to serve the health needs of the community by regulating the distribution of potentially harmful articles. It is plain that Massachusetts had no such purpose in mind before the enactment of § 21A. As the Court of Appeals remarked, "Consistent with the fact that the statute was contained in a chapter dealing with 'Crimes Against Chastity, Morality, Decency and Good Order,' it was cast only in terms of morals. A physician was forbidden to prescribe contraceptives even when needed for the protection of health." Nor did the Court of Appeals "believe that the legislature [in enacting § 21A] suddenly reversed its field and developed an interest in health. Rather, it merely made what it thought to be the precise accommodation necessary to escape the *Griswold* ruling."

Again, we must agree with the Court of Appeals. If health were the rationale of § 21A, the statute would be both discriminatory and overbroad. Dissenting in Commonwealth v. Baird, 355 Mass., at 758, Justices Whittemore and Cutter stated that they saw "in § 21 and § 21A, read together, no public health purpose. If there is need to have a physician prescribe (and a pharmacist dispense) contraceptives, that need is as great for unmarried persons as for married persons." The Court of Appeals added: "If the prohibition [on distribution to unmarried persons] ... is to be taken to mean that the same physician who can prescribe for married patients does not have sufficient skill to protect the health of patients who lack a marriage certificate, or who may be currently divorced, it is illogical to the point of irrationality." Furthermore, we must join the Court of Appeals in noting that not all contraceptives are potentially dangerous. As a result, if the Massachusetts statute were a health measure, it would not only invidiously discriminate against the unmarried, but also be overbroad with respect to the married....

But if further proof that the Massachusetts statute is not a health measure is necessary, the argument of Justice Spiegel, who also dissented in Commonwealth v. Baird, 355 Mass., at 759, is conclusive: "It is at best a strained conception to say that the Legislature intended to prevent the distribution of articles 'which may have undesirable, if not dangerous, physical consequences.' If that was the Legislature's goal, § 21 is not required" in view of the federal and state laws *already* regulating the distribution of harmful drugs. See Federal Food, Drug, and Cosmetic Act, § 503, 52 Stat. 1051, as amended, 21 U.S.C. § 353; Mass.Gen. Laws Ann., c. 94, § 187A, as amended. We conclude, accordingly, that, despite the statute's superficial earmarks as a health measure, health, on the face of the statute, may no more reasonably be regarded as its purpose than the deterrence of premarital sexual relations.

Third. If the Massachusetts statute cannot be upheld as a deterrent to fornication or as a health measure, may it, nevertheless, be sustained simply as a prohibition on contraception? The Court of Appeals analysis "led inevitably to the conclusion that, so far as morals are concerned, it is contraceptives per se that are considered immoral—to the extent that *Griswold* will permit such a declaration." The Court of Appeals went on to hold:

> "To say that contraceptives are immoral as such, and are to be forbidden to unmarried persons who will nevertheless persist in having intercourse, means that such persons must risk for themselves an unwanted pregnancy, for the child, illegitimacy, and for society, a possible obligation of support. Such a view of morality is not only the very mirror image of sensible legislation; we consider that it conflicts with fundamental human rights. In the absence of demonstrated harm, we hold it is beyond the competency of the state."

We need not and do not, however, decide that important question in this case because, whatever the rights of the individual to access to contraceptives may be, the rights must be the same for the unmarried and the married alike.

If under *Griswold* the distribution of contraceptives to married persons cannot be prohibited, a ban on distribution to unmarried persons would be equally impermissible. It is true that in *Griswold* the right of privacy in question inhered in the marital relationship. Yet the marital couple is not an independent entity with a mind and heart of its own, but an association of two individuals each with a separate intellectual and emotional makeup. If the right of privacy means anything, it is the right of the *individual*, married or single, to be free from unwarranted governmental intrusion into matters so fundamentally affecting a person as the decision whether to bear or beget a child.

On the other hand, if *Griswold* is no bar to a prohibition on the distribution of contraceptives, the State could not, consistently with the Equal Protection Clause, outlaw distribution to unmarried but not to married persons. In each case the evil, as perceived by the State, would be identical, and the underinclusion would be invidious....

We hold that by providing dissimilar treatment for married and unmarried persons who are similarly situated, Massachusetts General Laws Ann., c. 272, §§ 21 and 21A, violate the Equal Protection Clause....

Mr. Justice WHITE, with whom Mr. Justice BLACKMUN joins, concurring in the result.

....

Given Griswold v. Connecticut, and absent proof of the probable hazards of using vaginal foam, we could not sustain appellee's conviction had it been for selling or giving away foam to a married person. Just as in *Griswold*, where the right of married persons to use contraceptives was 'diluted or adversely affected' by permitting a conviction for giving advice as to its exercise, so here, to sanction a medical restriction upon distribution of a contraceptive not proved hazardous to health would impair the exercise of the constitutional right.

That Baird could not be convicted for distributing Emko to a married person disposes of this case. Assuming, *arguendo*, that the result would be otherwise had the recipient been unmarried, nothing has been placed in the record to indicate her marital status. The State has maintained that marital status is irrelevant because an unlicensed person cannot legally dispense vaginal foam either to married or unmarried persons. This approach is plainly erroneous and requires the reversal of Baird's conviction; for on the facts of this case, it deprives us of knowing whether Baird was in fact convicted for making a constitutionally protected distribution of Emko to a married person....

Because this case can be disposed of on the basis of settled constitutional doctrine, I perceive no reason for reaching the novel constitutional question whether a State may restrict or forbid the distribution of contraceptives to the unmarried.

[The concurring opinion of Justice Douglas, and the dissenting opinion of Chief Justice Burger, are omitted.]

Notes and Questions

1. In his opinion in *Griswold*, Justice Douglas characterizes *Meyer* and *Pierce* as cases applying the First Amendment against the states via the Fourteenth Amendment. But neither *Meyer* nor *Pierce* even once cited the First Amendment. Indeed, at the time those cases were decided, the Court had not yet "incorporated" the First Amendment and deemed it applicable to the states via the Fourteenth Amendment. *See McDonald v. City of Chi.*, 130 S. Ct. 3020, 3034 n.12 (2010).

Moreover, despite the *Meyer* Court's broad statement regarding the right "to marry, establish a home and bring up children," it was — as Justice Black notes in his dissent — fundamentally an economic substantive due process case, focused on the rights of the teachers and the parents to contract with one another for services. *See Meyer*, 262 U.S. at 401 ("Plaintiff in error taught this language in school as part of his occupation. His right thus to teach and the right of parents to engage him so to instruct their children, we think, are within the liberty of the amendment.").

2. In *Griswold*, Justice Douglas tries mightily to avoid reliance on the Due Process Clause, given the stigma associated with the *Lochner*-era cases. But how successful is he in doing so? As indicated in the previous note, he relies on two *Lochner*-era cases, *Meyer* and *Pierce*. But beyond that, even accepting that the right to privacy is located within the penumbras of the Bill of Rights, he still needs a vehicle for applying that penumbral right against the states. After all, if the Bill of Rights does not apply directly against the states without the aid of "incorporation" via the Due Process Clause of the Fourteenth Amendment, how could the penumbras of the Bill of Rights apply against the states?

3. How persuasive is Justice Douglas's argument in *Griswold* that, collectively, the First, Third, Fourth, Fifth and Ninth Amendments provide a more general constitutional right to "privacy"? Indeed, doesn't the fact that the framers provided protection for privacy in discrete circumstances suggest quite the opposite: that they did *not* intend to recognize a broader right to privacy?

In any event, even accepting that there exists a constitutional right to privacy, what limits are there on that right, and how are courts to determine those boundaries? After all, murder, sexual assault, and child abuse often occur in private — are those protected by the right to privacy? If not, what principle does Justice Douglas provide for deciding what is and is not protected?

4. If one is looking for textual support for the proposition that unenumerated constitutional rights exist, isn't Justice Goldberg exactly right in his concurring opinion in *Griswold* to focus on the Ninth Amendment? If the Ninth Amendment does not mean what Justice Goldberg represents it to mean, what, exactly, does it stand for?

5. In Justice Goldberg's view, what, exactly, is the *source* of the right at issue? On the one hand, he appears to reject the idea that he is incorporating the Ninth Amendment via the Fourteenth Amendment and applying it against the states. But is he not incorporating *something* and applying it against the states, and if so, what is that something?

6. To emphasize his point that a fundamental right to use contraception exists, Justice Goldberg sets forth a hypothetical in which the government *mandates* sterilization after two children have been born to a couple, and says the logic of the dissents in *Griswold* would support such a law. In evaluating the strength of this argument, of what significance is it that, in *Buck v. Bell*, 274 U.S. 200 (1927), the Court rejected a substantive due process challenge to a state law mandating sterilization of "mental defectives," reasoning as follows:

> It is better for all the world, if instead of waiting to execute degenerate offspring for crime, or to let them starve for their imbecility, society can prevent those who are manifestly unfit from continuing their kind. The principle that sustains compulsory vaccination is broad enough to cover cutting the Fallopian tubes. Three generations of imbeciles are enough.

Id. at 207.

7. How broad is the right to privacy recognized by Justices Douglas and Goldberg in *Griswold*? Justice Douglas speaks of the "privacy surrounding the marriage relationship"; does that mean the right to sexual privacy is not available to unmarried couples, whether same-sex or opposite-sex?

Although Justice Douglas does not provide any direct answers to these questions, Justice Goldberg does, making clear in his concurring opinion that states retain the ability to criminalize fornication (sexual intercourse engaged in by an unmarried person), adultery, and homosexuality, as well as the power to decide *who* may marry. What principled basis is there for drawing the line Justice Goldberg draws? Is that line still viable after *Eisenstadt*? After cases such as *Loving v. Virginia*, 388 U.S. 1 (1967) — examined in detail in Chapter 5 — which struck down as unconstitutional on equal protection and due process grounds laws banning interracial marriage?

8. Although the focus of Justice Douglas's opinion is on marital privacy, and the fear that the police would "search the sacred precincts of marital bedrooms for telltale signs of the use of contraceptives," no such invasion of marital privacy occurred in this case. After all, the conduct at issue in this case — giving information, instruction, and medical advice about preventing contraception — did not take place within the privacy of the marital bedroom. That means, does it not, that not only do the specific guarantees of the Bill of Rights have penumbras, but the penumbras themselves have penumbras?

9. Both Justices Goldberg and White focus in their opinions in *Griswold* on the *level* of scrutiny that applies under the Due Process Clause when a fundamental right is involved, namely, strict scrutiny. Justice Goldberg contrasts this with the normal level of scrutiny — rational basis — that is applicable for run-of-the mill substantive due process cases, as articulated in *Carolene Products* and *Williamson v. Lee Optical of Oklahoma*. Note that there are two key differences between rational basis and strict scrutiny: the importance of the state's interest in enacting and enforcing the law, and the fit between the end the government seeks to achieve and the means used to accomplish it.

As laid out in their opinions, strict scrutiny requires a very strong state interest underlying the law — a "compelling" one — as well as a close ends-means fit, one that is "necessary" to accomplishing the goal. In contrast, rational basis scrutiny requires a minimal state interest — it need only be a "legitimate" or "proper" one — and the ends-means fit need only be "rational."

10. Isn't Justice Black right to note in his dissenting opinion in *Griswold* that the tests set forth by Justices Douglas, Goldberg, and Harlan are too open-ended to place any constraints on the Court? How, for example, can one tell whether something is so rooted in the traditions and collective conscience of the people so as to be ranked as fundamental? What does it mean to be "implicit in the concept of ordered liberty"? Indeed, why is this any different from the *Dred Scott* or *Lochner* Courts' invocation of substantive due process?

11. Is *Eisenstadt* an equal protection case, a substantive due process case, or both? Asked somewhat differently, do you suppose the case would have turned out differently if a "lesser" right were at issue? After all, government discriminates against unmarried

couples in all sorts of ways, such as by denying them the income tax advantages given to married couples. If the Court had before it a challenge to the income tax preference for married couples, do you think the decision would have come out the same way?

12. Is *Eisenstadt* applying rational basis scrutiny or some form of heightened scrutiny? In this regard, consider whether the Court's analysis of the statute's constitutionality is more akin to the standard employed in *Lochner* or to that employed in *Williamson v. Lee Optical of Oklahoma*.

Roe v. Wade
410 U.S. 113 (1973)

Mr. Justice BLACKMUN delivered the opinion of the Court.

This Texas federal appeal and its Georgia companion, Doe v. Bolton, 410 U.S. 179, present constitutional challenges to state criminal abortion legislation. The Texas statutes under attack here are typical of those that have been in effect in many States for approximately a century. The Georgia statutes, in contrast, have a modern cast and are a legislative product that, to an extent at least, obviously reflects the influences of recent attitudinal change, of advancing medical knowledge and techniques, and of new thinking about an old issue.

We forthwith acknowledge our awareness of the sensitive and emotional nature of the abortion controversy, of the vigorous opposing views, even among physicians, and of the deep and seemingly absolute convictions that the subject inspires. One's philosophy, one's experiences, one's exposure to the raw edges of human existence, one's religious training, one's attitudes toward life and family and their values, and the moral standards one establishes and seeks to observe, are all likely to influence and to color one's thinking and conclusions about abortion.

In addition, population growth, pollution, poverty, and racial overtones tend to complicate and not to simplify the problem.

Our task, of course, is to resolve the issue by constitutional measurement, free of emotion and of predilection. We seek earnestly to do this, and, because we do, we have inquired into, and in this opinion place some emphasis upon, medical and medical-legal history and what that history reveals about man's attitudes toward the abortion procedure over the centuries. We bear in mind, too, Mr. Justice Holmes' admonition in his now-vindicated dissent in Lochner v. New York, 198 U.S. 45, 76 (1905):

> "[The Constitution] is made for people of fundamentally differing views, and the accident of our finding certain opinions natural and familiar, or novel, and even shocking, ought not to conclude our judgment upon the question whether statutes embodying them conflict with the Constitution of the United States."

I

The Texas statutes that concern us here … make it a crime to "procure an abortion," as therein defined, or to attempt one, except with respect to "an abortion procured or attempted by medical advice for the purpose of saving the life of the mother." Similar statutes are in existence in a majority of the States.

Texas first enacted a criminal abortion statute in 1854. This was soon modified into language that has remained substantially unchanged to the present time. The final article in each of these compilations provided the same exception, as does the present Article 1196, for an abortion by "medical advice for the purpose of saving the life of the mother."

II

Jane Roe,[4] a single woman who was residing in Dallas County, Texas, instituted this federal action in March 1970 against the District Attorney of the county. She sought a declaratory judgment that the Texas criminal abortion statutes were unconstitutional on their face, and an injunction restraining the defendant from enforcing the statutes.

Roe alleged that she was unmarried and pregnant; that she wished to terminate her pregnancy by an abortion "performed by a competent, licensed physician, under safe, clinical conditions"; that she was unable to get a "legal" abortion in Texas because her life did not appear to be threatened by the continuation of her pregnancy; and that she could not afford to travel to another jurisdiction in order to secure a legal abortion under safe conditions. She claimed that the Texas statutes were unconstitutionally vague and that they abridged her right of personal privacy, protected by the First, Fourth, Fifth, Ninth, and Fourteenth Amendments. By an amendment to her complaint Roe purported to sue "on behalf of herself and all other women" similarly situated.

James Hubert Hallford, a licensed physician, sought and was granted leave to intervene in Roe's action. In his complaint he alleged that he had been arrested previously for violations of the Texas abortion statutes and that two such prosecutions were pending against him. He described conditions of patients who came to him seeking abortions, and he claimed that for many cases he, as a physician, was unable to determine whether they fell within or outside the exception recognized by Article 1196. He alleged that, as a consequence, the statutes were vague and uncertain, in violation of the Fourteenth Amendment, and that they violated his own and his patients' rights to privacy in the doctor-patient relationship and his own right to practice medicine, rights he claimed were guaranteed by the First, Fourth, Fifth, Ninth, and Fourteenth Amendments.

John and Mary Doe,[5] a married couple, filed a companion complaint to that of Roe. They also named the District Attorney as defendant, claimed like constitutional deprivations, and sought declaratory and injunctive relief. The Does alleged that they were a childless couple; that Mrs. Doe was suffering from a "neural-chemical" disorder; that her physician had "advised her to avoid pregnancy until such time as her condition has materially improved" (although a pregnancy at the present time would not present "a serious risk" to her life); that, pursuant to medical advice, she had discontinued use of birth control pills; and that if she should become pregnant, she would want to terminate the pregnancy by an abortion performed by a competent, licensed physician under safe, clinical conditions. By an amendment to their complaint, the Does purported to sue "on behalf of themselves and all couples similarly situated."

The two actions were consolidated and heard together by a duly convened three-judge district court. The suits thus presented the situations of the pregnant single woman, the childless couple, with the wife not pregnant, and the licensed practicing physician, all joining in the attack on the Texas criminal abortion statutes. Upon the filing of affidavits, motions were made for dismissal and for summary judgment. The court held that Roe and members of her class, and Dr. Hallford, had standing to sue and presented justiciable controversies, but that the Does had failed to allege facts sufficient to state a present controversy and did not have standing. It concluded that, with respect to the requests for a declaratory judgment, abstention was not warranted. On the merits, the

---

4. The name is a pseudonym.
5. These names are pseudonyms.

District Court held that the "fundamental right of single women and married persons to choose where to have children is protected by the Ninth Amendment, through the Fourteenth Amendment," and that the Texas criminal abortion statutes were void on their face because they were both unconstitutionally vague and constituted an overbroad infringement of the plaintiffs' Ninth Amendment rights. The court then held that abstention was warranted with respect to the requests for an injunction. It therefore dismissed the Does' complaint, declared the abortion statutes void, and dismissed the application for injunctive relief....

IV

We are next confronted with issues of justiciability, standing, and abstention....

A. *Jane Roe.* Despite the use of the pseudonym, no suggestion is made that Roe is a fictitious person. For purposes of her case, we accept as true, and as established, her existence; her pregnant state, as of the inception of her suit in March 1970 and as late as May 21 of that year when she filed an alias affidavit with the District Court; and her inability to obtain a legal abortion in Texas.

Viewing Roe's case as of the time of its filing and thereafter until as late as May, there can be little dispute that it then presented a case or controversy and that, wholly apart from the class aspects, she, as a pregnant single woman thwarted by the Texas criminal abortion laws, had standing to challenge those statutes.... The "logical nexus between the status asserted and the claim sought to be adjudicated," and the necessary degree of contentiousness, are both present.

The appellee notes, however, that the record does not disclose that Roe was pregnant at the time of the District Court hearing on May 22, 1970, or on the following June 17 when the court's opinion and judgment were filed. And he suggests that Roe's case must now be moot because she and all other members of her class are no longer subject to any 1970 pregnancy.

The usual rule in federal cases is that an actual controversy must exist at stages of appellate or certiorari review, and not simply at the date the action is initiated.

But when, as here, pregnancy is a significant fact in the litigation, the normal 266-day human gestation period is so short that the pregnancy will come to term before the usual appellate process is complete. If that termination makes a case moot, pregnancy litigation seldom will survive much beyond the trial stage, and appellate review will be effectively denied. Our law should not be that rigid. Pregnancy often comes more than once to the same woman, and in the general population, if man is to survive, it will always be with us. Pregnancy provides a classic justification for a conclusion of nonmootness. It truly could be "capable of repetition, yet evading review."

We, therefore, agree with the District Court that Jane Roe had standing to undertake this litigation, that she presented a justiciable controversy, and that the termination of her 1970 pregnancy has not rendered her case moot.

B. *Dr. Hallford.* The doctor's position is different. He entered Roe's litigation as a plaintiff-intervenor, alleging in his complaint that he:

> "[I]n the past has been arrested for violating the Texas Abortion Laws and at the present time stands charged by indictment with violating said laws in the Criminal District Court of Dallas County, Texas to-wit: (1) The State of Texas vs. James H. Hallford, No. C-69-5307-IH, and (2) The State of Texas vs. James H. Hallford, No. C-69-2524-H. In both cases the defendant is charged with abortion …"

....

Dr. Hallford is, therefore, in the position of seeking, in a federal court, declaratory and injunctive relief with respect to the same statutes under which he stands charged in criminal prosecutions simultaneously pending in state court. Although he stated that he has been arrested in the past for violating the State's abortion laws, he makes no allegation of any substantial and immediate threat to any federally protected right that cannot be asserted in his defense against the state prosecutions. Neither is there any allegation of harassment or bad-faith prosecution. In order to escape the rule articulated in the cases cited in the next paragraph of this opinion that, absent harassment and bad faith, a defendant in a pending state criminal case cannot affirmatively challenge in federal court the statutes under which the State is prosecuting him, Dr. Hallford seeks to distinguish his status as a present state defendant from his status as a "potential future defendant" and to assert only the latter for standing purposes here.

We see no merit in that distinction. Our decision in Samuels v. Mackell, 401 U.S. 66 (1971), compels the conclusion that the District Court erred when it granted declaratory relief to Dr. Hallford instead of refraining from so doing. The court, of course, was correct in refusing to grant injunctive relief to the doctor. The reasons supportive of that action, however, are those expressed in Samuels v. Mackell and in Younger v. Harris, 401 U.S. 37 (1971)....

Dr. Hallford's complaint in intervention, therefore, is to be dismissed. He is remitted to his defenses in the state criminal proceedings against him....

C. *The Does.* In view of our ruling as to Roe's standing in her case, the issue of the Does' standing in their case has little significance. The claims they assert are essentially the same as those of Roe, and they attack the same statutes. Nevertheless, we briefly note the Does' posture.

Their pleadings present them as a childless married couple, the woman not being pregnant, who have no desire to have children at this time because of their having received medical advice that Mrs. Doe should avoid pregnancy, and for "other highly personal reasons." But they "fear ... they may face the prospect of becoming parents." And if pregnancy ensues, they "would want to terminate" it by an abortion. They assert an inability to obtain an abortion legally in Texas and, consequently, the prospect of obtaining an illegal abortion there or of going outside Texas to some place where the procedure could be obtained legally and competently.

We thus have as plaintiffs a married couple who have, as their asserted immediate and present injury, only an alleged "detrimental effect upon [their] marital happiness" because they are forced to "the choice of refraining from normal sexual relations or of endangering Mary Doe's health through a possible pregnancy." Their claim is that sometime in the future Mrs. Doe might become pregnant because of possible failure of contraceptive measures, and at that time in the future she might want an abortion that might then be illegal under the Texas statutes.

This very phrasing of the Does' position reveals its speculative character. Their alleged injury rests on possible future contraceptive failure, possible future pregnancy, possible future unpreparedness for parenthood, and possible future impairment of health. Any one or more of these several possibilities may not take place and all may not combine. In the Does' estimation, these possibilities might have some real or imagined impact upon their marital happiness. But we are not prepared to say that the bare allegation of so indirect an injury is sufficient to present an actual case or controversy.

The Does therefore are not appropriate plaintiffs in this litigation....

V

The principal thrust of appellant's attack on the Texas statutes is that they improperly invade a right, said to be possessed by the pregnant woman, to choose to terminate her pregnancy. Appellant would discover this right in the concept of personal 'liberty' embodied in the Fourteenth Amendment's Due Process Clause; or in personal marital, familial, and sexual privacy said to be protected by the Bill of Rights or its penumbras, see Griswold v. Connecticut, 381 U.S. 479 (1965); Eisenstadt v. Baird, 405 U.S. 438 (1972); *id.*, at 460 (White, J., concurring in result); or among those rights reserved to the people by the Ninth Amendment, Griswold v. Connecticut, 381 U.S., at 486 (Goldberg, J., concurring). Before addressing this claim, we feel it desirable briefly to survey, in several aspects, the history of abortion, for such insight as that history may afford us, and then to examine the state purposes and interests behind the criminal abortion laws.

VI

It perhaps is not generally appreciated that the restrictive criminal abortion laws in effect in a majority of States today are of relatively recent vintage. Those laws, generally proscribing abortion or its attempt at any time during pregnancy except when necessary to preserve the pregnant woman's life, are not of ancient or even of common-law origin. Instead, they derive from statutory changes effected, for the most part, in the latter half of the 19th century.

[The Court reviews ancient attitudes toward abortion as well as those contained in the Hippocratic Oath.]

3. *The common law.* It is undisputed that at common law, abortion performed *before* "quickening"—the first recognizable movement of the fetus *in utero*, appearing usually from the 16th to the 18th week of pregnancy—was not an indictable offense. The absence of a common-law crime for pre-quickening abortion appears to have developed from a confluence of earlier philosophical, theological, and civil and canon law concepts of when life begins. These disciplines variously approached the question in terms of the point at which the embryo or fetus became "formed" or recognizably human, or in terms of when a "person" came into being, that is, infused with a "soul" or "animated." A loose consensus evolved in early English law that these events occurred at some point between conception and live birth. This was "mediate animation." Although Christian theology and the canon law came to fix the point of animation at 40 days for a male and 80 days for a female, a view that persisted until the 19th century, there was otherwise little agreement about the precise time of formation or animation. There was agreement, however, that prior to this point the fetus was to be regarded as part of the mother, and its destruction, therefore, was not homicide. Due to continued uncertainty about the precise time when animation occurred, to the lack of any empirical basis for the 40–80-day view, and perhaps to Aquinas' definition of movement as one of the two first principles of life, Bracton focused upon quickening as the critical point. The significance of quickening was echoed by later common-law scholars and found its way into the received common law in this country.

Whether abortion of a quick fetus was a felony at common law, or even a lesser crime, is still disputed....

[The Court reviews the English common law's attitudes toward abortion.]

5. *The American law.* In this country, the law in effect in all but a few States until mid-19th century was the pre-existing English common law. Connecticut, the first State to enact abortion legislation, adopted in 1821 that part of Lord Ellenborough's Act that re-

lated to a woman "quick with child." The death penalty was not imposed. Abortion before quickening was made a crime in that State only in 1860. In 1828, New York enacted legislation that, in two respects, was to serve as a model for early anti-abortion statutes. First, while barring destruction of an unquickend fetus as well as a quick fetus, it made the former only a misdemeanor, but the latter second-degree manslaughter. Second, it incorporated a concept of therapeutic abortion by providing that an abortion was excused if it "shall have been necessary to preserve the life of such mother, or shall have been advised by two physicians to be necessary for such purpose." By 1840, when Texas had received the common law, only eight American States had statutes dealing with abortion. It was not until after the War Between the States that legislation began generally to replace the common law. Most of these initial statutes dealt severely with abortion after quickening but were lenient with it before quickening. Most punished attempts equally with completed abortions. While many statutes included the exception for an abortion thought by one or more physicians to be necessary to save the mother's life, that provision soon disappeared and the typical law required that the procedure actually be necessary for that purpose.

Gradually, in the middle and late 19th century the quickening distinction disappeared from the statutory law of most States and the degree of the offense and the penalties were increased. By the end of the 1950's a large majority of the jurisdictions banned abortion, however and whenever performed, unless done to save or preserve the life of the mother. The exceptions, Alabama and the District of Columbia, permitted abortion to preserve the mother's health. Three States permitted abortions that were not "unlawfully" performed or that were not "without lawful justification," leaving interpretation of those standards to the courts. In the past several years, however, a trend toward liberalization of abortion statutes has resulted in adoption, by about one-third of the States, of less stringent laws....

It is thus apparent that at common law, at the time of the adoption of our Constitution, and throughout the major portion of the 19th century, abortion was viewed with less disfavor than under most American statutes currently in effect. Phrasing it another way, a woman enjoyed a substantially broader right to terminate a pregnancy than she does in most States today. At least with respect to the early stage of pregnancy, and very possibly without such a limitation, the opportunity to make this choice was present in this country well into the 19th century. Even later, the law continued for some time to treat less punitively an abortion procured in early pregnancy.

[The Court proceeds to summarize the positions of the American Medical Association, the American Public Health Association, and the American Bar Association.]

VII

Three reasons have been advanced to explain historically the enactment of criminal abortion laws in the 19th century and to justify their continued existence.

It has been argued occasionally that these laws were the product of a Victorian social concern to discourage illicit sexual conduct. Texas, however, does not advance this justification in the present case, and it appears that no court or commentator has taken the argument seriously. The appellants and *amici* contend, moreover, that this is not a proper state purpose at all and suggest that, if it were, the Texas statutes are overbroad in protecting it since the law fails to distinguish between married and unwed mothers.

A second reason is concerned with abortion as a medical procedure. When most criminal abortion laws were first enacted, the procedure was a hazardous one for the woman. This was particularly true prior to the development of antisepsis. Antiseptic techniques, of course, were based on discoveries by Lister, Pasteur, and others first announced in 1867, but were not generally accepted and employed until about the turn of the century. Abortion mortality was high. Even after 1900, and perhaps until as late as the development of antibiotics in the 1940's, standard modern techniques such as dilation and curettage were not nearly so safe as they are today. Thus, it has been argued that a State's real concern in enacting a criminal abortion law was to protect the pregnant woman, that is, to restrain her from submitting to a procedure that placed her life in serious jeopardy.

Modern medical techniques have altered this situation. Appellants and various *amici* refer to medical data indicating that abortion in early pregnancy, that is, prior to the end of the first trimester, although not without its risk, is now relatively safe. Mortality rates for women undergoing early abortions, where the procedure is legal, appear to be as low as or lower than the rates for normal childbirth. Consequently, any interest of the State in protecting the woman from an inherently hazardous procedure, except when it would be equally dangerous for her to forgo it, has largely disappeared. Of course, important state interests in the areas of health and medical standards do remain. The State has a legitimate interest in seeing to it that abortion, like any other medical procedure, is performed under circumstances that insure maximum safety for the patient. This interest obviously extends at least to the performing physician and his staff, to the facilities involved, to the availability of after-care, and to adequate provision for any complication or emergency that might arise. The prevalence of high mortality rates at illegal "abortion mills" strengthens, rather than weakens, the State's interest in regulating the conditions under which abortions are performed. Moreover, the risk to the woman increases as her pregnancy continues. Thus, the State retains a definite interest in protecting the woman's own health and safety when an abortion is proposed at a late stage of pregnancy,

The third reason is the State's interest — some phrase it in terms of duty — in protecting prenatal life. Some of the argument for this justification rests on the theory that a new human life is present from the moment of conception. The State's interest and general obligation to protect life then extends, it is argued, to prenatal life. Only when the life of the pregnant mother herself is at stake, balanced against the life she carries within her, should the interest of the embryo or fetus not prevail. Logically, of course, a legitimate state interest in this area need not stand or fall on acceptance of the belief that life begins at conception or at some other point prior to life birth. In assessing the State's interest, recognition may be given to the less rigid claim that as long as at least *potential* life is involved, the State may assert interests beyond the protection of the pregnant woman alone.

Parties challenging state abortion laws have sharply disputed in some courts the contention that a purpose of these laws, when enacted, was to protect prenatal life. Pointing to the absence of legislative history to support the contention, they claim that most state laws were designed solely to protect the woman. Because medical advances have lessened this concern, at least with respect to abortion in early pregnancy, they argue that with respect to such abortions the laws can no longer be justified by any state interest. There is some scholarly support for this view of original purpose. The few state courts called upon to interpret their laws in the late 19th and early 20th centuries did focus on the State's interest in protecting the woman's health rather than in preserving the embryo and fetus. Proponents of this view point out that in many States, including Texas, by statute or judicial interpretation, the pregnant woman herself could not be prosecuted for self-abortion or for cooperating in an abortion performed upon her by another. They claim that adoption of the "quickening" distinction through received common law and state statutes tacitly recognizes the greater health hazards inherent in late abortion and impliedly repudiates the theory that life begins at conception.

It is with these interests, and the weight to be attached to them, that this case is concerned.

VIII

The Constitution does not explicitly mention any right of privacy. In a line of decisions, however … the Court has recognized that a right of personal privacy, or a guarantee of certain areas or zones of privacy, does exist under the Constitution.… These decisions make it clear that only personal rights that can be deemed "fundamental" or "implicit in the concept of ordered liberty," Palko v. Connecticut, 302 U.S. 319, 325 (1937), are included in this guarantee of personal privacy. They also make it clear that the right has some extension to activities relating to marriage, Loving v. Virginia, 388 U.S. 1, 12 (1967); procreation, Skinner v. Oklahoma, 316 U.S. 535, 541–542 (1942); contraception, Eisenstadt v. Baird, 405 U.S., at 453–454; id., at 460, 463–465 (White, J., concurring in result); family relationships, Prince v. Massachusetts, 321 U.S. 158, 166 (1944); and child rearing and education, Pierce v. Society of Sisters, 268 U.S. 510, 535 (1925), Meyer v. Nebraska.

This right of privacy, whether it be founded in the Fourteenth Amendment's concept of personal liberty and restrictions upon state action, as we feel it is, or, as the District Court determined, in the Ninth Amendment's reservation of rights to the people, is broad enough to encompass a woman's decision whether or not to terminate her pregnancy. The detriment that the State would impose upon the pregnant woman by denying this choice altogether is apparent. Specific and direct harm medically diagnosable even in early pregnancy may be involved. Maternity, or additional offspring, may force upon the woman a distressful life and future. Psychological harm may be imminent. Mental and physical health may be taxed by child care. There is also the distress, for all concerned, associated with the unwanted child, and there is the problem of bringing a child into a family already unable, psychologically and otherwise, to care for it. In other cases, as in this one, the additional difficulties and continuing stigma of unwed motherhood may be involved. All these are factors the woman and her responsible physician necessarily will consider in consultation.

On the basis of elements such as these, appellant and some *amici* argue that the woman's right is absolute and that she is entitled to terminate her pregnancy at whatever time, in whatever way, and for whatever reason she alone chooses. With this we do not agree. Appellant's arguments that Texas either has no valid interest at all in regulating the abortion decision, or no interest strong enough to support any limitation upon the woman's sole determination, are unpersuasive. The Court's decisions recognizing a right of privacy also acknowledge that some state regulation in areas protected by that right is appropriate. As noted above, a State may properly assert important interests in safeguarding health, in maintaining medical standards, and in protecting potential life. At some point in pregnancy, these respective interests become sufficiently compelling to sustain regulation of the factors that govern the abortion decision. The privacy right involved, therefore, cannot be said to be absolute. In fact, it is not clear to us that the claim asserted by some *amici* that one has an unlimited right to do with one's body as one pleases bears a close relationship to the right of privacy previously articulated in the Court's decisions. The Court has refused to recognize an unlimited right of this kind in the past.

We, therefore, conclude that the right of personal privacy includes the abortion decision, but that this right is not unqualified and must be considered against important state interests in regulation.…

Where certain "fundamental rights" are involved, the Court has held that regulation limiting these rights may be justified only by a "compelling state interest," and that legislative enactments must be narrowly drawn to express only the legitimate state interests at stake.…

IX

....

A. The appellee and certain *amici* argue that the fetus is a "person" within the language and meaning of the Fourteenth Amendment. In support of this, they outline at length and in detail the well-known facts of fetal development. If this suggestion of personhood is established, the appellant's case, of course, collapses, for the fetus' right to life would then be guaranteed specifically by the Amendment....

The Constitution does not define "person" in so many words. Section 1 of the Fourteenth Amendment contains three references to "person." The first, in defining "citizens," speaks of "persons born or naturalized in the United States." The word also appears both in the Due Process Clause and in the Equal Protection Clause. "Person" is used in other places in the Constitution: in the listing of qualifications for Representatives and Senators, Art. I, § 2, cl. 2, and § 3, cl. 3; in the Apportionment Clause, Art. I, § 2, cl. 3; in the Migration and Importation provision, Art. I, § 9, cl. 1; in the Emolument Clause, Art, I, § 9, cl. 8; in the Electros provisions, Art. II, § 1, cl. 2, and the superseded cl. 3; in the provision outlining qualifications for the office of President, Art. II, § 1, cl. 5; in the Extradition provisions, Art. IV, § 2, cl. 2, and the superseded Fugitive Slave Clause 3; and in the Fifth, Twelfth, and Twenty-second Amendments, as well as in §§ 2 and 3 of the Fourteenth Amendment. But in nearly all these instances, the use of the word is such that it has application only postnatally. None indicates, with any assurance, that it has any possible prenatal application.[54]

All this, together with our observation, *supra*, that throughout the major portion of the 19th century prevailing legal abortion practices were far freer than they are today, persuades us that the word "person," as used in the Fourteenth Amendment, does not include the unborn....

B. The pregnant woman cannot be isolated in her privacy. She carries an embryo and, later, a fetus, if one accepts the medical definitions of the developing young in the human uterus. The situation therefore is inherently different from marital intimacy, or bedroom possession of obscene material, or marriage, or procreation, or education, with which *Eisenstadt* and *Griswold*, *Stanley*, *Loving*, *Skinner* and *Pierce* and *Meyer* were respectively concerned. As we have intimated above, it is reasonable and appropriate for a State to decide that at some point in time another interest, that of health of the mother or that of potential human life, becomes significantly involved. The woman's privacy is no longer sole and any right of privacy she possesses must be measured accordingly.

---

54. When Texas urges that a fetus is entitled to Fourteenth Amendment protection as a person, it faces a dilemma. Neither in Texas nor in any other State are all abortions prohibited. Despite broad proscription, an exception always exists. The exception contained in Art. 1196, for an abortion procured or attempted by medical advice for the purpose of saving the life of the mother, is typical. But if the fetus is a person who is not to be deprived of life without due process of law, and if the mother's condition is the sole determinant, does not the Texas exception appear to be out of line with the Amendment's command?

There are other inconsistencies between Fourteenth Amendment status and the typical abortion statute. It has already been pointed out that in Texas the woman is not a principal or an accomplice with respect to an abortion upon her. If the fetus is a person, why is the woman not a principal or an accomplice? Further, the penalty for criminal abortion specified by Art. 1195 is significantly less than the maximum penalty for murder prescribed by Art. 1257 of the Texas Penal Code. If the fetus is a person, may the penalties be different?

Texas urges that, apart from the Fourteenth Amendment, life begins at conception and is present throughout pregnancy, and that, therefore, the State has a compelling interest in protecting that life from and after conception. We need not resolve the difficult question of when life begins. When those trained in the respective disciplines of medicine, philosophy, and theology are unable to arrive at any consensus, the judiciary, at this point in the development of man's knowledge, is not in a position to speculate as to the answer.

It should be sufficient to note briefly the wide divergence of thinking on this most sensitive and difficult question. There has always been strong support for the view that life does not begin until live birth. This was the belief of the Stoics. It appears to be the predominant, though not the unanimous, attitude of the Jewish faith. It may be taken to represent also the position of a large segment of the Protestant community, insofar as that can be ascertained; organized groups that have taken a formal position on the abortion issue have generally regarded abortion as a matter for the conscience of the individual and her family. As we have noted, the common law found greater significance in quickening. Physicians and their scientific colleagues have regarded that event with less interest and have tended to focus either upon conception, upon live birth, or upon the interim point at which the fetus becomes "viable," that is, potentially able to live outside the mother's womb, albeit with artificial aid. Viability is usually placed at about seven months (28 weeks) but may occur earlier, even at 24 weeks. The Aristotelian theory of "mediate animation," that held sway throughout the Middle Ages and the Renaissance in Europe, continued to be official Roman Catholic dogma until the 19th century, despite opposition to this "ensoulment" theory from those in the Church who would recognize the existence of life from the moment of conception. The latter is now, of course, the official belief of the Catholic Church. As one brief *amicus* discloses, this is a view strongly held by many non-Catholics as well, and by many physicians. Substantial problems for precise definition of this view are posed, however, by new embryological data that purport to indicate that conception is a "process" over time, rather than an event, and by new medical techniques such as menstrual extraction, the "morning-after" pill, implantation of embryos, artificial insemination, and even artificial wombs.

In areas other than criminal abortion, the law has been reluctant to endorse any theory that life, as we recognize it, begins before live birth or to accord legal rights to the unborn except in narrowly defined situations and except when the rights are contingent upon live birth. For example, the traditional rule of tort law denied recovery for prenatal injuries even though the child was born alive. That rule has been changed in almost every jurisdiction. In most States, recovery is said to be permitted only if the fetus was viable, or at least quick, when the injuries were sustained, though few courts have squarely so held. In a recent development, generally opposed by the commentators, some States permit the parents of a stillborn child to maintain an action for wrongful death because of prenatal injuries. Such an action, however, would appear to be one to vindicate the parents' interest and is thus consistent with the view that the fetus, at most, represents only the potentiality of life. Similarly, unborn children have been recognized as acquiring rights or interests by way of inheritance or other devolution of property, and have been represented by guardians *ad litem*. Perfection of the interests involved, again, has generally been contingent upon live birth. In short, the unborn have never been recognized in the law as persons in the whole sense.

X

In view of all this, we do not agree that, by adopting one theory of life, Texas may override the rights of the pregnant woman that are at stake. We repeat, however, that the State does have an important and legitimate interest in preserving and protecting the health of the pregnant woman, whether she be a resident of the State or a non-resident who seeks medical consultation and treatment there, and that it has still *another* important and legitimate interest in protecting the potentiality of human life. These interests are separate and distinct. Each grows in substantiality as the woman approaches term and, at a point during pregnancy, each becomes "compelling."

With respect to the State's important and legitimate interest in the health of the mother, the "compelling" point, in the light of present medical knowledge, is at approximately the end of the first trimester. This is so because of the now-established medical fact … that until the end of the first trimester mortality in abortion may be less than mortality in normal childbirth. It follows that, from and after this point, a State may regulate the abortion procedure to the extent that the regulation reasonably relates to the preservation and protection of maternal health. Examples of permissible state regulation in this area are requirements as to the qualifications of the person who is to perform the abortion; as to the licensure of that person; as to the facility in which the procedure is to be performed, that is, whether it must be a hospital or may be a clinic or some other place of less-than-hospital status; as to the licensing of the facility; and the like.

This means, on the other hand, that, for the period of pregnancy prior to this "compelling" point, the attending physician, in consultation with his patient, is free to determine, without regulation by the State, that, in his medical judgment, the patient's pregnancy should be terminated. If that decision is reached, the judgment may be effectuated by an abortion free of interference by the State.

With respect to the State's important and legitimate interest in potential life, the "compelling" point is at viability. This is so because the fetus then presumably has the capability of meaningful life outside the mother's womb. State regulation protective of fetal life after viability thus has both logical and biological justifications. If the State is interested in protecting fetal life after viability, it may go so far as to proscribe abortion during that period, except when it is necessary to preserve the life or health of the mother.

Measured against these standards, Art. 1196 of the Texas Penal Code, in restricting legal abortions to those "procured or attempted by medical advice for the purpose of saving the life of the mother," sweeps too broadly. The statute makes no distinction between abortions performed early in pregnancy and those performed later, and it limits to a single reason, "saving" the mother's life, the legal justification for the procedure. The statute, therefore, cannot survive the constitutional attack made upon it here.…

XI

To summarize and to repeat:

1. A state criminal abortion statute of the current Texas type, that excepts from criminality only a *life-saving* procedure on behalf of the mother, without regard to pregnancy stage and without recognition of the other interests involved, is violative of the Due Process Clause of the Fourteenth Amendment.

(a) For the stage prior to approximately the end of the first trimester, the abortion decision and its effectuation must be left to the medical judgment of the pregnant woman's attending physician.

(b) For the stage subsequent to approximately the end of the first trimester, the State, in promoting its interest in the health of the mother, may, if it chooses, regulate the abortion procedure in ways that are reasonably related to maternal health.

(c) For the stage subsequent to viability, the State in promoting its interest in the potentiality of human life may, if it chooses, regulate, and even proscribe, abortion except where it is necessary, in appropriate medical judgment, for the preservation of the life or health of the mother.

2. The State may define the term "physician," as it has been employed in the preceding paragraphs of this Part XI of this opinion, to mean only a physician currently licensed by the State, and may proscribe any abortion by a person who is not a physician as so defined....

This holding, we feel, is consistent with the relative weights of the respective interests involved, with the lessons and examples of medical and legal history, with the lenity of the common law, and with the demands of the profound problems of the present day. The decision leaves the State free to place increasing restrictions on abortion as the period of pregnancy lengthens, so long as those restrictions are tailored to the recognized state interests. The decision vindicates the right of the physician to administer medical treatment according to his professional judgment up to the points where important state interests provide compelling justifications for intervention. Up to those points, the abortion decision in all its aspects is inherently, and primarily, a medical decision, and basic responsibility for it must rest with the physician. If an individual practitioner abuses the privilege of exercising proper medical judgment, the usual remedies, judicial and intra-professional, are available.

XII

Our conclusion that Art. 1196 is unconstitutional means, of course, that the Texas abortion statutes, as a unit, must fall. The exception of Art. 1196 cannot be struck down separately, for then the State would be left with a statute proscribing all abortion procedures no matter how medically urgent the case....

Mr. Justice REHNQUIST, dissenting.

....

I

The Court's opinion decides that a State may impose virtually no restriction on the performance of abortions during the first trimester of pregnancy. Our previous decisions indicate that a necessary predicate for such an opinion is a plaintiff who was in her first trimester of pregnancy at some time during the pendency of her lawsuit. While a party may vindicate his own constitutional rights, he may not seek vindication for the rights of others. The Court's statement of facts in this case makes clear, however, that the record in no way indicates the presence of such a plaintiff. We know only that plaintiff Roe at the time of filing her complaint was a pregnant woman; for aught that appears in this record, she may have been in her *last* trimester of pregnancy as of the date the complaint was filed.

Nothing in the Court's opinion indicates that Texas might not constitutionally apply its proscription of abortion as written to a woman in that stage of pregnancy. Nonetheless, the Court uses her complaint against the Texas statute as a fulcrum for deciding that States may impose virtually no restrictions on medical abortions performed during the *first* trimester of pregnancy. In deciding such a hypothetical lawsuit, the Court departs from the longstanding admonition that it should never "formulate a rule of constitutional law broader than is required by the precise facts to which it is to be applied."

II

....

If the Court means by the term "privacy" no more than that the claim of a person to be free from unwanted state regulation of consensual transactions may be a form of "liberty" protected by the Fourteenth Amendment, there is no doubt that similar claims have been upheld in our earlier decisions on the basis of that liberty. I agree ... that the "liberty," against deprivation of which without due process the Fourteenth Amendment protects, embraces more than the rights found in the Bill of Rights. But that liberty is not guaranteed absolutely against deprivation, only against deprivation without due process of law. The test traditionally applied in the area of social and economic legislation is whether or not a law such as that challenged has a rational relation to a valid state objective. Williamson v. Lee Optical Co., 348 U.S. 483, 491 (1955). The Due Process Clause of the Fourteenth Amendment undoubtedly does place a limit, albeit a broad one, on legislative power to enact laws such as this. If the Texas statute were to prohibit an abortion even where the mother's life is in jeopardy, I have little doubt that such a statute would lack a rational relation to a valid state objective under the test stated in *Williamson*. But the Court's sweeping invalidation of any restrictions on abortion during the first trimester is impossible to justify under that standard, and the conscious weighing of competing factors that the Court's opinion apparently substitutes for the established test is far more appropriate to a legislative judgment than to a judicial one.

The Court eschews the history of the Fourteenth Amendment in its reliance on the "compelling state interest" test. But the Court adds a new wrinkle to this test by transposing it from the legal considerations associated with the Equal Protection Clause of the Fourteenth Amendment to this case arising under the Due Process Clause of the Fourteenth Amendment. Unless I misapprehend the consequences of this transplanting of the "compelling state interest test," the Court's opinion will accomplish the seemingly impossible feat of leaving this area of the law more confused than it found it.

While the Court's opinion quotes from the dissent of Mr. Justice Holmes in Lochner v. New York, 198 U.S. 45, 74 (1905), the result it reaches is more closely attuned to the majority opinion of Mr. Justice Peckham in that case. As in *Lochner* and similar cases applying substantive due process standards to economic and social welfare legislation, the adoption of the compelling state interest standard will inevitably require this Court to examine the legislative policies and pass on the wisdom of these policies in the very process of deciding whether a particular state interest put forward may or may not be "compelling." The decision here to break pregnancy into three distinct terms and to outline the permissible restrictions the State may impose in each one, for example, partakes more of judicial legislation than it does of a determination of the intent of the drafters of the Fourteenth Amendment.

The fact that a majority of the States reflecting, after all the majority sentiment in those States, have had restrictions on abortions for at least a century is a strong indication, it seems to me, that the asserted right to an abortion is not "so rooted in the traditions and conscience of our people as to be ranked as fundamental," Snyder v. Massachusetts, 291 U.S. 97, 105 (1934)....

III

Even if one were to agree that the case that the Court decides were here, and that the enunciation of the substantive constitutional law in the Court's opinion were proper, the actual disposition of the case by the Court is still difficult to justify. The Texas statute is struck down *in toto*, even though the Court apparently concedes that at later periods of pregnancy Texas might impose these selfsame statutory limitations on abortion. My understanding of past practice is that a statute found to be invalid as applied to a particular plaintiff, but not unconstitutional as a whole, is not simply "struck down" but is, instead, declared unconstitutional as applied to the fact situation before the Court.

For all of the foregoing reasons, I respectfully dissent.

[The concurring opinions of Chief Justice Burger and Justices Douglas and Stewart, and the dissenting opinion of Justice White, are omitted.]

Notes and Questions

1. Can you articulate the *Roe* Court's test for determining the scope of unenumerated rights? In other words, in thinking about the application of *Roe* outside the context of abortion, what would its test be for determining whether to recognize other unenumerated rights?

2. How persuasive is the Court's decision to draw fixed lines at the ends of the first and second trimesters of pregnancy? To what extent are its conclusions based on then-existing technology, and if so, what impact would (or should) later advances in technology have on the Court's test?

3. Are there analogies between what the Court did in *Dred Scott* and what it did in *Roe*? Of course, as discussed above, both cases are known as substantive due process cases. But beyond that, both cases reject a claim of personhood as a way of resolving the claims raised in the cases. In other words, is it fair to note that, just as *Dred Scott* held that slaves and their descendents are not citizens under the constitution, so too *Roe* held that fetuses are not persons?

4. If the state has an interest in potential life, why does that interest not justify state interference in the abortion decision before the point of "viability"? Indeed, wouldn't a state interest in potential life justify the bans on contraception use at issue in cases such as *Griswold* and *Eisenstadt*?

5. The *Roe* Court, like the *Griswold* Court, grounds its holding in the right to privacy. Accepting that that there is a constitutionally protected zone of privacy, is the claim to "privacy" as strong in *Roe* as it was in *Griswold*? Does the Court's definition of privacy turn on where the conduct occurs? Who is present when the conduct occurs? Or is privacy defined solely by the type of conduct at issue, without regard to where or in whose presence it takes place? Or does the question whether something is protected by the right to privacy depend upon all of these factors considered collectively?

6. Does *Roe* necessarily follow from the line of substantive due process cases that precede it? Recall that in *Griswold*, the Court spoke of a right to *marital* privacy, and addressed the issue of contraception. Jane Roe, however, was an unmarried woman, and the act of abortion is different in kind, is it not, from the use of contraception? To what extent does the *Eisenstadt* decision aid in linking *Roe* to *Griswold*?

7. The laws at issue in both *Griswold* and *Eisenstadt* were to some extent outliers in that at the time of those decisions, those laws were inconsistent with the laws of virtually every other state. In contrast, at the time *Roe* was decided, nearly every state regulated or prohibited abortion in some way. Of what significance is that distinction? Stated somewhat differently, what role do history and tradition play in the Court's substantive due process analysis? To the extent they play a role, which historical time periods are relevant?

C. The First Sodomy Case

Bowers v. Hardwick
478 U.S. 186 (1986)

Justice WHITE delivered the opinion of the Court.

In August 1982, respondent Hardwick (hereafter respondent) was charged with violating the Georgia statute criminalizing sodomy[1] by committing that act with another adult male in the bedroom of respondent's home. After a preliminary hearing, the District Attorney decided not to present the matter to the grand jury unless further evidence developed.

Respondent then brought suit in the Federal District Court, challenging the constitutionality of the statute insofar as it criminalized consensual sodomy.[2] He asserted that he was a practicing homosexual, that the Georgia sodomy statute, as administered by the defendants, placed him in imminent danger of arrest, and that the statute for several reasons violates the Federal Constitution. The District Court granted the defendants' motion to dismiss for failure to state a claim, relying on *Doe v. Commonwealth's Attorney for the City of Richmond*, 403 F.Supp. 1199 (ED Va.1975), which this Court summarily affirmed, 425 U.S. 901 (1976).

A divided panel of the Court of Appeals for the Eleventh Circuit reversed. The court first held that, because *Doe* was distinguishable and in any event had been undermined by later decisions, our summary affirmance in that case did not require affirmance of the District Court. Relying on our decisions in *Griswold v. Connecticut*, 381 U.S. 479 (1965); *Eisenstadt v. Baird*, 405 U.S. 438 (1972); *Stanley v. Georgia*, 394 U.S. 557 (1969); and *Roe v. Wade*, 410 U.S. 113 (1973), the court went on to hold that the Georgia statute violated respondent's fundamental rights because his homosexual activity is a private and intimate association that is beyond the reach of state regulation by reason of the Ninth Amendment and the Due Process Clause of the Fourteenth Amendment. The case was remanded for trial, at which, to prevail, the State would have to prove that the statute is supported by a compelling interest and is the most narrowly drawn means of achieving that end.

Because other Courts of Appeals have arrived at judgments contrary to that of the Eleventh Circuit in this case, we granted the Attorney General's petition for certiorari questioning the holding that the sodomy statute violates the fundamental rights of ho-

---

1. Georgia Code Ann. § 16-6-2 (1984) provides, in pertinent part, as follows:
"(a) A person commits the offense of sodomy when he performs or submits to any sexual act involving the sex organs of one person and the mouth or anus of another....
"(b) A person convicted of the offense of sodomy shall be punished by imprisonment for not less than one nor more than 20 years...."
2. John and Mary Doe were also plaintiffs in the action. They alleged that they wished to engage in sexual activity proscribed by § 16-6-2 in the privacy of their home, and that they had been "chilled and deterred" from engaging in such activity by both the existence of the statute and Hardwick's arrest. The District Court held, however, that because they had neither sustained, nor were in immediate danger of sustaining, any direct injury from the enforcement of the statute, they did not have proper standing to maintain the action. The Court of Appeals affirmed the District Court's judgment dismissing the Does' claim for lack of standing, and the Does do not challenge that holding in this Court.
The only claim properly before the Court, therefore, is Hardwick's challenge to the Georgia statute as applied to consensual homosexual sodomy. We express no opinion on the constitutionality of the Georgia statute as applied to other acts of sodomy.

mosexuals. We agree with petitioner that the Court of Appeals erred, and hence reverse its judgment.[4]

This case does not require a judgment on whether laws against sodomy between consenting adults in general, or between homosexuals in particular, are wise or desirable. It raises no question about the right or propriety of state legislative decisions to repeal their laws that criminalize homosexual sodomy, or of state-court decisions invalidating those laws on state constitutional grounds. The issue presented is whether the Federal Constitution confers a fundamental right upon homosexuals to engage in sodomy and hence invalidates the laws of the many States that still make such conduct illegal and have done so for a very long time. The case also calls for some judgment about the limits of the Court's role in carrying out its constitutional mandate.

We first register our disagreement with the Court of Appeals and with respondent that the Court's prior cases have construed the Constitution to confer a right of privacy that extends to homosexual sodomy and for all intents and purposes have decided this case. The reach of this line of cases was sketched in *Carey v. Population Services International,* 431 U.S. 678, 685 (1977). *Pierce v. Society of Sisters,* 268 U.S. 510 (1925), and *Meyer v. Nebraska,* 262 U.S. 390 (1923), were described as dealing with child rearing and education; *Prince v. Massachusetts,* 321 U.S. 158 (1944), with family relationships; *Skinner v. Oklahoma ex rel. Williamson,* 316 U.S. 535 (1942), with procreation; *Loving v. Virginia,* 388 U.S. 1 (1967), with marriage; *Griswold v. Connecticut, supra,* and *Eisenstadt v. Baird, supra,* with contraception; and *Roe v. Wade,* 410 U.S. 113 (1973), with abortion. The latter three cases were interpreted as construing the Due Process Clause of the Fourteenth Amendment to confer a fundamental individual right to decide whether or not to beget or bear a child. *Carey v. Population Services International, supra,* 431 U.S., at 688–689.

Accepting the decisions in these cases and the above description of them, we think it evident that none of the rights announced in those cases bears any resemblance to the claimed constitutional right of homosexuals to engage in acts of sodomy that is asserted in this case. No connection between family, marriage, or procreation on the one hand and homosexual activity on the other has been demonstrated, either by the Court of Appeals or by respondent. Moreover, any claim that these cases nevertheless stand for the proposition that any kind of private sexual conduct between consenting adults is constitutionally insulated from state proscription is unsupportable....

Precedent aside, however, respondent would have us announce, as the Court of Appeals did, a fundamental right to engage in homosexual sodomy. This we are quite unwilling to do. It is true that despite the language of the Due Process Clauses of the Fifth and Fourteenth Amendments, which appears to focus only on the processes by which life, liberty, or property is taken, the cases are legion in which those Clauses have been interpreted to have substantive content, subsuming rights that to a great extent are immune from federal or state regulation or proscription. Among such cases are those recognizing rights that have little or no textual support in the constitutional language. *Meyer, Prince,* and *Pierce* fall in this category, as do the privacy cases from *Griswold* to *Carey.*

Striving to assure itself and the public that announcing rights not readily identifiable in the Constitution's text involves much more than the imposition of the Justices' own choice of values on the States and the Federal Government, the Court has sought to identify the

---

4. Petitioner also submits that the Court of Appeals erred in holding that the District Court was not obligated to follow our summary affirmance in *Doe.* We need not resolve this dispute, for we prefer to give plenary consideration to the merits of this case rather than rely on our earlier action in *Doe.*

nature of the rights qualifying for heightened judicial protection. In *Palko v. Connecticut,* 302 U.S. 319, 325, 326 (1937), it was said that this category includes those fundamental liberties that are "implicit in the concept of ordered liberty," such that "neither liberty nor justice would exist if [they] were sacrificed." A different description of fundamental liberties appeared in *Moore v. East Cleveland,* 431 U.S. 494, 503 (1977) (opinion of POWELL, J.), where they are characterized as those liberties that are "deeply rooted in this Nation's history and tradition." *Id.,* at 503 (POWELL, J.). See also *Griswold v. Connecticut,* 381 U.S., at 506.

It is obvious to us that neither of these formulations would extend a fundamental right to homosexuals to engage in acts of consensual sodomy. Proscriptions against that conduct have ancient roots. Sodomy was a criminal offense at common law and was forbidden by the laws of the original thirteen States when they ratified the Bill of Rights. In 1868, when the Fourteenth Amendment was ratified, all but 5 of the 37 States in the Union had criminal sodomy laws. In fact, until 1961, all 50 States outlawed sodomy, and today, 24 States and the District of Columbia continue to provide criminal penalties for sodomy performed in private and between consenting adults. Against this background, to claim that a right to engage in such conduct is "deeply rooted in this Nation's history and tradition" or "implicit in the concept of ordered liberty" is, at best, facetious.

Nor are we inclined to take a more expansive view of our authority to discover new fundamental rights imbedded in the Due Process Clause. The Court is most vulnerable and comes nearest to illegitimacy when it deals with judge-made constitutional law having little or no cognizable roots in the language or design of the Constitution. That this is so was painfully demonstrated by the face-off between the Executive and the Court in the 1930's, which resulted in the repudiation of much of the substantive gloss that the Court had placed on the Due Process Clauses of the Fifth and Fourteenth Amendments. There should be, therefore, great resistance to expand the substantive reach of those Clauses, particularly if it requires redefining the category of rights deemed to be fundamental. Otherwise, the Judiciary necessarily takes to itself further authority to govern the country without express constitutional authority. The claimed right pressed on us today falls far short of overcoming this resistance.

Respondent, however, asserts that the result should be different where the homosexual conduct occurs in the privacy of the home. He relies on *Stanley v. Georgia,* 394 U.S. 557 (1969), where the Court held that the First Amendment prevents conviction for possessing and reading obscene material in the privacy of one's home: "If the First Amendment means anything, it means that a State has no business telling a man, sitting alone in his house, what books he may read or what films he may watch." *Id.,* at 565.

Stanley did protect conduct that would not have been protected outside the home, and it partially prevented the enforcement of state obscenity laws; but the decision was firmly grounded in the First Amendment. The right pressed upon us here has no similar support in the text of the Constitution, and it does not qualify for recognition under the prevailing principles for construing the Fourteenth Amendment. Its limits are also difficult to discern. Plainly enough, otherwise illegal conduct is not always immunized whenever it occurs in the home. Victimless crimes, such as the possession and use of illegal drugs, do not escape the law where they are committed at home. *Stanley* itself recognized that its holding offered no protection for the possession in the home of drugs, firearms, or stolen goods. And if respondent's submission is limited to the voluntary sexual conduct between consenting adults, it would be difficult, except by fiat, to limit the claimed right to homosexual conduct while leaving exposed to prosecution adultery, incest, and other sexual crimes even though they are committed in the home. We are unwilling to start down that road.

Even if the conduct at issue here is not a fundamental right, respondent asserts that there must be a rational basis for the law and that there is none in this case other than the presumed belief of a majority of the electorate in Georgia that homosexual sodomy is immoral and unacceptable. This is said to be an inadequate rationale to support the law. The law, however, is constantly based on notions of morality, and if all laws representing essentially moral choices are to be invalidated under the Due Process Clause, the courts will be very busy indeed. Even respondent makes no such claim, but insists that majority sentiments about the morality of homosexuality should be declared inadequate. We do not agree, and are unpersuaded that the sodomy laws of some 25 States should be invalidated on this basis.[8]

Accordingly, the judgment of the Court of Appeals is

Reversed.

Chief Justice BURGER, concurring.

I join the Court's opinion, but I write separately to underscore my view that in constitutional terms there is no such thing as a fundamental right to commit homosexual sodomy.

As the Court notes, the proscriptions against sodomy have very "ancient roots." Decisions of individuals relating to homosexual conduct have been subject to state intervention throughout the history of Western civilization. Condemnation of those practices is firmly rooted in Judaeo-Christian moral and ethical standards. Homosexual sodomy was a capital crime under Roman law. During the English Reformation when powers of the ecclesiastical courts were transferred to the King's Courts, the first English statute criminalizing sodomy was passed. Blackstone described "the infamous *crime against nature*" as an offense of "deeper malignity" than rape, a heinous act "the very mention of which is a disgrace to human nature," and "a crime not fit to be named." The common law of England, including its prohibition of sodomy, became the received law of Georgia and the other Colonies. In 1816 the Georgia Legislature passed the statute at issue here, and that statute has been continuously in force in one form or another since that time. To hold that the act of homosexual sodomy is somehow protected as a fundamental right would be to cast aside millennia of moral teaching.

This is essentially not a question of personal "preferences" but rather of the legislative authority of the State. I find nothing in the Constitution depriving a State of the power to enact the statute challenged here.

Justice POWELL, concurring.

I join the opinion of the Court. I agree with the Court that there is no fundamental right—*i.e.,* no substantive right under the Due Process Clause—such as that claimed by respondent Hardwick, and found to exist by the Court of Appeals. This is not to suggest, however, that respondent may not be protected by the Eighth Amendment of the Constitution. The Georgia statute at issue in this case, Ga.Code Ann. § 16-6-2 (1984), authorizes a court to imprison a person for up to 20 years for a single private, consensual act of sodomy. In my view, a prison sentence for such conduct—certainly a sentence of long duration—would create a serious Eighth Amendment issue. Under the Georgia statute a single act of sodomy, even in the private setting of a home, is a felony comparable in terms of the possible sentence imposed to serious felonies such as aggravated battery, § 16-5-24, first-degree arson, § 16-7-60, and robbery, § 16-8-40.

---

8. Respondent does not defend the judgment below based on the Ninth Amendment, the Equal Protection Clause, or the Eighth Amendment.

In this case, however, respondent has not been tried, much less convicted and sentenced.[2] Moreover, respondent has not raised the Eighth Amendment issue below. For these reasons this constitutional argument is not before us.

Justice BLACKMUN, with whom Justice BRENNAN, Justice MARSHALL, and Justice STEVENS join, dissenting.

This case is no more about "a fundamental right to engage in homosexual sodomy," as the Court purports to declare, than *Stanley v. Georgia*, 394 U.S. 557 (1969), was about a fundamental right to watch obscene movies, or *Katz v. United States*, 389 U.S. 347 (1967), was about a fundamental right to place interstate bets from a telephone booth. Rather, this case is about "the most comprehensive of rights and the right most valued by civilized men," namely, "the right to be let alone." *Olmstead v. United States*, 277 U.S. 438, 478 (1928) (Brandeis, J., dissenting).

The statute at issue, Ga.Code Ann. § 16-6-2 (1984), denies individuals the right to decide for themselves whether to engage in particular forms of private, consensual sexual activity. The Court concludes that § 16-6-2 is valid essentially because "the laws of ... many States ... still make such conduct illegal and have done so for a very long time." But the fact that the moral judgments expressed by statutes like § 16-6-2 may be "'natural and familiar ... ought not to conclude our judgment upon the question whether statutes embodying them conflict with the Constitution of the United States.'" *Roe v. Wade*, 410 U.S. 113, 117 (1973), quoting *Lochner v. New York*, 198 U.S. 45, 76 (1905) (Holmes, J., dissenting). Like Justice Holmes, I believe that "[i]t is revolting to have no better reason for a rule of law than that so it was laid down in the time of Henry IV. It is still more revolting if the grounds upon which it was laid down have vanished long since, and the rule simply persists from blind imitation of the past." I believe we must analyze Hardwick's claim in the light of the values that underlie the constitutional right to privacy. If that right means anything, it means that, before Georgia can prosecute its citizens for making choices about the most intimate aspects of their lives, it must do more than assert that the choice they have made is an "'abominable crime not fit to be named among Christians.'"

I

In its haste to reverse the Court of Appeals and hold that the Constitution does not "confe[r] a fundamental right upon homosexuals to engage in sodomy," the Court relegates the actual statute being challenged to a footnote and ignores the procedural posture of the case before it. A fair reading of the statute and of the complaint clearly reveals that the majority has distorted the question this case presents.

First, the Court's almost obsessive focus on homosexual activity is particularly hard to justify in light of the broad language Georgia has used. Unlike the Court, the Georgia Legislature has not proceeded on the assumption that homosexuals are so different from other citizens that their lives may be controlled in a way that would not be tolerated if it limited the choices of those other citizens. Rather, Georgia has provided that "[a] person commits the offense of sodomy when he performs or submits to any sexual act involving

---

2. It was conceded at oral argument that, prior to the complaint against respondent Hardwick, there had been no reported decision involving prosecution for private homosexual sodomy under this statute for several decades. Moreover, the State has declined to present the criminal charge against Hardwick to a grand jury, and this is a suit for declaratory judgment brought by respondents challenging the validity of the statute. The history of nonenforcement suggests the moribund character today of laws criminalizing this type of private, consensual conduct....

the sex organs of one person and the mouth or anus of another." Ga.Code Ann. § 16-6-2(a) (1984). The sex or status of the persons who engage in the act is irrelevant as a matter of state law. In fact, to the extent I can discern a legislative purpose for Georgia's 1968 enactment of § 16-6-2, that purpose seems to have been to broaden the coverage of the law to reach heterosexual as well as homosexual activity.[1] I therefore see no basis for the Court's decision to treat this case as an "as applied" challenge to § 16-6-2, or for Georgia's attempt, both in its brief and at oral argument, to defend § 16-6-2 solely on the grounds that it prohibits homosexual activity. Michael Hardwick's standing may rest in significant part on Georgia's apparent willingness to enforce against homosexuals a law it seems not to have any desire to enforce against heterosexuals. But his claim that § 16-6-2 involves an unconstitutional intrusion into his privacy and his right of intimate association does not depend in any way on his sexual orientation.

Second, I disagree with the Court's refusal to consider whether § 16-6-2 runs afoul of the Eighth or Ninth Amendments or the Equal Protection Clause of the Fourteenth Amendment. Respondent's complaint expressly invoked the Ninth Amendment, and he relied heavily before this Court on *Griswold v. Connecticut,* 381 U.S. 479, 484 (1965), which identifies that Amendment as one of the specific constitutional provisions giving "life and substance" to our understanding of privacy. More importantly, the procedural posture of the case requires that we affirm the Court of Appeals' judgment if there is *any* ground on which respondent may be entitled to relief. This case is before us on petitioner's motion to dismiss for failure to state a claim, Fed.Rule Civ.Proc. 12(b)(6).... Thus, even if respondent did not advance claims based on the Eighth or Ninth Amendments, or on the Equal Protection Clause, his complaint should not be dismissed if any of those provisions could entitle him to relief.... The Court's cramped reading of the issue before it makes for a short opinion, but it does little to make for a persuasive one.

II

"Our cases long have recognized that the Constitution embodies a promise that a certain private sphere of individual liberty will be kept largely beyond the reach of government." *Thornburgh v. American College of Obstetricians & Gynecologists,* 476 U.S. 747, 772 (1986). In construing the right to privacy, the Court has proceeded along two somewhat distinct, albeit complementary, lines. First, it has recognized a privacy interest with reference to certain *decisions* that are properly for the individual to make. *E.g., Roe v. Wade,* 410 U.S. 113 (1973); *Pierce v. Society of Sisters,* 268 U.S. 510 (1925). Second, it has recognized a privacy interest with reference to certain *places* without regard for the particular activities in which the individuals who occupy them are engaged. The case before us implicates both the decisional and the spatial aspects of the right to privacy.

A

The Court concludes today that none of our prior cases dealing with various decisions that individuals are entitled to make free of governmental interference "bears any resemblance to the claimed constitutional right of homosexuals to engage in acts of sodomy that is asserted in this case." While it is true that these cases may be characterized by their

---

1. Until 1968, Georgia defined sodomy as "the carnal knowledge and connection against the order of nature, by man with man, or in the same unnatural manner with woman." Ga.Crim.Code § 26-5901 (1933). In *Thompson v. Aldredge,* 187 Ga. 467 (1939), the Georgia Supreme Court held that § 26-5901 did not prohibit lesbian activity. And in *Riley v. Garrett,* 219 Ga. 345 (1963), the Georgia Supreme Court held that § 26-5901 did not prohibit heterosexual cunnilingus. Georgia passed the act-specific statute currently in force "perhaps in response to the restrictive court decisions such as *Riley,*" Note, The Crimes Against Nature, 16 J.Pub.L. 159, 167, n. 47 (1967).

connection to protection of the family, the Court's conclusion that they extend no further than this boundary ignores the warning in *Moore v. East Cleveland,* 431 U.S. 494, 501 (1977) (plurality opinion), against "clos[ing] our eyes to the basic reasons why certain rights associated with the family have been accorded shelter under the Fourteenth Amendment's Due Process Clause." We protect those rights not because they contribute, in some direct and material way, to the general public welfare, but because they form so central a part of an individual's life.... And so we protect the decision whether to marry precisely because marriage "is an association that promotes a way of life, not causes; a harmony in living, not political faiths; a bilateral loyalty, not commercial or social projects." *Griswold v. Connecticut,* 381 U.S., at 486. We protect the decision whether to have a child because parenthood alters so dramatically an individual's self-definition, not because of demographic considerations or the Bible's command to be fruitful and multiply. And we protect the family because it contributes so powerfully to the happiness of individuals, not because of a preference for stereotypical households....

Only the most willful blindness could obscure the fact that sexual intimacy is "a sensitive, key relationship of human existence, central to family life, community welfare, and the development of human personality." The fact that individuals define themselves in a significant way through their intimate sexual relationships with others suggests, in a Nation as diverse as ours, that there may be many "right" ways of conducting those relationships, and that much of the richness of a relationship will come from the freedom an individual has to *choose* the form and nature of these intensely personal bonds.

In a variety of circumstances we have recognized that a necessary corollary of giving individuals freedom to choose how to conduct their lives is acceptance of the fact that different individuals will make different choices. For example, in holding that the clearly important state interest in public education should give way to a competing claim by the Amish to the effect that extended formal schooling threatened their way of life, the Court declared: "There can be no assumption that today's majority is 'right' and the Amish and others like them are 'wrong.' A way of life that is odd or even erratic but interferes with no rights or interests of others is not to be condemned because it is different." *Wisconsin v. Yoder,* 406 U.S. 205, 223–224 (1972). The Court claims that its decision today merely refuses to recognize a fundamental right to engage in homosexual sodomy; what the Court really has refused to recognize is the fundamental interest all individuals have in controlling the nature of their intimate associations with others.

B

The behavior for which Hardwick faces prosecution occurred in his own home, a place to which the Fourth Amendment attaches special significance. The Court's treatment of this aspect of the case is symptomatic of its overall refusal to consider the broad principles that have informed our treatment of privacy in specific cases. Just as the right to privacy is more than the mere aggregation of a number of entitlements to engage in specific behavior, so too, protecting the physical integrity of the home is more than merely a means of protecting specific activities that often take place there. Even when our understanding of the contours of the right to privacy depends on "reference to a 'place,'" "the essence of a Fourth Amendment violation is 'not the breaking of [a person's] doors, and the rummaging of his drawers,' but rather is 'the invasion of his indefeasible right of personal security, personal liberty and private property.'"

The Court's interpretation of the pivotal case of *Stanley v. Georgia,* 394 U.S. 557 (1969), is entirely unconvincing. *Stanley* held that Georgia's undoubted power to punish the public distribution of constitutionally unprotected, obscene material did not permit the State to punish the private possession of such material. According to the majority here, *Stanley* relied entirely on the First Amendment, and thus, it is claimed, sheds no light on cases not involving printed materials. But that is not what *Stanley* said. Rather, the *Stanley* Court anchored its holding in the Fourth Amendment's special protection for the individual in his home....

The central place that *Stanley* gives Justice Brandeis' dissent in *Olmstead,* a case raising *no* First Amendment claim, shows that *Stanley* rested as much on the Court's understanding of the Fourth Amendment as it did on the First. Indeed, in *Paris Adult Theatre I v. Slaton,* 413 U.S. 49 (1973), the Court suggested that reliance on the Fourth Amendment not only supported the Court's outcome in *Stanley* but actually was *necessary* to it: "If obscene material unprotected by the First Amendment in itself carried with it a 'penumbra' of constitutionally protected privacy, this Court would not have found it necessary to decide *Stanley* on the narrow basis of the 'privacy of the home,' which was hardly more than a reaffirmation that 'a man's home is his castle.'" "The right of the people to be secure in their ... houses," expressly guaranteed by the Fourth Amendment, is perhaps the most "textual" of the various constitutional provisions that inform our understanding of the right to privacy, and thus I cannot agree with the Court's statement that "[t]he right pressed upon us here has no ... support in the text of the Constitution." Indeed, the right of an individual to conduct intimate relationships in the intimacy of his or her own home seems to me to be the heart of the Constitution's protection of privacy.

III

The Court's failure to comprehend the magnitude of the liberty interests at stake in this case leads it to slight the question whether petitioner, on behalf of the State, has justified Georgia's infringement on these interests. I believe that neither of the two general justifications for § 16-6-2 that petitioner has advanced warrants dismissing respondent's challenge for failure to state a claim.

First, petitioner asserts that the acts made criminal by the statute may have serious adverse consequences for "the general public health and welfare," such as spreading communicable diseases or fostering other criminal activity. Inasmuch as this case was dismissed by the District Court on the pleadings, it is not surprising that the record before us is barren of any evidence to support petitioner's claim. In light of the state of the record, I see no justification for the Court's attempt to equate the private, consensual sexual activity at issue here with the "possession in the home of drugs, firearms, or stolen goods," to which *Stanley* refused to extend its protection. None of the behavior so mentioned in *Stanley* can properly be viewed as "[v]ictimless": drugs and weapons are inherently dangerous, and for property to be "stolen," someone must have been wrongfully deprived of it. Nothing in the record before the Court provides any justification for finding the activity forbidden by § 16-6-2 to be physically dangerous, either to the persons engaged in it or to others.[4]

---

4. Although I do not think it necessary to decide today issues that are not even remotely before us, it does seem to me that a court could find simple, analytically sound distinctions between certain private, consensual sexual conduct, on the one hand, and adultery and incest (the only two vaguely specific "sexual crimes" to which the majority points, *ante,* at 2846), on the other. For example, marriage, in addition to its spiritual aspects, is a civil contract that entitles the contracting parties to a variety of governmentally provided benefits. A State might define the contractual commitment necessary to become eligible for these benefits to include a commitment of fidelity and then punish individuals for breaching that contract. Moreover, a State might conclude that adultery is likely to injure third persons, in particular, spouses and children of persons who engage in extramarital affairs. With respect to incest, a court might well agree with respondent that the nature of familial relationships ren-

The core of petitioner's defense of § 16-6-2, however, is that respondent and others who engage in the conduct prohibited by § 16-6-2 interfere with Georgia's exercise of the "'right of the Nation and of the States to maintain a decent society.'" Essentially, petitioner argues, and the Court agrees, that the fact that the acts described in § 16-6-2 "for hundreds of years, if not thousands, have been uniformly condemned as immoral" is a sufficient reason to permit a State to ban them today.

I cannot agree that either the length of time a majority has held its convictions or the passions with which it defends them can withdraw legislation from this Court's scrutiny. See, *e.g., Roe v. Wade*, 410 U.S. 113 (1973); *Loving v. Virginia*, 388 U.S. 1 (1967); *Brown v. Board of Education*, 347 U.S. 483 (1954).[5]....

It is precisely because the issue raised by this case touches the heart of what makes individuals what they are that we should be especially sensitive to the rights of those whose choices upset the majority.

The assertion that "traditional Judeo-Christian values proscribe" the conduct involved cannot provide an adequate justification for § 16-6-2. That certain, but by no means all, religious groups condemn the behavior at issue gives the State no license to impose their judgments on the entire citizenry. The legitimacy of secular legislation depends instead on whether the State can advance some justification for its law beyond its conformity to religious doctrine. Thus, far from buttressing his case, petitioner's invocation of Leviticus, Romans, St. Thomas Aquinas, and sodomy's heretical status during the Middle Ages undermines his suggestion that § 16-6-2 represents a legitimate use of secular coercive power. A State can no more punish private behavior because of religious intolerance than it can punish such behavior because of racial animus. "The Constitution cannot control such prejudices, but neither can it tolerate them. Private biases may be outside the reach of the law, but the law cannot, directly or indirectly, give them effect." *Palmore v. Sidoti*, 466 U.S. 429, 433 (1984). No matter how uncomfortable a certain group may make the majority of this Court, we have held that "[m]ere public intolerance or animosity cannot constitutionally justify the deprivation of a person's physical liberty." *O'Connor v. Donaldson*, 422 U.S. 563, 575 (1975). See also *Cleburne v. Cleburne Living Center, Inc.*, 473 U.S. 432 (1985); *United States Dept. of Agriculture v. Moreno*, 413 U.S. 528, 534 (1973).

Nor can § 16-6-2 be justified as a "morally neutral" exercise of Georgia's power to "protect the public environment," *Paris Adult Theatre I*, 413 U.S., at 68–69. Certainly, some

---

ders true consent to incestuous activity sufficiently problematical that a blanket prohibition of such activity is warranted. Notably, the Court makes no effort to explain why it has chosen to group private, consensual homosexual activity with adultery and incest rather than with private, consensual heterosexual activity by unmarried persons or, indeed, with oral or anal sex within marriage.

5. The parallel between *Loving* and this case is almost uncanny. There, too, the State relied on a religious justification for its law. Compare 388 U.S., at 3, 87 S.Ct., at 1819 (quoting trial court's statement that "Almighty God created the races white, black, yellow, malay and red, and he placed them on separate continents.... The fact that he separated the races shows that he did not intend for the races to mix"), with Brief for Petitioner 20–21 (relying on the Old and New Testaments and the writings of St. Thomas Aquinas to show that "traditional Judeo-Christian values proscribe such conduct"). There, too, defenders of the challenged statute relied heavily on the fact that when the Fourteenth Amendment was ratified, most of the States had similar prohibitions. There, too, at the time the case came before the Court, many of the States still had criminal statutes concerning the conduct at issue. Yet the Court held, not only that the invidious racism of Virginia's law violated the Equal Protection Clause, but also that the law deprived the Lovings of due process by denying them the "freedom of choice to marry" that had "long been recognized as one of the vital personal rights essential to the orderly pursuit of happiness by free men."

private behavior can affect the fabric of society as a whole. Reasonable people may differ about whether particular sexual acts are moral or immoral, but "we have ample evidence for believing that people will not abandon morality, will not think any better of murder, cruelty and dishonesty, merely because some private sexual practice which they abominate is not punished by the law." Petitioner and the Court fail to see the difference between laws that protect public sensibilities and those that enforce private morality. Statutes banning public sexual activity are entirely consistent with protecting the individual's liberty interest in decisions concerning sexual relations: the same recognition that those decisions are intensely private which justifies protecting them from governmental interference can justify protecting individuals from unwilling exposure to the sexual activities of others. But the mere fact that intimate behavior may be punished when it takes place in public cannot dictate how States can regulate intimate behavior that occurs in intimate places.

This case involves no real interference with the rights of others, for the mere knowledge that other individuals do not adhere to one's value system cannot be a legally cognizable interest, let alone an interest that can justify invading the houses, hearts, and minds of citizens who choose to live their lives differently.

IV

It took but three years for the Court to see the error in its analysis in *Minersville School District v. Gobitis*, 310 U.S. 586 (1940), and to recognize that the threat to national cohesion posed by a refusal to salute the flag was vastly outweighed by the threat to those same values posed by compelling such a salute. I can only hope that here, too, the Court soon will reconsider its analysis and conclude that depriving individuals of the right to choose for themselves how to conduct their intimate relationships poses a far greater threat to the values most deeply rooted in our Nation's history than tolerance of nonconformity could ever do. Because I think the Court today betrays those values, I dissent.

Justice STEVENS, with whom Justice BRENNAN and Justice MARSHALL join, dissenting.

Like the statute that is challenged in this case, the rationale of the Court's opinion applies equally to the prohibited conduct regardless of whether the parties who engage in it are married or unmarried, or are of the same or different sexes.[2] Sodomy was condemned as an odious and sinful type of behavior during the formative period of the common law. That condemnation was equally damning for heterosexual and homosexual sodomy. Moreover, it provided no special exemption for married couples. The license to cohabit and to produce legitimate offspring simply did not include any permission to engage in sexual conduct that was considered a "crime against nature."

The history of the Georgia statute before us clearly reveals this traditional prohibition of heterosexual, as well as homosexual, sodomy. Indeed, at one point in the 20th century, Georgia's law was construed to permit certain sexual conduct between homosexual women even though such conduct was prohibited between heterosexuals. The history of the statutes cited by the majority as proof for the proposition that sodomy is not constitutionally protected, similarly reveals a prohibition on heterosexual, as well as homosexual, sodomy.

---

2. The Court states that the "issue presented is whether the Federal Constitution confers a fundamental right upon homosexuals to engage in sodomy and hence invalidates the laws of the many States that still make such conduct illegal and have done so for a very long time." In reality, however, it is the indiscriminate prohibition of sodomy, heterosexual as well as homosexual, that has been present "for a very long time." Moreover, the reasoning the Court employs would provide the same support for the statute as it is written as it does for the statute as it is narrowly construed by the Court.

Because the Georgia statute expresses the traditional view that sodomy is an immoral kind of conduct regardless of the identity of the persons who engage in it, I believe that a proper analysis of its constitutionality requires consideration of two questions: First, may a State totally prohibit the described conduct by means of a neutral law applying without exception to all persons subject to its jurisdiction? If not, may the State save the statute by announcing that it will only enforce the law against homosexuals? The two questions merit separate discussion.

I

Our prior cases make two propositions abundantly clear. First, the fact that the governing majority in a State has traditionally viewed a particular practice as immoral is not a sufficient reason for upholding a law prohibiting the practice; neither history nor tradition could save a law prohibiting miscegenation from constitutional attack.[9] Second, individual decisions by married persons, concerning the intimacies of their physical relationship, even when not intended to produce offspring, are a form of "liberty" protected by the Due Process Clause of the Fourteenth Amendment. *Griswold v. Connecticut,* 381 U.S. 479 (1965). Moreover, this protection extends to intimate choices by unmarried as well as married persons. *Carey v. Population Services International,* 431 U.S. 678 (1977); *Eisenstadt v. Baird,* 405 U.S. 438 (1972).

In consideration of claims of this kind, the Court has emphasized the individual interest in privacy, but its decisions have actually been animated by an even more fundamental concern. As I wrote some years ago:

> "These cases do not deal with the individual's interest in protection from unwarranted public attention, comment, or exploitation. They deal, rather, with the individual's right to make certain unusually important decisions that will affect his own, or his family's, destiny. The Court has referred to such decisions as implicating 'basic values,' as being 'fundamental,' and as being dignified by history and tradition. The character of the Court's language in these cases brings to mind the origins of the American heritage of freedom — the abiding interest in individual liberty that makes certain state intrusions on the citizen's right to decide how he will live his own life intolerable. Guided by history, our tradition of respect for the dignity of individual choice in matters of conscience and the restraints implicit in the federal system, federal judges have accepted the responsibility for recognition and protection of these rights in appropriate cases."

Society has every right to encourage its individual members to follow particular traditions in expressing affection for one another and in gratifying their personal desires. It, of course, may prohibit an individual from imposing his will on another to satisfy his own selfish interests. It also may prevent an individual from interfering with, or violating, a legally sanctioned and protected relationship, such as marriage. And it may explain the relative advantages and disadvantages of different forms of intimate expression. But when individual married couples are isolated from observation by others, the way in which they voluntarily choose to conduct their intimate relations is a matter for them — not the State — to decide.[10] The essential "liberty" that animated the develop-

---

9. See *Loving v. Virginia,* 388 U.S. 1 (1967). Interestingly, miscegenation was once treated as a crime similar to sodomy.

10. Indeed, the Georgia Attorney General concedes that Georgia's statute would be unconstitutional if applied to a married couple. Significantly, Georgia passed the current statute three years after the Court's decision in *Griswold.*

ment of the law in cases like *Griswold, Eisenstadt,* and *Carey* surely embraces the right to engage in nonreproductive, sexual conduct that others may consider offensive or immoral.

Paradoxical as it may seem, our prior cases thus establish that a State may not prohibit sodomy within "the sacred precincts of marital bedrooms," *Griswold,* 381 U.S., at 485, or, indeed, between unmarried heterosexual adults. *Eisenstadt,* 405 U.S., at 453. In all events, it is perfectly clear that the State of Georgia may not totally prohibit the conduct proscribed by § 16-6-2 of the Georgia Criminal Code.

II

If the Georgia statute cannot be enforced as it is written—if the conduct it seeks to prohibit is a protected form of liberty for the vast majority of Georgia's citizens—the State must assume the burden of justifying a selective application of its law. Either the persons to whom Georgia seeks to apply its statute do not have the same interest in "liberty" that others have, or there must be a reason why the State may be permitted to apply a generally applicable law to certain persons that it does not apply to others.

The first possibility is plainly unacceptable. Although the meaning of the principle that "all men are created equal" is not always clear, it surely must mean that every free citizen has the same interest in "liberty" that the members of the majority share. From the standpoint of the individual, the homosexual and the heterosexual have the same interest in deciding how he will live his own life, and, more narrowly, how he will conduct himself in his personal and voluntary associations with his companions. State intrusion into the private conduct of either is equally burdensome.

The second possibility is similarly unacceptable. A policy of selective application must be supported by a neutral and legitimate interest—something more substantial than a habitual dislike for, or ignorance about, the disfavored group. Neither the State nor the Court has identified any such interest in this case. The Court has posited as a justification for the Georgia statute "the presumed belief of a majority of the electorate in Georgia that homosexual sodomy is immoral and unacceptable." But the Georgia electorate has expressed no such belief—instead, its representatives enacted a law that presumably reflects the belief that *all sodomy* is immoral and unacceptable. Unless the Court is prepared to conclude that such a law is constitutional, it may not rely on the work product of the Georgia Legislature to support its holding. For the Georgia statute does not single out homosexuals as a separate class meriting special disfavored treatment.

Nor, indeed, does the Georgia prosecutor even believe that all homosexuals who violate this statute should be punished. This conclusion is evident from the fact that the respondent in this very case has formally acknowledged in his complaint and in court that he has engaged, and intends to continue to engage, in the prohibited conduct, yet the State has elected not to process criminal charges against him. As Justice POWELL points out, moreover, Georgia's prohibition on private, consensual sodomy has not been enforced for decades. The record of nonenforcement, in this case and in the last several decades, belies the Attorney General's representations about the importance of the State's selective application of its generally applicable law.

Both the Georgia statute and the Georgia prosecutor thus completely fail to provide the Court with any support for the conclusion that homosexual sodomy, *simpliciter,* is considered unacceptable conduct in that State, and that the burden of justifying a selective application of the generally applicable law has been met.

III

The Court orders the dismissal of respondent's complaint even though the State's statute prohibits all sodomy; even though that prohibition is concededly unconstitutional with respect to heterosexuals; and even though the State's *post hoc* explanations for selective application are belied by the State's own actions. At the very least, I think it clear at this early stage of the litigation that respondent has alleged a constitutional claim sufficient to withstand a motion to dismiss.

I respectfully dissent.

Notes and Questions

1. During deliberations on *Bowers v. Hardwick*, Justice Powell changed his vote, initially voting to strike down the law on Eighth Amendment grounds, but later changing his mind. One of Justice Powell's law clerks at the time was gay, but never disclosed that fact to the Justice. During the clerk's discussions with Justice Powell, the Justice said, "I don't believe I've ever met a homosexual," to which his gay clerk replied, "Certainly you have, but you just don't know that they are." *See* John C. Jeffries, Jr., Justice Lewis F. Powell, Jr. 511–29 (1994). Four years after *Bowers* was decided, Justice Powell publicly stated that he "probably made a mistake" in *Bowers. See id.* at 530. Would the outcome have been different had his clerk come out to him, and if so, *should* it have impacted the outcome?

2. Recall from Chapter 2 that the lower court in *Bowers* held that there was standing to adjudicate the case. Should the U.S. Supreme Court have accepted that holding? To what extent, do you suppose, was the Court's willingness to uphold the law made easier by the fact that nobody was facing a criminal conviction in this case? At the very least, to what extent did that impact Justice Powell? In this regard, consider Justice Rehnquist's statement in *Valley Forge* that the requirement of Article III standing "tends to assure that the legal questions presented to the court will be resolved, not in the rarified atmosphere of a debating society, but in a concrete factual context conducive to a realistic appreciation of the consequences of judicial action." For an argument that Hardwick did not have standing, and that the lack of actual consequences to him made it easier for the Court to rule against him on his constitutional claim, *see* Donald A. Dripps, Bowers v. Hardwick *and the Law of Standing: Noncases Make Bad Law*, 44 Emory L.J. 1417 (1995).

3. To what extent is the outcome in *Bowers* pre-determined by the way in which Justice White frames both the right identified in its prior cases and the right claimed by Hardwick in this case? Note, in contrast, the way in which Justice Blackmun frames the right claimed and the right previously recognized. Compare as well the way in which the *Roe* Court framed the right at issue in that case. What are the advantages and disadvantages of each approach?

4. What is the role of history in *Bowers*? How does it compare with the role history played in *Roe*?

5. Justice White criticizes the *Meyer*, *Prince*, and *Pierce* cases, along with the privacy cases from *Griswold* to *Carey*, as "recognizing rights that have little or no textual support." He leaves out two other cases in the list immediately preceding this criticism: *Loving v. Virginia* and *Skinner v. Oklahoma*. Why are those two cases left off of the list? Is he perhaps re-characterizing those cases, or instead maybe undoing an earlier re-characterization of those cases by the Court? Reconsider this question after reading Chapter 5, where *Loving* is examined in greater detail.

6. In rejecting a more broadly framed right that encompasses voluntary sexual conduct between consenting adults in the home, Justice White notes that it would be difficult to distinguish homosexual conduct from adultery, incest, and other sexual crimes. How persuasive is this claim? Wouldn't a principle that focused on whether there was harm to others—as suggested by Justice Blackmun in note 4 of his dissent—serve to distinguish homosexual conduct from Justice White's list? Indeed, wouldn't such a principle make *Bowers* an easier case than *Roe*, which arguably involved harm to others (i.e., the unborn fetus) in a way that *Bowers* did not?

7. To the extent that the unenumerated right at issue is "privacy," isn't the claim to "privacy" at least as strong, if not stronger, in *Bowers* than it was in *Roe*? To what extent does this turn on the definition of "privacy"?

8. Justice White rather easily concludes that majority sentiments regarding morality suffice to justify the sodomy law. Is this consistent with the Court's earlier decisions in *Eisenstadt* and *Roe*, which each quickly dismissed morality-based rationales for the laws at issue in those cases? Perhaps the difference between *Roe* and *Bowers* can be explained by the level of scrutiny (strict versus rational basis), but what about the difference between *Eisenstadt* and *Bowers*, both of which purport to apply rational basis? Is it possible that morality can serve as a rational basis in due process but not equal protection challenges?

9. In Justice Blackmun's dissent, he brushes to one side a rationale for criminalizing sodomy raised by the state: preventing the spread of communicable diseases. Is that such an unsound rationale for the law? Might it have been more sound if, say, limited to anal intercourse and supported by scientific evidence indicating increased risks of disease transmission? To what extent was this concern likely on the minds of the Justices, who decided this case in the mid-1980s, at the height of the AIDS crisis in the United States?

10. Justices White and Blackmun both cite to the Court's earlier decision in *Moore v. City of East Cleveland*, 431 U.S. 494 (1977). In that case, the Court invalidated—on substantive due process grounds—a housing ordinance that criminalized living arrangements other than those consisting of a nuclear family. In striking down the ordinance, the Court distinguished its earlier decision in *Belle Terre v. Boraas*, 416 U.S. 1 (1974), upholding a housing ordinance prohibiting unrelated persons from living together:

> [O]ne overriding factor sets this case apart from *Belle Terre*. The ordinance there affected only *unrelated* individuals. It expressly allowed all who were related by "blood, adoption, or marriage" to live together, and in sustaining the ordinance we were careful to note that it promoted "family needs" and "family values." East Cleveland, in contrast, has chosen to regulate the occupancy of its housing by slicing deeply into the family itself.... In particular, it makes a crime of a grandmother's choice to live with her grandson in circumstances like those presented here....

> Ours is by no means a tradition limited to respect for the bonds uniting the members of the nuclear family. The tradition of uncles, aunts, cousins, and especially grandparents sharing a household along with parents and children has roots equally venerable and equally deserving of constitutional recognition.

Moore, 431 U.S. at 498–99, 504.

11. What do you make of the approach to the question that Justice Stevens takes in his dissent? Is it not akin to the reasoning employed by Justice Brennan in *Eisenstadt*? Under his approach, are due process and equal protection working independently or as a team?

12. As indicated by Justice White in note 8 of his opinion for the Court, the opinion does not address the question whether the statute violates the Equal Protection Clause.

What would be the Equal Protection Clause claim, given that the statute, in terms, applies equally to sodomy performed between same-sex and opposite-sex couples? Might a claim akin to that made in *Eisenstadt* succeed? The efficacy of Equal Protection Clause challenges to sodomy laws will be examined in Chapter 4.

13. In light of post-*Bowers* case law holding that the Eighth Amendment has a "narrow proportionality principle" in noncapital cases, *see Ewing v. California*, 538 U.S. 11 (2003) (upholding California's "three strikes" law imposing sentence of 25 years to life for third felony involving theft of golf clubs), the Eighth Amendment challenge to Georgia's sodomy law raised by Justice Powell's concurrence would not likely be accepted by the Court today.

However, the Eighth Amendment has served as a useful vehicle for transgendered prison inmates seeking hormone treatment or sex reassignment surgery. Characterizing gender identity disorder as a serious medical need of prisoners, some federal courts have held that a refusal to provide treatment where medically necessary violates the Eighth Amendment's ban on cruel and unusual punishment. *E.g.*, *Fields v. Smith*, 653 F.3d 550, 554–59 (7th Cir. 2011).

E. The In-Between Years

Far from definitively settling the issues before them, *Roe* and *Bowers* spawned decades of legislative and litigation battles regarding the criminalization of abortion and sodomy.

Gay rights activists turned their attention to the state legislatures and state courts, lobbying for legislative repeal of sodomy laws as well as the invalidation of sodomy laws based on state constitutional provisions. This two-pronged approach proved successful, and resulted in the repeal or invalidation of sodomy laws in twelve different states, reducing the total number of states with criminal sodomy laws to just over a dozen. Indeed, twelve years after the U.S. Supreme Court decided *Bowers*, the Georgia Supreme Court held — in *Powell v. State*, 510 S.E.2d 18 (Ga. 1998) — that the very same law at issue in *Bowers* violated the Due Process Clause of the Georgia Constitution.

At the same time, proponents and opponents of abortion litigated the scope of *Roe*, contesting such matters as the constitutionality of parental and spousal consent laws, informed consent requirements, waiting periods, and the like.

During the 1990s, the U.S. Supreme Court revisited its substantive due process line of cases in two decisions, excerpted below. The first of these decisions, *Planned Parenthood of Southeastern Pennsylvania v. Casey*, 505 U.S. 833 (1992), involved a state law regulating abortion, and the Court was asked by the United States (acting as *amicus curiae*) to overrule *Roe* on the ground that it was wrongly decided. The second of these decisions, *Washington v. Glucksberg*, 521 U.S. 702 (1997) — an excerpt of which appeared at the start of this chapter — involved a challenge to the constitutionality of a state law banning physician-assisted suicide.

As you read these two excerpts, consider the extent to which they modify or clarify the Court's prior line of substantive due process cases and the impact, if any, of that modification or clarification on the question whether *Bowers* was correctly decided.

Planned Parenthood of Southeastern Pennsylvania v. Casey
505 U.S. 833 (1992)

Justice O'CONNOR, Justice KENNEDY, and Justice SOUTER announced the judgment of the Court and delivered the opinion of the Court with respect to Parts I, II, III, V-A, V-C, and VI, an opinion with respect to Part V-E, in which Justice STEVENS joins, and an opinion with respect to Parts IV, V-B, and V-D.

I

Liberty finds no refuge in a jurisprudence of doubt. Yet 19 years after our holding that the Constitution protects a woman's right to terminate her pregnancy in its early stages, *Roe v. Wade*, 410 U.S. 113 (1973), that definition of liberty is still questioned. Joining the respondents as *amicus curiae,* the United States, as it has done in five other cases in the last decade, again asks us to overrule *Roe*....

[The Court describes the Pennsylvania abortion statute being challenged in the case, which contains: (a) an informed consent provision with a 24-hour waiting period; (b) a parental consent provision for minors seeking an abortion (with a judicial bypass option); (c) a spousal notification provision for adult women seeking an abortion; and (d) a provision imposing certain reporting requirements on facilities that provide abortion services.]

After considering the fundamental constitutional questions resolved by *Roe*, principles of institutional integrity, and the rule of *stare decisis,* we are led to conclude this: the essential holding of *Roe v. Wade* should be retained and once again reaffirmed.

It must be stated at the outset and with clarity that *Roe*'s essential holding, the holding we reaffirm, has three parts. First is a recognition of the right of the woman to choose to have an abortion before viability and to obtain it without undue interference from the State. Before viability, the State's interests are not strong enough to support a prohibition of abortion or the imposition of a substantial obstacle to the woman's effective right to elect the procedure. Second is a confirmation of the State's power to restrict abortions after fetal viability, if the law contains exceptions for pregnancies which endanger the woman's life or health. And third is the principle that the State has legitimate interests from the outset of the pregnancy in protecting the health of the woman and the life of the fetus that may become a child. These principles do not contradict one another; and we adhere to each.

II

Constitutional protection of the woman's decision to terminate her pregnancy derives from the Due Process Clause of the Fourteenth Amendment. It declares that no State shall "deprive any person of life, liberty, or property, without due process of law." The controlling word in the cases before us is "liberty." ....

It is tempting, as a means of curbing the discretion of federal judges, to suppose that liberty encompasses no more than those rights already guaranteed to the individual against federal interference by the express provisions of the first eight Amendments to the Constitution. But of course this Court has never accepted that view.

It is also tempting, for the same reason, to suppose that the Due Process Clause protects only those practices, defined at the most specific level, that were protected against government interference by other rules of law when the Fourteenth Amendment was ratified. But such a view would be inconsistent with our law. It is a promise of the Constitution that there is a realm of personal liberty which the government may not enter. We have vindicated this principle before. Marriage is mentioned nowhere in the Bill of Rights and interracial marriage was illegal in most States in the 19th century, but the Court was no doubt correct in finding it to be an aspect of liberty protected against state interference by the substantive component of the Due Process Clause in *Loving v. Virginia,* 388 U.S. 1, 12 (1967)....

Neither the Bill of Rights nor the specific practices of States at the time of the adoption of the Fourteenth Amendment marks the outer limits of the substantive sphere of liberty which the Fourteenth Amendment protects. See U.S. Const., Amdt. 9....

It is settled now, as it was when the Court heard arguments in *Roe v. Wade,* that the Constitution places limits on a State's right to interfere with a person's most basic decisions about family and parenthood, as well as bodily integrity....

Our law affords constitutional protection to personal decisions relating to marriage, procreation, contraception, family relationships, child rearing, and education. Our cases recognize "the right of the *individual,* married or single, to be free from unwarranted governmental intrusion into matters so fundamentally affecting a person as the decision whether to bear or beget a child." *Eisenstadt v. Baird,* 405 U.S., at 453 (emphasis in original). Our precedents "have respected the private realm of family life which the state cannot enter." *Prince v. Massachusetts,* 321 U.S. 158, 166 (1944). These matters, involving the most intimate and personal choices a person may make in a lifetime, choices central to personal dignity and autonomy, are central to the liberty protected by the Fourteenth Amendment. At the heart of liberty is the right to define one's own concept of existence, of meaning, of the universe, and of the mystery of human life. Beliefs about these matters could not define the attributes of personhood were they formed under compulsion of the State.

These considerations begin our analysis of the woman's interest in terminating her pregnancy but cannot end it, for this reason: though the abortion decision may originate within the zone of conscience and belief, it is more than a philosophic exercise. Abortion is a unique act. It is an act fraught with consequences for others: for the woman who must live with the implications of her decision; for the persons who perform and assist in the procedure; for the spouse, family, and society which must confront the knowledge that these procedures exist, procedures some deem nothing short of an act of violence against innocent human life; and, depending on one's beliefs, for the life or potential life that is aborted. Though abortion is conduct, it does not follow that the State is entitled to proscribe it in all instances. That is because the liberty of the woman is at stake in a sense unique to the human condition and so unique to the law. The mother who carries a child to full term is subject to anxieties, to physical constraints, to pain that only she must bear. That these sacrifices have from the beginning of the human race been endured by woman with a pride that ennobles her in the eyes of others and gives to the infant a bond of love cannot alone be grounds for the State to insist she make the sacrifice. Her suffering is too intimate and personal for the State to insist, without more, upon its own vision of the woman's role, however dominant that vision has been in the course of our history and our culture. The destiny of the woman must be shaped to a large extent on her own conception of her spiritual imperatives and her place in society.

It should be recognized, moreover, that in some critical respects the abortion decision is of the same character as the decision to use contraception, to which *Griswold v. Connecticut, Eisenstadt v. Baird,* and *Carey v. Population Services International* afford constitutional protection. We have no doubt as to the correctness of those decisions. They support the reasoning in *Roe* relating to the woman's liberty because they involve personal decisions concerning not only the meaning of procreation but also human responsibility and respect for it.…

It was this dimension of personal liberty that *Roe* sought to protect, and its holding invoked the reasoning and the tradition of the precedents we have discussed, granting protection to substantive liberties of the person. *Roe* was, of course, an extension of those cases.…

III

A

[I]t is common wisdom that the rule of *stare decisis* is not an "inexorable command," and certainly it is not such in every constitutional case. Rather, when this Court reexamines a prior holding, its judgment is customarily informed by a series of prudential and pragmatic considerations designed to test the consistency of overruling a prior decision with the ideal of the rule of law, and to gauge the respective costs of reaffirming and overruling a prior case. Thus, for example, we may ask whether the rule has proven to be intolerable simply in defying practical workability; whether the rule is subject to a kind of reliance that would lend a special hardship to the consequences of overruling and add inequity to the cost of repudiation; whether related principles of law have so far developed as to have left the old rule no more than a remnant of abandoned doctrine; or whether facts have so changed, or come to be seen so differently, as to have robbed the old rule of significant application or justification.…

1

Although *Roe* has engendered opposition, it has in no sense proven "unworkable," representing as it does a simple limitation beyond which a state law is unenforceable. While *Roe* has, of course, required judicial assessment of state laws affecting the exercise of the choice guaranteed against government infringement, and although the need for such review will remain as a consequence of today's decision, the required determinations fall within judicial competence.

2

The inquiry into reliance counts the cost of a rule's repudiation as it would fall on those who have relied reasonably on the rule's continued application....

[F]or two decades of economic and social developments, people have organized intimate relationships and made choices that define their views of themselves and their places in society, in reliance on the availability of abortion in the event that contraception should fail. The ability of women to participate equally in the economic and social life of the Nation has been facilitated by their ability to control their reproductive lives. The Constitution serves human values, and while the effect of reliance on *Roe* cannot be exactly measured, neither can the certain cost of overruling *Roe* for people who have ordered their thinking and living around that case be dismissed.

3

No evolution of legal principle has left *Roe* 's doctrinal footings weaker than they were in 1973. No development of constitutional law since the case was decided has implicitly or explicitly left *Roe* behind as a mere survivor of obsolete constitutional thinking....

4

We have seen how time has overtaken some of *Roe*'s factual assumptions: advances in maternal health care allow for abortions safe to the mother later in pregnancy than was true in 1973, and advances in neonatal care have advanced viability to a point somewhat earlier. But these facts go only to the scheme of time limits on the realization of competing interests, and the divergences from the factual premises of 1973 have no bearing on the validity of *Roe*'s central holding, that viability marks the earliest point at which the State's interest in fetal life is constitutionally adequate to justify a legislative ban on nontherapeutic abortions. The soundness or unsoundness of that constitutional judgment in no sense turns on whether viability occurs at approximately 28 weeks, as was usual at the time of *Roe,* at 23 to 24 weeks, as it sometimes does today, or at some moment even slightly earlier in pregnancy, as it may if fetal respiratory capacity can somehow be enhanced in the future. Whenever it may occur, the attainment of viability may continue to serve as the critical fact, just as it has done since *Roe* was decided; which is to say that no change in *Roe* 's factual underpinning has left its central holding obsolete, and none supports an argument for overruling it....

B

In a less significant case, *stare decisis* analysis could, and would, stop at the point we have reached. But the sustained and widespread debate *Roe* has provoked calls for some comparison between that case and others of comparable dimension that have responded to national controversies and taken on the impress of the controversies addressed....

C

....

Where, in the performance of its judicial duties, the Court decides a case in such a way as to resolve the sort of intensely divisive controversy reflected in *Roe* and those rare, comparable cases, its decision has a dimension that the resolution of the normal case does not carry. It is the dimension present whenever the Court's interpretation of the Constitution calls the contending sides of a national controversy to end their national division by accepting a common mandate rooted in the Constitution.

The Court is not asked to do this very often, having thus addressed the Nation only twice in our lifetime, in the decisions of *Brown* [*v. Board of Education*] and *Roe*. But when the Court does act in this way, its decision requires an equally rare precedential force to counter the inevitable efforts to overturn it and to thwart its implementation. Some of those efforts may be mere unprincipled emotional reactions; others may proceed from principles worthy of profound respect. But whatever the premises of opposition may be, only the most convincing justification under accepted standards of precedent could suffice to demonstrate that a later decision overruling the first was anything but a surrender to political pressure, and an unjustified repudiation of the principle on which the Court staked its authority in the first instance. So to overrule under fire in the absence of the most compelling reason to reexamine a watershed decision would subvert the Court's legitimacy beyond any serious question. . . .

IV

From what we have said so far it follows that it is a constitutional liberty of the woman to have some freedom to terminate her pregnancy. We conclude that the basic decision in *Roe* was based on a constitutional analysis which we cannot now repudiate. The woman's liberty is not so unlimited, however, that from the outset the State cannot show its concern for the life of the unborn, and at a later point in fetal development the State's interest in life has sufficient force so that the right of the woman to terminate the pregnancy can be restricted. . . .

We conclude the line should be drawn at viability, so that before that time the woman has a right to choose to terminate her pregnancy. . . .

Roe established a trimester framework to govern abortion regulations. Under this elaborate but rigid construct, almost no regulation at all is permitted during the first trimester of pregnancy; regulations designed to protect the woman's health, but not to further the State's interest in potential life, are permitted during the second trimester; and during the third trimester, when the fetus is viable, prohibitions are permitted provided the life or health of the mother is not at stake. . . .

We reject the trimester framework, which we do not consider to be part of the essential holding of *Roe*. . . . The trimester framework suffers from these basic flaws: in its formulation it misconceives the nature of the pregnant woman's interest; and in practice it undervalues the State's interest in potential life, as recognized in *Roe*. . . .

Numerous forms of state regulation might have the incidental effect of increasing the cost or decreasing the availability of medical care, whether for abortion or any other medical procedure. The fact that a law which serves a valid purpose, one not designed to strike at the right itself, has the incidental effect of making it more difficult or more expensive to procure an abortion cannot be enough to invalidate it. Only where state regulation imposes an undue burden on a woman's ability to make this decision does the power of the State reach into the heart of the liberty protected by the Due Process Clause. . . .

The very notion that the State has a substantial interest in potential life leads to the conclusion that not all regulations must be deemed unwarranted. Not all burdens on the right to decide whether to terminate a pregnancy will be undue. In our view, the undue burden standard is the appropriate means of reconciling the State's interest with the woman's constitutionally protected liberty. . . .

A finding of an undue burden is a shorthand for the conclusion that a state regulation has the purpose or effect of placing a substantial obstacle in the path of a woman seeking an abortion of a nonviable fetus. A statute with this purpose is invalid because the means chosen by the State to further the interest in potential life must be calculated to inform the woman's free choice, not hinder it. And a statute which, while furthering the interest in potential life or some other valid state interest, has the effect of placing a substantial obstacle in the path of a woman's choice cannot be considered a permissible means of serving its legitimate ends....

Some guiding principles should emerge. What is at stake is the woman's right to make the ultimate decision, not a right to be insulated from all others in doing so. Regulations which do no more than create a structural mechanism by which the State, or the parent or guardian of a minor, may express profound respect for the life of the unborn are permitted, if they are not a substantial obstacle to the woman's exercise of the right to choose. Unless it has that effect on her right of choice, a state measure designed to persuade her to choose childbirth over abortion will be upheld if reasonably related to that goal. Regulations designed to foster the health of a woman seeking an abortion are valid if they do not constitute an undue burden....

[Applying the "undue burden" standard, the Court proceeds to strike down the spousal consent provision, but upholds all other portions of the Pennsylvania statute.]

[The opinions of Justices Stevens, Blackmun, Scalia, and Chief Justice Rehnquist, concurring in part and dissenting in part, are omitted.]

Washington v. Glucksberg
521 U.S. 702 (1997)

Chief Justice REHNQUIST delivered the opinion of the Court.

[The Chief Justice summarizes the facts of the case, which involves a group of physicians and terminally ill patients as well as a nonprofit organization bringing suit against the State of Washington, seeking a declaration that its law banning physician-assisted suicide violates the Due Process Clause of the Fourteenth Amendment.]

II

Our established method of substantive-due-process analysis has two primary features: First, we have regularly observed that the Due Process Clause specially protects those fundamental rights and liberties which are, objectively, "deeply rooted in this Nation's history and tradition," and "implicit in the concept of ordered liberty," such that "neither liberty nor justice would exist if they were sacrificed." Second, we have required in substantive-due-process cases a "careful description" of the asserted fundamental liberty interest....

Turning to the claim at issue here, the Court of Appeals stated that "[p]roperly analyzed, the first issue to be resolved is whether there is a liberty interest in determining the time and manner of one's death," or, in other words, "[i]s there a right to die?" Similarly, respondents assert a "liberty to choose how to die" and a right to "control of one's final days," and describe the asserted liberty as "the right to choose a humane, dignified death," and "the liberty to shape death." As noted above, we have a tradition of carefully formulating the interest at stake in substantive-due-process cases. For example, although *Cruzan* [*v. Director, Mo. Dept. of Health*] is often described as a "right to die" case, we were, in fact, more precise: We assumed that the Constitution granted competent persons a "constitutionally protected right to refuse lifesaving hydration and nutrition." The Washington statute at issue in this case prohibits "aid[ing] another person to attempt suicide," and, thus, the question before us is whether the "liberty" specially protected by the Due

Process Clause includes a right to commit suicide which itself includes a right to assistance in doing so.

We now inquire whether this asserted right has any place in our Nation's traditions. Here … we are confronted with a consistent and almost universal tradition that has long rejected the asserted right, and continues explicitly to reject it today, even for terminally ill, mentally competent adults. To hold for respondents, we would have to reverse centuries of legal doctrine and practice, and strike down the considered policy choice of almost every State.…

Respondents contend, however, that the liberty interest they assert *is* consistent with this Court's substantive-due-process line of cases, if not with this Nation's history and practice. Pointing to *Casey* and *Cruzan*, respondents read our jurisprudence in this area as reflecting a general tradition of "self-sovereignty," and as teaching that the "liberty" protected by the Due Process Clause includes "basic and intimate exercises of personal autonomy," see *Casey*, 505 U.S., at 847 ("It is a promise of the Constitution that there is a realm of personal liberty which the government may not enter"). According to respondents, our liberty jurisprudence, and the broad, individualistic principles it reflects, protects the "liberty of competent, terminally ill adults to make end-of-life decisions free of undue government interference." The question presented in this case, however, is whether the protections of the Due Process Clause include a right to commit suicide with another's assistance. With this "careful description" of respondents' claim in mind, we turn to *Casey* and *Cruzan*.

In *Cruzan*, we considered whether Nancy Beth Cruzan, who had been severely injured in an automobile accident and was in a persistive vegetative state, "ha[d] a right under the United States Constitution which would require the hospital to withdraw life-sustaining treatment" at her parents' request. We began with the observation that "[a]t common law, even the touching of one person by another without consent and without legal justification was a battery." We then discussed the related rule that "informed consent is generally required for medical treatment." After reviewing a long line of relevant state cases, we concluded that "the common-law doctrine of informed consent is viewed as generally encompassing the right of a competent individual to refuse medical treatment." Next, we reviewed our own cases on the subject, and stated that "[t]he principle that a competent person has a constitutionally protected liberty interest in refusing unwanted medical treatment may be inferred from our prior decisions." Therefore, "for purposes of [that] case, we assume[d] that the United States Constitution would grant a competent person a constitutionally protected right to refuse lifesaving hydration and nutrition." We concluded that, notwithstanding this right, the Constitution permitted Missouri to require clear and convincing evidence of an incompetent patient's wishes concerning the withdrawal of life-sustaining treatment.…

The right assumed in *Cruzan* … was not simply deduced from abstract concepts of personal autonomy. Given the common-law rule that forced medication was a battery, and the long legal tradition protecting the decision to refuse unwanted medical treatment, our assumption was entirely consistent with this Nation's history and constitutional traditions. The decision to commit suicide with the assistance of another may be just as personal and profound as the decision to refuse unwanted medical treatment, but it has never enjoyed similar legal protection.…

Respondents also rely on *Casey*.… [R]espondents emphasize the statement in *Casey* that:

> "At the heart of liberty is the right to define one's own concept of existence, of meaning, of the universe, and of the mystery of human life. Beliefs about these

matters could not define the attributes of personhood were they formed under compulsion of the State."

By choosing this language, the Court's opinion in *Casey* described, in a general way and in light of our prior cases, those personal activities and decisions that this Court has identified as so deeply rooted in our history and traditions, or so fundamental to our concept of constitutionally ordered liberty, that they are protected by the Fourteenth Amendment. The opinion moved from the recognition that liberty necessarily includes freedom of conscience and belief about ultimate considerations to the observation that "though the abortion decision may originate within the zone of conscience and belief, it is *more than a philosophic exercise.*" That many of the rights and liberties protected by the Due Process Clause sound in personal autonomy does not warrant the sweeping conclusion that any and all important, intimate, and personal decisions are so protected, and *Casey* did not suggest otherwise.

The history of the law's treatment of assisted suicide in this country has been and continues to be one of the rejection of nearly all efforts to permit it. That being the case, our decisions lead us to conclude that the asserted "right" to assistance in committing suicide is not a fundamental liberty interest protected by the Due Process Clause....

[The concurring opinions of Justices Souter, O'Connor, Stevens, Ginsburg and Breyer are omitted.]

Notes and Questions

1. Recall that in *Griswold*, *Roe*, and *Bowers*, the Court spoke about a right to "privacy." Does the term "privacy" appear anywhere within the excerpts from *Casey* or *Glucksberg*? How, if at all, is the switch in terminology relevant?

2. As contrasted with the "strict scrutiny" standard employed in *Roe*, how protective is the "undue burden" standard of the abortion right articulated in *Casey*? In this regard, consider that the Court had—after *Roe* but prior to *Casey*—struck down informed consent provisions and waiting periods. *See Akron v. Akron Ctr. for Reprod. Health, Inc.*, 462 U.S. 416 (1983).

3. *Casey* uses breathtakingly broad language to describe the scope of the due process right at issue in the case. How does that compare with the more narrow focus of *Bowers*, which preceded it? With *Glucksberg*, which follows it? Are these three decisions reconcilable?

4. In *Casey*, the Court sets forth a series of factors to consider in deciding whether to overturn existing precedent. If the Court were asked to reconsider *Bowers*, in which way would these factors point?

5. In between its decisions in *Casey* and *Glucksberg*, the U.S. Supreme Court, in *Romer v. Evans*, 517 U.S. 620 (1996), struck down as violative of the Equal Protection Clause of the Fourteenth Amendment a 1992 amendment to the Colorado Constitution that both repealed local ordinances banning discrimination on the basis of sexual orientation and prohibited all levels of state government from enacting any laws outlawing discrimination on that basis. In so holding, the majority made no mention whatsoever of its earlier decision in *Bowers*, a point made by Justice Scalia in dissent. *See id.* at 640 (Scalia, J., dissenting) ("The case most relevant to the issue before us today is not even mentioned in the Court's opinion: In *Bowers v. Hardwick*, 478 U.S. 186 (1986), we held that the Constitution does not prohibit what virtually all States had done from the founding of the Republic until very recent years—making homo-

sexual conduct a crime."). The *Romer* decision is examined in greater detail in Chapter 4. To what extent, if any, does *Romer* (an equal protection case) cast doubt on *Bowers'* efficacy?

F. The Second Sodomy Case

Lawrence v. Texas
539 U.S. 558 (2003)

Justice KENNEDY delivered the opinion of the Court.

Liberty protects the person from unwarranted government intrusions into a dwelling or other private places. In our tradition the State is not omnipresent in the home. And there are other spheres of our lives and existence, outside the home, where the State should not be a dominant presence. Freedom extends beyond spatial bounds. Liberty presumes an autonomy of self that includes freedom of thought, belief, expression, and certain intimate conduct. The instant case involves liberty of the person both in its spatial and in its more transcendent dimensions.

I

The question before the Court is the validity of a Texas statute making it a crime for two persons of the same sex to engage in certain intimate sexual conduct.

In Houston, Texas, officers of the Harris County Police Department were dispatched to a private residence in response to a reported weapons disturbance. They entered an apartment where one of the petitioners, John Geddes Lawrence, resided. The right of the police to enter does not seem to have been questioned. The officers observed Lawrence and another man, Tyron Garner, engaging in a sexual act. The two petitioners were arrested, held in custody overnight, and charged and convicted before a Justice of the Peace.

The complaints described their crime as "deviate sexual intercourse, namely anal sex, with a member of the same sex (man)." The applicable state law is Tex. Penal Code Ann. § 21.06(a) (2003). It provides: "A person commits an offense if he engages in deviate sexual intercourse with another individual of the same sex." The statute defines "[d]eviate sexual intercourse" as follows:

"(A) any contact between any part of the genitals of one person and the mouth or anus of another person; or

"(B) the penetration of the genitals or the anus of another person with an object." § 21.01(1).

The petitioners exercised their right to a trial *de novo* in Harris County Criminal Court. They challenged the statute as a violation of the Equal Protection Clause of the Fourteenth Amendment and of a like provision of the Texas Constitution. Tex. Const., Art. 1, § 3a. Those contentions were rejected. The petitioners, having entered a plea of *nolo contendere,* were each fined $200 and assessed court costs of $141.25.

The Court of Appeals for the Texas Fourteenth District considered the petitioners' federal constitutional arguments under both the Equal Protection and Due Process Clauses of the Fourteenth Amendment. After hearing the case en banc the court, in a divided opinion, rejected the constitutional arguments and affirmed the convictions. The majority opinion indicates that the Court of Appeals considered our decision in *Bowers v. Hard-*

wick, 478 U.S. 186 (1986), to be controlling on the federal due process aspect of the case. *Bowers* then being authoritative, this was proper.

We granted certiorari to consider three questions:

1. Whether petitioners' criminal convictions under the Texas 'Homosexual Conduct' law—which criminalizes sexual intimacy by same-sex couples, but not identical behavior by different-sex couples—violate the Fourteenth Amendment guarantee of equal protection of the laws.

2. Whether petitioners' criminal convictions for adult consensual sexual intimacy in the home violate their vital interests in liberty and privacy protected by the Due Process Clause of the Fourteenth Amendment.

3. Whether *Bowers v. Hardwick, supra,* should be overruled.

The petitioners were adults at the time of the alleged offense. Their conduct was in private and consensual.

II

We conclude the case should be resolved by determining whether the petitioners were free as adults to engage in the private conduct in the exercise of their liberty under the Due Process Clause of the Fourteenth Amendment to the Constitution. For this inquiry we deem it necessary to reconsider the Court's holding in *Bowers.*

There are broad statements of the substantive reach of liberty under the Due Process Clause in earlier cases, including *Pierce v. Society of Sisters,* 268 U.S. 510 (1925), and *Meyer v. Nebraska,* 262 U.S. 390 (1923); but the most pertinent beginning point is our decision in *Griswold v. Connecticut,* 381 U.S. 479 (1965).

In *Griswold* the Court invalidated a state law prohibiting the use of drugs or devices of contraception and counseling or aiding and abetting the use of contraceptives. The Court described the protected interest as a right to privacy and placed emphasis on the marriage relation and the protected space of the marital bedroom.

After *Griswold* it was established that the right to make certain decisions regarding sexual conduct extends beyond the marital relationship. In *Eisenstadt v. Baird,* 405 U.S. 438 (1972), the Court invalidated a law prohibiting the distribution of contraceptives to unmarried persons. The case was decided under the Equal Protection Clause; but with respect to unmarried persons, the Court went on to state the fundamental proposition that the law impaired the exercise of their personal rights. It quoted from the statement of the Court of Appeals finding the law to be in conflict with fundamental human rights, and it followed with this statement of its own:

> "It is true that in *Griswold* the right of privacy in question inhered in the marital relationship.... If the right of privacy means anything, it is the right of the *individual,* married or single, to be free from unwarranted governmental intrusion into matters so fundamentally affecting a person as the decision whether to bear or beget a child."

The opinions in *Griswold* and *Eisenstadt* were part of the background for the decision in *Roe v. Wade,* 410 U.S. 113 (1973). As is well known, the case involved a challenge to the Texas law prohibiting abortions, but the laws of other States were affected as well. Although the Court held the woman's rights were not absolute, her right to elect an abortion did have real and substantial protection as an exercise of her liberty under the Due Process Clause. The Court cited cases that protect spatial freedom and cases that go well beyond it. *Roe* recognized the right of a woman to make certain fundamental decisions affecting her destiny and confirmed once more that the protection of liberty under the Due Process Clause has a substantive dimension of fundamental significance in defining the rights of the person.

In *Carey v. Population Services Int'l,* 431 U.S. 678 (1977), the Court confronted a New York law forbidding sale or distribution of contraceptive devices to persons under 16 years of age. Although there was no single opinion for the Court, the law was invalidated. Both *Eisenstadt* and *Carey,* as well as the holding and rationale in *Roe,* confirmed that the reasoning of *Griswold* could not be confined to the protection of rights of married adults. This was the state of the law with respect to some of the most relevant cases when the Court considered *Bowers v. Hardwick.*

The facts in *Bowers* had some similarities to the instant case. A police officer, whose right to enter seems not to have been in question, observed Hardwick, in his own bedroom, engaging in intimate sexual conduct with another adult male. The conduct was in violation of a Georgia statute making it a criminal offense to engage in sodomy. One difference between the two cases is that the Georgia statute prohibited the conduct whether or not the participants were of the same sex, while the Texas statute, as we have seen, applies only to participants of the same sex. Hardwick was not prosecuted, but he brought an action in federal court to declare the state statute invalid. He alleged he was a practicing homosexual and that the criminal prohibition violated rights guaranteed to him by the Constitution. The Court, in an opinion by Justice White, sustained the Georgia law. Chief Justice Burger and Justice Powell joined the opinion of the Court and filed separate, concurring opinions. Four Justices dissented.

The Court began its substantive discussion in *Bowers* as follows: "The issue presented is whether the Federal Constitution confers a fundamental right upon homosexuals to engage in sodomy and hence invalidates the laws of the many States that still make such conduct illegal and have done so for a very long time." That statement, we now conclude, discloses the Court's own failure to appreciate the extent of the liberty at stake. To say that the issue in *Bowers* was simply the right to engage in certain sexual conduct demeans the claim the individual put forward, just as it would demean a married couple were it to be said marriage is simply about the right to have sexual intercourse. The laws involved in *Bowers* and here are, to be sure, statutes that purport to do no more than prohibit a particular sexual act. Their penalties and purposes, though, have more far-reaching consequences, touching upon the most private human conduct, sexual behavior, and in the most private of places, the home. The statutes do seek to control a personal relationship that, whether or not entitled to formal recognition in the law, is within the liberty of persons to choose without being punished as criminals.

This, as a general rule, should counsel against attempts by the State, or a court, to define the meaning of the relationship or to set its boundaries absent injury to a person or abuse of an institution the law protects. It suffices for us to acknowledge that adults may choose to enter upon this relationship in the confines of their homes and their own private lives and still retain their dignity as free persons. When sexuality finds overt expression in intimate conduct with another person, the conduct can be but one element in a personal bond that is more enduring. The liberty protected by the Constitution allows homosexual persons the right to make this choice.

Having misapprehended the claim of liberty there presented to it, and thus stating the claim to be whether there is a fundamental right to engage in consensual sodomy, the *Bowers* Court said: "Proscriptions against that conduct have ancient roots." In academic writings, and in many of the scholarly *amicus* briefs filed to assist the Court in this case, there are fundamental criticisms of the historical premises relied upon by the majority and concurring opinions in *Bowers*. We need not enter this debate in the attempt to reach a definitive historical judgment, but the following considerations counsel against adopting the definitive conclusions upon which *Bowers* placed such reliance.

At the outset it should be noted that there is no longstanding history in this country of laws directed at homosexual conduct as a distinct matter. Beginning in colonial times there were prohibitions of sodomy derived from the English criminal laws passed in the first instance by the Reformation Parliament of 1533. The English prohibition was understood to include relations between men and women as well as relations between men and men. Nineteenth-century commentators similarly read American sodomy, buggery, and crime-against-nature statutes as criminalizing certain relations between men and women and between men and men. The absence of legal prohibitions focusing on homosexual conduct may be explained in part by noting that according to some scholars the concept of the homosexual as a distinct category of person did not emerge until the late 19th century. Thus early American sodomy laws were not directed at homosexuals as such but instead sought to prohibit nonprocreative sexual activity more generally. This does not suggest approval of homosexual conduct. It does tend to show that this particular form of conduct was not thought of as a separate category from like conduct between heterosexual persons.

Laws prohibiting sodomy do not seem to have been enforced against consenting adults acting in private. A substantial number of sodomy prosecutions and convictions for which there are surviving records were for predatory acts against those who could not or did not consent, as in the case of a minor or the victim of an assault. As to these, one purpose for the prohibitions was to ensure there would be no lack of coverage if a predator committed a sexual assault that did not constitute rape as defined by the criminal law. Thus the model sodomy indictments presented in a 19th-century treatise, addressed the predatory acts of an adult man against a minor girl or minor boy. Instead of targeting relations between consenting adults in private, 19th-century sodomy prosecutions typically involved relations between men and minor girls or minor boys, relations between adults involving force, relations between adults implicating disparity in status, or relations between men and animals.

To the extent that there were any prosecutions for the acts in question, 19th-century evidence rules imposed a burden that would make a conviction more difficult to obtain even taking into account the problems always inherent in prosecuting consensual acts committed in private. Under then-prevailing standards, a man could not be convicted of sodomy based upon testimony of a consenting partner, because the partner was considered an accomplice. A partner's testimony, however, was admissible if he or she had not consented to the act or was a minor, and therefore incapable of consent. The rule may explain in part the infrequency of these prosecutions. In all events that infrequency makes it difficult to say that society approved of a rigorous and systematic punishment of the consensual acts committed in private and by adults. The longstanding criminal prohibition of homosexual sodomy upon which the *Bowers* decision placed such reliance is as consistent with a general condemnation of nonprocreative sex as it is with an established tradition of prosecuting acts because of their homosexual character.

The policy of punishing consenting adults for private acts was not much discussed in the early legal literature. We can infer that one reason for this was the very private nature of the conduct. Despite the absence of prosecutions, there may have been periods in which there was public criticism of homosexuals as such and an insistence that the criminal laws be enforced to discourage their practices. But far from possessing "ancient roots," American laws targeting same-sex couples did not develop until the last third of the 20th century. The reported decisions concerning the prosecution of consensual, homosexual sodomy between adults for the years 1880–1995 are not always clear in the details, but a significant number involved conduct in a public place.

It was not until the 1970's that any State singled out same-sex relations for criminal prosecution, and only nine States have done so. Post-*Bowers* even some of these States did not adhere to the policy of suppressing homosexual conduct. Over the course of the last decades, States with same-sex prohibitions have moved toward abolishing them.

In summary, the historical grounds relied upon in *Bowers* are more complex than the majority opinion and the concurring opinion by Chief Justice Burger indicate. Their historical premises are not without doubt and, at the very least, are overstated.

It must be acknowledged, of course, that the Court in *Bowers* was making the broader point that for centuries there have been powerful voices to condemn homosexual conduct as immoral. The condemnation has been shaped by religious beliefs, conceptions of right and acceptable behavior, and respect for the traditional family. For many persons these are not trivial concerns but profound and deep convictions accepted as ethical and moral principles to which they aspire and which thus determine the course of their lives. These considerations do not answer the question before us, however. The issue is whether the majority may use the power of the State to enforce these views on the whole society through operation of the criminal law. "Our obligation is to define the liberty of all, not to mandate our own moral code." *Planned Parenthood of Southeastern Pa. v. Casey*, 505 U.S. 833, 850 (1992).

Chief Justice Burger joined the opinion for the Court in *Bowers* and further explained his views as follows: "Decisions of individuals relating to homosexual conduct have been subject to state intervention throughout the history of Western civilization. Condemnation of those practices is firmly rooted in Judeao-Christian moral and ethical standards." As with Justice White's assumptions about history, scholarship casts some doubt on the sweeping nature of the statement by Chief Justice Burger as it pertains to private homosexual conduct between consenting adults. In all events we think that our laws and traditions in the past half century are of most relevance here. These references show an emerging awareness that liberty gives substantial protection to adult persons in deciding how to conduct their private lives in matters pertaining to sex. "[H]istory and tradition are the starting point but not in all cases the ending point of the substantive due process inquiry."

This emerging recognition should have been apparent when *Bowers* was decided. In 1955 the American Law Institute promulgated the Model Penal Code and made clear that it did not recommend or provide for "criminal penalties for consensual sexual relations conducted in private." It justified its decision on three grounds: (1) The prohibitions undermined respect for the law by penalizing conduct many people engaged in; (2) the statutes regulated private conduct not harmful to others; and (3) the laws were arbitrarily enforced and thus invited the danger of blackmail. In 1961 Illinois changed its laws to conform to the Model Penal Code. Other States soon followed.

In *Bowers* the Court referred to the fact that before 1961 all 50 States had outlawed sodomy, and that at the time of the Court's decision 24 States and the District of Columbia had sodomy laws. Justice Powell pointed out that these prohibitions often were being ignored, however. Georgia, for instance, had not sought to enforce its law for decades.

The sweeping references by Chief Justice Burger to the history of Western civilization and to Judeo-Christian moral and ethical standards did not take account of other authorities pointing in an opposite direction. A committee advising the British Parliament recommended in 1957 repeal of laws punishing homosexual conduct. Parliament enacted the substance of those recommendations 10 years later.

Of even more importance, almost five years before *Bowers* was decided the European Court of Human Rights considered a case with parallels to *Bowers* and to today's case. An adult male resident in Northern Ireland alleged he was a practicing homosexual who desired to engage in consensual homosexual conduct. The laws of Northern Ireland forbade him that right. He alleged that he had been questioned, his home had been searched, and he feared criminal prosecution. The court held that the laws proscribing the conduct were invalid under the European Convention on Human Rights. *Dudgeon v. United Kingdom,* 45 Eur. Ct. H.R. (1981) & ¶ 52. Authoritative in all countries that are members of the Council of Europe (21 nations then, 45 nations now), the decision is at odds with the premise in *Bowers* that the claim put forward was insubstantial in our Western civilization.

In our own constitutional system the deficiencies in *Bowers* became even more apparent in the years following its announcement. The 25 States with laws prohibiting the relevant conduct referenced in the *Bowers* decision are reduced now to 13, of which 4 enforce their laws only against homosexual conduct. In those States where sodomy is still proscribed, whether for same-sex or heterosexual conduct, there is a pattern of nonenforcement with respect to consenting adults acting in private. The State of Texas admitted in 1994 that as of that date it had not prosecuted anyone under those circumstances.

Two principal cases decided after *Bowers* cast its holding into even more doubt. In *Planned Parenthood of Southeastern Pa. v. Casey,* 505 U.S. 833 (1992), the Court reaffirmed the substantive force of the liberty protected by the Due Process Clause. The *Casey* decision again confirmed that our laws and tradition afford constitutional protection to personal decisions relating to marriage, procreation, contraception, family relationships, child rearing, and education. In explaining the respect the Constitution demands for the autonomy of the person in making these choices, we stated as follows:

> "These matters, involving the most intimate and personal choices a person may make in a lifetime, choices central to personal dignity and autonomy, are central to the liberty protected by the Fourteenth Amendment. At the heart of liberty is the right to define one's own concept of existence, of meaning, of the universe, and of the mystery of human life. Beliefs about these matters could not define the attributes of personhood were they formed under compulsion of the State."

Persons in a homosexual relationship may seek autonomy for these purposes, just as heterosexual persons do. The decision in *Bowers* would deny them this right.

The second post-*Bowers* case of principal relevance is *Romer v. Evans,* 517 U.S. 620 (1996). There the Court struck down class-based legislation directed at homosexuals as a violation of the Equal Protection Clause. *Romer* invalidated an amendment to Colorado's Constitution which named as a solitary class persons who were homosexuals, lesbians, or bisexual either by "orientation, conduct, practices or relationships," and deprived them of protection under state antidiscrimination laws. We concluded that the provision was "born of animosity toward the class of persons affected" and further that it had no rational relation to a legitimate governmental purpose.

As an alternative argument in this case, counsel for the petitioners and some *amici* contend that *Romer* provides the basis for declaring the Texas statute invalid under the Equal Protection Clause. That is a tenable argument, but we conclude the instant case requires us to address whether *Bowers* itself has continuing validity. Were we to hold the statute invalid under the Equal Protection Clause some might question whether a prohibition would be valid if drawn differently, say, to prohibit the conduct both between same-sex and different-sex participants.

Equality of treatment and the due process right to demand respect for conduct protected by the substantive guarantee of liberty are linked in important respects, and a decision on the latter point advances both interests. If protected conduct is made criminal and the law which does so remains unexamined for its substantive validity, its stigma might remain even if it were not enforceable as drawn for equal protection reasons. When homosexual conduct is made criminal by the law of the State, that declaration in and of itself is an invitation to subject homosexual persons to discrimination both in the public and in the private spheres. The central holding of *Bowers* has been brought in question by this case, and it should be addressed. Its continuance as precedent demeans the lives of homosexual persons.

The stigma this criminal statute imposes, moreover, is not trivial. The offense, to be sure, is but a class C misdemeanor, a minor offense in the Texas legal system. Still, it remains a criminal offense with all that imports for the dignity of the persons charged. The petitioners will bear on their record the history of their criminal convictions.... We are advised that if Texas convicted an adult for private, consensual homosexual conduct under the statute here in question the convicted person would come within the registration laws of at least four States were he or she to be subject to their jurisdiction. This underscores the consequential nature of the punishment and the state-sponsored condemnation attendant to the criminal prohibition. Furthermore, the Texas criminal conviction carries with it the other collateral consequences always following a conviction, such as notations on job application forms, to mention but one example.

The foundations of *Bowers* have sustained serious erosion from our recent decisions in *Casey* and *Romer.* When our precedent has been thus weakened, criticism from other sources is of greater significance. In the United States criticism of *Bowers* has been substantial and continuing, disapproving of its reasoning in all respects, not just as to its historical assumptions. The courts of five different States have declined to follow it in interpreting provisions in their own state constitutions parallel to the Due Process Clause of the Fourteenth Amendment.

To the extent *Bowers* relied on values we share with a wider civilization, it should be noted that the reasoning and holding in *Bowers* have been rejected elsewhere. The European Court of Human Rights has followed not *Bowers* but its own decision in *Dudgeon v. United Kingdom.* Other nations, too, have taken action consistent with an affirmation of the protected right of homosexual adults to engage in intimate, consensual conduct. The right the petitioners seek in this case has been accepted as an integral part of human freedom in many other countries. There has been no showing that in this country the governmental interest in circumscribing personal choice is somehow more legitimate or urgent.

The doctrine of *stare decisis* is essential to the respect accorded to the judgments of the Court and to the stability of the law. It is not, however, an inexorable command. In *Casey* we noted that when a court is asked to overrule a precedent recognizing a constitutional liberty interest, individual or societal reliance on the existence of that liberty cautions with particular strength against reversing course. 505 U.S., at 855–856; see also *id.,* at 844 ("Liberty finds no refuge in a jurisprudence of doubt"). The holding in *Bowers,* however, has not induced detrimental reliance comparable to some instances where recognized individual rights are involved. Indeed, there has been no individual or societal reliance on *Bowers* of the sort that could counsel against overturning its holding once there are compelling reasons to do so. *Bowers* itself causes uncertainty, for the precedents before and after its issuance contradict its central holding.

The rationale of *Bowers* does not withstand careful analysis. In his dissenting opinion in Bowers Justice STEVENS came to these conclusions:

> "Our prior cases make two propositions abundantly clear. First, the fact that the governing majority in a State has traditionally viewed a particular practice as immoral is not a sufficient reason for upholding a law prohibiting the practice; neither history nor tradition could save a law prohibiting miscegenation from constitutional attack. Second, individual decisions by married persons, concerning the intimacies of their physical relationship, even when not intended to produce offspring, are a form of 'liberty' protected by the Due Process Clause of the Fourteenth Amendment. Moreover, this protection extends to intimate choices by unmarried as well as married persons."

Justice STEVENS' analysis, in our view, should have been controlling in *Bowers* and should control here.

Bowers was not correct when it was decided, and it is not correct today. It ought not to remain binding precedent. *Bowers v. Hardwick* should be and now is overruled.

The present case does not involve minors. It does not involve persons who might be injured or coerced or who are situated in relationships where consent might not easily be refused. It does not involve public conduct or prostitution. It does not involve whether the government must give formal recognition to any relationship that homosexual persons seek to enter. The case does involve two adults who, with full and mutual consent from each other, engaged in sexual practices common to a homosexual lifestyle. The petitioners are entitled to respect for their private lives. The State cannot demean their existence or control their destiny by making their private sexual conduct a crime. Their right to liberty under the Due Process Clause gives them the full right to engage in their conduct without intervention of the government. "It is a promise of the Constitution that there is a realm of personal liberty which the government may not enter." The Texas statute furthers no legitimate state interest which can justify its intrusion into the personal and private life of the individual.

Had those who drew and ratified the Due Process Clauses of the Fifth Amendment or the Fourteenth Amendment known the components of liberty in its manifold possibilities, they might have been more specific. They did not presume to have this insight. They knew times can blind us to certain truths and later generations can see that laws once thought necessary and proper in fact serve only to oppress. As the Constitution endures, persons in every generation can invoke its principles in their own search for greater freedom.

The judgment of the Court of Appeals for the Texas Fourteenth District is reversed, and the case is remanded for further proceedings not inconsistent with this opinion.

It is so ordered.

[The concurring opinion of Justice O'Connor is omitted here, but will be examined in Chapter 4.]

Justice SCALIA, with whom THE CHIEF JUSTICE and Justice THOMAS join, dissenting.

"Liberty finds no refuge in a jurisprudence of doubt." *Planned Parenthood of Southeastern Pa. v. Casey*, 505 U.S. 833, 844 (1992). That was the Court's sententious response, barely more than a decade ago, to those seeking to overrule *Roe v. Wade*, 410 U.S. 113 (1973).

The Court's response today, to those who have engaged in a 17-year crusade to overrule *Bowers v. Hardwick,* 478 U.S. 186 (1986), is very different. The need for stability and certainty presents no barrier.

Most of the rest of today's opinion has no relevance to its actual holding—that the Texas statute "furthers no legitimate state interest which can justify" its application to petitioners under rational-basis review. Though there is discussion of "fundamental proposition[s]," and "fundamental decisions," nowhere does the Court's opinion declare that homosexual sodomy is a "fundamental right" under the Due Process Clause; nor does it subject the Texas law to the standard of review that would be appropriate (strict scrutiny) if homosexual sodomy *were* a "fundamental right." Thus, while overruling the *outcome* of *Bowers,* the Court leaves strangely untouched its central legal conclusion: "[R]espondent would have us announce ... a fundamental right to engage in homosexual sodomy. This we are quite unwilling to do." Instead the Court simply describes petitioners' conduct as "an exercise of their liberty"—which it undoubtedly is—and proceeds to apply an unheard-of form of rational-basis review that will have far-reaching implications beyond this case.

I

I begin with the Court's surprising readiness to reconsider a decision rendered a mere 17 years ago in *Bowers v. Hardwick.* I do not myself believe in rigid adherence to *stare decisis* in constitutional cases; but I do believe that we should be consistent rather than manipulative in invoking the doctrine. Today's opinions in support of reversal do not bother to distinguish—or indeed, even bother to mention—the paean to *stare decisis* coauthored by three Members of today's majority in *Planned Parenthood v. Casey.* There, when *stare decisis* meant preservation of judicially invented abortion rights, the widespread criticism of *Roe* was strong reason to *reaffirm* it:

> "Where, in the performance of its judicial duties, the Court decides a case in such a way as to resolve the sort of intensely divisive controversy reflected in *Roe* [,] ... its decision has a dimension that the resolution of the normal case does not carry.... [T]o overrule under fire in the absence of the most compelling reason ... would subvert the Court's legitimacy beyond any serious question." 505 U.S., at 866–867.

Today, however, the widespread opposition to *Bowers,* a decision resolving an issue as "intensely divisive" as the issue in *Roe,* is offered as a reason in favor of *overruling* it. Gone, too, is any "enquiry" (of the sort conducted in *Casey*) into whether the decision sought to be overruled has "proven 'unworkable.'"

Today's approach to *stare decisis* invites us to overrule an erroneously decided precedent (including an "intensely divisive" decision) *if:* (1) its foundations have been "ero[ded]" by subsequent decisions; (2) it has been subject to "substantial and continuing" criticism; and (3) it has not induced "individual or societal reliance" that counsels against overturning. The problem is that *Roe* itself—which today's majority surely has no disposition to overrule—satisfies these conditions to at least the same degree as *Bowers.*

(1) A preliminary digressive observation with regard to the first factor: The Court's claim that *Planned Parenthood v. Casey, supra,* "casts some doubt" upon the holding in *Bowers* (or any other case, for that matter) does not withstand analysis. As far as its holding is concerned, *Casey* provided a *less* expansive right to abortion than did *Roe, which was already on the books when* Bowers *was decided.* And if the Court is referring not to the holding of *Casey,* but to the dictum of its famed sweet-mystery-of-life passage ("'At the heart of liberty is the right to define one's own concept of existence, of meaning, of the

universe, and of the mystery of human life'"): That "casts some doubt" upon either the totality of our jurisprudence or else (presumably the right answer) nothing at all. I have never heard of a law that attempted to restrict one's "right to define" certain concepts; and if the passage calls into question the government's power to regulate *actions based on* one's self-defined "concept of existence, etc.," it is the passage that ate the rule of law.

I do not quarrel with the Court's claim that *Romer v. Evans,* 517 U.S. 620 (1996), "eroded" the "foundations" of *Bowers'* rational-basis holding. See *Romer, supra,* at 640–643 (SCALIA, J., dissenting). But *Roe* and *Casey* have been equally "eroded" by *Washington v. Glucksberg,* 521 U.S. 702, 721 (1997), which held that *only* fundamental rights which are "'deeply rooted in this Nation's history and tradition'" qualify for anything other than rational-basis scrutiny under the doctrine of "substantive due process." *Roe* and *Casey,* of course, subjected the restriction of abortion to heightened scrutiny without even attempting to establish that the freedom to abort *was* rooted in this Nation's tradition.

(2) *Bowers,* the Court says, has been subject to "substantial and continuing [criticism], disapproving of its reasoning in all respects, not just as to its historical assumptions." Exactly what those nonhistorical criticisms are, and whether the Court even agrees with them, are left unsaid, although the Court does cite two books. Of course, *Roe* too (and by extension *Casey*) had been (and still is) subject to unrelenting criticism, including criticism from the two commentators cited by the Court today.

(3) That leaves, to distinguish the rock-solid, unamendable disposition of *Roe* from the readily overrulable *Bowers,* only the third factor. "[T]here has been," the Court says, "no individual or societal reliance on *Bowers* of the sort that could counsel against overturning its holding...." It seems to me that the "societal reliance" on the principles confirmed in *Bowers* and discarded today has been overwhelming. Countless judicial decisions and legislative enactments have relied on the ancient proposition that a governing majority's belief that certain sexual behavior is "immoral and unacceptable" constitutes a rational basis for regulation. State laws against bigamy, same-sex marriage, adult incest, prostitution, masturbation, adultery, fornication, bestiality, and obscenity are likewise sustainable only in light of *Bowers'* validation of laws based on moral choices. Every single one of these laws is called into question by today's decision; the Court makes no effort to cabin the scope of its decision to exclude them from its holding. The impossibility of distinguishing homosexuality from other traditional "morals" offenses is precisely why *Bowers* rejected the rational-basis challenge. "The law," it said, "is constantly based on notions of morality, and if all laws representing essentially moral choices are to be invalidated under the Due Process Clause, the courts will be very busy indeed."

What a massive disruption of the current social order, therefore, the overruling of *Bowers* entails. Not so the overruling of *Roe,* which would simply have restored the regime that existed for centuries before 1973, in which the permissibility of, and restrictions upon, abortion were determined legislatively State by State. *Casey,* however, chose to base its *stare decisis* determination on a different "sort" of reliance. "[P]eople," it said, "have organized intimate relationships and made choices that define their views of themselves and their places in society, in reliance on the availability of abortion in the event that contraception should fail." This falsely assumes that the consequence of overruling *Roe* would have been to make abortion unlawful. It would not; it would merely have *permitted* the States to do so. Many States would unquestionably have declined to prohibit abortion, and others would not have prohibited it within six months (after which the most significant reliance interests would have expired). Even for persons in States other than these, the choice would not have been between abortion and childbirth, but between abortion nearby and abortion in a neighboring State.

To tell the truth, it does not surprise me, and should surprise no one, that the Court has chosen today to revise the standards of *stare decisis* set forth in *Casey*. It has thereby exposed *Casey's* extraordinary deference to precedent for the result-oriented expedient that it is.

II

Having decided that it need not adhere to *stare decisis,* the Court still must establish that *Bowers* was wrongly decided and that the Texas statute, as applied to petitioners, is unconstitutional.

Texas Penal Code Ann. § 21.06(a) (2003) undoubtedly imposes constraints on liberty. So do laws prohibiting prostitution, recreational use of heroin, and, for that matter, working more than 60 hours per week in a bakery. But there is no right to "liberty" under the Due Process Clause, though today's opinion repeatedly makes that claim. The Fourteenth Amendment *expressly allows* States to deprive their citizens of "liberty," *so long as "due process of law" is provided:*

> "No state shall … deprive any person of life, liberty, or property, *without due process of law."*

Our opinions applying the doctrine known as "substantive due process" hold that the Due Process Clause prohibits States from infringing *fundamental* liberty interests, unless the infringement is narrowly tailored to serve a compelling state interest. We have held repeatedly, in cases the Court today does not overrule, that *only* fundamental rights qualify for this so-called "heightened scrutiny" protection—that is, rights which are "'deeply rooted in this Nation's history and tradition.'"[3] All other liberty interests may be abridged or abrogated pursuant to a validly enacted state law if that law is rationally related to a legitimate state interest.

Bowers held, first, that criminal prohibitions of homosexual sodomy are not subject to heightened scrutiny because they do not implicate a "fundamental right" under the Due Process Clause. Noting that "[p]roscriptions against that conduct have ancient roots," that "[s]odomy was a criminal offense at common law and was forbidden by the laws of the original 13 States when they ratified the Bill of Rights," and that many States had retained their bans on sodomy, *Bowers* concluded that a right to engage in homosexual sodomy was not "'deeply rooted in this Nation's history and tradition.'"

The Court today does not overrule this holding. Not once does it describe homosexual sodomy as a "fundamental right" or a "fundamental liberty interest," nor does it subject the Texas statute to strict scrutiny. Instead, having failed to establish that the right to homosexual sodomy is "'deeply rooted in this Nation's history and tradition,'" the Court concludes that the application of Texas's statute to petitioners' conduct fails the rational-basis test, and overrules *Bowers'* holding to the contrary. "The Texas statute furthers no legitimate state interest which can justify its intrusion into the personal and private life of the individual."

---

3. The Court is quite right that "'[h]istory and tradition are the starting point but not in all cases the ending point of the substantive due process inquiry.'" An asserted "fundamental liberty interest" must not only be "'deeply rooted in this Nation's history and tradition,'" but it must *also* be "'implicit in the concept of ordered liberty,'" so that "'neither liberty nor justice would exist if [it] were sacrificed.'" Moreover, liberty interests unsupported by history and tradition, though not deserving of "heightened scrutiny," are *still* protected from state laws that are not rationally related to any legitimate state interest. As I proceed to discuss, it is this latter principle that the Court applies in the present case.

I shall address that rational-basis holding presently. First, however, I address some aspersions that the Court casts upon *Bowers'* conclusion that homosexual sodomy is not a "fundamental right"—even though, as I have said, the Court does not have the boldness to reverse that conclusion.

III

The Court's description of "the state of the law" at the time of *Bowers* only confirms that *Bowers* was right. The Court points to *Griswold v. Connecticut,* 381 U.S. 479 (1965). But that case *expressly disclaimed* any reliance on the doctrine of "substantive due process," and grounded the so-called "right to privacy" in penumbras of constitutional provisions *other than* the Due Process Clause. *Eisenstadt v. Baird,* 405 U.S. 438 (1972), likewise had nothing to do with "substantive due process"; it invalidated a Massachusetts law prohibiting the distribution of contraceptives to unmarried persons solely on the basis of the Equal Protection Clause. Of course *Eisenstadt* contains well-known dictum relating to the "right to privacy," but this referred to the right recognized in *Griswold*—a right penumbral to the *specific* guarantees in the Bill of Rights, and not a "substantive due process" right.

Roe v. Wade recognized that the right to abort an unborn child was a "fundamental right" protected by the Due Process Clause. The *Roe* Court, however, made no attempt to establish that this right was "'deeply rooted in this Nation's history and tradition'"; instead, it based its conclusion that "the Fourteenth Amendment's concept of personal liberty ... is broad enough to encompass a woman's decision whether or not to terminate her pregnancy" on its own normative judgment that antiabortion laws were undesirable. We have since rejected *Roe's* holding that regulations of abortion must be narrowly tailored to serve a compelling state interest, see *Planned Parenthood v. Casey,* 505 U.S., at 876 (joint opinion of O'CONNOR, KENNEDY, and SOUTER, JJ.); *id.,* at 951–953 (REHNQUIST, C. J., concurring in judgment in part and dissenting in part)—and thus, by logical implication, *Roe's* holding that the right to abort an unborn child is a "fundamental right."

After discussing the history of antisodomy laws, the Court proclaims that, "it should be noted that there is no longstanding history in this country of laws directed at homosexual conduct as a distinct matter." This observation in no way casts into doubt the "definitive [historical] conclusio[n]," on which *Bowers* relied: that our Nation has a longstanding history of laws prohibiting *sodomy in general*—regardless of whether it was performed by same-sex or opposite-sex couples....

It is (as *Bowers* recognized) entirely irrelevant whether the laws in our long national tradition criminalizing homosexual sodomy were "directed at homosexual conduct as a distinct matter." Whether homosexual sodomy was prohibited by a law targeted at same-sex sexual relations or by a more general law prohibiting both homosexual and heterosexual sodomy, the only relevant point is that it *was* criminalized—which suffices to establish that homosexual sodomy is not a right "deeply rooted in our Nation's history and tradition." The Court today agrees that homosexual sodomy was criminalized and thus does not dispute the facts on which *Bowers actually* relied.

Next the Court makes the claim, again unsupported by any citations, that "[l]aws prohibiting sodomy do not seem to have been enforced against consenting adults acting in private." The key qualifier here is "acting in private"—since the Court admits that sodomy laws *were* enforced against consenting adults (although the Court contends that prosecutions were "infrequen[t]"). I do not know what "acting in private" means; surely consensual sodomy, like heterosexual intercourse, is rarely performed on stage.

If all the Court means by "acting in private" is "on private premises, with the doors closed and windows covered," it is entirely unsurprising that evidence of enforcement would be hard to come by. (Imagine the circumstances that would enable a search warrant to be obtained for a residence on the ground that there was probable cause to believe that consensual sodomy was then and there occurring.) Surely that lack of evidence would not sustain the proposition that consensual sodomy on private premises with the doors closed and windows covered was regarded as a "fundamental right," even though all other consensual sodomy was criminalized. There are 203 prosecutions for consensual, adult homosexual sodomy reported in the West Reporting system and official state reporters from the years 1880–1995. There are also records of 20 sodomy prosecutions and 4 executions during the colonial period. *Bowers'* conclusion that homosexual sodomy is not a fundamental right "deeply rooted in this Nation's history and tradition" is utterly unassailable.

Realizing that fact, the Court instead says: "[W]e think that our laws and traditions in the past half century are of most relevance here. These references show *an emerging awareness* that liberty gives substantial protection to adult persons in deciding how to conduct their private lives *in matters pertaining to sex.*" Apart from the fact that such an "emerging awareness" does not establish a "fundamental right," the statement is factually false. States continue to prosecute all sorts of crimes by adults "in matters pertaining to sex": prostitution, adult incest, adultery, obscenity, and child pornography. Sodomy laws, too, have been enforced "in the past half century," in which there have been 134 reported cases involving prosecutions for consensual, adult, homosexual sodomy. In relying, for evidence of an "emerging recognition," upon the American Law Institute's 1955 recommendation not to criminalize "'consensual sexual relations conducted in private,'" the Court ignores the fact that this recommendation was "a point of resistance in most of the states that considered adopting the Model Penal Code."

In any event, an "emerging awareness" is by definition not "deeply rooted in this Nation's history and tradition[s]," as we have said "fundamental right" status requires. Constitutional entitlements do not spring into existence because some States choose to lessen or eliminate criminal sanctions on certain behavior. Much less do they spring into existence, as the Court seems to believe, because *foreign nations* decriminalize conduct. The *Bowers* majority opinion *never* relied on "values we share with a wider civilization," but rather rejected the claimed right to sodomy on the ground that such a right was not "'deeply rooted in *this Nation's* history and tradition,'" 478 U.S., at 193–194 (emphasis added). *Bowers'* rational-basis holding is likewise devoid of any reliance on the views of a "wider civilization," see *id.,* at 196. The Court's discussion of these foreign views (ignoring, of course, the many countries that have retained criminal prohibitions on sodomy) is therefore meaningless dicta. Dangerous dicta, however, since "this Court ... should not impose foreign moods, fads, or fashions on Americans."

IV

I turn now to the ground on which the Court squarely rests its holding: the contention that there is no rational basis for the law here under attack. This proposition is so out of accord with our jurisprudence—indeed, with the jurisprudence of *any* society we know— that it requires little discussion.

The Texas statute undeniably seeks to further the belief of its citizens that certain forms of sexual behavior are "immoral and unacceptable,"—the same interest furthered by criminal laws against fornication, bigamy, adultery, adult incest, bestiality, and obscenity. *Bowers* held that this *was* a legitimate state interest. The Court today reaches the opposite conclusion. The Texas statute, it says, "furthers *no legitimate state interest* which can justify its intrusion into the personal and private life of the individual." The Court embraces instead Justice STEVENS' declaration in his *Bowers* dissent, that "'the fact that the governing majority in a State has traditionally viewed a particular practice as immoral is not a sufficient reason for upholding a law prohibiting the practice.'" This effectively decrees the end of all morals legislation. If, as the Court asserts, the promotion of majoritarian sexual morality is not even a *legitimate* state interest, none of the above-mentioned laws can survive rational-basis review....

* * *

Today's opinion is the product of a Court, which is the product of a law-profession culture, that has largely signed on to the so-called homosexual agenda, by which I mean the agenda promoted by some homosexual activists directed at eliminating the moral opprobrium that has traditionally attached to homosexual conduct. I noted in an earlier opinion the fact that the American Association of Law Schools (to which any reputable law school *must* seek to belong) excludes from membership any school that refuses to ban from its job-interview facilities a law firm (no matter how small) that does not wish to hire as a prospective partner a person who openly engages in homosexual conduct. See *Romer, supra,* at 653.

One of the most revealing statements in today's opinion is the Court's grim warning that the criminalization of homosexual conduct is "an invitation to subject homosexual persons to discrimination both in the public and in the private spheres." It is clear from this that the Court has taken sides in the culture war, departing from its role of assuring, as neutral observer, that the democratic rules of engagement are observed. Many Americans do not want persons who openly engage in homosexual conduct as partners in their business, as scoutmasters for their children, as teachers in their children's schools, or as boarders in their home. They view this as protecting themselves and their families from a lifestyle that they believe to be immoral and destructive. The Court views it as "discrimination" which it is the function of our judgments to deter. So imbued is the Court with the law profession's anti-anti-homosexual culture, that it is seemingly unaware that the attitudes of that culture are not obviously "mainstream"; that in most States what the Court calls "discrimination" against those who engage in homosexual acts is perfectly legal; that proposals to ban such "discrimination" under Title VII have repeatedly been rejected by Congress; that in some cases such "discrimination" is *mandated* by federal statute, see 10 U.S.C. §654(b)(1) (mandating discharge from the Armed Forces of any service member who engages in or intends to engage in homosexual acts); and that in some cases such "discrimination" is a constitutional right, see *Boy Scouts of America v. Dale,* 530 U.S. 640 (2000).

Let me be clear that I have nothing against homosexuals, or any other group, promoting their agenda through normal democratic means. Social perceptions of sexual and other morality change over time, and every group has the right to persuade its fellow citizens that its view of such matters is the best. That homosexuals have achieved some success in that enterprise is attested to by the fact that Texas is one of the few remaining States that criminalize private, consensual homosexual acts. But persuading one's fellow citizens is one thing, and imposing one's views in absence of democratic majority will is something else. I would no more *require* a State to criminalize homosexual acts—or, for that matter, display *any* moral disapprobation of them—than I would *forbid* it to do so. What Texas has chosen to do is well within the range of traditional democratic action, and its hand should not be stayed through the invention of a brand-new "constitutional right" by a Court that is impatient of democratic change. It is indeed true that "later generations can see that laws once thought necessary and proper in fact serve only to oppress"; and when that happens, later generations can repeal those laws. But it is the premise of our system that those judgments are to be made by the people, and not imposed by a governing caste that knows best.

One of the benefits of leaving regulation of this matter to the people rather than to the courts is that the people, unlike judges, need not carry things to their logical conclusion. The people may feel that their disapprobation of homosexual conduct is strong enough to disallow homosexual marriage, but not strong enough to criminalize private homosexual acts — and may legislate accordingly. The Court today pretends that it possesses a similar freedom of action, so that we need not fear judicial imposition of homosexual marriage, as has recently occurred in Canada (in a decision that the Canadian Government has chosen not to appeal). At the end of its opinion — after having laid waste the foundations of our rational-basis jurisprudence — the Court says that the present case "does not involve whether the government must give formal recognition to any relationship that homosexual persons seek to enter." Do not believe it. More illuminating than this bald, unreasoned disclaimer is the progression of thought displayed by an earlier passage in the Court's opinion, which notes the constitutional protections afforded to "personal decisions relating to *marriage,* procreation, contraception, family relationships, child rearing, and education," and then declares that "[p]ersons in a homosexual relationship may seek autonomy for these purposes, just as heterosexual persons do" (emphasis added). Today's opinion dismantles the structure of constitutional law that has permitted a distinction to be made between heterosexual and homosexual unions, insofar as formal recognition in marriage is concerned. If moral disapproval of homosexual conduct is "no legitimate state interest" for purposes of proscribing that conduct; and if, as the Court coos (casting aside all pretense of neutrality), "[w]hen sexuality finds overt expression in intimate conduct with another person, the conduct can be but one element in a personal bond that is more enduring"; what justification could there possibly be for denying the benefits of marriage to homosexual couples exercising "[t]he liberty protected by the Constitution"? Surely not the encouragement of procreation, since the sterile and the elderly are allowed to marry. This case "does not involve" the issue of homosexual marriage only if one entertains the belief that principle and logic have nothing to do with the decisions of this Court. Many will hope that, as the Court comfortingly assures us, this is so.

The matters appropriate for this Court's resolution are only three: Texas's prohibition of sodomy neither infringes a "fundamental right" (which the Court does not dispute), nor is unsupported by a rational relation to what the Constitution considers a legitimate state interest, nor denies the equal protection of the laws. I dissent.

Justice THOMAS, dissenting.

I join Justice SCALIA's dissenting opinion. I write separately to note that the law before the Court today "is … uncommonly silly." *Griswold v. Connecticut,* 381 U.S. 479, 527 (1965) (Stewart, J., dissenting). If I were a member of the Texas Legislature, I would vote to repeal it. Punishing someone for expressing his sexual preference through noncommercial consensual conduct with another adult does not appear to be a worthy way to expend valuable law enforcement resources.

Notwithstanding this, I recognize that as a Member of this Court I am not empowered to help petitioners and others similarly situated. My duty, rather, is to "decide cases 'agreeably to the Constitution and laws of the United States.'" *Id.,* at 530. And, just like Justice Stewart, I "can find [neither in the Bill of Rights nor any other part of the Constitution a] general right of privacy," or as the Court terms it today, the "liberty of the person both in its spatial and more transcendent dimensions."

Notes and Questions

1. In what ways were the facts and laws at issue in *Bowers* and *Lawrence* similar? To what extent were they different? What impact, if any, did those differences likely have on the outcome of the case?

2. Is *Lawrence* a fundamental rights substantive due process case applying strict scrutiny, or a run-of-the-mill substantive due process case applying rational basis? Or is it applying something more akin to the "undue burden" standard of *Casey*?

3. After *Lawrence*, can public moral disapproval ever suffice to justify a law when challenged on substantive due process grounds? If not, is Justice Scalia right in suggesting that the decision casts doubt on the constitutionality of laws criminalizing or banning bigamy, same-sex marriage, adult incest, prostitution, masturbation (!), adultery, fornication, bestiality, and obscenity? Or are there ways to distinguish these laws from laws criminalizing consensual sexual activity between two persons of the same sex?

4. In one sense, the majority opinion in *Lawrence*—like that in *Casey*—is breathtakingly broad, describing the right at issue in sweeping terms. Yet other aspects of the majority opinion appear to substantially constrain its scope. From the standpoint of the Court, what are the advantages of this framework coupled with its silence on the level of scrutiny being applied? From the standpoint of those seeking to litigate future gay rights cases (or other cases falling within the zone of liberty identified in *Lawrence*), what disadvantages are there with this approach?

5. *Lawrence* differs from *Bowers* in two key ways: it frames the right claimed and its prior holdings in much broader terms, and history plays a different role. How does this compare with the Court's earlier decision in *Glucksberg*? Does *Lawrence* overrule *Glucksberg sub silentio*? If not, how can the two cases be reconciled?

6. In his opinion in *Lawrence*, Justice Kennedy notes that "the concept of the homosexual as a distinct category of person did not emerge until the late 19th century." In the next chapter, you will consider Equal Protection Clause claims based on discrimination against a given class of persons. If homosexuals as a distinct category of persons did not emerge until the late 19th century, can laws that predate that emergence ever be deemed to violate the Equal Protection Clause? In this regard, consider a key limitation on the scope of the Equal Protection Clause that will be explored in greater detail in the next chapter: it only encompasses discrimination that is *intentional*; it does not encompass discrimination that merely has a disparate impact on a given group.

7. Justice O'Connor provided a sixth vote in favor of overturning Texas's sodomy statute, but she wrote a separate concurring opinion. In that opinion, Justice O'Connor declined to overrule *Bowers*, but instead argued that the Texas sodomy statute was distinguishable from the Georgia one and that it should be invalidated on equal protection grounds for its differential treatment of same-sex and opposite-sex sodomy. Justice O'Connor's opinion will be examined in Chapter 4.

8. Is the *Lawrence* Court's decision to overrule *Bowers* consistent with the *Casey* Court's decision *not* to overrule *Roe*?

9. What is the relationship between equal protection and due process in the entire line of cases studied in this chapter? In this regard, recall that *Skinner*, *Eisenstadt*, and *Romer* were all formally decided on equal protection grounds.

G. A Closer Look at *Lawrence*

As the previous materials suggest, the only thing certain about the Supreme Court's decision in *Lawrence v. Texas* is that it is unconstitutional for a state to criminalize consensual sexual activity that occurs in private between two adults. Since *Lawrence*, lower courts have struggled to discern its meaning when applied outside the narrow context at issue in *Lawrence* itself. The materials that follow are designed to help you begin to explore the potential reach and outer limits of *Lawrence*, as well as the tension between that decision and the Court's decision in *Glucksberg*.

Problem 3-A: Scoping Out Lawrence*'s Scope*

Assess the constitutionality of the following laws in light of *Lawrence* and the cases that follow interpreting it:

(1) A law that makes it a crime for two soldiers of equal rank to engage in consensual sodomy.

(2) A law that makes it a crime to commit adultery as applied in the following contexts: (a) the offending spouse and his wife have children; (b) the offending spouse and her husband have no children, and the husband consented to her engaging in adultery; (c) the offender is a single man in the military, and the act involved the wife of another soldier.

(3) A state law that criminalizes solicitation to commit sodomy, applied in the situation in which the defendant approaches an undercover officer in a public restroom and proposes that they go back to his place to engage in sexual activity.

(4) A law that makes it a crime to engage in consensual sexual acts that involve the infliction of pain or injury.

(5) A law that limits marriage to one man and one woman, applied to a man and two women (all adults) who seek to marry one another.

(6) A law that makes it a crime for three or more individuals to engage in sexual activity together.

(7) A law that makes it a crime to engage in sexual activity with an animal.

(8) A law that makes it a crime for first cousins to have sexual intercourse with one another.

(9) A law that makes it a crime to engage in prostitution.

Williams v. Attorney General of Alabama
378 F.3d 1232 (11th Cir. 2004)

BIRCH, Circuit Judge:

....

I. BACKGROUND

Alabama's Anti-Obscenity Enforcement Act prohibits, among other things, the commercial distribution of "any device designed or marketed as useful primarily for the stimulation of human genital organs for any thing of pecuniary value."

The Alabama statute proscribes a relatively narrow bandwidth of activity. It prohibits only the sale—but not the use, possession, or gratuitous distribution—of sexual devices (in fact, the users involved in this litigation acknowledge that they already possess multiple sex toys). The law does not affect the distribution of a number of other sexual products such as ribbed condoms or virility drugs. Nor does it prohibit Alabama residents from purchasing sexual devices out of state and bringing them back into Alabama. Moreover, the statute permits the sale of ordinary vibrators and body massagers that, although useful as sexual aids, are not "designed or marketed . . . primarily" for that particular purpose. Finally, the statute exempts sales of sexual devices "for a bona fide medical, scientific, educational, legislative, judicial, or law enforcement purpose." . . . .

This case, which is now before us on appeal for the second time, involves a challenge to the constitutionality of the Alabama statute. The ACLU, on behalf of various individual users and vendors of sexual devices, initially filed suit seeking to enjoin the statute on 29 July 1998, a month after the statute took effect. The ACLU argued that the statute burdens and violates sexual-device users' right to privacy and personal autonomy under the Fourteenth Amendment to the United States Constitution. . . .

II. DISCUSSION

....

A. Asserted Right

....

The ACLU invokes "privacy" and "personal autonomy" as if such phrases were constitutional talismans. In the abstract, however, there is no fundamental right to either. *See, e.g., Glucksberg*, 521 U.S. at 725 (fundamental rights are "not simply deduced from abstract concepts of personal autonomy"). Undoubtedly, many fundamental rights currently recognized under Supreme Court precedent touch on matters of personal autonomy and privacy. However, "[t]hat many of the rights and liberties protected by the Due Process Clause sound in personal autonomy does not warrant the sweeping conclusion that any and all important, intimate, and personal decisions are so protected." *Id.* at 727. Such rights have been denominated "fundamental" not simply because they implicate deeply personal and private considerations, but because they have been identified as "deeply rooted in this Nation's history and tradition and implicit in the concept of ordered liberty, such that neither liberty nor justice would exist if they were sacrificed." *Id.* at 720–21. . . .

Nor, contrary to the ACLU's assertion, have the Supreme Court's substantive-due-process precedents recognized a free-standing "right to sexual privacy." . . . . Although many of the Court's "privacy" decisions have implicated sexual matters, *see, e.g., Planned Parenthood v. Casey*, 505 U.S. 833 (1992) (abortion); *Carey*, 431 U.S. at 678 (contraceptives), the Court has never indicated that the mere fact that an activity is sexual and private entitles it to protection as a fundamental right.

The Supreme Court's most recent opportunity to recognize a fundamental right to sexual privacy came in *Lawrence v. Texas,* where petitioners and *amici* expressly invited the court to do so. That the *Lawrence* Court had declined the invitation was this court's conclusion in our recent decision in *Lofton v. Sec. of Dept. of Children and Family Servs.,* 358 F.3d 804, 815–16 (11th Cir.2004). In *Lofton,* we addressed in some detail the "question of whether *Lawrence* identified a new fundamental right to private sexual intimacy." We concluded that, although *Lawrence* clearly established the unconstitutionality of criminal prohibitions on consensual adult sodomy, "it is a strained and ultimately incorrect reading of *Lawrence* to interpret it to announce a new fundamental right"—whether to homosexual sodomy specifically or, more broadly, to all forms of sexual intimacy. We noted in particular that the *Lawrence* opinion did not employ fundamental-rights analysis and that it ultimately applied rational-basis review, rather than strict scrutiny, to the challenged statute.[6]

The dissent seizes on scattered *dicta* from *Lawrence* to argue that *Lawrence* recognized a *substantive* due process right of consenting adults to engage in private intimate sexual conduct, such that all infringements of this right must be subjected to strict scrutiny. As we noted in *Lofton,* we are not prepared to infer a new fundamental right from an opinion that never employed the usual *Glucksberg* analysis for identifying such rights. Nor are we prepared to assume that *Glucksberg*—a precedent that *Lawrence* never once mentions—is overruled by implication.

The dissent in turn argues that the right recognized in *Lawrence* was a longstanding right that preexisted *Lawrence,* thus obviating the need for any *Glucksberg*-type fundamental rights analysis. But the dissent never identifies the source, textual or precedential, of such a preexisting right to sexual privacy. It does cite *Griswold, Eisenstadt, Roe,* and *Carey.* However, although these precedents recognize various substantive rights *closely related* to sexual intimacy, none of them recognize the overarching right to sexual privacy asserted here.... As we noted above, in the most recent of these decisions, *Carey,* the Court

---

6. *Lofton* stated in relevant part:
   We are particularly hesitant to infer a new fundamental liberty interest from an opinion whose language and reasoning are inconsistent with standard fundamental-rights analysis. The Court has noted that it must "exercise the utmost care whenever [it is] asked to break new ground" in the field of fundamental rights, which is precisely what the *Lawrence* petitioners and their *amici curiae* had asked the Court to do. That the Court declined the invitation is apparent from the absence of the "two primary features" of fundamental-rights analysis in its opinion. First, the *Lawrence* opinion contains virtually no inquiry into the question of whether the petitioners' asserted right is one of "those fundamental rights and liberties which are, objectively, deeply rooted in this Nation's history and tradition and implicit in the concept of ordered liberty, such that neither liberty nor justice would exist if they were sacrificed." Second, the opinion notably never provides the "'careful description' of the asserted fundamental liberty interest" that is to accompany fundamental-rights analysis. Rather, the constitutional liberty interests on which the Court relied were invoked, not with "careful description," but with sweeping generality. Most significant, however, is the fact that the *Lawrence* Court never applied strict scrutiny, the proper standard when fundamental rights are implicated, but instead invalidated the Texas statute on rational-basis grounds, holding that it "furthers no legitimate state interest which can justify its intrusion into the personal and private life of the individual."

specifically observed that it had not answered the question of whether there is a constitutional right to private sexual conduct.[8] Moreover, nearly two decades later, the *Glucksberg* Court, listing the current catalog of fundamental rights, did not include such a right.

In short, we decline to extrapolate from *Lawrence* and its *dicta* a right to sexual privacy triggering strict scrutiny. To do so would be to impose a fundamental-rights interpretation on a decision that rested on rational-basis grounds, that never engaged in *Glucksberg* analysis, and that never invoked strict scrutiny. Moreover, it would be answering questions that the *Lawrence* Court appears to have left for another day. Of course, the Court may in due course expand *Lawrence's* precedent in the direction anticipated by the dissent. But for us preemptively to take that step would exceed our mandate as a lower court.[9]

B. *Glucksberg* Analysis

Because the ACLU is seeking recognition of a right neither mentioned in the Constitution nor encompassed within the reach of the Supreme Court's existing fundamental-right precedents, we must turn to the two-step analytical framework that the Court has established for evaluating new fundamental-rights claims. *See Glucksberg*, 521 U.S. at 720–21. First, in analyzing a request for recognition of a new fundamental right, or extension of an existing one, we "must begin with a careful description of the asserted right." Second, and most critically, we must determine whether this asserted right, carefully described, is one of "those fundamental rights and liberties which are, objectively, deeply rooted in this Nation's history and tradition, and implicit in the concept of ordered liberty, such that neither liberty nor justice would exist if they were sacrificed."

This analysis, as the Supreme Court has stressed, must proceed with "utmost care" because of the dangers inherent in the process of elevating extra-textual rights to constitutional status, thereby removing them from the democratic field of play....

---

8. Contrary to the dissent's accusation that "[t]he majority refuses ... to acknowledge *why* the Court in *Lawrence* held that criminal prohibitions on consensual sodomy are unconstitutional," we have refused to do no such thing. What we have refused to do, as we suggest the dissent has done, is to create a rationale that was not articulated as to the "why" for the ruling. The operative legal conclusion that we come to as a basis for the decision in *Lawrence* is that Texas's sodomy prohibition did not further a legitimate state interest....

The dissent also flatly states that the *Lawrence* Court rejected public morality as a legitimate state interest that can justify criminalizing private consensual sexual conduct, but this conclusion ignores the obvious difference in what this statute forbids and the prohibitions of the Texas statute. There is nothing "private" or "consensual" about the advertising and sale of a dildo. And such advertising and sale is just as likely to be exhibited to children as to "consenting adults." Moreover, the Supreme Court has noted on repeated occasions that laws can be based on moral judgments.... One would expect the Supreme Court to be manifestly more specific and articulate than it was in *Lawrence* if now such a traditional and significant jurisprudential princip[le] has been jettisoned wholesale (with all due respect to Justice Scalia's ominous dissent notwithstanding).

9. The dissent indicates that "even under the majority's own constrained interpretation of *Lawrence*, we are, at a bare minimum, obliged to revisit [our] previous conclusion in *Williams v. Pryor*, 240 F.3d 944 (11th Cir.2001) ('*Williams II*')" that this law has a rational basis in light of *Lawrence's* overruling of *Bowers* and our reliance in *Williams II* "on the now defunct *Bowers* to conclude that public morality provides a legitimate state interest." We agree with the dissent that, on remand, the district court, after considering the appropriate submissions of the parties, may examine "whether our holding in *Williams II* that Alabama's law has a rational basis (e.g., public morality) remains good law now that *Bowers* has been overruled." We save for a later day consideration of [] Justice Scalia's (perhaps ominous) predication that public morality may no longer serve as a rational basis for legislation after *Lawrence*.

1. *Careful Description*

As we noted in *Williams II,* the district court's initial opinion "narrowly framed the analysis as the question whether the concept of a constitutionally protected right to privacy protects an individual's liberty to use sexual devices when engaging in lawful, private, sexual activity." On appeal, we affirmed this formulation, stating that "the district court correctly framed the fundamental rights analysis in this case." However, on remand, the district court abandoned its initial, careful framing of the issue and instead characterized the asserted right more broadly as a generalized "right to sexual privacy."

. . . .

The sole limitation provided by the district court's ruling was that the right would extend only to *consenting adults.* The consenting-adult formula, of course, is a corollary to John Stuart Mill's celebrated "harm principle," which would allow the state to proscribe only conduct that causes identifiable harm to another. *See generally* John Stuart Mill, *On Liberty* (Elizabeth Rapaport ed., Hackett Pub. Co. 1978) (1859). Regardless of its force as a policy argument, however, it does not translate *ipse dixit* into a constitutionally cognizable standard.

If we were to accept the invitation to recognize a right to sexual intimacy, this right would theoretically encompass such activities as prostitution, obscenity, and adult incest—even if we were to limit the right to consenting adults. This in turn would require us to subject all infringements on such activities to strict scrutiny. In short, by framing our inquiry so broadly as to look for a general right to sexual intimacy, we would be answering many questions not before us on the present facts.

Indeed, the requirement of a "careful description" is designed to prevent the reviewing court from venturing into vaster constitutional vistas than are called for by the facts of the case at hand. . . .

Glucksberg and *Flores,* cases in which the Court was asked to expand certain substantive due process rights, are instructive examples. In *Glucksberg,* the lower court and the petitioners had variously characterized the asserted right as "a liberty interest in determining the time and manner of one's death," "a liberty to choose how to die and a right to control one's final days," and the "liberty of competent, terminally ill adults to make end-of-life decisions free of undue government interference." The Court rejected these characterizations as overbroad, noting its "tradition of carefully formulating the interest at stake in substantive-due-process cases." Then, looking to the specific statute under challenge—a ban on assisted suicide—the Court recast the asserted right as "a right to commit suicide which itself includes a right to assistance in doing so," or as "a right to commit suicide with another's assistance."

Under challenge in *Flores* was an immigration regulation that governed the detention and release of alien juveniles. The respondents, a class of detained alien juveniles, argued that the regulation violated their "fundamental right to freedom from physical restraint." The Supreme Court, emphasizing the importance of beginning substantive-due-process analysis with a "careful description," rejected respondents' broad formulation of the implicated liberty interests. The Court then restated the putative right—by careful reference to the challenged regulation:

> The "freedom from physical restraint" invoked by respondents is not at issue in this case. . . . Nor is the right asserted the right of a child to be released from all other custody into the custody of its parents, legal guardian, or even close relatives: The challenged regulation requires such release when it is sought. Rather,

> the right at issue is the alleged right of a child who has no available parent, close relative, or legal guardian, and for whom the government is responsible, to be placed in the custody of a willing-and-able private custodian rather than of a government-operated or government-selected child-care institution.

As in *Glucksberg* and *Flores,* the scope of the liberty interest at stake here must be defined in reference to the scope of the Alabama statute. We begin by observing that the broad rights to "privacy" and "sexual privacy" invoked by the ACLU are not at issue. The statute invades the privacy of Alabama residents in their bedrooms no more than does any statute restricting the availability of commercial products for use in private quarters as sexual enhancements.[12] Instead, the challenged Alabama statute bans the commercial distribution of sexual devices. At a minimum, therefore, the putative right at issue is the right to sell and purchase sexual devices.

It is more than that, however. For purposes of constitutional analysis, restrictions on the ability to purchase an item are tantamount to restrictions on the use of that item. Thus it was that the *Glucksberg* Court analyzed a ban on *providing* suicide assistance as a burden on the right to *receive* suicide assistance. Similarly, prohibitions on the *sale* of contraceptives have been analyzed as burdens on the *use* of contraceptives. Because a prohibition on the distribution of sexual devices would burden an individual's ability to use the devices, our analysis must be framed not simply in terms of whether the Constitution protects a right to *sell* and *buy* sexual devices, but whether it protects a right to *use* such devices.

2. *"History and Tradition" and "Implicit in the Concept of Ordered Liberty"*

With this "careful description" in mind, we turn now to the second prong of the fundamental-rights inquiry. The crucial inquiry under this prong is whether the right to use sexual devices when engaging in lawful, private sexual activity is (1) "objectively, deeply rooted in this Nation's history and tradition" and (2) "implicit in the concept of ordered liberty, such that neither liberty nor justice would exist if [it] were sacrificed." *Glucksberg,* 521 U.S. at 721. Although the district court never addressed the second part of this inquiry, it answered the "history and tradition" question in the affirmative.

We find that the district court, in reaching this conclusion, erred on four levels. The first error relates back to the district court's over-broad framing of the asserted right in question. Having framed the relevant right as a generalized "right to sexual privacy," the district court's history and tradition analysis consisted largely of an irrelevant exploration of the history of sex in America. Second, we find that this analysis placed too much weight on contemporary practice and attitudes with respect to sexual conduct and sexual devices. Third, rather than look for a history and tradition of *protection* of the asserted right, the district court asked whether there was a history and tradition of state *non-interference* with the right. Finally, we find that the district court's uncritical reliance on certain expert declarations in interpreting the historical record was flawed and that its reliance on certain putative "concessions" was unfounded....

---

12. The mere fact that a product is used within the privacy of the bedroom, or that it enhances intimate conduct, does not in itself bring the use of that article within the right to privacy. If it were otherwise, individuals whose sexual gratification requires other types of material or instrumentalities—perhaps hallucinogenic substances, depictions of child pornography or bestiality, or the services of a willing prostitute—likewise would have a colorable argument that prohibitions on such activities and materials interfere with their privacy in the bedchamber. Under this theory, all such sexual-enhancement paraphernalia (as long as it was used only in consensual encounters between adults) would also be encompassed within the right to privacy—and any burden thereon subject to strict scrutiny.

In reaching its holding, the district court relied heavily on "contemporary practice," emphasizing the "contemporary trend of legislative and societal liberalization of attitudes toward consensual, adult sexual activity."

. . . .

The district court justified this emphasis by noting that the *Glucksberg* Court had relied on contemporary practice in reaching its determination that assisted suicide is not a constitutional right. This gloss, however, considerably overstates that Court's reliance on contemporary attitudes. What the *Glucksberg* Court did was to note that democratic action in many states had recently reaffirmed assisted-suicide bans, thus buttressing the Court's conclusion that assisted suicide is not deeply rooted in the history and traditions of the nation. But the existence of this contemporary practice was never essential to that conclusion. That is, the Court never suggested that a lack of contemporary *reinforcement* of the prohibition on assisted suicide would have led it to a contrary conclusion.

The district court's interpretation also overlooks the context of *Glucksberg*'s contemporary practice analysis. The Court began its examination of history and tradition by inquiring "whether this asserted right has *any place* in our Nation's traditions." Having found that it did not, the Court had no need to proceed to the further question of whether that right was *deeply rooted* in those traditions (nor whether it was "implicit in the concept of ordered liberty"). Part of the reason the Court was able to dismiss the asserted right so summarily was because it found that the prohibition on assisted suicide "continues explicitly" to the present. In short, the democratic action cited by *Glucksberg* was merely one factor among many disproving the claim that assisted suicide is a "deeply rooted" right. . . .

The district court's central holding—its discovery of a constitutional "right to use sexual devices like . . . vibrators, dildos, anal beads, and artificial vaginas"—was not based on any evidence of a history and tradition of *affirmative protection* of this right. The district court's lengthy opinion cites no reference to such a right in the usual repositories of our freedoms, such as federal and state constitutional provisions, constitutional doctrines, statutory provisions, common-law doctrines, and the like. Instead, the critical evidence for the district court was the relative scarcity of statutes explicitly banning sexual devices and the rarity of reported cases of sexual-devices prosecutions—along with various factual assertions from declarations by the ACLU's experts. From this, the district court inferred "that history and contemporary practice demonstrate a conscious avoidance of regulation of [sexual] devices by the states."

This negative inference essentially inverted *Glucksberg*'s history and tradition inquiry. The district court—rather than requiring a showing that the right to use sexual devices is "deeply rooted in this Nation's history and tradition,"—looked for a showing that *proscriptions* against sexual devices are deeply rooted in history and tradition. Under this approach, the freedom to smoke, to pollute, to engage in private discrimination, to commit marital rape—at one time or another—all could have been elevated to fundamental-rights status. Moreover, it would create the perverse incentive for legislatures to regulate every area within their plenary power for fear that their restraint in any area might give rise to a right of constitutional proportions.

Beyond these obvious objections, the most significant flaw in the district court's analysis is its misreading of *Glucksberg*. Admittedly, the *Glucksberg* Court, in declining to extend constitutional protection to assisted suicide, cited the extensive history of laws forbidding or discouraging suicide. But the context of this inquiry was the Court's attempt to determine whether a right to suicide, and particularly assisted suicide, was deeply rooted in American history and tradition. Naturally, prohibitions on suicide were particularly competent evidence of the absence of such a history and tradition. The *Glucksberg* Court, however, never suggested that the reviewing court must find a history of proscription of a given activity before declining to recognize a new constitutional right to engage in that activity.

In short, nothing in *Glucksberg* indicates that an absence of historical *prohibition* is tantamount, for purposes of fundamental-rights analysis, to an historical record of *protection* under the law. To the contrary, the *Glucksberg* standard expressly requires a showing that the asserted right is "deeply rooted in this Nation's history and tradition" and "implicit in the concept of ordered liberty, such that neither liberty nor justice would exist if [it] were sacrificed." Not only does the record before us fail to evidence such a deeply rooted right, but it suggests that, to the extent that sex toys historically have attracted the attention of the law, it has been in the context of proscription, not protection....

Even if these prohibitions on sexual devices were not widespread or vigorously enforced, their mere existence significantly undermines the argument that sexual devices historically have been free from state interference. Moreover, the lack of statutory references to sexual devices is relatively meaningless without evidence that commerce in these devices was sufficiently widespread, or sufficiently in the public eye, to merit legislative attention, at least beyond general anti-obscenity laws. Likewise, the focus on searches of federal case reporters for references to "vibrators" or "dildos" assumes, unjustifiably, that reported cases are reliable proxies for actual prosecutions, the vast majority of which would have never appeared in the court reporters (it also overlooks the possibility of prosecutions under *state* law). It also overlooks the possibility that traditional sensibilities and mores restrained courts from explicitly mentioning particular sexual devices in the text of judicial opinions.

In light of these realities, the negative inference drawn by the district court—that the scarcity of explicit reference to sexual devices in statutory schemes and reported cases reflects a "deliberate non-interference,"—is too speculative a basis for constitutionalizing a hitherto unrecognized right. This is especially true given the lack of any indicia of affirmative protection under the law. In short, there is no competent evidence in the record before us indicating that the lack of explicit and aggressive proscription of sex toys was, as the district court surmised, "conscious avoidance of regulation of these devices by the states."

    ....

III. CONCLUSION

Hunting expeditions that seek trophy game in the fundamental-rights forest must heed the maxim "look before you shoot." Such excursions, if embarked upon recklessly, endanger the very ecosystem in which such liberties thrive—our republican democracy. Once elevated to constitutional status, a right is effectively removed from the hands of the people and placed into the guardianship of unelected judges. We are particularly mindful of this fact in the delicate area of morals legislation. One of the virtues of the democratic process is that, unlike the judicial process, it need not take matters to their logical conclusion. If the people of Alabama in time decide that a prohibition on sex toys is misguided, or ineffective, or just plain silly, they can repeal the law and be finished with the matter. On the other hand, if we today craft a new fundamental right by which to invalidate the law, we would be bound to give that right full force and effect in all future cases—including, for example, those involving adult incest, prostitution, obscenity, and the like....

BARKETT, Circuit Judge, dissenting:

The majority's decision rests on the erroneous foundation that there is no substantive due process right to adult consensual sexual intimacy in the home and erroneously assumes that the promotion of public morality provides a rational basis to criminally burden such private intimate activity. These premises directly conflict with the Supreme Court's holding in *Lawrence v. Texas,* 539 U.S. 558 (2003).

This case is not, as the majority's demeaning and dismissive analysis suggests, about sex or about sexual devices. It is about the tradition of American citizens from the inception of our democracy to value the constitutionally protected right to be left alone in the privacy of their bedrooms and personal relationships....

The majority claims that *Lawrence,* like *Bowers v. Hardwick,* 478 U.S. 186 (1986), failed to recognize the substantive due process right of consenting adults to engage in private sexual conduct. Conceding that *Lawrence* must have done *something,* the majority acknowledges that *Lawrence* "established the unconstitutionality of criminal prohibitions on consensual adult sodomy." The majority refuses, however, to acknowledge *why* the Court in *Lawrence* held that criminal prohibitions on consensual sodomy are unconstitutional. This failure underlies the majority's flawed conclusion in this case.

As explained more fully below, *Lawrence* held that a state may not criminalize sodomy because of the existence of the very right to private sexual intimacy that the majority refuses to acknowledge. *Lawrence* reiterated that its prior fundamental rights cases protected individual choices "concerning the intimacies of [a] physical relationship." Because of this precedent, the *Lawrence* Court overruled *Bowers,* concluding that *Bowers* had "misapprehended the claim of liberty there presented" as involving a particular sexual act rather than the broader right of adult sexual privacy. Instead of heeding the Supreme Court's instruction regarding *Bowers'* error, the majority *repeats* it, ignoring *Lawrence*'s teachings about how to correctly frame a liberty interest affecting sexual privacy.

Compounding this error, the majority also ignores *Lawrence*'s holding that although history and tradition may be used as a "starting point," they are not the "ending point" of a substantive due process inquiry. In cases solely involving adult consensual sexual privacy, the Court has never required that there be a long-standing history of *affirmative* legal protection of *specific conduct* before a right can be recognized under the Due Process Clause. To the contrary, because of the fundamental nature of this liberty interest, this right has been protected by the Court despite historical, legislative *restrictions* on private sexual conduct. Applying the analytical framework of *Lawrence* compels the conclusion that the Due Process Clause protects a right to sexual privacy that encompasses the use of sexual devices.

Finally, even under the majority's own constrained and erroneous interpretation of *Lawrence,* we are, at a bare minimum, obliged to revisit this Court's previous conclusion in *Williams v. Pryor,* 240 F.3d 944 (11th Cir.2001) ("*Williams II*"), that Alabama's law survives the most basic level of review, that of rational basis. That decision explicitly depended upon the finding in *Bowers* that the promotion of public morality provided a rational basis to restrict private sexual activity. *Id.* While the majority recognizes that *Bowers* has been overruled, it inexplicably fails to offer any explanation whatsoever for why public morality provides a rational basis to criminalize the private sexual activity in this case, when it was clearly not found to be a legitimate state interest in *Lawrence.*

For all of these reasons, which are amplified below, I dissent.

I. Lawrence Recognized a Substantive Due Process Right to Sexual Privacy.

There is no question that *Lawrence* was decided on substantive due process grounds. The doctrine of substantive due process requires, first, that *every* law must address in a relevant way only a legitimate governmental purpose. In other words, no law may be arbitrary and capricious but rather must address a permissible state interest in a way that is rationally related to that interest. As a consequence, any law challenged as violating a substantive due process right must survive rational-basis review.

However, the Supreme Court has found that some decisions are so fundamental and central to human liberty that they are protected as part of a right to privacy under the Due Process Clause, and the government may constitutionally restrict these decisions only if it has *more* than an ordinary run-of-the-mill governmental purpose. In such cases, the Court subjects these governmental restrictions to a heightened scrutiny, requiring that legislation be "narrowly drawn" to achieve a "compelling state interest." Included within this right to privacy is the ability to make decisions about intimate sexual matters....

The *Lawrence* Court noted in its opinion that it had granted certiorari specifically to consider "[w]hether Petitioners' criminal convictions for *adult consensual sexual intimacy in the home* violate their *vital interests in liberty and privacy protected by the Due Process Clause of the Fourteenth Amendment?*" While the Court also granted certiorari to address whether Texas's sodomy statute violated the Equal Protection Clause, the Court explicitly decided to rest its holding on a substantive due process analysis because it found that if a sodomy law "remain[ed] unexamined for its substantive validity, its stigma might remain even if it were not enforceable as drawn for equal protection reasons." The Court stated that the "case should be resolved by determining whether the petitioners were free as adults to engage in the private [sexual] conduct in the exercise of their liberty under the Due Process Clause of the Fourteenth Amendment."

In resolving this issue of whether the petitioners were "free as adults" to engage in "private [sexual] conduct," the Court retraced its substantive due process jurisprudence by discussing the fundamental rights cases of *Griswold, Eisenstadt, Roe,* and *Carey* and emphasized the breadth of their holdings as involving private decisions regarding intimate physical relationships. Beginning with *Griswold,* the *Lawrence* Court found that its prior decisions confirmed "that the protection of liberty under the Due Process Clause has a substantive dimension of fundamental significance in defining the rights of the person" and "that the right to make certain decisions regarding sexual conduct extends beyond the marital relationship."

Because of the existence of this right to make private decisions regarding sexual conduct, the *Lawrence* Court was compelled to overrule the anomaly of *Bowers,* which had failed to acknowledge this right in permitting Georgia to criminalize sodomy. *Lawrence* found that at the time of the *Bowers* decision the Court's prior holdings had already made "abundantly clear" that individuals have a substantive due process right to make decisions "concerning the intimacies of their physical relationship[s], even when not intended to produce offspring." The *Lawrence* Court therefore concluded that "*Bowers* was not correct *when it was decided.*"

Given these statements in *Lawrence,* I fail to understand the majority's reliance on a footnote from the Supreme Court's 1977 decision in *Carey,* where the Court indicated in dicta that it had not "definitively answered" the extent to which the Due Process Clause protects the private sexual conduct of consenting adults. Obviously, *Carey* does not resolve in any way the meaning of a case that comes twenty-six years later. Nor does it prevent *Lawrence* from answering the very question posed in *Carey*'s footnote. *Lawrence* does precisely this in affirming the right of consenting adults to make private sexual decisions. Moreover, this could not have been a new right. *Carey*'s footnote notwithstanding, the *Lawrence* Court determined that its pre-*Bowers* decisions had already recognized a right to sexual privacy. This is the only way to make sense of the *Lawrence* Court's statements that *Bowers* was "not correct when it was decided," and that its decisions before *Bowers* had already made "abundantly clear" that adults have a right to make decisions "concerning the intimacies of their physical relationship[s]."

....

II. The Majority Ignores <u>Lawrence</u>'s Teaching Regarding the Proper Framing of a Liberty Interest and the Appropriate Use of History.

....

Regardless of the majority's belief that *Lawrence* did not recognize a substantive due process right, it cannot then simply conduct an analysis that ignores *Lawrence*'s clear statements about the erroneous analytical framework of *Bowers* and repeat that methodology here. Even if *Lawrence* were not itself a fundamental rights decision, it remains the case that *Bowers* conducted a fundamental rights analysis that *Lawrence* found to be deeply flawed. *Lawrence*'s repudiation of *Bowers*' substantive due process approach cannot be dismissed as dicta, since overruling *Bowers* was necessary to the disposition of the decision in *Lawrence*. Therefore, *Lawrence,* coming after *Glucksberg,* must be read as providing binding guidance about how to properly analyze a liberty interest affecting sexual privacy.

A. The Proper Framing of a Liberty Interest

Just as the *Bowers* Court framed the question before it as "whether the Federal Constitution confers a fundamental right upon homosexuals to engage in sodomy," the majority also mistakenly reduces the asserted liberty interest here to a particular sexual act, asking not whether consenting adults have a right to sexual privacy, but whether an Alabama citizen has the right to use sex toys. The *Lawrence* Court explained that the narrow framing of the question in *Bowers* "demean[ed] the claim" set forth and "disclose[d] the Court's own failure to appreciate the extent of the liberty at stake" in that case. The *Lawrence* Court further explained that "[t]he laws involved in *Bowers* and here are, to be sure, statutes that *purport to do no more than prohibit a particular sexual act.* Their penalties and purposes, though, have more far-reaching consequences, touching upon the most private human conduct, sexual behavior, and in the most private of places, the home." In exactly the same manner, the majority's characterization of the right at issue here as involving the right to use certain sexual devices severely discounts the extent of the liberty at stake in this case. Alabama's law not only restricts the sale of certain sexual devices, but, like the statute in *Lawrence,* burdens private adult sexual activity within the home.

B. The Use of History and Tradition

....

Contrary to the majority's claim, neither *Glucksberg* nor any other relevant Supreme Court precedent supports the requirement that there must be a history of affirmative legislative protection before a right can be judicially protected. The majority simply invents this requirement, effectively redefining the doctrine of substantive due process to protect only those rights that are *already* explicitly protected by law. Such a requirement ignores not only *Lawrence* but also a complete body of Supreme Court jurisprudence. Had the Supreme Court required affirmative governmental protection of an asserted liberty interest, all of the Court's privacy cases would have been decided differently. For instance, there was no lengthy tradition of protecting abortion and the use of contraceptives, yet both were found to be protected by a right to privacy under the Due Process Clause. In its analysis, the trial court here correctly considered the history of non-interference by government. Its analysis was expressly validated by *Lawrence,* in which there was no history of affirmatively protecting the right to engage in consensual sodomy. In overruling *Bowers,* the *Lawrence* Court noted with approval Justice Powell's observation in *Bowers* that "*[t]he history of nonenforcement* [of sodomy laws] suggests the moribund character today of laws criminalizing this type of private, consensual conduct." Therefore, the majority is plainly incorrect that there must be a history and tradition of laws protecting the right to use sex toys.

Moreover, while history and tradition can be important factors, they are not the only relevant considerations in a substantive due process inquiry related to sexual privacy. As the *Lawrence* Court emphasized, "[h]istory and tradition are the starting point but not in all cases the ending point of the substantive due process inquiry." Furthermore, like the district court in this case, *Lawrence* looked to modern trends and practices. The *Lawrence* Court wrote:

> [W]e think that *our laws and traditions in the past half century are of most relevance here.* These references show an emerging awareness that liberty gives substantial protection to adult persons in deciding how to *conduct their private lives in matters pertaining to sex.*

Given this unequivocal statement, the majority cannot legitimately criticize the district court for its attention to "contemporary practice and attitudes with respect to sexual conduct and sexual devices." In light of all relevant Supreme Court precedents, the trial court—not the majority—strikes the proper balance between a concern with history and contemporary practice, and articulates a careful and correct description of the asserted liberty interest.

III. Under Lawrence, *"Public Morality" Cannot Be Deemed a Legitimate Governmental Purpose for Criminalizing Private Sexual Activity.*

The majority states that *Lawrence* held that sodomy laws fail rational-basis review. However, the majority neglects to address whether Alabama's statute has a rational basis even though Alabama relies upon the same justification for criminalizing private sexual activity rejected by *Lawrence*—public morality. In *Lawrence,* Texas had explicitly relied upon public morality as a rational basis for its sodomy law. *Lawrence* summarily rejected Texas's argument, holding that the sodomy law "further[ed] *no* legitimate state interest which can justify its intrusion into the personal and private life of the individual." In *Williams II,* this Court previously upheld Alabama's law on rational basis grounds, relying on the now defunct *Bowers* to conclude that public morality provides a legitimate state interest. Obviously, now that *Bowers* has been overruled, this proposition is no longer good law and we must, accordingly, revisit our holding in *Williams II.* Yet despite the *Lawrence* Court's rejection of public morality as a legitimate state interest that can justify criminalizing private consensual sexual conduct, the majority, although acknowledging that the district court will have to do so, never once addresses how our holding in *Williams II* can remain good law. Justice Scalia, in his *Lawrence* dissent, specifically noted that the principles we relied upon in our decision in *Williams II* have been "discarded" by *Lawrence:*

> It seems to me that the "societal reliance" on the principles confirmed in Bowers and *discarded today* has been overwhelming. Countless judicial decisions and legislative enactments have relied on the ancient proposition that a governing majority's belief that certain sexual behavior is "immoral and unacceptable" constitutes a rational basis for regulation. *See, e.g., Williams v. Pryor,* 240 F.3d 944,

949 (C.A.11 2001) (citing *Bowers* in upholding Alabama's prohibition on the sale of sex toys on the ground that "[t]he crafting and safeguarding of public morality ... indisputably is a legitimate government interest under rational basis scrutiny").

....

IV. Conclusion

For all the reasons explicated above, Alabama's statute should be invalidated because it violates a substantive due process right of adults to engage in private consensual sexual activity and because the state's reliance on public morality fails to provide even a rational basis for its law. Ignoring *Lawrence,* the majority turns a reluctance to expand substantive due process into a stubborn unwillingness to consider relevant Supreme Court authority. I dissent.

Williams v. Morgan

478 F.3d 1316 (11th Cir. 2007)

WILSON, Circuit Judge:

This case comes to us for the third time, arising from a constitutional challenge to a provision of the Alabama Code prohibiting the commercial distribution of devices "primarily for the stimulation of human genital organs." Ala.Code § 13A-12-200.2(a)(1). The only question remaining before us is whether public morality remains a sufficient rational basis for the challenged statute after the Supreme Court's decision in *Lawrence v. Texas,* 539 U.S. 558 (2003)....

In *Lawrence* the Supreme Court held that the Texas sodomy statute challenged in that case "further[ed] no legitimate state interest which can justify its intrusion into the personal and private life of the individual." In so holding, the *Lawrence* majority relied on Justice Stevens's analysis in his *Bowers* dissent: "[T]he fact that the governing majority in a State has traditionally viewed a particular practice as immoral is not a sufficient reason for upholding a law prohibiting the practice...." The Court applied Justice Stevens's analysis in overruling *Bowers* and in holding that the Texas sodomy statute was unconstitutional.

The ACLU argues that the Alabama statute at issue in this case, like the Texas sodomy statute at issue in *Lawrence,* intrudes into personal and private decisions about sexual intimacy. It argues that "this law intrudes just as deeply into the sphere of individual decision-making about sexuality as the law struck down in *Lawrence.*" Thus, the ACLU argues, this case is indistinguishable from *Lawrence*—just as in that case, in this case there is no legitimate state interest, including public morality, that supports the challenged Alabama statute. Therefore, it argues that the statute cannot survive constitutional scrutiny under *Lawrence.*

However, while the statute at issue in *Lawrence* criminalized *private* sexual conduct, the statute at issue in this case forbids *public, commercial* activity. To the extent *Lawrence* rejects public morality as a legitimate government interest, it invalidates only those laws that target conduct that is *both* private *and* non-commercial. *Lawrence,* 539 U.S. at 578 ("The present case does not involve minors. It does not involve persons who might be injured or coerced or who are situated in relationships where consent might not easily be refused. *It does not involve public conduct* or prostitution.") (emphasis added). Unlike *Lawrence,* the activity regulated here is *neither* private *nor* non-commercial.[6]

---

6. The ACLU emphasizes language in *Williams IV* where we stated that "for purposes of constitutional analysis, restrictions on the ability to purchase an item are tantamount to restrictions on the

This statute targets *commerce* in sexual devices, an inherently public activity, whether it occurs on a street corner, in a shopping mall, or in a living room. As the majority in *Williams IV* so colorfully put it: "There is nothing 'private' or 'consensual' about the advertising and sale of a dildo." The challenged statute does not target possession, use, or even the gratuitous distribution of sexual devices. In fact, plaintiffs here continue to possess and use such devices. States have traditionally had the authority to regulate commercial activity they deem harmful to the public. Thus, while public morality was an insufficient government interest to sustain the Texas sodomy statute, because the challenged statute in this case does not target private activity, but public, commercial activity, the state's interest in promoting and preserving public morality remains a sufficient rational basis.

Furthermore, we do not read *Lawrence,* the overruling of *Bowers,* or the *Lawrence* court's reliance on Justice Stevens's dissent, to have rendered public morality altogether illegitimate as a rational basis. The principle that "[t]he law ... is constantly based on notions of morality," *Bowers,* 478 U.S. at 196, was not announced for the first time in *Bowers* and remains in force today.... As we noted in *Williams IV,* the Supreme Court has affirmed on repeated occasions that laws can be based on moral judgments. *Williams IV,* 378 F.3d at 1238 n. 8....

We have also noted: "One would expect the Supreme Court to be manifestly more specific and articulate than it was in *Lawrence* if now such a traditional and significant jurisprudential princip[le] has been jettisoned wholesale...." *Williams IV,* 378 F.3d at 1238 n. 8.

Accordingly, we find that public morality survives as a rational basis for legislation even after *Lawrence,* and we find that in this case the State's interest in the preservation of public morality remains a rational basis for the challenged statute....

Reliable Consultants, Inc. v. Earle
517 F.3d 738 (5th Cir. 2008)

REAVLEY, Circuit Judge:

This case assesses the constitutionality of a Texas statute making it a crime to promote or sell sexual devices....

In essence, the statute criminalizes the selling, advertising, giving, or lending of a device designed or marketed for sexual stimulation unless the defendant can prove that the device was sold, advertised, given, or lent for a statutorily-approved purpose. The statute, however, does not prohibit the use or possession of sexual devices for any purpose....

The Plaintiffs' claim is predicated upon the individual right under the Fourteenth Amendment to engage in private intimate conduct in the home without government intrusion. Because the asserted governmental interests for the law do not meet the applicable constitutional standard announced in *Lawrence v. Texas,* the statute cannot be constitutionally enforced.

The State argues that Plaintiffs, who distribute sexual devices for profit, cannot assert the individual rights of their customers. This argument fails under the Supreme Court prece-

---

use of that item." However, the *Williams IV* court connected the sale of sexual devices with their use only in the limited context of framing the scope of the liberty interest at stake under the fundamental rights analysis of *Washington v. Glucksberg,* 521 U.S. 702 (1997). We were clear in *Williams IV,* that the challenged statute did not implicate private or consensual activity.

dent holding that (1) bans on commercial transactions involving a product can unconstitutionally burden individual substantive due process rights and (2) lawsuits making this claim may be brought by providers of the product. In the landmark 1965 case of *Griswold v. Connecticut*, which invalidated a ban on the *use* of contraceptives, the Court recognized that the plaintiff pharmacists "have standing to raise the constitutional rights of the married people with whom they had a professional relationship." Other Supreme Court cases hold that businesses can assert the rights of their customers and that restricting the ability to purchase an item is tantamount to restricting that item's use. In line with these cases, the statute must be scrutinized for impermissible burdens on the constitutional rights of those who wish to use sexual devices.

To determine the constitutional standard applicable to this claim, we must address what right is at stake. Plaintiffs claim that the right at stake is the individual's substantive due process right to engage in private intimate conduct free from government intrusion. The State proposes a different right for the Plaintiffs: "the right to stimulate one's genitals for non-medical purposes unrelated to procreation or outside of an interpersonal relationship." The Court in *Lawrence*—where it overruled its decision in *Bowers v. Hardwick* and struck down Texas's sodomy ban—guides our decision:

> To say that the issue in *Bowers* was simply the right to engage in certain sexual conduct demeans the claim the individual put forward, just as it would demean a married couple were it to be said marriage is simply about the right to have sexual intercourse. The laws involved in *Bowers* and here are, to be sure, statutes that purport to do no more than prohibit a particular sexual act. Their penalties and purposes, though, have more far-reaching consequences, touching upon the most private human conduct, sexual behavior, and in the most private of places, the home.

The right the Court recognized was not simply a right to engage in the sexual act itself, but instead a right to be free from governmental intrusion regarding "the most private human contact, sexual behavior." That *Lawrence* recognized this as a constitutional right is the only way to make sense of the fact that the Court explicitly chose to answer the following question in the affirmative: "We granted certiorari ... [to resolve whether] petitioners' criminal convictions for *adult consensual sexual intimacy* in the home violate their vital interests in liberty and privacy protected by the Due Process Clause of the Fourteenth Amendment."

....

Because of *Lawrence*, the issue before us is whether the Texas statute impermissibly burdens the individual's substantive due process right to engage in private intimate conduct of his or her choosing. Contrary to the district court's conclusion, we hold that the Texas law burdens this constitutional right. An individual who wants to legally use a safe sexual device during private intimate moments alone or with another is unable to legally purchase a device in Texas, which heavily burdens a constitutional right. This conclusion is consistent with the decisions in *Carey* and *Griswold*, where the Court held that restricting commercial transactions unconstitutionally burdened the exercise of individual rights. Indeed, under this statute it is even illegal to "lend" or "give" a sexual device to another person. This further restricts the exercise of the constitutional right to engage in private intimate conduct in the home free from government intrusion. It also undercuts any argument that the statute only affects public conduct.

The dissent relegates the burden on this right to rational basis review. The State says we have two alternatives: (1) strict scrutiny if *Lawrence* established this right as a fundamental right or (2) rational basis review if *Lawrence* did not. There has been debate about this and the Eleventh Circuit concluded that *Lawrence* did not establish a fundamental right.

The Supreme Court did not address the classification, nor do we need to do so, because the Court expressly held that "individual decisions by married persons, concerning the intimacies of their physical relationship, even when not intended to produce offspring, are a form of 'liberty' protected by the Due Process Clause of the Fourteenth Amendment. Moreover, this protection extends to intimate choices by unmarried as well as married persons." The Court also carefully delineated the types of governmental interests that are constitutionally insufficient to sustain a law that infringes on this substantive due process right. Therefore, our responsibility as an inferior federal court is mandatory and straightforward. We must apply *Lawrence* to the Texas statute.[32]

The State's primary justifications for the statute are "morality based." The asserted interests include "discouraging prurient interests in autonomous sex and the pursuit of sexual gratification unrelated to procreation and prohibiting the commercial sale of sex."

These interests in "public morality" cannot constitutionally sustain the statute after *Lawrence.* To uphold the statute would be to ignore the holding in *Lawrence* and allow the government to burden consensual private intimate conduct simply by deeming it morally offensive. In *Lawrence,* Texas's only argument was that the anti-sodomy law reflected the moral judgment of the legislature. The Court expressly rejected the State's rationale by adopting Justice Stevens' view in *Bowers* as "controlling" and quoting Justice Stevens' statement that "'the fact that the governing majority in a State has traditionally viewed a particular practice as immoral is not a sufficient reason for upholding a law prohibiting the practice.'" Thus, if in *Lawrence* public morality was an insufficient justification for a law that restricted "adult consensual intimacy in the home," then public morality also cannot serve as a rational basis for Texas's statute, which also regulates private sexual intimacy.[36]

Perhaps recognizing that public morality is an insufficient justification for the statute after *Lawrence,* the State asserts that an interest the statute serves is the "protection of minors and unwilling adults from exposure to sexual devices and their advertisement." It is undeniable that the government has a compelling interest in protecting children from improper sexual expression. However, the State's generalized concern for children does not justify such a heavy-handed restriction on the exercise of a constitutionally protected individual right. Ultimately, because we can divine no rational connection between the statute and the protection of children, and because the State offers none, we cannot sustain the law under this justification.

The alleged governmental interest in protecting "unwilling adults" from exposure to sexual devices is even less convincing. The Court has consistently refused to burden individual rights out of concern for the protection of "unwilling recipients." Furthermore, this asserted interest bears no rational relation to the restriction on sales of sexual devices because an adult cannot buy a sexual device without making the affirmative decision to visit a store and make the purchase.

---

32. *Lawrence* did not categorize the right to sexual privacy as a fundamental right, and we do not purport to do so here. Instead, we simply follow the precise instructions from *Lawrence* and hold that the statute violates the right to sexual privacy, however it is otherwise described.

36. The State offers cases for the general proposition that protecting morality is a legitimate governmental interest. Our holding in no way overtly expresses or implies that public morality can never be a constitutional justification for a law. We merely hold that after *Lawrence* it is not a constitutional justification for this statute.

The State argues that if this statute, which proscribes the distribution of sexual devices, is struck down, it is equivalent to extending substantive due process protection to the "commercial sale of sex." Not so. The sale of a device that an individual may choose to use during intimate conduct with a partner in the home is not the "sale of sex" (prostitution). Following the State's logic, the sale of contraceptives would be equivalent to the sale of sex because contraceptives are intended to be used for the pursuit of sexual gratification unrelated to procreation. This argument cannot be accepted as a justification to limit the sale of contraceptives. The comparison highlights why the focus of our analysis is on the burden the statute puts on the individual's right to make private decisions about consensual intimate conduct. Furthermore, there are justifications for criminalizing prostitution other than public morality, including promoting public safety and preventing injury and coercion.[40]

Just as in *Lawrence,* the State here wants to use its laws to enforce a public moral code by restricting private intimate conduct. The case is not about public sex. It is not about controlling commerce in sex. It is about controlling what people do in the privacy of their own homes because the State is morally opposed to a certain type of consensual private intimate conduct. This is an insufficient justification for the statute after *Lawrence.*

It follows that the Texas statute cannot define sexual devices themselves as obscene and prohibit their sale.... Whatever one might think or believe about the use of these devices, government interference with their personal and private use violates the Constitution....

[The opinion of Judge Barksdale, concurring in part and dissenting in part, is omitted.]

United States v. Marcum

60 M.J. 198 (C.A.A.F. 2004)

Judge BAKER delivered the opinion of the Court.

....

Appellant, a cryptologic linguist, technical sergeant (E-6), and the supervising noncommissioned officer in a flight of Persian-Farsi speaking intelligence analysts, was stationed at Offutt Air Force Base, Nebraska. His duties included training and supervising airmen newly assigned to the Operations Training Flight.

While off-duty Appellant socialized with airmen from his flight at parties. According to the testimony of multiple members of his unit, airmen "often" spent the night at Appellant's off-base home following these parties. The charges in this case resulted from allegations by some of these subordinate airmen that Appellant engaged in consensual and nonconsensual sexual activity with them.

Among other offenses, Appellant was charged with the forcible sodomy of Senior Airman (SrA) H (E-4)....

A panel of officers and enlisted members found Appellant "not guilty of forcible sodomy" but guilty of non-forcible sodomy in violation of Article 125....

---

40. To guide future courts, the Court in *Lawrence* delineated what the right is not about: "The present case does not involve minors. It does not involve persons who might be injured or coerced or who are situated in relationships where consent might not easily be refused. It does not involve public conduct or prostitution." Instead, the right at issue in *Lawrence* dealt with two adults engaging in consensual sexual conduct.

Discussion

A. *Article 125 Text*

Article 125 states:

> (a) Any person subject to this chapter who engages in unnatural carnal copulation with another person of the same or opposite sex or with an animal is guilty of sodomy. Penetration, however slight, is sufficient to complete the offense.

> (b) Any person found guilty of sodomy shall be punished as a court-martial may direct.

As we stated in *United States v. Scoby*,

> By its terms, Article 125 prohibits every kind of unnatural carnal intercourse, whether accomplished by force or fraud, or with consent. Similarly, the article does not distinguish between an act committed in the privacy of one's home, with no person present other than the sexual partner, and the same act committed in a public place in front of a group of strangers, who fully apprehend in the nature of the act.

5 M.J. 160, 163 (C.M.A.1978). Thus, Article 125 forbids sodomy whether it is consensual or forcible, heterosexual or homosexual, public or private.

B. *Arguments*

Appellant challenges his conviction on the ground that *Lawrence* recognized a constitutional liberty interest in sexual intimacy between consenting adults in private. Appellant argues that Article 125 suffers from the same constitutional deficiencies as the Texas statute in *Lawrence* because both statutes criminalize private consensual acts of sodomy between adults....

The amici curiae, arguing in support of Appellant's position, assert that Article 125 is unconstitutional on its face.... As with other fundamental rights, the amici contend that a statute purporting to criminalize a fundamental right must be narrowly tailored to accomplish a compelling government interest. The amici argue that Article 125 is not narrowly tailored because it reaches, among other conduct, the private, consensual, off-base, intimate activity of married military persons and their civilian spouses. Arguing in the alternative, quoting *Lawrence,* the amici do not "dispute that the interests in good order and discipline, and in national security, are important. But the importance of those interests is irrelevant, because there is simply no basis to conclude that they are even rationally related to Article 125...."

The Government argues that *Lawrence* is not applicable in the military environment due to the distinct and separate character of military life from civilian life as recognized by the Supreme Court in *Parker v. Levy,* 417 U.S. 733 (1974). The Government further argues that because the Supreme Court did not expressly state that engaging in homosexual sodomy is a fundamental right, this Court should analyze Article 125 using the rational basis standard of review. Utilizing this standard, the Government contends Article 125 is constitutional because it is rationally related to a legitimate state interest. Specifically, the Government maintains that Article 125 criminalizes conduct that "create[s] an unacceptable risk to the high standards of morale, good order and discipline, and unit cohesion" within the military as recognized by Congress in 10 U.S.C. §654(a)(15)....

C. The *Lawrence* Decision

....

(1) Standard of Constitutional Review

. . . .

Although particular sentences within the Supreme Court's opinion may be culled in support of the Government's argument, other sentences may be extracted to support Appellant's argument. On the one hand, the opinion incorporates some of the legal nomenclature typically associated with the rational basis standard of review. For example, as the Government notes, the Supreme Court declared "[t]he Texas statute furthers no legitimate state interest[.]" This is the counter-weight applied in the rational basis analysis. Moreover, the Supreme Court did not apply the nomenclature associated with strict scrutiny, i.e., identification of a compelling state interest and narrow tailoring of the statute to accomplish that interest.

On the other hand, the Supreme Court placed *Lawrence* within its liberty line of cases resting on the *Griswold* foundation. These cases treated aspects of liberty and privacy as fundamental rights, thereby, subjecting them to the compelling interest analysis. With regard to the Supreme Court's use of language attributed to the rational basis review, Appellant and the amici argue the Supreme Court is simply stating that the Texas statute does not even accomplish a legitimate interest, let alone a compelling one.

Indeed, in response to the Supreme Court's decision in *Lawrence,* some courts have applied the rational basis standard of review while other courts have applied strict scrutiny. . . .

The focus by the Government and Appellant on the nature of the Supreme Court's constitutional test in *Lawrence* is understandable. Utilization of either the rational basis test or strict scrutiny might well prove dispositive of a facial challenge to Article 125. On the one hand, the interests in military readiness, combat effectiveness, or national security arguably would qualify as either rational or compelling governmental interests. On the other hand, it is less certain that Article 125 is narrowly tailored to accomplish these interests.

The Supreme Court did not expressly state which test it used. The Court did place the liberty interest in *Lawrence* within the *Griswold* line of cases. *Griswold* and *Carey* address fundamental rights. However, the Supreme Court has not determined that all liberty or privacy interests are fundamental rights. In *Lawrence,* the Court did not expressly identify the liberty interest as a fundamental right. Therefore, we will not presume the existence of such a fundamental right in the military environment when the Supreme Court declined in the civilian context to expressly identify such a fundamental right.

What *Lawrence* requires is searching constitutional inquiry. This inquiry may require a court to go beyond a determination as to whether the activity at issue falls within column A—conduct of a nature to bring it within the liberty interest identified in *Lawrence,* or within column B—factors identified by the Supreme Court as outside its *Lawrence* analysis. The Court's analysis reached beyond the immediate facts of the case presented. This is reflected by the Court's decision to rule on the grounds of due process as opposed to equal protection. "Were we to hold the statute invalid under the Equal Protection Clause," the Supreme Court noted, "some might question whether a prohibition would be valid if drawn differently, say, to prohibit the conduct both between same-sex and different-sex participants." The Supreme Court also acknowledged "an emerging awareness that liberty gives substantial protection to adult persons in deciding how to conduct their private lives in matters pertaining to sex."

At the same time the Court identified factors, which it did not delimit, that might place conduct outside the *Lawrence* zone of liberty. Thus, the door is held open for lower courts to address the scope and nature of the right identified in *Lawrence,* as well as its limitations, based on contexts and factors the Supreme Court may not have anticipated or chose not to address in *Lawrence*. In our view, this framework argues for contextual, as applied analysis, rather than facial review. This is particularly apparent in the military context.

(2) *Lawrence* in the Military Context

The Supreme Court and this Court have long recognized that "[m]en and women in the Armed Forces do not leave constitutional safeguards and judicial protection behind when they enter military service." .... As a result, this Court has consistently applied the Bill of Rights to members of the Armed Forces, except in cases where the express terms of the Constitution make such application inapposite.

At the same time, these constitutional rights may apply differently to members of the armed forces than they do to civilians. *See Parker,* 417 U.S. at 743. "The military is, by necessity, a specialized society." Thus, when considering how the First Amendment and Fourth Amendment apply in the military context, this Court has relied on Supreme Court civilian precedent, but has also specifically addressed contextual factors involving military life. In light of the military mission, it is clear that servicemembers, as a general matter, do not share the same autonomy as civilians.

While the Government does not contest the general proposition that the Constitution applies to members of the Armed Forces, it argues that *Lawrence* only applies to civilian conduct. Moreover, with respect to the military, the Government contends that Congress definitively addressed homosexual sodomy by enacting 10 U.S.C. § 654 (2000). According to the Government, pursuant to Congress's Article I authority to make rules and regulations for the Armed Forces, Congress not only prohibited sodomy through Article 125, but with Article 125 as a backdrop, determined in 1993 through 10 U.S.C. § 654 that homosexuality, and, therefore, sodomy was incompatible with military service. In enacting § 654, Congress determined that "[t]he presence in the armed forces of persons who demonstrate a propensity or intent to engage in homosexual acts would create an unacceptable risk to the high standards of morale, good order and discipline, and unit cohesion that are the essence of military capability." 10 U.S.C. § 654(a)(15). Thus, according to the Government, this Court should apply traditional principles of deference to Congress's exercise of its Article I authority and not apply *Lawrence* to the military.

The military landscape, however, is less certain than the Government suggests. The fog of constitutional law settles on separate and shared powers where neither Congress nor the Supreme Court has spoken authoritatively. Congress has indeed exercised its Article I authority to address homosexual sodomy in the Armed Forces, but this occurred prior to the Supreme Court's constitutional decision and analysis in *Lawrence* and at a time when *Bowers* served as the operative constitutional backdrop. Moreover, the Supreme Court did not accept the Government's present characterization of the right as one of homosexual sodomy....

Constitutional rights identified by the Supreme Court generally apply to members of the military unless by text or scope they are plainly inapplicable. Therefore, we consider the application of *Lawrence* to Appellant's conduct. However, we conclude that its application must be addressed in context and not through a facial challenge to Article 125. This view is consistent with the principle that facial challenges to criminal statutes are "best when infrequent" and are "especially to be discouraged." *Sabri v. United States,* 541 U.S. 600 (2004). In the military setting, as this case demonstrates, an understanding of military culture and mission cautions against sweeping constitutional pronouncements that may not account for the nuance of military life. This conclusion is also supported by this Court's general practice of addressing constitutional questions on an as applied basis where national security and constitutional rights are both paramount interests. Further, because Article 125 addresses both forcible and non-forcible sodomy, a facial challenge reaches too far. Clearly, the *Lawrence* analysis is not at issue with respect to forcible sodomy.

Thus, this case presents itself to us as a challenge to a discrete criminal conviction based on a discrete set of facts. The question this Court must ask is whether Article 125 is constitutional as applied to Appellant's conduct. This as-applied analysis requires consideration of three questions. First, was the conduct that the accused was found guilty of committing of a nature to bring it within the liberty interest identified by the Supreme Court? Second, did the conduct encompass any behavior or factors identified by the Supreme Court as outside the analysis in *Lawrence*? Third, are there additional factors relevant solely in the military environment that affect the nature and reach of the *Lawrence* liberty interest?

D. Is Article 125 Constitutional as Applied to Appellant?

Appellant was charged with dereliction of duty, three specifications of forcible sodomy, three specifications of indecent assault, and two specifications of committing an indecent act. With regard to the charge addressed on appeal, the members found Appellant "not guilty of forcible sodomy, but guilty of non-forcible sodomy." As part of Appellant's contested trial, the following additional facts surrounding his conduct were elicited: The act of sodomy occurred in Appellant's off-base apartment during off-duty hours; no other members of the military were present at the time of the conduct; Appellant was an E-6 and the supervising noncommissioned officer in his flight. His duties included training and supervising airmen. SrA H, an E-4, was one of the airmen Appellant supervised. As a result, SrA H was subordinate to, and directly within, Appellant's chain of command.

The first question we ask is whether Appellant's conduct was of a nature to bring it within the *Lawrence* liberty interest. Namely, did Appellant's conduct involve private, consensual sexual activity between adults? In the present case, the members determined Appellant engaged in non-forcible sodomy. This sodomy occurred off-base in Appellant's apartment and it occurred in private. We will assume without deciding that the jury verdict of non-forcible sodomy in this case satisfies the first question of our as applied analysis.

The second question we ask is whether Appellant's conduct nonetheless encompassed any of the behavior or factors that were identified by the Supreme Court as not involved in *Lawrence*. For instance, did the conduct involve minors? Did it involve public conduct or prostitution? Did it involve persons who might be injured or coerced or who are situated in relationships where consent might not easily be refused?

When evaluating whether Appellant's conduct involved persons who might be injured or coerced or who were situated in relationships where consent might not easily be refused, the nuance of military life is significant. An Air Force instruction applicable to Appellant at the time of the offenses included the following proscriptions.

> Unduly familiar relationships between members in which one member exercises supervisory or command authority over the other can easily be or become unprofessional. Similarly, as differences in grade increase, even in the absence of a command or supervisory relationship, there may be more risk that the relationship will be, or be perceived to be unprofessional because senior members in military organizations normally exercise authority or some direct or indirect organizational influence over more junior members.

> Relationships are unprofessional, whether pursued on or off-duty, when they detract from the authority of superiors or result in, or reasonably create the appearance of, favoritism, misuse of office or position, or the abandonment of organizational goals for personal interests.

Dep't. of the Air Force Instruction, 36-2909 Professional and Unprofessional Relationships, paras. 2.2, 3.1 (May 1, 1996).

For these reasons, the military has consistently regulated relationships between servicemembers based on certain differences in grade in an effort to avoid partiality, preferential treatment, and the improper use of one's rank. Indeed, Dep't of the Air Force Instruction 36-2909 is subject to criminal sanction through operation of Article 92, UCMJ. As both the Supreme Court and this Court have recognized elsewhere, "The fundamental necessity for obedience and the consequent necessity for imposition of discipline, may render permissible within the military that which would be constitutionally impermissible outside it." *Parker,* 417 U.S. at 758. While servicemembers clearly retain a liberty interest to engage in certain intimate sexual conduct, "this right must be tempered in a military setting based on the mission of the military, the need for obedience of orders, and civilian supremacy."

In light of Air Force Instructions at the time, Appellant might have been charged with a violation of Article 92 for failure to follow a lawful order. However, the Government chose to proceed under Article 125. Nonetheless, the fact that Appellant's conduct might have violated Article 92 informs our analysis as to whether Appellant's conduct fell within the *Lawrence* zone of liberty.

As the supervising noncommissioned officer, Appellant was in a position of responsibility and command within his unit with respect to his fellow airmen. He supervised and rated SrA H. Appellant also testified that he knew he should not engage in a sexual relationship with someone he supervised. Under such circumstances, which Appellant acknowledged was prohibited by Air Force policy, SrA H, a subordinate airman within Appellant's chain of command, was a person "who might be coerced" or who was "situated in [a] relationship[] where consent might not easily be refused." *Lawrence,* 539 U.S. at 578. Thus, based on this factor, Appellant's conduct fell outside the liberty interest identified by the Supreme Court. As a result, we need not consider the third step in our *Lawrence* analysis. Nor, given our determination that Appellant's conduct fell outside the liberty interest identified in *Lawrence,* need we decide what impact, if any, 10 U.S.C. § 654 would have on the constitutionality of Article 125 as applied in other settings....

[The opinion of Chief Judge Crawford, concurring in part and dissenting in part, is omitted.]

Singson v. Commonwealth of Virginia

621 S.E.2d 682 (Va. Ct. App. 2005)

ROBERT J. HUMPHREYS, Judge.

Appellant Joel Dulay Singson ("Singson") appeals his conviction, following a conditional guilty plea, for solicitation to commit oral sodomy, in violation of Code §§ 18.2-29 (criminal solicitation) and 18.2-361 (crimes against nature). Based on the holding of the United States Supreme Court in *Lawrence v. Texas,* 539 U.S. 558 (2003), Singson contends that Code § 18.2-361 is facially unconstitutional because it prohibits private acts of consensual sodomy, in violation of the Due Process Clause of the Fourteenth Amendment. Thus, Singson argues that he cannot be convicted for attempting, through solicitation, to violate that statute....

I. BACKGROUND

The relevant facts are not in dispute. At approximately 4:00 p.m. on March 20, 2003, Singson walked into a men's restroom located in a department store. The restroom is freely accessible to members of the public, including children. Once in the restroom, Singson entered the handicapped bathroom stall and remained in that stall for approximately thirty minutes. Singson then left the handicap bathroom stall and approached a stall occupied by an undercover police officer. Singson "stopped in front of the stall, leaned forward," and "peered into [the] stall through the crack in the stall door." The undercover police officer, who was in "a state of undress," asked Singson "What's up?" and "What are you looking for?" Singson replied, "Cock." The officer then asked "What do you want to do," and Singson replied, "I want to suck cock." The undercover officer asked if Singson wanted to suck his penis, and Singson responded, "Yes." When the officer asked, "Do you want to do it in here," Singson nodded towards the handicap stall. The officer then asked if Singson wanted to suck his penis in the handicap stall, and Singson responded, "Yes."

A grand jury indicted Singson for "command[ing], entreat[ing] or otherwise attempt[ing] to persuade another to commit a felony other than murder," specifically, "Crimes Against Nature," in violation of Code §§ 18.2-29 and 18.2-361. Singson moved to dismiss the indictment, arguing that Code § 18.2-361 "is overbroad and vague, [and] violates the defendant's rights to Due Process under the United States Constitution as outlined in the recent U.S. Supreme Court opinion in [*Lawrence v. Texas,* 539 U.S. 558 (2003)]."

The trial court overruled the motion to dismiss, reasoning that *Lawrence* did not apply because "the restrooms within [s]tores open to the public are not within the zone of privacy as contemplated by the United States Supreme Court." The court further noted that it could not "imagine too much more [of a] public place than a restroom in a shopping mall." Singson entered a conditional guilty plea, and the trial court, noting Singson's extensive criminal history of prior, similar behavior, imposed a sentence of three years in prison. The court suspended two and one-half years of Singson's sentence, resulting in a total active sentence of six months.

II. ANALYSIS

. . . .

A. *Whether Code § 18.2-361 is Facially Unconstitutional Because it Encompasses Conduct Protected Under the Due Process Clause of the Fourteenth Amendment*

Citing the United States Supreme Court's decision in *Lawrence v. Texas,* 539 U.S. 558 (2003), Singson initially contends that Code § 18.2-361 is facially unconstitutional because it encompasses private acts of consensual sodomy, thus offending the Due Process Clause of the Fourteenth Amendment. However, because Singson's conduct occurred in a public place — not a private location — we hold that he lacks standing to challenge the constitutionality of Code § 18.2-361 on this ground. Accordingly, we do not reach the issue of whether, applying *Lawrence,* Code § 18.2-361 is facially unconstitutional under the Fourteenth Amendment because it encompasses private — as well as public — acts of consensual sodomy. And, because application of Code § 18.2-361 under the circumstances of this case neither implicates nor violates Singson's constitutional right to due process of law, we conclude that this assignment of error has no merit. . . .

2. *Appellant's Standing to Mount a Facial Challenge on Due Process Grounds*

Singson argues ... that Code § 18.2-361 is facially unconstitutional because, in light of the United States Supreme Court's holding in *Lawrence,* the statute — as applied to private, consensual acts of sodomy — violates the Due Process Clause of the Fourteenth Amendment. Because the statute is facially unconstitutional, Singson reasons that, even though his public conduct falls within the ambit of Code § 18.2-361, the statute cannot be enforced against him.

However, a litigant "has standing to challenge the constitutionality of a statute only insofar as it has an adverse impact on his own rights." *County Court of Ulster County v. Allen,* 442 U.S. 140 (1979). Thus, "[a]s a general rule, if there is no constitutional defect in the application of the statute to the litigant, he does not have standing to argue that it would be unconstitutional if applied to third parties in hypothetical situations." *Id.* at 155.[2]

For example, in *DePriest v. Commonwealth,* 33 Va.App. 754 (2000), the appellants challenged their convictions for solicitation to commit oral sodomy, in violation of the exact statutes at issue in this appeal. The appellants contended — as does Singson — that Code § 18.2-361 was "unconstitutional on its face," reasoning that the statute, *inter alia,* "denies the fundamental right to privacy guaranteed by the Constitution of Virginia." We held, however, that appellants lacked standing to mount a facial challenge to Code § 18.2-361, reasoning that the appellants fell "within the general rule that a party attacking the constitutionality of a statute must demonstrate that his own, rather than a third party's, rights are constitutionally infringed." Thus, we addressed the constitutionality of Code § 18.2-361 "only as it applie[d] to the appellants in [that] case and to the[ ] conduct that underlay their convictions."

Similarly, in *Santillo,* the appellant challenged the constitutionality of Code § 18.2-361 on substantially similar grounds, contending that the statute "abridge[d] his constitutional right to privacy" because it prohibited "consensual heterosexual sex." Before conducting a constitutional analysis, we noted that, "generally, a litigant may challenge the constitutionality of a law only as it applies to him or her." We further explained that whether "'the statute may apply unconstitutionally to another is irrelevant; one cannot raise third party rights.'"

Accordingly, as in *DePriest* and *Santillo,* we hold that Singson lacks standing to mount a facial challenge to Code § 18.2-361. Rather, this Court is constrained to deciding whether Code § 18.2-361 is constitutional as applied to the circumstances of this case. And, for the reasons that follow, we hold that application of Code § 18.2-361 to Singson's proposed conduct does not offend the Due Process Clause of the Fourteenth Amendment.

3. *Whether Code § 18.2-361 is Constitutional as Applied to the Circumstances of this Case*

.... The issue presented in *Lawrence* was "whether the petitioners were free as adults to engage in the private conduct in the exercise of their liberty under the Due Process Clause of the Fourteenth Amendment to the Constitution." The *Lawrence* Court overruled its earlier decision in *Bowers v. Hardwick,* 478 U.S. 186 (1986), and invalidated the Texas statute, concluding that the government cannot make "private sexual con-

---

2. The only recognized exceptions to this rule are "First Amendment challenges" and vagueness challenges that "touch[ ] First Amendment concerns." ....

duct a crime" because the "right to liberty under the Due Process Clause gives [individuals] the full right to engage in [that] conduct without intervention of the government."

However, in *Lawrence*, the Supreme Court explicitly noted that the case being decided on appeal did not "involve public conduct or prostitution." The Court, therefore, only addressed the constitutionality of criminalizing "adult consensual sexual intimacy in the home," leaving undisturbed the states' authority to prohibit sexual conduct that occurs in a public—rather than private—arena.

Singson argues, however, that, in *Lawrence*, the Supreme Court effectively declared all sodomy statutes facially unconstitutional. Singson points to the Court's statement that "*Bowers* was not correct when it was decided, and it is not correct today," as evidencing the Supreme Court's belief that no statute encompassing private acts of sodomy can survive scrutiny under the Due Process Clause. We disagree.

In *Bowers*, the appellant was prosecuted for engaging in homosexual acts of sodomy in the privacy of his own home. After the indictment was dismissed, the appellant brought a suit in federal district court seeking, in essence, a declaratory judgment that the Georgia statute was unconstitutional "as applied to consensual homosexual sodomy." The *Bowers* majority carefully stated that its decision "express[ed] no opinion on the constitutionality of the Georgia statute as applied to other acts of sodomy," later noting that the issue being resolved in the appeal involved the continuing imposition of "criminal penalties for sodomy performed in private and between consenting adults." Similarly, the principal dissent in *Bowers* noted that the issue being decided concerned "the right of an individual to conduct intimate relationships in the intimacy of his or her own home." Thus, despite Singson's argument to the contrary, *Bowers* did not involve a facial challenge to the Georgia sodomy statute. At best, then, the *dicta* in *Lawrence* indicates that the as-applied challenge in *Bowers* should have been upheld, and the statement does not—as Singson contends—announce a *per se* rule that all sodomy statutes are facially unconstitutional....

Thus, to the extent that Code § 18.2-361 prohibits individuals from engaging in *public* acts of sodomy, the statute survives constitutional scrutiny under the Due Process Clause. And, because Singson's proposed conduct occurred in a public location, application of Code § 18.2-361 under the circumstances of this case does not implicate Singson's constitutionally-protected right to engage in private, consensual acts of sodomy.

Our decision in *DePriest* is instructive on this point. In *DePriest*, we affirmed the appellants' convictions for solicitation to commit oral sodomy, holding that application of Code § 18.2-361 under the circumstances of that case did not "infringe [ ] [the appellants'] right to privacy" because "the appellants' conduct was not private." The appellants in *DePriest* approached "strangers in public parks" and "proposed to commit sodomy in the public parks." We held that "[t]he appellants' acts and their proposed conduct were clothed with no circumstance giving rise to a supportable claim of privacy," reasoning that, "[w]hatever may be the constitutional privacy rights of one who engages in sodomy in private, those rights do not attach to one who does the same thing in public."

Similarly, here, Singson's proposed conduct was "clothed with no circumstances giving rise to a supportable claim of privacy." Specifically, Singson approached a stranger in a public restroom in a public department store during business hours, and he proposed to commit sodomy in that restroom. Because Singson's proposed conduct involved a public rather than private location, application of Code § 18.2-361 under the circumstances of this case does not implicate the narrow liberty interest recognized in *Lawrence*.[6]

....

State v. Lowe

861 N.E.2d 512 (Ohio 2007)

LANZINGER, J.

In this case, accepted on a discretionary appeal, we consider R.C. 2907.03(A)(5), Ohio's incest statute, and hold that the statute is constitutional as applied to the consensual sexual conduct between a stepparent and adult stepchild.

Case Procedure

The Stark County Grand Jury indicted defendant-appellant, Paul Lowe, on one count of sexual battery, a felony violation of R.C. 2907.03(A)(5), as a result of his consensual sex with his 22-year-old stepdaughter, the biological daughter of his wife, on March 19, 2003. Lowe pleaded not guilty and filed a motion to dismiss, claiming that the facts alleged in the indictment did not constitute an offense under R.C. 2907.03(A)(5), because the use of the term "stepchild" in the statute signified a "clear legislative intent to have the law apply to children, not adults." In the alternative, Lowe argued that the statute was unconstitutional as applied to his case because the government has no legitimate interest in regulating sex between consenting adults.

After the trial court overruled his motion, Lowe changed his plea to no contest, was convicted, and was sentenced to 120 days of incarceration and three years of community control. The trial court also classified him as a sexually oriented offender. The Fifth District Court of Appeals upheld Lowe's conviction, holding that R.C. 2907.03(A)(5) clearly and unambiguously prohibits sexual conduct between a stepparent and stepchild regardless of the stepchild's age. The court of appeals also held that Lowe "does not have a constitutionally protected right to engage in sex with his stepdaughter."

We accepted the case on a discretionary appeal. Lowe argues that in enacting R.C. 2907.03(A)(5), the General Assembly intended to protect *children* against adults in positions of authority who harmed them. He claims that the statute is unconstitutional when applied to consensual sexual conduct between adults related only by affinity. We will address these arguments in order.

---

6. As noted by one federal court,

   > there are many activities that the law recognizes a person may constitutionally engage in in his home that could be made criminal if done in public. For instance, a person is free to drink alcohol to the point of inebriation in his home, but could be cited for public intoxication if he left the house. A person can possess a firearm without a license in his home, but could be cited for carrying that same item in public. A person can walk around naked in his home, but could be cited for public indecency if he left his house in that condition.

   United States v. Extreme Assocs., Inc., 352 F.Supp.2d 578, 594 (W.D.Pa.2005). Similarly, although individuals may engage in private, consensual acts of sodomy free from government intrusion, the Commonwealth remains free to criminalize that conduct if—as here—it occurs in a public location.

Ohio's Incest Statute

R.C. 2907.03(A) states:

"No person shall engage in sexual conduct with another, not the spouse of the offender, when any of the following apply:

" * * *

"(5) The offender is the other person's natural or adoptive parent, or a stepparent, or guardian, custodian, or person in loco parentis of the other person."

. . . .

The statute does not limit its reach to children, as Lowe argues. R.C. 2907.03(A)(5) states that "[n]o person shall engage in sexual conduct *with another,* not the spouse of the offender when any of the following apply * * *." The statute goes on to list guardians and custodians as well as natural and adoptive parents and persons in loco parentis. Thus, the statute is not limited to protecting minors from those in a position of authority over them. In the 1973 Legislative Service Commission Comments to the statute, the commission explained:

"This section forbids sexual conduct with a person other than the offender's spouse in a variety of situations where the offender takes unconscionable advantage of the victim.

" * * * Incestuous conduct is also included, though defined in broader terms than formerly, so as to include not only sexual conduct by a parent with his child, but also sexual conduct by a stepparent with his stepchild, a guardian with his ward, or a custodian or person in loco parentis with his charge."

In other words, although the statute does indeed protect minor children from adults with authority over them, it also protects the family unit more broadly....

Lowe would have the statute's prohibition against sexual conduct be limited to conduct with minors.... But the plain language of R.C. 2907.03(A)(5) clearly prohibits sexual conduct with one's stepchild while the stepparent-stepchild relationship exists. It makes no exception for consent of the stepchild or the stepchild's age.

Constitutional Discussion

Lowe argues that he has a fundamental right to engage in sexual activity with a consenting adult and that his conduct was private conduct protected by the Constitution. He therefore argues that, as applied to him, R.C. 2907.03(A)(5) violates the Fourteenth Amendment to the United States Constitution, which protects him against deprivation of "life, liberty, or property, without due process of law."

. . . .

There are two tests used to assess the constitutionality of a statute under the Due Process Clause: strict scrutiny or rational-basis scrutiny. When the law restricts the exercise of a fundamental right, the strict-scrutiny test is used. See *Washington v. Glucksberg* (1997), 521 U.S. 702, 721. A statute survives strict scrutiny if it is narrowly tailored to serve a compelling state interest. Yet this heightened test is available only when fundamental rights are implicated. Where there is no fundamental right at issue, a rational-basis test is used to protect liberty interests. *Glucksberg,* 521 U.S. at 722. Under the rational-basis test, a statute survives if it is reasonably related to a legitimate government interest.

Therefore, first we must determine whether Lowe is guaranteed a fundamental right to engage in sexual intercourse with his consenting adult stepdaughter....

Lowe cites *Lawrence v. Texas,* 539 U.S. 558, to argue that he has a constitutionally protected liberty interest to engage in private, consensual, adult sexual conduct with his stepdaughter when that activity does not involve minors or persons who may be easily injured or coerced. In *Lawrence,* a Texas statute criminalizing homosexual conduct was held to be unconstitutional as applied to adult males who had engaged in private and consensual acts of sodomy. Lowe contends that *Lawrence* named a new fundamental right to engage in consensual sex in the privacy of one's home.

However, the statute in *Lawrence* was subjected to a rational-basis rather than a strict-scrutiny test, with the court concluding that the Texas statute furthered no legitimate state interest that could justify intrusion into an individual's personal and private life. In using a rational-basis test to strike down the Texas statute, the court declined to announce a new fundamental right arising from the case.

In addition to emphasizing that the court in using a rational-basis test did not name a new fundamental right, the state in this case distinguishes *Lawrence* as being limited to consensual sexual conduct between unrelated adults. Lowe and his stepdaughter were not unrelated. The state argues that since Lowe has no fundamental right in this case, and the state has a legitimate interest in prohibiting incestuous relations and in protecting the family unit and family relationships, the rational-basis test should apply. Lowe argues for strict scrutiny of R.C. 2907.03(A)(5) and contends that Ohio's incest statute is not the least restrictive means for protecting the state's interest.

We agree with the state that a rational-basis test should be used to analyze the statute. *Lawrence* did not announce a "fundamental" right to all consensual adult sexual activity, let alone consensual sex with one's adult children or stepchildren. Because Lowe's claimed liberty interest in sexual activity with his stepdaughter is not a fundamental right, the statute affecting it need only have a reasonable relationship to some legitimate governmental interest.

Using the rational-basis test, we conclude that, as applied in this case, Ohio's statute serves the legitimate state interest of protecting the family unit and family relationships. While it is not enough under the rational-basis test for the government to just announce a noble purpose behind a statute, the statute will pass if it is reasonably related to any legitimate state purpose. Ohio has a tradition of acknowledging the "importance of maintaining the family unit." A sexual relationship between a parent and child or a stepparent and stepchild is especially destructive to the family unit. R.C. 2907.03(A)(5) was designed to protect the family unit by criminalizing incest in Ohio. Stepchildren and adopted children have been included as possible victims of the crime of incest because society is concerned with the integrity of the family, including step and adoptive relationships as well as blood relationships, and sexual activity is equally disruptive, whatever the makeup of the family. As the "traditional family unit has become less and less traditional, * * * the legislature wisely recognized that the parental role can be assumed by persons other than biological parents, and that sexual conduct by someone assuming that role can be just as damaging to a child." This reasoning applies not only to minor children, but to adult children as well. Moreover, parents do not cease being parents—whether natural parents, stepparents, or adoptive parents—when their minor child reaches the age of majority.

Accordingly, as applied in this case, R.C. 2907.03(A)(5) bears a rational relationship to the legitimate state interest in protecting the family, because it reasonably advances its goal of protection of the family unit from the destructive influence of sexual relationships between parents or stepparents and their children or stepchildren. If Lowe divorced his wife and no longer was a stepparent to his wife's daughter, the stepparent-stepchild relationship would be dissolved. The statute would no longer apply in that case.

We hold that R.C. 2907.03(A)(5) is constitutional as applied to consensual sexual conduct between a stepparent and adult stepchild, because it bears a rational relationship to the state's legitimate interest in protecting the family....

[The dissenting opinion of Judge Pfeifer is omitted.]

State v. Holm

137 P.3d 726 (Utah 2006)

DURRANT, Justice:

. . . .

BACKGROUND

[Rodney Hans] Holm was legally married to Suzie Stubbs in 1986. Subsequent to this marriage, Holm, a member of the Fundamentalist Church of Jesus Christ of Latter-day Saints (the "FLDS Church"), participated in a religious marriage ceremony with Wendy Holm. Then, when Rodney Holm was thirty-two, he participated in another religious marriage ceremony with then-sixteen-year-old Ruth Stubbs, Suzie Stubbs's sister. After the ceremony, Ruth moved into Holm's house, where her sister Suzie Stubbs, Wendy Holm, and their children also resided. By the time Ruth turned eighteen, she had conceived two children with Holm, the second of which was born approximately three months after her eighteenth birthday.

Holm was subsequently arrested in Utah and charged with three counts of unlawful sexual conduct with a sixteen- or seventeen-year-old, in violation of Utah Code section 76-5-401.2 (2003), and one count of bigamy, in violation of Utah Code section 76-7-101 (2003)—all third degree felonies....

The jury returned a guilty verdict on each of the charges....

2. Holm's Conviction Does Not Offend the Due Process Clause of the Fourteenth Amendment

Holm argues that the State of Utah is foreclosed from criminalizing polygamous behavior because the freedom to engage in such behavior is a fundamental liberty interest that can be infringed only for compelling reasons and that the State has failed to identify a sufficiently compelling justification for its criminalization of polygamy. We disagree and conclude that there is no fundamental liberty interest to engage in the type of polygamous behavior at issue in this case.

In arguing that his behavior is constitutionally protected as a fundamental liberty interest, Holm relies primarily on the United States Supreme Court's decision in *Lawrence v. Texas*, 539 U.S. 558 (2003). In that case, the United States Supreme Court struck down a Texas statute criminalizing homosexual sodomy, concluding that private, consensual sexual behavior is protected by the Due Process Clause of the Fourteenth Amendment. Holm argues that the liberty interest discussed in *Lawrence* is sufficiently broad to shield the type of behavior that he engages in from the intruding hand of the state. Holm misconstrues the breadth of the *Lawrence* opinion.

Despite its use of seemingly sweeping language, the holding in *Lawrence* is actually quite narrow. Specifically, the Court takes pains to limit the opinion's reach to decriminalizing private and intimate acts engaged in by consenting adult gays and lesbians. In fact, the Court went out of its way to exclude from protection conduct that causes "injury to a person or abuse of an institution the law protects." Further, after announcing its holding, the Court noted the following: "The present case does not involve minors. It does not involve persons who might be injured or coerced or who are situated in relationships where consent might not easily be refused. It does not involve public conduct...."

In marked contrast to the situation presented to the Court in *Lawrence,* this case implicates the public institution of marriage, an institution the law protects, and also involves a minor. In other words, this case presents the exact conduct identified by the Supreme Court in *Lawrence* as outside the scope of its holding.

First, the behavior at issue in this case is not confined to personal decisions made about sexual activity, but rather raises important questions about the State's ability to regulate marital relationships and prevent the formation and propagation of marital forms that the citizens of the State deem harmful.

> Sexual intercourse ... is the most intimate behavior in which the citizenry engages. [*Lawrence*] spoke to this discreet, personal activity. Marriage, on the other hand, includes both public and private conduct. Within the privacy of the home, marriage means essentially whatever the married individuals wish it to mean. Nonetheless, marriage extends beyond the confines of the home to our society.

Joseph Bozzuti, Note, *The Constitutionality of Polygamy Prohibitions After Lawrence v. Texas: Is Scalia a Punchline or a Prophet?,* 43 Catholic Law. 409, 435 (Fall 2004).

The very "concept of marriage possesses 'undisputed social value.'" Utah's own constitution enshrines a commitment to prevent polygamous behavior. That commitment has undergirded this State's establishment of "a vast and convoluted network of ... laws ... based exclusively upon the practice of monogamy as opposed to plural marriage." Our State's commitment to monogamous unions is a recognition that decisions made by individuals as to how to structure even the most personal of relationships are capable of dramatically affecting public life.

The dissent states quite categorically that the State of Utah has no interest in the commencement of an intimate personal relationship so long as the participants do not present their relationship as being state-sanctioned. On the contrary, the formation of relationships that are marital in nature is of great interest to this State, no matter what the participants in or the observers of that relationship venture to name the union. We agree with the dissent's statement that any two people may make private pledges to each other and that these relationships do not receive legal recognition unless a legal adjudication of marriage is sought.[11] That does not, however, prevent the legislature from having a substantial interest in criminalizing such behavior when there is an existing marriage.

As the dissent recognizes, a marriage license significantly alters the bond between two people because the State becomes a third party to the marital contract. It is precisely that third-party contractual relationship that gives the State a substantial interest in prohibiting unlicensed marriages when there is an existing marriage. Without this contractual relationship, the State would be unable to enforce important marital rights and obliga-

---

11. Utah Code section 30-1-4.5 (Supp.2005) allows a court to order that an unsolemnized marriage is a legal and valid marriage so long as the relationship is between a man and a woman who are capable of giving consent and marrying, have cohabited, have mutually assumed marital rights, duties, and obligations, and have held themselves out as husband and wife.

tions. In situations where there is no existing marriage, the Legislature has developed a mechanism for legally determining that a marriage did in fact exist, even where the couple did not seek legal recognition of that marriage, so that the State may enforce marital obligations such as spousal support or prevent welfare abuse. There is no such mechanism for protecting the State's interest in situations where there is an existing marriage because, under any interpretation of the bigamy statute, a party cannot seek a legal adjudication of a second marriage. Thus, the State has a substantial interest in criminalizing such an unlicensed second marriage.

Moreover, marital relationships serve as the building blocks of our society. The State must be able to assert some level of control over those relationships to ensure the smooth operation of laws and further the proliferation of social unions our society deems beneficial while discouraging those deemed harmful. The people of this State have declared monogamy a beneficial marital form and have also declared polygamous relationships harmful. As the Tenth Circuit stated in *Potter,* Utah "is justified, by a compelling interest, in upholding and enforcing its ban on plural marriage to protect the monogamous marriage relationship."

Further, this case features another critical distinction from *Lawrence;* namely, the involvement of a minor. Stubbs was sixteen years old at the time of her betrothal, and evidence adduced at trial indicated that she and Holm regularly engaged in sexual activity. Further, it is not unreasonable to conclude that this case involves behavior that warrants inquiry into the possible existence of injury and the validity of consent.

Given the above, we conclude that *Lawrence* does not prevent our Legislature from prohibiting polygamous behavior. The distinction between private, intimate sexual conduct between consenting adults and the public nature of polygamists' attempts to extralegally redefine the acceptable parameters of a fundamental social institution like marriage is plain. The contrast between the present case and *Lawrence* is even more dramatic when the minority status of Stubbs is considered. Given the critical differences between the two cases, and the fact that the United States Supreme Court has not extended its jurisprudence to such a degree as to protect the formation of polygamous marital arrangements, we conclude that the criminalization of the behavior engaged in by Holm does not run afoul of the personal liberty interests protected by the Fourteenth Amendment....

[The concurring opinion of Justice Nehring is omitted.]

DURHAM, Chief Justice, concurring in part and dissenting in part:

I join the majority in upholding Holm's conviction for unlawful sexual conduct with a minor. As to the remainder of its analysis, I respectfully dissent....

III. FOURTEENTH AMENDMENT DUE PROCESS CLAIM

Because I conclude that Holm's bigamy conviction violates the Utah Constitution's religious freedom guarantees, my dissenting vote is not based on the majority's analysis of Holm's federal constitutional claims. I do, however, wish to register my disagreement with the majority's treatment of Holm's claim that his conviction violates his Fourteenth Amendment right under the Due Process Clause to individual liberty, as recognized by the United States Supreme Court in *Lawrence v. Texas,* 539 U.S. 558 (2003). As the majority acknowledges, the Court in *Lawrence* stated the principle that "absent injury to a person or abuse of an institution the law protects," adults are free to choose the nature of their relationships "in the confines of their homes and their own private lives." The majority concludes that the private consensual behavior of two individuals who did not claim legal recognition of their relationship somehow constitutes an abuse of the institution of marriage, thus rendering *Lawrence* inapplicable. On that basis,[34] the majority summarily rejects Holm's due process claim as beyond the scope of *Lawrence's* holding. I disagree with this analysis.

As I have discussed extensively above, I do not believe that the conduct at issue threatens the institution of marriage, and I therefore cannot agree that it constitutes an "abuse" of that institution. The majority fails to offer a persuasive justification for its view to the contrary. It asserts that "the behavior at issue in this case" implicates "the state's ability to regulate marital relationships." According to the majority, this regulation includes the state's ability to impose a legal marriage on an individual against his or her will in order to enforce spousal support obligations or prevent welfare abuse. In regard to spousal support, I am unpersuaded that the potential interests of consenting adults who voluntarily enter legally unrecognized relationships despite the financial risks they might face in the future justify the imposition of criminal penalties on the parties to those relationships. Under the majority's rationale, the state would be justified in imposing criminal penalties on unmarried persons who enter same-sex relationships simply because the state, under the applicable constitutional and statutory provisions, is unable to hold them legally married. In regard to welfare abuse, I find it difficult to understand how those in polygamous relationships that are ineligible to receive legal sanction are committing welfare abuse when they seek benefits available to unmarried persons.

The majority also offers the view that "[t]he state must be able to … further the proliferation of social unions our society deems beneficial while discouraging those deemed harmful." The Supreme Court in *Lawrence,* however, rejected the very notion that a state can criminalize behavior merely because the majority of its citizens prefers a different form of personal relationship. Striking down Texas's criminal sodomy statute as unconstitutional, the Court in *Lawrence* recognized that the Fourteenth Amendment's individual liberty guarantee "gives substantial protection to adult persons in deciding how to conduct their private lives in matters pertaining to sex." As described in *Lawrence,* this protection encompasses not merely the consensual act of sex itself but the "autonomy of the person" in making choices "relating to … family relationships." The sodomy statute was thus held unconstitutional because it sought "to control a personal relationship that, whether or not entitled to formal recognition in the law, is within the liberty of persons to choose without being punished as criminals."

I agree with the majority that marriage, when understood as a legal union, qualifies as "an institution the law protects." However, the Court's statement in *Lawrence* that a state may interfere when such an institution is "abuse[d]," together with its holding that the sodomy statute was unconstitutional, leads me to infer that, in the Court's view, sexual acts between consenting adults and the private personal relationships within which these acts occur, do not "abuse" the institution of marriage simply because they take place outside its confines. In the wake of *Lawrence,* the Virginia Supreme Court has come to the same conclusion, striking down its state law criminalizing fornication. *Martin v. Ziherl,* 607 S.E.2d 367, 371 (2005). In my opinion, these holdings correctly recognize that individuals in today's society may make varied choices regarding the organization of their family and personal relationships without fearing criminal punishment.

---

34. The majority could have limited its rejection of Holm's liberty claim to the fact that Holm's behavior involved a minor. That fact alone, in my view, justifies the conclusion that Holm's bigamy conviction does not violate his right to individual liberty under the Due Process Clause of the Fourteenth Amendment to the United States Constitution.

The majority does not adequately explain how the institution of marriage is abused or state support for monogamy threatened simply by an individual's choice to participate in a religious ritual with more than one person outside the confines of legal marriage. Rather than offering such an explanation, the majority merely proclaims that "the public nature of polygamists' attempts to extralegally redefine the acceptable parameters of a fundamental social institution like marriage is plain." It is far from plain to me.

I am concerned that the majority's reasoning may give the impression that the state is free to criminalize any and all forms of personal relationships that occur outside the legal union of marriage. While under *Lawrence* laws criminalizing isolated acts of sodomy are void, the majority seems to suggest that the relationships within which these acts occur may still receive criminal sanction. Following such logic, nonmarital cohabitation might also be considered to fall outside the scope of federal constitutional protection. Indeed, the act of living alone and unmarried could as easily be viewed as threatening social norms.

In my view, any such conclusions are foreclosed under *Lawrence*. Essentially, the Court's decision in *Lawrence* simply reformulates the longstanding principle that, in order to "secure individual liberty, ... certain kinds of highly personal relationships" must be given "a substantial measure of sanctuary from unjustified interference by the State." *Roberts v. U.S. Jaycees*, 468 U.S. 609, 618 (1984). Whether referred to as a right of "intimate" or "intrinsic" association, as in *Roberts*, 468 U.S. at 618, a right to "privacy," as in *Griswold v. Connecticut*, 381 U.S. 479, 485 (1965), and *Eisenstadt v. Baird*, 405 U.S. 438, 453 (1972), a right to make "choices concerning family living arrangements," as in *Moore v. City of East Cleveland*, 431 U.S. 494, 499 (1977) (plurality), or a right to choose the nature of one's personal relationships, as in *Lawrence*, 539 U.S. at 574, this individual liberty guarantee essentially draws a line around an individual's home and family and prevents governmental interference with what happens inside, as long as it does not involve injury or coercion or some other form of harm to individuals or to society. As the Court in *Lawrence* recognized:

> [F]or centuries there have been powerful voices to condemn [certain private] conduct as immoral. The condemnation has been shaped by religious beliefs, conceptions of right and acceptable behavior, and respect for the traditional family. For many persons these are not trivial concerns but profound and deep convictions accepted as ethical and moral principles to which they aspire and which thus determine the course of their lives. These considerations do not answer the question before us, however. The issue is whether the majority may use the power of the State to enforce these views on the whole society through operation of the criminal law.

The Court determined that when "adults ... with full and mutual consent from each other" enter into particular personal relationships with no threat of injury or coercion, a state may not criminalize the relationships themselves or the consensual intimate conduct that occurs within them.

In conclusion, I agree with the majority that because Holm's conduct in this case involved a minor, he is unable to prevail on his individual liberty claim under the Due Process Clause. However, I disagree with the majority's implication that the same result would apply where an individual enters a private relationship with another adult....

Notes and Questions

1. Setting aside your personal view of what the right *outcome* should be, which court—the Eleventh Circuit in *Williams v. Attorney General of Alabama* or the Fifth Circuit in

Reliable Consultants—is more consistent with *Lawrence*? Or are both approaches more or less equally consistent with *Lawrence*?

2. What basis was there for the majority in *Williams v. Attorney General of Alabama* to demand "affirmative protection" of a right historically, as opposed to historical non-interference with a right? Was there "affirmative protection" of the right to use contraceptives, to procure an abortion, or to engage in acts of consensual sodomy in *Griswold*, *Roe*, and *Lawrence*, respectively?

3. In *Williams v. Attorney General of Alabama*, the court cites its prior decision in *Lofton* for the proposition that *Lawrence* did not identify a fundamental right to private sexual intimacy. The *Lofton* case—which upheld a substantive due process and equal protection challenge to a Florida law banning "practicing homosexuals" from adopting children—is examined in full in Chapter 5.

4. To what extent was the difference in rank between the soldiers decisive to the outcome in *Marcum*? In other words, would the sodomy law violate *Lawrence* as applied to consensual sodomy between two soldiers of equal rank? *Compare United States v. Barber*, 2004 WL 5862927, at *7 (A. Ct. Crim. App. 2004) (when both are of equal rank, not within the *Lawrence* exception), *and United States v. Meno*, 2005 WL 6520748, at *4 (A. Ct. Crim. App. 2005) (same), *with United States v. Smith*, 66 M.J. 556 (C.G. Ct. Crim. App. 2008) (holding that even though the situation is within the right protected by *Lawrence*, the third *Marcum* factor—"additional factors relevant solely in the military environment"—comes into play, specifically, those of discipline and order).

5. As the *Marcum* court indicates—and as you previewed in the *Meinhold* case in Chapter 1—the U.S. Supreme Court has held that although constitutional safeguards apply in the military context, they are often applied differently. More specifically, the Court will often give greater deference to the importance of the government interests identified by the military in support of their policies. The extent of this deference is examined in greater detail in Chapters 4 through 6.

6. When adultery occurs in private between two consenting adults, is that equivalent to the sort of conduct at issue in *Lawrence*? Or does adultery involve the interests of more than the two adults engaging in the conduct? *Compare Thong v. Andre Chreky Salon*, 634 F. Supp. 2d 40, 46–47 (D.D.C. 2009) (suggesting that logic of *Lawrence* might apply to adultery statutes since they involve private sexual conduct between two consenting adults), *with United States v. Orellana*, 62 M.J. 595, 598 (N-M. Ct. Crim. App. 2005) (relying on the fact that in military context, adultery is harmful to good order and discipline, and also noting that government has an interest in preserving marriages so that members of military and spouses left behind during deployments are not affected by concerns over integrity of marriage), *and* Mary Ann Case, *Of "This" and "That" in* Lawrence v. Texas, 55 SUP. CT. REV. 75, 140–41 (2003) (relying on *Lawrence*'s reference to "abuse of an institution that the law protects" to refer to the continuing interest of the state in prohibiting adultery even when there is consent of the other spouse). *See generally* Peter Nicolas, *The Lavender Letter: Applying the Law of Adultery to Same-Sex Couples and Same-Sex Conduct*, 63 FLA. L. REV. 97 (2011) (surveying the modern law of adultery and considering its application to married same-sex couples).

7. Much is made in *Lawrence* about the fact that the conduct at issue occurred in *private*. In distinguishing *Lawrence*, the two *Williams* decisions and the *Singson* decision thus make much of the fact that the conduct occurred in public. The *Williams* court noted that "[t]here is nothing 'private' or 'consensual' about the advertising and sale of a dildo." And the *Singson* court emphasized the fact that the prohibited sexual conduct was to

occur in public. How do these decisions relate to the situation in which the *proposal* to engage in the conduct occurs in public but the proposal is to engage in the conduct in *private*?

8. Consent appears to be a necessary condition for falling within the scope of the liberty identified in *Lawrence*, but is it a *sufficient* condition as well? In other words, does the substantive guarantee of liberty include the liberty to engage in painful or harmful forms of sexual activity? *Compare State v. Jensen*, 118 P.3d 762 (N.M. Ct. App. 2005) (Robinson, J., concurring in part and dissenting in part) (suggesting that, after *Lawrence*, it may be unconstitutional for the state to criminalize consensual "rough sex" between two adults), *with People v. Febrissy*, 2006 WL 2006161, at *5 (Cal. Ct. App. 2006) (leaving open question whether *Lawrence* reaches "bondage, discipline, and sadomasochistic sexuality," but noting *Lawrence*'s caveat that the case did not "involve persons *who might be injured*"), *and State v. Van*, 688 N.W.2d 600, 615 (Neb. 2004) ("The *Lawrence* Court did not extend constitutional protection to any conduct which occurs in the context of a consensual sexual relationship. Rather, the Court indicated that State regulation of such conduct was inappropriate 'absent injury to a person or abuse of an institution the law protects.' In addition, it specifically noted that the case it was deciding did not involve 'persons who might be injured.'").

9. Is the right recognized in *Lawrence* limited to sexual activity involving *two* persons? Might there be a government interest in regulating sexual activity involving multiple persons, akin to the interests that might justify limiting marriage to two persons? *See United States v. Kowalski*, 69 M. J. 705, 710 n.5 (C.G. Ct. Crim. App. 2010) (suggesting *Lawrence* is distinguishable where three individuals are involved, since it made specific reference to the fact that the case "involve[s] *two* adults").

10. What reasons are there for prohibiting sexual activity with animals? Might one argue that they lack the ability to consent, and thus that the activity is outside the scope of *Lawrence*? (Of course, they probably also don't consent to being eaten, yet that happens with some frequency!) Might there be government interests other than the lack of consent? *See Kuch v. Rapelje*, 2010 WL 3419823, at *10 (E.D. Mich. 2010) (noting public health concern of disease spreading from animals to humans).

11. What are the reasons for prohibiting incest? Do all types of incest raise the same concerns, and if so, are there some for which public morality is the only justification? Consider the following:

> There are many varieties of the crime called "incest," and each variety should be subjected to its own harm analysis. The typical harm justification for incest rests on the risks of genetic abnormalities and of coercion and abuse. But some forms of incest, such as incest between first cousins, adopted children, in-laws, and uncles and nieces, may not raise substantial risks of harm.... Nonetheless, studies show that most people have an instinctive negative response to incest, even where the risks of harm are not present. Such responses, long common among substantial majorities with respect to interracial marriage and homosexual activity, should not suffice. Other forms of legitimate harm may exist, including the risk of coercion and abuse, but *Lawrence* requires that these harms be documented in order to justify a criminal statute.

J. Kelly Strader, Lawrence's *Criminal Law*, 16 Berkeley J. Crim. L. 41, 103-04 (2011).

In *Lowe*, the court notes that the incest statute would not, in terms, apply to the stepparent-stepchild relationship after that relationship is dissolved by divorce. What *if* the statute were amended by the state legislature to apply even in that situation? Would it still be constitutional post-*Lawrence*?

12. What reasons, other than public morality, justify laws criminalizing prostitution? The *Reliable Consultants* case identifies the interests of "promoting public safety and preventing injury and coercion." In addition, prostitution creates public health risks, such as the spread of communicable diseases. *See* J. Kelly Strader, Lawrence's *Criminal Law*, 16 BERKELEY J. CRIM. L. 41, 102 n.332 (2011).

13. What would have been the consequence in the cases and hypotheticals in this section had the *Lawrence* Court formally recognized the right at issue as a *fundamental* one subject to strict scrutiny? To what extent was that likely on the minds of Justice Kennedy and those who signed onto his majority opinion?

Chapter 4

Equal Protection

A. Background

The Equal Protection Clause of the Fourteenth Amendment commands:

> No State shall ... deny to any person within its jurisdiction the equal protection of the laws.

Unlike the Due Process Clause of the Fourteenth Amendment, the Equal Protection Clause—in terms—finds no counterpart in the Fifth Amendment, or indeed any other part of the U.S. Constitution applicable to the federal government.

The clause has long posed an interpretive quandary for courts. Taken at face value, it could be viewed as a command for *strict* equality, meaning that government could *never* draw distinctions amongst people, but would have to treat everyone precisely the same. While at first glance that might seem like a positive, consider for just a moment the many ways in which government *routinely* classifies people and treats people in those classes differently:

- *Classifications based on age*—Government routinely draws lines on the basis of age, establishing a minimum age for obtaining a driver's license, purchasing or consuming tobacco products or alcohol, or obtaining social security and other governmental benefits.

- *Classifications based on income*—Government routinely draws lines on the basis of income, imposing differential income tax rates depending upon income and providing public assistance benefits only for those below certain income thresholds.

- *Classifications based on intellectual ability*—Government routinely draws lines on the basis of ability, admitting into state colleges and universities only those whose grade-point averages and standardized test scores exceed certain thresholds, and providing differential financial aid in the form of merit scholarships based on ability.

- *Classifications based on physical ability*—Government routinely specifies certain types of physical characteristics (height, weight, strength) for performing certain types of jobs, such as those in law enforcement or the military.

If the term "equal" as used in the Equal Protection Clause were to command strict equality, all such government classifications would be deemed unconstitutional, even though virtually everyone would agree that the sorts of line drawing described seem very sensible. The U.S. Supreme Court has thus acknowledged that "[t]he Fourteenth Amendment's promise that no person shall be denied the equal protection of the laws must coexist with the practical necessity that most legislation classifies for one purpose or another, with resulting disadvantage to various groups or persons," and its case law has sought to "reconcile the principle with the reality." *Romer v. Evans*, 517 U.S. 620, 631 (1996).

Indeed, in its first decision interpreting the Equal Protection Clause, the Court suggested a limitation based on the history that motivated Congress to enact it and the States to ratify it:

> We doubt very much whether any action of a State not directed by way of discrimination against the negroes as a class, or on account of their race, will ever be held to come within the purview of this provision. It is so clearly a provision for that race and that emergency, that a strong case would be necessary for its application to any other.

Slaughter-House Cases, 83 U.S. 36, 81 (1873).

Even within the realm of racial discrimination, the Court—in its early decisions—invoked history as a basis for interpreting the command of "equal" treatment in a rather narrow fashion. Thus, in *Plessy v. Ferguson*, 163 U.S. 537 (1896), the Court held the doctrine of "separate but equal" to be consistent with the Equal Protection Clause:

> The object of the amendment was undoubtedly to enforce the absolute equality of the two races before the law, but, in the nature of things, it could not have been intended to abolish distinctions based upon color, or to enforce social, as distinguished from political, equality, or a commingling of the two races upon terms unsatisfactory to either. Laws permitting, and even requiring, their separation, in places where they are liable to be brought into contact, do not necessarily imply the inferiority of either race to the other, and have been generally, if not universally, recognized as within the competency of the state legislatures in the exercise of their police power. The most common instance of this is connected with the establishment of separate schools for white and colored children, which have been held to be a valid exercise of the legislative power even by courts of states where the political rights of the colored race have been longest and most earnestly enforced....
>
> Laws forbidding the intermarriage of the two races may be said in a technical sense to interfere with the freedom of contract, and yet have been universally recognized as within the police power of the state.
>
> The distinction between laws interfering with the political equality of the negro and those requiring the separation of the two races in schools, theaters, and railway carriages has been frequently drawn by this court....
>
> In this connection, it is also suggested by the learned counsel for the plaintiff in error that the same argument that will justify the state legislature in requiring railways to provide separate accommodations for the two races will also authorize them to require separate cars to be provided for people whose hair is of a certain color, or who are aliens, or who belong to certain nationalities, or to enact laws requiring colored people to walk upon one side of the street, and white people upon the other, or requiring white men's houses to be painted white, and colored men's black, or their vehicles or business signs to be of different colors, upon the theory that one side of the street is as good as the other, or that a house or vehicle of one color is as good as one of another color. The reply to all this is that every exercise of the police power must be reasonable, and extend only to such laws as are enacted in good faith for the promotion of the public good, and not for the annoyance or oppression of a particular class....
>
> So far, then, as a conflict with the fourteenth amendment is concerned, the case reduces itself to the question whether the statute of Louisiana is a reason-

able regulation, and with respect to this there must necessarily be a large discretion on the part of the legislature. In determining the question of reasonableness, it is at liberty to act with reference to the established usages, customs, and traditions of the people, and with a view to the promotion of their comfort, and the preservation of the public peace and good order. Gauged by this standard, we cannot say that a law which authorizes or even requires the separation of the two races in public conveyances is unreasonable, or more obnoxious to the fourteenth amendment than the acts of congress requiring separate schools for colored children in the District of Columbia, the constitutionality of which does not seem to have been questioned, or the corresponding acts of state legislatures.

We consider the underlying fallacy of the plaintiff's argument to consist in the assumption that the enforced separation of the two races stamps the colored race with a badge of inferiority. If this be so, it is not by reason of anything found in the act, but solely because the colored race chooses to put that construction upon it. The argument necessarily assumes that if, as has been more than once the case, and is not unlikely to be so again, the colored race should become the dominant power in the state legislature, and should enact a law in precisely similar terms, it would thereby relegate the white race to an inferior position. We imagine that the white race, at least, would not acquiesce in this assumption. The argument also assumes that social prejudices may be overcome by legislation, and that equal rights cannot be secured to the negro except by an enforced commingling of the two races. We cannot accept this proposition. If the two races are to meet upon terms of social equality, it must be the result of natural affinities, a mutual appreciation of each other's merits, and a voluntary consent of individuals.... If the civil and political rights of both races be equal, one cannot be inferior to the other civilly or politically. If one race be inferior to the other socially, the constitution of the United States cannot put them upon the same plane.

Id. at 544–52.

In the years and decades immediately following *Plessy*, litigants and the Court switched their focus away from the equality based arguments of the Equal Protection Clause to the rights-based arguments of the Due Process Clause. Indeed, just one year after *Plessy* was decided, the Court kicked off the so-called *Lochner* era—discussed in the previous chapter—with its decision in *Allgeyer v. Louisiana,* 165 U.S. 578 (1897).

To be sure, litigants continued to invoke the Equal Protection Clause during the *Lochner* era, yet they continued to be rebuffed. Indicative of the Court's view of the Equal Protection Clause was the Court's 1927 decision upholding the constitutionality of a state law authorizing the sterilization of mentally retarded persons living in institutions. In his opinion for the Court, Justice Holmes quickly brushed to one side the equal protection claim, describing it as "the usual last resort of constitutional arguments" and concluding that "the law does all that is needed when it does all that it can, indicates a policy, applies it to all within the lines, and seeks to bring within the lines all similarly situated so far and so fast as its means allow." *Buck v. Bell*, 274 U.S. 200, 208 (1927).

At the close of the *Lochner* era, the Court, in *United States v. Carolene Products Co.*, 304 U.S. 144 (1938) rejected a substantive due process challenge to a federal statute prohibiting the shipment of "filled milk" in interstate commerce, applying the permissive post-*Lochner* standard of rational basis review. The Court went on to describe the rather loose standard by which it would assess an Equal Protection Clause challenge to such a statute:

The Fifth Amendment has no equal protection clause, and even that of the Fourteenth, applicable only to the states, does not compel their Legislatures to prohibit all like evils, or none. A Legislature may hit at an abuse which it has found, even though it has failed to strike at another.

Id. at 151.

Yet in what has been termed "the most celebrated footnote in constitutional law," Lewis F. Powell, Jr., *Carolene Products Revisited*, 82 Colum. L. Rev. 1087, 1087 (1982), the Court went on to state, in pertinent part, as follows:

It is unnecessary to consider now whether legislation which restricts those political processes which can ordinarily be expected to bring about repeal of undesirable legislation, is to be subjected to more exacting judicial scrutiny under the general prohibitions of the Fourteenth Amendment than are most other types of legislation. [The Court here cites cases addressing the constitutionality of restrictions upon the right to vote; restraints upon the dissemination of information; interferences with political organizations; and prohibitions of peaceable assembly.] Nor need we enquire whether similar considerations enter into the review of statutes directed at particular religious, or national, or racial minorities: whether prejudice against discrete and insular minorities may be a special condition, which tends seriously to curtail the operation of those political processes ordinarily to be relied upon to protect minorities, and which may call for a correspondingly more searching judicial inquiry.

United States v. Carolene Prods. Co., 304 U.S. 144, 152 n.4 (1938).

As the cases that follow will demonstrate, the Court—in a series of post-*Carolene Products* decisions—has developed a multi-tiered framework for assessing Equal Protection Clause claims in which the level of scrutiny varies depending upon the type of classification (race versus age, for example) as well as the type of right involved.

The materials in this first section of the chapter demonstrate the two extremes of the multi-tiered framework: rational basis review and strict scrutiny. In comparing the two approaches, note both the different standard that the Court applies to the *ends* the government seeks to achieve as well as the *means* employed to achieve those ends. The materials in the two sections that follow examine the Court's standard for determining which types of classification merit heightened scrutiny under the Equal Protection Clause, as well as the question whether to recognize other levels of scrutiny in between the extremes of rational basis and strict scrutiny. Finally, the last section examines the application of these principles in cases involving discrimination on the basis of sexual orientation or gender identity.

Federal Communications Commission v. Beach Communications, Inc.

508 U.S. 307 (1993)

Justice THOMAS delivered the opinion of the Court.

....

I

The Cable Communications Policy Act of 1984 (Cable Act) amended the Communications Act of 1934 to establish a national framework for regulating cable television.... Congress provided for the franchising of cable systems by local governmental authorities, and prohibited any person from operating a cable system without a franchise, subject to certain exceptions. Section 602(7) of the Communications Act ... determines the reach of the franchise requirement by defining the operative term "cable system." A cable system means any facility designed to provide video programming to multiple subscribers through "closed transmission paths," but does not include, *inter alia,*

> "a facility that serves only subscribers in 1 or more multiple unit dwellings under common ownership, control, or management, unless such facility or facilities us[e] any public right-of-way" § 602(7)(B), 47 U.S.C. § 522(7)(B) (1988 ed., Supp. V).

....

This case arises out of an FCC proceeding clarifying the agency's interpretation of the term "cable system" as it is used in the Cable Act. In this proceeding, the Commission addressed the application of the exemption codified in § 602(7)(B) to satellite master antenna television (SMATV) facilities. Unlike a traditional cable television system, which delivers video programming to a large community of subscribers through coaxial cables laid under city streets or along utility lines, an SMATV system typically receives a signal from a satellite through a small satellite dish located on a rooftop and then retransmits the signal by wire to units within a building or complex of buildings. The Commission ruled that an SMATV system that serves multiple buildings via a network of interconnected physical transmission lines is a cable system, unless it falls within the § 602(7)(B) exemption. Consistent with the plain terms of the statutory exemption, the Commission concluded that such an SMATV system is subject to the franchise requirement if its transmission lines interconnect separately owned and managed buildings or if its lines use or cross any public right-of-way.

Respondents Beach Communications, Inc., Maxtel Limited Partnership, Pacific Cablevision, and Western Cable Communications, Inc. — SMATV operators that would be subject to franchising under the Cable Act as construed by the Commission — petitioned the Court of Appeals for review. The Court of Appeals rejected respondents' statutory challenge to the Commission's interpretation, but a majority of the court found merit in the claim that § 602(7) violates the implied equal protection guarantee of the Due Process Clause. In the absence of what it termed "the predominant rationale for local franchising" (use of public rights-of-way), the court saw no rational basis "[o]n the record," and was "unable to imagine" any conceivable basis, for distinguishing between those facilities exempted by the statute and those SMATV cable systems that link separately owned and managed buildings. The court remanded the record and directed the FCC to provide "additional 'legislative facts'" to justify the distinction.

A report subsequently filed by the Commission failed to satisfy the Court of Appeals.... In a second opinion, the majority ... held that "the Cable Act violates the equal protection component of the Fifth Amendment, insofar as it imposes a discriminatory franchising requirement....

II

Whether embodied in the Fourteenth Amendment or inferred from the Fifth, equal protection is not a license for courts to judge the wisdom, fairness, or logic of legislative choices. In areas of social and economic policy, a statutory classification that neither proceeds along suspect lines nor infringes fundamental constitutional rights must be upheld against equal protection challenge if there is any reasonably conceivable state of facts that could provide a rational basis for the classification. See *Sullivan v. Stroop,* 496 U.S. 478, 485 (1990); *Bowen v. Gilliard,* 483 U.S. 587, 600–603 (1987); *United States Railroad Re-*

tirement Bd. v. Fritz, 449 U.S. 166, 174–179 (1980); *Dandridge v. Williams,* 397 U.S. 471, 484–485 (1970). Where there are "plausible reasons" for Congress' action, "our inquiry is at an end." *United States Railroad Retirement Bd. v. Fritz, supra,* 449 U.S., at 179. This standard of review is a paradigm of judicial restraint. "The Constitution presumes that, absent some reason to infer antipathy, even improvident decisions will eventually be rectified by the democratic process and that judicial intervention is generally unwarranted no matter how unwisely we may think a political branch has acted." *Vance v. Bradley,* 440 U.S. 93, 97 (1979).

On rational-basis review, a classification in a statute such as the Cable Act comes to us bearing a strong presumption of validity, see *Lyng v. Automobile Workers,* 485 U.S. 360, 370 (1988), and those attacking the rationality of the legislative classification have the burden "to negative every conceivable basis which might support it," *Lehnhausen v. Lake Shore Auto Parts Co.,* 410 U.S. 356, 364 (1973). Moreover, because we never require a legislature to articulate its reasons for enacting a statute, it is entirely irrelevant for constitutional purposes whether the conceived reason for the challenged distinction actually motivated the legislature. *United States Railroad Retirement Bd. v. Fritz, supra,* 449 U.S., at 179. Thus, the absence of "'legislative facts'" explaining the distinction "[o]n the record," 294 U.S.App.D.C., at 389, has no significance in rational-basis analysis. See *Nordlinger v. Hahn,* 505 U.S. 1, 15 (1992) (equal protection "does not demand for purposes of rational-basis review that a legislature or governing decision-maker actually articulate at any time the purpose or rationale supporting its classification"). In other words, a legislative choice is not subject to courtroom fact-finding and may be based on rational speculation unsupported by evidence or empirical data. See *Vance v. Bradley, supra,* 440 U.S., at 111. "'Only by faithful adherence to this guiding principle of judicial review of legislation is it possible to preserve to the legislative branch its rightful independence and its ability to function.'" *Lehnhausen, supra,* 410 U.S., at 365.

These restraints on judicial review have added force "where the legislature must necessarily engage in a process of line-drawing." *United States Railroad Retirement Bd. v. Fritz,* 449 U.S., at 179. Defining the class of persons subject to a regulatory requirement—much like classifying governmental beneficiaries—"inevitably requires that some persons who have an almost equally strong claim to favored treatment be placed on different sides of the line, and the fact [that] the line might have been drawn differently at some points is a matter for legislative, rather than judicial, consideration." The distinction at issue here represents such a line: By excluding from the definition of "cable system" those facilities that serve commonly owned or managed buildings without using public rights-of-way, §602(7)(B) delineates the bounds of the regulatory field. Such scope-of-coverage provisions are unavoidable components of most economic or social legislation. In establishing the franchise requirement, Congress had to draw the line somewhere; it had to choose which facilities to franchise. This necessity renders the precise coordinates of the resulting legislative judgment virtually unreviewable, since the legislature must be allowed leeway to approach a perceived problem incrementally. See, *e.g., Williamson v. Lee Optical of Okla., Inc.,* 348 U.S. 483 (1955):

> "The problem of legislative classification is a perennial one, admitting of no doctrinaire definition. Evils in the same field may be of different dimensions and proportions, requiring different remedies. Or so the legislature may think. Or the reform may take one step at a time, addressing itself to the phase of the problem which seems most acute to the legislative mind. The legislature may select one phase of one field and apply a remedy there, neglecting the others. The

prohibition of the Equal Protection Clause goes no further than the invidious discrimination."[7]

Applying these principles, we conclude that the common-ownership distinction is constitutional. There are at least two possible bases for the distinction; either one suffices. First, Congress borrowed § 602(7)(B) from pre-Cable Act regulations, and although the existence of a prior administrative scheme is certainly not necessary to the rationality of the statute, it is plausible that Congress also adopted the FCC's earlier rationale. Under that rationale, common ownership was thought to be indicative of those systems for which the costs of regulation would outweigh the benefits to consumers. Because the number of subscribers was a similar indicator, the Commission also exempted cable facilities that served fewer than 50 subscribers. In explaining both exemptions, the Commission stated:

> "[N]ot all [systems] can be subject to effective regulation with the resources available nor is regulation necessarily needed in every instance. A sensible regulatory program requires that a division between the regulated and unregulated be made in a manner which best conserves regulatory energies and allows the most cost effective use of available resources. In attempting to make this division, we have focused on subscriber numbers as well as the multiple unit dwelling indicia on the theory that the very small are inefficient to regulate and can safely be ignored in terms of their potential for impact on broadcast service to the public and on multiple unit dwelling facilities on the theory that this effectively establishes certain maximum size limitations."

This regulatory-efficiency model ... provides a conceivable basis for the common-ownership exemption. A legislator might rationally assume that systems serving only commonly owned or managed buildings without crossing public rights-of-way would typically be limited in size or would share some other attribute affecting their impact on the welfare of cable viewers such that regulators could "safely ignor[e]" these systems.

Respondents argue that Congress did not intend common ownership to be a surrogate for small size, since Congress simultaneously rejected the FCC's 50-subscriber exemption by omitting it from the Cable Act. Whether the posited reason for the challenged distinction actually motivated Congress is "constitutionally irrelevant," *United States Railroad Retirement Bd. v. Fritz, supra,* 449 U.S., at 179, and, in any event, the FCC's explanation indicates that both common ownership and number of subscribers were considered indicia of "very small" cable systems....

Furthermore, small size is only one plausible ownership-related factor contributing to consumer welfare. Subscriber influence is another. Where an SMATV system serves a complex of buildings under common ownership or management, individual subscribers could conceivably have greater bargaining power vis-à-vis the cable operator (even if the number of dwelling units were large), since all the subscribers could negotiate with one voice through the common owner or manager. Such an owner might have substantial leverage, because he could withhold permission to operate the SMATV system on his property. He would also have an incentive to guard the interests of his tenants. Thus,

---

7. See also *Dandridge v. Williams,* 397 U.S. 471, 485 (1970) (classification does not violate equal protection simply because it "is not made with mathematical nicety or because in practice it results in some inequality"); *Metropolis Theatre Co. v. Chicago,* 228 U.S. 61, 69–70 (1913) ("The problems of government are practical ones and may justify, if they do not require, rough accommodations — illogical, it may be, and unscientific"); *Heath & Milligan Mfg. Co. v. Worst,* 207 U.S. 338, 354 (1907) ("logical appropriateness of the inclusion or exclusion of objects or persons" and "exact wisdom and nice adaptation of remedies are not required").

there could be less need to establish regulatory safeguards for subscribers in commonly owned complexes. Respondents acknowledge such possibilities, and we certainly cannot say that these assumptions would be irrational.

There is a second conceivable basis for the statutory distinction. Suppose competing SMATV operators wish to sell video programming to subscribers in a group of contiguous buildings, such as a single city block, which can be interconnected by wire without crossing a public right-of-way. If all the buildings belong to one owner or are commonly managed, that owner or manager could freely negotiate a deal for all subscribers on a competitive basis. But if the buildings are separately owned and managed, the first SMATV operator who gains a foothold by signing a contract and installing a satellite dish and associated transmission equipment on one of the buildings would enjoy a powerful cost advantage in competing for the remaining subscribers: He could connect additional buildings for the cost of a few feet of cable, whereas any competitor would have to recover the cost of his own satellite headend facility. Thus, the first operator could charge rates well above his cost and still undercut the competition. This potential for effective monopoly power might theoretically justify regulating the latter class of SMATV systems and not the former.

III

The Court of Appeals quite evidently believed that the crossing or use of a public right-of-way is the only conceivable basis upon which Congress could rationally require local franchising of SMATV systems. As we have indicated, however, there are plausible rationales unrelated to the use of public rights-of-way for regulating cable facilities serving separately owned and managed buildings. The assumptions underlying these rationales may be erroneous, but the very fact that they are "arguable" is sufficient, on rational-basis review, to "immuniz[e]" the congressional choice from constitutional challenge. *Vance v. Bradley,* 440 U.S., at 112....

[The concurring opinion of Justice Stevens is omitted.]

Adarand Constructors, Inc. v. Peña
515 U.S. 200 (1995)

Justice O'CONNOR announced the judgment of the Court and delivered an opinion with respect to Parts I, II, III-A, III-B, III-D, and IV, which is for the Court except insofar as it might be inconsistent with the views expressed in Justice SCALIA's concurrence, and an opinion with respect to Part III-C in which Justice KENNEDY joins.

Petitioner Adarand Constructors, Inc., claims that the Federal Government's practice of giving general contractors on Government projects a financial incentive to hire subcontractors controlled by "socially and economically disadvantaged individuals," and in particular, the Government's use of race-based presumptions in identifying such individuals, violates the equal protection component of the Fifth Amendment's Due Process Clause....

III

....

Adarand's claim arises under the Fifth Amendment to the Constitution, which provides that "No person shall ... be deprived of life, liberty, or property, without due process of law." Although this Court has always understood that Clause to provide some measure of protection against *arbitrary* treatment by the Federal Government, it is not as explicit a guarantee of *equal* treatment as the Fourteenth Amendment, which provides that "No *State* shall ... deny to any person within its jurisdiction the equal protection of the laws" (emphasis added). Our cases have accorded varying degrees of significance to the difference in the language of those two Clauses. We think it necessary to revisit the issue here.

A

Through the 1940's, this Court had routinely taken the view in non-race-related cases that, "[u]nlike the Fourteenth Amendment, the Fifth contains no equal protection clause and it provides no guaranty against discriminatory legislation by Congress." *Detroit Bank v. United States,* 317 U.S. 329, 337 (1943). When the Court first faced a Fifth Amendment equal protection challenge to a federal racial classification, it adopted a similar approach, with most unfortunate results. In *Hirabayashi v. United States,* 320 U.S. 81 (1943), the Court considered a curfew applicable only to persons of Japanese ancestry. The Court.... cited *Detroit Bank* for the proposition that the Fifth Amendment "restrains only such discriminatory legislation by Congress as amounts to a denial of due process," and upheld the curfew because "circumstances within the knowledge of those charged with the responsibility for maintaining the national defense afforded a rational basis for the decision which they made."

....

In *Bolling v. Sharpe,* 347 U.S. 497 (1954), the Court for the first time explicitly questioned the existence of any difference between the obligations of the Federal Government and the States to avoid racial classifications. *Bolling* did note that "[t]he 'equal protection of the laws' is a more explicit safeguard of prohibited unfairness than 'due process of law.'" But *Bolling* then concluded that, "[i]n view of [the] decision that the Constitution prohibits the states from maintaining racially segregated public schools, it would be unthinkable that the same Constitution would impose a lesser duty on the Federal Government."

....

Later cases in contexts other than school desegregation did not distinguish between the duties of the States and the Federal Government to avoid racial classifications....

[I]n 1975, the Court stated explicitly that "[t]his Court's approach to Fifth Amendment equal protection claims has always been precisely the same as to equal protection claims under the Fourteenth Amendment." *Weinberger v. Wiesenfeld,* 420 U.S. 636, 638, n. 2....

B

Most of the cases discussed above involved classifications burdening groups that have suffered discrimination in our society. In 1978, the Court confronted the question whether race-based governmental action designed to *benefit* such groups should also be subject to "the most rigid scrutiny." *Regents of Univ. of Cal. v. Bakke,* 438 U.S. 265, involved an equal protection challenge to a state-run medical school's practice of reserving a number of spaces in its entering class for minority students. The petitioners argued that "strict scrutiny" should apply only to "classifications that disadvantage 'discrete and insular minorities.'" *Id.,* at 287–288 (opinion of Powell, J.) (citing *United States v. Carolene Products Co.,* 304 U.S. 144, 152, n. 4 (1938)). *Bakke* did not produce an opinion for the Court, but Justice Powell's opinion announcing the Court's judgment rejected the argument. In a passage joined by Justice White, Justice Powell wrote that "[t]he guarantee of equal protection cannot mean one thing when applied to one individual and something else when applied to a person of another color." He concluded that "[r]acial and ethnic distinctions of any sort are inherently suspect and thus call for the most exacting judicial examination." On the other hand, four Justices in *Bakke* would have applied a less stringent standard of review to racial classifications "designed to further remedial purposes," see *id.,* at 359 (Brennan, White, Marshall, and Blackmun, JJ., concurring in judgment in part and dissenting in part). And four Justices thought the case should be decided on statutory grounds. *Id.,* at 411–412 (STEVENS, J., joined by Burger, C.J., and Stewart and REHNQUIST, JJ., concurring in judgment in part and dissenting in part)....

The Court's failure to produce a majority opinion in *Bakke* [as well as in subsequent cases] left unresolved the proper analysis for remedial race-based governmental action....

The Court resolved the issue, at least in part, in 1989. *Richmond v. J.A. Croson Co.,* 488 U.S. 469 (1989), concerned a city's determination that 30% of its contracting work should go to minority-owned businesses. A majority of the Court in *Croson* held that "the standard of review under the Equal Protection Clause is not dependent on the race of those burdened or benefited by a particular classification," and that the single standard of review for racial classifications should be "strict scrutiny." ....

With *Croson,* the Court finally agreed that the Fourteenth Amendment requires strict scrutiny of all race-based action by state and local governments. But *Croson* of course had no occasion to declare what standard of review the Fifth Amendment requires for such action taken by the Federal Government....

Despite lingering uncertainty in the details, however, the Court's cases through *Croson* had established three general propositions with respect to governmental racial classifications. First, skepticism: "'Any preference based on racial or ethnic criteria must necessarily receive a most searching examination.'" Second, consistency: "[T]he standard of review under the Equal Protection Clause is not dependent on the race of those burdened or benefited by a particular classification," *i.e.,* all racial classifications reviewable under the Equal Protection Clause must be strictly scrutinized. And third, congruence: "Equal protection analysis in the Fifth Amendment area is the same as that under the Fourteenth Amendment." Taken together, these three propositions lead to the conclusion that any person, of whatever race, has the right to demand that any governmental actor subject to the Constitution justify any racial classification subjecting that person to unequal treatment under the strictest judicial scrutiny....

A year later, however, the Court took a surprising turn. *Metro Broadcasting, Inc. v. FCC,* involved a Fifth Amendment challenge to two race-based policies of the Federal Communications Commission (FCC). In *Metro Broadcasting,* the Court repudiated the long-held notion that "it would be unthinkable that the same Constitution would impose a lesser duty on the Federal Government" than it does on a State to afford equal protection of the laws, *Bolling, supra,* at 500. It did so by holding that "benign" federal racial classifications need only satisfy intermediate scrutiny, even though *Croson* had recently concluded that such classifications enacted by a State must satisfy strict scrutiny. "[B]enign" federal racial classifications, the Court said, "— even if those measures are not 'remedial' in the sense of being designed to compensate victims of past governmental or societal discrimination — are constitutionally permissible to the extent that they serve *important* governmental objectives within the power of Congress and are *substantially related* to achievement of those objectives." *Metro Broadcasting,* 497 U.S., at 564–565 (emphasis added)....

By adopting intermediate scrutiny as the standard of review for congressionally mandated "benign" racial classifications, *Metro Broadcasting* departed from prior cases in two significant respects. First, it turned its back on *Croson's* explanation of why strict scrutiny of all governmental racial classifications is essential:

"Absent searching judicial inquiry into the justification for such race-based measures, there is simply no way of determining what classifications are 'benign' or
'remedial' and what classifications are in fact motivated by illegitimate notions
of racial inferiority or simple racial politics. Indeed, the purpose of strict scrutiny
is to 'smoke out' illegitimate uses of race by assuring that the legislative body is
pursuing a goal important enough to warrant use of a highly suspect tool. The
test also ensures that the means chosen 'fit' this compelling goal so closely that
there is little or no possibility that the motive for the classification was illegitimate racial prejudice or stereotype."

We adhere to that view today, despite the surface appeal of holding "benign" racial classifications to a lower standard, because "it may not always be clear that a so-called preference is in fact benign." *Bakke, supra,* at 298 (opinion of Powell, J.)....

Second, *Metro Broadcasting* squarely rejected one of the three propositions established
by the Court's earlier equal protection cases, namely, congruence between the standards
applicable to federal and state racial classifications, and in so doing also undermined the
other two — skepticism of all racial classifications and consistency of treatment irrespective of the race of the burdened or benefited group....

The three propositions undermined by *Metro Broadcasting* all derive from the basic
principle that the Fifth and Fourteenth Amendments to the Constitution protect *persons,*
not *groups.* It follows from that principle that all governmental action based on race — a
group classification long recognized as "in most circumstances irrelevant and therefore
prohibited," *Hirabayashi,* 320 U.S., at 100 — should be subjected to detailed judicial inquiry to ensure that the *personal* right to equal protection of the laws has not been infringed.
These ideas have long been central to this Court's understanding of equal protection, and
holding "benign" state and federal racial classifications to different standards does not
square with them.... Accordingly, we hold today that all racial classifications, imposed by
whatever federal, state, or local governmental actor, must be analyzed by a reviewing
court under strict scrutiny. In other words, such classifications are constitutional only if
they are narrowly tailored measures that further compelling governmental interests....

In dissent, Justice STEVENS criticizes us for "deliver[ing] a disconcerting lecture about
the evils of governmental racial classifications." With respect, we believe his criticisms reflect a serious misunderstanding of our opinion.

Justice STEVENS concurs in our view that courts should take a skeptical view of all governmental racial classifications. He also allows that "[n]othing is inherently wrong with
applying a single standard to fundamentally different situations, as long as that standard
takes relevant differences into account." What he fails to recognize is that strict scrutiny
does take "relevant differences" into account — indeed, that is its fundamental purpose.
The point of carefully examining the interest asserted by the government in support of a
racial classification, and the evidence offered to show that the classification is needed, is
precisely to distinguish legitimate from illegitimate uses of race in governmental decision
making. And Justice STEVENS concedes that "some cases may be difficult to classify"; all
the more reason, in our view, to examine all racial classifications carefully. Strict scrutiny
does not "trea[t] dissimilar race-based decisions as though they were equally objectionable"; to the contrary, it evaluates carefully all governmental race-based decisions *in order
to decide* which are constitutionally objectionable and which are not. By requiring strict
scrutiny of racial classifications, we require courts to make sure that a governmental classification based on race, which "so seldom provide[s] a relevant basis for disparate treatment," is legitimate, before permitting unequal treatment based on race to proceed.

Justice STEVENS chides us for our "supposed inability to differentiate between 'invidious' and 'benign' discrimination," because it is in his view sufficient that "people understand the difference between good intentions and bad." But, as we have just explained, the point of strict scrutiny is to "differentiate between" permissible and impermissible governmental use of race....

Perhaps it is not the standard of strict scrutiny itself, but our use of the concepts of "consistency" and "congruence" in conjunction with it, that leads Justice STEVENS to dissent. According to Justice STEVENS, our view of consistency "equate[s] remedial preferences with invidious discrimination," and ignores the difference between "an engine of oppression" and an effort "to foster equality in society," or, more colorfully, "between a 'No Trespassing' sign and a welcome mat." It does nothing of the kind. The principle of consistency simply means that whenever the government treats any person unequally because of his or her race, that person has suffered an injury that falls squarely within the language and spirit of the Constitution's guarantee of equal protection. It says nothing about the ultimate validity of any particular law; that determination is the job of the court applying strict scrutiny. The principle of consistency explains the circumstances in which the injury requiring strict scrutiny occurs. The application of strict scrutiny, in turn, determines whether a compelling governmental interest justifies the infliction of that injury.

Consistency *does* recognize that any individual suffers an injury when he or she is disadvantaged by the government because of his or her race, whatever that race may be....

D

....

Some have questioned the importance of debating the proper standard of review of race-based legislation.... We think that requiring strict scrutiny is the best way to ensure that courts will consistently give racial classifications that kind of detailed examination, both as to ends and as to means....

Finally, we wish to dispel the notion that strict scrutiny is "strict in theory, but fatal in fact." The unhappy persistence of both the practice and the lingering effects of racial discrimination against minority groups in this country is an unfortunate reality, and government is not disqualified from acting in response to it.... When race-based action is necessary to further a compelling interest, such action is within constitutional constraints if it satisfies the "narrow tailoring" test this Court has set out in previous cases....

Justice SCALIA, concurring in part and concurring in the judgment.

I join the opinion of the Court, except Part III-C, and except insofar as it may be inconsistent with the following: In my view, government can never have a "compelling interest" in discriminating on the basis of race in order to "make up" for past racial discrimination in the opposite direction. Individuals who have been wronged by unlawful racial discrimination should be made whole; but under our Constitution there can be no such thing as either a creditor or a debtor race. That concept is alien to the Constitution's focus upon the individual. To pursue the concept of racial entitlement—even for the most admirable and benign of purposes—is to reinforce and preserve for future mischief the way of thinking that produced race slavery, race privilege and race hatred. In the eyes of government, we are just one race here. It is American.

It is unlikely, if not impossible, that the challenged program would survive under this understanding of strict scrutiny, but I am content to leave that to be decided on remand.

[The concurring opinion of Justice Thomas and the dissenting opinions of Justices Stevens, Souter, and Ginsburg are omitted.]

Kramer v. Union Free School District No. 15

395 U.S. 621 (1969)

Mr. Chief Justice WARREN delivered the opinion of the Court.

In this case we are called on to determine whether § 2012 of the New York Education Law, McKinney's Consol.Laws, c. 16, is constitutional. The legislation provides that in certain New York school districts residents who are otherwise eligible to vote in state and federal elections may vote in the school district election only if they (1) own (or lease) taxable real property within the district, or (2) are parents (or have custody of) children enrolled in the local public schools. Appellant, a bachelor who neither owns nor leases taxable real property, filed suit in federal court claiming that § 2012 denied him equal protection of the laws in violation of the Fourteenth Amendment....

II.

....

"In determining whether or not a state law violates the Equal Protection Clause, we must consider the facts and circumstances behind the law, the interests which the State claims to be protecting, and the interests of those who are disadvantaged by the classification." Williams v. Rhodes, 393 U.S. 23, 30 (1968). And, in this case, we must give the statute a close and exacting examination. "[S]ince the right to exercise the franchise in a free and unimpaired manner is preservative of other basic civil and political rights, any alleged infringement of the right of citizens to vote must be carefully and meticulously scrutinized." Reynolds v. Sims, 377 U.S. 533, 562 (1964). This careful examination is necessary because statutes distributing the franchise constitute the foundation of our representative society. Any unjustified discrimination in determining who may participate in political affairs or in the selection of public officials undermines the legitimacy of representative government.

Thus, state apportionment statutes, which may *dilute* the effectiveness of some citizens' votes, receive close scrutiny from this Court. Reynolds v. Sims, *supra*. No less rigid an examination is applicable to statutes *denying* the franchise to citizens who are otherwise qualified by residence and age. Statutes granting the franchise to residents on a selective basis always pose the danger of denying some citizens any effective voice in the governmental affairs which substantially affect their lives. Therefore, if a challenged state statute grants the right to vote to some bona fide residents of requisite age and citizenship and denies the franchise to others, the Court must determine whether the exclusions are necessary to promote a compelling state interest.

And, for these reasons, the deference usually given to the judgment of legislators does not extend to decisions concerning which resident citizens may participate in the election of legislators and other public officials. Those decisions must be carefully scrutinized by the Court to determine whether each resident citizen has, as far as is possible, an equal voice in the selections. Accordingly, when we are reviewing statutes which deny some residents the right to vote, the general presumption of constitutionality afforded state statutes and the traditional approval given state classifications if the Court can conceive of a "rational basis" for the distinctions made are not applicable. See Harper v. Virginia State Bd. of Elections, 383 U.S. 663, 670 (1966). The presumption of constitutionality and the approval given "rational" classifications in other types of enactments[9] are based on an assumption that the institutions of state government are structured so as to represent fairly all the people. However, when the challenge to the statute is in effect a challenge of this basic assumption, the assumption can no longer serve as the basis for presuming constitutionality. And, the assumption is no less under attack because the legislature which decides who may participate at the various levels of political choice is fairly elected. Legislation which delegates decision making to bodies elected by only a portion of those eligible to vote for the legislature can cause unfair representation. Such legislation can exclude a minority of voters from any voice in the decisions just as effectively as if the decisions were made by legislators the minority had no voice in selecting.

The need for exacting judicial scrutiny of statutes distributing the franchise is undiminished simply because, under a different statutory scheme, the offices subject to election might have been filled through appointment.[11] States do have latitude in determining whether certain public officials shall be selected by election or chosen by appointment and whether various questions shall be submitted to the voters. In fact, we have held that where a county school board is an administrative, not legislative, body, its members need not be elected. Sailors v. Kent County Bd. of Education, 387 U.S. 105, 108 (1967). However, "once the franchise is granted to the electorate, lines may not be drawn which are inconsistent with the Equal Protection Clause of the Fourteenth Amendment." Harper v. Virginia Bd. of Elections, *supra*, 383 U.S., at 665.

Nor is the need for close judicial examination affected because the district meetings and the school board do not have "general" legislative powers. Our exacting examination is

---

9. Of course, we have long held that if the basis of classification is inherently suspect, such as race, the statute must be subjected to an exacting scrutiny, regardless of the subject matter of the legislation.

11. Similarly, no less a showing of a compelling justification for disenfranchising residents is required merely because the questions scheduled for the election need not have been submitted to the voters.

not necessitated by the subject of the election; rather, it is required because some resident citizens are permitted to participate and some are not. For example, a city charter might well provide that the elected city council appoint a mayor who would have broad administrative powers. Assuming the council were elected consistent with the commands of the Equal Protection Clause, the delegation of power to the mayor would not call for this Court's exacting review. On the other hand, if the city charter made the office of mayor subject to an election in which only some resident citizens were entitled to vote, there would be presented a situation calling for our close review.

III.

Besides appellant and others who similarly live in their parents' homes, the statute also disenfranchises the following persons (unless they are parents or guardians of children enrolled in the district public school): senior citizens and others living with children or relatives; clergy, military personnel, and others who live on tax-exempt property; boarders and lodgers; parents who neither own nor lease qualifying property and whose children are too young to attend school; parents who neither own nor lease qualifying property and whose children attend private schools....

We turn[ ] to [the] question whether the exclusion is necessary to promote a compelling state interest. First appellees argue that the State has a legitimate interest in limiting the franchise in school district elections to "members of the community of interest" — those "primarily interested in such elections." Second, appellees urge that the State may reasonably and permissibly conclude that "property taxpayers" (including lessees of taxable property who share the tax burden through rent payments) and parents of the children enrolled in the district's schools are those "primarily interested" in school affairs.

We do not understand appellees to argue that the State is attempting to limit the franchise to those "subjectively concerned" about school matters. Rather, they appear to argue that the State's legitimate interest is in restricting a voice in school matters to those "directly affected" by such decisions. The State apparently reasons that since the schools are financed in part by local property taxes, persons whose out-of-pocket expenses are "directly" affected by property tax changes should be allowed to vote. Similarly, parents of children in school are thought to have a "direct" stake in school affairs and are given a vote.

Appellees argue that it is necessary to limit the franchise to those "primarily interested" in school affairs because "the ever increasing complexity of the many interacting phases of the school system and structure make it extremely difficult for the electorate fully to understand the whys and wherefores of the detailed operations of the school system." Appellees say that many communications of school boards and school administrations are sent home to the parents through the district pupils and are "not broadcast to the general public"; thus, nonparents will be less informed than parents. Further, appellees argue, those who are assessed for local property taxes (either directly or indirectly through rent) will have enough of an interest "through the burden on their pocketbooks, to acquire such information as they may need."

We need express no opinion as to whether the State in some circumstances might limit the exercise of the franchise to those "primarily interested" or "primarily affected." Of course, we therefore do not reach the issue of whether these particular elections are of the type in which the franchise may be so limited. For, assuming, *arguendo*, that New York legitimately might limit the franchise in these school district elections to those "primarily interested in school affairs," close scrutiny of the §2012 classifications demonstrates that they do not accomplish this purpose with sufficient precision to justify denying appellant the franchise.

Whether classifications allegedly limiting the franchise to those resident citizens "primarily interested" deny those excluded equal protection of the laws depends, *inter alia*, on whether all those excluded are in fact substantially less interested or affected than those the statute includes. In other words, the classifications must be tailored so that the exclusion of appellant and members of his class is necessary to achieve the articulated state goal.[14] Section 2012 does not meet the exacting standard of precision we require of statutes which selectively distribute the franchise. The classifications in § 2012 permit inclusion of many persons who have, at best, a remote and indirect interest, in school affairs and, on the other hand, exclude others who have a distinct and direct interest in the school meeting decisions.[15]

Nor do appellees offer any justification for the exclusion of seemingly interested and informed residents—other than to argue that the § 2012 classifications include those "whom the State could understandably deem to be the most intimately interested in actions taken by the school board," and urge that "the task of * * * balancing the interest of the community in the maintenance of orderly school district elections against the interest of any individual in voting in such elections should clearly remain with the Legislature." But the issue is not whether the legislative judgments are rational. A more exacting standard obtains. The issue is whether the § 2012 requirements do in fact sufficiently further a compelling state interest to justify denying the franchise to appellant and members of his class. The requirements of § 2012 are not sufficiently tailored to limiting the franchise to those "primarily interested" in school affairs to justify the denial of the franchise to appellant and members of his class. . . .

[The dissenting opinion of Justice Stewart is omitted.]

Notes and Questions

1. As noted at the start of this chapter, in terms, the Equal Protection Clause of the Fourteenth Amendment applies only to the states, and there is no analogous clause in any portion of the U.S. Constitution that governs the actions of the federal government. Yet, both the *Beach Communications* and *Adarand* Courts acknowledge that the Due Process Clause of the Fifth Amendment has an "equal protection" component that subjects the federal government to the same scrutiny that states are subjected to under the Equal Protection Clause.

As *Adarand* notes, the Court first explicitly so held in *Bolling v. Sharpe*, 347 U.S. 497 (1954), the companion case to *Brown v. Board of Education*, 347 U.S. 483 (1954). The *Bolling* Court reasoned as follows:

> We have this day held that the Equal Protection Clause of the Fourteenth Amendment prohibits the states from maintaining racially segregated public schools. The legal problem in the District of Columbia is somewhat different, however. The Fifth Amendment, which is applicable in the District of Columbia, does not contain an equal protection clause as does the Fourteenth

---

14. Of course, if the exclusions are necessary to promote the articulated state interest, we must then determine whether the interest promoted by limiting the franchise constitutes a compelling state interest. We do not reach that issue in this case.

15. For example, appellant resides with his parents in the school district, pays state and federal taxes and is interested in and affected by school board decisions; however, he has no vote. On the other hand, an uninterested unemployed young man who pays no state or federal taxes, but who rents an apartment in the district, can participate in the election.

Amendment which applies only to the states. But the concepts of equal protection and due process, both stemming from our American ideal of fairness, are not mutually exclusive. The "equal protection of the laws" is a more explicit safeguard of prohibited unfairness than "due process of law," and, therefore, we do not imply that the two are always interchangeable phrases. But, as this Court has recognized, discrimination may be so unjustifiable as to be violative of due process....

In view of our decision that the Constitution prohibits the states from maintaining racially segregated public schools, it would be unthinkable that the same Constitution would impose a lesser duty on the Federal Government. We hold that racial segregation in the public schools of the District of Columbia is a denial of the due process of law guaranteed by the Fifth Amendment to the Constitution.

Id. at 498–500.

Recall from the introduction to Chapter 3 that the Court has held that the Due Process Clause of the Fourteenth Amendment "incorporated" virtually all provisions of the Bill of Rights (which was ratified *before* the Fourteenth Amendment). In contrast, the holding in *Bolling* is often referred to as "reverse incorporation" in that the Court is holding that the Due Process Clause of the Fifth Amendment, in effect, "incorporates" the Equal Protection Clause of the Fourteenth Amendment, even though the latter was ratified long *after* the former. Is the concept of "reverse incorporation" as sound as the concept of incorporation? Would it really be "unthinkable" to hold the federal and state governments to different duties under the U.S. Constitution, and if so, is that enough to ignore the textual limitations found in it? Finally, do cases such as *Bolling*—when considered in conjunction with cases such as *Eisenstadt* and *Skinner* from the previous chapter—suggest that the "equal protection" and "due process" guarantees are not so much distinct constitutional rights but provisions that work in tandem to protect individual rights?

2. If taken seriously, how useful are the tests for rational basis and strict scrutiny set forth in *Beach Communications* and *Adarand*, respectively? Stated somewhat differently, can you imagine any law that would fail the rational basis test articulated in *Beach Communications*? And despite Justice O'Connor's protestations in *Adarand* to the contrary, do you think that many laws will be able to survive strict scrutiny?

3. What distinguishes the law in *Beach Communications* on the one hand from those in *Adarand* and *Kramer* on the other such that the former is subject only to rational basis scrutiny while the latter are subject to strict scrutiny? Which test would apply to laws drawing distinctions based on age? Based on sex? Based on sexual orientation?

4. Note that *Adarand* holds that the Court's focus under equal protection is not the specific *class* discriminated against (e.g., African Americans, women, gays and lesbians) but instead the *classification* used to discriminate (race, sex, sexual orientation). Does the focus on suspect classifications as opposed to suspect classes make sense, particularly in light of the statement in *Carolene Products* that a more searching form of judicial review may be appropriate where "prejudice against discrete and insular minorities" is involved? In light of the Court's statement in the *Slaughter-House Cases* that "[w]e doubt very much whether any action of a State not directed by way of discrimination against the negroes as a class, or on account of their race, will ever be held to come within the purview of this provision"?

5. Later in this chapter, you will examine the factors that the Court takes into account in deciding whether or not to apply a heightened level of scrutiny under the Equal Pro-

tection Clause. Once you review those materials, reconsider the question whether *Adarand*'s focus on classifications is sound.

6. Recall from Chapter 3 that the substantive component of the Due Process Clauses protects "fundamental rights," and typically subjects infringements on such rights to strict scrutiny. Yet, as demonstrated by the cases in this section, the Equal Protection Clause (and the equal protection component of the Fifth Amendment's Due Process Clause) also protects "fundamental rights" and subjects infringements of such rights to strict scrutiny. What, then, is the difference, if any, between "fundamental rights" under the substantive component of the Due Process Clause and "fundamental rights" under the Equal Protection Clause? Consider the following:

> The major difference between due process and equal protection as the basis for protecting fundamental rights is in how the constitutional arguments are phrased. If a right is safeguarded under due process, the constitutional issue is whether the government's interference is justified by a sufficient purpose. But if the right is protected under equal protection, the issue is whether the government's discrimination as to who can exercise the right is justified by a sufficient purpose. Although the difference is generally just semantics and phrasing, there can be a real distinction: If a law denies the right to everyone, then due process would be the best grounds for analysis; but if a law denies a right to some, while allowing it to others, the discrimination can be challenged as offending equal protection or the violation of the right can be objected to under due process.

Erwin Chemerinsky, Constitutional Law: Principles and Policies § 7.1, at 523 (2d ed. 2002).

In this regard, consider what right, exactly, the Court in *Kramer* is recognizing: is it recognizing a free-standing right to vote for certain types of government officials or issues, or merely an equal right to vote for those officials *if* the government decides to put those officials or issues to a vote? In contrast, what sort of right was recognized in cases such as *Griswold*?

7. A key limitation on the reach of the Equal Protection Clause (and the equal protection component of the Fifth Amendment's Due Process Clause) is the requirement that the discrimination be *intentional*. In other words, it is not enough to show that a law has a disparate impact (or discriminatory effect) on a class of individuals; rather, one must also show that the law was enacted with the *intent* to do so. The Court first made this requirement explicit in *Washington v. Davis*, 426 U.S. 229 (1976). In that case, the Court held that a qualifying test for positions of police officers was not subject to strict scrutiny merely because it was alleged to have a disparate impact on African Americans:

> [O]ur cases have not embraced the proposition that a law or other official act, without regard to whether it reflects a racially discriminatory purpose, is unconstitutional *solely* because it has a racially disproportionate impact.
>
> Almost 100 years ago, *Strauder v. West Virginia*, 100 U.S. 303 (1880), established that the exclusion of Negroes from grand and petit juries in criminal proceedings violated the Equal Protection Clause, but the fact that a particular jury or a series of juries does not statistically reflect the racial composition of the community does not in itself make out an invidious discrimination forbidden by the Clause. "A purpose to discriminate must be present which may be proven by systematic exclusion of eligible jurymen of the proscribed race or by unequal application of the law to such an extent as to show intentional discrimination." *Akins v. Texas*, 325 U.S. 398, 403–404 (1945)....

The school desegregation cases have also adhered to the basic equal protection principle that the invidious quality of a law claimed to be racially discriminatory must ultimately be traced to a racially discriminatory purpose. That there are both predominantly black and predominantly white schools in a community is not alone violative of the Equal Protection Clause. The essential element of *de jure* segregation is "a current condition of segregation resulting from intentional state action. *Keyes v. School Dist. No. 1*, 413 U.S. 189, 205 (1973). The differentiating factor between *de jure* segregation and so-called *de facto* segregation ... is *purpose* or *intent* to segregate." *Id.*, at 208. ...

This is not to say that the necessary discriminatory racial purpose must be express or appear on the face of the statute, or that a law's disproportionate impact is irrelevant in cases involving Constitution-based claims of racial discrimination. A statute, otherwise neutral on its face, must not be applied so as invidiously to discriminate on the basis of race. *Yick Wo v. Hopkins*, 118 U.S. 356 (1886). ...

Necessarily, an invidious discriminatory purpose may often be inferred from the totality of the relevant facts, including the fact, if it is true, that the law bears more heavily on one race than another. It is also not infrequently true that the discriminatory impact in the jury cases for example, the total or seriously disproportionate exclusion of Negroes from jury venires may for all practical purposes demonstrate unconstitutionality because in various circumstances the discrimination is very difficult to explain on nonracial grounds. Nevertheless, we have not held that a law, neutral on its face and serving ends otherwise within the power of government to pursue, is invalid under the Equal Protection Clause simply because it may affect a greater proportion of one race than of another. Disproportionate impact is not irrelevant, but it is not the sole touchstone of an invidious racial discrimination forbidden by the Constitution. Standing alone, it does not trigger the rule that racial classifications are to be subjected to the strictest scrutiny and are justifiable only by the weightiest of considerations.

Id. at 239–42.

The following year, the Court made clear that the discriminatory purpose need not be the sole, dominant, or even primary purpose behind a law or official governmental action; rather, it suffices that it was a "motivating factor." *See Vill. of Arlington Heights v. Metro. Hous. Dev. Corp.*, 429 U.S. 252, 265–66 (1977). It went on to suggest ways in which a court could determine discriminatory purpose when a law was neutral on its face:

Determining whether invidious discriminatory purpose was a motivating factor demands a sensitive inquiry into such circumstantial and direct evidence of intent as may be available. The impact of the official action whether it "bears more heavily on one race than another," *Washington v. Davis, supra*, 426 U.S., at 242 may provide an important starting point. Sometimes a clear pattern, unexplainable on grounds other than race, emerges from the effect of the state action even when the governing legislation appears neutral on its face. The evidentiary inquiry is then relatively easy. But such cases are rare. Absent a pattern as stark as that in *Gomillion* or *Yick Wo*, impact alone is not determinative, and the Court must look to other evidence.

The historical background of the decision is one evidentiary source, particularly if it reveals a series of official actions taken for invidious purposes. The specific sequence of events leading up the challenged decision also may shed some light on the decisionmaker's purposes. For example, if the property involved here always had been zoned R-5 but suddenly was changed to R-3 when the town learned of MHDC's plans to erect integrated housing, we would have a far different case. Departures from the normal procedural sequence also might afford evidence that improper purposes are playing a role. Substantive departures too may be relevant, particularly if the factors usually considered important by the decisionmaker strongly favor a decision contrary to the one reached.

The legislative or administrative history may be highly relevant, especially where there are contemporary statements by members of the decision making body, minutes of its meetings, or reports. In some extraordinary instances the members might be called to the stand at trial to testify concerning the purpose of the official action, although even then such testimony frequently will be barred by privilege.

The foregoing summary identifies, without purporting to be exhaustive, subjects of proper inquiry in determining whether racially discriminatory intent existed.

Id. at 266–68.

Two years later, the Court clarified that the phrase "discriminatory purpose" is defined in a very narrow and specific way. In *Personnel Administrator of Massachusetts v. Feeney*, 442 U.S. 256 (1979), the Court addressed the question whether a veterans' preference in hiring that had a disparate impact on women (since 98 percent of veterans in the state were men) violated the Equal Protection Clause:

The decision to grant a preference to veterans was of course "intentional." So, necessarily, did an adverse impact upon nonveterans follow from that decision. And it cannot seriously be argued that the Legislature of Massachusetts could have been unaware that most veterans are men. It would thus be disingenuous to say that the adverse consequences of this legislation for women were unintended, in the sense that they were not volitional or in the sense that they were not foreseeable.

"Discriminatory purpose," however, implies more than intent as volition or intent as awareness of consequences. It implies that the decisionmaker, in this case a state legislature, selected or reaffirmed a particular course of action at least in part "because of," not merely "in spite of," its adverse effects upon an identifiable group. Yet, nothing in the record demonstrates that this preference for veterans was originally devised or subsequently re-enacted because it would accomplish the collateral goal of keeping women in a stereotypic and predefined place in the Massachusetts Civil Service.

Id. at 278–79.

8. As indicated in the excerpt from *Washington v. Davis*, *Yick Wo* stands for the proposition that a facially neutral law that is administered in a discriminatory manner runs afoul of the equal protection clause:

Though the law itself be fair on its face, and impartial in appearance, yet, if it is applied and administered by public authority with an evil eye and an unequal hand, so as practically to make unjust and illegal discriminations between persons in similar circumstances, material to their rights, the denial of equal justice is still within the prohibition of the constitution.

Yick Wo v. Hopkins, 118 U.S. 356, 373–74 (1886).

9. Proof of intent to discriminate is required only when the statute is facially neutral: "A showing of discriminatory intent is not necessary when the equal protection claim is

based on an overtly discriminatory classification." *Wayte v. United States*, 470 U.S. 598, 608 n.10 (1985) (citing *Strauder v. West Virginia*, 100 U.S. 303 (1880)).

10. The *Gomillion* and *Yick Wo* cases cited in *Village of Arlington Heights* are sufficiently extreme in their facts that the caveat regarding such starkly discriminatory patterns is unlikely to arise in most cases. In *Yick Wo*, a facially neutral statute required laundries to be located in certain types of buildings absent a waiver. Every Chinese applicant was denied a waiver, while all but one non-Chinese applicant was granted a waiver. *See Yick Wo v. Hopkins*, 118 U.S. 356 (1886). And in *Gomillion*, the Alabama legislature redrew the boundaries of the City of Tuskegee so as to create an oddly shaped twenty-eight sided figure that had the effect of removing all but a handful of African-American voters from the city without removing a single Caucasian voter. *See Gomillion v. Lightfoot*, 364 U.S. 339, 341 (1960).

11. What if a legislative scheme draws lines not based on the class itself, but something highly correlated with the class? In *Geduldig v. Aiello*, 417 U.S. 484 (1974), the U.S. Supreme Court considered the constitutionality of a state disability insurance program that did not provide coverage for loss of work resulting from pregnancy. The Court rejected an argument that this was a form of sex discrimination:

> The California insurance program does not exclude anyone from benefit eligibility because of gender but merely removes one physical condition — pregnancy — from the list of compensable disabilities. While it is true that only women can become pregnant it does not follow that every legislative classification concerning pregnancy is a sex-based classification.... Normal pregnancy is an objectively identifiable physical condition with unique characteristics. Absent a showing that distinctions involving pregnancy are mere pretexts designed to effect an invidious discrimination against the members of one sex or the other, lawmakers are constitutionally free to include or exclude pregnancy from the coverage of legislation such as this on any reasonable basis, just as with respect to any other physical condition. The lack of identity between the excluded disability and gender as such under this insurance program becomes clear upon the most cursory analysis. The program divides potential recipients into two groups — pregnant women and nonpregnant persons. While the first group is exclusively female, the second includes members of both sexes. The fiscal and actuarial benefits of the program thus accrue to members of both sexes.

Id. at 496 n.20.

On the same day *Geduldig* was decided, the Court also rejected an argument that a federal policy providing an employment preference in the Bureau of Indian Affairs for those who are "one-fourth or more degree Indian blood and [] a member of a Federally-recognized tribe" constituted impermissible racial discrimination violating the equal protection guarantee of the Fifth Amendment's Due Process Clause:

> The preference is not directed towards a "racial" group consisting of "Indians"; instead, it applies only to members of "federally recognized" tribes. This operates to exclude many individuals who are racially to be classified as "Indians." In this sense, the preference is political rather than racial in nature.

Morton v. Mancari, 417 U.S. 535, 553 n.24 (1974).

In a similar vein, consider *Hernandez v. New York*, 500 U.S. 352 (1991), in which the Supreme Court upheld as race-neutral a prosecutor's decision to exercise peremptory challenges to strike two prospective Latino jurors. The prosecutor contended that he struck the jurors not because they were Latino, but because they spoke Spanish and did not indicate — to the prosecutor's satisfaction — that they would be able to defer to the court interpreter's translation of Spanish testimony into English. The Court held:

> Petitioner argues that Spanish-language ability bears a close relation to ethnicity, and that, as a consequence, it violates the Equal Protection Clause to exercise a peremptory challenge on the ground that a Latino potential juror speaks Spanish. He points to the high correlation between Spanish-language ability and ethnicity in New York, where the case was tried. We need not address that argument here, for the prosecutor did not rely on language ability without more, but explained that the specific responses and the demeanor of the two individuals during *voir dire* caused him to doubt their ability to defer to the official translation of Spanish-language testimony. . . .
>
> Just as shared language can serve to foster community, language differences can be a source of division. Language elicits a response from others, ranging from admiration and respect, to distance and alienation, to ridicule and scorn. Reactions of the latter type all too often result from or initiate racial hostility. In holding that a race-neutral reason for a peremptory challenge means a reason other than race, we do not resolve the more difficult question of the breadth with which the concept of race should be defined for equal protection purposes. We would face a quite different case if the prosecutor had justified his peremptory challenges with the explanation that he did not want Spanish-speaking jurors. It may well be, for certain ethnic groups and in some communities, that proficiency in a particular language, like skin color, should be treated as a surrogate for race under an equal protection analysis. And, as we make clear, a policy of striking all who speak a given language, without regard to the particular circumstances of the trial or the individual responses of the jurors, may be found by the trial judge to be a pretext for racial discrimination. But that case is not before us.

Id. at 360, 371–72.

Does this line of cases completely shut the door to equal protection claims grounded on discriminating on the basis of qualities highly associated with specific classes of people? In this regard, reconsider the excerpts from *Lawrence v. Texas*, *Hernandez v. Robles*, and *In re Marriage Cases* in Chapter 1, which address the question whether laws criminalizing sodomy between two persons of the same sex or laws banning same-sex marriage in fact discriminate on the basis of sexual orientation.

B. The Sex and Legitimacy Cases

Reed v. Reed
404 U.S. 71 (1971)

Mr. Chief Justice BURGER delivered the opinion of the Court.

Richard Lynn Reed, a minor, died intestate in Ada County, Idaho, on March 29, 1967. . . . Approximately seven months after Richard's death, his mother, appellant Sally Reed, filed a petition in the Probate Court of Ada County, seeking appointment as administratrix of her son's estate. Prior to the date set for a hearing on the mother's petition, appellee Cecil Reed, the father of the decedent, filed a competing petition seeking to have himself appointed administrator of the son's estate. The probate court held a joint hearing on the two petitions and thereafter ordered that letters of administration be issued to appellee Cecil Reed upon his taking the oath and filing the bond required by law. The court treated §§ 15-312 and 15-314 of the Idaho Code as the controlling statutes and read those sections as compelling a preference for Cecil Reed because he was a male.

Section 15-312 designates the persons who are entitled to administer the estate of one who dies intestate. In making these designations, that section lists 11 classes of persons who are so entitled and provides, in substance, that the order in which those classes are listed in the section shall be determinative of the relative rights of competing applicants for letters of administration. One of the 11 classes so enumerated is "[t]he father or mother" of the person dying intestate. Under this section then appellant and appellee, being members of the same entitlement class, would seem to have been equally entitled to administer their son's estate. Section 15-314 provides, however, that

> "[o]f several persons claiming and equally entitled (under § 15-312) to administer, males must be preferred to females, and relatives of the whole to those of the half blood."

[The decision was appealed and eventually affirmed by the Idaho Supreme Court.]

Sally Reed thereupon appealed for review by this Court.... Having examined the record and considered the briefs and oral arguments of the parties, we have concluded that the arbitrary preference established in favor of males by § 15-314 of the Idaho Code cannot stand in the face of the Fourteenth Amendment's command that no State deny the equal protection of the laws to any person within its jurisdiction....

Section 15-314 is restricted in its operation to those situations where competing applications for letters of administration have been filed by both male and female members of the same entitlement class established by § 15-312. In such situations, § 15-314 provides that different treatment be accorded to the applicants on the basis of their sex; it thus establishes a classification subject to scrutiny under the Equal Protection Clause.

In applying that clause, this Court has consistently recognized that the Fourteenth Amendment does not deny to States the power to treat different classes of persons in different ways. The Equal Protection Clause of that amendment does, however, deny to States the power to legislate that different treatment be accorded to persons placed by a statute into different classes on the basis of criteria wholly unrelated to the objective of that statute. A classification "must be reasonable, not arbitrary, and must rest upon some ground of difference having a fair and substantial relation to the object of the legislation, so that all persons similarly circumstanced shall be treated alike." *Royster Guano Co. v. Virginia*, 253 U.S. 412, 415 (1920). The question presented by this case, then, is whether a difference in the sex of competing applicants for letters of administration bears a rational relationship to a state objective that is sought to be advanced by the operation of §§ 15-312 and 15-314.

In upholding the latter section, the Idaho Supreme Court concluded that its objective was to eliminate one area of controversy when two or more persons, equally entitled under § 15-312, seek letters of administration and thereby present the probate court "with the issue of which one should be named." The court also concluded that where such persons are not of the same sex, the elimination of females from consideration "is neither an illogical nor arbitrary method devised by the legislature to resolve an issue that would otherwise require a hearing as to the relative merits * * * of the two or more petitioning relatives * * *."

Clearly the objective of reducing the workload on probate courts by eliminating one class of contests is not without some legitimacy. The crucial question, however, is whether § 15-314 advances that objective in a manner consistent with the command of the Equal Protection Clause. We hold that it does not. To give a mandatory preference to members of either sex over members of the other, merely to accomplish the elimination of hearings on the merits, is to make the very kind of arbitrary legislative choice forbidden by the Equal Protection Clause of the Fourteenth Amendment; and whatever may be said as to the positive values of avoiding intrafamily controversy, the choice in this context may not lawfully be mandated solely on the basis of sex....

Weber v. Aetna Casualty & Surety Co.
406 U.S. 164 (1972)

Mr. Justice POWELL delivered the opinion of the Court.

....

I

For purposes of recovery under workmen's compensation, Louisiana law defines children to include "only legitimate children, stepchildren, posthumous children, adopted children, and illegitimate children acknowledged under the provisions of Civil Code Articles 203, 204, and 205." Thus, legitimate children and acknowledged illegitimates may recover on an equal basis. Unacknowledged illegitimate children, however, are relegated to the lesser status of "other dependents" under § 1232(8) of the workmen's compensation statute and may recover *only* if there are not enough surviving dependents in the preceding classifications to exhaust the maximum allowable benefits. Both the Louisiana Court of Appeal and a divided Louisiana Supreme Court sustained these statutes over petitioner's constitutional objections, holding that our decision in *Levy* was not controlling.

We disagree. In *Levy*, the Court held invalid as denying equal protection of the laws, a Louisiana statute which barred an illegitimate child from recovering for the wrongful death of its mother when such recoveries by legitimate children were authorized. The Court there decided that the fact of a child's birth out of wedlock bore no reasonable relation to the purpose of wrongful-death statutes which compensate children for the death of a mother. As the Court said in *Levy*:

> "Legitimacy or illegitimacy of birth has no relation to the nature of the wrong allegedly inflicted on the mother. These children, though illegitimate, were dependent on her; she cared for them and nurtured them; they were indeed hers in the biological and in the spiritual sense; in her death they suffered wrong in the sense that any dependent would." Levy v. Louisiana, 391 U.S., at 72.

.... Here, as in *Levy*, there is impermissible discrimination. An unacknowledged illegitimate child may suffer as much from the loss of a parent as a child born within wedlock or an illegitimate later acknowledged. So far as this record shows, the dependency and natural affinity of the unacknowledged illegitimate children for their father were as great as those of the four legitimate children whom Louisiana law has allowed to recover. The legitimate children and the illegitimate children all lived in the home of the deceased and were equally dependent upon him for maintenance and support....

II

Having determined that *Levy* is the applicable precedent we briefly reaffirm here the reasoning which produced that result. The tests to determine the validity of state statutes under the Equal Protection Clause have been variously expressed, but this Court requires, at a minimum, that a statutory classification bear some rational relationship to a legitimate state purpose. Though the latitude given state economic and social regulation is necessarily broad, when state statutory classifications approach sensitive and fundamental personal rights, this Court exercises a stricter scrutiny, Brown v. Board of Education, 347 U.S. 483 (1954); Harper v. Virginia State Board of Elections, 383 U.S. 663 (1966). The essential inquiry in all the foregoing cases is, however, inevitably a dual one: What legitimate state interest does the classification promote? What fundamental personal rights might the classification endanger?

The Louisiana Supreme Court emphasized strongly the State's interest in protecting "legitimate family relationships," and the regulation and protection of the family unit have indeed been a venerable state concern. We do not question the importance of that interest; what we do question is how the challenged statute will promote it. As was said in *Glona*:

> "[W]e see no possible rational basis ... for assuming that if the natural mother is allowed recovery for the wrongful death of her illegitimate child, the cause of illegitimacy will be served. It would, indeed, be farfetched to assume that women have illegitimate children so that they can be compensated in damages for their death." Glona v. American Guarantee & Liability Insurance Co., 391 U.S., at 75.

Nor can it be thought here that persons will shun illicit relations because the offspring may not one day reap the benefits of workmen's compensation.

It may perhaps be said that statutory distinctions between the legitimate and illegitimate reflect closer family relationships in that the illegitimate is more often not under care in the home of the father nor even supported by him. The illegitimate, so this argument runs, may thus be made less eligible for the statutory recoveries and inheritances reserved for those more likely to be within the ambit of familial care and affection. Whatever the merits elsewhere of this contention, it is not compelling in a statutory compensation scheme where dependency on the deceased is a prerequisite to anyone's recovery, and where the acknowledgment so necessary to equal recovery rights may be unlikely to occur or legally impossible to effectuate even where the illegitimate child may be nourished and loved.

Finally, we are mindful that States have frequently drawn arbitrary lines in workmen's compensation and wrongful death statutes to facilitate potentially difficult problems of proof. Nothing in our decision would impose on state court systems a greater burden in this regard. By limiting recovery to dependents of the deceased, Louisiana substantially lessens the possible problems of locating illegitimate children and of determining uncertain claims of parenthood. Our decision fully respects Louisiana's choice on this matter. It will not expand claimants for workmen's compensation beyond those in a direct blood and dependency relationship with the deceased and it avoids altogether diffuse questions of affection and affinity which pose difficult probative problems. Our ruling requires equality of treatment between two classes of persons the genuineness of whose claims the State might in any event be required to determine.

The state interest in legitimate family relationships is not served by the statute; the state interest in minimizing problems of proof is not significantly disturbed by our decision. The inferior classification of dependent unacknowledged illegitimates bears, in this instance, no significant relationship to those recognized purposes of recovery which workmen's compensation statutes commendably serve.

The status of illegitimacy has expressed through the ages society's condemnation of irresponsible liaisons beyond the bonds of marriage. But visiting this condemnation on the head of an infant is illogical and unjust. Moreover, imposing disabilities on the illegitimate child is contrary to the basic concept of our system that legal burdens should bear some relationship to individual responsibility or wrongdoing. Obviously, no child is responsible for his birth and penalizing the illegitimate child is an ineffectual — as well as an unjust — way of deterring the parent. Courts are powerless to prevent the social opprobrium suffered by these hapless children, but the Equal Protection Clause does enable us to strike down discriminatory laws relating to status of birth where — as in this case — the classification is justified by no legitimate state interest, compelling or otherwise....

[The concurring opinion of Justice Blackmun and the dissenting opinion of Justice Rehnquist are omitted.]

Notes and Questions

1. Both *Reed* and the cases collected in *Weber* (and arguably *Weber* itself) purport to be applying rational basis review to assess the constitutionality of the laws at issue in those cases. Yet, are they applying rational basis review with the same degree of deference as did the *Beach Communications* Court?

2. Assuming that the "rational basis" review employed in *Reed* and *Weber* is less deferential than that employed in *Beach Communications*, are there sound reasons for treating the classifications in the former pair of cases less deferentially than that in the latter case?

3. Are classifications based on sex and legitimacy *akin* to racial classifications? Are they *precisely* like racial classifications? To what extent do the answers to these questions impact the level of scrutiny that should be employed?

4. If *Reed* and *Weber* are in fact employing some form of heightened scrutiny, why don't they explicitly state that they are doing so? From the standpoint of the Court, what are the advantages of not, in terms, applying a heightened level of scrutiny?

Frontiero v. Richardson
411 U.S. 677 (1973)

Mr. Justice BRENNAN announced the judgment of the Court in an opinion in which Mr. Justice DOUGLAS, Mr. Justice WHITE, and Mr. Justice MARSHALL join.

The question before us concerns the right of a female member of the uniformed services to claim her spouse as a "dependent" for the purposes of obtaining increased quarters allowances and medical and dental benefits under 37 U.S.C. §§ 401, 403, and 10 U.S.C. §§ 1072, 1076, on an equal footing with male members. Under these statutes, a serviceman may claim his wife as a "dependent" without regard to whether she is in fact dependent upon him for any part of her support. A servicewoman, on the other hand, may not claim her husband as a "dependent" under these programs unless he is in fact dependent upon her for over one-half of his support. Thus, the question for decision is whether this difference in treatment constitutes an unconstitutional discrimination against servicewomen in violation of the Due Process Clause of the Fifth Amendment....

I

. . . .

Appellant Sharron Frontiero, a lieutenant in the United States Air Force, sought increased quarters allowances, and housing and medical benefits for her husband, appellant Joseph Frontiero, on the ground that he was her "dependent." Although such benefits would automatically have been granted with respect to the wife of a male member of the uniformed services, appellant's application was denied because she failed to demonstrate that her husband was dependent on her for more than one-half of his support. Appellants then commenced this suit, contending that, by making this distinction, the statutes unreasonably discriminate on the basis of sex in violation of the Due Process Clause of the Fifth Amendment.[5] In essence, appellants asserted that the discriminatory impact of the statutes is twofold: first, as a procedural matter, a female member is required to demonstrate her spouse's dependency, while no such burden is imposed upon male members; and, second, as a substantive matter, a male member who does not provide more than one-half of his wife's support receives benefits, while a similarly situated female member is denied such benefits. Appellants therefore sought a permanent injunction against the continued enforcement of these statutes and an order directing the appellees to provide Lieutenant Frontiero with the same housing and medical benefits that a similarly situated male member would receive.

Although the legislative history of these statutes sheds virtually no light on the purposes underlying the differential treatment accorded male and female members, a majority of the three-judge District Court surmised that Congress might reasonably have concluded that, since the husband in our society is generally the "breadwinner" in the family—and the wife typically the "dependent" partner—"it would be more economical to require married female members claiming husbands to prove actual dependency than to extend the presumption of dependency such members." Indeed, given the fact that approximately 99% of all members of the uniformed services are male, the District Court speculated that such differential treatment might conceivably lead to a "considerable saving of administrative expense and manpower."

II

At the outset, appellants contend that classifications based upon sex, like classifications based upon race, alienage, and national origin, are inherently suspect and must therefore be subjected to close judicial scrutiny. We agree and, indeed, find at least implicit support for such an approach in our unanimous decision only last Term in Reed v. Reed, 404 U.S. 71 (1971).

In *Reed*, the Court considered the constitutionality of an Idaho statute providing that, when two individuals are otherwise equally entitled to appointment as administrator of an estate, the male applicant must be preferred to the female. Appellant, the mother of the deceased, and appellee, the father, filed competing petitions for appointment as administrator of their son's estate. Since the parties, as parents of the deceased, were members of the same entitlement class the statutory preference was invoked and the father's petition was therefore granted. Appellant claimed that this statute, by giving a mandatory preference to males over females without regard to their individual qualifications, violated the Equal Protection Clause of the Fourteenth Amendment.

---

5. "[W]hile the Fifth Amendment contains no equal protection clause, it does forbid discrimination that is 'so unjustifiable as to be violative of due process.'" Schneider v. Rusk, 377 U.S. 163, 168 (1964); see Shapiro v. Thompson, 394 U.S. 618, 641–642 (1969); Bolling v. Sharpe, 347 U.S. 497 (1954).

The Court noted that the Idaho statute "provides that different treatment be accorded to the applicants on the basis of their sex; it thus establishes a classification subject to scrutiny under the Equal Protection Clause." Under "traditional" equal protection analysis, a legislative classification must be sustained unless it is "patently arbitrary" and bears no rational relationship to a legitimate governmental interest.

In an effort to meet this standard, appellee contended that the statutory scheme was a reasonable measure designed to reduce the workload on probate courts by eliminating one class of contests. Moreover, appellee argued that the mandatory preference for male applicants was in itself reasonable since "men [are] as a rule more conversant with business affairs than ... women."[10] Indeed, appellee maintained that "it is a matter of common knowledge, that women still are not engaged in politics, the professions, business or industry to the extent that men are."[11] And the Idaho Supreme Court, in upholding the constitutionality of this statute, suggested that the Idaho Legislature might reasonably have "concluded that in general men are better qualified to act as an administrator than are women."

Despite these contentions, however, the Court held the statutory preference for male applicants unconstitutional. In reaching this result, the Court implicitly rejected appellee's apparently rational explanation of the statutory scheme, and concluded that, by ignoring the individual qualifications of particular applicants, the challenged statute provide "dissimilar treatment for men and women who are ... similarly situated." The Court therefore held that, even though the State's interest in achieving administrative efficiency "is not without some legitimacy," "[t]o give a mandatory preference to members of either sex over members of the other, merely to accomplish the elimination of hearings on the merits, is to make the very kind of arbitrary legislative choice forbidden by the [Constitution]...." This departure from "traditional" rational-basis analysis with respect to sex-based classifications is clearly justified.

There can be no doubt that our Nation has had a long and unfortunate history of sex discrimination. Traditionally, such discrimination was rationalized by an attitude of "romantic paternalism" which, in practical effect, put women, not on a pedestal, but in a cage. Indeed, this paternalistic attitude became so firmly rooted in our national consciousness that, 100 years ago, a distinguished Member of this Court was able to proclaim:

> "Man is, or should be, women's protector and defender. The natural and proper timidity and delicacy which belongs to the female sex evidently unfits it for many of the occupations of civil life. The constitution of the family organization, which is founded in the divine ordinance, as well as in the nature of things, indicates the domestic sphere as that which properly belongs to the domain and functions of womanhood. The harmony, not to say identity, of interests and views which belong, or should belong, to the family institution is repugnant to the idea of a woman adopting a distinct and independent career from that of her husband....

> "... The paramount destiny and mission of woman are to fulfil the noble and benign offices of wife and mother. This is the law of the Creator." Bradwell v. State of Illinois, 16 Wall. 130, 141 (1873) (Bradley, J., concurring).

As a result of notions such as these, our statute books gradually became laden with gross, stereotyped distinctions between the sexes and, indeed, throughout much of the 19th century the position of women in our society was, in many respects, comparable to that

---

10. Brief for Appellee in No. 70-4, O.T. 1971, Reed v. Reed, p. 12.
11. *Id.*, at 12–13.

of blacks under the pre-Civil War slave codes. Neither slaves nor women could hold office, serve on juries, or bring suit in their own names, and married women traditionally were denied the legal capacity to hold or convey property or to serve as legal guardians of their own children. And although blacks were guaranteed the right to vote in 1870, women were denied even that right—which is itself "preservative of other basic civil and political rights"—until adoption of the Nineteenth Amendment half a century later.

It is true, of course, that the position of women in America has improved markedly in recent decades. Nevertheless, it can hardly be doubted that, in part because of the high visibility of the sex characteristic, women still face pervasive, although at times more subtle, discrimination in our educational institutions, in the job market and, perhaps most conspicuously, in the political arena.[17]

Moreover, since sex, like race and national origin, is an immutable characteristic determined solely by the accident of birth, the imposition of special disabilities upon the members of a particular sex because of their sex would seem to violate "the basic concept of our system that legal burdens should bear some relationship to individual responsibility...." Weber v. Aetna Casualty & Surety Co., 406 U.S. 164, 175 (1972). And what differentiates sex from such non-suspect statuses as intelligence or physical disability, and aligns it with the recognized suspect criteria, is that the sex characteristic frequently bears no relation to ability to perform or contribute to society. As a result, statutory distinctions between the sexes often have the effect of invidiously relegating the entire class of females to inferior legal status without regard to the actual capabilities of its individual members.

We might also note that, over the past decade, Congress has itself manifested an increasing sensitivity to sex-based classifications. In Tit. VII of the Civil Rights Act of 1964, for example, Congress expressly declared that no employer, labor union, or other organization subject to the provisions of the Act shall discriminate against any individual on the basis of "race, color, religion, *sex*, or national origin." Similarly, the Equal Pay Act of 1963 provides that no employer covered by the Act "shall discriminate ... between employees on the basis of sex." And § 1 of the Equal Rights Amendment, passed by Congress on March 22, 1972, and submitted to the legislatures of the States for ratification, declares that "[e]quality of rights under the law shall not be denied or abridged by the United States or by any State on account of sex." Thus, Congress itself has concluded that classifications based upon sex are inherently invidious, and this conclusion of a coequal branch of Government is not without significance to the question presently under consideration.

With these considerations in mind, we can only conclude that classifications based upon sex, like classifications based upon race, alienage, or national origin, are inherently suspect, and must therefore be subjected to strict judicial scrutiny. Applying the analysis mandated by that stricter standard of review, it is clear that the statutory scheme now before us is constitutionally invalid.

III

The sole basis of the classification established in the challenged statutes is the sex of the individuals involved. Thus, under 37 U.S.C. §§ 401, 403, and 10 U.S.C. §§ 2072, 2076, a

---

17. It is true, of course, that when viewed in the abstract, women do not constitute a small and powerless minority. Nevertheless, in part because of past discrimination, women are vastly underrepresented in this Nation's decision making councils. There has never been a female President, nor a female member of this Court. Not a single woman presently sits in the United States Senate, and only 14 women hold seats in the House of Representatives. And, as appellants point out, this underrepresentation is present throughout all levels of our State and Federal Government.

female member of the uniformed services seeking to obtain housing and medical benefits for her spouse must prove his dependency in fact, whereas no such burden is imposed upon male members. In addition, the statutes operate so as to deny benefits to a female member, such as appellant Sharron Frontiero, who provides less than one-half of her spouse's support, while at the same time granting such benefits to a male member who likewise provides less than one-half of his spouse's support. Thus, to this extent at least, it may fairly be said that these statutes command "dissimilar treatment for men and women who are … similarly situated." Reed v. Reed, 404 U.S., at 77.

Moreover, the Government concedes that the differential treatment accorded men and women under these statutes serves no purpose other than mere "administrative convenience." In essence, the Government maintains that, as an empirical matter, wives in our society frequently are dependent upon their husbands, while husbands rarely are dependent upon their wives. Thus, the Government argues that Congress might reasonably have concluded that it would be both cheaper and easier simply conclusively to presume that wives of male members are financially dependent upon their husbands, while burdening female members with the task of establishing dependency in fact.[22]

The Government offers no concrete evidence, however, tending to support its view that such differential treatment in fact saves the Government any money. In order to satisfy the demands of strict judicial scrutiny, the Government must demonstrate, for example, that it is actually cheaper to grant increased benefits with respect to all male members, than it is to determine which male members are in fact entitled to such benefits and to grant increased benefits only to those members whose wives actually meet the dependency requirement. Here, however, there is substantial evidence that, if put to the test, many of the wives of male members would fail to qualify for benefits.[23] And in light of the fact that the dependency determination with respect to the husbands of female members is presently made solely on the basis of affidavits rather than through the more costly hearing process, the Government's explanation of the statutory scheme is, to say the least, questionable.

In any case, our prior decisions make clear that, although efficacious administration of governmental programs is not without some importance, "the Constitution recognizes higher values than speed and efficiency." And when we enter the realm of "strict judicial scrutiny," there can be no doubt that "administrative convenience" is not a shibboleth, the mere recitation of which dictates constitutionality. On the contrary, any statutory scheme which draws a sharp line between the sexes, *solely* for the purpose of achieving administrative convenience, necessarily commands "dissimilar treatment for men and women who are … similarly situated," and therefore involves the "very kind of arbitrary legislative choice forbidden by the [Constitution]…." Reed v. Reed, 404 U.S., at 77. We therefore conclude that, by according differential treatment to male and female members

---

22. It should be noted that these statutes are not in any sense designed to rectify the effects of past discrimination against women. On the contrary, these statutes seize upon a group—women—who have historically suffered discrimination in employment, and rely on the effects of this past discrimination as a justification for heaping on additional economic disadvantages.

23. In 1971, 43% of all women over the age of 16 were in the labor force, and 18% of all women worked full time 12 months per year. Moreover, 41.5% of all married women are employed. It is also noteworthy that, while the median income of a male member of the armed forces is approximately $3,686, the median income for all women over the age of 14, including those who are not employed, is approximately $2,237. Applying the statutory definition of "dependency" to these statistics, it appears that in the "median" family, the wife of a male member must have personal expenses of approximately $4,474, or about 75% of the total family income, in order to qualify as a "dependent."

of the uniformed services for the sole purpose of achieving administrative convenience, the challenged statutes violate the Due Process Clause of the Fifth Amendment insofar as they require a female member to prove the dependency of her husband.

Reversed.

Mr. Justice STEWART concurs in the judgment, agreeing that the statutes before us work an invidious discrimination in violation of the Constitution. Reed v. Reed, 404 U.S. 71.

Mr. Justice REHNQUIST dissents for the reasons stated by Judge Rives in his opinion for the District Court, Frontiero v. Laird, 341 F.Supp. 201 (1972).

Mr. Justice POWELL, with whom THE CHIEF JUSTICE and Mr. Justice BLACKMUN join, concurring in the judgment.

I agree that the challenged statutes constitute an unconstitutional discrimination against servicewomen in violation of the Due Process Clause of the Fifth Amendment, but I cannot join the opinion of Mr. Justice BRENNAN, which would hold that all classifications based upon sex, "like classifications based upon race, alienage, and national origin," are "inherently suspect and must therefore be subjected to close judicial scrutiny." It is unnecessary for the Court in this case to characterize sex as a suspect classification, with all of the far-reaching implications of such a holding. Reed v. Reed, 404 U.S. 71 (1971), which abundantly supports our decision today, did not add sex to the narrowly limited group of classifications which are inherently suspect. In my view, we can and should decide this case on the authority of *Reed* and reserve for the future any expansion of its rationale.

There is another, and I find compelling, reason for deferring a general categorizing of sex classifications as invoking the strictest test of judicial scrutiny. The Equal Rights Amendment, which if adopted will resolve the substance of this precise question, has been approved by the Congress and submitted for ratification by the States. If this Amendment is duly adopted, it will represent the will of the people accomplished in the manner prescribed by the Constitution. By acting prematurely and unnecessarily, as I view it, the Court has assumed a decisional responsibility at the very time when state legislatures, functioning within the traditional democratic process, are debating the proposed Amendment. It seems to me that this reaching out to pre-empt by judicial action a major political decision which is currently in process of resolution does not reflect appropriate respect for duly prescribed legislative processes.

There are times when this Court, under our system, cannot avoid a constitutional decision on issues which normally should be resolved by the elected representatives of the people. But democratic institutions are weakened, and confidence in the restraint of the Court is impaired, when we appear unnecessarily to decide sensitive issues of broad social and political importance at the very time they are under consideration within the prescribed constitutional processes.

Notes and Questions

1. Note that, in *Frontiero*, only four justices signed onto the plurality opinion holding that laws that discriminate on the basis of gender are subject to strict scrutiny. In *Craig v. Boren*, the Court, citing its prior decisions (including *Reed* and *Frontiero*), described the standard by which it would review classifications based on gender in terms now associated with so-called intermediate scrutiny: "classifications by gender must serve important governmental objectives and must be substantially related to achievement of those objectives." *Craig v. Boren*, 429 U.S. 190 (1976) (striking down state law setting a minimum

General, you have it
backwards: classifications based
on gender are "inherently suspect".
Women are not.

drinking age of 18 years for females and 21 years for males). In dissent, Justice Rehnquist responded as follows:

> I would think we have had enough difficulty with the two standards of review which our cases have recognized — the norm of "rational basis," and the "compelling state interest" required where a "suspect classification" is involved — so as to counsel weightily against the insertion of still another "standard" between those two. How is this Court to divine what objectives are important? How is it to determine whether a particular law is "substantially" related to the achievement of such objective, rather than related in some other way to its achievement? Both of the phrases used are so diaphanous and elastic as to invite subjective judicial preferences or prejudices relating to particular types of legislation, masquerading as judgments whether such legislation is directed at "important" objectives or, whether the relationship to those objectives is "substantial" enough.

Id. at 220–21 (Rehnquist, J., dissenting).

2. More recently, the Court has summarized its cases dealing with gender discrimination as follows:

> Without equating gender classifications, for all purposes, to classifications based on race or national origin, the Court, in post-*Reed* decisions, has carefully inspected official action that closes a door or denies opportunity to women (or to men). To summarize the Court's current directions for cases of official classification based on gender: Focusing on the differential treatment for denial of opportunity for which relief is sought, the reviewing court must determine whether the proffered justification is "exceedingly persuasive." The burden of justification is demanding and it rests entirely on the State. The State must show "at least that the [challenged] classification serves 'important governmental objectives and that the discriminatory means employed' are 'substantially related to the achievement of those objectives.'" The justification must be genuine, not hy-

pothesized or invented *post hoc* in response to litigation. And it must not rely on overbroad generalizations about the different talents, capacities, or preferences of males and females.

The heightened review standard our precedent establishes does not make sex a proscribed classification. Supposed "inherent differences" are no longer accepted as a ground for race or national origin classifications. Physical differences between men and women, however, are enduring....

"Inherent differences" between men and women, we have come to appreciate, remain cause for celebration, but not for denigration of the members of either sex or for artificial constraints on an individual's opportunity. Sex classifications may be used to compensate women "for particular economic disabilities [they have] suffered," to "promot[e] equal employment opportunity," to advance full development of the talent and capacities of our Nation's people. But such classifications may not be used, as they once were, to create or perpetuate the legal, social, and economic inferiority of women....

United States v. Virginia, 518 U.S. 515, 532–34 (1996).

3. Is the *Reed-Frontiero-Craig-Virginia* line of cases about *sex* discrimination, *gender* discrimination, or both? To what extent do you suppose that the Justices in these cases understood the nuanced distinctions between sex and gender discussed in cases such as *Littleton v. Prange* and *In re Heilig* from Chapter 1?

More generally, might one think of all types of discrimination based on sexual orientation or gender identity as subsets of sex or gender discrimination? After all, if you discriminate against individuals because they are gay or transgendered, are you not discriminating against them because of their failure to live up to stereotypes of how a man or a woman *should* behave? For example, isn't a gay man being gender non-conforming when he dates a man instead of a woman?

4. As with the sex discrimination cases, the Court eventually settled on intermediate scrutiny for discrimination on the basis of legitimacy: "Between the[] extremes of rational basis review and strict scrutiny lies a level of intermediate scrutiny, which generally has been applied to discriminatory classifications based on sex or illegitimacy. To withstand intermediate scrutiny, a statutory classification must be substantially related to an important governmental objective." *Clark v. Jeter*, 486 U.S. 456, 461 (1988).

5. Cases such as *Reed* and *Weber* might be classified as "transitional rational basis plus" cases, meaning that the Court uses the language of rational basis while in fact applying some form of heightened scrutiny, and eventually explicitly holds that laws discriminating on that basis are subject to heightened scrutiny.

6. What is it about sex and legitimacy discrimination that caused the Court to select intermediate, as opposed to strict, scrutiny? Is government more justified in discriminating on these bases than on race, and if so, why? What would be the consequences of applying strict scrutiny to classifications based on sex or legitimacy, particularly in light of *Adarand*? In this regard, consider the following critique by Justice Stevens of *Adarand*'s consistency principle:

[T]he Court may find that its new "consistency" approach to race-based classifications is difficult to square with its insistence upon rigidly separate categories for discrimination against different classes of individuals. For example, as the law currently stands, the Court will apply "intermediate scrutiny" to cases of invidious gender discrimination and "strict scrutiny" to cases of invidious race discrimination, while applying the same standard for benign classifications as for invidious ones. If this remains the law, then today's lecture about "consistency" will produce the anomalous result that the Government can more easily enact affirmative-action programs to remedy discrimination against women than it can enact affirmative-action programs to remedy discrimination against African-Americans — even though the primary purpose of the Equal Protection Clause was to end discrimination against the former slaves.

Adarand Constructors, Inc. v. Peña, 515 U.S. 200, 247 (1995) (Stevens, J., dissenting).

7. The *Frontiero* Court identified a number of factors for deciding whether or not to apply heightened scrutiny to a given type of classification under the Equal Protection Clause. Where do these factors come from, and to what extent, if at all, do they relate to the theory of footnote 4 of *Carolene Products*? Assuming that sexual orientation and gender identity discrimination are *not* merely a subset of sex discrimination, how do the *Frontiero* factors stack up for these two types of classifications?

8. Do the *Frontiero* factors make any sense in light of *Adarand*'s holding that the focus of equal protection analysis is on the classification and not the class discriminated against? After all, don't the *Frontiero* factors — with their focus on a history of discrimination, political powerlessness, and the like — necessarily call for a focus on the class discriminated against? Are the *Frontiero* factors valid post-*Adarand* for determining whether to apply heightened scrutiny? In this regard, consider the application of the *Frontiero* factors to the question whether sexual orientation discrimination should be subjected to heightened scrutiny. If the case involves a challenge brought by a heterosexual individual against a law that discriminates in *favor* of gays and lesbians, is the plaintiff required to show that *heterosexuals* are politically powerless and have faced a history of discrimination, or is it enough to show that sexual orientation classifications have been used against those who are politically powerless and who have faced a history of discrimination? Or must a heterosexual plaintiff first wait for a gay person to successfully invoke the *Frontiero* factors to obtain heightened scrutiny, and only then invoke *Adarand* to get equal scrutiny for laws that discriminate against heterosexuals?

In contemplating the answer to this, consider the fact that *Craig* — which followed *Frontiero* and which involved a law that discriminated against men — did not reconsider the factors identified in *Frontiero*, but merely recharacterized the *Reed-Frontiero* line of cases as standing for the proposition that discrimination on the basis of sex was subject to intermediate scrutiny (a standard which the Court announced for the first time in *Craig* itself).

9. Given *Craig*, which subjected laws discriminating against men to the same heightened scrutiny as laws discriminating against women, is the "consistency" principle announced in *Adarand* decades later in the context of race discrimination less surprising? Or are there sound reasons to treat sex and race discrimination differently? In this regard, reconsider a case such as *Frontiero*: is it obvious whether the discrimination in that case is against men or women? Does it turn on whether you view the servicemember or their spouse as the victim of the discrimination?

10. To what extent might the rationale for heightened scrutiny underlying the legitimacy cases provide support for heightened scrutiny against laws that discriminate against the *children* of sexual minorities? In a related vein, consider the Court's decision in *Plyler v. Doe*, 457 U.S. 202 (1982), in which it applied a heightened form of scrutiny to laws discriminating against the children of undocumented aliens while acknowledging that discrimination against the parents would not be subject to heightened review:

Persuasive arguments support the view that a State may withhold its beneficence from those whose very presence within the United States is the product of their own unlawful conduct. These arguments do not apply with the same force to classifications imposing disabilities on the minor *children* of such illegal entrants. At the least, those who elect to enter our territory by stealth and in violation of our law should be prepared to bear the consequences, including, but not limited to, deportation. But the children of those illegal entrants are not comparably situated. Their "parents have the ability to conform their conduct to societal norms," and presumably the ability to remove themselves from the State's jurisdiction; but the children who are plaintiffs in these cases "can affect neither their parents' conduct nor their own status." Even if the State found it expedient to control the conduct of adults by acting against their children, legislation directing the onus of a parent's misconduct against his children does not comport with fundamental conceptions of justice.

> "[V]isiting ... condemnation on the head of an infant is illogical and unjust. Moreover, imposing disabilities on the ... child is contrary to the basic concept of our system that legal burdens should bear some relationship to individual responsibility or wrongdoing. Obviously, no child is responsible for his birth and penalizing the ... child is an ineffectual—as well as unjust—way of deterring the parent." *Weber v. Aetna Casualty & Surety Co.*, 406 U.S. 164, 175 (1972).

Plyler v. Doe, 457 U.S. 202, 219–20 (1982).

11. Under the tiered system that the Court has established for equal protection claims, as one moves from rational basis to intermediate to strict scrutiny, the Court's scrutiny of both the *end* furthered by a law and the *means* employed to achieve that end increases, as illustrated by the following table:

Level of Scrutiny	Means-End Fit	Interest Furthered
Strict	*Narrowly tailored*	*Compelling*
Intermediate	*Substantially Related*	*Important*
Rational Basis	*Rationally Related*	*Legitimate*

Moreover, under rational basis review, as *Beach Communications* holds, the legitimate interest justifying a law need not even be the actual motivation for the law, but can be one conceived for purposes of defending the statute when challenged. In contrast, where intermediate or strict scrutiny are involved, "[t]he justification must be genuine, not hypothesized or invented *post hoc* in response to litigation." *United States v. Virginia*, 518 U.S. 515, 533 (1996).

C. The "Second Order" Rational Basis Cases

United States Department of Agriculture v. Moreno
413 U.S. 528 (1973)

Mr. Justice BRENNAN delivered the opinion of the Court.

This case requires us to consider the constitutionality of § 3(e) of the Food Stamp Act of 1964, which, with certain exceptions, excludes from participation in the food stamp program any household containing an individual who is unrelated to any other member of the household. In practical effect, § 3(e) creates two classes of persons for food stamp purposes: one class is composed of those individuals who live in households all of whose members are related to one another, and the other class consists of those individuals who live in households containing one or more members who are unrelated to the rest. The latter class of persons is denied federal food assistance....

I

....

As initially enacted, § 3(e) defined a "household" as "a group of *related or non-related* individuals, who are not residents of an institution or boarding house, but are living as one economic unit sharing common cooking facilities and for whom food is customarily purchased in common."[1] In January 1971, however Congress redefined the term "household" so as to include only groups of related individuals. Pursuant to this amendment, the Secretary of Agriculture promulgated regulations rendering ineligible for participation in the program any "household" whose members are not "all related to each other."

Appellees in this case consist of several groups of individuals who allege that, although they satisfy the income eligibility requirements for federal food assistance, they have nevertheless been excluded from the program solely because the persons in each group are not "all related to each other." ....

These and two other groups of appellees instituted a class action against the Department of Agriculture, its Secretary, and two other departmental officials, seeking declaratory and injunctive relief against the enforcement of the 1971 amendment of § 3(e) and its implementing regulations. In essence, appellees contend, and the District Court held, that the "unrelated person" provision of § 3(e) creates an irrational classification in violation of the equal protection component of the Due Process Clause of the Fifth Amendment. We agree.

II

Under traditional equal protection analysis, a legislative classification must be sustained, if the classification itself is rationally related to a legitimate governmental interest. The purposes of the Food Stamp Act were expressly set forth in the congressional "declaration of policy":

> "It is hereby declared to be the policy of Congress ... to safeguard the health and well-being of the Nation's population and raise levels of nutrition among low-income households. The Congress hereby finds that the limited food purchasing power of low-income households contributes to hunger and malnutrition among members of such households. The Congress further finds that increased utilization of food in establishing and maintaining adequate national levels of nutrition will promote the distribution in a beneficial manner of our agricultural abundances and will strengthen our agricultural economy, as well as result in more orderly marketing and distribution of food. To alleviate such hunger and malnutrition, a food stamp program is herein authorized which will permit low-income households to purchase a nutritionally adequate diet through normal channels of trade."

---

1. The act provided further that "[t]he term 'household' shall also mean a single individual living alone who has cooking facilities and who purchases and prepares food for home consumption."

The challenged statutory classification (households of related persons versus households containing one or more unrelated persons) is clearly irrelevant to the stated purposes of the Act. As the District Court recognized, "[t]he relationships among persons constituting one economic unit and sharing cooking facilities have nothing to do with their abilities to stimulate the agricultural economy by purchasing farm surpluses, or with their personal nutritional requirements."

Thus, if it is to be sustained, the challenged classification must rationally further some legitimate governmental interest other than those specifically stated in the congressional "declaration of policy." Regrettably, there is little legislative history to illuminate the purposes of the 1971 amendment of § 3(e). The legislative history that does exist, however, indicates that that amendment was intended to prevent so-called "hippies" and "hippie communes" from participating in the food stamp program. The challenged classification clearly cannot be sustained by reference to this congressional purpose. For if the constitutional conception of "equal protection of the laws" means anything, it must at the very least mean that a bare congressional desire to harm a politically unpopular group cannot constitute a *legitimate* governmental interest. As a result, "[a] purpose to discriminate against hippies cannot, in and of itself and without reference to (some independent) considerations in the public interest, justify the 1971 amendment."

Although apparently conceding this point, the Government maintains that the challenged classification should nevertheless be upheld as rationally related to the clearly legitimate governmental interest in minimizing fraud in the administration of the food stamp program.[7] In essence, the Government contends that, in adopting the 1971 amendment, Congress might rationally have thought (1) that households with one or more unrelated members are more likely than "fully related" households to contain individuals who abuse the program by fraudulently failing to report sources of income or by voluntarily remaining poor; and (2) that such households are "relatively unstable," thereby increasing the difficulty of detecting such abuses. But even if we were to accept as rational the Government's wholly unsubstantiated assumptions concerning the differences between "related" and "unrelated" households we still could not agree with the Government's conclusion that the denial of essential federal food assistance to *all* otherwise eligible households containing unrelated members constitutes a rational effort to deal with these concerns.

At the outset, it is important to note that the Food Stamp Act itself contains provisions, wholly independent of § 3(e), aimed specifically at the problems of fraud and of the voluntarily poor. For example, with certain exceptions, § 5(c) of the Act renders ineligible for assistance any household containing "an able-bodied adult person between the ages of eighteen and sixty-five" who fails to register for, and accept, offered employment. Similarly, § 14(b) and (c) specifically impose strict criminal penalties upon any individ-

---

7. The Government initially argued to the District Court that the challenged classification might be justified as a means to foster "morality." In rejecting that contention, the District Court noted that "interpreting the amendment as an attempt to regulate morality would raise serious constitutional questions." Indeed, citing this Court's decisions in Griswold v. Connecticut, 381 U.S. 479 (1965), Stanley v. Georgia, 394 U.S. 557 (1969), and Eisenstadt v. Baird, 405 U.S. 438 (1972), the District Court observed that it was doubtful at best, whether Congress, "in the name of morality," could "infringe the rights to privacy and freedom of association in the home." Moreover, the court also pointed out that the classification established in § 3(e) was not rationally related "to prevailing notions of morality, since it in terms disqualifies all households of unrelated individuals, without reference to whether a particular group contains both sexes." The Government itself has now abandoned the "morality" argument.

ual who obtains or uses food stamps fraudulently. The existence of these provisions necessarily casts considerable doubt upon the proposition that the 1971 amendment could rationally have been intended to prevent those very same abuses. See Eisenstadt v. Baird, 405 U.S. 438, 452 (1972).

Moreover, in practical effect, the challenged classification simply does not operate so as rationally to further the prevention of fraud. As previously noted, § 3(e) defines an eligible "household" as "a group of related individuals ... [1] living as one economic unit [2] sharing common cooking facilities [and 3] for whom food is customarily purchased in common." Thus, two *unrelated* persons living together and meeting all three of these conditions would constitute a single household ineligible for assistance. If financially feasible, however, these same two individuals can legally avoid the "unrelated person" exclusion simply by altering their living arrangements so as to eliminate any one of the three conditions. By so doing, they effectively create two separate "households" both of which are eligible for assistance. Indeed, as the California Director of Social Welfare has explained:

> "The 'related household' limitations will eliminate many households from eligibility in the Food Stamp Program. It is my understanding that the Congressional intent of the new regulations are specifically aimed at the 'hippies' and 'hippie communes.' Most people in this category can and will alter their living arrangements in order to remain eligible for food stamps. However, the AFDC mothers who try to raise their standard of living by sharing housing will be affected. They will not be able to utilize the altered living patterns in order to continue to be eligible without giving up their advantage of shared housing costs."

Thus, in practical operation, the 1971 amendment excludes from participation in the food stamp program, *not* those persons who are "likely to abuse the program," but, rather, *only* those persons who are so desperately in need of aid that they cannot even afford to alter their living arrangements so as to retain their eligibility. Traditional equal protection analysis does not require that every classification be drawn with precise "'mathematical nicety.'" Dandridge v. Williams, 397 U.S., at 485. But the classification here in issue is not only "imprecise", it is wholly without any rational basis. The judgment of the District Court holding the 'unrelated person' provision invalid under the Due Process Clause of the Fifth Amendment is therefore affirmed.

Mr. Justice DOUGLAS, concurring.

. . . .

The test of equal protection is whether the legislative line that is drawn bears "some rational relationship to a legitimate" governmental purpose....

But for the constitutional aspects of the problem, the "unrelated" person provision of the Act might well be sustained as a means to prevent fraud. Fraud is a concern of the Act. Able-bodied persons must register and accept work or lose their food stamp rights. I could not say that this "unrelated" person provision has no "rational" relation to control of fraud. We deal here, however, with the right of association, protected by the First Amendment. People who are desperately poor but unrelated come together and join hands with the aim better to combat the crises of poverty. The need of those living together better to meet those crises is denied, while the need of households made up of relatives that is no more acute is serviced....

Dandridge v. Williams, 397 U.S. 471, is not opposed. It sustained a Maryland grant of welfare, against the claim of violation of equal protection, which placed an upper limit on the monthly amount any single family could receive. The claimants had large families so that their standard of need exceeded the actual grants. Their claim was that the grants of aid considered in light of the size of their families created an invidious discrimination against them and in favor of small needy families. The claim was rejected on the basis that state economic or social legislation had long been judged by a less strict standard than comes into play when constitutionally protected rights are involved. Laws touching social and economic matters can pass muster under the Equal Protection Clause though they are imperfect, the test being whether the classification has some "reasonable basis." *Dandridge* held that "the Fourteenth Amendment gives the federal courts no power to impose upon the States their views of what constitutes wise economic or social policy." But for the First Amendment aspect of the case, Dandridge would control here.

Dandridge, however, did not reach classifications touching on associational rights that lie in the penumbra of the First Amendment. Since the "unrelated" person provision is not directed to the maintenance of the family as a unit but treats impoverished households composed of relatives more favorably than impoverished households having a single unrelated person, it draws a line that can be sustained only on a showing of a "compelling" governmental interest....

Mr. Justice REHNQUIST, with whom THE CHIEF JUSTICE concurs, dissenting.

....

The Court's opinion would make a very persuasive congressional committee report arguing against the adoption of the limitation in question. Undoubtedly, Congress attacked the problem with a rather blunt instrument and, just as undoubtedly, persuasive arguments may be made that what we conceive to be its purpose will not be significantly advanced by the enactment of the limitation. But questions such as this are for Congress, rather than for this Court; our role is limited to the determination of whether there is any rational basis on which Congress could decide that public funds made available under the food stamp program should not go to a household containing an individual who is unrelated to any other member of the household.

I do not believe that asserted congressional concern with the fraudulent use of food stamps is, when interpreted in the light most favorable to sustaining the limitation, quite as irrational as the Court seems to believe. A basic unit which Congress has chosen for determination of availability for food stamps is the "household," a determination which is not criticized by the Court. By the limitation here challenged, it has singled out households which contain unrelated persons and made such households ineligible. I do not think it is unreasonable for Congress to conclude that the basic unit which it was willing to support with federal funding through food stamps is some variation on the family as we know it—a household consisting of related individuals. This unit provides a guarantee which is not provided by households containing unrelated individuals that the household exists for some purpose other than to collect federal food stamps.

Admittedly, as the Court points out, the limitation will make ineligible many households which have not been formed for the purpose of collecting federal food stamps, and will at the same time not wholly deny food stamps to those households which may have been formed in large part to take advantage of the program. But, as the Court concedes, "[t]raditional equal protection analysis does not require that every classification be drawn with precise 'mathematical nicety.'" ....

The limitation which Congress enacted could, in the judgment of reasonable men, conceivably deny food stamps to members of households which have been formed solely for the purpose of taking advantage of the food stamp program. Since the food stamp program is not intended to be a subsidy for every individual who desires low-cost food, this was a permissible congressional decision quite consistent with the underlying policy of the Act. The fact that the limitation will have unfortunate and perhaps unintended consequences beyond this does not make it unconstitutional.

City of Cleburne v. Cleburne Living Center, Inc.

473 U.S. 432 (1985)

Justice WHITE delivered the opinion of the Court.

     . . . .

I

In July 1980, respondent Jan Hannah purchased a building at 201 Featherston Street in the city of Cleburne, Texas, with the intention of leasing it to Cleburne Living Center, Inc. (CLC), for the operation of a group home for the mentally retarded. It was anticipated that the home would house 13 retarded men and women, who would be under the constant supervision of CLC staff members. The house had four bedrooms and two baths, with a half bath to be added. CLC planned to comply with all applicable state and federal regulations.

The city informed CLC that a special use permit would be required for the operation of a group home at the site, and CLC accordingly submitted a permit application. In response to a subsequent inquiry from CLC, the city explained that under the zoning regulations applicable to the site, a special use permit, renewable annually, was required for the construction of "[h]ospitals for the insane or feeble-minded, or alcoholic [sic] or drug addicts, or penal or correctional institutions." The city had determined that the proposed group home should be classified as a "hospital for the feebleminded." After holding a public hearing on CLC's application, the City Council voted 3 to 1 to deny a special use permit.

CLC then filed suit in Federal District Court against the city and a number of its officials, alleging, *inter alia,* that the zoning ordinance was invalid on its face and as applied because it discriminated against the mentally retarded in violation of the equal protection rights of CLC and its potential residents.... Concluding that no fundamental right was implicated and that mental retardation was neither a suspect nor a quasi-suspect classification, the court employed the minimum level of judicial scrutiny applicable to equal protection claims. The court deemed the ordinance, as written and applied, to be rationally related to the city's legitimate interests in "the legal responsibility of CLC and its residents, ... the safety and fears of residents in the adjoining neighborhood," and the number of people to be housed in the home.

The Court of Appeals for the Fifth Circuit reversed, determining that mental retardation was a quasi-suspect classification and that it should assess the validity of the ordinance under intermediate-level scrutiny. Because mental retardation was in fact relevant to many legislative actions, strict scrutiny was not appropriate. But in light of the history of "unfair and often grotesque mistreatment" of the retarded, discrimination against them was "likely to reflect deep-seated prejudice." In addition, the mentally retarded lacked political power, and their condition was immutable. The court considered heightened scrutiny to be particularly appropriate in this case, because the city's ordinance withheld a benefit which, although not fundamental, was very important to the mentally retarded. Without group homes, the court stated, the retarded could never hope to integrate themselves into the community. Applying the test that it considered appropriate, the court held that the ordinance was invalid on its face because it did not substantially further any important governmental interests. The Court of Appeals went on to hold that the ordinance was also invalid as applied....

II

The Equal Protection Clause of the Fourteenth Amendment commands that no State shall "deny to any person within its jurisdiction the equal protection of the laws," which is essentially a direction that all persons similarly situated should be treated alike. *Plyler v. Doe,* 457 U.S. 202, 216 (1982). Section 5 of the Amendment empowers Congress to enforce this mandate, but absent controlling congressional direction, the courts have themselves devised standards for determining the validity of state legislation or other official action that is challenged as denying equal protection. The general rule is that legislation is presumed to be valid and will be sustained if the classification drawn by the statute is rationally related to a legitimate state interest. When social or economic legislation is at issue, the Equal Protection Clause allows the States wide latitude, and the Constitution presumes that even improvident decisions will eventually be rectified by the democratic processes.

The general rule gives way, however, when a statute classifies by race, alienage, or national origin. These factors are so seldom relevant to the achievement of any legitimate state interest that laws grounded in such considerations are deemed to reflect prejudice and antipathy — a view that those in the burdened class are not as worthy or deserving as others. For these reasons and because such discrimination is unlikely to be soon rectified by legislative means, these laws are subjected to strict scrutiny and will be sustained only if they are suitably tailored to serve a compelling state interest. Similar oversight by the courts is due when state laws impinge on personal rights protected by the Constitution.

Legislative classifications based on gender also call for a heightened standard of review. That factor generally provides no sensible ground for differential treatment. "[W]hat differentiates sex from such nonsuspect statuses as intelligence or physical disability ... is that the sex characteristic frequently bears no relation to ability to perform or contribute to society." *Frontiero v. Richardson,* 411 U.S. 677, 686 (1973) (plurality opinion). Rather than resting on meaningful considerations, statutes distributing benefits and burdens between the sexes in different ways very likely reflect outmoded notions of the relative capabilities of men and women. A gender classification fails unless it is substantially related to a sufficiently important governmental interest. *Mississippi University for Women v. Hogan,* 458 U.S. 718 (1982); *Craig v. Boren,* 429 U.S. 190 (1976). Because illegitimacy is beyond the individual's control and bears "no relation to the individual's ability to participate in and contribute to society," *Mathews v. Lucas,* 427 U.S. 495, 505 (1976), official discriminations resting on that characteristic are also subject to somewhat heightened review. Those restrictions "will survive equal protection scrutiny to the extent they are substantially related to a legitimate state interest." *Mills v. Habluetzel,* 456 U.S. 91, 99 (1982).

We have declined, however, to extend heightened review to differential treatment based on age:

> "While the treatment of the aged in this Nation has not been wholly free of discrimination, such persons, unlike, say, those who have been discriminated against on the basis of race or national origin, have not experienced a 'history of purposeful unequal treatment' or been subjected to unique disabilities on the basis of stereotyped characteristics not truly indicative of their abilities." *Massachusetts Board of Retirement v. Murgia,* 427 U.S. 307, 313 (1976).

The lesson of *Murgia* is that where individuals in the group affected by a law have distinguishing characteristics relevant to interests the State has the authority to implement, the courts have been very reluctant, as they should be in our federal system and with our respect for the separation of powers, to closely scrutinize legislative choices as to whether, how, and to what extent those interests should be pursued. In such cases, the Equal Protection Clause requires only a rational means to serve a legitimate end.

III

Against this background, we conclude for several reasons that the Court of Appeals erred in holding mental retardation a quasi-suspect classification calling for a more exacting standard of judicial review than is normally accorded economic and social legislation. First, it is undeniable, and it is not argued otherwise here, that those who are mentally retarded have a reduced ability to cope with and function in the everyday world. Nor are they all cut from the same pattern: as the testimony in this record indicates, they range from those whose disability is not immediately evident to those who must be constantly cared for. They are thus different, immutably so, in relevant respects, and the States' interest in dealing with and providing for them is plainly a legitimate one.[10] How this large and diversified group is to be treated under the law is a difficult and often a technical matter, very much a task for legislators guided by qualified professionals and not by the perhaps ill-informed opinions of the judiciary. Heightened scrutiny inevitably involves substantive judgments about legislative decisions, and we doubt that the predicate for such judicial oversight is present where the classification deals with mental retardation.

Second, the distinctive legislative response, both national and state, to the plight of those who are mentally retarded demonstrates not only that they have unique problems, but also that the lawmakers have been addressing their difficulties in a manner that belies a continuing antipathy or prejudice and a corresponding need for more intrusive oversight by the judiciary. Thus, the Federal Government has not only outlawed discrimination against the mentally retarded in federally funded programs, but it has also provided the retarded with the right to receive "appropriate treatment, services, and habilitation" in a setting that is "least restrictive of [their] personal liberty." In addition, the Government has conditioned federal education funds on a State's assurance that retarded children will enjoy an education that, "to the maximum extent appropriate," is integrated with that of nonmentally retarded children. The Government has also facilitated the hiring of the mentally retarded into the federal civil service by exempting them from the requirement of competitive examination. The State of Texas has similarly enacted legislation that acknowledges the special status of the mentally retarded by conferring certain rights upon them, such as "the right to live in the least restrictive setting appropriate to [their] individual needs and abilities," including "the right to live … in a group home."

Such legislation thus singling out the retarded for special treatment reflects the real and undeniable differences between the retarded and others. That a civilized and decent society expects and approves such legislation indicates that governmental consideration

---

10. As Dean Ely has observed:

"Surely one has to feel sorry for a person disabled by something he or she can't do anything about, but I'm not aware of any reason to suppose that elected officials are unusually unlikely to share that feeling. Moreover, classifications based on physical disability and intelligence are typically accepted as legitimate, even by judges and commentators who assert that immutability is relevant. The explanation, when one is given, is that *those* characteristics (unlike the one the commentator is trying to render suspect) are often relevant to legitimate purposes. At that point there's not much left of the immutability theory, is there?" J. Ely, Democracy and Distrust 150 (1980) (footnote omitted). See also *id.*, at 154–155.

of those differences in the vast majority of situations is not only legitimate but also desirable. It may be, as CLC contends, that legislation designed to benefit, rather than disadvantage, the retarded would generally withstand examination under a test of heightened scrutiny. The relevant inquiry, however, is whether heightened scrutiny is constitutionally mandated in the first instance. Even assuming that many of these laws could be shown to be substantially related to an important governmental purpose, merely requiring the legislature to justify its efforts in these terms may lead it to refrain from acting at all. Much recent legislation intended to benefit the retarded also assumes the need for measures that might be perceived to disadvantage them. The Education of the Handicapped Act, for example, requires an "appropriate" education, not one that is equal in all respects to the education of nonretarded children; clearly, admission to a class that exceeded the abilities of a retarded child would not be appropriate. Similarly, the Developmental Disabilities Assistance Act and the Texas Act give the retarded the right to live only in the "least restrictive setting" appropriate to their abilities, implicitly assuming the need for at least some restrictions that would not be imposed on others. Especially given the wide variation in the abilities and needs of the retarded themselves, governmental bodies must have a certain amount of flexibility and freedom from judicial oversight in shaping and limiting their remedial efforts.

Third, the legislative response, which could hardly have occurred and survived without public support, negates any claim that the mentally retarded are politically powerless in the sense that they have no ability to attract the attention of the lawmakers. Any minority can be said to be powerless to assert direct control over the legislature, but if that were a criterion for higher level scrutiny by the courts, much economic and social legislation would now be suspect.

Fourth, if the large and amorphous class of the mentally retarded were deemed quasi-suspect for the reasons given by the Court of Appeals, it would be difficult to find a principled way to distinguish a variety of other groups who have perhaps immutable disabilities setting them off from others, who cannot themselves mandate the desired legislative responses, and who can claim some degree of prejudice from at least part of the public at large. One need mention in this respect only the aging, the disabled, the mentally ill, and the infirm. We are reluctant to set out on that course, and we decline to do so.

Doubtless, there have been and there will continue to be instances of discrimination against the retarded that are in fact invidious, and that are properly subject to judicial correction under constitutional norms. But the appropriate method of reaching such instances is not to create a new quasi-suspect classification and subject all governmental action based on that classification to more searching evaluation. Rather, we should look to the likelihood that governmental action premised on a particular classification is valid as a general matter, not merely to the specifics of the case before us. Because mental retardation is a characteristic that the government may legitimately take into account in a wide range of decisions, and because both State and Federal Governments have recently committed themselves to assisting the retarded, we will not presume that any given legislative action, even one that disadvantages retarded individuals, is rooted in considerations that the Constitution will not tolerate.

Our refusal to recognize the retarded as a quasi-suspect class does not leave them entirely unprotected from invidious discrimination. To withstand equal protection review, legislation that distinguishes between the mentally retarded and others must be rationally related to a legitimate governmental purpose. This standard, we believe, affords government the latitude necessary both to pursue policies designed to assist the retarded in realizing their full potential, and to freely and efficiently engage in activities that burden the retarded in what is essentially an incidental manner. The State may not rely on a classification whose relationship to an asserted goal is so attenuated as to render the distinction arbitrary or irrational. See *Zobel v. Williams,* 457 U.S. 55, 61–63 (1982); *United States Dept. of Agriculture v. Moreno,* 413 U.S. 528, 535 (1973). Furthermore, some objectives—such as "a bare … desire to harm a politically unpopular group," *id.,* at 534—are not legitimate state interests. Beyond that, the mentally retarded, like others, have and retain their substantive constitutional rights in addition to the right to be treated equally by the law.

IV

We turn to the issue of the validity of the zoning ordinance insofar as it requires a special use permit for homes for the mentally retarded. We inquire first whether requiring a special use permit for the Featherston home in the circumstances here deprives respondents of the equal protection of the laws. If it does, there will be no occasion to decide whether the special use permit provision is facially invalid where the mentally retarded are involved, or to put it another way, whether the city may never insist on a special use permit for a home for the mentally retarded in an R-3 zone. This is the preferred course of adjudication since it enables courts to avoid making unnecessarily broad constitutional judgments.

The constitutional issue is clearly posed. The city does not require a special use permit in an R-3 zone for apartment houses, multiple dwellings, boarding and lodging houses, fraternity or sorority houses, dormitories, apartment hotels, hospitals, sanitariums, nursing homes for convalescents or the aged (other than for the insane or feebleminded or alcoholics or drug addicts), private clubs or fraternal orders, and other specified uses. It does, however, insist on a special permit for the Featherston home, and it does so, as the District Court found, because it would be a facility for the mentally retarded. May the city require the permit for this facility when other care and multiple-dwelling facilities are freely permitted?

It is true, as already pointed out, that the mentally retarded as a group are indeed different from others not sharing their misfortune, and in this respect they may be different from those who would occupy other facilities that would be permitted in an R-3 zone without a special permit. But this difference is largely irrelevant unless the Featherston home and those who would occupy it would threaten legitimate interests of the city in a way that other permitted uses such as boarding houses and hospitals would not. Because in our view the record does not reveal any rational basis for believing that the Featherston home would pose any special threat to the city's legitimate interests, we affirm the judgment below insofar as it holds the ordinance invalid as applied in this case.

The District Court found that the City Council's insistence on the permit rested on several factors. First, the Council was concerned with the negative attitude of the majority of property owners located within 200 feet of the Featherston facility, as well as with the fears of elderly residents of the neighborhood. But mere negative attitudes, or fear, unsubstantiated by factors which are properly cognizable in a zoning proceeding, are not permissible bases for treating a home for the mentally retarded differently from apartment houses, multiple dwellings, and the like. It is plain that the electorate as a whole, whether by referendum or otherwise, could not order city action violative of the Equal Protection Clause, and the City may not avoid the strictures of that Clause by deferring to the wishes or objections of some fraction of the body politic. "Private biases may be outside the reach of the law, but the law cannot, directly or indirectly, give them effect." *Palmore v. Sidoti*, 466 U.S. 429, 433 (1984).

Second, the Council had two objections to the location of the facility. It was concerned that the facility was across the street from a junior high school, and it feared that the students might harass the occupants of the Featherston home. But the school itself is attended by about 30 mentally retarded students, and denying a permit based on such vague, undifferentiated fears is again permitting some portion of the community to validate what would otherwise be an equal protection violation. The other objection to the home's location was that it was located on "a five hundred year flood plain." This concern with the possibility of a flood, however, can hardly be based on a distinction between the Featherston home and, for example, nursing homes, homes for convalescents or the aged, or sanitariums or hospitals, any of which could be located on the Featherston site without obtaining a special use permit. The same may be said of another concern of the Council—doubts about the legal responsibility for actions which the mentally retarded might take. If there is no concern about legal responsibility with respect to other uses that would be permitted in the area, such as boarding and fraternity houses, it is difficult to believe that the groups of mildly or moderately mentally retarded individuals who would live at 201 Featherston would present any different or special hazard.

Fourth, the Council was concerned with the size of the home and the number of people that would occupy it. The District Court found, and the Court of Appeals repeated, that "[i]f the potential residents of the Featherston Street home were not mentally retarded, but the home was the same in all other respects, its use would be permitted under the city's zoning ordinance." Given this finding, there would be no restrictions on the number of people who could occupy this home as a boarding house, nursing home, family dwelling, fraternity house, or dormitory. The question is whether it is rational to treat the mentally retarded differently. It is true that they suffer disability not shared by others; but why this difference warrants a density regulation that others need not observe is not at all apparent. At least this record does not clarify how, in this connection, the characteristics of the intended occupants of the Featherston home rationally justify denying to those occupants what would be permitted to groups occupying the same site for different purposes. Those who would live in the Featherston home are the type of individuals who, with supporting staff, satisfy federal and state standards for group housing in the community; and there is no dispute that the home would meet the federal square-footage-per-resident requirement for facilities of this type. In the words of the Court of Appeals, "[t]he City never justifies its apparent view that other people can live under such 'crowded' conditions when mentally retarded persons cannot."

In the courts below the city also urged that the ordinance is aimed at avoiding concentration of population and at lessening congestion of the streets. These concerns obviously fail to explain why apartment houses, fraternity and sorority houses, hospitals and the like, may freely locate in the area without a permit. So, too, the expressed worry about fire hazards, the serenity of the neighborhood, and the avoidance of danger to other residents fail rationally to justify singling out a home such as 201 Featherston for the special use permit, yet imposing no such restrictions on the many other uses freely permitted in the neighborhood.

The short of it is that requiring the permit in this case appears to us to rest on an irrational prejudice against the mentally retarded, including those who would occupy the Featherston facility and who would live under the closely supervised and highly regulated conditions expressly provided for by state and federal law.

The judgment of the Court of Appeals is affirmed insofar as it invalidates the zoning ordinance as applied to the Featherston home. The judgment is otherwise vacated, and the case is remanded.

Justice STEVENS, with whom THE CHIEF JUSTICE joins, concurring.

The Court of Appeals disposed of this case as if a critical question to be decided were which of three clearly defined standards of equal protection review should be applied to a legislative classification discriminating against the mentally retarded. In fact, our cases have not delineated three—or even one or two—such well-defined standards. Rather, our cases reflect a continuum of judgmental responses to differing classifications which have been explained in opinions by terms ranging from "strict scrutiny" at one extreme to "rational basis" at the other. I have never been persuaded that these so-called "standards" adequately explain the decisional process. Cases involving classifications based on alienage, illegal residency, illegitimacy, gender, age, or—as in this case—mental retardation, do not fit well into sharply defined classifications.

"I am inclined to believe that what has become known as the [tiered] analysis of equal protection claims does not describe a completely logical method of deciding cases, but rather is a method the Court has employed to explain decisions that actually apply a single standard in a reasonably consistent fashion." *Craig v. Boren,* 429 U.S. 190, 212 (1976) (STEVENS, J., concurring). In my own approach to these cases, I have always asked myself whether I could find a "rational basis" for the classification at issue. The term "rational," of course, includes a requirement that an impartial lawmaker could logically believe that the classification would serve a legitimate public purpose that transcends the harm to the members of the disadvantaged class. Thus, the word "rational"—for me at least—includes elements of legitimacy and neutrality that must always characterize the performance of the sovereign's duty to govern impartially.

The rational-basis test, properly understood, adequately explains why a law that deprives a person of the right to vote because his skin has a different pigmentation than that of other voters violates the Equal Protection Clause. It would be utterly irrational to limit the franchise on the basis of height or weight; it is equally invalid to limit it on the basis of skin color. None of these attributes has any bearing at all on the citizen's willingness or ability to exercise that civil right. We do not need to apply a special standard, or to apply "strict scrutiny," or even "heightened scrutiny," to decide such cases.

In every equal protection case, we have to ask certain basic questions. What class is harmed by the legislation, and has it been subjected to a "tradition of disfavor" by our laws? What is the public purpose that is being served by the law? What is the characteristic of the disadvantaged class that justifies the disparate treatment? In most cases the answer to these questions will tell us whether the statute has a "rational basis." The answers will result in the virtually automatic invalidation of racial classifications and in the validation of most economic classifications, but they will provide differing results in cases involving classifications based on alienage, gender, or illegitimacy. But that is not because we apply an "intermediate standard of review" in these cases; rather it is because the characteristics of these groups are sometimes relevant and sometimes irrelevant to a valid public purpose, or, more specifically, to the purpose that the challenged laws purportedly intended to serve.

Every law that places the mentally retarded in a special class is not presumptively irrational. The differences between mentally retarded persons and those with greater mental capacity are obviously relevant to certain legislative decisions. An impartial lawmaker—

indeed, even a member of a class of persons defined as mentally retarded—could rationally vote in favor of a law providing funds for special education and special treatment for the mentally retarded. A mentally retarded person could also recognize that he is a member of a class that might need special supervision in some situations, both to protect himself and to protect others. Restrictions on his right to drive cars or to operate hazardous equipment might well seem rational even though they deprived him of employment opportunities and the kind of freedom of travel enjoyed by other citizens. "That a civilized and decent society expects and approves such legislation indicates that governmental consideration of those differences in the vast majority of situations is not only legitimate but also desirable."

Even so, the Court of Appeals correctly observed that through ignorance and prejudice the mentally retarded "have been subjected to a history of unfair and often grotesque mistreatment." The discrimination against the mentally retarded that is at issue in this case is the city's decision to require an annual special use permit before property in an apartment house district may be used as a group home for persons who are mildly retarded. The record convinces me that this permit was required because of the irrational fears of neighboring property owners, rather than for the protection of the mentally retarded persons who would reside in respondent's home.

Although the city argued in the Court of Appeals that legitimate interests of the neighbors justified the restriction, the court unambiguously rejected that argument. In this Court, the city has argued that the discrimination was really motivated by a desire to protect the mentally retarded from the hazards presented by the neighborhood. Zoning ordinances are not usually justified on any such basis, and in this case, for the reasons explained by the Court, I find that justification wholly unconvincing. I cannot believe that a rational member of this disadvantaged class could ever approve of the discriminatory application of the city's ordinance in this case.

Accordingly, I join the opinion of the Court.

Justice MARSHALL, with whom Justice BRENNAN and Justice BLACKMUN join, concurring in the judgment in part and dissenting in part.

    ....

I

At the outset, two curious and paradoxical aspects of the Court's opinion must be noted. First, because the Court invalidates Cleburne's zoning ordinance on rational-basis grounds, the Court's wide-ranging discussion of heightened scrutiny is wholly superfluous to the decision of this case....

Second, the Court's heightened-scrutiny discussion is even more puzzling given that Cleburne's ordinance is invalidated only after being subjected to precisely the sort of probing inquiry associated with heightened scrutiny. To be sure, the Court does not label its handiwork heightened scrutiny, and perhaps the method employed must hereafter be called "second order" rational-basis review rather than "heightened scrutiny." But however labeled, the rational basis test invoked today is most assuredly not the rational-basis test of *Williamson v. Lee Optical of Oklahoma, Inc.,* 348 U.S. 483 (1955), *Allied Stores of Ohio, Inc. v. Bowers,* 358 U.S. 522 (1959), and their progeny.

The Court, for example, concludes that legitimate concerns for fire hazards or the serenity of the neighborhood do not justify singling out respondents to bear the burdens of these concerns, for analogous permitted uses appear to pose similar threats. Yet under the traditional and most minimal version of the rational-basis test, "reform may take one step at a time, addressing itself to the phase of the problem which seems most acute to the legislative mind." *Williamson v. Lee Optical of Oklahoma, Inc., supra,* 348 U.S., at 489. The "record" is said not to support the ordinance's classifications, but under the traditional standard we do not sift through the record to determine whether policy decisions are squarely supported by a firm factual foundation. Finally, the Court further finds it "difficult to believe" that the retarded present different or special hazards inapplicable to other groups. In normal circumstances, the burden is not on the legislature to convince the Court that the lines it has drawn are sensible; legislation is presumptively constitutional, and a State "is not required to resort to close distinctions or to maintain a precise, scientific uniformity with reference" to its goals.

I share the Court's criticisms of the overly broad lines that Cleburne's zoning ordinance has drawn. But if the ordinance is to be invalidated for its imprecise classifications, it must be pursuant to more powerful scrutiny than the minimal rational-basis test used to review classifications affecting only economic and commercial matters. The same imprecision in a similar ordinance that required opticians but not optometrists to be licensed to practice, see *Williamson v. Lee Optical of Oklahoma, Inc.,* or that excluded new but not old businesses from parts of a community, see *New Orleans v. Dukes,* would hardly be fatal to the statutory scheme.

The refusal to acknowledge that something more than minimum rationality review is at work here is, in my view, unfortunate in at least two respects.[4] The suggestion that the traditional rational-basis test allows this sort of searching inquiry creates precedent for this Court and lower courts to subject economic and commercial classifications to similar and searching "ordinary" rational-basis review—a small and regrettable step back toward the days of *Lochner v. New York,* 198 U.S. 45 (1905). Moreover, by failing to articulate the factors that justify today's "second order" rational-basis review, the Court provides no principled foundation for determining when more searching inquiry is to be invoked. Lower courts are thus left in the dark on this important question, and this Court remains unaccountable for its decisions employing, or refusing to employ, particularly searching scrutiny. Candor requires me to acknowledge the particular factors that justify invalidating Cleburne's zoning ordinance under the careful scrutiny it today receives....

Notes and Questions

1. As with "transitional rational basis plus" cases such as *Reed* and *Weber,* it seems clear (as Justice Marshall notes in his *Cleburne* dissent) that *Moreno* and *Cleburne* are also applying a more stringent form of rational basis review than is traditionally employed. Yet, unlike *Reed* and *Weber,* the *Moreno* and *Cleburne* cases are *not* transitional, for the Court *never* goes on to subsequently hold that the classifications employed therein (hippies and

---

4. The two cases the Court cites in its rational-basis discussion, *Zobel v. Williams,* 457 U.S. 55 (1982), and *United States Dept. of Agriculture v. Moreno,* 413 U.S. 528 (1973), expose the special nature of the rational-basis test employed today. As two of only a handful of modern equal protection cases striking down legislation under what purports to be a rational-basis standard, these cases must be and generally have been viewed as intermediate review decisions masquerading in rational-basis language.

the mentally retarded, respectively) are, as a general rule, subject to heightened scrutiny. Accordingly, these cases are best thought of as "fleeting rational basis plus" cases, meaning that the Court applies a heightened form of scrutiny in a given case based on its specific facts.

2. What fact or set of facts triggered the heightened scrutiny in *Moreno* and *Cleburne*? Can you articulate a general rule for when these cases would call for "fleeting rational basis plus" review?

3. Recall from Chapter 3 that there is an open question whether majoritarian views regarding morality can justify a law when challenged on substantive due process grounds. In *Moreno*, the Court in footnote 7 references (but does not assess) an argument that the denial of food stamp assistance to households containing unrelated persons is justified by majoritarian notions of morality. Are there reasons why majoritarian views regarding morality might serve as legitimate governmental interests under due process but not under equal protection? What distinction, if any, is there between moral disapproval of a group and "a bare … desire to harm a politically unpopular group"?

4. What do the *Moreno* and *Cleburne* Courts mean by the term "harm" as used in the phrase "a bare … desire to harm a politically unpopular group"? Is a desire to harm a group the same as a desire not to help that group? Did the government actors in *Moreno* and *Cleburne* affirmatively desire to injure hippies and the mentally retarded, respectively?

5. Re-examine the table on page 269. In what way does "fleeting rational basis plus" review differ from traditional rational basis review? Does it require a tighter means-end fit? A stronger governmental interest? A real—as opposed to a hypothetical—governmental interest?

6. Note that the *Cleburne* Court treats at least some of the *Frontiero* factors as authoritative in deciding whether or not to apply heightened scrutiny to laws discriminating on the basis of mental retardation. Are you persuaded by the Court's application of the *Frontiero* factors and the stated rationales for not applying heightened scrutiny generally to such laws? To what extent does *Cleburne* modify the list of factors set forth in *Frontiero*?

7. One of the justifications Justice White gives in *Cleburne* for *not* treating mental retardation as a suspect classification is that doing so would mean that laws designed to *benefit* the mentally retarded would likewise be subject to heightened scrutiny. Does this make the Court's announcement in *Adarand* of the "consistency" principle less surprising, given that *Cleburne* pre-dates *Adarand* by ten years?

8. In his concurring opinion in *Cleburne*, Justice Stevens argues that the tiered system used by the Court to analyze equal protection claims is better characterized as a single standard in which the Court demands a "rational basis" for the law. Pretty clearly, Justice Stevens has in mind a rational basis test very different from that used in *Beach Communications*. Can you articulate the standard that Justice Stevens advocates for? Is it sufficiently structured to avoid the risk of result-oriented decision making, or does the structured appearance of the tiered system merely mask the discretion that judges actually exercise when deciding equal protection claims?

9. What do you make of Justice Marshall's twin concerns regarding the *Cleburne* Court's use of "'second order' rational-basis review"? Is he right to contend that the Court is both aggrandizing its own power *Lochner*-style and leaving lower courts confused about the appropriate standard of review? To what extent are there parallels between what is going on in cases such as these and what the Court did with substantive due process review in *Lawrence*?

D. The Gay & Transgender Rights Cases

1. The Argument for Heightened Scrutiny

Watkins v. United States Army
875 F.2d 699 (9th Cir. 1989) (en banc)

PREGERSON, Circuit Judge:

The United States Army denied Sgt. Perry J. Watkins reenlistment solely because he is a homosexual. The Army refused to reenlist Watkins, a 14-year veteran, even though he had been completely candid about his homosexuality from the start of his Army career, even though he is in all respects an outstanding soldier, and even though the Army, with full knowledge of his homosexuality, had repeatedly permitted him to reenlist in the past. The Army did so despite its longstanding policy that homosexuality was a nonwaivable disqualification for reenlistment. The issue before the en banc court is whether the Army may deny reenlistment to Watkins solely because of his acknowledged homosexuality.

[The majority opinion avoids addressing the constitutionality of the policy, holding instead that the Army is equitably estopped—based on its prior acquiescence—from refusing to reenlist Watkins based on his acknowledged sexual orientation.]

NORRIS, Circuit Judge, concurring in the judgment:

I

I concur in the judgment requiring the Army to reconsider Sgt. Watkins' reenlistment application without regard to his homosexuality. I cannot join the majority's opinion, however, because I agree with the dissent that the judgment cannot rest on the doctrine of equitable estoppel. The Supreme Court has declined to approve the invocation of equitable estoppel against the government even in cases where the facts are no less sympathetic than the facts in Sgt. Watkins' case. Indeed, the Supreme Court has expressed uncertainty as to whether equitable estoppel can ever be invoked against the government. In any event, I see no justification for invoking the doctrine on the facts of this case....

I now turn to Watkins' claim that the Army's regulations deny him equal protection of the laws in violation of the Fifth Amendment. Watkins argues that the Army's regulations constitute an invidious discrimination based on sexual orientation.[3] To evaluate this claim I must engage in a three-stage inquiry. First, I must decide whether the regulations in fact discriminate on the basis of sexual orientation. Second, I must decide which level of judicial scrutiny applies by asking whether discrimination based on sexual orientation

---

3. In this opinion I use the term "sexual orientation" to refer to the orientation of an individual's sexual preference, not to his actual sexual conduct. Individuals whose sexual orientation creates in them a desire for sexual relationships with persons of the opposite sex have a heterosexual orientation. Individuals whose sexual orientation creates in them a desire for sexual relationships with persons of the same sex have a homosexual orientation.

In contrast, I use the terms "homosexual conduct" and "homosexual acts" to refer to sexual activity between two members of the same sex whether their orientations are homosexual, heterosexual, or bisexual, and we use the terms "heterosexual conduct" and "heterosexual acts" to refer to sexual activity between two members of the opposite sex whether their orientations are homosexual, heterosexual, or bisexual.

Throughout this opinion, the terms "gay" and "homosexual" will be used synonymously to denote persons of homosexual orientation.

burdens a suspect or quasi-suspect class, which would make it subject, respectively, to strict or intermediate scrutiny. *See City of Cleburne v. Cleburne Living Center,* 473 U.S. 432, 439–41 (1985). If the discrimination burdens no such class, it is subject to ordinary rationality review. *Id.* Finally, I must decide whether the challenged regulations survive the applicable level of scrutiny by deciding whether, under strict scrutiny, the legal classification is necessary to serve a compelling governmental interest; whether, under intermediate scrutiny, the classification is substantially related to an important governmental interest; or whether, under rationality review, the classification is rationally related to a legitimate governmental interest. *See id.*

II

I turn first to the threshold question raised by Watkins' equal protection claim: Do the Army's regulations discriminate on the basis of sexual orientation? The portion of the Army's reenlistment regulation that bars homosexuals from reenlisting states in full:

> Applicants to whom the disqualifications below apply are ineligible for RA [Regular Army] reenlistment at any time and requests for waiver or exception to policy will not be submitted....
>
> c. Persons of questionable moral character and a history of antisocial behavior, sexual perversion or homosexuality. A person who has committed homosexual acts or is an admitted homosexual but as to whom there is no evidence that they have engaged in homosexual acts either before or during military services is included. (See note 1)....
>
> k. Persons being discharged under AR 635-200 for homosexuality....
>
> *Note:* Homosexual acts consist of bodily contact between persons of the same sex, actively undertaken or passively permitted, with the intent of obtaining or giving sexual satisfaction, or any proposal, solicitation, or attempt to perform such an act. Persons who have been involved in homosexual acts in an apparently isolated episode, stemming solely from immaturity, curiousity [sic], or intoxication, and in the absence of other evidence that the person is a homosexual, normally will not be excluded from reenlistment. A homosexual is a person, regardless of sex, who desires bodily contact between persons of the same sex, actively undertaken or passively permitted, with the intent to obtain or give sexual gratification. Any official, private, or public profession of homosexuality, may be considered in determining whether a person is an admitted homosexual.

AR 601-280, ¶ 2-21. Although worded in somewhat greater detail, the Army's regulation mandating the separation of homosexual soldiers from service (discharge), AR 635-200, is essentially the same in substance.

On their face, these regulations discriminate against homosexuals on the basis of their sexual orientation. Under the regulations any homosexual act or statement of homosexuality gives rise to a presumption of homosexual orientation, and anyone who fails to rebut that presumption is conclusively barred from Army service. In other words, the regulations target homosexual orientation itself. The homosexual acts and statements are merely relevant, and rebuttable, indicators of that orientation.

In spite of these facial appearances, the Army argues that its regulations target homosexual conduct rather than orientation. I cannot agree. A close reading of the complex regulations leaves no room for doubt that the regulations target orientation rather than conduct.

Under the Army's regulations, "homosexuality," not sexual conduct, is clearly the operative trait for disqualification. AR 601-280, ¶ 2-21(c); *see also* AR 635-200, ¶ 15-1(a) (articulating the same goal). For example, the regulations ban homosexuals who have done nothing more than acknowledge their homosexual orientation even in the absence of evidence that the persons ever engaged in any form of sexual conduct. The reenlistment regulation disqualifies any "admitted homosexual"—a status that can be proved by "[a]ny official, private, or public profession of homosexuality" even if "there is no evidence that they have engaged in homosexual acts either before or during military service." AR 601-280, ¶ 2-21(c) & note; *see also* AR 635-200, ¶ 15-3(b). Since the regulations define a "homosexual" as "a person, regardless of sex, who *desires* bodily contact between persons of the same sex, actively undertaken or passively permitted, with the intent to obtain or give sexual gratification," a person can be deemed homosexual under the regulations without ever engaging in a homosexual act. 601-280, ¶ 2-21(c) & note (emphasis added); *see also* A.R. 635-200, 15-2(a) (same desire sufficient to make one homosexual). Thus, no matter what statements a person has made, and what conduct he or she has engaged in, the ultimate evidentiary issue is whether he or she has a homosexual orientation. Under the reenlistment regulation, persons are disqualified from reenlisting only if, based on any "profession of homosexuality" they have made, they are found to have a homosexual orientation. AR 601-280, ¶ 2-21(c) & note. Similarly, under the discharge regulation a soldier must be discharged if "[t]he soldier has stated that he or she is a homosexual or bisexual, *unless* there is a further finding that the soldier is not a homosexual or bisexual." AR 635-200, ¶ 15-3(b) (emphasis added). In short, the regulations do not penalize all statements of sexual desire, or even only statements of homosexual desire; they penalize only homosexuals who declare their homosexual orientation.

True, a "person who has committed homosexual acts" is also presumptively "included" under the reenlistment regulation as a person excludable for "homosexuality." AR 601-280, ¶ 2-21(c); *see also* AR 635-200, ¶ 15-3(a). But it is clear that this provision is merely designed to round out the possible evidentiary grounds for inferring a homosexual orientation. The regulations define "homosexual acts" to encompass any "bodily contact between persons of the same sex, actively undertaken or passively permitted, with the intent of obtaining or giving sexual satisfaction, or any proposal, solicitation, or attempt to perform such an act." AR 601-280, ¶ 2-21(c) & note; *see also* AR 635-200, ¶¶ 15-2(c) & 15-3(a) (stating the same in slightly different order). Thus, the regulations barring homosexuals from the Army cover any form of bodily contact between persons of the same sex that gives sexual satisfaction—from oral and anal intercourse to holding hands, kissing, caressing and any number of other sexual acts. Indeed, in this case the Army tried to prove at Watkins' discharge proceedings that he had committed a homosexual act described as squeezing the knee of a male soldier, but failed to prove it was Watkins who did the alleged knee-squeezing. Moreover, even non-sexual conduct can trigger a presumption of homosexuality: The regulations provide for the discharge of soldiers who have "married or attempted to marry a person known to be of the same sex ... *unless* there are further findings that the soldier is not a homosexual or bisexual." AR 635-200, ¶ 15-3(c) (emphasis added). With all the acts and statements that can serve as presumptive evidence of homosexuality under the regulations, it is hard to think of any grounds for inferring homosexual orientation that are *not* included.[6] The fact remains, however, that homosexual orientation, not homosexual conduct, is plainly the object of the Army's regulations.

---

6. In stark contrast to the breadth and focus of the regulations, the only statute Congress has enacted regulating the private consensual sexual activity of military personnel covers only sodomy, not other forms of sexual conduct, and covers sodomy whether engaged in by homosexuals or heterosexuals. 10 U.S.C. § 925 (1982) provides:

Moreover, under the regulations a person is not automatically disqualified from Army service just because he or she committed a homosexual act. Persons may still qualify for the Army despite their homosexual conduct if they prove to the satisfaction of Army officials that their *orientation* is heterosexual rather than homosexual. To illustrate, the discharge regulation provides that a soldier who engages in homosexual acts can escape discharge if he can show that the conduct was "a departure from the soldier's usual and customary behavior" that "is unlikely to recur because it is shown, for example, that the act occurred because of immaturity, intoxication, coercion, or a desire to avoid military service" *and* that the "soldier does not desire to engage in or intend to engage in homosexual acts." AR 635-200, ¶ 15-3(a). The regulation expressly states, "The intent of this policy is to permit retention *only* of *nonhomosexual* soldiers who, because of extenuating circumstances engaged in, attempted to engage in, or solicited a homosexual act." *Id.* at note (emphasis in original). Similarly, the Army's ban on reenlisting persons who have committed homosexual acts does not apply to "[p]ersons who have been involved in homosexual acts in an apparently isolated episode, stemming solely from immaturity, curiousity [sic], or intoxication, and in the absence of other evidence that the person is a homosexual." AR 601-280, ¶ 2-21 note. If a straight soldier and a gay soldier of the same sex engage in homosexual acts because they are drunk, immature or curious, the straight soldier may remain in the Army while the gay soldier is automatically terminated. In short, the regulations do not penalize soldiers for engaging in homosexual acts; they penalize soldiers who have engaged in homosexual acts only when the Army decides that those soldiers are actually gay.

In sum, the discrimination against homosexual orientation under these regulations is about as complete as one could imagine. The regulations make any act or statement that might conceivably indicate a homosexual orientation evidence of homosexuality; that evidence is in turn weighed against any evidence of a heterosexual orientation. It is thus clear in answer to my threshold equal protection inquiry that the regulations directly burden the class consisting of persons of homosexual orientation.

III

A

Before reaching the question of the level of scrutiny applicable to discrimination based on sexual orientation and the question whether the Army's regulations survive the applicable level of scrutiny, I first address the Army's argument that *Bowers v. Hardwick,* 478 U.S. 186 (1986), forecloses Watkins' equal protection claim. In *Hardwick,* the Court rejected a claim by a homosexual that a Georgia statute criminalizing sodomy deprived him of his liberty without due process of law in violation of the Fourteenth Amendment. More specifically, the Court held that the constitutionally protected right to privacy — recognized in cases such as *Griswold v. Connecticut,* 381 U.S. 479 (1965), and *Eisenstadt*

(a) Any person subject to this chapter who engages in unnatural carnal copulation with another person of the same or opposite sex or with an animal is guilty of sodomy. Penetration, however slight, is sufficient to complete the offense.

(b) Any person found guilty of sodomy shall be punished as a court-martial may direct.
Although the statute does not define "sodomy" or "unnatural carnal copulation," the statute does require proof of "penetration," which apparently limits sodomy to oral and anal copulation. *See United States v. Harris,* 8 M.J. 52, 53–59 (C.M.A.1979).

The Army has never made a finding that Watkins ever engaged in an act of sodomy in violation of section 925. Indeed, the Army twice investigated Watkins for allegedly committing sodomy in violation of section 925 and had to drop both investigations because of "insufficient evidence."

v. Baird, 405 U.S. 438 (1972)—does not extend to acts of consensual homosexual sodomy. The Court's holding was limited to this due process question. The parties did not argue and the Court explicitly did not decide the question whether the Georgia sodomy statute might violate the equal protection clause. *See id.* at 196, n. 8.

The Army nonetheless argues that it would be "incongruous" to hold that its regulations deprive gays of equal protection of the laws when *Hardwick* holds that there is no constitutionally protected privacy right to engage in homosexual sodomy. I could not disagree more. First, while *Hardwick* does indeed hold that the due process clause provides no substantive privacy protection for acts of private homosexual sodomy, nothing in *Hardwick* suggests that the state may penalize gays merely for their sexual orientation. *Cf. Robinson v. California,* 370 U.S. 660 (1962) (holding that state violated due process by criminalizing the status of narcotics addiction, even though the state could criminalize the use of the narcotics—conduct in which narcotics addicts by definition are prone to engage). In other words, the class of persons involved in *Hardwick*—those who engage in homosexual sodomy—is not congruous with the class of persons targeted by the Army's regulations—those with a homosexual orientation. *Hardwick* was a "conduct" case; Watkins' is an "orientation" case.

Second, and more importantly, *Hardwick* does not foreclose Watkins' claim because Hardwick was a *due process,* not an *equal protection* case. Although the Army acknowledges, as it must, that *Hardwick* does not discuss equal protection explicitly, the Army nonetheless argues that *Hardwick's* discussion of due process has equal protection implications. Specifically, the Army argues that the *Hardwick* Court, in holding that the criminalization of homosexual sodomy does not violate due process, decided *sub silentio* that the criminalization of *heterosexual* sodomy *would* violate due process. The Army concludes from this that *Hardwick* is controlling precedent that the government may discriminate against homosexuals without violating equal protection.

Both the premise and the conclusion of the Army's argument are mistaken. In the first place, *Hardwick* did not decide *sub silentio* that heterosexual sodomy is constitutionally protected. Indeed, the Court expressly refused to take a position on whether heterosexual sodomy was protected by the due process clause. Second, even if we accept, *arguendo,* the Army's premise that the *Hardwick* Court drew a distinction between homosexual sodomy and heterosexual sodomy for due process purposes, such a distinction under the *due process* clause would have no bearing on whether the *equal protection* clause nonetheless prohibits official discrimination against homosexuals. I discuss these points in turn.

Implicit in the Army's position is the proposition that the Court in *Hardwick* somehow *did* decide that the due process clause prohibits a state from criminalizing heterosexual sodomy. That is, the Army reads Justice White's opinion in *Hardwick* as extending the zone of privacy first recognized in *Griswold* to heterosexual sodomy, thus drawing a due process line between heterosexual and homosexual sodomy. That reading of *Hardwick* flies directly in the face of footnote 2, which expressly reserves the question of the constitutionality of the Georgia statute as applied to heterosexual sodomy.[13]

Even apart from the Court's express reservation of this question, the Army's reading of *Hardwick* is untenable. I see no basis for reading *Hardwick* as holding *sub silentio* that a right to engage in heterosexual sodomy is "deeply rooted in this Nation's history and tra-

---

13. "The only claim properly before the Court … is Hardwick's challenge to the Georgia statute as applied to consensual homosexual sodomy. *We express no opinion on the constitutionality of the Georgia statute as applied to other acts of sodomy.*" *Hardwick,* 478 U.S. at 188 n. 2 (emphasis added).

dition" or "implicit in the concept of ordered liberty"—which would be necessary for heterosexual sodomy to qualify for due process protection under *Hardwick*'s analysis. Note that when the Court found the suggestion that homosexual sodomy qualified for due process protection to be "at best, facetious," it relied upon the historical fact that sodomy was a criminal offense at common law, under the laws of all 13 colonies, and, until 1961, under the laws of all 50 states. Note further that the Court did *not* find it significant that these laws, as Justice Stevens pointed out in his dissent, drew no distinction between homosexual and heterosexual sodomy. They outlawed all acts of sodomy, both homosexual and heterosexual.

In light of the historical record relied upon by the Court, there is no way to read *Hardwick* as establishing that heterosexual sodomy is "deeply rooted in this Nation's history and tradition" while homosexual sodomy is not. I find it untenable, then, to interpret *Hardwick* as extending due process protection to heterosexual conduct while denying such protection to homosexual conduct. It is hard to imagine that the Court in *Hardwick* intended to suggest that acts of heterosexual sodomy implicate higher constitutional values than acts of homosexual sodomy.

Even if, as the Army implicitly argues, *Hardwick* did in fact extend constitutional protection to heterosexual sodomy while denying it to homosexual sodomy, such a differentiation between heterosexual and homosexual sodomy for *due process* purposes would have no bearing—none—on the entirely separate question whether official discrimination against homosexuals violates the *equal protection* clause. The relevant inquiry in equal protection jurisprudence is fundamentally different from the relevant due process inquiry. The due process clause, as the Court recognized in *Hardwick,* protects practices which are "deeply rooted in this Nation's history and tradition." The equal protection clause, in contrast, protects minorities from discriminatory treatment at the hands of the majority. Its purpose is not to protect traditional values and practices, but to *call into question* such values and practices when they operate to burden disadvantaged minorities. As Professor Sunstein puts it:

> From its inception, the Due Process Clause has been interpreted largely (though not exclusively) to protect traditional practices against short-run departures. The clause has therefore been associated with a particular conception of judicial review, one that sees the courts as safeguards against novel developments brought about by temporary majorities who are insufficiently sensitive to the claims of history.
>
> The Equal Protection Clause, by contrast, has been understood as an attempt to protect disadvantaged groups from discriminatory practices, however deeply engrained and longstanding. The Due Process Clause often looks backward; it is highly relevant to the Due Process issue whether an existing or time-honored convention, described at the appropriate level of generality, is violated by the practice under attack. By contrast, the Equal Protection Clause looks forward, serving to invalidate practices that were widespread at the time of its ratification and that were expected to endure. The two clauses therefore operate along different tracks.

The Supreme Court did not decide in *Hardwick*—and indeed has never decided in any case—whether discrimination against homosexuals violates equal protection. All *Hardwick* decided is that homosexual sodomy is not a practice so "deeply rooted in this Nation's history and tradition" that it falls within the zone of personal privacy protected by the due process clause. It is perfectly consistent to say that homosexual sodomy is not a practice so deeply rooted in our traditions as to merit due process protection, and at the same time to say, for example, that because homosexuals have historically been subject to invidious discrimination, laws which burden homosexuals as a class should be subjected to heightened scrutiny under the equal protection clause. Indeed, the two propositions may be complementary: In all probability, homosexuality is not considered a deeply-rooted part of our traditions *precisely because* homosexuals have historically been subjected to invidious discrimination. In any case, homosexuals do not become "fair game" for discrimination simply because their sexual practices are not considered part of our mainstream traditions....

The Army also argues that *Hardwick*'s concern "about the limits of the Court's role in carrying out its constitutional mandate," should prevent courts from holding that equal protection doctrine protects homosexuals from discrimination. To be sure, the Court in *Hardwick* justified its decision to cabin the right to privacy largely by pointing to the problems allegedly created when judges recognize constitutional "rights not readily identifiable in the Constitution's text" and "having little or no cognizable roots in the language or design of the Constitution." The Court stressed its concern that such rights might be perceived as involving "the imposition of the Justices' own choice of values on the States and the Federal Government" and that this antidemocratic perception might undermine the legitimacy of the Court. Finally, the Court expressed the more specific concern about potential difficulties in defining the contours of the right to privacy.

Whatever one might think about the *Hardwick* Court's concerns about substantive due process in general and the right of privacy in particular, these concerns have little if any relevance to equal protection doctrine. The right to equal protection of the laws has a clear basis in the text of the Constitution. This principle of equal treatment, when imposed against majoritarian rule, arises from the Constitution itself, not from judicial fiat. Moreover, equal protection doctrine does not prevent the majority from enacting laws based on its substantive value choices. Equal protection simply requires that the majority apply its values evenhandedly. Indeed, equal protection doctrine plays an important role in perfecting, rather than frustrating, the democratic process. The constitutional requirement of evenhandedness advances the political legitimacy of majority rule by safeguarding minorities from majoritarian oppression. The requirement of evenhandedness also facilitates a representation of minorities in government that advances the operation of representative democracy. Finally, the practical difficulties of defining the requirements imposed by equal protection, while not insignificant, do not involve the judiciary in the same degree of value-based line-drawing that the Supreme Court in *Hardwick* found so troublesome in defining the contours of substantive due process. In sum, the driving force behind *Hardwick* is the Court's ongoing concern with the expansion of rights under substantive due process, not an unbounded antipathy toward a disfavored group....

IV

I now address the merits of Watkins' argument that the Army's regulations must be subjected to strict scrutiny because homosexuals constitute a suspect class under equal protection jurisprudence. The Supreme Court has identified several factors that guide our suspect class inquiry. I now turn to each of these factors.

The first factor the Supreme Court generally considers is whether the group at issue has suffered a history of purposeful discrimination. *See, e.g., Cleburne,* 473 U.S. at 441; *Massachusetts Bd. of Retirement v. Murgia,* 427 U.S. 307, 313 (1976); *Rodriguez,* 411 U.S. at 28; *Frontiero,* 411 U.S. at 684–85 (plurality). As the Army concedes, it is indisputable that "homosexuals have historically been the object of pernicious and sustained hostility."

Rowland v. Mad River Local School Dist., 470 U.S. 1009, 1014 (1985) (Brennan, J., dissenting from denial of cert.)....

Discrimination against homosexuals has been pervasive in both the public and private sectors. Legislative bodies have excluded homosexuals from certain jobs and schools, and have prevented homosexual[] marriage. In the private sphere, homosexuals continue to face discrimination in jobs, housing and churches. Moreover, reports of violence against homosexuals have become commonplace in our society. In sum, the discrimination faced by homosexuals is plainly no less pernicious or intense than the discrimination faced by other groups already treated as suspect classes, such as aliens or people of a particular national origin.

The second factor that the Supreme Court considers in suspect class analysis is difficult to capsulize and may in fact represent a cluster of factors grouped around a central idea—whether the discrimination embodies a gross unfairness that is sufficiently inconsistent with the ideals of equal protection to term it "invidious." Consideration of this additional factor makes sense. After all, discrimination exists against some groups because the animus is warranted—no one could seriously argue that burglars form a suspect class. In giving content to this concept of gross unfairness, the Court has considered (1) whether the disadvantaged class is defined by a trait that "frequently bears no relation to ability to perform or contribute to society," *Frontiero,* 411 U.S. at 686 (plurality); (2) whether the class has been saddled with unique disabilities because of prejudice or inaccurate stereotypes; and (3) whether the trait defining the class is immutable. *See Cleburne,* 473 U.S. at 440–44; *Plyler,* 457 U.S. at 216 n. 14, 219 n. 19, 220, 223; *Murgia,* 427 U.S. at 313; *Frontiero,* 411 U.S. at 685–87 (plurality). I consider these questions in turn.

Sexual orientation plainly has no relevance to a person's "ability to perform or contribute to society." Sergeant Watkins' exemplary record of military service stands as a testament to quite the opposite. Moreover, as the Army itself concluded, there is not a scintilla of evidence that Watkins' avowed homosexuality "had either a degrading effect upon unit performance, morale or discipline, or upon his own job performance." ER at 26c.

This irrelevance of sexual orientation to the quality of a person's contribution to society also suggests that classifications based on sexual orientation reflect prejudice and inaccurate stereotypes—the second indicium of a classification's gross unfairness. *See Cleburne,* 473 U.S. at 440–441. I agree with Justice Brennan that "discrimination against homosexuals is 'likely ... to reflect deep-seated prejudice rather than ... rationality.'" *Rowland,* 470 U.S. at 1014 (Brennan, J., dissenting from denial of cert.) (quoting *Plyler,* 457 U.S. at 216 n. 14).

The Army suggests that the opprobrium directed towards gays does not constitute prejudice in the pejorative sense of the word, but rather is simply appropriate public disapproval of persons who engage in immoral behavior. The Army equates homosexuals with sodomists and justifies its regulations as simply reflecting a rational bias against a class of persons who engage in criminal acts of sodomy. In essence, the Army argues that homosexuals, like burglars, cannot form a suspect class because they are criminals.

The Army's argument rests on two false premises. First, as I have noted throughout this opinion, the class burdened by the regulations at issue in this case is defined by the sexual *orientation* of its members, not by their sexual conduct. To my knowledge, homosexual orientation itself has never been criminalized in this country. Moreover, any attempt to criminalize the status of an individual's sexual orientation would present grave constitutional problems. *See generally Robinson v. California,* 370 U.S. 660 (1962).

Second, little of the homosexual *conduct* covered by the regulations is criminal. The regulations reach many forms of homosexual conduct other than sodomy such as kissing, hand-holding, caressing, and hand-genital contact. Yet, sodomy is the only consensual adult sexual conduct that Congress has criminalized, 10 U.S.C. §925. Indeed, the Army points to no law, federal or state, which criminalizes any form of private consensual homosexual behavior other than sodomy. The Army's argument that its regulations merely ban a class of criminals might be relevant, although not necessarily persuasive, if the class at issue were limited to sodomists. But the class banned from Army service is not comprised of sodomists, or even of homosexual sodomists; the class is comprised of persons of homosexual orientation whether or not they have engaged in sodomy.

Finally, I turn to immutability as an indicator of gross unfairness. The Supreme Court has never held that only classes with immutable traits can be deemed suspect. *Cf., e.g., Cleburne,* 473 U.S. at 442 n. 10 (casting doubt on immutability theory); *id.* at 440–441 (stating the defining characteristics of suspect classes without mentioning immutability); *Murgia,* 427 U.S. at 313 (same); *Rodriguez,* 411 U.S. at 28 (same). I nonetheless consider immutability because the Supreme Court has often focused on immutability, *see, e.g., Plyler,* 457 U.S. at 220; *Frontiero,* 411 U.S. at 686 (plurality), and has sometimes described the recognized suspect classes as having immutable traits, *see, e.g., Parham v. Hughes,* 441 U.S. 347, 351 (1979) (plurality opinion) (describing race, national origin, alienage, illegitimacy, and gender as immutable).

It is clear that by "immutability" the Court has never meant strict immutability in the sense that members of the class must be physically unable to change or mask the trait defining their class. People can have operations to change their sex. Aliens can ordinarily become naturalized citizens. The status of illegitimate children can be changed. People can frequently hide their national origin by changing their customs, their names, or their associations. Lighter skinned blacks can sometimes "pass" for white, as can Latinos for Anglos, and some people can even change their racial appearance with pigment injections. *See* J. Griffin, Black Like Me (1977). At a minimum, then, the Supreme Court is willing to treat a trait as effectively immutable if changing it would involve great difficulty, such as requiring a major physical change or a traumatic change of identity. Reading the case law in a more capacious manner, "immutability" may describe those traits that are so central to a person's identity that it would be abhorrent for government to penalize a person for refusing to change them, regardless of how easy that change might be physically. Racial discrimination, for example, would not suddenly become constitutional if medical science developed an easy, cheap, and painless method of changing one's skin pigment.

With these principles in mind, I have no trouble concluding that sexual orientation is immutable for the purposes of equal protection doctrine. Although the causes of homosexuality are not fully understood, scientific research indicates that we have little control over our sexual orientation and that, once acquired, our sexual orientation is largely impervious to change. Scientific proof aside, it seems appropriate to ask whether heterosexuals feel capable of changing *their* sexual orientation. Would heterosexuals living in a city that passed an ordinance burdening those who engaged in or desired to engage in sex with persons of the *opposite* sex find it easy not only to abstain from heterosexual activity but also to shift the object of their sexual desires to persons of the same sex? It may be that some heterosexuals and homosexuals can change their sexual orientation through extensive therapy, neurosurgery or shock treatment. But the possibility of such a difficult and traumatic change does not make sexual orientation "mutable" for equal protection purposes. To express the same idea under the alternative formulation, I conclude that allowing the government to penalize the failure to change such a central aspect of individual and group identity would be abhorrent to the values animating the constitutional ideal of equal protection of the laws.

The final factor the Supreme Court considers in suspect class analysis is whether the group burdened by official discrimination lacks the political power necessary to obtain redress from the political branches of government. *See, e.g., Cleburne,* 473 U.S. at 441; *Plyler,* 457 U.S. at 216 n. 14; *Rodriguez,* 411 U.S. at 28. Courts are understandably reluctant to extend heightened protection under equal protection doctrine to groups fully capable of securing their rights through the political process. It cannot be seriously disputed, however, that homosexuals as a group cannot protect their right to be free from invidious discrimination by appealing to the political branches.

The very fact that homosexuals have historically been underrepresented in and victimized by political bodies is itself strong evidence that they lack the political power necessary to ensure fair treatment at the hands of government. In addition, homosexuals as a group are handicapped by structural barriers that operate to make effective political participation unlikely if not impossible. First, the social, economic, and political pressures to conceal one's homosexuality operate to discourage gays from openly protesting anti-homosexual governmental action. Ironically, by "coming out of the closet" to protest against discriminatory legislation and practices, homosexuals expose themselves to the very discrimination they seek to eliminate. As a result, the voices of many homosexuals are not even heard, let alone counted. "Because of the immediate and severe opprobrium often manifested against homosexuals once so identified publicly, members of this group are particularly powerless to pursue their rights openly in the political arena." *Rowland,* 470 U.S. at 1014 (Brennan, J., dissenting from denial of cert.).

Even when gays do come out of the closet to participate openly in politics, the general animus towards homosexuality may render this participation ineffective. Many heterosexuals, including elected officials, find it difficult to empathize with and take seriously the arguments advanced by homosexuals, in large part because of the lack of meaningful interaction between the heterosexual majority and the homosexual minority. Most people have little exposure to gays, both because they rarely encounter gays[29] and because—as I noted above—homosexuals are often pressured into concealing their sexual identity. Thus, elected officials sensitive to public prejudice and ignorance, and insensitive to the needs of the homosexual constituency, may refuse to even consider legislation that even appears to be pro-homosexual. Indeed, the Army itself argues that its regulations are justified by the need to "maintain the public acceptability of military service," AR 635-200, ¶ 15-2(a), because "toleration of homosexual conduct ... might be understood as tacit approval" and "the existence of homosexual units might well be a source of ridicule and notoriety." These barriers to the exercise of political power both reinforce and are reinforced by the underrepresentation of avowed homosexuals in the decision making bodies of government and the inability of homosexuals to prevent legislation hostile to their group interests.[30] *See Frontiero,* 411 U.S. at 686 & n. 17 (plurality) (un-

---

29. Because homosexuals are a minority and are frequently excluded from jobs, schools, churches, and heterosexual social circles, *see supra,* heterosexuals generally have relatively few opportunities to meet homosexuals and overcome their stereotypical thinking about homosexuality.

30. The Army claims that homosexuals cannot be politically powerless because two states, Wisconsin and California, have passed statutes prohibiting discrimination against homosexuals. Two state statutes do not overcome the long and extensive history of laws discriminating against homosexuals in all fifty states. Moreover, at the national level—the relevant political level for seeking protection from military discrimination—homosexuals have been wholly unsuccessful in getting legislation

derrepresentation of women in government caused in part by history of discrimination); *Cleburne,* 473 U.S. at 445 (reasoning that the existence of legislation responsive to the needs of the mentally disabled belied the claim that they were politically powerless).

In sum, all of the relevant factors drive me to the conclusion that homosexuals constitute a suspect class for equal protection purposes. Moreover, the principles that animate equal protection doctrine—the principles that gave rise to these factors in the first place—reinforce that conclusion....

V

Having concluded that homosexuals constitute a suspect class, I now must subject the Army's regulations facially discriminating against homosexuals to strict scrutiny. Consequently, I may uphold the regulations only if they are "'*necessary* to promote a *compelling* governmental interest.'" The requirement of necessity means that no less restrictive alternative is available to promote the compelling governmental interest.

I recognize that even under strict scrutiny, my review of military regulations must be more deferential than comparable review of laws governing civilians. *See Goldman v. Weinberger,* 475 U.S. 503 (1986). While the Supreme Court does not "purport to apply a different equal protection test because of the military context, [it does] stress the deference due congressional choices among alternatives in exercising the congressional authority to raise and support armies and make rules for their governance." *Rostker v. Goldberg,* 453 U.S. 57, 71 (1981) (citing *Schlesinger v. Ballard,* 419 U.S. 498 (1975))....

In any case, even granting special deference to the policy choices of the military, I must reject many of the Army's asserted justifications because they illegitimately cater to private biases. For example, the Army argues that it has a valid interest in maintaining morale and discipline by avoiding hostilities and "'tensions between known homosexuals and other members [of the armed services] who despise/detest homosexuality.'"[31] The Army also expresses its "'doubts concerning a homosexual officer's ability to command the respect and trust of the personnel he or she commands'" because many lower-ranked heterosexual soldiers despise and detest homosexuality. Finally, the Army argues that the presence of gays in its ranks "might well be a source of ridicule and notoriety, harmful to the Army's recruitment efforts" and to its public image.

---

passed that protects them from discrimination.

The Army also argues that the repeal of sodomy statutes by many states proves that homosexuals are not politically powerless. However, sodomy statutes restrict the sexual freedom of heterosexuals as well as homosexuals. The repeal of sodomy statutes may thus reflect the liberalization of attitudes about heterosexual behavior more than it reflects the political power of homosexuals.

31. A somewhat different rationale conceivably could also underlie certain cryptic statements the Army makes about its concerns regarding "close conditions affording minimal privacy," "'potential for difficulties arising out of possible close confinement,'" and "the intimacy of barrack's [*sic*] life." Conceivably, the Army could be concerned in part that the presence of gays in the ranks will create *sexual* tensions—as distinguished from tensions arising from prejudice—because of the practical necessity of housing gays with personnel of the same sex. The Army, however, never articulates this concern. Thus it gives no indication that it regards this concern as compelling or that it believes that weeding *all* homosexuals out of the military—even soldiers as exemplary as Sergeant Watkins—is necessary to advance a compelling military interest in reducing sexual tensions. Indeed, at points in its argument the Army implies that it is concerned about the close confinement of soldiers only insofar as such confinement might exacerbate hostilities and tensions assertedly created by the prejudice some heterosexuals have against homosexuals. Even if the Army had raised the argument that excluding homosexuals from barracks reduces sexual tension and had shown that reducing sexual tension serves a compelling interest, nothing in the record even suggests that a per se rule banning all homosexuals from the Army would be the least restrictive method of advancing this interest.

These concerns strike an all-too-familiar chord. For much of our history, the military's fear of racial tension kept black soldiers separated from whites. As recently as World War II both the Army chief of staff and the Secretary of the Navy justified racial segregation in the ranks as necessary to maintain efficiency, discipline, and morale.[32] Today, it is unthinkable that the judiciary would defer to the Army's prior "professional" judgment that black and white soldiers had to be segregated to avoid interracial tensions. Indeed, the Supreme Court has decisively rejected the notion that private prejudice against minorities can ever justify official discrimination, even when those private prejudices create real and legitimate problems. *See Palmore v. Sidoti*, 466 U.S. 429 (1984).

In *Palmore*, a state granted custody of a child to her father because her white mother had remarried a black man. The state rested its decision on the best interests of the child, reasoning that, despite improvements in race relations, the social reality was that the child would likely suffer social stigmatization if she had parents of different races. A unanimous Court, in an opinion by Chief Justice Burger, conceded the importance of the state's interest in the welfare of the child, but nonetheless reversed with the following reasoning:

> It would ignore reality to suggest that racial and ethnic prejudices do not exist or that all manifestations of those prejudices have been eliminated.... The question, however, is whether the reality of private biases and the possible injury they might inflict are permissible considerations for removal of an infant child from the custody of its natural mother. We have little difficulty concluding that they are not. The Constitution cannot control such prejudices but neither can it tolerate them. Private biases may be outside the reach of the law, but the law cannot, directly or indirectly, give them effect.

Thus, *Palmore* forecloses the Army from justifying its ban on homosexuals on the ground that private prejudice against homosexuals would somehow undermine the strength of our armed forces if homosexuals were permitted to serve. *See also Cleburne*, 473 U.S. at 448 (even under rationality review of discrimination against group that is neither suspect nor quasi-suspect, catering to private prejudice is not a cognizable state interest).

The Army's defense of its regulations, however, goes beyond its professed fear of prejudice in the ranks. Apparently, the Army believes that its regulations rooting out persons with certain sexual tendencies are not merely a response to prejudice, but are also grounded in legitimate moral norms. In other words, the Army believes that its ban against homosexuals simply codifies society's moral consensus that homosexuality is evil. Yet, even accepting *arguendo* this proposition that anti-homosexual animus is grounded in morality (as opposed to prejudice masking as morality), and assuming further that the Army is an appropriate governmental body to articulate moral norms, equal protection doctrine does not permit notions of majoritarian morality to serve as compelling justification for laws that discriminate against suspect classes.

A similar principle animates *Loving v. Virginia*, 388 U.S. 1 (1967), in which the Supreme Court struck down a Virginia statute outlawing marriages between whites and blacks. Although the Virginia legislature may have adopted this law in the sincere belief that miscegenation — the mixing of racial blood lines — was evil, this moral judgment could not justify the statute's discrimination on the basis of race. Like the Army's regulations proscribing sexual acts only when committed by homosexual couples, the Virginia statute

---

32. It took an Executive Order in 1945 by President Truman, issued against the advice of almost every admiral and general, to integrate our armed forces. It is also interesting to note that during World War II the Army deliberately minimized any publicity about the existence of black soldiers because it feared that such publicity would tarnish the Army's public image.

proscribed marriage only when undertaken by mixed-race couples. In both cases, the government did not prohibit certain conduct, it prohibited certain conduct selectively—only when engaged in by certain classes of people. Although courts may sometimes have to accept society's moral condemnation as a justification even when the morally condemned activity causes no harm to interests outside notions of morality, *see Hardwick,* 478 U.S. at 196 (accepting moral condemnation as justification under rationality review), our deference to majoritarian notions of morality must be tempered by the equal protection principles which require that those notions be applied evenhandedly. Laws that limit the acceptable focus of one's sexual desires to members of the opposite sex, like laws that limit one's choice of spouse (or sexual partner) to members of the same race, cannot withstand constitutional scrutiny absent a compelling governmental justification. This requirement would be reduced to a nullity if the government's assertion of moral objections only to interracial couples or only to homosexual couples could itself serve as a tautological basis for the challenged classification.

The Army's remaining justifications for discriminating against homosexuals may not be illegitimate, but they bear little relation to the regulations at issue. For example, the Army argues that military discipline might be undermined if emotional relationships developed between homosexuals of different military rank. Although this concern might be a compelling and legitimate military interest, the Army's regulations are poorly tailored to advance that interest. No one would suggest that heterosexuals are any less likely to develop emotional attachments within military ranks than homosexuals. Yet the Army's regulations do not address the problem of emotional attachments between male and female personnel, which presumably subjects military di[s]cipline to similar stress. Surely, the Army's interest in preventing emotional relationships that could erode military discipline would be advanced much more directly by a ban on all sexual contact between members of the same unit, whether between persons of the same or opposite sex. *Cf. Cleburne,* 473 U.S. at 449–50 (rejecting certain asserted justifications under *rationality* review where the justification would extend to other groups but the challenged classification did not). Here the Army's regulations disqualify all homosexuals whether or not they have developed any emotional or sexual relationships with other soldiers.

Also bearing little relation to the regulations is the Army's professed concern with breaches of security. Certainly the Army has a compelling interest in excluding persons who may be susceptible to blackmail. It is evident, however, that homosexuality poses a special risk of blackmail only if a homosexual is secretive about his or her sexual orientation. The Army's regulations do nothing to lessen this problem. Quite the opposite, the regulations ban homosexuals only after they have declared their homosexuality or have engaged in known homosexual acts. The Army's concern about security risks among gays could be addressed in a more sensible and less restrictive manner by adopting a regulation banning only those gays who had lied about or failed to admit their sexual orientation.[34] In that way, the Army would *encourage,* rather than discourage, declarations of homosexuality, thereby reducing the number of closet homosexuals who might indeed pose a security risk. Moreover, even if banning homosexuals could lessen security risks, there appears to be no reason for treating homosexuality as a nonwaivable disqualification from military service while treating other more seri-

---

34. Watkins has forthrightly reported his homosexuality since his induction in 1967, and his homosexuality was always a matter of common knowledge. There is no suggestion in the record before us that Watkins ever feared public disclosure of his homosexuality.

ous potential sources of blackmail as waivable disqualifications. *See* AR 635-200, ¶ 14-12(c) & (d) (making drug abuse and the commission of other serious military offenses waivable disqualifications).

CONCLUSION

The Army's regulations violate the constitutional guarantee of equal protection of the laws because they discriminate against persons of homosexual orientation, a suspect class, and because the regulations are not necessary to promote a legitimate compelling governmental interest. I would thus reverse the district court's rulings denying Watkins' motion for summary judgment and granting summary judgment in favor of the Army, and remand with instructions to enter a declaratory judgment that the Army Regulations A.R. 635-200, Chapter 15, and 601-280, ¶ 2-21(c), are constitutionally void on their face, and to enter an injunction requiring the Army to consider Watkins' reenlistment application without regard to his sexual orientation.

CANBY, Circuit Judge, concurring:

I concur wholeheartedly in Judge Pregerson's majority opinion. My concurrence indicates no retreat, however, from my conviction that the Army's discrimination against Watkins because of his homosexual orientation denies him equal protection of the laws. I joined Judge Norris' eloquent opinion so holding in *Watkins II*, and I agree with everything Judge Norris says today on the equal protection point. Because we are en banc, and the constitutional issue is a recurring one, I think I may appropriately reach it even though equitable estoppel may dispose of the case.

[The dissenting opinion of Judge Hall is omitted.]

High Tech Gays v. Defense Industrial Security Clearance Office

895 F.2d 563 (9th Cir. 1990)

BRUNETTI, Circuit Judge:

The plaintiffs-appellees challenge whether the Department of Defense's (DoD) policy of subjecting all homosexual applicants for Secret and Top Secret clearances to expanded investigations and mandatory adjudications, and whether the alleged DoD policy and practice of refusing to grant security clearances to known or suspected gay applicants, violates the equal protection component of the Fifth Amendment's Due Process Clause....

I.

Background

A.

This appeal involves a class action challenging the mandatory investigation of all homosexual applicants seeking a Secret or Top Secret clearance. The clearance process begins when the defense contractor forwards an individual's name to the DoD for Secret or Top Secret clearance. For a Secret clearance, the Defense Industrial Security Clearance Organization (DISCO) conducts a National Agency Check (NAC), which consists at a minimum of a record check of the Federal Bureau of Investigation and the Defense Central Intelligence Index, but may also include a record check of the Office of Personnel Management, the Immigration and Naturalization Service, the State Department, and the Central Intelligence Agency. For Top Secret clearance, the Defense Investigative Service (DIS) completes a Background Investigation (BI) for each applicant, which consists of a NAC, local records check, and interviews with personal sources.

DISCO will grant a Secret clearance if no adverse or questionable information is developed by the NAC. If adverse information arises from the NAC, DIS conducts an expanded investigation to substantiate or disprove the adverse or questionable information and conducts a personal interview of the applicant. If information obtained from the expanded investigation resolves the question of potentially adverse information, DISCO grants the Secret clearance. Similarly, for a Top Secret clearance application, if the BI resolves any potentially derogatory information that may have arisen during the investigation, DISCO grants the clearance. The Department of Defense Personnel Security Program provides guidelines for DISCO in determining whether there is significant adverse information that prevents the granting of a clearance.

For both Secret and Top Secret clearances, if DISCO cannot find that granting the security clearance would be clearly consistent with the national interest, the case is referred to the Directorate for Industrial Security Clearance Review (DISCR) for review and adjudication. DISCR evaluates the application under the standards and criteria set forth in the DoD directives and determines whether or not to grant a clearance.

> The personnel security standard that must be applied to determine whether a person is eligible for access to classified information or assignment to sensitive duties is whether, based on all available information, the person's loyalty, reliability, and trustworthiness are such that entrusting the person with classified information or assigning the person to sensitive duties is clearly consistent with the interests of national security....

Section 154.7 provides a list of criteria for determining eligibility for a clearance under this standard. These criteria are further explained in 32 C.F.R. pt. 154, appendices D and H. In appendix D, number 2, acts of sexual misconduct under 32 C.F.R. § 154.7(q) are defined to include "all indications of moral turpitude, heterosexual promiscuity, aberrant, deviant or bizarre sexual conduct or behavior, transvestitism [sic], transsexualism, indecent exposure, rape, contributing to the delinquency of a minor, child molestation, wife-swapping, window peeping, and similar situations from whatever source."

In appendix H, each category is further broken down into sections describing disqualifying factors and mitigating factors. The disqualifying factors under sexual misconduct include conduct involving acts performed in open or in public places; acts performed with minors or animals; acts involving inducement, force, coercion, or violence; prostitution; sexual harassment; self-mutilation; spouse swapping or group sex orgies; adultery that is recent, frequent and likely to continue and has adverse effect in the work place; conduct determined to be criminal in the locale in which it occurred; and deviant or perverted sexual behavior which may indicate a mental or personality disorder (e.g., transsexualism, transvestism, exhibitionism, incest, child molestation, voyeurism, bestiality, or sodomy). The disqualifying factors also include whether such conduct has been recent; whether it increases the applicant's vulnerability to blackmail, coercion or pressure; and whether the applicant is likely to repeat the conduct in the future. Mitigating factors include whether the conduct occurred on an isolated basis, the age of the applicant at the time of the act, whether the applicant has completed professional therapy, and whether the sexual misconduct can no longer form the basis for vulnerability to blackmail, coercion or pressure.

The DIS Manual for Personnel Security Investigations (DIS 20-1-M) establishes operational and investigative policy and procedural guidance for conducting personnel security investigations. According to the DIS 20-1-M, the DIS will not ordinarily "investigate allegations of heterosexual conduct between consenting adults." If circumstances warrant, the DIS will expand the investigation "to determine if the SUBJECT, through his or her activities is susceptible to coercion and blackmail has committed criminal acts, or engaged in reckless and irresponsible conduct." Extramarital sexual relations are considered a legitimate concern when the potential for undue influence or duress exists. Other sexual conduct including homosexuality, bestiality, fetishism, exhibitionism, sadism, masochism, transvestism, necrophilia, nymphomania or satyriasis, pedophilia and voyeurism is considered a "relevant consideration in circumstances in which deviant conduct indicates a personality disorder or could result in exposing the individual to direct or indirect blackmail or coercion."

. . . .

While DIS will expand an investigation with a heterosexual if circumstances warrant, it is undisputed that for both Secret and Top Secret clearances, DISCO refers all homosexual applicants to DISCR for an expanded investigation and adjudication. However, the DIS 20-1-M states that

> [m]atters pertaining to sex are not in themselves relevant to a security determination, unless they are indicative of irresponsibility, are criminal, in nature, or create a situation making the SUBJECT vulnerable to blackmail. A SUBJECT will not be asked specific questions about sex unless: (a) the SUBJECT introduces the matter or it has been developed through other sources ... or prior investigation; and (b) questioning is necessary to determine the SUBJECT'S susceptibility to pressure or blackmail, or to explore criminality or irresponsible behavior.

. . . .

III.

Equal Protection

"The Equal Protection Clause of the Fourteenth Amendment commands that no State shall deny to any person within its jurisdiction the equal protection of the laws, which is essentially a direction that all persons similarly situated should be treated alike." *City of Cleburne v. Cleburne Living Center,* 473 U.S. 432, 439 (1985).

In *Bolling v. Sharpe,* 347 U.S. 497 (1954), the Supreme Court held that while the Equal Protection Clause of the Fourteenth Amendment prohibited states from maintaining racially segregated public schools, *see Brown v. Board of Education,* 347 U.S. 483 (1954), only the Fifth Amendment, not the Fourteenth, was applicable in the District of Columbia. The Court noted that the Fifth Amendment "does not contain an equal protection clause as does the Fourteenth Amendment which applies only to the states," and held that racial segregation in the District of Columbia public schools violated the Due Process Clause of the Fifth Amendment. The Court believed that in light of their decision in *Brown* that the Constitution prohibits states from maintaining racially segregated schools, "it would be unthinkable that the same Constitution would impose a lesser duty on the Federal Government." The Court also noted that

> the concepts of equal protection and due process, both stemming from our American ideal of fairness, are not mutually exclusive. The "equal protection of the laws" is a more explicit safeguard of prohibited unfairness than "due process of law," and, therefore, we do not imply that the two are always interchangeable phrases. [However], discrimination may be so unjustifiable as to be violative of due process.

It is thus clear that there is an equal protection component of the Due Process Clause of the Fifth Amendment which applies to the federal government.

In this case, the plaintiffs challenge the validity of the DoD Security Clearance Regulations under the equal protection component of the Fifth Amendment; specifically, that the DoD security clearance regulations discriminate against gay people. In considering such Fifth Amendment claims, the Supreme Court has held:

> While the Fifth Amendment contains no equal protection clause, it does forbid discrimination that is so unjustifiable as to be violative of due process. This Court's approach to Fifth Amendment equal protection claims has always been precisely the same as to equal protection claims under the Fourteenth Amendment.

Wiesenfeld, 420 U.S. at 638 n. 2.

It is well established that there are three standards we may apply in reviewing the plaintiffs' equal protection challenge to the DoD Security Clearance Regulations: strict scrutiny, heightened scrutiny, and rational basis review. *See Cleburne,* 473 U.S. at 440–41. The plaintiffs assert that homosexuality should be added to the list of suspect or quasi-suspect classifications requiring strict or heightened scrutiny. We disagree and hold that the district court erred in applying heightened scrutiny to the regulations at issue and that the proper standard is rational basis review.

The Supreme Court has ruled that homosexual activity is not a fundamental right protected by substantive due process and that the proper standard of review under the Fifth Amendment is rational basis review. *Bowers v. Hardwick,* 478 U.S. 186, 194–96 (1986). The Court explained that the right to privacy inheres only in family relationships, marriage and procreation, and does not extend to all private sexual conduct between consenting adults. The Court specifically characterized "fundamental liberties" under the Constitution "as those liberties that are deeply rooted in this Nation's history and tradition." In holding that the Constitution does not confer a fundamental right upon homosexuals to engage in consensual sodomy, the Court stated:

> There should be, therefore, great resistance to expand the substantive reach of [the Due Process Clauses of the Fifth and Fourteenth Amendments], particularly if it requires redefining the category of rights deemed to be fundamental. Otherwise, the Judiciary necessarily takes to itself further authority to govern the country without express constitutional authority.

There has been a repudiation of much of the substantive gloss that the Court has placed on the Due Process Clauses of the Fifth and Fourteenth Amendments. If for federal analysis we must reach equal protection of the Fourteenth Amendment by the Due Process Clause of the Fifth Amendment, *see Bolling,* 347 U.S. at 499, and if there is no fundamental right to engage in homosexual sodomy under the Due Process Clause of the Fifth Amendment, *see Hardwick,* 478 U.S. at 194, it would be incongruous to expand the reach of equal protection to find a fundamental right of homosexual conduct under the equal protection component of the Due Process Clause of the Fifth Amendment. *See Bolling,* 347 U.S. at 500.

Other circuits are in accord and have held that although the Court in *Hardwick* analyzed the constitutionality of the sodomy statute on a due process rather than equal protection basis, by the *Hardwick* majority holding that the Constitution confers no fundamental right upon homosexuals to engage in sodomy, and because homosexual conduct can thus be criminalized, homosexuals cannot constitute a suspect or quasi-suspect class entitled to greater than rational basis review for equal protection purposes....

[T]he majority in our recent *Watkins* en banc case did not rule that homosexuality is subject to heightened scrutiny. *See Watkins v. United States Army*, 875 F.2d 699, 705 (9th Cir.1989) (en banc) (*Watkins II*).[9]

. . . .

It is apparent that while the Supreme Court has identified that legislative classifications based on race, alienage, or national origin are subject to strict scrutiny and that classifications based upon gender or illegitimacy call for a heightened standard, the Court has never held homosexuality to a heightened standard of review.

To be a "suspect" or "quasi-suspect" class, homosexuals must 1) have suffered a history of discrimination; 2) exhibit obvious, immutable, or distinguishing characteristics that define them as a discrete group; and 3) show that they are a minority or politically powerless, or alternatively show that the statutory classification at issue burdens a fundamental right.

While we do agree that homosexuals have suffered a history of discrimination, we do not believe that they meet the other criteria. Homosexuality is not an immutable characteristic; it is behavioral and hence is fundamentally different from traits such as race, gender, or alienage, which define already existing suspect and quasi-suspect classes. The behavior or conduct of such already recognized classes is irrelevant to their identification.

Moreover, legislatures have addressed and continue to address the discrimination suffered by homosexuals on account of their sexual orientation through the passage of anti-discrimination legislation. Thus, homosexuals are not without political power; they have the ability to and do "attract the attention of the lawmakers," as evidenced by such legislation. *See Cleburne*, 473 U.S. at 445. Lastly, as previously noted, homosexual conduct is not a fundamental right.

Our review compels us to agree with the other circuits that have ruled on this issue and to hold that homosexuals do not constitute a suspect or quasi-suspect class entitled to greater than rational basis scrutiny under the equal protection component of the Due Process Clause of the Fifth Amendment. . . .

Holloway v. Arthur Andersen & Co.

566 F.2d 659 (9th Cir. 1977)

NIELSEN, District Judge:

Appellant, Ramona Holloway, a transsexual, claims that appellee, Arthur Andersen and Company, an accounting firm, discriminated against her in employment on account

---

9. In *Watkins II*, the majority specifically declined to reach the constitutional equal protection issues concerning homosexuality raised by the panel opinion. We instead relied upon equitable estoppel, holding that the Army was estopped from refusing to reenlist Watkins on the basis of his homosexuality.

Judge Norris' concurrence in *Watkins II*, joined by Judge Canby, expresses the opinion that homosexuals constitute a suspect class, arguing that the *Hardwick* Court's concerns about substantive due process have little or no relevance to equal protection doctrine. We disagree.

As discussed in the main text of this case, under *Bolling* the equal protection guarantees of the Fourteenth Amendment are applied to federal statutes, regulations, and actions through the Fifth Amendment's Due Process Clause. The two are thus intertwined for purposes of equal protection analyses of federal action. . . .

The *Watkins II* concurring opinion's conclusion that homosexuals constitute a suspect class is also based in part on an analysis distinguishing *Hardwick* as a "conduct" rather than an "orientation" case. However, this differentiation is not relevant to this case, as the DoD regulations challenged by the plaintiffs all relate to conduct.

of her sex and has therefore violated Title VII of the Civil Rights Act of 1964, 42 U.S.C. § 2000e *et seq.* . . .

I

Holloway was first employed by Arthur Andersen in 1969 and was then known as Robert Holloway. In 1970, appellant began to receive female hormone treatments. In February of 1974, appellant was promoted to the position of Head Multilith Operator. At this time, appellant informed Marion D. Passard, her supervisor, that appellant was undergoing treatment in preparation for anatomical sex change surgery. In June of 1974, during annual review, an official of the company suggested that appellant would be happier at a new job where her transsexualism would be unknown. However, Holloway was still given a pay raise.

In November, 1974, at her request, Holloway's records were changed to reflect her present first name. Shortly thereafter, on November 18, 1974, Holloway was terminated.

After exhausting her administrative remedies, Holloway filed a complaint alleging that she was fired for her transsexuality. . . . the district court issued a memorandum decision which held that transsexualism was not encompassed within the definition of "sex" as the term appears in 42 U.S.C. § 2000e-2(a)(1). Therefore, the court concluded that it lacked jurisdiction, so that judgment issued in defendant's favor. . . .

II

[The court holds that the term "sex" as used in Title VII does not encompass claims of discrimination based on transsexuality.]

III

The Fourteenth Amendment provides that "No State shall … deprive any person of life, liberty, or property, without due process of law; nor deny to any person within its jurisdiction the equal protection of the laws." The Constitution contains no specific equal protection guarantee against the federal government; but the substance of such a guarantee has been implied in the Fifth Amendment Due Process Clause. *Bolling v. Sharpe*, 347 U.S. 497, 499 (1954).

Appellant contends that had Congress chosen to expressly exclude transsexuals from the coverage of Title VII, there would be a violation of equal protection. Appellant further claims that a restrictive interpretation of the language of Title VII acts to exclude transsexuals as a class and "at the very least necessarily" raises equal protection problems. Therefore, argues appellant, because the narrow interpretation of the language of Title VII raises such equal protection issues, we must follow the "cardinal principle" of statutory construction as expressed by Justice Brandeis in *Ashwander v. Tennessee Valley Authority*, 297 U.S. 288, 347 (1936). That principle is that one must construe statutes so that constitutional questions may be avoided if at all possible. Therefore, the proper construction of Title VII, according to appellant, is that transsexuals are protected, thus avoiding all possible equal protection problems.

Assuming briefly that appellant has properly raised an equal protection argument, we find no merit to it. Normally, any rational classification or discrimination is presumed valid. That is, a statute is constitutional if the classification or discrimination it contains has some rational relationship to a legitimate government interest, unless the statute is based upon an inherently suspect classification, in which case the statute requires close judicial scrutiny. *Graham v. Richardson*, 403 U.S. 365, 371–72 (1971).

This court cannot conclude that transsexuals are a suspect class. Examining the traditional indicia of suspect classification, we find that transsexuals are not necessarily a "discrete and insular minority," *Graham v. Richardson*, 403 U.S. 365, 372 (1971); nor has it been established that transsexuality is an "immutable characteristic determined solely by the accident of birth" like race or national origin. *Frontiero v. Richardson*, 411 U.S. 677, 686 (1973). Furthermore, the complexities involved merely in defining the term "transsexual" would prohibit a determination of suspect classification for transsexuals. Thus, the rational relationship test is the standard to apply. In applying this standard to this statute, it can be said without question that the prohibition of employment discrimination between males and females and on the basis of race, religion or national origin is rationally related to a legitimate governmental interest.

An equal protection argument is clearly not appropriate here, however. Pursuant to this court's construction, Title VII remedies are equally available to all individuals for employment discrimination based on race, religion, sex, or national origin. Indeed, consistent with the determination of this court, transsexuals claiming discrimination because of their sex, male or female, would clearly state a cause of action under Title VII. Holloway has not claimed to have treated discriminatorily because she is male or female, but rather because she is a transsexual who chose to change her sex. This type of claim is not actionable under Title VII and is certainly not in violation of the doctrines of Due Process and Equal Protection....

[The dissenting opinion of Judge Goodwin is omitted.]

Brown v. Zavaras

63 F.3d 967 (10th Cir. 1995)

HENRY, Circuit Judge.

Pro se plaintiff Josephine Brown appeals the summary judgment order of the district court dismissing his 42 U.S.C. § 1983 civil rights action.[1] ....

I. BACKGROUND

Mr. Brown is an inmate at the Limon Correctional Facility, a Colorado state prison. In his complaint against two corrections officials, Mr. Brown states that he is a transsexual. The medical term for transsexuality is "gender dysphoria," and gender dysphoria is a medically recognized psychological disorder resulting from the "disjunction between sexual identity and sexual organs."

Mr. Brown alleged in his complaint that the defendants have violated his Eighth Amendment right to be free from cruel and unusual punishment and his Fourteenth Amendment equal protection rights. Specifically, he alleged that defendants have withheld medical care with deliberate indifference to his serious medical needs by not providing him with the female hormone estrogen and other medical treatment....

II. DISCUSSION

[The court first holds that the district court on remand must consider whether the alleged denial of estrogen treatment for Brown violated the Eighth Amendment's ban on cruel and unusual punishment.]

---

1. Although plaintiff identifies his true gender as female, plaintiff is biologically male and refers to himself with masculine pronouns throughout his pleadings. As is our practice, we refer to litigants as the record suggests they prefer to be addressed.

C. Equal Protection

Mr. Brown also asserts that he is being denied the equal protection of the laws because *some* prisoners receive estrogen treatment. In this case, the district court observed that transsexuals are not a protected class and dismissed Mr. Brown's equal protection claim.

The Ninth Circuit has held that transsexuals are not a protected class. *Holloway v. Arthur Andersen & Co.,* 566 F.2d 659, 663 (9th Cir.1977). In *Holloway,* the court reasoned that transsexuality did not meet the traditional indicia of a suspect classification because transsexuals are not a discrete and insular minority, and because the plaintiff did not establish that "'transsexuality is an immutable characteristic determined solely by the accident of birth' like race, or national origin." *Id.* (quoting *Frontiero v. Richardson,* 411 U.S. 677, 686 (1973)). A number of courts have adopted the *Holloway* court's holding.

Recent research concluding that sexual identity may be biological suggests reevaluating *Holloway. See Equality Found. v. City of Cincinnati,* 860 F.Supp. 417, 437 (S.D.Ohio 1994) (concluding that sexual orientation is an issue beyond individual control), *aff'd in part and vacated in part,* 54 F.3d 261 (6th Cir.1995); *Dahl v. Secretary of the United States Navy,* 830 F.Supp. 1319, 1324 n. 5 (E.D.Cal.1993) (collecting research suggesting that sexual identity is biological). However, we decline to make such an evaluation in this case because Mr. Brown's allegations are too conclusory to allow proper analysis of this legal question. We therefore follow *Holloway* and hold that Mr. Brown is not a member of a protected class in this case. When the plaintiff is not a member of a protected class and does not assert a fundamental right, we determine only whether government classifications have a rational basis....

Notes and Questions

1. Both the concurring opinion by Judge Norris in *Watkins* and the court in *High Tech Gays* purport to apply the *Frontiero* factors, but reach different conclusions on two of the factors, immutability and political power. Which decision is more persuasive? Asked somewhat differently, is sexual orientation any less immutable than sex or the other classifications that are subject to heightened scrutiny? Was the political power of gays and lesbians any greater at the time *Watkins* and *High Tech Gays* were decided than that of women at the time *Frontiero* was decided?

2. Note the extent to which the U.S. Supreme Court's holding in *Bowers* — a substantive due process case — influences how lower court judges approach the ostensibly distinct equal protection claim. Specifically, to get around *Bowers,* Judge Norris distinguishes between homosexual status or orientation on the one hand and homosexual conduct on the other. How persuasive is this distinction? How does it compare with the definition of sexual orientation that you found most persuasive in Chapter 1? Indeed, isn't it an even more forced distinction than the Latino/Spanish-speaking and female/pregnancy lines discussed in *Hernandez* and *Feeney,* respectively?

On the other hand, the *High Tech Gays* court views *Bowers* as foreclosing any argument for heightened scrutiny under the Equal Protection Clause. Yet in so holding, the court relies on the fact that "equal protection" as applied to the federal government is a subset of due process, and thus that an "equal protection" case decided under the Fifth Amendment's Due Process Clause should come out the same way as a "substantive due process" case decided under that same clause. But is this not in tension with *Adarand*'s "congruence" principle, which holds that the "equal protection" component of the Fifth Amendment's Due Process Clause is identical to the reach of the Fourteenth Amendment's Equal Protection Clause?

3. What do you make of the *High Tech Gays* court's statement that homosexuality is "behavioral and hence is fundamentally different from traits such as race, gender, or alienage"? Do you agree that being male or female, black or white, or a citizen or alien is something you just *are*, while being gay or straight is something you *do*? To what extent does the answer to that question turn on which definition of homosexuality you employ? Are the definitions of homosexuality employed by the laws being challenged in *Watkins* and *High Tech Gays* identical, or can one be characterized as focused on status and the other on conduct?

4. Recall the hypothesis raised earlier in the chapter: that majoritarian views regarding morality might justify a law when challenged on due process grounds, but not when challenged on equal protection grounds. Does the opinion by Judge Norris in *Watkins*, which distinguishes due process as backward-looking and equal protection as forward-looking, provide support for that hypothesis?

5. As with the cases involving sexual orientation, those involving gender identity tend to falter on the question of immutability. To what extent do more modern cases—such as those excerpted in Chapter 1—shed light on the question of immutability?

On another level, to what extent does the very existence of transgendered persons cast doubt on the *Frontiero* Court's conclusion that sex is an immutable characteristic? Of course, that depends on what the *Reed-Frontiero-Craig-Virginia* line of cases mean when they refer to "sex" or "gender." If the Court means to refer to visible characteristics, such as secondary sex characteristics and genitalia, then "sex" is not really immutable, is it? If, on the other hand, the Court means to refer to characteristics such as chromosomes or psychological gender identity, then "sex" is immutable, right?

2. A Subset of Sex Discrimination?

Baker v. State
744 A.2d 864 (Vt. 1999)

[Same-sex couples bring suit in Vermont state court, contending that denying them the right to marry violates the Vermont Constitution. The majority holds that denying same-sex couples the benefits associated with marriage violates the Common Benefits Clause of the Vermont Constitution.]

JOHNSON, J., concurring in part and dissenting in part.

....

II.

Although I concur with the majority's conclusion that Vermont law unconstitutionally excludes same-sex couples from the benefits of marriage, I write separately to state my belief that this is a straightforward case of sex discrimination.

As I argue below, the marriage statutes establish a classification based on sex. Whether such classification is legally justifiable should be analyzed under our common-benefits jurisprudence, which until today, has been closely akin to the federal equal-protection analysis under the Fourteenth Amendment. Therefore, the State must show that the classification is narrowly tailored to further important, if not compelling, interests. Not only do the rationalizations advanced by the State fail to pass constitutional muster under this or any other form of heightened scrutiny, they fail to satisfy the rational-basis test as articulated under the Common Benefits Clause.

"We have held that the Common Benefits Clause in the Vermont Constitution, see ch. I, art. 7, is generally coextensive with the equivalent guarantee in the United States Constitution, and imports similar methods of analysis." Where the statutory scheme affects a fundamental constitutional right or involves a suspect classification, "the State must demonstrate that any discrimination occasioned by the law serves a compelling governmental interest, and is narrowly tailored to serve that objective." Otherwise, classifications are constitutional if they are "reasonably related to the promotion of a valid public purpose."

As the majority states, the marriage "statutes, read as a whole, reflect the common understanding that marriage under Vermont law consists of a union between a man and a woman." Thus, the statutes impose a sex-based classification. A woman is denied the right to marry another woman because her would-be partner is a woman, not because one or both are lesbians. Similarly, a man is denied the right to marry another man because his would-be partner is a man, not because one or both are gay. Thus, an individual's right to marry a person of the same sex is prohibited solely on the basis of sex, not on the basis of sexual orientation. Indeed, sexual orientation does not appear as a qualification for marriage under the marriage statutes. The State makes no inquiry into the sexual practices or identities of a couple seeking a license.

The State advances two arguments in support of its position that Vermont's marriage laws do not establish a sex-based classification. The State first contends that the marriage statutes merely acknowledge that marriage, by its very nature, cannot be comprised of two persons of the same sex. Thus, in the State's view, it is the *definition* of marriage, not the statutes, that restricts marriage to two people of the opposite sex. This argument is circular. It is the State that defines civil marriage under its statute. The issue before us today is whether the State may continue to deprive same-sex couples of the benefits of marriage. This question is not resolved by resorting to a historical definition of marriage; it is that very definition that is being challenged in this case.

The State's second argument, also propounded by the majority, is that the marriage statutes do not discriminate on the basis of sex because they treat similarly situated males the same as similarly situated females. Under this argument, there can be no sex discrimination here because "[i]f a man wants to marry a man, he is barred; a woman seeking to marry a woman is barred in precisely the same way. For this reason, women and men are not treated differently." But consider the following example. Dr. A and Dr. B both want to marry Ms. C, an X-ray technician. Dr. A may do so because Dr. A is a man. Dr. B may not because Dr. B is a woman. Dr. A and Dr. B are people of opposite sexes who are similarly situated in the sense that they both want to marry a person of their choice. The statute disqualifies Dr. B from marriage solely on the basis of her sex and treats her differently from Dr. A, a man. This is sex discrimination.[10]

I recognize, of course, that although the classification here is sex-based on its face, its most direct impact is on lesbians and gay men, the class of individuals most likely to seek same-sex marriage. Viewing the discrimination as sex-based, however, is important. Although the *original* purpose of the marriage statutes was not to exclude same-sex couples, for the simple reason that same-sex marriage was very likely not on the minds of the Legislature when it passed the licensing statute, the *preservation* of the sex-based classification deprives lesbians and gay men of the right to marry the life partner of their choice.

---

10. Under the State's analysis, a statute that required courts to give custody of male children to fathers and female children to mothers would not be sex discrimination. Although such a law would not treat men and women differently, I believe it would discriminate on the basis of sex....

If, as I argue below, the sex-based classification contained in the marriage laws is unrelated to any valid purpose, but rather is a vestige of sex-role stereotyping that applies to both men and women, the classification is still unlawful sex discrimination even if it applies equally to men and women. See *MacCallum,* 165 Vt. at 459 (Constitution does not permit law to give effect, either directly or indirectly, to private biases; when government itself makes the classification, it is obliged to afford all persons equal protection of the law); *Loving v. Virginia,* 388 U.S. 1, 8–9, 11 (1967) (statute prohibiting racial intermarriage violates Equal Protection Clause although it applies equally to Whites and Blacks because classification was designed to maintain White Supremacy.)

Although Vermont has not had occasion to consider the question, most, if not all, courts have held that the denial of rights or benefits on the basis of sex subject the state's action to some level of heightened scrutiny.[12] This is so because the sex of an individual "frequently bears no relation to ability to perform or contribute to society." *Frontiero v. Richardson,* 411 U.S. 677, 686 (1973) (plurality opinion). Moreover, in some cases, such as here, sex-based classifications "very likely reflect outmoded notions of the relative capabilities of men and women." *City of Cleburne v. Cleburne Living Ctr., Inc.,* 473 U.S. 432, 441 (1985).

I do not believe that it is necessary to reach the question in this case, however, because in my view, the justifications asserted by the State do not satisfy even our rational-basis standard under the Common Benefits Clause....

[The majority opinion of Chief Justice Amestoy and the concurring opinion of Justice Dooley are omitted.]

Glenn v. Brumby
663 F.3d 1312 (11th Cir. 2011)

BARKETT, Circuit Judge:

Sewell R. Brumby appeals from an adverse summary judgment in favor of Vandiver Elizabeth Glenn on her complaint seeking declaratory and injunctive relief pursuant to 42 U.S.C. § 1983 for alleged violations of her rights under the Equal Protection Clause of the Fourteenth Amendment of the U.S. Constitution. Glenn claimed that Brumby fired her from her job as an editor in the Georgia General Assembly's Office of Legislative Counsel ("OLC") because of sex discrimination, thus violating the Equal Protection Clause....

Vandiver Elizabeth Glenn was born a biological male. Since puberty, Glenn has felt that she is a woman, and in 2005, she was diagnosed with [Gender Identity Disorder ("GID")], a diagnosis listed in the American Psychiatric Association's Diagnostic and Statistical Manual of Mental Disorders.

Starting in 2005, Glenn began to take steps to transition from male to female under the supervision of health care providers. This process included living as a woman outside of the workplace, which is a prerequisite to sex reassignment surgery. In October 2005, then known as Glenn Morrison and presenting as a man, Glenn was hired as an editor

---

12. See, e.g., *United States v. Virginia,* 518 U.S. 515, 533 (1996) (concluding that sex-based classifications are subject to heightened standard of review less rigorous than that imposed for race or national origin classifications); *Frontiero,* 411 U.S. at 684, 686 (plurality opinion) (concluding that sex is suspect classification under two-part test inquiring whether class is defined by immutable characteristic and whether there is history of invidious discrimination against class)....

by the Georgia General Assembly's OLC. Sewell Brumby is the head of the OLC and is responsible for OLC personnel decisions, including the decision to fire Glenn.

In 2006, Glenn informed her direct supervisor, Beth Yinger, that she was a transsexual and was in the process of becoming a woman. On Halloween in 2006, when OLC employees were permitted to come to work wearing costumes, Glenn came to work presenting as a woman. When Brumby saw her, he told her that her appearance was not appropriate and asked her to leave the office. Brumby deemed her appearance inappropriate "[b]ecause he was a man dressed as a woman and made up as a woman." Brumby stated that "it's unsettling to think of someone dressed in women's clothing with male sexual organs inside that clothing," and that a male in women's clothing is "unnatural." Following this incident, Brumby met with Yinger to discuss Glenn's appearance on Halloween of 2006 and was informed by Yinger that Glenn intended to undergo a gender transition.

In the fall of 2007, Glenn informed Yinger that she was ready to proceed with gender transition and would begin coming to work as a woman and was also changing her legal name. Yinger notified Brumby, who subsequently terminated Glenn because "Glenn's intended gender transition was inappropriate, that it would be disruptive, that some people would view it as a moral issue, and that it would make Glenn's coworkers uncomfortable."

Glenn sued, alleging ... discrimination under the Equal Protection Clause.... Glenn alleged that Brumby "discriminat[ed] against her because of her sex, including her female gender identity and her failure to conform to the sex stereotypes associated with the sex Defendant[ ] perceived her to be." ...

I. Equal Protection and Sex Stereotyping

    ....

The Equal Protection Clause requires the State to treat all persons similarly situated alike or, conversely, to avoid all classifications that are "arbitrary or irrational" and those that reflect "a bare ... desire to harm a politically unpopular group." *City of Cleburne v. Cleburne Living Ctr., Inc.*, 473 U.S. 432, 446–47 (1985). States are presumed to act lawfully, and therefore state action is generally upheld if it is rationally related to a legitimate governmental purpose. *Id.* at 440. However, more than a rational basis is required in certain circumstances. In describing generally the contours of the Equal Protection Clause, the Supreme Court noted its application to this issue, referencing both gender and sex, using the terms interchangeably:

> Legislative classifications based on gender also call for a heightened standard of review. That factor generally provides no sensible ground for differential treatment. [W]hat differentiates sex from such nonsuspect statuses as intelligence or physical disability ... is that the sex characteristic frequently bears no relation to ability to perform or contribute to society. Rather than resting on meaningful considerations, statutes distributing benefits and burdens between the sexes in different ways very likely reflect outmoded notions of the relative capabilities of men and women. A gender classification fails unless it is substantially related to a sufficiently important governmental interest.

Id. at 440–41. In *United States v. Virginia*, the Supreme Court reaffirmed its prior holdings that sex-based discrimination is subject to intermediate scrutiny under the Equal Protection Clause. 518 U.S. 515, 555 (1996). This standard requires the government to show that its "gender classification ... is substantially related to a sufficiently important government interest." *Cleburne*, 473 U.S. at 441. Moreover, this test requires a "genuine" justification, not one that is "hypothesized or invented *post hoc* in response to litigation." *Virginia*, 518 U.S. at 533. In *Virginia*, the state's policy of excluding women from the Virginia Military Institute failed this test because the state could not rely on generalizations about different aptitudes of males and females to support the exclusion of women. *Id.* at 542. "State actors controlling gates to opportunity, we have instructed, may not exclude qualified individuals based on 'fixed notions concerning the roles and abilities of males and females.'" *Id.* at 541 (quoting *Mississippi Univ. for Women v. Hogan*, 458 U.S. 718, 725 (1982)).

The question here is whether discriminating against someone on the basis of his or her gender non-conformity constitutes sex-based discrimination under the Equal Protection Clause. For the reasons discussed below, we hold that it does.

In *Price Waterhouse v. Hopkins*, 490 U.S. 228 (1989), the Supreme Court held that discrimination on the basis of gender stereotype is sex-based discrimination. In that case, the Court considered allegations that a senior manager at Price Waterhouse was denied partnership in the firm because she was considered "macho," and "overcompensated for being a woman." *Id.* at 235. Six members of the Supreme Court agreed that such comments were indicative of gender discrimination and held that Title VII barred not just discrimination because of biological sex, but also gender stereotyping—failing to act and appear according to expectations defined by gender. *Id.* at 250–51 (plurality opinion); *id.* at 258–61 (White, J., concurring); *id.* at 272–73 (O'Connor, J., concurring). The Court noted that "[a]s for the legal relevance of sex stereotyping, we are beyond the day when an employer could evaluate employees by assuming or insisting that they matched the stereotypes associated with their group...." *Id.* at 251.

A person is defined as transgender precisely because of the perception that his or her behavior transgresses gender stereotypes.... There is thus a congruence between discriminating against transgender and transsexual individuals and discrimination on the basis of gender-based behavioral norms.

Accordingly, discrimination against a transgender individual because of her gender-nonconformity is sex discrimination, whether it's described as being on the basis of sex or gender....

All persons, whether transgender or not, are protected from discrimination on the basis of gender stereotype. For example, courts have held that plaintiffs cannot be discriminated against for wearing jewelry that was considered too effeminate, carrying a serving tray too gracefully, or taking too active a role in child-rearing. An individual cannot be punished because of his or her perceived gender-nonconformity. Because these protections are afforded to everyone, they cannot be denied to a transgender individual. The nature of the discrimination is the same; it may differ in degree but not in kind, and discrimination on this basis is a form of sex-based discrimination that is subject to heightened scrutiny under the Equal Protection Clause. Ever since the Supreme Court began to apply heightened scrutiny to sex-based classifications, its consistent purpose has been to eliminate discrimination on the basis of gender stereotypes.

In *Frontiero v. Richardson*, the Court struck down legislation requiring only female service members to prove that their spouses depended upon them financially in order to receive certain benefits for married couples. *See* 411 U.S. 677, 691 (1973) (plurality opinion). The plurality applied heightened scrutiny to sex-based classifications by referring to the pervasiveness of gender stereotypes, *see id.* at 683–86 (noting a tradition of "'romantic paternalism'" that "put women [ ] not on a pedestal, but in a cage"), and held that gender-based classifications are "inherently suspect," *id.* at 688, because they are often animated by "stereotyped distinctions between the sexes," *id.* at 685. Two years later, the Court applied this heightened level of scrutiny to a Utah statute setting a lower age of majority for women and concluded that the statute could not be sustained by the stereotypical assumption that women tend to marry earlier than men. *See Stanton v. Stanton*, 421 U.S. 7, 14 (1975). The Court again rejected gender stereotypes, holding that "'old notions'" about men and women's behavior provided no support for the State's classification. *Id.* at 14. That same year, the Court confronted a provision of the Social Security Act that allowed certain benefits to widows while denying them to widowers. *See Weinberger v. Wiesenfeld*, 420 U.S. 636, 637 (1975). The Court again used heightened scrutiny to strike at gender stereotype, concluding that "the Constitution also forbids gender-based differentiation" premised on the stereotypical assumption that a husband's income is always more important to the wife than is the wife's to the husband. *Id.* at 645.

In each of these foundational cases, the Court concluded that discriminatory state action could not stand on the basis of gender stereotypes. *See also Craig v. Boren*, 429 U.S. 190, 199 (1976) (explaining that "the weak congruence between gender and the characteristic or trait that gender purported to represent" necessitated applying heightened scrutiny); *Orr v. Orr*, 440 U.S. 268, 282 (1979) ("Legislative classifications which distribute benefits and burdens on the basis of gender carry the risk of reinforcing stereotypes about the 'proper place' of women...."). The Court's more recent cases reiterate that the Equal Protection Clause does not tolerate gender stereotypes. *See Mississippi Univ. for Women v. Hogan*, 458 U.S. 718, 726 (1982) (explaining that "the purpose" of heightened scrutiny is to ensure that sex-based classifications rest upon "reasoned analysis rather than ... traditional, often inaccurate, assumptions about the proper roles of men and women."); *see also Virginia*, 518 U.S. at 533 ("[The government] must not rely on overbroad generalizations about the different talents, capacities, or preferences of males and females.") Accordingly, governmental acts based upon gender stereotypes — which presume that men and women's appearance and behavior will be determined by their sex — must be subjected to heightened scrutiny because they embody "the very stereotype the law condemns." *J.E.B. v. Alabama*, 511 U.S. 127, 138 (1994) (internal quotation marks omitted) (declaring unconstitutional a government attorney's use of peremptory juror strikes based on the presumption that potential jurors' views would correspond to their sexes).

We conclude that a government agent violates the Equal Protection Clause's prohibition of sex-based discrimination when he or she fires a transgender or transsexual employee because of his or her gender non-conformity.

II. Glenn's Termination

We now turn to whether Glenn was fired on the basis of gender stereotyping. The first inquiry is whether Brumby acted on the basis of Glenn's gender-nonconformity. *See Vill. of Arlington Heights v. Metro. Hous. Dev. Corp.*, 429 U.S. 252, 266 (1977) (requiring proof of discriminatory intent). If so, we must then apply heightened scrutiny to decide whether that action was substantially related to a sufficiently important governmental interest.

A plaintiff can show discriminatory intent through direct or circumstantial evidence. In this case, Brumby testified at his deposition that he fired Glenn because he considered it "inappropriate" for her to appear at work dressed as a woman and that he found it "unsettling" and "unnatural" that Glenn would appear wearing women's clothing. Brumby testified that his decision to dismiss Glenn was based on his perception of Glenn as "a man dressed as a woman and made up as a woman," and Brumby admitted that his decision to fire Glenn was based on "the sheer fact of the transition." Brumby's testimony provides ample direct evidence to support the district court's conclusion that Brumby acted on the basis of Glenn's gender non-conformity.

If this were a Title VII case, the analysis would end here. However, because Glenn's claim is based on the Equal Protection Clause, we must, under heightened scrutiny, consider whether Brumby succeeded in showing an "exceedingly persuasive justification," *Virginia*, 518 U.S. at 546, that is, that there was a "sufficiently important governmental interest" for his discriminatory conduct, *Cleburne*, 473 U.S. at 441. This burden "is demanding and it rests entirely on the State." *Virginia*, 518 U.S. at 533. The defendant's burden cannot be met by relying on a justification that is "hypothesized or invented post hoc in response to litigation." *Id.*

On appeal, Brumby advances only one putative justification for Glenn's firing: his purported concern that other women might object to Glenn's restroom use. However, Brumby presented insufficient evidence to show that he was actually motivated by concern over litigation regarding Glenn's restroom use. To support the justification that he now argues, Brumby points to a single statement in his deposition where he referred to a speculative concern about lawsuits arising if Glenn used the women's restroom. The district court recognized that this single reference, based on speculation, was overwhelmingly contradicted by specific evidence of Brumby's intent, and we agree. Indeed, Brumby testified that he viewed the possibility of a lawsuit by a co-worker if Glenn were retained as unlikely and the record indicates that the OLC, where Glenn worked, had only single-occupancy restrooms. Brumby advanced this argument before the district court only as a *conceivable* explanation for his decision to fire Glenn under rational basis review. The fact that such a hypothetical justification may have been sufficient to withstand rational-basis scrutiny, however, is wholly irrelevant to the heightened scrutiny analysis that is required here.

Brumby has advanced no other reason that could qualify as a governmental purpose, much less an "important" governmental purpose, and even less than that, a "sufficiently important governmental purpose" that was achieved by firing Glenn because of her gender non-conformity. *Cleburne*, 473 U.S. at 441.

We therefore **AFFIRM** the judgment of the district court granting summary judgment in favor of Glenn on her sex-discrimination claim....

Notes and Questions

1. Recall that, under *Washington v. Davis* and its progeny, to make out an equal protection claim, one must show either: (a) that the law, on its face, discriminates against a class of persons; (b) the law is neutral on its face, but is applied in a discriminatory manner against a class of persons; or (c) the law is neutral on its face, but was enacted for the purpose of having a discriminatory impact on a class of persons. Recall further that, in *Hernandez v. Robles* (Chapter 1), Judge Graffeo's concurring opinion relied on this line of cases to hold that there was not a valid equal protection claim based on sexual orientation discrimination because the marriage statutes do not, in terms, draw distinctions based on sexual orientation, and that there was no evidence that the marriage statutes were enacted for the purpose of having a discriminatory impact on gays and lesbians.

Accepting as valid the *Hernandez* court's application of the *Washington v. Davis* line of cases, isn't the logical consequence of the court's holding *exactly* what Justice Johnson holds in her concurring opinion in *Baker v. State*, to wit, that the marriage statutes are a form of facial sex discrimination? And if that is so, the plaintiffs are entitled to intermediate scrutiny without the need to invoke the *Frontiero* factors to seek heightened scrutiny for sexual orientation discrimination.

2. Is a valid counter to Justice Johnson's argument in *Baker v. State* that the law does not discriminate on the basis of sex because men and women are *equally* disadvantaged by the statute? In other words — as the state argued in *Baker* — men and women are *both* barred from marrying people of the same sex, and thus there is no sex discrimination. Justice Johnson arrives at a different answer by switching the focus from men and women as groups to specific individuals (Dr. A, Dr. B, and Ms. C). Which focus — that on groups or that on individuals — is the correct focus for equal protection purposes? What light, if any, does *Adarand* shed on this issue?

3. Recall from Chapters 1 and 3 that the Texas law at issue in *Lawrence v. Texas* only criminalized acts of oral or anal sex committed between two persons of the same sex. When the case was heard *en banc* by the Court of Appeals of Texas, Justice Anderson, writing in dissent, contended that the statute was subject to heightened scrutiny under the Equal Protection Clause because it discriminated on the basis of sex:

> That 21.06 is not gender neutral is manifest based on application of the statute to the following events:
>
>> There are three people in a room: Alice, Bob, and Cathy. Bob approaches Alice, and with her consent, engages with her in several varieties of "deviate sexual intercourse," the conduct at issue here. Bob then leaves the room. Cathy approaches Alice, and with her consent, engages with her in several kinds of "deviate sexual intercourse." Cathy is promptly arrested for violating section 21.06.
>
> I have indulged in this tableau to demonstrate one important point: one person simply committed a sex act while another committed a crime. While the acts were exactly the same, the gender of the actors was different, and it was this difference alone that determined the criminal nature of the conduct. In other words, because he is a man, Bob committed no crime and may freely indulge his predilection for "deviate sexual intercourse," but because she is a woman, Cathy is a criminal. Thus, women are treated differently in this scenario, and therefore, are discriminated against by the explicit gender-based prohibition of section 21.06, and to suggest otherwise is disingenuous at best.

Lawrence v. State, 41 S.W.3d 349, 368 (Tex. App. 2001) (Anderson, J., dissenting).

4. The *Glenn* case reads the *Reed-Frontiero-Craig-Virginia* line of cases as standing for the proposition that discriminating against individuals because of their gender non-conformity is sex discrimination subject to intermediate scrutiny under equal protection jurisprudence. Is that a fair read of that line of cases? If so, does that not mean that all claims of discrimination on the basis of sexual orientation and gender identity are subsets of sex discrimination, since almost any form of discrimination on those bases can be characterized as punishment for a form of gender non-conformity?

5. As the *Glenn* case demonstrates, a key advantage for plaintiffs of heightened scrutiny is not only the requirement of a tighter means-end fit and a stronger governmental interest for the discrimination, but also the requirement of a real as opposed to a hypothesized rationale for justifying the law. In *Glenn*, the court refused to consider the rationale raised by the defendant — the concern of other women regarding restroom use — because there was no evidence that this was the real motivation behind the discriminatory action. Yet suppose that, in *Glenn*, the defendant *had* in fact relied on that rationale from the start. How would that rationale stand up under intermediate scrutiny?

In this regard, consider the Supreme Court's statement in *Palmore v. Sidoti*, 466 U.S. 429, 433 (1984) that "[p]rivate biases may be outside the reach of the law, but the law cannot, directly or indirectly, give them effect," or the Court's statement in *City of Cleburne v. Cleburne Living Center*, 473 U.S. 432, 448 (1985) rejecting reliance on "mere negative attitudes, or fear, unsubstantiated by factors which are properly cognizable." In any event, even assuming that the concern is a legitimate or important one, are there more narrowly tailored solutions that could be employed to address it?

3. Second Order Rational Basis Review?

Romer v. Evans
517 U.S. 620 (1996)

Justice KENNEDY delivered the opinion of the Court.

One century ago, the first Justice Harlan admonished this Court that the Constitution "neither knows nor tolerates classes among citizens." *Plessy v. Ferguson,* 163 U.S. 537, 559 (1896) (dissenting opinion). Unheeded then, those words now are understood to state a commitment to the law's neutrality where the rights of persons are at stake. The Equal Protection Clause enforces this principle and today requires us to hold invalid a provision of Colorado's Constitution.

I

The enactment challenged in this case is an amendment to the Constitution of the State of Colorado, adopted in a 1992 statewide referendum. The parties and the state courts refer to it as "Amendment 2," its designation when submitted to the voters. The impetus for the amendment and the contentious campaign that preceded its adoption came in large part from ordinances that had been passed in various Colorado municipalities. For example, the cities of Aspen and Boulder and the city and County of Denver each had enacted ordinances which banned discrimination in many transactions and activities, including housing, employment, education, public accommodations, and health and welfare services. What gave rise to the statewide controversy was the protection the ordinances afforded to persons discriminated against by reason of their sexual orientation. Amendment 2 repeals these ordinances to the extent they prohibit discrimination on the basis of "homosexual, lesbian or bisexual orientation, conduct, practices or relationships."

Yet Amendment 2, in explicit terms, does more than repeal or rescind these provisions. It prohibits all legislative, executive or judicial action at any level of state or local government designed to protect the named class, a class we shall refer to as homosexual persons or gays and lesbians. The amendment reads:

> "No Protected Status Based on Homosexual, Lesbian or Bisexual Orientation. Neither the State of Colorado, through any of its branches or departments, nor any of its agencies, political subdivisions, municipalities or school districts, shall enact, adopt or enforce any statute, regulation, ordinance or policy whereby homosexual, lesbian or bisexual orientation, conduct, practices or relationships shall constitute or otherwise be the basis of or entitle any person or class of persons to have or claim any minority status, quota preferences, protected status or claim of discrimination. This Section of the Constitution shall be in all respects self-executing."

Soon after Amendment 2 was adopted, this litigation to declare its invalidity and enjoin its enforcement was commenced in the District Court for the City and County of Denver. Among the plaintiffs (respondents here) were homosexual persons, some of them government employees. They alleged that enforcement of Amendment 2 would subject them to immediate and substantial risk of discrimination on the basis of their sexual orientation. Other plaintiffs (also respondents here) included the three municipalities whose ordinances we have cited and certain other governmental entities which had acted earlier to protect homosexuals from discrimination but would be prevented by Amendment 2 from continuing to do so. Although Governor Romer had been on record opposing the adoption of Amendment 2, he was named in his official capacity as a defendant, together with the Colorado Attorney General and the State of Colorado.

The trial court granted a preliminary injunction to stay enforcement of Amendment 2, and an appeal was taken to the Supreme Court of Colorado. Sustaining the interim injunction and remanding the case for further proceedings, the State Supreme Court held that Amendment 2 was subject to strict scrutiny under the Fourteenth Amendment because it infringed the fundamental right of gays and lesbians to participate in the political process. *Evans v. Romer,* 854 P.2d 1270 (Colo.1993) *(Evans I)*. To reach this conclusion, the state court relied on our voting rights cases, and on our precedents involving discriminatory restructuring of governmental decision making. On remand, the State advanced various arguments in an effort to show that Amendment 2 was narrowly tailored to serve compelling interests, but the trial court found none sufficient. It enjoined enforcement of Amendment 2, and the Supreme Court of Colorado, in a second opinion, affirmed the ruling. 882 P.2d 1335 (1994) *(Evans II)*. We granted certiorari, and now affirm the judgment, but on a rationale different from that adopted by the State Supreme Court.

II

The State's principal argument in defense of Amendment 2 is that it puts gays and lesbians in the same position as all other persons. So, the State says, the measure does no more than deny homosexuals special rights. This reading of the amendment's language is implausible. We rely not upon our own interpretation of the amendment but upon the authoritative construction of Colorado's Supreme Court. The state court, deeming it unnecessary to determine the full extent of the amendment's reach, found it invalid even on a modest reading of its implications. The critical discussion of the amendment, set out in *Evans I,* is as follows:

> "The immediate objective of Amendment 2 is, at a minimum, to repeal existing statutes, regulations, ordinances, and policies of state and local entities that barred discrimination based on sexual orientation.

> "The 'ultimate effect' of Amendment 2 is to prohibit any governmental entity from adopting similar, or more protective statutes, regulations, ordinances, or policies in the future unless the state constitution is first amended to permit such measures."

Sweeping and comprehensive is the change in legal status effected by this law. So much is evident from the ordinances the Colorado Supreme Court declared would be void by operation of Amendment 2. Homosexuals, by state decree, are put in a solitary class with respect to transactions and relations in both the private and governmental spheres. The amendment withdraws from homosexuals, but no others, specific legal protection from the injuries caused by discrimination, and it forbids reinstatement of these laws and policies.

The change Amendment 2 works in the legal status of gays and lesbians in the private sphere is far reaching, both on its own terms and when considered in light of the structure and operation of modern anti-discrimination laws. That structure is well illustrated by contemporary statutes and ordinances prohibiting discrimination by providers of public accommodations. "At common law, innkeepers, smiths, and others who 'made profession of a public employment,' were prohibited from refusing, without good reason, to serve a customer." *Hurley v. Irish-American Gay, Lesbian and Bisexual Group of Boston, Inc.,* 515 U.S. 557, 571 (1995). The duty was a general one and did not specify protection for particular groups. The common-law rules, however, proved insufficient in many instances, and it was settled early that the Fourteenth Amendment did not give Congress a general power to prohibit discrimination in public accommodations, *Civil Rights Cases,* 109 U.S. 3, 25 (1883). In consequence, most States have chosen to counter discrimination by enacting detailed statutory schemes.

Colorado's state and municipal laws typify this emerging tradition of statutory protection and follow a consistent pattern. The laws first enumerate the persons or entities subject to a duty not to discriminate. The list goes well beyond the entities covered by the common law. The Boulder ordinance, for example, has a comprehensive definition of entities deemed places of "public accommodation." They include "any place of business engaged in any sales to the general public and any place that offers services, facilities, privileges, or advantages to the general public or that receives financial support through solicitation of the general public or through governmental subsidy of any kind." The Denver ordinance is of similar breadth, applying, for example, to hotels, restaurants, hospitals, dental clinics, theaters, banks, common carriers, travel and insurance agencies, and "shops and stores dealing with goods or services of any kind."

These statutes and ordinances also depart from the common law by enumerating the groups or persons within their ambit of protection. Enumeration is the essential device used to make the duty not to discriminate concrete and to provide guidance for those who must comply. In following this approach, Colorado's state and local governments have not limited antidiscrimination laws to groups that have so far been given the protection of heightened equal protection scrutiny under our cases. Rather, they set forth an extensive catalog of traits which cannot be the basis for discrimination, including age, military status, marital status, pregnancy, parenthood, custody of a minor child, political affiliation, physical or mental disability of an individual or of his or her associates—and, in recent times, sexual orientation.

Amendment 2 bars homosexuals from securing protection against the injuries that these public-accommodations laws address. That in itself is a severe consequence, but there is more. Amendment 2, in addition, nullifies specific legal protections for this targeted class in all transactions in housing, sale of real estate, insurance, health and welfare services, private education, and employment.

Not confined to the private sphere, Amendment 2 also operates to repeal and forbid all laws or policies providing specific protection for gays or lesbians from discrimination by every level of Colorado government. The State Supreme Court cited two examples of protections in the governmental sphere that are now rescinded and may not be reintroduced. The first is Colorado Executive Order D0035 (1990), which forbids employment discrimination against "'all state employees, classified and exempt' on the basis of sexual orientation." Also repealed, and now forbidden, are "various provisions prohibiting discrimination based on sexual orientation at state colleges." The repeal of these measures and the prohibition against their future reenactment demonstrate that Amendment 2 has the same force and effect in Colorado's governmental sector as it does elsewhere and that it applies to policies as well as ordinary legislation.

Amendment 2's reach may not be limited to specific laws passed for the benefit of gays and lesbians. It is a fair, if not necessary, inference from the broad language of the amendment that it deprives gays and lesbians even of the protection of general laws and poli-

cies that prohibit arbitrary discrimination in governmental and private settings. See, *e.g.,*
Colo.Rev.Stat. §24-4-106(7) (1988) (agency action subject to judicial review under arbitrary and capricious standard); §18-8-405 (making it a criminal offense for a public servant knowingly, arbitrarily, or capriciously to refrain from performing a duty imposed on him by law); §10-3-1104(1)(f) (prohibiting "unfair discrimination" in insurance); 4 Colo.Code of Regulations 801-1, Policy 11-1 (1983) (prohibiting discrimination in state employment on grounds of specified traits or "other non-merit factor"). At some point in the systematic administration of these laws, an official must determine whether homosexuality is an arbitrary and, thus, forbidden basis for decision. Yet a decision to that effect would itself amount to a policy prohibiting discrimination on the basis of homosexuality, and so would appear to be no more valid under Amendment 2 than the specific prohibitions against discrimination the state court held invalid.

If this consequence follows from Amendment 2, as its broad language suggests, it would compound the constitutional difficulties the law creates. The state court did not decide whether the amendment has this effect, however, and neither need we. In the course of rejecting the argument that Amendment 2 is intended to conserve resources to fight discrimination against suspect classes, the Colorado Supreme Court made the limited observation that the amendment is not intended to affect many anti-discrimination laws protecting nonsuspect classes. In our view that does not resolve the issue. In any event, even if, as we doubt, homosexuals could find some safe harbor in laws of general application, we cannot accept the view that Amendment 2's prohibition on specific legal protections does no more than deprive homosexuals of special rights. To the contrary, the amendment imposes a special disability upon those persons alone. Homosexuals are forbidden the safeguards that others enjoy or may seek without constraint. They can obtain specific protection against discrimination only by enlisting the citizenry of Colorado to amend the State Constitution or perhaps, on the State's view, by trying to pass helpful laws of general applicability. This is so no matter how local or discrete the harm, no matter how public and widespread the injury. We find nothing special in the protections Amendment 2 withholds. These are protections taken for granted by most people either because they already have them or do not need them; these are protections against exclusion from an almost limitless number of transactions and endeavors that constitute ordinary civic life in a free society.

III

The Fourteenth Amendment's promise that no person shall be denied the equal protection of the laws must coexist with the practical necessity that most legislation classifies for one purpose or another, with resulting disadvantage to various groups or persons. We have attempted to reconcile the principle with the reality by stating that, if a law neither burdens a fundamental right nor targets a suspect class, we will uphold the legislative classification so long as it bears a rational relation to some legitimate end. See, *e.g., Heller v. Doe,* 509 U.S. 312, 319–320 (1993).

Amendment 2 fails, indeed defies, even this conventional inquiry. First, the amendment has the peculiar property of imposing a broad and undifferentiated disability on a single named group, an exceptional and, as we shall explain, invalid form of legislation. Second, its sheer breadth is so discontinuous with the reasons offered for it that the amendment seems inexplicable by anything but animus toward the class it affects; it lacks a rational relationship to legitimate state interests.

Taking the first point, even in the ordinary equal protection case calling for the most deferential of standards, we insist on knowing the relation between the classification adopted and the object to be attained. The search for the link between classification and objective gives substance to the Equal Protection Clause; it provides guidance and discipline for the legislature, which is entitled to know what sorts of laws it can pass; and it marks the limits of our own authority. In the ordinary case, a law will be sustained if it can be said to advance a legitimate government interest, even if the law seems unwise or works to the disadvantage of a particular group, or if the rationale for it seems tenuous. See *New Orleans v. Dukes,* 427 U.S. 297 (1976) (tourism benefits justified classification favoring pushcart vendors of certain longevity); *Williamson v. Lee Optical of Okla., Inc.,* 348 U.S. 483 (1955) (assumed health concerns justified law favoring optometrists over opticians); *Railway Express Agency, Inc. v. New York,* 336 U.S. 106 (1949) (potential traffic hazards justified exemption of vehicles advertising the owner's products from general advertising ban); *Kotch v. Board of River Port Pilot Comm'rs for Port of New Orleans,* 330 U.S. 552 (1947) (licensing scheme that disfavored persons unrelated to current river boat pilots justified by possible efficiency and safety benefits of a closely knit pilotage system). The laws challenged in the cases just cited were narrow enough in scope and grounded in a sufficient factual context for us to ascertain some relation between the classification and the purpose it served. By requiring that the classification bear a rational relationship to an independent and legitimate legislative end, we ensure that classifications are not drawn for the purpose of disadvantaging the group burdened by the law. See *Railroad Retirement Bd. v. Fritz,* 449 U.S. 166, 181 (1980) (STEVENS, J., concurring) ("If the adverse impact on the disfavored class is an apparent aim of the legislature, its impartiality would be suspect").

Amendment 2 confounds this normal process of judicial review. It is at once too narrow and too broad. It identifies persons by a single trait and then denies them protection across the board. The resulting disqualification of a class of persons from the right to seek specific protection from the law is unprecedented in our jurisprudence. The absence of precedent for Amendment 2 is itself instructive; "[d]iscriminations of an unusual character especially suggest careful consideration to determine whether they are obnoxious to the constitutional provision." *Louisville Gas & Elec. Co. v. Coleman,* 277 U.S. 32, 37–38 (1928).

It is not within our constitutional tradition to enact laws of this sort. Central both to the idea of the rule of law and to our own Constitution's guarantee of equal protection is the principle that government and each of its parts remain open on impartial terms to all who seek its assistance. "'Equal protection of the laws is not achieved through indiscriminate imposition of inequalities.'" *Sweatt v. Painter,* 339 U.S. 629, 635 (1950) (quoting *Shelley v. Kraemer,* 334 U.S. 1, 22 (1948)). Respect for this principle explains why laws singling out a certain class of citizens for disfavored legal status or general hardships are rare. A law declaring that in general it shall be more difficult for one group of citizens than for all others to seek aid from the government is itself a denial of equal protection of the laws in the most literal sense. "The guaranty of 'equal protection of the laws is a pledge of the protection of equal laws.'" *Skinner v. Oklahoma ex rel. Williamson,* 316 U.S. 535, 541 (1942) (quoting *Yick Wo v. Hopkins,* 118 U.S. 356, 369 (1886)).

Davis v. Beason, 133 U.S. 333 (1890), not cited by the parties but relied upon by the dissent, is not evidence that Amendment 2 is within our constitutional tradition, and any reliance upon it as authority for sustaining the amendment is misplaced. In *Davis,* the Court approved an Idaho territorial statute denying Mormons, polygamists, and advocates of polygamy the right to vote and to hold office because, as the Court construed the statute, it "simply excludes from the privilege of voting, or of holding any office of honor, trust or profit, those who have been convicted of certain offences, and those who advocate a practical resistance to the laws of the Territory and justify and approve the commission of crimes forbidden by it." To the extent *Davis* held that persons advocating a certain practice may be denied the right to vote, it is no longer good law. *Brandenburg v. Ohio,* 395 U.S. 444 (1969) *(per curiam)*. To the extent it held that the groups designated in the statute may be deprived of the right to vote because of their status, its ruling could not stand without surviving strict scrutiny, a most doubtful outcome. To the extent *Davis* held that a convicted felon may be denied the right to vote, its holding is not implicated by our decision and is unexceptionable. See *Richardson v. Ramirez,* 418 U.S. 24 (1974).

A second and related point is that laws of the kind now before us raise the inevitable inference that the disadvantage imposed is born of animosity toward the class of persons affected. "[I]f the constitutional conception of 'equal protection of the laws' means anything, it must at the very least mean that a bare ... desire to harm a politically unpopular group cannot constitute a *legitimate* governmental interest." *Department of Agriculture v. Moreno,* 413 U.S. 528, 534 (1973). Even laws enacted for broad and ambitious purposes often can be explained by reference to legitimate public policies which justify the incidental disadvantages they impose on certain persons. Amendment 2, however, in making a general announcement that gays and lesbians shall not have any particular protections from the law, inflicts on them immediate, continuing, and real injuries that outrun and belie any legitimate justifications that may be claimed for it. We conclude that, in addition to the far-reaching deficiencies of Amendment 2 that we have noted, the principles it offends, in another sense, are conventional and venerable; a law must bear a rational relationship to a legitimate governmental purpose, and Amendment 2 does not.

The primary rationale the State offers for Amendment 2 is respect for other citizens' freedom of association, and in particular the liberties of landlords or employers who have personal or religious objections to homosexuality. Colorado also cites its interest in conserving resources to fight discrimination against other groups. The breadth of the amendment is so far removed from these particular justifications that we find it impossible to credit them. We cannot say that Amendment 2 is directed to any identifiable legitimate purpose or discrete objective. It is a status-based enactment divorced from any factual context from which we could discern a relationship to legitimate state interests; it is a classification of persons undertaken for its own sake, something the Equal Protection Clause does not permit. "[C]lass legislation ... [is] obnoxious to the prohibitions of the Fourteenth Amendment...." *Civil Rights Cases,* 109 U.S., at 24.

We must conclude that Amendment 2 classifies homosexuals not to further a proper legislative end but to make them unequal to everyone else. This Colorado cannot do. A State cannot so deem a class of persons a stranger to its laws. Amendment 2 violates the Equal Protection Clause, and the judgment of the Supreme Court of Colorado is affirmed.

It is so ordered.

Justice SCALIA, with whom THE CHIEF JUSTICE and Justice THOMAS join, dissenting.

The Court has mistaken a Kulturkampf for a fit of spite. The constitutional amendment before us here is not the manifestation of a "'bare ... desire to harm'" homosexuals, but is rather a modest attempt by seemingly tolerant Coloradans to preserve traditional sexual mores against the efforts of a politically powerful minority to revise those mores through use of the laws. That objective, and the means chosen to achieve it, are not only unimpeachable under any constitutional doctrine hitherto pronounced (hence the opinion's heavy reliance upon principles of righteousness rather than judicial holdings); they have been specifically approved by the Congress of the United States and by this Court.

In holding that homosexuality cannot be singled out for disfavorable treatment, the Court contradicts a decision, unchallenged here, pronounced only 10 years ago, see *Bowers v. Hardwick,* 478 U.S. 186 (1986), and places the prestige of this institution behind the proposition that opposition to homosexuality is as reprehensible as racial or religious bias. Whether it is or not is *precisely* the cultural debate that gave rise to the Colorado constitutional amendment (and to the preferential laws against which the amendment was directed). Since the Constitution of the United States says nothing about this subject, it is left to be resolved by normal democratic means, including the democratic adoption of provisions in state constitutions. This Court has no business imposing upon all Americans the resolution favored by the elite class from which the Members of this institution are selected, pronouncing that "animosity" toward homosexuality is evil. I vigorously dissent.

I

Let me first discuss Part II of the Court's opinion, its longest section, which is devoted to rejecting the State's arguments that Amendment 2 "puts gays and lesbians in the same position as all other persons," and "does no more than deny homosexuals special rights." The Court concludes that this reading of Amendment 2's language is "implausible" under the "authoritative construction" given Amendment 2 by the Supreme Court of Colorado.

In reaching this conclusion, the Court considers it unnecessary to decide the validity of the State's argument that Amendment 2 does not deprive homosexuals of the "protection [afforded by] general laws and policies that prohibit arbitrary discrimination in governmental and private settings." I agree that we need not resolve that dispute, because the Supreme Court of Colorado has resolved it for us. In the case below, the Colorado court stated:

> "[I]t is significant to note that Colorado law currently proscribes discrimination against persons who are not suspect classes, including discrimination based on age, § 24-34-402(1)(a), 10A C.R.S. (1994 Supp.); marital or family status, § 24-34-502(1)(a), 10A C.R.S. (1994 Supp.); veterans' status, § 28-3-506, 11B C.R.S. (1989); and for any legal, off-duty conduct such as smoking tobacco, § 24-34-402.5, 10A C. R.S. (1994 Supp.). *Of course Amendment 2 is not intended to have any effect on this legislation, but seeks only to prevent the adoption of antidiscrimination laws intended to protect gays, lesbians, and bisexuals." Id.,* at 1346, n. 9 (emphasis added).

The Court utterly fails to distinguish this portion of the Colorado court's opinion. Colorado Rev. Stat. § 24-34-402.5 (Supp.1995), which this passage authoritatively declares *not* to be affected by Amendment 2, was respondents' primary example of a generally applicable law whose protections would be unavailable to homosexuals under Amendment 2. The clear import of the Colorado court's conclusion that it is not affected is that "general laws and policies that prohibit arbitrary discrimination" would continue to prohibit discrimination on the basis of homosexual conduct as well. This analysis, which is fully in accord with (indeed, follows inescapably from) the text of the constitutional provision, lays to rest such horribles, raised in the course of oral argument, as the prospect that assaults upon homosexuals could not be prosecuted. The amendment prohibits *special treatment* of homosexuals, and nothing more. It would not affect, for example, a requirement of state law that pensions be paid to all retiring state employees with a certain length of service; homosexual employees, as well as others, would be entitled to that benefit. But it would prevent the State or any municipality from making death-benefit payments to the "life partner" of a homosexual when it does not make such payments to the long-time roommate of a nonhomosexual employee. Or again, it does not affect the requirement of the State's general insurance laws that customers be afforded coverage without discrimination unrelated to anticipated risk. Thus, homosexuals could not be denied coverage, or charged a greater premium, with respect to auto collision insurance; but neither the State nor any municipality could require that distinctive health insurance risks associated with homosexuality (if there are any) be ignored.

Despite all of its hand wringing about the potential effect of Amendment 2 on general antidiscrimination laws, the Court's opinion ultimately does not dispute all this, but assumes it to be true. The only denial of equal treatment it contends homosexuals have suffered is this: They may not obtain *preferential* treatment without amending the State Constitution. That is to say, the principle underlying the Court's opinion is that one who is accorded equal treatment under the laws, but cannot as readily as others obtain *preferential* treatment under the laws, has been denied equal protection of the laws. If merely stating this alleged "equal protection" violation does not suffice to refute it, our constitutional jurisprudence has achieved terminal silliness.

The central thesis of the Court's reasoning is that any group is denied equal protection when, to obtain advantage (or, presumably, to avoid disadvantage), it must have recourse to a more general and hence more difficult level of political decision making than others. The world has never heard of such a principle, which is why the Court's opinion is so long on emotive utterance and so short on relevant legal citation. And it seems to me most unlikely that any multilevel democracy can function under such a principle. For *whenever* a disadvantage is imposed, or conferral of a benefit is prohibited, at one of the higher levels of democratic decision making (*i.e.,* by the state legislature rather than local government, or by the people at large in the state constitution rather than the legislature), the affected group has (under this theory) been denied equal protection. To take the simplest of examples, consider a state law prohibiting the award of municipal contracts to relatives of mayors or city councilmen. Once such a law is passed, the group composed of such relatives must, in order to get the benefit of city contracts, persuade the state legislature—unlike all other citizens, who need only persuade the municipality. It is ridiculous to consider this a denial of equal protection, which is why the Court's theory is unheard of.

The Court might reply that the example I have given is *not* a denial of equal protection only because the same "rational basis" (avoidance of corruption) which renders constitutional the *substantive discrimination* against relatives (*i.e.,* the fact that they alone cannot obtain city contracts) also automatically suffices to sustain what might be called the *electoral-procedural discrimination* against them (*i.e.,* the fact that they must go to the state level to get this changed). This is of course a perfectly reasonable response, and would explain why "electoral-procedural discrimination" has not hitherto been heard of: A law that is valid in its substance is automatically valid in its level of enactment. But the Court cannot afford to make this argument, for as I shall discuss next, there is no doubt of a rational basis for the substance of the prohibition at issue here. The Court's entire novel theory rests upon the proposition that there is something *special*—something that cannot be justified by normal "rational basis" analysis—in making a disadvantaged group (or a nonpreferred group) resort to a higher decision making level. That proposition finds no support in law or logic.

II

I turn next to whether there was a legitimate rational basis for the substance of the constitutional amendment—for the prohibition of special protection for homosexuals.[1]

---

1. The Court evidently agrees that "rational basis"—the normal test for compliance with the Equal Protection Clause—is the governing standard. The trial court rejected respondents' argument

It is unsurprising that the Court avoids discussion of this question, since the answer is so obviously yes. The case most relevant to the issue before us today is not even mentioned in the Court's opinion: In *Bowers v. Hardwick,* 478 U.S. 186 (1986), we held that the Constitution does not prohibit what virtually all States had done from the founding of the Republic until very recent years—making homosexual conduct a crime. That holding is unassailable, except by those who think that the Constitution changes to suit current fashions. But in any event it is a given in the present case: Respondents' briefs did not urge overruling *Bowers,* and at oral argument respondents' counsel expressly disavowed any intent to seek such overruling. If it is constitutionally permissible for a State to make homosexual conduct criminal, surely it is constitutionally permissible for a State to enact other laws merely *disfavoring* homosexual conduct. (As the Court of Appeals for the District of Columbia Circuit has aptly put it: "If the Court [in *Bowers*] was unwilling to object to state laws that criminalize the behavior that defines the class, it is hardly open … to conclude that state sponsored discrimination against the class is invidious. After all, there can hardly be more palpable discrimination against a class than making the conduct that defines the class criminal." *Padula v. Webster,* 822 F.2d 97, 103 (1987).) And *a fortiori* it is constitutionally permissible for a State to adopt a provision *not even* disfavoring homosexual conduct, but merely prohibiting all levels of state government from bestowing *special protections* upon homosexual conduct. Respondents (who, unlike the Court, cannot afford the luxury of ignoring inconvenient precedent) counter *Bowers* with the argument that a greater-includes-the-lesser rationale cannot justify Amendment 2's application to individuals who do not engage in homosexual acts, but are merely of homosexual "orientation." Some Courts of Appeals have concluded that, with respect to laws of this sort at least, that is a distinction without a difference….

But assuming that, in Amendment 2, a person of homosexual "orientation" is someone who does not engage in homosexual conduct but merely has a tendency or desire to do so, *Bowers* still suffices to establish a rational basis for the provision. If it is rational to criminalize the conduct, surely it is rational to deny special favor and protection to those with a self-avowed tendency or desire to engage in the conduct. Indeed, where criminal sanctions are not involved, homosexual "orientation" is an acceptable stand-in for homosexual conduct. A State "does not violate the Equal Protection Clause merely because the classifications made by its laws are imperfect," *Dandridge v. Williams,* 397 U.S. 471 (1970). Just as a policy barring the hiring of methadone users as transit employees does not violate equal protection simply because *some* methadone users pose no threat to passenger safety, see *New York City Transit Authority v. Beazer,* 440 U.S. 568 (1979), and just as a mandatory retirement age of 50 for police officers does not violate equal protection even though it prematurely ends the careers of many policemen over 50 who still have the capacity to do the job, see *Massachusetts Bd. of Retirement v. Murgia,* 427 U.S. 307 (1976) *(per curiam),* Amendment 2 is not constitutionally invalid simply because it could have been drawn more precisely so as to withdraw special antidiscrimination protections only from those of homosexual "orientation" who actually engage in homosexual conduct. As Justice KENNEDY wrote, when he was on the Court of Appeals, in a case involving discharge of homosexuals from the Navy: "Nearly any statute which classifies people may be irrational as applied in particular cases. Discharge of the particular plaintiffs before us would be rational, under minimal scrutiny, not because their particular cases present the

---

that homosexuals constitute a "suspect" or "quasi-suspect" class, and respondents elected not to appeal that ruling to the Supreme Court of Colorado. And the Court implicitly rejects the Supreme Court of Colorado's holding that Amendment 2 infringes upon a "fundamental right" of "independently identifiable class[es]" to "participate equally in the political process."

dangers which justify Navy policy, but instead because the general policy of discharging all homosexuals is rational." *Beller v. Middendorf,* 632 F.2d 788, 808–809, n. 20 (C.A.9 1980) (citation omitted).

Moreover, even if the provision regarding homosexual "orientation" *were* invalid, respondents' challenge to Amendment 2—which is a facial challenge—must fail. "A facial challenge to a legislative Act is, of course, the most difficult challenge to mount successfully, since the challenger must establish that no set of circumstances exists under which the Act would be valid." *United States v. Salerno,* 481 U.S. 739, 745 (1987). It would not be enough for respondents to establish (if they could) that Amendment 2 is unconstitutional as applied to those of homosexual "orientation"; since, under *Bowers,* Amendment 2 is unquestionably constitutional as applied to those who engage in homosexual conduct, the facial challenge cannot succeed. Some individuals of homosexual "orientation" who do not engage in homosexual acts might successfully bring an as-applied challenge to Amendment 2, but so far as the record indicates, none of the respondents is such a person.

III

The foregoing suffices to establish what the Court's failure to cite any case remotely in point would lead one to suspect: No principle set forth in the Constitution, nor even any imagined by this Court in the past 200 years, prohibits what Colorado has done here. But the case for Colorado is much stronger than that. What it has done is not only unprohibited, but eminently reasonable, with close, congressionally approved precedent in earlier constitutional practice.

First, as to its eminent reasonableness. The Court's opinion contains grim, disapproving hints that Coloradans have been guilty of "animus" or "animosity" toward homosexuality, as though that has been established as un-American. Of course it is our moral heritage that one should not hate any human being or class of human beings. But I had thought that one could consider certain conduct reprehensible—murder, for example, or polygamy, or cruelty to animals—and could exhibit even "animus" toward such conduct. Surely that is the only sort of "animus" at issue here: moral disapproval of homosexual conduct, the same sort of moral disapproval that produced the centuries-old criminal laws that we held constitutional in *Bowers.* The Colorado amendment does not, to speak entirely precisely, prohibit giving favored status to people who are *homosexuals;* they can be favored for many reasons—for example, because they are senior citizens or members of racial minorities. But it prohibits giving them favored status *because of their homosexual conduct*—that is, it prohibits favored status *for homosexuality.*

But though Coloradans are, as I say, *entitled* to be hostile toward homosexual conduct, the fact is that the degree of hostility reflected by Amendment 2 is the smallest conceivable. The Court's portrayal of Coloradans as a society fallen victim to pointless, hate-filled "gay-bashing" is so false as to be comical. Colorado not only is one of the 25 States that have repealed their antisodomy laws, but was among the first to do so. But the society that eliminates criminal punishment for homosexual acts does not necessarily abandon the view that homosexuality is morally wrong and socially harmful; often, abolition simply reflects the view that enforcement of such criminal laws involves unseemly intrusion into the intimate lives of citizens.

There is a problem, however, which arises when criminal sanction of homosexuality is eliminated but moral and social disapprobation of homosexuality is meant to be retained. The Court cannot be unaware of that problem; it is evident in many cities of the country, and occasionally bubbles to the surface of the news, in heated political disputes over such matters as the introduction into local schools of books teaching that homosexuality is an optional and fully acceptable "alternative life style." The problem (a problem, that is, for those who wish to retain social disapprobation of homosexuality) is that, because those who engage in homosexual conduct tend to reside in disproportionate numbers in certain communities, and, of course, care about homosexual-rights issues much more ardently than the public at large, they possess political power much greater than their numbers, both locally and statewide. Quite understandably, they devote this political power to achieving not merely a grudging social toleration, but full social acceptance, of homosexuality.

By the time Coloradans were asked to vote on Amendment 2, their exposure to homosexuals' quest for social endorsement was not limited to newspaper accounts of happenings in places such as New York, Los Angeles, San Francisco, and Key West. Three Colorado cities — Aspen, Boulder, and Denver — had enacted ordinances that listed "sexual orientation" as an impermissible ground for discrimination, equating the moral disapproval of homosexual conduct with racial and religious bigotry. The phenomenon had even appeared statewide: The Governor of Colorado had signed an executive order pronouncing that "in the State of Colorado we recognize the diversity in our pluralistic society and strive to bring an end to discrimination in any form," and directing state agency-heads to "ensure non-discrimination" in hiring and promotion based on, among other things, "sexual orientation." I do not mean to be critical of these legislative successes; homosexuals are as entitled to use the legal system for reinforcement of their moral sentiments as is the rest of society. But they are subject to being countered by lawful, democratic countermeasures as well.

That is where Amendment 2 came in. It sought to counter both the geographic concentration and the disproportionate political power of homosexuals by (1) resolving the controversy at the statewide level, and (2) making the election a single-issue contest for both sides. It put directly, to all the citizens of the State, the question: Should homosexuality be given special protection? They answered no. The Court today asserts that this most democratic of procedures is unconstitutional. Lacking any cases to establish that facially absurd proposition, it simply asserts that it *must* be unconstitutional, because it has never happened before.

> "[Amendment 2] identifies persons by a single trait and then denies them protection across the board. The resulting disqualification of a class of persons from the right to seek specific protection from the law is unprecedented in our jurisprudence. The absence of precedent for Amendment 2 is itself instructive....
>
> "It is not within our constitutional tradition to enact laws of this sort. Central both to the idea of the rule of law and to our own Constitution's guarantee of equal protection is the principle that government and each of its parts remain open on impartial terms to all who seek its assistance."

As I have noted above, this is proved false every time a state law prohibiting or disfavoring certain conduct is passed, because such a law prevents the adversely affected group — whether drug addicts, or smokers, or gun owners, or motorcyclists — from changing the policy thus established in "each of [the] parts" of the State. What the Court says is even demonstrably false at the constitutional level. The Eighteenth Amendment to the Federal Constitution, for example, deprived those who drank alcohol not only of the power to alter the policy of prohibition *locally* or through *state legislation,* but even of the power to alter it through *state constitutional amendment* or *federal legislation.* The Establishment Clause of the First Amendment prevents theocrats from having their way by converting their fellow citizens at the local, state, or federal statutory level; as does the Republican Form of Government Clause prevent monarchists.

But there is a much closer analogy, one that involves precisely the effort by the majority of citizens to preserve its view of sexual morality statewide, against the efforts of a geographically concentrated and politically powerful minority to undermine it. The Constitutions of the States of Arizona, Idaho, New Mexico, Oklahoma, and Utah *to this day* contain provisions stating that polygamy is "forever prohibited." Polygamists, and those who have a polygamous "orientation," have been "singled out" by these provisions for much more severe treatment than merely denial of favored status; and that treatment can only be changed by achieving amendment of the state constitutions. The Court's disposition today suggests that these provisions are unconstitutional, and that polygamy must be permitted in these States on a state-legislated, or perhaps even local-option, basis — unless, of course, polygamists for some reason have fewer constitutional rights than homosexuals.

The United States Congress, by the way, *required* the inclusion of these antipolygamy provisions in the Constitutions of Arizona, New Mexico, Oklahoma, and Utah, as a condition of their admission to statehood. (For Arizona, New Mexico, and Utah, moreover, the Enabling Acts required that the antipolygamy provisions be "irrevocable without the consent of the United States and the people of said State" — so that not only were "each of [the] parts" of these States not "open on impartial terms" to polygamists, but even the States as a whole were not; polygamists would have to persuade the whole country to their way of thinking.) Idaho adopted the constitutional provision on its own, but the 51st Congress, which admitted Idaho into the Union, found its Constitution to be "republican in form *and … in conformity with the Constitution of the United States.*" Act of Admission of Idaho, 26 Stat. 215 (emphasis added). Thus, this "singling out" of the sexual practices of a single group for statewide, democratic vote — so utterly alien to our constitutional system, the Court would have us believe — has not only happened, but has received the explicit approval of the United States Congress.

I cannot say that this Court has explicitly approved any of these state constitutional provisions; but it has approved a territorial statutory provision that went even further, depriving polygamists of the ability even to achieve a constitutional amendment, by depriving them of the power to vote. In *Davis v. Beason,* 133 U.S. 333 (1890), Justice Field wrote for a unanimous Court:

> "In our judgment, § 501 of the Revised Statutes of Idaho Territory, which provides that 'no person … who is a bigamist or polygamist or who teaches, advises, counsels, or encourages any person or persons to become bigamists or polygamists, or to commit any other crime defined by law, or to enter into what is known as plural or celestial marriage, or who is a member of any order, organization or association which teaches, advises, counsels, or encourages its members or devotees or any other persons to commit the crime of bigamy or polygamy, or any other crime defined by law … is permitted to vote at any election, or to hold any position or office of honor, trust, or profit within this Territory,' *is not open to any constitutional or legal objection.*" *Id.,* at 346–347 (emphasis added).

To the extent, if any, that this opinion permits the imposition of adverse consequences upon mere abstract advocacy of polygamy, it has, of course, been overruled by later cases. See *Brandenburg v. Ohio,* 395 U.S. 444 (1969) *(per curiam).* But the proposition that polygamy can be criminalized, and those engaging in that crime deprived of the vote, remains good law. See *Richardson v. Ramirez,* 418 U.S. 24, 53 (1974). *Beason* rejected the argument that "such discrimination is a denial of the equal protection of the laws." Among the Justices joining in that rejection were the two whose views in other cases the Court today treats as equal protection lodestars—Justice Harlan, who was to proclaim in *Plessy v. Ferguson,* 163 U.S. 537, 559 (1896) (dissenting opinion), that the Constitution "neither knows nor tolerates classes among citizens," and Justice Bradley, who had earlier declared that "class legislation ... [is] obnoxious to the prohibitions of the Fourteenth Amendment," *Civil Rights Cases,* 109 U.S. 3, 24 (1883).[3]

This Court cited *Beason* with approval as recently as 1993, in an opinion authored by the same Justice who writes for the Court today.... It remains to be explained how § 501 of the Idaho Revised Statutes was not an "impermissible targeting" of polygamists, but (the much more mild) Amendment 2 is an "impermissible targeting" of homosexuals. Has the Court concluded that the perceived social harm of polygamy is a "legitimate concern of government," and the perceived social harm of homosexuality is not?

IV

I strongly suspect that the answer to the last question is yes, which leads me to the last point I wish to make: The Court today, announcing that Amendment 2 "defies ... conventional [constitutional] inquiry," and "confounds [the] normal process of judicial review," employs a constitutional theory heretofore unknown to frustrate Colorado's reasonable effort to preserve traditional American moral values. The Court's stern disapproval of "animosity" towards homosexuality might be compared with what an earlier Court (including the revered Justices Harlan and Bradley) said in *Murphy v. Ramsey,* 114 U.S. 15 (1885), rejecting a constitutional challenge to a United States statute that denied the franchise in federal territories to those who engaged in polygamous cohabitation:

> "[C]ertainly no legislation can be supposed more wholesome and necessary in the founding of a free, self-governing commonwealth, fit to take rank as one of the coordinate States of the Union, than that which seeks to establish it on the basis of the idea of the family, as consisting in and springing from the union for life of one man and one woman in the holy estate of matrimony; the sure foundation of all that is stable and noble in our civilization; the best guaranty of that reverent morality which is the source of all beneficent progress in social and political improvement."

I would not myself indulge in such official praise for heterosexual monogamy, because I think it no business of the courts (as opposed to the political branches) to take sides in this culture war.

---

3. The Court labors mightily to get around *Beason,* but cannot escape the central fact that this Court found the statute at issue—which went much further than Amendment 2, denying polygamists not merely special treatment but the right *to vote*—"not open to any constitutional or legal objection," rejecting the appellant's argument (much like the argument of respondents today) that the statute impermissibly "single[d] him out." The Court adopts my conclusions that (a) insofar as *Beason* permits the imposition of adverse consequences based upon mere advocacy, it has been overruled by subsequent cases, and (b) insofar as *Beason* holds that convicted felons may be denied the right to vote, it remains good law. To these conclusions, it adds something new: the claim that "[t]o the extent [*Beason*] held that the groups designated in the statute may be deprived of the right to vote because of their status, its ruling could not stand without surviving strict scrutiny, a most doubtful outcome." But if that is so, it is only because we have declared the right *to vote* to be a "fundamental political right," deprivation of which triggers strict scrutiny. Amendment 2, of course, does not deny the fundamental right to vote, and the Court rejects the Colorado court's view that there exists a fundamental right to participate in the political process. Strict scrutiny is thus not in play here. Finally, the Court's suggestion that § 501 of the Revised Statutes of Idaho, and Amendment 2, deny rights on account of "status" (rather than conduct) opens up a broader debate involving the significance of *Bowers* to this case, a debate which the Court is otherwise unwilling to join.

But the Court today has done so, not only by inventing a novel and extravagant constitutional doctrine to take the victory away from traditional forces, but even by verbally disparaging as bigotry adherence to traditional attitudes. To suggest, for example, that this constitutional amendment springs from nothing more than "'a bare ... desire to harm a politically unpopular group,'" quoting *Department of Agriculture v. Moreno*, 413 U.S. 528, 534 (1973), is nothing short of insulting. (It is also nothing short of preposterous to call "politically unpopular" a group which enjoys enormous influence in American media and politics, and which, as the trial court here noted, though composing no more than 4% of the population had the support of 46% of the voters on Amendment 2.)

When the Court takes sides in the culture wars, it tends to be with the knights rather than the villeins—and more specifically with the Templars, reflecting the views and values of the lawyer class from which the Court's Members are drawn. How that class feels about homosexuality will be evident to anyone who wishes to interview job applicants at virtually any of the Nation's law schools. The interviewer may refuse to offer a job because the applicant is a Republican; because he is an adulterer; because he went to the wrong prep school or belongs to the wrong country club; because he eats snails; because he is a womanizer; because she wears real-animal fur; or even because he hates the Chicago Cubs. But if the interviewer should wish not to be an associate or partner of an applicant because he disapproves of the applicant's homosexuality, *then* he will have violated the pledge which the Association of American Law Schools requires all its member schools to exact from job interviewers: "assurance of the employer's willingness" to hire homosexuals. By-laws of the Association of American Law Schools, Inc. §6-4(b); Executive Committee Regulations of the Association of American Law Schools §6.19, in 1995 Handbook, Association of American Law Schools. This law-school view of what "prejudices" must be stamped out may be contrasted with the more plebeian attitudes that apparently still prevail in the United States Congress, which has been unresponsive to repeated attempts to extend to homosexuals the protections of federal civil rights laws, see, *e.g.*, Employment Non-Discrimination Act of 1994, S. 2238, 103d Cong., 2d Sess. (1994); Civil Rights Amendments of 1975, H.R. 5452, 94th Cong., 1st Sess. (1975), and which took the pains to exclude them specifically from the Americans with Disabilities Act of 1990, see 42 U.S.C. §12211(a) (1988 ed., Supp. V).

* * *

Today's opinion has no foundation in American constitutional law, and barely pretends to. The people of Colorado have adopted an entirely reasonable provision which does not even disfavor homosexuals in any substantive sense, but merely denies them preferential treatment. Amendment 2 is designed to prevent piecemeal deterioration of the sexual morality favored by a majority of Coloradans, and is not only an appropriate means to that legitimate end, but a means that Americans have employed before. Striking it down is an act, not of judicial judgment, but of political will. I dissent.

Lawrence v. Texas
539 U.S. 558 (2003)

[At issue in this case is a challenge to the constitutionality of a Texas statute that criminalized same-sex, but not opposite-sex, sodomy. The majority opinion—which struck the statute down on substantive due process grounds—as well as most of Justice Scalia's dissent and the dissent by Justice Thomas, can be found in Chapter 3. Excerpted below is Justice O'Connor's concurring opinion and Justice Scalia's response to the same.]

Justice O'CONNOR, concurring in the judgment.

The Court today overrules *Bowers v. Hardwick*, 478 U.S. 186 (1986). I joined *Bowers*, and do not join the Court in overruling it. Nevertheless, I agree with the Court that Texas' statute banning same-sex sodomy is unconstitutional. Rather than relying on the substantive component of the Fourteenth Amendment's Due Process Clause, as the Court does, I base my conclusion on the Fourteenth Amendment's Equal Protection Clause.

The Equal Protection Clause of the Fourteenth Amendment "is essentially a direction that all persons similarly situated should be treated alike." Under our rational basis standard of review, "legislation is presumed to be valid and will be sustained if the classification drawn by the statute is rationally related to a legitimate state interest."

Laws such as economic or tax legislation that are scrutinized under rational basis review normally pass constitutional muster, since "the Constitution presumes that even improvident decisions will eventually be rectified by the democratic processes." We have consistently held, however, that some objectives, such as "a bare ... desire to harm a politically unpopular group," are not legitimate state interests. *Department of Agriculture v. Moreno, supra,* at 534. See also *Cleburne v. Cleburne Living Center, supra,* at 446–447; *Romer v. Evans, supra,* at 632. When a law exhibits such a desire to harm a politically unpopular group, we have applied a more searching form of rational basis review to strike down such laws under the Equal Protection Clause.

We have been most likely to apply rational basis review to hold a law unconstitutional under the Equal Protection Clause where, as here, the challenged legislation inhibits personal relationships. In *Department of Agriculture v. Moreno,* for example, we held that a law preventing those households containing an individual unrelated to any other member of the household from receiving food stamps violated equal protection because the purpose of the law was to "'discriminate against hippies.'" The asserted governmental interest in preventing food stamp fraud was not deemed sufficient to satisfy rational basis review. In *Eisenstadt v. Baird,* 405 U.S. 438, 447–455 (1972), we refused to sanction a law that discriminated between married and unmarried persons by prohibiting the distribution of contraceptives to single persons. Likewise, in *Cleburne v. Cleburne Living Center,* we held that it was irrational for a State to require a home for the mentally disabled to obtain a special use permit when other residences—like fraternity houses and apartment buildings—did not have to obtain such a permit. And in *Romer v. Evans,* we disallowed a state statute that "impos[ed] a broad and undifferentiated disability on a single named group"—specifically, homosexuals.

The statute at issue here makes sodomy a crime only if a person "engages in deviate sexual intercourse with another individual of the same sex." Tex. Penal Code Ann. § 21.06(a) (2003). Sodomy between opposite-sex partners, however, is not a crime in Texas. That is, Texas treats the same conduct differently based solely on the participants. Those harmed by this law are people who have a same-sex sexual orientation and thus are more likely to engage in behavior prohibited by § 21.06.

The Texas statute makes homosexuals unequal in the eyes of the law by making particular conduct—and only that conduct—subject to criminal sanction. It appears that prosecutions under Texas' sodomy law are rare. This case shows, however, that prosecutions under § 21.06 *do* occur. And while the penalty imposed on petitioners in this case was relatively minor, the consequences of conviction are not. It appears that petitioners' convictions, if upheld, would disqualify them from or restrict their ability to engage in a variety of professions, including medicine, athletic training, and interior design. Indeed, were petitioners to move to one of four States, their convictions would require them to register as sex offenders to local law enforcement.

And the effect of Texas' sodomy law is not just limited to the threat of prosecution or consequence of conviction. Texas' sodomy law brands all homosexuals as criminals, thereby making it more difficult for homosexuals to be treated in the same manner as everyone else. Indeed, Texas itself has previously acknowledged the collateral effects of the law, stipulating in a prior challenge to this action that the law "legally sanctions discrimination against [homosexuals] in a variety of ways unrelated to the criminal law," including in the areas of "employment, family issues, and housing." *State v. Morales,* 826 S.W.2d 201, 203 (Tex.App.1992).

Texas attempts to justify its law, and the effects of the law, by arguing that the statute satisfies rational basis review because it furthers the legitimate governmental interest of the promotion of morality. In *Bowers,* we held that a state law criminalizing sodomy as applied to homosexual couples did not violate substantive due process. We rejected the argument that no rational basis existed to justify the law, pointing to the government's interest in promoting morality. The only question in front of the Court in *Bowers* was whether the substantive component of the Due Process Clause protected a right to engage in homosexual sodomy. *Bowers* did not hold that moral disapproval of a group is a rational basis under the Equal Protection Clause to criminalize homosexual sodomy when heterosexual sodomy is not punished.

This case raises a different issue than *Bowers:* whether, under the Equal Protection Clause, moral disapproval is a legitimate state interest to justify by itself a statute that bans homosexual sodomy, but not heterosexual sodomy. It is not. Moral disapproval of this group, like a bare desire to harm the group, is an interest that is insufficient to satisfy rational basis review under the Equal Protection Clause. See, *e.g., Department of Agriculture v. Moreno,* 413 U.S., at 534; *Romer v. Evans,* 517 U.S., at 634–635. Indeed, we have never held that moral disapproval, without any other asserted state interest, is a sufficient rationale under the Equal Protection Clause to justify a law that discriminates among groups of persons.

Moral disapproval of a group cannot be a legitimate governmental interest under the Equal Protection Clause because legal classifications must not be "drawn for the purpose of disadvantaging the group burdened by the law." *Id.,* at 633. Texas' invocation of moral disapproval as a legitimate state interest proves nothing more than Texas' desire to criminalize homosexual sodomy. But the Equal Protection Clause prevents a State from creating "a classification of persons undertaken for its own sake." *Id.,* at 635. And because Texas so rarely enforces its sodomy law as applied to private, consensual acts, the law serves more as a statement of dislike and disapproval against homosexuals than as a tool to stop criminal behavior. The Texas sodomy law "raise[s] the inevitable inference that the disadvantage imposed is born of animosity toward the class of persons affected." *Id.,* at 634.

Texas argues, however, that the sodomy law does not discriminate against homosexual persons. Instead, the State maintains that the law discriminates only against homosexual conduct. While it is true that the law applies only to conduct, the conduct targeted by this law is conduct that is closely correlated with being homosexual. Under such circumstances, Texas' sodomy law is targeted at more than conduct. It is instead directed toward gay persons as a class. "After all, there can hardly be more palpable discrimination against a class than making the conduct that defines the class criminal." *Id.,* at 641 (SCALIA, J., dissenting). When a State makes homosexual conduct criminal, and not "deviate sexual intercourse" committed by persons of different sexes, "that declaration in and of itself is an invitation to subject homosexual persons to discrimination both in the public and in the private spheres."

Indeed, Texas law confirms that the sodomy statute is directed toward homosexuals as a class. In Texas, calling a person a homosexual is slander *per se* because the word "homosexual" "impute[s] the commission of a crime." The State has admitted that because of the sodomy law, *being* homosexual carries the presumption of being a criminal. Texas' sodomy law therefore results in discrimination against homosexuals as a class in an array of areas outside the criminal law. In *Romer v. Evans,* we refused to sanction a law that singled out homosexuals "for disfavored legal status." The same is true here. The Equal Protection Clause "'neither knows nor tolerates classes among citizens.'"

A State can of course assign certain consequences to a violation of its criminal law. But the State cannot single out one identifiable class of citizens for punishment that does not apply to everyone else, with moral disapproval as the only asserted state interest for the law. The Texas sodomy statute subjects homosexuals to "a lifelong penalty and stigma. A legislative classification that threatens the creation of an underclass ... cannot be reconciled with" the Equal Protection Clause. *Plyler v. Doe,* 457 U.S., at 239 (Powell, J., concurring).

Whether a sodomy law that is neutral both in effect and application, see *Yick Wo v. Hopkins,* 118 U.S. 356 (1886), would violate the substantive component of the Due Process Clause is an issue that need not be decided today. I am confident, however, that so long as the Equal Protection Clause requires a sodomy law to apply equally to the private consensual conduct of homosexuals and heterosexuals alike, such a law would not long stand in our democratic society. In the words of Justice Jackson:

> "The framers of the Constitution knew, and we should not forget today, that there is no more effective practical guaranty against arbitrary and unreasonable government than to require that the principles of law which officials would impose upon a minority be imposed generally. Conversely, nothing opens the door to arbitrary action so effectively as to allow those officials to pick and choose only a few to whom they will apply legislation and thus to escape the political retribution that might be visited upon them if larger numbers were affected." *Railway Express Agency, Inc. v. New York,* 336 U.S. 106, 112–113 (1949) (concurring opinion).

That this law as applied to private, consensual conduct is unconstitutional under the Equal Protection Clause does not mean that other laws distinguishing between heterosexuals and homosexuals would similarly fail under rational basis review. Texas cannot assert any legitimate state interest here, such as national security or preserving the traditional institution of marriage. Unlike the moral disapproval of same-sex relations—the asserted state interest in this case—other reasons exist to promote the institution of marriage beyond mere moral disapproval of an excluded group.

A law branding one class of persons as criminal based solely on the State's moral disapproval of that class and the conduct associated with that class runs contrary to the values of the Constitution and the Equal Protection Clause, under any standard of review. I therefore concur in the Court's judgment that Texas' sodomy law banning "deviate sexual intercourse" between consenting adults of the same sex, but not between consenting adults of different sexes, is unconstitutional.

Justice SCALIA, with whom THE CHIEF JUSTICE and Justice THOMAS join, dissenting.

....

V

Finally, I turn to petitioners' equal-protection challenge, which no Member of the Court save Justice O'CONNOR (opinion concurring in judgment), embraces: On its face § 21.06(a) applies equally to all persons. Men and women, heterosexuals and homosexuals, are all subject to its prohibition of deviate sexual intercourse with someone of the same sex. To be sure, § 21.06 does distinguish between the sexes insofar as concerns the partner with whom the sexual acts are performed: men can violate the law only with other men, and women only with other women. But this cannot itself be a denial of equal protection, since it is precisely the same distinction regarding partner that is drawn in state laws prohibiting marriage with someone of the same sex while permitting marriage with someone of the opposite sex.

The objection is made, however, that the antimiscegenation laws invalidated in *Loving v. Virginia,* 388 U.S. 1, 8 (1967), similarly were applicable to whites and blacks alike, and only distinguished between the races insofar as the *partner* was concerned. In *Loving,* however, we correctly applied heightened scrutiny, rather than the usual rational-basis review, because the Virginia statute was "designed to maintain White Supremacy." *Id.,* at 6, 11. A racially discriminatory purpose is always sufficient to subject a law to strict scrutiny, even a facially neutral law that makes no mention of race. See *Washington v. Davis,* 426 U.S. 229, 241–242 (1976). No purpose to discriminate against men or women as a class can be gleaned from the Texas law, so rational-basis review applies. That review is readily satisfied here by the same rational basis that satisfied it in *Bowers*—society's belief that certain forms of sexual behavior are "immoral and unacceptable." This is the same justification that supports many other laws regulating sexual behavior that make a distinction based upon the identity of the partner—for example, laws against adultery, fornication, and adult incest, and laws refusing to recognize homosexual marriage.

Justice O'CONNOR argues that the discrimination in this law which must be justified is not its discrimination with regard to the sex of the partner but its discrimination with regard to the sexual proclivity of the principal actor.

> "While it is true that the law applies only to conduct, the conduct targeted by this law is conduct that is closely correlated with being homosexual. Under such circumstances, Texas' sodomy law is targeted at more than conduct. It is instead directed toward gay persons as a class."

Of course the same could be said of any law. A law against public nudity targets "the conduct that is closely correlated with being a nudist," and hence "is targeted at more than conduct"; it is "directed toward nudists as a class." But be that as it may. Even if the Texas law *does* deny equal protection to "homosexuals as a class," that denial *still* does not need to be justified by anything more than a rational basis, which our cases show is satisfied by the enforcement of traditional notions of sexual morality.

Justice O'CONNOR simply decrees application of "a more searching form of rational basis review" to the Texas statute. The cases she cites do not recognize such a standard, and reach their conclusions only after finding, as required by conventional rational-basis analysis, that no conceivable legitimate state interest supports the classification at issue. Nor does Justice O'CONNOR explain precisely what her "more searching form" of rational-basis review consists of. It must at least mean, however, that laws exhibiting "a desire to harm a politically unpopular group" are invalid *even though* there may be a conceivable rational basis to support them.

This reasoning leaves on pretty shaky grounds state laws limiting marriage to opposite-sex couples. Justice O'CONNOR seeks to preserve them by the conclusory statement that "preserving the traditional institution of marriage" is a legitimate state interest. But "preserving the traditional institution of marriage" is just a kinder way of describing the State's *moral disapproval* of same-sex couples. Texas's interest in § 21.06 could be recast in similarly euphemistic terms: "preserving the traditional sexual mores of our society." In the jurisprudence Justice O'CONNOR has seemingly created, judges can validate laws by characterizing them as "preserving the traditions of society" (good); or invalidate them by characterizing them as "expressing moral disapproval" (bad)....

Notes and Questions

1. As with most other cases in which the Court strikes down a law under the rational basis standard, the form of rational basis applied in *Romer* does not seem like that applied in cases such as *Beach Communications*. Thus far, we have identified two types of "rational basis plus": transitional (e.g., *Reed* and *Weber*) and fleeting (e.g., *Moreno* and *Cleburne*). Which of these forms of rational basis plus seems to be at play here? Does Justice Kennedy suggest an answer to that question in *Romer*? Does Justice O'Connor suggest an answer to that question in her concurring opinion in *Lawrence*?

2. Justice Scalia is quick to limit the reach of *Romer*, making clear that the majority only applied rational basis scrutiny, and did not hold that sexual orientation is a suspect or quasi-suspect classification. Of course, the Court does not actually foreclose the possibility of heightened scrutiny for sexual orientation discrimination, does it?

3. Is it possible that the *Romer* Court is neither applying transitional nor fleeting rational basis plus review, but is instead ushering in a new era of equal protection review

in which the Court applies a single standard of "rational basis," akin to that advocated by Justice Stevens in *Cleburne*? In other words, is it possible that, just as *Lawrence* arguably kicks off a new method for assessing substantive due process claims, so *Romer* kicks off a new method for assessing equal protection clause claims?

In thinking about this possibility, consider this: the Court has not identified *any* new classifications subject to heightened scrutiny since it recognized intermediate scrutiny for sex and legitimacy classifications. Moreover, as indicated earlier in this chapter, the *Frontiero* factors are in significant tension with the *Adarand* approach to equal protection. Might this new method be a way of resolving that tension?

4. Justice O'Connor's concurring opinion in *Lawrence* is important because it is the only Supreme Court opinion — save for Justice Marshall's separate opinion in *Cleburne* — to acknowledge the existence of "a more searching form of rational basis review." Yet, does she articulate how, exactly, that form of rational basis review differs from traditional rational basis review?

5. As the majority notes in *Romer*, the Colorado Supreme Court relied on the U.S. Supreme Court's decisions treating voting as a fundamental right, coupled with its cases involving discriminatory restructuring of governmental decisionmaking, to conclude that strict scrutiny applied to Amendment 2.

The case law treating voting as a fundamental right under the Equal Protection Clause was examined at the start of this chapter. The cases involving discriminatory restructuring of governmental decisionmaking — all of which arose in the context of race — applied strict scrutiny to laws that made it harder for racial minorities to repeal legislation that negatively impacted their interests:

> [W]hen the political process or the decisionmaking mechanism used to *address* racially conscious legislation — and only such legislation — is singled out for peculiar and disadvantageous treatment, the governmental action plainly "rests on 'distinctions based on race.'" And when the State's allocation of power places unusual burdens on the ability of racial groups to enact legislation specifically designed to overcome the "special condition" of prejudice, the governmental action seriously "curtail[s] the operation of those political processes ordinarily to be relied upon to protect minorities." *United States v. Carolene Products Co.*, 304 U.S. 144, 153 n. 4 (1938). In a most direct sense, this implicates the judiciary's special role in safeguarding the interests of those groups that are "relegated to such a position of political powerlessness as to command extraordinary protection from the majoritarian political process."

Washington v. Seattle Sch. Dist. No. 1, 458 U.S. 457, 485–86 (1982). *See also Hunter v. Erickson*, 393 U.S. 385 (1969) (striking down city charter amendment preventing city council from implementing any ordinance dealing with racial discrimination in housing without voter approval, and concluding that "[e]ven though Akron might have proceeded by majority vote at town meeting on all its municipal legislation, it has instead chosen a more complex system. Having done so, the State may no more disadvantage any particular group by making it more difficult to enact legislation in its behalf than it may dilute any person's vote or give any group a smaller representation than another of comparable size.")

Is it clear from the quoted language whether the Court in these cases is applying heightened scrutiny because a *racial* classification is involved, because the political process has been restricted so as to make it harder to repeal undesirable legislation, or because *both* are involved? Does *Carolene Products* suggest that the latter alone is a free-standing basis for heightened scrutiny? Might that lack of clarity explain the *Romer* Court's unwillingness to affirm on that ground? In this regard, consider Justice Scalia's example of a law making it harder for smokers to repeal undesirable legislation by preempting local laws and making the issue a statewide one. Doesn't the Court still have to apply some sort of sliding scale of equal protection review in applying the discriminatory restructuring of governmental decisionmaking line of cases? If so, is a necessary precondition to applying this line of precedents to cases involving the rights of sexual minorities resolution of the question whether discrimination on the basis of sexual orientation or gender identity is subject to heightened scrutiny in the first instance? In this regard, note that where race (or some other suspect or quasi-suspect classification) was not explicitly or implicitly involved, the Court has declined to apply heightened scrutiny where similar restructuring of governmental decisionmaking has occurred. *See, e.g., James v. Valtierra*, 402 U.S. 137 (1971). Would heightened scrutiny be appropriate for discriminatory restructuring of governmental decisionmaking that appeared to be motivated in a given case by a desire to harm a politically unpopular group, relying on the *Moreno-Cleburne* line of cases?

6. Both Justice Scalia (in his dissenting opinions in *Romer* and *Lawrence*) and Justice O'Connor in her concurring opinion in *Lawrence* reject the idea of drawing a distinction—for equal protection purposes—between homosexual conduct on the one hand and homosexual orientation or status on the other. Is this thus a tacit acceptance of the idea, raised in *Hernandez v. New York*, that something can be so closely correlated with a class that discrimination on that basis is tantamount to discrimination against that class? To what extent, if any, does that help to resolve the question whether bans on same-sex marriage are a form of sexual orientation discrimination?

7. What counts as unconstitutional "animus" under *Romer*? After all, isn't Justice Scalia correct to note that numerous types of criminal laws are grounded in a form of animus towards certain types of individuals, namely those who commit heinous crimes such as murder or child molestation? How is a court to determine what forms of animus are permissible and what forms are not?

8. Which resolution of *Lawrence* do you find more satisfying, the majority's application of rational basis review under the Due Process Clause examined in Chapter 3, or Justice O'Connor's application of "a more searching form of rational basis review" under the Equal Protection Clause? Had Justice O'Connor's approach been the approach adopted by the majority, how would the Court have resolved a challenge to a sodomy law—akin to that in *Bowers*—that criminalized both same-sex and opposite-sex sodomy? In this regard, consider Justice O'Connor's citation to *Yick Wo v. Hopkins*, 118 U.S. 356 (1886).

9. Justice O'Connor treats moral disapproval differently for due process and equal protection purposes, deeming it a legitimate governmental interest under the former but not under the latter. Although the majority in *Lawrence* held—or at least strongly implied—that moral disapproval was not a legitimate governmental interest for due process purposes (as explored in Chapter 3), it did not address its legitimacy under equal protection. Nonetheless, do you see why Justice O'Connor's conclusion that moral disapproval is never a legitimate governmental interest is a necessary conclusion if equal protection is to have any meaning?

10. In contrast to Justice O'Connor's application of "a more searching form of rational basis review" in *Lawrence*, the Supreme Court of Missouri—just months after the U.S. Supreme Court's decision in *Bowers*—applied the following line of reasoning to uphold a state law criminalizing only same-sex, but not opposite-sex, sodomy:

§ 566.090.1(3) is rationally related to the State's concededly legitimate interest in protecting the public health. The State has argued that forbidding homosexual activity will inhibit the spread of sexually communicable diseases like acquired immuneo-deficiency syndrome (AIDS).

Respondent counters that "No one, including the Missouri Legislature was aware of AIDS in 1977 when this statute was enacted," and "AIDS is and can be acquired through numerous forms of conduct other than homosexual activity."

We reject both arguments. A legislative enactment will be upheld if "any state of facts reasonably can be conceived that would sustain it * * *" and notwithstanding that "it is not made with mathematical nicety * * *." *See, Lindsley v. National Carbonic Gas Co.*, 220 U.S. 61, 79 (1911). That AIDS was not discovered until after the enactment of § 566.090.1(3) does not affect its present validity. It would be an idle exercise indeed to strike down this statute, upon the grounds urged, only to have it reenacted ostensibly based on current data. Moreover, we believe the public health aspect of § 566.090.1(3) need not be limited to the threat of AIDS. The General Assembly could well have considered that the acts proscribed presented other threats to public health. We need not refer to medical literature to suggest, for example, that there might rationally be health ramifications to anal intercourse and/or oral-genital sex. Finally, the General Assembly could have reasonably concluded that the general promiscuity characteristic of the homosexual lifestyle made such acts among homosexuals particularly deserving of regulation, thus rationally distinguishing such acts within a heterosexual context. "We cannot say that that judgment is not an allowable one. * * * It is no requirement of equal protection that all evils of the same genus be eradicated or none at all." *Railway Express Agency v. New York*, 336 U.S. 106, 110 (1949). Accordingly, we hold that § 566.090.1(3) is rationally related to the State's legitimate interest in public health.

State v. Walsh, 713 S.W.2d 508, 512–13 (Mo. 1986).

11. In *Lawrence*, both the majority and Justice O'Connor seek to cabin the reach of their holdings, alluding to such issues as same-sex marriage and Don't Ask, Don't Tell and noting that the decision does not address those issues. Yet, as Justice Scalia points out in his dissent, the Court cannot draw a principled line between the issue before it and those other issues. To be sure, had the Court come out and held in either *Romer* or *Lawrence* that intermediate or strict scrutiny applied to sexual orientation discrimination, it would have virtually answered the question whether bans on same-sex marriage and military service are constitutional, would it not? Might this be the virtue (or vice, depending upon your perspective) of not clearly articulating which standard of review is being applied?

12. In his dissenting opinion in *Lawrence*, Justice Scalia makes clear his view that the law at issue in *Lawrence* does not discriminate on the basis of *sex* because it treats men and women alike in that both are equally prohibited from engaging in sexual intercourse with someone of the same sex. Recall, in contrast, that Justice Johnson, in her concurring opinion in *Baker*, viewed the ban on same-sex marriage as a clear-cut form of facial sex discrimination. Both Justices Scalia and Johnson cite *Loving v. Virginia*, 388 U.S. 1 (1967)—which declared unconstitutional state laws banning interracial marriage—in support of their conclusions. The *Loving* decision will be examined in great detail in Chapter 5. When you read *Loving*, return to the arguments of Justices Scalia and Johnson and determine who you believe has the better of the argument.

Problem 4-A: Domestic Partnership Benefits

Under Michigan law, same-sex couples are not permitted to marry, nor is there any official recognition of same-sex relationships at the state level. For some time, however, a number of municipalities in Michigan have provided domestic partnership benefits to the same-sex domestic partners of their employees.

On December 22, 2011, a new state law went into effect that prohibits all public employers in the state from providing medical or other fringe benefits to an individual currently residing in the same residence as the public employee unless that individual is either married to the employee, a dependent of the employee as defined by the Internal Revenue Code, or otherwise eligible to inherit from the employee under the laws of intestate succession in the state.

It is clear that same-sex domestic partners are not dependents under the Internal Revenue Code, and that they are not eligible to inherit under the laws of intestate succession in Michigan.

Assess the constitutionality of the statute if challenged on equal protection grounds (if more information is required, indicate what that information would be and how it would matter).

Kansas v. Limon

122 P.3d 22 (Kan. 2005)

The opinion was delivered by LUCKERT, J.:

The principal issue presented in this case is whether the Kansas unlawful voluntary sexual relations statute violates the equal protection provision of the Fourteenth Amendment to the United States Constitution. Matthew Limon argues that the United States Supreme Court decision in *Lawrence v. Texas,* 539 U.S. 558 (2003), requires this court to find the statute unconstitutional because it results in a punishment for unlawful voluntary sexual conduct between members of the opposite sex that is less harsh than the punishment for the same conduct between members of the same sex.

The statute subject to this challenge, commonly referred to as the Romeo and Juliet statute, applies to voluntary sexual intercourse, sodomy, or lewd touching when, at the time of the incident, (1) the victim is a child of 14 or 15; (2) the offender is less than 19 years of age and less than 4 years older than the victim; (3) the victim and offender are the only ones involved; and (4) the victim and offender are members of the opposite sex. Limon's conduct meets all of the elements of the Romeo and Juliet statute except the one limiting application to acts between members of the opposite sex.

When the Romeo and Juliet statute applies, prison terms are shorter and other consequences, such as postrelease supervision periods and sex offender registration requirements, are less harsh than when general rape, sodomy, and lewd touching statutes apply. Because these disparities are based upon the homosexual nature of Limon's conduct, he argues the Romeo and Juliet statute creates a classification which violates the equal protection principles announced by the United States Supreme Court. Limon suggests we apply a strict level of scrutiny when reviewing his claim, but asserts that even if the rational basis test applies, under the guidance of *Lawrence,* the classification bears no rational relationship to legitimate State interests.

We agree that the United States Supreme Court's decision in *Lawrence* controls our analysis and, when considered in conjunction with several equal protection decisions of the United States Supreme Court, requires us to hold that the State does not have a rational basis for the statutory classification created in the Romeo and Juliet statute.…

Factual and Procedural Background

Limon was convicted of criminal sodomy pursuant to K.S.A. 21-3505(a)(2) after a bench trial on stipulated facts. The stipulation established that on February 16, 2000, Limon had consensual oral contact with the genitalia of M.A.R. Both Limon and M.A.R. are male. Limon turned 18 years of age just 1 week before the incident; his date of birth is February 9, 1982. He was less than 4 years older than M.A.R., who turned 15 years of age the month following the incident. M.A.R.'s date of birth is March 17, 1985.…

The contact occurred at a school for developmentally disabled children where Limon and M.A.R. were residents. Although there is a discrepancy between Limon's and M.A.R.'s functioning, the difference is minor. Intellectually, Limon falls between the ranges described as borderline intellectual functioning and mild mental retardation. M.A.R. functions in the upper limits of the range of mild mental retardation. M.A.R. consented to the sexual contact, and when he asked Limon to stop, Limon did so.

[The trial court rejected Limon's equal protection challenge, and this holding was affirmed by the Kansas courts on appellate review.]

Limon then filed a petition for writ of certiorari to the United States Supreme Court. While his petition was pending, the Supreme Court issued its decision in *Lawrence v. Texas*.…

One day after issuing this decision, the Supreme Court granted Limon's petition, vacated the judgment, and remanded the case to the Kansas Court of Appeals "for further consideration in light of *Lawrence v. Texas*." .…

Analysis

In this appeal, Limon primarily argues that to punish criminal voluntary sexual conduct between teenagers of the same sex more harshly than criminal voluntary sexual conduct between teenagers of the opposite sex is a violation of the equal protection provision of the United States Constitution.…

Limon's arguments are constructed entirely upon the precedent of United States Supreme Court cases, and those precedents command our decision in this case. However, Limon also cites § 1 of the Kansas Constitution Bill of Rights and, thus, preserves a state constitutional claim.

Sections 1 and 2 of the Kansas Constitution Bill of Rights "are given much the same effect as the clauses of the Fourteenth Amendment relating to due process and equal protection of the law." *Farley v. Engelken,* 241 Kan. 663, 667 (1987).…

Traditionally, when analyzing an equal protection claim, the United States and Kansas Supreme Courts employ three levels of scrutiny: strict scrutiny, intermediate scrutiny, and the rational basis test. The level of scrutiny applied by the court depends on the nature of the legislative classification and the rights affected by that classification. *Romer v. Evans*, 517 U.S. 620, 632 (1996). The general rule is that a law will be subject to the rational basis test unless the legislative classification targets a suspect class or burdens a fundamental right.…

Thus, when an equal protection claim is made, the first step of the analysis is to determine the nature of the legislative classification and the rights which are affected by the classification. That determination will dictate the level of scrutiny which applies. The final step of the analysis requires determining whether the classification withstands the scrutiny.

Classification

In the first step, we must examine the nature of the classification created by the Romeo and Juliet statute. The State argues that the statute applies only to conduct and does not discriminate against any class of individual, in particular against homosexual persons. The State also argues that nothing in the record establishes that either Limon or M.A.R. is homosexual.

Indeed, there is no per se classification of homosexuals, bisexuals, or heterosexuals in the statute, nor do we know which classification applies to Limon or M.A.R. However, that does not mean that Limon's argument fails. As Justice Scalia noted in his dissent in *Romer,* "there can hardly be more palpable discrimination against a class than making the *conduct* that defines the class criminal" (emphasis added). 517 U.S. at 641. The majority in *Lawrence* similarly noted that making homosexual conduct criminal and not legislating against "deviate sexual intercourse" committed by persons of different sexes "in and of itself is an invitation to subject homosexual persons to discrimination both in the public and in the private spheres." Throughout the *Lawrence* opinion, the majority refers to the stigmatizing and demeaning effect of criminalizing conduct commonly engaged in by homosexuals and concludes that a state may not "demean their existence or control their destiny." Additionally, *Lawrence* makes it clear that *Romer* applies to "persons who were homosexuals, lesbians, or bisexual either by 'orientation, conduct, practices or relationships.'" *Lawrence,* 539 U.S. at 574 (quoting *Romer,* 517 U.S. at 624).

This case is different from *Lawrence,* where homosexual conduct was criminal and heterosexual conduct was not. The *Lawrence* Court focused upon the "stigma" the criminal statute imposed which it characterized as "not trivial." 539 U.S. at 575. Here, both types of conduct are criminalized and, thus, stigma attaches to the heterosexual conduct covered by the Romeo and Juliet statute. However, there is an enormous escalation in the severity of punishment for those punished under the general rape, sodomy, and lewd act statutes....

There is also the distinction that Limon faces the stigma of sex offender registration; those convicted under the Romeo and Juliet statute do not.

Furthermore, the demeaning and stigmatizing effect upon which the *Lawrence* Court focused is at least equally applicable to teenagers, both the victim and the offender, as it is to adults and, according to some, the impact is greater upon a teen.

Based upon these considerations we conclude there is a discriminatory classification requiring us to examine the level of scrutiny to be applied in testing the constitutionality of the classification.

Level of Scrutiny

The next step of our analysis is to determine the appropriate level of scrutiny to apply. Limon argues that under the holding in *Lawrence* the highest level of scrutiny should apply because the statute creates a classification of homosexuals which the *Lawrence* Court recognized as suspect. Contrary to this argument, the United States Supreme Court has not recognized homosexuals as a suspect classification. In addition, as Justice Scalia notes in his dissenting opinion in *Lawrence,* "Though there is discussion of 'fundamental proposition[s]' and 'fundamental decisions,' nowhere does the Court's opinion declare that homosexual sodomy is a 'fundamental right.'" 539 U.S. at 586 (Scalia, J., dissenting). Thus, strict scrutiny does not apply to our analysis of whether the Romeo and Juliet provision unconstitutionally discriminates based upon sexual orientation.

Justice O'Connor, in her concurring opinion in *Lawrence*, suggests "a more searching form of rational basis review" applies when a law exhibits a "desire to harm a politically unpopular group." 539 U.S. at 580 (O'Connor, J., concurring). Her suggestion was not discussed by the *Lawrence* majority, which did not analyze the Texas statute on equal protection grounds. The majority did note that the "alternative" argument that the Texas statute was invalid under the Equal Protection Clause

> "is a tenable argument, but we conclude the instant case requires us to address whether *Bowers* itself has continuing validity. Were we to hold the statute invalid under the Equal Protection Clause some might question whether a prohibition would be valid if drawn differently, say, to prohibit the conduct both between same-sex and different-sex participants." 539 U.S. at 574–75.

Despite not deciding the case on equal protection grounds and never explicitly identifying the standard utilized for its due process analysis, the *Lawrence* majority, by approvingly citing and discussing the equal protection analysis in *Romer,* at least implied that the rational basis test is the appropriate standard when a statute is attacked because of its classification of homosexual conduct.... In *Lawrence,* the Court summarized the *Romer* decision, noting that the amendment named a "solitary class ... and deprived them of protection under state antidiscrimination laws. We concluded that the provision was 'born of animosity toward the class of persons affected' and further that it had no rational relation to a legitimate governmental purpose." 539 U.S. at 574.

The *Lawrence* opinion contains another oblique indication that the rational basis test would apply, stating: "The Texas statute furthers no *legitimate* state interest which can justify its intrusion into the personal and private life of the individual" 539 U.S. at 578 (emphasis added). Typically, a search for a legitimate interest signifies a rational basis analysis.

Hence, we apply the rational basis test to determine whether the Romeo and Juliet statute is unconstitutional because of its exclusion of homosexual conduct.

Rational Basis Test

The Court of Appeals applied the rational basis test and upheld the statute upon finding minimal congruence between the classifying means and the one legislative end upon which the two judges who comprised the majority could agree: public health.

As the Court of Appeals noted, the basic contours of the rational basis test are well-defined: "For a statute to pass constitutional muster under the rational basis standard, it therefore must meet a two-part test: (1) It must implicate legitimate goals, and (2) the means chosen by the legislature must bear a rational relationship to those goals."

In explaining the test, the United States Supreme Court has said that, although the rational basis test is "the most deferential of standards, we insist on knowing the relation between the classification adopted and the object obtained." *Romer,* 517 U.S. at 632. The Court observed that the "search for the link between classification and objective gives substance to the Equal Protection Clause; it provides guidance and discipline for the legislature ... ; and it marks the limits of our own authority." 517 U.S. at 632. The Court continued: "By requiring that the classification bear a rational relationship to an independent and legitimate legislative end, we ensure that classifications are not drawn for the purpose of disadvantaging the group burdened by the law.... 'If the adverse impact on the disfavored class is an apparent aim of the legislature, its impartiality would be suspect.'" 517 U.S. at 633 (quoting *U.S. Railroad Retirement Bd. v. Fritz,* 449 U.S. 166, 181 [1980]) (Stevens, J., concurring).

Romer and other United States Supreme Court decisions instruct that we must examine the scope of the classification. Over-inclusiveness, where the legislation burdens a wider range of individuals than necessary given the State's interest, may be particularly invidious and unconstitutional. Likewise, a failure to create a classification which is sufficiently broad to effectively accommodate the State's interest, *i.e.*, the creation of an under-inclusive class, may evidence an animus toward those burdened. *Cleburne*, 473 U.S. at 450. Paradoxically, a class may be both under- and over-inclusive; Limon argues the Romeo and Juliet statute creates such a class.

Justice O'Connor, in her concurring opinion in *Lawrence*, cites and synthesizes four cases which illustrate these points:

> "In *Department of Agriculture v. Moreno*, for example, we held that a law preventing those households containing an individual unrelated to any other member of the household from receiving food stamps violated equal protection because the purpose of the law was to '"discriminate against hippies."' The asserted governmental interest in preventing food stamp fraud was not deemed sufficient to satisfy rational basis review. In *Eisenstadt v. Baird*, we refused to sanction a law that discriminated between married and unmarried persons by prohibiting the distribution of contraceptives to single persons. Likewise, in *Cleburne v. Cleburne Living Center*, we held that it was irrational for a State to require a home for the mentally disabled to obtain a special use permit when other residences—like fraternity houses and apartment buildings—did not have to obtain such a permit. And in *Romer v. Evans*, we disallowed a state statute that 'impos[ed] a broad and undifferentiated disability on a single named group'—specifically, homosexuals."

Of the four cases Justice O'Connor discusses, two are particularly analogous to this case. As Justice O'Connor indicated, in *Eisenstadt v. Baird*, the Court invalidated on rational basis grounds a Massachusetts statute banning the distribution of contraceptives to unmarried persons. The state's highest court had found the legislative purpose to be "the State's interest in protecting the health of its citizens" by "preventing the distribution of articles designed to prevent conception which may have undesirable, if not dangerous, physical consequences" and "to protect morals" by discouraging premarital sexual intercourse. Addressing the purpose of preventing premarital sex, the Supreme Court concluded: "'The rationality of this justification is dubious, particularly in light of the admitted widespread availability to all persons..., unmarried as well as married, of birth-control devices for the prevention of disease, as distinguished from the prevention of contraception.'" The Court concluded that "the Massachusetts statute is thus so riddled with exceptions that deterrence of premarital sex cannot reasonably be regarded as its aim."

The *Eisenstadt* Court also explained, if the State genuinely considered contraceptives to pose a health risk, it would have banned their use by both married and unmarried persons. Protecting only single persons from the alleged dangers of contraceptives, and even then only when used to prevent pregnancy rather than the spread of disease, was "both discriminatory and overbroad" and "illogical to the point of irrationality."

In the other case cited by Justice O'Connor which is particularly analogous, *Romer*, the Court was reviewing the Colorado constitutional amendment which the State argued protected the associational rights of landlords and employers with moral objections to homosexuality and furthered the State's interest in "conserving resources to fight discrimination against other groups." The Court found it "impossible to credit" these proffered purposes. Noting that rational basis inquiry was meant to "ensure that classifications are not drawn for the purpose of disadvantaging the group burdened by the law," the Court held that "[e]ven laws enacted for broad and ambitious purposes often can be explained by reference to legitimate public policies which justify the incidental disadvantages they impose on certain persons. Amendment 2, however, in making a general announcement that gays and lesbians shall not have any particular protections from the law, inflicts on them immediate, continuing, and real injuries that outrun and belie any legitimate justification that may be claimed for it."

The Court faulted the Colorado constitutional amendment for imposing a "broad and undifferentiated disability on a single named group." The Court further condemned the statute because "its sheer breadth is so discontinuous with the reasons offered for it that the amendment seems inexplicable by anything but animus toward the class it affects." Additionally, the amendment was "a status-based enactment divorced from any factual context from which we could discern a relationship to legitimate state interests." Because of these faults, the Court reached "the inevitable inference that the disadvantage imposed is born of animosity toward the class of persons affected." "'[D]esire to harm a politically unpopular group cannot constitute a *legitimate* governmental interest.'" 517 U.S. at 634 (quoting *U.S. Department of Agriculture v. Moreno*, 413 U.S. 528, 534 [1973]). The result of these deficiencies was that, whatever else might be said of the amendment, it "offended" the "conventional and venerable" principle that "a law must bear a rational relationship to a legitimate governmental purpose."

With these holdings to direct us, we begin our search for a rational basis for the harshly disparate sentencing treatment of those 18 years old and younger who engage in voluntary sex with an underage teenager of the same sex....

Although the legislative history does not suggest the State's interest in including the phrase "and are members of the opposite sex," the State argues several possibilities. In addition, we must consider the rationales utilized by the Court of Appeals majority. These various possible State interests can be categorized as: (1) the protection and preservation of the traditional sexual mores of society; (2) preservation of the historical notions of appropriate sexual development of children; (3) protection of teenagers against coercive relationships; (4) protection of teenagers from the increased health risks that accompany sexual activity; (5) promotion of parental responsibility and procreation; and (6) protection of those in group homes.

Traditional Sexual Mores and Development

Limon counters this theoretical justification by arguing that the State's moral disapproval of homosexuality is an illegitimate justification for discrimination.

The *Lawrence* decision rejected a morality-based rationale as a legitimate State interest. The Court recognized that many people condemn homosexuality as immoral....

However, the Court continued by stating: "These considerations do not answer the question before us." 539 U.S. at 571. The Court framed the issue as "whether the majority may use the power of the State to enforce these views on the whole society through operation of the criminal law. 'Our obligation is to define the liberty of all, not to mandate our own moral code.' *Planned Parenthood of Southeastern Pa. v. Casey*, 505 U.S. 833, 850 (1992)."

Thus, when Texas argued that its anti-sodomy law furthered the promotion of morality, the Court in *Lawrence* rejected the argument and adopted the following reasoning from Justice Stevens' dissent in *Bowers:* "'[T]he fact that the governing majority in a State has traditionally viewed a particular practice as immoral is not a sufficient reason for upholding a law prohibiting the practice.'"

This holding followed the precedent of *Casey, Eisenstadt, Romer,* and other cases. The Court in *Romer* explained that our laws are often morality-based which, in and of itself, is not objectionable if the laws are applied fairly to all. However, the right to equal protection of those laws is offended when legal classifications are drawn for the purpose of invoking moral disapproval with "the purpose of disadvantaging the group burdened by the law."

The Court of Appeals majority would dismiss this analysis in *Lawrence* because of the due process context in which the discussion was made. The *Lawrence* majority, however, signaled application of the principles to equal protection analysis: "Equality of treatment and the due process right to demand respect for conduct protected by the substantive guarantee of liberty are linked in important respects, and a decision on the latter point advances both interests." In essence, the *Lawrence* decision recognized that the substantive due process analysis at issue in that case and the equal protection analysis necessary in this case are inevitably linked....

Thus, we are directed in our equal protection analysis by the United States Supreme Court's holding in *Lawrence* that moral disapproval of a group cannot be a legitimate governmental interest.

Historical Notions of Appropriate Sexual Development of Children

The Court of Appeals also determined the *Lawrence* holding did not apply to this case because *Lawrence* involved adults and this case involved an adult in a relationship with a minor. Likewise, the State focuses its argument on the State's interest in the moral and sexual development of children.

Undoubtedly, the State has broad powers to protect minors. This point was noted by the United States Supreme Court in *Carey v. Population Services International,* 431 U.S. 678 (1977). *Carey* involved a constitutional challenge to a prohibition on distribution of contraceptives to persons under 16 years of age. The appellants argued that the free availability of contraceptives might encourage sexual activity among minors and the State had a legitimate interest in discouraging such behavior. In response, the appellees argued that minors as well as adults had a privacy right to engage in consensual sexual behavior. The *Carey* court noted that "in the area of sexual mores, as in other areas, the scope of permissible state regulation is broader as to minors than as to adults." 431 U.S. at 694 n. 17.

However, *Carey* held that "the right to privacy in connection with decisions affecting procreation extends to minors as well as adults" and invalidated the prohibition in question. The Court noted that "State restrictions inhibiting privacy rights of minors are valid only if they serve 'any significant state interest ... that is not present in the case of an adult.'"

Although this case does not involve the fundamental right to privacy in connection with decisions affecting procreation or legislation which inhibits the rights of minors, the *Carey* rationale suggests that even when the articulated interest is the protection of minors, there still must be a connection between the State's interest and the classification and, if the burden would not be allowed if placed upon an adult, the State's interest must be unique to children. So, unless the justifications for criminalizing homosexual activity between teenagers more severely than heterosexual activity between teenagers are somehow different than the justifications for criminalizing adult homosexual activity, those justifications must fail.

Neither the Court of Appeals nor the State cites any scientific research or other evidence justifying the position that homosexual sexual activity is more harmful to minors than adults.

After this court accepted review of the Court of Appeals decision, the National Association of Social Workers and the Kansas Chapter of the National Association of Social

Workers filed an *amici* brief which specifically questions the Court of Appeals' conclusion that the exclusion of gay teens from the application of the unlawful sexual relations statute protects the traditional sexual development of children. That brief cites a number of studies indicating that sexual orientation is already settled by the time a child turns 14, that sexual orientation is not affected by the sexual experiences teenagers have, and that efforts to pressure teens into changing their sexual orientation are not effective.

We conclude, as the United States Supreme Court stated in *Romer,* the "status-based enactment [is so] divorced from any factual context" we cannot "discern a relationship" to the espoused State interest that the law preserves the sexual development of children consistent with traditional sexual mores. Additionally, we again recognize the *Lawrence* Court's conclusion that moral disapproval of a group cannot be a legitimate governmental interest.

Coercive Effect Upon Minors

The State at various times refers to the coercive effect often existing in a relationship between an adult and a child. Certainly, the State has a significant interest in prohibiting sex between adults and minors, not only because of the potentially coercive effect of an adult's influence but also because of concern regarding the minor's ability to arrive at an informed consent. These concerns are addressed by and form the fundamental policy rationale of statutory rape provisions. Limon's argument accepts and supports this State interest; he agrees he deserves punishment. He simply disputes that he should be punished more severely for having sex with a member of the same sex.

Additionally, the policy decision made by the legislature in enacting the Romeo and Juliet statute undercuts this argument. The legislature determined, at least as to those in a heterosexual relationship, that a mutual relationship between teenagers is less likely to involve the same coercion that a relationship between an older adult and a child might and is more likely to be one where the minor's participation is voluntary, although not legally consensual.

This, however, begs the question of whether there is a rational basis to distinguish between a class of those 18 years old and younger who engage in voluntary sex with minors aged 14 or 15 who are of the same sex and a class of those 18 years old and younger who engage in voluntary sex with such minors of the opposite sex. We see no basis to determine that as a class one group or the other would have a higher tendency to be coercive. A distinction on this basis has no factual support....

Public Health

As to the public health justification, Limon argues that excluding gay teenagers from the lesser penalties of the Romeo and Juliet law has no connection with the State's interest in reducing the spread of sexually transmitted diseases. Specifically, the State focuses upon the risks of HIV and in support of its argument cites briefs filed before the United States Supreme Court in the *Lawrence* case.

We first note that there is no basis to determine that public health risks for minors engaging in same-gender sexual relations is greater than the risk for adults. That *Lawrence* did not discuss the often-cited justifications of public health and morality tells us that those interests are either not legitimate interests at all, or more likely, that they are not sufficient to overcome an individual's right to liberty and privacy.

At a minimum, we cannot distinguish between the health risks for the adults involved in *Lawrence* and the minor involved in this case. Additionally, we find persuasive Limon's argument that for this justification to be rational, the prohibited sexual activities would have to be more likely to transmit disease when engaged in by homosexuals than by heterosexuals; however, this proposition is not grounded in fact.

Again, we have the benefit of additional arguments, including the *amici curiae* brief of a number of public health organizations which provided scientific and statistical information. These studies persuade us that the Romeo and Juliet statute presents one of those seemingly paradoxical situations where the classification is both over- and under-inclusive.

Using statistics from the United States Centers for Disease Control and Prevention (CDC) and other studies, the *amici* support the argument that the Court of Appeals majority and the State focus on the wrong population in citing the statistics regarding the incidence of HIV infection in adult homosexual males. Significantly, they point to the CDC's Basic Statistics which reflect that among the population of HIV-positive young people ages 13–19, which includes the age range covered by the Romeo and Juliet statute, 61 percent are female. Yet, the risk of transmission of the HIV infection through female to female contact is negligible. Recognizing that HIV is transmitted through intravenous drug use of shared needles and other mechanisms besides sexual transmission, the gravest risk of sexual transmission for females is through heterosexual intercourse.

There is a near-zero chance of acquiring the HIV infection through the conduct which gave rise to this case, oral sex between males, or through cunnilingus. And, although the statute grants a lesser penalty for heterosexual anal sex, the risk of HIV transmission during anal sex with an infected partner is the same for heterosexuals and homosexuals.

The legislative history reveals that the concern of conferees was more focused upon teenage pregnancy. Obviously, this public health risk is not addressed through this legislation. According to the Kansas Department of Health and Environment's Teenage Pregnancy Report for 2003, there were 1,559 pregnancies in Kansas teens age 15 to 17. In contrast, the same agency reports that from 2000 to 2002 there were two cases of AIDS in Kansas among teenagers 13–19 years old.

Dissenting Judge Pierron cited several scenarios in which the statute did not protect against activities which raise a public health risk. In part, he stated:

> "[U]nder the law a female infected with every venereal disease yet identified, and engaging in acts quite likely to infect or actually infecting a male minor, will receive a much lighter sentence. A disease-free male engaging in sex with another male in a manner not likely to spread disease if it was present will receive a much heavier sentence. Perversely, under the law, a male with a venereal disease who infects and impregnates an underage female will also receive a much lighter sentence."

In essence, the Romeo and Juliet statute is over-inclusive because it increases penalties for sexual relations which are unlikely to transmit HIV and other sexually transmitted diseases. Thus, the statute burdens a wider range of individuals than necessary for public health purposes. Simultaneously, the provision is under-inclusive because it lowers the penalty for heterosexuals engaging in high-risk activities. In other words, the statute proscribes conduct unrelated to a public health purpose and does not proscribe conduct which is detrimental to public health.

Thus, the conclusions of the *Romer* Court are, again, particularly salient. The status-based distinction in the Kansas Romeo and Juliet statute is so broad and so divorced from supporting facts that we cannot discern a relationship to the facially legitimate interest of protecting public health and "its sheer breadth is so discontinuous with the reasons offered for it that the amendment seems inexplicable by anything but animus toward the class it affects." 517 U.S. at 632. The "statute's superficial earmarks as a health measure" (*Eisenstadt,* 405 U.S. at 452) do not satisfy scrutiny under the rational basis test.

Promoting Parental Responsibility and Procreation

Limon also contends that there is no rational connection between the classification and the Court of Appeals' parental responsibility and procreation justifications. The Court of Appeals stated that the legislature might have determined that lengthy incarceration of a young adult offender who has become a parent as a result of a heterosexual relationship with a minor would be counterproductive to that young adult's duty to support his or her child. But, because same-sex relationships do not lead to unplanned pregnancies, the need to release a same-sex offender from incarceration is absent.

Limon argues this justification and Judge Green's findings regarding the State's interest in relationships which lead to procreation make no sense since the State's interest is to discourage teen pregnancies, not encourage them. Further, the statute does not reduce penalties solely for conduct that results in pregnancy, but also for heterosexual intercourse which does not result in pregnancy, *i.e.,* sodomy and lewd contact. Again, the relationship between the objective and the classification is so strained that we cannot conclude it is rational.

Protection of Those in Group Homes

The State also makes an argument that the State has an interest in gender segregation in group homes. The Romeo and Juliet statute has no limitation related to living arrangements or disability. If the statute punished similar behavior in segregated group homes for juveniles, the State's argument could conceivably justify a harsher penalty. However, the statute is not limited in this manner. If the legislative purpose is to protect those in group homes, the statute's overbreadth in covering situations both inside and outside residential living environments suggests animus toward teenagers who engage in homosexual sex. See *Romer,* 517 U.S. at 632.

No Rational Basis

We conclude that ... the Kansas unlawful voluntary sexual relations statute, does not pass rational basis scrutiny under the United States Constitution Equal Protection Clause or, because we traditionally apply the same analysis to our state constitution, under the Kansas Constitution Equal Protection Clause. The Romeo and Juliet statute suffers the same faults as found by the United States Supreme Court in *Romer* and *Eisenstadt;* adding the phrase "and are members of the opposite sex" created a broad, overreaching, and undifferentiated status-based classification which bears no rational relationship to legitimate State interests. Paraphrasing the United States Supreme Court's decision in *Romer,* the statute inflicts immediate, continuing, and real injuries that outrun and belie any legitimate justification that may be claimed for it. Furthermore, the State's interests fail under the holding in *Lawrence* that moral disapproval of a group cannot be a legitimate governmental interest. As Justice Scalia stated: "If, as the [United States Supreme] Court asserts, the promotion of majoritarian sexual morality is not even a *legitimate* state interest," the statute cannot "survive rational-basis review." 539 U.S. at 599 (Scalia, J., dissenting).

Because we determine the statute violates constitutional equal protection guarantees based upon a rational basis analysis, we need not reach Limon's other arguments that strict scrutiny should be applied, including his argument that the statute discriminates based on sex....

Conclusion of Equal Protection Analysis

We hold [the Romeo and Juliet statute] unconstitutional as violating the equal protection provisions of the United States and Kansas Constitutions and strike from the statute the words "and are members of the opposite sex." ....

We further grant Limon's requested remedy of imposing a time limit upon further proceedings in this case and order that the State will have 30 days in which to: (1) charge Limon under the provisions of [the Romeo and Juliet statute] without the words "members of the opposite sex" or (2) take other action....

Doe v. Jindal

2012 WL 1068776 (E.D. La. 2012)

MARTIN L.C. FELDMAN, District Judge.

....

At issue in this case is a first and defining principle of our struggle as a nation that finally resolved in the Fourteenth Amendment to the Constitution: Equal Protection before the Law....

In Louisiana, the solicitation of oral or anal sex for compensation can be prosecuted under two different statutes: the solicitation for compensation provision of the Prostitution statute, and the Crime Against Nature by Solicitation statute.[2] Nine anonymous plaintiffs, all of whom were convicted of violating Louisiana's Crime Against Nature by Solicitation statute based on their agreement to engage in oral sex for compensation prior to August 15, 2011, bring this civil rights suit. They challenge that statute's requirement that, as a result of their conviction, they must register as sex offenders under Louisiana's sex offender registry law. They complain that if, instead, they had been convicted of solicitation of sex for money under the state Prostitution law, they would not have been required to register as sex offenders....

The plaintiffs trace the history of the Crime Against Nature by Solicitation statute and suggest that history supports their theory that no rational basis exists for treating them differently from those convicted of participating in identical conduct under the Prostitution statute:[10] Since 1805, Louisiana's Crime Against Nature statute has criminalized the commission of "unnatural carnal copulation."[11]

In 1982, Louisiana expanded the Crime Against Nature statute to specifically criminalize "solicitation by a human being of another with the intent to engage in any unnatural car-

---

2. The solicitation provision of the Prostitution statute outlaws "[t]he solicitation by one person of another with the intent to engage in indiscriminate sexual intercourse with the latter for compensation." La.R.S. 14:82(A)(2). The Prostitution statute defines "sexual intercourse" as "anal, oral, or vaginal sexual intercourse." La.R.S. 14:82(B). The Crime Against Nature by Solicitation statute forbids "solicitation by a human being of another with the intent to engage in any unnatural carnal copulation for compensation." La.R.S. 14:89.2(A). "Unnatural carnal copulation" is also defined as oral or anal sexual intercourse.

10. The Court need not consider this argument in reaching its decision. Plaintiffs draw attention to what they characterize as the State's history of bias toward gays and lesbians. But neither side seems to raise a question about whether one needs to establish animus to succeed in an Equal Protection challenge. And case literature is mixed. *Compare Personnel Admin. of Massachusetts v. Feeney,* 442 U.S. 256 (1979) *with Eisenstadt v. Baird,* 405 U.S. 438 (1972); *see also Stefanoff v. Hays County, Texas,* 154 F.3d 523 (5th Cir.1998).

11. Much of the Crime Against Nature statute has been held unconstitutional by the United States Supreme Court in *Lawrence v. Texas,* 539 U.S. 558 (2003). *Lawrence* does not speak to the solicitation of sex for money, and has little precedential force here.

nal copulation for compensation."[12] In so doing, Louisiana apparently became the first and only state in the nation to adopt a freestanding statute that specifically criminalizes offering or agreeing to engage in oral or anal sex for a fee in addition to its prostitution laws. While other states have general provisions criminalizing solicitation and prostitution-related offenses,[13] until recently Louisiana also singled out solicitation of oral and anal sex for money for harsher punishment and for sex offender registration....

To prove an Equal Protection violation ... the plaintiffs must show that they have been treated differently by the state from others similarly situated, and that there is no rational basis for the difference in treatment. They have done so as a matter of law. The plaintiffs contend that they have demonstrated a violation of the Equal Protection Clause: they observe that an examination of the two statutes reflects that they treat differently identically-situated individuals, because plaintiffs are required to register as sex offenders simply because they were convicted of Crime Against Nature by Solicitation, rather than solicitation of Prostitution (conduct chargeable by and covered under either statute). Plaintiffs draw the conclusion that the statutory classification drawn between individuals convicted of Crime Against Nature by Solicitation and those convicted of Prostitution is not rationally related to achieving any legitimate state interest.[23] The Court agrees.

The plaintiffs contend that their Equal Protection claim turns on the obvious situation that, because the Crime Against Nature by Solicitation and the solicitation provision of the Prostitution statute have identical elements and punish, as to them, identical conduct, the State cannot point to any constitutionally acceptable rationale for requiring those convicted of Crime Against Nature by Solicitation, but not Prostitution, to register as sex offenders. The plaintiffs correctly lean heavily on *Eisenstadt v. Baird,* 405 U.S. 438, 454 (1972), which they argue supports their assertion that the State cannot have a legitimate interest in imposing a sanction on one group of people and not another when the "evil, as perceived by the State, [is] identical." The Court finds that *Eisenstadt* supports their contentions and is binding here.

In *Eisenstadt,* the Supreme Court invalidated a Massachusetts law that criminalized the distribution of contraception to unmarried persons because of the different statutory treatment of married persons, who were allowed access to contraception. In so doing, the high court rejected various arguments that the government offered for treating these groups differently. The Court announced that "whatever the rights of the individual to access to contraceptives may be, the rights must be the same for the unmarried and the married alike." Those words resonate here. For example, the Supreme Court rejected the asserted public health purpose of the law, on the ground that such a purpose would apply equally to married people not subject to the restriction and, also, that any concern over the dangerousness of the contraceptives themselves was already addressed by federal and state public health regulations in place. In holding that criminally outlawing the distribution of contraceptives to unmarried persons but not the distribution to married persons violated the Equal Protection Clause, the Supreme Court explained: "the evil, as

---

12. The Crime Against Nature by Solicitation statute was adopted in 1982. The Prostitution statute was already in effect.

13. Louisiana's Prostitution statute outlaws the solicitation and commission of "indiscriminate sexual intercourse", including vaginal, oral, and anal intercourse, for compensation. Quite obviously, the scope of the Prostitution is broader — but it also encompasses all of the sex acts criminalized by the Crime Against Nature by Solicitation statute.

23. The parties concede that no fundamental right has been infringed, nor any suspect classification is involved; accordingly, the parties agree that the classification need only bear a rational relationship to some legitimate objective....

perceived by the State, would be identical, and the underinclusion would be invidious." *Eisenstadt* reaches far into this dispute and the State unconvincingly seeks to run from it.

The Court finds that the plaintiffs have demonstrated entitlement to judgment as a matter of law: First, the State has created two classifications of similarly (in fact, identical) situated individuals who were treated differently (only one class is subject to mandatory sex offender registration). Second, the classification has no rational relation to any legitimate government objective: there is no legitimating rationale in the record to justify targeting only those convicted of Crime Against Nature by Solicitation for mandatory sex offender registration. The defendants' arguments fail, as the similar ones did under *Eisenstadt*. The very same public health and moral purposes apply to both statutes....

[T]he defendants assert that requiring sex offender registration protects the public's safety, health, and welfare. They insist that conviction is an imperfect indicator of the underlying charge and, because Crime Against Nature by Solicitation is a lesser offense to which other registrable offenses can be pleaded down to, it is possible that prosecutors pleaded down "more heinous" solicitation charges (such as solicitation of persons under 17, human trafficking, and intentional exposure to the AIDS virus if the exposure occurred during the course of a commercial sex act). The Court has no duty to indulge such patent hypothetical speculation; no suggestion exists in the record that the state legislature's purpose for requiring those convicted of Crime Against Nature by Solicitation to register as sex offenders was anchored to a legislative desire that prosecutors plead down other registrable offenses. The defendants add that requiring individuals convicted of Crime Against Nature by Solicitation protects public morality. But the Court has already observed that public health and moral concerns apply equally to prostitution. The defendants fail to credibly serve up even one unique legitimating governmental interest that can rationally explain the registration requirement imposed on those convicted of Crime Against Nature by Solicitation. The Court is left with no other conclusion but that the relationship between the classification is so shallow as to render the distinction wholly arbitrary. *See City of Cleburne, Texas v. Cleburne Living Ctr.,* 473 U.S. 432, 446 (1985).

For all of these reasons, stripped of all political theater and with a concern solely to fidelity to the simple and clear injunction of the Fourteenth Amendment, the Court finds that the plaintiffs have demonstrated that the record, taken as a whole, leads to no rational basis for what the state legislature has done.[30]

....

Diaz v. Brewer

656 F.3d 1008 (9th Cir. 2011)

SCHROEDER, Circuit Judge:

....

In April of 2008, the State of Arizona administratively adopted amendments to Section 101 of Chapter 5 of Title 2 of the Arizona Administrative Code to offer access to health-

---

30. The Supreme Court has held, albeit in a factually distinguishable context, that imposing different restrictions on those who committed the same type of offense violates the Equal Protection Clause. *Skinner v. Okla. ex rel. Williamson,* 316 U.S. 535, 542 (1942) ("When the law lays an unequal hand on those who have committed intrinsically the same quality of offense ... it has made an invidious a discrimination as if it had selected a particular race or nationality for oppressive treatment"; "The equal protection clause would ... be a formula of empty words if such conspicuously artificial lines could be drawn.").

care benefits for qualified opposite-sex and same-sex domestic partners of state employees. Prior to 2008, when state employees chose to participate in the State's health insurance program, they only had the option to include their spouses and children within the defined parameters of the term "dependent." In 2008, the amendments expanded the definition of "dependent" to include qualified "domestic partners," who could be of either sex.

In November of 2008, however, the Arizona voters approved Proposition 102, also known as the *Marriage Protection Amendment,* which amended the Arizona Constitution to define marriage as between one man and one woman.... On September 4, 2009, the governor of Arizona signed House Bill 2013, which included a statutory provision, Ariz.Rev.Stat. § 38-651(O) ("Section O") that redefined "dependants" as "spouses," and thus would eliminate coverage for domestic partners....

After a number of adjustments not at issue here, the new definition of "dependent" was slated to take effect on January 1, 2011.

A group of gay and lesbian state employees ("Plaintiffs") filed a complaint ... seeking injunctive and declaratory relief to redress Section O's claimed violation of their equal protection and substantive due process rights under the Fourteenth Amendment to the U.S. Constitution....

In a careful order, the court considered each of the possible state interests the law might be said to further and ruled that the law and the record negated each of them. Although plaintiffs argued heightened scrutiny was required, the district court applied rational basis review, but noting that such review is more searching when a classification adversely affects unpopular groups. *Collins,* 727 F.Supp.2d at 804 (citing *Lawrence v. Texas,* 539 U.S. 558, 580 (2003) (O'Connor, J., concurring)). We do not need to decide whether heightened scrutiny might be required.

While the district court noted that Section O was not discriminatory on its face, because it affected both same-sex and different-sex couples, the court held that Section O had a discriminatory effect. This is because, under Arizona law, different-sex couples could retain their health coverage by marrying, but same-sex couples could not. Therefore, the district court granted plaintiffs' request for a preliminary injunction on equal protection grounds....

This appeal by the defendants followed....

The defendants ... contend that the district court's order impermissibly recognized a constitutional right to healthcare.... [T]his contention rests on a misunderstanding of the court's decision. The court held that the withholding of benefits for same-sex couples was a denial of equal protection. The state is correct in asserting that state employees and their families are not constitutionally entitled to health benefits. But when a state chooses to provide such benefits, it may not do so in an arbitrary or discriminatory manner that adversely affects particular groups that may be unpopular. The most instructive Supreme Court case involving arbitrary restriction of benefits for a particular group perceived as unpopular is *U.S. Department of Agriculture v. Moreno,* 413 U.S. 528 (1973). In that case, Plaintiffs challenged the constitutionality of an amendment to the Food Stamp Act of 1964, which redefined the term "household" to limit the program's eligible recipients to groups of related individuals. *Id.* at 529–30. While noting the "little legislative history" available on the amendment, the Court concluded that the legislation was aimed at groups that were unpopular. The "amendment was intended to prevent so-called 'hippies' and 'hippie communes' from participating in the food stamp program." *Id.* at 534.

In defending the amendment under rational basis review, the government contended that Congress might rationally have thought that the amendment would prevent fraud given the relative instability of households with unrelated individuals. *Id.* at 535. The Court rejected both justifications. The Court held that the "practical operation" of the amendment would allow the hippies, with means, who were allegedly abusing the program, to rearrange their housing status to retain eligibility, while excluding those who were financially unable to do so, i.e., "only those persons who are so desperately in need of aid that they cannot even afford to alter their living arrangements so as to retain their eligibility." *Id.* at 538. Those excluded were like the same-sex partners in this case who, because they cannot marry, are unable to alter their living arrangements to retain eligibility. The Court concluded that the "hippie" amendment's classification was "wholly without any rational basis." *Id.* We must reach the same conclusion.

Here, as in *Moreno,* the legislature amended a benefits program in order to limit eligibility. Since in this case eligibility was limited to married couples, different-sex couples wishing to retain their current family health benefits could alter their status—marry—to do so. The Arizona Constitution, however, prohibits same-sex couples from doing so. Thus, this case may present a more compelling scenario, since the plaintiffs in *Moreno* were prevented by financial circumstances from adjusting their status to gain eligibility, while same-sex couples in Arizona are prevented by operation of law.

Defendants nevertheless contend on appeal that this law is rationally related to the state's interests in cost savings and reducing administrative burdens. As the district court observed, however, the savings depend upon distinguishing between homosexual and heterosexual employees, similarly situated, and such a distinction cannot survive rational basis review. The Supreme Court in *Eisenstadt v. Baird,* 405 U.S. 438 (1972), was well aware of this principle when it quoted the eloquent words of Justice Robert H. Jackson, decrying the selective application of legislation to a small group:

> The framers of the Constitution knew, and we should not forget today, that there is no more effective practical guaranty against arbitrary and unreasonable government than to require that the principles of law which officials would impose upon a minority must be imposed generally. Conversely, nothing opens the door to arbitrary action so effectively as to allow those officials to pick and choose only a few to whom they will apply legislation and thus to escape the political retribution that might be visited upon them if larger numbers were affected. Courts can take no better measure to assure that laws will be just than to require that laws be equal in operation.

Eisenstadt, 405 U.S. at 454 (quoting *Ry. Express Agency v. New York,* 336 U.S. 106, 112–113 (1949) (Jackson, J., concurring)).

The state has also argued that the statute promotes marriage by eliminating benefits for domestic partners, but the plaintiffs negated that as a justification. The district court properly concluded that the denial of benefits to same-sex domestic partners cannot promote marriage, since such partners are ineligible to marry. On appeal, the state has not seriously advanced this justification.

In sum, the district court correctly recognized that barring the state of Arizona from discriminating against same-sex couples in its distribution of employee health benefits does not constitute the recognition of a new constitutional right to such benefits. Rather, it is consistent with long standing equal protection jurisprudence holding that "some objectives, such as 'a bare … desire to harm a politically unpopular group,' are not legitimate state interests." *Lawrence,* 539 U.S. at 580 (O'Connor, J., concurring) (quoting *Moreno,* 413 U.S. at 534) (alteration in the original); *see also City of Cleburne v. Cleburne Living Center, Inc.,* 473 U.S. 432, 447 (1985). Moreover, the district court properly rejected the state's claimed legislative justification because the record established that the statute was not rationally related to furthering such interests. Contrary to the state's assertions, the court did not place the burden on the state to prove a legitimate interest. After concluding that neither the law nor the record could sustain any of the interests the state suggested, the district court considered whether it could conceive of any additional interests Section O might further and concluded it could not. On appeal, the state does not suggest any interests it or the district court may have overlooked. The court ruled the plaintiffs had established a likelihood of success in showing the statute furthered no legitimate interest....

Notes and Questions

1. The *Limon* decision rather easily concludes that the law draws distinctions against homosexuals as a class, relying on the apparent rejection of the status-conduct distinction in the various opinions in *Romer* and *Lawrence*. Is that a fair reading of those opinions? Is the status-conduct distinction, which historically has proven to be of great importance so far as equal protection claims for sexual minorities are involved, moribund post-*Lawrence*?

In *Christian Legal Society Chapter of the University of California, Hastings College of the Law v. Martinez*, 130 S.Ct. 2971 (2010) — a case examined in greater detail in Chapter 6 — the Court appeared to expressly reject the status-conduct distinction:

> CLS contends that it does not exclude individuals because of sexual orientation, but rather "on the basis of a conjunction of conduct and the belief that the conduct is not wrong." Our decisions have declined to distinguish between status and conduct in this context. See *Lawrence v. Texas*, 539 U.S. 558, 575 (2003) ("When homosexual *conduct* is made criminal by the law of the State, that declaration in and of itself is an invitation to subject homosexual *persons* to discrimination" (emphasis added)); *id.*, at 583 (O'Connor, J., concurring in judgment) ("While it is true that the law applies only to conduct, the conduct targeted by this law is conduct that is closely correlated with being homosexual. Under such circumstances, [the] law is targeted at more than conduct. It is instead directed toward gay persons as a class.").

Id. at 2990.

2. Is *Limon* blurring the lines between equal protection and due process? The case was sent back to the Kansas Supreme Court for reconsideration of its earlier opinion upholding the statute after the U.S. Supreme Court decided *Lawrence*. Yet the Kansas Supreme Court, while relying on *Lawrence* heavily, decides the case on equal protection grounds. Or is it the U.S. Supreme Court itself that has blurred the lines between equal protection and due process?

3. The *Limon* court purports to apply rational basis review, and in so doing, raises concerns about the over- and under-inclusiveness of the law. Of course, under the *Beach Communications* form of rational basis review, even significant over- and under-inclusiveness is not cause for deeming a law unconstitutional. In what way — if at all — does the *Romer* form of "rational basis plus" review narrow the traditional rational basis fit requirement?

4. In *Jindal*, the court alludes to a claim that the statutory scheme may entail a form of sexual orientation discrimination, but it finds it unnecessary to reach that issue. Had the court directly addressed that issue, what would be the likely result? How, if at all, would the fact that prostitutes engaging in sex acts with persons of the opposite sex were *always* prosecuted under the Prostitution statute — even if the acts included oral or anal

sex—impact your analysis? Even in the absence of such data, could the statute still be viewed as a form of sexual orientation discrimination without regard to the actual enforcement practices?

In *State v. Baxley*, 656 So.2d 973 (La. 1995), the Louisiana Supreme Court rejected such a challenge to the statute, reasoning as follows:

> [W]e find no legislative classification on the face of the statute. To the contrary, the statute, on its face, is neutral. It applies equally to all individuals—male, female, heterosexual and homosexual. The statute punishes *conduct*—solicitation with the intent to engage in oral sex or anal sex for compensation. The statute does not single out gay men or lesbians for punishment....
>
> A statute, though facially neutral, may still be challenged as constitutionally infirm if the challenger can prove that the statute was enacted because of a discriminatory purpose. *Personnel Admin. of Massachusetts v. Feeney*, 442 U.S. 256, 272 (1979). "'Discriminatory purpose'... implies more than intent as volition or intent as awareness of the consequences.... It implies that the decisionmaker, in this case a state legislature, selected or reaffirmed a particular course of action at least in part 'because of,' not merely 'in spite of,' its adverse effects upon an identifiable group." *Id.* at 279. Disparate impact upon the identifiable group, while relevant, is not dispositive of this issue. That disparate impact must be traced to a discriminatory purpose to support a claim that the statute is unconstitutional under the equal protection clause. Given the presumption of the constitutionality of legislation which does not classify on its face, it is incumbent upon the challenger of the legislation to prove the discriminatory purpose. In the present case, the record is devoid of any evidence that the crime against nature statute was enacted for the purpose of discriminating against gay men and lesbians. Therefore, the statute is not constitutionally infirm on these grounds....
>
> Both statutes apply to heterosexuals and homosexuals equally. They simply punish two types of *conduct* differently. The prostitution statute punishes "indiscriminate sexual intercourse" while the crime against nature statute punishes "unnatural carnal copulation." The conduct punished by La.R.S. 14:89(A)(2) is not unique to gay men and lesbians. Heterosexuals can be, and are, convicted under this statute.

Id. at 978–79.

Does the status-conduct divide arguably make more sense in the context of criminal prosecutions for prostitution and solicitation than it does in other contexts, such as criminal prosecutions for consensual sodomy or laws banning same-sex marriage? Indeed, would it arguably make sense if the law only criminalized *same-sex* prostitution or sodomy? In other words, while the desire to engage in consensual sodomy or marry someone of the same sex may be intertwined with one's sexual orientation, engaging in sex acts for pay may be less connected with one's sexual orientation.

5. In *Jindal*, the significant overlap between the Prostitution and Crime Against Nature by Solicitation statutes made the court's task relatively simple. But what if that overlap were absent in the statutory scheme? In other words, suppose that the Prostitution statute *only* criminalized the solicitation of vaginal sex, while the Crime Against Nature by Solicitation statute only criminalized solicitation of oral and anal sex. Would the disposition of the case be as straightforward?

6. Of what significance was it that *Limon* and *Jindal* involved *criminal* sanctions? Are there reasons why a court might apply the rational basis test more robustly in that circumstance?

7. Note that the *Diaz* court speaks not of the law as distinguishing between heterosexual and homosexual individuals, but instead as distinguishing between opposite-sex and same-sex couples. Is that a better way to characterize laws such as those banning same-sex marriage or same-sex sodomy? To be sure, it sidesteps the *Davis v. Washington* question about whether these laws are intentionally discriminating on the basis of sexual orientation. On the other hand, if one seeks to argue for heightened scrutiny based on the *Frontiero* factors, which characterization is more likely to bear fruit? Moreover, is the focus on couples consistent with the Court's characterization of the equal protection right in *Adarand* as an individual rather than a group right?

Even accepting the *Diaz* court's focus on same-sex couples, is there still potentially a *Davis v. Washington* problem? The *Diaz* court notes that although the statute at issue is facially neutral (in that it harmed both same-sex and opposite-sex couples), it had a "discriminatory effect" on same-sex couples. Yet, under *Davis v. Washington* and its progeny, discriminatory effect, standing alone, is insufficient to state an equal protection clause claim. What, then, is the basis for treating this as discrimination against same-sex couples for equal protection purposes?

In answering this question, consider first whether it is fair to characterize the statute at issue as facially neutral. Can an argument be made that the statute—when considered in tandem with the 2008 Amendment to the Arizona Constitution—cannot realistically be viewed as facially neutral?

Assuming that it is nonetheless treated as facially neutral, and assuming that there is no "smoking gun" legislative history suggesting an intent to target either same-sex couples or gays and lesbians, can an analogy be drawn between this case and the *Gomillion* or *Yick Wo* scenarios discussed in *Village of Arlington Heights*? To what extent does the answer to that question turn on whether the court views the classification as same-sex couples versus opposite-sex couples instead of heterosexual versus homosexual individuals?

8. Of what significance is it in *Diaz* that same-sex couples initially received benefits, and that the benefits were subsequently taken away? Is that constitutionally significant? If not, does *Diaz* stand for the proposition that every state that bans same-sex marriage is constitutionally required to extend benefits to those in same-sex relationships?

4. True Rational Basis Review?

Equality Foundation of Greater Cincinnati, Inc. v. City of Cincinnati
128 F.3d 289 (6th Cir. 1997)

KRUPANSKY, Circuit Judge.

This court previously disposed of this cause in *Equality Foundation of Greater Cincinnati, Inc. v. City of Cincinnati ("Equality Foundation I"),* 54 F.3d 261 (6th Cir.1995), *vacated,* 518 U.S. 1001 (1996). It has been remanded for reconsideration by the United States Supreme Court consequent to its decision in *Romer v. Evans,* 517 U.S. 620 (1996).

In case numbers 94-3855/3973, defendant/appellant the City of Cincinnati ("the City"), and intervening defendants/appellants Equal Rights Not Special Rights ("ERNSR"), Mark Miller, Thomas E. Brinkman, Jr., and Albert Moore (collectively denominated "the defendants"), challenged the lower court's invalidation of an amendment to the City Charter of Cincinnati ("the Charter") for purported constitutional infirmities, and its permanent injunction restraining implementation of that measure. As a result of an initiative petition, the subject amendment had appeared on the November 2, 1993 local ballot as "Issue 3" and was enacted by 62% of the ballots cast, thereby becoming Article XII of the Charter (hereinafter "the Cincinnati Charter Amendment" or "Article XII"). Article XII read:

> *NO SPECIAL CLASS STATUS MAY BE GRANTED BASED UPON SEXUAL ORIENTATION, CONDUCT OR RELATIONSHIPS.*
>
> The City of Cincinnati and its various Boards and Commissions may not enact, adopt, enforce or administer any ordinance, regulation, rule or policy which provides that homosexual, lesbian, or bisexual orientation, status, conduct, or relationship constitutes, entitles, or otherwise provides a person with the basis to have any claim of minority or protected status, quota preference or other preferential treatment. This provision of the City Charter shall in all respects be self-executing. Any ordinance, regulation, rule or policy enacted before this amendment is adopted that violates the foregoing prohibition shall be null and void and of no force or effect.

Defendant ERNSR had drafted and initiated Issue 3 in response to the prior adoption by the Cincinnati City Council ("Council") of two city ordinances. On March 13, 1991, Council enacted Ordinance No. 79-1991, commonly known as the "Equal Employment Opportunity Ordinance," which mandated that the City could not discriminate in its own hiring practices on the basis of

> classification factors such as race, color, sex, handicap, religion, national or ethnic origin, age, *sexual orientation,* HIV status, Appalachian regional ancestry, and marital status (emphasis added).

Subsequently, Council on November 25, 1992 adopted Ordinance No. 490-1992 (commonly referred to as the "Human Rights Ordinance") which prohibited private discrimination in employment, housing, or public accommodation for reasons of sexual orientation. The opening paragraph of the Human Rights Ordinance expressed the intent of this legislation as:

> PROHIBITING unlawful discriminatory practices in the City of Cincinnati based on race, gender, age, color, religion, disability status, *sexual orientation,* marital status, or ethnic, national or Appalachian regional origin, in *employment, housing,* and *public accommodations* by ordaining Chapter 914, Cincinnati Municipal Code (emphases added).

The new law created a complaint and hearing procedure for seeking redress from purported sexual orientation discrimination, and exposed offenders to civil and criminal penalties....

Applying the Supreme Court's longstanding, traditional tripartite equal protection analysis, this court initially considered if the newly enacted Cincinnati Charter Amendment uniquely disabled any "suspect class" or "quasi-suspect class," or invaded any person's "fundamental right(s)." In so doing, it resolved that, under *Bowers v. Hardwick,* 478 U.S. 186 (1986) (directing that homosexuals possessed no fundamental substantive due process right to engage in homosexual conduct or constitutional protection against criminalization of that activity) and its progeny, homosexuals did not constitute either a "suspect class" or a "quasi-suspect class" because the conduct which defined them as homosexuals was constitutionally proscribable. This court further observed that any attempted identification of homosexuals by non-behavioral attributes could have no meaning, because the law could not successfully categorize persons "by subjective and unapparent characteristics such as innate desires, drives, and thoughts." Additionally, this court denied the existence of any all-inclusive fundamental constitutional right to "participate fully in the political process" which could be impaired by the Cincinnati Charter Amendment....

Accordingly, because the Cincinnati Charter Amendment targeted no suspect class or quasi-suspect class, and divested no one of any fundamental right, it was not subject to either form of heightened constitutional scrutiny (namely "strict scrutiny" or "intermediate scrutiny"). Rather, it should have been assessed under the most common and least rigorous equal protection norm (the "rational relationship" test), which directed that challenged legislation must stand if it rationally furthers any conceivable legitimate governmental interest. In *Equality Foundation I,* this court observed that the Cincinnati Charter Amendment advanced a variety of valid community interests, including enhanced associational liberty for its citizenry, conservation of public resources, and augmentation of individual autonomy imbedded in personal conscience and morality. Thus, Article XII satisfied minimal constitutional requirements....

On May 20, 1996, the United States Supreme Court decided *Romer v. Evans,* 517 U.S. 620 (1996)....

Although the United States Supreme Court in *Romer* affirmed the Colorado Supreme Court's decision striking down Colorado Amendment 2, it rejected the reasoning of that court which had posited the existence of a fundamental constitutional right to participate in the political process and then concluded that, under "strict scrutiny" review, Colorado Amendment 2 deprived homosexuals in Colorado of that fundamental right. By contrast, the United States Supreme Court did not assess Colorado Amendment 2 under "strict scrutiny" or "intermediate scrutiny" standards, but instead ultimately applied "rational relationship" strictures to that enactment and resolved that the Colorado state constitutional provision did not invade any fundamental right and did not target any suspect class or quasi-suspect class. In so ruling, the Court, *inter alia,* (1) reconfirmed the traditional tripartite equal protection assessment of legislative measures; and (2) resolved that the deferential "rational relationship" test, that declared the constitutional validity of a statute or ordinance if it rationally furthered any conceivable valid public interest, was the correct point of departure for the evaluation of laws which uniquely burdened the interests of homosexuals.

Nonetheless, the *Romer* Court invalidated Colorado Amendment 2 because it was deemed invidiously discriminatory and not rationally connected to the advancement of any legitimate state objective. Subsequently, on June 17, 1996, the Supreme Court granted the plaintiffs' petition for a writ of certiorari in the case *sub judice,* vacated this court's judgment in *Equality Foundation I,* and remanded the cause to this forum "for further consideration in light of *Romer v. Evans,* 517 U.S. 620 (1996)." *Equality Foundation of Greater Cincinnati v. City of Cincinnati,* 518 U.S. 1001 (1996). Upon remand, this court ordered rebriefing by the parties and full rehearing (conducted on March 19, 1997).

Although this circuit, in *Equality Foundation I,* and the Supreme Court, in *Romer,* each applied "rational relationship" scrutiny to a popularly enacted measure which negatively impacted the interests of homosexuals, this court concluded that the Cincinnati Charter Amendment withstood a constitutional equal protection attack, whereas the Supreme Court resolved that Colorado Amendment 2 did not. An exacting comparative analysis of *Romer* with the facts and circumstances of this case disclose that these contrary results were reached because the two cases involved substantially different enactments of entirely distinct scope and impact, which conceptually and analytically distinguished the constitutional posture of the two measures. As developed herein, the salient operative factors which motivated the *Romer* analysis and result were unique to that case and were not implicated in *Equality Foundation I.*

The *Romer* Court, prior to undertaking the conventional "rational relationship" equal protection inquiry, initially characterized Colorado Amendment 2 as facially objectionable because it removed municipally legislated special legal protection from gays and precluded the relegislation of special legal rights for them at every level of state government....

The Court additionally observed that Colorado Amendment 2 could be read to divest homosexuals of all state law government protection available to all other citizens....

However, the *Romer* Court did not rely upon that potential universally exclusive effect to invalidate the measure, but instead ultimately construed Colorado Amendment 2 only to remove and prohibit special legal rights for homosexuals under state law:

> If this consequence [withdrawal of all state law rights from homosexuals] follows from Amendment 2, as its broad language suggests, it would compound the constitutional difficulties the law creates. The state court did not decide whether the amendment had this effect, however, and neither do we.

The more restricted reach of the Cincinnati Charter Amendment, as compared to the actual and potential sweep of Colorado Amendment 2, is noteworthy. Colorado's Amendment 2 provided:

> **No Protected Status** Based on Homosexual, Lesbian, or Bisexual Orientation. Neither the State of Colorado, through any of its branches or departments, nor any of its agencies, political subdivisions, municipalities or school districts, shall enact, adopt or enforce any statute, regulation, ordinance or policy whereby homosexual, lesbian or bisexual orientation, conduct, practices or relationships shall constitute or otherwise be the basis of or entitle any person or class of persons to have or claim **any** minority status, quota preferences, **protected status** or **claim of discrimination**. This Section of the Constitution shall be in all respects self-executing.

Romer, 116 S.Ct. at 1623 (boldface added). By contrast, Cincinnati's Article XII pronounced:

> *NO SPECIAL CLASS STATUS MAY BE GRANTED BASED UPON SEXUAL ORIENTATION, CONDUCT OR RELATIONSHIPS.*

> The City of Cincinnati and its various Boards and Commissions may not enact, adopt, enforce or administer any ordinance, regulation, rule or policy which provides that homosexual, lesbian, or bisexual orientation, status, conduct, or relationship constitutes, entitles, or otherwise provides a person with the basis to have any claim of minority or protected status, quota preference **or other preferential treatment**. This provision of the City Charter shall in all respects be self-executing. Any ordinance, regulation, rule or policy enacted before this amendment is adopted that violates the foregoing prohibition shall be null and void and of no force or effect.

Equality Foundation I, 54 F.3d at 264 (boldface added).

Accordingly, the language of the Cincinnati Charter Amendment, read in its full context, merely prevented homosexuals, as homosexuals, from obtaining special privileges and preferences (such as affirmative action preferences or the legally sanctioned power to force employers, landlords, and merchants to transact business with them) from the City. In stark contrast, Colorado Amendment 2's far broader language could be construed to exclude homosexuals from the protection of every Colorado state law, including laws generally applicable to all other Coloradans, thus rendering gay people without recourse to any state authority at any level of government for any type of victimization or abuse which they might suffer by either private or public actors. *Romer,* 116 S.Ct. at 1625–27. Whereas Colorado Amendment 2 ominously threatened to reduce an entire segment of the state's population to the status of virtual non-citizens (or even non-persons) without legal rights under any and every type of state law, the Cincinnati Charter Amendment had no such sweeping and conscience-shocking effect, because (1) it applied only at the lowest (municipal) level of government and thus could not dispossess gay Cincinnatians of any rights derived from any higher level of state law and enforced by a superior apparatus of state government, and (2) its narrow, restrictive language could not be construed to deprive homosexuals of all legal protections even under municipal law, but instead eliminated only "special class status" and "preferential treatment" for gays as gays under Cincinnati ordinances and policies, leaving untouched the application, to gay citizens, of any and all legal rights generally accorded by the municipal government to all persons as persons.

At bottom, the Supreme Court in *Romer* found that a state constitutional proviso which deprived a politically unpopular minority, but no others, of the political ability to obtain special legislation at every level of state government, including within local jurisdictions having pro-gay rights majorities, with the only possible recourse available through surmounting the formidable political obstacle of securing a rescinding amendment to the state constitution, was simply so obviously and fundamentally inequitable, arbitrary, and oppressive that it literally violated basic equal protection values. Thus, the Supreme Court directed that the ordinary three-part equal protection query was rendered irrelevant. *See Romer,* 116 S.Ct. at 1627 (noting that Colorado Amendment 2 "defies" conventional equal protection analysis).

This "extra-conventional" application of equal protection principles can have no pertinence to the case *sub judice.* The low level of government at which Article XII becomes operative is significant because the opponents of that strictly local enactment need not undertake the monumental political task of procuring an amendment to the Ohio Constitution as a precondition to achievement of a desired change in the local law, but instead may either seek local repeal of the subject amendment through ordinary municipal political processes, or pursue relief from every higher level of Ohio government including but not limited to Hamilton County, state agencies, the Ohio legislature, or the voters themselves via a statewide initiative.

Moreover, unlike Colorado Amendment 2, which interfered with the expression of local community preferences in that state, the Cincinnati Charter Amendment constituted a direct expression of the local community will on a subject of direct consequences to the voters. Patently, a local measure adopted by direct franchise, designed in part to preserve community values and character, which does not impinge upon any fundamental right or the interests of any suspect or quasi-suspect class, carries a formidable presumption of legitimacy and is thus entitled to the highest degree of deference from the courts.

As the product of direct legislation by the people, a popularly enacted initiative or referendum occupies a special posture in this nation's constitutional tradition and jurisprudence. An expression of the popular will expressed by majority plebiscite, especially at the lowest level of government (which is the level of government closest to the people), must not be cavalierly disregarded.[9]

---

9. This court underscores that the constitutional concerns which anchor *Romer* are not implicated when previously adopted special legal protection at the local level is rescinded, and its rein-

In any event, *Romer* should not be construed to forbid local electorates the authority, via initiative, to instruct their elected city council representatives, or their elected or appointed municipal officers, to withhold special rights, privileges, and protections from homosexuals, or to prospectively remove the authority of such public representatives and officers to accord special rights, privileges, and protections to any non-suspect and non-quasi-suspect group. Such a reading would disenfranchise the voters of their most fundamental right which is the very foundation of the democratic form of government, even through the lowest (and most populist) organs and avenues of state government, to vote to override or preempt any policy or practice implemented or contemplated by their subordinate civil servants to bestow special rights, protections, and/or privileges upon a group of people who do not comprise a suspect or a quasi-suspect class and hence are not constitutionally entitled to any special favorable legal status. *Romer* dealt with a statewide constitutional amendment that denied homosexuals access to every level and instrumentality of state government as possible sources of special legal protection. *Romer* supplied no rationale for subjecting a purely local measure of modest scope, which simply refused special privileges under local law for a non-suspect and non-quasi-suspect group of citizens, to any equal protection assessment other than the traditional "rational relationship" test.

The *Romer* Court, after concluding that the sweeping effect of Colorado Amendment 2 literally offended basic equal protection standards without the necessity of performing the traditional three-tiered equal protection analysis, then mandated that, even under traditional equal protection strictures, Colorado Amendment 2 could not survive "rational relationship" review....

Accordingly, the *Romer* majority's rejection of rational relationship assessment hinged upon the wide breadth of Colorado Amendment 2, which deprived a politically unpopular minority of the opportunity to secure special rights at every level of state law. The uniqueness of Colorado Amendment 2's sweeping scope and effect differentiated it from the "ordinary case" in which a law adversely affects a discern[i]ble group in a relatively discrete manner and limited degree. In this context, the Court found that the rationales

---

statement precluded, irrespective of whether the prohibition is enacted by the voters directly, by the city's elected representatives, or by some other competent instrumentality such as a local department supervisor. Unlike a state government, which is composed of discrete and quasi-independent levels and entities such as cities, counties, and the general state government, a municipality is a unitary local political subdivision or unit comprised, fundamentally, of the territory and residents within its geographical boundaries. The citizens of the City of Cincinnati have instituted a charter form of government whereby day to day management is delegated to an elected city council, which in turn delegates specific tasks to various departments and agents. But the citizenry as a whole remains the ultimate authority in this discrete political subdivision, and it can, by charter amendment, alter the authority and powers it delegated to its council.

No logically sound construction of the components of a municipal polity could compartmentalize the City's citizens, elected representatives, and administrative departments into conceptually separate levels of local government, in the way that municipalities and other local entities are distinct levels of state government as compared to the state entity itself. Hence, it would be irrational to argue that the adoption of a gay rights regulation by a municipal department could not constitutionally be eliminated, and its reintroduction barred, by the city council or the city's voters, on the theory that it would be more difficult for proponents of gay rights to lobby the city council or the city's electorate than to lobby the pertinent department chief, because the city's voters, elected council, and departments and employees are all components, with varying degrees and spheres of authority, of the same (municipal) level of state government. Stated differently, it would be illogical to conclude that city council would be powerless to void a rule or regulation promulgated by one of the city's departments or department heads on the theory that it would be more difficult to lobby council for a change than the department administrators.

proffered by the state in support of Colorado Amendment 2 could not be justified, because the scope and effect of Colorado Amendment 2 "raise the inevitable inference that the disadvantage imposed is born of animosity toward the class of persons affected." Therefore, the *Romer* Court rejected the state's argument that Colorado Amendment 2, as drafted, rationally advanced its legitimate public interests in furthering "respect for other citizens' freedom of association, and in particular of landlords or employers who have personal or religious objections to homosexuality" and "conserving resources to fight discrimination against other groups." The Court found:

> The breadth of the Amendment is so far removed from these particular justifications that we find it impossible to credit them. We cannot say that Amendment 2 is directed to any identifiable legitimate purpose or discrete objective.

In essence, the high Court resolved that a state constitutional amendment which denied homosexuals any opportunity to attain state law protection, even from municipalities or other local entities within that state which desired to accord them special legal rights, could not be justified by the proffered public interests purportedly advanced by that state enactment, namely enhancement of the associational liberty of the state's residents and the conservation of public resources, because the citizens of the affected subordinate bodies politic had elected, or otherwise would elect, to forgo those identified public interests in favor of guaranteeing, through local governmental instrumentalities, nondiscriminatory treatment of the gay citizens of their local governmental units.

A state law which prevents local voters or their representatives, against their will, from granting special rights to gays, cannot be rationally justified by cost savings and associational liberties which the majority of citizens in those communities do not want. Clearly, the financial interests and associational liberties of the citizens of the state as a whole are not implicated if a municipality creates special legal protections for homosexuals applicable only within that jurisdiction and implements those protections solely via local governmental apparatuses. For this reason, the justifications proffered by Colorado for Colorado Amendment 2 insufficiently supported that provision, and implied that no reason other than a bare desire to harm homosexuals, rather than to advance the individual and collective interests of the majority of Colorado's citizens, motivated the state's voters to adopt Colorado Amendment 2.

In contradistinction, as evolved herein, the Cincinnati Charter Amendment constituted local legislation of purely local scope. As such, the City's voters had clear, actual, and direct individual and collective interests in that measure, and in the potential cost savings and other contingent benefits which could result from that local law. Beyond contradiction, passage of the Cincinnati Charter Amendment was not facially animated solely by an impermissible naked desire of a majority of the City's residents to injure an unpopular group of citizens, rather than to legally actualize their individual and collective interests and preferences. Clearly, the Cincinnati Charter Amendment implicated at least one issue of direct, actual, and practical importance to those who voted it into law, namely whether those voters would be legally compelled by municipal ordinances to expend their own public and private resources to guarantee and enforce nondiscrimination against gays in local commercial transactions and social intercourse.

Unquestionably, the Cincinnati Charter Amendment's removal of homosexuals from the ranks of persons protected by municipal antidiscrimination ordinances, and its preclusion of restoring that group to protected status, would eliminate and forestall the substantial public costs that accrue from the investigation and adjudication of sexual orientation discrimination complaints, which costs the City alone would otherwise bear because no coextensive protection exists under federal or state law. Moreover, the elimination of actionable special rights extended by city ordinances, and prevention of the reinstatement of such ordinances, would effectively advance the legitimate governmental interest of reducing the exposure of the City's residents to protracted and costly litigation by eliminating a municipally-created class of legal claims and charges, thus necessarily saving the City and its citizens, including property owners and employers, the costs of defending against such actions. Although the *Romer* Court never rejected associational liberty and the expression of community moral disapproval of homosexuality as rational bases supporting an enactment denying privileged treatment to homosexuals, it concluded that under the facts and circumstances of *Romer,* the state's argument in support of Colorado Amendment 2 was not credible. Because the valid interests of the Cincinnati electorate in conserving public and private financial resources is, standing alone, of sufficient weight to justify the City's Charter Amendment under a rational basis analysis, discussion of equally justifiable community interests, including the application of associational liberty and community moral disapproval of homosexuality, is unnecessary to sustain the Charter Amendment's viability.

In summary, the Cincinnati Charter Amendment did not disempower a group of citizens from attaining special protection at all levels of state government, but instead merely removed municipally enacted special protection from gays and lesbians. Unlike Colorado Amendment 2, the Cincinnati Charter Amendment cannot be characterized as an irrational measure fashioned only to harm an unpopular segment of the population in a sweeping and unjustifiable manner....

Citizens for Equal Protection v. Bruning

455 F.3d 859 (8th Cir. 2006)

LOKEN, Chief Judge.

In November 2000, Nebraska voters passed by a large majority a constitutional amendment, codified as Article I, § 29 of the Nebraska Constitution, providing:

> Only marriage between a man and a woman shall be valid or recognized in Nebraska. The uniting of two persons of the same sex in a civil union, domestic partnership, or other similar same-sex relationship shall not be valid or recognized in Nebraska.

Three public interest groups whose members include gay and lesbian citizens of Nebraska commenced this action against the Governor and the Attorney General in their official capacities seeking an order declaring that § 29 violates the Equal Protection Clause....

II. Equal Protection

....

Relying primarily on *Romer,* Appellees argue that § 29 violates the Equal Protection Clause because it raises an insurmountable political barrier to same-sex couples obtaining the many governmental and private sector benefits that are based upon a legally valid marriage relationship. Appellees do not assert a right to marriage or same-sex unions. Rather, they seek "a level playing field, an equal opportunity to convince the people's elected representatives that same-sex relationships deserve legal protection." The argument turns on the fact that § 29 is an amendment to the Nebraska Constitution. Unlike state-wide legislation restricting marriage to a man and a woman, a constitutional amendment deprives gays and lesbians of "equal footing in the political arena" because state and local government officials now lack the power to address issues of importance to this minority.[2]

The district court agreed, concluding "that Section 29 is indistinguishable from the Colorado constitutional amendment at issue in *Romer.*" In this part of its opinion, the district court purported to apply conventional, "rational-basis" equal protection analysis— "If a legislative classification or distinction neither burdens a fundamental right nor targets a suspect class, we will uphold it so long as it bears a rational relation to some legitimate [government] end." But the court in its discussion applied the same strict scrutiny analysis applied by the Colorado Supreme Court, but not by the United States Supreme Court, in *Romer.* Like the Colorado Court, the district court based its heightened scrutiny on Appellees' "fundamental right of access to the political process."

As Supreme Court decisions attest, the level of judicial scrutiny to be applied in determining the validity of state legislative and constitutional enactments under the Fourteenth Amendment is a subject of continuing debate and disagreement among the Justices. Though the most relevant precedents are murky, we conclude for a number of reasons that §29 should receive rational-basis review under the Equal Protection Clause, rather than a heightened level of judicial scrutiny.

While voting rights and apportionment cases establish the fundamental right to access the political process, it is not an absolute right. In a multi-tiered democracy, it is inevitable that interest groups will strive to make it more difficult for competing interest groups to achieve contrary legislative objectives. This can be done, for example, by having the state legislature repeal a local ordinance, or by having the electorate adopt a constitutional amendment barring future legislation. As the Supreme Court said in upholding a state constitutional amendment in *James v. Valtierra,* 402 U.S. 137, 141–43 (1971):

> Provisions for referendums demonstrate devotion to democracy, not to bias, discrimination, or prejudice. Nonetheless, appellees contend that Article XXXIV denies them equal protection because ... it hampers persons desiring public housing from achieving their objective when no such roadblock faces other groups seeking to influence other public decisions to their advantage.... Under any such holding, presumably a State would not be able to require referendums on any subject unless referendums were required on all, because they would always disadvantage some group. And this Court would be required to analyze governmental structures to determine whether a gubernatorial veto provision or a filibuster rule is likely to 'disadvantage' any of the diverse and shifting groups that make up the American people.

Similarly, Justice Scalia's discussion of the anti-polygamy provisions in many state constitutions illustrates the chaos that would result if all enactments that allegedly deprive a group of "equal" political access must survive the rigors of strict judicial scrutiny. *Romer,* 517 U.S. at 648–51 (Scalia, J., dissenting). No doubt for these reasons, although the majority opinion in *Romer* contained broad language condemning the Colorado enactment for making it "more difficult for one group of citizens than for all others to

---

2. Constitutional provisions that prohibit certain activities disadvantage the class of persons who wish to engage in the activity. For example, Article III, §24, of the Nebraska Constitution forbids "games of chance." Does §24 deny casino operators equal protection because they, unlike other businesses, must repeal a constitutional amendment to legalize the activities they wish to conduct? Note, too, that the equal-access theory urged by Appellees would likewise apply to a state statute that limits the policies and laws municipalities may adopt.

seek aid from the government," the Court's conclusion was that the enactment "lacks a rational relationship to legitimate state interests." That is the core standard of rational-basis review.

If sexual orientation, like race, were a "suspect classification" for purposes of the Equal Protection Clause, then Appellees' focus on the political burden erected by a constitutional amendment would find support in cases like *Reitman v. Mulkey,* 387 U.S. 369 (1967), *Hunter v. Erickson,* 393 U.S. 385 (1969), and *Washington v. Seattle Sch. Dist. No. 1,* 458 U.S. 457 (1982). But the Supreme Court has never ruled that sexual orientation is a suspect classification for equal protection purposes. The Court's general standard is that rational-basis review applies "where individuals in the group affected by a law have distinguishing characteristics relevant to interests the State has the authority to implement." *City of Cleburne v. Cleburne Living Center,* 473 U.S. 432, 441 (1985). As we will explain, that is the case here, and therefore Appellees are not entitled to strict scrutiny review on this ground.

Rational-basis review is highly deferential to the legislature or, in this case, to the electorate that directly adopted § 29 by the initiative process. "In areas of social and economic policy, a statutory classification that neither proceeds along suspect lines nor infringes fundamental constitutional rights must be upheld against equal protection challenge if there is any reasonably conceivable state of facts that could provide a rational-basis for the classification." *F.C.C. v. Beach Communications, Inc.,* 508 U.S. 307, 313 (1993). Thus, the classification created by § 29 and other laws defining marriage as the union between one man and one woman is afforded a "strong presumption of validity." *Heller v. Doe,* 509 U.S. 312, 319 (1993). The Equal Protection Clause "is not a license for courts to judge the wisdom, fairness, or logic of [the voters'] choices." *Beach Communications,* 508 U.S. at 313.

Our rational-basis review begins with an historical fact — the institution of marriage has always been, in our federal system, the predominant concern of state government. The Supreme Court long ago declared, and recently reaffirmed, that a State "has absolute right to prescribe the conditions upon which the marriage relation between its own citizens shall be created, and the causes for which it may be dissolved." *Pennoyer v. Neff,* 95 U.S. 714, 734–35 (1878), quoted in *Sosna v. Iowa,* 419 U.S. 393, 404 (1975). This necessarily includes the power to classify those persons who may validly marry. "Surely, for example, a State may legitimately say that no one can marry his or her sibling, that no one can marry who is not at least 14 years old, that no one can marry without first passing an examination for venereal disease, or that no one can marry who has a living husband or wife." *Zablocki v. Redhail,* 434 U.S. 374, 392 (1978) (Stewart, J., concurring). In this constitutional environment, rational-basis review must be particularly deferential.

The State argues that the many laws defining marriage as the union of one man and one woman and extending a variety of benefits to married couples are rationally related to the government interest in "steering procreation into marriage." By affording legal recognition and a basket of rights and benefits to married heterosexual couples, such laws "encourage procreation to take place within the socially recognized unit that is best situated for raising children." The State and its supporting amici cite a host of judicial decisions and secondary authorities recognizing and upholding this rationale. The argument is based in part on the traditional notion that two committed heterosexuals are the optimal partnership for raising children, which modern-day homosexual parents understandably decry. But it is also based on a "responsible procreation" theory that justifies conferring the inducements of marital recognition and benefits on opposite-sex couples, who can otherwise produce children by accident, but not on same-sex couples, who cannot. Whatever our personal views regarding this political and sociological debate, we cannot conclude that the State's justification "lacks a rational relationship to legitimate state interests." *Romer,* 517 U.S. at 632.

The district court rejected the State's justification as being "at once too broad and too narrow." But under rational-basis review, "Even if the classification ... is to some extent both underinclusive and overinclusive, and hence the line drawn ... imperfect, it is nevertheless the rule that ... perfection is by no means required." *Vance v. Bradley,* 440 U.S. 93 (1979). Legislatures are permitted to use generalizations so long as "the question is at least debatable." *Heller,* 509 U.S. at 326. The package of government benefits and restrictions that accompany the institution of formal marriage serve a variety of other purposes. The legislature — or the people through the initiative process — may rationally choose not to expand in wholesale fashion the groups entitled to those benefits. "We accept such imperfection because it is in turn rationally related to the secondary objective of legislative convenience." *Vance,* 440 U.S. at 109, 99 S.Ct. 939.

We likewise reject the district court's conclusion that the Colorado enactment at issue in *Romer* is indistinguishable from § 29. The Colorado enactment repealed all existing and barred all future preferential policies based on "orientation, conduct, practices, or relationships." The Supreme Court struck it down based upon this "unprecedented" scope. Here, § 29 limits the class of people who may validly enter into marriage and the legal equivalents to marriage emerging in other States — civil unions and domestic partnerships. This focus is not so broad as to render Nebraska's reasons for its enactment "inexplicable by anything but animus" towards same-sex couples.

Appellees argue that § 29 does not rationally advance this purported state interest because "prohibiting protection for gay people's relationships" does not steer procreation into marriage. This demonstrates, Appellees argue, that § 29's only purpose is to disadvantage gay people. But the argument disregards the expressed intent of traditional marriage laws — to encourage heterosexual couples to bear and raise children in committed marriage relationships. Appellees attempt to isolate § 29 from other state laws limiting marriage to heterosexual couples. But as we have explained, there is no fundamental right to be free of the political barrier a validly enacted constitutional amendment erects. If the many state laws limiting the persons who may marry are rationally related to a legitimate government interest, so is the reinforcing effect of § 29....

Problem 4-B: Affirmative Action for Sexual Minorities

Assume that a public medical school — concerned with its low percentage of openly gay, lesbian, bisexual, or transgendered students (hereinafter, "sexual minorities") — decides to establish an affirmative action program designed to address this concern. The rationale for the program is a belief that sexual minorities have special health concerns that are often misunderstood or undervalued by doctors, and that increasing the number of sexual minorities who are doctors will alleviate this problem, both because these individuals will naturally be more attuned to these concerns when they serve patients from their respective groups, and because they will raise these issues in their medical school classes, thus exposing other future doctors to these concerns.

Under the school's current admissions scheme, every applicant receives an index score ranging from 0–100 based on a composite of their grade-point average and MCAT score, with those with the highest index scores being admitted. Under the new affirmative action program, 15 points are added to the index score of applicants who are sexual minorities.

David Preston, a heterosexual who applied for and was denied admission in the year following the adoption of the new policy, decides to bring an equal protection challenge to the constitutionality of the affirmative action policy.

Assess the likelihood that David will succeed on his equal protection challenge. How, if at all, would your answer be impacted if there were a recording of the faculty meeting at which the policy was adopted in which one faculty member stated — immediately prior to the vote — that "the best thing about this policy is that I will no longer have to stare into a sea of straight people each time I walk into a classroom," followed by a mix of laughter and applause by some members of the faculty?

Irizarry v. Board of Education of the City of Chicago
251 F.3d 604 (7th Cir. 2001)

POSNER, Circuit Judge.

Although Milagros Irizarry has lived with the same man for more than two decades and they have two (now adult) children, they have never married. As an employee of the Chicago public school system, she receives health benefits but he does not, even though he is her "domestic partner" (the term for persons who are cohabiting with each other in a relationship similar to marriage), though he would if he were her husband. In July 1999, the Chicago Board of Education extended spousal health benefits to domestic partners — but only if the domestic partner was of the same sex as the employee, which excluded Irizarry's domestic partner, an exclusion that she contends is unconstitutional.

Besides being of the same sex, applicants for domestic-partner status must be unmarried, unrelated, at least 18 years old, and "each other's sole domestic partner, responsible for each other's common welfare." They must satisfy two of the following four additional conditions as well: that they have been living together for a year; that they jointly own their home; that they jointly own other property of specified kinds; that the domestic partner is the primary beneficiary named in the employee's will. Although the board's purpose in entitling domestic partners so defined to spousal benefits was to extend such benefits to homosexual employees, homosexual marriage not being recognized by Illinois, entitlement to the benefits does not require proof of sexual orientation.

Irizarry's domestic partner satisfies all the conditions for domestic-partner benefits except being of the same sex. She argues that the board's policy denies equal protection....

The board of education makes two arguments for treating homosexual couples differently from unmarried heterosexual couples. First, since homosexual marriage is not possible in Illinois (or anywhere else in the United States, though it is now possible in the Netherlands), and heterosexual marriage of course is, the recognition of a domestic-partnership surrogate is more important for homosexual than for heterosexual couples, who can obtain the benefits simply by marrying. Second, the board wants to attract homosexual teachers in order to provide support for homosexual students. According to its brief, the board "believes that lesbian and gay male school personnel who have a healthy acceptance of their own sexuality can act as role models and provide emotional support for lesbian and gay students.... They can support students who are questioning their sexual identities or who are feeling alienated due to their minority sexual orientation. They can also encourage all students to be tolerant and accepting of lesbians and gay males, and discourage violence directed at these groups."

This line of argument will shock many people even today; it was not that long ago when homosexual teachers were almost universally considered a public menace likely to seduce or recruit their students into homosexuality, then regarded with unmitigated horror. The plaintiff does not argue, however, that the Chicago Board of Education is irrational in having turned the traditional attitude toward homosexual teachers upside down. It is not for a federal court to decide whether a local government agency's policy of tolerating or even endorsing homosexuality is sound. Even if the judges consider such a policy morally repugnant—even dangerous—they may not interfere with it unless convinced that it lacks even minimum rationality, which is a permissive standard. It is a fact that some school children are homosexual, and the responsibility for dealing with that fact is lodged in the school authorities, and (if they are public schools) ultimately in the taxpaying public, rather than in the federal courts.

The efficacy of the policy may be doubted. Although it had been in effect for a year and a half when the appeal was argued, only nine employees out of some 45,000 had signed up for domestic-partner benefits and none of the nine indicated whether he or she was homosexual; they may not all have been, as we shall see—perhaps none were. Nor is there any indication that any of the nine are new employees attracted to teach in the Chicago public schools by the availability of health benefits for same-sex domestic partners. Maybe it's too early, though, to assess the efficacy of the policy. No matter; limited efficacy does not make the policy irrational—not even if we think limited efficacy evidence that the policy is more in the nature of a political gesture than a serious effort to improve the lot of homosexual students—if only because with limited efficacy comes limited cost. Because homosexuals are a small fraction of the population, because the continuing stigma of homosexuality discourages many of them from revealing their sexual orientation, and because nowadays a significant number of heterosexuals substitute cohabitation for marriage in response to the diminishing stigma of cohabitation, extending domestic-partner benefits to mixed-sex couples would greatly increase the expense of the program.

Irizarry argues that the child of an unmarried couple ought equally to be entitled to the mentoring and role-model benefits of having teachers who live in the same way the student's parents do. Cost considerations to one side, the argument collides with a nationwide policy in favor of marriage. True, it is no longer widely popular to try to pressure homosexuals to marry persons of the opposite sex. But so far as heterosexuals are concerned, the evidence that on average married couples live longer, are healthier, earn more, have lower rates of substance abuse and mental illness, are less likely to commit suicide, and report higher levels of happiness—that marriage civilizes young males, confers economies of scale and of joint consumption, minimizes sexually transmitted disease, and provides a stable and nourishing framework for child rearing—refutes any claim that policies designed to promote marriage are irrational. The Chicago Board of Education cannot be faulted, therefore, for not wishing to encourage heterosexual cohabitation; and, though we need not decide the point, the refusal to extend domestic-partner benefits to heterosexual cohabitators could be justified on the basis of the policy favoring marriage for heterosexuals quite apart from the reasons for wanting to extend the spousal fringe benefits to homosexual couples.

Of course, self-selection is important; people are more likely to marry who believe they have characteristics favorable to a long-term relationship. But the Chicago Board of Education would not be irrational (though it might be incorrect) in assigning some causal role to the relationship itself. Linda J. Waite, "Does Marriage Matter?" 32 *Demography* 483, 498–99 (1995), finds that cohabitants are much less likely than married couples to pool financial resources, more likely to assume that each partner is responsible for supporting himself or herself financially, more likely to spend free time separately, and less likely to agree on the future of the relationship. This makes both investment in the relationship and specialization with this partner much riskier than in marriage, and so reduces them. Whereas marriage connects individuals to other important social institutions, such as organized religion, cohabitation seems to distance them from these institutions.

Irizarry and her domestic partner may, given the unusual duration of their relationship, be an exception to generalizations about the benefits of marriage. We are not aware of an extensive scholarly literature comparing marriage to long-term cohabitation. This may be due to the fact that long-term cohabitation is rare — only ten percent of such relationships last for five years or more. But there is evidence that the widespread substitution of cohabitation for marriage in Sweden has given that country the highest rate of family dissolution and single parenting in the developed world. It is well known that divorce is harmful to children, and presumably the same is true for the dissolution of a cohabitation — and a cohabitation is more likely to dissolve than a marriage. True, Irizarry's cohabitation has not dissolved; but law and policy are based on the general rather than the idiosyncratic, as the Supreme Court noted with reference to other benefits tied to marital status in *Califano v. Jobst*, 434 U.S. 47, 53–54 (1977). Nor is it entirely clear that this couple ought to be considered an exception to the general concern with heterosexuals who choose to have a family outside of marriage. For when asked at argument why the couple had never married, Irizarry's counsel replied that he had asked his client that question and she had told him that "it just never came up." There may be good reasons why a particular couple would not marry even after producing children, but that the thought of marriage would not even occur to them is disquieting.

The Lambda Legal Defense and Education Fund has filed an amicus curiae brief surprisingly urging reversal — surprisingly because Lambda is an organization for the promotion of homosexual rights, and if it is the law that domestic-partnership benefits must be extended to heterosexual couples, the benefits are quite likely to be terminated for everyone lest the extension to heterosexual cohabitors impose excessive costs and invite criticism as encouraging heterosexual cohabitation and illegitimate births and discouraging marriage and legitimacy. But Lambda is concerned with the fact that state and national policy encourages (heterosexual) marriage in all sorts of ways that domestic-partner health benefits cannot begin to equalize. Lambda wants to knock marriage off its perch by requiring the board of education to treat unmarried heterosexual couples as well as it treats married ones, so that marriage will lose some of its luster.

This is further evidence of the essentially symbolic or political rather than practical significance of the board's policy. Lambda is not jeopardizing a substantial benefit for homosexuals because very few of them want or will seek the benefit. In any event, it would not be proper for judges to use the vague concept of "equal protection" to undermine marriage just because it is a heterosexual institution. The desire of the board of education to increase the employment of homosexual teachers is admittedly a striking manifestation of the sexual revolution that has characterized, some would say convulsed, the United States in the last forty years. The courts did not try to stop the revolution. On the contrary, they spurred it on, most pertinently to this case by their decisions removing legal disabilities of birth out of wedlock, disabilities that if they still existed might have induced Ms. Irizarry and the father of her children to marry in order to remove those disabilities from their children. Likewise relevant are cases such as *Stanley v. Illinois*, 405 U.S. 645 (1972), that confer constitutional rights on unwed fathers. But no court has gone so far as to deem marriage a suspect classification because government provides benefits to married persons that it withholds from cohabiting couples. That would be a bizarre extension of case law already criticized as having carried the courts well beyond the point at which the Constitution might be thought to provide guidance to social policy.

To the board's argument that it has extended spousal benefits to the domestic partners of homosexual employees because homosexual marriage is not a status available to its employees, Irizarry replies that the argument depends on the board's groundless decision to provide benefits to spouses, rather than domestic partners, of its employees. She says that all the board has to do to purge the constitutional violation is to condition all nonemployee fringe benefits on satisfaction of its domestic-partnership conditions other than that the domestic partner be of the same sex as the employee; and then the "discrimination" in favor of heterosexuals that the extension of spousal benefits to homosexual domestic partners was intended to erase will be eliminated without discrimination against heterosexual domestic partners. She points to Chicago's Human Rights Ordinance, which forbids discrimination on the basis of marital status. But the purpose, at least the primary purpose, of such a prohibition is surely not to dethrone marriage; it is to prevent discrimination against married women, who employers might think have divided loyalties. Such laws are pro-marriage, not anti- as the plaintiff suggests.

All other considerations to one side, the board reaps cost savings by basing dependent benefits on marital status—savings distinct from those discussed earlier that depend simply on the much smaller number of homosexuals than heterosexuals likely to seek or qualify for domestic-partner benefits. It is easier to determine whether the claimant is married to an employee than to determine whether the claimant satisfies the multiple criteria for domestic partnership. Earlier we took for granted that cost is an admissible consideration in evaluating the rationality of a classification; here we add that the cases so hold. And we do not understand the plaintiff to be arguing that the board of education must have anything more than a rational basis for its action in order to defeat the plaintiff's equal protection claim. Only when the plaintiff in an equal protection case is complaining of a form of discrimination that is suspect because historically it was irrational or invidious is there a heavier burden of justifying a difference in treatment than merely showing that it is rational. Heterosexuals cohabiting outside of marriage are not such a class. There is a history of disapproval of (nonmarital) cohabitation, and some states still criminalize it—as indeed Illinois did until 1990. But the disapproval is not necessarily irrational or invidious, given the benefits of marriage discussed earlier. It was rational for the board to refuse to extend domestic-partnership benefits to persons who can if they wish marry and by doing so spare the board from having to make a factual inquiry into the nature of their relationship.

The least rational feature of the board's policy, though not emphasized by the plaintiff, is that although[]domestic-partner benefits are confined to persons of the same sex, the partners need not be homosexual. They could be roommates who have lived together for a year and own some property jointly and for want of relatives are each other's "sole domestic-partner," and if so they would be entitled to domestic-partner benefits under the board of education's policy. To distinguish between roommates of the same and of different sexes, as the policy implicitly does, cannot be justified on the ground that the latter but not the former could marry each other!

So the policy does not make a very close fit between end and means. But it doesn't have to, provided there is a rational basis for the loose fit. This follows from our earlier point that cost is a rational basis for treating people differently. Economy is one of the principal reasons for using rules rather than standards to govern conduct. Rules single out one or a few facts from the welter of possibly relevant considerations and make that one or those few facts legally determinative, thus dispensing with inquiry into the other considerations. A standard that takes account of all relevant considerations will produce fewer arbitrary differences in outcome, but at a cost in uncertainty, administrative burden, and sometimes even—as here—in invading people's privacy. It is easy to see why the board of education does not want to put applicants to the proof of their sexual preference. That would be resented. The price of avoiding an inquiry that would be costly because it would be obnoxious is that a few roommates may end up with windfall benefits. We cannot say that the board is being irrational in deciding to pay that price rather than snoop into people's sex lives.

If the result is, as it may be, that none of the nine employees who have opted for domestic-partner benefits is homosexual (or at least that none is willing to acknowledge his homosexuality publicly, for that is not required by the board's policy though it would seem implicit in the board's desire to attract homosexuals who have "a healthy acceptance of their own sexuality"), this would lend a note of irony to the board's policy and would reinforce our earlier conjecture that the purpose is to make a statement rather than to confer actual monetary benefits. But "making a statement" is a common purpose of legislation and does not condemn it as irrational....

Notes and Questions

1. *Equality Foundation* and *Bruning* engage in what might be described as vertical and horizontal distinguishing of *Romer*, respectively. Thus, *Equality Foundation* focuses on the level of government at which the barrier to repealing undesirable legislation has been placed—municipal versus state—treating the former as less burdensome and thus constitutionally permissible. In contrast, *Bruning* focuses on the scope of the deprivation, treating the surgical elimination of a single right for gays and lesbians as less burdensome than the evident across-the-board denial of rights at issue in *Romer*.

Are the distinctions identified by *Equality Foundation* and *Bruning* artificial, or are they a sound application of the rational basis standard applied in *Romer*? In all events, are results such as these the likely consequence of the Court's unwillingness to explicitly apply heightened scrutiny in *Romer*? Do decisions such as these confirm the concerns raised by Justice Marshall in his opinion concurring in part and dissenting in part in *Cleburne*?

2. In assessing vertical distinctions of *Romer*, is there a difference in kind between legislation on the one hand and amendments to governing documents such as constitutions and city charters on the other? In other words, is it relevant that legislation can be reversed by lobbying the state legislature or city council, respectively, while constitutional and charter amendments require a vote of the public? In this regard, consider whether a state statute, enacted by the legislature, which preempted local anti-discrimination ordinances prohibiting discrimination on the basis of sexual orientation and gender identity would be unconstitutional under *Romer*. For an example of such legislation, *see* Nebraska LB 912 (Jan. 10, 2012).

3. In assessing the *Equality Foundation* court's effort to distinguish *Romer*, consider the following dissent from a petition to rehear the case *en banc*:

> In a pre-*Romer* decision, this court upheld Issue Three under rational basis review. Over the dissent of three justices, the Supreme Court granted certiorari and remanded the case for reconsideration in light of *Romer*.

On remand, the panel sought to distinguish *Romer* on a number of grounds, each of which ultimately had its genesis in the rationale proffered by the *dissenting* justices in the order remanding this case for further consideration. As a majority of the Supreme Court obviously did not share the views of the dissent, using the dissent's rationale is itself suspect. Moreover, the distinctions drawn by the dissent and later articulated by the panel appear to be either refuted by the facts or the principle of law announced in *Romer*.

The panel first began by noting that "the salient operative factors which motivated the *Romer* analysis and result were *unique* to that case and were not implicated in" this case. The panel acknowledged that the *Romer* Court struck down Amendment 2 on the narrowest reading advocated for the measure, *i.e.,* the withdrawal of special rights for homosexuals. The panel nevertheless opined that Amendment 2's true constitutional infirmity rested with the "ominous" possibility that it could be read broadly to withdraw from homosexuals the protection afforded to all of Colorado's citizens. Since the panel construed Issue Three to only divest homosexuals of special rights, it is allegedly distinguishable from Amendment 2. The panel's analysis appears faulty, however, because the Supreme Court expressly declined to decide the case based on such a possibility. ("If this consequence [the withholding of protection provided by statutes of general application] follows from Amendment 2, as its broad language suggests, it would compound the constitutional difficulties the law creates. The state court did not decide whether the amendment has this effect, however, *and neither need we.*" *Romer,* 116 S.Ct. at 1626 (emphasis added)).

The panel then noted that the Supreme Court struck down Amendment 2 because the only avenue through which homosexuals could seek redress after Amendment 2 was by "the formidable political obstacle of securing a rescinding amendment to the state constitution." Because homosexuals could "seek local repeal [of Issue Three] through ordinary municipal political processes," the panel declared Issue Three did not impose as onerous a burden as Amendment 2. This distinction is unpersuasive, however, given that the Supreme Court expressly declined to rest its holding on the political restructuring cases, such as *Hunter v. Erickson,* where such distinctions are normally used. Therefore, the fact that it is easier for a group to seek the repeal of a city charter amendment as opposed to a state constitutional amendment is of no consequence as far as the essential rationale of *Romer* is concerned.

The panel also stated that the Supreme Court employed an "extra-conventional" application of equal protection principles in *Romer* because Amendment 2 was passed by people living outside the municipalities that had passed anti-discrimination ordinances. It opined that since the voters in Colorado were not directly affected by the ordinances they sought to repeal through Amendment 2, no rational relationship to a legitimate state interest existed. The panel's hypothesis, while novel, ignores the facts in *Romer*. Amendment 2 not only invalidated city ordinances; it also rescinded a section of the state's insurance code, an executive order signed by the state's governor, and various anti-discrimination policies adopted by state run universities. Therefore, the citizens of Colorado were indeed directly affected by the measures they sought to repeal when they passed Amendment 2.

Finally, the panel makes the sweeping statement that "[i]n any event, *Romer* should not be construed to forbid local electorates the authority, via initiative, to instruct their elected ... representatives ... to withhold special rights." *Romer,* however, was decided on equal protection grounds, which applies to local as well as state governmental action. Therefore, the fact that Issue Three is a local as opposed to a state measure is of no controlling significance for purposes of the Equal Protection Clause. *See City of Cleburne v. Cleburne Living Ctr.,* 473 U.S. 432 (1985).

Whether or not we agree with the majority decision in *Romer,* we are of course obligated by law to give rulings of the Supreme Court full force and effect. We believe the panel decision in this case draws "distinctions without a difference" and fails to abide by the key ruling in *Romer* that "A law declaring that in general it shall be more difficult for one group of citizens than for all others to seek aid from the government is itself a denial of equal protection of the laws in the most literal sense."

Equal. Found. of Greater Cincinnati, Inc. v. City of Cincinnati, 1998 WL 101701, at *4–*5 (6th Cir. 1998) (Gilman, J., dissenting from denial of petition to rehear en banc).

4. The U.S. Supreme Court declined to grant certiorari to review *Equality Foundation* after the remand. Although the Court typically does not state its reasons for denying review, Justice Stevens, joined by Justices Souter and Ginsburg, wrote a brief opinion in which they stated as follows:

As I have pointed out on more than one occasion, the denial of a petition for a writ of certiorari is not a ruling on the merits. Sometimes such an order reflects nothing more than a conclusion that a particular case may not constitute an appropriate forum in which to decide a significant issue. In this case, the Sixth Circuit held that the city charter "merely removed municipally enacted special protection from gays and lesbians." This construction differs significantly, although perhaps not dispositively, from the reading advocated by the petitioners. They construe the charter as an enactment that "bars antidiscrimination protections only for gay, lesbian and bisexual citizens."

This Court does not normally make an independent examination of state-law questions that have been resolved by a court of appeals. Thus, the confusion over the proper construction of the city charter counsels against granting the petition for certiorari. The Court's action today should not be interpreted either as an independent construction of the charter or as an expression of its views about the underlying issues that the parties have debated at length.

Equal. Found. of Greater Cincinnati, Inc. v. City of Cincinnati, 525 U.S. 943 (1998).

5. Why did the *Irizarry* court consider cost savings and administrative burdens a justification for giving domestic partnership benefits to same-sex couples but not to opposite-sex couples, while the *Diaz* court rejected those rationales for allowing married opposite-sex couples but not unmarried same-sex couples to receive health benefits? Are they applying the same type of rational basis review? Or are there factual differences between the two scenarios that justify treating them differently?

6. As *Irizarry* demonstrates, the downside of rational basis scrutiny when you seek to challenge a law that discriminates against a class to which you belong has advantages when you seek to defend a law that discriminates in favor of the class to which you belong. As a general rule, is a traditionally disadvantaged group better served with rational basis, intermediate, or strict scrutiny? In answering this question, consider the fact that nearly all modern race-based equal protection cases have involved Caucasian plaintiffs

challenging affirmative action laws designed to benefit racial minorities, and that many of the sex-based equal protection cases have involved lawsuits brought by men challenging laws designed to benefit women as a class.

7. Where *race*-based affirmative action is involved, the U.S. Supreme Court has held that under strict scrutiny review, awarding extra "points" in the admissions process to racial minorities does not satisfy the narrow tailoring standard. *See Grutter v. Bollinger*, 539 U.S. 306, 334–35 (2003); *Gratz v. Bollinger*, 539 U.S. 244, 270–76 (2003). Thus, if strict scrutiny were applied to the facts of Problem 4-B, it would without question be struck down as unconstitutional. Would a similar outcome follow where intermediate or rational basis review is involved?

8. Assuming that the plaintiff in *Irizarry* (or in Problem 4-B) were to seek heightened scrutiny for discrimination on the basis of sexual orientation, how would they successfully invoke the *Frontiero* factors to establish heightened scrutiny?

9. The "fleeting rational basis plus" cases appear to be triggered by evidence of "a bare ... desire to harm a politically unpopular group." Can the "fleeting rational basis plus" standard be invoked by a member of a *majority* group? Thus, for example, even if sexual orientation is not subject to heightened scrutiny generally under the equal protection clause, if a law favoring gays and lesbians over heterosexuals appears to be motivated by animus, will the law be subject to heightened rational basis review?

Chapter 5

Due Process and Equal Protection in Tandem: Marriage, Parenting, and Public Employment

A. Introduction

Chapters 3 and 4 separately presented the U.S. Supreme Court's substantive due process and equal protection cases through *Lawrence* and *Romer*, respectively, as well as lower federal and state court decisions exploring the uncertain contours of those two decisions.

As a formal matter, due process and equal protection serve as independent bases for challenging the constitutionality of a law. A good example of this can be found in *Lawrence v. Texas*, where the defendants separately invoked equal protection and due process as independent reasons to challenge the statute criminalizing same-sex sodomy. There, Justice Kennedy's majority opinion decided the case on due process grounds, while Justice O'-Connor's concurring opinion decided it on equal protection grounds.

Yet as you also observed, the Court has often blurred the line between its equal protection and due process lines of cases, sometimes citing cases from one line of cases in a decision involving the other line of cases. Thus, for example, cases such as *Skinner v. Oklahoma* and *Eisenstadt v. Baird* were formally equal protection cases but later were subsumed within the Court's substantive due process line of cases. And the majority opinion in *Lawrence*, while grounding itself in due process, viewed *Romer*—an equal protection decision—as pertinent in deciding that the foundations of *Bowers*—a due process decision—had been eroded. And of course, the "reverse incorporation" cases blurred the line between the two by treating the Fifth Amendment's Due Process Clause as encompassing within its scope an "equal protection" guarantee.

The cases in this chapter take a closer look at constitutional challenges to restrictions on the rights of sexual minorities in three substantive areas in which those rights have most frequently been litigated in recent years. First, Section B examines the right of same-sex couples to marry. That is followed in Section C by a look at laws restricting the right of sexual minorities to parent, such as through bans on adoption. Finally, Section D examines challenges to laws restricting public employment opportunities for sexual minorities, specifically, the right to serve in the U.S. military.

In each of these three substantive areas, separate equal protection and due process claims are raised as bases for challenging the laws. As you read the decisions, consider the extent to which equal protection and due process are working separately and the extent to which they are working as a team.

B. Marriage

1. The Foundational Marriage Cases

One of the most litigated civil rights issues in recent decades has been over the right of same-sex couples to marry. The legal battle over bans on same-sex marriage has much in common with the legal battle over sodomy laws that culminated in the Court's decision in *Lawrence*. First, just as sodomy was at one point criminalized in every state in the United States, so for most of U.S. history, *no* state has permitted same-sex couples to marry. Moreover, both the sodomy laws and the restrictions on same-sex marriage are open to being challenged on both substantive due process as well as equal protection grounds, since they both arguably infringe upon a fundamental right and draw classifications based on sex and/or sexual orientation.

For much of U.S. history, however, legislatures have exercised plenary power over the rules of entry into and exit from marriage. Thus, as the Supreme Court indicated in *Maynard v. Hill*, 125 U.S. 190, 205 (1888):

> Marriage, as creating the most important relation in life, as having more to do with the morals and civilization of a people than any other institution, has always been subject to the control of the legislature. That body prescribes the age at which parties may contract to marry, the procedure or form essential to constitute marriage, the duties and obligations it creates, its effects upon the property rights of both, present and prospective, and the acts which may constitute grounds for its dissolution.

Not mentioned in *Maynard* is one of the more pernicious historical restrictions on entry into marriage: the race of the participants. For much of American history, states have not only banned, but criminalized, interracial marriage. Indeed, a few years after *Maynard*, the Supreme Court, in *Plessy v. Ferguson*, 163 U.S. 537, 545 (1896)—after upholding against an equal protection challenge a state law requiring "equal but separate" railway carriages for "white and colored" persons—noted in dicta that "[l]aws forbidding the intermarriage of the two races ... have been universally recognized as within the police power of the state."

In addition, a few years before *Maynard*, the U.S. Supreme Court upheld against an equal protection challenge a pair of statutes that punished interracial fornication and adultery more severely than fornication and adultery between people of the same race. In *Pace v. Alabama*, 106 U.S. 583, 585 (1883), the Court reasoned that such a statutory scheme did not actually discriminate at all on the basis of race:

> The defect in the argument of counsel consists in his assumption that any discrimination is made by the laws of Alabama.... The one prescribes, generally, a punishment for an offense committed between persons of different sexes; the other prescribes a punishment for an offense which can only be committed where the two sexes are of different races. There is in neither section any discrimination against either race. Section 4184 equally includes the offense when the persons of the two sexes are both white and when they are both black. Section 4189 applies the same punishment to both offenders, the white and the black.... Whatever discrimination is made in the punishment prescribed in the two sections is directed against the offense designated and not against the person of any particular color or race. The punishment of each offending person, whether white or black, is the same.

Thus, together, *Maynard*, *Plessy*, and *Pace* provided slim hope to those seeking to challenge the constitutionality of laws prohibiting interracial marriage.

Yet as the twentieth century progressed, a number of cases were decided that provided support for challenging such laws both on the grounds that they infringed upon a fundamental right and because they denied equal protection.

First, in *Meyer v. Nebraska*, 262 U.S. 390, 399 (1923), the Court stated that the Fourteenth Amendment's Due Process Clause guaranteed "the right of the individual ... to marry." Then, in *Skinner v. Oklahoma*, 316 U.S. 535, 541 (1942), the Court — in considering an Equal Protection Clause challenge to a law requiring the forced sterilization of those convicted of certain crimes — referred to "[m]arriage and procreation" as "fundamental," and applied strict scrutiny to the law because it infringed on the right to procreate.

Then, in 1954, the U.S. Supreme Court held that segregated schools violated the Equal Protection Clause, concluding that "in the field of public education the doctrine of 'separate but equal' has no place." *Brown v. Board of Education*, 347 U.S. 483, 495 (1954). The following year, Virginia's high court distinguished *Brown* in a case challenging the constitutionality of that state's prohibition on interracial marriage, *see Naim v. Naim*, 87 S.E.2d 749 (Va. 1955). The U.S. Supreme Court initially signaled that the decision might be incorrect and vacated it, *Naim v. Naim*, 350 U.S. 891 (1955), but ultimately let the decision stand and opted not to review it, *Naim v. Naim*, 350 U.S. 985 (1956).

Eight years later, the Court struck down on equal protection grounds a law similar to the Alabama law it upheld in *Pace*. In *McLaughlin v. State of Florida*, 379 U.S. 184 (1964), the Court struck down a Florida law that criminalized only interracial cohabitation. In so doing, the Court stated that "*Pace* represents a limited view of the Equal Protection Clause which has not withstood analysis in the subsequent decisions of this Court" and that "[j]udicial inquiry under the Equal Protection Clause ... does not end with a showing of equal application among the members of the class defined by the legislation." *Id.* at 188, 191. Applying strict scrutiny, it struck the statute down, while making clear it was not reaching "the question of the validity of the State's prohibition against interracial marriage." *Id.* at 195.

The next case, decided three years after *McLaughlin*, provided the Court with another opportunity to assess the constitutionality of Virginia's ban on interracial marriage.

Loving v. Virginia
388 U.S. 1 (1967)

Mr. Chief Justice WARREN delivered the opinion of the Court.

This case presents a constitutional question never addressed by this Court: whether a statutory scheme adopted by the State of Virginia to prevent marriages between persons solely on the basis of racial classifications violates the Equal Protection and Due Process Clauses of the Fourteenth Amendment. For reasons which seem to us to reflect the central meaning of those constitutional commands, we conclude that these statutes cannot stand consistently with the Fourteenth Amendment.

In June 1958, two residents of Virginia, Mildred Jeter, a Negro woman, and Richard Loving, a white man, were married in the District of Columbia pursuant to its laws. Shortly after their marriage, the Lovings returned to Virginia and established their marital abode in Caroline County. At the October Term, 1958, of the Circuit Court of Caroline County, a grand jury issued an indictment charging the Lovings with violating Virginia's ban on interracial marriages. On January 6, 1959, the Lovings pleaded guilty to the charge and were sentenced to one year in jail; however, the trial judge suspended the sentence for a period of 25 years on the condition that the Lovings leave the State and not return to Virginia together for 25 years. He stated in an opinion that:

> "Almighty God created the races white, black, yellow, malay and red, and he placed them on separate continents. And but for the interference with his arrangement there would be no cause for such marriages. The fact that he separated the races shows that he did not intend for the races to mix."

After their convictions, the Lovings took up residence in the District of Columbia. On November 6, 1963, they filed a motion in the state trial court to vacate the judgment and set aside the sentence on the ground that the statutes which they had violated were repugnant to the Fourteenth Amendment. The motion not having been decided by October 28, 1964, the Lovings instituted a class action in the United States District Court for the Eastern District of Virginia requesting that a three-judge court be convened to declare the Virginia antimiscegenation statutes unconstitutional and to enjoin state officials from enforcing their convictions. On January 22, 1965, the state trial judge denied the motion to vacate the sentences, and the Lovings perfected an appeal to the Supreme Court of Appeals of Virginia. On February 11, 1965, the three-judge District Court continued the case to allow the Lovings to present their constitutional claims to the highest state court.

The Supreme Court of Appeals upheld the constitutionality of the antimiscegenation statutes and, after modifying the sentence, affirmed the convictions. The Lovings appealed this decision, and we noted probable jurisdiction on December 12, 1966.

The two statutes under which appellants were convicted and sentenced are part of a comprehensive statutory scheme aimed at prohibiting and punishing interracial marriages. The Lovings were convicted of violating § 20-58 of the Virginia Code:

> "*Leaving State to evade law.* — If any white person and colored person shall go out of this State, for the purpose of being married, and with the intention of returning, and be married out of it, and afterwards return to and reside in it, cohabiting as man and wife, they shall be punished as provided in § 20-59, and the marriage shall be governed by the same law as if it had been solemnized in this State. The fact of their cohabitation here as man and wife shall be evidence of their marriage."

Section 20-59, which defines the penalty for miscegenation, provides:

> "*Punishment for marriage.* — If any white person intermarry with a colored person, or any colored person intermarry with a white person, he shall be guilty of a felony and shall be punished by confinement in the penitentiary for not less than one nor more than five years."

Other central provisions in the Virginia statutory scheme are § 20-57, which automatically voids all marriages between "a white person and a colored person" without any judicial proceeding, and §§ 20-54 and 1-14 which, respectively, define "white persons" and "colored persons and Indians" for purposes of the statutory prohibitions.[4] The Lovings have

---

4. Section 20-54 of the Virginia Code provides:

"*Intermarriage prohibited; meaning of term 'white persons.'* — It shall hereafter be unlawful for any white person in this State to marry any save a white person, or a person with no other admixture of blood than white and American Indian. For the purpose of this chapter, the term 'white person' shall apply only to such person as has no trace whatever of any blood other than Caucasian; but persons who have one-sixteenth or less of the blood of the American Indian and have no other non-Caucasic blood shall be deemed to be white per-

never disputed in the course of this litigation that Mrs. Loving is a "colored person" or that Mr. Loving is a "white person" within the meanings given those terms by the Virginia statutes.

Virginia is now one of 16 States which prohibit and punish marriages on the basis of racial classifications. Penalties for miscegenation arose as an incident to slavery and have been common in Virginia since the colonial period. The present statutory scheme dates from the adoption of the Racial Integrity Act of 1924, passed during the period of extreme nativism which followed the end of the First World War. The central features of this Act, and current Virginia law, are the absolute prohibition of a "white person" marrying other than another "white person," a prohibition against issuing marriage licenses until the issuing official is satisfied that the applicants' statements as to their race are correct, certificates of "racial composition" to be kept by both local and state registrars, and the carrying forward of earlier prohibitions against racial intermarriage.

I.

In upholding the constitutionality of these provisions in the decision below, the Supreme Court of Appeals of Virginia referred to its 1955 decision in Naim v. Naim, as stating the reasons supporting the validity of these laws. In *Naim*, the state court concluded that the State's legitimate purposes were "to preserve the racial integrity of its citizens," and to prevent "the corruption of blood," "a mongrel breed of citizens," and "the obliteration of racial pride," obviously an endorsement of the doctrine of White Supremacy. The court also reasoned that marriage has traditionally been subject to state regulation without federal intervention, and, consequently, the regulation of marriage should be left to exclusive state control by the Tenth Amendment.

While the state court is no doubt correct in asserting that marriage is a social relation subject to the State's police power, Maynard v. Hill, 125 U.S. 190 (1888), the State does not contend in its argument before this Court that its powers to regulate marriage are unlimited notwithstanding the commands of the Fourteenth Amendment. Nor could it do so in light of Meyer v. State of Nebraska, 262 U.S. 390 (1923), and Skinner v. State of Oklahoma, 316 U.S. 535 (1942). Instead, the State argues that the meaning of the Equal Protection Clause, as illuminated by the statements of the Framers, is only that state penal laws containing an interracial element as part of the definition of the offense must apply equally to whites and Negroes in the sense that members of each race are punished to the same degree. Thus, the State contends that, because its miscegenation statutes punish equally both the white and the Negro participants in an interracial marriage, these statutes, despite their reliance on racial classifications do not constitute an invidious discrimination based upon race. The second argument advanced by the State assumes the validity

---

sons. All laws heretofore passed and now in effect regarding the intermarriage of white and colored persons shall apply to marriages prohibited by this chapter."
The exception for persons with less than one-sixteenth "of the blood of the American Indian" is apparently accounted for, in the words of a tract issued by the Registrar of the State Bureau of Vital Statistics, by "the desire of all to recognize as an integral and honored part of the white race the descendants of John Rolfe and Pocahontas * * *."
Section 1-14 of the Virginia Code provides:
  ["]*Colored persons and Indians defined.* — Every person in whom there is ascertainable any Negro blood shall be deemed and taken to be a colored person, and every person not a colored person having one fourth or more of American Indian blood shall be deemed an American Indian; except that members of Indian tribes existing in this Commonwealth having one fourth or more of Indian blood and less than one sixteenth of Negro blood shall be deemed tribal Indians."

of its equal application theory. The argument is that, if the Equal Protection Clause does not outlaw miscegenation statutes because of their reliance on racial classifications, the question of constitutionality would thus become whether there was any rational basis for a State to treat interracial marriages differently from other marriages. On this question, the State argues, the scientific evidence is substantially in doubt and, consequently, this Court should defer to the wisdom of the state legislature in adopting its policy of discouraging interracial marriages.

Because we reject the notion that the mere "equal application" of a statute containing racial classifications is enough to remove the classifications from the Fourteenth Amendment's proscription of all invidious racial discriminations, we do not accept the State's contention that these statutes should be upheld if there is any possible basis for concluding that they serve a rational purpose. The mere fact of equal application does not mean that our analysis of these statutes should follow the approach we have taken in cases involving no racial discrimination where the Equal Protection Clause has been arrayed against a statute discriminating between the kinds of advertising which may be displayed on trucks in New York City, Railway Express Agency, Inc. v. People of State of New York, 336 U.S. 106 (1949), or an exemption in Ohio's ad valorem tax for merchandise owned by a non-resident in a storage warehouse, Allied Stores of Ohio, Inc. v. Bowers, 358 U.S. 522 (1959). In these cases, involving distinctions not drawn according to race, the Court has merely asked whether there is any rational foundation for the discriminations, and has deferred to the wisdom of the state legislatures. In the case at bar, however, we deal with statutes containing racial classifications, and the fact of equal application does not immunize the statute from the very heavy burden of justification which the Fourteenth Amendment has traditionally required of state statutes drawn according to race.

The State argues that statements in the Thirty-ninth Congress about the time of the passage of the Fourteenth Amendment indicate that the Framers did not intend the Amendment to make unconstitutional state miscegenation laws. Many of the statements alluded to by the State concern the debates over the Freedmen's Bureau Bill, which President Johnson vetoed, and the Civil Rights Act of 1866, 14 Stat. 27, enacted over his veto. While these statements have some relevance to the intention of Congress in submitting the Fourteenth Amendment, it must be understood that they pertained to the passage of specific statutes and not to the broader, organic purpose of a constitutional amendment. As for the various statements directly concerning the Fourteenth Amendment, we have said in connection with a related problem, that although these historical sources "cast some light" they are not sufficient to resolve the problem; "[a]t best, they are inconclusive. The most avid proponents of the post-War Amendments undoubtedly intended them to remove all legal distinctions among 'all persons born or naturalized in the United States.' Their opponents, just as certainly, were antagonistic to both the letter and the spirit of the Amendments and wished them to have the most limited effect." Brown v. Board of Education of Topeka, 347 U.S. 483, 489 (1954). See also Strauder v. State of West Virginia, 100 U.S. 303, 310 (1880). We have rejected the proposition that the debates in the Thirty-ninth Congress or in the state legislatures which ratified the Fourteenth Amendment supported the theory advanced by the State, that the requirement of equal protection of the laws is satisfied by penal laws defining offenses based on racial classifications so long as white and Negro participants in the offense were similarly punished. McLaughlin v. State of Florida, 379 U.S. 184 (1964).

The State finds support for its "equal application" theory in the decision of the Court in Pace v. State of Alabama, 106 U.S. 583 (1883). In that case, the Court upheld a conviction under an Alabama statute forbidding adultery or fornication between a white person and a Negro which imposed a greater penalty than that of a statute proscribing similar conduct by members of the same race. The Court reasoned that the statute could not be said to discriminate against Negroes because the punishment for each participant in the offense was the same. However, as recently as the 1964 Term, in rejecting the reasoning of that case, we stated "*Pace* represents a limited view of the Equal Protection Clause which has not withstood analysis in the subsequent decisions of this Court." McLaughlin v. Florida, supra, 379 U.S. at 188. As we there demonstrated, the Equal Protection Clause requires the consideration of whether the classifications drawn by any statute constitute an arbitrary and invidious discrimination. The clear and central purpose of the Fourteenth Amendment was to eliminate all official state sources of invidious racial discrimination in the States.

There can be no question but that Virginia's miscegenation statutes rest solely upon distinctions drawn according to race. The statutes proscribe generally accepted conduct if engaged in by members of different races. Over the years, this Court has consistently repudiated "[d]istinctions between citizens solely because of their ancestry" as being "odious to a free people whose institutions are founded upon the doctrine of equality." Hirabayashi v. United States, 320 U.S. 81, 100 (1943). At the very least, the Equal Protection Clause demands that racial classifications, especially suspect in criminal statutes, be subjected to the "most rigid scrutiny," Korematsu v. United States, 323 U.S. 214, 216 (1944), and, if they are ever to be upheld, they must be shown to be necessary to the accomplishment of some permissible state objective, independent of the racial discrimination which it was the object of the Fourteenth Amendment to eliminate. Indeed, two members of this Court have already stated that they "cannot conceive of a valid legislative purpose * * * which makes the color of a person's skin the test of whether his conduct is a criminal offense." McLaughlin v. Florida, supra, 379 U.S. at 198 (Stewart, J., joined by Douglas, J., concurring).

There is patently no legitimate overriding purpose independent of invidious racial discrimination which justifies this classification. The fact that Virginia prohibits only interracial marriages involving white persons demonstrates that the racial classifications must stand on their own justification, as measures designed to maintain White Supremacy.[11] We have consistently denied the constitutionality of measures which restrict the rights of citizens on account of race. There can be no doubt that restricting the freedom to marry solely because of racial classifications violates the central meaning of the Equal Protection Clause.

II.

These statutes also deprive the Lovings of liberty without due process of law in violation of the Due Process Clause of the Fourteenth Amendment. The freedom to marry has long been recognized as one of the vital personal rights essential to the orderly pursuit of happiness by free men.

Marriage is one of the "basic civil rights of man," fundamental to our very existence and survival. Skinner v. State of Oklahoma, 316 U.S. 535, 541 (1942). See also Maynard

---

11. Appellants point out that the State's concern in these statutes, as expressed in the words of the 1924 Act's title, "An Act to Preserve Racial Integrity," extends only to the integrity of the white race. While Virginia prohibits whites from marrying any nonwhite (subject to the exception for the descendants of Pocahontas), Negroes, Orientals, and any other racial class may intermarry without statutory interference. Appellants contend that this distinction renders Virginia's miscegenation statutes arbitrary and unreasonable even assuming the constitutional validity of an official purpose to preserve "racial integrity." We need not reach this contention because we find the racial classifications in these statutes repugnant to the Fourteenth Amendment, even assuming an even-handed state purpose to protect the "integrity" of all races.

v. Hill, 125 U.S. 190 (1888). To deny this fundamental freedom on so unsupportable a basis as the racial classifications embodied in these statutes, classifications so directly subversive of the principle of equality at the heart of the Fourteenth Amendment, is surely to deprive all the State's citizens of liberty without due process of law. The Fourteenth Amendment requires that the freedom of choice to marry not be restricted by invidious racial discriminations. Under our Constitution, the freedom to marry or not marry, a person of another race resides with the individual and cannot be infringed by the State.

These convictions must be reversed. It is so ordered.

Reversed.

Mr. Justice STEWART, concurring.

I have previously expressed the belief that "it is simply not possible for a state law to be valid under our Constitution which makes the criminality of an act depend upon the race of the actor." McLaughlin v. State of Florida, 379 U.S. 184, 198 (concurring opinion). Because I adhere to that belief, I concur in the judgment of the Court.

Notes and Questions

1. At issue in *Loving* is a statute that imposes *criminal* sanctions for those who enter into interracial marriages. How critical is the imposition of criminal sanctions to the decision? The Court does note that such racial classifications are "especially suspect in criminal statutes." *Loving*, 388 U.S. at 11. Moreover, *McLaughlin v. Florida*, 379 U.S. 184, 192 (1964), in striking down Florida's interracial cohabitation statute, noted that "[w]e deal here with a racial classification embodied in a criminal statute. In this context, where the power of the State weighs most heavily upon the individual or the group, we must be especially sensitive to the policies of the Equal Protection Clause." Thus, if seeking to invoke *Loving* as a basis to strike down modern-day bans on same-sex marriage, is it relevant that those laws do not impose criminal sanctions on people who enter into same-sex marriages, but only refuse to recognize them?

Setting the specific issue of marriage to one side, note the parallels between the criminalization of interracial relationships and that of same-sex relationships: just as the sodomy laws were used historically to criminalize the latter, so the marriage, fornication, and adultery laws were used historically to criminalize the former.

2. After rejecting the "equal application" theory of *Pace*, the *Loving* Court proceeds to hold the antimiscegenation statute unconstitutional on equal protection grounds, applying strict scrutiny because the classification is race-based. As seen in Chapter 4, most courts have rejected heightened scrutiny for classifications based on sexual orientation. However, does *Loving*'s rejection of *Pace*, coupled with heightened scrutiny for *sex*-based classifications, provide support for applying at least intermediate scrutiny to laws banning same-sex marriage?

3. In the alternative, the *Loving* Court finds the antimiscegenation statute to be constitutionally infirm because it infringes upon a "fundamental" right. Is the Court saying that it is a "due process" fundamental right, an "equal protection" fundamental right, or both, and what is the significance of holding it to be one or the other? Moreover, what does the Court mean by "marriage"? Does the Court mean merely that the state must provide couples with official recognition of their relationships, or must the state also use the term "marriage" in recognizing those relationships?

Moreover, what, exactly, does the Court mean by the right to marry? After all, Virginia law did not say that Mildred Jeter and Richard Loving could not get married to *someone*; it was just that they could not get married to someone of the opposite race. Thus, does the Court mean the right to marry the person of your choosing? What if someone chooses to marry a person to whom they are related? A child? Someone who is already married to another person? Someone of the same sex? How would laws restricting any of these types of marriages fare under strict scrutiny?

4. One of the justifications given by the state in *Loving* was the preservation of racial integrity. The Court, however, notes that it is only the integrity of the white race that the statute actually protects, and thus describes the statute as being "designed to maintain White Supremacy." *Loving*, 388 U.S. at 11. How important is that finding to the Court's conclusion? What if the statute had, in fact, been more even-handed? In footnote 11, the Court states that "[w]e need not reach this contention because we find the racial classifications in these statutes repugnant to the Fourteenth Amendment, even assuming an even-handed state purpose to protect the 'integrity' of all races." What does the Court mean by this statement?

stus.com

Zablocki v. Redhail
434 U.S. 374 (1978)

Mr. Justice MARSHALL delivered the opinion of the Court.

At issue in this case is the constitutionality of a Wisconsin statute, Wis.Stat. §§ 245.10(1), (4), (5) (1973), which provides that members of a certain class of Wisconsin residents may not marry, within the State or elsewhere, without first obtaining a court order granting permission to marry. The class is defined by the statute to include any "Wisconsin resident having minor issue not in his custody and which he is under obligation to support by any court order or judgment." The statute specifies that court permission cannot be granted unless the marriage applicant submits proof of compliance with the support obligation and, in addition, demonstrates that the children covered by the support order "are not then and are not likely thereafter to become public charges." No marriage license may lawfully be issued in Wisconsin to a person covered by the statute, except upon court order; any marriage entered into without compliance with § 245.10 is declared void; and persons acquiring marriage licenses in violation of the section are subject to criminal penalties....

I

Appellee Redhail is a Wisconsin resident who, under the terms of § 245.10, is unable to enter into a lawful marriage in Wisconsin or elsewhere so long as he maintains his Wisconsin residency....

On September 27, 1974, appellee filed an application for a marriage license with appellant Zablocki, the County Clerk of Milwaukee County, and a few days later the application was denied on the sole ground that appellee had not obtained a court order granting him permission to marry, as required by § 245.10. Although appellee did not petition a state court thereafter, it is stipulated that he would not have been able to satisfy either of the statutory prerequisites for an order granting permission to marry....

On December 24, 1974, appellee filed his complaint in the District Court, on behalf of himself and the class of all Wisconsin residents who had been refused a marriage license pursuant to § 245.10(1) by one of the county clerks in Wisconsin.... The statute was attacked on the grounds that it deprived appellee, and the class he sought to represent of equal protection and due process rights secured by the First, Fifth, Ninth, and Fourteenth Amendments to the United States Constitution.

A three-judge court was convened pursuant to 28 U.S.C. §§ 2281, 2284....

On the merits, the three-judge panel analyzed the challenged statute under the Equal Protection Clause and concluded that "strict scrutiny" was required because the classification created by the statute infringed upon a fundamental right, the right to marry. The court then proceeded to evaluate the interests advanced by the State to justify the statute, and, finding that the classification was not necessary for the achievement of those interests, the court held the statute invalid and enjoined the county clerks from enforcing it.

Appellant brought this direct appeal pursuant to 28 U.S.C. § 1253, claiming that the three-judge court erred in finding §§ 245.10(1), (4), (5) invalid under the Equal Protection Clause. Appellee defends the lower court's equal protection holding and, in the alternative, urges affirmance of the District Court's judgment on the ground that the statute does not satisfy the requirements of substantive due process. We agree with the District Court that the statute violates the Equal Protection Clause.

II

In evaluating §§ 245.10(1), (4), (5) under the Equal Protection Clause, "we must first determine what burden of justification the classification created thereby must meet, by looking to the nature of the classification and the individual interests affected." *Memorial Hospital v. Maricopa County*, 415 U.S. 250, 253 (1974). Since our past decisions make clear that the right to marry is of fundamental importance, and since the classification at issue here significantly interferes with the exercise of that right, we believe that "critical examination" of the state interests advanced in support of the classification is required. *Massachusetts Board of Retirement v. Murgia*, 427 U.S. 307, 312, 314 (1976); see, *e. g.*, *San Antonio Independent School Dist. v. Rodriguez*, 411 U.S. 1, 17 (1973).

The leading decision of this Court on the right to marry is *Loving v. Virginia*, 388 U.S. 1 (1967). In that case, an interracial couple who had been convicted of violating Virginia's miscegenation laws challenged the statutory scheme on both equal protection and due process grounds. The Court's opinion could have rested solely on the ground that the statutes discriminated on the basis of race in violation of the Equal Protection Clause. But the Court went on to hold that the laws arbitrarily deprived the couple of a fundamental liberty protected by the Due Process Clause, the freedom to marry....

Although *Loving* arose in the context of racial discrimination, prior and subsequent decisions of this Court confirm that the right to marry is of fundamental importance for all individuals. Long ago, in *Maynard v. Hill*, 125 U.S. 190 (1888), the Court characterized marriage as "the most important relation in life," and as "the foundation of the family and of society, without which there would be neither civilization nor progress." In *Meyer v. Nebraska*, 262 U.S. 390 (1923), the Court recognized that the right "to marry, establish a home and bring up children" is a central part of the liberty protected by the Due Process Clause, and in *Skinner v. Oklahoma ex rel. Williamson, supra*, 316 U.S. 535 (1942), marriage was described as "fundamental to the very existence and survival of the race."

More recent decisions have established that the right to marry is part of the fundamental "right of privacy" implicit in the Fourteenth Amendment's Due Process Clause. In *Griswold v. Connecticut*, 381 U.S. 479 (1965), the Court observed:

> "We deal with a right of privacy older than the Bill of Rights—older than our political parties, older than our school system. Marriage is a coming together for better or for worse, hopefully enduring, and intimate to the degree of being sacred. It is an association that promotes a way of life, not causes; a harmony in living, not political faiths; a bilateral loyalty, not commercial or social projects. Yet it is an association for as noble a purpose as any involved in our prior decisions."

Cases subsequent to *Griswold* and *Loving* have routinely categorized the decision to marry as among the personal decisions protected by the right of privacy. For example, last Term in *Carey v. Population Services International*, 431 U.S. 678 (1977), we declared:

> "While the outer limits of [the right of personal privacy] have not been marked by the Court, it is clear that among the decisions that an individual may make without unjustified government interference are personal decisions 'relating to marriage, *Loving v. Virginia*, 388 U.S. 1, 12 (1967); procreation, *Skinner v. Oklahoma ex rel. Williamson*, 316 U.S. 535, 541–542 (1942); contraception, *Eisenstadt v. Baird*, 405 U.S. [438], at 453–454; *id.*, at 460, 463–465 (White, J., concurring in result); family relationships, *Prince v. Massachusetts*, 321 U.S. 158, 166 (1944); and child rearing and education, *Pierce v. Society of Sisters*, 268 U.S. 510, 535 (1925); *Meyer v. Nebraska*, [262 U.S. 390, 399 (1923)].'" *Id.*, at 684–685, quoting *Roe v. Wade*, 410 U.S. 113, 152–153 (1973).

It is not surprising that the decision to marry has been placed on the same level of importance as decisions relating to procreation, childbirth, child rearing, and family relationships. As the facts of this case illustrate, it would make little sense to recognize a right of privacy with respect to other matters of family life and not with respect to the decision to enter the relationship that is the foundation of the family in our society. The woman whom appellee desired to marry had a fundamental right to seek an abortion of their expected child, see *Roe v. Wade, supra*, or to bring the child into life to suffer the myriad social, if not economic, disabilities that the status of illegitimacy brings. Surely, a decision to marry and raise the child in a traditional family setting must receive equivalent protection. And, if appellee's right to procreate means anything at all, it must imply some right to enter the only relationship in which the State of Wisconsin allows sexual relations legally to take place.[11]

By reaffirming the fundamental character of the right to marry, we do not mean to suggest that every state regulation which relates in any way to the incidents of or prerequisites for marriage must be subjected to rigorous scrutiny. To the contrary, reasonable regulations that do not significantly interfere with decisions to enter into the marital relationship may legitimately be imposed. The statutory classification at issue here, however, clearly does interfere directly and substantially with the right to marry.

Under the challenged statute, no Wisconsin resident in the affected class may marry in Wisconsin or elsewhere without a court order, and marriages contracted in violation of the statute are both void and punishable as criminal offenses. Some of those in the affected class, like appellee, will never be able to obtain the necessary court order, because they either lack the financial means to meet their support obligations or cannot prove that their children will not become public charges. These persons are absolutely prevented from getting married. Many others, able in theory to satisfy the statute's requirements, will be sufficiently burdened by having to do so that they will in effect be coerced into forgoing their right to marry. And even those who can be persuaded to meet the statute's requirements suffer a serious intrusion into their freedom of choice in an area in which we have held such freedom to be fundamental.

III

When a statutory classification significantly interferes with the exercise of a fundamental right, it cannot be upheld unless it is supported by sufficiently important state interests and is closely tailored to effectuate only those interests. Appellant asserts that two interests are served by the challenged statute: the permission-to-marry proceeding furnishes an opportunity to counsel the applicant as to the necessity of fulfilling his prior support obligations; and the welfare of the out-of-custody children is protected. We may accept for present purposes that these are legitimate and substantial interests, but, since the means selected by the State for achieving these interests unnecessarily impinge on the right to marry, the statute cannot be sustained.

There is evidence that the challenged statute, as originally introduced in the Wisconsin Legislature, was intended merely to establish a mechanism whereby persons with support obligations to children from prior marriages could be counseled before they entered into new marital relationships and incurred further support obligations. Court permission to marry was to be required, but apparently permission was automatically to be granted after counseling was completed. The statute actually enacted, however, does not expressly require or provide for any counseling whatsoever, nor for any automatic granting of permission to marry by the court, and thus it can hardly be justified as a means for ensuring counseling of the persons within its coverage. Even assuming that counseling does take place — a fact as to which there is no evidence in the record — this interest obviously cannot support the withholding of court permission to marry once counseling is completed.

With regard to safeguarding the welfare of the out-of-custody children, appellant's brief does not make clear the connection between the State's interest and the statute's requirements. At argument, appellant's counsel suggested that, since permission to marry

---

11. Wisconsin punishes fornication as a criminal offense:
"Whoever has sexual intercourse with a person not his spouse may be fined not more than $200 or imprisoned not more than 6 months or both." Wis.Stat. § 944.15 (1973).

cannot be granted unless the applicant shows that he has satisfied his court-determined support obligations to the prior children and that those children will not become public charges, the statute provides incentive for the applicant to make support payments to his children. This "collection device" rationale cannot justify the statute's broad infringement on the right to marry.

First, with respect to individuals who are unable to meet the statutory requirements, the statute merely prevents the applicant from getting married, without delivering any money at all into the hands of the applicant's prior children. More importantly, regardless of the applicant's ability or willingness to meet the statutory requirements, the State already has numerous other means for exacting compliance with support obligations, means that are at least as effective as the instant statute's and yet do not impinge upon the right to marry. Under Wisconsin law, whether the children are from a prior marriage or were born out of wedlock, court-determined support obligations may be enforced directly via wage assignments, civil contempt proceedings, and criminal penalties. And, if the State believes that parents of children out of their custody should be responsible for ensuring that those children do not become public charges, this interest can be achieved by adjusting the criteria used for determining the amounts to be paid under their support orders.

There is also some suggestion that § 245.10 protects the ability of marriage applicants to meet support obligations to prior children by preventing the applicants from incurring new support obligations. But the challenged provisions of § 245.10 are grossly underinclusive with respect to this purpose, since they do not limit in any way new financial commitments by the applicant other than those arising out of the contemplated marriage. The statutory classification is substantially overinclusive as well: Given the possibility that the new spouse will actually better the applicant's financial situation, by contributing income from a job or otherwise, the statute in many cases may prevent affected individuals from improving their ability to satisfy their prior support obligations. And, although it is true that the applicant will incur support obligations to any children born during the contemplated marriage, preventing the marriage may only result in the children being born out of wedlock, as in fact occurred in appellee's case. Since the support obligation is the same whether the child is born in or out of wedlock, the net result of preventing the marriage is simply more illegitimate children.

The statutory classification created by §§ 245.10(1), (4), (5) thus cannot be justified by the interests advanced in support of it....

Mr. Justice STEWART, concurring in the judgment.

I cannot join the opinion of the Court. To hold, as the Court does, that the Wisconsin statute violates the Equal Protection Clause seems to me to misconceive the meaning of that constitutional guarantee. The Equal Protection Clause deals not with substantive rights or freedoms but with invidiously discriminatory classifications....

Like almost any law, the Wisconsin statute now before us affects some people and does not affect others. But to say that it thereby creates "classifications" in the equal protection sense strikes me as little short of fantasy. The problem in this case is not one of discriminatory classifications, but of unwarranted encroachment upon a constitutionally protected freedom. I think that the Wisconsin statute is unconstitutional because it exceeds the bounds of permissible state regulation of marriage, and invades the sphere of liberty protected by the Due Process Clause of the Fourteenth Amendment.

I

....

A State may not only "significantly interfere with decisions to enter into marital relationship," but may in many circumstances absolutely prohibit it. Surely, for example, a State may legitimately say that no one can marry his or her sibling, that no one can marry who is not at least 14 years old, that no one can marry without first passing an examination for venereal disease, or that no one can marry who has a living husband or wife. But, just as surely, in regulating the intimate human relationship of marriage, there is a limit beyond which a State may not constitutionally go....

II

In an opinion of the Court half a century ago, Mr. Justice Holmes described an equal protection claim as "the usual last resort of constitutional arguments." *Buck v. Bell*, 274 U.S. 200, 208. Today equal protection doctrine has become the Court's chief instrument for invalidating state laws. Yet, in a case like this one, the doctrine is no more than substantive due process by another name.

Although the Court purports to examine the bases for legislative classifications and to compare the treatment of legislatively defined groups, it actually erects substantive limitations on what States may do. Thus, the effect of the Court's decision in this case is not to require Wisconsin to draw its legislative classifications with greater precision or to afford similar treatment to similarly situated persons. Rather, the message of the Court's opinion is that Wisconsin may not use its control over marriage to achieve the objectives of the state statute. Such restrictions on basic governmental power are at the heart of substantive due process.

The Court is understandably reluctant to rely on substantive due process. See *Roe v. Wade*, 410 U.S., at 167–168 (concurring opinion). But to embrace the essence of that doctrine under the guise of equal protection serves no purpose but obfuscation. "[C]ouched in slogans and ringing phrases," the Court's equal protection doctrine shifts the focus of the judicial inquiry away from its proper concerns, which include "the nature of the individual interest affected, the extent to which it is affected, the rationality of the connection between legislative means and purpose, the existence of alternative means for effectuating the purpose, and the degree of confidence we may have that the statute reflects the legislative concern for the purpose that would legitimately support the means chosen." *Williams v. Illinois, supra*, 399 U.S., at 260 (Harlan, J., concurring in result).

To conceal this appropriate inquiry invites mechanical or thoughtless application of misfocused doctrine. To bring it into the open forces a healthy and responsible recognition of the nature and purpose of the extreme power we wield when, in invalidating a state law in the name of the Constitution, we invalidate *pro tanto* the process of representative democracy in one of the sovereign States of the Union.

Mr. Justice POWELL, concurring in the judgment.

I concur in the judgment of the Court that Wisconsin's restrictions on the exclusive means of creating the marital bond, erected by Wis.Stat. §§ 245.10(1), (4), and (5) (1973), cannot meet applicable constitutional standards. I write separately because the majority's rationale sweeps too broadly in an area which traditionally has been subject to pervasive state regulation. The Court apparently would subject all state regulation which "directly and substantially" interferes with the decision to marry in a traditional family setting to "critical examination" or "compelling state interest" analysis. Presumably, "reasonable regulations that do not significantly interfere with decisions to enter into the marital relationship may legitimately be imposed." The Court does not present, however, any principled means for distinguishing between the two types of regulations. Since state regulation in this area typically takes the form of a prerequisite or barrier to marriage or divorce, the degree of "direct" interference with the decision to marry or to divorce is unlikely to provide either guidance for state legislatures or a basis for judicial oversight.

I

On several occasions, the Court has acknowledged the importance of the marriage relationship to the maintenance of values essential to organized society. "This Court has long recognized that freedom of personal choice in matters of marriage and family life is one of the liberties protected by the Due Process Clause of the Fourteenth Amendment." *Cleveland Board of Education v. LaFleur*, 414 U.S. 632, 639–640 (1974)....

Thus, it is fair to say that there is a right of marital and familial privacy which places some substantive limits on the regulatory power of government. But the Court has yet to hold that all regulation touching upon marriage implicates a "fundamental right" triggering the most exacting judicial scrutiny.

The principal authority cited by the majority is *Loving v. Virginia*, 388 U.S. 1 (1967). Although *Loving* speaks of the "freedom to marry" as "one of the vital personal rights essential to the orderly pursuit of happiness by free men," the Court focused on the miscegenation statute before it.... Thus, *Loving* involved a denial of a "fundamental freedom" on a wholly unsupportable basis — the use of classifications "directly subversive of the principle of equality at the heart of the Fourteenth Amendment...." It does not speak to the level of judicial scrutiny of, or governmental justification for, "supportable" restrictions on the "fundamental freedom" of individuals to marry or divorce.

In my view, analysis must start from the recognition of domestic relations as "an area that has long been regarded as a virtually exclusive province of the States." *Sosna v. Iowa*, 419 U.S. 393, 404 (1975).... State regulation has included bans on incest, bigamy, and homosexuality, as well as various preconditions to marriage, such as blood tests. Likewise, a showing of fault on the part of one of the partners traditionally has been a prerequisite to the dissolution of an unsuccessful union. A "compelling state purpose" inquiry would cast doubt on the network of restrictions that the States have fashioned to govern marriage and divorce....

Mr. Justice REHNQUIST, dissenting.

I substantially agree with my Brother POWELL's reasons for rejecting the Court's conclusion that marriage is the sort of "fundamental right" which must invariably trigger the strictest judicial scrutiny. I disagree with his imposition of an "intermediate" standard of review, which leads him to conclude that the statute, though generally valid as an "additional collection mechanism" offends the Constitution by its "failure to make provision for those without the means to comply with child-support obligations." For similar reasons, I disagree with my Brother STEWART's conclusion that the statute is invalid for its failure to exempt those persons who "simply cannot afford to meet the statute's financial requirements." I would view this legislative judgment in the light of the traditional presumption of validity. I think that under the Equal Protection Clause the statute need pass only the "rational basis test," *Dandridge v. Williams*, 397 U.S. 471, 485 (1970), and that under the Due Process Clause it need only be shown that it bears a rational relation to a constitutionally permissible objective. *Williamson v. Lee Optical Co.*, 348 U.S. 483, 491 (1955); *Ferguson v. Skrupa*, 372 U.S. 726, 733 (1963) (Harlan, J., concurring). The statute so viewed is a permissible exercise of the State's power to regulate family life and to assure the support of minor children, despite its possible imprecision in the extreme cases envisioned in the concurring opinions....

[The concurring opinions of Chief Justice Burger and Justice Stevens are omitted.]

Turner v. Safley
482 U.S. 78 (1987)

Justice O'CONNOR delivered the opinion of the Court.

This case requires us to determine the constitutionality of regulations promulgated by the Missouri Division of Corrections relating to inmate marriages....

I

....

The challenged marriage regulation, which was promulgated while this litigation was pending, permits an inmate to marry only with the permission of the superintendent of the prison, and provides that such approval should be given only "when there are compelling reasons to do so." The term "compelling" is not defined, but prison officials testified at trial that generally only a pregnancy or the birth of an illegitimate child would be considered a compelling reason. Prior to the promulgation of this rule, the applicable regulation did not obligate Missouri Division of Corrections officials to assist an inmate who wanted to get married, but it also did not specifically authorize the superintendent of an institution to prohibit inmates from getting married....

The [District] court, relying on *Procunier v. Martinez*, 416 U.S. 396, 413–414 (1974), applied a strict scrutiny standard. It held the marriage regulation to be an unconstitutional infringement upon the fundamental right to marry because it was far more restrictive than was either reasonable or essential for the protection of the State's interests in security and rehabilitation....

The Court of Appeals for the Eighth Circuit affirmed. The Court of Appeals held that the District Court properly used strict scrutiny....

We granted certiorari.

II

We begin, as did the courts below, with our decision in *Procunier v. Martinez, supra,* which described the principles that necessarily frame our analysis of prisoners' constitutional claims. The first of these principles is that federal courts must take cognizance of the valid constitutional claims of prison inmates. Prison walls do not form a barrier separating prison inmates from the protections of the Constitution. Hence, for example, prisoners retain the constitutional right to petition the government for the redress of grievances; they are protected against invidious racial discrimination by the Equal Protection Clause of the Fourteenth Amendment; and they enjoy the protections of due process. Because prisoners retain these rights, "[w]hen a prison regulation or practice offends a fundamental constitutional guarantee, federal courts will discharge their duty to protect constitutional rights." *Procunier v. Martinez*, 416 U.S., at 405–406.

A second principle identified in *Martinez*, however, is the recognition that "courts are ill equipped to deal with the increasingly urgent problems of prison administration and reform." As the *Martinez* Court acknowledged, "the problems of prisons in America are complex and intractable, and, more to the point, they are not readily susceptible of resolution by decree." Running a prison is an inordinately difficult undertaking that requires expertise, planning, and the commitment of resources, all of which are peculiarly within the province of the legislative and executive branches of government. Prison administration is, moreover, a task that has been committed to the responsibility of those branches, and separation of powers concerns counsel a policy of judicial restraint. Where a state penal system is involved, federal courts have, as we indicated in *Martinez,* additional reason to accord deference to the appropriate prison authorities.

Our task, then, as we stated in *Martinez,* is to formulate a standard of review for prisoners' constitutional claims that is responsive both to the "policy of judicial restraint regarding prisoner complaints and [to] the need to protect constitutional rights." As the Court of Appeals acknowledged, *Martinez* did not itself resolve the question that it framed. *Martinez* involved mail censorship regulations proscribing statements that "unduly complain," "magnify grievances," or express "inflammatory political, racial, religious or other views." In that case, the Court determined that the proper standard of review for prison restrictions on correspondence between prisoners and members of the general public could be decided without resolving the "broad questions of 'prisoners' rights.'" The *Martinez* Court based its ruling striking down the content-based regulation on the First Amendment rights of those who are not prisoners, stating that "[w]hatever the status of a prisoner's claim to uncensored correspondence with an outsider, it is plain that the latter's interest is grounded in the First Amendment's guarantee of freedom of speech." Our holding therefore turned on the fact that the challenged regulation caused a "consequential restriction on the First and Fourteenth Amendment rights of those who are *not* prisoners." We expressly reserved the question of the proper standard of review to apply in cases "involving questions of 'prisoners' rights.'"

. . . .

If [our post-*Martinez* cases] have not already resolved the question posed in *Martinez,* we resolve it now: when a prison regulation impinges on inmates' constitutional rights, the regulation is valid if it is reasonably related to legitimate penological interests. In our view, such a standard is necessary if "prison administrators . . . , and not the courts, [are] to make the difficult judgments concerning institutional operations." *Jones v. North Carolina Prisoners' Union,* 433 U.S., at 128. Subjecting the day-to-day judgments of prison officials to an inflexible strict scrutiny analysis would seriously hamper their ability to anticipate security problems and to adopt innovative solutions to the intractable problems of prison administration. The rule would also distort the decision making process, for every administrative judgment would be subject to the possibility that some court somewhere would conclude that it had a less restrictive way of solving the problem at hand. Courts inevitably would become the primary arbiters of what constitutes the best solution to every administrative problem, thereby "unnecessarily perpetuat[ing] the involvement of the federal courts in affairs of prison administration." *Procunier v. Martinez,* 416 U.S., at 407.

. . . [S]everal factors are relevant in determining the reasonableness of the regulation at issue. First, there must be a "valid, rational connection" between the prison regulation and the legitimate governmental interest put forward to justify it. Thus, a regulation cannot be sustained where the logical connection between the regulation and the asserted goal is so remote as to render the policy arbitrary or irrational. Moreover, the governmental objective must be a legitimate and neutral one. . . .

A second factor relevant in determining the reasonableness of a prison restriction . . . is whether there are alternative means of exercising the right that remain open to prison inmates. Where "other avenues" remain available for the exercise of the asserted right, courts should be particularly conscious of the "measure of judicial deference owed to corrections officials . . . in gauging the validity of the regulation."

A third consideration is the impact accommodation of the asserted constitutional right will have on guards and other inmates, and on the allocation of prison resources generally. In the necessarily closed environment of the correctional institution, few changes will have no ramifications on the liberty of others or on the use of the prison's limited resources for preserving institutional order. When accommodation of an asserted right will have a significant "ripple effect" on fellow inmates or on prison staff, courts should be particularly deferential to the informed discretion of corrections officials.

Finally, the absence of ready alternatives is evidence of the reasonableness of a prison regulation. By the same token, the existence of obvious, easy alternatives may be evidence that the regulation is not reasonable, but is an "exaggerated response" to prison concerns. This is not a "least restrictive alternative" test: prison officials do not have to set up and then shoot down every conceivable alternative method of accommodating the claimant's constitutional complaint. But if an inmate claimant can point to an alternative that fully accommodates the prisoner's rights at *de minimis* cost to valid penological interests, a court may consider that as evidence that the regulation does not satisfy the reasonable relationship standard.

III

. . . .

B

In support of the marriage regulation, petitioners first suggest that the rule does not deprive prisoners of a constitutionally protected right. They concede that the decision to marry is a fundamental right under *Zablocki v. Redhail,* 434 U.S. 374 (1978), and *Loving v. Virginia,* 388 U.S. 1 (1967), but they imply that a different rule should obtain "in ... a prison forum." Petitioners then argue that even if the regulation burdens inmates' constitutional rights, the restriction should be tested under a reasonableness standard. They urge that the restriction is reasonably related to legitimate security and rehabilitation concerns.

We disagree with petitioners that *Zablocki* does not apply to prison inmates. It is settled that a prison inmate "retains those [constitutional] rights that are not inconsistent with his status as a prisoner or with the legitimate penological objectives of the corrections system." The right to marry, like many other rights, is subject to substantial restrictions as a result of incarceration. Many important attributes of marriage remain, however, after taking into account the limitations imposed by prison life. First, inmate marriages, like others, are expressions of emotional support and public commitment. These elements are an important and significant aspect of the marital relationship. In addition, many religions recognize marriage as having spiritual significance; for some inmates and their spouses, therefore, the commitment of marriage may be an exercise of religious faith as well as an expression of personal dedication. Third, most inmates eventually will be released by parole or commutation, and therefore most inmate marriages are formed in the expectation that they ultimately will be fully consummated. Finally, marital status often is a precondition to the receipt of government benefits (*e.g.,* Social Security benefits), property rights (*e.g.,* tenancy by the entirety, inheritance rights), and other, less tangible benefits (*e.g.,* legitimation of children born out of wedlock). These incidents of marriage, like the religious and personal aspects of the marriage commitment, are unaffected by the fact of confinement or the pursuit of legitimate corrections goals.

Taken together, we conclude that these remaining elements are sufficient to form a constitutionally protected marital relationship in the prison context. Our decision in *Butler v. Wilson,* 415 U.S. 953 (1974), summarily affirming *Johnson v. Rockefeller,* 365 F.Supp. 377 (SDNY 1973), is not to the contrary. That case involved a prohibition on marriage only for inmates sentenced to life imprisonment; and, importantly, denial of the right was part of the punishment for crime.

The Missouri marriage regulation prohibits inmates from marrying unless the prison superintendent has approved the marriage after finding that there are compelling reasons for doing so. As noted previously, generally only pregnancy or birth of a child is considered a "compelling reason" to approve a marriage. In determining whether this regulation impermissibly burdens the right to marry, we note initially that the regulation prohibits marriages between inmates and civilians, as well as marriages between inmates. Although not urged by respondents, this implication of the interests of nonprisoners may support application of the *Martinez* standard, because the regulation may entail a "consequential restriction on the [constitutional] rights of those who are not prisoners." We need not reach this question, however, because even under the reasonable relationship test, the marriage regulation does not withstand scrutiny.

Petitioners have identified both security and rehabilitation concerns in support of the marriage prohibition. The security concern emphasized by petitioners is that "love triangles" might lead to violent confrontations between inmates. With respect to rehabilitation, prison officials testified that female prisoners often were subject to abuse at home or were overly dependent on male figures, and that this dependence or abuse was connected to the crimes they had committed. The superintendent at Renz, petitioner William Turner, testified that in his view, these women prisoners needed to concentrate on developing skills of self-reliance, and that the prohibition on marriage furthered this rehabilitative goal. Petitioners emphasize that the prohibition on marriage should be understood in light of Superintendent Turner's experience with several ill-advised marriage requests from female inmates.

We conclude that on this record, the Missouri prison regulation, as written, is not reasonably related to these penological interests. No doubt legitimate security concerns may require placing reasonable restrictions upon an inmate's right to marry, and may justify requiring approval of the superintendent. The Missouri regulation, however, represents an exaggerated response to such security objectives. There are obvious, easy alternatives to the Missouri regulation that accommodate the right to marry while imposing a *de minimis* burden on the pursuit of security objectives. See, *e.g.,* 28 CFR § 551.10 (1986) (marriage by inmates in federal prison generally permitted, but not if warden finds that it presents a threat to security or order of institution, or to public safety). We are aware of no place in the record where prison officials testified that such ready alternatives would not fully satisfy their security concerns. Moreover, with respect to the security concern emphasized in petitioners' brief—the creation of "love triangles"—petitioners have pointed to nothing in the record suggesting that the marriage regulation was viewed as preventing such entanglements. Common sense likewise suggests that there is no logical connection between the marriage restriction and the formation of love triangles: surely in prisons housing both male and female prisoners, inmate rivalries are as likely to develop without a formal marriage ceremony as with one. Finally, this is not an instance where the "ripple effect" on the security of fellow inmates and prison staff justifies a broad restriction on inmates' rights— indeed, where the inmate wishes to marry a civilian, the decision to marry (apart from the logistics of the wedding ceremony) is a completely private one.

Nor, on this record, is the marriage restriction reasonably related to the articulated rehabilitation goal. First, in requiring refusal of permission absent a finding of a compelling reason to allow the marriage, the rule sweeps much more broadly than can be explained by petitioners' penological objectives. Missouri prison officials testified that generally they had experienced no problem with the marriage of male inmates, and the District Court found that such marriages had routinely been allowed as a matter of practice at Missouri correctional institutions prior to adoption of the rule. The proffered justification thus does not explain the adoption of a rule banning marriages by these inmates. Nor does it account for the prohibition on inmate marriages to civilians. Missouri prison officials testified that generally they had no objection to inmate-civilian marriages, and Superintendent Turner testified that he usually did not object to the marriage of either male or female prisoners to civilians. The rehabilitation concern appears from the record to have been centered almost exclusively on female inmates marrying other inmates or ex-felons; it does not account for the ban on inmate-civilian marriages.

Moreover, although not necessary to the disposition of this case, we note that on this record the rehabilitative objective asserted to support the regulation itself is suspect. Of the several female inmates whose marriage requests were discussed by prison officials at trial, only one was refused on the basis of fostering excessive dependency. The District Court found that the Missouri prison system operated on the basis of excessive paternalism in that the proposed marriages of *all* female inmates were scrutinized carefully even before adoption of the current regulation—only one was approved at Renz in the period from 1979–1983—whereas the marriages of male inmates during the same period were routinely approved. That kind of lopsided rehabilitation concern cannot provide a justification for the broad Missouri marriage rule.

It is undisputed that Missouri prison officials may regulate the time and circumstances under which the marriage ceremony itself takes place. On this record, however, the almost complete ban on the decision to marry is not reasonably related to legitimate penological objectives. We conclude, therefore, that the Missouri marriage regulation is facially invalid....

[The opinion of Justice Stevens, concurring in part and dissenting in part, is omitted.]

Notes and Questions

1. In *Loving*, the Court could arrive at the same conclusion regardless of whether a fundamental right was involved, because the racial nature of the classification would result in strict scrutiny either way. In that sense, the *Loving* Court's discussion of the right to marry as fundamental was unnecessary to its conclusion. Yet in *Zablocki*, the Court had to reach the question whether marriage was a fundamental right in order to apply heightened scrutiny, since no suspect classifications were involved in that case.

2. In holding that marriage is a fundamental right, does *Zablocki* make clear whether it is an "equal protection" fundamental right, a "due process" one, or both? To what extent does *Turner* help to clarify that question?

3. Recall the question in the notes following *Loving* regarding the scope of the right to marry. If the right *really* encompasses the right to marry the person of one's choice, then shouldn't any restriction on that choice trigger strict scrutiny, even if the marriage would be incestuous, polygamous, to someone of the same sex, or to someone who is under-age? How do the separate opinions of Justices Stewart and Powell address these concerns?

4. Recall that in *Skinner v. Oklahoma*, the reference to marriage was in the context of a law requiring sterilization of those convicted of certain crimes, and the Court spoke of "marriage and procreation" as "fundamental." Was the *Skinner* Court conceptualizing marriage as a free-standing right, or as one linked to the right to procreate? In other words, given that for much of U.S. history, the only way to procreate lawfully was to do so within a marital relationship, is "marriage" only a fundamental right because the state traditionally imposed marriage as a prerequisite for lawful procreation? In this regard, of what significance is footnote 11 in *Zablocki*? Moreover, to what extent is that conceptualization of

the fundamental right at stake reinforced or reconceptualized by the *Turner* Court? And of what significance is this to the current legal battles regarding same-sex marriage?

2. The First Same-Sex Marriage Case

The Supreme Court's 1967 decision in *Loving v. Virginia* opened the door to challenging bans on marriage between people of the same sex. After all, one could find in *Loving* at least two different bases for striking down such laws. First, a class-based equal protection claim, contending that such laws discriminate on the basis of sexual orientation and/or sex. And second, a fundamental rights claim because of the infringement on the right to marry.

The first case to challenge a state's refusal to permit a same-sex couple to marry was initiated in a state court in Minnesota. The Minnesota case raised federal equal protection and due process claims, and—as you saw in Chapter 2—made its way to the U.S. Supreme Court under its then-existing mandatory appellate jurisdiction, which dismissed it "for want of a substantial federal question." The opinion of the Minnesota Supreme Court in that case follows.

Baker v. Nelson
191 N.W.2d 185 (Minn. 1971)

OPINION

PETERSON, Justice.

The questions for decision are whether a marriage of two persons of the same sex is authorized by state statutes and, if not, whether state authorization is constitutionally compelled.

Petitioners, Richard John Baker and James Michael McConnell, both adult male persons, made application to respondent, Gerald R. Nelson, clerk of Hennepin County District Court, for a marriage license, pursuant to Minn.St. 517.08. Respondent declined to issue the license on the sole ground that petitioners were of the same sex, it being undisputed that there were otherwise no statutory impediments to a heterosexual marriage by either petitioner.

The trial court, quashing an alternative writ of mandamus, ruled that respondent was not required to issue a marriage license to petitioners and specifically directed that a marriage license not be issued to them. This appeal is from those orders. We affirm.

1. Petitioners contend, first, that the absence of an express statutory prohibition against same-sex marriages evinces a legislative intent to authorize such marriages. We think, however, that a sensible reading of the statute discloses a contrary intent.

Minn.St. c. 517, which governs "marriage," employs that term as one of common usage, meaning the state of union between persons of the opposite sex.[1] It is unrealistic to think

---

1. Webster's Third New International Dictionary (1966) p. 1384 gives this primary meaning to marriage: "1 a: the state of being united to a person of the opposite sex as husband or wife."

Black, Law Dictionary (4 ed.) p. 1123 states this definition: "Marriage * * * is the civil status, condition, or relation of one man and one woman united in law for life, for the discharge to each other and the community of the duties legally incumbent on those whose association is founded on the distinction of sex."

that the original draftsmen of our marriage statutes, which date from territorial days, would have used the term in any different sense. The term is of contemporary significance as well, for the present statute is replete with words of heterosexual import such as "husband and wife" and "bride and groom" (the latter words inserted by L.1969, c. 1145, §3, subd. 3).

We hold, therefore, that Minn.St. c. 517 does not authorize marriage between persons of the same sex and that such marriages are accordingly prohibited.

2. Petitioners contend, second, that Minn.St. c. 517, so interpreted, is unconstitutional. There is a dual aspect to this contention: The prohibition of a same-sex marriage denies petitioners a fundamental right guaranteed by the Ninth Amendment to the United States Constitution, arguably made applicable to the states by the Fourteenth Amendment, and petitioners are deprived of liberty and property without due process and are denied the equal protection of the laws, both guaranteed by the Fourteenth Amendment.[2]

These constitutional challenges have in common the assertion that the right to marry without regard to the sex of the parties is a fundamental right of all persons and that restricting marriage to only couples of the opposite sex is irrational and invidiously discriminatory. We are not independently persuaded by these contentions and do not find support for them in any decisions of the United States Supreme Court.

The institution of marriage as a union of man and woman, uniquely involving the procreation and rearing of children within a family, is as old as the book of Genesis. Skinner v. Oklahoma ex rel. Williamson, 316 U.S. 535, 541 (1942), which invalidated Oklahoma's Habitual Criminal Sterilization Act on equal protection grounds, stated in part: "Marriage and procreation are fundamental to the very existence and survival of the race." This historic institution manifestly is more deeply founded than the asserted contemporary concept of marriage and societal interests for which petitioners contend. The Due Process Clause of the Fourteenth Amendment is not a charter for restructuring it by judicial legislation.

Griswold v. Connecticut, 381 U.S. 479 (1965), upon which petitioners rely, does not support a contrary conclusion. A Connecticut criminal statute prohibiting the use of contraceptives by married couples was held invalid, as violating the Due Process Clause of the Fourteenth Amendment. The basic premise of that decision, however, was that the state, having authorized marriage, was without power to intrude upon the right of privacy inherent in the marital relationship. Mr. Justice Douglas, author of the majority opinion, wrote that this criminal statute "operates directly on an intimate relation of husband and wife," 381 U.S. 482, and that the very idea of its enforcement by police search of "the sacred precincts of marital bedrooms for telltale signs of the use of contraceptives * * * is repulsive to the notions of privacy surrounding the marriage relationship," 381 U.S. 485. In a separate opinion for three justices, Mr. Justice Goldberg similarly abhorred this state disruption of "the traditional relation of the family — a relation as old and as fundamental as our entire civilization." 381 U.S. 496.[3]

The equal protection clause of the Fourteenth Amendment, like the Due Process Clause, is not offended by the state's classification of persons authorized to marry. There is no ir-

---

2. We dismiss without discussion petitioners' additional contentions that the statute contravenes the First Amendment and Eighth Amendment of the United States Constitution.

3. The difference between the majority opinion of Mr. Justice Douglas and the concurring opinion of Mr. Justice Goldberg was that the latter wrote extensively concerning this right of marital privacy as one preserved to the individual by the Ninth Amendment. He stopped short, however, of an implication that the Ninth Amendment was made applicable against the states by the Fourteenth Amendment.

rational or invidious discrimination. Petitioners note that the state does not impose upon heterosexual married couples a condition that they have a proved capacity or declared willingness to procreate, posing a rhetorical demand that this court must read such condition into the statute if same-sex marriages are to be prohibited. Even assuming that such a condition would be neither unrealistic nor offensive under the Griswold rationale, the classification is no more than theoretically imperfect. We are reminded, however, that "abstract symmetry" is not demanded by the Fourteenth Amendment.

Loving v. Virginia, 388 U.S. 1 (1967), upon which petitioners additionally rely, does not militate against this conclusion. Virginia's antimiscegenation statute, prohibiting interracial marriages, was invalidated solely on the grounds of its patent racial discrimination. As Mr. Chief Justice Warren wrote for the court:

> "Marriage is one of the 'basic civil rights of man,' fundamental to our very existence and survival. Skinner v. Oklahoma, 316 U.S. 535, 541 (1942). See also Maynard v. Hill, 125 U.S. 190 (1888). To deny this fundamental freedom on so unsupportable a basis as the racial classifications embodied in these statutes, classifications so directly subversive of the principle of equality at the heart of the Fourteenth Amendment, is surely to deprive all the State's citizens of liberty without due process of law. The Fourteenth Amendment requires that the freedom of choice to marry not be restricted by invidious racial discriminations.[5]"

Loving does indicate that not all state restrictions upon the right to marry are beyond reach of the Fourteenth Amendment. But in commonsense and in a constitutional sense, there is a clear distinction between a marital restriction based merely upon race and one based upon the fundamental difference in sex.

We hold, therefore, that Minn.St. c. 517 does not offend the First, Eighth, Ninth, or Fourteenth Amendments to the United States Constitution.

Affirmed.

Notes and Questions

1. At the time *Baker* was decided, virtually no state had an *explicit* ban on same-sex marriage. Accordingly, the first question facing the court was a question of statutory interpretation, namely, do the state marriage laws actually limit marriage to persons of the opposite sex. Are you persuaded by the court's conclusions regarding the legislative intent? A traditional canon of statutory interpretation in the federal courts (that some state courts also employ) is the canon of constitutional doubt: "where an otherwise acceptable construction of a statute would raise serious constitutional problems, the Court will construe the statute to avoid such problems unless such construction is plainly contrary to the intent of Congress." *Edward J. DeBartolo Corp. v. Fla. Gulf Coast Bldg. & Const. Trades Council*, 485 U.S. 568, 575 (1988). Assuming that the Minnesota courts employ a similar canon, would the failure to invoke it be based on the conclusion that the legislature's intent was clear, or that the constitutional issues raised were not serious? Assuming these challenges had instead been filed in federal court, what would a federal court have likely done in the face of the unclear question of statutory interpretation?

---

5. See, also, McLaughlin v. Florida, 379 U.S. 184 (1964), in which the United States Supreme Court, for precisely the same reason of classification based only upon race, struck down a Florida criminal statute which proscribed and punished habitual cohabitation only if one of an unmarried couple was white and the other black.

2. In rejecting the fundamental rights claim, the *Baker* court acknowledges *Loving*'s statement that marriage is a fundamental right, but concludes that "in commonsense and in a constitutional sense, there is a clear distinction between a marital restriction based merely upon race and one based upon the fundamental difference in sex." What is that clear distinction? Is the answer found in the Court's citation to *Skinner*?

3. The *Baker* court acknowledges that not all opposite-sex couples can or will procreate, yet it deems procreative capacity a sufficient reason to uphold the statutory distinction between same-sex and opposite-sex couples for equal protection purposes. To what extent does the court's holding in this regard turn on the level of scrutiny applied to the claims? To the extent that fostering procreation is deemed to be a purpose of marriage, such a distinction arguably would pass rational basis scrutiny. But what about intermediate or strict scrutiny?

4. *Baker* was decided only a few years after *Loving*, and without the benefit of either the *Zablocki* or *Turner* decisions. To what extent would *Zablocki* and *Turner* have made it harder for the *Baker* court to distinguish *Loving* in the way that it did?

5. Might the plaintiffs in *Baker* have done well to invoke the *Loving* Court's rejection of the "equal application" theory of *Pace v. State of Alabama* in support of an argument that the statutory scheme involved sex discrimination? How helpful would this have been, given that in 1971—when *Baker* was decided—the Court was still subjecting sex-based classifications to rational basis scrutiny?

6. Not only did the litigants in *Baker* lose their case, one of them also was denied public employment for his role in the litigation. McConnell (one of the two plaintiffs in *Baker*) was denied employment at the University of Minnesota, and that decision was upheld when challenged in federal court. *See McConnell v. Anderson*, 451 F.2d 193 (8th Cir. 1971).

3. The Modern Same-Sex Marriage Cases

In the decades following *Baker*, cases challenging bans on same-sex marriage were brought sporadically, but the challenges all failed, with courts often relying on the reasoning of the *Baker* decision.

But in 1993, for the first time, a state high court—the Hawaii Supreme Court—held the state's ban on same-sex marriage to violate the state constitution's own equal protection guarantee. *See Baehr v. Lewin*, 852 P.2d 44 (Haw. 1993). However, Hawaiian same-sex couples never got a chance to marry, as voters in that state amended the state's constitution to give the legislature the exclusive power to define marriage. Moreover, the Hawaii decision led to a panic in state legislatures and in Congress, resulting not only in most states explicitly prohibiting same-sex marriage through state statutes and constitutional amendments, but also the enactment of the Federal Defense of Marriage Act, which both defined marriage for federal purposes as the union of one man and one woman, and amended the Full Faith and Credit Act to provide that states need not recognize same-sex marriages performed in other states.

Then, in 1999, Vermont's Supreme Court interpreted the Vermont Constitution to require that same-sex couples be given all of the rights associated with marriage, either by extending to them the right to marry or through the creation of a parallel statutory scheme. *See Baker v. State*, 744 A.2d 864 (Vt. 1999). The Vermont legislature enacted a civil union scheme for same-sex couples, which took effect in 2000.

In 2003, ten years after the Hawaii Supreme Court's decision and just a few months after the U.S. Supreme Court's decision in *Lawrence v. Texas*, the Massachusetts high court interpreted the equal protection and due process provisions of the Massachusetts Constitution to require the extension of marriage rights to same-sex couples. *See Goodridge v. Dep't of Pub. Health*, 798 N.E.2d 941 (Mass. 2003). Despite significant efforts to block the decision from taking effect, it ultimately was enforced, and in 2004, Massachusetts became the first state to permit same-sex couples to marry.

The materials that follow examine the various legal arguments in favor of and against same-sex marriage in these and other modern cases challenging bans on same-sex marriage. Rather than merely examining the decisions in chronological order, this section breaks down and separately analyzes the many legal issues that arise in litigating the constitutionality of banning same-sex marriage.

Sub-section "a" examines the threshold question of what sort of classification for equal protection purposes—sexual orientation or sex—laws banning same-sex marriage create. Sub-section "b" addresses the question whether bans on same-sex marriage satisfy even the lowest level of review, rational basis, when challenged on either equal protection or due process grounds. Sub-section "c" examines the question whether bans on same-sex marriage should be subject to strict scrutiny under either the Equal Protection or Due Process Clauses because they infringe upon a fundamental right. Sub-section "d" examines the question whether bans on same-sex marriage should be subject to heightened scrutiny on the ground that sexual orientation is a suspect classification. Sub-section "e" addresses the question whether giving same-sex couples the right to an alternative to marriage, such as domestic partnerships or civil unions, satisfies the constitutional command of equal treatment. Sub-section "f" examines the question whether taking away marriage rights from same-sex couples or blocking them from going into effect via a voter referendum raises a separate constitutional claim wholly independent from the underlying question whether same-sex couples have a right to marry. Finally, sub-section "g" examines the constitutionality of the federal Defense of Marriage Act, considering not only 14th Amendment challenges to it, but also those raised under the Full Faith and Credit Clause and the 10th Amendment.

a. The Nature of the Classification

A threshold question for assessing equal protection claims is to determine the nature of the classification—if any—made by the law being challenged. The materials that follow assess two possible ways of characterizing the nature of the classification involved in laws banning same-sex marriage: as a form of sexual orientation discrimination, or as a form of sex discrimination.

Baehr v. Lewin
852 P.2d 44 (Haw. 1993)

[Same-sex couples who applied for and were denied marriage licenses brought suit, contending that denying them the right to marry violates, *inter alia*, the equal protection guarantee of the Hawaii Constitution.]

LEVINSON, Judge, in which MOON, Chief Judge, joins.

    ....

[T]he applicant couples contend that they have been denied the equal protection of the laws as guaranteed by article I, section 5 of the Hawaii Constitution....

Rudimentary principles of statutory construction render manifest the fact that, by its plain language, HRS § 572-1 restricts the marital relation to a male and a female.... Accordingly, on its face and (as Lewin admits) as applied, HRS § 572-1 denies same-sex couples access to the marital status and its concomitant rights and benefits. It is the state's regulation of access to the status of married persons, on the basis of the applicants' sex, that gives rise to the question whether the applicant couples have been denied the equal protection of the laws in violation of article I, section 5 of the Hawaii Constitution....

[The Court goes on to hold that, under the Hawaii Constitution, sex-based classifications are subject to strict scrutiny.]

It therefore follows, and we so hold, that (1) HRS § 572-1 is presumed to be unconstitutional (2) unless Lewin, as an agent of the State of Hawaii, can show that (a) the statute's sex-based classification is justified by compelling state interests and (b) the statute is narrowly drawn to avoid unnecessary abridgements of the applicant couples' constitutional rights....

We understand that Judge Heen disagrees with our view in this regard based on his belief that "HRS § 572-1 treats everyone alike and applies equally to both sexes[,]," with the result that "neither sex is being *granted* a right or benefit the other does not have, and neither sex is being *denied* a right or benefit that the other has." The rationale underlying Judge Heen's belief, however, was expressly considered and rejected in *Loving*:

> Thus, the State contends that, because its miscegenation statutes punish equally both the white and the Negro participants in an interracial marriage, these statutes, despite their reliance on racial classifications do not constitute an invidious discrimination based upon race.... [W]e reject the notion that the mere "equal application" of a statute containing racial classifications is enough to remove the classifications from the Fourteenth Amendment's proscriptions of all invidious discriminations.... In the case at bar, ... we deal with statutes containing racial classifications, and the fact of equal application does not immunize the statute from the very heavy burden of justification which the Fourteenth Amendment has traditionally required of state statutes drawn according to race.

388 U.S. at 8. Substitution of "sex" for "race" and article I, section 5 for the fourteenth amendment yields the precise case before us together with the conclusion that we have reached....

[The concurring opinion of Chief Judge Burns and the dissenting opinion of Judge Heen are omitted.]

Hernandez v. Robles

855 N.E.2d 1 (N.Y. 2006)

[Same-sex couples who applied for and were denied marriage licenses brought suit, contending that denying them the right to marry violates, *inter alia*, the equal protection guarantee of the New York Constitution.]

R.S. SMITH, J.

....

By limiting marriage to opposite-sex couples, New York is not engaging in sex discrimination. The limitation does not put men and women in different classes, and give one class a benefit not given to the other. Women and men are treated alike—they are permitted to marry people of the opposite sex, but not people of their own sex. This is not the kind of sham equality that the Supreme Court confronted in *Loving*; the statute there, prohibiting black and white people from marrying each other, was in substance anti-black legislation. Plaintiffs do not argue here that the legislation they challenge is designed to subordinate either men to women or women to men as a class.

However, the legislation does confer advantages on the basis of sexual preference. Those who prefer relationships with people of the opposite sex and those who prefer relationships with people of the same sex are not treated alike, since only opposite-sex relationships may gain the status and benefits associated with marriage....

GRAFFEO, J. (concurring).

....

Plaintiffs argue that the Domestic Relations Law creates a classification based on gender that requires intermediate scrutiny because a woman cannot marry another woman due to her gender and a man cannot marry another man due to his gender. Respondents counter that the marriage laws are neutral insofar as gender is concerned because they treat all males and females equally—neither gender can marry a person of the same sex and both can marry persons of the opposite sex.

Respondents' interpretation more closely comports with the analytical framework for gender discrimination applied by this Court and the Supreme Court. The precedent establishes that gender discrimination occurs when men and women are not treated equally and one gender is benefitted or burdened as opposed to the other....

Plaintiffs cite *Loving* for the proposition that a statute can discriminate even if it treats both classes identically. This misconstrues the *Loving* analysis because the antimiscegenation statute did not treat blacks and whites identically—it restricted who whites could marry (but did not restrict intermarriage between non-whites) for the purpose of promoting white supremacy. Virginia's antimiscegenation statute was the quintessential example of invidious racial discrimination as it was intended to advantage one race and disadvantage all others, which is why the Supreme Court applied strict scrutiny and struck it down as violating the core interest of the Equal Protection Clause.

In contrast, neither men nor women are disproportionately disadvantaged or burdened by the fact that New York's Domestic Relations Law allows only opposite-sex couples to marry—both genders are treated precisely the same way. As such, there is no gender classification triggering intermediate scrutiny.

Nor does the statutory scheme create a classification based on sexual orientation. In this respect, the Domestic Relations Law is facially neutral: individuals who seek marriage licenses are not queried concerning their sexual orientation and are not precluded from marrying if they are not heterosexual. Regardless of sexual orientation, any person can marry a person of the opposite sex. Certainly, the marriage laws create a classification that distinguishes between opposite-sex and same-sex couples and this has a disparate impact on gays and lesbians. However, a claim that a facially-neutral statute enacted without an invidious discriminatory intent has a disparate impact on a class (even a suspect class, such as one defined by race) is insufficient to establish an equal protection violation (*see Washington v. Davis*, 426 U.S. 229, 240 [1976]). Plaintiffs concede that the Domestic Relations Law was not enacted with an invidiously discriminatory intent—the Legislature did not craft the marriage laws for the purpose of disadvantaging gays and lesbians (*cf. Romer v. Evans*, 517 U.S. 620 [1996]). Hence, there is no basis to address plaintiffs' argument that classifications based on sexual orientation should be subjected to intermediate scrutiny....

[The dissenting opinion of Chief Judge Kaye is omitted.]

In re Marriage Cases
183 P.3d 384 (Cal. 2008)

[Same-sex couples who applied for and were denied marriage licenses brought suit, contending that denying them the right to marry violates, *inter alia*, the equal protection guarantee of the California Constitution.]

GEORGE, C.J.

....

Plaintiffs initially contend that the relevant California statutes, by drawing a distinction between couples consisting of a man and a woman and couples consisting of two persons of the same sex or gender, discriminate on the basis of sex and for that reason should be subjected to strict scrutiny under the state equal protection clause. Although the governing California cases long have established that statutes that discriminate on the basis of sex or gender are subject to strict scrutiny under the California Constitution, we conclude that the challenged statutes cannot properly be viewed as discriminating on the basis of sex or gender for purposes of the California equal protection clause.

In drawing a distinction between opposite-sex couples and same-sex couples, the challenged marriage statutes do not treat men and women differently. Persons of either gender are treated equally and are permitted to marry only a person of the opposite gender. In light of the equality of treatment between genders, the distinction prescribed by the relevant statutes plainly does not constitute discrimination on the basis of sex as that concept is commonly understood.

Plaintiffs contend, however, that the statutory distinction nonetheless should be viewed as sex or gender discrimination because the statutory limitation upon marriage in a particular case is dependent upon an individual person's sex or gender. Plaintiffs argue that because a woman who wishes to marry another woman would be permitted to do so if she were a man rather than a woman, and a man who wishes to marry another man would be permitted to do so if he were a woman rather than a man, the statutes must be seen as embodying discrimination on the basis of sex. Plaintiffs rely on the decisions in *Perez, supra,* 32 Cal.2d 711, and *Loving v. Virginia, supra,* 388 U.S. 1, in which this court and subsequently the United States Supreme Court found that the antimiscegenation statutes at issue in those cases discriminated on the basis of race, even though the statutes prohibited White persons from marrying Black persons and Black persons from marrying White persons.

The decisions in *Perez* and *Loving v. Virginia*, however, are clearly distinguishable from this case, because the antimiscegenation statutes at issue in those cases plainly treated members of minority races differently from White persons, prohibiting only intermarriage that involved White persons in order to prevent (in the undisguised words of the defenders of the statute in *Perez*) "the Caucasian race from being contaminated by races whose members are by nature physically and mentally inferior to Caucasians." (*Perez, supra,* 32 Cal.2d at p. 722; see also *Loving, supra,* 388 U.S. at p. 11 ["The fact that Virginia prohibits only interracial marriages involving white persons demonstrates that the racial classifications must stand on their own justification, as measures designed to maintain White Supremacy"].) Under these circumstances, there can be no doubt that the reference to race in the statutes at issue in *Perez* and *Loving* unquestionably reflected the kind of racial discrimination that always has been recognized as calling for strict scrutiny under equal protection analysis.

In *Perez, Loving,* and a number of other decisions (see, e.g., *McLaughlin v. Florida* (1964) 379 U.S. 184, 192), courts have recognized that a statute that treats a couple differently based upon whether the couple consists of persons of the same race or of different races generally reflects a policy disapproving of the integration or close relationship of individuals of different races in the setting in question, and as such properly is viewed as embodying an instance of *racial discrimination* with respect to the interracial couple and both of its members. By contrast, past judicial decisions, in California and elsewhere, virtually uniformly hold that a statute or policy that treats men and women equally but that accords differential treatment either to a couple based upon whether it consists of persons of the same sex rather than opposite sexes, or to an individual based upon whether he or she generally is sexually attracted to persons of the same gender rather than the opposite gender, is more accurately characterized as involving differential treatment on the basis of *sexual orientation* rather than an instance of *sex discrimination,* and properly should be analyzed on the *former* ground. These cases recognize that, in realistic terms, a statute or policy that treats same-sex couples differently from opposite-sex couples, or that treats individuals who are sexually attracted to persons of the same gender differently from individuals who are sexually attracted to persons of the opposite gender, does not treat an individual man or an individual woman differently *because of* his or her *gender* but rather accords differential treatment *because of* the individual's *sexual orientation....*

Although plaintiffs further contend that the difference in treatment prescribed by the relevant statutes should be treated as sex discrimination for equal protection purposes because the differential treatment reflects illegitimate gender-related stereotyping based on the view that men are attracted to women and women are attracted to men, this argument again improperly conflates two concepts — discrimination on the basis of sex, and discrimination on the basis of sexual orientation — that traditionally have been viewed as distinct phenomena. Under plaintiffs' argument, discrimination on the basis of sexual orientation always would constitute a subset of discrimination on the basis of sex.

For purposes of determining the applicable standard of judicial review under the California equal protection clause, we conclude that discrimination on the basis of sexual orientation cannot appropriately be viewed as a subset of, or subsumed within, discrimination on the basis of sex. The seminal California decisions that address the question of which equal protection standard should apply to statutory classifications that discriminate on the basis of sex or gender, and that explain why under the California Constitution the strict scrutiny standard is applicable to such classifications, look to (1) whether a person's *gender* (rather than sexual orientation) does or does not bear a relation to one's ability to perform or contribute to society, and (2) the long history of societal and legal discrimination against *women* (rather than against gay individuals). Each of these seminal California decisions addressed instances in which the applicable statutes favored one gender over another, or prescribed different treatment for one gender as compared to the other based upon a stereotype relating to one particular gender, rather than instances in which a statute treated the genders equally but imposed differential treatment based upon whether or not an individual was of the same gender as his or her sexual partner. In light of the reasoning underlying these rulings, we conclude that the type of discrimination or differential treatment between same-sex and opposite-sex couples reflected in the challenged marriage statutes cannot fairly be viewed as embodying the same type of discrimination at issue in the California decisions establishing that the strict scrutiny standard applies to statutes that discriminate on the basis of sex.

Accordingly, we conclude that in the context of California's equal protection clause, the differential treatment prescribed by the relevant statutes cannot properly be found to constitute discrimination on the basis of sex, and thus that the statutory classification embodied in the marriage statutes is not subject to strict scrutiny on that ground....

Plaintiffs next maintain that even if the applicable California statutes do not discriminate on the basis of sex or gender, they do so on the basis of sexual orientation....

In arguing that the marriage statutes do not discriminate on the basis of sexual orientation, defendants rely upon the circumstance that these statutes, on their face, do not refer explicitly to sexual orientation and do not prohibit gay individuals from marrying a person of the opposite sex. Defendants contend that under these circumstances, the marriage statutes should not be viewed as directly classifying or discriminating on the basis of sexual orientation but at most should be viewed as having a "disparate impact" on gay persons.

In our view, the statutory provisions restricting marriage to a man and a woman cannot be understood as having merely a disparate impact on gay persons, but instead properly must be viewed as directly classifying and prescribing distinct treatment on the basis of sexual orientation. By limiting marriage to opposite-sex couples, the marriage statutes, realistically viewed, operate clearly and directly to impose different treatment on gay individuals because of their sexual orientation. By definition, gay individuals are persons who are sexually attracted to persons of the same sex and thus, if inclined to enter into a marriage relationship, would choose to marry a person of their own sex or gender.[59] A statute that limits marriage to a union of persons of opposite sexes, thereby placing marriage outside the reach of couples of the same sex, unquestionably imposes different treatment on the basis of sexual orientation. In our view, it is sophistic to suggest that this conclusion is avoidable by reason of the circumstance that the marriage statutes permit a gay man or a lesbian to marry someone of the opposite sex, because making such a choice would require the negation of the person's sexual orientation. Just as a statute that

---

59. As explained in the amicus curiae brief filed by a number of leading mental health organizations, including the American Psychological Association and the American Psychiatric Association: "Sexual orientation is commonly discussed as a characteristic of the *individual*, like biological sex, gender identity, or age. This perspective is incomplete because sexual orientation is always defined in relational terms and necessarily involves relationships with other individuals. Sexual acts and romantic attractions are categorized as homosexual or heterosexual according to the biological sex of the individuals involved in them, relative to each other. Indeed, it is by acting — or desiring to act — with another person that individuals express their heterosexuality, homosexuality, or bisexuality.... Thus, sexual orientation is integrally linked to the intimate personal relationships that human beings form with others to meet their deeply felt needs for love, attachment, and intimacy. In addition to sexual behavior, these bonds encompass nonsexual physical affection between partners, shared goals and values, mutual support, and ongoing commitment. [¶] Consequently, sexual orientation is not merely a personal characteristic that can be defined in isolation. Rather, one's sexual orientation defines the universe of persons with whom one is likely to find the satisfying and fulfilling relationships that, for many individuals, comprise an essential component of personal identity."

restricted marriage only to couples of the same sex would discriminate against heterosexual persons on the basis of their heterosexual orientation, the current California statutes realistically must be viewed as discriminating against gay persons on the basis of their homosexual orientation....

[The concurring opinion of Justice Kennard and the dissenting opinions of Justices Baxter and Corrigan are omitted.]

Conaway v. Deane
932 A.2d 571 (Md. 2007)

BATTAGLIA, J., dissenting.

[Same-sex couple wishing to marry brought suit seeking a declaration that a state law limiting marriage to opposite sex couples violated, *inter alia*, the equal protection guarantee set forth in the Maryland Constitution.]

Although the majority asserts that Family Law Section 2-201 draws classifications based on sexual orientation, on its face the statute actually classifies on the basis of sex, not sexual orientation. Section 2-201 does not prohibit homosexuals from marrying; in fact, a homosexual male may marry either a heterosexual or homosexual female, and a homosexual female may marry either a heterosexual or homosexual male. Only by virtue of a person's sex is he or she prohibited from marrying a person of the same sex. Clearly, Section 2-201 draws distinctions based on sex and thus, the issue of sexual orientation simply does not enter into an ERA analysis.

The Appellees in the present case allege that Section 2-201 has a discriminatory effect, regardless of its alleged facial neutrality, and that the landmark Supreme Court decision in *Loving*, 388 U.S. at 1, should control the outcome here. *Loving* involved the State assertion of an analogous allegedly neutral, generally applicable statute prohibiting miscegenation. The Court applied strict scrutiny to the Virginia statute despite its ostensibly equal application to both races. *Id.* at 9. Not only did the Court weigh the long history of white supremacy and racial segregation heavily against the State, but the Court found the antimiscegenation statute applied only to interracial marriages involving whites, and thus, was not facially neutral as asserted by Virginia. The Court reached its holding independently of the issue of discriminatory intent, however, "find[ing] the racial classifications in these statutes repugnant to the Fourteenth Amendment, even assuming an even-handed state purpose to protect the 'integrity' of all races." *Id.* at 11 n. 11. Clearly, the Court found no legitimate purpose in the racial classifications themselves, regardless of the proffered justification.

The State attempts to distinguish *Loving* from the instant case on the basis that the same-sex marriage ban does not evince the intent to impose segregation based on sex. The State's position is reinforced by *amici*, The Maryland Catholic Conference, who argue that "anti-miscegenation statutes were intended to keep persons of *different* races *separate;* marriage statutes, on the other hand, are intended to bring persons of the *opposite* sex *together.*" This argument begs the question whether Family Law Section 2-201 is facially neutral; it is well-settled that the question of discriminatory intent does not arise unless the threshold question of facial neutrality is answered in the affirmative.

Here, there is no plausible assertion that Section 2-201 accrues only to the benefit of either men or women as a class.... [H]owever, there is sex discrimination at the level of the *individual* who wishes to marry but is precluded from doing so because of the statute. Thus, a man who wishes to marry another man is prevented from choosing his marriage partner purely on the basis of sex; likewise, a woman who wishes to marry another woman is prevented from choosing her marriage partner purely on the basis of sex. Manifestly, Section 2-201 classifies on the basis of sex; because it would be necessary to consider the underlying legislative intent only if the same-sex marriage ban did not draw sex-based distinctions, the question of legislative intent is irrelevant. Just as in *Loving*, it is the *nature of the classifications themselves* that implicates strict scrutiny....

[The majority opinion of Judge Harrell, the concurring opinion of Judge Raker, and the dissenting opinion of Chief Judge Bell are omitted.]

Notes and Questions

1. Given *Loving*'s rejection of the "equal application" theory, one would think that the sex discrimination argument would be a slam dunk in same-sex marriage litigation. Yet to date, only the Hawaii Supreme Court and a handful of concurring and dissenting judges in other cases have accepted the argument, with other courts distinguishing *Loving* on the ground that the Virginia statute was tainted by "White Supremacy" and that it was in fact designed only to protect the purity of the Caucasian race. But in so holding, aren't these courts—as Judge Battaglia suggests in his dissent in *Conaway*—ignoring the *Loving* Court's statement in footnote 11 that "we find the racial classifications in these statutes repugnant to the Fourteenth Amendment, even assuming an even-handed state purpose to protect the 'integrity' of all races"?

On the other hand, even if characterized as sex discrimination, is it possible that the reasons justifying limiting marriage to people of opposite sexes might pass *intermediate* scrutiny even if an interest in "racial integrity" would not pass *strict* scrutiny?

2. If the statutes challenged in these cases cannot be viewed as discriminating on the basis of sex, must they not clearly be viewed as discriminating on the basis of sexual orientation? Judge Graffeo, however, reminds us in *Hernandez* that under equal protection jurisprudence, for discrimination to be actionable, it must be intentional. Thus, where, as here, the laws are facially neutral, they can be challenged only if they are either enforced in a discriminatory manner or were designed with the purpose of discriminating against a given class; those facially neutral laws that merely have a discriminatory effect on a given class do not present a viable equal protection claim.

As Judge Graffeo further indicates, the plaintiffs conceded that the law was not designed with the intent of discriminating against gays and lesbians. In this regard, does it make sense to distinguish between older marriage statutes such as those at issue in cases such as *Hernandez* that were enacted long before legislatures gave any thought at all about gays and lesbians and more recent statutes that have a clear legislative record evincing an intent to prevent gays and lesbians from marrying? Is it thus conceivable—as Judge Graffeo holds—that for equal protection purposes these laws do not discriminate on the basis of either sex or sexual orientation?

3. Is it perhaps more appropriate to say that the line drawn is not between heterosexual and homosexual *individuals* but rather between same-sex and opposite-sex *couples*, as the court in *Diaz v. Brewer* (Chapter 4) did in assessing the constitutionality of Arizona's decision to eliminate health benefits for domestic partners of public employees? The Massachusetts Supreme Judicial Court so characterized the state's marriage laws in its decision holding them to be unconstitutional for preventing same-sex couples from marrying:

> We use the terms "same sex" and "opposite sex" when characterizing the couples in question, because these terms are more accurate in this context than the terms "homosexual" or "heterosexual," although at times we use those terms when we consider them appropriate. Nothing in our marriage law precludes people who identify themselves (or who are identified by others) as gay, lesbian, or bisexual from marrying persons of the opposite sex.

Goodridge v. Dep't of Pub. Health, 798 N.E.2d 941, 953 n.11 (Mass. 2003). How, if at all, does this characterization of the law alter the equal protection analysis?

4. Recall from Chapter 4 that in *Hernandez v. New York*, the Court held that a characteristic may be so closely associated with a class that it may be possible to treat a law targeting that characteristic as a surrogate for targeting the class itself. To what extent does that case provide support for the argument that what is at play in these statutes is sexual orientation discrimination?

b. Is It "Rational" to Deny Same-Sex Couples the Right to Marry?

Recall from Chapters 3 and 4 that if a law neither burdens a fundamental right nor draws suspect or quasi-suspect lines, it is subject only to rational basis review when challenged on either due process or equal protection grounds. Recall as well how deferential that standard is: it allows for substantial over- and under-inclusiveness, does not require an actual but merely a hypothetical rationale, and places the burden on the challenger.

In the two cases that follow, the Massachusetts and New York high courts apply rational basis review to equal protection and due process challenges to their states' laws permitting only opposite-sex couples to marry. In the Massachusetts case, the court does so because it finds that the laws cannot even satisfy rational basis scrutiny, while in the New York case, the court concludes that the law neither burdens a fundamental right nor draws suspect or quasi-suspect lines.

Goodridge v. Department of Public Health
798 N.E.2d 941 (Mass. 2003)

MARSHALL, C.J.

[Same-sex couples who applied for and were denied marriage licenses brought suit, contending that denying them the right to marry violates the equal protection and due process guarantees of the Massachusetts Constitution.]

II

. . . .

The plaintiffs argue that because nothing in that licensing law specifically prohibits marriages between persons of the same sex, we may interpret the statute to permit "qualified same sex couples" to obtain marriage licenses, thereby avoiding the question whether the law is constitutional. This claim lacks merit.

We interpret statutes to carry out the Legislature's intent, determined by the words of a statute interpreted according to "the ordinary and approved usage of the language." The everyday meaning of "marriage" is "[t]he legal union of a man and woman as husband and wife," Black's Law Dictionary 986 (7th ed.1999), and the plaintiffs do not argue that the term "marriage" has ever had a different meaning under Massachusetts law. This definition of marriage, as both the department and the Superior Court judge point out, derives from the common law. Far from being ambiguous, the undefined word "marriage," as used in G.L. c. 207, confirms the General Court's intent to hew to the term's common-law and quotidian meaning concerning the genders of the marriage partners.

The intended scope of G.L. c. 207 is also evident in its consanguinity provisions. Sections 1 and 2 of G.L. c. 207 prohibit marriages between a man and certain female relatives and a woman and certain male relatives, but are silent as to the consanguinity of male-male or female-female marriage applicants. The only reasonable explanation is that the Legislature did not intend that same-sex couples be licensed to marry. We conclude, as did the judge, that G.L. c. 207 may not be construed to permit same-sex couples to marry.

III

A

The larger question is whether, as the department claims, government action that bars same-sex couples from civil marriage constitutes a legitimate exercise of the State's authority to regulate conduct, or whether, as the plaintiffs claim, this categorical marriage exclusion violates the Massachusetts Constitution. We have recognized the long-standing statutory understanding, derived from the common law, that "marriage" means the lawful union of a woman and a man. But that history cannot and does not foreclose the constitutional question.

The plaintiffs' claim that the marriage restriction violates the Massachusetts Constitution can be analyzed in two ways. Does it offend the Constitution's guarantees of equality before the law? Or do the liberty and due process provisions of the Massachusetts Constitution secure the plaintiffs' right to marry their chosen partner? In matters implicating marriage, family life, and the upbringing of children, the two constitutional concepts frequently overlap, as they do here. Much of what we say concerning one standard applies to the other....

B

For decades, indeed centuries, in much of this country (including Massachusetts) no lawful marriage was possible between white and black Americans. That long history availed not when the Supreme Court of California held in 1948 that a legislative prohibition against interracial marriage violated the due process and equality guarantees of the Fourteenth Amendment, *Perez v. Sharp,* 32 Cal.2d 711, 728 (1948), or when, nineteen years later, the United States Supreme Court also held that a statutory bar to interracial marriage violated the Fourteenth Amendment, *Loving v. Virginia,* 388 U.S. 1 (1967). As both *Perez* and *Loving* make clear, the right to marry means little if it does not include the right to marry the person of one's choice, subject to appropriate government restrictions in the interests of public health, safety, and welfare. In this case, as in *Perez* and *Loving,* a statute deprives individuals of access to an institution of fundamental legal, personal, and social significance—the institution of marriage—because of a single trait: skin color in *Perez* and *Loving,* sexual orientation here. As it did in *Perez* and *Loving,* history must yield to a more fully developed understanding of the invidious quality of the discrimination.[17]

---

17. Recently, the United States Supreme Court has reaffirmed that the Constitution prohibits a State from wielding its formidable power to regulate conduct in a manner that demeans basic human dignity, even though that statutory discrimination may enjoy broad public support. The Court struck down

The Massachusetts Constitution protects matters of personal liberty against government incursion as zealously, and often more so, than does the Federal Constitution, even where both Constitutions employ essentially the same language....

The individual liberty and equality safeguards of the Massachusetts Constitution protect both "freedom from" unwarranted government intrusion into protected spheres of life and "freedom to" partake in benefits created by the State for the common good. Both freedoms are involved here. Whether and whom to marry, how to express sexual intimacy, and whether and how to establish a family—these are among the most basic of every individual's liberty and due process rights. See, e.g., *Lawrence, supra* at 2481; *Planned Parenthood of Southeastern Pa. v. Casey*, 505 U.S. 833, 851 (1992); *Zablocki v. Redhail*, 434 U.S. 374, 384 (1978); *Roe v. Wade*, 410 U.S. 113, 152–153 (1973); *Eisenstadt v. Baird*, 405 U.S. 438, 453 (1972); *Loving v. Virginia, supra.* And central to personal freedom and security is the assurance that the laws will apply equally to persons in similar situations.... The liberty interest in choosing whether and whom to marry would be hollow if the Commonwealth could, without sufficient justification, foreclose an individual from freely choosing the person with whom to share an exclusive commitment in the unique institution of civil marriage.

The Massachusetts Constitution requires, at a minimum, that the exercise of the State's regulatory authority not be "arbitrary or capricious." Under both the equality and liberty guarantees, regulatory authority must, at very least, serve "a legitimate purpose in a rational way"; a statute must "bear a reasonable relation to a permissible legislative objective." Any law failing to satisfy the basic standards of rationality is void....

The department argues that no fundamental right or "suspect" class is at issue here,[21] and rational basis is the appropriate standard of review. For the reasons we explain below, we conclude that the marriage ban does not meet the rational basis test for either due process or equal protection. Because the statute does not survive rational basis review, we do not consider the plaintiffs' arguments that this case merits strict judicial scrutiny.

The department posits three legislative rationales for prohibiting same-sex couples from marrying: (1) providing a "favorable setting for procreation"; (2) ensuring the optimal setting for child rearing, which the department defines as "a two-parent family with one parent of each sex"; and (3) preserving scarce State and private financial resources. We consider each in turn.

The judge in the Superior Court endorsed the first rationale, holding that "the state's interest in regulating marriage is based on the traditional concept that marriage's primary purpose is procreation." This is incorrect. Our laws of civil marriage do not privilege procreative heterosexual intercourse between married people above every other form of adult intimacy and every other means of creating a family. General Laws c. 207 contains no requirement that the applicants for a marriage license attest to their ability or intention to conceive children by coitus. Fertility is not a condition of marriage, nor is it grounds for divorce. People who have never consummated their marriage, and never plan to, may be and stay married. People who cannot stir from their deathbed may marry. While it is certainly true that many, perhaps most, married couples have children together (assisted or unassisted), it is the exclusive and permanent commitment of the mar-

---

a statute criminalizing sodomy. See *Lawrence, supra* at 2478 ("The liberty protected by the Constitution allows homosexual persons the right to make this choice").

21. Article 1 of the Massachusetts Constitution specifically prohibits sex-based discrimination. We have not previously considered whether "sexual orientation" is a "suspect" classification. Our resolution of this case does not require that inquiry here.

riage partners to one another, not the begetting of children, that is the sine qua non of civil marriage.

Moreover, the Commonwealth affirmatively facilitates bringing children into a family regardless of whether the intended parent is married or unmarried, whether the child is adopted or born into a family, whether assistive technology was used to conceive the child, and whether the parent or her partner is heterosexual, homosexual, or bisexual. If procreation were a necessary component of civil marriage, our statutes would draw a tighter circle around the permissible bounds of nonmarital child bearing and the creation of families by noncoital means. The attempt to isolate procreation as "the source of a fundamental right to marry" overlooks the integrated way in which courts have examined the complex and overlapping realms of personal autonomy, marriage, family life, and child rearing. Our jurisprudence recognizes that, in these nuanced and fundamentally private areas of life, such a narrow focus is inappropriate.

The "marriage is procreation" argument singles out the one unbridgeable difference between same-sex and opposite-sex couples, and transforms that difference into the essence of legal marriage. Like "Amendment 2" to the Constitution of Colorado, which effectively denied homosexual persons equality under the law and full access to the political process, the marriage restriction impermissibly "identifies persons by a single trait and then denies them protection across the board." *Romer v. Evans,* 517 U.S. 620, 633 (1996). In so doing, the State's action confers an official stamp of approval on the destructive stereotype that same-sex relationships are inherently unstable and inferior to opposite-sex relationships and are not worthy of respect.

The department's first stated rationale, equating marriage with unassisted heterosexual procreation, shades imperceptibly into its second: that confining marriage to opposite-sex couples ensures that children are raised in the "optimal" setting. Protecting the welfare of children is a paramount State policy. Restricting marriage to opposite-sex couples, however, cannot plausibly further this policy. "The demographic changes of the past century make it difficult to speak of an average American family. The composition of families varies greatly from household to household." *Troxel v. Granville,* 530 U.S. 57, 63 (2000). Massachusetts has responded supportively to "the changing realities of the American family," *id.* at 64, and has moved vigorously to strengthen the modern family in its many variations....

The department has offered no evidence that forbidding marriage to people of the same sex will increase the number of couples choosing to enter into opposite-sex marriages in order to have and raise children. There is thus no rational relationship between the marriage statute and the Commonwealth's proffered goal of protecting the "optimal" child rearing unit. Moreover, the department readily concedes that people in same-sex couples may be "excellent" parents. These couples (including four of the plaintiff couples) have children for the reasons others do—to love them, to care for them, to nurture them. But the task of child rearing for same-sex couples is made infinitely harder by their status as outliers to the marriage laws. While establishing the parentage of children as soon as possible is crucial to the safety and welfare of children, same-sex couples must undergo the sometimes lengthy and intrusive process of second-parent adoption to establish their joint parentage. While the enhanced income provided by marital benefits is an important source of security and stability for married couples and their children, those benefits are denied to families headed by same-sex couples. While the laws of divorce provide clear and reasonably predictable guidelines for child support, child custody, and property division on dissolution of a marriage, same-sex couples who dissolve their relationships find themselves and their children in the highly unpredictable terrain of equity jurisdiction. Given the wide range of public benefits reserved only for married couples, we do not credit the department's contention that the absence of access to civil marriage amounts to little more than an inconvenience to same-sex couples and their children. Excluding same-sex couples from civil marriage will not make children of opposite-sex marriages more secure, but it does prevent children of same-sex couples from enjoying the immeasurable advantages that flow from the assurance of "a stable family structure in which children will be reared, educated, and socialized."

No one disputes that the plaintiff couples are families, that many are parents, and that the children they are raising, like all children, need and should have the fullest opportunity to grow up in a secure, protected family unit. Similarly, no one disputes that, under the rubric of marriage, the State provides a cornucopia of substantial benefits to married parents and their children. The preferential treatment of civil marriage reflects the Legislature's conclusion that marriage "is the foremost setting for the education and socialization of children" precisely because it "encourages parents to remain committed to each other and to their children as they grow."

In this case, we are confronted with an entire, sizeable class of parents raising children who have absolutely no access to civil marriage and its protections because they are forbidden from procuring a marriage license. It cannot be rational under our laws, and indeed it is not permitted, to penalize children by depriving them of State benefits because the State disapproves of their parents' sexual orientation.

The third rationale advanced by the department is that limiting marriage to opposite-sex couples furthers the Legislature's interest in conserving scarce State and private financial resources. The marriage restriction is rational, it argues, because the General Court logically could assume that same-sex couples are more financially independent than married couples and thus less needy of public marital benefits, such as tax advantages, or private marital benefits, such as employer-financed health plans that include spouses in their coverage.

An absolute statutory ban on same-sex marriage bears no rational relationship to the goal of economy. First, the department's conclusory generalization — that same-sex couples are less financially dependent on each other than opposite-sex couples — ignores that many same-sex couples, such as many of the plaintiffs in this case, have children and other dependents (here, aged parents) in their care. The department does not contend, nor could it, that these dependents are less needy or deserving than the dependents of married couples. Second, Massachusetts marriage laws do not condition receipt of public and private financial benefits to married individuals on a demonstration of financial dependence on each other; the benefits are available to married couples regardless of whether they mingle their finances or actually depend on each other for support.

The department suggests additional rationales for prohibiting same-sex couples from marrying, which are developed by some amici. It argues that broadening civil marriage to include same-sex couples will trivialize or destroy the institution of marriage as it has historically been fashioned. Certainly our decision today marks a significant change in the definition of marriage as it has been inherited from the common law, and understood by many societies for centuries. But it does not disturb the fundamental value of marriage in our society.

Here, the plaintiffs seek only to be married, not to undermine the institution of civil marriage. They do not want marriage abolished. They do not attack the binary nature of marriage, the consanguinity provisions, or any of the other gate-keeping provisions of the marriage licensing law. Recognizing the right of an individual to marry a person of the same sex will not diminish the validity or dignity of opposite-sex marriage, any more than recognizing the right of an individual to marry a person of a different race devalues the marriage of a person who marries someone of her own race. If anything, extending civil marriage to same-sex couples reinforces the importance of marriage to individuals and communities. That same-sex couples are willing to embrace marriage's solemn obligations of exclusivity, mutual support, and commitment to one another is a testament to the enduring place of marriage in our laws and in the human spirit. . . .

The history of constitutional law "is the story of the extension of constitutional rights and protections to people once ignored or excluded." *United States v. Virginia,* 518 U.S. 515, 557 (1996). This statement is as true in the area of civil marriage as in any other area of civil rights. . . . Alarms about the imminent erosion of the "natural" order of marriage were sounded over the demise of antimiscegenation laws, the expansion of the rights of married women, and the introduction of "no-fault" divorce. Marriage has survived all of these transformations, and we have no doubt that marriage will continue to be a vibrant and revered institution.

We also reject the argument suggested by the department, and elaborated by some amici, that expanding the institution of civil marriage in Massachusetts to include same-sex couples will lead to interstate conflict. We would not presume to dictate how another State should respond to today's decision. But neither should considerations of comity prevent us from according Massachusetts residents the full measure of protection available under the Massachusetts Constitution. The genius of our Federal system is that each State's Constitution has vitality specific to its own traditions, and that, subject to the minimum requirements of the Fourteenth Amendment, each State is free to address difficult issues of individual liberty in the manner its own Constitution demands.

Several amici suggest that prohibiting marriage by same-sex couples reflects community consensus that homosexual conduct is immoral. Yet Massachusetts has a strong affirmative policy of preventing discrimination on the basis of sexual orientation. See G.L. c. 151B (employment, housing, credit, services); G.L. c. 265, §39 (hate crimes); G.L. c. 272, §98 (public accommodation); G.L. c. 76, §5 (public education). See also, e.g., *Commonwealth v. Balthazar,* 366 Mass. 298 (1974) (decriminalization of private consensual adult conduct); *Doe v. Doe,* 16 Mass.App.Ct. 499, 503 (1983) (custody to homosexual parent not per se prohibited).

The department has had more than ample opportunity to articulate a constitutionally adequate justification for limiting civil marriage to opposite-sex unions. It has failed to do so. The department has offered purported justifications for the civil marriage restriction that are starkly at odds with the comprehensive network of vigorous, gender-neutral laws promoting stable families and the best interests of children. It has failed to identify any relevant characteristic that would justify shutting the door to civil marriage to a person who wishes to marry someone of the same sex.

The marriage ban works a deep and scarring hardship on a very real segment of the community for no rational reason. The absence of any reasonable relationship between, on the one hand, an absolute disqualification of same-sex couples who wish to enter into civil marriage and, on the other, protection of public health, safety, or general welfare, suggests that the marriage restriction is rooted in persistent prejudices against persons who are (or who are believed to be) homosexual. "The Constitution cannot control such prejudices but neither can it tolerate them. Private biases may be outside the reach of the law, but the law cannot, directly or indirectly, give them effect." *Palmore v. Sidoti,* 466 U.S. 429, 433 (1984) (construing Fourteenth Amendment). Limiting the protections, benefits, and obligations of civil marriage to opposite-sex couples violates the basic premises of individual liberty and equality under law protected by the Massachusetts Constitution....

SOSMAN, J. (dissenting, with whom Spina and Cordy, JJ., join).

....

Although ostensibly applying the rational basis test to the civil marriage statutes, it is abundantly apparent that the court is in fact applying some undefined stricter standard to assess the constitutionality of the marriage statutes' exclusion of same-sex couples. While avoiding any express conclusion as to any of the proffered routes by which that exclusion would be subjected to a test of strict scrutiny—infringement of a fundamental right, discrimination based on gender, or discrimination against gays and lesbians as a suspect classification—the opinion repeatedly alludes to those concepts in a prolonged and eloquent prelude before articulating its view that the exclusion lacks even a rational basis. In short, while claiming to apply a mere rational basis test, the court's opinion works up an enormous head of steam by repeated invocations of avenues by which to subject the statute to strict scrutiny, apparently hoping that that head of steam will generate momentum sufficient to propel the opinion across the yawning chasm of the very deferential rational basis test.

Shorn of these emotion-laden invocations, the opinion ultimately opines that the Legislature is acting irrationally when it grants benefits to a proven successful family structure while denying the same benefits to a recent, perhaps promising, but essentially untested alternate family structure. Placed in a more neutral context, the court would never find any irrationality in such an approach....

The issue is whether it is rational to reserve judgment on whether this change can be made at this time without damaging the institution of marriage or adversely affecting the critical role it has played in our society. Absent consensus on the issue (which obviously does not exist), or unanimity amongst scientists studying the issue (which also does not exist), or a more prolonged period of observation of this new family structure (which has not yet been possible), it is rational for the Legislature to postpone any redefinition of marriage that would include same-sex couples until such time as it is certain that that redefinition will not have unintended and undesirable social consequences....

As a matter of social history, today's opinion may represent a great turning point that many will hail as a tremendous step toward a more just society. As a matter of constitutional jurisprudence, however, the case stands as an aberration. To reach the result it does, the court has tortured the rational basis test beyond recognition. I fully appreciate the strength of the temptation to find this particular law unconstitutional—there is much to be said for the argument that excluding gay and lesbian couples from the benefits of civil marriage is cruelly unfair and hopelessly outdated; the inability to marry has a profound impact on the personal lives of committed gay and lesbian couples (and their children) to whom we are personally close (our friends, neighbors, family members, classmates, and co-workers); and our resolution of this issue takes place under the intense glare of national and international publicity. Speaking metaphorically, these factors have combined to turn the case before us into a "perfect storm" of a constitutional question. In my view, however, such factors make it all the more imperative that we adhere precisely and scrupulously to the established guideposts of our constitutional jurisprudence, a jurisprudence that makes the rational basis test an extremely deferential one that focuses on the rationality, not the persuasiveness, of the potential justifications for the classifications in the legislative scheme. I trust that, once this particular "storm" clears, we will return to the rational basis test as it has always been understood and applied. Applying that deferential test in the manner it is customarily applied, the exclusion of gay and lesbian couples from the institution of civil marriage passes constitutional muster. I respectfully dissent.

CORDY, J. (dissenting, with whom Spina and Sosman, JJ., join).

[Justice Cordy first concludes that rational basis is the appropriate level of scrutiny under both the equal protection and due process provisions of the Massachusetts Constitution.]

3. *Rational relationship.* The question we must turn to next is whether the statute, construed as limiting marriage to couples of the opposite sex, remains a rational way to further that purpose. Stated differently, we ask whether a conceivable rational basis exists on which the Legislature could conclude that continuing to limit the institution of civil marriage to members of the opposite sex furthers the legitimate purpose of ensuring, promoting, and supporting an optimal social structure for the bearing and raising of children.[21]

....

Taking all of [the] available information into account, the Legislature could rationally conclude that a family environment with married opposite-sex parents remains the optimal social structure in which to bear children, and that the raising of children by same-sex couples, who by definition cannot be the two sole biological parents of a child and cannot provide children with a parental authority figure of each gender, presents an alternative structure for child rearing that has not yet proved itself beyond reasonable scientific dispute to be as optimal as the biologically based marriage norm. Working from the assumption that a recognition of same-sex marriages will increase the number of children experiencing this alternative, the Legislature could conceivably conclude that declining to recognize same-sex marriages remains prudent until empirical questions about its impact on the upbringing of children are resolved.

The fact that the Commonwealth currently allows same-sex couples to adopt does not affect the rationality of this conclusion. The eligibility of a child for adoption presupposes that at least one of the child's biological parents is unable or unwilling, for some reason, to participate in raising the child. In that sense, society has "lost" the optimal setting in which to raise that child—it is simply not available. In these circumstances, the principal and overriding consideration is the "best interests of the child," considering his or her unique circumstances and the options that are available for that child. The objective is an individualized determination of the best environment for a particular child, where the normative social structure—a home with both the child's biological father and mother—is not an option. That such a focused determination may lead to the approval of a same-sex couple's adoption of a child does not mean that it would be irrational for a legislator, in fashioning statutory laws that cannot make such individualized determinations, to conclude generally that being raised by a same-sex

---

21. In support of its conclusion that the marriage statute does not satisfy the rational basis test, the court emphasizes that "[t]he department has offered no evidence that forbidding marriage to people of the same sex will increase the number of couples choosing to enter into opposite-sex marriages in order to have and raise children." This surprising statement misallocates the burden of proof in a constitutional challenge to the rational basis of a statute. It is the plaintiffs who must prove that supporting and promoting one form of relationship by providing (as is pointed out) literally hundreds of benefits, could not conceivably affect the decision-making of anyone considering whether to bear and raise a child. The department is not required to present "evidence" of anything.

couple has not yet been shown to be the absolute equivalent of being raised by one's married biological parents.

That the State does not preclude different types of families from raising children does not mean that it must view them all as equally optimal and equally deserving of State endorsement and support. For example, single persons are allowed to adopt children, but the fact that the Legislature permits single-parent adoption does not mean that it has endorsed single parenthood as an optimal setting in which to raise children or views it as the equivalent of being raised by both of one's biological parents. The same holds true with respect to same-sex couples—the fact that they may adopt children means only that the Legislature has concluded that they may provide an acceptable setting in which to raise children who cannot be raised by both of their biological parents. The Legislature may rationally permit adoption by same-sex couples yet harbor reservations as to whether parenthood by same-sex couples should be affirmatively encouraged to the same extent as parenthood by the heterosexual couple whose union produced the child.

In addition, the Legislature could conclude that redefining the institution of marriage to permit same-sex couples to marry would impair the State's interest in promoting and supporting heterosexual marriage as the social institution that it has determined best normalizes, stabilizes, and links the acts of procreation and child rearing. While the plaintiffs argue that they only want to take part in the same stabilizing institution, the Legislature conceivably could conclude that permitting their participation would have the unintended effect of undermining to some degree marriage's ability to serve its social purpose.

So long as marriage is limited to opposite-sex couples who can at least theoretically procreate, society is able to communicate a consistent message to its citizens that marriage is a (normatively) necessary part of their procreative endeavor; that if they are to procreate, then society has endorsed the institution of marriage as the environment for it and for the subsequent rearing of their children; and that benefits are available explicitly to create a supportive and conducive atmosphere for those purposes. If society proceeds similarly to recognize marriages between same-sex couples who cannot procreate, it could be perceived as an abandonment of this claim, and might result in the mistaken view that civil marriage has little to do with procreation: just as the potential of procreation would not be necessary for a marriage to be valid, marriage would not be necessary for optimal procreation and child rearing to occur. In essence, the Legislature could conclude that the consequence of such a policy shift would be a diminution in society's ability to steer the acts of procreation and child rearing into their most optimal setting.[35]

    ....

[The concurring opinion of Justice Greaney and the dissenting opinion of Justice Spina are omitted.]

---

35. Although the marriage statute is overinclusive because it comprehends within its scope infertile or voluntarily nonreproductive opposite-sex couples, this overinclusiveness does not make the statute constitutionally infirm. See *Massachusetts Fed'n of Teachers v. Board of Educ.*, 436 Mass. 763, 778 (2002) ("Some degree of overinclusiveness or underinclusiveness is constitutionally permissible ..."). The overinclusiveness present here is constitutionally permissible because the Commonwealth has chosen, reasonably, not to test every prospective married couple for fertility and not to demand of fertile prospective married couples whether or not they will procreate. It is satisfied, rather, to allow every couple whose biological opposition makes procreation theoretically possible to join the institution.

Hernandez v. Robles

855 N.E.2d 1 (N.Y. 2006)

R.S. SMITH, J.

[Same-sex couples who applied for and were denied marriage licenses brought suit, contending that denying them the right to marry violates the equal protection and due process guarantees of the New York Constitution.]

    ....

II

We approach plaintiffs' claims by first considering, in section III below, whether the challenged limitation can be defended as a rational legislative decision. The answer to this question, as we show in section IV below, is critical at every stage of the due process and equal protection analysis.

III

It is undisputed that the benefits of marriage are many....

The critical question is whether a rational legislature could decide that these benefits should be given to members of opposite-sex couples, but not same-sex couples.... We conclude, however, that there are at least two grounds that rationally support the limitation on marriage that the Legislature has enacted....

First, the Legislature could rationally decide that, for the welfare of children, it is more important to promote stability, and to avoid instability, in opposite-sex than in same-sex relationships. Heterosexual intercourse has a natural tendency to lead to the birth of children; homosexual intercourse does not. Despite the advances of science, it remains true that the vast majority of children are born as a result of a sexual relationship between a man and a woman, and the Legislature could find that this will continue to be true. The Legislature could also find that such relationships are all too often casual or temporary. It could find that an important function of marriage is to create more stability and permanence in the relationships that cause children to be born. It thus could choose to offer an inducement — in the form of marriage and its attendant benefits — to opposite-sex couples who make a solemn, long-term commitment to each other.

The Legislature could find that this rationale for marriage does not apply with comparable force to same-sex couples. These couples can become parents by adoption, or by artificial insemination or other technological marvels, but they do not become parents as a result of accident or impulse. The Legislature could find that unstable relationships between people of the opposite sex present a greater danger that children will be born into or grow up in unstable homes than is the case with same-sex couples, and thus that promoting stability in opposite-sex relationships will help children more. This is one reason why the Legislature could rationally offer the benefits of marriage to opposite-sex couples only.

There is a second reason: The Legislature could rationally believe that it is better, other things being equal, for children to grow up with both a mother and a father. Intuition and experience suggest that a child benefits from having before his or her eyes, every day, living models of what both a man and a woman are like. It is obvious that there are exceptions to this general rule — some children who never know their fathers, or their mothers, do far better than some who grow up with parents of both sexes — but the Legislature could find that the general rule will usually hold.

Plaintiffs, and amici supporting them, argue that the proposition asserted is simply untrue: that a home with two parents of different sexes has no advantage, from the point of view of raising children, over a home with two parents of the same sex. Perhaps they are right, but the Legislature could rationally think otherwise.

To support their argument, plaintiffs and amici supporting them refer to social science literature reporting studies of same-sex parents and their children. Some opponents of same-sex marriage criticize these studies, but we need not consider the criticism, for the studies on their face do not establish beyond doubt that children fare equally well in same-sex and opposite-sex households. What they show, at most, is that rather limited observation has detected no marked differences. More definitive results could hardly be expected, for until recently few children have been raised in same-sex households, and there has not been enough time to study the long-term results of such child-rearing.

Plaintiffs seem to assume that they have demonstrated the irrationality of the view that opposite-sex marriages offer advantages to children by showing there is no scientific evidence to support it. Even assuming no such evidence exists, this reasoning is flawed. In the absence of conclusive scientific evidence, the Legislature could rationally proceed on the commonsense premise that children will do best with a mother and father in the home. And a legislature proceeding on that premise could rationally decide to offer a special inducement, the legal recognition of marriage, to encourage the formation of opposite-sex households.

In sum, there are rational grounds on which the Legislature could choose to restrict marriage to couples of opposite sex. Plaintiffs have not persuaded us that this long-accepted restriction is a wholly irrational one, based solely on ignorance and prejudice against homosexuals....

[The concurring opinion of Judge Graffeo and the dissenting opinion of Chief Judge Kaye are omitted.]

Notes and Questions

1. Is the *Goodridge* majority *really* applying rational basis review, or is the criticism by Judge Sosman well-taken? Isn't the majority requiring a greater ends-means fit than rational basis review requires? And is it in fact placing the burden on the challenger? Is it perhaps applying "transitional rational basis plus" or "fleeting rational basis plus" review?

2. Judge Sosman describes the many citations to cases employing strict scrutiny to "work[] up a head of steam." In this regard, note the many citations to U.S. Supreme Court cases interpreting the federal constitution, such as *Loving, Lawrence, Casey, Zablocki*, and *Eisenstadt*. The plaintiffs in this case only challenged the marriage laws on state constitutional grounds. Is it clear, in reading the opinion, that the case was decided on an "adequate and *independent* state ground"?

3. Why would the majority be reluctant to openly apply heightened scrutiny by either treating sexual orientation as a suspect classification, characterizing the statute as discriminating on the basis of sex, or holding that it infringes upon a fundamental right? While the *Romer* and *Lawrence* Courts may have been reluctant to openly apply heightened scrutiny for fear that so doing would effectively decide the same-sex marriage question, why should the Massachusetts high court be concerned if it is doing so in the context of a case that actually is deciding the same-sex marriage question? What unintended consequences might a ruling for intermediate or strict scrutiny on one of those alternative bases entail?

4. How persuasive are the various rationales for the law posited in the *Goodridge* dissents and the *Hernandez* majority opinion? Remember, to satisfy rational basis review, a law needs only *one* supporting reason, and it does not have to be a terribly persuasive one. Regardless of your own personal views on the constitutionality of laws prohibiting same-sex marriage, can it really be said that none of the hypothesized rationales satisfy the traditional rational basis standard under equal protection and due process jurisprudence?

5. Note how much discussion there is in the majority opinion in *Goodridge* about the negative impact that bans on same-sex marriage have on the *children* of same-sex couples. Does this not suggest that the more appropriate plaintiffs in such cases might be the *children* of same-sex couples rather than their parents? Is there an argument—based on the legitimacy cases as well as the Court's decision in *Plyler* (applying heightened scrutiny to laws targeting the *children* of illegal immigrants)—that these laws should be subject to heightened scrutiny when analyzed from the perspective of the children of gays and lesbians even if heightened scrutiny is inapplicable when viewed from the perspective of their parents?

c. Are Laws Banning Same-Sex Marriage Subject to Strict Scrutiny because They Infringe upon a Fundamental Right?

Problem 5-A: The "Fundamental Right" to Marry

In which of the following scenarios, if any, is there a viable argument that the state is unconstitutionally infringing upon the "fundamental right" to marry?

(1) A state permits opposite-sex couples to marry but does not permit same-sex couples to marry or otherwise receive legal recognition of their relationships (gay people are still free to marry someone of the opposite sex).

(2) A state permits opposite-sex couples to marry but only permits same-sex couples to enter into civil unions that come with all the rights, responsibilities, and privileges associated with marriage.

(3) A state eliminates marriage for all couples and replaces it with civil unions for same-sex as well as opposite-sex couples.

(4) A state eliminates marriage for all couples and provides no legal recognition of any relationships, same-sex or opposite-sex.

(5) Same as scenario (1), except that state law prevents transgendered persons (defined as "those who have attempted to alter their sex as assigned at birth through surgery or hormone treatment") from marrying anyone.

As seen in Part B.3.a, most courts have rejected the *Loving* analogy so far as sex-based equal protection challenges to laws prohibiting same-sex marriage are concerned. But recall that *Loving* also held that Virginia's antimiscegenation laws were independently subject to strict scrutiny on the ground that they infringed upon the fundamental right to marry. The first same-sex marriage case—*Baker v. Nelson*—rejected the fundamental right argument, but that court also did not have the benefit of the U.S. Supreme Court's subsequent decisions in *Zablocki* and *Turner*. The materials that follow consider the argument for applying heightened scrutiny to laws prohibiting same-sex marriage on the ground that they interfere with a fundamental right.

Baehr v. Lewin

852 P.2d 44 (Haw. 1993)

LEVINSON, Judge, in which MOON, Chief Judge, joins.

[Same-sex couples who applied for and were denied marriage licenses brought suit, contending that denying them the right to marry violates, *inter alia*, the due process guarantee of the Hawaii Constitution.]

[T]here is no doubt that, at a minimum, article I, section 6 of the Hawaii Constitution encompasses all of the fundamental rights expressly recognized as being subsumed within the privacy protections of the United States Constitution. In this connection, the United States Supreme Court has declared that "the right to marry is part of the fundamental 'right of privacy' implicit in the Fourteenth Amendment's Due Process Clause." *Zablocki v. Redhail*, 434 U.S. 374, 384 (1978)....

The United States Supreme Court first characterized the right of marriage as fundamental in *Skinner v. Oklahoma ex rel. Williamson*, 316 U.S. 535 (1942). In *Skinner,* the right to marry was inextricably linked to the right of procreation. The dispute before the Court arose out of an Oklahoma statute that allowed the state to sterilize "habitual criminals" without their consent. In striking down the statute, the *Skinner* court indicated that it was "dealing ... with legislation which involve[d] *one of the basic civil rights of man. Marriage and procreation are fundamental to the very existence and survival of the race." Id.* at 541 (emphasis added). Whether the Court viewed marriage and procreation as a single indivisible right, the least that can be said is that it was obviously contemplating unions between men and women when it ruled that the right to marry was fundamental. This is hardly surprising inasmuch as none of the United States sanctioned any other marriage configuration at the time.

The United States Supreme Court has set forth its most detailed discussion of the fundamental right to marry in *Zablocki, supra,* which involved a Wisconsin statute that prohibited any resident of the state with minor children "not in his custody and which he is under obligation to support" from obtaining a marriage license until the resident demonstrated to a court that he was in compliance with his child support obligations. The *Zablocki* court held that the statute burdened the fundamental right to marry; applying the "strict scrutiny" standard to the statute, the Court invalidated it as violative of the fourteenth amendment to the United States Constitution. In so doing, the *Zablocki* court delineated its view of the evolution of the federally recognized fundamental right of marriage as follows:

> Long ago, in *Maynard v. Hill,* 125 U.S. 190 (1888), the Court characterized marriage as "the most important relation in life," and as "the foundation of the family and of society, without which there would be neither civilization nor progress." In *Meyer v. Nebraska,* 262 U.S. 390 (1923), the Court recognized that the right "to marry, establish a home and bring up children" is a central part of the liberty protected by the Due Process Clause, and in *Skinner v. Oklahoma ex rel. Williamson, supra,* ... marriage was described as "fundamental to the very existence and survival of the race."
>
> ....
>
> It is not surprising that the decision to marry has been placed on the same level of importance as decisions relating to procreation, childbirth, child rearing, and family relationships. As the facts of this case illustrate, it would make little sense to recognize a right of privacy with respect to other matters of family life and not with respect to the decision to enter the relationship that is the foundation

> of the family in our society. The woman whom appellee desired to marry had a fundamental right to seek an abortion of their expected child, see *Roe v. Wade, supra,* or to bring the child into life to suffer the myriad social, if not economic, disabilities that the status of illigitimacy brings.... Surely, a decision to marry and raise the child in a traditional family setting must receive equivalent protection. And, if appellee's right to procreate means anything at all, it must imply some right to enter the only relationship in which the State of Wisconsin allows sexual relations legally to take place.

Implicit in the *Zablocki* court's link between the right to marry, on the one hand, and the fundamental rights of procreation, childbirth, abortion, and child rearing, on the other, is the assumption that the one is simply the logical predicate of the others.

The foregoing case law demonstrates that the federal construct of the fundamental right to marry—subsumed within the right to privacy implicitly protected by the United States Constitution—presently contemplates unions between men and women....

[W]e do not believe that a right to same-sex marriage is so rooted in the traditions and collective conscience of our people that failure to recognize it would violate the fundamental principles of liberty and justice that lie at the base of all our civil and political institutions. Neither do we believe that a right to same-sex marriage is implicit in the concept of ordered liberty, such that neither liberty nor justice would exist if it were sacrificed. Accordingly, we hold that the applicant couples do not have a fundamental constitutional right to same-sex marriage arising out of the right to privacy or otherwise....

[The concurring opinion of Judge Burns and the dissenting opinion of Judge Heen are omitted.]

Hernandez v. Robles

855 N.E.2d 1 (N.Y. 2006)

R.S. SMITH, J.

[Same-sex couples who applied for and were denied marriage licenses brought suit, contending that denying them the right to marry violates, *inter alia,* the due process guarantee of the New York Constitution.]

In deciding the validity of legislation under the Due Process Clause, courts first inquire whether the legislation restricts the exercise of a fundamental right, one that is "deeply rooted in this Nation's history and tradition" (*Washington v. Glucksberg,* 521 U.S. 702, 721 [1997], quoting *Moore v. East Cleveland,* 431 U.S. 494, 503 [1977] [plurality op.]; *Hope v. Perales,* 83 N.Y.2d 563, 575 [1994]). In this case, whether the right in question is "fundamental" depends on how it is defined. The right to marry is unquestionably a fundamental right (*Loving,* 388 U.S. at 12; *Zablocki v. Redhail,* 434 U.S. 374, 384 [1978]; *Cooper,* 49 N.Y.2d at 79). The right to marry someone of the same sex, however, is not "deeply rooted"; it has not even been asserted until relatively recent times. The issue then becomes whether the right to marry must be defined to include a right to same-sex marriage.

Recent Supreme Court decisions show that the definition of a fundamental right for due process purposes may be either too narrow or too broad. In *Lawrence v. Texas,* 539 U.S. 558, 566 (2003), the Supreme Court criticized its own prior decision in *Bowers v. Hardwick,* 478 U.S. 186, 190 (1986) for defining the right at issue as the right of "homosexuals to engage in sodomy." The *Lawrence* court plainly thought the right should have been defined more broadly, as a right to privacy in intimate relationships. On the other hand, in *Washington v. Glucksberg*, 521 U.S. at 722, 723, the Court criticized a lower federal court for defining the right at issue too broadly as a "right to die"; the right at issue in *Glucksberg*, the Court said, was really the "right to commit suicide" and to have assistance in doing so.

The difference between *Lawrence* and *Glucksberg* is that in *Glucksberg* the relatively narrow definition of the right at issue was based on rational line-drawing. In *Lawrence*, by contrast, the court found the distinction between homosexual sodomy and intimate relations generally to be essentially arbitrary. Here, there are, as we have explained, rational grounds for limiting the definition of marriage to opposite-sex couples. This case is therefore, in the relevant way, like *Glucksberg* and not at all like *Lawrence*. Plaintiffs here do not, as the petitioners in *Lawrence* did, seek protection against state intrusion on intimate, private activity. They seek from the courts access to a state-conferred benefit that the Legislature has rationally limited to opposite-sex couples. We conclude that, by defining marriage as it has, the New York Legislature has not restricted the exercise of a fundamental right....

[The concurring opinion of Judge Graffeo and the dissenting opinion of Chief Judge Kaye are omitted.]

In re Marriage Cases

183 P.3d 384 (Cal. 2008)

[Same-sex couples who applied for and were denied marriage licenses brought suit, contending that denying them the right to marry violates, *inter alia*, the due process guarantee of the California Constitution.]

GEORGE, C.J.

....

Although all parties in this proceeding agree that the right to marry constitutes a fundamental right protected by the state Constitution, there is considerable disagreement as to the scope and content of this fundamental state constitutional right....

Plaintiffs challenge the Court of Appeal's characterization of the constitutional right they seek to invoke as the right to same-sex marriage, and on this point we agree with plaintiffs' position. In *Perez v. Sharp*, 32 Cal.2d 711—this court's 1948 decision holding that the California statutory provisions prohibiting interracial marriage were unconstitutional—the court did not characterize the constitutional right that the plaintiffs in that case sought to obtain as "a right to interracial marriage" and did not dismiss the plaintiffs' constitutional challenge on the ground that such marriages never had been permitted in California. Instead, the *Perez* decision focused on the *substance* of the constitutional right at issue—that is, the importance to an individual of the freedom "to join in marriage *with the person of one's choice*"—in determining whether the statute impinged upon the plaintiffs' fundamental constitutional right.... And, in addressing a somewhat analogous point, the United States Supreme Court in *Lawrence v. Texas* (2003) 539 U.S. 558 concluded that its prior decision in *Bowers v. Hardwick* (1986) 478 U.S. 186 had erred in narrowly characterizing the constitutional right sought to be invoked in that case as the right to engage in intimate *homosexual* conduct, determining instead that the constitutional right there at issue properly should be understood in a broader and more neutral fashion so as to focus upon the substance of the interests that the constitutional right is intended to protect.[33]

The flaw in characterizing the constitutional right at issue as the right to same-sex marriage rather than the right to marry goes beyond mere semantics. It is important both analytically and from the standpoint of fairness to plaintiffs' argument that we recognize they are not seeking to create a new constitutional right—the right to "same-sex marriage"—or to change, modify, or (as some have suggested) "deinstitutionalize" the existing institution of marriage. Instead, plaintiffs contend that, properly interpreted, the state constitutional right to marry affords same-sex couples the same rights and benefits—accompanied by the same mutual responsibilities and obligations—as this constitutional right affords to opposite-sex couples....

In discussing the constitutional right to marry in *Perez v. Sharp, supra,* 32 Cal.2d 711 (*Perez*), then Justice Traynor in the lead opinion quoted the seminal passage from the United States Supreme Court's decision in *Meyer v. Nebraska, supra,* 262 U.S. 390. There the high court, in describing the scope of the "liberty" protected by the due process clause of the federal Constitution, stated that "'[w]ithout doubt, it denotes not merely freedom from bodily restraint, but also the right of the individual to contract, to engage in any of the common occupations of life, to acquire useful knowledge, *to marry, establish a home and bring up children,* to worship God according to the dictates of one's own conscience, *and, generally, to enjoy those privileges long recognized at common law as essential to the orderly pursuit of happiness by free men.*'" The *Perez* decision continued: "*Marriage is thus something more than a civil contract subject to regulation by the state; it is a fundamental right of free men.*"

Like *Perez,* subsequent California decisions discussing the nature of marriage and the right to marry have recognized repeatedly the linkage between marriage, establishing a home, and raising children in identifying civil marriage as the means available to an individual to establish, with a loved one of his or her choice, an officially recognized *family* relationship....

If civil marriage were an institution whose *only* role was to serve the interests of society, it reasonably could be asserted that the state should have full authority to decide whether to establish or abolish the institution of marriage (and any similar institution, such as domestic partnership). In recognizing, however, that the right to marry is a basic, *constitutionally protected* civil right—"a fundamental right of free men [and women]" (*Perez, supra,* 32 Cal.2d 711, 714)—the governing California cases establish that this right embodies fundamental interests of an individual that are protected from abrogation or elimination by the state. Because our cases make clear that the right to marry is an integral component of an individual's interest in *personal autonomy* protected by the privacy provision of article I, section 1, and of the *liberty* interest protected by the due process clause of article I, section 7, it is apparent under the California Constitution that the right to marry—like the right to establish a home and raise children—has independent *substantive* content, and cannot properly be understood as simply the right to enter into such a relationship *if (but only if)* the Legislature chooses to establish and retain it.[42]

---

33. Similarly, in addressing under the federal Constitution the validity of a prison rule that permitted a prisoner to marry only if the superintendent of the prison found there were compelling reasons to permit the marriage, the high court did not characterize the constitutional right at issue as "the right to inmate marriage," but rather considered whether the purposes and attributes of the general fundamental right to marry were applicable in the prison context. (*Turner v. Safley* (1987) 482 U.S. 78, 95–96.)

42. One legal commentator has suggested that the federal constitutional right to marry simply "comprises a right of access to the expressive and material benefits that the state affords to the institution of marriage ... [and that] states may abolish marriage without offending the Constitution."

One very important aspect of the substantive protection afforded by the California constitutional right to marry is, of course, an individual's right to be free from undue governmental intrusion into (or interference with) integral features of this relationship—that is, the right of marital or familial privacy. The substantive protection embodied in the constitutional right to marry, however, goes beyond what is sometimes characterized as simply a "negative" right insulating the couple's relationship from overreaching governmental intrusion or interference, and includes a "positive" right to have the state take at least some affirmative action to acknowledge and support the family unit.

Although the constitutional right to marry clearly does not obligate the state to afford specific tax or other governmental benefits on the basis of a couple's family relationship, the right to marry does obligate the state to take affirmative action to grant official, public recognition to the couple's relationship as a family, as well as to protect the core elements of the family relationship from at least some types of improper interference by others....

In light of the fundamental nature of the substantive rights embodied in the right to marry—and their central importance to an individual's opportunity to live a happy, meaningful, and satisfying life as a full member of society—the California Constitution properly must be interpreted to guarantee this basic civil right to *all* individuals and couples, without regard to their sexual orientation....

In reaching the contrary conclusion that the right to marry guaranteed by the California Constitution should be understood as protecting only an individual's right to enter into an officially recognized family relationship with a person of the opposite sex, the Court of Appeal relied upon a number of decisions that have cautioned against defining at too high a level of generality those constitutional rights that are protected as part of the substantive due process doctrine.

None of the foregoing decisions—in emphasizing the importance of undertaking a "'careful description' of the asserted fundamental liberty interest" (*Washington v. Glucksberg, supra,* 521 U.S. 702, 721)—suggests, however, that it is appropriate to define a fundamental constitutional right or interest in so narrow a fashion that the basic protections afforded by the right are withheld from a class of persons—composed of individuals sharing a personal characteristic such as a particular sexual orientation—who historically have been denied the benefit of such rights. As noted above, our decision in *Perez, supra,* 32 Cal.2d 711, declining to define narrowly the right to marry, did not consider the fact that discrimination against interracial marriage was "sanctioned by the state for many years" to be a reason to reject the plaintiffs' claim in that case. Instead the court looked to the essence and substance of the right to marry, a right itself deeply rooted in the history and tradition of our state and nation, to determine whether the challenged statute impinged upon the plaintiffs' constitutional right. For similar reasons, it is apparent that history alone does not provide a justification for interpreting the constitutional right to

---

(Sunstein, *The Right to Marry* (2005) 26 Cardozo L.Rev. 2081, 2083–2084.) The article in question concedes, however, that its suggested view of the right to marry is inconsistent with the governing federal cases that identify the right to marry as an integral feature of the liberty interest protected by the due process clause, and further acknowledges that even "[i]f official marriage was abolished, the Due Process Clause might give people a right to some of the benefits and arrangements to which married people are ordinarily entitled under existing law." As explained above, in light of the governing cases identifying the source and explaining the significance of the state constitutional right to marry, we conclude that under the California Constitution this constitutional right properly must be viewed as having substantive content.

marry as protecting only one's ability to enter into an officially recognized family relationship with a person of the opposite sex. In this regard, we agree with the view expressed by Chief Judge Kaye of the New York Court of Appeals in her dissenting opinion in *Hernandez v. Robles, supra,* 855 N.E.2d 1, 23: "[F]undamental rights, once recognized, cannot be denied to particular groups on the ground that these groups have historically been denied those rights."

. . . .

The Proposition 22 Legal Defense Fund and the Campaign agree that the constitutional right to marry is integrally related to the right of two persons to join together to establish an officially recognized family, but they contend that the only family that possibly can be encompassed by the constitutional right to marry is a family headed by a man and a woman. Pointing out that past cases often have linked marriage and procreation, these parties argue that because only a man and a woman can produce children biologically with one another, the constitutional right to marry necessarily is limited to opposite-sex couples.

This contention is fundamentally flawed for a number of reasons. To begin with, although the legal institution of civil marriage may well have originated in large part to promote a stable relationship for the procreation and raising of children, and although the right to marry and to procreate often are treated as closely related aspects of the privacy and liberty interests protected by the state and federal Constitutions, the constitutional right to marry never has been viewed as the sole preserve of individuals who are physically capable of having children. Men and women who desire to raise children with a loved one in a recognized family but who are physically unable to conceive a child with their loved one never have been excluded from the right to marry. Although the Proposition 22 Legal Defense Fund and the Campaign assert that the circumstance that marriage has not been limited to those who can bear children can be explained and justified by reference to the state's reluctance to intrude upon the privacy of individuals by inquiring into their fertility, if that were an accurate and adequate explanation for the absence of such a limitation it would follow that in instances in which the state is able to make a determination of an individual's fertility without such an inquiry, it would be constitutionally permissible for the state to preclude an individual who is incapable of bearing children from entering into marriage. There is, however, no authority whatsoever to support the proposition that an individual who is physically incapable of bearing children does not possess a fundamental constitutional right to marry. Such a proposition clearly is untenable. A person who is physically incapable of bearing children still has the potential to become a parent and raise a child through adoption or through means of assisted reproduction, and the constitutional right to marry ensures the individual the opportunity to raise children in an officially recognized family with the person with whom the individual has chosen to share his or her life. Thus, although an important purpose underlying marriage may be to channel procreation into a stable family relationship, that purpose cannot be viewed as limiting the constitutional right to marry to couples who are capable of biologically producing a child together. . . .

Furthermore, although promoting and facilitating a stable environment for the procreation and raising of children is unquestionably one of the vitally important purposes underlying the institution of marriage and the constitutional right to marry, past cases make clear that this right is not confined to, or restrictively defined by, that purpose alone. As noted above, our past cases have recognized that the right to marry is the right to enter into a relationship that is "the center of the personal affections that ennoble and enrich human life"—a relationship that is "at once the most socially productive and individually fulfilling relationship that one can enjoy in the course of a lifetime." The personal enrichment afforded by the right to marry may be obtained by a couple whether or not they choose to have children, and the right to marry never has been limited to those who plan or desire to have children. Indeed, in *Griswold v. Connecticut, supra*, 381 U.S. 479—one of the seminal federal cases striking down a state law as violative of the federal constitutional right of privacy—the high court upheld a married couple's right to use contraception *to prevent procreation*, demonstrating quite clearly that the promotion of procreation is not the sole or defining purpose of marriage. Similarly, in *Turner v. Safley, supra*, 482 U.S. 78, the court held that the constitutional right to marry extends to an individual confined in state prison—even a prisoner who has no right to conjugal visits with his would-be spouse—emphasizing that "[m]any important attributes of marriage remain … after taking into account the limitations imposed by prison life … [including the] expressions of emotional support and public commitment [that] are an important and significant aspect of the marital relationship." Although *Griswold* and *Turner* relate to the right to marry under the federal Constitution, they accurately reflect the scope of the state constitutional right to marry as well. Accordingly, this right cannot properly be defined by or limited to the state's interest in fostering a favorable environment for the procreation and raising of children.…

[The concurring opinion of Justice Kennard and the dissenting opinions of Justices Baxter and Corrigan are omitted.]

Notes and Questions

1. Recall the discussion in Chapter 3 regarding the tension that exists between *Lawrence* and *Glucksberg* as to how narrowly or broadly to define the right at issue for substantive due process purposes. Resolving that tension is decisive, is it not, to determining the question whether the fundamental right to marry encompasses same-sex marriage? How good of a job do the *Hernandez* and *In re Marriage Cases* courts do in attempting to resolve the conflict?

In a case pre-dating both *Lawrence* and *Glucksberg*, some U.S. Supreme Court Justices raised but did not resolve the framing issue so far as the fundamental right to marry is concerned. In his plurality opinion in *Michael H. v. Gerald D.*, 491 U.S. 110 (1989), Justice Scalia wrote that when conducting substance due process analysis, the Court must define the right at issue with a high degree of specificity. *See id.* at 127 n.6. Justice O'Connor, joined by Justice Kennedy, wrote a separate concurring opinion refusing to join this portion of Justice Scalia's plurality opinion:

> I concur in all but footnote 6 of Justice SCALIA's opinion. This footnote sketches a mode of historical analysis to be used when identifying liberty interests protected by the Due Process Clause of the Fourteenth Amendment that may be somewhat inconsistent with our past decisions in this area. On occasion the Court has characterized relevant traditions protecting asserted rights at levels of generality that might not be "the most specific level" available. *See Loving v. Virginia*, 388 U.S. 1, 12 (1967); *Turner v. Safley*, 482 U.S. 78, 94 (1987). I would not foreclose the unanticipated by the prior imposition of a single mode of historical analysis.

Id. at 132 (O'Connor, J., concurring in part).

2. As discussed earlier in this chapter and discussed in the *Baehr* and *Hernandez* cases, it is possible to characterize the federal due process right to marry as little more than a proxy for the right to procreate. Thus, to the extent that, historically, marriage was the only lawful gateway to engaging in procreative activity (since states often criminalized

sexual intercourse between unmarried persons), marriage was "fundamental" in the sense that denying people the right to marry was tantamount to denying them the right to procreate. Yet, given that the Court's due process decisions through *Lawrence* no longer would permit a state to prevent unmarried persons from engaging in procreative sexual intercourse, is there really much to the argument that there is a free-standing substantive due process right to "marry" separate from the right to procreate?

3. Is it clear from the *Loving-Zablocki-Turner* line of cases whether the fundamental right to marry is a substantive due process fundamental right, an equal protection fundamental right, or both? Is it possible that to the extent that marriage serves as a gateway to procreation, it is a substantive due process right, but to the extent it merely involves official state recognition of the relationship (and the associated benefits), it is an equal protection right? If so, what leeway would a state have to eliminate "marriage" and either replace it with an alternative scheme (such as civil unions) or to eliminate completely formal recognition of relationships? What does the *In re Marriage Cases* court suggest about the nature of the right under the California Constitution?

d. Is Sexual Orientation a Suspect Classification, thus Requiring Heightened Equal Protection Scrutiny of Laws Banning Same-Sex Marriage?

The cases in Chapter 4 examined the so-called "*Frontiero* factors" for determining whether to recognize a group as suspect or quasi-suspect for equal protection purposes, including: whether the group has suffered a history of discrimination; whether the defining characteristic bears any relationship to their ability to perform or contribute to society; whether the characteristic is "immutable"; and whether the group is politically powerless.

Chapter 4 previewed cases applying the *Frontiero* factors to sexual orientation. Typical of these cases was *High Tech Gays v. Defense Industrial Security Clearance Office*, 895 F.2d 563 (9th Cir. 1990). Like *High Tech Gays*, most federal and state cases, while having no difficulty concluding that gays and lesbians have suffered from a history of discrimination and that one's sexual orientation has little to do with ability to perform or contribute to society, have traditionally rejected arguments for heightened scrutiny for sexual orientation classifications on the grounds that gays and lesbians are not politically powerless and that it is not clear that sexual orientation is immutable.

Accordingly, many state courts that have been confronted with equal protection challenges to state laws prohibiting same-sex marriage have rejected claims for heightened scrutiny for sexual orientation classifications. However, in 2008 and 2009 several state high courts — including those in California, Connecticut, and Iowa — held that sexual orientation was either a suspect or quasi-suspect classification. The following decision from Connecticut is representative.

Kerrigan v. Commissioner of Public Health

957 A.2d 407 (Conn. 2008)

PALMER, J.

[Same-sex couples challenge scheme whereby they are permitted to enter into civil unions (with all the rights, benefits, and responsibilities associated with marriage), but are not permitted to marry, contending that it violates, *inter alia*, the equal protection guarantee of the Connecticut Constitution.]

....

IV
QUASI-SUSPECT CLASSIFICATIONS UNDER THE STATE CONSTITUTION

Although this court has indicated that a group may be entitled to heightened protection under the state constitution because of its status as a quasi-suspect class, we previously have not articulated the specific criteria to be considered in determining whether recognition as a quasi-suspect class is warranted. The United States Supreme Court, however, consistently has identified two factors that must be met, for purposes of the federal constitution, if a group is to be accorded such status. These two required factors are: (1) the group has suffered a history of invidious discrimination; and (2) the characteristics that distinguish the group's members bear "no relation to [their] ability to perform or contribute to society." The United States Supreme Court also has cited two other considerations that, in a given case, may be relevant in determining whether statutory provisions pertaining to a particular group are subject to heightened scrutiny. These two additional considerations are: (1) the characteristic that defines the members of the class as a discrete group is immutable or otherwise not within their control; and (2) the group is "a minority or politically powerless."

To date, the United States Supreme Court has recognized two quasi-suspect classes, namely, sex and illegitimacy. The court, however, has rejected claims that the aged and the mentally disadvantaged are quasi-suspect classes, principally because the defining characteristic of each group does in fact bear a substantial relationship to the group's ability to participate in and contribute to society.

Because of the evident correlation between the indicia of suspectness identified by the United States Supreme Court and the issue of whether a class that has been singled out by the state for unequal treatment is entitled to heightened protection under the federal constitution, we conclude that those factors also are pertinent to the determination of whether a group comprises a quasi-suspect class for purposes of the state constitution. It bears emphasis, however, that the United States Supreme Court has placed far greater weight — indeed, it invariably has placed dispositive weight — on the first two factors, that is, whether the group has been the subject of long-standing and invidious discrimination and whether the group's distinguishing characteristic bears no relation to the ability of the group members to perform or function in society. In circumstances in which a group has been subject to such discrimination and its distinguishing characteristic does not bear any relation to such ability, the court inevitably has employed heightened scrutiny in reviewing statutory classifications targeting those groups....

It is evident, moreover, that immutability and minority status or political powerlessness are subsidiary to the first two primary factors because, as we explain more fully hereinafter, the United States Supreme Court has granted suspect class status to a group whose distinguishing characteristic is not immutable; see *Nyquist v. Mauclet,* 432 U.S. 1, 9 n. 11 (1977) (rejecting immutability requirement in treating group of resident aliens as suspect class despite their ability to opt out of class voluntarily); and has accorded quasi-suspect status to a group that had not been a minority or truly politically powerless. See *Frontiero v. Richardson,* supra, 411 U.S. at 686 n. 17 (plurality opinion) (according women heightened protection despite court's acknowledgment that women "do not constitute a small and powerless minority"). We do not doubt, moreover, that the court has accorded little weight to a group's political power because that factor, in contrast to the other criteria, frequently is not readily discernible by reference to objective standards. Thus, an attempt to quantify a group's political influence often will involve a myriad of complex and interrelated considerations of a kind not readily susceptible to judicial fact-finding. Nevertheless, because the court has identified the immutability of the group's distinguishing characteristic and the group's minority status or relative lack of political power as potentially relevant factors to the determination of whether heightened judicial protection is appropriate, we, too, shall consider those factors for purposes of our inquiry under the state constitution.

Finally, we note that courts generally have applied the same criteria to determine whether a classification is suspect, quasi-suspect or neither. Just as there is no uniformly applied formula for determining whether a group is entitled to heightened protection under the constitution, there also is no clear test for determining whether a group that deserves such protection is entitled to designation as a suspect class or as a quasi-suspect class.... [A]lthough the same factors are relevant for the purpose of identifying both suspect and quasi-suspect classes, we apply those factors less stringently with respect to groups claiming quasi-suspect class status because the intermediate scrutiny applicable to a statutory classification that discriminates on the basis of quasi-suspect status is less rigorous or demanding than the strict scrutiny to which laws burdening a suspect class are subject. With these principles in mind, we consider the plaintiffs' contention that they are entitled to recognition as a quasi-suspect class.

V
STATUS OF GAY PERSONS AS A QUASI-SUSPECT CLASS

For the reasons that follow, we agree with the plaintiffs' claim that sexual orientation meets all of the requirements of a quasi-suspect classification....

A
History of Discrimination

The defendants do not dispute that gay persons historically have been, and continue to be, the target of purposeful and pernicious discrimination due solely to their sexual orientation. For centuries, the prevailing attitude toward gay persons has been "one of strong disapproval, frequent ostracism, social and legal discrimination, and at times ferocious punishment."

. . . .

Of course, gay persons have been subjected to such severe and sustained discrimination because of our culture's long-standing intolerance of intimate homosexual conduct.... Until not long ago, gay persons were widely regarded as deviants in need of treatment to deal with their sexual orientation. Moreover, until 2003, when the United States Supreme Court concluded, contrary to its earlier holding in *Bowers* that consensual homosexual conduct is protected under the due process clause of the fourteenth amendment; see *Lawrence v. Texas,* supra, at 578; such conduct carried criminal penalties in over one quarter of the states. Connecticut did not repeal its anti-sodomy law until 1969; and, as late as 1986, the court in *Bowers* noted that twenty-four states and the District of Columbia "still [made] such conduct illegal and ha [d] done so for a very long time." *Bowers v. Hardwick,* supra, at 190. It therefore is not surprising that no court ever has refused to treat gay persons as a suspect or quasi-suspect class on the ground that they have not suffered a history of invidious discrimination....

B
Whether Sexual Orientation Is Related to a Person's Ability to
Participate in or Contribute to Society

The defendants also concede that sexual orientation bears no relation to a person's ability to participate in or contribute to society, a fact that many courts have acknowledged, as well. In this critical respect, gay persons stand in stark contrast to other groups that have been denied suspect or quasi-suspect class recognition, despite a history of discrimination, because the distinguishing characteristics of those groups adversely affect their ability or capacity to perform certain functions or to discharge certain responsibilities in society. See, e.g., *Cleburne v. Cleburne Living Center, Inc.,* supra, 473 U.S. at 442 (for purposes of federal constitution, mental retardation is not quasi-suspect classification because, inter alia, "it is undeniable … that those who are mentally retarded have a reduced ability to cope with and function in the everyday world"); *Massachusetts Board of Retirement v. Murgia,* supra, 427 U.S. at 315 (age is not suspect classification because, inter alia, "physical ability generally declines with age"); see also *Gregory v. Ashcroft,* 501 U.S. 452, 472 (1991) ("[i]t is an unfortunate fact of life that physical [capacity] and mental capacity sometimes diminish with age").

Unlike the characteristics unique to those groups, however, "homosexuality bears no relation at all to [an] individual's ability to contribute fully to society." Indeed, because an individual's homosexual orientation "implies no impairment in judgment, stability, reliability or general social or vocational capabilities," the observation of the United States Supreme Court that race, alienage and national origin—all suspect classes entitled to the highest level of constitutional protection—"are so seldom relevant to the achievement of any legitimate state interest that laws grounded in such considerations are deemed to reflect prejudice and antipathy"; *Cleburne v. Cleburne Living Center, Inc.,* supra, 473 U.S. at 440; is no less applicable to gay persons.

It is highly significant, moreover, that it is the public policy of this state that sexual orientation bears no relation to an individual's ability to raise children; to an individual's capacity to enter into relationships analogous to marriage; and to an individual's ability otherwise to participate fully in every important economic and social institution and activity that the government regulates. These statutory provisions constitute an acknowledgment by the state that homosexual orientation is no more relevant to a person's ability to perform and contribute to society than is heterosexual orientation. It therefore is clear that the plaintiffs have satisfied this second and final required prong for determining whether a group is entitled to recognition as a quasi-suspect or suspect class.

C
Immutability of the Group's Distinguishing Characteristic

A third factor that courts have considered in determining whether the members of a class are entitled to heightened protection for equal protection purposes is whether the attribute or characteristic that distinguishes them is immutable or otherwise beyond their control. Of course, the characteristic that distinguishes gay persons from others and qualifies them for recognition as a distinct and discrete group is the characteristic that historically has resulted in their social and legal ostracism, namely, their attraction to persons of the same sex.

On a number of occasions, in connection with its consideration of a claim that a particular group is entitled to suspect or quasi-suspect class status, the United States Supreme Court has considered whether the group's distinguishing characteristic is immutable. Immutability has been deemed to be a relevant consideration because it "make[s] discrimination more clearly unfair." "Immutability may be considered important because it would be pointless to try to deter membership in the immutable group, or because individual group members cannot be blamed for their status, or because immutability heightens the sense of stigma associated with membership.…" Put differently, "[t]he degree to which an individual controls, or cannot avoid, the acquisition of a defining trait, and the relative ease or difficulty with which a trait can be changed, are relevant to whether a classi-fication is 'suspect' or 'quasi-suspect' because this inquiry is one way of asking whether someone, rather than being victimized, has voluntarily joined a persecuted group and thereby invited the discrimination."

A number of courts that have considered this factor have rejected the claim that sex-ual orientation is an immutable characteristic. Other courts, however, as well as many, if not most, scholarly commentators, have reached a contrary conclusion. Although we do not doubt that sexual orientation — heterosexual or homosexual — is highly resistant to change, it is not necessary for us to decide whether sexual orientation is immutable in the same way and to the same extent that race, national origin and gender are immutable, because, even if it is not, the plaintiffs nonetheless have established that they fully satisfy this consideration.

Sexual intimacy is "a sensitive, key relationship of human existence, central to ... the development of human personality...." Thus, the United States Supreme Court has rec-ognized that, because "the protected right of homosexual adults to engage in intimate, con-sensual conduct ... [represents] an integral part of human freedom"; *Lawrence v. Texas,* supra, 539 U.S. at 576–77; individual decisions by consenting adults concerning the in-timacies of their physical relationships are entitled to constitutional protection. Indeed, it is indisputable that sexual orientation "forms a significant part of a person's identity." It is equally apparent that, "[b]ecause a person's sexual orientation is so integral an aspect of one's identity, it is not appropriate to require a person to repudiate or change his or her sexual orientation in order to avoid discriminatory treatment." *In re Marriage Cases,* supra, 43 Cal.4th at 842.

In view of the central role that sexual orientation plays in a person's fundamental right to self-determination, we fully agree with the plaintiffs that their sexual orientation rep-resents the kind of distinguishing characteristic that defines them as a discrete group for purposes of determining whether that group should be afforded heightened protection under the equal protection provisions of the state constitution. This prong of the sus-pectness inquiry surely is satisfied when, as in the present case, the identifying trait is "so central to a person's identity that it would be abhorrent for government to penalize a per-son for refusing to change [it]...." *Watkins v. United States Army,* supra, 875 F.2d at 726 (Norris, J., concurring in the judgment). To decide otherwise would be to penalize some-one for being unable or unwilling to "change ... a central aspect of individual and group identity"; *Watkins v. United States Army,* supra, at 726 (Norris, J., concurring in the judg-ment); a result repugnant "to the values animating the constitutional ideal of equal pro-tection of the laws."

D
Whether the Group Is a Minority or Lacking in Political Power

The final factor that bears consideration is whether the group is "a minority or polit-ically powerless." We therefore turn to that prong of the test.

1

We commence our analysis by noting that, in previous cases involving groups seek-ing heightened protection under the federal equal protection clause, the United States Supreme Court described this factor without reference to the minority status of the sub-ject group, focusing instead on the group's lack of political power. In its most recent formulation of the test for determining whether a group is entitled to suspect or quasi-suspect classification, however, the court has indicated that this factor is satisfied upon a showing *either* that the group is a minority *or* that it lacks political power.... This disjunctive test properly recognizes that a group may warrant heightened protection even though it does not fit the archetype of a discrete and insular minority. The test also properly recognizes that legislation singling out a true minority that meets the first three prongs of the suspectness inquiry must be viewed with skepticism because, under such circumstances, there exists an undue risk that legislation involving the historically disfavored group has been motivated by improper considerations borne of prejudice or animosity.

When this approach is applied to the present case, there is no doubt that gay persons clearly comprise a distinct minority of the population.[30] Consequently, they clearly satisfy the first part of the disjunctive test and, thus, may be deemed to satisfy this prong of the suspectness inquiry on that basis alone.

2

The defendants nevertheless maintain that gay persons should not receive recognition as a quasi-suspect group because they are not politically powerless. In light of this claim, which represents the defendants' primary challenge to the plaintiffs' contention that they are entitled to quasi-suspect class status, and because some courts have applied that component of the suspectness inquiry to deny gay persons protected status even though they represent a minority of the population, we consider the defendants' contention....

We commence our analysis by considering what the term "political powerlessness" actually means for purposes of the suspectness inquiry. Unfortunately, "in most cases the [United States] Supreme Court has no more than made passing reference to the 'political power' factor without actually analyzing it. In view of this fact, and because the extent to which a group possesses or lacks political power is neither readily discernible nor easily measurable, this facet of the suspectness inquiry aptly has been characterized as "ill-defined...." Our task is further complicated by the fact that, to our knowledge, no other court has undertaken a thorough analysis of this factor. The defendants are correct, of course, that gay persons are not entirely without political power, both because the legislature has been persuaded of the need for laws prohibiting sexual orientation discrimination and because some gay persons serve openly in public office. We agree with the plaintiffs, however, that they need not demonstrate that gay persons are politically powerless in any literal sense of that term in order to satisfy this component of the suspectness inquiry.

This conclusion is compelled by United States Supreme Court jurisprudence. We commence our review of that jurisprudence with *Frontiero v. Richardson* (plurality opinion) ... [T]he [*Frontiero*] court concluded that classifications based on sex, like classifications based on race, alienage or national origin, are inherently suspect, and therefore must be subject to heightened judicial review.

In reaching its conclusion, the court observed, first, that "the position of women in America has improved markedly in recent decades." Despite this improvement, however, the court also explained that "women still face[d] pervasive, although at times more subtle, discrimination in our educational institutions, in the job market and, perhaps most conspicuously, in the political arena."

---

30. It is difficult to discern precisely the percentage of homosexuals in the population. Studies conducted by Alfred C. Kinsey in the mid-twentieth century indicated that approximately one out of every ten men was gay. Although these figures received widespread acceptance for many years, subsequent research suggests that the percentage of homosexuals in the population likely is lower.

The court nevertheless recognized the significant political advances that had been made toward gender equality, observing that "Congress ha[d] … manifested an increasing sensitivity to sex-based classifications. In [Title] VII of the Civil Rights Act of 1964, for example, Congress expressly declared that no employer, labor union, or other organization subject to the provisions of the [a]ct shall discriminate against any individual on the basis of race, color, religion, sex, or national origin. Similarly, the Equal Pay Act of 1963 provides that no employer covered by the [a]ct shall discriminate … between employees on the basis of sex. And § 1 of the [e]qual [r]ights [a]mendment, passed by Congress on March 22, 1972, and submitted to the legislatures of the [s]tates for ratification, declares that [e]quality of rights under the law shall not be denied or abridged by the United States or by any [s]tate on account of sex."

In light of these significant protections, the court also acknowledged that, "when viewed in the abstract, *women do not constitute a small and powerless minority*" (emphasis added). Id., at 686 n. 17. The court further observed, however, that, in large part because of past discrimination, women were "vastly under-represented in []this [n]ation's decision making councils."[32] Thus, after explaining that women reasonably could not be characterized as politically powerless in the literal sense of that term, the court nevertheless concluded that women are entitled to enhanced judicial protection because the discrimination to which they had been subjected was irrational and unlikely to be eliminated solely by the enactment of remedial legislation. In other words, as the court since has explained, heightened scrutiny of certain classifications, including gender, is warranted because those classifications "are so seldom relevant to the achievement of any legitimate state interest that laws grounded in such considerations are deemed to reflect prejudice and antipathy … *and because such discrimination is unlikely to be soon rectified by legislative means.…*" (emphasis added.) *Cleburne v. Cleburne Living Center, Inc.,* supra, 473 U.S. at 440.

Women have continued to make significant political progress in the years following the court's decision in *Frontiero*. Indeed, because females outnumber males in this country, they do not constitute a minority, let alone a relatively powerless one. Nevertheless, the United States Supreme Court repeatedly has applied heightened scrutiny to statutory classifications based on sex and continues to do so. Moreover, despite significant political gains by racial and ethnic minorities since they first were accorded treatment as a suspect class, both in terms of the enactment of antidiscrimination laws and electoral success, courts also continue to apply strict scrutiny to statutes that draw distinctions on the basis of such classifications.

It is apparent, then, that the political powerlessness aspect of the suspectness inquiry does not require a showing that the group seeking recognition as a protected class is, in fact, without political power. As we have explained, women were not politically powerless in an absolute sense when they first were accorded heightened constitutional protection in the early 1970s; indeed, prior to the recognition of women as a quasi-suspect class, gender discrimination had been prohibited statutorily—much like discrimination on the basis of sexual orientation has been barred by statute in this state—and Congress had adopted a joint resolution that caused the proposed equal rights amendment to the United States constitution to be presented to the states for

---

32. As examples, the court noted that, as of the date of its decision in 1973, no woman ever had been elected president of the United States or appointed to the United States Supreme Court. *Frontiero v. Richardson,* supra, 411 U.S. at 686 n. 17 (plurality opinion). The court also noted that, at that time, no woman was serving in the United States Senate, and only fourteen women were serving in the United States House of Representatives.

ratification. Today, women, like African-Americans, continue to receive heightened protection under the equal protection clause even though they are a potent and growing political force. The term "political powerlessness," therefore, is clearly a misnomer. We apply this facet of the suspectness inquiry not to ascertain whether a group that has suffered invidious discrimination borne of prejudice or bigotry is devoid of political power but, rather, for the purpose of determining whether the group lacks sufficient political strength to bring a prompt end to the prejudice and discrimination through traditional political means. Consequently, a group satisfies the political powerlessness factor if it demonstrates that, because of the pervasive and sustained nature of the discrimination that its members have suffered, there is a risk that that discrimination will not be rectified, sooner rather than later, merely by resort to the democratic process. Applying this standard, we have little difficulty in concluding that gay persons are entitled to heightened constitutional protection despite some recent political progress.

First, the discrimination that gay persons have suffered has been so pervasive and severe—even though their sexual orientation has no bearing at all on their ability to contribute to or perform in society—that it is highly unlikely that legislative enactments alone will suffice to eliminate that discrimination. As we previously have noted, prejudice against gay persons is long-standing and deeply rooted, in this state and throughout the nation. In fact, until recently, gay persons were widely deemed to be mentally ill and their intimate conduct was subject to criminal sanctions. It is impossible to overestimate the stigma that attaches in such circumstances....

That prejudice against gay persons is so widespread and so deep-seated is due, in large measure, to the fact that many people in our state and nation sincerely believe that homosexuality is morally reprehensible. Indeed, homosexuality is contrary to the teachings of more than a few religions.... Feelings and beliefs predicated on such profound religious and moral principles are likely to be enduring, and persons and groups adhering to those views undoubtedly will continue to exert influence over public policy makers.

Beyond moral disapprobation, gay persons also face virulent homophobia that rests on nothing more than feelings of revulsion toward gay persons and the intimate sexual conduct with which they are associated.... Such visceral prejudice is reflected in the large number of hate crimes that are perpetrated against gay persons.... In fact, the bigotry and hatred that gay persons have faced are akin to, and, in certain respects, perhaps even more severe than, those confronted by some groups that have been accorded heightened judicial protection. This fact provides further reason to doubt that such prejudice soon can be eliminated and underscores the reality that gay persons face unique challenges to their political and social integration.

Insofar as gay persons play a role in the political process, it is apparent that their numbers reflect their status as a small and insular minority. It recently has been noted that, of the more than one-half million people who hold a political office at the local, state and national level, only about 300 are openly gay persons. No openly gay person ever has been appointed to a United States Cabinet position or to any federal appeals court.[41] In addition, no openly gay person has served in the United States Senate, and only two currently serve in the United States House of Representatives. Gay persons also lack representation in the highest levels of business, industry and academia. For example, no openly

---

41. Indeed, as far as we know, there is only one openly gay or lesbian federal judge in the entire nation.

gay person heads a Fortune 500 company, and it has been estimated that there are only fourteen openly gay college and university presidents or chancellors, a number that represents only one half of 1 percent of such positions nationwide.

In this state, no openly gay person ever has been elected to *statewide* office, and only five of the 187 members of the state legislature are openly gay or lesbian. No openly gay man or lesbian ever has been appointed to the state Supreme Court or Appellate Court, and we are aware of only one openly gay or lesbian judge of the Superior Court. By contrast, this state's current governor, comptroller and secretary of the state are women, as are the current chief justice and two associate justices of the state Supreme Court, and other women now hold and previously have held statewide office and positions in the United States House of Representatives. By any standard, therefore, gay persons "remain a political underclass in our [state and] nation."

In recent years, our legislature has taken substantial steps to address discrimination against gay persons. These efforts are most notably reflected in this state's gay rights law.... Other statutes also seek to prohibit discrimination against same sex couples and gay persons. These antidiscrimination provisions, along with the civil union law, reflect the fact that gay persons are able to exert some degree of political influence in the state.

Notwithstanding these provisions, however, the legislature expressly has stated that the gay rights law shall *not* be "deemed or construed (1) to mean the state of Connecticut condones homosexuality or bisexuality or any equivalent lifestyle, (2) to authorize the promotion of homosexuality or bisexuality in educational institutions or require the teaching in educational institutions of homosexuality or bisexuality as an acceptable lifestyle, (3) to authorize or permit the use of numerical goals or quotas, or other types of affirmative action programs, with respect to homosexuality or bisexuality in the administration or enforcement of the [state's antidiscrimination laws], (4) to authorize the recognition of or the right of marriage between persons of the same sex, or (5) to establish sexual orientation as a specific and separate cultural classification in society." General Statutes § 46a-81r. By singling out same sex relationships in this manner—there is, of course, no such statutory disclaimer for opposite sex relationships—the legislature effectively has proclaimed, as a matter of state policy, that same sex relationships are disfavored. That policy, which is unprecedented among the various antidiscrimination measures enacted in this state, represents a kind of state-sponsored disapproval of same sex relationships and, consequently, serves to undermine the legitimacy of homosexual relationships, to perpetuate feelings of personal inferiority and inadequacy among gay persons, and to diminish the effect of the laws barring discrimination against gay persons. Indeed, the purposeful description of homosexuality as a "lifestyle" not condoned by the state stigmatizes gay persons and equates their identity with conduct that is disfavored by the state. Furthermore, although the legislature eventually enacted the gay rights law, its enactment was preceded by nearly a decade of numerous, failed attempts at passage. In addition, the bill that did become law provides more limited protection than the proposals that had preceded it, all of which would have added sexual orientation to the existing nondiscrimination laws and would have treated the classification in the same manner as other protected classes. Finally, as we have explained, the legislation that ultimately emerged from this process passed only after a compromise was reached that resulted in, inter alia, an unprecedented proviso expressing the position of the legislature that it does not condone homosexuality. Thus, to the extent that those civil rights laws, as well as the civil union law, reflect the fact that gay persons wield a measure of political power, the public policy articulated in § 46a-81r is clear evidence of the limits of that political influence.

Finally, although state law provides certain protections to gay persons, the United States Supreme Court has explained that such protective legislation, while indicative that the subject group possesses at least some political power also is a factor *supporting* the conclusion that the subject group is in need of heightened constitutional protection. In particular, in *Frontiero v. Richardson* (plurality opinion), the court observed that Congress had taken significant steps, both statutory and otherwise, to eliminate gender discrimination. The court further explained that, in undertaking those efforts, Congress had manifested its determination that gender classifications are "inherently invidious" and that that "conclusion of a coequal branch of [g]overnment" was significant for the purpose of deciding whether gender constituted a suspect class for equal protection purposes. Thus, the court viewed the enactment of remedial legislation aimed at protecting women from discrimination not as reason to deny them protected class status but, rather, as a justification for granting them such treatment, because it reflected the determination of Congress that gender based classifications are likely to be founded on prejudice and stereotype....

The antidiscrimination provisions of our gay rights law, no less than the provisions that Congress had enacted prior to *Frontiero* to counter gender discrimination; see *Frontiero v. Richardson,* supra, 411 U.S. at 687 (plurality opinion) (citing Title VII of Civil Rights Act of 1964, Equal Pay Act of 1963 and proposed equal rights amendment to United States constitution); represent a legislative consensus that sexual orientation discrimination, like gender discrimination several decades ago, is widespread, invidious and resistant to change.

Gay persons, moreover, continue to "face an uphill battle in pursuing political success. The awareness of public hatred and the fear of violence that often accompanies it undermine efforts to develop an effective gay political identity. [Gay persons] are disinclined to risk retaliation by open identification with the movement, and potential allies from outside the gay [and lesbian] community may think twice about allying their fortunes with such a despised population. That may explain why many gay [and lesbian] officials hide their sexual orientation until they have built up considerable public trust, or why gay [and lesbian] candidates have not been elected to public office in due proportion to the size of the gay [and lesbian] community or [have not] enjoyed the same level of political success as blacks, Latinos, and other minority groups."

With respect to the comparative political power of gay persons, they presently have no greater political power—in fact, they undoubtedly have a good deal less such influence—than women did in 1973, when the United States Supreme Court, in *Frontiero,* held that women are entitled to heightened judicial protection. After all, at that time, women were not a true minority, and they had begun to flex their political muscle on the national scene. Indeed, the court in *Frontiero* accorded women protected status even though gender discrimination *already* was broadly prohibited by federal legislation—just as sexual orientation discrimination is statutorily prohibited in this state. Moreover, when *Frontiero* was decided, the proposed equal rights amendment to the United States constitution, which would have accorded women suspect class status, had broad support in Congress, where it passed overwhelmingly, and among the states, where it nearly achieved the votes necessary for adoption. In addition, "both major political parties ha[d] repeatedly supported [the amendment] in their national party platforms" and it had been endorsed by Presidents Eisenhower, Kennedy, Johnson and Nixon, along with an extraordinary array of civic, labor and legal organizations. In 1974, a nationwide poll indicated overwhelming public support for the amendment. In view of the conclusion of the court in *Frontiero* that women were entitled to heightened judicial protection despite their emergence as a growing political force and despite the widespread, bipartisan support for the equal rights amendment — the imminent ratification of which seemed all but assured — we see no justification for depriving gay persons of such protection. Tellingly, the defendants have proffered no justification for applying a different standard to gay persons under the state constitution than the court in *Frontiero* applied to women for purposes of the federal constitution.

We also note that, despite the likelihood of ratification when *Frontiero* was decided in 1973, the equal rights amendment ultimately did not muster enough support among the states, and it therefore never was adopted. Thus, one of the lessons to be learned from *Frontiero* and its treatment of the equal rights amendment — an initiative that seemed far more likely to succeed nationally than any current effort to enact a gay marriage law in this state — is that, because support for particular legislation may ebb or flow at any time, the adjudication of the rights of a disfavored minority cannot depend solely on such an eventuality.

Finally, gay persons clearly lack the political power that African-Americans and women possess today. Yet political gains by African-Americans and women have not been found to obviate the need for heightened judicial scrutiny of legislation that draws distinctions on the basis of race or gender. We therefore agree fully with the California Supreme Court's recent observation in recognizing gay persons as a suspect class under the California constitution: "[I]f a group's *current* political powerlessness were a prerequisite to a characteristic's being considered a constitutionally suspect basis for differential treatment, it would be impossible to justify the numerous decisions that continue to treat sex, race, and religion as suspect [or quasi-suspect] classifications. Instead, [the relevant case law] make[s] clear that the most important factors in deciding whether a characteristic should be considered a constitutionally suspect basis for classification are whether the class of persons who exhibit a certain characteristic historically has been subjected to invidious and prejudicial treatment, and whether society now recognizes that the characteristic in question generally bears no relationship to the individual's ability to perform or contribute to society" (emphasis in original). *In re Marriage Cases,* supra, 43 Cal.4th at 843. Under the standard for political powerlessness that the defendants advocate, however, African-Americans and women necessarily would have lost their protected status. The fact that courts have not seen fit to remove those groups from that status, even though they wield considerable political power, leads inexorably to the conclusion that gay persons cannot be deprived of heightened judicial protection merely because of their relatively limited political influence....

[The court proceeded to apply intermediate scrutiny, and concluded that none of the reasons that actually motivated the legislature to enact the prohibition on same-sex marriage satisfy that standard.]

[The dissenting opinions of Justices Borden, Vertefeuille, and Zarella are omitted.]

Notes and Questions

1. As the *Kerrigan* court notes, the U.S. Supreme Court's precedents have not provided very clear guidance for distinguishing between whether to treat a classification as suspect or quasi-suspect. Yet, as a practical matter, for purposes of assessing the constitutionality of prohibitions on same-sex marriage, does it make much difference whether sexual orientation classifications are subjected to intermediate or strict scrutiny? After all, if decisions such as *Goodridge* hold that one cannot even hypothesize reasons that will satisfy rational basis review, how likely is it that a state will come up with an *actual* reason — as

is required for intermediate or strict scrutiny — that will satisfy the tighter means-end fit requirements of even intermediate scrutiny? Won't almost any rationale necessarily be too over- and/or under-inclusive?

2. As indicated in Chapter 4, it is unclear whether application of the *Frontiero* factors — with their focus on the history of discrimination and political powerless of the class being discriminated against — make any sense in light of *Adarand*'s holding that the focus of equal protection analysis is on the classification and not the class discriminated against. Might this explain why most courts — at least most federal courts — have been reluctant to recognize new suspect classifications, including sexual orientation, post-*Adarand*? Indeed, in addressing the "political powerlessness" factor, the *Kerrigan* Court noted that it clearly does not require that a group be "wholly lacking in political influence," in this regard noting that heightened scrutiny applies to laws that discriminate against men or Caucasians. *See Kerrigan*, 957 A.2d at 441.

e. Is the Difference between Granting Same-Sex Couples "Marriage" Rights versus Its Functional Equivalent Constitutionally Significant?

In recent years, a number of states have sought to balance the demands from advocates for gay and lesbian equality with the objections of religious conservatives to same-sex marriage by creating alternative, parallel schemes for same-sex couples — typically entitled domestic partnerships or civil unions — that provide them with all of the same rights and responsibilities of marriage but without the name "marriage."

To be sure, were these states to eliminate marriage for same-sex and opposite-sex couples alike and replace it with civil unions or domestic partnerships for all couples, no class-based equal protection claim would remain (although, depending on what is meant by the "fundamental" right to marry, as discussed in Part B.3.c, a substantive due process challenge for same-sex and opposite-sex couples might still be viable). However, to date, no state has eliminated its marriage statutes entirely, instead continuing to allow opposite-sex couples to marry while relegating same-sex couples to civil unions or domestic partnerships.

The question thus arises: if same-sex couples are given all of the rights and responsibilities associated with marriage, is denying them the official designation of "marriage" — when that designation is granted to opposite-sex couples — constitutionally significant for equal protection purposes?

Lewis v. Harris
908 A.2d 196 (N.J. 2006)

Justice ALBIN delivered the opinion of the Court.

[The court first holds that the equal protection guarantee of the New Jersey Constitution requires that same-sex couples receive the same rights and benefits enjoyed by married opposite-sex couples. It then turns to consideration of the appropriate remedy.]

The equal protection requirement of Article I, Paragraph 1 leaves the Legislature with two apparent options. The Legislature could simply amend the marriage statutes to include same-sex couples, or it could create a separate statutory structure, such as a civil union, as Connecticut and Vermont have done.

Plaintiffs argue that even equal social and financial benefits would not make them whole unless they are allowed to call their committed relationships by the name of marriage. They maintain that a parallel legal structure, called by a name other than marriage, which provides the social and financial benefits they have sought, would be a separate-but-equal classification that offends Article I, Paragraph 1. From plaintiffs' standpoint, the title of marriage is an intangible right, without which they are consigned to second-class citizenship. Plaintiffs seek not just legal standing, but also social acceptance, which in their view is the last step toward true equality. Conversely, the State asserts that it has a substantial interest in preserving the historically and almost universally accepted definition of marriage as the union of a man and a woman. For the State, if the age-old definition of marriage is to be discarded, such change must come from the crucible of the democratic process. The State submits that plaintiffs seek by judicial decree "a fundamental change in the meaning of marriage itself," when "the power to define marriage rests with the Legislature, the branch of government best equipped to express the judgment of the people on controversial social questions."

Raised here is the perplexing question — "what's in a name?" — and is a name itself of constitutional magnitude after the State is required to provide full statutory rights and benefits to same-sex couples? We are mindful that in the cultural clash over same-sex marriage, the word marriage itself — independent of the rights and benefits of marriage — has an evocative and important meaning to both parties. Under our equal protection jurisprudence, however, plaintiffs' claimed right to the name of marriage is surely not the same now that equal rights and benefits must be conferred on committed same-sex couples.

We do not know how the Legislature will proceed to remedy the equal protection disparities that currently exist in our statutory scheme. The Legislature is free to break from the historical traditions that have limited the definition of marriage to heterosexual couples or to frame a civil union style structure, as Vermont and Connecticut have done. Whatever path the Legislature takes, our starting point must be to presume the constitutionality of legislation.... Because this State has no experience with a civil union construct that provides equal rights and benefits to same-sex couples, we will not speculate that identical schemes called by different names would create a distinction that would offend Article I, Paragraph 1. We will not presume that a difference in name alone is of constitutional magnitude....

If the Legislature creates a separate statutory structure for same-sex couples by a name other than marriage, it probably will state its purpose and reasons for enacting such legislation. To be clear, it is not our role to suggest whether the Legislature should either amend the marriage statutes to include same-sex couples or enact a civil union scheme. Our role here is limited to constitutional adjudication, and therefore we must steer clear of the swift and treacherous currents of social policy when we have no constitutional compass with which to navigate.

Despite the extraordinary remedy crafted in this opinion extending equal rights to same-sex couples, our dissenting colleagues are willing to part ways from traditional principles of judicial restraint to reach a constitutional issue that is not before us. Before the Legislature has been given the opportunity to act, the dissenters are willing to substitute their judicial definition of marriage for the statutory definition, for the definition that has reigned for centuries, for the definition that is accepted in forty-nine states and in the vast majority of countries in the world. Although we do not know whether the Legislature will choose the option of a civil union statute, the dissenters presume in advance that our legislators cannot give any reason to justify retaining the definition of marriage solely for opposite-sex couples. A proper respect for a coordinate branch of government counsels that we defer until it has spoken. Unlike our colleagues who are prepared immediately to overthrow the long established definition of marriage, we believe that our democratically elected representatives should be given a chance to address the issue under the constitutional mandate set forth in this opinion.

We cannot escape the reality that the shared societal meaning of marriage—passed down through the common law into our statutory law—has always been the union of a man and a woman. To alter that meaning would render a profound change in the public consciousness of a social institution of ancient origin. When such change is not compelled by a constitutional imperative, it must come about through civil dialogue and reasoned discourse, and the considered judgment of the people in whom we place ultimate trust in our republican form of government. Whether an issue with such far-reaching social implications as how to define marriage falls within the judicial or the democratic realm, to many, is debatable. Some may think that this Court should settle the matter, insulating it from public discussion and the political process. Nevertheless, a court must discern not only the limits of its own authority, but also when to exercise forbearance, recognizing that the legitimacy of its decisions rests on reason, not power. We will not short-circuit the democratic process from running its course.

New language is developing to describe new social and familial relationships, and in time will find its place in our common vocabulary. Through a better understanding of those new relationships and acceptance forged in the democratic process, rather than by judicial fiat, the proper labels will take hold. However the Legislature may act, same-sex couples will be free to call their relationships by the name they choose and to sanctify their relationships in religious ceremonies in houses of worship.

The institution of marriage reflects society's changing social mores and values. In the last two centuries, that institution has undergone a great transformation, much of it through legislative action. The Legislature broke the grip of the dead hand of the past and repealed the common law decisions that denied a married woman a legal identity separate from that of her husband. Through the passage of statutory laws, the Legislature gave women the freedom to own property, to contract, to incur debt, and to sue. The Legislature has played a major role, along with the courts, in ushering marriage into the modern era.

Our decision today significantly advances the civil rights of gays and lesbians. We have decided that our State Constitution guarantees that every statutory right and benefit conferred to heterosexual couples through civil marriage must be made available to committed same-sex couples. Now the Legislature must determine whether to alter the long accepted definition of marriage. The great engine for social change in this country has always been the democratic process. Although courts can ensure equal treatment, they cannot guarantee social acceptance, which must come through the evolving ethos of a maturing society. Plaintiffs' quest does not end here. Their next appeal must be to their fellow citizens whose voices are heard through their popularly elected representatives....

[The opinion of Chief Justice Poritz, concurring in part and dissenting in part, is omitted.]

Kerrigan v. Commissioner of Public Health
957 A.2d 407 (Conn. 2008)

PALMER, J.

[In this suit brought by same-sex couples challenging the state excluding them from marriage, the state contends that, as a threshold matter, the plaintiffs have suffered no legally cognizable harm because the state already allows same-sex couples to enter civil unions that have all of the rights and responsibilities of marriage.]

The plaintiffs challenge the trial court's conclusion that the distinction between marriage and civil unions is merely one of nomenclature. They contend that marriage is not simply a term denominating a bundle of legal rights. Rather, they contend that it is an institution of unique and enduring importance in our society, one that carries with it a special status. The plaintiffs therefore contend that their claim of unequal treatment cannot be dismissed solely because same sex couples who enter into a civil union enjoy the same rights under state law as married couples. The plaintiffs also claim that we must consider the legislature's decision to create civil unions for same sex couples in the context of the historical condemnation and discrimination that gay persons have suffered. We agree with the plaintiffs that, despite the legislature's recent establishment of civil unions, the restriction of marriage to opposite sex couples implicates the constitutional rights of gay persons who wish to marry a person of the same sex.

A cognizable constitutional claim arises whenever the government singles out a group for differential treatment. The legislature has subjected gay persons to precisely that kind of differential treatment by creating a separate legal classification for same sex couples who, like opposite sex couples, wish to have their relationship recognized under the law....

Especially in light of the long and undisputed history of invidious discrimination that gay persons have suffered, we cannot discount the plaintiffs' assertion that the legislature, in establishing a statutory scheme consigning same sex couples to civil unions, has relegated them to an inferior status, in essence, declaring them to be unworthy of the institution of marriage. In other words, "[b]y excluding same-sex couples from civil marriage, the [s]tate declares that it is legitimate to differentiate between their commitments and the commitments of heterosexual couples. Ultimately, the message is that what same-sex couples have is not as important or as significant as 'real' marriage, that such lesser relationships cannot have the name of marriage."[14] *Lewis v. Harris,* 188 N.J. 415, 467 (2006) (Poritz, C.J., concurring and dissenting); see also *In re Marriage Cases,* 43 Cal.4th 757, 830–31 (2008) ("[t]he current statutes—by drawing a distinction between the name assigned to the family relationship available to opposite-sex couples and the name assigned to the family relationship available to same-sex couples, and by reserving the historic and highly respected designation of marriage exclusively to opposite-sex couples while offering same-sex couples only the new and unfamiliar designation of domestic partnership—pose a serious risk of denying the official family relationship of same-sex couples the equal dignity and respect that is a core element of the constitutional right to marry"); *Opinions of the Justices to the Senate,* 440 Mass. 1201, 1207 (2004) ("[t]he dissimilitude between the terms 'civil marriage' and 'civil union' is not innocuous; it is a considered choice of language that reflects a demonstrable assigning of same-sex, largely homosexual, couples to second-class status"). Although the legislature has determined that same sex couples are entitled to "all the same benefits, protections and responsibilities ... [that] are granted to spouses in a marriage"; General Statutes § 46b-38nn; the legislature nonetheless created an entirely separate and distinct legal entity for same sex

---

14. We agree with the following point made by the Lambda Legal Defense and Education Fund, Inc., in its amicus brief: "Any married couple [reasonably] would feel that they had lost something precious and irreplaceable if the government were to tell them that they no longer were 'married' and instead were in a 'civil union.' The sense of being 'married'—what this conveys to a couple and their community, and the security of having others clearly understand the fact of their marriage and all it signifies—would be taken from them. These losses are part of what same sex couples are denied when government assigns them a 'civil union' status. If the tables were turned, very few heterosexuals would countenance being told that they could enter only civil unions and that marriage is reserved for lesbian and gay couples. Surely there is [a] constitutional injury when the majority imposes on the minority that which it would not accept for itself."

couples even though it readily could have made those same rights available to same sex couples by permitting them to marry. In view of the exalted status of marriage in our society, it is hardly surprising that civil unions are perceived to be inferior to marriage. We therefore agree with the plaintiffs that "[m]aintaining a second-class citizen status for same-sex couples by excluding them from the institution of civil marriage *is* the constitutional infirmity at issue" (emphasis in original). *Opinions of the Justices to the Senate,* supra, at 1209.

Accordingly, we reject the trial court's conclusion that marriage and civil unions are "separate" but "equal" legal entities and that it therefore "would be the elevation of form over substance" to conclude that the constitutional rights of same sex couples are implicated by a statutory scheme that restricts them to civil unions. Although marriage and civil unions do embody the same legal rights under our law, they are by no means "equal." As we have explained, the former is an institution of transcendent historical, cultural and social significance, whereas the latter most surely is not. Even though the classifications created under our statutory scheme result in a type of differential treatment that generally may be characterized as symbolic or intangible, this court correctly has stated that such treatment nevertheless "is every bit as restrictive as naked exclusions" because it is no less real than more tangible forms of discrimination, at least when, as in the present case, the statute singles out a group that historically has been the object of scorn, intolerance, ridicule or worse.

We do not doubt that the civil union law was designed to benefit same sex couples by providing them with legal rights that they previously did not have. If, however, the intended effect of a law is to treat politically unpopular or historically disfavored minorities differently from persons in the majority or favored class, that law cannot evade constitutional review under the separate but equal doctrine. See, e.g., *Brown v. Board of Education,* 347 U.S. 483, 495 (1954). In such circumstances, the very existence of the classification gives credence to the perception that separate treatment is warranted for the same illegitimate reasons that gave rise to the past discrimination in the first place. Despite the truly laudable effort of the legislature in equalizing the legal rights afforded same sex and opposite sex couples, there is no doubt that civil unions enjoy a lesser status in our society than marriage. We therefore conclude that the plaintiffs have alleged a constitutionally cognizable injury, that is, the denial of the right to marry a same sex partner....

[The dissenting opinions of Justices Borden, Vertefeuille, and Zarella are omitted.]

In re Marriage Cases
183 P.3d 384 (Cal. 2008)

GEORGE, C.J.

[In this suit brought by same-sex couples challenging the state excluding them from marriage, the state contends that the plaintiffs have suffered no legally cognizable harm because the state already allows same-sex couples to enter domestic partnerships that have all of the rights and responsibilities of marriage.]

Maintaining that "under the domestic partnership system, the word 'marriage' is all that the state is denying to registered domestic partners," the Attorney General asserts that "[t]he fundamental right to marry can no more be the basis for same-sex couples to compel the state to denominate their committed relationships 'marriage' than it could be the basis for anyone to prevent the state legislature from changing the name of the marital institution itself to 'civil unions.'" Accordingly, the Attorney General argues that in light of the rights afforded to same-sex couples by the Domestic Partner Act, the current California statutes cannot be found to violate the right of same-sex couples to marry.

We have no occasion in this case to determine whether the state constitutional right to marry necessarily affords all couples the constitutional right to require the state to designate their official family relationship a "marriage," or whether, as the Attorney General suggests, the Legislature would not violate a couple's constitutional right to marry if—perhaps in order to emphasize and clarify that this civil institution is distinct from the religious institution of marriage—it were to assign a name other than marriage as the official designation of the family relationship for *all* couples. The current California statutes, of course, do not assign a name other than marriage for *all* couples, but instead reserve exclusively to opposite-sex couples the traditional designation of marriage, and assign a different designation—domestic partnership—to the only official family relationship available to same-sex couples.

Whether or not the name "marriage," in the abstract, is considered a core element of the state constitutional right to marry, one of the core elements of this fundamental right is the right of same-sex couples to have their official family relationship accorded the same dignity, respect, and stature as that accorded to all other officially recognized family relationships. The current statutes—by drawing a distinction between the name assigned to the family relationship available to opposite-sex couples and the name assigned to the family relationship available to same-sex couples, and by reserving the historic and highly respected designation of marriage exclusively to opposite-sex couples while offering same-sex couples only the new and unfamiliar designation of domestic partnership—pose a serious risk of denying the official family relationship of same-sex couples the equal dignity and respect that is a core element of the constitutional right to marry. As observed by the City at oral argument, this court's conclusion in *Perez, supra,* 32 Cal.2d 711, that the statutory provision barring interracial marriage was unconstitutional, undoubtedly would have been the same even if alternative nomenclature, such as "transracial union," had been made available to interracial couples....

[The concurring opinion of Justice Kennard, and the dissenting opinions of Justices Baxter and Corrigan, are omitted.]

Notes and Questions

1. Do you agree with the analogy that the *Kerrigan* and *In re Marriage Cases* courts draw to interracial marriage and segregated public schools, with their invocation of the "separate but equal" doctrine prior to *Brown v. Board of Education* and the suggestion that upholding the distinction would have been akin to the *Loving* Court approving the use of the phrase "transracial union" in lieu of marriage for relationships between people of different races? Or is the *Lewis* court right to draw a distinction between formal equality and social equality?

Note in this regard how surprisingly similar the *Lewis* court's distinction between formal equality and social equality is to the distinction made by the Supreme Court in *Plessy v. Ferguson*, 163 U.S. 537 (1896), when the Court first explicitly held the doctrine of "separate but equal" to be consistent with the Equal Protection Clause (which *Brown* and its progeny collectively overturned):

> We consider the underlying fallacy of the plaintiff's argument to consist in the assumption that the enforced separation of the two races stamps the colored race

with a badge of inferiority. If this be so, it is not by reason of anything found in the act, but solely because the colored race chooses to put that construction upon it. The argument necessarily assumes that if, as has been more than once the case, and is not unlikely to be so again, the colored race should become the dominant power in the state legislature, and should enact a law in precisely similar terms, it would thereby relegate the white race to an inferior position. We imagine that the white race, at least, would not acquiesce in this assumption. The argument also assumes that social prejudices may be overcome by legislation, and that equal rights cannot be secured to the negro except by an enforced commingling of the two races. We cannot accept this proposition. If the two races are to meet upon terms of social equality, it must be the result of natural affinities, a mutual appreciation of each other's merits, and a voluntary consent of individuals.... If the civil and political rights of both races be equal, one cannot be inferior to the other civilly or politically. If one race be inferior to the other socially, the constitution of the United States cannot put them upon the same plane.

Plessy, 163 U.S. at 551–52.

2. In *Lewis*, the plaintiffs raised only state constitutional claims. A subsequent lawsuit, which was pending at the time this book went to press, raises a federal Fourteenth Amendment challenge to the state's refusal to let same-sex couples marry. *See Garden State Equal. v. Dow*, 2012 WL 540608 (N.J. 2012).

3. In *Perry v. Brown*, 671 F.3d 1052 (9th Cir. 2012), a federal appeals court considering a challenge to the constitutionality of California's Proposition 8—which amended California's Constitution to prohibit same-sex marriage and thus effectively nullified *In re Marriage Cases* so far as marriage rights for same-sex couples are concerned—agreed that the distinction between "marriage" and "domestic partnerships" was constitutionally significant:

> [W]e emphasize the extraordinary significance of the official designation of 'marriage.' That designation is important because 'marriage' is the name that society gives to the relationship that matters most between two adults. A rose by any other name may smell as sweet, but to the couple desiring to enter into a committed lifelong relationship, a marriage by the name of 'registered domestic partnership' does not.... As Proponents have admitted, "the word 'marriage' has a unique meaning," and "there is a significant symbolic disparity between domestic partnership and marriage." It is the designation of 'marriage' itself that expresses validation, by the state and the community, and that serves as a symbol, like a wedding ceremony or a wedding ring, of something profoundly important.

> We need consider only the many ways in which we encounter the word 'marriage' in our daily lives and understand it, consciously or not, to convey a sense of significance. We are regularly given forms to complete that ask us whether we are "single" or "married." Newspapers run announcements of births, deaths, and marriages. We are excited to see someone ask, "Will you marry me?", whether on bended knee in a restaurant or in text splashed across a stadium Jumbotron. Certainly it would not have the same effect to see "Will you enter into a registered domestic partnership with me?" Groucho Marx's one-liner, "Marriage is a wonderful institution ... but who wants to live in an institution?" would lack its punch if the word 'marriage' were replaced with the alternative phrase. So too with Shakespeare's "A young man married is a man that's marr'd," Lincoln's "Marriage is neither heaven nor hell, it is simply purgatory," and Sinatra's "A man doesn't know what happiness is until he's married. By then it's too late." We see tropes like "mar-

rying for love" versus "marrying for money" played out again and again in our films and literature because of the recognized importance and permanence of the marriage relationship. Had Marilyn Monroe's film been called *How to Register a Domestic Partnership with a Millionaire*, it would not have conveyed the same meaning as did her famous movie, even though the underlying drama for same-sex couples is no different. The *name* 'marriage' signifies the unique recognition that society gives to harmonious, loyal, enduring, and intimate relationships.

The official, cherished status of 'marriage' is distinct from the incidents of marriage, such as those listed in the California Family Code. The incidents are both elements of the institution and manifestations of the recognition that the State affords to those who are in stable and committed lifelong relationships. We allow spouses but not siblings or roommates to file taxes jointly, for example, because we acknowledge the financial interdependence of those who have entered into an "enduring" relationship. The incidents of marriage, standing alone, do not, however, convey the same governmental and societal recognition as does the designation of 'marriage' itself. We do not celebrate when two people merge their bank accounts; we celebrate when a couple marries. The designation of 'marriage' is the status that we recognize. It is the principal manner in which the State attaches respect and dignity to the highest form of a committed relationship and to the individuals who have entered into it.

Id. at 1078–79. The *Perry* decision is examined in closer detail in the section that follows.

f. Does Taking Away Marriage Rights for Same-Sex Couples via the Referendum Process Create an Independent Equal Protection Claim?

Problem 5-B: The People's Choice

In recent years, legislatures in several states have voted to amend their marriage laws to permit same-sex couples to marry.

Each of these states gives citizens the option to put newly enacted legislation on hold and to require a citizen vote on the issue before such laws can go into effect by collecting a statutorily defined number of signatures. If the requisite number of signatures are collected by the deadline, the law does not take effect until a public vote on the issue is held.

In none of these states do these voter drives have the effect of amending the state constitution to ban same-sex marriage, and in none of these states is the legislature categorically barred from re-enacting similar legislation in the future. Moreover, if the requisite number of signatures are collected, in none of these states is there a period of time prior to the public vote when same-sex couples are actually able to marry.

In 2009, such a signature drive blocked Maine's new marriage law from taking effect. Currently, efforts are underway to block similar marriage laws recently enacted in other states.

Assuming that same-sex couples have no free-standing due process or equal protection right to marry, is there nonetheless a viable constitutional challenge that can be brought against such repeal votes?

In the *In re Marriage Cases* decision, excerpted in several places in this and other chapters, the California Supreme Court held that the due process, privacy, and equal protection guarantees of the California Constitution mandated that same-sex couples be given the right to marry. The decision went into effect in June 2008, and same-sex couples began to marry in that state.

But in November 2008, voters in California approved Proposition 8, which amended the state's constitution to prohibit marriages between people of the same sex. With no viable state constitutional claims left to pursue, proponents of same-sex marriage in California filed suit in federal court, challenging the constitutionality of Proposition 8 on equal protection and due process grounds. The trial court ruled in the plaintiffs' favor on both grounds, using reasoning analogous to the state court decisions excerpted above. When the decision reached the Ninth Circuit, the appeals court affirmed, but relying on reasons rather different from those examined above.

Perry v. Brown
671 F.3d 1052 (9th Cir. 2012)

REINHARDT, Circuit Judge:

Prior to November 4, 2008, the California Constitution guaranteed the right to marry to opposite-sex couples and same-sex couples alike. On that day, the People of California adopted Proposition 8, which amended the state constitution to eliminate the right of same-sex couples to marry. We consider whether that amendment violates the Fourteenth Amendment to the United States Constitution. We conclude that it does....

V

....

A

The district court held Proposition 8 unconstitutional for two reasons: first, it deprives same-sex couples of the fundamental right to marry, which is guaranteed by the Due Process Clause; and second, it excludes same-sex couples from state-sponsored marriage while allowing opposite-sex couples access to that honored status, in violation of the Equal Protection Clause. Plaintiffs elaborate upon those arguments on appeal.

Plaintiffs and Plaintiff-Intervenor San Francisco also offer a third argument: Proposition 8 singles out same-sex couples for unequal treatment by *taking away* from them alone the right to marry, and this action amounts to a distinct constitutional violation because the Equal Protection Clause protects minority groups from being targeted for the deprivation of an existing right without a legitimate reason. *Romer,* 517 U.S. at 634–35. Because this third argument applies to the specific history of same-sex marriage in California, it is the narrowest ground for adjudicating the constitutional questions before us, while the first two theories, if correct, would apply on a broader basis. Because courts generally decide constitutional questions on the narrowest ground available, we consider the third argument first.

B

Proposition 8 worked a singular and limited change to the California Constitution: it stripped same-sex couples of the right to have their committed relationships recognized by the State with the designation of 'marriage,' which the state constitution had previously guaranteed them, while leaving in place all of their other rights and responsibilities as partners — rights and responsibilities that are identical to those of married spouses and form an integral part of the marriage relationship. In determining that the law had this effect, "[w]e rely not upon our own interpretation of the amendment but upon the authoritative construction of [California's] Supreme Court." *Romer,* 517 U.S. at 626. . . .

Both before and after Proposition 8, same-sex partners could enter into an official, state-recognized relationship that affords them "the same rights, protections, and benefits" as an opposite-sex union and subjects them "to the same responsibilities, obligations, and duties under law, whether they derive from statutes, administrative regulations, court rules, government policies, common law, or any other provisions or sources of law, as are granted to and imposed upon spouses." . . . .

In adopting the amendment, the People simply took the designation of 'marriage' away from lifelong same-sex partnerships, and with it the State's authorization of that official status and the societal approval that comes with it. . . .

We set this forth because we must evaluate Proposition 8's constitutionality in light of its actual and specific effects on committed same-sex couples desiring to enter into an officially recognized lifelong relationship. Before Proposition 8, California guaranteed gays and lesbians both the incidents and the status and dignity of marriage. Proposition 8 left the incidents but took away the status and the dignity. . . . The question we therefore consider is this: did the People of California have legitimate reasons for enacting a constitutional amendment that serves only to take away from same-sex couples the right to have their lifelong relationships dignified by the official status of 'marriage,' and to compel the State and its officials and all others authorized to perform marriage ceremonies to substitute the label of 'domestic partnership' for their relationships?

. . . .

Even were we not bound by the state court's explanation, we would be obligated to consider Proposition 8 in light of its actual effect, which was, as the voters were told, to "*eliminate* the right of same-sex couples to marry in California." The context matters. Withdrawing from a disfavored group the right to obtain a designation with significant societal consequences is different from declining to extend that designation in the first place, regardless of whether the right was withdrawn after a week, a year, or a decade. The action of changing something suggests a more deliberate purpose than does the inaction of leaving it as it is. . . . Whether or not it is a historical accident, as Proponents argue, that Proposition 8 postdated the *Marriage Cases* rather than predating and thus preempting that decision, the relative timing of the two events is a fact, and we must decide this case on its facts.

C

1

This is not the first time the voters of a state have enacted an initiative constitutional amendment that reduces the rights of gays and lesbians under state law. In 1992, Colorado adopted Amendment 2 to its state constitution, which prohibited the state and its political subdivisions from providing any protection against discrimination on the basis of sexual orientation. Amendment 2 was proposed in response to a number of local ordinances that had banned sexual-orientation discrimination in such areas as housing, employment, education, public accommodations, and health and welfare services. The effect of Amendment 2 was "to repeal" those local laws and "to prohibit any governmental entity from adopting similar, or more protective statutes, regulations, ordinances, or policies in the future." The law thus "withdr[ew] from homosexuals, but no others, specific legal protection…, and it forb[ade] reinstatement of these laws and policies." *Romer,* 517 U.S. at 627.

The Supreme Court held that Amendment 2 violated the Equal Protection Clause because "[i]t is not within our constitutional tradition to enact laws of this sort"—laws that "singl[e] out a certain class of citizens for disfavored legal status," which "raise the inevitable inference that the disadvantage imposed is born of animosity toward the class of persons affected." *Id.* at 633–34. The Court considered possible justifications for Amendment 2 that might have overcome the "inference" of animus, but it found them all lacking. It therefore concluded that the law "classifie[d] homosexuals not to further a proper legislative end but to make them unequal to everyone else." *Id.* at 635.[13]

Proposition 8 is remarkably similar to Amendment 2. Like Amendment 2, Proposition 8 "single[s] out a certain class of citizens for disfavored legal status…." *Id.* at 633. Like Amendment 2, Proposition 8 has the "peculiar property," *id.* at 632, of "withdraw[ing] from homosexuals, but no others," an existing legal right—here, access to the official designation of 'marriage'—that had been broadly available, notwithstanding the fact that the Constitution did not compel the state to confer it in the first place. *Id.* at 627. Like Amendment 2, Proposition 8 denies "equal protection of the laws in the most literal sense," *id.* at 633, because it "carves out" an "exception" to California's equal protection clause, by removing equal access to marriage, which gays and lesbians had previously enjoyed, from the scope of that constitutional guarantee. Like Amendment 2, Proposition 8 "by state decree … put[s] [homosexuals] in a solitary class with respect to" an important aspect of human relations, and accordingly "imposes a special disability upon [homosexuals] alone." *Romer,* 517 U.S. at 627, 631. And like Amendment 2, Proposition 8 constitutionalizes that disability, meaning that gays and lesbians may overcome it "only by enlisting the citizenry of [the state] to amend the State Constitution" for a second time. *Id.* at 631. As we explain below, *Romer* compels that we affirm the judgment of the district court.

To be sure, there are some differences between Amendment 2 and Proposition 8. Amendment 2 "impos[ed] a broad and undifferentiated disability on a single named group" by "identif[ying] persons by a single trait and then den[ying] them protection across the board." *Romer,* 517 U.S. at 632–33. Proposition 8, by contrast, excises with surgical precision one specific right: the right to use the designation of 'marriage' to describe a couple's officially recognized relationship. Proponents argue that Proposition 8 thus merely "restor[es] the traditional definition of marriage while otherwise leaving undisturbed the manifold rights and protections California law provides gays and lesbians," making it unlike Amendment 2, which eliminated various substantive rights.

These differences, however, do not render *Romer* less applicable. It is no doubt true that the "special disability" that Proposition 8 "imposes upon" gays and lesbians has a less sweeping effect on their public and private transactions than did Amendment 2. Nevertheless, Proposition 8 works a meaningful harm to gays and lesbians, by denying to their committed lifelong relationships the societal status conveyed by the designation of 'mar-

---

13. *Romer* did not apply heightened scrutiny to Amendment 2, even though the amendment targeted gays and lesbians. Instead, *Romer* found that Amendment 2 "fail[ed], indeed defie[d], even [the] conventional inquiry" for non-suspect classes, concerning whether a "legislative classification … bears a rational relation to some legitimate end." *Romer,* 517 U.S. at 631–32. Amendment 2 amounted to "a classification of persons undertaken for its own sake, something the Equal Protection Clause does not permit." *Id.* at 635. We follow this approach and reach the same conclusion as to Proposition 8. *See also High Tech Gays v. Defense Indus. Sec. Clearance Office,* 895 F.2d 563, 574 (9th Cir.1990) (declining to apply heightened scrutiny).

riage,' and this harm must be justified by some legitimate state interest. *Romer,* 517 U.S. at 631. Proposition 8 is no less problematic than Amendment 2 merely because its effect is narrower; to the contrary, the surgical precision with which it excises a right belonging to gay and lesbian couples makes it even more suspect. A law that has no practical effect except to strip one group of the right to use a state-authorized and socially meaningful designation is all the more "unprecedented" and "unusual" than a law that imposes broader changes, and raises an even stronger "inference that the disadvantage imposed is born of animosity toward the class of persons affected," *id.* at 633–34. In short, *Romer* governs our analysis notwithstanding the differences between Amendment 2 and Proposition 8.

There is one further important similarity between this case and *Romer.* Neither case requires that the voters have stripped the state's gay and lesbian citizens of any federal constitutional right. In *Romer,* Amendment 2 deprived gays and lesbians of statutory protections against discrimination; here, Proposition 8 deprived same-sex partners of the right to use the designation of 'marriage.' There is no necessity in either case that the privilege, benefit, or protection at issue be a constitutional right. We therefore need not and do not consider whether same-sex couples have a fundamental right to marry, or whether states that fail to afford the right to marry to gays and lesbians must do so. Further, we express no view on those questions.

Ordinarily, "if a law neither burdens a fundamental right nor targets a suspect class, we will uphold the legislative classification so long as it bears a rational relation to some legitimate end." *Romer,* 517 U.S. at 631. Such was the case in *Romer,* and it is the case here as well. The end must be one that is legitimate for the *government* to pursue, not just one that would be legitimate for a private actor. *See id.* at 632, 635. The question here, then, is whether California had any more legitimate justification for withdrawing from gays and lesbians its constitutional protection with respect to the official designation of 'marriage' than Colorado did for withdrawing from that group all protection against discrimination generally.

Proposition 8, like Amendment 2, enacts a "'[d]iscrimination[ ] of an unusual character,'" which requires "'careful consideration to determine whether [it] [is] obnoxious to the'" Constitution. *Id.* at 633. As in *Romer,* therefore, we must consider whether any *legitimate* state interest constitutes a rational basis for Proposition 8; otherwise, we must infer that it was enacted with only the constitutionally illegitimate basis of "animus toward the class it affects." *Romer,* 517 U.S. at 632.

2

Before doing so, we briefly consider one other objection that Proponents raise to this analysis: the argument that because the Constitution "is not simply a one-way ratchet that forever binds a State to laws and policies that go beyond what the Fourteenth Amendment would otherwise require," the State of California—"'having gone beyond the requirements of the Federal Constitution'" in extending the right to marry to same-sex couples—"'was free to return ... to the standard prevailing generally throughout the United States.'" Proponents appear to suggest that unless the Fourteenth Amendment actually requires that the designation of 'marriage' be given to same-sex couples in the first place, there can be no constitutional infirmity in taking the designation away from that group of citizens, whatever the People's reason for doing so.

Romer forecloses this argument. The rights that were repealed by Amendment 2 included protections against discrimination on the basis of sexual orientation in the private sphere. Those protections, like any protections against private discrimination, were not compelled by the Fourteenth Amendment. Rather, "[s]tates ha[d] *chosen* to counter discrimination by enacting detailed statutory schemes" prohibiting discrimination in employment and public accommodations, among other contexts, and certain Colorado jurisdictions had chosen to extend those protections to gays and lesbians. *Romer,* 517 U.S. at 628 (emphasis added). It was these elective protections that Amendment 2 withdrew and forbade. The relevant inquiry in *Romer* was not whether the *state of the law* after Amendment 2 was constitutional; there was no doubt that the Fourteenth Amendment did not require antidiscrimination protections to be afforded to gays and lesbians. The question, instead, was whether the *change in the law* that Amendment 2 effected could be justified by some legitimate purpose.

The Supreme Court's answer was "no"—there was no legitimate reason to take away broad legal protections from gays and lesbians alone, and to inscribe that deprivation of equality into the state constitution, once those protections had already been provided. We therefore need not decide whether a state may decline to provide the right to marry to same-sex couples. To determine the validity of Proposition 8, we must consider only whether the *change* in the law that it effected—eliminating by constitutional amendment the right of same-sex couples to have the official designation and status of 'marriage' bestowed upon their relationships, while maintaining that right for opposite-sex couples— was justified by a legitimate reason.

This does not mean that the Constitution is a "one-way ratchet," as Proponents suggest. It means only that the Equal Protection Clause requires the state to have a legitimate reason for withdrawing a right or benefit *from one group but not others,* whether or not it was required to confer that right or benefit in the first place. Thus, when Congress, having chosen to provide food stamps to the poor in the Food Stamp Act of 1964, amended the Act to exclude households of unrelated individuals, such as "hippies" living in "hippie communes," the Supreme Court held the amendment unconstitutional because "a bare congressional desire to harm a politically unpopular group cannot constitute a *legitimate* governmental interest." *U.S. Dep't of Agric. v. Moreno,* 413 U.S. 528, 534 (1973). In both *Romer* and *Moreno,* the constitutional violation that the Supreme Court identified was not the failure to confer a right or benefit in the first place; Congress was no more obligated to provide food stamps than Colorado was to enact antidiscrimination laws. Rather, what the Supreme Court forbade in each case was the targeted exclusion of a group of citizens from a right or benefit that they had enjoyed on equal terms with all other citizens. The constitutional injury that *Romer* and *Moreno* identified—and that serves as a basis of our decision to strike down Proposition 8—has little to do with the substance of the right or benefit from which a group is excluded, and much to do with the act of exclusion itself....

Following *Romer,* we must therefore decide whether a legitimate interest exists that justifies the People of California's action in taking away from same-sex couples the right to use the official designation and enjoy the status of 'marriage'—a legitimate interest that suffices to overcome the "inevitable inference" of animus to which Proposition 8's discriminatory effects otherwise give rise.

D

We first consider four possible reasons offered by Proponents or amici to explain why Proposition 8 might have been enacted.... To be credited, these rationales "must find some footing in the realities of the subject addressed by the legislation." *Heller v. Doe,* 509 U.S. 312, 321 (1993). They are, conversely, not to be credited if they "could not reasonably be conceived to be true by the governmental decisionmaker." *Vance v. Bradley,* 440 U.S. 93, 111 (1979). Because Proposition 8 did not further any of these interests, we conclude that they cannot have been rational bases for this measure, whether or not they are legitimate state interests.

1

The primary rationale Proponents offer for Proposition 8 is that it advances California's interest in responsible procreation and childrearing. This rationale appears to comprise two distinct elements. The first is that children are better off when raised by two biological parents and that society can increase the likelihood of that family structure by allowing only potential biological parents—one man and one woman—to marry. The second is that marriage reduces the threat of "irresponsible procreation"—that is, unintended pregnancies out of wedlock—by providing an incentive for couples engaged in potentially procreative sexual activity to form stable family units. Because same-sex couples are not at risk of "irresponsible procreation" as a matter of biology, Proponents argue, there is simply no need to offer such couples the same incentives. Proposition 8 is not rationally related, however, to either of these purported interests, whether or not the interests would be legitimate under other circumstances.

We need not decide whether there is any merit to the sociological premise of Proponents' first argument—that families headed by two biological parents are the best environments in which to raise children—because even if Proponents are correct, Proposition 8 had absolutely no effect on the ability of same-sex couples to become parents or the manner in which children are raised in California. As we have explained, Proposition 8 in no way modified the state's laws governing parentage, which are distinct from its laws governing marriage. Both before and after Proposition 8, committed opposite-sex couples ("spouses") and same-sex couples ("domestic partners") had identical rights with regard to forming families and raising children. Similarly, Proposition 8 did not alter the California adoption or presumed-parentage laws, which continue to apply equally to same-sex couples. In order to be rationally related to the purpose of funneling more childrearing into families led by two biological parents, Proposition 8 would have had to modify these laws in some way. It did not do so.... We will not credit a justification for Proposition 8 that is totally inconsistent with the measure's actual effect and with the operation of California's family laws both before and after its enactment.

Proponents' second argument is that there is no need to hold out the designation of 'marriage' as an encouragement for same-sex couples to engage in responsible procreation, because unlike opposite-sex couples, same-sex couples pose no risk of procreating accidentally. Proponents contend that California need not extend marriage to same-sex couples when the State's interest in responsible procreation would not be advanced by doing so, even if the interest would not be harmed, either. *See Johnson v. Robison*, 415 U.S. 361, 383 (1974) ("When ... the inclusion of one group promotes a legitimate governmental purpose, and the addition of other groups would not, we cannot say that the statute's classification of beneficiaries and nonbeneficiaries is invidiously discriminatory."). But Plaintiffs do not ask that marriage be *extended* to anyone. As we have by now made clear, the question is whether there is a legitimate governmental interest in *withdrawing* access to marriage from same-sex couples. We therefore need not decide whether, under *Johnson*, California would be justified in not extending the designation of 'marriage' to same-sex couples; that is not what Proposition 8 did. *Johnson* concerns decisions not to *add* to a legislative scheme a group that is unnecessary to the purposes of that scheme, but Proposition 8 *subtracted* a disfavored group from a scheme of which it already was a part.

Under *Romer,* it is no justification for taking something away to say that there was no need to provide it in the first place; instead, there must be some legitimate reason for the act of taking it away, a reason that overcomes the "inevitable inference that the disadvantage imposed is born of animosity toward the class of persons affected." *Romer,* 517 U.S. at 634. In order to explain how *rescinding* access to the designation of 'marriage' is rationally related to the State's interest in responsible procreation, Proponents would have had to argue that opposite-sex couples were *more* likely to procreate accidentally or irresponsibly when same-sex couples were allowed access to the designation of 'marriage.' We are aware of no basis on which this argument would be even conceivably plausible. There is no rational reason to think that taking away the designation of 'marriage' from same-sex couples would advance the goal of encouraging California's opposite-sex couples to procreate more responsibly. The *Johnson* argument, to put it mildly, does not help Proponents' cause.

Given the realities of California law, and of human nature, both parts of Proponents' primary rationale simply "find [no] footing in the realities of the subject addressed by the legislation," and thus cannot be credited as rational. *Heller,* 509 U.S. at 321. Whatever sense there may be in preferring biological parents over other couples—and we need not decide whether there is any—California law clearly does not recognize such a preference, and Proposition 8 did nothing to change that circumstance. The same is true for Proponents' argument that it is unnecessary to extend the right to use the designation of 'marriage' to couples who cannot procreate, because the purpose of the designation is to reward couples who procreate responsibly or to encourage couples who wish to procreate to marry first. Whatever merit this argument may have—and again, we need not decide whether it has any—the argument is addressed to a failure to afford the use of the designation of 'marriage' to same-sex couples in the first place; it is irrelevant to a measure *withdrawing* from them, and only them, use of that designation.

The same analysis applies to the arguments of some amici curiae that Proposition 8 not only promotes responsible procreation and childrearing as a general matter but promotes the single best family structure for such activities. As discussed above, Proposition 8 in no way alters the state laws that govern childrearing and procreation. It makes no change with respect to the laws regarding family structure. As before Proposition 8, those laws apply in the same way to same-sex couples in domestic partnerships and to married couples. Only the designation of 'marriage' is withdrawn and only from one group of individuals.

We in no way mean to suggest that Proposition 8 would be constitutional if only it had gone further—for example, by also repealing same-sex couples' equal parental rights or their rights to share community property or enjoy hospital visitation privileges. Only if Proposition 8 had actually had any effect on childrearing or "responsible procreation" would it be necessary or appropriate for us to *consider* the legitimacy of Proponents' primary rationale for the measure. Here, given all other pertinent aspects of California law, Proposition 8 simply could not have the effect on procreation or childbearing that Proponents claim it might have been intended to have. Accordingly, an interest in responsible procreation and childbearing cannot provide a rational basis for the measure.

We add one final note. To the extent that it has been argued that withdrawing from same-sex couples access to the designation of 'marriage'—without in any way altering the substantive laws concerning their rights regarding childrearing or family formation—will encourage heterosexual couples to enter into matrimony, or will strengthen their matrimonial bonds, we believe that the People of California "could not reasonably" have "conceived" such an argument "to be true." *Vance,* 440 U.S. at 111. It is implausible to think that denying two men or two women the right to call themselves married could somehow bolster the stability of families headed by one man and one woman. While deferential, the rational-basis standard "is not a toothless one." *Mathews v. Lucas,* 427 U.S. 495, 510 (1976). "[E]ven the standard of rationality ... must find some footing in the realities of the subject addressed by the legislation." *Heller,* 509 U.S. at 321. Here, the argument that withdrawing the designation of 'marriage' from same-sex couples could on its own promote the strength or stability of opposite-sex marital relationships lacks any such footing in reality.

2

Proponents offer an alternative justification for Proposition 8: that it advances California's interest in "proceed[ing] with caution" when considering changes to the definition of marriage. But this rationale, too, bears no connection to the reality of Proposition 8. The amendment was enacted *after* the State had provided same-sex couples the right to marry and *after* more than 18,000 couples had married (and remain married even after Proposition 8).

Perhaps what Proponents mean is that California had an interest in pausing at 18,000 married same-sex couples to evaluate whether same-sex couples should continue to be allowed to marry, or whether the same-sex marriages that had already occurred were having any adverse impact on society. Even if that were so, there could be no rational connection between the asserted purpose of "*proceeding* with caution" and the enactment of an absolute ban, unlimited in time, on same-sex marriage in the state constitution. To enact a constitutional prohibition is to adopt a fundamental barrier: it means that the legislative process, by which incremental policymaking would normally proceed, is completely foreclosed. *Cf. Williamson v. Lee Optical of Okla., Inc.,* 348 U.S. 483, 489 (1955) (observing that legislatures may rationally reform policy "one step at a time"). Once Proposition 8 was enacted, any future steps forward, however cautious, would require "enlisting the citizenry of [California] to amend the State Constitution" once again. *Romer,* 517 U.S. at 631.

Had Proposition 8 imposed not a total ban but a time-specific moratorium on same-sex marriages, during which the Legislature would have been authorized to consider the question in detail or at the end of which the People would have had to vote again to renew the ban, the amendment might plausibly have been designed to "proceed with caution." In that case, we would have had to consider whether the objective of "proceed[ing] with caution" was a legitimate one. But that is not what Proposition 8 did. The amendment superseded the *Marriage Cases* and then went further, by prohibiting the Legislature or even the People (except by constitutional amendment) from choosing to make the designation of 'marriage' available to same-sex couples in the future. Such a permanent ban cannot be rationally related to an interest in proceeding with caution.

In any event, in light of the express purpose of Proposition 8 and the campaign to enact it, it is not credible to suggest that "proceed[ing] with caution" was the reason the voters adopted the measure. The purpose and effect of Proposition 8 was "to *eliminate* the right of same-sex couples to marry in California"—not to "suspend" or "study" that right. The voters were told that Proposition 8 would "overturn[ ]" the *Marriage Cases* "to RESTORE the meaning of marriage." The avowed purpose of Proposition 8 was to return with haste to a time when same-sex couples were barred from using the official designation of 'marriage,' not to study the matter further before deciding whether to make the designation more equally available.

3

We briefly consider two other potential rationales for Proposition 8, not raised by Proponents but offered by amici curiae. First is the argument that Proposition 8 advanced the State's interest in protecting religious liberty. There is no dispute that even before Proposition 8, "no religion [was] required to change its religious policies or practices with regard to same-sex couples, and no religious officiant [was] required to solemnize a marriage in contravention of his or her religious beliefs." Rather, the religious-liberty interest that Proposition 8 supposedly promoted was to decrease the likelihood that religious organizations would be penalized, under California's antidiscrimination laws and other government policies concerning sexual orientation, for refusing to provide services to families headed by same-sex spouses. But Proposition 8 did nothing to affect those laws. To the extent that California's antidiscrimination laws apply to various activities of religious organizations, their protections apply in the same way as before. Amicus's argument is thus more properly read as an appeal to the Legislature, seeking reform of the State's antidiscrimination laws to include greater accommodations for religious organizations. This argument is in no way addressed by Proposition 8 and could not have been the reason for Proposition 8.

Second is the argument, prominent during the campaign to pass Proposition 8, that it would "protect[ ] our children from being taught in public schools that 'same-sex marriage' is the same as traditional marriage." Yet again, California law belies the premise of this justification. Both before and after Proposition 8, schools have not been required to teach anything about same-sex marriage. . . . Both before and after Proposition 8, schools have retained control over the content of such lessons. And both before and after Proposition 8, schools and individual teachers have been prohibited from giving any instruction that discriminates on the basis of sexual orientation; now as before, students could not be taught the superiority or inferiority of either same- or opposite-sex marriage or other "committed relationships." The *Marriage Cases* therefore did not weaken, and Proposition 8 did not strengthen, the rights of schools to control their curricula and of parents to control their children's education.

There is a limited sense in which the extension of the designation 'marriage' to same-sex partnerships might alter the content of the lessons that schools choose to teach. Schools teach about the world as it is; when the world changes, lessons change. A shift in the State's marriage law may therefore affect the content of classroom instruction just as would the election of a new governor, the discovery of a new chemical element, or the adoption of a new law permitting no-fault divorce: students learn about these as empirical facts of the world around them. But to protest the teaching of these facts is little different from protesting their very existence; it is like opposing the election of a particular governor on the ground that students would learn about his holding office, or opposing the legitimation of no-fault divorce because a teacher might allude to that fact if a course in societal structure were taught to graduating seniors. The prospect of children learning about the laws of the State and society's assessment of the legal rights of its members does not provide an *independent* reason for stripping members of a disfavored group of those rights they presently enjoy.

4

Proposition 8's only effect, we have explained, was to withdraw from gays and lesbians the right to employ the designation of 'marriage' to describe their committed relationships and thus to deprive them of a societal status that affords dignity to those relationships. Proposition 8 could not have reasonably been enacted to promote childrearing by biological parents, to encourage responsible procreation, to proceed with caution in social change, to protect religious liberty, or to control the education of schoolchildren. Simply taking away the designation of 'marriage,' while leaving in place all the substantive rights and responsibilities of same-sex partners, did not do any of the things its Proponents now suggest were its purposes. Proposition 8 "is so far removed from these particular justifications that we find it impossible to credit them." *Romer,* 517 U.S. at 635. We therefore need not, and do not, decide whether any of these purported rationales for the law would be "legitimate," *id.* at 632, or would suffice to justify Proposition 8 if the amendment actually served to further them.

E

1

We are left to consider why else the People of California might have enacted a constitutional amendment that takes away from gays and lesbians the right to use the designation of 'marriage.' One explanation is the desire to revert to the way things were prior to the *Marriage Cases,* when 'marriage' was available only to opposite-sex couples, as had been the case since the founding of the State and in other jurisdictions long before that. This purpose is one that Proposition 8 actually did accomplish: it "restore[d] the traditional definition of marriage as referring to a union between a man and a woman." But tradition alone is not a justification for *taking away* a right that had already been granted, even though that grant was in derogation of tradition. In *Romer,* it did not matter that at common law, gays and lesbians were afforded no protection from discrimination in the private sphere; Amendment 2 could not be justified on the basis that it simply repealed positive law and restored the "traditional" state of affairs. 517 U.S. at 627–29. Precisely the same is true here.

Laws may be repealed and new rights taken away if they have had unintended consequences or if there is some conceivable affirmative good that revocation would produce, but new rights may not be stripped away solely *because* they are new. Tradition is a legitimate consideration in policymaking, of course, but it cannot be an end unto itself. "[T]he fact that the governing majority in a State has traditionally viewed a particular practice as immoral is not a sufficient reason for upholding a law prohibiting the practice; neither history nor tradition could save a law prohibiting miscegenation from constitutional attack." *Lawrence v. Texas,* 539 U.S. 558, 577–78 (2003); *see Loving v. Virginia,* 388 U.S. 1 (1967) (noting the historical pedigree of bans on interracial marriage but not even considering tradition as a possible justification for Virginia's law). If tradition alone is insufficient to justify *maintaining* a prohibition with a discriminatory effect, then it is necessarily insufficient to justify *changing* the law to revert to a previous state. A preference for the way things were before same-sex couples were allowed to marry, without any identifiable good that a return to the past would produce, amounts to an impermissible preference against same-sex couples themselves, as well as their families.

Absent any legitimate purpose for Proposition 8, we are left with "the inevitable inference that the disadvantage imposed is born of animosity toward," or, as is more likely with respect to Californians who voted for the Proposition, mere disapproval of, "the class of persons affected." *Romer,* 517 U.S. at 634. We do not mean to suggest that Proposition 8 is the result of ill will on the part of the voters of California. "Prejudice, we are beginning to understand, rises not from malice or hostile animus alone." Disapproval may also be the product of longstanding, sincerely held private beliefs. Still, while "[p]rivate biases may be outside the reach of the law, … the law cannot, directly or indirectly, give them effect." *Palmore v. Sidoti,* 466 U.S. 429, 433 (1984). Ultimately, the "inevitable inference" we must draw in this circumstance is not one of ill will, but rather one of disapproval of gays and lesbians as a class. "[L]aws singling out a certain class of citizens for disfavored legal status or general hardships are rare." *Romer,* 517 U.S. at 633. Under *Romer,* we must infer from Proposition 8's effect on California law that the People took away from gays and lesbians the right to use the official designation of 'marriage'—and the societal status that accompanies it—because they disapproved of these individuals *as a class* and did not wish them to receive the same official recognition and societal approval of their committed relationships that the State makes available to opposite-sex couples.

It will not do to say that Proposition 8 was intended only to disapprove of same-sex marriage, rather than to pass judgment on same-sex couples as people. Just as the criminalization of "homosexual conduct … is an invitation to subject homosexual persons to discrimination both in the public and in the private spheres," *Lawrence,* 539 U.S. at 575, so too does the elimination of the right to use the official designation of 'marriage' for the relationships of committed same-sex couples send a message that gays and lesbians are of lesser worth as a class—that they enjoy a lesser societal status. Indeed, because laws affecting gays and lesbians' rights often regulate individual conduct—what sexual activity people may undertake in the privacy of their own homes, or who is permitted to marry whom—as much as they regulate status, the Supreme Court has "declined to distinguish between status and conduct in [the] context" of sexual orientation. *Christian Legal Soc'y v. Martinez,* 130 S.Ct. 2971, 2990, 177 L.Ed.2d 838 (2010). By withdrawing the availability of the recognized designation of 'marriage,' Proposition 8 enacts nothing more or less than a judgment about the worth and dignity of gays and lesbians as a class.

Just as a "desire to harm … cannot constitute a *legitimate* governmental interest," *Moreno,* 413 U.S. at 534, neither can a more basic disapproval of a class of people. *Romer,* 517 U.S. at 633–35. "The issue is whether the majority may use the power of the State to enforce these views on the whole society" through a law that abridges minority individuals' rights. *Lawrence,* 539 U.S. at 571. It may not. Without more, "[m]oral disapproval of [a] group, like a bare desire to harm the group, is an interest that is insufficient to satisfy rational basis review under the Equal Protection Clause." *Id.* at 582 (O'Connor, J., concurring). Society does sometimes draw classifications that likely are rooted partially in disapproval, such as a law that grants educational benefits to veterans but denies them to conscientious objectors who engaged in alternative civilian service. *See Johnson,* 415 U.S. at 362–64. Those classifications will not be invalidated so long as they can be justified by reference to some *independent* purpose they serve; in *Johnson,* they could provide an incentive for military service and direct assistance to those who needed the most help in readjusting to post-war life, *see id.* at 376–83. Enacting a rule into law based solely on the disapproval of a group, however, "is a classification of persons undertaken for its own sake, something the Equal Protection Clause does not permit." *Romer,* 517 U.S. at 635. Like Amendment 2, Proposition 8 is a classification of gays and lesbians undertaken for its own sake.

2

The "inference" that Proposition 8 was born of disapproval of gays and lesbians is heightened by evidence of the context in which the measure was passed. The district court found that "[t]he campaign to pass Proposition 8 relied on stereotypes to show that same-sex relationships are inferior to opposite-sex relationships." Television and print advertisements "focused on … the concern that people of faith and religious groups would somehow be harmed by the recognition of gay marriage" and "conveyed a message that gay people and relationships are inferior, that homosexuality is undesirable and that children need to be protected from exposure to gay people and their relationships." These messages were not crafted accidentally. The strategists responsible for the campaign in favor of Proposition 8 later explained their approach: "'[T]here were limits to the degree of tolerance Californians would afford the gay community. They would entertain allowing gay marriage, but not if doing so had significant implications for the rest of society,'" such as what children would be taught in school. Nor were these messages new; for decades, ballot measures regarding homosexuality have been presented to voters in terms designed to appeal to stereotypes of gays and lesbians as predators, threats to children, and practitioners of a deviant "lifestyle." The messages presented here mimic those presented to Colorado voters in support of Amendment 2, such as, "Homosexual indoctrination in the schools? IT'S HAPPENING IN COLORADO!"

When directly enacted legislation "singl[es] out a certain class of citizens for disfavored legal status," we must "insist on knowing the relation between the classification adopted and the object to be attained," so that we may ensure that the law exists "to further a proper legislative end" rather than "to make the[ ] [class] unequal to everyone else." *Romer,* 517 U.S. at 632–33, 635. Proposition 8 fails this test. Its sole purpose and effect is "to eliminate the right of same-sex couples to marry in California"—to dishonor a disfavored group by taking away the official designation of approval of their committed relationships and the accompanying societal status, and nothing more. "It is at once too narrow and too broad," for it changes the law far too little to have any of the effects it purportedly was intended to yield, yet it dramatically reduces the societal standing of gays and lesbians and diminishes their dignity. *Romer,* 517 U.S. at 633. Proposition 8 did not result from a legitimate "Kulturkampf" concerning the structure of families in California, because it had no effect on family structure, but in order to strike it down, we need not go so far as to find that it was enacted in "a fit of spite." *Id.* at 636 (Scalia, J., dissenting). It is enough to say that Proposition 8 operates with no apparent purpose but to impose on gays and lesbians, through the public law, a majority's private disapproval of them and their relationships, by taking away from them the official designation of 'marriage,' with its societally recognized status. Proposition 8 therefore violates the Equal Protection Clause....

N.R. SMITH, Circuit Judge, concurring in part and dissenting in part.

    ....

III.

The majority concludes that "*Romer* governs our analysis notwithstanding the differences between Amendment 2 and Proposition 8," because of the similarities between the measures at issue in *Romer* and in the present case. However, the differences between Amendment 2 and Proposition 8 indicate that *Romer* does not directly control our analysis of the constitutionality of Proposition 8....

B.

There are several ways to distinguish *Romer* from the present case. First, in *Romer,* the Supreme Court stated that "[t]he change Amendment 2 works in the legal status of gays and lesbians in the private sphere is far reaching, both on its own terms and when considered in light of the structure and operation of modern anti-discrimination laws." *Id.* at 627. Here, "Proposition 8 reasonably must be interpreted in a limited fashion as eliminating only the right of same-sex couples to equal access to the designation of marriage, and as not otherwise affecting the constitutional right of those couples to establish an officially recognized family relationship." Thus, *Romer* is inapposite, because Proposition 8 eliminates the right of access to the designation of marriage from same-sex couples, rather than working a far reaching change in their legal status.

Second, Amendment 2's "sheer breadth is so discontinuous with the reasons offered for it that the amendment seems inexplicable by anything but animus toward the class it affects." *Romer*, 517 U.S. at 632. Again, Proposition 8 "carves out a narrow and limited exception to [the] state constitutional rights" of privacy and due process. Proposition 8 therefore lacks the "sheer breadth" that prompted the Supreme Court to raise the inference of animus in *Romer.*

The effect of animus is also unclear. In *Romer,* the Supreme Court stated that "laws of the kind now before us raise the inevitable inference that the disadvantage imposed is born of animosity towards the class of persons affected." 517 U.S. at 634. The Supreme Court indicated that Amendment 2 was constitutionally invalid, because its only purpose was animus; Amendment 2 was not "directed to any identifiable legitimate purpose or discrete objective." *Id.* at 635. In short, *Romer* was a case where the only basis for the measure at issue was animus. However, in a case where the measure at issue was prompted both by animus and by some independent legitimate purpose, the measure may still be constitutionally valid. The Supreme Court has stated that while "negative attitudes," "fear" or other biases "may often accompany irrational (and therefore unconstitutional) discrimination, their presence alone does not a constitutional violation make." *Bd. of Trustees of Univ. of Ala. v. Garrett,* 531 U.S. 356, 367 (2001) (discussing *Cleburne,* 473 U.S. at 448). If "animus" is one such bias, its presence alone may not make Proposition 8 invalid if the measure also rationally relates to a legitimate governmental interest.

Finally, gays and lesbians were burdened by Amendment 2, because it "operate[d] to repeal and forbid all laws or policies providing specific protection for gays or lesbians from discrimination by every level of Colorado government." *Romer,* 517 U.S. at 629. In contrast, "although Proposition 8 eliminates the ability of same-sex couples to enter into an official relationship designated 'marriage,' in all other respects those couples continue to possess, under the state constitutional privacy and due process clauses, the core set of basic *substantive* legal rights and attributes traditionally associated with marriage...." Put otherwise, Proposition 8 does not burden gays and lesbians to the same extent Amendment 2 burdened gays and lesbians in Colorado....

Notes and Questions

1. How persuasive is the *Perry* court's efforts to analogize the case before it to *Romer*? After all, isn't Judge Smith's contention in dissent that *Romer* is distinguishable sound given the contrast between the "sheer breadth" of Colorado's Amendment 2 and the rather limited scope of Proposition 8?

2. How critical is it to the *Perry* court's decision that there was actually a period of time when same-sex couples could marry before that right was taken away? That the method of taking that right away came by means of a constitutional amendment? To the extent that the *Perry* court is relying on *Romer,* how critical is the answer to the second question?

In this regard, recall the cases involving discriminatory restructuring of governmental decisionmaking examined in Chapter 4. In those cases, the Court repeatedly emphasized that mere repeal of a law extending rights to minorities does not constitute an equal protection violation. Rather, it is the "comparative structural burden" placed on "future attempts" to reenact similar legislation that constitutes the equal protection clause violation. *See Washington v. Seattle Sch. Dist. No. 1*, 458 U.S. 457, 474 n.17, 483 (1982); *Hunter v. Erickson*, 393 U.S. 385, 390 n.5 (1969).

3. The *Perry* court is rather clearly trying to write a very narrow decision that does not definitively decide the question whether same-sex couples have a free-standing equal protection right to marry. But how persuasive is the court's effort to distinguish the taking away of a right from the refusal to grant it in the first place? Stated somewhat differently, if the various rationales for the law that the court raises and shoots down are insufficient to justify the decision to repeal marriage rights for same-sex couples, how could those same rationales justify not extending marriage rights to same-sex couples in the first instance?

4. One of the rationales given in support of Proposition 8 was the interest in "proceeding with caution." A similar rationale was raised and rejected in one of the race-based cases involving discriminatory restructuring of governmental decisionmaking:

> Characterizing it simply as a public decision to move slowly in the delicate area of race relations emphasizes the impact and burden of § 137, but does not justify it. The amendment was unnecessary either to implement a decision to go slowly, or to allow the people of Akron to participate in that decision.

Hunter v. Erickson, 393 U.S. 385, 392 (1969). In support of the finding that § 137 was unnecessary to further this interest, the Court noted that under the existing city charter, citizens had the ability to repeal legislation enacted by the council via the referendum process. *See id.* at 392 n.7; *see also id.* at 390 n.6. Does this, when coupled with the distinction discussed in note 2 between "mere repeal" and placing a "comparative structural burden" on future legislation suggest that *Perry* would have been decided differently had it involved a referendum repealing a legislatively enacted extension of the right to marry to same-sex couples?

g. *The Defense of Marriage Act*

As indicated earlier in the chapter, after the Hawaii Supreme Court's decision in *Baehr v. Lewin*, there was a widespread fear among federal and state legislators that same-sex couples nationwide would travel to Hawaii and get married, and that their marriages would have to be recognized when those couples returned to their home states.

This belief was grounded in two doctrines. The first was that, as a general rule, most states in the United States have adopted—either by statute or as a matter of common law—the so-called place-of-celebration rule for determining the validity of marriages. Under this traditional choice-of-law rule, a state will recognize a marriage as valid if it was valid in the state where the marriage was performed, *even if* the marriage could not have been entered into in the state in which recognition is sought. And the second was a belief that the Full Faith and Credit Clause of the U.S. Constitution *requires* states to recognize marriages performed in sister states.

Although applied as a general rule, the place-of-celebration rule has always been subject to both statutory and common law exceptions. Thus, for example, many states enacted "evasion" statutes under which a marriage would not be recognized if citizens from that state traveled to a sister state as a way of evading the state's marriage restrictions, such as where an underage couple traveled to a state with a lower minimum age to marry. Moreover, states would also refuse to recognize out-of-state marriages that violated a strong public policy of the state, such as a policy against incestuous and—in an earlier era, interracial—marriages. Moreover, as demonstrated below, the common belief regarding the effect of the Full Faith and Credit Clause on interstate marriage recognition is overstated.

Congress reacted to the *Baehr* decision in 1996 by enacting the Defense of Marriage Act (DOMA), which contains two key substantive sections. Section 2 of the Act purports to relieve states of the obligation to recognize marriages entered into in other states, providing as follows:

> No State, territory, or possession of the United States, or Indian tribe, shall be required to give effect to any public act, record, or judicial proceeding of any other State, territory, possession, or tribe respecting a relationship between persons of the same sex that is treated as a marriage under the laws of such other State, territory, possession, or tribe, or a right or claim arising from such relationship.

Section 3 of DOMA sets forth a federal definition of marriage that excludes same-sex marriages, providing as follows:

> In determining the meaning of any Act of Congress, or of any ruling, regulation, or interpretation of the various administrative bureaus and agencies of the United States, the word 'marriage' means only a legal union between one man and one woman as husband and wife, and the word 'spouse' refers only to a person of the opposite sex who is a husband or a wife.

There are currently several cases pending in federal courts nationwide challenging the constitutionality of both substantive sections of the Defense of Marriage Act. As these courts have noted, these lawsuits do not really involve the question whether marriage is a fundamental right, since the couples in these cases *are* married; instead, what they seek is recognition of their marriage by either the federal government or a sister state. *See, e.g.,* *Golinski v. U.S. Office of Pers. Mgmt.*, 824 F. Supp. 2d 968, 982 n.5 (N.D. Cal. 2012). Accordingly, the materials that follow explore possible challenges to Sections 2 and 3 of DOMA on other grounds, including equal protection, the 10th Amendment, and the Full Faith and Credit Clause.

Letter from Eric H. Holder, Attorney General of the United States, to John A. Boehner, Speaker of the U.S. House of Representatives

(February 23, 2011)

Dear Mr. Speaker:

After careful consideration, including review of a recommendation from me, the President of the United States has made the determination that Section 3 of the Defense of Marriage Act ("DOMA"), as applied to same-sex couples who are legally married under state law, violates the equal protection component of the Fifth Amendment....

[T]he President and I have concluded that classifications based on sexual orientation warrant heightened scrutiny and that, as applied to same-sex couples legally married under state law, Section 3 of DOMA is unconstitutional.

Standard of Review

The Supreme Court has yet to rule on the appropriate level of scrutiny for classifications based on sexual orientation. It has, however, rendered a number of decisions that set forth the criteria that should inform this and any other judgment as to whether heightened scrutiny applies: (1) whether the group in question has suffered a history of discrimination; (2) whether individuals "exhibit obvious, immutable, or distinguishing characteristics that define them as a discrete group"; (3) whether the group is a minority or is politically powerless; and (4) whether the characteristics distinguishing the group have little relation to legitimate policy objectives or to an individual's "ability to perform or contribute to society."

Each of these factors counsels in favor of being suspicious of classifications based on sexual orientation. First and most importantly, there is, regrettably, a significant history of purposeful discrimination against gay and lesbian people, by governmental as well as private entities, based on prejudice and stereotypes that continue to have ramifications today. Indeed, until very recently, states have "demean[ed] the[] existence" of gays and lesbians "by making their private sexual conduct a crime." *Lawrence v. Texas*, 539 U.S. 558, 578 (2003).

Second, while sexual orientation carries no visible badge, a growing scientific consensus accepts that sexual orientation is a characteristic that is immutable, *see* Richard A. Posner, Sex and Reason 101 (1992); it is undoubtedly unfair to require sexual orientation to be hidden from view to avoid discrimination, *see* Don't Ask, Don't Tell Repeal Act of 2010, Pub. L. No. 111-321, 124 Stat. 3515 (2010).

Third, the adoption of laws like those at issue in *Romer v. Evans*, 517 U.S. 620 (1996), and *Lawrence*, the longstanding ban on gays and lesbians in the military, and the absence of federal protection for employment discrimination on the basis of sexual orientation show the group to have limited political power and "ability to attract the [favorable] attention of the lawmakers." *Cleburne*, 473 U.S. at 445. And while the enactment of the Matthew Shepard Act and pending repeal of Don't Ask, Don't Tell indicate that the political process is not closed *entirely* to gay and lesbian people, that is not the standard by which the Court has judged "political powerlessness." Indeed, when the Court ruled that gender-based classifications were subject to heightened scrutiny, women already had won major political victories such as the Nineteenth Amendment (right to vote) and protection under Title VII (employment discrimination).

Finally, there is a growing acknowledgment that sexual orientation "bears no relation to ability to perform or contribute to society." *Frontiero v. Richardson*, 411 U.S. 677, 686 (1973) (plurality). Recent evolutions in legislation (including the pending repeal of Don't Ask, Don't Tell), in community practices and attitudes, in case law (including the Supreme Court's holdings in *Lawrence* and *Romer*), and in social science regarding sexual orientation all make clear that sexual orientation is not a characteristic that generally bears on legitimate policy objectives. *See, e.g.,* Statement by the President on the Don't Ask, Don't Tell Repeal Act of 2010 ("It is time to recognize that sacrifice, valor and integrity are no more defined by sexual orientation than they are by race or gender, religion or creed.")

To be sure, there is substantial circuit court authority applying rational basis review to sexual-orientation classifications. We have carefully examined each of those decisions. Many of them reason only that if consensual same-sex sodomy may be criminalized under *Bowers v. Hardwick*, then it follows that no heightened review is appropriate—a line of reasoning that does not survive the overruling of *Bowers* in *Lawrence v. Texas*, 538 U.S. 558 (2003). Others rely on claims regarding "procreational responsibility" that the Department has disavowed already in litigation as unreasonable, or claims regarding the immutability of sexual orientation that we do not believe can be reconciled with more recent social science understandings. And none engages in an examination of all the factors that the Supreme Court has identified as relevant to a decision about the appropriate level of scrutiny. Finally, many of the more recent decisions have relied on the fact that the Supreme Court has not recognized that gays and lesbians constitute a suspect class or the fact that the Court has applied rational basis review in its most recent decisions addressing classifications based on sexual orientation, *Lawrence* and *Romer*. But neither of those decisions reached, let alone resolved, the level of scrutiny issue because in both the Court concluded that the laws could not even survive the more deferential rational basis standard.

Application to Section 3 of DOMA

In reviewing a legislative classification under heightened scrutiny, the government must establish that the classification is "substantially related to an important government objective." *Clark v. Jeter*, 486 U.S. 456, 461 (1988). Under heightened scrutiny, "a tenable justification must describe actual state purposes, not rationalizations for actions in fact differently grounded." *United States v. Virginia*, 518 U.S. 515, 535–36 (1996). "The justification must be genuine, not hypothesized or invented post hoc in response to litigation." *Id.* at 533.

In other words, under heightened scrutiny, the United States cannot defend Section 3 by advancing hypothetical rationales, independent of the legislative record, as it has done in circuits where precedent mandates application of rational basis review. Instead, the United States can defend Section 3 only by invoking Congress' actual justifications for the law.

Moreover, the legislative record underlying DOMA's passage contains discussion and debate that undermines any defense under heightened scrutiny. The record contains numerous expressions reflecting moral disapproval of gays and lesbians and their intimate and family relationships—precisely the kind of stereotype-based thinking and animus the Equal Protection Clause is designed to guard against. *See Cleburne*, 473 U.S. at 448 ("mere negative attitudes, or fear" are not permissible bases for discriminatory treatment); *see also Romer*, 517 U.S. at 635 (rejecting rationale that law was supported by "the liberties of landlords or employers who have personal or religious objections to homosexuality"); *Palmore v. Sidotti*, 466 U.S. 429, 433 (1984) ("Private biases may be outside the reach of the law, but the law cannot, directly or indirectly, give them effect.").

Application to Second Circuit Cases

After careful consideration, including a review of my recommendation, the President has concluded that given a number of factors, including a documented history of discrimination, classifications based on sexual orientation should be subject to a heightened standard of scrutiny. The President has also concluded that Section 3 of DOMA, as applied to legally married same-sex couples, fails to meet that standard and is therefore unconstitutional. Given that conclusion, the President has instructed the Department not to defend the statute in *Windsor* and *Pedersen*, now pending in the Southern District of New York and the District of Connecticut. I concur in this determination....

Sincerely yours,

Eric H. Holder, Jr.
Attorney General

Commonwealth of Massachusetts v.
United States Department of Health and Human Services
682 F.3d 1 (1st Cir. 2012)

BOUDIN, Circuit Judge.

These appeals present constitutional challenges to section 3 of the Defense of Marriage Act ("DOMA"), 1 U.S.C. §7, which denies federal economic and other benefits to same-sex couples lawfully married in Massachusetts and to surviving spouses from couples thus married. Rather than challenging the right of states to define marriage as they see fit, the appeals contest the right of Congress to undercut the choices made by same-sex couples and by individual states in deciding who can be married to whom....

DOMA affects a thousand or more generic cross-references to marriage in myriad federal laws. In most cases, the changes operate to the disadvantage of same-sex married couples in the half dozen or so states that permit same-sex marriage.... Further, DOMA has potentially serious adverse consequences, hereafter described, for states that choose to legalize same-sex marriage.

In *Gill v. OPM*, No. 10-2207, seven same-sex couples married in Massachusetts and three surviving spouses of such marriages brought suit in federal district court to enjoin pertinent federal agencies and officials from enforcing DOMA to deprive the couples of federal benefits available to opposite-sex married couples in Massachusetts. The Commonwealth brought a companion case, *Massachusetts v. DHHS*, No. 10-2204, concerned that DOMA will revoke federal funding for programs tied to DOMA's opposite-sex marriage definition — such as Massachusetts' state Medicaid program and veterans' cemeteries.

By combining the income of individuals in same-sex marriages, Massachusetts' Medicaid program is noncompliant with DOMA, and the Department of Health and Human Services, through its Centers for Medicare and Medicaid Services, has discretion to rescind Medicaid funding to noncomplying states. Burying a veteran with his or her same-sex spouse removes federal "veterans' cemetery" status and gives the Department of Veterans' Affairs discretion to recapture all federal funding for the cemetery.

The Department of Justice defended DOMA in the district court but, on July 8, 2010, that court found section 3 unconstitutional under the Equal Protection Clause. In the companion case, the district court accepted the Commonwealth's argument that section 3 violated the Spending Clause and the Tenth Amendment....

The Justice Department filed a brief in this court defending DOMA against all constitutional claims. Thereafter, altering its position, the Justice Department filed a revised brief arguing that the equal protection claim should be assessed under a "heightened scrutiny" standard and that DOMA failed under that standard. It opposed the separate Spending Clause and Tenth Amendment claims pressed by the Commonwealth. The *Gill* plaintiffs defend the district court judgment on all three grounds.

A delay in proceedings followed the Justice Department's about face while defense of the statute passed to a group of Republican leaders of the House of Representatives — the Bipartisan Legal Advisory Group ("the Legal Group") — who retained counsel and intervened in the appeal to support section 3....

This case is difficult because it couples issues of equal protection and federalism with the need to assess the rationale for a congressional statute passed with minimal hearings and lacking in formal findings. In addition, Supreme Court precedent offers some help to each side, but the rationale in several cases is open to interpretation. We have done our best to discern the direction of these precedents, but only the Supreme Court can finally decide this unique case.

Although our decision discusses equal protection and federalism concerns separately, it concludes that governing precedents under both heads combine — not to create some new category of "heightened scrutiny" for DOMA under a prescribed algorithm, but rather to require a closer than usual review based in part on discrepant impact among married couples and in part on the importance of state interests in regulating marriage. Our decision then tests the rationales offered for DOMA, taking account of Supreme Court precedent limiting which rationales can be counted and of the force of certain rationale.

Equal Protection. The Legal Group says that any equal protection challenge to DOMA is foreclosed at the outset by *Baker v. Nelson*, 409 U.S. 810 (1972). There, a central claim made was that a state's refusal to recognize same-sex marriage violated federal equal protection principles. Minnesota had, like DOMA, defined marriage as a union of persons of the opposite sex, and the state supreme court had upheld the statute. On appeal, the Supreme Court dismissed summarily for want of a substantial federal question. *Id.*

Baker is precedent binding on us unless repudiated by subsequent Supreme Court precedent. *Hicks v. Miranda*, 422 U.S. 332, 344 (1975). Following *Baker*, "gay rights" claims prevailed in several well known decisions, *Lawrence v. Texas*, 539 U.S. 558 (2003), and *Romer v. Evans*, 517 U.S.620 (1996),[4] but neither mandates that the Constitution requires states to permit same-sex marriages. A Supreme Court summary dismissal "prevent[s] lower courts from coming to opposite conclusions on the precise issues presented and necessarily decided by those actions." *Mandel v. Bradley*, 432 U.S. 173, 176 (1977) (per curiam). *Baker* does not resolve our own case but it does limit the arguments to ones that do not presume or rest on a constitutional right to same-sex marriage.

Central to this appeal is Supreme Court case law governing equal protection analysis. The *Gill* plaintiffs say that DOMA fails under the so-called rational basis test, traditionally used in cases not involving "suspect" classifications. The federal defendants said that DOMA would survive such rational basis scrutiny but now urge, instead, that DOMA fails under so-called intermediate scrutiny. In our view, these competing formulas are inadequate fully to describe governing precedent.

Certain suspect classifications—race, alienage and national origin—require what the Court calls strict scrutiny, which entails both a compelling governmental interest and narrow tailoring. Gender-based classifications invoke intermediate scrutiny and must be substantially related to achieving an important governmental objective. Both are far more demanding than rational basis review as conventionally applied in routine matters of commercial, tax and like regulation.

Equal protection claims tested by this rational basis standard, famously called by Justice Holmes the "last resort of constitutional argument," *Buck v. Bell*, 274 U.S. 200, 208 (1927), rarely succeed. Courts accept as adequate any plausible factual basis, *Williamson v. Lee Optical of Oklahoma, Inc.*, 348 U.S. 483, 487–88 (1955), without regard to Congress' actual motives. *Beach Commc'ns*, 508 U.S. at 314. Means need not be narrowly drawn to meet—or even be entirely consistent with—the stated legislative ends. *Lee Optical*, 348 U.S. at 487–88.

Under such a rational basis standard, the *Gill* plaintiffs cannot prevail. Consider only one of the several justifications for DOMA offered by Congress itself, namely, that broadening the definition of marriage will reduce tax revenues and increase social security payments. This is the converse of the very advantages that the *Gill* plaintiffs are seeking, and

---

4. *Lawrence* struck down Texas' statute forbidding homosexual sodomy and *Romer* overturned a Colorado constitutional amendment that curtailed the right of communities to enact laws to prevent discrimination against gays and lesbians. Although *Lawrence* rested on substantive due process precedent and not equal protection, precedents under the two rubrics use somewhat related tests as to levels of scrutiny—applied to liberty interests under the former and discrimination claims under the latter. *Lawrence*, 539 U.S. at 575–76, 578; *Romer*, 517 U.S. at 632, 635.

Congress could rationally have believed that DOMA would reduce costs, even if newer studies of the actual economic effects of DOMA suggest that it may in fact raise costs for the federal government.

The federal defendants conceded that rational basis review leaves DOMA intact but now urge this court to employ the so-called intermediate scrutiny test used by Supreme Court for gender discrimination. Some similarity exists between the two situations along with some differences. But extending intermediate scrutiny to sexual preference classifications is not a step open to us.

First, this court in *Cook v. Gates*, 528 F.3d 42 (1st Cir. 2008), has already declined to create a major new category of "suspect classification" for statutes distinguishing based on sexual preference. *Cook* rejected an equal protection challenge to the now-superceded "Don't Ask, Don't Tell" policy adopted by Congress for the military, pointing out that *Romer* itself avoided the suspect classification label. This binds the panel.

Second, to create such a new suspect classification for same-sex relationships would have far-reaching implications—in particular, by implying an overruling of *Baker*, which we are neither empowered to do nor willing to predict. Nothing indicates that the Supreme Court is about to adopt this new suspect classification when it conspicuously failed to do so in *Romer*—a case that could readily have been disposed by such a demarche. That such a classification could overturn marriage laws in a huge majority of individual states underscores the implications.

However, that is not the end of the matter. Without relying on suspect classifications, Supreme Court equal protection decisions have both intensified scrutiny of purported justifications where minorities are subject to discrepant treatment and have limited the permissible justifications. And (as we later explain), in areas where state regulation has traditionally governed, the Court may require that the federal government interest in intervention be shown with special clarity.

In a set of equal protection decisions, the Supreme Court has now several times struck down state or local enactments without invoking any suspect classification. In each, the protesting group was historically disadvantaged or unpopular, and the statutory justification seemed thin, unsupported or impermissible. It is these decisions—not classic rational basis review—that the *Gill* plaintiffs and the Justice Department most usefully invoke in their briefs (while seeking to absorb them into different and more rigid categorical rubrics).

The oldest of the decisions, *U.S. Dept. of Agric. v. Moreno*, 413 U.S. 528 (1973), invalidated Congress' decision to exclude from the food stamp program households containing unrelated individuals. Disregarding purported justifications that such households were more likely to under-report income and to evade detection, the Court closely scrutinized the legislation's fit—finding both that the rule disqualified many otherwise-eligible and particularly needy households, and a "bare congressional desire to harm a politically unpopular group." *Id.* at 534, 537–38.

The second, *City of Cleburne v. Cleburne Living Ctr.*, 473 U.S. 432 (1985), overturned a local ordinance as applied to the denial of a special permit for operating a group home for the mentally disabled. The Court found unconvincing interests like protecting the inhabitants against the risk of flooding, given that nursing or convalescent homes were allowed without a permit; mental disability too had no connection to alleged concerns about population density. All that remained were "mere negative attitudes, or fear, unsubstantiated by factors which are properly cognizable in a zoning proceeding." *Id.* at 448.

Finally, in *Romer v. Evans*, 517 U.S. 620 (1996), the Court struck down a provision in Colorado's constitution prohibiting regulation to protect homosexuals from discrimination. The Court, calling "unprecedented" the "disqualification of a class of persons from the right to seek specific protection from the law," deemed the provision a "status-based enactment divorced from any factual context from which we could discern a relationship to legitimate state interests." *Id.* at 632–33, 635.

These three decisions did not adopt some new category of suspect classification or employ rational basis review in its minimalist form; instead, the Court rested on the case-specific nature of the discrepant treatment, the burden imposed, and the infirmities of the justifications offered.... There is nothing remarkable about this: categories are often approximations and are themselves constructed by weighing of underlying elements.

All three of the cited cases—*Moreno*, *City of Cleburne* and *Romer*—stressed the historic patterns of disadvantage suffered by the group adversely affected by the statute. As with the women, the poor and the mentally impaired, gays and lesbians have long been the subject of discrimination. *Lawrence*, 539 U.S. at 571. The Court has in these cases undertaken a more careful assessment of the justifications than the light scrutiny offered by conventional rational basis review.

As for burden, the combined effect of DOMA's restrictions on federal benefits will not prevent same-sex marriage where permitted under state law; but it will penalize those couples by limiting tax and social security benefits to opposite-sex couples in their own and all other states. For those married same-sex couples of which one partner is in federal service, the other cannot take advantage of medical care and other benefits available to opposite-sex partners in Massachusetts and everywhere else in the country.

These burdens are comparable to those the Court found substantial in *Moreno*, *City of Cleburne*, and *Romer*. *Moreno*, like this case, involved meaningful economic benefits; *City of Cleburne* involved the opportunity to secure housing; *Romer*, the chance to secure equal protection of the laws on the same terms as other groups. Loss of survivor's social security, spouse-based medical care and tax benefits are major detriments on any reckoning; provision for retirement and medical care are, in practice, the main components of the social safety net for vast numbers of Americans.

Accordingly, we conclude that the extreme deference accorded to ordinary economic legislation in cases like *Lee Optical* would not be extended to DOMA by the Supreme Court; and without insisting on "compelling" or "important" justifications or "narrow tailoring," the Court would scrutinize with care the purported bases for the legislation. Before providing such scrutiny, a separate element absent in *Moreno*, *City of Cleburne*, and *Romer*—federalism—must be considered.

Federalism. In assailing DOMA, the plaintiffs and especially the Commonwealth rely directly on limitations attributed to the Spending Clause of the Constitution and the Tenth Amendment.... In our view, neither the Tenth Amendment nor the Spending Clause invalidates DOMA; but Supreme Court precedent relating to federalism-based challenges to federal laws reinforce the need for closer than usual scrutiny of DOMA's justifications and diminish somewhat the deference ordinarily accorded.

It is true that DOMA intrudes extensively into a realm that has from the start of the nation been primarily confided to state regulation—domestic relations and the definition and incidents of lawful marriage—which is a leading instance of the states' exercise of their broad police-power authority over morality and culture....

Nevertheless, Congress surely has an interest in who counts as married. The statutes and programs that section 3 governs are federal regimes such as social security, the Internal Revenue Code and medical insurance for federal workers; and their benefit structure requires deciding who is married to whom. That Congress has traditionally looked to state law to determine the answer does not mean that the Tenth Amendment or Spending Clause require it to do so.

Supreme Court interpretations of the Tenth Amendment have varied over the years but those in force today have struck down statutes only where Congress sought to commandeer state governments or otherwise directly dictate the *internal operations* of state government. *Printz v. United States*, 521 U.S. 898, 935 (1997); *New York v. United States*, 505 U.S. 144, 188 (1992). Whatever its spin-off effects, section 3 governs only federal programs and funding, and does not share these two vices of commandeering or direct command.

Neither does DOMA run afoul of the "germaneness" requirement that conditions on federal funds must be related to federal purposes. *South Dakota v. Dole*, 483 U.S. 203, 207–08 (1987). The requirement is not implicated where, as here, Congress merely defines the terms of the federal benefit. In *Dole*, the Supreme Court upheld a condition by which federal funds for highway construction depended on a state's adoption of a minimum drinking age for all driving on state roadways. DOMA merely limits the use of federal funds to prescribed purposes.

However, the denial of federal benefits to same-sex couples lawfully married does burden the choice of states like Massachusetts to regulate the rules and incidents of marriage; notably, the Commonwealth stands both to assume new administrative burdens and to lose funding for Medicaid or veterans' cemeteries solely on account of its same-sex marriage laws. These consequences do not violate the Tenth Amendment or Spending Clause, but Congress' effort to put a thumb on the scales and influence a state's decision as to how to shape its own marriage laws does bear on how the justifications are assessed.

In *United States v. Morrison*, 529 U.S. 598 (2000), and *United States v. Lopez*, 514 U.S. 549 (1995), the Supreme Court scrutinized with special care federal statutes intruding on matters customarily within state control. The lack of adequate and persuasive findings led the Court in both cases to invalidate the statutes under the Commerce Clause even though nothing more than rational basis review is normally afforded in such cases....

Given that DOMA intrudes broadly into an area of traditional state regulation, a closer examination of the justifications that would prevent DOMA from violating equal protection (and thus from exceeding federal authority) is uniquely reinforced by federalism concerns.

DOMA's Rationales. Despite its ramifying application throughout the U.S. Code, only one day of hearings was held on DOMA, and none of the testimony concerned DOMA's effects on the numerous federal programs at issue....

The statute, only a few paragraphs in length, is devoid of the express prefatory findings commonly made in major federal laws. Accordingly, in discerning and assessing Congress' basis for DOMA our main resort is the House Committee report and, in lesser measure, to variations of its themes advanced in the briefs before us. The committee report stated:

> [T]he Committee briefly discusses four of the governmental interests advanced by this legislation: (1) defending and nurturing the institution of traditional,

heterosexual marriage; (2) defending traditional notions of morality; (3) protecting state sovereignty and democratic self-governance; and (4) preserving scarce government resources.

H.R. Rep. No. 104-664, at 12 (1996).

The penultimate reason listed above was not directed to section 3—indeed, is antithetical to it—but was concerned solely with section 2, which reserved a state's power not to recognize same-sex marriages performed in other states. Thus, we begin with the others, reserving for separate consideration the claim strongly pressed by the *Gill* plaintiffs that DOMA should be condemned because its unacknowledged but alleged central motive was hostility to homosexuality.

First, starting with the most concrete of the cited reasons—"preserving scarce government resources"—it is said that DOMA will save money for the federal government by limiting tax savings and avoiding social security and other payments to spouses....

But, where the distinction is drawn against a historically disadvantaged group and has no other basis, Supreme Court precedent marks this as a reason undermining rather than bolstering the distinction. *Plyler v. Doe*, 457 U.S. 202, 227 (1982); *Romer*, 517 U.S. at 635. The reason, derived from equal protection analysis, is that such a group has historically been less able to protect itself through the political process. *Plyler*, 457 U.S. at 218 n.14; *United States v. Carolene Prods. Co.*, 304 U.S. 144, 152 n.4 (1938).

A second rationale of a pragmatic character, advanced by the Legal Group's brief and several others, is to support child-rearing in the context of stable marriage. The evidence as to child rearing by same-sex couples is the subject of controversy, but we need not enter the debate. Whether or not children raised by opposite-sex marriages are on average better served, DOMA cannot preclude same-sex couples in Massachusetts from adopting children or prevent a woman partner from giving birth to a child to be raised by both partners.

Although the House Report is filled with encomia to heterosexual marriage, DOMA does not increase benefits to opposite-sex couples—whose marriages may in any event be childless, unstable or both—or explain how denying benefits to same-sex couples will reinforce heterosexual marriage. Certainly, the denial will not affect the gender choices of those seeking marriage. This is not merely a matter of poor fit of remedy to perceived problem, but a lack of any demonstrated connection between DOMA's treatment of same-sex couples and its asserted goal of strengthening the bonds and benefits to society of heterosexual marriage.

A third reason, moral disapproval of homosexuality, is one of DOMA's stated justifications:

Civil laws that permit only heterosexual marriage reflect and honor a collective moral judgment about human sexuality. This judgment entails both *moral disapproval of homosexuality*, and a moral conviction that heterosexuality better comports with traditional (especially Judeo-Christian) morality.

H.R. Rep. No. 104-664, at 15–16 (emphasis added); *see also, e.g.*, 142 Cong. Rec. 16,972 (1996) (statement of Rep. Coburn) (homosexuality "morally wrong").

For generations, moral disapproval has been taken as an adequate basis for legislation, although usually in choices made by state legislators to whom general police power is entrusted. But, speaking directly of same-sex preferences, *Lawrence* ruled that moral disapproval alone cannot justify legislation discriminating on this basis. Moral judgments can hardly be avoided in legislation, but *Lawrence* and *Romer* have undercut *this* basis. Cf. *Palmore v. Sidoti*, 466 U.S. 429, 433 (1984).

Finally, it has been suggested by the Legal Group's brief that, faced with a prospective change in state marriage laws, Congress was entitled to "freeze" the situation and reflect. But the statute was not framed as a temporary time-out; and it has no expiration date, such as one that Congress included in the Voting Rights Act. The House Report's own arguments — moral, prudential and fiscal — make clear that DOMA was not framed as a temporary measure.

Congress did emphasize a related concern, based on the Hawaii Supreme Court's decision in *Baehr*, that state judges would impose same-sex marriage on unwilling states. But almost all states have readily amended constitutions, as well as elected judges, and can protect themselves against what their citizens may regard as overreaching. The fear that Hawaii could impose same-sex marriage on sister states through the Full Faith and Credit Clause relates solely to section 2 of DOMA, which is not before us.

We conclude, without resort to suspect classifications or any impairment of *Baker*, that the rationales offered do not provide adequate support for section 3 of DOMA. Several of the reasons given do not match the statute and several others are diminished by specific holdings in Supreme Court decisions more or less directly on point. If we are right in thinking that disparate impact on minority interests and federalism concerns both require somewhat more in this case than almost automatic deference to Congress' will, this statute fails that test. . . .

In reaching our judgment, we do not rely upon the charge that DOMA's hidden but dominant purpose was hostility to homosexuality. The many legislators who supported DOMA acted from a variety of motives, one central and expressed aim being to preserve the heritage of marriage as traditionally defined over centuries of Western civilization. Preserving this institution is not the same as "mere moral disapproval of an excluded group," *Lawrence*, 539 U.S. at 585 (O'Connor, J., concurring), and that is singularly so in this case given the range of bipartisan support for the statute.

The opponents of section 3 point to selected comments from a few individual legislators; but the motives of a small group cannot taint a statute supported by large majorities in both Houses and signed by President Clinton. Traditions are the glue that holds society together, and many of our own traditions rest largely on belief and familiarity — not on benefits firmly provable in court. The desire to retain them is strong and can be honestly held.

For 150 years, this desire to maintain tradition would alone have been justification enough for almost any statute. . . . But Supreme Court decisions in the last fifty years call for closer scrutiny of government action touching upon minority group interests and of federal action in areas of traditional state concern.

To conclude, many Americans believe that marriage is the union of a man and a woman, and most Americans live in states where that is the law today. One virtue of federalism is that it permits this diversity of governance based on local choice, but this applies as well to the states that have chosen to legalize same-sex marriage. Under current Supreme Court authority, Congress' denial of federal benefits to same-sex couples lawfully married in Massachusetts has not been adequately supported by any permissible federal interest. . . .

Franchise Tax Board of California v. Hyatt

538 U.S. 488 (2003)

Justice O'CONNOR delivered the opinion of the Court.

[Individual filed tort action against the California Franchise Tax Board (CFTB) in a Nevada state court for torts allegedly committed by CFTB in Nevada. CFTB contended that under the Full Faith and Credit Clause, the Nevada courts were required to apply a California statute immunizing CFTB from liability, but the Nevada courts applied Nevada law instead.]

The Constitution's Full Faith and Credit Clause provides: "Full Faith and Credit shall be given in each State to the public Acts, Records, and judicial Proceedings of every other State. And the Congress may by general Laws prescribe the Manner in which such Acts, Records and Proceedings shall be proved, and the Effect thereof." Art. IV, § 1. As we have explained, "[o]ur precedent differentiates the credit owed to laws (legislative measures and common law) and to judgments." *Baker v. General Motors Corp.*, 522 U.S. 222, 232 (1998). Whereas the full faith and credit command "is exacting" with respect to "[a] final judgment ... rendered by a court with adjudicatory authority over the subject matter and persons governed by the judgment," *id.*, at 233, it is less demanding with respect to choice of laws. We have held that the Full Faith and Credit Clause does not compel "'a state to substitute the statutes of other states for its own statutes dealing with a subject matter concerning which it is competent to legislate.'" *Sun Oil Co. v. Wortman*, 486 U.S. 717, 722 (1988) (quoting *Pacific Employers Ins. Co. v. Industrial Accident Comm'n*, 306 U.S. 493, 501 (1939)).

The State of Nevada is undoubtedly "competent to legislate" with respect to the subject matter of the alleged intentional torts here, which, it is claimed, have injured one of its citizens within its borders. "'[F]or a State's substantive law to be selected in a constitutionally permissible manner, that State must have a significant contact or significant aggregation of contacts, creating state interests, such that choice of its law is neither arbitrary nor fundamentally unfair.'" *Phillips Petroleum Co. v. Shutts*, 472 U.S. 797, 818 (1985) (quoting *Allstate Ins. Co. v. Hague*, 449 U.S. 302, 312–313 (1981) (plurality opinion)); see 472 U.S., at 822–823. Such contacts are manifest in this case: the plaintiff claims to have suffered injury in Nevada while a resident there; and it is undisputed that at least some of the conduct alleged to be tortious occurred in Nevada....

We have recognized ... that "it is frequently the case under the Full Faith and Credit Clause that a court can lawfully apply either the law of one State or the contrary law of another." *Sun Oil Co. v. Wortman, supra*, at 727. We thus have held that a State need not "substitute the statutes of other states for its own statutes dealing with a subject matter concerning which it is competent to legislate." *Pacific Employers Ins. Co. v. Industrial Accident Comm'n, supra*, at 501; see *Baker v. General Motors Corp., supra*, at 232; *Sun Oil Co. v. Wortman, supra*, at 722; *Phillips Petroleum Co. v. Shutts, supra*, at 818–819....

Wilson v. Ake

354 F. Supp. 2d 1298 (M.D. Fla. 2005)

MOODY, District Judge.

[Same-sex couple from Florida—who married one another in Massachusetts after that state's decision in *Goodridge*—filed suit, contending that a Florida statute providing for non-recognition of same-sex marriages, as well as Section 2 of DOMA, violate the Full Faith and Credit Clause.]

Plaintiffs' Complaint asserts that DOMA conflicts with the Constitution's Full Faith and Credit Clause. Article IV, Section I of the Constitution provides:

> Full Faith and Credit shall be given in each State to the public Acts, Records, and Judicial Proceedings of every other State; And the Congress may by general Laws

prescribe the Manner in which such Acts, Records and Proceedings shall be proved, and the Effect thereof.

Plaintiffs argue that "[o]nce Massachusetts sanctioned legal same-gender marriage, all other states should be constitutionally required to uphold the validity of the marriage." Plaintiffs believe that the differences in individuals' rights to enter into same-sex marriages among the States, such as Florida and Massachusetts, is exactly what the Full Faith and Credit Clause prohibits. They also assert that DOMA is beyond the scope of Congress' legislative power under the Full Faith and Credit Clause because Congress may only regulate what effect a law may have, it may not dictate that the law has no effect at all.

This Court disagrees with Plaintiff's interpretation of the Full Faith and Credit Clause. Congress' actions in adopting DOMA are exactly what the Framers envisioned when they created the Full Faith and Credit Clause. DOMA is an example of Congress exercising its powers under the Full Faith and Credit Clause to determine the effect that "any public act, record, or judicial proceeding of any other State, territory, possession, or tribe respecting a relationship between persons of the same sex that is treated as a marriage" has on the other States. 28 U.S.C. § 1738C. Congress' actions are an appropriate exercise of its power to regulate conflicts between the laws of two different States, in this case, conflicts over the validity of same-sex marriages.

Adopting Plaintiffs' rigid and literal interpretation of the Full Faith and Credit would create a license for a single State to create national policy. *See Nevada v. Hall,* 440 U.S. 410, 423–24 (1979) ("Full Faith and Credit does not . . . enable one state to legislate for the other or to project its laws across state lines so as to preclude the other from prescribing for itself the legal consequences of acts within it.") (quoting *Pacific Ins. Co. v. Industrial Accident Comm'n,* 306 U.S. 493, 504–05 (1939)); *Williams v. North Carolina,* 317 U.S. 287, 296 (1942) ("Nor is there any authority which lends support to the view that the full faith and credit clause compels the courts of one state to subordinate the local policy of that state, as respects its domiciliaries, to the statutes of any other state."). The Supreme Court has clearly established that "the Full Faith and Credit Clause does not require a State to apply another State's law in violation of its own legitimate public policy." *Hall,* 440 U.S. at 422 (citing *Pacific Ins. Co.,* 306 U.S. at 493). Florida is not required to recognize or apply Massachusetts' same-sex marriage law because it clearly conflicts with Florida's legitimate public policy of opposing same-sex marriage.[6]

. . . .

Notes and Questions

1. After the Obama Administration announced that it would no longer defend Section 3 of the Defense of Marriage Act when challenged on equal protection grounds, Congress hired its own counsel to defend the statute when challenged in federal court.

Is it appropriate for the President to refuse to defend a law's constitutionality? In this regard, consider the arguments raised in Chapter 2 regarding the refusal of the State of California to defend the constitutionality of Proposition 8. Would you feel differently had Congress enacted a statute prohibiting employment discrimination based on sexual orientation or gender identity, or hate crimes motivated by the victim's sexual orientation

---

6. Under Plaintiffs' interpretation of the clause, a single State could mandate that all the States recognize bigamy, polygamy, marriages between blood relatives or marriages involving minor children.

or gender identity, and when their constitutionality was challenged in court, the President refused to defend those laws?

2. As demonstrated by the *Franchise Tax* and *Wilson* cases, as a general rule, Full Faith and Credit Clause challenges to either Section 2 of DOMA or a state's refusal to recognize a marriage validly entered into in another state are unlikely to succeed. However, in two narrow instances, the license granted by Section 2 may run afoul of the Full Faith and Credit Clause.

First, in a few, narrow instances, it is possible for a state's courts to have sufficient "minimum contacts" for due process purposes to exercise personal jurisdiction over the case, but insufficient contacts to apply its own law to the dispute under the *Phillips Petroleum* and *Allstate* cases cited in *Franchise Tax*. The paradigmatic example of this is when personal jurisdiction is based on the defendant's transient presence in the jurisdiction. To the extent that a question regarding the validity of an out-of-state same-sex marriage arose in the litigation, it would likely violate the Full Faith and Credit Clause for the state to apply its own law to deny recognition.

Second, as indicated in *Franchise Tax*, the Full Faith and Credit command where *judgments* are involved is *exacting*. Thus, for example, suppose that one partner in a same-sex marriage was killed, and his surviving spouse sued for wrongful death in their home state, where the marriage is valid. If they sought to enforce the judgment in another state—where the defendant had assets—the "exacting" command of the Full Faith and Credit Clause would require that the sister state enforce the judgment, even if normally it would refuse to recognize the validity of out-of-state same-sex marriages.

For a thorough analysis of the Full Faith and Credit Clause in this context, see Jeffrey L. Rensberger, *Same-Sex Marriages and the Defense of Marriage Act: A Deviant View of an Experiment in Full Faith and Credit*, 32 CREIGHTON L. REV. 409 (1998).

3. To what extent must one state recognize a sister state's adjudication that someone is male or female? *See* David B. Cruz, *Sexual Judgments: Full Faith and Credit and the Relational Character of Legal Sex*, 46 HARV. C.R.-C.L. L. REV. 51 (2011) (contending that each state is entitled to define "male" and "female" differently for purposes of applying their own laws, and thus that although sister states are required to recognize judgments that are based on an underlying finding regarding the person's sex for the specific matter decided retrospectively in the earlier case, they need not recognize such judgments *prospectively*, such as in deciding what sex the person is for purposes of marrying under the law of the state in which enforcement of the prior judgment is sought).

C. Parenting

Problem 5-C: Best Interests of the Embryo

Under Florida law, surrogacy contracts are binding only if the couple seeking the assistance of the surrogate is "legally married." *See* FLA. STAT. ANN. § 742.15. Under Florida law, same-sex marriages are not permitted, nor are out-of-state same-sex marriages recognized as valid.

A same-sex couple who wishes to have a child through surrogacy seeks to challenge the statute's constitutionality.

What are the best arguments in favor of and against the constitutionality of the Florida statute?

In the same-sex marriage cases, the fitness of gays and lesbians to raise children played an indirect role, with states defending their prohibitions on same-sex marriage by contending that marriage and child-rearing are linked, and that the state has an interest in promoting the optimal setting for raising children. In light of the fact that the bans on same-sex marriage did not in any way prevent same-sex couples from adopting or having children, however, many courts rejected this justification as a rational basis for the law.

In the case that follows, the fitness of gays and lesbians to raise children plays a direct role. At issue in the case is the constitutionality of a Florida law banning "homosexual" persons from adopting children—the same law you previewed in Chapter 1.

Lofton v. Secretary of the Department of Children & Family Services
358 F.3d 804 (11th Cir. 2004)

BIRCH, Circuit Judge:

....

I. BACKGROUND

A. *The Challenged Florida Statute*

Since 1977, Florida's adoption law has contained a codified prohibition on adoption by any "homosexual" person. For purposes of this statute, Florida courts have defined the term "homosexual" as being "limited to applicants who are known to engage in current, voluntary homosexual activity," thus drawing "a distinction between homosexual orientation and homosexual activity." *Fla. Dep't of Health & Rehab. Servs. v. Cox*, 627 So.2d 1210, 1215 (Fla.Dist.Ct.App.1993), *aff'd in relevant part*, 656 So.2d 902, 903 (Fla.1995). During the past twelve years, several legislative bills have attempted to repeal the statute, and three separate legal challenges to it have been filed in the Florida courts. To date, no attempt to overturn the provision has succeeded. We now consider the most recent challenge to the statute.

B. *The Litigants*

Six plaintiffs-appellants bring this case. The first, Steven Lofton, is a registered pediatric nurse who has raised from infancy three Florida foster children, each of whom tested positive for HIV at birth. By all accounts, Lofton's efforts in caring for these children have been exemplary, and his story has been chronicled in dozens of news stories and editorials as well as on national television.... John Doe, also named as a plaintiff-appellant in this litigation, was born on 29 April 1991. Testing positive at birth for HIV and cocaine, Doe immediately entered the Florida foster care system. Shortly thereafter, Children's Home Society, a private agency, placed Doe in foster care with Lofton, who has extensive experience treating HIV patients. At eighteen months, Doe sero-reverted and has since tested HIV negative. In September of 1994, Lofton filed an application to adopt Doe but refused to answer the application's inquiry about his sexual preference and also failed to disclose Roger Croteau, his cohabiting partner, as a member of his household. After Lofton refused requests from the Department of Children and

Families ("DCF") to supply the missing information, his application was rejected pursuant to the homosexual adoption provision.... Two years later, in light of the length of Doe's stay in Lofton's household, DCF offered Lofton the compromise of becoming Doe's legal guardian. This arrangement would have allowed Doe to leave the foster care system and DCF supervision. However, because it would have cost Lofton over $300 a month in lost foster care subsidies and would have jeopardized Doe's Medicaid coverage, Lofton declined the guardianship option unless it was an interim stage toward adoption. Under Florida law, DCF could not accommodate this condition, and the present litigation ensued.

Plaintiff-appellant Douglas E. Houghton, Jr., is a clinical nurse specialist and legal guardian of plaintiff-appellant John Roe, who is eleven years old. Houghton has been Roe's caretaker since 1996 when Roe's biological father, suffering from alcohol abuse and frequent unemployment, voluntarily left Roe, then four years old, with Houghton. That same year, Houghton was appointed co-guardian of Roe along with one Robert Obeso (who otherwise has no involvement in this case). After Roe's biological father consented to termination of his parental rights, Houghton attempted to adopt Roe. Because of Houghton's homosexuality, however, he did not receive a favorable preliminary home study evaluation, which precluded him from filing the necessary adoption petition in state circuit court.

Plaintiff-appellants Wayne Larue Smith and Daniel Skahen, an attorney and real estate broker residing together in Key West, became licensed DCF foster parents after completing a requisite ten-week course in January of 2000. Since then, they have cared for three foster children, none of whom has been available for adoption. On 1 May 2000, Smith and Skahen submitted applications with DCF to serve as adoptive parents. On their adoption applications, both Smith and Skahen indicated that they are homosexuals. On 15 May 2000, they received notices from DCF stating that their applications had been denied because of their homosexuality....

II. DISCUSSION

....

C. *Appellants' Due Process Challenges*

1. Fundamental Right to "Family Integrity"

Neither party disputes that there is no fundamental right to adopt, nor any fundamental right to be adopted. R4-124 at 10 (Joint Pre-trial Stipulation); *see also Mullins v. Oregon,* 57 F.3d 789, 794 (9th Cir.1995) ("[W]hatever claim a prospective adoptive parent may have to a child, we are certain that it does not rise to the level of a fundamental liberty interest."); *Lindley,* 889 F.2d at 131 ("[W]e are constrained to conclude that there is no fundamental right to adopt.").... Because there is no fundamental right to adopt or to be adopted, it follows that there can be no fundamental right to apply for adoption.

Nevertheless, appellants argue that, by prohibiting homosexual adoption, the state is refusing to recognize and protect constitutionally protected parent-child relationships between Lofton and Doe and between Houghton and Roe. Noting that the Supreme Court has identified "the interest of parents in the care, custody, and control of their children" as "perhaps the oldest of the fundamental liberty interests recognized by this Court," *Troxel,* 530 U.S. at 65, appellants argue that they are entitled to a similar constitutional liberty interest because they share deeply loving emotional bonds that are as close as those between a natural parent and child. They further contend that this liberty interest is significantly burdened by the Florida statute, which prevents them from obtaining permanency in their relationships and creates uncertainty about the future integrity of their families. Only by being given the opportunity to adopt, appellants assert, will they be able to protect their alleged right to "family integrity."

Although the text of the Constitution contains no reference to familial or parental rights, Supreme Court precedent has long recognized that "the Due Process Clause of the Fourteenth Amendment protects the fundamental right of parents to make decisions concerning the care, custody, and control of their children." *Id.* at 66. A corollary to this right is the "private realm of family life which the state cannot enter that has been afforded both substantive and procedural protection." *Smith v. Org. of Foster Families for Equal. & Reform,* 431 U.S. 816, 842 (1977). Historically, the Court's family and parental-rights holdings have involved biological families. *See, e.g., Troxel,* 530 U.S. 57 (2000); *Wisconsin v. Yoder,* 406 U.S. 205 (1972); *Stanley v. Illinois,* 405 U.S. 645 (1972); *Pierce v. Soc'y of Sisters,* 268 U.S. 510 (1925); *Meyer v. Nebraska,* 262 U.S. 390 (1923). The Court itself has noted that "the usual understanding of 'family' implies biological relationships, and most decisions treating the relation between parent and child have stressed this element." *Smith,* 431 U.S. at 843. Appellants, however, seize on a few lines of *dicta* from *Smith,* in which the Court acknowledged that "biological relationships are not [the] exclusive determination of the existence of a family," *id.,* and noted that "[a]doption, for instance, is recognized as the legal equivalent of biological parenthood," *id.* at 844 n. 51. Extrapolating from *Smith,* appellants argue that parental and familial rights should be extended to individuals such as foster parents and legal guardians and that the touchstone of this liberty interest is not biological ties or official legal recognition, but the emotional bond that develops between and among individuals as a result of shared daily life.

We do not read *Smith* so broadly. In *Smith,* the Court considered whether the appellee foster families possessed a constitutional liberty interest in "the integrity of their family unit" such that the state could not disrupt the families without procedural due process. *Id.* at 842. Although the Court found it unnecessary to resolve that question, Justice Brennan, writing for the majority, did note that the importance of familial relationships stems not merely from blood relationships, but also from "the emotional attachments that derive from the intimacy of daily association." *Id.* at 844. The *Smith* Court went on, however, to discuss the "important distinctions between the foster family and the natural family," particularly the fact that foster families have their genesis in state law. *Id.* at 845. The Court stressed that the parameters of whatever potential liberty interest such families might possess would be defined by state law and the justifiable expectations it created. *Id.* at 845–46. The Court found that the expectations created by New York law—which accorded only limited recognition to foster families—supported only "the most limited constitutional 'liberty' in the foster family." *Id.* at 846. Basing its holding on other grounds, the Court concluded that the procedures provided under New York law were "adequate to protect whatever liberty interest appellees may have." *Id.* at 856.

In *Drummond v. Fulton County Dep't of Family & Children's Servs.,* the former Fifth Circuit construed *Smith*'s *dicta* in considering due process and equal protection claims brought by white foster parents challenging Georgia's refusal to permit them to adopt their mixed-race foster child, whom they had parented for two years. 563 F.2d 1200, 1206 (5th Cir.1977) (en banc). Arguing that theirs was a "psychological family," the foster parents advanced a theory identical to that of present appellants....

Relying on *Smith,* the *Drummond* court rejected plaintiffs' argument. Examining state law to determine the extent of plaintiffs' constitutional interests, the court found that "[t]here is no basis in the Georgia law, which creates the foster relationship, for a justifiable expectation that the relationship will be left undisturbed." *Id.* at 1207. The *Drummond* court stated:

The very fact that the relationship before us is a creature of state law, as well as the fact that it has never been recognized as equivalent to either the natural family or the adoptive family by any court, demonstrates that it is not a protected liberty interest, but an interest limited by the very laws which create it.

Id.; *accord Mullins,* 57 F.3d at 794 (holding that biological grandparents possessed no liberty interest in adopting two of their grandchildren who were available for adoption); *Procopio v. Johnson,* 994 F.2d 325, 329 (7th Cir.1993) (relying on *Smith* and holding that "[n]otwithstanding the preference that state law grants to foster families seeking to adopt their foster children, this priority does not rise to the level of an entitlement or expectancy").

Neither *Smith* nor *Drummond,* however, categorically foreclosed the possibility that, under exceptional circumstances, a foster family could possess some degree of constitutional protection if state law created a "justifiable expectation" of family unit permanency. *Drummond,* 563 F.2d at 1207. Here, we find that under Florida law neither a foster parent nor a legal guardian could have a justifiable expectation of a permanent relationship with his or her child free from state oversight or intervention. Under Florida law, foster care is designed to be a short-term arrangement while the state attempts to find a permanent adoptive home.... [T]he state is not interfering with natural family units that exist independent of its power, but is regulating ones created by it. Lofton and Houghton entered into relationships to be a foster parent and legal guardian, respectively, with an implicit understanding that these relationships would not be immune from state oversight and would be permitted to continue only upon state approval. The emotional connections between Lofton and his foster child and between Houghton and his ward originate in arrangements that have been subject to state oversight from the outset. We conclude that Lofton, Doe, Houghton, and Roe could have no justifiable expectation of permanency in their relationships. Nor could Lofton and Houghton have developed expectations that they would be allowed to adopt, in light of the adoption provision itself.

Even if Florida law did create an expectation of permanency, appellants misconstrue the nature of the liberty interest that it would confer upon them. The resulting liberty interest at most would provide *procedural* due process protection in the event the state were to attempt to remove Doe or Roe. Such a procedural right does not translate, however, into a substantive right to be free from state inference. Nor does it create an affirmative right to be accorded official recognition as "parent" and "child." In sum, Florida's statute by itself poses no threat to whatever hypothetical constitutional protection foster families and guardian-ward relationships may possess.

We conclude that appellants' right-to-family-integrity argument fails to state a claim. There is no precedent for appellants' novel proposition that long-term foster care arrangements and guardianships are entitled to constitutional protection akin to that accorded to natural and adoptive families. Moreover, we decline appellants' invitation to recognize a new fundamental right to family integrity for groups of individuals who have formed deeply loving and interdependent relationships. Under appellants' theory, any collection of individuals living together and enjoying strong emotional bonds could claim a right to legal recognition of their family unit, and every removal of a child from a long-term foster care placement—or simply the state's failure to give long-term foster parents the opportunity to adopt—would give rise to a constitutional claim....

2. Fundamental Right to "Private Sexual Intimacy"

Laws that burden the exercise of a fundamental right require strict scrutiny and are sustained only if narrowly tailored to further a compelling government interest. Appellants argue that the Supreme Court's recent decision in *Lawrence v. Texas,* 539 U.S. 558

(2003), which struck down Texas's sodomy statute, identified a hitherto unarticulated fundamental right to private sexual intimacy. They contend that the Florida statute, by disallowing adoption to any individual who chooses to engage in homosexual conduct, impermissibly burdens the exercise of this right.

We begin with the threshold question of whether *Lawrence* identified a new fundamental right to private sexual intimacy. *Lawrence*'s holding was that substantive due process does not permit a state to impose a criminal prohibition on private consensual homosexual conduct. The effect of this holding was to establish a greater respect than previously existed in the law for the right of consenting adults to engage in private sexual conduct. Nowhere, however, did the Court characterize this right as "fundamental." Nor did the Court locate this right directly in the Constitution, but instead treated it as the by-product of several different constitutional principles and liberty interests.

We are particularly hesitant to infer a new fundamental liberty interest from an opinion whose language and reasoning are inconsistent with standard fundamental-rights analysis. The Court has noted that it must "exercise the utmost care whenever [it is] asked to break new ground" in the field of fundamental rights, *Washington v. Glucksberg*, 521 U.S. 702, 720 (1997), which is precisely what the *Lawrence* petitioners and their *amici curiae* had asked the Court to do. That the Court declined the invitation is apparent from the absence of the "two primary features" of fundamental-rights analysis in its opinion. First, the *Lawrence* opinion contains virtually no inquiry into the question of whether the petitioners' asserted right is one of "those fundamental rights and liberties which are, objectively, deeply rooted in this Nation's history and tradition and implicit in the concept of ordered liberty, such that neither liberty nor justice would exist if they were sacrificed."[15] Second, the opinion notably never provides the "'careful description' of the asserted fundamental liberty interest" that is to accompany fundamental-rights analysis. Rather, the constitutional liberty interests on which the Court relied were invoked, not with "careful description," but with sweeping generality. Most significant, however, is the fact that the *Lawrence* Court never applied strict scrutiny, the proper standard when fundamental rights are implicated, but instead invalidated the Texas statute on rational-basis grounds, holding that it "furthers no legitimate state interest which can justify its intrusion into the personal and private life of the individual."

We conclude that it is a strained and ultimately incorrect reading of *Lawrence* to interpret it to announce a new fundamental right. Accordingly, we need not resolve ... appellants' fundamental-rights argument: whether exclusion from the statutory privilege of adoption because of appellants' sexual conduct creates an impermissible burden on the exercise of their asserted right to private sexual intimacy.

Moreover, the holding of *Lawrence* does not control the present case. Apart from the shared homosexuality component, there are marked differences in the facts of the two cases. The Court itself stressed the limited factual situation it was addressing in *Lawrence*:

> The present case does not involve minors. It does not involve persons who might
> be injured or coerced or who are situated in relationships where consent might

---

15. The Court did devote considerable attention to history and tradition. This examination, however, was for the purpose of challenging the historical premises relied upon by the *Bowers* Court, and it focused on whether there has been a history of enacting, and regularly enforcing, laws specifically directed at private homosexual conduct. Notably absent from this discussion was the critical inquiry for purposes of fundamental-rights analysis: whether there has been a deeply rooted tradition and history of *protecting* the right to homosexual sodomy or the right to private sexual intimacy.

not easily be refused. It does not involve public conduct or prostitution. It does not involve whether the government must give formal recognition to any relationship that homosexual persons seek to enter. The case does involve two adults who, with full and mutual consent from each other, engaged in sexual practices common to a homosexual lifestyle.

Here, the involved actors are not only consenting adults, but minors as well. The relevant state action is not criminal prohibition, but grant of a statutory privilege. And the asserted liberty interest is not the negative right to engage in private conduct without facing criminal sanctions, but the affirmative right to receive official and public recognition. Hence, we conclude that the *Lawrence* decision cannot be extrapolated to create a right to adopt for homosexual persons.

D. *Appellants' Equal Protection Challenge*

1. Rational-Basis Review

The Equal Protection Clause of the Fourteenth Amendment proclaims that "[n]o State shall ... deny to any person within its jurisdiction the equal protection of laws." U.S. Const. amend. XIV, § 1.... Equal protection, however, does not forbid legislative classifications.... Unless the challenged classification burdens a fundamental right or targets a suspect class, the Equal Protection Clause requires only that the classification be rationally related to a legitimate state interest. *Romer v. Evans,* 517 U.S. 620, 631 (1996). As we have explained, Florida's statute burdens no fundamental rights. Moreover, all of our sister circuits that have considered the question have declined to treat homosexuals as a suspect class. Because the present case involves neither a fundamental right nor a suspect class, we review the Florida statute under the rational-basis standard.

Rational-basis review, "a paradigm of judicial restraint," does not provide "a license for courts to judge the wisdom, fairness, or logic of legislative choices." *F.C.C. v. Beach Communications, Inc.,* 508 U.S. 307, 313–14 (1993). The question is simply whether the challenged legislation is rationally related to a legitimate state interest. *Heller v. Doe,* 509 U.S. 312, 320 (1993). Under this deferential standard, a legislative classification "is accorded a strong presumption of validity," *id.* at 319, and "must be upheld against equal protection challenge if there is any reasonably conceivable state of facts that could provide a rational basis for the classification," *id.* at 320. This holds true "even if the law seems unwise or works to the disadvantage of a particular group, or if the rationale for it seems tenuous." *Romer,* 517 U.S. at 632. Moreover, a state has "no obligation to produce evidence to sustain the rationality of a statutory classification." *Heller,* 509 U.S. at 320. Rather, "the burden is on the one attacking the legislative arrangement to negative every conceivable basis which might support it, whether or not the basis has a foundation in the record." *Id.* at 320–21.

2. Florida's Asserted Rational Bases

Cognizant of the narrow parameters of our review, we now analyze the challenged Florida law. Florida contends that the statute is only one aspect of its broader adoption policy, which is designed to create adoptive homes that resemble the nuclear family as closely as possible. Florida argues that the statute is rationally related to Florida's interest in furthering the best interests of adopted children by placing them in families with married mothers and fathers. Such homes, Florida asserts, provide the stability that marriage affords and the presence of both male and female authority figures, which it considers critical to optimal childhood development and socialization. In particular, Florida emphasizes a vital role that dual-gender parenting plays in shaping sexual and gender identity and in providing heterosexual role modeling. Florida argues that disallowing adoption into homosexual households, which are necessarily motherless or fatherless and lack the stability that comes with marriage, is a rational means of furthering Florida's interest in promoting adoption by marital families.[17]

Florida clearly has a legitimate interest in encouraging a stable and nurturing environment for the education and socialization of its adopted children. It is chiefly from parental figures that children learn about the world and their place in it, and the formative influence of parents extends well beyond the years spent under their roof, shaping their children's psychology, character, and personality for years to come. In time, children grow up to become full members of society, which they in turn influence, whether for good or ill. The adage that "the hand that rocks the cradle rules the world" hardly overstates the ripple effect that parents have on the public good by virtue of their role in raising their children. It is hard to conceive an interest more legitimate and more paramount for the state than promoting an optimal social structure for educating, socializing, and preparing its future citizens to become productive participants in civil society—particularly when those future citizens are displaced children for whom the state is standing *in loco parentis*.

More importantly for present purposes, the state has a legitimate interest in encouraging this optimal family structure by seeking to place adoptive children in homes that have both a mother and father. Florida argues that its preference for adoptive marital families is based on the premise that the marital family structure is more stable than other household arrangements and that children benefit from the presence of both a father and mother in the home. Given that appellants have offered no competent evidence to the contrary, we find this premise to be one of those "unprovable assumptions" that nevertheless can provide a legitimate basis for legislative action. Although social theorists from Plato to Simone de Beauvoir have proposed alternative child-rearing arrangements, none has proven as enduring as the marital family structure, nor has the accumulated wisdom of several millennia of human experience discovered a superior model. Against this "sum of experience," it is rational for Florida to conclude that it is in the best interests of adoptive children, many of whom come from troubled and unstable backgrounds, to be placed in a home anchored by both a father and a mother.

3. Appellants' Arguments

Appellants offer little to dispute whether Florida's preference for marital adoptive families is a legitimate state interest. Instead, they maintain that the statute is not rationally related to this interest. Arguing that the statute is both overinclusive and underinclusive, appellants contend that the real motivation behind the statute cannot be the best interest of adoptive children.

In evaluating this argument, we note from the outset that "it is entirely irrelevant for constitutional purposes whether the conceived reason for the challenged distinction ac-

---

17. Florida also asserts that the statute is rationally related to its interest in promoting public morality both in the context of child rearing and in the context of determining which types of households should be accorded legal recognition as families. Appellants respond that public morality cannot serve as a legitimate state interest. Because of our conclusion that Florida's interest in promoting married-couple adoption provides a rational basis, it is unnecessary for us to resolve the question. We do note, however, the Supreme Court's conclusion that there is not only a legitimate interest, but "a substantial government interest in protecting order and morality," *Barnes v. Glen Theatre, Inc.,* 501 U.S. 560, 569 (1991), and its observation that "[i]n a democratic society legislatures, not courts, are constituted to respond to the will and consequently the moral values of the people." *Gregg v. Georgia,* 428 U.S. 153, 175 (1976) (plurality opinion).

We also note that our own recent precedent has unequivocally affirmed the furtherance of public morality as a legitimate state interest.

tually motivated the legislature." *Beach Communications,* 508 U.S. at 315. Instead, the question before us is whether the Florida legislature *could* have reasonably believed that prohibiting adoption into homosexual environments would further its interest in placing adoptive children in homes that will provide them with optimal developmental conditions. Unless appellants' evidence, which we view on summary judgment review in the light most favorable to appellants, can negate every plausible rational connection between the statute and Florida's interest in the welfare of its children, we are compelled to uphold the statute. We turn now to appellants' specific arguments.

a. Adoption by Unmarried Heterosexual Persons

Appellants note that Florida law permits adoption by unmarried individuals and that, among children coming out the Florida foster care system, 25% of adoptions are to parents who are currently single. Their argument is that homosexual persons are similarly situated to unmarried persons with regard to Florida's asserted interest in promoting married-couple adoption. According to appellants, this disparate treatment lacks a rational basis and, therefore, disproves any rational connection between the statute and Florida's asserted interest in promoting adoption into married homes. Citing *City of Cleburne v. Cleburne Living Ctr., Inc.,* 473 U.S. 432 (1985), appellants argue that the state has not satisfied *Cleburne*'s threshold requirement that it demonstrate that homosexuals pose a unique threat to children that others similarly situated in relevant respects do not.

We find appellants' reading of *Cleburne* to be an unwarranted interpretation. In *Cleburne,* the Supreme Court invalidated under the rational-basis test a municipal zoning ordinance requiring a group home for the mentally retarded to obtain a special use permit. The municipality argued that it had a legitimate interest in (1) protecting the residents of the home from a nearby flood plain, (2) limiting potential liability for acts of residents of the home, (3) maintaining low-density land uses in the neighborhood, (4) reducing congestion in neighborhood streets, and (5) avoiding fire hazards. The Court, however, found that the municipality failed to distinguish how these concerns applied particularly to mentally retarded residents of the home and not to a number of other persons who could freely occupy the identical structure without a permit, such as boarding houses, fraternity houses, and nursing homes. The Court concluded that the purported justifications for the ordinance made no sense in light of how it treated other groups similarly situated. Appellants have overstated *Cleburne*'s holding by asserting that it places a burden on the State of Florida to show that homosexuals pose a greater threat than other unmarried adults who are allowed to adopt. The *Cleburne* Court reasserted the unremarkable principle that, when a statute imposes a classification on a particular group, its failure to impose the same classification on "other groups similarly situated in relevant respects" can be probative of a lack of a rational basis. *Bd. of Trustees of the Univ. of Alabama v. Garrett,* 531 U.S. 356, 366 n. 4 (2001) (explaining *Cleburne*'s rationale).

This case is distinguishable from *Cleburne.* The Florida legislature could rationally conclude that homosexuals and heterosexual singles are not "similarly situated in relevant respects." It is not irrational to think that heterosexual singles have a markedly greater probability of eventually establishing a married household and, thus, providing their adopted children with a stable, dual-gender parenting environment. Moreover, as the state noted, the legislature could rationally act on the theory that heterosexual singles, even if they never marry, are better positioned than homosexual individuals to provide adopted children with education and guidance relative to their sexual development throughout pubescence and adolescence.[19] In a previous challenge to Florida's statute, a Florida appellate court observed:

> [W]hatever causes a person to become a homosexual, it is clear that the state cannot know the sexual preferences that a child will exhibit as an adult. Statistically, the state does know that a very high percentage of children available for adoption will develop heterosexual preferences. As a result, those children will need education and guidance after puberty concerning relationships with the opposite sex. In our society, we expect that parents will provide this education to teenagers in the home. These subjects are often very embarrassing for teenagers and some aspects of the education are accomplished by the parents telling stories about their own adolescence and explaining their own experiences with the opposite sex. It is in the best interests of a child if his or her parents can personally relate to the child's problems and assist the child in the difficult transition to heterosexual adulthood. Given that adopted children tend to have some developmental problems arising from adoption or from their experiences prior to adoption, it is perhaps more important for adopted children than other children to have a stable heterosexual household during puberty and the teenage years.

Cox, 627 So.2d at 1220. "It could be that the assumptions underlying these rationales are erroneous, but the very fact that they are arguable is sufficient, on rational-basis review, to immunize the legislative choice from constitutional challenge." *Heller,* 509 U.S. at 333. Although the influence of environmental factors in forming patterns of sexual behavior and the importance of heterosexual role models are matters of ongoing debate, they ultimately involve empirical disputes not readily amenable to judicial resolution—as well as policy judgments best exercised in the legislative arena. For our present purposes, it is sufficient that these considerations provide a reasonably conceivable rationale for Florida to preclude all homosexuals, but not all heterosexual singles, from adopting.

The possibility, raised by appellants, that some homosexual households, including those of appellants, would provide a better environment than would some heterosexual single-parent households does not alter our analysis. The Supreme Court repeatedly has instructed that neither the fact that a classification may be overinclusive or underinclusive nor the fact that a generalization underlying a classification is subject to exceptions renders the classification irrational. "[C]ourts are compelled under rational-basis review to accept a legislature's generalizations even when there is an imperfect fit between means and ends." *Id.* at 321. We conclude that there are plausible rational reasons for the disparate treatment of homosexuals and heterosexual singles under Florida adoption law and that, to the extent that the classification may be imperfect, that imperfection does not rise to the level of a constitutional infraction.

b. Current Foster Care Population

Appellants make much of the fact that Florida has over three thousand children who are currently in foster care and, consequently, have not been placed with permanent adop-

---

19. The New Hampshire Supreme Court, in considering the constitutionality of a similar prohibition on homosexual adoption, concluded that the prohibition was rationally related to the state's desire "to provide appropriate role models for children" in the development of their sexual and gender identities. *In re Op. of the Justices,* 530 A.2d 21, 25 (1987). That court noted that "the source of sexual orientation is still inadequately understood and is thought to be a combination of genetic and environmental influences. Given the reasonable possibility of environmental influences, we believe that the legislature can rationally act on the theory that a role model can influence the child's developing sexual identity."

tive families. According to appellants, because excluding homosexuals from the pool of prospective adoptive parents will not create more eligible married couples to reduce the backlog, it is impossible for the legislature to believe that the statute advances the state's interest in placing children with married couples.

We do not agree that the statute does not further the state's interest in promoting nuclear-family adoption because it may delay the adoption of some children. Appellants misconstrue Florida's interest, which is not simply to place children in a permanent home as quickly as possible, but, when placing them, to do so in an optimal home, i.e., one in which there is a heterosexual couple or the potential for one. According to appellants' logic, every restriction on adoptive-parent candidates, such as income, in-state residency, and criminal record — none of which creates more available married couples — are likewise constitutionally suspect as long as Florida has a backlog of unadopted foster children. The best interests of children, however, are not automatically served by adoption into *any* available home merely because it is permanent. Moreover, the legislature could rationally act on the theory that not placing adoptees in homosexual households increases the probability that these children eventually will be placed with married-couple families, thus furthering the state's goal of optimal placement. Therefore, we conclude that Florida's current foster care backlog does not render the statute irrational.

c. Foster Care and Legal Guardianship

Noting that Florida law permits homosexuals to become foster parents and permanent guardians, appellants contend that this fact demonstrates that Florida must not truly believe that placement in a homosexual household is not in a child's best interests. We do not find that the fact that Florida has permitted homosexual foster homes and guardianships defeats the rational relationship between the statute and the state's asserted interest.... Indeed, it bears a rational relationship to Florida's interest in promoting the nuclear-family model of adoption since foster care and guardianship have neither the permanence nor the societal, cultural, and legal significance as does adoptive parenthood, which is the legal equivalent of natural parenthood.

Foster care and legal guardianship are designed to address a different situation than permanent adoption, and "the legislature must be allowed leeway to approach a perceived problem incrementally." *Beach Communications,* 508 U.S. at 316. The fact that "[t]he legislature may select one phase of one field and apply a remedy there, neglecting the others," does not render the legislative solution invalid. *Id.*; *Heller,* 509 U.S. at 321 ("The problems of government are practical ones and may justify, if they do not require, rough accommodations — illogical, it may be, and unscientific."). We conclude that the rationality of the statute is not defeated by the fact that Florida permits homosexual persons to serve as foster parents and legal guardians.

d. Social Science Research

Appellants cite recent social science research and the opinion of mental health professionals and child welfare organizations as evidence that there is no child welfare basis for excluding homosexuals from adopting. They argue that the cited studies show that the parenting skills of homosexual parents are at least equivalent to those of heterosexual parents and that children raised by homosexual parents suffer no adverse outcomes. Appellants also point to the policies and practices of numerous adoption agencies that permit homosexual persons to adopt.

In considering appellants' argument, we must ask not whether the latest in social science research and professional opinion *support* the decision of the Florida legislature, but whether that evidence is so well established and so far beyond dispute that it would be irrational for the Florida legislature to believe that the interests of its children are best served by not permitting homosexual adoption. Also, we must credit any conceivable rational reason that the legislature might have for choosing not to alter its statutory scheme in response to this recent social science research. We must assume, for example, that the legislature might be aware of the critiques of the studies cited by appellants—critiques that have highlighted significant flaws in the studies' methodologies and conclusions, such as the use of small, self-selected samples; reliance on self-report instruments; politically driven hypotheses; and the use of unrepresentative study populations consisting of disproportionately affluent, educated parents. Alternatively, the legislature might consider and credit other studies that have found that children raised in homosexual households fare differently on a number of measures, doing worse on some of them, than children raised in similarly situated heterosexual households. Or the legislature might consider, and even credit, the research cited by appellants, but find it premature to rely on a very recent and still developing body of research, particularly in light of the absence of longitudinal studies following child subjects into adulthood and of studies of adopted, rather than natural, children of homosexual parents.

We do not find any of these possible legislative responses to be irrational. Openly homosexual households represent a very recent phenomenon, and sufficient time has not yet passed to permit any scientific study of how children raised in those households fare as adults. Scientific attempts to study homosexual parenting in general are still in their nascent stages and so far have yielded inconclusive and conflicting results. Thus, it is hardly surprising that the question of the effects of homosexual parenting on childhood development is one on which even experts of good faith reasonably disagree. Given this state of affairs, it is not irrational for the Florida legislature to credit one side of the debate over the other. Nor is it irrational for the legislature to proceed with deliberate caution before placing adoptive children in an alternative, but unproven, family structure that has not yet been conclusively demonstrated to be equivalent to the marital family structure that has established a proven track record spanning centuries. Accordingly, we conclude that appellants' proffered social science evidence does not disprove the rational basis of the Florida statute.

e. *Romer v. Evans*

Finally, we disagree with appellants' contention that *Romer* requires us to strike down the Florida statute. In *Romer,* the Supreme Court invalidated Amendment 2 to the Colorado state constitution, which prohibited all legislative, executive, or judicial action designed to protect homosexual persons from discrimination. 517 U.S. 620, 624 (1996). The constitutional defect in Amendment 2 was the disjunction between the "[s]weeping and comprehensive" classification it imposed on homosexuals and the state's asserted bases for the classification—respect for freedom of association and conservation of resources to fight race and gender discrimination. The Court concluded that the Amendment's "sheer breadth is so discontinuous with the reasons offered for it that the amendment seems inexplicable by anything but animus toward the class it affects."

Unlike Colorado's Amendment 2, Florida's statute is not so "[s]weeping and comprehensive" as to render Florida's rationales for the statute "inexplicable by anything but animus" toward its homosexual residents. Amendment 2 deprived homosexual persons of "protections against exclusion from an almost limitless number of transactions and endeavors that constitute ordinary civic life in a free society." In contrast to this "broad and undifferentiated disability," the Florida classification is limited to the narrow and discrete context of access to the statutory privilege of adoption and, more importantly, has a plausible connection with the state's asserted interest. Moreover, not only is the effect of Florida's classification dramatically smaller, but the classification itself is narrower. Whereas Amendment 2's classification encompassed both conduct *and* status, Florida's adoption prohibition is limited to conduct. Thus, we conclude that *Romer*'s unique factual situation and narrow holding are inapposite to this case. . . .

Lofton v. Secretary of the Department of Children & Family Services

377 F.3d 1275 (11th Cir. 2004) (en banc)

BY THE COURT:

The Court having been polled at the request of one of the members of the Court and a majority of the Circuit Judges who are in regular active service not having voted in favor of it (Rule 35, Federal Rules of Appellate Procedures; Eleventh Circuit Rule 35-5), the Petition for Rehearing En Banc is DENIED.

. . . .

BARKETT, Circuit Judge, Dissenting from the Denial of Rehearing En Banc:

. . . .

I. EQUAL PROTECTION

A. The Rational Basis Test Established in the Analogous Cases of <u>Romer</u>, <u>Cleburne</u>, <u>Moreno</u>, *and* <u>Eisenstadt</u> *Requires that We Invalidate this Statute.*

. . . .

As will be explained more fully below, the classification at issue in this case burdens personal relationships and exudes animus against a politically unpopular group. Under these circumstances, statutes have consistently failed rational basis review. Summarizing these cases, Justice O'Connor observed in her concurrence in *Lawrence* that

> [l]aws such as economic or tax legislation that are scrutinized under rational basis review normally pass constitutional muster, since the Constitution presumes that even improvident decisions will eventually be rectified by the democratic processes. We have consistently held, however, that some objectives, such as a bare . . . desire to harm a politically unpopular group, are not legitimate state interests. *When a law exhibits such a desire to harm a politically unpopular group, we have applied a more searching form of rational basis review to strike down such laws under the Equal Protection Clause.*

Lawrence, 539 U.S. at 580 (O'Connor, J., concurring) (emphasis added). Justice O'Connor went on to explain how this principle has been applied by the Court in prior equal protection cases:

> *We have been most likely to apply rational basis review to hold a law unconstitutional under the Equal Protection Clause where, as here, the challenged legislation inhibits personal relationships. . . .*

All four of these precedents involved legislation targeting politically unpopular groups to varying degrees: "hippies" (*Moreno*), unmarried users of birth control (*Eisenstadt*), the mentally disabled (*Cleburne*), and homosexuals (*Romer*). Moreover, in each case, the

Court invalidated a law that had the effect of inhibiting personal relationships of one sort or another: among mentally disabled or unrelated persons who wished to share a common living space (*Cleburne* and *Moreno*); among unmarried individuals who wished to engage in intimate relations (*Eisenstadt*); and among individuals who wished to live without fear of state-sanctioned discrimination prompted solely by their attachment to persons of the same sex (*Romer*)....

In all four cases, the Court concluded that the asserted justifications were not rationally related to the classification. Thus, the Court *inferred* that animus was the motivation behind the legislation and established that such a motivation could not constitute a legitimate state interest....

B. Subjected to the Identical Analysis Used in Eisenstadt, Cleburne, Moreno, *and* Romer, *the Florida Ban Would be Unconstitutional.*

Like the justifications for the statutes in the cases discussed above, Florida's proffered justifications for the categorical ban here are false, do not rationally relate to the best interests of children, and are simply pretexts for impermissible animus and prejudice against homosexuals. The panel in *Lofton* credits the state's assertion that the statutory ban is

> designed to create adoptive homes that resemble the *nuclear family* as closely as possible. Florida argues that the statute is rationally related to Florida's interest in furthering the best interests of adopted children by placing them in *families with married mothers and fathers.* Such homes, Florida asserts, provide the *stability that marriage affords* and the presence of both male and female authority figures, which it considers critical to optimal childhood development and socialization. In particular, Florida emphasizes a *vital role that dual-gender parenting plays in shaping sexual and gender identity and in providing heterosexual role modeling.* Florida argues that disallowing adoption into homosexual households, which are necessarily motherless or fatherless and *lack the stability that comes with marriage,* is a rational means of furthering Florida's interest in promoting adoption by marital families.

358 F.3d at 818–19 (emphasis added).

This rhetoric boils down to the argument that Florida prohibits homosexuals from being considered as adoptive parents because it wishes to place children with married couples. It wishes to do so for two alleged reasons: (1) to provide "stability" in the home, which the panel apparently believes can only be provided by married couples representing the "nuclear" family model; and (2) to properly shape heterosexual "sexual and gender identity," which the panel asserts should be accomplished by married couples.

Like the proffered reasons in *Eisenstadt,* which were "so riddled with exceptions" that the state's asserted goal could not "reasonably be regarded as its aim," 405 U.S. at 449, the state's proffered rational basis for the statute here (providing adopted children with married couples as parents) cannot be legitimately credited because it fails the equal protection requirement that "all persons similarly situated should be treated alike." *Cleburne,* 473 U.S. at 439.... [I]t is plainly false that Florida has established a preference for "married mothers and fathers" as adoptive parents. The 1977 statute prohibiting homosexual adoption expresses no preference whatsoever for married couples, expressly permitting an "unmarried adult" to adopt. Moreover, the DCF administrative regulations that are inextricably tied to Florida's adoption statutes do not prefer married over single candidates for adoption. In short, the Florida legislature never did, and the Florida executive no longer does, express a preference for married over unmarried couples or singles in the area of adoption. The fact that Florida places children for adoption with single parents directly and explicitly contradicts Florida's post hoc assertion that the ban is justified by the state's wish to place children for adoption only with "families with married mothers and fathers." This contradiction alone is enough to prove that the state's alleged reasons are "illogical to the point of irrationality." *Eisenstadt*, 405 U.S. at 451.

However, instead of acknowledging this glaring gap between the ban on homosexual adoption and the state's purported justification, as did the Supreme Court in invalidating the statutes in *Eisenstadt, Moreno, Cleburne,* and *Romer,* the *Lofton* panel stretches mightily to construct a hypothetical to bridge this gap. "It is not irrational," the panel opines, "to think that heterosexual singles have a markedly greater probability of eventually establishing a married household and, thus, providing their adopted children with a stable, dual-gender parenting environment." The panel's contrived hypothetical offering blatantly ignores not only the absence of any preference in Florida's statute for married couples but also the realities of the adoption process. Evaluations of prospective parents are based on present, not "eventual," status and conditions. Florida does not ask for a commitment of plans to marry someday in the future and permits single adults to adopt without making inquiry into whether they have immediate, or even long-range, marriage plans or prospects. Indeed, that many individuals choose to adopt outside of marriage is an indication that adoption and commitment to a permanent adult relationship are completely separate decisions. Moreover, experience leads one to believe that single heterosexuals who adopt are less likely to marry in the future, not more likely. Finally, this speculative hypothesis also fails to take account of "non-practicing homosexuals" who are not likely to marry but can adopt under Florida law. The Supreme Court found the state's arguments in *Eisenstadt* to be a futile and transparent move to escape the reach of the Court's decision in *Griswold*. The hypothetical posited by the *Lofton* panel demonstrates a comparable and equally transparent attempt to ignore the equal protection cases applicable here.

In addition to its failure to meaningfully distinguish homosexuals from single heterosexuals, the panel never explains why it is rational to believe that homosexuals, as a class, are unable to provide stable homes and appropriate role models for children. With respect to the first of these arguments, there is absolutely no record evidence to show that homosexuals are incapable of providing the permanent family life sought by Florida. To the contrary, as the facts in this case suggest, many children throughout the country are lovingly and successfully cared for by homosexuals in their capacity as biological parents, foster parents, or legal guardians. Furthermore, it is not marriage that guarantees a stable, caring environment for children but the character of the individual caregiver. Indeed, given the reality of foster care in Florida, the statute actually operates to impede, rather than promote, the placement of a child into a permanent family. Florida's statute expresses a clear intent "to protect and promote the well-being of persons being adopted ... and to provide to all children who can benefit by it a permanent family life." Fla. Stat. §63.022(3) (2003). Yet, Florida's foster care system has a backlog of more than 3,400 children in it, far more than the number of married couples eligible to adopt. Given this backlog, the state's ban on gay adoption does nothing to increase the number of children being adopted, whether by married couples or anyone else. The state is evidently willing to allow children to live with the potential uncertainties of several foster-care placements rather than enjoy the security and certainty of an adoptive home with one or two caring parents who are also homosexual.

Nor does the panel offer a reason for why it is rational to credit the state's second argument: that homosexuals are incapable of providing good role models. The panel claims that "[heterosexual] children will need education and guidance after puberty concerning relationships with the opposite sex.... It is in the best interests of a child if his or her parents can personally relate to the child's problems and assist the child in the difficult transition to heterosexual adulthood." Is the panel suggesting that heterosexual parents are necessary in order to tell children about their own dating experiences after puberty? For anyone who has been a parent, this will no doubt seem a very strange, even faintly comical, claim. There is certainly no evidence that the ability to share one's adolescent dating experiences (or lack thereof) is an important, much less essential, facet of parenting. The difficult transition to adulthood is a common human experience, not an experience unique to human beings of a particular race, gender, or sexual orientation. It is downright silly to argue that parents must have experienced everything that a child will experience in order to guide them. Indeed, that will generally not be the case. For example, immigrant parents help their children adjust to a world and culture they have not known. It cannot be suggested that such individuals are unfit to parent any more than it could be suggested that a mother is unfit to parent a son or that a white person is unfit to parent an African-American child.[22] Furthermore, the panel's argument completely neglects to consider the situation of gay children of heterosexual parents. Children simply need parents who will love and support them.

In addition to this contrived argument about teenage dating advice, the panel suggests that placing children with homosexual parents may make it more likely that children will become homosexual, referring cryptically to the "vital role that dual-gender parenting plays in *shaping sexual and gender identity* and in providing heterosexual role modeling." In our democracy, however, it is not the province of the State, even if it were *able* to do so, to dictate or even attempt to influence how its citizens should develop their sexual and gender identities. This approach views homosexuality in and of itself as a social harm that must be discouraged, and so demeans the dignity of homosexuals, something that *Lawrence* specifically proscribes.

Finally, the panel also intimates in dicta that Florida has a legitimate interest in defending public morality by expressing disapproval of homosexuality. But moral disapproval of disfavored groups "is an interest that is insufficient to satisfy rational basis review under the Equal Protection Clause." *Lawrence*, 539 U.S. at 581 (O'Connor, J., concurring). *Moreno* established that "if the constitutional conception of 'equal protection of the laws' means anything, it must at the very least mean that a bare ... desire to harm a politically unpopular group cannot constitute a legitimate government interest." 413 U.S. at 534....

Nor may the state hide behind a suggestion that it is attempting to protect children from disapproval at large in society. Florida courts have specifically rejected moral disapprobation of homosexuality as a justification for granting custody of a child to one or another biological parent. *See Maradie v. Maradie*, 680 So.2d 538 (Fla.Dist.Ct.App.1996) (holding that a lower court's finding as to the effect of a homosexual environment on a child is not a proper subject of judicial notice, and that it requires reversal and remand for a new custody determination); *Jacoby v. Jacoby*, 763 So.2d 410 (Fla.Dist.Ct.App.2000) (citing *Palmore v. Sidoti*, 466 U.S. 429, 433 (1984), and holding that a lower court's reliance on perceived biases against homosexuality is an improper basis for a residential custody determination).

Ultimately, the breadth of the categorical adoption ban "outrun[s] and belie[s]" the state's asserted justifications. *Romer*, 517 U.S. at 635. As *Moreno* discounted the state's asserted reason of protecting the public from fraud because the state had adequate antifraud provisions with strict penalties, Florida's rationale should likewise be discounted, given that Florida has explicitly tailored provisions to protect children placed in adoptive homes. Florida Statute § 63.092(3) (2003) requires a preliminary and thorough

---

22. Nor, for example, could anyone responsibly suggest that priests must be married in order to provide marriage counseling, or that psychiatrists must have suffered every ill they treat.

home study of prospective adoptive parents and the state uses its full power to screen all applicants and bar adoption by anyone not deemed to be a fit parent. The adoption statute accords everyone other than homosexuals the benefit of an individualized consideration that is directed toward the best interests of the child. Child abusers, terrorists, drug dealers, rapists and murderers are not categorically barred by the adoption statute from consideration for adoptive parenthood in Florida. On the other hand, individuals who take children into their care, including unwanted children, such as those who are HIV-positive, and who have raised them with loving care for years are categorically barred from adopting if they happen to be homosexual. In the context of adoption, this disparity of treatment on the face of the statute amounts to the purest form of irrationality....

When there is no reason to believe that the disadvantaged class is different, in relevant respects, from similarly situated classes, the Supreme Court has held that irrational prejudice can be inferred as the basis for a classification. *Cleburne*, 473 U.S. at 449–50.... Moreover, when all the proffered rationales for a law are clearly and manifestly implausible, a reviewing court may infer that animus is the only explicable basis. *Romer*, 517 U.S. at 632, 635.... Unsurprisingly, animus is just what the legislative history of Florida's ban confirms.

C. Legislative History

The Florida statute was enacted after an organized and relentless anti-homosexual campaign led by Anita Bryant, a pop singer who sought to repeal a January 1977 ordinance of the Dade County Metropolitan Commission prohibiting discrimination against homosexuals in the areas of housing, public accommodations, and employment. Bryant organized a drive that collected the 10,000 signatures needed to force a public referendum on the ordinance. In the course of her campaign, which the Miami Herald described as creating a "witch-hunting hysteria more appropriate to the 17th century than the 20th," Bryant referred to homosexuals as "human garbage." She also promoted the insidious myth that schoolchildren were vulnerable to molestation at the hands of homosexual schoolteachers who would rely on the ordinance to avoid being dismissed from their positions.

In response to Bryant's efforts, Senator Curtis Peterson introduced legislation in the Florida Senate banning both adoptions by and marriage between homosexuals. The legislative history reveals the very close and utterly transparent connection between Bryant's campaign and the Peterson bills. At the May 3, 1977 hearings of the Senate Judiciary Civil Committee, for example, Senator Peterson observed that "it is a possible problem, constantly in the news." Senator George Firestone commented that "this [gay rights controversy] has totally polarized [my] community unnecessarily." And Senator Don Chamberlin explicitly tied the Bryant campaign to the proposed ban on homosexual adoption, arguing that the latter would never have arisen without the ruckus over the Dade County antidiscrimination ordinance. The impetus for Florida's adoption ban exactly parallels the impetus for the state constitutional amendment struck down in *Romer*.

The Florida legislature's intention to stigmatize and demean homosexuals is further confirmed by the passage, on May 30, 1977, of a House amendment that allowed for public disclosure of the reasons for a denial of an application for adoption. The explicit purpose of this amendment was to protect non-homosexual prospective parents whose applications were denied for reasons other than sexual orientation from the stigma of being thought to be homosexual. The Senate provided added coverage against stigmatization for non-homosexual applicants with its May 31 amendment requiring courts, when dismissing a petition for adoption, to state with specificity the reasons for doing so.

Throughout all of these proceedings, it could hardly be said that there was any discussion of the "best interests of the child" standard. The only legislator who bothered to inject the concept was Senator Chamberlin, who tried to block the bill, noting that there was no incompatibility at all between homosexuals and the best interests of children. Another senator simply stated that "we have a responsibility to provide children with a wholesome atmosphere."

As the House and Senate gave their final approval to the Peterson bills on May 31, Senator Peterson stated that his bills were a message to homosexuals that "[w]e're really tired of you. We wish you would go back into the closet." On June 8, 1977, exactly one day after Dade County voters repealed the antidiscrimination ordinance, the Governor of Florida signed the Peterson bills into law, in what can only be seen as a deliberate acknowledgment of the orchestration between Bryant's campaign and the legislature's actions. In short, the legislative history shows that anti-gay animus was the major factor — indeed the sole factor — behind the law's promulgation, thereby confirming that the standard of review in this case is controlled by *Eisenstadt, Cleburne, Romer,* and *Moreno.*

Whereas the Texas sodomy statute struck down in *Lawrence* treated homosexuals as criminals, Florida's ban on gay adoption treats criminals with more dignity than homosexuals. Nothing more clearly raises the "inevitable inference that the disadvantage imposed is born of animosity toward the class of persons affected," *Romer,* 517 U.S. at 634, than this disparity of treatment.

II. SUBSTANTIVE DUE PROCESS

....

A. Lawrence Reaffirmed a Fundamental Right or Liberty Interest to Engage in Private Intimate Sexual Conduct.

....

In invalidating the sodomy statute at issue in *Lawrence,* the Court reaffirmed this right of sexual privacy, finding that private homosexual conduct is likewise encompassed within it....

In resolving this issue, the Court retraced its substantive due process jurisprudence by discussing the fundamental rights cases of *Griswold, Eisenstadt, Roe,* and *Carey* and emphasized the breadth of their holdings as involving private decisions regarding intimate physical relationships. Beginning with *Griswold,* the *Lawrence* Court found that its prior decisions confirmed "that the protection of liberty under the Due Process Clause has a substantive dimension of fundamental significance in defining the rights of the person" and "that the right to make certain decisions regarding sexual conduct extends beyond the marital relationship."

Because of the existence of this right to make private decisions regarding sexual conduct, the *Lawrence* Court was compelled to overrule the anomaly of *Bowers,* which had failed to acknowledge this right in permitting Georgia to criminalize sodomy....

Without defining what other kind of right it could be, *Lofton* maintains that "it is a strained and ultimately incorrect reading of *Lawrence* to interpret it to announce a new fundamental right." Indeed, *Lawrence* did not establish a *new* fundamental right. Rather, given the Court's statement that *Bowers* was not correct when it was decided, the *Lawrence* Court *reiterated the longstanding right* of consenting adults to engage in private sexual conduct.

B. Lofton's Arguments for Why Lawrence is a Rational Basis Case are Unsupported by any Supreme Court Precedents.

....

The panel's ... argument that *Lawrence* did not provide the "careful description" of the right required by *Glucksberg* is ... untenable given that the *Lawrence* Court was at pains to describe how *Bowers* had misframed the question in that case in terms of whether there was a fundamental right to engage in consensual homosexual sodomy.... Thus, *Lawrence* demonstrates that the "careful description" of a liberty interest required by *Glucksberg* will not necessarily be synonymous with framing the liberty interest in the most narrow fashion possible. The panel has ignored this important clarification of the *Glucksberg* analysis required by the Court's subsequent decision in *Lawrence*....

[T]he panel further ignores how *Lawrence* clarifies *Glucksberg*'s treatment of the role of history and tradition in identifying a fundamental right or liberty interest. The panel mis-reads *Glucksberg* to say that the only relevant historical inquiry is whether there has been a tradition of laws affirmatively protecting the conduct at issue. The panel then argues that while *Lawrence* "devote[d] considerable attention to history and tradition," it did so only to demonstrate that there had not been a "history of enacting, and regularly enforc-ing, laws specifically directed at private homosexual conduct." Apparently in the panel's view, this was a superfluous inquiry, devoid of legal meaning. According to the panel, the Supreme Court should have asked "whether there has been a deeply rooted tradition and history of *protecting* the right to homosexual sodomy or the right to private sexual intimacy."

The panel's belief that a history of state non-interference in the private sexual lives of homosexual adults cannot, as a matter of law, serve as the basis for recognizing a right to sexual privacy is entirely unsupported by any Supreme Court case. The panel has sim-ply made up a new constitutional requirement that there must be a history of affirmative legislative protection before a right can be judicially protected under the Due Process Clause. Such a requirement ignores not only *Lawrence,* but an entire body of Supreme Court jurisprudence. Had the Supreme Court required affirmative governmental protection of an asserted liberty interest, all of the Court's privacy cases would have been decided dif-ferently.[49] Equally significantly, the panel fails to heed the *Lawrence* Court's instruction that "[h]istory and tradition are the starting point but not in all cases the ending point of the substantive due process inquiry." As *Lawrence* stated:

> [W]e think that our laws and traditions in the past half century are of most rel-evance here. These references show an emerging awareness that liberty gives sub-stantial protection to adult persons in deciding how to conduct their private lives in matters pertaining to sex.

Thus, *Lawrence* elucidates the *Glucksberg* discussion of the proper use of history and tra-dition in more than one sense. In addition to clarifying that history and tradition do not themselves resolve the due process inquiry, *Lawrence* establishes that recent trends and prac-tices are as important as more distant ones in defining the existence and scope of a lib-erty interest....

[T]he panel insists that, no matter how hard *Lawrence* tries, it cannot have involved a liberty interest that requires heightened scrutiny because of a single reference to the

---

49. For instance, there was no lengthy tradition of protecting abortion and the use of contracep-tives, yet both were found to be protected by a right to privacy under the Due Process Clause. In *Roe,* the Court's historical analysis of Anglo-American statutory and common law served to provide evi-dence of the relatively recent (late nineteenth-century) vintage of state restrictions on abortion, not to demonstrate a tradition of affirmative protection of the right to an abortion. 410 U.S. at 132–41. Despite the lack of a history of protecting the right to abortion, the *Roe* Court nevertheless held that the "right of privacy ... is broad enough to encompass a woman's decision whether or not to termi-nate her pregnancy." *Id.* at 153.

phrase "legitimate state interest" towards the end of the *Lawrence* opinion. . . . The mere presence of the phrase "legitimate state interest" does not mean that heightened scrutiny is not applicable. . . . Once the *Lawrence* Court found that the Texas sodomy statute completely proscribed the petitioners' substantive right under the Due Process Clause, and that the law lacked any legitimate purpose, its inquiry was at an end. Heightened scrutiny requires a compelling state interest. The *Lawrence* Court clearly found that there was not even a conceivable legitimate state interest that could have sustained the Texas law.

The only way to avoid the conclusion that *Lawrence* recognized a fundamental right or liberty interest that requires heightened scrutiny is to deliberately refuse to give meaning to the overwhelming bulk of the words, phrases, sentences, and paragraphs used in *Lawrence.* Under the panel's view, *Lawrence* is a one-sentence opinion with pages and pages of irrelevant *dicta.* . . .

C. Florida's Adoption Ban is Subject to Heightened Scrutiny Because It Significantly Burdens the Right Identified in <u>Lawrence</u>.

Every precedent teaches that when the government directly burdens a fundamental right or liberty interest of the nature affirmed in *Lawrence,* heightened scrutiny applies. *See, e.g., Roe,* 410 U.S. at 155; *Zablocki v. Redhail,* 434 U.S. 374, 387–88 (1978) (heightened scrutiny applies to direct and substantial burdens on due process right). This heightened scrutiny requires that legislation be "narrowly drawn" to achieve a "compelling state interest." *Roe,* 410 U.S. at 155.[53]

The panel argues essentially that, even if *Lawrence* affirmed a fundamental right or liberty interest, heightened scrutiny is not appropriate here ... because Florida's ban is the product of a civil rather than a criminal law. . . .

The need to closely scrutinize Florida's justifications for burdening this right is not diminished because the burden in this case is the product of a civil statute, rather than a criminal law. Once a fundamental right or liberty interest has been established, the Supreme Court has stated that heightened scrutiny applies not only when a state punishes its exercise by means of a criminal statute, but also when a civil law directly and substantially burdens that protected right.

For example, the Court in *Zablocki* applied heightened scrutiny in striking down a civil law that prevented individuals who had not made child support payments from receiving a marriage license. . . .

Similarly, in *Shapiro,* the Court struck down the civil laws of various jurisdictions which required that residents live within the jurisdiction for a year before receiving welfare benefits. Even though the laws involved the receipt of a government benefit (welfare payments) rather than a right, the Court expressly rejected the application of rational-basis review. Instead, because the law "penalized" the fundamental right to interstate travel, the Court asked whether the law was "necessary" to achieve a "compelling governmental interest."

Together, *Zablocki* and *Shapiro* stand for the proposition that a court must analyze a civil law under heightened scrutiny when it either penalizes or severely burdens the ex-

---

53. The only sexual privacy case where the Court did not use this language was *Casey,* where it analyzed civil burdens on a woman's right to abortion, not an outright criminal ban. The Court found that a state regulation that had "the purpose or effect of placing a substantial obstacle in the path of a woman seeking an abortion of a nonviable fetus" would place an "undue burden" on the right to abortion and therefore be unconstitutional. *Casey,* 505 U.S. at 869.

ercise of a fundamental right. I submit that if heightened scrutiny was required given the nature of the civil burdens in *Zablocki* and *Shapiro,* then such scrutiny must, a fortiori, apply in this case. After all, in *Zablocki,* a person could marry after making his or her delinquent child support payment. And in *Shapiro,* a resident would be eligible to receive welfare payments (a government benefit like the ability to adopt) after living in the relevant jurisdiction for a year. But a person exercising his or her *Lawrence* right in Florida may *never* adopt. The categorical nature of this ban, which burdens the right to form intimate relationships only when it is exercised by homosexuals, requires the same close analysis that the Court gave to the laws analyzed in *Zablocki* and *Shapiro* and warrants the very same result.[56]....

The statute in this case imposes a direct, substantial and severe burden on the right recognized in *Lawrence.* Florida's adoption ban forces a choice between the right to participate in a consensual, private, intimate relationship and consideration for parenthood through adoption. In effect, under the Florida statute, homosexual men and women must forgo the consideration given to all others to be adoptive parents in order to engage in conduct protected by the Fourteenth Amendment. The Constitution does not permit such a choice unless, under heightened scrutiny, a compelling and narrowly tailored justification has been found. As demonstrated above, not only is there no compelling interest to justify the Florida adoption ban, but the law is not even rationally related to the governmental purposes asserted. As such, Florida's ban on homosexual adoption fails both heightened scrutiny and rational basis review.

[The opinion of Judge Birch, specially concurring in the denial of rehearing en banc, and the opinions of Judges Anderson and Marcus, dissenting in the denial of rehearing en banc, are omitted.]

Notes and Questions

1. The *Lofton* case is a paradigmatic example of the consequences of the Supreme Court's unwillingness to openly embrace heightened review under the Equal Protection and Due Process Clauses in its decisions in *Romer* and *Lawrence.* After all, is not the *Lofton* court's application of those cases perfectly reasonable, given what the Court actually held in those cases? On the other hand, Judge Barkett's reading of *Romer* and *Lawrence* is equally plausible, is it not? Might this be the very sort of case that the Supreme Court did not wish to effectively decide by announcing heightened scrutiny under either the Due Process or Equal Protection Clauses?

2. In *Lofton,* the court cites *Barnes v. Glen Theatre, Inc.*, 501 U.S. 560, 569 (1991) in footnote 17 of its opinion for the proposition that furthering morality is a "substantial government interest." *Barnes* involved a First Amendment challenge to a public indecency statute. Yet in support of that conclusion, the *Barnes* Court cited *Bowers v. Hardwick.* To what extent is that statement in *Barnes* thus undercut by *Lawrence*?

---

56. In *Zablocki* and *Shapiro,* the Court applied heightened scrutiny using an equal protection analysis. This made sense given that the government had burdened the right of poor people to marry (*Zablocki*), and had discriminated against new residents exercising their right to travel (*Shapiro*). Likewise, Florida's statute creates two classes of citizens: one of whom (heterosexuals) is allowed to form intimate relationships without any penalties, while the other (homosexuals) must choose between being considered as an adoptive parent and the ability to enter or remain in an intimate relationship. Therefore, *Zablocki* and *Shapiro* demonstrate that Florida's law can be analyzed using heightened scrutiny under *either* the Equal Protection or Due Process clauses.

In any event, *Lofton* raises public morality in the section of its opinion addressing the equal protection challenge. Even assuming that public morality remains a legitimate governmental interest when a law is challenged on due process (or perhaps, as in the case of *Barnes*, First Amendment) grounds, are there sound reasons—consistent with Justice O'Connor's concurring opinion in *Lawrence*—why public morality should not suffice as a legitimate governmental interest when a law is challenged on equal protection grounds?

3. The petition to rehear the case *en banc* failed by a tie vote of 6–6, with the sixth vote against rehearing the case provided by a recess appointment (one made without Senate confirmation) by then-President George W. Bush.

4. As the *Lofton* court noted, this was not the first time the Florida law's constitutionality was challenged in court and, as it turns out, not the last. Six years after the *Lofton* decision, a Florida appeals court held the statute to be unconstitutional. *See Fla. Dep't of Children & Families v. Adoption of X.X.G. & N.R.G.*, 45 So. 3d 79 (Fla. Dist. Ct. App. 2010). The court, applying rational basis review under the equal protection guarantee of the Florida Constitution, found that none of the reasons offered by the state satisfied rational basis review, particularly when considered in light of the fact that the state permitted gays and lesbians to serve as foster parents or guardians on a temporary or permanent basis. The state decided to forgo an appeal to the Florida Supreme Court.

5. In 2008, voters in Arkansas approved a ballot initiative that prohibited people "cohabiting with a sexual partner outside of a marriage that is valid under the Arkansas Constitution and the laws of this state" from adopting or serving as foster parents. The Arkansas Supreme Court, relying on its own pre-*Lawrence* decision striking down the state's sodomy law as violating the fundamental right to privacy implicit in the Arkansas Constitution, deemed the ballot initiative unconstitutional for burdening the exercise of that fundamental right. *See Ark. Dep't of Human Servs. v. Cole*, 2011 Ark. 145 (2011).

6. As *Lofton* indicates, numerous cases have held that there is no fundamental right under the due process clause to *adopt* a child. *See, e.g., Adar v. Smith*, 639 F.3d 146, 162 (5th Cir. 2011) (en banc); *Mullins v. Oregon*, 57 F.3d 789, 794 (9th Cir. 1995); *Lindley v. Sullivan*, 889 F.2d 124, 131 (7th Cir. 1989).

Yet if a state were to prohibit people from entering into surrogacy contracts or using other forms of assisted reproductive technology, might that not arguably infringe upon the right to *procreate* identified in *Skinner*? *See J.R. v. Utah*, 261 F. Supp. 2d 1268 (D. Utah 2002) (relying on *Skinner* to declare unconstitutional a state law providing that the surrogate is automatically granted the legal status of mother, on the ground that it interferes with the fundamental right of the biological parents to procreate). *See also T.M.H. v. D.M.T.*, 79 So.3d 787, 817–21 (Fla. Dist. Ct. App. 2011) (Lawson, J., dissenting) (collecting sources contending that *Skinner* can be broadly construed to encompass assisted reproduction or narrowly construed to be limited to "natural" procreation).

7. If an adoption decree is issued by a court in one state, must sister states recognize the validity of the adoption decree, even if it involves an adoption by two people of the same sex that would not be valid if entered into in the state in which enforcement of the decree is sought? In answering this question, recall from the previous section the distinction under the Full Faith and Credit Clause between out-of-state *laws* and out-of-state *judgments*. *See Finstuen v. Crutcher*, 496 F.3d 1139 (10th Cir. 2007) (relying on this distinction to conclude that final adoption orders and decrees are judgments that are entitled to recognition by all other states under the Full Faith and Credit Clause). *But see Adar v. Smith*, 639 F.3d 146, 158–61 (5th Cir. 2011) (en banc) (distinguishing in dicta between *recognition* and *enforcement* under the Full Faith and Credit

Clause, and noting that although sister states are required to recognize the validity of the adoption, they need not enforce it in a way that is inconsistent with the state's own law, such as by reissuing a new birth certificate with the names of two unmarried persons as parents).

D. Public Employment

As you previewed in earlier chapters, one of the most pervasive forms of public employment discrimination against sexual minorities in recent years has been the exclusion of openly gay, lesbian, and bisexual persons — as well as all transgendered persons — from military service.

Regarding gay, lesbian, and bisexual persons, earlier versions of the policy called for outright exclusion due merely to the person's sexual orientation, while a later version of the policy — "Don't Ask, Don't Tell" (DADT) — called for exclusion based on homosexual *conduct*, with statements regarding one's orientation serving as evidence of that conduct (thus, effectively barring openly gay, lesbian, or bisexual persons from serving in the military). In 2011, that policy was repealed as well, allowing for service by openly gay, lesbian, or bisexual persons, although a separate policy disqualifying transgendered persons from serving due to a medical disqualification remains undisturbed.

The challenges to the military's exclusion of sexual minorities from the military that you previewed in earlier chapters predated the U.S. Supreme Court's decision in *Lawrence v. Texas*, as well as more recent decisions suggesting or holding that discrimination based on sexual orientation is subject to heightened equal protection scrutiny.

In 2008, two federal appeals courts revisited the constitutionality of the military's Don't Ask, Don't Tell policy in light of these developments. Although the decisions are not directly relevant today given the policy's repeal, they shed light on how these courts might approach other laws that either draw distinctions based on sexual orientation or that burden the right identified in *Lawrence*.

Witt v. Department of the Air Force
527 F.3d 806 (9th Cir. 2008)

GOULD, Circuit Judge:

....

I

Major Witt entered the Air Force in 1987. She was commissioned as a Second Lieutenant that same year and promoted to First Lieutenant in 1989, to Captain in 1991, and to Major in 1999. In 1995, she transferred from active to reserve duty and was assigned to McChord Air Force Base in Tacoma, Washington.

By all accounts, Major Witt was an outstanding Air Force officer. She received medals for her service, including the Meritorious Service Medal, the Air Medal, the Aerial Achievement Medal, the Air Force Commendation Medal, and numerous others. Her annual "Officer Performance Reviews" commended her accomplishments and abilities. Major Witt was made an Air Force "poster child" in 1993, when the Air Force featured her in recruitment materials; photos of her appeared in Air Force promotional materials for more than a decade.

Major Witt was in a committed and long-term relationship with another woman from July 1997 through August 2003. Major Witt's partner was never a member nor a civilian employee of any branch of the armed forces, and Major Witt states that she never had sexual relations while on duty or while on the grounds of any Air Force base. During their relationship, Major Witt and her partner shared a home in Spokane, Washington, about 250 miles away from McChord Air Force Base. While serving in the Air Force, Major Witt never told any member of the military that she was homosexual.

In July 2004, Major Witt was contacted by Major Adam Torem, who told her that he had been assigned to investigate an allegation that she was homosexual. She declined to make any statement to him. An Air Force chaplain contacted her thereafter to discuss her homosexuality, but she declined to speak to him, as well. In November 2004, Major Witt's Air Force superiors told her that they were initiating formal separation proceedings against her on account of her homosexuality. This was confirmed in a memorandum that Major Witt received on November 9, 2004. That memorandum also stated that she could not engage in any "pay or point activity pending resolution" of the separation proceedings. Stated another way, she could not be paid as a reservist, she could not earn points toward promotion, and she could not earn retirement benefits. When she received this memorandum, Major Witt was less than one year short of twenty years of service for the Air Force, at which time she would have earned a right to a full Air Force retirement pension.

Sixteen months later, on March 6, 2006, Major Witt received another memorandum notifying her that a discharge action was being initiated against her on account of her homosexuality. It also advised her of her right to request an administrative hearing, which she promptly did. On April 12, 2006, Major Witt filed this suit in the United States District Court for the Western District of Washington, seeking declaratory and injunctive relief from the discharge proceedings.

A military hearing was held on September 28–29, 2006. The military board found that Major Witt had engaged in homosexual acts and had stated that she was a homosexual in violation of DADT. It recommended that she be honorably discharged from the Air Force Reserve. The Secretary of the Air Force acted on this recommendation on July 10, 2007, ordering that Major Witt receive an honorable discharge.

Major Witt is well regarded in her unit, and she believes that she would continue to be so regarded even if the entire unit was made aware that she is homosexual. She also contends that the proceedings against her have had a negative effect on unit cohesion and morale, and that there is currently a shortage of nurses in the Air Force of her rank and ability. We must presume those facts to be true for the purposes of this appeal.

II

A

. . . .

Major Witt argues that DADT violates substantive due process, the Equal Protection Clause, and procedural due process. The Ninth Circuit has considered and rejected similar claims in the past, *see, e.g., Holmes v. Cal. Army Nat'l Guard,* 124 F.3d 1126, 1136 (9th Cir.1997) (rejecting an Equal Protection Clause challenge to DADT under rational basis review); *Philips v. Perry,* 106 F.3d 1420, 1425–26 (9th Cir.1997) (same); *Beller v. Middendorf,* 632 F.2d 788, 805–12 (9th Cir.1980) (rejecting procedural due process and substantive due process challenges to a Navy regulation forbidding homosexual service in the Navy). However, Major Witt argues that *Holmes, Philips,* and

Beller are no longer dispositive in light of *Lawrence v. Texas,* 539 U.S. 558 (2003), in which the Supreme Court struck down a Texas statute that banned homosexual sodomy. Accordingly, to resolve this appeal, we must consider the effect of *Lawrence* on our prior precedents....

III

To evaluate Major Witt's substantive due process claim, we first must determine the proper level of scrutiny to apply. In previous cases, we have applied rational basis review to DADT and predecessor policies. However, Major Witt argues that *Lawrence* effectively overruled those cases by establishing a fundamental right to engage in adult consensual sexual acts. The Air Force disagrees. Having carefully considered *Lawrence* and the arguments of the parties, we hold that *Lawrence* requires something more than traditional rational basis review and that remand is therefore appropriate....

B

Major Witt argues that *Lawrence* recognized a fundamental right to engage in private, consensual, homosexual conduct and therefore requires us to subject DADT to heightened scrutiny. The Air Force argues that *Lawrence* applied only rational basis review, and that the Ninth Circuit's decisions in *Holmes, Philips,* and *Beller* remain binding law on DADT's validity. Because *Lawrence* is, perhaps intentionally so, silent as to the level of scrutiny that it applied, both parties draw upon language from *Lawrence* that supports their views.

Major Witt argues that the "plain language" of *Lawrence* demonstrates that heightened scrutiny is required here. She notes that, in *Lawrence,* the Supreme Court relied on *Griswold,* 381 U.S. 479, *Roe v. Wade,* 410 U.S. 113 (1973), and *Carey v. Population Services International,* 431 U.S. 678 (1977), all of which are fundamental rights cases. She also observes that the language of *Lawrence* emphasizes the importance of the right at issue and refers to "substantial protections" afforded "adult persons in deciding how to conduct their private lives in matters pertaining to sex." "Substantial protections" are not afforded under rational basis review, Major Witt argues, because rational basis review considers only whether the challenged policy is rationally related to a legitimate state interest.

In response, the Air Force argues that the same "plain language" implies only rational basis review. In particular, the Air Force stresses the passage in *Lawrence* that states that the challenged statute "further[ed] no *legitimate state interest* which can justify its intrusion into the personal and private life of the individual," 539 U.S. at 578 (emphasis added). According to the Air Force, legitimate interests are the hallmark of rational basis review. The Air Force also notes that *Lawrence* never stated that it was applying anything other than rational basis review, so, the Air Force concludes, it surely was not.

1

As a preliminary matter, the Air Force argues that no court to date has held that *Lawrence* applied a heightened level of scrutiny. However, the situation is more complex than that presented by the Air Force. Although the Air Force argues that "every Article III court to have decided th[e] question [whether *Lawrence* applied heightened scrutiny], including three courts of appeals, agreed with the District Court in this case that Lawrence applied rational-basis review, meaning that the case did not implicate a fundamental right," that is not the case. As we see it, only one court of appeals has directly considered the issue....

In *Lofton v. Secretary of the Department of Children & Family Services,* 358 F.3d 804, 817 (11th Cir.2004), the Eleventh Circuit upheld a law that forbade homosexuals from adopting children, explicitly holding that *Lawrence* did not apply strict scrutiny. Otherwise, our sister circuits are silent.…

One other court of note has considered the implications of *Lawrence.* In *United States v. Marcum,* 60 M.J. 198 (C.A.A.F.2004), the United States Court of Appeals for the Armed Forces considered a challenge to an Air Force sodomy law brought by a serviceman who had been convicted of consensual sodomy with a man of inferior rank within his chain of command. That court concluded that the application of *Lawrence* must be addressed "in context and not through a facial challenge." *Lawrence,* the court concluded, did not identify a fundamental right; however, it required "searching constitutional inquiry." The court distilled this inquiry into a three-step analysis:

> First, was the conduct that the accused was found guilty of committing of a nature to bring it within the liberty interest identified by the Supreme Court? Second, did the conduct encompass any behavior or factors identified by the Supreme Court as outside the analysis in *Lawrence?* Third, are there additional factors relevant solely in the military environment that affect the nature and reach of the *Lawrence* liberty interest?

The Court of Appeals for the Armed Forces, in our view, applied a heightened level of scrutiny. By considering whether the policy applied properly to a particular litigant, rather than whether there was a permissible application of the statute, the court necessarily required more than hypothetical justification for the policy—all that is required under rational basis review. The court also required consideration of "additional factors" that might justify the policy, which might be viewed as a corollary to the requirement that a challenged policy serve a "compelling" or "important" government interest under traditional forms of heightened scrutiny.

With this mixed background, we now turn to our analysis of *Lawrence.*

2

The parties urge us to pick through *Lawrence* with a fine-toothed comb and to give credence to the particular turns of phrase used by the Supreme Court that best support their claims. But given the studied limits of the verbal analysis in *Lawrence,* this approach is not conclusive. Nor does a review of our circuit precedent answer the question; as the Court of Appeals for the Armed Forces stated in *Marcum,* 60 M.J. at 204, "[a]lthough particular sentences within the Supreme Court's opinion may be culled in support of the Government's argument, other sentences may be extracted to support Appellant's argument." In these ambiguous circumstances, we analyze *Lawrence* by considering what the Court actually *did,* rather than by dissecting isolated pieces of text. In so doing, we conclude that the Supreme Court applied a heightened level of scrutiny in *Lawrence.*

We cannot reconcile what the Supreme Court did in *Lawrence* with the minimal protections afforded by traditional rational basis review. First, the Court overruled *Bowers,* an earlier case in which the Court had upheld a Georgia sodomy law under rational basis review. If the Court was undertaking rational basis review, then *Bowers* must have been wrong because it failed under that standard; namely, it must have lacked "any reasonably conceivable state of facts that could provide a rational basis for the classification." *FCC v. Beach Commc'ns, Inc.,* 508 U.S. 307, 313 (1993). But the Court's criticism of *Bowers* had nothing to do with the basis for the law; instead, the Court rejected *Bowers* because of the "Court's own failure to appreciate the extent of the liberty at stake." *Lawrence,* 539 U.S. at 567.

The criticism that the Court in *Bowers* had misapprehended "the extent of the liberty at stake" does not sound in rational basis review. Under rational basis review, the Court determines whether governmental action is so arbitrary that a rational basis for the action cannot even be conceived *post hoc.* If the Court was applying that standard—"a paradigm of judicial restraint," *Beach,* 508 U.S. at 314—it had no reason to consider the extent of the liberty involved. Yet it did, ultimately concluding that the ban on homosexual sexual conduct sought to "control a personal relationship that, whether or not entitled to formal recognition in the law, is within the liberty of persons to choose without being punished as criminals." *Lawrence,* 539 U.S. at 567. This is inconsistent with rational basis review.

Second, the cases on which the Supreme Court explicitly based its decision in *Lawrence* are based on heightened scrutiny. As Major Witt pointed out, those cases include *Griswold, Roe,* and *Carey.* Moreover, the Court stated that *Casey,* a post-*Bowers* decision, cast its holding in *Bowers* into doubt. *Lawrence,* 539 U.S. at 573–74. Notably, the Court did not mention or apply the post-*Bowers* case of *Romer v. Evans,* 517 U.S. 620 (1996), in which the Court applied rational basis review to a law concerning homosexuals. Instead, the Court overturned *Bowers* because "[i]ts continuance as precedent demeans the lives of homosexual persons." *Lawrence,* 539 U.S. at 575.

Third, the *Lawrence* Court's rationale for its holding—the inquiry analysis that it was applying—is inconsistent with rational basis review. The Court declared: "The Texas statute furthers no legitimate state interest *which can justify its intrusion into the personal and private life of the individual." Id.* at 578 (emphasis added). Were the Court applying rational basis review, it would not identify a legitimate state interest to "justify" the particular intrusion of liberty at issue in *Lawrence;* regardless of the liberty involved, any hypothetical rationale for the law would do.

We therefore conclude that *Lawrence* applied something more than traditional rational basis review. This leaves open the question whether the Court applied strict scrutiny, intermediate scrutiny, or another heightened level of scrutiny. Substantive due process cases typically apply strict scrutiny in the case of a fundamental right and rational basis review in all other cases. When a fundamental right is recognized, substantive due process forbids the infringement of that right "at all, no matter what process is provided, unless the infringement is narrowly tailored to serve a compelling state interest." *Reno v. Flores,* 507 U.S. 292, 301–02 (1993) (emphasis omitted). Few laws survive such scrutiny, and DADT most likely would not.[5] However, we hesitate to apply strict scrutiny when the Supreme Court did not discuss narrow tailoring or a compelling state interest in *Lawrence,* and we do not address the issue here.

Instead, we look to another recent Supreme Court case that applied a heightened level of scrutiny to a substantive due process claim—a scrutiny that resembles and expands upon the analysis performed in *Lawrence.* In *Sell v. United States,* 539 U.S. 166, 179 (2003), the Court considered whether the Constitution permits the government to forcibly administer antipsychotic drugs to a mentally-ill defendant in order to render that defendant competent to stand trial. The Court held that the defendant has a "significant constitutionally protected liberty interest" at stake, so the drugs could be administered

---

5. The rationale for DADT is found at 10 U.S.C. §654(a)(15), which states Congress's finding that:

> The presence in the armed forces of persons who demonstrate a propensity or intent to engage in homosexual acts would create an unacceptable risk to the high standards of morale, good order and discipline, and unit cohesion that are the essence of military capability.

forcibly "only if the treatment is medically appropriate, is substantially unlikely to have side effects that may undermine the fairness of the trial, and, taking account of less intrusive alternatives, is necessary significantly to further important governmental trial-related interests."

Although the Court's holding in *Sell* is specific to the context of forcibly administering medication, the scrutiny employed by the Court to reach that holding is instructive. The Court recognized a "significant" liberty interest — the interest "in avoiding the unwanted administration of antipsychotic drugs" — and balanced that liberty interest against the "legitimate" and "important" state interest "in providing appropriate medical treatment to reduce the danger that an inmate suffering from a serious mental disorder represents to himself or others."[7] To balance those two interests, the Court required the state to justify its intrusion into an individual's recognized liberty interest against forcible medication — just as *Lawrence* determined that the state had failed to "justify its intrusion into the personal and private life of the individual." *Lawrence*, 539 U.S. at 578.

The heightened scrutiny applied in *Sell* consisted of four factors: First, a court must find that *important* governmental interests are at stake....

> Courts, however, must consider the facts of the individual case in evaluating the Government's interest.... Special circumstances may lessen the importance of that interest....
>
> Second, the court must conclude that involuntary medication will *significantly further* those concomitant state interests....
>
> Third, the court must conclude that involuntary medication is *necessary* to further those interests. The court must find that any alternative, less intrusive treatments are unlikely to achieve substantially the same results....
>
> Fourth, ... the court must conclude that administration of the drugs is *medically appropriate*....

539 U.S. at 180–81. The fourth factor is specific to the medical context of *Sell*, but the first three factors apply equally here. We thus take our direction from the Supreme Court and adopt the first three heightened-scrutiny *Sell* factors as the heightened scrutiny balancing analysis required under *Lawrence*. We hold that when the government attempts to intrude upon the personal and private lives of homosexuals, in a manner that implicates the rights identified in *Lawrence*, the government must advance an important governmental interest, the intrusion must significantly further that interest, and the intrusion must be necessary to further that interest. In other words, for the third factor, a less intrusive means must be unlikely to achieve substantially the government's interest.

In addition, we hold that this heightened scrutiny analysis is as-applied rather than facial. "This is the preferred course of adjudication since it enables courts to avoid making unnecessarily broad constitutional judgments." *City of Cleburne v. Cleburne Living Ctr. Inc.*, 473 U.S. 432, 447 (1985). In *Cleburne*, the Court employed a "type of 'active' rational basis review," *Pruitt*, 963 F.2d at 1165–66, in requiring the city to justify its zoning ordinance as applied to the specific plaintiffs in that case. And *Sell* required courts to "consider the facts of the individual case in evaluating the Government's interest." 539 U.S. at 180. Under this review, we must determine not whether DADT has some hypothetical, posthoc rationalization in general, but whether a justification exists for the ap-

---

7. This inquiry is similar to intermediate scrutiny in equal protection cases.

plication of the policy as applied to Major Witt. This approach is necessary to give meaning to the Supreme Court's conclusion that "liberty gives substantial protection to adult persons in deciding how to conduct their private lives in matters pertaining to sex." *Lawrence*, 539 U.S. at 572....

Here, applying heightened scrutiny to DADT in light of current Supreme Court precedents, it is clear that the government advances an important governmental interest. DADT concerns the management of the military, and "judicial deference to ... congressional exercise of authority is at its apogee when legislative action under the congressional authority to raise and support armies and make rules and regulations for their governance is challenged." *Rostker v. Goldberg*, 453 U.S. 57, 70 (1981). Notably, "deference does not mean abdication." *Id.* "Congress, of course, is subject to the requirements of the Due Process Clause when legislating in the area of military affairs...." *Weiss v. United States*, 510 U.S. 163, 176 (1994).

However, it is unclear on the record before us whether DADT, as applied to Major Witt, satisfies the second and third factors. The Air Force attempts to justify the policy by relying on congressional findings regarding "unit cohesion" and the like, but that does not go to whether the application of DADT specifically to Major Witt significantly furthers the government's interest and whether less intrusive means would achieve substantially the government's interest.[11] Remand therefore is required for the district court to develop the record on Major Witt's substantive due process claim. Only then can DADT be measured against the appropriate constitutional standard.

IV

We next turn to Major Witt's Equal Protection Clause claim. She argues that DADT violates equal protection because the Air Force has a mandatory rule discharging those who engage in homosexual activities but not those "whose presence may also cause discomfort among other service members," such as child molesters. However, *Philips* clearly held that DADT does not violate equal protection under rational basis review, 106 F.3d at 1424–25, and that holding was not disturbed by *Lawrence*, which declined to address equal protection, *see* 539 U.S. at 574–75 (declining to reach the equal protection argument and, instead, addressing "whether *Bowers* itself ha[d] continuing validity"). We thus affirm the district court's dismissal of Major Witt's equal protection claims....

CANBY, Circuit Judge, concurring in part and dissenting in part:

The majority has written an opinion that is very praiseworthy as far as it goes. I concur in Parts I and II. I also concur in the first portion of Part III, to the end of subdivision (1). Beyond that, I agree substantially with the majority's discussion leading to the conclusion that the Supreme Court in *Lawrence v. Texas*, 539 U.S. 558 (2003), applied something more rigorous than traditional rational basis review in striking down Texas's criminalization of sexual relations between members of the same sex. Finally, I agree that the district court erred in dismissing the complaint for failure to state a substantive due process claim, and that we must remand for further proceedings. Unlike the majority, however, I would also reverse the dismissal of the equal protection claim. But where I differ most from the majority is in the level of scrutiny to be applied to both claims. In

---

11. Indeed, the facts as alleged by Major Witt indicate the contrary. Major Witt was a model officer whose sexual activities hundreds of miles away from base did not affect her unit until the military initiated discharge proceedings under DADT and, even then, it was her suspension pursuant to DADT, not her homosexuality, that damaged unit cohesion.

my view, the so-called "Don't Ask, Don't Tell" statute,[1] 10 U.S.C. §654, must be subjected to strict scrutiny. Under that standard, the Air Force must demonstrate that the statute's restriction of liberty, and its adverse classification of homosexuals, are "narrowly tailored to serve a compelling state interest." *Reno v. Flores,* 507 U.S. 292, 301–02 (1993).

Substantive Due Process

As the majority opinion correctly recognizes, the Supreme Court's opinion in *Lawrence* never unambiguously states what standard of review it is applying. The *Lawrence* opinion leaves no doubt at all, however, about the importance of the right it is protecting. In discussing the flaws of *Bowers v. Hardwick,* 478 U.S. 186 (1986), which it was overruling, *Lawrence* explained:

> To say that the issue in *Bowers* was simply the right to engage in certain sexual conduct demeans the claim the individual put forward, just as it would demean a married couple were it to be said marriage is simply about the right to have sexual intercourse. The laws involved in *Bowers* and here are, to be sure, statutes that purport to do no more than prohibit a particular sexual act. Their penalties and purposes, though, have more far-reaching consequences, touching upon the most private human conduct, sexual behavior, and in the most private of places, the home. The statutes do seek to control *a personal relationship that, whether or not entitled to formal recognition in the law, is within the liberty of persons to choose without being punished as criminals.*
>
> This, as a general rule, should counsel against attempts by the State, or a court, to define the meaning of the relationship or to set its boundaries absent injury to a person or abuse of an institution the law protects. It suffices for us to acknowledge that adults may choose to enter upon this relationship in the confines of their homes and their own private lives and still retain their dignity as free persons. When sexuality finds overt expression in intimate conduct with another person, the conduct can be but one element in a personal bond that is more enduring. *The liberty protected by the Constitution allows homosexual persons the right to make this choice.*

Lawrence, 539 U.S. at 567 (emphases added). Two points shine forth from this passage and its context in *Lawrence:* first, the right to choose to engage in private, consensual sexual relations with another adult is a human right of the first order and, second, that right is firmly protected by the substantive guarantee of privacy—autonomy of the Due Process Clause. Thus, even though the Court did not expressly characterize the right as "fundamental," it certainly treated it as such. It is this treatment, and the important individual values of liberty it recognizes, that require strict scrutiny of governmental encroachment on that right. In my view, therefore, *Lawrence* itself mandates strict scrutiny of the "Don't Ask, Don't Tell" statute.

In order to apply strict scrutiny, however, we do not need to satisfy ourselves that *Lawrence* commands or expressly adopts that standard of review.... In the present context, it is enough that the question is an open one. As the majority opinion recognizes, *Lawrence* avoids (carefully, it seems) stating what standard of review the Court was applying. Certainly nothing in *Lawrence* can reasonably be read as *forbidding* the application of strict scrutiny to statutes attaching severe consequences to homosexual behavior. The question of the standard of scrutiny in this case is therefore an open

---

1. Under the facts alleged in the complaint, the statute's popular name appears to be a misnomer as applied to Major Witt. She did not tell, but the Air Force asked.

one, and we must address it according to our best understanding of the individual constitutional rights and governmental action involved. For reasons that should already be apparent from my quotation and discussion of *Lawrence,* I have no difficulty concluding that the right to engage in homosexual relationships and related private sexual conduct is a personal right of a high constitutional order, and that the "Don't Ask, Don't Tell" statute so penalizes that relationship and conduct that it must be subjected to strict scrutiny.

Equal Protection

Major Witt presented an equal protection claim to the district court, but acknowledges here that such a claim was rejected by our court in *Philips v. Perry,* 106 F.3d 1420 (9th Cir.1997). Although she does not pursue it before our three-judge panel, she does preserve her right to assert the claim in the event she seeks en banc review of our decision; she has not abandoned the claim.

I do not believe that *Philips* ties our hands. *Philips* applied rational basis review to an equal protection attack on the "Don't Ask, Don't Tell" policy of the Navy. It did so on the authority of our earlier decision in *High Tech Gays v. Defense Industrial Security Clearance Office,* 895 F.2d 563 (9th Cir.1990). *High Tech Gays,* however, was based on the proposition that it would be inappropriate to apply strict scrutiny to classifications targeting homosexuals when the Supreme Court had held in *Bowers* that homosexual conduct could be made a crime. Because *Lawrence* unequivocally overruled *Bowers,* it "undercut the theory [and] reasoning underlying" *High Tech Gays* and *Philips* "in such a way that the cases are clearly irreconcilable." *Miller v. Gammie,* 335 F.3d 889, 900 (9th Cir.2003) (en banc). I am therefore convinced that *Philips* is no longer controlling.

An equal protection analysis applying strict scrutiny to the "Don't Ask, Don't Tell" statute is accordingly open to us. There are two different approaches to strict scrutiny under equal protection analysis, and both should be followed in this case.

The most direct path to strict scrutiny of the statute under the equal protection principle is to hold that classifications discriminating against homosexuals are "suspect," like classifications based on race. I have long been convinced that classifications against homosexuals are suspect in the equal protection sense, but I was unable to persuade a majority of my colleagues to embark on en banc review to establish that proposition. As I have already explained, however, the overruling of *Bowers* by *Lawrence* has undermined *High Tech Gays.* We accordingly are free to revisit the question whether the adverse classification of homosexuals is "suspect" under equal protection analysis. My reasons for concluding that such classifications are suspect are fully set out in my dissent from denial of en banc review in *High Tech Gays,* and I will not belabor the matter here. Suffice it to say that homosexuals have "experienced a history of purposeful unequal treatment [and] been subjected to unique disabilities on the basis of stereotyped characteristics not truly indicative of their abilities." *Mass. Bd. of Ret. v. Murgia,* 427 U.S. 307, 313 (1976). They also "exhibit obvious, immutable, or distinguishing characteristics that define them as a discrete group; and they are [ ] a minority." *Lyng v. Castillo,* 477 U.S. 635, 638 (1986). In short, they are a group deserving of protection against the prejudices and power of an often-antagonistic majority.

The Supreme Court's decision in *Romer v. Evans,* 517 U.S. 620 (1996), is not a barrier to a suspect classification, strict scrutiny approach. In that case, the Court struck down a Colorado constitutional provision prohibiting, among other things, any anti-discrimination legislation protecting homosexuals. The Supreme Court noted that most laws involve a classification and that, if no fundamental right or suspect class is involved, statutes are subject only to rational basis review. The Court then stated that the Colorado provision

> fails, indeed defies, *even this* conventional inquiry. First, the amendment has the peculiar property of imposing a broad and undifferentiated disability on a single named group, an exceptional and, as we shall explain, invalid form of legislation.

Id. at 632 (emphasis added). Thus the Court had no need to address whether homosexuals constituted a suspect class because the Colorado provision failed "even" rational basis review. That ruling does not negate the application of higher levels of scrutiny on similar classifications. Indeed, the strong language of *Romer* suggests that the invidiousness of the legislation would have supported any standard of review as a path to its invalidation. *Romer,* like *Lawrence,* does not forbid the application of strict scrutiny, even though it may have found that level of scrutiny unnecessary to invalidate the legislation before the Court in that case.

In addition to the avenue of a suspect classification, there is another path to strict scrutiny under equal protection analysis. Classifications that impinge on a fundamental right are subject to strict scrutiny when challenged as a violation of equal protection. As I have already explained, *Lawrence* effectively establishes a fundamental right without so labeling it. At the very least, *Lawrence* leaves the question open, to permit us to recognize the fundamental right to homosexual relations as I have already insisted we must. Even though that right justifies strict scrutiny under a theory of substantive due process, there are good reasons for adding an equal protection analysis in this case. It is true that, in *Lawrence,* the Supreme Court elected not to employ an equal protection theory. It recognized, however, that equal protection provided a "tenable" basis for declaring the statute invalid, and conceded that a decision recognizing a liberty interest in certain conduct advanced the cause of equality as well as due process. The reason why the Court in *Lawrence* did not employ an equal protection analysis was itself protective. The Court stated that it would not sufficiently establish the right to intimate homosexual relations if only equal protection were invoked, because a state might frustrate the right by denying heterosexuals as well as homosexuals the right to non-marital sexual relations.

The danger of an end-run remedy of equal treatment is not severe in our case, however. I doubt that the armed services are likely to respond to an invalidation of the "Don't Ask, Don't Tell" statute as a violation of equal protection by decreeing the automatic discharge of any member, heterosexual or homosexual, who is found to have engaged in sexual relations outside of marriage. In any event, we can guard against any such result by retaining our substantive due process analysis along with an equal protection approach.

The reason for including an equal protection analysis is that there is a very clear element of discrimination in the whole "Don't Ask, Don't Tell" apparatus, and an equal protection analysis focuses the inquiry sharply on a question that should not be ignored: what compelling interest of the Air Force is narrowly served by discharging homosexuals but not others who engage in sexual relations privately off duty, off base, and with persons unconnected to the military? It is no answer to such a question that the known presence of a sexually active homosexual in a military unit necessarily creates sexual tensions (if indeed that could be shown), unless it were also demonstrated that the presence of heterosexuals in a military unit created no comparable tensions. It is also not a sufficient answer that many military personnel are biased against homosexuals. *See Pruitt v. Cheney,* 963 F.2d 1160, 1165 (9th Cir.1992); *see also Palmore v. Sidoti,* 466 U.S. 429, 433

(1984) ("The Constitution cannot control such prejudices but neither can it tolerate them. Private biases may be outside the reach of the law, but the law cannot, directly or indirectly, give them effect."); *Romer,* 517 U.S. at 634–35. There are other requirements of narrow tailoring that would apply during further proceedings applying strict scrutiny, but the point now is that part of the inquiry should address the clear discrimination between homosexuals and heterosexuals, and determine whether that discrimination is necessary to serve a compelling governmental interest and sweeps no more broadly than necessary.

Order of Inquiry in Further Proceedings

The inquiry on remand should focus first on the Air Force's justification for its impingement on the right to private intimate sexual relations and the compelling nature of any interest that is served by that measure. The Air Force should be required to identify a compelling interest with sufficient specificity so that the relation between the "Don't Ask, Don't Tell" statute and that policy can be evaluated. It is difficult to accomplish that goal if the compelling interest is as broadly stated as "management of the military" or, say, "winning wars." Moreover, under strict scrutiny, it is not enough that the interest be merely "served" by the challenged legislation; the legislation must be *necessary* to that purpose, and must sweep no more broadly than is essential to serve the governmental purpose.

Thus, as a matter of due process, the Air Force can be required to show why there is a compelling need to discharge homosexuals who have been sexually active outside of their duty station with persons unconnected to the military and why the measure it has adopted is narrowly tailored to the satisfaction of that compelling need. As a matter of equal protection, the Air Force can be asked to show what compelling need is narrowly served by treating homosexuals who are sexually active off duty and outside the military context differently from heterosexuals who are sexually active off duty and outside the military context. These requirements are case-specific in that they reflect the alleged facts that Major Witt conducted all of her relations with her female partner off-base, and her partner was alleged not to be in or employed by the military. If the Air Force cannot meet these requirements, the statute must be invalidated in such applications.

There are clear advantages to addressing the Air Force's justifications first, before any inquiry into the personal characteristics and situation of Major Witt in her unit. First, requiring the Air Force to make the requisite showing as a threshold matter may end the case.

Second, the inquiry directed toward the Air Force is less potentially disruptive than a focus on Major Witt herself and, particularly, the allegedly favorable attitude toward her on the part of other members of her unit. To require unit members to testify or submit affidavits concerning the degree to which they do or do not consider themselves adversely affected by the presence of a known, sexually active homosexual, may constitute a distraction from regular duties. It is better to employ such an inquiry only as a last resort. Finally, requiring the Air Force to justify the application of the statute to a generic service member who carries on a homosexual relationship and intimate conduct away from the duty station and its personnel provides more protection of the constitutional right set forth in *Lawrence.* Because the right to choose to engage in private, intimate sexual conduct is a constitutional right of a high order, it must be protected not just for the outstanding service member like Major Witt, but also for the run-of-the-mill airman or soldier. It is thus the general application of the statute to the generic service member that the Air Force must be required to justify. In *Lawrence,* after all, the Supreme Court struck down the statute as applied to anyone engaging in homosexual conduct; it did not find it necessary or relevant to inquire into whether the individual conduct of which the petitioners had been convicted was more or less offensive to the interests of the State under the circumstances of its occurrence.…

Cook v. Gates
528 F.3d 42 (1st Cir. 2008)

HOWARD, Circuit Judge.

In 1993, Congress enacted a statute regulating the service of homosexual persons in the United States military. The Act, known as "Don't Ask, Don't Tell," provides for the separation of members of the military who engage, attempt to engage, intend to engage, or have a propensity to engage in a homosexual act. In the aftermath of this congressional action, several members of the military brought constitutional challenges, claiming the Act violated the due process and equal protection components of the Fifth Amendment and the free speech clause of the First Amendment. These challenges were rejected in other circuits.

In 2003, the United States Supreme Court invalidated, on substantive due process grounds, two convictions under a Texas law criminalizing sodomy between consenting homosexual adults. *Lawrence v. Texas*, 539 U.S. 558 (2003). *Lawrence* has reinvigorated the debate over the Act's constitutionality. This case is the second post-*Lawrence* challenge to the Act to be decided by a federal court of appeals.…

V. *Discussion*

….

A. Due Process

We agree with the parties and the district court that interpreting *Lawrence* is the critical first step in evaluating the plaintiffs' substantive due process claim. Prior to *Lawrence*, the courts of appeals, relying on the Supreme Court's holding in *Bowers v. Hardwick*, 478 U.S. 186 (1986) that homosexuals did not possess a substantive due process interest in engaging in sodomy, considered due process challenges to the Act under rational basis review. But *Lawrence* overruled *Bowers*, so the post-*Lawrence* standard for reviewing a substantive due process challenge to the Act is unclear.…

Courts and commentators interpreting *Lawrence* diverge over the doctrinal approach employed to invalidate the petitioners' convictions. Some have read *Lawrence* to apply a rational basis approach. Others see the case as applying strict scrutiny. And a third group view the case as applying a balancing of state and individual interests that cannot be characterized as strict scrutiny or rational basis. *Lawrence*'s doctrinal approach is "difficult to pin down." But we are persuaded that *Lawrence* did indeed recognize a protected liberty interest for adults to engage in private, consensual sexual intimacy and applied a balancing of constitutional interests that defies either the strict scrutiny or rational basis label.

There are at least four reasons for reading *Lawrence* as recognizing a protected liberty interest. First, *Lawrence* relies on the following due process cases for doctrinal support: *Griswold*, *Eisenstadt*, *Roe*, *Carey*, and *Casey*. Each case resulted in the Supreme Court recognizing a due process right to make personal decisions related to sexual conduct that mandated the application of heightened judicial scrutiny. It would be strange indeed to interpret *Lawrence* as not recognizing a protected liberty interest when virtually every case it relied upon for support recognized such an interest.

Second, the language employed throughout *Lawrence* supports the recognition of a protected liberty interest. *Lawrence* associated the right at issue with the core constitutional rights of "freedom of thought, belief, and expression," rights which undoubtedly mandate special protection under the Constitution. It also stated that "liberty gives *substantial* protection to adult persons in deciding how to conduct their private lives in matters pertaining to sex." And it concluded its analysis by stating that the "right to liberty under the Due Process Clause" allowed the petitioners to engage in "private sexual conduct" because "'[i]t is a promise of the Constitution that there is a realm of personal liberty which the government may not enter.'" Such language strongly suggests that *Lawrence* identified a protected liberty interest.

Third, in overruling *Bowers*, *Lawrence* relied on Justice Stevens' *Bowers* dissent as stating the controlling principles. The passage of Justice Stevens' dissent quoted in *Lawrence* stated that "individual decisions by married persons, concerning the intimacies of their physical relationship, even when not intended to produce offspring, are a form of liberty protected by the Due Process Clause.... Moreover, this protection extends to intimate choices by unmarried as well as married persons." In support of this proposition, Justice Stevens cited *Griswold, Eisenstadt* and *Carey*. As discussed above, these are due process cases that recognize protected liberty interests. Furthermore, in the very next passage of Justice Stevens' dissent, he described these cases as establishing rights that are "fundamental" and placed the right of adults to engage in private intimate conduct in the same category. It is impossible to read *Lawrence* as declining to recognize a protected liberty interest without ignoring the Court's statement that Justice Stevens' *Bowers* dissent was controlling.

Finally, if *Lawrence* had applied traditional rational basis review (the appropriate standard if no protected liberty interest was at stake), the convictions under the Texas statute would have been sustained. The governmental interest in prohibiting immoral conduct was the only state interest that Texas offered to justify the statute. It is well established that a "legislature [can] legitimately act ... to protect the societal interest in order and morality." *Barnes v. Glen Theatre, Inc.,* 501 U.S. 560, 569 (1991) (quoting *Paris Adult Theatre I v. Slaton,* 413 U.S. 49, 61 (1973)). Thus, *Lawrence's* holding can only be squared with the Supreme Court's acknowledgment of morality as a rational basis by concluding that a protected liberty interest was at stake, and therefore a rational basis for the law was not sufficient.

Taking into account the precedent relied on by *Lawrence,* the tenor of its language, its special reliance on Justice Stevens' *Bowers* dissent, and its rejection of morality as an adequate basis for the law in question, we are convinced that *Lawrence* recognized that adults maintain a protected liberty interest to engage in certain "consensual sexual intimacy in the home." The district court, relying on cases from other circuits, read *Lawrence* as applying rational basis review. We, however, do not find any of the four primary reasons supporting this view persuasive.

First, the argument has been made that *Lawrence* nowhere explicitly stated that the right at issue was "fundamental" and therefore the opinion cannot be read as recognizing a fundamental right under the due process clause. While it is true that *Lawrence* nowhere used the word "fundamental" to describe the interest at stake, there are several Supreme Court cases that have recognized protected liberty interests without using this word. For example, in *Washington v. Harper,* 494 U.S. 210, 223 (1990), the Supreme Court held that a state prisoner "retains a significant liberty interest" under the due process clause to avoid the unwanted administration of certain drugs. And in *Parham v. J.R.,* 442 U.S. 584, 600 (1979), the Court described a child's "substantial liberty interest" in not being confined unnecessarily for medical treatment. *See also Casey,* 505 U.S. at 851 (describing the interest as a "protected liberty"); *Cruzan v. Director of Mo. Dept. of Health,* 497 U.S. 261, 278 (1990) (describing the interest as a "constitutionally protected liberty interest"); *Youngberg v. Romeo,* 457 U.S. 307, 315 (1982) (describing the interests as "liberty interests"). It is thus clear that the Supreme Court does not always use the word "fundamental" when it wishes to identify an interest protected by substantive due process.

Second, it has been maintained that *Lawrence* could not have identified a protected liberty interest because the Supreme Court did not engage in a thorough analysis of the "Nation's history and tradition" as required under *Glucksberg.* This argument is based on the mistaken premise that the only history relevant to the substantive due process inquiry is a history demonstrating affirmative government action to protect the right in question. But *Glucksberg* does not establish such a requirement. *Lawrence* engaged in a thorough historical analysis identifying the lack of a long history of government action to punish the private consensual, intimate conduct of homosexuals. This sort of historical analysis is not inconsistent with Supreme Court precedent in this area. Indeed, if affirmative government action protecting a right were required to trigger substantive due process protection, at least some of the due process cases recognizing a liberty interest would have come out differently because there was no established history of government protection for the right to have an abortion or to use contraception. *See Roe,* 410 U.S. at 132–41 (reviewing history of abortion law to show that laws restricting abortion are of recent vintage but not showing any history of affirmative government action to protect the right to an abortion).

Moreover, to the extent that *Lawrence* did not adhere to the *Glucksberg* approach of locating the right to private, consensual adult intimacy in the Nation's history and tradition, it explicitly disavowed the exclusivity of this approach. *See Lawrence,* 539 U.S. at 572 ("history and tradition are the starting but not in all cases the ending point of the substantive due process inquiry."). In this regard, the *Lawrence* Court stated:

> [W]e think that our laws and traditions in the past half century are of most relevance here. These references show an emerging awareness that liberty gives substantial protection to adult persons in deciding how to conduct their private lives in matters pertaining to sex.

Thus, *Lawrence* recognized that, in at least some circumstances, the consideration of recent trends and practices is relevant to defining the scope of protected liberty.

Third, it has been suggested that the *Lawrence* majority's refusal to respond to Justice Scalia's *Lawrence* dissent, in which he argued that the majority had not recognized a protected liberty interest, indicates that the majority agreed with the dissent's analysis. The district court relied heavily on this point, observing that "it might be expected that if [Justice Scalia's dissent] wrongly characterized a principal holding of the case, the majority would have answered and corrected it."

This is a possible explanation for the majority's silence, but it is not the only explanation. It is equally possible that the *Lawrence* majority believed that the text of its opinion stood for itself and that there was little to be gained by debating Justice Scalia on this point. Given the equally possible, but conflicting, inferences that can be drawn from the majority's lack of response to Justice Scalia's dissent, we think that there is little to be gleaned about *Lawrence*'s meaning from it.

Finally, it has been claimed that *Lawrence*'s conclusion that "[t]he Texas statute furthers *no legitimate state interest* which can justify its intrusion into the personal and private life of the individual" indicates that *Lawrence* did not recognize a protected liberty interest. This argument is premised on the notion that the words "legitimate state interest" indicate the application of rational basis review, which is not the proper standard where a protected liberty interest is implicated. As the district court stated, "[t]he use of the appropriate adjective is telltale to constitutional lawyers. If the *Lawrence* court had been evaluating the constitutionality of the Texas statute under the more exacting standard where fundamental interests are at stake, it would instead have asked whether the state interest was compelling, rather than whether it was legitimate."

We take a different view. A law survives rational basis review so long as the law is rationally related to a legitimate governmental interest. Rational basis review does *not* permit consideration of the strength of the individual's interest or the extent of the intrusion on that interest caused by the law; the focus is entirely on the rationality of the state's reason for enacting the law. Thus, the argument that *Lawrence* did not recognize a protected liberty interest because it used the words "legitimate state interest" divorces these word from context—a context which shows that *Lawrence* did not employ traditional rational basis review since the *Lawrence* Court's analysis focused on the individual's liberty interest. This view is supported by Supreme Court cases that have recognized protected liberty interests in the face of "legitimate state interests." *Casey,* 505 U.S. at 853 (recognizing that even though protected liberty interest was at stake, "the separate States could act in some degree to further their own legitimate interests in protecting prenatal life"); *Addington v. Texas,* 441 U.S. 418, 425–26 (1979) (balancing the "individual's interest in not being involuntarily confined indefinitely" against the state's "legitimate interest under its *parens patriae* powers in providing care to its citizens who are unable because of emotional disorders to care for themselves").

To say, as we do, that *Lawrence* recognized a protected liberty interest for adults to engage in consensual sexual intimacy in the home does not mean that the Court applied strict scrutiny to invalidate the convictions. Several pre-*Lawrence* cases that have recognized protected liberty interests did not mandate that the challenged law be "narrowly tailored to serve a compelling state interest"—the strict scrutiny standard. For example, in *Sell v. United States,* 539 U.S. 166, 179 (2003), the Court recognized a "constitutionally protected liberty interest [for a criminal defendant] in avoiding the unwanted administration of antipsychotic drugs" and then applied a standard of review less demanding than strict scrutiny by asking whether administering the drugs was "necessary significantly to further important governmental trial-related interests." And similarly, in *Casey,* the Supreme Court reaffirmed a woman's fundamental right to choose to have an abortion but applied the "undue burden" test which balanced the state's legitimate interest in potential human life against the extent of the imposition on the woman's liberty interest.

Lawrence is, in our view, another in this line of Supreme Court authority that identifies a protected liberty interest and then applies a standard of review that lies between strict scrutiny and rational basis. In invalidating the convictions, the *Lawrence* Court determined that there was no legitimate state interest that was adequate to "justify" the intrusion on liberty worked by the law. In other words, *Lawrence* balanced the strength of the state's asserted interest in prohibiting immoral conduct against the degree of intrusion into the petitioners' private sexual life caused by the statute in order to determine whether the law was unconstitutionally applied.

Having defined the nature of the constitutional review mandated by *Lawrence,* we now consider whether the plaintiffs' facial due process challenge to the Act can survive a motion to dismiss.

"A facial challenge to a legislative Act is, of course, the most difficult challenge to mount successfully, since the challenger must establish that no set of circumstances exists under which the Act would be valid. The fact that [an Act] might operate unconstitutionally under some conceivable set of circumstances is insufficient to render it wholly invalid...." *United States v. Salerno*, 481 U.S. 739, 745 (1987). The Supreme Court has recently emphasized the limits on facial challenges in the substantive due process context. *See Gonzales v. Carhart*, 550 U.S. 124, (2007).

The plaintiffs' facial challenge fails. *Lawrence* did not identify a protected liberty interest in all forms and manner of sexual intimacy. *Lawrence* recognized only a narrowly defined liberty interest in adult consensual sexual intimacy in the confines of one's home and one's own private life. The Court made it abundantly clear that there are many types of sexual activity that are beyond the reach of that opinion. Here, the Act includes such other types of sexual activity. The Act provides for the separation of a service person who engages in a public homosexual act or who coerces another person to engage in a homosexual act. Both of these forms of conduct are expressly excluded from the liberty interest recognized by *Lawrence*.

The plaintiffs' as-applied challenge, on the other hand, presents a more difficult question. The plaintiffs point out that the Act could apply to some conduct that falls within the zone of protected liberty identified by *Lawrence*. The Act, for example, could cover homosexual conduct occurring off base between two consenting adults in the privacy of their home.

Before addressing the significance of this observation, we pause to recognize the unique context in which the liberty interest at stake in this case arises. We are reviewing an exercise of Congressional judgment in the area of military affairs. The deferential approach courts take when doing so is well-established.

The Supreme Court has articulated essentially two reasons for this deference. The first involves institutional competence. The Court has remarked:

> It is difficult to conceive of an area of governmental activity in which courts have less competence. The complex, subtle, and professional decisions as to the composition, training, equipping and control of a military force are essentially professional military judgments, subject always to civilian control of the Legislative and Executive Branches.

Gilligan v. Morgan, 413 U.S. 1, 10 (1973); *see also N.D. v. United States*, 495 U.S. 423, 443 (1990) (noting that where confronted with questions relating to military operations the Court "properly defer[s] to the judgment of those who must lead our Armed Forces in battle").

The second relates to the constitutional power of Congress to "raise and support armies and to make all laws necessary and proper to that end." *United States v. O'Brien*, 391 U.S. 367, 377 (1968). The Court has described this power as "broad and sweeping," *id.*, and has further noted Congress' accompanying responsibility for "the delicate task of balancing the rights of servicemen against the needs of the military." *Solorio v. United States*, 483 U.S. 435, 447 (1987).

It is unquestionable that judicial deference to congressional decision-making in the area of military affairs heavily influences the analysis and resolution of constitutional challenges that arise in this context. The Court's examination of the equal protection challenge leveled in *Rostker* provides an example. That case concerned a statute that required only males to register for selective service. The lower court had invalidated the statute as unlawful gender discrimination. In reversing, the Court focused its analysis entirely on the legislative record that led to Congress' action. The Court discussed, in detail, the process Congress employed in considering the issue, its consultation with all interested parties, its serious consideration of the issues, including the constitutional implications, and its clear articulation of the basis for its decision. The Court then declared the district court's analysis striking down the law "quite wrong" because the district court undertook "an independent evaluation of evidence rather than adopting an appropriately deferential examination of Congress' evaluation of the evidence."

The Court's treatment of First Amendment and Due Process challenges brought in this area similarly manifests this deference to congressional judgment. In *Parker v. Levy,* 417 U.S. 733 (1974), a case involving vagueness and overbreadth challenges to provisions of the Uniform Code of Military Justice, the Court stated that "Congress is permitted to legislate both with greater breadth and with greater flexibility when the statute governs military society." In *Weiss,* the Court reemphasized that when dealing with due process challenges "the tests and limitations [associated with those challenges] may differ because of the military context."[9]

Fully apprised of the constraints on our constitutional inquiry when considering constitutional challenges in the military context, we now examine both the process by which Congress passed the Act and the rationale Congress advanced for it.

Congress' process for developing the Act was involved and it included sustained consideration of the Act's necessity and its impact on constitutional rights. After President Clinton was inaugurated, he directed the Secretary of Defense to submit a draft Executive Order "ending discrimination on the basis of sexual orientation in determining who may serve in the Armed Services." The President instructed the Secretary to consult with the military's professional leadership and others concerned with the issue. While this review was in progress, an interim policy was imposed that ended the practice of asking new recruits to confirm that they were heterosexual.

Congress quickly intervened. A few weeks after President Clinton was sworn in, Congress passed a provision calling for a review of the military's approach to homosexuals serving in the military by the Secretary of Defense and the Senate Armed Services Committee.

Subsequently, the Department and congressional committees engaged in an exhaustive policy review. The Senate and House Armed Services Committees conducted fourteen days of hearings, heard more than fifty witnesses, and traveled to military facilities to investigate the issue. The Committees heard from witnesses with a wide range of views and various backgrounds, including the Secretary of Defense, the Chairman of the Joint Chiefs of Staff, military and legal experts, enlisted personnel, officers, and public policy activists.

While this congressional review was ongoing, the Department conducted its own review. The Department convened a military working group comprised of senior officers, commissioned a RAND Corporation study, studied the history of the military's response to social change, and consulted legal experts.

In July 1993, President Clinton announced a new policy for the service of homosexuals in the military. Under the policy, applicants for military service would not be asked

---

9. Other examples of the deferential approach the Court has taken when analyzing constitutional challenges in the military context include: *Goldman v. Weinberger,* 475 U.S. 503, 508 (1986) (free exercise of religion); *Chappell v. Wallace,* 462 U.S. 296, 300–05 (1983) (racial discrimination); *Brown v. Glines,* 444 U.S. 348, 357–60 (1980) (free expression); *Middendorf v. Henry,* 425 U.S. 25, 43 (1976) (right to counsel in summary court-martial proceeding).

their sexual orientation but, once inducted into service, a member could be separated for homosexual conduct.

A few weeks after the President's announcement, the House and Senate Armed Services Committees proposed to codify the military's policy. The Senate Report, in support of this effort, stated that the Committee was acting only after it had considered "a wide range of experiences, including those of current and former servicemembers who have publicly identified themselves as gay or lesbian" and after having "carefully considered all points of view." Similarly, the House Committee reported that its recommendation was based on "an extensive hearing record as well as full consideration of the extended public debate on this issue . . ." The Senate Report also focused explicitly on the effect that the Act could have on constitutional rights of homosexuals, concluding that "if the Supreme Court should reverse its ruling in *Bowers* and hold that private consensual homosexual acts between adults may not be prosecuted in civilian society, this would not alter the committee's judgment as to the effect of homosexual conduct in the armed forces."

Prior to the enactment of the Act, the full House and Senate debated the measure and considered floor amendments. In particular, each house rejected amendments that would have permitted the military to develop whatever policy it deemed appropriate and would have allowed the Department to resume asking applicants to state their sexual orientation. The Act became law in November 1993, and ... the Act expressly identified its purpose as preserving "high standards of morale, good order and discipline, and unit cohesion" in the military. 10 U.S.C. §654(a)(15).

The circumstances surrounding the Act's passage lead to the firm conclusion that Congress and the Executive studied the issues intensely and from many angles, including by considering the constitutional rights of gay and lesbian service members. Congress ultimately concluded that the voluminous evidentiary record supported adopting a policy of separating certain homosexuals from military service to preserve the "high morale, good order and discipline, and unit cohesion" of the troops.

Acknowledging the government interest identified in this case, one that our deferential posture requires us to take at face value, as-applied challenges to the Act must fail as well.

Here, as in *Rostker,* there is a detailed legislative record concerning Congress' reasons for passing the Act. This record makes plain that Congress concluded, after considered deliberation, that the Act was necessary to preserve the military's effectiveness as a fighting force, and thus, to ensure national security. This is an exceedingly weighty interest and one that unquestionably surpasses the government interest that was at stake in *Lawrence. See Lawrence,* 539 U.S. at 585 (O'Connor, J., concurring).

Every as-applied challenge brought by a member of the armed forces against the Act, at its core, implicates this interest. Every member of the armed forces has one fact in common—at a moment's notice he or she may be deployed to a combat area. The conditions of service in such an area bring into play the animating concerns behind the Act, namely, maintaining the morale and unit cohesion that the military deems essential to an effective fighting force. Accordingly, we have no choice but to dismiss the plaintiffs' as-applied challenge.

To be sure, deference to Congressional judgment in this area does not mean abdication. But where Congress has articulated a substantial government interest for a law, and where the challenges in question implicate that interest, judicial intrusion is simply not warranted.

B. Equal Protection

In addition to their due process claim, the plaintiffs assert that the Act is unconstitutional under equal protection principles. Unlike the due process claim, which is premised on the constitutional protection afforded all citizens to engage in certain sexual conduct, the equal protection claim is based on the Act's differential treatment of homosexual military members versus heterosexual military members. The district court rejected this claim under rational basis review.

Under equal protection jurisprudence, a governmental classification aimed at a "suspect class" is subject to heightened judicial scrutiny. Classifications that target non-suspect classes are subject only to rational basis review. The plaintiffs contend that the district court erred by applying rational basis review because the Supreme Court's decisions in *Romer v. Evans*, 517 U.S. 620 (1996), and *Lawrence* mandate a more demanding standard.

In *Romer*, the Supreme Court invalidated, on equal protection grounds, a Colorado constitutional amendment which prohibited the enactment of any measure designed to protect individuals due to their sexual orientation. The Court analyzed the constitutionality of the amendment through the prism of rational basis, asking whether the classification bore "a rational relation to some legitimate end." Applying this standard, the Court concluded that the amendment was unconstitutional because the only possible justification for the amendment was "animosity toward the class of persons affected," which does not constitute even "a legitimate governmental interest."

Romer, by its own terms, applied rational basis review.... *Romer* nowhere suggested that the Court recognized a new suspect class. Absent additional guidance from the Supreme Court, we join our sister circuits in declining to read *Romer* as recognizing homosexuals as a suspect class for equal protection purposes.

Lawrence does not alter this conclusion. As discussed earlier, *Lawrence* was a substantive due process decision that recognized a right in all adults, regardless of sexual orientation, to engage in certain intimate conduct. Indeed, the *Lawrence* Court explicitly declined to base its ruling on equal protection principles, even though that issue was presented. Thus, there is no basis for arguing that *Lawrence* changed the standard of review applicable to a legislative classification based on sexual orientation.

As neither *Romer* nor *Lawrence* mandate heightened scrutiny of the Act because of its classification of homosexuals, the district court was correct to analyze the plaintiffs' equal protection claim under the rational basis standard. As stated earlier, an enactment survives this level of scrutiny so long as the "classification drawn by the statute is rationally related to a legitimate state interest." *City of Cleburne, Tex. v. Cleburne Living Ctr.*, 473 U.S. 432, 440 (1985).

The plaintiffs maintain that, even under this standard, their claim survives because they will be able to demonstrate that the Act was based on irrational animus and therefore is invalid under *Romer*. We disagree. Congress has put forward a non-animus based explanation for its decision to pass the Act. Given the substantial deference owed Congress' assessment of the need for the legislation, the Act survives rational basis review.

In sum, the district court was correct to reject the plaintiffs' equal protection claim because homosexuals are not a suspect class and the legitimate interests Congress put forward are rationally served by the Act....

[The opinion of Judge Saris, concurring in part and dissenting in part, is omitted.]

Notes and Questions

1. Both *Witt* and *Cook* involve the military context. As the opinions take care to note, Supreme Court precedent requires a greater degree of judicial deference when laws re-

lated to the armed forces are challenged on equal protection or due process grounds. Setting their impact to one side so far as the military setting is concerned, to what extent do these decisions provide support for challenging laws prohibiting same-sex couples from marrying or adopting children?

2. Is the panel in *Witt* as deferential to the military as the Supreme Court's precedents typically require? Dissenting from the denial to rehear the case *en banc*, Judge Kleinfeld wrote as follows:

> Quite a few constitutional rights do not apply to the military as they do in civilian life. For example, though mandatory conscription is not currently in force, men but not women must register for the draft, and an equal protection challenge may be ruled out by *Rostker v. Goldberg*. When men are drafted, they are not free to decline the employment on Thirteenth Amendment grounds, as civilians are. And soldiers may be vigorously prosecuted for desertion, though civilians are generally free to leave an employment. If a new Secretary in, say, the Department of Education issued an order that all employees must stand and salute when a higher ranking employee enters the room, no doubt a First Amendment challenge would succeed, perhaps with an *a fortiori* reference to the proposition that even a child need not salute the flag in school during wartime, yet it is hard to imagine a soldier defeating an insubordination charge on the ground that he had a First Amendment right to express his true feeling of disrespect and not make a false show of respect for a superior officer who entered the room.
>
> This case should be treated as an *a fortiori* application of the Supreme Court's holding in *Goldman v. Weinberger*. An Orthodox Jewish rabbi serving as a clinical psychologist in a base hospital was recommended for non-retention because he wore a yarmulke (5 1/2" circle of dark cloth) on his head on duty. The right to free exercise of religion is certainly as protected by the Constitution as whatever right to sexual liberty *Lawrence* may create, and the military headgear policy was merely a regulation, not a statute, yet the Court rejected Captain Goldman's Free Exercise challenge to application of the rule. The Court relied on its well established general principle that "'the military is, by necessity, a specialized society separate from civilian society,'" and "'must insist on a respect for duty and a discipline without counterpart in civilian life.'" The Court went so far as to say that "[t]he essence of military service 'is the subordination of the desires and interests of the individual to the needs of the service,'" while defining the service's "needs" to embrace pretty much whatever the military thought desirable to promote "discipline" and "uniformity."
>
> Congress picked up the language from *Goldman* in its findings in the statute before us, that "the armed forces ... exist as a specialized society ... characterized by ... numerous restrictions on personal behavior, that would not be acceptable in civilian society." It is more difficult to imagine threats to order and discipline from the wearing of a yarmulke by a clinical psychologist in an on-shore base hospital, than from the emotions stirred up by sexual conduct, and free exercise of religion is among the most fundamental constitutional rights, yet religion gives way to the military interest in discipline and uniformity. If a man does not have a constitutional right to wear an unobtrusive 5" circle of dark cloth on his head as his religion requires, because of the threat to discipline and uniformity, it is hard to see how an individual could nevertheless be entitled to practice or declare a sexual orientation that the military, Congress, and the President have concluded endangers military effectiveness.

Witt v. Dep't of the Air Force, 548 F.3d 1264, 1278–79 (9th Cir. 2008) (en banc) (Kleinfeld, J., dissenting).

3. Recall from the earlier two sections the question whether the Supreme Court's privacy line of cases call for greater scrutiny only where *criminal* sanctions are involved. In his dissent from the Ninth Circuit's refusal to rehear the *Witt* case *en banc*, Judge O'Scannlain focused on this distinction:

> All the statutes *Lawrence* cites in explaining its actual holding are criminal statutes. Indeed, almost all of the substantive due process cases the Court cites at the start of its analysis for the most general propositions in the opinion also dealt with criminal statutes. *See id.* at 564–67 (summarizing the reasoning of *Griswold v. Connecticut*, 381 U.S. 479 (1965) (invalidating statute criminalizing the use of contraceptives); *Eisenstadt v. Baird*, 405 U.S. 438 (1972) (invalidating statute criminalizing the distribution of contraceptives to unmarried persons); and *Carey v. Population Services International*, 431 U.S. 678 (1977) (invalidating statute criminalizing the sale or distribution of contraceptives to persons younger than sixteen years old)).
>
> Furthermore, in explaining why the Texas statute offended the Constitution, the Court focused like a laser on its *criminal* consequences. *See, e.g., id.* at 571 ("The issue is whether the majority may use the power of the State to enforce[moral] views on the whole society through operation of the *criminal* law" (emphasis added)); *id.* at 575 ("When homosexual conduct is made *criminal* by the law of the State, that declaration in and of itself is an invitation to subject homosexual persons to discrimination...." (emphasis added)); *id.* ("The stigma this *criminal statute* imposes ... is not trivial. The offense to be sure, is but a Class C misdemeanor.... [but] *it remains a criminal offense* with all that imports for the dignity of the persons charged. The petitioners will bear on their record the history of their *criminal convictions*" (emphases added)); *id.* ("[I]f *Texas convicted an adult* for private, consensual homosexual conduct under the statute here in question the *convicted* person would come within the registration laws of at least four States...." (emphases added)); *id.* at 576 (noting "the *consequential nature of the punishment* and the state-sponsored condemnation *attendant to the criminal prohibition*.... [and that] *the Texas criminal conviction* carries with it the other *collateral consequences always following a conviction*" (emphases added)). These sentences form much of the reasoning preceding the holding that the Court summarized at the end of its opinion, namely that "[t]he State cannot demean [homosexuals'] existence or control their destiny by making their private sexual conduct *a crime.*" *Id.* at 578 (emphasis added).

Witt v. Dep't of the Air Force, 548 F.3d 1264, 1270 (9th Cir. 2008) (en banc) (O'Scannlain, J., dissenting). Does the *Witt* court's rejection of the criminal-civil distinction suggest that it would likewise reject efforts to invoke that distinction in a case challenging a prohibition on same-sex marriage or adoption by gays and lesbians?

4. To what extent might decisions addressing the constitutionality of Don't Ask, Don't Tell provide support for challenging the military's current ban on military service by transgendered persons? Is there an argument for greater scrutiny under the Equal Protection Clause by relying on cases such as *Glenn v. Brumby*, 663 F.3d 1312 (11th Cir. 2011), which—as you saw in Chapter 4—characterized discrimination against transgendered persons as a form of gender discrimination subject to intermediate scrutiny under the Equal Protection Clause?

As indicated in the introduction to this section, the disqualification on military service by transgendered persons is treated as a *medical* disqualification: those who have not undergone sex reassignment surgery will be deemed ineligible to serve due to "[c]urrent or history of psychosexual conditions, including but not limited to transsexualism," while those who have undergone sex reassignment surgery will be deemed ineligible to serve due to a "[h]istory of major abnormalities or defects of the genitalia such as change of sex." *See* Department of Defense Instruction 6130.3: Medical Standards for Appointment, Enlistment, or Induction in the Military Services, Enclosure 4, ¶¶ 14(f), 15(r), 29(r) (Sept. 13, 2011).

To date, court challenges to the military's ban are few and far between, and those that do exist have suggested extreme deference to the military's position, focusing on the *medical* nature of the disqualification:

> Several cases have held that a service secretary's determination of fitness for duty of a servicemember is beyond the competence of the judiciary to review and, thus, nonjusticiable....

> Thus, the medical qualifications for military service are usually considered a matter within the discretion of the military, and courts will not substitute their judgment for the military regarding whether an individual is qualified to serve. Thus, although regulations may be challenged as facially unconstitutional and servicemembers may challenge a decision as procedurally defective (*i.e.*, the military did not follow its own regulations), a challenge to the medical qualifications for active duty service is not justiciable.

DeGroat v. Townsend, 495 F. Supp. 2d 845, 851 n.7 (S.D. Ohio 2007).

But should the government be able to avoid serious scrutiny of its policies by characterizing something as a "medical" disqualification? After all, for many decades, the psychiatric profession—and in turn the military—treated homosexuality as a medical disorder as well.

5. Note that the military's Don't Ask, Don't Tell policy targets *speech* regarding one's sexual orientation and is thus arguably subject to challenge on First Amendment grounds as well. The portion of *Cook v. Gates* in which the court considers a challenge on this ground is excerpted in the following chapter of the book, which explores the relevance of the First Amendment in cases involving the rights of sexual minorities.

6. Outside the context of military employment—where special deference is not required—lower courts have held that firing, refusing to hire, or harassing a public employee simply because of their sexual orientation violates the Equal Protection Clause even under rational basis review:

> Several Courts have recently considered the question of Equal Protection and sexual orientation and applied the "rational basis test" utilized in *Romer*. These cases, which typically analyzed the constitutionality of the United States Military's "Don't Ask, Don't Tell" policy, examined whether the forced separation from service of individuals who engage in a homosexual act or who state that they are homosexual violates the Equal Protection Clause. In concluding that the policy does not violate the Equal Protection Clause, these Courts have relied on the uniqueness of the military setting and the deference accorded to military decisions. Nevertheless, as in *Romer*, these Courts recognized that government action in a civil rather than a military setting cannot survive a rational basis review when it is motivated by irrational fear and prejudice towards homosexuals.

> Under the above cases, and viewing the proof in a light most favorable to Quinn, the plaintiff has introduced more than sufficient evidence to support a claim for

an Equal Protection violation based on a workplace environment that transcended hostile, coarse and boorish behavior, and which was motivated by an invidious, irrational fear and prejudice towards homosexuals.... Like the enactment at issue in *Romer*, conduct by police department officers, supervisors and policy makers contributing to, failing to address, and outright condoning harassment of homosexuals amounts to impermissible "status-based [conduct and policy] divorced from any factual context from which we could discern a relationship to legitimate state interests." Such harassment by Nassau County Police Department personnel cannot survive a rational basis review when it is motivated by irrational fear and prejudice towards homosexuals. The "inevitable inference" from the Quinn's mistreatment is that it was "born of animosity toward the class of persons affected," namely, homosexuals.

Quinn v. Nassau Cnty. Police Dep't, 53 F. Supp. 2d 347, 357–58 (E.D.N.Y. 1999). *See also Miguel v. Guess*, 51 P.3d 89, 97 (Wash. Ct. App. 2002) (holding "that a state actor violates a homosexual employee's right of equal protection when it treats that person differently than it treats heterosexual employees, based solely upon the employee's sexual orientation.").

Chapter 6

The First Amendment

A. Background

The First Amendment to the U.S. Constitution provides:

> Congress shall make no law respecting an establishment of religion, or prohibiting the free exercise thereof; or abridging the freedom of speech, or of the press; or the right of the people peaceably to assemble, and to petition the Government for a redress of grievances.

As with so many other provisions of the U.S. Constitution, the U.S. Supreme Court has not interpreted the First Amendment literally. Thus, although in terms the First Amendment applies only to "Congress," the Court has held it to be applicable to restrictions on speech imposed by the other branches of the federal government, and has held it applicable to the states by "incorporating" it via the Due Process Clause of the Fourteenth Amendment. And although one might well construe the phrase "shall make *no law*" to state an absolute command, the U.S. Supreme Court has developed a series of tests—including balancing tests—for assessing governmental action that infringes upon the rights protected by the First Amendment.

Often, the Court's decisions—particularly the more recent ones—employ a categorical approach whereby speech is presumptively protected by the First Amendment unless it falls into a category of historically exempted expression, such as obscenity, defamation, true threats, and the like.

In addition, the Court's decisions will scrutinize restrictions on speech differently depending on the location or context in which the speech is made, employing different tests to evaluate the strength of the government interest underlying the law and the fit between that end and the means employed to achieve it. In some instances, the Court will use tests like the familiar "strict scrutiny" test employed for equal protection and due process claims, such as when it evaluates restrictions on speech occurring in a traditional public forum, like public streets and parks. Yet more frequently, the Court will employ location or context-specific balancing or factor-based tests that are typically referred to not by general level of scrutiny but rather the case in which the particular test was established, such as *Pickering* balancing for speech by government employees or the *Tinker* "substantial disruption" test for speech occurring in a public schools setting.

Moreover, other First Amendment doctrines will sometimes "trump" a specific First Amendment principle. For example, as a general rule, restrictions on speech that are content-based or viewpoint-based (i.e., those that distinguish favored speech from disfavored speech based on the topic discussed or viewpoint expressed) are subject to strict scrutiny. Accordingly, even if speech falls within a category that the Court has held can normally be restricted by the government—such as "true threats"—if the restriction at issue draws distinctions depending upon the viewpoint expressed, it will be subject to the strict level of scrutiny associated with viewpoint discrimination.

In the context of GLBT rights, First Amendment claims differ in an important way from equal protection and due process claims. The latter, with few exceptions, are nearly always invoked by sexual minorities in attacking governmental discrimination. In contrast, while the First Amendment is sometimes invoked by sexual minorities, it is at least as often invoked by opponents of gay and transgendered rights as a means of invalidating antidiscrimination laws and other laws enacted to protect the rights of sexual minorities.

The First Amendment is a complex area of constitutional law, and many books and courses are devoted entirely to studying the various rights it contains in all of the contexts in which they arise. Although cases regarding GLBT rights can be found in which all of the First Amendment freedoms—speech, assembly, press, petition for the redress of grievances, and religion—are involved, the lion's share of the case law involves freedom of speech.

Accordingly, the focus of this chapter is on freedom of speech, examined in six different contexts. Section B examines the constitutionality of laws punishing "hate crimes" or "hate speech" targeting sexual minorities. Section C examines the freedom of individuals to associate with one another to engage in expressive conduct. Section D examines laws restricting the freedom of government employees to engage in speech or expressive conduct related to sexual orientation or gender identity. Section E examines laws restricting the freedom of students to engage in similar speech or expressive conduct. Section F examines the freedom to speak anonymously, considered in the context of political campaigns involving rights for sexual minorities. Finally, Section G revisits two types of laws with speech elements that were explored in earlier chapters—the military's Don't Ask, Don't Tell policy and laws banning the solicitation of sodomy—and examines the First Amendment as an alternative vehicle for challenging the constitutionality of such laws.

B. Hate Crimes and Hate Speech

In recent years, there has been much discussion and focus on hate speech and hate crimes directed at sexual minorities. Yet to what extent can government punish speech, even hateful speech, directed at sexual minorities? Moreover, to the extent that one's speech is used as evidence of one's hateful intent when inflicting harm on sexual minorities, to what extent does that evidentiary use of speech implicate First Amendment concerns?

Problem 6-A: I Hate You!

Every year, a one-day gay pride festival takes place in a local park in the City of New Condon.

Lisa, who holds very strong anti-gay views, visits the park on the day of the gay pride festival, and is disgusted by what she sees as flagrant exhibits of homosexuality. As she walks through the park, she approaches any gay couples who are holding hands and yells epithets at them such as, "You will burn in hell for your sins!" and "God will afflict you with AIDS as punishment for your homosexual ways!"

Lisa is arrested and charged with violating the state's felony harassment statute, which makes it a crime to engage in intentional conduct—including spoken statements—that would cause a reasonable person under the circumstances to feel oppressed or persecuted.

Lisa's attorney defends on the ground that the harassment statute, if construed to encompass Lisa's conduct, violates her First Amendment rights.

How should the court rule on Lisa's constitutional claim?

Problem 6-B: Evidence That I Hate You!

The State of New Condon enacts a hate crimes statute that provides for enhanced criminal penalties for acts of violence, including murder, if the victim was selected because of their race, religion, national origin, sex, or sexual orientation.

David is indicted on charges of violating the hate crimes statute in connection with a physical assault on John. At trial, the prosecution seeks to offer into evidence: (a) testimony by John that just before attacking him, David yelled, "I'm going to kill you, you goddamn faggot!"; and (b) evidence that, several months before the crime at issue, David posted entries on a blog stating that "homosexuality is against God's will and it is the responsibility of all people of faith to eradicate and punish homosexuality whenever and wherever they see it."

David objects to the admission of the evidence, contending that its admission against him violates his First Amendment rights.

How should the court rule on David's constitutional claim?

Virginia v. Black
538 U.S. 343 (2003)

Justice O'CONNOR announced the judgment of the Court and delivered the opinion of the Court with respect to Parts I, II, and III, and an opinion with respect to Parts IV and V, in which THE CHIEF JUSTICE, Justice STEVENS, and Justice BREYER join.

....

I

Respondents Barry Black, Richard Elliott, and Jonathan O'Mara were convicted separately of violating Virginia's cross-burning statute, § 18.2-423. That statute provides:

"It shall be unlawful for any person or persons, with the intent of intimidating any person or group of persons, to burn, or cause to be burned, a cross on the property of another, a highway or other public place. Any person who shall violate any provision of this section shall be guilty of a Class 6 felony.

"Any such burning of a cross shall be prima facie evidence of an intent to intimidate a person or group of persons."

On August 22, 1998, Barry Black led a Ku Klux Klan rally in Carroll County, Virginia. Twenty-five to thirty people attended this gathering, which occurred on private property with the permission of the owner, who was in attendance. The property was located on an open field just off Brushy Fork Road (State Highway 690) in Cana, Virginia.

When the sheriff of Carroll County learned that a Klan rally was occurring in his county, he went to observe it from the side of the road....

At the conclusion of the rally, the crowd circled around a 25- to 30-foot cross. The cross was between 300 and 350 yards away from the road. According to the sheriff, the cross "then all of a sudden ... went up in a flame." As the cross burned, the Klan played Amazing Grace over the loudspeakers....

On May 2, 1998, respondents Richard Elliott and Jonathan O'Mara, as well as a third individual, attempted to burn a cross on the yard of James Jubilee. Jubilee, an African-American, was Elliott's next-door neighbor in Virginia Beach, Virginia. Four months prior to the incident, Jubilee and his family had moved from California to Virginia Beach. Before the cross burning, Jubilee spoke to Elliott's mother to inquire about shots being fired from behind the Elliott home. Elliott's mother explained to Jubilee that her son shot firearms as a hobby, and that he used the backyard as a firing range.

On the night of May 2, respondents drove a truck onto Jubilee's property, planted a cross, and set it on fire. Their apparent motive was to "get back" at Jubilee for complaining about the shooting in the backyard. Respondents were not affiliated with the Klan....

II

....

The first Ku Klux Klan began in Pulaski, Tennessee, in the spring of 1866. Although the Ku Klux Klan started as a social club, it soon changed into something far different. The Klan fought Reconstruction and the corresponding drive to allow freed blacks to participate in the political process....

Often, the Klan used cross burnings as a tool of intimidation and a threat of impending violence....

Throughout the history of the Klan, cross burnings have also remained potent symbols of shared group identity and ideology. The burning cross became a symbol of the Klan itself and a central feature of Klan gatherings....

At Klan gatherings across the country, cross burning became the climax of the rally or the initiation. Posters advertising an upcoming Klan rally often featured a Klan member holding a cross....

To this day, regardless of whether the message is a political one or whether the message is also meant to intimidate, the burning of a cross is a "symbol of hate." And while cross burning sometimes carries no intimidating message, at other times the intimidating message is the *only* message conveyed. For example, when a cross burning is directed at a particular person not affiliated with the Klan, the burning cross often serves as a message of intimidation, designed to inspire in the victim a fear of bodily harm. Moreover, the history of violence associated with the Klan shows that the possibility of injury or death is not just hypothetical. The person who burns a cross directed at a particular person often is making a serious threat, meant to coerce the victim to comply with the Klan's wishes unless the victim is willing to risk the wrath of the Klan. Indeed, as the cases of respondents Elliott and O'Mara indicate, individuals without Klan affiliation who wish to threaten or menace another person sometimes use cross burning because of this association between a burning cross and violence.

In sum, while a burning cross does not inevitably convey a message of intimidation, often the cross burner intends that the recipients of the message fear for their lives. And when a cross burning is used to intimidate, few if any messages are more powerful.

III

A

The First Amendment, applicable to the States through the Fourteenth Amendment, provides that "Congress shall make no law ... abridging the freedom of speech." The hallmark of the protection of free speech is to allow "free trade in ideas"—even ideas that the overwhelming majority of people might find distasteful or discomforting.... The First Amendment affords protection to symbolic or expressive conduct as well as to actual speech.

The protections afforded by the First Amendment, however, are not absolute, and we have long recognized that the government may regulate certain categories of expression consistent with the Constitution. See, *e.g., Chaplinsky v. New Hampshire,* 315 U.S. 568, 571–572 (1942). The First Amendment permits "restrictions upon the content of speech in a few limited areas, which are 'of such slight social value as a step to truth that any benefit that may be derived from them is clearly outweighed by the social interest in order and morality.'" *R.A.V. v. City of St. Paul, supra,* at 382–383 (quoting *Chaplinsky v. New Hampshire, supra,* at 572).

Thus, for example, a State may punish those words "which by their very utterance inflict injury or tend to incite an immediate breach of the peace." *Chaplinsky v. New Hampshire, supra,* at 572. We have consequently held that fighting words—"those personally abusive epithets which, when addressed to the ordinary citizen, are, as a matter of common knowledge, inherently likely to provoke violent reaction"—are generally proscribable under the First Amendment. Furthermore, "the constitutional guarantees of free speech and free press do not permit a State to forbid or proscribe advocacy of the use of force or of law violation except where such advocacy is directed to inciting or producing imminent lawless action and is likely to incite or produce such action." *Brandenburg v. Ohio,* 395 U.S. 444, 447 (1969) *(per curiam).* And the First Amendment also permits a State to ban a "true threat." *Watts v. United States,* 394 U.S. 705, 708 (1969) *(per curiam).*

"True threats" encompass those statements where the speaker means to communicate a serious expression of an intent to commit an act of unlawful violence to a particular individual or group of individuals. See *Watts v. United States, supra,* at 708 ("political hyperbole" is not a true threat); *R.A.V. v. City of St. Paul,* 505 U.S., at 388. The speaker need not actually intend to carry out the threat. Rather, a prohibition on true threats "protect[s] individuals from the fear of violence" and "from the disruption that fear engenders," in addition to protecting people "from the possibility that the threatened violence will occur." *Ibid.* Intimidation in the constitutionally proscribable sense of the word is a type of true threat, where a speaker directs a threat to a person or group of persons with the intent of placing the victim in fear of bodily harm or death. Respondents do not contest that some cross burnings fit within this meaning of intimidating speech, and rightly so. As noted in Part II, *supra,* the history of cross burning in this country shows that cross burning is often intimidating, intended to create a pervasive fear in victims that they are a target of violence.

B

The Supreme Court of Virginia ruled that in light of *R.A.V. v. City of St. Paul, supra,* even if it is constitutional to ban cross burning in a content-neutral manner, the Virginia cross-burning statute is unconstitutional because it discriminates on the basis of content and viewpoint. It is true, as the Supreme Court of Virginia held, that the burning of a cross is symbolic expression. The reason why the Klan burns a cross at its rallies, or individuals place a burning cross on someone else's lawn, is that the burning cross represents the message that the speaker wishes to communicate. Individuals burn crosses as opposed to other means of communication because cross burning carries a message in an effective and dramatic manner.

The fact that cross burning is symbolic expression, however, does not resolve the constitutional question. The Supreme Court of Virginia relied upon *R.A.V. v. City of St. Paul, supra,* to conclude that once a statute discriminates on the basis of this type of content, the law is unconstitutional. We disagree.

In *R.A.V.,* we held that a local ordinance that banned certain symbolic conduct, including cross burning, when done with the knowledge that such conduct would "'arouse anger, alarm or resentment in others on the basis of race, color, creed, religion or gender'" was unconstitutional. We held that the ordinance did not pass constitutional muster because it discriminated on the basis of content by targeting only those individuals who "provoke violence" on a basis specified in the law. The ordinance did not cover "[t]hose who wish to use 'fighting words' in connection with other ideas—to express hostility, for example, on the basis of political affiliation, union membership, or homosexuality." This content-based discrimination was unconstitutional because it allowed the city "to impose special prohibitions on those speakers who express views on disfavored subjects."

We did not hold in *R.A.V.* that the First Amendment prohibits *all* forms of content-based discrimination within a proscribable area of speech. Rather, we specifically stated that some types of content discrimination did not violate the First Amendment:

> "When the basis for the content discrimination consists entirely of the very reason the entire class of speech at issue is proscribable, no significant danger of idea or viewpoint discrimination exists. Such a reason, having been adjudged neutral enough to support exclusion of the entire class of speech from First Amendment protection, is also neutral enough to form the basis of distinction within the class."

Indeed, we noted that it would be constitutional to ban only a particular type of threat: "[T]he Federal Government can criminalize only those threats of violence that are directed against the President ... since the reasons why threats of violence are outside the First Amendment ... have special force when applied to the person of the President." And a State may "choose to prohibit only that obscenity which is the most patently offensive *in its prurience—i.e.,* that which involves the most lascivious displays of sexual activity." Consequently, while the holding of *R.A.V.* does not permit a State to ban only obscenity based on "offensive *political* messages," or "only those threats against the President that mention his policy on aid to inner cities," the First Amendment permits content discrimination "based on the very reasons why the particular class of speech at issue ... is proscribable."

Similarly, Virginia's statute does not run afoul of the First Amendment insofar as it bans cross burning with intent to intimidate. Unlike the statute at issue in *R.A.V.,* the Virginia statute does not single out for opprobrium only that speech directed toward "one of the specified disfavored topics." It does not matter whether an individual burns a cross with intent to intimidate because of the victim's race, gender, or religion, or because of the victim's "political affiliation, union membership, or homosexuality." Moreover, as a factual matter it is not true that cross burners direct their intimidating conduct solely to racial or religious minorities....

The First Amendment permits Virginia to outlaw cross burnings done with the intent to intimidate because burning a cross is a particularly virulent form of intimidation. Instead of prohibiting all intimidating messages, Virginia may choose to regulate this subset of intimidating messages in light of cross burning's long and pernicious history as a signal of impending violence. Thus, just as a State may regulate only that obscenity which is the most obscene due to its prurient content, so too may a State choose to prohibit only those forms of intimidation that are most likely to inspire fear of bodily harm. A ban on cross burning carried out with the intent to intimidate is fully consistent with our holding in *R.A.V.* and is proscribable under the First Amendment.

IV

The Supreme Court of Virginia ruled in the alternative that Virginia's cross-burning statute was unconstitutionally overbroad due to its provision stating that "[a]ny such burning of a cross shall be prima facie evidence of an intent to intimidate a person or group of persons." ....

The jury in the case of Richard Elliott did not receive any instruction on the prima facie evidence provision, and the provision was not an issue in the case of Jonathan O'-Mara because he pleaded guilty. The court in Barry Black's case, however, instructed the jury that the provision means: "The burning of a cross, by itself, is sufficient evidence from which you may infer the required intent." ....

The prima facie evidence provision, as interpreted by the jury instruction, renders the statute unconstitutional.... As construed by the jury instruction, the prima facie provision strips away the very reason why a State may ban cross burning with the intent to intimidate. The prima facie evidence provision permits a jury to convict in every cross-burning case in which defendants exercise their constitutional right not to put on a defense. And even where a defendant like Black presents a defense, the prima facie evidence provision makes it more likely that the jury will find an intent to intimidate regardless of the particular facts of the case. The provision permits the Commonwealth to arrest, prosecute, and convict a person based solely on the fact of cross burning itself.

It is apparent that the provision as so interpreted "'would create an unacceptable risk of the suppression of ideas.'" The act of burning a cross may mean that a person is engaging in constitutionally proscribable intimidation. But that same act may mean only that the person is engaged in core political speech. The prima facie evidence provision in this statute blurs the line between these two meanings of a burning cross. As interpreted by the jury instruction, the provision chills constitutionally protected political speech because of the possibility that the Commonwealth will prosecute—and potentially convict—somebody engaging only in lawful political speech at the core of what the First Amendment is designed to protect.

As the history of cross burning indicates, a burning cross is not always intended to intimidate. Rather, sometimes the cross burning is a statement of ideology, a symbol of group solidarity. It is a ritual used at Klan gatherings, and it is used to represent the Klan itself. Thus, "[b]urning a cross at a political rally would almost certainly be protected expression." *R.A.V. v. St. Paul,* 505 U.S., at 402, n. 4 (White, J., concurring in judgment). Indeed, occasionally a person who burns a cross does not intend to express either a statement of ideology or intimidation. Cross burnings have appeared in movies such as Mississippi Burning, and in plays such as the stage adaptation of Sir Walter Scott's The Lady of the Lake.

The prima facie provision makes no effort to distinguish among these different types of cross burnings. It does not distinguish between a cross burning done with the purpose of creating anger or resentment and a cross burning done with the purpose of threatening or intimidating a victim. It does not distinguish between a cross burning at a public rally or a cross burning on a neighbor's lawn. It does not treat the cross burning directed at an individual differently from the cross burning directed at a group of like-minded be-lievers. It allows a jury to treat a cross burning on the property of another with the owner's acquiescence in the same manner as a cross burning on the property of another without the owner's permission....

It may be true that a cross burning, even at a political rally, arouses a sense of anger or hatred among the vast majority of citizens who see a burning cross. But this sense of anger or hatred is not sufficient to ban all cross burnings.... The prima facie evidence provision in this case ignores all of the contextual factors that are necessary to decide whether a particular cross burning is intended to intimidate. The First Amendment does not permit such a shortcut.

For these reasons, the prima facie evidence provision, as interpreted through the jury instruction and as applied in Barry Black's case, is unconstitutional on its face. We rec-ognize that the Supreme Court of Virginia has not authoritatively interpreted the mean-ing of the prima facie evidence provision. Unlike Justice SCALIA, we refuse to speculate on whether *any* interpretation of the prima facie evidence provision would satisfy the First Amendment. Rather, all we hold is that because of the interpretation of the prima facie evidence provision given by the jury instruction, the provision makes the statute fa-cially invalid at this point. We also recognize the theoretical possibility that the court, on remand, could interpret the provision in a manner different from that so far set forth in order to avoid the constitutional objections we have described. We leave open that pos-sibility....

[The concurring opinion of Justice Stevens, the opinions of Justices Scalia and Souter, concurring in part and dissenting in part, and the dissenting opinion of Justice Thomas are omitted.]

Snyder v. Phelps

131 S. Ct. 1207 (2011)

Chief Justice ROBERTS delivered the opinion of the Court.

    ....

I

A

Fred Phelps founded the Westboro Baptist Church in Topeka, Kansas, in 1955. The church's congregation believes that God hates and punishes the United States for its toler-ance of homosexuality, particularly in America's military. The church frequently communicates its views by picketing, often at military funerals. In the more than 20 years that the mem-bers of Westboro Baptist have publicized their message, they have picketed nearly 600 funerals.

Marine Lance Corporal Matthew Snyder was killed in Iraq in the line of duty. Lance Corporal Snyder's father selected the Catholic church in the Snyders' hometown of West-minster, Maryland, as the site for his son's funeral. Local newspapers provided notice of the time and location of the service.

Phelps became aware of Matthew Snyder's funeral and decided to travel to Maryland with six other Westboro Baptist parishioners (two of his daughters and four of his grand-children) to picket....

The church had notified the authorities in advance of its intent to picket at the time of the funeral, and the picketers complied with police instructions in staging their demonstration. The picketing took place within a 10-by-25-foot plot of public land adjacent to a public street, behind a temporary fence. That plot was approximately 1,000 feet from the church where the funeral was held. Several buildings separated the picket site from the church. The Westboro picketers displayed their signs for about 30 minutes before the funeral began and sang hymns and recited Bible verses. None of the picketers entered church property or went to the cemetery. They did not yell or use profanity, and there was no violence associated with the picketing.

The funeral procession passed within 200 to 300 feet of the picket site. Although Snyder testified that he could see the tops of the picket signs as he drove to the funeral, he did not see what was written on the signs until later that night, while watching a news broadcast covering the event.

B

Snyder filed suit against Phelps, Phelps's daughters, and the Westboro Baptist Church (collectively Westboro or the church) in the United States District Court for the District of Maryland under that court's diversity jurisdiction....

A jury found for Snyder on the intentional infliction of emotional distress, intrusion upon seclusion, and civil conspiracy claims, and held Westboro liable for $2.9 million in compensatory damages and $8 million in punitive damages....

II

.... The Free Speech Clause of the First Amendment—"Congress shall make no law ... abridging the freedom of speech"—can serve as a defense in state tort suits, including suits for intentional infliction of emotional distress.[3]

Whether the First Amendment prohibits holding Westboro liable for its speech in this case turns largely on whether that speech is of public or private concern, as determined by all the circumstances of the case....

"'[N]ot all speech is of equal First Amendment importance,'" however, and where matters of purely private significance are at issue, First Amendment protections are often less rigorous. That is because restricting speech on purely private matters does not implicate the same constitutional concerns as limiting speech on matters of public interest: "[T]here is no threat to the free and robust debate of public issues; there is no potential interference with a meaningful dialogue of ideas"; and the "threat of liability" does not pose the risk of "a reaction of self-censorship" on matters of public import....

Speech deals with matters of public concern when it can "be fairly considered as relating to any matter of political, social, or other concern to the community," or when it "is a subject of legitimate news interest; that is, a subject of general interest and of value and concern to the public." ....

Deciding whether speech is of public or private concern requires us to examine the "'content, form, and context'" of that speech, "'as revealed by the whole record.'" .... In considering content, form, and context, no factor is dispositive, and it is necessary to evaluate all the circumstances of the speech, including what was said, where it was said, and how it was said.

---

3. The dissent attempts to draw parallels between this case and hypothetical cases involving defamation or fighting words. But, as the court below noted, there is "no suggestion that the speech at issue falls within one of the categorical exclusions from First Amendment protection, such as those for obscenity or 'fighting words.'"

The "content" of Westboro's signs plainly relates to broad issues of interest to society at large, rather than matters of "purely private concern." The placards read "God Hates the USA/Thank God for 9/11," "America is Doomed," "Don't Pray for the USA," "Thank God for IEDs," "Fag Troops," "Semper Fi Fags," "God Hates Fags," "Maryland Taliban," "Fags Doom Nations," "Not Blessed Just Cursed," "Thank God for Dead Soldiers," "Pope in Hell," "Priests Rape Boys," "You're Going to Hell," and "God Hates You." While these messages may fall short of refined social or political commentary, the issues they highlight — the political and moral conduct of the United States and its citizens, the fate of our Nation, homosexuality in the military, and scandals involving the Catholic clergy — are matters of public import. The signs certainly convey Westboro's position on those issues, in a manner designed ... to reach as broad a public audience as possible. And even if a few of the signs — such as "You're Going to Hell" and "God Hates You" — were viewed as containing messages related to Matthew Snyder or the Snyders specifically, that would not change the fact that the overall thrust and dominant theme of Westboro's demonstration spoke to broader public issues.

Apart from the content of Westboro's signs, Snyder contends that the "context" of the speech — its connection with his son's funeral — makes the speech a matter of private rather than public concern. The fact that Westboro spoke in connection with a funeral, however, cannot by itself transform the nature of Westboro's speech. Westboro's signs, displayed on public land next to a public street, reflect the fact that the church finds much to condemn in modern society....

Snyder argues that the church members in fact mounted a personal attack on Snyder and his family, and then attempted to "immunize their conduct by claiming that they were actually protesting the United States' tolerance of homosexuality or the supposed evils of the Catholic Church." We are not concerned in this case that Westboro's speech on public matters was in any way contrived to insulate speech on a private matter from liability. Westboro had been actively engaged in speaking on the subjects addressed in its picketing long before it became aware of Matthew Snyder, and there can be no serious claim that Westboro's picketing did not represent its "honestly believed" views on public issues. There was no preexisting relationship or conflict between Westboro and Snyder that might suggest Westboro's speech on public matters was intended to mask an attack on Snyder over a private matter.

Snyder goes on to argue that Westboro's speech should be afforded less than full First Amendment protection "not only because of the words" but also because the church members exploited the funeral "as a platform to bring their message to a broader audience." There is no doubt that Westboro chose to stage its picketing at the Naval Academy, the Maryland State House, and Matthew Snyder's funeral to increase publicity for its views and because of the relation between those sites and its views — in the case of the military funeral, because Westboro believes that God is killing American soldiers as punishment for the Nation's sinful policies.

Westboro's choice to convey its views in conjunction with Matthew Snyder's funeral made the expression of those views particularly hurtful to many, especially to Matthew's father. The record makes clear that the applicable legal term — "emotional distress" — fails to capture fully the anguish Westboro's choice added to Mr. Snyder's already incalculable grief. But Westboro conducted its picketing peacefully on matters of public concern at a public place adjacent to a public street. Such space occupies a "special position in terms of First Amendment protection." *United States v. Grace,* 461 U.S. 171, 180 (1983). "[W]e have repeatedly referred to public streets as the archetype of a traditional public forum," noting that "'[t]ime out of mind' public streets and sidewalks have been used for public assembly and debate." *Frisby v. Schultz,* 487 U.S. 474, 480 (1988).

That said, "[e]ven protected speech is not equally permissible in all places and at all times." Westboro's choice of where and when to conduct its picketing is not beyond the Government's regulatory reach—it is "subject to reasonable time, place, or manner restrictions" that are consistent with the standards announced in this Court's precedents. *Clark v. Community for Creative Non-Violence,* 468 U.S. 288, 293 (1984). Maryland now has a law imposing restrictions on funeral picketing, as do 43 other States and the Federal Government. To the extent these laws are content neutral, they raise very different questions from the tort verdict at issue in this case. Maryland's law, however, was not in effect at the time of the events at issue here, so we have no occasion to consider how it might apply to facts such as those before us, or whether it or other similar regulations are constitutional.

We have identified a few limited situations where the location of targeted picketing can be regulated under provisions that the Court has determined to be content neutral. In *Frisby,* for example, we upheld a ban on such picketing "before or about" a particular residence, 487 U.S., at 477. In *Madsen v. Women's Health Center, Inc.,* we approved an injunction requiring a buffer zone between protesters and an abortion clinic entrance. 512 U.S. 753, 768 (1994). The facts here are obviously quite different, both with respect to the activity being regulated and the means of restricting those activities.

Simply put, the church members had the right to be where they were. Westboro alerted local authorities to its funeral protest and fully complied with police guidance on where the picketing could be staged. The picketing was conducted under police supervision some 1,000 feet from the church, out of the sight of those at the church. The protest was not unruly; there was no shouting, profanity, or violence.

The record confirms that any distress occasioned by Westboro's picketing turned on the content and viewpoint of the message conveyed, rather than any interference with the funeral itself. A group of parishioners standing at the very spot where Westboro stood, holding signs that said "God Bless America" and "God Loves You," would not have been subjected to liability. It was what Westboro said that exposed it to tort damages.

Given that Westboro's speech was at a public place on a matter of public concern, that speech is entitled to "special protection" under the First Amendment. Such speech cannot be restricted simply because it is upsetting or arouses contempt....

The jury here was instructed that it could hold Westboro liable for intentional infliction of emotional distress based on a finding that Westboro's picketing was "outrageous." "Outrageousness," however, is a highly malleable standard with "an inherent subjectiveness about it which would allow a jury to impose liability on the basis of the jurors' tastes or views, or perhaps on the basis of their dislike of a particular expression." In a case such as this, a jury is "unlikely to be neutral with respect to the content of [the] speech," posing "a real danger of becoming an instrument for the suppression of … 'vehement, caustic, and sometimes unpleasan[t]'" expression. Such a risk is unacceptable; "in public debate [we] must tolerate insulting, and even outrageous, speech in order to provide adequate 'breathing space' to the freedoms protected by the First Amendment." What Westboro said, in the whole context of how and where it chose to say it, is entitled to "special protection" under the First Amendment, and that protection cannot be overcome by a jury finding that the picketing was outrageous.

For all these reasons, the jury verdict imposing tort liability on Westboro for intentional infliction of emotional distress must be set aside.

III

The jury also found Westboro liable for the state law torts of intrusion upon seclusion and civil conspiracy....

Snyder argues that even assuming Westboro's speech is entitled to First Amendment protection generally, the church is not immunized from liability for intrusion upon seclusion because Snyder was a member of a captive audience at his son's funeral. We do not agree. In most circumstances, "the Constitution does not permit the government to decide which types of otherwise protected speech are sufficiently offensive to require protection for the unwilling listener or viewer. Rather, … the burden normally falls upon the viewer to avoid further bombardment of [his] sensibilities simply by averting [his] eyes." ….

As a general matter, we have applied the captive audience doctrine only sparingly to protect unwilling listeners from protected speech. For example, we have upheld a statute allowing a homeowner to restrict the delivery of offensive mail to his home, see *Rowan v. Post Office Dept.,* 397 U.S. 728, 736–738 (1970), and an ordinance prohibiting picketing "before or about" any individual's residence, *Frisby,* 487 U.S., at 484–485.

Here, Westboro stayed well away from the memorial service. Snyder could see no more than the tops of the signs when driving to the funeral. And there is no indication that the picketing in any way interfered with the funeral service itself. We decline to expand the captive audience doctrine to the circumstances presented here.…

IV

Our holding today is narrow. We are required in First Amendment cases to carefully review the record, and the reach of our opinion here is limited by the particular facts before us.…

Westboro believes that America is morally flawed; many Americans might feel the same about Westboro. Westboro's funeral picketing is certainly hurtful and its contribution to public discourse may be negligible. But Westboro addressed matters of public import on public property, in a peaceful manner, in full compliance with the guidance of local officials. The speech was indeed planned to coincide with Matthew Snyder's funeral, but did not itself disrupt that funeral, and Westboro's choice to conduct its picketing at that time and place did not alter the nature of its speech.

Speech is powerful. It can stir people to action, move them to tears of both joy and sorrow, and—as it did here—inflict great pain. On the facts before us, we cannot react to that pain by punishing the speaker. As a Nation we have chosen a different course—to protect even hurtful speech on public issues to ensure that we do not stifle public debate. That choice requires that we shield Westboro from tort liability for its picketing in this case.…

[The concurring opinion of Justice Breyer and the dissenting opinion of Justice Alito are omitted.]

Wisconsin v. Mitchell

508 U.S. 476 (1993)

Chief Justice REHNQUIST delivered the opinion of the Court.

Respondent Todd Mitchell's sentence for aggravated battery was enhanced because he intentionally selected his victim on account of the victim's race. The question presented in this case is whether this penalty enhancement is prohibited by the First and Fourteenth Amendments. We hold that it is not.

On the evening of October 7, 1989, a group of young black men and boys, including Mitchell, gathered at an apartment complex in Kenosha, Wisconsin. Several members of the group discussed a scene from the motion picture "Mississippi Burning," in which a white man beat a young black boy who was praying. The group moved outside and Mitchell asked them: "'Do you all feel hyped up to move on some white people?'" Shortly thereafter, a young white boy approached the group on the opposite side of the street where they were standing. As the boy walked by, Mitchell said: "'You all want to fuck somebody up? There goes a white boy; go get him.'" Mitchell counted to three and pointed in the boy's direction. The group ran toward the boy, beat him severely, and stole his tennis shoes. The boy was rendered unconscious and remained in a coma for four days.

After a jury trial in the Circuit Court for Kenosha County, Mitchell was convicted of aggravated battery. That offense ordinarily carries a maximum sentence of two years' imprisonment. But because the jury found that Mitchell had intentionally selected his victim because of the boy's race, the maximum sentence for Mitchell's offense was increased to seven years under § 939.645. That provision enhances the maximum penalty for an offense whenever the defendant "[i]ntentionally selects the person against whom the crime … is committed … because of the race, religion, color, disability, sexual orientation, national origin or ancestry of that person.…" § 939.645(1)(b). The Circuit Court sentenced Mitchell to four years' imprisonment for the aggravated battery.…

The State argues that the statute does not punish bigoted thought, as the Supreme Court of Wisconsin said, but instead punishes only conduct. While this argument is literally correct, it does not dispose of Mitchell's First Amendment challenge. To be sure, our cases reject the "view that an apparently limitless variety of conduct can be labeled 'speech' whenever the person engaging in the conduct intends thereby to express an idea." *United States v. O'Brien,* 391 U.S. 367, 376 (1968). Thus, a physical assault is not by any stretch of the imagination expressive conduct protected by the First Amendment.

But the fact remains that under the Wisconsin statute the same criminal conduct may be more heavily punished if the victim is selected because of his race or other protected status than if no such motive obtained. Thus, although the statute punishes criminal conduct, it enhances the maximum penalty for conduct motivated by a discriminatory point of view more severely than the same conduct engaged in for some other reason or for no reason at all. Because the only reason for the enhancement is the defendant's discriminatory motive for selecting his victim, Mitchell argues (and the Wisconsin Supreme Court held) that the statute violates the First Amendment by punishing offenders' bigoted beliefs.

Traditionally, sentencing judges have considered a wide variety of factors in addition to evidence bearing on guilt in determining what sentence to impose on a convicted defendant. The defendant's motive for committing the offense is one important factor. Thus, in many States the commission of a murder, or other capital offense, for pecuniary gain is a separate aggravating circumstance under the capital sentencing statute.

But it is equally true that a defendant's abstract beliefs, however obnoxious to most people, may not be taken into consideration by a sentencing judge. *Dawson v. Delaware,* 503 U.S. 159 (1992). In *Dawson,* the State introduced evidence at a capital sentencing hearing that the defendant was a member of a white supremacist prison gang. Because "the evidence proved nothing more than [the defendant's] abstract beliefs," we held that its admission violated the defendant's First Amendment rights. *Id.,* at 167. In so holding, however, we emphasized that "the Constitution does not erect a *per se* barrier to the admission of evidence concerning one's beliefs and associations at sentencing simply because those beliefs and associations are protected by the First Amendment." *Id.,* at 165. Thus, in *Barclay v. Florida,* 463 U.S. 939 (1983) (plurality opinion), we allowed the sentencing judge to take into account the defendant's racial animus towards his victim. The evidence in that case showed that the defendant's membership in the Black Liberation

Army and desire to provoke a "race war" were related to the murder of a white man for which he was convicted. See *id.,* at 942–944. Because "the elements of racial hatred in [the] murder" were relevant to several aggravating factors, we held that the trial judge permissibly took this evidence into account in sentencing the defendant to death. *Id.,* at 949, and n. 7.

Mitchell suggests that *Dawson* and *Barclay* are inapposite because they did not involve application of a penalty-enhancement provision. But in *Barclay* we held that it was permissible for the sentencing court to consider the defendant's racial animus in determining whether he should be sentenced to death, surely the most severe "enhancement" of all. And the fact that the Wisconsin Legislature has decided, as a general matter, that bias-motivated offenses warrant greater maximum penalties across the board does not alter the result here....

Mitchell argues that the Wisconsin penalty-enhancement statute is invalid because it punishes the defendant's discriminatory motive, or reason, for acting. But motive plays the same role under the Wisconsin statute as it does under federal and state antidiscrimination laws, which we have previously upheld against constitutional challenge. See *Roberts v. United States Jaycees, supra,* 468 U.S., at 628; *Hishon v. King & Spalding,* 467 U.S. 69, 78 (1984); *Runyon v. McCrary,* 427 U.S. 160, 176 (1976). Title VII of the Civil Rights Act of 1964, for example, makes it unlawful for an employer to discriminate against an employee "*because of* such individual's race, color, religion, sex, or national origin." 42 U.S.C. § 2000e-2(a)(1) (emphasis added). In *Hishon,* we rejected the argument that Title VII infringed employers' First Amendment rights. And more recently, in *R.A.V. v. St. Paul,* 505 U.S., at 389–390, we cited Title VII (as well as 18 U.S.C. § 242 and 42 U.S.C. §§ 1981 and 1982) as an example of a permissible content-neutral regulation of conduct.

Nothing in our decision last Term in *R.A.V.* compels a different result here. That case involved a First Amendment challenge to a municipal ordinance prohibiting the use of "'fighting words' that insult, or provoke violence, 'on the basis of race, color, creed, religion or gender.'" Because the ordinance only proscribed a class of "fighting words" deemed particularly offensive by the city—*i.e.,* those "that contain ... messages of 'bias-motivated' hatred," we held that it violated the rule against content-based discrimination. But whereas the ordinance struck down in *R.A.V.* was explicitly directed at expression (*i.e.,* "speech" or "messages"), the statute in this case is aimed at conduct unprotected by the First Amendment.

Moreover, the Wisconsin statute singles out for enhancement bias-inspired conduct because this conduct is thought to inflict greater individual and societal harm. For example, according to the State and its *amici,* bias-motivated crimes are more likely to provoke retaliatory crimes, inflict distinct emotional harms on their victims, and incite community unrest. The State's desire to redress these perceived harms provides an adequate explanation for its penalty-enhancement provision over and above mere disagreement with offenders' beliefs or biases....

Finally, there remains to be considered Mitchell's argument that the Wisconsin statute is unconstitutionally overbroad because of its "chilling effect" on free speech. Mitchell argues (and the Wisconsin Supreme Court agreed) that the statute is "overbroad" because evidence of the defendant's prior speech or associations may be used to prove that the defendant intentionally selected his victim on account of the victim's protected status. Consequently, the argument goes, the statute impermissibly chills free expression with respect to such matters by those concerned about the possibility of enhanced sentences if they should in the future commit a criminal offense covered by the statute. We find no merit in this contention.

The sort of chill envisioned here is far more attenuated and unlikely than that contemplated in traditional "overbreadth" cases. We must conjure up a vision of a Wisconsin citizen suppressing his unpopular bigoted opinions for fear that if he later commits an offense covered by the statute, these opinions will be offered at trial to establish that he selected his victim on account of the victim's protected status, thus qualifying him for penalty enhancement. To stay within the realm of rationality, we must surely put to one side minor misdemeanor offenses covered by the statute, such as negligent operation of a motor vehicle; for it is difficult, if not impossible, to conceive of a situation where such offenses would be racially motivated. We are left, then, with the prospect of a citizen suppressing his bigoted beliefs for fear that evidence of such beliefs will be introduced against him at trial if he commits a more serious offense against person or property. This is simply too speculative a hypothesis to support Mitchell's overbreadth claim.

The First Amendment, moreover, does not prohibit the evidentiary use of speech to establish the elements of a crime or to prove motive or intent. Evidence of a defendant's previous declarations or statements is commonly admitted in criminal trials subject to evidentiary rules dealing with relevancy, reliability, and the like. Nearly half a century ago, in *Haupt v. United States,* 330 U.S. 631 (1947), we rejected a contention similar to that advanced by Mitchell here. Haupt was tried for the offense of treason, which, as defined by the Constitution (Art. III, §3), may depend very much on proof of motive. To prove that the acts in question were committed out of "adherence to the enemy" rather than "parental solicitude," the Government introduced evidence of conversations that had taken place long prior to the indictment, some of which consisted of statements showing Haupt's sympathy with Germany and Hitler and hostility towards the United States. We rejected Haupt's argument that this evidence was improperly admitted. While "[s]uch testimony is to be scrutinized with care to be certain the statements are not expressions of mere lawful and permissible difference of opinion with our own government or quite proper appreciation of the land of birth," we held that "these statements ... clearly were admissible on the question of intent and adherence to the enemy." *Id.,* at 642. See also *Price Waterhouse v. Hopkins,* 490 U.S. 228, 251–252 (1989) (plurality opinion) (allowing evidentiary use of defendant's speech in evaluating Title VII discrimination claim); *Street v. New York,* 394 U.S. 576, 594 (1969)....

Notes and Questions

1. As indicated in *Black*, the Court has recognized that it is constitutionally permissible for a state to punish the use of so-called "fighting words," defined as "those personally abusive epithets which, when addressed to the ordinary citizen, are, as a matter of common knowledge, inherently likely to provoke violent reaction." *Cohen v. California*, 403 U.S. 15, 20 (1971) (citing *Chaplinsky v. New Hampshire*, 315 U.S. 568 (1942)).

How easy is it to determine whether someone's statement constitutes "fighting words"? In addition to making a finding that the words are "inherently likely to prove violent reaction," courts, as a general rule, are likely to find statements to constitute fighting words only when directed toward a specific individual or small group of individuals, not when directed more broadly toward a larger group. *See Gilles v. Davis*, 427 F.3d 197, 205–06 (3d Cir. 2005) ("Of Gilles' questionable speech, some was derogatory language generically directed to the crowd (*e.g.,* 'by definition, there are thousands of fornicators on this campus,' 'drunkards are everywhere on this campus'). This type of language, when not personally directed at a particular member of the audience, is not likely to incite an immediate breach of the peace.... Nonetheless, Gilles' epithets directed at the woman who identified herself as a Christian and a lesbian ('Christian lesbo,' 'lesbian for Jesus,' 'do you lay down with dogs,' 'are you a bestiality lover') were especially abusive and constituted fighting words."); *State v. Machholz*, 574 N.W.2d 415, 422 (Minn. 1998) (man riding horse through park during gay pride event yelling, "You're giving us AIDS!"; "You're spreading your filth!"; "There are no homosexuals in heaven!"; and "You're corrupting our children!" not deemed to be fighting words, with court noting that the statements were "not directed at a specific individual"); *Gilles v. State*, 531 N.E.2d 220, 222–23 (Ind. Ct. App. 1988) (deeming epithets "whores," "queers," and "AIDS people" to be fighting words, noting that "[t]o be fighting words the words must be spoken as a face-to-face personal insult," and after finding that they were, concluding that, "In terms generally considered some of the most offensive in our culture, Gilles placed his listeners in categories defined by sexual activity, sexual orientation, and sexually transmitted disease. This language was inherently likely to provoke a violent reaction.").

2. The *Black* Court, citing *Watts v. United States*, 394 U.S. 705, 708 (1969), distinguishes between punishing "true threats" (permissible) and mere "political hyperbole" (impermissible). In *Watts*, the U.S. Supreme Court overturned a conviction under a statute prohibiting threats on the life of the President, finding that the speaker was not making a true threat but only engaging in political hyperbole when he said, during a protest of the draft, "If they ever make me carry a rifle the first man I want to get in my sights is L.B.J."

3. Is the standard for determining whether something is a "true threat" a subjective or objective one? *Compare United States v. Mabie*, 663 F.3d 322, 332–33 (8th Cir. 2011) (objective only), *with United States v. Bagdasarian*, 652 F.3d 1113, 1116–17 (9th Cir. 2011) (subjective, and sometimes subjective and objective). Does *Black* provide clear guidance on this question?

4. In *Black*, the Court cites *Brandenburg v. Ohio*, 395 U.S. 444, 449 (1969) for the proposition that the government can prohibit speech that amounts to an "incitement to imminent lawless action." Prior to the U.S. Supreme Court's decision in *Lawrence v. Texas* deeming unconstitutional laws prohibiting private, consensual sodomy, lower courts rejected efforts to restrict the establishment of organizations advocating for the repeal of such laws on the ground that such organizations were engaged in "incitement to imminent lawless action," distinguishing between advocacy to repeal undesirable laws (permissible) and advocacy to imminently engage in unlawful conduct, i.e., sodomy (impermissible). *See Nat'l Gay Task Force v. Bd. of Educ.*, 729 F.2d 1270, 1274 (10th Cir. 1984); *Gay Lesbian Bisexual Alliance v. Pryor*, 110 F.3d 1543 (11th Cir. 1997); *Gay Student Servs. v. Tex. A & M Univ.*, 737 F.2d 1317, 1328 (5th Cir. 1984); *Gay Lib v. Univ. of Mo.*, 558 F.2d 848, 856 (8th Cir. 1977); *Gay Alliance of Students v. Matthews*, 544 F.2d 162 (4th Cir. 1976).

5. In what ways are the categories of "fighting words," "true threats," and statements tending to incite "imminent lawless action" similar? In what ways are they different? Consider the following explanation:

> [D]espite superficial similarities, threats are not, for First Amendment purposes, treated identically with either fighting words or expression tending to incite imminent lawless action. Both fighting words and incitement have expressive value, the former as provocative communication of a most effective sort, the latter as communication aimed at moving the listener to act. The First Amendment protects the inherent communicative value in each of the two kinds of expression up to the point at which the state's compelling interest in maintaining order

must outweigh the speaker's freedom of expression. This is the purpose served by the rule in *Brandenburg* that to forfeit constitutional protection the speech must be "directed to inciting … imminent lawless action" and must be likely to do so, and the corresponding rule of *Chaplinsky* that fighting words lose First Amendment protection only when, by their very utterance, they "inflict injury or tend to incite an immediate breach of the peace."

Violence and threats of violence, by contrast, fall outside the protection of the First Amendment because they coerce by unlawful *conduct*, rather than persuade by expression, and thus play no part in the "marketplace of ideas." As such, they are punishable because of the state's interest in protecting individuals from the fear of violence, the disruption fear engenders and the possibility the threatened violence will occur. As long as the threat reasonably appears to be a serious expression of intention to inflict bodily harm, and its circumstances are such that there is a reasonable tendency to produce in the victim a fear the threat will be carried out, the fact the threat may be contingent on some future event (e.g., "If you don't move out of the neighborhood by Sunday, I'll kill you") does not cloak it in constitutional protection.

In re M.S., 896 P.2d 1365, 1373–74 (Cal. 1995).

6. In *Black*, the Court, citing *R.A.V. v. City of St. Paul*, 505 U.S. 377 (1992), distinguishes between permissible and impermissible content-discrimination. What, exactly, is the distinction? Consider the following excerpt from *R.A.V.*:

The proposition that a particular instance of speech can be proscribable on the basis of one feature (*e.g.*, obscenity) but not on the basis of another (*e.g.*, opposition to the city government) is commonplace and has found application in many contexts. We have long held, for example, that nonverbal expressive activity can be banned because of the action it entails, but not because of the ideas it expresses—so that burning a flag in violation of an ordinance against outdoor fires could be punishable, whereas burning a flag in violation of an ordinance against dishonoring the flag is not. Similarly, we have upheld reasonable "time, place, or manner" restrictions, but only if they are "justified without reference to the content of the regulated speech." And just as the power to proscribe particular speech on the basis of a noncontent element (*e.g.*, noise) does not entail the power to proscribe the same speech on the basis of a content element; so also, the power to proscribe it on the basis of *one* content element (*e.g.*, obscenity) does not entail the power to proscribe it on the basis of *other* content elements.

In other words, the exclusion of "fighting words" from the scope of the First Amendment simply means that, for purposes of that Amendment, the unprotected features of the words are, despite their verbal character, essentially a "nonspeech" element of communication. Fighting words are thus analogous to a noisy sound truck: Each is, as Justice Frankfurter recognized, a "mode of speech"; both can be used to convey an idea; but neither has, in and of itself, a claim upon the First Amendment. As with the sound truck, however, so also with fighting words: The government may not regulate use based on hostility—or favoritism—towards the underlying message expressed.

R.A.V. v. City of St. Paul, 505 U.S. 377, 385–86 (1992).

7. As noted in *Snyder*, the Court has, in a series of decisions, upheld neutral "time, place, and manner" restrictions that govern the choice of where and when to conduct

picketing. Indeed, in *Hill v. Colorado*, 530 U.S. 703 (2000), the Supreme Court up-held, against a First Amendment challenge, a state statute that made it a crime, within 100 feet of the entrance to any health care facility, to approach another person within eight feet of that person, without their consent, for the purpose of passing a leaflet or handbill to them; displaying a sign to them; or engaging in oral protest, education, or counseling.

As the Court also notes, many states have enacted laws limiting protests at funerals, re-quiring protesters to remain several hundred feet away for a certain period of time im-mediately before and after the funeral. Are such statutes constitutional? *See Phelps-Roper v. Strickland*, 539 F.3d 356 (6th Cir. 2008) (upholding a statute prohibiting picketing or other protest activities within 300 feet of a funeral or burial service from one hour before until one hour after the service). *See also Phelps-Roper v. Troutman*, 662 F.3d 485 (8th Cir. 2011) (Murphy, J., concurring and Beam, J., concurring in the judgment) (noting that together, *Hill v. Colorado* and *Snyder v. Phelps* provide support for upholding the consti-tutionality of such statutes).

8. The Matthew Shepard and James Byrd, Jr., Hate Crimes Prevention Act, adopted in 2009, makes it a federal crime to intentionally cause bodily injury to another person when the injury was motivated by, *inter alia*, the actual or perceived sexual orientation of the victim. *See* 18 U.S.C. § 249(a)(2). In *Glenn v. Holder*, 738 F.Supp.2d 718, 728 (E.D. Mich. 2010), *aff'd on other grounds*, 2012 WL 3115683 (6th Cir. 2012) the Court—relying on *Wisconsin v. Mitchell*—rejected a First Amendment overbreadth challenge contending that the statute would chill constitutionally protected speech, deeming the claim too spec-ulative to support standing to challenge the statute.

9. In light of the general principles set forth in this section, courts have struck down laws designed to establish "speech codes" prohibiting derogatory statements based on one's race, sex, sexual orientation, or other factors. *See Davis Next Friend LaShonda D. v. Monroe Cnty. Bd. of Educ.* 526 U.S. 629, 667 (1999) (Kennedy, J., dissenting) (collect-ing cases); *DeJohn v. Temple Univ.*, 537 F.3d 301 (3d Cir. 2008).

Yet if this is so, how is it that sexual harassment claims are actionable even though often based on speech? Consider the following explanation:

> Another valid basis for according differential treatment to even a content-defined subclass of proscribable speech is that the subclass happens to be associated with particular "secondary effects" of the speech, so that the regulation is "*justified* without reference to the content of the … speech." *Renton v. Playtime Theatres, Inc.*, 475 U.S. 41, 48 (1986). A State could, for example, permit all obscene live performances except those involving minors. Moreover, since words can in some circumstances violate laws directed not against speech but against conduct (a law against treason, for example, is violated by telling the enemy the Nation's defense secrets), a particular content-based subcategory of a proscribable class of speech can be swept up incidentally within the reach of a statute directed at conduct rather than speech. Thus, for example, sexually derogatory "fighting words," among other words, may produce a violation of Title VII's general prohibition against sexual discrimination in employment practices. Where the government does not target conduct on the basis of its expressive content, acts are not shielded from regulation merely because they express a discriminatory idea or philosophy.

R.A.V. v. City of St. Paul, 505 U.S. 377, 389–90 (1992). *But see id.* at 409–10 (White, J., dissenting) (noting that it is difficult to distinguish the "secondary effects" associated with banning sexual harassment specifically rather than harassment generally from those associated with banning cross-burning and other types of symbolic conduct intended to express hostility on the basis of race, color, creed, religion or gender specifically rather than engaging in that conduct generally).

C. Freedom of Expressive Association

As you saw in Chapter 3, the equal protection guarantee found in the Fourteenth Amendment and implied from the Fifth Amendment's Due Process Clause has served as a vehicle for limiting the ability of governmental bodies to discriminate on the basis of race, sex, and sexual orientation. However, because the equal protection guarantee applies only to discrimination by *governmental* actors, it provides no relief to those who suffer discrimination at the hands of private actors.

In time, federal, state, and local governments began enacting anti-discrimination statutes banning discrimination in employment, housing, and public accommodations on the basis of race, sex, sexual orientation, and other bases.

One effect of such laws is to require people to associate with others that they would prefer not to associate with. Of course, in terms, the Constitution nowhere refers to any right to "freedom of association." However, in two separate lines of cases, the U.S. Supreme Court has recognized that such a right exists. First, in its substantive due process cases, the Court has recognized a right to "intimate association." And second, the Court's First Amendment cases have recognized a right to "expressive association."

The first case in this section, *Roberts v. United States Jaycees*, 468 U.S. 609 (1984), delineates the difference between these two different rights to association. The cases that follow explore the application of the second right, that of expressive association, where sexual minorities are involved.

Problem 6-C: Play Ball!

The North American Gay Amateur Athletic Alliance (NAGAAA) is a national organization that "promotes amateur sports competition, particularly softball, for all persons regardless of age, sexual orientation or preference, with special emphasis on the participation of members of the gay, lesbian, bisexual and transgender (GLBT) community." Among other things, NAGAAA oversees an annual softball competition.

NAGAAA rules provide that teams may have no more than two heterosexuals on their teams, defined as those "having a predominant sexual interest in a member or members of the opposite sex."

Plaintiffs, a Seattle-based team that seeks to enter the competition with a team containing more than two heterosexual players, file suit in state court, contending that the organization's rule violates the state's public accommodation laws, which prohibit discrimination on the basis of sexual orientation.

NAGAAA defends on the ground that the state public accommodations law, as applied to NAGAAA, violates its rights under the First Amendment.

How should the court rule on NAGAAA's constitutional defense?

Roberts v. United States Jaycees

468 U.S. 609 (1984)

Justice BRENNAN delivered the opinion of the Court.

This case requires us to address a conflict between a State's efforts to eliminate gender-based discrimination against its citizens and the constitutional freedom of association asserted by members of a private organization. In the decision under review, the Court of Appeals for the Eighth Circuit concluded that, by requiring the United States Jaycees to admit women as full voting members, the Minnesota Human Rights Act violates the First and Fourteenth Amendment rights of the organization's members....

II

Our decisions have referred to constitutionally protected "freedom of association" in two distinct senses. In one line of decisions, the Court has concluded that choices to enter into and maintain certain intimate human relationships must be secured against undue intrusion by the State because of the role of such relationships in safeguarding the individual freedom that is central to our constitutional scheme. In this respect, freedom of association receives protection as a fundamental element of personal liberty. In another set of decisions, the Court has recognized a right to associate for the purpose of engaging in those activities protected by the First Amendment — speech, assembly, petition for the redress of grievances, and the exercise of religion. The Constitution guarantees freedom of association of this kind as an indispensable means of preserving other individual liberties.

The intrinsic and instrumental features of constitutionally protected association may, of course, coincide. In particular, when the State interferes with individuals' selection of those with whom they wish to join in a common endeavor, freedom of association in both of its forms may be implicated. The Jaycees contend that this is such a case. Still, the nature and degree of constitutional protection afforded freedom of association may vary depending on the extent to which one or the other aspect of the constitutionally protected liberty is at stake in a given case. We therefore find it useful to consider separately the effect of applying the Minnesota statute to the Jaycees on what could be called its members' freedom of intimate association and their freedom of expressive association.

A

The Court has long recognized that, because the Bill of Rights is designed to secure individual liberty, it must afford the formation and preservation of certain kinds of highly personal relationships a substantial measure of sanctuary from unjustified interference by the State. *E.g., Pierce v. Society of Sisters*, 268 U.S. 510, 534–535 (1925); *Meyer v. Nebraska*, 262 U.S. 390, 399 (1923). Without precisely identifying every consideration that may underlie this type of constitutional protection, we have noted that certain kinds of personal bonds have played a critical role in the culture and traditions of the Nation by cultivating and transmitting shared ideals and beliefs; they thereby foster diversity and act as critical buffers between the individual and the power of the State. Moreover, the constitutional shelter afforded such relationships reflects the realization that individuals draw much of their emotional enrichment from close ties with others. Protecting these relationships from unwarranted state interference therefore safeguards the ability independently to define one's identity that is central to any concept of liberty.

The personal affiliations that exemplify these considerations, and that therefore suggest some relevant limitations on the relationships that might be entitled to this sort of constitutional protection, are those that attend the creation and sustenance of a family—marriage, *e.g., Zablocki v. Redhail*; childbirth, *e.g., Carey v. Population Services International*; the raising and education of children, *e.g., Smith v. Organization of Foster Families*; and cohabitation with one's relatives, *e.g., Moore v. East Cleveland*. Family relationships, by their nature, involve deep attachments and commitments to the necessarily few other individuals with whom one shares not only a special community of thoughts, experiences, and beliefs but also distinctively personal aspects of one's life. Among other things, therefore, they are distinguished by such attributes as relative smallness, a high degree of selectivity in decisions to begin and maintain the affiliation, and seclusion from others in critical aspects of the relationship. As a general matter, only relationships with these sorts of qualities are likely to reflect the considerations that have led to an understanding of freedom of association as an intrinsic element of personal liberty. Conversely, an association lacking these qualities—such as a large business enterprise—seems remote from the concerns giving rise to this constitutional protection. Accordingly, the Constitution undoubtedly imposes constraints on the State's power to control the selection of one's spouse that would not apply to regulations affecting the choice of one's fellow employees. Compare *Loving v. Virginia*, 388 U.S. 1, 12 (1967), with *Railway Mail Assn. v. Corsi*, 326 U.S. 88, 93–94 (1945).

Between these poles, of course, lies a broad range of human relationships that may make greater or lesser claims to constitutional protection from particular incursions by the State. Determining the limits of state authority over an individual's freedom to enter into a particular association therefore unavoidably entails a careful assessment of where that relationship's objective characteristics locate it on a spectrum from the most intimate to the most attenuated of personal attachments. We need not mark the potentially significant points on this terrain with any precision. We note only that factors that may be relevant include size, purpose, policies, selectivity, congeniality, and other characteristics that in a particular case may be pertinent. In this case, however, several features of the Jaycees clearly place the organization outside of the category of relationships worthy of this kind of constitutional protection.

The undisputed facts reveal that the local chapters of the Jaycees are large and basically unselective groups.... Apart from age and sex, neither the national organization nor the local chapters employ any criteria for judging applicants for membership.... Furthermore, despite their inability to vote, hold office, or receive certain awards, women affiliated with the Jaycees attend various meetings, participate in selected projects, and engage in many of the organization's social functions. Indeed, numerous non-members of both genders regularly participate in a substantial portion of activities central to the decision of many members to associate with one another....

Accordingly, we conclude that the Jaycees chapters lack the distinctive characteristics that might afford constitutional protection to the decision of its members to exclude women. We turn therefore to consider the extent to which application of the Minnesota statute to compel the Jaycees to accept women infringes the group's freedom of expressive association.

B

An individual's freedom to speak, to worship, and to petition the government for the redress of grievances could not be vigorously protected from interference by the State unless a correlative freedom to engage in group effort toward those ends were not also guaranteed. According protection to collective effort on behalf of shared goals is especially important in preserving political and cultural diversity and in shielding dissident expression from suppression by the majority. Consequently, we have long understood as implicit in the right to engage in activities protected by the First Amendment a corresponding right to associate with others in pursuit of a wide variety of political, social, economic, educational, religious, and cultural ends. In view of the various protected activities in which the Jaycees engages, that right is plainly implicated in this case.

Government actions that may unconstitutionally infringe upon this freedom can take a number of forms. Among other things, government may seek to impose penalties or withhold benefits from individuals because of their membership in a disfavored group; it may attempt to require disclosure of the fact of membership in a group seeking anonymity; and it may try to interfere with the internal organization or affairs of the group. By requiring the Jaycees to admit women as full voting members, the Minnesota Act works an infringement of the last type. There can be no clearer example of an intrusion into the internal structure or affairs of an association than a regulation that forces the group to accept members it does not desire. Such a regulation may impair the ability of the original members to express only those views that brought them together. Freedom of association therefore plainly presupposes a freedom not to associate.

The right to associate for expressive purposes is not, however, absolute. Infringements on that right may be justified by regulations adopted to serve compelling state interests, unrelated to the suppression of ideas, that cannot be achieved through means significantly less restrictive of associational freedoms. We are persuaded that Minnesota's compelling interest in eradicating discrimination against its female citizens justifies the impact that application of the statute to the Jaycees may have on the male members' associational freedoms.

On its face, the Minnesota Act does not aim at the suppression of speech, does not distinguish between prohibited and permitted activity on the basis of viewpoint, and does not license enforcement authorities to administer the statute on the basis of such constitutionally impermissible criteria. Nor does the Jaycees contend that the Act has been applied in this case for the purpose of hampering the organization's ability to express its views. Instead, as the Minnesota Supreme Court explained, the Act reflects the State's strong historical commitment to eliminating discrimination and assuring its citizens equal access to publicly available goods and services. That goal, which is unrelated to the suppression of expression, plainly serves compelling state interests of the highest order.

The Minnesota Human Rights Act at issue here is an example of public accommodations laws that were adopted by some States beginning a decade before enactment of their federal counterpart, the Civil Rights Act of 1875. Indeed, when this Court invalidated that federal statute in the *Civil Rights Cases*, 109 U.S. 3 (1883), it emphasized the fact that state laws imposed a variety of equal access obligations on public accommodations. In response to that decision, many more States, including Minnesota, adopted statutes prohibiting racial discrimination in public accommodations. These laws provided the primary means for protecting the civil rights of historically disadvantaged groups until the Federal Government reentered the field in 1957. Like many other States, Minnesota has progressively broadened the scope of its public accommodations law in the years since it was first enacted, both with respect to the number and type of covered facilities and with respect to the groups against whom discrimination is forbidden....

By prohibiting gender discrimination in places of public accommodation, the Minnesota Act protects the State's citizenry from a number of serious social and personal harms. In the context of reviewing state actions under the Equal Protection Clause, this Court has frequently noted that discrimination based on archaic and overbroad assumptions about the relative needs and capacities of the sexes forces individuals to labor under stereotypical notions that often bear no relationship to their actual abilities. It thereby both deprives persons of their individual dignity and denies society the benefits of wide participation in political, economic, and cultural life. These concerns are strongly implicated with respect to gender discrimination in the allocation of publicly available goods and services. Thus, in upholding Title II of the Civil Rights Act of 1964, which forbids race discrimination in public accommodations, we emphasized that its "fundamental object ... was to vindicate 'the deprivation of personal dignity that surely accompanies denials of equal access to public establishments.'" *Heart of Atlanta Motel, Inc. v. United States*, 379 U.S. 241, 250 (1964). That stigmatizing injury, and the denial of equal opportunities that accompanies it, is surely felt as strongly by persons suffering discrimination on the basis of their sex as by those treated differently because of their race.

Nor is the state interest in assuring equal access limited to the provision of purely tangible goods and services. Like many States and municipalities, Minnesota has adopted a functional definition of public accommodations that reaches various forms of public, quasi-commercial conduct. This expansive definition reflects a recognition of the changing nature of the American economy and of the importance, both to the individual and to society, of removing the barriers to economic advancement and political and social integration that have historically plagued certain disadvantaged groups, including women....

In applying the Act to the Jaycees, the State has advanced those interests through the least restrictive means of achieving its ends. Indeed, the Jaycees has failed to demonstrate that the Act imposes any serious burdens on the male members' freedom of expressive association. To be sure, as the Court of Appeals noted, a "not insubstantial part" of the Jaycees' activities constitutes protected expression on political, economic, cultural, and social affairs. Over the years, the national and local levels of the organization have taken public positions on a number of diverse issues, and members of the Jaycees regularly engage in a variety of civic, charitable, lobbying, fundraising, and other activities worthy of constitutional protection under the First Amendment. There is, however, no basis in the record for concluding that admission of women as full voting members will impede the organization's ability to engage in these protected activities or to disseminate its preferred views. The Act requires no change in the Jaycees' creed of promoting the interests of young men, and it imposes no restrictions on the organization's ability to exclude individuals with ideologies or philosophies different from those of its existing members. Moreover, the Jaycees already invites women to share the group's views and philosophy and to participate in much of its training and community activities. Accordingly, any claim that admission of women as full voting members will impair a symbolic message conveyed by the very fact that women are not permitted to vote is attenuated at best.

While acknowledging that "the specific content of most of the resolutions adopted over the years by the Jaycees has nothing to do with sex," the Court of Appeals nonetheless entertained the hypothesis that women members might have a different view or agenda with respect to these matters so that, if they are allowed to vote, "some change in the Jaycees' philosophical cast can reasonably be expected." It is similarly arguable that, insofar as the Jaycees is organized to promote the views of young men whatever those views happen to be, admission of women as voting members will change the message communicated by the group's speech because of the gender-based assumptions of the audience. Neither supposition, however, is supported by the record. In claiming that women might have a different attitude about such issues as the federal budget, school prayer, voting rights, and foreign relations, or that the organization's public positions would have a different effect if the group were not "a purely young men's association," the Jaycees relies solely on unsupported generalizations about the relative interests and perspectives of men and women. Although such generalizations may or may not have a statistical basis in fact with respect to particular positions adopted by the Jaycees, we have repeatedly condemned legal decision making that relies uncritically on such assumptions. In the absence of a showing far more substantial than that attempted by the Jaycees, we decline to indulge in the sexual stereotyping that underlies appellee's contention that, by allowing women to vote, application of the Minnesota Act will change the content or impact of the organization's speech.

In any event, even if enforcement of the Act causes some incidental abridgment of the Jaycees' protected speech, that effect is no greater than is necessary to accomplish the State's legitimate purposes. As we have explained, acts of invidious discrimination in the distribution of publicly available goods, services, and other advantages cause unique evils that government has a compelling interest to prevent—wholly apart from the point of view such conduct may transmit. Accordingly, like violence or other types of potentially expressive activities that produce special harms distinct from their communicative impact, such practices are entitled to no constitutional protection. In prohibiting such practices, the Minnesota Act therefore "responds precisely to the substantive problem which legitimately concerns" the State and abridges no more speech or associational freedom than is necessary to accomplish that purpose....

Justice REHNQUIST concurs in the judgment.

THE CHIEF JUSTICE and Justice BLACKMUN took no part in the decision of this case.

[The opinion of Justice O'Connor, concurring in part and concurring in the judgment, is omitted.]

Hurley v. Irish-American Gay, Lesbian & Bisexual Group of Boston
515 U.S. 557 (1995)

Justice SOUTER delivered the opinion of the Court.

[Each year, since 1947, the petitioner, South Boston Allied War Veterans Council ("Council"), was the sole applicant for a permit to hold a St. Patrick's Day parade along a given route that typically includes thousands of participants and nearly a million observers. In 1992 and again in 1993, GLIB—an organization consisting of gay, lesbian, and bisexual descendants of Irish immigrants—sought inclusion in the parade organized by the Council, but their request was rejected. GLIB sued the Council in state court, relying on the state's public accommodation law, which bans discrimination on the basis of, *inter alia*, sexual orientation. The Council contended that application of the law to them violated their right to expressive association under the First Amendment, but the state courts, relying on *Roberts v. United States Jaycees*, rejected the Council's claim.]

III

A

If there were no reason for a group of people to march from here to there except to reach a destination, they could make the trip without expressing any message beyond the fact of the march itself. Some people might call such a procession a parade, but it would not be much of one.... Hence, we use the word "parade" to indicate marchers who are making some sort of collective point, not just to each other but to bystanders along the way.... Parades are thus a form of expression, not just motion, and the inherent expressiveness of marching to make a point explains our cases involving protest marches....

The protected expression that inheres in a parade is not limited to its banners and songs, however, for the Constitution looks beyond written or spoken words as mediums of expression. Noting that "[s]ymbolism is a primitive but effective way of communicating ideas," *West Virginia Bd. of Ed. v. Barnette,* 319 U.S. 624, 632 (1943), our cases have recognized that the First Amendment shields such acts as saluting a flag (and refusing to do so), *id.,* at 632, 642, wearing an armband to protest a war, *Tinker v. Des Moines Independent Community School Dist.,* 393 U.S. 503, 505–506 (1969), displaying a red flag, *Stromberg v. California,* 283 U.S. 359, 369 (1931), and even "[m]arching, walking or parading" in uniforms displaying the swastika, *National Socialist Party of America v. Skokie,* 432 U.S. 43 (1977). As some of these examples show, a narrow, succinctly articulable message is not a condition of constitutional protection, which if confined to expressions conveying a "particularized message," would never reach the unquestionably shielded painting of Jackson Pollock, music of Arnold Schöenberg [sic], or Jabberwocky verse of Lewis Carroll.

Not many marches, then, are beyond the realm of expressive parades, and the South Boston celebration is not one of them.... To be sure, we agree with the state courts that in spite of excluding some applicants, the Council is rather lenient in admitting participants. But a private speaker does not forfeit constitutional protection simply by combining multifarious voices, or by failing to edit their themes to isolate an exact message as the exclusive subject matter of the speech. Nor, under our precedent, does First Amendment protection require a speaker to generate, as an original matter, each item featured in the communication. Cable operators, for example, are engaged in protected speech activities even when they only select programming originally produced by others. *Turner Broadcasting System, Inc. v. FCC,* 512 U.S. 622, 636 (1994). For that matter, the presentation of an edited compilation of speech generated by other persons is a staple of most newspapers' opinion pages, which, of course, fall squarely within the core of First Amendment security, *Miami Herald Publishing Co. v. Tornillo,* 418 U.S. 241, 258 (1974), as does even the simple selection of a paid noncommercial advertisement for inclusion in a daily paper, see *New York Times,* 376 U.S., at 265–266. The selection of contingents to make a parade is entitled to similar protection.

Respondents' participation as a unit in the parade was equally expressive. GLIB was formed for the very purpose of marching in it, as the trial court found, in order to celebrate its members' identity as openly gay, lesbian, and bisexual descendants of the Irish immigrants, to show that there are such individuals in the community, and to support the like men and women who sought to march in the New York parade.... GLIB understandably seeks to communicate its ideas as part of the existing parade, rather than staging one of its own.

B

The Massachusetts public accommodations law under which respondents brought suit has a venerable history. At common law, innkeepers, smiths, and others who "made profession of a public employment," were prohibited from refusing, without good reason, to serve a customer....

After the Civil War, the Commonwealth of Massachusetts was the first State to codify this principle to ensure access to public accommodations regardless of race.... As with many public accommodations statutes across the Nation, the legislature continued to broaden the scope of legislation, to the point that the law today prohibits discrimination on the basis of "race, color, religious creed, national origin, sex, sexual orientation..., deafness, blindness or any physical or mental disability or ancestry" in "the admission of any person to, or treatment in any place of public accommodation, resort or amusement." Provisions like these are well within the State's usual power to enact when a legislature has reason to believe that a given group is the target of discrimination, and they do not, as a general matter, violate the First or Fourteenth Amendments. See, *e.g., New York State Club Assn., Inc. v. City of New York,* 487 U.S. 1, 11–16 (1988); *Roberts v. United States Jaycees,* 468 U.S., at 624–626; *Heart of Atlanta Motel, Inc. v. United States,* 379 U.S. 241, 258–262 (1964). Nor is this statute unusual in any obvious way, since it does not, on its face, target speech or discriminate on the basis of its content, the focal point of its prohibition being rather on the act of discriminating against individuals in the provision of publicly available goods, privileges, and services on the proscribed grounds.

C

In the case before us, however, the Massachusetts law has been applied in a peculiar way. Its enforcement does not address any dispute about the participation of openly gay, lesbian, or bisexual individuals in various units admitted to the parade. Petitioners disclaim any intent to exclude homosexuals as such, and no individual member of GLIB claims to have been excluded from parading as a member of any group that the Council has approved to march. Instead, the disagreement goes to the admission of GLIB as its own parade unit carrying its own banner. Since every participating unit affects the message conveyed by the private organizers, the state courts' application of the statute produced an order essentially requiring petitioners to alter the expressive content of their parade. Although the state courts spoke of the parade as a place of public accommodation, once the expressive character of both the parade and the marching GLIB contingent is understood, it becomes apparent that the state courts' application of the statute had the effect of declaring the sponsors' speech itself to be the public accommodation. Under this approach any contingent of protected individuals with a message would have the right to participate in petitioners' speech, so that the communication produced by the private organizers would be shaped by all those protected by the law who wished to join in with some expressive demonstration of their own. But this use of the State's power violates the fundamental rule of protection under the First Amendment, that a speaker has the autonomy to choose the content of his own message.

"Since *all* speech inherently involves choices of what to say and what to leave unsaid," *Pacific Gas & Electric Co. v. Public Utilities Comm'n of Cal.*, 475 U.S. 1, 11 (1986) (plurality opinion), one important manifestation of the principle of free speech is that one who chooses to speak may also decide "what not to say," *id.*, at 16. Although the State may at times "prescribe what shall be orthodox in commercial advertising" by requiring the dissemination of "purely factual and uncontroversial information," *Zauderer v. Office of Disciplinary Counsel of Supreme Court of Ohio*, 471 U.S. 626, 651 (1985), outside that context it may not compel affirmance of a belief with which the speaker disagrees, see *Barnette*, 319 U.S., at 642. Indeed this general rule, that the speaker has the right to tailor the speech, applies not only to expressions of value, opinion, or endorsement, but equally to statements of fact the speaker would rather avoid, subject, perhaps, to the permissive law of defamation. Nor is the rule's benefit restricted to the press, being enjoyed by business corporations generally and by ordinary people engaged in unsophisticated expression as well as by professional publishers. Its point is simply the point of all speech protection, which is to shield just those choices of content that in someone's eyes are misguided, or even hurtful.

Petitioners' claim to the benefit of this principle of autonomy to control one's own speech is as sound as the South Boston parade is expressive. Rather like a composer, the Council selects the expressive units of the parade from potential participants, and though the score may not produce a particularized message, each contingent's expression in the Council's eyes comports with what merits celebration on that day. Even if this view gives the Council credit for a more considered judgment than it actively made, the Council clearly decided to exclude a message it did not like from the communication it chose to make, and that is enough to invoke its right as a private speaker to shape its expression by speaking on one subject while remaining silent on another. The message it disfavored is not difficult to identify. Although GLIB's point (like the Council's) is not wholly articulate, a contingent marching behind the organization's banner would at least bear witness to the fact that some Irish are gay, lesbian, or bisexual, and the presence of the organized marchers would suggest their view that people of their sexual orientations have as much claim to unqualified social acceptance as heterosexuals and indeed as members of parade units organized around other identifying characteristics. The parade's organizers may not believe these facts about Irish sexuality to be so, or they may object to unqualified social acceptance of gays and lesbians or have some other reason for wishing to keep GLIB's message out of the parade. But whatever the reason, it boils down to the choice of a speaker not to propound a particular point of view, and that choice is presumed to lie beyond the government's power to control.

Respondents argue that any tension between this rule and the Massachusetts law falls short of unconstitutionality, citing the most recent of our cases on the general subject of compelled access for expressive purposes, *Turner Broadcasting System, Inc. v. FCC*, 512 U.S. 622 (1994). There we reviewed regulations requiring cable operators to set aside channels for designated broadcast signals, and applied only intermediate scrutiny. Respondents contend on this authority that admission of GLIB to the parade would not threaten the core principle of speaker's autonomy because the Council, like a cable operator, is merely "a conduit" for the speech of participants in the parade "rather than itself a speaker." But this metaphor is not apt here, because GLIB's participation would likely be perceived as having resulted from the Council's customary determination about a unit admitted to the parade, that its message was worthy of presentation and quite possibly of support as well. A newspaper, similarly, "is more than a passive receptacle or conduit for news, comment, and advertising," and we have held that "[t]he choice of material ... and the decisions made as to limitations on the size and content ... and treatment of public issues ... — whether fair or unfair — constitute the exercise of editorial control and judgment" upon which the State can not intrude. *Tornillo,* 418 U.S., at 258. Indeed, in *Pacific Gas & Electric,* we invalidated coerced access to the envelope of a private utility's bill and newsletter because the utility "may be forced either to appear to agree with [the intruding leaflet] or to respond." The plurality made the further point that if "the government [were] freely able to compel ... speakers to propound political messages with which they disagree, ... protection [of a speaker's freedom] would be empty, for the government could require speakers to affirm in one breath that which they deny in the next." Thus, when dissemination of a view contrary to one's own is forced upon a speaker intimately connected with the communication advanced, the speaker's right to autonomy over the message is compromised.

In *Turner Broadcasting,* we found this problem absent in the cable context, because "[g]iven cable's long history of serving as a conduit for broadcast signals, there appears little risk that cable viewers would assume that the broadcast stations carried on a cable system convey ideas or messages endorsed by the cable operator." We stressed that the viewer is frequently apprised of the identity of the broadcaster whose signal is being received via cable and that it is "common practice for broadcasters to disclaim any identity of viewpoint between the management and the speakers who use the broadcast facility."

Parades and demonstrations, in contrast, are not understood to be so neutrally presented or selectively viewed. Unlike the programming offered on various channels by a cable network, the parade does not consist of individual, unrelated segments that happen to be transmitted together for individual selection by members of the audience. Although each parade unit generally identifies itself, each is understood to contribute something to a common theme, and accordingly there is no customary practice whereby private sponsors disavow "any identity of viewpoint" between themselves and the selected participants. Practice follows practicability here, for such disclaimers would be quite curious in a moving parade. Cf. *PruneYard Shopping Center v. Robins,* 447 U.S. 74, 87 (1980) (owner of shopping mall "can expressly disavow any connection with the message by simply posting signs in the area where the speakers or handbillers stand"). Without deciding on the precise significance of the likelihood of misattribution, it nonetheless becomes clear that in the context of an expressive parade, as with a protest march, the parade's overall message is distilled from the individual presentations along the way, and each unit's expression is perceived by spectators as part of the whole.

An additional distinction between *Turner Broadcasting* and this case points to the fundamental weakness of any attempt to justify the state-court order's limitation on the Council's autonomy as a speaker. A cable is not only a conduit for speech produced by others and selected by cable operators for transmission, but a franchised channel giving monopolistic opportunity to shut out some speakers. This power gives rise to the Government's interest in limiting monopolistic autonomy in order to allow for the survival of broadcasters who might otherwise be silenced and consequently destroyed. The Government's interest in *Turner Broadcasting* was not the alteration of speech, but the survival of speakers. In thus identifying an interest going beyond abridgment of speech itself, the defenders of the law at issue in *Turner Broadcasting* addressed the threshold requirement of any review under the Speech Clause, whatever the ultimate level of scrutiny, that a challenged restriction on speech serve a compelling, or at least important, governmental object.

In this case, of course, there is no assertion comparable to the *Turner Broadcasting* claim that some speakers will be destroyed in the absence of the challenged law. True, the size and success of petitioners' parade makes it an enviable vehicle for the dissemination of GLIB's views, but that fact, without more, would fall far short of supporting a claim that petitioners enjoy an abiding monopoly of access to spectators. Considering that GLIB presumably would have had a fair shot (under neutral criteria developed by the city) at obtaining a parade permit of its own, respondents have not shown that petitioners enjoy the capacity to "silence the voice of competing speakers," as cable operators do with respect to program providers who wish to reach subscribers. Nor has any other legitimate interest been identified in support of applying the Massachusetts statute in this way to expressive activity like the parade....

On its face, the object of the law is to ensure by statute for gays and lesbians desiring to make use of public accommodations what the old common law promised to any member of the public wanting a meal at the inn, that accepting the usual terms of service, they will not be turned away merely on the proprietor's exercise of personal preference. When the law is applied to expressive activity in the way it was done here, its apparent object is simply to require speakers to modify the content of their expression to whatever extent beneficiaries of the law choose to alter it with messages of their own. But in the absence of some further, legitimate end, this object is merely to allow exactly what the general rule of speaker's autonomy forbids.

It might, of course, have been argued that a broader objective is apparent: that the ultimate point of forbidding acts of discrimination toward certain classes is to produce a society free of the corresponding biases. Requiring access to a speaker's message would thus be not an end in itself, but a means to produce speakers free of the biases, whose expressive conduct would be at least neutral toward the particular classes, obviating any future need for correction. But if this indeed is the point of applying the state law to expressive conduct, it is a decidedly fatal objective.... Our tradition of free speech commands that a speaker who takes to the street corner to express his views in this way should be free from interference by the State based on the content of what he says. The very idea that a noncommercial speech restriction be used to produce thoughts and statements acceptable to some groups or, indeed, all people, grates on the First Amendment, for it amounts to nothing less than a proposal to limit speech in the service of orthodox expression. The Speech Clause has no more certain antithesis. While the law is free to promote all sorts of conduct in place of harmful behavior, it is not free to interfere with speech for no better reason than promoting an approved message or discouraging a disfavored one, however enlightened either purpose may strike the government.

Far from supporting GLIB, then, *Turner Broadcasting* points to the reasons why the present application of the Massachusetts law can not be sustained. So do the two other principal authorities GLIB has cited. In *PruneYard Shopping Center v. Robins,* to be sure, we sustained a state law requiring the proprietors of shopping malls to allow visitors to solicit signatures on political petitions without a showing that the shopping mall owners would otherwise prevent the beneficiaries of the law from reaching an audience. But we found in that case that the proprietors were running "a business establishment that is open to the public to come and go as they please," that the solicitations would "not likely be identified with those of the owner," and that the proprietors could "expressly disavow any connection with the message by simply posting signs in the area where the speakers or handbillers stand." 447 U.S., at 87. Also, in *Pacific Gas & Electric, supra,* at 12, we noted that *PruneYard* did not involve "any concern that access to this area might affect the shopping center owner's exercise of his own right to speak: the owner did not even allege that he objected to the content of the pamphlets...." The principle of speaker's autonomy was simply not threatened in that case.

New York State Club Assn. is also instructive by the contrast it provides. There, we turned back a facial challenge to a state antidiscrimination statute on the assumption that the expressive associational character of a dining club with over 400 members could be sufficiently attenuated to permit application of the law even to such a private organization, but we also recognized that the State did not prohibit exclusion of those whose views were at odds with positions espoused by the general club memberships. In other words, although the association provided public benefits to which a State could ensure equal access, it was also engaged in expressive activity; compelled access to the benefit, which was upheld, did not trespass on the organization's message itself. If we were to analyze this case strictly along those lines, GLIB would lose. Assuming the parade to be large enough and a source of benefits (apart from its expression) that would generally justify a mandated access provision, GLIB could nonetheless be refused admission as an expressive contingent with its own message just as readily as a private club could exclude an applicant whose manifest views were at odds with a position taken by the club's existing members....

Boy Scouts of America v. Dale
530 U.S. 640 (2000)

Chief Justice REHNQUIST delivered the opinion of the Court.

Petitioners are the Boy Scouts of America and the Monmouth Council, a division of the Boy Scouts of America (collectively, Boy Scouts). The Boy Scouts is a private, not-for-profit organization engaged in instilling its system of values in young people. The Boy Scouts asserts that homosexual conduct is inconsistent with the values it seeks to instill. Respondent is James Dale, a former Eagle Scout whose adult membership in the Boy Scouts was revoked when the Boy Scouts learned that he is an avowed homosexual and gay rights activist. The New Jersey Supreme Court held that New Jersey's public accommodations law requires that the Boy Scouts readmit Dale. This case presents the question whether applying New Jersey's public accommodations law in this way violates the Boy Scouts' First Amendment right of expressive association. We hold that it does....

II

....

The forced inclusion of an unwanted person in a group infringes the group's freedom of expressive association if the presence of that person affects in a significant way the group's ability to advocate public or private viewpoints. *New York State Club Assn., Inc. v. City of New York,* 487 U.S. 1, 13 (1988). But the freedom of expressive association, like many freedoms, is not absolute. We have held that the freedom could be overridden "by regulations adopted to serve compelling state interests, unrelated to the suppression of ideas, that cannot be achieved through means significantly less restrictive of associational freedoms." *Roberts, supra,* at 623.

To determine whether a group is protected by the First Amendment's expressive associational right, we must determine whether the group engages in "expressive association." The First Amendment's protection of expressive association is not reserved for advocacy groups. But to come within its ambit, a group must engage in some form of expression, whether it be public or private.

Because this is a First Amendment case where the ultimate conclusions of law are virtually inseparable from findings of fact, we are obligated to independently review the factual record to ensure that the state court's judgment does not unlawfully intrude on free expression....

[T]he general mission of the Boy Scouts is clear: "[T]o instill values in young people." The Boy Scouts seeks to instill these values by having its adult leaders spend time with the youth members, instructing and engaging them in activities like camping, archery, and fishing. During the time spent with the youth members, the scoutmasters and assistant scoutmasters inculcate them with the Boy Scouts' values—both expressly and by example. It seems indisputable that an association that seeks to transmit such a system of values engages in expressive activity.

Given that the Boy Scouts engages in expressive activity, we must determine whether the forced inclusion of Dale as an assistant scoutmaster would significantly affect the Boy Scouts' ability to advocate public or private viewpoints. This inquiry necessarily requires us first to explore, to a limited extent, the nature of the Boy Scouts' view of homosexuality.

The values the Boy Scouts seeks to instill are "based on" those listed in the Scout Oath and Law. The Boy Scouts explains that the Scout Oath and Law provide "a positive moral code for living; they are a list of 'do's' rather than 'don'ts.'" The Boy Scouts asserts that homosexual conduct is inconsistent with the values embodied in the Scout Oath and Law, particularly with the values represented by the terms "morally straight" and "clean."

Obviously, the Scout Oath and Law do not expressly mention sexuality or sexual orientation. And the terms "morally straight" and "clean" are by no means self-defining. Different people would attribute to those terms very different meanings. For example, some people may believe that engaging in homosexual conduct is not at odds with being "morally straight" and "clean." And others may believe that engaging in homosexual conduct is contrary to being "morally straight" and "clean." The Boy Scouts says it falls within the latter category....

The Boy Scouts asserts that it "teach[es] that homosexual conduct is not morally straight," and that it does "not want to promote homosexual conduct as a legitimate form of behavior." We accept the Boy Scouts' assertion. We need not inquire further to determine the nature of the Boy Scouts' expression with respect to homosexuality....

We must then determine whether Dale's presence as an assistant scoutmaster would significantly burden the Boy Scouts' desire to not "promote homosexual conduct as a legitimate form of behavior." As we give deference to an association's assertions regarding the nature of its expression, we must also give deference to an association's view of what would impair its expression. That is not to say that an expressive association can erect a shield against antidiscrimination laws simply by asserting that mere acceptance of a member from a particular group would impair its message. But here Dale, by his own admission, is one of a group of gay Scouts who have "become leaders in their community and are open and honest about their sexual orientation." Dale was the copresident of a gay and lesbian organization at college and remains a gay rights activist. Dale's presence in the Boy Scouts would, at the very least, force the organization to send a message, both to the youth members and the world, that the Boy Scouts accepts homosexual conduct as a legitimate form of behavior.

Hurley is illustrative on this point.... Here, we have found that the Boy Scouts believes that homosexual conduct is inconsistent with the values it seeks to instill in its youth members; it will not "promote homosexual conduct as a legitimate form of behavior." As the presence of GLIB in Boston's St. Patrick's Day parade would have interfered with the parade organizers' choice not to propound a particular point of view, the presence of Dale as an assistant scoutmaster would just as surely interfere with the Boy Scouts' choice not to propound a point of view contrary to its beliefs.

The New Jersey Supreme Court determined that the Boy Scouts' ability to disseminate its message was not significantly affected by the forced inclusion of Dale as an assistant scoutmaster because of the following findings:

> "Boy Scout members do not associate for the purpose of disseminating the belief that homosexuality is immoral; Boy Scouts discourages its leaders from disseminating *any* views on sexual issues; and Boy Scouts includes sponsors and members who subscribe to different views in respect of homosexuality."

We disagree with the New Jersey Supreme Court's conclusion drawn from these findings.

First, associations do not have to associate for the "purpose" of disseminating a certain message in order to be entitled to the protections of the First Amendment. An association must merely engage in expressive activity that could be impaired in order to be entitled to protection. For example, the purpose of the St. Patrick's Day parade in *Hurley* was not to espouse any views about sexual orientation, but we held that the parade organizers had a right to exclude certain participants nonetheless.

Second, even if the Boy Scouts discourages Scout leaders from disseminating views on sexual issues—a fact that the Boy Scouts disputes with contrary evidence—the First Amendment protects the Boy Scouts' method of expression. If the Boy Scouts wishes Scout leaders to avoid questions of sexuality and teach only by example, this fact does not negate the sincerity of its belief discussed above.

Third, the First Amendment simply does not require that every member of a group agree on every issue in order for the group's policy to be "expressive association." The Boy Scouts takes an official position with respect to homosexual conduct, and that is sufficient for First Amendment purposes. In this same vein, Dale makes much of the claim that the Boy Scouts does not revoke the membership of heterosexual Scout leaders that openly disagree with the Boy Scouts' policy on sexual orientation. But if this is true, it is irrelevant. The presence of an avowed homosexual and gay rights activist in an assistant scoutmaster's uniform sends a distinctly different message from the presence of a heterosexual assistant scoutmaster who is on record as disagreeing with Boy Scouts policy. The Boy Scouts has a First Amendment right to choose to send one message but not the other. The fact that the organization does not trumpet its views from the housetops, or that it tolerates dissent within its ranks, does not mean that its views receive no First Amendment protection.

Having determined that the Boy Scouts is an expressive association and that the forced inclusion of Dale would significantly affect its expression, we inquire whether the application of New Jersey's public accommodations law to require that the Boy Scouts accept Dale as an assistant scoutmaster runs afoul of the Scouts' freedom of expressive association. We conclude that it does.

State public accommodations laws were originally enacted to prevent discrimination in traditional places of public accommodation—like inns and trains. Over time, the public accommodations laws have expanded to cover more places.[2] New Jersey's statutory de-

---

2. Public accommodations laws have also broadened in scope to cover more groups; they have expanded beyond those groups that have been given heightened equal protection scrutiny under our cases. See *Romer*, 517 U.S., at 629. Some municipal ordinances have even expanded to cover criteria

finition of "'[a] place of public accommodation'" is extremely broad. The term is said to "include, but not be limited to," a list of over 50 types of places. Many on the list are what one would expect to be places where the public is invited. For example, the statute includes as places of public accommodation taverns, restaurants, retail shops, and public libraries. But the statute also includes places that often may not carry with them open invitations to the public, like summer camps and roof gardens. In this case, the New Jersey Supreme Court went a step further and applied its public accommodations law to a private entity without even attempting to tie the term "place" to a physical location. As the definition of "public accommodation" has expanded from clearly commercial entities, such as restaurants, bars, and hotels, to membership organizations such as the Boy Scouts, the potential for conflict between state public accommodations laws and the First Amendment rights of organizations has increased.

We recognized in cases such as *Roberts* and *Duarte* that States have a compelling interest in eliminating discrimination against women in public accommodations. But in each of these cases we went on to conclude that the enforcement of these statutes would not materially interfere with the ideas that the organization sought to express. In *Roberts,* we said "[i]ndeed, the Jaycees has failed to demonstrate . . . any serious burdens on the male members' freedom of expressive association." In *Duarte,* we said:

> "[I]mpediments to the exercise of one's right to choose one's associates can violate the right of association protected by the First Amendment. In this case, however, the evidence fails to demonstrate that admitting women to Rotary Clubs will affect in any significant way the existing members' ability to carry out their various purposes." 481 U.S., at 548.

We thereupon concluded in each of these cases that the organizations' First Amendment rights were not violated by the application of the States' public accommodations laws.

In *Hurley,* we said that public accommodations laws "are well within the State's usual power to enact when a legislature has reason to believe that a given group is the target of discrimination, and they do not, as a general matter, violate the First or Fourteenth Amendments." But we went on to note that in that case "the Massachusetts [public accommodations] law has been applied in a peculiar way" because "any contingent of protected individuals with a message would have the right to participate in petitioners' speech, so that the communication produced by the private organizers would be shaped by all those protected by the law who wished to join in with some expressive demonstration of their own." And in the associational freedom cases such as *Roberts, Duarte,* and *New York State Club Assn.,* after finding a compelling state interest, the Court went on to examine whether or not the application of the state law would impose any "serious burden" on the organization's rights of expressive association. So in these cases, the associational interest in freedom of expression has been set on one side of the scale, and the State's interest on the other. . . .

In *Hurley,* we applied traditional First Amendment analysis to hold that the application of the Massachusetts public accommodations law to a parade violated the First Amendment rights of the parade organizers. Although we did not explicitly deem the parade in *Hurley* an expressive association, the analysis we applied there is similar to the analysis we apply here. We have already concluded that a state requirement that the Boy Scouts retain Dale as an assistant scoutmaster would significantly burden the organiza-

---

such as prior criminal record, prior psychiatric treatment, military status, personal appearance, source of income, place of residence, and political ideology.

tion's right to oppose or disfavor homosexual conduct. The state interests embodied in New Jersey's public accommodations law do not justify such a severe intrusion on the Boy Scouts' rights to freedom of expressive association. That being the case, we hold that the First Amendment prohibits the State from imposing such a requirement through the application of its public accommodations law....

[The dissenting opinions of Justices Stevens and Souter are omitted.]

Notes and Questions

1. In *Rumsfeld v. Forum for Academic and Institutional Rights, Inc. ("FAIR")*, 547 U.S. 47 (2006), a group of law schools and law faculties sought to invoke *Dale* as a way to challenge the constitutionality of the Solomon Amendment, which conditioned a university's receipt of certain federal funds on all units of campus providing access to military recruiters. Because Don't Ask, Don't Tell was still in force at the time, the law schools objected to the military recruiting law students, as it was contrary to their anti-discrimination policies. The Court, however, rejected the law schools' expressive association claim:

> FAIR argues that the Solomon Amendment violates law schools' freedom of expressive association. According to FAIR, law schools' ability to express their message that discrimination on the basis of sexual orientation is wrong is significantly affected by the presence of military recruiters on campus and the schools' obligation to assist them....
>
> In *Dale,* we held that the Boy Scouts' freedom of expressive association was violated by New Jersey's public accommodations law, which required the organization to accept a homosexual as a scoutmaster. After determining that the Boy Scouts was an expressive association, that "the forced inclusion of Dale would significantly affect its expression," and that the State's interests did not justify this intrusion, we concluded that the Boy Scouts' First Amendment rights were violated.
>
> The Solomon Amendment, however, does not similarly affect a law school's associational rights. To comply with the statute, law schools must allow military recruiters on campus and assist them in whatever way the school chooses to assist other employers. Law schools therefore "associate" with military recruiters in the sense that they interact with them. But recruiters are not part of the law school. Recruiters are, by definition, outsiders who come onto campus for the limited purpose of trying to hire students—not to become members of the school's expressive association. This distinction is critical. Unlike the public accommodations law in *Dale,* the Solomon Amendment does not force a law school "'to accept members it does not desire.'" [*Dale*, 530 U.S.] at 648 (quoting *Roberts, supra,* at 623). The law schools *say* that allowing military recruiters equal access impairs their own expression by requiring them to associate with the recruiters, but just as saying conduct is undertaken for expressive purposes cannot make it symbolic speech, so too a speaker cannot "erect a shield" against laws requiring access "simply by asserting" that mere association "would impair its message." 530 U.S., at 653.
>
> FAIR correctly notes that the freedom of expressive association protects more than just a group's membership decisions. For example, we have held laws unconstitutional that require disclosure of membership lists for groups seeking anonymity, *Brown v. Socialist Workers '74 Campaign Comm. (Ohio),* 459 U.S. 87, 101–102 (1982), or impose penalties or withhold benefits based on membership

in a disfavored group, *Healy v. James*, 408 U.S. 169, 180–184 (1972). Although these laws did not directly interfere with an organization's composition, they made group membership less attractive, raising the same First Amendment concerns about affecting the group's ability to express its message.

The Solomon Amendment has no similar effect on a law school's associational rights. Students and faculty are free to associate to voice their disapproval of the military's message; nothing about the statute affects the composition of the group by making group membership less desirable. The Solomon Amendment therefore does not violate a law school's First Amendment rights. A military recruiter's mere presence on campus does not violate a law school's right to associate, regardless of how repugnant the law school considers the recruiter's message.

Id. at 68–70.

2. *Hurley* cites *Roberts* and in turn is cited by *Dale*. Are all three cases dealing with the same type of First Amendment claim? On the one hand, the cross-citation suggests that they are, but subsequent cases by the U.S. Supreme Court suggest that they might in fact be dealing with two distinct types of claims, with *Roberts* and *Dale* being expressive association cases and *Hurley* being part of the Court's compelled-speech line of cases, which includes *Pacific Gas & Electric Co. v. Public Utility Commission of California*, 475 U.S. 1 (1986), and *Miami Herald Publishing Co. v. Tornillo*, 418 U.S. 241 (1974), both of which were cited and discussed in *Hurley*.

In *Rumsfeld* (discussed in the previous note), the U.S. Supreme Court addressed the claim that the Solomon Amendment violated the First Amendment because it was a form of compelled speech, in that the schools were required to provide the same services to military recruiters that they provided to other recruiters, which included the "speech" of sending out emails or posting notices on the employer's behalf:

> Our compelled-speech cases are not limited to the situation in which an individual must personally speak the government's message. We have also in a number of instances limited the government's ability to force one speaker to host or accommodate another speaker's message. See *Hurley v. Irish-American Gay, Lesbian and Bisexual Group of Boston, Inc.*, 515 U.S. 557, 566 (1995) (state law cannot require a parade to include a group whose message the parade's organizer does not wish to send); *Pacific Gas & Elec. Co. v. Public Util. Comm'n of Cal.*, 475 U.S. 1, 20–21 (1986) (plurality opinion); accord, *id.*, at 25 (Marshall, J., concurring in judgment) (state agency cannot require a utility company to include a third-party newsletter in its billing envelope); *Miami Herald Publishing Co. v. Tornillo*, 418 U.S. 241, 258 (1974) (right-of-reply statute violates editors' right to determine the content of their newspapers). Relying on these precedents, the Third Circuit concluded that the Solomon Amendment unconstitutionally compels law schools to accommodate the military's message "[b]y requiring schools to include military recruiters in the interviews and recruiting receptions the schools arrange."

The compelled-speech violation in each of our prior cases, however, resulted from the fact that the complaining speaker's own message was affected by the speech it was forced to accommodate. The expressive nature of a parade was central to our holding in *Hurley*. We concluded that because "every participating unit affects the message conveyed by the [parade's] private organizers," a law dictating that a particular group must be included in the parade "alter[s] the expressive content of th[e] parade." As a result, we held that the State's public accommodation law, as applied to a private parade, "violates the fundamental rule of protection under the First Amendment, that a speaker has the autonomy to choose the content of his own message."

The compelled-speech violations in *Tornillo* and *Pacific Gas* also resulted from interference with a speaker's desired message. In *Tornillo*, we recognized that "the compelled printing of a reply ... tak[es] up space that could be devoted to other material the newspaper may have preferred to print," and therefore concluded that this right-of-reply statute infringed the newspaper editors' freedom of speech by altering the message the paper wished to express. The same is true in *Pacific Gas*. There, the utility company regularly included its newsletter, which we concluded was protected speech, in its billing envelope. Thus, when the state agency ordered the utility to send a third-party newsletter four times a year, it interfered with the utility's ability to communicate its own message in its newsletter. A plurality of the Court likened this to the situation in *Tornillo* and held that the forced inclusion of the other newsletter interfered with the utility's own message.

In this case, accommodating the military's message does not affect the law schools' speech, because the schools are not speaking when they host interviews and recruiting receptions. Unlike a parade organizer's choice of parade contingents, a law school's decision to allow recruiters on campus is not inherently expressive. Law schools facilitate recruiting to assist their students in obtaining jobs. A law school's recruiting services lack the expressive quality of a parade, a newsletter, or the editorial page of a newspaper; its accommodation of a military recruiter's message is not compelled speech because the accommodation does not sufficiently interfere with any message of the school.

The schools respond that if they treat military and nonmilitary recruiters alike in order to comply with the Solomon Amendment, they could be viewed as sending the message that they see nothing wrong with the military's policies, when they do. We rejected a similar argument in *PruneYard Shopping Center v. Robins*, 447 U.S. 74 (1980). In that case, we upheld a state law requiring a shopping center owner to allow certain expressive activities by others on its property. We explained that there was little likelihood that the views of those engaging in the expressive activities would be identified with the owner, who remained free to disassociate himself from those views and who was "not ... being compelled to affirm [a] belief in any governmentally prescribed position or view."

The same is true here. Nothing about recruiting suggests that law schools agree with any speech by recruiters, and nothing in the Solomon Amendment restricts what the law schools may say about the military's policies....

Rumsfeld v. Forum for Academic & Institutional Rights, Inc., 547 U.S. 47, 63–65 (2006). *See also Christian Legal Soc'y Chapter of the Univ. of Cal, Hastings Coll. of the Law v. Martinez*, 130 S. Ct. 2971, 2986 n.14 (2010) (raising the question whether "*Hurley* is best conceptualized as a speech or association case (or both)").

3. In *Christian Legal Society Chapter of the University of California, Hastings College of the Law v. Martinez*, 130 S. Ct. 2971 (2010), the U.S. Supreme Court upheld a public law school's rule conditioning official recognition of student groups on their compliance with a non-discrimination policy that required groups to accept all students. The Christian Legal Society sought an exemption from the policy so that it could exclude those who engaged in "unrepentant homosexual conduct" as well as those who held religious convictions inconsistent with those of the group, but their request was rejected. The group challenged

the policy, invoking the right to expressive association recognized in cases such as *Dale* and *Hurley*. However, in determining the appropriate level of scrutiny to apply to the law, the Court invoked a separate line of cases, its forum analysis line of cases, which the Court uses "to determine when a governmental entity, in regulating property in its charge, may place limitations on speech." *Id.* at 2984. It summarized that line of cases as follows:

> In conducting forum analysis, our decisions have sorted government property into three categories. First, in traditional public forums, such as public streets and parks, "any restriction based on the content of … speech must satisfy strict scrutiny, that is, the restriction must be narrowly tailored to serve a compelling government interest." *Pleasant Grove City v. Summum*, 129 S.Ct. 1125, 1132 (2009). Second, governmental entities create designated public forums when "government property that has not traditionally been regarded as a public forum is intentionally opened up for that purpose"; speech restrictions in such a forum "are subject to the same strict scrutiny as restrictions in a traditional public forum." *Id.* at 1127. Third, governmental entities establish limited public forums by opening property "limited to use by certain groups or dedicated solely to the discussion of certain subjects." *Ibid.* As noted in text, "[i]n such a forum, a governmental entity may impose restrictions on speech that are reasonable and viewpoint-neutral."

Id. at 2984 n.11. After concluding that the law school, through its official recognition program, had established a limited public forum, the Court concluded that the school's policy satisfied the less onerous requirement that the restrictions be "reasonable and viewpoint-neutral." In so doing, it distinguished cases such as *Hurley*, which "involved the application of a statewide public-accommodations law to the most traditional of public forums: the street," *id.* at 2986 n.14. Moreover, it distinguished *Dale* and *Roberts*, which involved regulations that *compelled* a group to accept members with no choice to opt out, from the case before it, which left the group free to exclude members for any reason by foregoing the benefits of official recognition. *Id.* at 2986.

4. Reconsider the facts of Problem 6-A. If a gay rights organization obtains a permit to hold a gay pride festival in a park or a neighborhood, can the local government exclude speakers and protesters with an anti-gay message from circulating within the boundaries of the festival area, on the theory that participation by such individuals interferes with the gay rights organization's right to expressive association in the same way that GLIB interfered with the right of the South Boston Allied War Veterans Council? Cases addressing this issue have distinguished *Hurley* in this context, and recognized the First Amendment rights of the protesters to be present:

> *Hurley* is as distinguishable from the situation presented here as was the decision in *Turner* from *Hurley*. As the *Hurley* Court noted, Turner upheld regulations that required cable operators to set aside channels for designated broadcast signals because cable had long served as a conduit for broadcast signals, and there was little risk that cable viewers would assume that the cable operator endorsed the ideas or messages carried on the broadcast stations.

> The situation in *Hurley* would be comparable to that presented here if Repent America had sought a stage area or a vendor booth, because such participation in Out-Fest "would likely be perceived as having resulted from [Philly Pride's] customary determination about a unit admitted to [participate in OutFest's activities], that its message was worthy of presentation and quite possibly of support as well." However, that is not the issue in this case. Instead, the question presented is whether *Hurley* authorizes exclusion of Appellants from attending OutFest, a private-

sponsored event in a public forum that was free and open to the general public. We hold that it does not.

Although the *Hurley* parade took place on a public thoroughfare, nothing in the opinion suggests that GLIB could be excluded from the streets after the parade had passed. To the contrary, the Court noted that GLIB was free to seek its own parade permit. There is no basis to read *Hurley* as circumscribing the long line of authority upholding free access by the general public to street festivals and other events held in traditional public fora.

In *Hague v. C.I.O.*, 307 U.S. 496, 515 (1939), Justice Owen J. Roberts wrote, streets and parks "have immemorially been held in trust for the use of the public and, time out of mind, have been used for purposes of assembly, communicating thoughts between citizens, and discussing public questions." That principle has been reiterated in case after case, and neither the grant of a permit nor anything in *Hurley* alters that still viable principle....

... OutFest took place in the streets and sidewalks of Philadelphia, an undisputed quintessential public forum. The issuance of a permit to use this public forum does not transform its status as a public forum. "In places which by long tradition or by government fiat have been devoted to assembly and debate, the rights of the State to limit expressive activity are sharply circumscribed." *Perry*, 460 U.S. at 45. In such traditional public fora the state may not prohibit all communicative activity. *Perry*, 460 U.S. at 45. Indeed, "[s]treets, sidewalks, parks, and other similar public places are so historically associated with the exercise of First Amendment rights that access to them for the purpose of exercising such rights cannot constitutionally be denied broadly and absolutely." *Carey v. Brown*, 447 U.S. 455, 460 (1980).

Startzell v. City of Phila., 533 F.3d 183, 194–96 (3d Cir. 2008). *Accord Gay-Lesbian-Bisexual-Transgender Pride/Twin Cities v. Minneapolis Park & Recreation Bd.*, 721 F. Supp. 2d 866 (D. Minn. 2010).

5. How persuasive is the distinction between *Roberts* and *Dale*? In *Roberts*, the Court asserts that the state's interest is compelling, and that application of the state antidiscrimination law will not impair the ability of the group to disseminate its preferred views. In contrast, the *Dale* Court accepts at face value the Boy Scouts' assertion that admitting Dale will impair their ability to disseminate their preferred views, and clearly does not view the state's interest as sufficiently compelling. Does the difference turn on the characteristic at issue (sex versus sexual orientation)? Stated somewhat differently, in deciding that the state's interest in eradicating sex discrimination in *Roberts* is sufficiently compelling, while effectively deciding that the state's interest in eradicating sexual orientation discrimination is not sufficiently compelling in *Dale*, does the Court have in the back of its mind the distinction between sex and sexual orientation for equal protection purposes?

6. In deciding that Dale's inclusion in the Boy Scouts was inconsistent with the organization's expressive association rights, was the Court moved merely by the fact that Dale was gay? That he was openly gay? Or that—in the words of the Court—he was "an avowed homosexual and gay rights activist"? What does the Court mean by this description? In this regard, consider the Court's summary of Dale's pre-discharge conduct:

> After arriving at Rutgers, Dale first acknowledged to himself and others that he is gay. He quickly became involved with, and eventually became the copresident of, the Rutgers University Lesbian/Gay Alliance. In 1990, Dale attended a seminar addressing the psychological and health needs of lesbian and gay teenagers.

A newspaper covering the event interviewed Dale about his advocacy of homosexual teenagers' need for gay role models. In early July 1990, the newspaper published the interview and Dale's photograph over a caption identifying him as the copresident of the Lesbian/Gay Alliance.

Boy Scouts of Am. v. Dale, 530 U.S. 640 (2000).

7. What would the consequences have been had *Dale* been decided differently? In this regard, consider whether a *pro*-gay rights organization should be required to admit those with visibly anti-gay views, or whether a *pro*-abortion rights organization should be required to admit those who are visibly opposed to abortion.

8. Soon after the *Dale* decision came down, school districts across the United States who opposed the Boy Scouts' discriminatory policy responded by denying the Boy Scouts access to school facilities. Congress responded by enacting the Boy Scouts of America Equal Access Act, 20 U.S.C. § 7905. The Act, which is analogous to the Solomon Amendment, conditions the receipt of federal funds to school districts on their agreement to grant the Boy Scouts of America "equal access" to school facilities.

9. For a case based on the facts of Problem 6-C, *see Apilado v. N. Am. Gay Amateur Athletic Alliance*, 2011 WL 5563206 (W.D. Wash. 2011); *Apilado v. N. Am. Gay Amateur Athletic Alliance*, 792 F. Supp. 2d 1151 (W.D. Wash. 2011).

10. In recent years, another common First Amendment defense raised to the application of anti-discrimination statutes is a "free exercise" claim that such statutes—to the extent they require someone to do something that conflicts with their religious beliefs—are unconstitutional. Could a medical provider whose religious beliefs teach that homosexuality is immoral refuse to provide assisted reproductive services to a gay or lesbian individual or couple despite a state law requiring non-discrimination on the basis of, *inter alia*, sexual orientation, in the provision of public accommodations or services?

The U.S. Supreme Court has held that the First Amendment right to free exercise of religion does not relieve individuals of the obligation to comply with a law that is neutral and of general applicability, even if it has the incidental effect of burdening a particular religious practice. *See Church of the Lukumi Babalu Aye, Inc. v. City of Hialeah*, 508 U.S. 520, 531 (1993); *Emp. Div., Dep't of Human Res. of Or. v. Smith*, 494 U.S. 872, 879 (1990). In *North Coast Women's Care Medical Group, Inc. v. San Diego County Superior Court*, 189 P.3d 959 (Cal. 2008), the California Supreme Court relied on these precedents to conclude that a medical provider engaged in the practice of assisted reproduction was obligated to comply with the state's anti-discrimination law, and thus could not refuse to provide such services to a patient because she was a lesbian.

D. Government Employment

As indicated in the background section of this chapter, when the government seeks to regulate speech by members of the general public, the Court's precedents have, as a general rule, imposed significant hurdles for the government to overcome.

However, the Court has acknowledged that the government has more leeway where it seeks to regulate, not speech by the public generally, but instead that of its employees. In *Pickering v. Board of Education*, 391 U.S. 563 (1968), the U.S. Supreme Court, while emphasizing that the government cannot condition public employment on relinquishment of one's First Amendment freedoms, nevertheless acknowledged the difference between government as mere regulator and government as employer in the First Amendment context:

> At the same time it cannot be gainsaid that the State has interests as an employer in regulating the speech of its employees that differ significantly from those it possesses in connection with regulation of the speech of the citizenry in general. The problem in any case is to arrive at a balance between the interests of the [employee], as a citizen, in commenting upon matters of public concern and the interest of the State, as an employer, in promoting the efficiency of the public services it performs through its employees.

Id. at 568. More recently, the Court has clarified *Pickering*'s meaning:

> *Pickering* and the cases decided in its wake identify two inquiries to guide interpretation of the constitutional protections accorded to public employee speech. The first requires determining whether the employee spoke as a citizen on a matter of public concern. If the answer is no, the employee has no First Amendment cause of action based on his or her employer's reaction to the speech. If the answer is yes, then the possibility of a First Amendment claim arises. The question becomes whether the relevant government entity had an adequate justification for treating the employee differently from any other member of the general public. This consideration reflects the importance of the relationship between the speaker's expressions and employment. A government entity has broader discretion to restrict speech when it acts in its role as employer, but the restrictions it imposes must be directed at speech that has some potential to affect the entity's operations....

> When a citizen enters government service, the citizen by necessity must accept certain limitations on his or her freedom. Government employers, like private employers, need a significant degree of control over their employees' words and actions; without it, there would be little chance for the efficient provision of public services. Public employees, moreover, often occupy trusted positions in society. When they speak out, they can express views that contravene governmental policies or impair the proper performance of governmental functions.

> At the same time, the Court has recognized that a citizen who works for the government is nonetheless a citizen. The First Amendment limits the ability of a public employer to leverage the employment relationship to restrict, incidentally or intentionally, the liberties employees enjoy in their capacities as private citizens. So long as employees are speaking as citizens about matters of public concern, they must face only those speech restrictions that are necessary for their employers to operate efficiently and effectively.

Garcetti v. Ceballos, 547 U.S. 410, 418–19 (2006). In *Garcetti*, the Court went on to hold that the speech by the government employee in that case—a deputy district attorney who alleged wrongdoing by a deputy sheriff in a memo to his supervisor—was not entitled to First Amendment protection because he was not speaking "as a citizen" when he wrote it:

> We hold that when public employees make statements pursuant to their official duties, the employees are not speaking as citizens for First Amendment purposes, and the Constitution does not insulate their communications from employer discipline.

> Ceballos wrote his disposition memo because that is part of what he, as a calendar deputy, was employed to do. It is immaterial whether he experienced some per-

sonal gratification from writing the memo; his First Amendment rights do not depend on his job satisfaction. The significant point is that the memo was written pursuant to Ceballos' official duties. Restricting speech that owes its existence to a public employee's professional responsibilities does not infringe any liberties the employee might have enjoyed as a private citizen. It simply reflects the exercise of employer control over what the employer itself has commissioned or created. Contrast, for example, the expressions made by the speaker in *Pickering*, whose letter to the newspaper had no official significance and bore similarities to letters submitted by numerous citizens every day....

This result is consistent with our precedents' attention to the potential societal value of employee speech. Refusing to recognize First Amendment claims based on government employees' work product does not prevent them from participating in public debate. The employees retain the prospect of constitutional protection for their contributions to the civic discourse. This prospect of protection, however, does not invest them with a right to perform their jobs however they see fit.

Id. at 421–22.

The cases that follow consider the application of *Pickering* balancing in the context of employee speech that is in some way related to sexual orientation or gender identity. In some of the cases, the government seeks to suppress pro-GLBT speech, while in others, it seeks to suppress anti-GLBT speech.

Problem 6-D: To Whom It May Concern ...

Tom, an Assistant Attorney General in the State of New Condon, is a gay man in a same-sex relationship who strongly favors same-sex marriage.

When the legislature in New Condon decides to take up a bill legalizing same-sex marriage, Tom decides to write a letter to the editor in support of passage. Among other things, he writes that the current law banning same-sex marriage is clearly unconstitutional under both the federal and state constitutions.

When New Condon's Attorney General learns of the letter's publication, he fires Tom.

Tom files a lawsuit, contending that being fired for writing the letter violates his First Amendment rights.

How should the court rule on Tom's claim? Of what significance, if any, would it be that (a) Tom did or did not include his job title in the letter to the editor; (b) Tom did or did not work in the division of the Attorney General's office responsible for defending the constitutionality of the state's marriage laws; (c) Tom was not an Assistant Attorney General, but instead a secretary in the Attorney General's office?

Shahar v. Bowers
114 F.3d 1097 (11th Cir. 1997) (en banc)

EDMONDSON, Circuit Judge:

In this government-employment case, Plaintiff-Appellant contends that the Attorney General of the State of Georgia violated her federal constitutional rights by revoking an employment offer because of her purported "marriage"[1] to another woman. The district court concluded that Plaintiff's rights had not been violated. We affirm.

Given the culture and traditions of the Nation, considerable doubt exists that Plaintiff has a constitutionally protected federal right to be "married" to another woman: the question about the right of intimate association. Given especially that Plaintiff's religion requires a woman neither to "marry" another female — even in the case of lesbian couples — nor to marry at all, considerable doubt also exists that she has a constitutionally protected federal right to be "married" to another woman to engage in her religion: the question about the right of expressive association.

Because even a favorable decision on these constitutional questions would entitle Plaintiff to no relief in this case, powerful considerations of judicial restraint call upon us not to decide these constitutional issues. So, today we do stop short of making a final decision about such claimed rights. Instead, we assume (for the sake of argument only) that Plaintiff has these rights; but we conclude that the Attorney General's act — as an employer — was still lawful.

I.

The facts are not much in dispute; but we accept Plaintiff's view when there is uncertainty. Plaintiff Robin Joy Shahar is a woman who has "married" another woman in a ceremony performed by a rabbi within the Reconstructionist Movement of Judaism. According to Shahar, though the State of Georgia does not recognize her "marriage" and she does not claim that the "marriage" has legal effect, she and her partner consider themselves to be "married."

Since August 1981, Defendant-Appellee Michael J. Bowers has been the Attorney General of the State of Georgia, a statewide elective office. He has been elected to the office four times. As the Attorney General, Bowers is the chief legal officer of the State of Georgia and head of the Georgia Department of Law (the "Department"). His responsibilities include enforcing the laws of the State by acting as a prosecutor in certain criminal actions; conducting investigations; representing Georgia, its agencies and officials in all civil litigation (including habeas corpus matters); and providing legal advice (including advice on the proper interpretation of Georgia law) to Georgia's executive branch.

While a law student, Shahar spent the summer of 1990 as a law clerk with the Department. In September 1990, the Attorney General offered Shahar the position of Staff Attorney when she graduated from law school. Shahar accepted the offer and was scheduled to begin work in September 1991.

In the summer of 1990, Shahar began making plans for her "wedding." Her rabbi announced the expected "wedding" to the congregation at Shahar's synagogue in Atlanta. Shahar and her partner invited approximately 250 people, including two Department employees, to the "wedding." The written invitations characterized the ceremony as a "Jewish, lesbian-feminist, out-door wedding." The ceremony took place in a public park in South Carolina in June 1991.

In November 1990, Shahar filled out the required application for a Staff Attorney position. In response to the question on "marital status," Shahar indicated that she was "engaged." She altered "spouse's name" to read "future spouse's name" and filled in her

---

1. For clarity's sake, we use the words "marriage" and "wedding" (in quotation marks) to refer to Shahar's relationship with her partner; we use the word marriage (absent quotation marks) to indicate legally recognized heterosexual marriage.

partner's name: "Francine M. Greenfield." In response to the question "Do any of your relatives work for the State of Georgia?" she filled in the name of her partner as follows: "Francine Greenfield, future spouse."

Sometime in the spring of 1991, Shahar and her partner were working on their "wedding" invitations at an Atlanta restaurant. While there, they ran into Elizabeth Rowe and Susan Rutherford. Rowe was employed by the Department as a paralegal, Rutherford as an attorney. Rowe was invited to, and did attend, Shahar's ceremony. The four women had a brief conversation, which included some discussion of the "wedding" preparations.

In June 1991, Shahar told Deputy Attorney General Robert Coleman that she was getting married at the end of July, changing her last name, taking a trip to Greece and, accordingly, would not be starting work with the Department until mid-to-late September. At this point, Shahar did not say that she was "marrying" another woman. Senior Assistant Attorney General Jeffrey Milsteen, who had been co-chair of the summer clerk committee, was in Coleman's office at the time and heard Coleman congratulate Shahar. Milsteen later mentioned to Rutherford that Shahar was getting married. Rutherford then told Milsteen that Shahar was planning on "marrying" another woman. This revelation caused a stir.

Senior aides to the Attorney General became concerned about what they viewed as potential problems in the office resulting from the Department's employment of a Staff Attorney who purported to be part of a same-sex "marriage." As the Attorney General was out of the office that week, the five aides held several meetings among themselves to discuss the situation.

Upon the Attorney General's return to the office, he was informed of the situation. He held discussions with the senior aides, as well as a few other lawyers within the Department. After much discussion, the Attorney General decided, with the advice of his senior lawyers, to withdraw Shahar's job offer. In July 1991, he did so in writing. The pertinent letter stated that the withdrawal of Shahar's offer:

> has become necessary in light of information which has only recently come to my attention relating to a purported marriage between you and another woman. As chief legal officer of this state, inaction on my part would constitute tacit approval of this purported marriage and jeopardize the proper functioning of this office.

The Attorney General and his staff have also indicated (in depositions taken in the present action) that, after weighing the facts and relevant considerations, they concluded that Shahar's same-sex "marriage" would create the appearance of conflicting interpretations of Georgia law and affect public credibility about the Department's interpretations; interfere with the Department's ability to handle controversial matters; interfere with the Department's ability to enforce Georgia's sodomy law; and, in general, create difficulties maintaining the supportive working relationship among the office lawyers that is necessary for the proper functioning of the Department. Also, following her decision to participate in a controversial same-sex "wedding," the Attorney General and his staff had serious doubts about the quality of Shahar's judgment in general.

Shahar brought the present action against the Attorney General, individually and in his official capacity, seeking both damages and injunctive relief (including "reinstatement")....

II.

Even when we assume, for argument's sake, that either the right to intimate association or the right to expressive association or both are present, we know they are not absolute. Georgia and its elected Attorney General also have rights and duties which must be taken into account, especially where (as here) the State is acting as employer. We also know that because the government's role as employer is different from its role as sovereign, we review its acts differently in the different contexts. In reviewing Shahar's claim, we stress that this case is about the government acting as employer.

A.

Shahar argues that we must review the withdrawal of her job offer under strict scrutiny....

In *Board of Comm'rs, Wabaunsee Cty. v. Umbehr,* 518 U.S. 668 (1996), the Court held that government contractors are protected from termination or failure to renew their contracts for exercising their free speech rights and that the *Pickering* balancing test is the appropriate standard for determining whether a First Amendment violation has occurred. The Court specifically rejected the contractor's argument that "on proof of viewpoint-based retaliation for contractors' political speech, the government should be required to justify its actions as narrowly tailored to serve a compelling state interest," and wrote as follows:

> [Contractor] is correct that if the Board had exercised sovereign power against him as a citizen in response to his political speech, it would be required to demonstrate that its action was narrowly tailored to serve a compelling governmental interest. But in this case, as in government employment cases, the Board exercised contractual power, and its interests as a public service provider, including its interest in being free from intensive judicial supervision of its daily management functions, are potentially indicated. Deference is therefore due to the government's reasonable assessment of its interest *as contractor.*

We conclude that the appropriate test for evaluating the constitutional implications of the State of Georgia's decision — as an employer — to withdraw Shahar's job offer based on her "marriage" is the same test as the test for evaluating the constitutional implications of a government employer's decision based on an employee's exercise of her right to free speech, that is, the *Pickering* balancing test.

B.

We have previously pointed out that government employees who have access to their employer's confidences or who act as spokespersons for their employers, as well as those employees with some policy-making role, are in a special class of employees and might seldom prevail under the First Amendment in keeping their jobs when they conflict with their employers.

Put differently, the government employer's interest in staffing its offices with persons the employer fully trusts is given great weight when the pertinent employee helps make policy, handles confidential information or must speak or act — for others to see — on the employer's behalf. Staff Attorneys inherently do (or must be ready to do) important things, which require the capacity to exercise good sense and discretion (as the Attorney General, using his considered judgment, defines those qualities): advise about policy; have access to confidential information (for example, litigation strategies); speak, write and act on behalf of the Attorney General and for the State.

In a case such as this one, the employee faces a difficult situation. In fact, we know of no federal appellate decision in which a subordinate prosecutor, state's attorney or like lawyer has prevailed in keeping his job over the chief lawyer's objection. We conclude that the Attorney General — who is an elected official with great duties and with no job security except that which might come from his office's performing well — may properly limit the lawyers on his professional staff to persons in whom he has trust.

As both parties acknowledge, this case arises against the backdrop of an ongoing controversy in Georgia about homosexual sodomy, homosexual marriages, and other related issues, including a sodomy prosecution—in which the Attorney General's staff was engaged—resulting in the well-known Supreme Court decision in *Bowers v. Hardwick,* 478 U.S. 186, 190–92 (1986) (criminal prosecution of homosexual sodomy does not violate substantive due process).[16] When the Attorney General viewed Shahar's decision to "wed" openly—complete with changing her name—another woman (in a large "wedding") against this background of ongoing controversy, he saw her acts as having a realistic likelihood to affect her (and, therefore, the Department's) credibility, to interfere with the Department's ability to handle certain kinds of controversial matters (such as claims to same-sex marriage licenses, homosexual parental rights, employee benefits, insurance coverage of "domestic partners"), to interfere with the Department's efforts to enforce Georgia's laws against homosexual sodomy,[17] and to create other difficulties within the Department which would be likely to harm the public perception of the Department.

In addition, because of Shahar's decision to participate in such a controversial same-sex "wedding" and "marriage" and the fact that she seemingly did not appreciate the importance of appearances and the need to avoid bringing "controversy" to the Department, the Attorney General lost confidence in her ability to make good judgments for the Department.

Whatever our individual, personal estimates might be, we—as we observe throughout this opinion—cannot say that the Attorney General's worries and view of the circumstances that led him to take the adverse personnel action against Shahar are beyond the broad range of reasonable assessments of the facts.

C.

We must decide whether Shahar's interests outweigh the disruption and other harm the Attorney General believes her employment could cause. *Pickering* balancing is never a

---

16. The controversy in the State of Georgia and the Attorney General's involvement at the heart of that controversy, both as the State's litigator and its legal advisor, have not let up since the Attorney General's 1991 decision to revoke the offer to Shahar. *See In re R.E.W.,* 267 Ga. 62, 472 S.E.2d 295 (1996) (three-judge dissent from denial of certiorari to review court of appeal decision holding restriction on father's visitation rights inappropriate where based on his homosexual relationship); *Christensen v. State,* 266 Ga. 474, 468 S.E.2d 188, 190 (1996) (in case involving same-sex solicitation in public rest area, upholding—against challenge based on state constitution—statute criminalizing solicitation of sodomy); *City of Atlanta v. McKinney,* 265 Ga. 161, 454 S.E.2d 517, 521 (1995) (striking down portion of Atlanta ordinance mandating provision of benefits to registered "Domestic Partners"); *Van Dyck v. Van Dyck,* 262 Ga. 720, 425 S.E.2d 853 (1993) (live-in lover statute inapplicable to attempt to modify alimony where former spouse lived in meretricious same-sex relationship); Op. Att'y. Gen 96-7, 1996 WL 180274 (Ga.A.G.) (Attorney General called on to advise whether state college newspaper may refuse to publish advertisements suggesting that homosexuals are not "born gay" and "[t]here is another way out" and containing text which "might be perceived to 'derogatorily describe homosexuals'"); Op. Att'y Gen. 94-14 (1994 Ops. Att'y Gen. Ga. 32 (Darby 1994)) (Attorney General called on to advise Insurance Commissioner as to approval of proposed policy amendment affording group accident and health coverage to "domestic partners"); Op. Att'y Gen. 93-26 (1993 Ops. Att'y Gen. Ga. 72 (Darby 1993)) (Attorney General called on to advise Insurance Commissioner regarding "group health insurance provided pursuant to municipal ordinances which create the status of domestic partnership").

17. About public perception, we accept that the fact the Shahars are professed lesbians and see themselves as "married" does not prove beyond reasonable doubt that either of them has engaged in sodomy within the meaning of Georgia law. But we also accept that, when two people say of themselves that they are "married" to each other, it is reasonable for others to think those two people engage in marital relations....

precise mathematical process: it is a method of analysis by which a court compares the *relative* values of the things before it. A person often knows that "x" outweighs "y" even without first determining exactly what either "x" or "y" weighs. And it is this common experience that illustrates the workings of a *Pickering* balance.

To decide this case, we are willing to accord Shahar's claimed associational rights (which we have assumed to exist) substantial weight. But, we know that the weight due intimate associational rights, such as, those involved in even a state-authorized marriage, can be overcome by a government employer's interest in maintaining the effective functioning of his office. *See McCabe v. Sharrett,* 12 F.3d 1558, 1569–1570 (11th Cir.1994) (upholding transfer of sheriff's secretary to less desirable job based on her marriage to an officer in sheriff's department).

In weighing her interest in her associational rights, Shahar asks us also to consider the "non-employment related context" of her "wedding" and "marriage" and that "[s]he took no action to transform her intimate association into a public or political statement." In addition, Shahar says that we should take into account that she has affirmatively disavowed a right to benefits from the Department based on her "marriage."

To the extent that Shahar disclaims benefits bestowed by the State based on marriage, she is merely acknowledging what is undisputed, that Georgia law does not and has not recognized homosexual marriage. We fail to see how that technical acknowledgment counts for much in the balance.

If Shahar is arguing that she does not hold herself out as "married," the undisputed facts are to the contrary. Department employees, among many others, were invited to a "Jewish, lesbian-feminist, out-door wedding" which included exchanging wedding rings: the wearing of a wedding ring is an outward sign of having entered into marriage. Shahar listed her "marital status" on her employment application as "engaged" and indicated that her future spouse was a woman. She and her partner have both legally changed their family name to Shahar by filing a name change petition with the Fulton County Superior Court. They sought and received the married rate on their insurance. And, they, together, own the house in which they cohabit. These things were not done secretly, but openly.

Even if Shahar is not married to another woman, she, for appearance purposes, might as well be. We suppose that Shahar could have done more to "transform" her intimate relationship into a public statement. But after (as she says) "sanctifying" the relationship with a large "wedding" ceremony by which she became — and remains for all to see — "married," she has done enough to warrant the Attorney General's concern. He could conclude that her acts would give rise to a likelihood of confusion in the minds of members of the public: confusion about her marital status and about his attitude on same-sex marriage and related issues.

As for disruption within the Department, Shahar argues that we may discount the potential harm based on (what she sees as) the weakness of the Attorney General's predictions. Shahar overstates the Attorney General's "evidentiary burden."

In *Connick v. Myers,* 461 U.S. 138, 103 S.Ct. 1684, 75 L.Ed.2d 708 (1983), the Supreme Court upheld the termination of an assistant district attorney based on her exercise of her free speech rights. In so doing, the Court noted the close working relationship involved in a district attorney's office (which we think is similar to the Department) and held as follows:

> When close working relationships are essential to fulfilling public responsibilities, a wide degree of deference to the employer's judgment is appropriate. Fur-

thermore, we do not see the necessity for an employer to allow events to unfold to the extent that the disruption of the office and the destruction of working relationships is manifest before taking action.

As we have already written, the Attorney General's worry about his office being involved in litigation in which Shahar's special personal interest might appear to be in conflict with the State's position has been borne out in fact. This worry is not unreasonable. In addition, the Department, when the job offer was withdrawn, had already engaged in and won a recent battle about homosexual sodomy — highly visible litigation in which its lawyers worked to uphold the lawful prohibition of homosexual sodomy. This history makes it particularly reasonable for the Attorney General to worry about the internal consequences for his professional staff (for example, loss of morale, loss of cohesiveness and so forth) of allowing a lawyer, who openly — for instance, on her employment application and in statements to coworkers — represents herself to be "married" to a person of the same sex, to become part of his staff. Doubt and uncertainty of purpose can undo an office; he is not unreasonable to guard against that potentiality.

Shahar also argues that, at the Department, she would have handled mostly death penalty appeals and that the *Pickering* test requires evidence of potential interference with these particular duties. Even assuming Shahar is correct about her likely assignment within the Department, a particularized showing of interference with the provision of public services is not required....

D.

As we have already touched upon, the Attorney General, for balancing purposes, has pointed out, among other things, his concern about the public's reaction — the public that elected him and that he serves — to his having a Staff Attorney who is part of a same-sex "marriage." Shahar argues that he may not justify his decision by reference to perceived public hostility to her "marriage." We have held otherwise about the significance of public perception when law enforcement is involved. In *McMullen v. Carson,* 754 F.2d 936 (11th Cir.1985), we held that a sheriff's clerical employee's First Amendment interest in an off-duty statement that he was employed by the sheriff's office and also was a recruiter for the Ku Klux Klan was outweighed by the sheriff's interest in esprit de corps and credibility in the community the sheriff policed. More important, we relied, in large part, on public perceptions of the employee's constitutionally protected act.

In *McMullen,* both public perception and the anticipated effect that the employee's constitutionally protected activity would have on cohesion within the office were crucial in tipping the scales in the sheriff's favor. Nothing indicates that the employee had engaged in a criminal act or that he had joined an organization (he had joined the Invisible Empire) that had engaged in any criminal act. Given that it was additionally undisputed that neither the employee's statements nor his protected expressive association hindered his ability to perform his clerical duties and that the specific clerk "performed his duties in exemplary fashion," the two factors — public perception and anticipated effect — seemed to be the only ones weighing on the sheriff's side of the scale. But that was enough.

This case is different from *McMullen* in some ways, but *McMullen* guides us about the significance of "public perception." In this case, the Attorney General was similarly entitled to consider any "deleterious effect on [his] ability to enforce the law of the community," and that "[u]nder our system of Government, that duty [law enforcement] can be performed only with the consent of the vast majority.... Efficient law enforcement requires mutual respect, trust and support."

The Attorney General was also entitled to conclude that the public may think that employment of a Staff Attorney who openly purports to be part of a same-sex "marriage" is, at best, inconsistent with the other positions taken or likely to be taken by the Attorney General as the state's chief legal officer. The Attorney General has a right to take steps to protect the public from confusion about his stand and the Law Department's stand on controversial matters, such as same-sex marriage.

Public perception is important; but, at the same time, it is not knowable precisely. That the public (which we know is rarely monolithic) would not draw the Attorney General's anticipated inferences from Shahar's "marriage" or, at least, would not attribute such perceptions to the Department or the Attorney General is a possibility. But assessing what the public perceives about the Attorney General and the Law Department is a judgment for the Attorney General to make in the day-to-day course of filling his proper role as the elected head of the Department, not for the federal judiciary to make with hindsight or from a safe distance away from the distress and disturbance that might result if the decision was mistaken. We must defer to Georgia's Attorney General's judgment about what Georgians might perceive unless his judgment is definitely outside of the broad range of reasonable views. Nothing that either the Supreme Court or this circuit has held in applying the *Pickering* test leads us to a different conclusion.

Shahar says that by taking into account these concerns about public reaction, the Attorney General impermissibly discriminated against homosexuals; and she refers us to the Supreme Court's recent decision in *Romer v. Evans,* 517U.S. 620, 116 S.Ct. 1620, 134 L.Ed.2d 855 (1996). In *Romer,* the Supreme Court struck down an amendment to a state constitution as irrational because the amendment's sole purpose was to disadvantage a particular class of people (to "den[y] them protection across the board") and because the government engaged in "classification of persons undertaken for its own sake, something the Equal Protection Clause does not permit."

Romer is about people's condition; this case is about a person's conduct.[25] And, *Romer* is no employment case. Considering (in deciding to revoke a job offer) public reaction to a future Staff Attorney's conduct in taking part in a same-sex "wedding" and subsequent "marriage" is not the same kind of decision as an across-the-board denial of legal protection to a group because of their condition, that is, sexual orientation or preference.

III

This case is about the powers of government as an employer, powers which are far broader than government's powers as sovereign. In addition, the employment in this case is of a special kind: employment involving access to the employer's confidences, acting as the employer's spokesperson, and helping to make policy. This kind of employment is one in which the employer's interest has been given especially great weight in the past. Furthermore, the employment in this case is employment with responsibilities directly impacting on the enforcement of a state's laws: a kind of employment in which appearances and public perceptions and public confidence count a lot.

Particularly considering this Attorney General's many years of experience and Georgia's recent legal history, we cannot say that he was unreasonable to think that Shahar's acts were likely to cause the public to be confused and to question the Law Department's

---

25. We also note that in deciding *Romer,* the Court did not overrule or disapprove (or even mention) *Bowers v. Hardwick,* 478 U.S. 186 (1986), which was similarly about conduct in that it held that the State of Georgia did not violate "substantive due process" in prosecuting homosexual sodomy as a crime.

credibility; to interfere with the Law Department's ability to handle certain controversial matters, including enforcing the law against homosexual sodomy; and to endanger working relationships inside the Department. We also cannot say that the Attorney General was unreasonable to lose confidence in Shahar's ability to make good judgments as a lawyer for the Law Department.

We stress in this case the sensitive nature of the pertinent professional employment. And we hold that the Attorney General's interest—that is, the State of Georgia's interest—as an employer in promoting the efficiency of the Law Department's important public service does outweigh Shahar's personal associational interests....

[The concurring opinion of Judge Tjoflat, and the dissenting opinions of Judges Godbold, Kravitch, Birch, and Barkett are omitted.]

Dixon v. University of Toledo

842 F. Supp. 2d 1044 (N.D. Ohio 2012)

KATZ, District Judge.

....

I. BACKGROUND

At the beginning of 2008, Plaintiff was the interim Associate Vice President for Human Resources for all campuses at the University of Toledo. She had previously served as the permanent Associate Vice President for Human Resources for the Health Science Campus. Under either position, she reported directly to Logie, the Vice President of Human Resources and Campus Safety, and to Jacobs, the University President. On April 15, 2008, Logie prepared paperwork to present to Jacobs to make Plaintiff's position over all campuses permanent.

As Associate Vice President for Human Resources, Plaintiff was an "appointing authority" at the University, which means she had the power to hire and fire employees. Her work reviews from Logie had always been positive and praised her in the area of diversity. Logie clearly knew of her views on homosexuality due to an interoffice memo she had written years earlier.

The University had an Equal Opportunity Policy which prohibited discrimination based on sexual orientation. Further, the University has taken explicit steps to reach out to homosexuals and make them feel welcome.

On April 4, 2008, the *Toledo Free Press* ran an opinion by Michael Miller which Plaintiff felt compared the modern movement toward increased tolerance and rights for homosexuals to the historical struggles of the African-American civil rights movement and which noted that one University of Toledo campus offered domestic partner benefits and the other did not. Due to her religious conviction, Plaintiff, an African-American woman, felt the need to respond. The *Toledo Free Press* ran her response on April 18, 2008. In it she objected to the idea that homosexuals are "civil rights victims," asserted that homosexuality is purely a choice, and noted that the inter-campus benefits disparities involved all employees, not just those interested in domestic partner benefits. Plaintiff identified herself as "an alumnus of the University of Toledo's Graduate School, an employee and business owner" and signed only her name, though she used her University photograph. She did not mention her title or duties within the University. Since she intended to write as an unaffiliated citizen, she did not tell her superiors that she was writing an opinion or present it to them for approval.

Because of the response to her article, Plaintiff was immediately placed on administrative leave. However, the University could not proceed at that time because Jacobs was
out of the country.

In early May, shortly after he returned, the *Toledo Free Press* ran an opinion by Jacobs
in which he repudiated Plaintiff's opinion on the behalf of the University and noted the
University's stance on diversity. He also noted Plaintiff's position within the University.
On May 5, 2008, Jacobs held a disciplinary hearing concerning Plaintiff's actions. Logie
was not present. She appeared and read a statement, which she also distributed to those
attending. In that statement Plaintiff did not state that her opinion had been misinter-
preted, but claimed that she had never discriminated based on sexual orientation, noted
the treatment and behavior of others (including Logie), and complained about the response her opinion had generated from the public and media. On May 12, she received
a letter from Jacobs dated May 8, terminating her employment.

Plaintiff filed this suit against Logie, Jacobs, and the University....

III. ANALYSIS

The primary issue presented by this case is the distinction between how a government
entity relates to its employees and how it relates to citizens in general. The Supreme Court
has long held that, though "a public employee does not relinquish First Amendment rights
to comment on matters of public interest by virtue of government employment ... the
State's interests as an employer in regulating the speech of its employees 'differ significantly from those it possesses in connection with regulation of the speech of the citizenry
in general.'" *Connick v. Myers,* 461 U.S. 138, 140 (1983) (quoting *Pickering v. Bd. of Educ.,*
391 U.S. 563, 568 (1968))....

In a First Amendment Free Speech employment retaliation claim filed under 42 U.S.C.
§ 1983, a plaintiff must show that the speech was constitutionally protected, that the retaliation at issue would deter an individual of "ordinary firmness," and that the speech
motivated the employer's "retaliation." *Evans-Marshall v. Bd. of Educ.,* 624 F.3d 332, 337
(6th Cir.2010). Whether a plaintiff's speech is protected is a purely legal question for the
Court to decide. This question is further parsed into three elements: a plaintiff must show
that the speech involved "matters of public concern," that the state employer's interest
"'as an employer, in promoting the efficiency of the public services it performs through
its employees'... [does] not outweigh [plaintiff's] desire to 'contribute to public debate'
like any other citizen," and that the speech was not made "pursuant to" the duties of plaintiff's employment. *Evans-Marshall,* 624 F.3d at 337–38 (quoting *Pickering,* 391 U.S. at
568–73). In weighing the government interest as employer, the Court must consider
"whether the statement impairs discipline by superiors or harmony among co-workers,
has a detrimental impact on close working relationships for which personal loyalty and
confidence are necessary, or impedes the performance of the speaker's duties or interferes with the regular operation of the enterprise." *Rankin v. McPherson,* 483 U.S. 378,
388 (1987) (citing *Pickering,* 391 U.S. at 570–73). While the balancing factor incorporates the level of public concern as weight for Plaintiff, Defendants need not have "allow[ed]
events to unfold to the extent that the disruption of the office and the destruction of
working relationships is manifest before taking action." *Connick,* 461 U.S. at 152.

Defendants present three theories justifying Plaintiff's termination in the face of her
free speech rights. They argue that she spoke pursuant to her job duties, that she occupied a position demanding special loyalty, and that the University's interest outweighed
her interest in saying what she said; they do not contest any of the other elements. Two
of these theories are highly persuasive.

First, the Court will consider Defendants' theory based on the most recent permutation of the law on free speech for government employees: the First Amendment does not prohibit discipline for speech made "pursuant to official responsibilities." *Garcetti v. Ceballos*, 547 U.S. 410, 424 (2006). Defendants support this theory by arguing that Plaintiff depended on her job to support her opinion. However, they do not argue that Plaintiff's job required that she write her article, a situation which may be clearly contrasted with Jacobs' article.

Essentially, Defendants' theory expands "pursuant to official responsibilities" to "in relation to official responsibilities." The Sixth Circuit has already rejected a similar expansion in *Westmoreland v. Sutherland*, 622 F.3d 714 (6th Cir. 2011). In that case, an off-duty firefighter appeared at a public meeting, identified himself as a Fire Department employee, and railed against a policy regarding the Fire Department. The Sixth Circuit held that merely identifying himself as a public employee and speaking regarding his public employment did not place the firefighter's speech within the *Garcetti* test. To satisfy that test speech must be "made pursuant to a task that was within the scope of his official duties" rather than merely in regard to such official duties.

Here, there is factual dispute over whether Plaintiff identified herself to the same extent as the firefighter in *Westmoreland*, but Defendants have not presented any job duty she was attempting to satisfy. Indeed, the evidence clearly demonstrates that Plaintiff was not attempting to fulfill any job duty in writing her article, but to present a personal opinion. Even if she attempted to give herself credence with the public by identifying herself, this does not satisfy the *Garcetti* test. Thus, Defendants' theory that Plaintiff spoke pursuant to her job duties does not defeat her First Amendment claim.

Defendants present two arguments concerning the balancing factor. First, they argue that Plaintiff's specific authority automatically tips the balance in their favor. Second, they assert the specific weights and balances presented by this case demonstrate that the University's interest outweighs Plaintiff's.

The first argument relies on the Sixth Circuit's statement that when certain employees "speak on job-related issues in a manner contrary to the position of [their] employer" they have been insubordinate and a presumption arises that the balance weighs in the favor of the employer. *Rose v. Stephens*, 291 F.3d 917, 923 (6th Cir. 2002). Thus, "when an employee is in a policymaking or confidential position and is terminated for speech related to his or her political or policy views, there is a presumption that the *Pickering* balance favors the government." *Silberstein v. City of Dayton*, 440 F.3d 306, 319 (6th Cir. 2006)....

[T]he presumption of insubordination will only apply if her statement related her policy view on a matter related to her employment. Plaintiff stated that she did not think homosexuals were civil rights victims. Not only does this statement directly contradict the University's policies granting homosexuals civil rights protections (such as the Equal Opportunity Policy), but as an appointing authority, Plaintiff was charged with ensuring that the University maintained those protections in employment actions. Thus, the *Rose* insubordination presumption applies.... Because the presumption holds, the balance of employee and employer concerns automatically tips in the employer's favor.

Defendants further argue that even if the *Rose* presumption does not apply, the actual weighing of employee versus employer interests in this case would clearly favor them. Plaintiff counters by asserting that her speech should be afforded the greatest protection.

In demonstrating the employer's interests in this case, Defendants again emphasize Plaintiff's position. As such, they emphasize her authority over employment actions and further note that even she has testified that she was serving as "an ambassador" for the University. Given her position, her statements against the rights of homosexuals could have done very serious damage to the University in three ways (all of which Defendants cited and stated multiple times, including in the termination letter). Though all three may be speculative and concern only what might happen, as noted above, the law does not require Defendants to wait for damage to occur.

First, her statements could disrupt the Human Resources Department by making homosexual employees uncomfortable or disgruntled. Though it did not enter into the actual consideration, Erich Stolz's letter to Defendants clearly demonstrated that effect: he stated that her letter not only made him individually uncomfortable, but it also reduced his respect for her professionalism. Plaintiff responds that mere offense is insufficient to justify her termination. That might be an appropriate response to Defendants' offense, but it does not address loss of cohesion in the Human Resources Department as a legitimate interest of her employer. Further, this addresses only the least of the three feared effects.

Second, Plaintiff's public statements could have interfered with the University's interest in diversity. Because of her statements, homosexual prospective employees might reconsider applications they knew she would review or withdraw them altogether. This concern removes a significant portion of Plaintiff's rebuttal that she has only acted fairly because she has not demonstrated how any applicants would know. Plaintiff also complains about consideration of the value of diversity as opposed to focus on teaching capacity alone. However, not only is that an overly simple description of the University's interest, any decrease in the capability of the University workforce could have an impact on instruction. If fewer qualified people apply, because some are homosexuals who know that the head of Human Resources (Plaintiff) does not think they deserve civil rights, then it could be that the quality of the eventual workforce will decline. Further, Plaintiff has not rebutted the concept that diversity itself (even with regard to non-faculty positions) improves the teaching function.

Third, as the termination letter stated, Plaintiff's public position could lead to challenges to her personnel decisions. In other words, Defendants feared lawsuits from homosexuals alleging sexual orientation or sexual harassment discrimination. This fear is clearly appropriate as her statement could be offered in a suit for either direct evidence of discrimination or for evidence of pretext (in rebuttal to a non-discriminatory reason). Further, Plaintiff's article could also lead to additional suits and grievances as people realize they may have a claim or the statement could be just enough to cause someone to decide to sue who otherwise might not have undertaken the expense and effort. Thus, Plaintiff's statements could subject the University to significant expense through more litigation or more difficult litigation (or other employment action challenges).

In response to these concerns, other than by emphasizing the value of her speech, Plaintiff primarily relies on the prior knowledge of her opinions and her history of behaving in a non-discriminatory manner. Neither of these actually addresses concerns over how others will react to Plaintiff, especially since her claims relate to facts which are not public. In other words, contrary to her assertion, she was not terminated due to Defendants discovering her views, but due to the public discovering them....

Next, Plaintiff claims that her article stated that she did not discriminate. Though she may have intended to imply this with some of her religious statements, her article never states that people should be treated without discrimination. Further, she claims that her article was merely meant to refute the comparison between historical racial and gender civil rights struggles and modern sexual orientation struggles. However, her article is far from clear on these points: she objects to homosexuals as "civil rights victims," not directly to the comparison of the movements. At her disciplinary hearing she had the opportunity to claim that she had been misunderstood and instead chose to defend her speech, claim that she did not discriminate, and complain about the complaints. Those very complaints she protested should have alerted her to the fact that it was not perceived as though she had said that she did not discriminate or that she was merely contrasting historical movements, yet she did not suggest that such perceptions were inaccurate, instead calling them intolerant. She cannot inject now what she had the opportunity to clarify then.

Plaintiff then invokes academic freedom. However, her speech "was not related to classroom instruction and was only loosely, if at all, related to academic scholarship" and thus deserves no extra protection. Further, Plaintiff did not even have any responsibilities related to classroom instruction or academic scholarship. Thus, this claim adds no weight to her interests.

Finally, Plaintiff claims that her termination impedes diversity. She claims that accepting Defendants' employer interest arguments would prevent any conservative Christians from holding managerial positions at the University of Toledo. Plaintiff's claim is far too broad in two important ways. First, Defendants' arguments only restrict those who cannot hold their tongues about their beliefs (or fail to submit their beliefs anonymously). Plus, the position would likewise restrict liberal atheists as well. Second, Plaintiff ignores that Defendants' arguments are very specific to her position at the top of the Human Resources Department with only one person between her and the President.

Thus, the balance of Plaintiff's interest in making a comment of public concern is clearly outweighed by the University's interest as her employer in carrying out its own objectives. Therefore, Plaintiff has failed to establish that her speech was protected....

Piggee v. Carl Sandburg College
464 F.3d 667 (7th Cir. 2006)

WOOD, Circuit Judge.

In September 2002, Martha Louise Piggee, who was then a part-time instructor of cosmetology at Carl Sandburg College, gave a gay student two religious pamphlets on the sinfulness of homosexuality. The student was offended and complained to college officials. After the college looked into the matter, it found that Piggee had sexually harassed the student. It admonished her in a letter to cease such behavior, and the following semester it chose not to retain her. Piggee sued the college, the members of its board of trustees, and various college administrators....

I

Carl Sandburg College ("the college") is a public community college located in downtown Galesburg, Illinois. Its cosmetology department requires its students to undertake a combination of classroom and clinical work in a facility that operates as an ordinary beauty salon open to the public. Jason Ruel was a student in the program. He enrolled in June 2002, and Piggee was his instructor for several classes. At some point, Ruel became aware that Piggee was a Christian and she realized that he was gay. On September 5, 2002, Piggee placed two pamphlets in Ruel's smock during clinical instruction time, as he was preparing to leave for the day. She told him to read the materials later and invited him to discuss them with her.

The next day, Ruel glanced at the pamphlets, both of which used a comic-book format. The first was entitled "Sin City." It tells the story of a man who tries to persuade gay pride advocates that homosexuality is an abomination. He is beaten when he tries to stop a gay pride parade; he is arrested by the police; a demon urges on a minister who preaches that God loves even gay people; the man then asks about Sodom and Gomorrah; and eventually the minister repents his sin (which apparently is supporting gay pride). The second pamphlet was entitled "Doom Town." Its message is similar. It begins by showing a group of homosexuals headed by a speaker, who states that a certain number of children will wind up homosexual. She threatens that all gay males will pollute the blood supply with HIV-positive blood unless people give more money for AIDS research. A Christian observing this recounts the story of Sodom and Gomorrah. One scene implies that an evil man is about to assault a frightened boy sexually; another indicates that some angels being sheltered by Lot are about to be raped. God, however, intervenes, stops the mob, and destroys the two sinful cities.

[Ruel filed a complaint about Piggee's conduct with the college. After investigating the matter, the college issued a formal warning to Piggee to stop proselytizing in the workplace, and subsequently decided not to renew her contract.]

II

. . . . Piggee's real complaint has to do with her ability to speak at the workplace, and in particular her ability to discuss matters of religious concern there. Since the oral argument in this case, the Supreme Court has spoken to these issues, in *Garcetti v. Ceballos*, 547 U.S. 410 (2006)....

[T]he [*Garcetti*] Court held that "when public employees make statements pursuant to their official duties, the employees are not speaking as citizens for First Amendment purposes, and the Constitution does not insulate their communications from employer discipline."

Application of these principles to the educational setting requires an appreciation of the way in which teachers, professors, or instructors communicate with their students. As we have recognized in the past, academic freedom has two aspects. We wrote in *Trejo v. Shoben*, 319 F.3d 878 (7th Cir.2003) that "the First Amendment protects the right of faculty members to engage in academic debates, pursuits, and inquiries" and to discuss ideas. *Id.* at 884. The idea of some kind of government-sponsored orthodoxy in the classroom is repugnant to our values. On the other hand, we have also recognized that a university's "ability to set a curriculum is as much an element of academic freedom as any scholar's right to express a point of view." *Webb v. Bd. of Trustees of Ball State Univ.*, 167 F.3d 1146, 1149 (7th Cir.1999). We added, in *Webb*, that "[u]niversities are entitled to insist that members of the faculty (and their administrative aides) devote their energies to promoting goals such as research and teaching." *Id.* at 1150. No college or university is required to allow a chemistry professor to devote extensive classroom time to the teaching of James Joyce's demanding novel *Ulysses*, nor must it permit a professor of mathematics to fill her class hours with instruction on the law of torts. Classroom or instructional speech, in short, is inevitably speech that is part of the instructor's official duties, even though at the same time the instructor's freedom to express her views on the assigned course is protected.

The examples we have just given illustrate why it is not very useful to focus on the fact that speech about religion, or speech about the pros and cons of homosexual behavior, plainly deals with a topic that richly deserves full public discussion. So, for that matter, does tort law, or *Ulysses* (which, recall, was initially banned in this country as obscene, see *United States v. One Book Entitled* Ulysses *by James Joyce,* 72 F.2d 705 (2d Cir.1934)). (The way to fit this conclusion into traditional *Pickering* analysis is to say that we assume, for purposes of this discussion, that Piggee's proselytizing is speech that qualifies as a matter of public concern; it certainly had nothing to do with how to style hair.) The real question, however, is whether the college had the right to insist that Piggee refrain from engaging in that particular speech while serving as an instructor of cosmetology.

Piggee's first effort to convince us that the college had no such right is to argue that the clinical beauty salon where she approached Ruel was just a store, like any other store. Had she come up to Ruel in a local grocery store and slipped the pamphlets into his pocket, we would have a different case. It is still possible that this might have raised concerns, because the instructor/student relationship does not end the moment the instructional period is over. If we conclude that the beauty salon where Ruel was working was part of the instructional environment, however, we need not reach the question of Piggee's responsibilities away from the college.

We have little trouble concluding that the beauty salon was, in fact, one of the places where cosmetology instruction was taking place. It is undisputed that students enrolled in this program must participate in two different kinds of instruction: classroom, and hands-on clinical work. This type of program is exceedingly common, especially for those learning some type of service. Law students almost universally have the opportunity to work in instructional clinics, which typically are open to the public and offer legal services to indigent clients; medical students begin supervised work with real patients in university-affiliated hospitals and clinics while they are still in medical school, even before they complete their formal education with a residency. The beauty clinic operated by Carl Sandburg College served exactly the same function: students were able to learn their trade by serving customers under the supervision of trained instructors like Piggee. Whether the customers themselves were chatting about religion, or the latest Chicago Cubs game, or the price of gasoline, the college was entitled to insist on a professional relationship between the students and the instructors.

The Supreme Court's decision in *Ceballos* is not directly relevant to our problem, but it does signal the Court's concern that courts give appropriate weight to the public employer's interests. In that case, the employer had an interest in the deputy district attorney's recommendations about prosecutions, in the face of a problematic search warrant affidavit. Here, the public employer is a university, and its interest is in the instructor's adherence to the subject matter of the course she has been hired to teach.... Here, the college had an interest in ensuring that its instructors stay on message while they were supervising the beauty clinic, just as it had an interest in ensuring that the instructors do the same while in the classroom.

Piggee's "speech," both verbal and through the pamphlets she put in Ruel's pocket, was not related to her job of instructing students in cosmetology. Indeed, if it did anything, it inhibited her ability to perform that job by undermining her relationship with Ruel and other students who disagreed with or were offended by her expressions of her beliefs. The record reflects that her actions disrupted Ruel's education: he testified that he "avoided her like the plague," that he was unhappy that he still had to go to a class that she taught, and that he felt unsafe because she was present. Furthermore, while Ruel was the only student who complained formally, Piggee herself testified that she gave various religious pamphlets to other students as part of her effort to "witness." Out of eight student evaluations of Piggee's performance from the fall semester of 2001, five spoke about Piggee's emphasis on religion. One student wrote "Mrs. Piggee usually inquires [sic] her religion into everyday. Some people don't always agree w/ what she feel. I think that if we are taught that we are not to speak of our religions in the salon, neither should she." Another commented "Mrs. Piggee is a great teacher, but I really do not appreciate religion being discussed in school. I do not believe the same way she does and don't want to hear how my religion is inferior to hers." A third said "Mrs. Piggee ... told me that I was not saved & that I have the devil in me. She also told me that she was going to get that devil out of me.... I just wish that she will [sic] keep her religion out of school." This evidence shows, at a minimum, that the college reasonably took the position that nongermane discussions of religion and other matters had no place in the classroom, because they could impede the school's educational mission....

Notes and Questions

1. Note that the *Shahar* majority *assumes* that Shahar had a constitutionally protected right to marry someone of the same sex, but nonetheless concludes that under *Pickering*, that right is outweighed by the government's interests in this case. Can that really be so? Would that not involve infringement on a fundamental right of the sort raised in the military cases at the end of Chapter 5? In *Shahar*, Judge Tjoflat wrote a concurring opinion in which he contended that it was necessary to reach the question whether she had such a right (which he concluded that she did not):

> When a court engages in *Pickering* balancing, it must identify the constitutional source of the right the employee exercised and assign weight to that right. Otherwise, balancing cannot occur. It cannot occur any more than the local butcher can weigh five pounds of hamburger without placing a five pound weight on the other side of the scale. In the case at hand, the court, with respect to each of Shahar's claims, assumes Shahar's exercise of a constitutional right without describing the right and telling us the weight it has assigned to it. It then places on the other side of the scale the Attorney General's interest in operating an efficient Department of Law that can command the public's respect, and concludes that such interest outweighs what the court has assumed and placed on Shahar's side of the scale....

> If Shahar's relationship is entitled to the same level of protection as is a heterosexual marriage, I doubt whether the public perception of that relationship, or the State of Georgia's public policy against according such relationships the same protections and privileges as heterosexual marriage, would be placed on the government's side of the scale. Even if those factors were weighed in the balance, it is difficult to imagine that they would outweigh Shahar's interest in her relationship.

> A hypothetical will illustrate the point. Suppose that Shahar had married a man of another race rather than "marrying" a woman. Such a relationship would clearly be protected as an intimate association. See *Roberts*, 468 U.S. at 620 (citing *Loving v. Com. of Virginia*, 388 U.S. 1, 12 (1967)). I believe that a court engaged in a *Pickering* balance would either (1) refuse to consider as government interests the public perception of such a relationship or any state policy positions hostile toward that relationship, or (2) conclude that such governmental interests do not prevail in the balance. In short, if the court accords Shahar's relationship the same constitutional value that the Supreme Court has assigned to heterosexual marriage, the Attorney General would face a heavy burden in prevailing in a *Pickering* balance.

Shahar v. Bowers, 114 F.3d 1097, 1113, 1116 (11th Cir. 1997) (en banc) (Tjoflat, J., concurring).

In support of its conclusion, the *Shahar* majority cites its earlier decision in *McCabe v. Sharrett*, 12 F.3d 1558 (11th Cir. 1994), in which the court held that a police chief could permissibly transfer his secretary to a less desirable job because she married a police officer within the department who was under the command of the police chief. The rationale for the transfer was the importance to the chief of having a secretary who was completely loyal to him and able to keep confidences about departmental matters, and the court concluded that "[i]t is a matter of common experience that spouses tend to possess a higher degree of loyalty to their marital partners than to their superiors, and often discuss workplace matters with one another, even matters that a superior has designated as confidential." *Id.* at 1572.

Even accepting that the employers' interests in *McCabe* and *Shahar* were comparable, is there not a significant difference between a transfer to a less desirable job (as occurred in *McCabe*) and complete loss of employment (as occurred in *Shahar*)? Would not an analogous solution be for Shahar to be prevented from working on cases related to same-sex marriage or sodomy laws? Is that not something law offices do all the time when one attorney within the organization has a potential conflict of interest?

2. In support of its holding, the *Shahar* court cites its earlier decision in *McMullen v. Carson*, 754 F.2d 936 (11th Cir. 1985). There, the court upheld the discharge of a clerical employee of a sheriff's office who was a recruiter for the Ku Klux Klan in a city in which a burning cross had recently been left in the yard of an African-American woman. Following the cross burning, the clerical employee went on television, identified himself as both a Klan recruiter and a Sheriff's office employee, and disclaimed Klan involvement in the cross-burning incident. The *Shahar* court describes the case before it as "different from *McMullen* in some ways," but nonetheless holds that it supports its conclusion regarding the significance of public perception. Is not the statement that the cases are different "in some ways" a bit of an understatement? Is the court really comparing self-identifying on television as both a member of the Ku Klux Klan and a sheriff's office employee on television with holding a same-sex marriage ceremony?

3. In *Rankin v. McPherson*, 483 U.S. 378 (1987), the Court considered a First Amendment challenge raised by a clerical employee who was fired from the county constable's office after she said to a coworker—during a private conversation and upon hearing of an attempt on the life of President Reagan—"If they go for him again, I hope they get him."

In holding that the employee's discharge violated her First Amendment rights, the Court discussed the appropriate factors to take into account in applying the *Pickering* balancing test as well as the impact of her low-level position within the organization:

> In performing the balancing, the statement will not be considered in a vacuum; the manner, time, and place of the employee's expression are relevant, as is the context in which the dispute arose. We have previously recognized as pertinent considerations whether the statement impairs discipline by superiors or harmony among co-workers, has a detrimental impact on close working relationships for which personal loyalty and confidence are necessary, or impedes the performance of the speaker's duties or interferes with the regular operation of the enterprise. *Pickering*, 391 U.S., at 570–573.

> These considerations, and indeed the very nature of the balancing test, make apparent that the state interest element of the test focuses on the effective functioning of the public employer's enterprise. Interference with work, personnel relationships, or the speaker's job performance can detract from the public employer's function; avoiding such interference can be a strong state interest. From this per-

spective, however, petitioners fail to demonstrate a state interest that outweighs McPherson's First Amendment rights. While McPherson's statement was made at the workplace, there is no evidence that it interfered with the efficient functioning of the office....

Nor was there any danger that McPherson had discredited the office by making her statement in public. McPherson's speech took place in an area to which there was ordinarily no public access; her remark was evidently made in a private conversation with another employee. There is no suggestion that any member of the general public was present or heard McPherson's statement....

[I]n weighing the State's interest in discharging an employee based on any claim that the content of a statement made by the employee somehow undermines the mission of the public employer, some attention must be paid to the responsibilities of the employee within the agency. The burden of caution employees bear with respect to the words they speak will vary with the extent of authority and public accountability the employee's role entails. Where, as here, an employee serves no confidential, policymaking, or public contact role, the danger to the agency's successful functioning from that employee's private speech is minimal. We cannot believe that every employee in Constable Rankin's office, whether computer operator, electrician, or file clerk, is equally required, on pain of discharge, to avoid any statement susceptible of being interpreted by the Constable as an indication that the employee may be unworthy of employment in his law enforcement agency. At some point, such concerns are so removed from the effective functioning of the public employer that they cannot prevail over the free speech rights of the public employee.

See id. at 388–91. However, in a footnote, the Court made clear—citing the *McMullen* case cited by the *Shahar* court—that even statements by clerical employees can result in their being fired under *Pickering*:

This is not to say that clerical employees are insulated from discharge where their speech, taking the acknowledged factors into account, truly injures the public interest in the effective functioning of the public employer. Cf. *McMullen v. Carson,* 754 F.2d 936 (CA11 1985) (clerical employee in sheriff's office properly discharged for stating on television news that he was an employee for the sheriff's office and a recruiter for the Ku Klux Klan).

Id. at 391 n.18.

4. What facts were critical in determining that it was constitutional to terminate Shahar? That she had a same-sex marriage ceremony? That it was a large ceremony? That she wore a wedding ring? That she changed her last name? That she listed her status as "engaged" and referred to her partner as her "future spouse" on her job application?

Stated somewhat differently, would the result have been the same if she had a small, private ceremony and someone happened to find out about it? In this regard, to what extent is the *Shahar* court—like the *Dale* Court—drawing a distinction between those who are gay and those who are *openly* gay?

5. How critical to the outcome in *Shahar* was the fact that *sodomy* laws were still on the books? Would the case have come out differently a year later, when the Supreme Court of Georgia, in *Powell v. State*, 510 S.E.2d 18 (Ga. 1998), struck down the state's sodomy law as unconstitutional under the due process clause of the Georgia Constitution?

6. The *Shahar* court, in distinguishing *Romer*, emphasizes that *Romer* was about *status* while this case is about *conduct*. Moreover, in footnote 25 of the opinion, the court

notes that *Romer* did not overrule *Bowers*, which it characterizes as also being a case about *conduct*.

To what extent does *Lawrence v. Texas* undermine the *Shahar* court's holding, both because of its overruling of *Bowers* and because of its evident rejection of the status/conduct divide between sexual orientation and expressions of that orientation?

7. The Shahar case was decided on May 30, 1997. Less than a week later—on June 6, 1997—Michael Bowers, the Attorney General who fired Shahar, publicly admitted that he had been carrying on an adulterous affair with a woman who once worked in his office. Under Georgia law at the time and still today, adultery is a criminal offense in the same chapter of the criminal code as Georgia's sodomy statute. *See* Ga. Code. Ann. § 16-6-19. Would that fact, if known to the *Shahar* court, have changed the outcome? Should it have made a difference?

8. Would the result in *Dixon* have been different if the plaintiff worked in Human Resources, but was a clerical worker instead of the Associate Vice President? What if she was the Vice President for Information Technology, or the Vice President for Finance? What if instead she wrote the following in her letter to the *Toledo Free Press*:

> As an African-American female, I was offended by the reference to homosexuals as "civil rights victims." While I harbor no ill will toward homosexuals and do not support discriminating against them, drawing analogies to the experience of African-Americans—in light of the history of slavery and severe racial discrimination in this country—diminishes the suffering of African-Americans.

9. Note that the *Piggee* Court treats the plaintiff's claim somewhat differently because of the academic context in which it arose. In *Garcetti*, the U.S. Supreme Court acknowledged that the constitutional analysis in this context may call for more weight to be given to the interests of the instructor-employee:

> There is some argument that expression related to academic scholarship or classroom instruction implicates additional constitutional interests that are not fully accounted for by this Court's customary employee-speech jurisprudence. We need not, and for that reason do not, decide whether the analysis we conduct today would apply in the same manner to a case involving speech related to scholarship or teaching.

Garcetti, 547 U.S. at 425.

E. The Public School Environment

Do students have First Amendment rights, and if so, do they have the right to express themselves in any manner they wish at any time while at school?

In *Tinker v. Des Moines Independent Community School District*, 393 U.S. 503 (1969), the U.S. Supreme Court addressed the constitutionality of a ban by a public high school and junior high school on the wearing of black armbands by students, which were worn by students as a way of protesting the Vietnam War.

In *Tinker*, the Court first emphasized that:

> First Amendment rights, applied in light of the special characteristics of the school environment, are available to teachers and students. It can hardly be ar-

gued that either students or teachers shed their constitutional rights to freedom of speech or expression at the schoolhouse gate.

Id. at 506. On the other side of the balance, the Court acknowledged the need for school officials "to prescribe and control conduct in the schools." *Id.* at 507. Accordingly, in what has come to be known as the *Tinker* "substantial disruption" test, the Court held that infringement upon the First Amendment rights of students can "be justified by a showing that the students' activities would materially and substantially disrupt the work and discipline of the school." *Id.* at 513.

In subsequent cases — examined in greater detail in the notes at the end of this section — the Court has refined and qualified the *Tinker* test. The cases that follow explore the application of the *Tinker* test both in cases in which schools seek to suppress pro-GLBT speech as well as those in which they seek to suppress anti-GLBT speech.

Problem 6-E: You Are So Gay!

Faced with the pervasive problem of student-on-student bullying, a school decides to enact a policy banning derogatory comments made by one student to another about, *inter alia*, the other student's actual or perceived sexual orientation.

Is the policy constitutional? In answering this question, how, if at all, would your answer be impacted by the following:

(a) *The policy is enacted by a high school*

(b) *The policy is enacted by a university*

(c) *The policy is enacted by an elementary school*

(d) *The policy is applied not only to comments made in the classroom, but also those made during recess*

(e) *The policy is applied to comments posted on the Internet — even if written by a student using his home computer — if the student could reasonably foresee that the comments would be seen by other students*

(f) *The policy is applied to statements made by one student to another off-campus during non-school hours*

Fricke v. Lynch

491 F. Supp. 381 (D.R.I. 1980)

OPINION

PETTINE, Chief Judge.

Most of the time, a young man's choice of a date for the senior prom is of no great interest to anyone other than the student, his companion, and, perhaps, a few of their classmates. But in Aaron Fricke's case, the school authorities actively disapprove of his choice, the other students are upset, the community is abuzz, and out-of-state newspapers consider the matter newsworthy. All this fuss arises because Aaron Fricke's intended escort is another young man. Claiming that the school's refusal to allow him to bring a male escort violates his first and fourteenth amendment rights, Fricke seeks a preliminary injunction ordering the school officials to allow him to attend with a male escort.

Two days of testimony have revealed the following facts. The senior reception at Cumberland High School is a formal dinner-dance sponsored and run by the senior class. It is held shortly before graduation but is not a part of the graduation ceremonies. This year the students have decided to hold the dance at the Pleasant Valley Country Club in Sutton, Massachusetts on Friday, May 30. All seniors except those on suspension are eligible to attend the dance; no one is required to go. All students who attend must bring an escort, although their dates need not be seniors or even Cumberland High School students. Each student is asked the name of his date at the time he buys the tickets.

The principal testified that school dances are chaperoned by him, two assistant principals, and one or two class advisers. They are sometimes joined by other teachers who volunteer to help chaperone; such teachers are not paid. Often these teachers will drop in for part of the dance. Additionally, police officers are on duty at the dance. Usually two officers attend; last year three plainclothes officers were at the junior prom.

The seeds of the present conflict were planted a year ago when Paul Guilbert, then a junior at Cumberland High School, sought permission to bring a male escort to the junior prom. The principal, Richard Lynch (the defendant here), denied the request, fearing that student reaction could lead to a disruption at the dance and possibly to physical harm to Guilbert. The request and its denial were widely publicized and led to widespread community and student reaction adverse to Paul. Some students taunted and spit at him, and once someone slapped him; in response, principal Lynch arranged an escort system, in which Lynch or an assistant principal accompanied Paul as he went from one class to the next. No other incidents or violence occurred. Paul did not attend the prom. At that time Aaron Fricke (plaintiff here) was a friend of Paul's and supported his position regarding the dance.

This year, during or after an assembly in April in which senior class events were discussed, Aaron Fricke, a senior at Cumberland High School, decided that he wanted to attend the senior reception with a male companion. Aaron considers himself a homosexual, and has never dated girls, although he does socialize with female friends. He has never taken a girl to a school dance. Until this April, he had not "come out of the closet" by publicly acknowledging his sexual orientation.

Aaron asked principal Lynch for permission to bring a male escort, which Lynch denied. A week later (during vacation), Aaron asked Paul Guilbert who now lives in New York to be his escort (if allowed), and Paul accepted. Aaron met again with Lynch, at which time they discussed Aaron's commitment to homosexuality; Aaron indicated that although it was possible he might someday be bisexual, at the present he is exclusively homosexual and could not conscientiously date girls. Lynch gave Aaron written reasons for his action; his prime concern was the fear that a disruption would occur and Aaron or, especially, Paul would be hurt. He indicated in court that he would allow Aaron to bring a male escort if there were no threat of violence.

After Aaron filed suit in this Court, an event reported by the Rhode Island and Boston papers, a student shoved and, the next day, punched Aaron. The unprovoked, surprise assault necessitated five stitches under Aaron's right eye. The assailant was suspended for nine days. After this, Aaron was given a special parking space closer to the school doors and has been provided with an escort (principal or assistant principal) between classes. No further incidents have occurred.

This necessarily brief account does not convey the obvious concern and good faith Lynch has displayed in his handling of the matter. Lynch sincerely believes that there is a significant possibility that some students will attempt to injure Aaron and Paul if they attend the dance. Moreover, Lynch's actions in school have displayed a concern for Aaron's safety while at school. Perhaps one cannot be at all sure a totally different approach by Lynch might have kept the matter from reaching its present proportions, but I am convinced that Lynch's actions have stemmed in significant part from a concern for disruption....

The starting point in my analysis of Aaron's first amendment free speech claim must be, of course, to determine whether the action he proposes to take has a "communicative content sufficient to bring it within the ambit of the first amendment." *Gay Students Organization v. Bonner*, 509 F.2d 652 (1st Cir. 1974) (hereinafter *Bonner*). As this Court has noted before, the "speech pure"/"speech plus" demarcation is problematic, both in logic and in practice. This normally difficult task is made somewhat easier here, however, by the precedent set in *Bonner, supra*. In that case, the University of New Hampshire prohibited the Gay Students' Organization (GSO) from holding dances and other social events. The first circuit explicitly rejected the idea that traditional first amendment rights of expression were not involved. The Court found that not only did discussion and exchange of ideas take place at informal social functions, but also that:

> beyond the specific communications at such events is the basic "message" GSO seeks to convey that homosexuals exist, that they feel repressed by existing laws and attitudes, that they wish to emerge from their isolation, and that public understanding of their attitudes and problems is desirable for society.

Here too the proposed activity has significant expressive content. Aaron testified that he wants to go because he feels he has a right to attend and participate just like all the other students and that it would be dishonest to his own sexual identity to take a girl to the dance. He went on to acknowledge that he feels his attendance would have a certain political element and would be a statement for equal rights and human rights. Admittedly, his explanation of his "message" was hesitant and not nearly as articulate as Judge Coffin's restatement of the GSO's message, cited above. Nevertheless, I believe Aaron's testimony that he is sincerely although perhaps not irrevocably committed to a homosexual orientation and that attending the dance with another young man would be a political statement. While mere communicative intent may not always transform conduct into speech, *United States v. O'Brien*, 391 U.S. 367, 376 (1968), *Bonner* makes clear that this exact type of conduct as a vehicle for transmitting this very message can be considered protected speech.

Accordingly, the school's action must be judged by the standards articulated in *United States v. O'Brien*, 391 U.S. 367 (1968), and applied in *Bonner*: (1) was the regulation within the constitutional power of the government; (2) did it further an important or substantial governmental interest; (3) was the governmental interest unrelated to the suppression of free expression; and (4) was the incidental restriction on alleged first amendment freedoms no greater than essential to the furtherance of that interest?

I need not dwell on the first two *O'Brien* requirements: the school unquestionably has an important interest in student safety and has the power to regulate students' conduct to ensure safety. As to the suppression of free expression, Lynch's testimony indicated that his personal views on homosexuality did not affect his decision, and that but for the threat of violence he would let the two young men go together. Thus the government's interest here is not in squelching a particular message because it objects to its content as such. On the other hand, the school's interest is in suppressing certain speech activity because of the reaction its message may engender. Surely this is still suppression of free expression.

It is also clear that the school's action fails to meet the last criterion set out in *O'Brien*, the requirement that the government employ the "least restrictive alternative" before curtailing speech. The plaintiff argues, and I agree, that the school can take appropriate security measures to control the risk of harm. Lynch testified that he did not know if adequate security could be provided, and that he would still need to sit down and make the necessary arrangements. In fact he has not made any effort to determine the need for and logistics of additional security. Although Lynch did not say that any additional security measures would be adequate, from the testimony I find that significant measures could be taken and would in all probability critically reduce the likelihood of any disturbance. As Lynch's own testimony indicates, police officers and teachers will be present at the dance, and have been quite successful in the past in controlling whatever problems arise, including unauthorized drinking. Despite the ever-present possibility of violence at sports events, adequate discipline has been maintained. From Lynch's testimony, I have every reason to believe that additional school or law enforcement personnel could be used to "shore up security" and would be effective. It should also be noted that Lynch testified that if he considered it impossible to provide adequate security he would move to cancel the dance. The Court appreciates that controlling high school students is no easy task. It is, of course, impossible to guarantee that no harm will occur, no matter what measures are taken. But only one student so far has attempted to harm Aaron, and no evidence was introduced of other threats. The measures taken already, especially the escort system, have been highly effective in preventing any further problems at school. Appropriate security measures coupled with a firm, clearly communicated attitude by the administration that any disturbance will not be tolerated appear to be a realistic, and less restrictive, alternative to prohibiting Aaron from attending the dance with the date of his choice.

The analysis so far has been along traditional first amendment lines, making no real allowance for the fact that this case arises in a high school setting. The most difficult problem this controversy presents is how this setting should affect the result. *Tinker v. Des Moines Independent Community School District*, 393 U.S. 503 (1969), makes clear that high school students do not "shed their constitutional rights to freedom of speech or expression at the schoolhouse gate." ....

Tinker did, however, indicate that there are limits on first amendment rights within the school:

> A student's rights, therefore, do not embrace merely the classroom hours. When he is in the cafeteria, or on the playing field, or on the campus during the authorized hours, he may express his opinions, even on controversial subjects like the conflict in Vietnam, if he does so without "materially and substantially interfer(ing) with the requirements of appropriate discipline in the operation of the school" and without colliding with the rights of others. *But conduct by the student, in class or out of it, which for any reason whether it stems from time, place or type of behavior materially disrupts classwork or involves substantial disorder or invasion of the rights of others is, of course, not immunized by the constitutional guarantee of freedom of speech.*

It seems to me that here, not unlike in *Tinker*, the school administrators were acting on "an undifferentiated fear or apprehension of disturbance." True, Aaron was punched and then security measures were taken, but since that incident he has not been threatened with violence nor has he been attacked. There has been no disruption at the school; classes have not been cancelled, suspended, or interrupted. In short, while the defendants have perhaps shown more of a basis for fear of harm than in *Tinker*, they have failed to make a "showing" that Aaron's conduct would "materially and substantially interfere" with school discipline. However, even if the Court assumes that there is justifiable fear and that Aaron's peaceful speech leads, or may lead, to a violent reaction from others, the question remains: may the school prohibit the speech, or must it protect the speaker?

It is certainly clear that outside of the classroom the fear however justified of a violent reaction is not sufficient reason to restrain such speech in advance, and an actual hostile reaction is rarely an adequate basis for curtailing free speech. Thus, the question here is whether the interest in school discipline and order, recognized in *Tinker*, requires a different approach.

After considerable thought and research, I have concluded that even a legitimate interest in school discipline does not outweigh a student's right to peacefully express his views in an appropriate time, place, and manner. To rule otherwise would completely subvert free speech in the schools by granting other students a "heckler's veto," allowing them to decide through prohibited and violent methods what speech will be heard. The first amendment does not tolerate mob rule by unruly school children. This conclusion is bolstered by the fact that any disturbance here, however great, would not interfere with the main business of school education. No classes or school work would be affected; at the very worst an optional social event, conducted by the students for their own enjoyment, would be marred. In such a context, the school does have an obligation to take reasonable measures to protect and foster free speech, not to stand helpless before unauthorized student violence.

This holding is supported by other cases that have considered the problem, although they were not actually confronted with a reasonable expectation of a disturbance. In *Butts v. Dallas Independent School District*, 436 F.2d 728, 732 (5th Cir. 1971), the fifth circuit protected the wearing of black armbands saying:

> we do not agree that the precedential value of the *Tinker* decision is nullified whenever a school system is confronted with disruptive activities or the possibility of them. Rather we believe that the Supreme Court has declared a constitutional right which school authorities must nurture and protect, not extinguish, unless they find the circumstances allow them no practical alternative.

Judge Goldberg's well reasoned and eloquent opinion in *Shanley v. Northeast Independent School District*, 462 F.2d 960, 973–74 (5th Cir. 1972), upholding the right of high school students to write and distribute a newspaper off school grounds, asserted:

> However, we must emphasize in the context of this case that even reasonably forecast disruption is not per se justification for prior restraint or subsequent punishment of expression afforded to students by the First Amendment. If the content of a student's expression could give rise to a disturbance from those who hold opposing views, then it is certainly within the power of the school administration to regulate the time, place, and manner of distribution with even greater latitude of discretion. And the administration should, of course, take all reasonable steps to control disturbances, however generated. We are simply taking note here of the fact that disturbances themselves can be wholly without reasonable or rational basis, and that those students who would reasonably exercise their freedom of expression should not be restrained or punishable at the threshold of their attempts at expression merely because a small, perhaps vocal or violent, group of students with differing views might or does create a disturbance.

The present case is so difficult because the Court is keenly sensitive to the testimony regarding the concerns of a possible disturbance, and of physical harm to Aaron or Paul. However, I am convinced that meaningful security measures are possible, and the first amendment requires that such steps be taken to protect rather than to stifle free expression. Some may feel that Aaron's attendance at the reception and the message he will thereby convey is trivial compared to other social debates, but to engage in this kind of a weighing in process is to make the content-based evaluation forbidden by the first amendment.

As to the other concern raised by *Tinker*, some people might say that Aaron Fricke's conduct would infringe the rights of the other students, and is thus unprotected by *Tinker*. This view is misguided, however. Aaron's conduct is quiet and peaceful; it demands no response from others and in a crowd of some five hundred people can be easily ignored. Any disturbance that might interfere with the rights of others would be caused by those students who resort to violence, not by Aaron and his companion, who do not want a fight.

Because the free speech claim is dispositive, I find it unnecessary to reach the plaintiff's right of association argument or to deal at length with his equal protection claim....

As a final note, I would add that the social problems presented by homosexuality are emotionally charged; community norms are in flux, and the psychiatric profession itself is divided in its attitude towards homosexuality. This Court's role, of course, is not to mandate social norms or impose its own view of acceptable behavior. It is instead, to interpret and apply the Constitution as best it can. The Constitution is not self-explanatory, and answers to knotty problems are inevitably inexact. All that an individual judge can do is to apply the legal precedents as accurately and as honestly as he can, uninfluenced by personal predilections or the fear of community reaction, hoping each time to disprove the legal maxim that "hard cases make bad law."

Doe v. Yunits

2000 WL 33162199 (Mass. Dist. Ct. 2000)

MEMORANDUM OF DECISION AND ORDER ON PLAINTIFF'S MOTION FOR PRELIMINARY INJUNCTION

GILES.

Plaintiff Pat Doe ("plaintiff"), a fifteen-year-old student, has brought this action by her next friend, Jane Doe, requesting that this court prohibit defendants from excluding the plaintiff from South Junior High School ("South Junior High"), Brockton, Massachusetts, on the basis of the plaintiff's sex, disability, or gender identity and expression. Plaintiff has been diagnosed with gender identity disorder, which means that, although plaintiff was born biologically male, she has a female gender identity. Plaintiff seeks to attend school wearing clothes and fashion accouterments that are consistent with her gender identity. Defendants have informed plaintiff that she could not enroll in school this academic year if she wore girls' clothes or accessories. After a hearing, and for the reasons stated below, plaintiff's motion for preliminary injunction is *ALLOWED*.

BACKGROUND

Plaintiff began attending South Junior High, a Brockton public school, in September 1998, as a 7th grader. In early 1999, plaintiff first began to express her female gender identity by wearing girls' make-up, shirts, and fashion accessories to school. South Junior High has a dress code which prohibits, among other things, "clothing which could be disruptive or distractive to the educational process or which could affect the safety of students." In early 1999, the principal, Kenneth Cardone ("Cardone"), would often send the plaintiff home to change if she arrived at school wearing girls' apparel. On some occasions, plaintiff would change and return to school; other times, she would remain home, too upset to return. In June 1999, after being referred to a therapist by the South Junior High, plaintiff was diagnosed with gender identity disorder. Plaintiff's treating therapist, Judith Havens ("Havens"), determined that it was medically and clinically necessary for plaintiff to wear clothing consistent with the female gender and that failure to do so could cause harm to plaintiff's mental health.

Plaintiff returned to school in September 1999, as an 8th grader, and was instructed by Cardone to come to his office every day so that he could approve the plaintiff's appearance. Some days the plaintiff would be sent home to change, sometimes returning to school dressed differently and sometimes remaining home. During the 1999–2000 school year, plaintiff stopped attending school, citing the hostile environment created by Cardone. Because of plaintiff's many absences during the 1999–2000 school year, plaintiff was required to repeat the 8th grade this year.

Over the course of the 1998–1999 and 1999–2000 school years, plaintiff sometimes arrived at school wearing such items as skirts and dresses, wigs, high-heeled shoes, and padded bras with tight shirts. The school faculty and administration became concerned because the plaintiff was experiencing trouble with some of her classmates. Defendants cite one occasion when the school adjustment counselor had to restrain a male student because he was threatening to punch the plaintiff for allegedly spreading rumors that the two had engaged in oral sex. Defendants also point to an instance when a school official had to break up a confrontation between the plaintiff and a male student to whom plaintiff persistently blew kisses. At another time, plaintiff grabbed the buttock of a male student in the school cafeteria. Plaintiff also has been known to primp, pose, apply make up, and flirt with other students in class. Defendants also advance that the plaintiff sometimes called attention to herself by yelling and dancing in the halls. Plaintiff has been suspended at least three times for using the ladies' restroom after being warned not to.

On Friday, September 1, 2000, Cardone and Dr. Kenneth Sennett ("Sennett"), Senior Director for Pupil Personnel Services, met with the plaintiff relative to repeating the 8th grade. At that meeting, Cardone and Sennett informed the plaintiff that she would not be allowed to attend South Junior High if she were to wear any outfits disruptive to the educational process, specifically padded bras, skirts or dresses, or wigs. On September 21, 2000, plaintiff's grandmother tried to enroll plaintiff in school and was told by Cardone and Sennett that plaintiff would not be permitted to enroll if she wore any girls' clothing or accessories. Defendants allege that they have not barred the plaintiff from school but have merely provided limits on the type of dress the plaintiff may wear. Defendants claim it is the plaintiff's own choice not to attend school because of the guidelines they have placed on her attire. Plaintiff is not currently attending school, but the school has provided a home tutor for her to allow her to keep pace with her classmates.

On September 26, 2000, the plaintiff filed a complaint in this court claiming ... a violation of her right to free expression as guaranteed by the [Massachusetts] Declaration of Rights. ...

DISCUSSION

....

A. Freedom of Expression, Massachusetts Declaration of Rights, Art. II and X

The Massachusetts Declaration of Rights ... provides, "[t]he right of free speech shall not be abridged." The analysis of this article is guided by federal free speech analysis. According to federal analysis, this court must first determine whether the plaintiff's symbolic acts constitute expressive speech. ... If the speech is expressive, the court must next determine if the defendants' conduct was impermissible because it was meant to suppress that speech. See *Texas v. Johnson,* 491 U.S. 397, 403 (1989), citing *United States v. O'Brien,*

391 U.S. 367, 377 (1968); see also *Spence v. Washington,* 418 U.S. 405, 414 n. 8 (1974). If the defendants' conduct is not related to the suppression of speech, furthers an important or substantial governmental interest, and is within the constitutional powers of the government, and if the incidental restriction on speech is no greater than necessary, the government's conduct is permissible. See *United States v. O'Brien, supra.* In addition, because this case involves public school students, suppression of speech that "materially and substantially interferes with the work of the school" is permissible. See *Tinker v. Des Moines Community School Dist.,* 393 U.S. 503, 739 (1969).

1. The Plaintiff's Conduct is Expressive Speech Which is Understood by Those Perceiving It

Symbolic acts constitute expression if the actor's intent to convey a particularized message is likely to be understood by those perceiving the message. See *Spence v. Washington,* 418 U.S. 405, 410–11 (1974) (finding that an upside-down flag with a peace symbol attached was protected speech because it was a purposeful message people could understand); see also *Chalifoux v. New Caney Independent School Dist.,* 976 F.Supp. 659 (S.D.Tex.1997) (students wearing rosary beads as a sign of their religious belief was likely to be understood by others and therefore protected).

Plaintiff in this case is likely to establish that, by dressing in clothing and accessories traditionally associated with the female gender, she is expressing her identification with that gender. In addition, plaintiff's ability to express herself and her gender identity through dress is important to her health and well-being, as attested to by her treating therapist. Therefore, plaintiff's expression is not merely a personal preference but a necessary symbol of her very identity. Contrast *Olesen v. Board of Education of School District No. 228,* 676 F.Supp. 820 (N.D.Ill.1987) (school's anti-gang policy of prohibiting males from wearing earrings, passed for safety reasons, was upheld because plaintiff's desire to wear an earring as an expression of his individuality and attractiveness to girls was a message not within the scope of the First Amendment).

This court must next determine if the plaintiff's message was understood by those perceiving it, i.e., the school faculty and plaintiff's fellow students. See *Bivens v. Albuquerque Public Schools,* 899 F.Supp. 556 (D.N.M.1995) (student failed to provide evidence that his wearing of sagging pants to express his identity as a black youth was understood by others and, therefore, such attire was not speech). In the case at bar, defendants contend that junior high school students are too young to understand plaintiff's expression of her female gender identity through dress and that "not every defiant act by a high school student is constitutionally protected speech." *Id.* at 558. However, unlike *Bivens,* here there is strong evidence that plaintiff's message is well understood by faculty and students. The school's vehement response and some students' hostile reactions are proof of the fact that the plaintiff's message clearly has been received. Moreover, plaintiff is likely to establish, through testimony, that her fellow students are well aware of the fact that she is a biological male more comfortable wearing traditionally "female"-type clothing because of her identification with that gender.

2. The Defendants' Conduct Was a Suppression of the Plaintiff's Speech

Plaintiff also will probably prevail on the merits of the second prong of the *Texas v. Johnson* test, that is, the defendants' conduct was meant to suppress plaintiff's speech. Defendants in this case have prohibited the plaintiff from wearing items of clothing that are traditionally labeled girls' clothing, such as dresses and skirts, padded bras, and wigs. This constitutes direct suppression of speech because biological females who wear items such as tight skirts to school are unlikely to be disciplined by school officials, as admitted by defendants' counsel at oral argument. See *Texas v. Johnson,* 491 U.S. 397, 408–16

(1989). Therefore, the test set out in *United States v. O'Brien,* which permits restrictions on speech where the government motivation is not directly related to the content of the speech, cannot apply here. Further, defendants' argument that the school's policy is a content-neutral regulation of speech is without merit because, as has been discussed, the school is prohibiting the plaintiff from wearing clothes a biological female would be allowed to wear. Therefore, the plaintiff has a likelihood of fulfilling the *Texas v. Johnson* test that her speech conveyed a particularized message understood by others and that the defendants' conduct was meant to suppress that speech.

3. Plaintiff's Conduct is not Disruptive

This court also must consider if the plaintiff's speech "materially and substantially interferes with the work of the school." *Tinker v. Des Moines Community School Dist., supra.* Defendants argue that they are merely preventing disruptive conduct on the part of the plaintiff by restricting her attire at school. Their argument is unpersuasive. Given the state of the record thus far, the plaintiff has demonstrated a likelihood of proving that defendants, rather than attempting to restrict plaintiff's wearing of distracting items of clothing, are seeking to ban her from donning apparel that can be labeled "girls' clothes" and to encourage more conventional, male-oriented attire. Defendants argue that any other student who came to school dressed in distracting clothing would be disciplined as the plaintiff was. However, defendants overlook the fact that, if a female student came to school in a frilly dress or blouse, make-up, or padded bra, she would go, and presumably has gone, unnoticed by school officials. Defendants do not find plaintiff's clothing distracting *per se,* but, essentially, distracting simply because plaintiff is a biological male.

In addition to the expression of her female gender identity through dress, however, plaintiff has engaged in behavior in class and towards other students that can be seen as detrimental to the learning process. This deportment, however, is separate from plaintiff's dress. Defendants vaguely cite instances when the principal became aware of threats by students to beat up the "boy who dressed like a girl" to support the notion that plaintiff's dress alone is disruptive. To rule in defendants' favor in this regard, however, would grant those contentious students a "heckler's veto." See *Fricke v. Lynch,* 491 F.Sup. 381, 387 (D.R.I. 1980). The majority of defendants' evidence of plaintiff's disruption is based on plaintiff's actions as distinct from her mode of dress. Some of these acts may be a further expression of gender identity, such as applying make-up in class; but many are instances of misconduct for which any student would be punished. Regardless of plaintiff's gender identity, any student should be punished for engaging in harassing behavior towards classmates. Plaintiff is not immune from such punishment but, by the same token, should not be punished on the basis of dress alone.

Plaintiff has framed this issue narrowly as a question of whether or not it is appropriate for defendants to restrict the manner in which she can dress. Defendants, on the other hand, appear unable to distinguish between instances of conduct connected to plaintiff's expression of her female gender identity, such as the wearing of a wig or padded bra, and separate from it, such as grabbing a male student's buttocks or blowing kisses to a male student. The line between expression and flagrant behavior can blur, thereby rendering this case difficult for the court. It seems, however, that expression of gender identity through dress can be divorced from conduct in school that warrants punishment, regardless of the gender or gender identity of the offender. Therefore, a school should not be allowed to bar or discipline a student because of gender-identified dress but should be permitted to ban clothing that would be inappropriate if worn by any student, such as a theatrical costume, and to punish conduct that would be deemed offensive if committed by any student, such as harassing, threatening, or obscene behavior. See *Bethel v. Fraser,* 478 U.S. 675 (1986)....

Zamecnik v. Indian Prairie School District No. 204

636 F.3d 874 (7th Cir. 2011)

POSNER, Circuit Judge.

These consolidated appeals (functionally one appeal, and we'll treat them as such) are a sequel to an appeal we decided almost three years ago, *Nuxoll v. Indian Prairie School Dist. # 204,* 523 F.3d 668 (7th Cir.2008). The plaintiffs, two students at Neuqua Valley High School, a large public high school in Naperville, Illinois, had sued the school district (and school officials, whom we can ignore — we'll call the defendants, collectively, "the school") for infringing their right of free speech by forbidding them to make a specific negative statement about homosexuality. They moved for a preliminary injunction, which the district judge denied. They appealed, and we reversed, directing the district judge to enter forthwith a preliminary injunction that would permit plaintiff Nuxoll (Zamecnik having graduated) to wear during school hours a T-shirt that recites "Be Happy, Not Gay." Nuxoll's right to wear it outside of school is not questioned.

A private group called the Gay, Lesbian, and Straight Education Network promotes an annual event called the Day of Silence that is intended to draw critical attention to harassment of homosexuals; the idea behind the name is that homosexuals are silenced by harassment and other discrimination. Students participate in the Day of Silence by remaining silent throughout the day except when called upon in class, though some teachers, as part of their own observance of the Day of Silence, will not call on students that day. Some students and faculty wear T-shirts on the Day of Silence that display slogans such as "Be Who You Are." None of the slogans criticizes heterosexuality or advocates homosexuality, though "Be Who You Are" carries the suggestion that persons who are homosexual should not be ashamed of the fact or try to change it.

The plaintiffs, who disapprove of homosexuality on religious grounds, participated (we use the past tense because both have now graduated) with other like-minded students in a Day of Truth held on the first school day after the Day of Silence. Plaintiff Zamecnik wore a shirt that read "*My* Day of Silence, Straight Alliance" on the front and "Be Happy, Not Gay" on the back. A school official inked out the phrase "Not Gay" and has banned display of the slogan as a violation of a school rule forbidding "derogatory comments," spoken or written, "that refer to race, ethnicity, religion, gender, *sexual orientation,* or disability" (emphasis added). He did not object to the slogan on the front of the shirt.

The plaintiffs assert a constitutional right to make negative statements about members of any group provided the statements are not inflammatory — that is, are not "fighting words," which means speech likely to provoke a violent response amounting to a breach of the peace. *Chaplinsky v. New Hampshire,* 315 U.S. 568, 572–73 (1942). They concede that they could not inscribe "homosexuals go to Hell" on their T-shirts because those are fighting words, at least in a high-school setting, and so could be prohibited despite the fact that they are speech, disseminating an opinion. *R.A.V. v. City of St. Paul,* 505 U.S. 377, 386 (1992).

When last this case was here, we expressed (and we repeat our expression of) sympathy (thought excessive by Judge Rovner in her concurring opinion, 523 F.3d at 676–80) for an expansive interpretation of the "fighting words" doctrine when the speech in question is that of students. We noted that the contribution that kids can make to the marketplace of ideas and opinions is modest (Judge Rovner disagreed) and we emphasized (overemphasized, in her view) a school's countervailing interest in protecting its students from offensive speech by their classmates that would interfere with the learning process —

though we added that because 18-year-olds can now vote, high-school students should not be "raised in an intellectual bubble," *American Amusement Machine Ass'n v. Kendrick,* 244 F.3d 572, 577 (7th Cir.2001), which would be the tendency of forbidding all discussion of public issues by such students during school hours. (Hence the younger the children, the more latitude the school authorities have in limiting expression. *Muller ex rel. Muller v. Jefferson Lighthouse School,* 98 F.3d 1530, 1538–39 (7th Cir.1996).)

Thus a school that permits advocacy of the rights of homosexual students cannot be allowed to stifle criticism of homosexuality. The school argued (and still argues) that banning "Be Happy, Not Gay" was just a matter of protecting the "rights" of the students against whom derogatory comments are directed. But people in our society do not have a legal right to prevent criticism of their beliefs or even their way of life. *R.A.V. v. City of St. Paul, supra,* 505 U.S. at 394; *Boos v. Barry,* 485 U.S. 312, 321 (1988). Although tolerance of homosexuality has grown, gay marriage remains highly controversial. Today's high school students may soon find themselves, as voters, asked to vote on whether to approve gay marriage, or to vote for candidates who approve of it, or ones who disapprove.

In asking for a preliminary injunction Nuxoll acknowledged that "Be Happy, Not Gay" was one of the "negative comments" about homosexuality that he thought himself entitled to make. But we said that unlike "homosexuals go to Hell," which he concedes are "fighting words" in the context of a school (and unlike "I will not accept what God has condemned" and "homosexuality is shameful"—terms held, perhaps questionably—unless euphemism is to be the only permitted mode of expressing a controversial opinion—to be fighting words in *Harper v. Poway Unified School District,* 445 F.3d 1166, 1171 (9th Cir.2006), *vacated as moot,* 549 U.S. 1262 (2007)), "Be Happy, Not Gay" is not an instance of fighting words. To justify prohibiting their display the school would have to present "facts which might reasonably lead school officials to forecast substantial disruption." *Tinker v. Des Moines Independent Community School District,* 393 U.S. 503, 514 (1969). Such facts might include a decline in students' test scores, an upsurge in truancy, or other symptoms of a sick school—but the school had presented no such facts in response to the motion for a preliminary injunction.

In this factual vacuum, we described "Be Happy, Not Gay" as "only tepidly negative," saying that "derogatory" or "demeaning" seemed too strong a characterization. As one would expect in a high school of more than 4,000 students, there had been incidents of harassment of homosexual students. But we thought it speculative that allowing the plaintiff to wear a T-shirt that said "Be Happy, Not Gay" "would have even a slight tendency to provoke such incidents, or for that matter to poison the educational atmosphere. Speculation that it might is, under the ruling precedents, and on the scanty record compiled thus far in the litigation, too thin a reed on which to hang a prohibition of the exercise of a student's free speech."

Not that *Tinker's* "substantial disruption" test has proved a model of clarity in its application. The cases have tended to rely on judicial intuition rather than on data, and the intuitions are sometimes out of date. For example, although it's been ruled that "lewd, vulgar, obscene, or plainly offensive speech" can be banned from a school, *Canady v. Bossier Parish School Bd.,* 240 F.3d 437, 442 (5th Cir.2001), the authority for the ruling—*Bethel School District No. 403 v. Fraser,* 478 U.S. 675, 680–82 (1986)—involved student speech that, from the perspective enabled by 25 years of erosion of refinement in the use of language, seems distinctly lacking in shock value (e.g., "I know a man who is firm—he's firm in his pants, he's firm in his shirt, his character is firm—but most ... of all, his belief in you, the students of Bethel, is firm," *id.* at 687 (concurring opinion)). An example of school censorship that courts have authorized on firmer grounds is forbidding display of the Confederate flag, as in *Defoe ex rel. Defoe v. Spiva,* 625 F.3d 324,

333–36 and n. 6 (6th Cir.2010); *Scott v. School Board of Alachua County*, 324 F.3d 1246, 1248–49 (11th Cir.2003) (per curiam), and *West v. Derby Unified School District No. 260*, 206 F.3d 1358, 1361, 1365–66 (10th Cir.2000)—cases in which serious racial tension had led to outbursts of violence even before the display of the flag, which is widely regarded as racist and incendiary. *Boroff v. Van Wert City Board of Education*, 220 F.3d 465, 467, 469–71 (6th Cir.2000), involved T-shirts that depicted a three-faced Jesus, accompanied by the words "See No Truth. Hear No Truth. Speak No Truth" and advocated, albeit obliquely, the use of illegal drugs, a form of advocacy in the school setting that can be prohibited without evidence of disruption. *Morse v. Frederick*, 551 U.S. 393, 406–10 (2007).

These cases, more extreme than ours, do not establish a generalized "hurt feelings" defense to a high school's violation of the First Amendment rights of its students. "A particular form of harassment or intimidation can be regulated ... only if ... the speech at issue gives rise to a well-founded fear of disruption or interference with the rights of others." *Sypniewski v. Warren Hills Regional Bd. of Education*, 307 F.3d 243, 264–65 (3d Cir.2002). The same court, in *Saxe v. State College Area School District*, 240 F.3d 200, 209 (3d Cir.2001), found "little basis for the District Court's sweeping assertion that 'harassment'—at least when it consists of speech targeted solely on the basis of its expressive content—'has never been considered to be protected activity under the First Amendment.' Such a categorical rule is without precedent in the decisions of the Supreme Court or this Court, and it belies the very real tension between anti-harassment laws and the Constitution's guarantee of freedom of speech." Severe harassment, however, blends insensibly into bullying, intimidation, and provocation, which can cause serious disruption of the decorum and peaceable atmosphere of an institution dedicated to the education of youth. School authorities are entitled to exercise discretion in determining when student speech crosses the line between hurt feelings and substantial disruption of the educational mission, because they have the relevant knowledge of and responsibility for the consequences.

As Judge Rovner explained in her concurring opinion in the previous appeal, "the statement ['Be Happy, Not Gay'] is clearly intended to derogate homosexuals. Teenagers today often use the word 'gay' as a generic term of disparagement. They might say, 'That sweater is so gay' as a way of insulting the look of the garment. In this way, Nuxoll's statement is really a double-play on words because 'gay' formerly meant 'happy' in common usage, and now 'gay,' in addition to meaning 'homosexual' is also often used as a general insult. Nuxoll's statement easily fits the school's definition of 'disparaging' and would meet that standard for most listeners.... [T]here is no doubt that the slogan is disparaging.... [But] it is not the kind of speech that would materially and substantially interfere with school activities. I suspect that similar uses of the word 'gay' abound in the halls of [Neuqua Valley High School] and virtually every other high school in the United States without causing any substantial interruption to the educational process." Judge Rovner warned that the fact that schools "are educating the young for citizenship is reason for scrupulous protection of Constitutional freedoms of the individual, if we are not to strangle the free mind at its source.... The First Amendment ... is consistent with the school's mission to teach by encouraging debate on controversial topics while also allowing the school to limit the debate when it becomes substantially disruptive. Nuxoll's slogan-adorned T-shirt comes nowhere near that standard."

The preliminary injunction issued on remand permitted Nuxoll to wear during school hours a T-shirt that recites "Be Happy, Not Gay." Pretrial discovery ensued. Eventually the district judge granted summary judgment in favor of the plaintiffs, awarded each of them $25 in damages for the infringement of their constitutional rights, and later entered a permanent injunction, which differs from the preliminary one in running in favor of any student and in not being limited to the display of the slogan on a T-shirt; for "T-shirt" the permanent injunction substitutes "clothing or personal items."

The judge had granted summary judgment against the school district on April 29, 2010, after classes had ended but before final exams. By the time he entered the permanent injunction, on May 20, Nuxoll was about to graduate. (Zamecnik was long gone.) All that remained for graduating seniors to do was to participate in a few ceremonial events culminating in the graduation ceremony on May 23. The school argues that injunctive relief was moot on May 20 because Nuxoll had no occasion to wear his "Be Happy, Not Gay" T-shirt at the ceremonial events, and did not. But remember that the injunction had been broadened to permit the display of the slogan on other clothing as well, and so he could by virtue of the injunction have displayed it on his graduation gown had he wanted to.

The school points out that the graduation wasn't held on school grounds and that the injunction doesn't apply to the display of the slogan elsewhere; that's because the school has never asserted a right to control speech off school property. But it would very much like to control it at the graduation ceremony, and so treats the venue of the ceremony as temporary school grounds, as by imposing a dress code on the graduating students and enforcing its school rules against drunkenness and other disruptive behavior—and it regards the display of the slogan "Be Happy, Not Gay" as disruptive.

The claim of mootness evaporates completely when one notes that the permanent injunction runs in favor of any student at the high school, not just Nuxoll; it is not unlikely that one or more of its 4,000-plus students may someday want to display the slogan. Injunctions often run in favor of unnamed members of a group, and this is proper as long as the group is specified....

The school's main argument is that the district judge entered summary judgment prematurely. He did if the school presented enough evidence to warrant an evidentiary hearing to determine whether the school had had a reasonable belief that it faced a threat of substantial disruption. To carry its burden it presented three types of evidence: incidents of harassment of homosexual students; incidents of harassment of plaintiff Zamecnik; and the report of an expert which concluded that the slogan "Be Happy, Not Gay" was "particularly insidious."

The first type of evidence was negligible: a handful of incidents years before the T-shirt was first worn, in a school with thousands of students. The evidence consists, moreover, of just the affidavit and deposition of a single school district official, which merely repeats statements by other, unidentified school officials repeating statements by unidentified students. The deponent described but could not confirm the details of the incidents— and admitted that because the allegations of harassment had not been confirmed, no students had been disciplined.

The second type of evidence was barred by the doctrine, unmentioned by the school, of the "heckler's veto." *Brown v. Louisiana,* 383 U.S. 131, 133 n. 1 (1966); *Tinker v. Des Moines Independent Community School District, supra,* 393 U.S. at 508–09; *Terminiello v. City of Chicago,* 337 U.S. 1, 4–5 (1949); *Hedges v. Wauconda Community Unit School Dist. No. 118,* 9 F.3d 1295, 1299–1300 (7th Cir.1993). Statements that while not fighting words are met by violence or threats or other unprivileged retaliatory conduct by persons offended by them cannot lawfully be suppressed because of that conduct. Otherwise free speech could be stifled by the speaker's opponents' mounting a riot, even though, because the speech had contained no fighting words, no reasonable person would have been moved to a riotous response. So the fact that homosexual students and their sympathizers harassed Zamecnik because of their disapproval of her message is not a permissible ground for banning it.

Two of the cases that endorse the doctrine of the heckler's veto, *Tinker* and *Hedges,* are school cases, but *Tinker* is also the source of the substantial disruption test of permissible school censorship. A city can protect an unpopular speaker from the violence of an angry audience by deploying police, but that is hardly an apt response to students enraged by a T-shirt. A school has legitimate responsibilities, albeit paternalistic in character, toward the immature captive audience that consists of its students, including the responsibility of protecting them from being seriously distracted from their studies by offensive speech during school hours.

But the anger engendered by Zamecnik's wearing a T-shirt that said "Be Happy, Not Gay" did not give rise to substantial disruption. It was not her wearing the shirt, but her filing this lawsuit, that engendered the creation of a Facebook group entitled "Be Happy! Not Heidi" (Zamecnik's first name) in which hundreds of comments were posted, many hostile to her. But only one was a threat ("someone tells me where she lives, i will fuck up her house, car, and whatever else i can find"), and it provoked a sensible comment from another student: "you sound [when making threats] just as stupid as she does." Many of the comments addressed substantial issues involving First Amendment claims, school policies, treatment of homosexual students, and the role of the media in the dispute; and apart from the obsessive use of expletives—a defining feature of modern American culture, by no means limited to teenagers—the discussion of the issues was substantive, and even, to a degree, thoughtful. Here are typical comments: "The social studies teachers are going to be having a department meeting right after Spring Break in order to be able to discuss this whole law suit in an educational way, to bring up some really meaningful discussion. More than anything, this case boils down to an issue of constitutional rights. And frankly, school rules override the constitutional rights of minors in the public school system. The school has the right to search and seizure at any time, despite constitutional law. Similarly, 'free speech' doesn't apply in public schools, because school rules are more specific"; "I'm very glad that so many people are banding together against discrimination, just please go about it in a classy and mature way; just like Ana said on the message board, don't stoop to her [Zamecnik's] level"; "Heidi isn't suing because she hates gays, she's suing because she was harassed for being active in what she believes in. I also think that if you were put in her situation, you'd fight tooth and nail to get whatever fucking point it is you are trying to get across. With every good, there is the bad. You have to take it in stride, not make up some stupid community making fun of someone. Heidi is actually a really nice person who is just misguided by religion and a closed mind."

Zamecnik's parents asked the school to allow a bodyguard to accompany her to class on the 2007 Day of Silence. Her mother said she was worried by the "threats that these particular students had made against Heidi expressing her view." The school did not allow the bodyguard but did have a female staff member escort Zamecnik from class to class on that day. She decided not to wear her "Be Happy, Not Gay" shirt. There were no serious incidents, though it is possible that a water bottle that was thrown and struck one of her friends had been aimed at her.

That leaves for consideration the expert's report. Stephen T. Russell has a Ph.D. in sociology and is a professor of family and consumer sciences at the University of Arizona. His 38-page report, 29 pages of which are devoted to his impressive curriculum vitae, establishes that he's qualified to give expert testimony on matters relating to the attitudes and behavior of teenagers, with special reference to teenagers who belong to minorities, including sexual minorities—including therefore homosexual high-school students. Yet the "analysis and opinions" section of his report, minus its bibliographical references, is less than two and a half pages long and can satisfy none of the requirements for admissible expert testimony that are set forth in Rule 702 of the Federal Rules of Evidence: "(1) the testimony is based upon sufficient facts or data, (2) the testimony is the product of reliable principles and methods, and (3) the witness has applied the principles and methods reliably to the facts of the case."

All that the report says, in seven numbered paragraphs, is that: (1) harassment, particularly verbal, of homosexual students is common in schools; (2) schools should therefore have anti-harassment policies; (3) harassed students "are at risk for negative educational and health outcomes"; (4) "homophobic slurs and derogatory remarks" create a risk of "disruptive behavior including student victimization and violence"; (5) school districts can lose state funding "when students miss school because of feeling unsafe due to anti-gay bullying"; (6) the Day of Silence does not "promote homosexual conduct" or "promote the idea that homosexual conduct should be endorsed by society"; (7) "the phrase 'be happy, not gay' is not 'tepid' in a public school setting" and indeed "is particularly insidious because it references a long-standing stereotype that gay people are unhappy, yet appears to be a simple play on words." Points 1 through 6 are plausible inferences from the research that Dr. Russell has either conducted or cites in his report, or so at least we'll assume, though he does not discuss any of that research — just lists citations.

Point 7, however, which is the punchline, comes out of nowhere. There is nothing in the report to indicate that Russell knows anything about Neuqua Valley High School, for there is no reference to the school in the report. No example is given of "particularly insidious" statements about homosexuals. No example is given of a "homophobic slur" or "derogatory remark" about them that has ever been uttered in any school, or elsewhere for that matter. Though the report calls "be happy, not gay" particularly insidious, it does not indicate what effects it would be likely to have on homosexual students. It gives no

stus.com

indication of what kind of data or study or model Russell uses or other researchers use to base a prediction of harm to homosexual students on particular "negative comments." No methodology is described. No similar research is described.

In the idiom of Rule 702, the expert's report contains no indication of the "facts or data" relied on, no indication that testimony based on the report would be "the product of reliable principles and methods," and no indication that in formulating his opinion the expert "applied the principles and methods reliably to the facts of the case." Dr. Russell is an expert, but fails to indicate, however sketchily, how he used his expertise to generate his conclusion. Mere conclusions, without a "hint of an inferential process," are useless to the court. Russell's is as thin an expert-witness report as we've seen....

Notes and Questions

1. As indicated in *Fricke*, the U.S. Supreme Court has articulated a relaxed standard of review where communicative *conduct* is involved. At issue in *United States v. O'Brien*, 391 U.S. 367 (1968), was a First Amendment challenge to a statute that made it a crime to knowingly destroy or mutilate Selective Service registration certificates (i.e., draft cards). In upholding a conviction under the statute of four people who burned their registration certificates on the steps of a courthouse in an apparent protest, the Court held that "when 'speech' and 'nonspeech' elements are combined in the same course of conduct, a sufficiently important governmental interest in regulating the nonspeech element can justify incidental limitations on First Amendment freedoms." *Id.* at 376. In what is today referred to as the *O'Brien* test, the Court held that:

> a government regulation is sufficiently justified if it is within the constitutional power of the Government; if it furthers an important or substantial governmental interest; if the governmental interest is unrelated to the suppression of free expression; and if the incidental restriction on alleged First Amendment freedoms is no greater than is essential to the furtherance of that interest.

Id. at 377.

2. In *Zamecnik*, the court makes reference to *Morse v. Frederick*, 551 U.S. 393 (2007). At issue in that case was the constitutionality of suspending a student for failing to comply with an order by the principal to take down a 14-foot banner bearing the phrase "BONG HiTS 4 JESUS" that the student had unfurled during a high school event. There, the Court noted that the "facts of *Tinker* are quite stark, implicating concerns at the heart of the First Amendment" in that "[t]he students sought to engage in political speech." *Morse*, 551 U.S. at 403. After determining that the speech at issue in *Morse* could reasonably be viewed by the principal as promoting illegal drug use (as opposed to political speech advocating the decriminalization of drugs), the *Morse* Court concluded that there was no need to employ *Tinker*'s "substantial disruption" test, reasoning as follows:

> This Court's next student speech case [after *Tinker*] was *Fraser*. Matthew Fraser was suspended for delivering a speech before a high school assembly in which he employed what this Court called "an elaborate, graphic, and explicit sexual metaphor." Analyzing the case under *Tinker,* the District Court and Court of Appeals found no disruption, and therefore no basis for disciplining Fraser. This Court reversed, holding that the "School District acted entirely within its permissible authority in imposing sanctions upon Fraser in response to his offensively lewd and indecent speech."

The mode of analysis employed in *Fraser* is not entirely clear. The Court was plainly attuned to the content of Fraser's speech, citing the "marked distinction between the political 'message' of the armbands in *Tinker* and the sexual content of [Fraser's] speech." But the Court also reasoned that school boards have the authority to determine "what manner of speech in the classroom or in school assembly is inappropriate."

We need not resolve this debate to decide this case. For present purposes, it is enough to distill from *Fraser* two basic principles. First, *Fraser's* holding demonstrates that "the constitutional rights of students in public school are not automatically coextensive with the rights of adults in other settings." Had Fraser delivered the same speech in a public forum outside the school context, it would have been protected. See *Cohen v. California*, 403 U.S. 15 (1971); *Fraser, supra*, at 682–683. In school, however, Fraser's First Amendment rights were circumscribed "in light of the special characteristics of the school environment." *Tinker, supra*, at 506. Second, *Fraser* established that the mode of analysis set forth in *Tinker* is not absolute. Whatever approach *Fraser* employed, it certainly did not conduct the "substantial disruption" analysis prescribed by *Tinker*.

Id. at 404–05. How, if at all, does *Morse* alter the results in the cases examined in this section, many of which predate *Morse*? Is the speech at issue in *Fricke, Yunits*, and *Zamecnik* more akin to the speech at issue in *Tinker* or that in *Morse*?

3. In *Morse*, the Supreme Court acknowledged a second case in which it had declined to apply the *Tinker* "substantial disruption" standard, *Hazelwood School District v. Kuhlmeier*, 484 U.S. 260 (1988). At issue in *Hazelwood* was the constitutionality of school officials exercising editorial control over the content of a school-sponsored student newspaper:

The question whether the First Amendment requires a school to tolerate particular student speech—the question that we addressed in *Tinker*—is different from the question whether the First Amendment requires a school affirmatively to promote particular student speech. The former question addresses educators' ability to silence a student's personal expression that happens to occur on the school premises. The latter question concerns educators' authority over school-sponsored publications, theatrical productions, and other expressive activities that students, parents, and members of the public might reasonably perceive to bear the imprimatur of the school....

Educators are entitled to exercise greater control over this second form of student expression to assure that participants learn whatever lessons the activity is designed to teach, that readers or listeners are not exposed to material that may be inappropriate for their level of maturity, and that the views of the individual speaker are not erroneously attributed to the school....

Accordingly, we conclude that the standard articulated in *Tinker* for determining when a school may punish student expression need not also be the standard for determining when a school may refuse to lend its name and resources to the dissemination of student expression. Instead, we hold that educators do not offend the First Amendment by exercising editorial control over the style and content of student speech in school-sponsored expressive activities so long as their actions are reasonably related to legitimate pedagogical concerns.

Id. at 270–73.

4. Where restrictions on speech by public school *teachers* is involved, is the *Tinker* "substantial disruption" standard or *Pickering* balancing the appropriate test? *See Johnson*

v. Poway Unified Sch. Dist., 658 F.3d 954, 961–64 (9th Cir. 2011) (collecting cases holding that the *Pickering* balancing test governs).

5. When students engage in *off-campus* speech, does the *Tinker* "substantial disruption" standard apply to efforts to regulate their speech, or are such regulations governed by general First Amendment law? In *Kowalski v. Berkeley Cnty. Sch.*, 652 F.3d 565 (4th Cir. 2011), a case involving a student who was suspended for creating a web page (which the student created using a computer off campus and not during school hours) that the school viewed as verbally bullying other students, the court held — in accordance with the prevailing view — that *Tinker* applies to off-campus speech where it is "reasonably foreseeable that the post would reach the school and create a substantial disruption there." *Id.* at 574. *But see J.S. ex rel. Snyder v. Blue Mountain Sch. Dist.*, 650 F.3d 915, 940 (3d Cir. 2011) (Smith, J., concurring) ("Regardless of its place of origin, speech *intentionally* directed towards a school is properly considered on-campus speech. On the other hand, speech originating off campus does not mutate into on-campus speech simply because it foreseeably makes its way onto campus. A bare foreseeability standard could be stretched too far, and would risk ensnaring any off-campus expression that happened to discuss school-related matters.") (emphasis added).

Are there dangers to interpreting *Tinker* to apply to off-campus conduct? In this regard, consider the following hypothetical:

> Suppose a high school student, while at home after school hours, were to write a blog entry defending gay marriage. Suppose further that several of the student's classmates got wind of the entry, took issue with it, and caused a significant disturbance at school. While the school could clearly punish the students who acted disruptively, if *Tinker* were held to apply to off-campus speech, the school could also punish the student whose blog entry brought about the disruption.

J.S. ex rel. Snyder, 650 F.3d at 939 (Smith, J., concurring).

6. The *Tinker* line of cases involved children in the public junior high school and high school environments. Does *Tinker* apply in the college and university setting as well? The U.S. Supreme Court's decisions have cited with approval *Tinker*'s "substantial disruption" test in the context of cases involving colleges and universities, *see Christian Legal Soc'y Chapter of the Univ. of Cal., Hastings Coll. of the Law v. Martinez*, 130 S. Ct. 2971, 2988 (2010); *Widmar v. Vincent*, 454 U.S. 263, 267 n.5 (1981); *Healy v. James*, 408 U.S. 169, 189 (1972), although they have at least left open the possibility that *Tinker* might apply differently in the latter setting. *See, e.g., Hazelwood Sch. Dist. v. Kuhlmeier*, 484 U.S. 260, 273 n.7 (1988) ("A number of lower federal courts have similarly recognized that educators' decisions with regard to the content of school-sponsored newspapers, dramatic productions, and other expressive activities are entitled to substantial deference. We need not now decide whether the same degree of deference is appropriate with respect to school-sponsored expressive activities at the college and university level.").

Some lower federal courts have drawn a distinction between the public elementary and high school setting on the one hand and the college and university setting on the other, reasoning as follows:

> [U]niversity students, unlike public elementary and high school students, often reside in dormitories on campus, so they remain subject to university rules at almost all hours of the day. The concept of the "schoolhouse gate," and the idea that students may lose some aspects of their First Amendment right to freedom of speech while in school, does not translate well to an environment where the student is constantly within the confines of the schoolhouse. "Under our Con-

stitution, free speech is not a right that is given only to be so circumscribed that it exists in principle but not in fact." Yet this is exactly what would occur for students residing on university campuses were we to grant public university administrators the speech-prohibiting power afforded to public elementary and high school administrators. Those students would constantly be subject to a circumscription of their free speech rights due to university rules....

Public universities have significantly less leeway in regulating student speech than public elementary or high schools. Admittedly, it is difficult to explain how this principle should be applied in practice and it is unlikely that any broad categorical rules will emerge from its application. At a minimum, the teachings of *Tinker, Fraser, Hazelwood, Morse,* and other decisions involving speech in public elementary and high schools, cannot be taken as gospel in cases involving public universities.

McCauley v. Univ. of the Virgin Islands, 618 F.3d 232, 247 (3d Cir. 2010). *Accord Bd. of Regents of the Univ. of Wis. Sys. v. Southworth*, 529 U.S. 217, 238 n.4 (2000) (Souter, J., concurring) ("Our ... cases dealing with the right of teaching institutions to limit expressive freedom of students have been confined to high schools, whose students and their schools' relation to them are different and at least arguably distinguishable from their counterparts in college education.")

On the flip side, some decisions have raised the question whether the *Tinker* standard or instead some more deferential standard applies in the *elementary or preschool* context. *See, e.g., Muller by Muller v. Jefferson Lighthouse Sch.*, 98 F.3d 1530, 1538–39 (7th Cir. 1996). In any event, the lower courts seem to agree that assuming *Tinker* applies, it is applied with much more deference to school administrators than in the middle or high school context in light of the differences in student age and maturity. *See Morgan v. Swanson*, 659 F.3d 359, 385–87 (5th Cir. 2011); *S.G. ex rel. A.G. v. Sayreville Bd. of Educ.*, 333 F.3d 417, 423 (3d Cir. 2003).

7. Where regulation of student speech is involved, does the level of scrutiny turn on whether the regulation is viewpoint or content based versus viewpoint and content neutral? A number of lower federal courts have held that the *Tinker* "substantial disruption" test applies where schools engage in regulation of speech that is content based, while a more deferential standard applies to regulations that are content and viewpoint neutral. *See M.A.L. ex re. M.L. v. Kinsland*, 543 F.3d 841, 849–50 (6th Cir. 2008) (collecting cases); *Jacobs v. Clark Cnty. Sch. Dist.*, 526 F.3d 419, 430–35 (9th Cir. 2008).

8. The *Fricke, Doe,* and *Zamecnik* cases all make reference to the idea that, as a general rule, the First Amendment does not countenance a "heckler's veto." But does not the *Tinker* "substantial disruption" test, by definition, arguably take the risk of a "heckler's veto" into account in deciding whether or not speech in schools can be banned?

9. The risk of mootness can often arise in school-related cases because an event — such as a prom — may pass or a student may graduate before a court has a chance to rule. How did the plaintiff in *Zamecnik* avoid a finding of mootness in that case? More generally, how should a prospective plaintiff structure their lawsuit so as to avoid the risk of mootness in such a case?

F. Freedom to Speak Anonymously

In a series of cases, the U.S. Supreme Court has established that the right to free speech guaranteed by the First Amendment includes a right to speak anonymously. Thus, in

Talley v. California, 362 U.S. 60, 64 (1960), the Court struck down a broad city ordinance banning the distribution of anonymous handbills, noting that "[p]ersecuted groups and sects from time to time throughout history have been able to criticize oppressive practices and laws either anonymously or not at all," and reasoning that "an identification requirement would tend to restrict freedom to distribute information and thereby freedom of expression."

Talley was followed by *McIntyre v. Ohio Elections Commission*, 514 U.S. 334 (1995), which assessed the constitutionality of a more narrowly drawn Ohio law that only banned those anonymous communications designed to influence voters in an election. The Court held that even such a narrowly drawn law is subject to "exacting scrutiny," and will be upheld "only if it is narrowly tailored to serve an overriding state interest," *id.* at 347, a standard which the Court determined was not satisfied by the Ohio law. This was followed by *Buckley v. American Constitutional Law Foundation, Inc.*, 525 U.S. 182 (1999), which struck down as inconsistent with the right to speak anonymously a Colorado law requiring individuals circulating initiative and referendum petitions to wear identification badges.

In recent years, groups opposed to same-sex marriage have initiated signature drives designed to either amend state laws or constitutions to ban same-sex marriage or to require a citizen referendum on efforts by legislatures to extend marriage or marriage-like rights to same-sex couples. Bolstered by decisions such as *McIntyre* and *Buckley*, proponents of such efforts have sought to shield the identity of individuals signing the petitions as well as those donating to their campaigns. In contrast, proponents of GLBT rights have sought to obtain and expose the identity of people signing the petitions and supporting the campaigns. The following materials explore judicial responses to those efforts.

John Doe No. 1 v. Reed
130 S. Ct. 2811 (2010)

Chief Justice ROBERTS delivered the opinion of the Court.

....

I

The Washington Constitution reserves to the people the power to reject any bill, with a few limited exceptions not relevant here, through the referendum process. To initiate a referendum, proponents must file a petition with the secretary of state that contains valid signatures of registered Washington voters equal to or exceeding four percent of the votes cast for the office of Governor at the last gubernatorial election. A valid submission requires not only a signature, but also the signer's address and the county in which he is registered to vote.

In May 2009, Washington Governor Christine Gregoire signed into law Senate Bill 5688, which "expand[ed] the rights and responsibilities" of state-registered domestic partners, including same-sex domestic partners. That same month, Protect Marriage Washington, one of the petitioners here, was organized as a "State Political Committee" for the purpose of collecting the petition signatures necessary to place a referendum on the ballot, which would give the voters themselves an opportunity to vote on SB 5688. If the referendum made it onto the ballot, Protect Marriage Washington planned to encourage voters to reject SB 5688.

On July 25, 2009, Protect Marriage Washington submitted to the secretary of state a petition containing over 137,000 signatures. The secretary of state then began the verification and canvassing process, as required by Washington law, to ensure that only legal signatures were counted. Some 120,000 valid signatures were required to place the referendum on the ballot. The secretary of state determined that the petition contained a sufficient number of valid signatures, and the referendum (R-71) appeared on the November 2009 ballot. The voters approved SB 5688 by a margin of 53% to 47%.

The PRA, makes all "public records" available for public inspection and copying.... Washington takes the position that referendum petitions are "public records."

By August 20, 2009, the secretary had received requests for copies of the R-71 petition from an individual and four entities, including Washington Coalition for Open Government (WCOG) and Washington Families Standing Together (WFST), two of the respondents here. Two entities, WhoSigned.org and KnowThyNeighbor.org, issued a joint press release stating their intention to post the names of the R-71 petition signers online, in a searchable format.

The referendum petition sponsor and certain signers filed a complaint and a motion for a preliminary injunction in the United States District Court for the Western District of Washington, seeking to enjoin the secretary of state from publicly releasing any documents that would reveal the names and contact information of the R-71 petition signers. Count I of the complaint alleges that "[t]he Public Records Act is unconstitutional as applied to referendum petitions." Count II of the complaint alleges that "[t]he Public Records Act is unconstitutional as applied to the Referendum 71 petition because there is a reasonable probability that the signatories of the Referendum 71 petition will be subjected to threats, harassment, and reprisals." Determining that the PRA burdened core political speech, the District Court held that plaintiffs were likely to succeed on the merits of Count I and granted them a preliminary injunction on that count, enjoining release of the information on the petition.

The United States Court of Appeals for the Ninth Circuit reversed....

II

It is important at the outset to define the scope of the challenge before us.... The District Court decision was based solely on Count I; the Court of Appeals decision reversing the District Court was similarly limited. Neither court addressed Count II.

The parties disagree about whether Count I is properly viewed as a facial or as-applied challenge. It obviously has characteristics of both: The claim is "as applied" in the sense that it does not seek to strike the PRA in all its applications, but only to the extent it covers referendum petitions. The claim is "facial" in that it is not limited to plaintiffs' particular case, but challenges application of the law more broadly to all referendum petitions.

The label is not what matters. The important point is that plaintiffs' claim and the relief that would follow — an injunction barring the secretary of state "from making referendum petitions available to the public" — reach beyond the particular circumstances of these plaintiffs. They must therefore satisfy our standards for a facial challenge to the extent of that reach.

III

A

The compelled disclosure of signatory information on referendum petitions is subject to review under the First Amendment. An individual expresses a view on a political matter when he signs a petition under Washington's referendum procedure. In most cases, the individual's signature will express the view that the law subject to the petition should be overturned. Even if the signer is agnostic as to the merits of the underlying law, his signature still expresses the political view that the question should be considered "by the whole electorate." In either case, the expression of a political view implicates a First Amendment right....

Respondents counter that signing a petition is a legally operative legislative act and therefore "does not involve any significant expressive element." It is true that signing a referendum petition may ultimately have the legal consequence of requiring the secretary of state to place the referendum on the ballot. But we do not see how adding such legal effect to an expressive activity somehow deprives that activity of its expressive component, taking it outside the scope of the First Amendment. Respondents themselves implicitly recognize that the signature expresses a particular viewpoint, arguing that one purpose served by disclosure is to allow the public to engage signers in a debate on the merits of the underlying law.

Petition signing remains expressive even when it has legal effect in the electoral process. But that is not to say that the electoral context is irrelevant to the nature of our First Amendment review. We allow States significant flexibility in implementing their own voting systems. To the extent a regulation concerns the legal effect of a particular activity in that process, the government will be afforded substantial latitude to enforce that regulation. Also pertinent to our analysis is the fact that the PRA is not a prohibition on speech, but instead a *disclosure* requirement....

We have a series of precedents considering First Amendment challenges to disclosure requirements in the electoral context. These precedents have reviewed such challenges under what has been termed "exacting scrutiny."

That standard "requires a 'substantial relation' between the disclosure requirement and a 'sufficiently important' governmental interest." To withstand this scrutiny, "the strength of the governmental interest must reflect the seriousness of the actual burden on First Amendment rights."

B

Respondents assert two interests to justify the burdens of compelled disclosure under the PRA on First Amendment rights: (1) preserving the integrity of the electoral process by combating fraud, detecting invalid signatures, and fostering government transparency and accountability; and (2) providing information to the electorate about who supports the petition. Because we determine that the State's interest in preserving the integrity of the electoral process suffices to defeat the argument that the PRA is unconstitutional with respect to referendum petitions in general, we need not, and do not, address the State's "informational" interest.

The State's interest in preserving the integrity of the electoral process is undoubtedly important.... The State's interest is particularly strong with respect to efforts to root out fraud, which not only may produce fraudulent outcomes, but has a systemic effect as well: It "drives honest citizens out of the democratic process and breeds distrust of our government." The threat of fraud in this context is not merely hypothetical; respondents and their *amici* cite a number of cases of petition-related fraud across the country to support the point.

But the State's interest in preserving electoral integrity is not limited to combating fraud. That interest extends to efforts to ferret out invalid signatures caused not by fraud but by simple mistake, such as duplicate signatures or signatures of individuals who are not registered to vote in the State. That interest also extends more generally to promoting transparency and accountability in the electoral process, which the State argues is "essential to the proper functioning of a democracy."

Plaintiffs contend that the disclosure requirements of the PRA are not "sufficiently related" to the interest of protecting the integrity of the electoral process. They argue that disclosure is not necessary because the secretary of state is already charged with verifying and canvassing the names on a petition, advocates and opponents of a measure can observe that process, and any citizen can challenge the secretary's actions in court. They also stress that existing criminal penalties reduce the danger of fraud in the petition process.

But the secretary's verification and canvassing will not catch all invalid signatures: The job is large and difficult (the secretary ordinarily checks "only 3 to 5% of signatures"), and the secretary can make mistakes, too. Public disclosure can help cure the inadequacies of the verification and canvassing process.

Disclosure also helps prevent certain types of petition fraud otherwise difficult to detect, such as outright forgery and "bait and switch" fraud, in which an individual signs the petition based on a misrepresentation of the underlying issue. The signer is in the best position to detect these types of fraud, and public disclosure can bring the issue to the signer's attention.

Public disclosure thus helps ensure that the only signatures counted are those that should be, and that the only referenda placed on the ballot are those that garner enough valid signatures. Public disclosure also promotes transparency and accountability in the electoral process to an extent other measures cannot. In light of the foregoing, we reject plaintiffs' argument and conclude that public disclosure of referendum petitions in general is substantially related to the important interest of preserving the integrity of the electoral process.

C

Plaintiffs' more significant objection is that "the strength of the governmental interest" does not "reflect the seriousness of the actual burden on First Amendment rights." According to plaintiffs, the objective of those seeking disclosure of the R-71 petition is not to prevent fraud, but to publicly identify those who had validly signed and to broadcast the signers' political views on the subject of the petition. Plaintiffs allege, for example, that several groups plan to post the petitions in searchable form on the Internet, and then encourage other citizens to seek out the R-71 signers.

Plaintiffs explain that once on the Internet, the petition signers' names and addresses "can be combined with publicly available phone numbers and maps," in what will effectively become a blueprint for harassment and intimidation. To support their claim that they will be subject to reprisals, plaintiffs cite examples from the history of a similar proposition in California, and from the experience of one of the petition sponsors in this case.

In related contexts, we have explained that those resisting disclosure can prevail under the First Amendment if they can show "a reasonable probability that the compelled disclosure [of personal information] will subject them to threats, harassment, or reprisals from either Government officials or private parties." The question before us, however, is not whether PRA disclosure violates the First Amendment with respect to those who signed the R-71 petition, or other particularly controversial petitions. The question instead is whether such disclosure in general violates the First Amendment rights of those who sign referendum petitions.

The problem for plaintiffs is that their argument rests almost entirely on the specific harm they say would attend disclosure of the information on the R-71 petition, or on similarly controversial ones. Voters care about such issues, some quite deeply—but there is no reason to assume that any burdens imposed by disclosure of typical referendum petitions would be remotely like the burdens plaintiffs fear in this case.

Plaintiffs have offered little in response. They have provided us scant evidence or argument beyond the burdens they assert disclosure would impose on R-71 petition signers or the signers of other similarly controversial petitions. Indeed, what little plaintiffs do offer with respect to typical petitions in Washington hurts, not helps: Several other petitions in the State "have been subject to release in recent years," plaintiffs tell us, but apparently that release has come without incident.

Faced with the State's unrebutted arguments that only modest burdens attend the disclosure of a typical petition, we must reject plaintiffs' broad challenge to the PRA. In doing so, we note—as we have in other election law disclosure cases—that upholding the law against a broad-based challenge does not foreclose a litigant's success in a narrower one. The secretary of state acknowledges that plaintiffs may press the narrower challenge in Count II of their complaint in proceedings pending before the District Court...

[The concurring opinions of Justices Breyer, Alito, Sotomayor, Stevens, and Scalia, and the dissenting opinion of Justice Thomas, are omitted.]

Notes and Questions

1. In *Reed*, Justice Alito concurred separately to express his view that the as-applied challenge (Count II) should succeed, given the relatively high burden on the plaintiffs' First Amendment rights that would result from disclosure due to intimidation and harassment by gay rights supporters coupled with the relative weakness of the state's asserted interests. *See John Doe No. 1 v. Reed*, 130 S. Ct. 2811, 2822–27 (2010) (Alito, J., concurring). In contrast, Justices Sotomayor and Justice Stevens wrote separately to suggest just the opposite. *See id.* at 2827–29 (Sotomayor, J., concurring); *id.* at 2829–32 (Stevens, J., concurring).

On remand, the trial court—relying in part on the concurring opinions by Justices Sotomayor and Stevens—rejected the as-applied challenge to the public disclosure of the signatures. *See Doe v. Reed*, 823 F. Supp. 2d 1195 (W.D. Wash. 2011). The petition signatures have since been posted for viewing online. *See* www.whosigned.org (last visited Aug. 29, 2012).

2. In his separate concurring opinion, Justice Scalia raised doubts about whether the act of signing a referendum petition qualifies as speech at all, viewing it instead as an act of legislating, which has historically been granted no First Amendment protection. *See John Doe No. 1 v. Reed*, 130 S. Ct. 2811, 2832–37. He concluded that "a society which ... exercises the direct democracy of initiative and referendum hidden from public scrutiny and protected from the accountability of criticism.... does not resemble the Home of the Brave." *Id.* at 2837.

In this regard, note the inconsistency of both the pro-gay rights and anti-gay rights sides in both *Reed* and in *Perry v. Brown*. In *Reed*, the pro-gay rights side characterized the proponents of the ballot initiative as quasi-legislators, while the anti-gay rights side resisted that characterization. Yet in *Perry*—for purposes of determining whether the proponents of Proposition 8 had standing to appeal the trial court's ruling—the anti-gay rights side characterized themselves as quasi-legislators while the pro-gay rights side resisted that characterization.

Are there reasons to think that the two issues necessarily rise or fall together? In other words, to the extent one seeks to have standing to represent the state's interests in a quasi-legislative capacity, must one also accept the loss of First Amendment protections that go along with that role?

3. Proponents of ballot initiatives seeking to ban marriage for same-sex couples have also challenged the constitutionality of state laws requiring disclosure of the names of contributors to such campaigns on First Amendment grounds. To date, lower courts have uniformly rejected such claims. *See, e.g., Nat'l Org. for Marriage, Inc. v. McKee,* 669 F.3d 34 (1st Cir. 2012); *ProtectMarriage.com v. Bowen,* 830 F. Supp. 2d 914 (E.D. Cal. 2011).

4. During the Proposition 8 litigation in California, the opponents of Proposition 8 sought disclosure of private communications among members of groups supporting Proposition 8. However, the Ninth Circuit upheld a First Amendment challenge to the disclosure, reasoning that it would chill the individuals' exercise of their right to associate. *See Perry v. Schwarzenegger,* 591 F.3d 1126 (9th Cir. 2009).

G. Don't Ask, Don't Tell and Sodomy Laws Revisited

Recall that in many of the cases examined in earlier chapters in which Don't Ask, Don't Tell was enforced, the precipitating factor was the fact that the servicemembers stated their sexual orientation. Indeed, the policy's name ("Don't Tell") discloses an effort to restrict speech, does it not? Moreover, the text of the statute calls for a member's separation if "the member has *stated* that he or she is a homosexual or bisexual." 10 U.S.C. § 654(b)(2) (emphasis added). Similarly, Chapter 3 examined the constitutionality of a statute that made it a crime to *solicit* an act of sodomy, which thus likewise would seem to be a restriction on one's speech.

The two cases that follow re-visit these now familiar laws and consider their impact on First Amendment free speech rights as a basis for challenging their constitutionality.

Cook v. Gates
528 F.3d 42 (1st Cir. 2008)

HOWARD, Circuit Judge.

In 1993, Congress enacted a statute regulating the service of homosexual persons in the United States military. The Act, known as "Don't Ask, Don't Tell," provides for the separation of members of the military who engage, attempt to engage, intend to engage, or have a propensity to engage in a homosexual act. In the aftermath of this congressional action, several members of the military brought constitutional challenges, claiming the Act violated the due process and equal protection components of the Fifth Amendment and the free speech clause of the First Amendment. These challenges were rejected in other circuits.

In 2003, the United States Supreme Court invalidated, on substantive due process grounds, two convictions under a Texas law criminalizing sodomy between consenting homosexual adults. *Lawrence v. Texas,* 539 U.S. 558 (2003). *Lawrence* has reinvigorated the debate over the Act's constitutionality. This case is the second post-*Lawrence* challenge to the Act to be decided by a federal court of appeals....

V. *Discussion*

[In this section of the opinion, excerpted in Chapter 5, the Court first rejects the plaintiffs' substantive due process and equal protection challenges to "Don't Ask, Don't Tell."]

C. First Amendment

The plaintiffs' final challenge attacks the portion of the Act that subjects a member to possible separation for making a statement identifying himself or herself as a homosexual. The plaintiffs assert that they have adequately stated a claim that this aspect of the Act violates the First Amendment because it subjects a member to separation for stating his or her sexual identity.[13] The plaintiffs maintain that this aspect of the Act is invalid because it restricts the content of the plaintiffs' speech and forces them to pretend that they are heterosexual.

There is no question that members of the military are engaging in speech when they state their sexual orientation. *See Hurley v. Irish-American Gay & Lesbian & Bisexual Group of Boston, Inc.,* 515 U.S. 557, 574–75 (1995). There is also no question that First Amendment protections apply to some degree in the military context. *See Goldman,* 475 U.S. at 503. But "our review of military regulations challenged on First Amendment grounds is far more deferential than constitutional review of similar laws or regulations designed for civilian society." *Id.* This limitation is rooted in the recognition that free expression can sometimes conflict with the military's compelling need to "foster instinctive obedience, unity, commitment, and espirit de corps" and that "the essence of military service is the subordination of the desires and interests of the individual to the needs of service." *Id.*

The Act does affect the right of military members to express their sexual orientation by establishing the possibility of adverse consequences from announcing their sexual orientation. But the Act's purpose is not to restrict this kind of speech. Its purpose is to identify those who have engaged or are likely to engage in a homosexual act as defined by the statute. The law is thus aimed at eliminating certain conduct or the possibility of certain conduct from occurring in the military environment, not at restricting speech. The Act relies on a member's speech only because a member's statement that he or she is homosexual will often correlate with a member who has a propensity to engage in a homosexual act.

The Supreme Court has held that the First Amendment "does not prohibit the evidentiary use of speech to establish" a claim "or to prove motive or intent." *Wisconsin v. Mitchell,* 508 U.S. 476, 489 (1993). As the Fourth Circuit explained in rejecting a challenge identical to the one presented here:

> There is no constitutional impediment … to the use of speech as relevant evidence of facts that may furnish a permissible basis for separation from military service. No First Amendment concern would arise, for instance, from the discharge of service members for declaring that they would refuse to follow orders, or that they were addicted to controlled substances. Such remarks provide evidence of activity that the military may validly proscribe.

Thomasson, 80 F.3d at 931.

---

13. For the first time on appeal, the plaintiffs contend that a wide variety of expressive activities could trigger discharge proceedings. They argue, "A service member might wave a rainbow flag or wear a pink triangle, or he might state that he opposes 'Don't Ask, Don't Tell.' Under §654 … these possibilities and more could force the service member—whether straight or gay—into discharge proceedings where he must prove that he has no propensity to engage in homosexual conduct." None of the plaintiffs contend that they were separated from service because they participated in expressive activities. Moreover, the explicit terms of the Act do not indicate that such activities could trigger separation proceedings and the government has stipulated they do not. In any event, we decline to reach this newly raised overbreadth argument on appeal.

We think that the Fourth Circuit has correctly analyzed this claim. To the extent that the Act may be constitutionally applied to circumscribe sexual conduct, the First Amendment does not bar the military from using a member's declaration of homosexuality as evidence of a violation of the Act. We therefore join the other courts that have rejected First Amendment challenges to the Act on this basis.

The plaintiffs argue that, after *Lawrence,* this analysis is "outmoded." We disagree. The Act does not punish a member for making a statement regarding sexual orientation; separation from service is mandated only because a member has engaged, intends to engage or has a propensity to engage in a homosexual act. This is still a question concerning conduct (or likely conduct); the member's speech continues to have only evidentiary significance in making this conduct-focused determination.

Citing *Dawson v. Delaware,* 503 U.S. 159 (1992), the plaintiffs also argue that the First Amendment nevertheless limits the kinds of statements that may be used by the government as evidence in an adversary proceeding. In *Dawson,* the Supreme Court held that the defendant's membership in a white supremacist group could not be introduced against him in a capital sentencing hearing because it violated the defendant's First Amendment right to associate. In reaching this conclusion, the Court emphasized that the admission violated the First Amendment because it had "no bearing on the issue being tried." No similar claim can be made here. A statement by a member that he or she is homosexual is undoubtedly relevant to the kind of conduct a member intends to engage in or has a propensity to engage in. Therefore, *Dawson* is inapposite.

Finally, plaintiffs argue that the Act's rebuttable presumption violates their First Amendment rights. The Act's rebuttable presumption works as follows. A military member may be separated from the armed forces if,

> the member has stated that he or she is a homosexual or bisexual, or words to that effect, *unless* there is a further finding, made and approved in accordance with procedures set forth in the regulations, that the member has demonstrated that he or she is not a person who engages in, attempts to engage in, has a propensity to engage in, or intends to engage in homosexual acts.

10 U.S.C. § 654(b)(2) (emphasis added).

The plaintiffs' attack on the rebuttable presumption is twofold. First, they claim that for homosexual military members, the rebuttable presumption is functionally impossible to rebut. Because they are homosexual within the meaning of section 654(f)(1), they cannot prove that they are not homosexual as section 654(b)(2) effectively requires. Second, the plaintiffs argue that even if section 654(b)(2) *did* offer a presumption capable of being rebutted by homosexual members, the existence of such a presumption "would still force [them] and other gay and lesbian service members to live in an environment that severely restricts and chills constitutionally protected speech." We deal with each contention in turn.

Each plaintiff has agreed that he or she is a person who "engages in, attempts to engage in, has a propensity to engage in, or intends to engage in homosexual acts." 10 U.S.C. § 654(f)(1). Because they admit they fall within section 654(f)(1)'s definition of homosexual, none of them could have proved at a separation proceeding that she or he was not a person who "engages in, attempts to engage in, has a propensity to engage in, or intends to engage in" prohibited conduct because, by definition, they are such a person. In that sense, for a military member who is homosexual as defined by 654(f)(1), the rebuttable presumption would be functionally impossible to rebut.

But that does not mean the Act violates the plaintiffs' First Amendment rights. As noted earlier, the government may use a member's statement that he or she is a homosexual as evidence that he or she "engages in, attempts to engage in, has a propensity to engage in, or intends to engage in homosexual acts." If a person cannot show otherwise, because in fact he or she does engage in or have such a propensity to engage in homosexual conduct, then the military is entitled to separate that person from the service. The military, in that scenario, is not punishing speech but conduct or propensity to engage in conduct.

Moreover, the contention that it is functionally impossible for a gay member to say "I am homosexual" and then rebut the presumption according to the terms of section 654(b)(2) is inaccurate on its face. A member's personal definition of "homosexuality" may not be co-extensive with the Act's. For example, a person may say he or she is homosexual even though the person does not engage in, attempt to engage in, have a propensity to engage in, or intend to engage in homosexual acts. In that scenario, there is a meaningful opportunity to rebut the presumption. The Ninth Circuit's opinion in *Holmes* provides examples.

> One female Naval officer admitted to her homosexuality but submitted a statement, in which she stated, *inter alia,* that she understands the rules against homosexual conduct and intended to obey those rules. Another female Naval officer stated that she was a lesbian but that the statement 'in no way, was meant to imply [ ] any propensity or intent or desire to engage in prohibited conduct.'

Of course, a situation may arise where a gay member triggers the rebuttable presumption by stating he is gay, proves he is not a person who "engages in, attempts to engage in, has a propensity to engage in, or intends to engage in homosexual acts," and yet is still separated from service. This member would have an administrative challenge available to him. *See* 5 U.S.C. § 701. No facts have been plead suggesting such a scenario arose in this case.

We now turn to the plaintiffs' alternative argument that the rebuttable presumption, even if capable of being rebutted by homosexual military members, chills their First Amendment rights. The plaintiffs suggest that the presumption is content based and thus unconstitutional. The Fourth Circuit rejected a similar argument in *Thomasson*. It observed:

> Whenever a provision prohibits certain acts, it necessarily chills speech that constitutes evidence of the acts. A regulation directed at acts thus inevitably restricts a certain type of speech; this policy is no exception. But effects of this variety do not establish a content-based restriction of speech.

Thomasson, 80 F.3d at 932.

As we explained, the Act's purpose is not to restrict military members from expressing their sexual orientation. Its purpose is to identify those who have engaged in or are likely to engage in a homosexual act. The fact that the Act may, in operation, have the effect of chilling speech does not change the analysis. *See Ward v. Rock Against Racism,* 491 U.S. 781, 791 (1989) (noting that regulation is … content-neutral so long as it is "'justified without reference to the content of the regulated speech'" even if it has an "effect on some speakers or messages but not others."). Ultimately, the Act is justified on a content-neutral, nonspeech basis; specifically, maintaining the military's effectiveness as a fighting force. "That the policy may hinge the commencement of administrative proceedings on a particular type of statement does not convert it into a content based enactment." *Thomasson,* 80 F.3d at 933.…

SARIS, United States District Judge, concurring and dissenting.

I concur with the majority opinion regarding the application of *Lawrence* to the "Don't Ask, Don't Tell" statute, 10 U.S.C. § 654 (the "Act"). I also concur with the majority's discussion of the plaintiffs' equal protection challenge. However, I respectfully dissent from the discussion of the plaintiffs' claim that 10 U.S.C. § 654(b)(2) violates the First Amendment.

The military calls the evidentiary presumption created by 10 U.S.C. § 654(b)(2) a "rebuttable" presumption. Because the plaintiffs dispute that the presumption is rebuttable, I adopt the phrasing used by the Second Circuit, and call the presumption the "statement presumption." *See Able v. United States*, 88 F.3d 1280, 1283 (2d Cir.1996).

1. *The Claims*

Plaintiffs argue that the statement presumption violates the First Amendment in two ways. *First,* they contend that the presumption is a dead letter in practice because, as applied, "it is functionally impossible for a gay service member to say 'I am gay' and then prove that he has no 'propensity' to engage in homosexual activity, even if the service member could show a track record of celibacy and an honest intent to refrain from prohibited conduct." In the plaintiffs' view, the only way to avoid discharge is to recant their sexual orientation. As such, the statement presumption is allegedly used to punish plaintiffs' speech concerning their own status as homosexuals.

Second, the plaintiffs argue that the statement presumption is an unconstitutional allocation of the burden of proof, which chills their own speech as well as a whole range of protected expression by both gay and straight service members. The plaintiffs argue that:

> The provision's burden falls on any speaker whose "[l]anguage or behavior" suggests to "a reasonable person" that the person "intended to convey" that he or she is gay. This broad definition could chill a whole range of protected expression: A service member might wave a rainbow flag or wear a pink triangle, or he might state that he opposes "Don't Ask, Don't Tell." Under § 654's burden-shifting mechanism, these possibilities and more could force the service member — whether straight or gay — into discharge proceedings where he must prove that he has no propensity to engage in homosexual conduct.

2. *Content Neutrality*

The starting point for the analysis is the difficult question of whether the statement presumption restricts speech based on its content or viewpoint. I ultimately agree with the majority's position that the statement presumption is content-neutral, but I believe that the issue is a much closer call.

"The First Amendment generally prevents government from proscribing speech, or even expressive conduct, because of disapproval of the ideas expressed. Content-based regulations are presumptively invalid." *R.A.V. v. City of St. Paul*, 505 U.S. 377, 382 (1992). A content-based restriction "can stand only if it satisfies strict scrutiny," and thus is only constitutional if it is "narrowly tailored to promote a compelling Government interest." *United States v. Playboy Entm't Group, Inc.*, 529 U.S. 803, 813 (2000).

However, "[a] restriction that on its face appears to be content-based, yet serves another purpose that by itself is not speech restrictive, may be constitutionally permitted." *Able*, 88 F.3d at 1294. Where a restriction does not "fit neatly into either the 'content-based' or 'content-neutral' category," the Supreme Court has held that the speech restriction is content-neutral so long as it is "*justified* without reference to the content of the regulated speech." *City of Renton v. Playtime Theatres, Inc.*, 475 U.S. 41, 47–48 (1986) (finding zoning ordinance that limits placement of adult theaters content-neutral because it was "aimed not at the *content* of the films shown ... but rather at the *secondary effects* of such theaters on the surrounding community").

Even a content-neutral statute, though, must pass First Amendment muster. A content-neutral regulation is permissible:

[1] if it is within the constitutional power of the Government;

[2] if it furthers an important or substantial governmental interest;

[3] if the governmental interest is unrelated to the suppression of free expression; and

[4] if the incidental restriction on alleged First Amendment freedoms is no greater than is essential to the furtherance of that interest.

Wayte v. United States, 470 U.S. 598, 611 (1985) (quoting *United States v. O'Brien,* 391 U.S. 367, 377 (1968)).

The four circuits that addressed the constitutionality of the Act soon after its passage (and before *Lawrence*) rejected First Amendment challenges to the statement presumption, but they did not fully agree on the appropriate categorization of the First Amendment restriction. In *Thomasson v. Perry,* 80 F.3d 915 (4th Cir.1996) (en banc), involving a First Amendment challenge to the Act both on its face and as-applied, the Fourth Circuit rejected an argument that the statement presumption suppressed speech on the basis of its content and viewpoint, holding:

> The statute does not target speech declaring homosexuality; rather it targets homosexual acts and the propensity or intent to engage in homosexual acts, and permissibly uses the speech as evidence. The use of speech as evidence in this manner does not raise a constitutional issue—"the First Amendment ... does not prohibit the evidentiary use of speech to establish the elements of a crime," or, as is the case here, "to prove motive or intent."

The Fourth Circuit pointed out that service members subject to proceedings under the statement presumption have, in the past, "successfully demonstrated that they lack a propensity or intent to engage in homosexual acts." The Fourth Circuit relied on opinions from two district courts to demonstrate that some service members had successfully rebutted the presumption of propensity.

Two circuits similarly held that the Act and its implementing DoD Directives do not target mere status or speech, but seek to identify and exclude those who are likely to engage in homosexual acts.

In a thoughtful opinion, the Second Circuit in *Able v. United States,* 88 F.3d 1280 (2d Cir.1996), addressed a facial challenge to the statement presumption claiming that it violated the First Amendment. Assuming, without deciding, that separation of a service member based on status alone would be unconstitutional, the Second Circuit discussed whether the statement presumption was content-neutral or content-based. The court never opted for one label or the other, holding instead that the statement presumption passed constitutional muster under both standards. The court emphasized that, under *United States v. Salerno,* 481 U.S. 739, 745 (1987), the plaintiffs failed to show that "no matter how the Act [was] read, it punish[ed] status not conduct." It reasoned:

> Contrary to the district court, we do not believe that, in the context of a facial challenge, we may conclude that the Act equates status with propensity. To be sure, in most cases a member who admits to a homosexual orientation will eventually be separated from the armed forces. But that is because the evidentiary value of the admission is strongly linked to what it is used to prove: a like-

lihood of engaging in homosexual acts. The plaintiffs cannot prove and the district court cannot credibly maintain that there are no instances in which a person will be retained, despite admitting to a homosexual status, because there is no likelihood that he will engage in such acts. The Directives promulgated by the DoD in accordance with the Act specifically contemplate that such an event may occur.

As the Supreme Court has held, when it is not clear whether a restriction is content-based or content-neutral, the controlling consideration is the governmental purpose in enacting the legislation. *Renton,* 475 U.S. at 48; *see also Ward v. Rock Against Racism,* 491 U.S. 781, 791 (1989). Here, the government insists that the purpose of the Act is to target conduct, not status, and points to DoD Directives that limit the Act to only those who engage in or are likely to engage in homosexual conduct. According to plaintiffs, given the vagueness of the term "propensity," the statement presumption can be interpreted to reach expressions of mere homosexual status.

While the question is close, I conclude that the statement presumption is better viewed as content-neutral because its primary purpose, as set forth by the government, is to target conduct, not speech. *But see Thomasson,* 80 F.3d at 934 (Luttig, J., concurring) (agreeing with plaintiff that the purpose of Congress in passing the Act was to mandate exclusion of all known homosexuals based on their orientation or status "regardless of whether they have actually engaged in homosexual conduct or are likely to engage in any such conduct").

Thus, under the standard that applies to content-neutral restrictions on speech, the critical remaining inquiries are "(1) whether the statement[ ] presumption furthers a substantial governmental interest, and (2) whether the statement[ ] presumption restricts the plaintiffs' speech *no more than is essential.*" *Able,* 88 F.3d at 1295 (emphasis added). For the reasons stated by the majority opinion with respect to the plaintiffs' other constitutional claims, the answer to the first of these inquiries is "yes." Accordingly, I now turn to the question of whether the statement presumption, as applied, is overly restrictive of the plaintiffs' speech.

3. *Dead Letter*

Undaunted by pre-*Lawrence* case law, the plaintiffs, who all admit they are homosexual within the meaning of Section 654(f)(1),[16] argue that the statement presumption burdens speech more than is essential because, as applied, it is "functionally impossible" to rebut the presumption short of recanting one's status. As such, plaintiffs allege that the statement presumption punishes service members who speak about their constitutionally protected homosexual status by requiring their discharge.

The government disagrees with plaintiffs' dead letter theory that the statement presumption is impossible to rebut in practice. The government points out that, although the Act broadly defines homosexual conduct to include a "propensity to engage in" homosexual conduct, 10 U.S.C. §654(f)(1), the implementing DoD Directives narrowly interpret "propensity to engage in" homosexual conduct to mean "more than an abstract

---

16. As the majority correctly points out, "[e]ach plaintiff has agreed that he or she is a person who 'engages in, attempts to engage in, has a propensity to engage in, or intends to engage in homosexual acts,'" as defined under the Act. Yet this concession by the plaintiffs does not end the matter because the plaintiffs also argue that the Act's definition of propensity improperly includes homosexual status. Thus, I do not understand the plaintiffs to be conceding that they could not have rebutted the statement presumption under §654(b)(2) if, as the government maintains in defending the Act, "propensity" was limited to a likelihood of engaging in prohibited homosexual acts while a service member.

preference or desire to engage in homosexual acts; it indicates a *likelihood* that a person engages in or will engage in homosexual acts." Accordingly, in the government's view, because a service member's personal definition of "homosexuality" may not coincide with the Act's definition, a service member may be able to successfully rebut the statement presumption if he can show that his statement "I am gay" is not indicative of a likelihood that the he will engage in proscribed homosexual conduct.

As several courts have pointed out, the line between "propensity" and "orientation" is razor-thin at best. *See, e.g., Able,* 880 F.Supp. at 975 (characterizing the distinction between "orientation" and "propensity" as "Orwellian"); *Thomasson,* 80 F.3d at 941–42 n. 8 (Luttig, J., concurring) ("I do not know what homosexual orientation is, if it is not the propensity to commit homosexual acts; indeed, I do not understand how one even knows that he has a homosexual orientation except by realizing that he has a propensity toward the commission of homosexual acts."). Emphasizing that "propensity" sweeps in everyone who is gay, plaintiffs allege that, in practice, gay and lesbian service members are routinely discharged despite evidence that there is no likelihood that they will engage in proscribed homosexual conduct while they are in military service. Accordingly, plaintiffs contend that any honest admission of a gay or lesbian service member's sexual orientation results in discharge.

In my view, if the Act were applied to punish statements about one's status as a homosexual, it would constitute a content-based speech restriction subject to strict scrutiny. *See Meinhold v. U.S. Dep't of Def.,* 34 F.3d 1469, 1476–80 (9th Cir.1994) (in an equal protection challenge to the military's pre-"Don't Ask, Don't Tell" homosexuality policy, construing the policy as only applying to conduct in order to avoid constitutional concerns that would arise if the policy punished service members for "mere propensity" or status alone). Indeed, as *Lawrence* articulates, "Liberty presumes an autonomy of self that includes freedom of thought, belief, expression, and certain intimate conduct." *Lawrence v. Texas,* 539 U.S. 558, 562 (2003).

It is telling that the government does not contend it has a substantial interest, let alone a compelling one, in separating a service member because of his or her status as a homosexual. Rather, the government protests that it is not punishing homosexual status, and insists that it has an interest only in identifying and proscribing homosexual *conduct* to further its substantial interest in morale, good order and discipline, and unit cohesion.

As proof that the statement presumption is in fact rebuttable, the government highlights opinions, in particular *Able* and *Holmes,* that have found that the statement presumption has been successfully rebutted in the past. However, in *Able,* the fact that some service members were successful was held to be sufficient to defeat a *facial* assault on the statute under the *Salerno* standard. Here, in contrast to *Able,* plaintiffs mount an as-applied challenge by alleging the presumption is now functionally impossible to rebut short of recanting. Although the government points to cases of the statement presumption being successfully rebutted, the cherry-picked examples are all well over twelve years old: In fact, some 11,000 service members have been discharged under the Act since 1993....

Finally, the government argues that even if the statement presumption is a dead letter in practice, any misapplication of the presumption can be cured by the availability of administrative review. It may be true that an individual service member may prevail in rebutting the presumption on administrative review short of recanting his status, by stating, for example, that he will refrain from engaging in prohibited homosexual conduct. However, the availability of an administrative remedy does not defeat a First Amendment claim that the government is systematically applying the Act in such a way that it unconstitutionally burdens protected speech.

Accordingly, when all reasonable inferences are drawn in their favor, the plaintiffs have alleged a viable cause of action that the burden placed by the government on gay and lesbian service members' speech is "greater than is essential" to the government's interest in preventing the occurrence of homosexual acts in the military.

4. Chill

Plaintiffs also argue that the statement presumption is an unconstitutional allocation of the burden of proof, which chills a whole range of protected expression. The majority treats the plaintiffs' chill claim as an "overbreadth" claim, although only Appellant Pietrangelo describes the claim in those terms. This designation by the majority is understandable because plaintiffs are unclear as to whether this is a facial challenge, an as-applied challenge, or both.

Because the plaintiffs have not expressly raised a facial challenge to the statement presumption, I will treat the claim as an as-applied challenge. The majority is correct to state that "[n]one of the plaintiffs contend that they were separated from service because they participated in expressive activities." However, the core of the plaintiffs' as-applied challenge is that they were *chilled* from engaging in protected speech, not that they were punished for engaging in such speech....

The government contends that the DoD Directives and Issuances specifically carve out protected speech, quoting Directives and Issuances that show that the presumption is not triggered by rumors, suspicions, or capricious claims of others, or by going to a gay or lesbian bar, possessing or reading homosexual publications, associating with gays and lesbians, or marching in a gay rights parade in civilian clothes.

Citing *Parker v. Levy,* 417 U.S. 733 (1974), the government argues that the military's need for obedience and necessity "may render permissible within the military that which would be constitutionally impermissible outside it." As the Supreme Court has held, its "review of military regulations challenged on First Amendment grounds is far more deferential than constitutional review of similar laws or regulations designed for civilian society." *Goldman v. Weinberger,* 475 U.S. 503, 507 (1986). Moreover, Congress is given the "highest deference" when legislating in the realm of military affairs.

While judicial deference is "at its apogee" when legislative action regarding military affairs is challenged, "deference does not mean abdication." *Rostker v. Goldberg,* 453 U.S. 57, 70 (1981). The Supreme Court has struck down restrictions on speech imposed by Congress on First Amendment grounds, even when military matters were involved. *See Schacht v. United States,* 398 U.S. 58, 60, 62–63 (1970) (striking down a statutory restriction that allowed the wearing of military uniforms by actors in civilian theatrical productions only when such productions would not "tend to discredit" the military).

The Supreme Court has afforded its strongest deference to the military for speech *in military settings. See, e.g., Goldman,* 475 U.S. at 507–10 (affording deference to regulation that prevented soldiers from wearing yarmulkes while on duty and in uniform); *Brown v. Glines,* 444 U.S. 348, 354–55 (1980) (affording deference to regulation that prevented soldiers from circulating petitions on air force bases). Even then, the deference is not absolute. In *Brown v. Glines,* for example, the Court held that the limitations on on-base petitions "restrict speech no more than is reasonably necessary" because it allowed for alternative channels of protest, such as through the United States mail, and the regulations "specifically prevent commanders from halting the distribution of materials that merely criticize the Government or its policies."

The most troubling aspect of the Act's statement presumption is that it covers purely private speech, and public speech made off base and off duty. By its own terms, the Act is "pervasive" in scope, applies "24 hours [a] day," and applies even to speech made "off base" and/or "off duty." Thus, as alleged in the complaint, the Act required the discharge of some of the plaintiffs based upon strictly private speech, such as confiding in a friend or words within a letter from a friend or family member. In addition, the amicus brief submitted by the constitutional law professors cites the example of an Arizona state representative who spoke about his homosexuality on the floor of the legislature. After the military discovered the speech through an anonymous complaint and initiated discharge proceedings against the representative, he negotiated a voluntary separation from the Army.

Plaintiffs argue that the statement presumption, as applied, chills speech because a service member will fear triggering a discharge proceeding, regardless of whether he or she could successfully rebut the presumption. As the Supreme Court explained when striking down a statement presumption in another context, "[t]he man who knows that he must bring forth proof and persuade another of the lawfulness of his conduct necessarily must steer far wider of the unlawful zone than if the State must bear these burdens." *Speiser v. Randall,* 357 U.S. 513, 526 (1958). As alleged, the Act's statement presumption chills individual service members from discussing homosexuality both privately and publicly even when they have no intent to engage in prohibited homosexual conduct.

In conclusion, the plaintiffs' burden is a tough one in light of the strong deference owed to Congress and the military seeking to protect unit cohesion. Yet, when all reasonable inferences are drawn in their favor, plaintiffs have made sufficient allegations that the burden that the statement presumption places on speech is greater than is essential, particularly in nonmilitary settings off base and off duty. Thus, I believe that the motion to dismiss should be denied. Because the majority holds otherwise, I respectfully dissent in this very difficult case.

Singson v. Commonwealth of Virginia
621 S.E.2d 682 (Va. Ct. App. 2005)

ROBERT J. HUMPHREYS, Judge.

[At issue in this case is the constitutionality of the defendant's conviction for solicitation to commit oral sodomy. The act of solicitation occurred in a public restroom, and the defendant was proposing to commit the act there as well. In an earlier section of the opinion, excerpted in Chapter 3, the court rejects a claim that the statute was invalid on substantive due process grounds after *Lawrence v. Texas.*]

....

B. *Whether Code § 18.2-361 is Unconstitutional Because it is Overbroad*

In the alternative, Singson contends that Code § 18.2-361 is constitutionally overbroad, reasoning that the statute "deters constitutionally protected conduct as well as unprotected conduct" because it, in conjunction with Code § 18.2-29, criminalizes "speech requesting legal acts." Specifically, Singson argues that, because private, consensual acts of sodomy are encompassed by the statutory language, Code § 18.2-361 chills protected speech because "the plain language of the solicitation law coupled with the sodomy law prohibits all discussions in which persons exercise their right to discuss private sodomy, including oral sex, and this undoubtedly reaches a substantial amount of speech."[7] For the reasons that follow, we disagree.[8]

The First Amendment mandates that the government "shall make no law ... abridging the freedom of speech." U.S. Const. amend. I. Although "[t]he government may violate this mandate in many ways," it is well settled that "a law imposing criminal penalties on protected speech is a stark example of speech suppression." *Ashcroft v. Free Speech Coalition*, 535 U.S. 234, 244 (2002). Similarly, laws that do not directly regulate speech but, instead, tend to chill constitutionally-protected forms of expression may also run afoul of the First Amendment. *See id.* ("The Constitution gives significant protection from overbroad laws that chill speech within the First Amendment's vast and privileged sphere."). Accordingly, if a statute chills "a substantial amount of protected expression," the statute is "unconstitutional on its face." *Id.* at 244, 252–53 (invalidating a federal statute that went "well beyond" the government interest in "prohibit[ing] illegal conduct" by also "restricting the speech available to law-abiding adults").

1. Whether Code § 18.2-361 is Overbroad Because it Criminalizes Constitutionally Protected Speech

Singson argues primarily that Code § 18.2-361 is constitutionally overbroad because it imposes criminal penalties on individuals who engage in constitutionally protected speech. Specifically, Singson reasons that Code § 18.2-361, in conjunction with Code § 18.2-29, directly prohibits speech proposing a private act of sodomy. For the reasons that follow, we disagree.

Initially, Code § 18.2-361 itself does not criminalize speech or *expressive* conduct. Rather, it only prohibits *sexual* conduct. Accordingly, Code § 18.2-361 does not, in and of itself, prohibit conduct potentially protected by the First Amendment.

Similarly, solicitation of a sexual act is not communicative speech, but rather, non-expressive conduct. As noted by the Virginia Supreme Court, "[l]aws prohibiting solicitation are not directed against words but against acts." *Pedersen v. Richmond*, 219 Va. 1061 (1979) (upholding ordinance prohibiting solicitation of sodomy). That is, "[so]licitation ... is the *act* of enticing or importuning on a personal basis for personal benefit or gain," and, as such, contains no element of expressive conduct. *District of Columbia v. Garcia*, 335 A.2d 217, 224 (D.C.1975) (emphasis added) (distinguishing solicitation of sodomy from "advocacy of sodomy as socially beneficial," reasoning that only the latter constitutes "an act of public expression" implicating the First Amendment).

---

7. We note at the outset that Code §§ 18.2-361 and 18.2-29 do not operate, even at their fullest extent, to prohibit "all" discussions regarding sodomy and oral sex. Rather, with respect to consenting adults, only those conversations during which a party actively requests participation in public commission of an act prohibited by Code § 18.2-361 would arguably fall within the scope of the statutes.

8. Although the statute, as applied to Singson, is constitutional, "[l]itigants ... are permitted to challenge a statute not because their own rights of free expression are violated, but because of a judicial prediction or assumption that the statute's very existence may cause others not before the court to refrain from constitutionally protected speech or expression." *Broadrick*, 413 U.S. at 612. Accordingly, Singson has standing, in the narrow context of his First Amendment arguments, to challenge the facial constitutionality of Code § 18.2-361.

To the extent that an individual may be held criminally liable for soliciting a violation of Code § 18.2-361, it is not the individual's speech that is being prohibited—rather, "'speech is merely the vehicle'" through which the solicitation occurs. *Dhingra,* 371 F.3d at 561 (quoting *United States v. Meek,* 366 F.3d 705, 721 (9th Cir.2004)). Because the prohibition against solicitation of sodomy criminalizes conduct, not expression, Code § 18.2-361— even in conjunction with Code § 18.2-29—does not directly prohibit speech or other forms of communicative conduct. Thus, we find no merit in Singson's argument that Code § 18.2-361 is constitutionally overbroad because it criminalizes constitutionally protected speech.

2. Whether Code § 18.2-361 Is Overbroad Because It "Chills" Constitutionally Protected Speech

Singson, however, also contends that Code § 18.2-361 is unconstitutional on its face because it chills protected speech, specifically, by deterring individuals from "exercis[ing] their right to discuss private sodomy...." Because Code § 18.2-361, in conjunction with Code § 18.2-29, does not chill "a substantial amount" of protected expression, *Free Speech Coalition,* 535 U.S. at 255, we disagree.

a. Whether Speech Soliciting an Act of Sodomy Is Protected by the First Amendment

Initially, we must consider whether the speech allegedly being chilled is, in fact, constitutionally protected. As noted by the United States Supreme Court, "[t]he freedom of speech has its limits; it does not embrace certain categories of speech, including defamation, incitement, obscenity, and pornography produced with real children." *Free Speech Coalition,* 535 U.S. at 245–46. Two of these categories of unprotected speech are potentially relevant here: obscenity and communications inciting another to commit a crime.

First, although speech inciting an individual to commit a crime is unprotected by the First Amendment, *see Pedersen,* 219 Va. at 1066, it is clear, in the wake of *Lawrence,* that private acts of sodomy between consenting adults cannot, pursuant to the Due Process Clause of the Fourteenth Amendment, be criminally punished. And, because private acts of consensual sodomy are constitutionally protected, speech proposing a private act of sodomy no longer qualifies as an "incitement" to commit a "crime."

Second, although discussions of the conduct prohibited by Code § 18.2-361 may border on obscenity, it is not clear that those communications would be "patently offensive in light of community standards." *Miller v. California,* 413 U.S. 15, 24 (1973) (holding that the government, to prove obscenity, must establish that the communication "appeals to the prurient interest" and is "patently offensive in light of community standards"). Accordingly, we cannot assume that speech proposing a private act of sodomy necessarily qualifies as "obscene."

As noted by the United States Supreme Court, "speech may not be prohibited [or chilled] because it concerns subjects offending our sensibilities." *Free Speech Coalition,* 535 U.S. at 245; *see also Reno v. ACLU,* 521 U.S. 844, 874 (1997) ("In evaluating the free speech right of adults, we have made it perfectly clear that sexual expression which is indecent but not obscene is protected by the First Amendment."); *FCC v. Pacifica Found.,* 438 U.S. 726, 745 (1978) ("The fact that society may find speech offensive is not a sufficient reason for suppressing it."). Thus, we cannot conclude that speech proposing a private act of sodomy entirely lacks First Amendment protection.

b. Whether Code § 18.2-361 Impermissibly "Chills" Constitutionally Protected Speech

The overbreadth doctrine "prohibits the Government from banning unprotected speech if a substantial amount of protected speech is prohibited or chilled in the process." *Free*

Speech Coalition, 535 U.S. at 255. To establish that Code § 18.2-361 is facially unconstitutional, Singson must therefore demonstrate, "'from the text of [the law] and from actual fact,'" *Virginia v. Hicks,* 539 U.S. 113, 122 (2003), that the criminal penalties for soliciting a violation of that statute chill "a substantial amount of protected speech," *Free Speech Coalition,* 535 U.S. at 255. Although Singson contends that Code § 18.2-361 is substantially overbroad because it could potentially deter consenting adults from proposing private acts of sodomy, we find his arguments unpersuasive.

"[F]acial overbreadth adjudication is an exception to our traditional rules of practice," and the rationale behind application of the overbreadth doctrine "attenuates as the otherwise unprotected behavior that it forbids the State to sanction moves from 'pure speech' toward conduct." *Broadrick v. Oklahoma,* 413 U.S. 601, 615 (1973). Moreover, courts are especially reluctant to invalidate a statute on facial overbreadth grounds when the prohibited conduct "falls within the scope of otherwise valid criminal laws that reflect legitimate state interests in maintaining comprehensive controls over harmful, constitutionally unprotected conduct." *Id.* Thus, although criminal laws,

> if too broadly worded, may deter protected speech to some unknown extent, there comes a point where that effect — at best a prediction — cannot, with confidence, justify invalidating a statute on its face and so prohibiting a State from enforcing the statute against conduct that is admittedly within its power to proscribe.

Broadrick, 413 U.S. at 615, 93 S.Ct. at 2917–18.

Moreover, "'the existence of a "chilling effect," even in the area of First Amendment rights, has never been considered a sufficient basis, in and of itself, for prohibiting state action.'" *Freeman v. Commonwealth,* 223 Va. 301, 310 (1982) (quoting *Younger v. Harris,* 401 U.S. 37, 51 (1971)). As a result,

> "[w]here a statute does not directly abridge free speech, but ... tends to have the incidental effect of inhibiting First Amendment rights, it is well settled that the statute can be upheld if the effect on speech is minor in relating to the need for control of the conduct and the lack of alternative means for doing so."

Id. (quoting *Younger,* 401 U.S. at 51).

Accordingly, where a statute regulates non-expressive conduct rather than speech, "the overbreadth of [the] statute must not only be real, but substantial as well, judged in relation to the statute's plainly legitimate sweep." *Broadrick,* 413 U.S. at 615. Also, when deciding whether a statute is overbroad because it chills a substantial amount of protected speech, this Court must be cognizant of the principle that "overbreadth scrutiny [is] somewhat less rigid in the context of statutes regulating conduct in the shadow of the First Amendment, but doing so in a neutral, noncensorial manner." *Id.* at 614.

As discussed above, Code § 18.2-361 does not criminalize speech or other expressive conduct. And, as noted by the United States Supreme Court, "rarely, if ever, will an overbreadth challenge succeed against a law or regulation that is not specifically addressed to speech or to conduct necessarily associated with speech (such as picketing or demonstrating)." *Hicks,* 539 U.S. at 124.

Moreover, to the extent that the statute, in conjunction with Code § 18.2-29, might "chill" an individual from requesting an act of private sodomy, speech arguably residing "in the shadow of the First Amendment," it does so "in a neutral, noncensorial manner." *Broadrick,* 413 U.S. at 614. Also, the statute's "legitimate sweep" encompasses not only public sodomy, but also other forms of conduct that lack constitutional protection, specifically, non-consensual sodomy, incestual sodomy, sodomy with a minor, committing sodomy in exchange for money, and engaging in acts of bestiality. In our view, the incidental, hypothetical effect of the statute on speech requesting an act of private, consensual sodomy "cannot, with confidence, justify invalidating [the] statute on its face and so prohibiting a State from enforcing the statute against conduct that is admittedly within its power to proscribe." *Id.* at 615; *see also Hicks*, 539 U.S. at 119–20 ("[T]here comes a point at which the chilling effect of an overbroad law, significant though it may be, cannot justify prohibiting all enforcement of that law," particularly when striking the statute down on its face would "block application of [the] law . . . to constitutionally unprotected conduct."); *Parker v. Levy*, 417 U.S. 733, 760 (1974) ("This Court has . . . repeatedly expressed its reluctance to strike down a statute on its face where there were a substantial number of situations to which it might be validly applied.").

For these reasons, we hold that Code § 18.2-361 is not substantially overbroad and, therefore, decline to strike it down as facially unconstitutional. . . .

Notes and Questions

1. In light of *Wisconsin v. Mitchell*'s holding that the mere *evidentiary* use of speech to prove motive or intent does not violate the First Amendment, how persuasive is the First Amendment argument against the Don't Ask, Don't Tell policy? After all, the policy does not technically punish speech, for a person who states that he is gay is not subject to discharge if he can rebut the presumption that follows from it that he engages in homosexual *conduct*. How persuasive are Judge Saris's counterarguments in *Cook*? What about the fact that the policy also requires the discharge of those with a "propensity" to engage in homosexual conduct (as contrasted with a homosexual "orientation")?

2. The *Cook* court rejects the argument that it is "functionally impossible" to rebut the presumption of homosexual conduct that arises from a statement that one is gay, citing to a handful of examples of people who successfully rebutted the presumption. Yet, as Judge Saris points out in her dissent, there are thousands of counterexamples.

One reason for this disparity in outcomes is the effect that the presumption had on the burden of proof in discharge proceedings under Don't Ask, Don't Tell. Normally, under Federal Rule of Evidence 301, a presumption shifts to the party against whom it is directed only the burden of *producing* evidence, with the ultimate burden of persuasion remaining with the party who bears the initial burden of persuasion. Thus, if discharges from the military were governed by Federal Rule of Evidence 301, the servicemember would not actually have to prove a negative, namely, that he did not engage in homosexual conduct. Rather, he would simply be required to produce some evidence that he does not engage in homosexual conduct, such as testimony by the servicemember or other evidence that, if believed by the trier of fact, would counter the presumption. The burden of *persuading* the trier of fact that the servicemember engaged in homosexual conduct, however, would remain with the party who bears the initial burden of persuasion in discharge proceedings: the military.

However, the military rules of evidence do not include a rule equivalent to Federal Rule of Evidence 301, and Department of Defense Directives in force at the time Don't Ask, Don't Tell was in place provided that the effect of the presumption was to shift not only the burden of production, but also the burden of *persuasion*, to the servicemember. *See* Peter Nicolas, *"They Say He's Gay": The Admissibility of Evidence of Sexual Orientation*, 37 Ga. L. Rev. 793, 887–91 (2003).

3. Recall from Section B that, in *Virginia v. Black*, the Court upheld a statute criminalizing the burning of a cross with the intent to intimidate a person or group of persons. However, the Court also deemed unconstitutional the "prima facie" evidence provision—which *allows* (but does not require) the jury to infer intent to intimidate from the mere act of burning a cross—concluding that it violates the First Amendment by unduly chilling constitutionally protected speech.

Does it not follow, then, that the presumption at issue in *Cook*—which does not merely allow but actually *requires* the trier of fact to conclude that a person who states he is gay engages in homosexual conduct unless he proves otherwise—is at least as problematic? If not, does the distinction turn on the stakes involved (criminal conviction versus discharge from the military)?

4. *Cook* involves the revised policy on gays in military, which focuses on conduct rather than status. Under the old policy, First Amendment challenges were likewise rejected:

> A central problem underlying Pruitt's first amendment argument is that it is based, understandably enough, on the classical dichotomy between the punishment of speech and the punishment of conduct. Because she was not discharged for her conduct, Pruitt concludes that she was discharged for her speech. The Army, however, is not discharging members just for homosexual conduct, or even primarily for homosexual conduct. It is discharging members because of their *status* as homosexuals.... [A]n officer who commits a homosexual act can remain in the service if he or she is not a homosexual, but must be separated if he or she is homosexual....
>
> That it was her homosexuality, and not her speech, that caused Pruitt to be discharged is apparent from the subsection of the regulation under which she was discharged.... Pruitt's admission, like most admissions, was made in speech, but that does not mean that the first amendment precludes the use of the admission as evidence of the facts admitted. Pruitt admitted homosexuality and was discharged for it. The question is not whether the Army is free to discharge her for her speech, because it did not do so. The question is whether the Army is entitled to discharge her for her homosexuality—an issue not encompassed by Pruitt's first amendment claim.

Pruitt v. Cheney, 963 F.2d 1160, 1163–64 (9th Cir. 1991).

5. Just as there is deference to the military in interpreting the reach of other constitutional provisions, as seen in Chapters 3, 4, and 5, so too is there deference in interpreting the reach of the First Amendment in the military context:

> Our review of military regulations challenged on First Amendment grounds is far more deferential than constitutional review of similar laws or regulations designed for civilian society. The military need not encourage debate or tolerate protest to the extent that such tolerance is required of the civilian state by the First Amendment; to accomplish its mission the military must foster instinctive obedience, unity, commitment, and esprit de corps....
>
> These aspects of military life do not, of course, render entirely nugatory in the military context the guarantees of the First Amendment. But "within the military community there is simply not the same [individual] autonomy as there is in the larger civilian community." In the context of the present case, when evaluating whether military needs justify a particular restriction on religiously motivated conduct, courts must give great deference to the professional judgment of mili-

tary authorities concerning the relative importance of a particular military inter-est. Not only are courts "'ill-equipped to determine the impact upon discipline that any particular intrusion upon military authority might have,'" but the mili-tary authorities have been charged by the Executive and Legislative Branches with carrying out our Nation's military policy. "[J]udicial deference ... is at its apogee when legislative action under the congressional authority to raise and support armies and make rules and regulations for their governance is challenged."

Goldman v. Weinberger, 475 U.S. 503, 507–08 (1986).

6. How persuasive is the effort to attack the constitutionality of laws criminalizing the solicitation of sodomy by way of First Amendment argument, rather than substantively attacking the constitutionality of criminalizing the underlying conduct?

The U.S. Supreme Court has made clear that statements offering to engage in unlaw-ful conduct lack First Amendment protection:

> Offers to engage in illegal transactions are categorically excluded from First Amendment protection....

> [T]he rationale for the categorical exclusion.... is based ... on the principle that offers to give or receive what it is unlawful to possess have no social value and thus, like obscenity, enjoy no First Amendment protection. Many long estab-lished criminal proscriptions—such as laws against conspiracy, incitement, and solicitation—criminalize speech (commercial or not) that is intended to induce or commence illegal activities....

United States v. Williams, 553 U.S. 285, 297–98 (2008).

7. Recall that the cases in Section B of this chapter indicated that it violates the First Amendment to ban organizations advocating repeal of sodomy laws. How does that speech differ from the speech at issue in cases such as *Singson*? Consider the following:

> The principle is well established "that the constitutional guarantees of free speech and free press do not permit a State to forbid or proscribe advocacy of the use of force or of law violation except where such advocacy is directed to inciting or producing imminent lawless action and is likely to incite or produce such ac-tion." However, there is a significant distinction between advocacy and solicita-tion of law violation in the context of freedom of expression. Advocacy is the act of "pleading for, supporting, or recommending; active espousal" and, as an act of public expression, is not readily disassociated from the arena of ideas and causes, whether political or academic. Solicitation, on the other hand, implies no ideological motivation but rather is the act of enticing or importuning on a personal basis for personal benefit or gain. Thus advocacy of sodomy as socially beneficial and solicitation to commit sodomy present entirely distinguishable threshold questions in terms of the First Amendment freedom of speech. The lat-ter, we hold, is not protected speech.

District of Columbia v. Garcia, 335 A.2d 217, 223–24 (D.C. 1975).

8. Note that in both *Cook* and *Singson*, the courts try to distinguish conduct from speech, much in the same way as the cases involving true threats in Section B of this chap-ter. How clear is the line between speech and conduct? Is it any less elusive than the dis-tinction between conduct and status examined in earlier chapters involving the Equal Protection Clause?